A CONCISE
ANGLO-SAXON DICTIONARY

A CONCISE
ANGLO-SAXON
DICTIONARY

BY

JOHN R. CLARK HALL
M.A., PH.D.

FOURTH EDITION
WITH A SUPPLEMENT BY
HERBERT D. MERITT

CAMBRIDGE
AT THE UNIVERSITY PRESS
1962

PUBLISHED BY
THE SYNDICS OF THE CAMBRIDGE UNIVERSITY PRESS

Bentley House, 200 Euston Road, London, N.W. 1
American Branch: 32 East 57th Street, New York 22, N.Y.
West African Office: P.O. Box 33, Ibadan, Nigeria

First Edition	1894
Second Edition,	
revised and enlarged	1916
Third Edition,	
further revised and enlarged	1931
Fourth Edition	
with Supplement	1960
Reprinted	1962

First printed in Great Britain
Reprinted by offset-lithography in U.S.A.

PREFACE TO THE SECOND EDITION

The first edition of this dictionary having been exhausted, it has been extensively revised, and certain new features and alterations have been introduced into it.

1. The principle of arranging all words according to their actual spelling has been to a considerable extent abandoned. It was admittedly an unscientific one, and opened the door to a good many errors and inconsistencies. The head form in this edition may be either a normalised form or one which actually occurs.

2. Words beginning with *ge-* have been distributed among the letters of the alphabet which follow that prefix, and the sign + has been employed instead of *ge-* in order to make the break in alphabetical continuity as little apparent to the eye as possible. The sign ± has been used where a word occurs both with and without the prefix.

3. References to Cook's translation of Sievers' *Anglo-Saxon Grammar*, and to the Grammatical Introduction to Sweet's *Reader* have been taken out, as Wright's or Wyatt's *Old English Grammar* will have taken their place with most English students.

4. A new feature which, it is hoped, will prove widely useful, is the introduction of references to all, or nearly all, the headings in the *New English Dictionary* under which quotations from Anglo-Saxon texts are to be found. A vast mass of valuable information as to the etymology, meaning and occurrence of Old English words is contained in that Dictionary, but is to a very large extent overlooked because it is to be found under the head of words which are now obsolete, so that unless one happens to know what was the last form which they had in Middle English, one does not know how to get at it. This information will be made readily available by the references in the present work, which will form a practically complete index to the Anglo-Saxon material in the larger dictionary and will at the same time put the student on the track of interesting Middle English examples of the use of Old English words. Besides directing the reader (by means of quotation marks) to the heading in the *New English Dictionary* where the relevant matter may be found, an indication has been given of the texts from which quotations are made therein, when these do not exceed four or five.

5. There have been many valuable contributions to Anglo-Saxon lexicography (by Napier, Swaen, Schlutter, Förster, Wülfing and

others) since the first edition of this Dictionary appeared, and these have been made use of, but (as before) unglossaried matter has not been systematically searched for words not hitherto recorded in Anglo-Saxon Dictionaries.

6. The number of references to passages has been very largely increased. All words occurring only in poetical texts have been marked. If they occur more than once they bear the sign †, if only once, a reference to the passage is generally given. If not they are marked ‡. As regards prose texts, the rule has been only to give references to particular passages in the case of rare words,—more especially ἅπαξ λεγόμενα. The references to AO, CP and Æ which were given in the earlier edition have been retained, as a useful indication that the word occurs in Early West Saxon or Late West Saxon prose, as the case may be.

7. By various devices it has been found possible, while much increasing the amount of matter in the book, to add very slightly to the number of pages, and at the same time to reduce the number of columns on a page from three to two. Most of these devices are more or less mechanical, but one method of saving space may be mentioned. Certain compound words, descriptive of places, which, as far as I know, occur only in charters and which may often be more correctly regarded as proper nouns, have not been separately inserted. Their meaning can however always be ascertained by referring to their components, and where the abbreviation Mdf is inserted the reader will understand that examples of words so compounded, or of the components, or of both, will be found in Birch's *Cartularium Saxonicum*, or in Earle's *Land Charters*, and that references to those examples are given in Middendorff's *Altenglisches Flurnamenbuch*.

8. In the List of Abbreviations, etc. at the commencement of the book, editions of texts which are furnished with a glossary have been specially indicated.

J. R. C. H.

January 1916

PREFACE TO THE THIRD EDITION

In this new edition account has been taken of the important publications concerned with Anglo-Saxon lexicography which have appeared
within the last sixteen years, and notably of the final instalments of
'*Bosworth-Toller*' (BT) and the *New English Dictionary* (NED). A
considerable number of words from twelfth-century texts, which
have not been recorded in BT, has been inserted in the Dictionary,
as there seemed to the writer that there was no sufficient ground for
their exclusion.

Generally speaking, the preface to the Second Edition still holds
good, except that a few words now marked † do not occur exclusively
in poetical texts but appear very rarely elsewhere, e.g. in glosses.
References to lines have been given in the case of all poetical words
which occur only once, the sign ‡ being thus rendered unnecessary;
and as regards prose words, references to page and line have usually
been limited to those occurring once, or very rarely, or to passages
which are not noted in other dictionaries.

In the same preface it was stated that references to the texts from
which quotations have been made in the NED have only been given
as a rule when the numbers did not exceed four or five. As regards
the cases in which the quotations contained in the NED are more
numerous, this has been indicated in the present edition by the NED
word being printed in small capitals, an asterisk being added where
inflectional or other forms are specially illustrated in that Dictionary
by examples.

For the rest, the number of references has again been materially
increased, an indication having often been given of one or two texts
in which the more common words are to be found. It may be added
that a few words have been given on the authority of BT, NED or
Sweet alone when I have not been able to trace their source, or to
verify the references given in those dictionaries.

J. R. C. H.

EASTBOURNE

April 1931

LIST OF SIGNS AND ABBREVIATIONS
WITH THEIR EXPLANATION

Note 1. Where references are in *italic type*, quotations from the texts indicated will be found in the *New English Dictionary*, under the head of the English word which is distinguished in the article by quotation marks (see Preface). When the quotations in the NED have been too numerous to allow of reference to them in this Dictionary, the Modern English word has been put in SMALL CAPITALS; and an asterisk is affixed to it when examples of inflectional or other forms of an Anglo-Saxon word are given in the NED. In references to special passages volumes have been marked off from pages by an inverted full stop, and lines or verses have been shown, *where they follow other numerals*, by small superior figures. Occasionally where lines have not been numbered in a quoted text, the mark ' has been inserted to show that the quotation is in the lower part of a page. References to page and line have, as a rule, been restricted to words only occurring once.

Note 2. In the following list the number (1) after an edition of a text indicates that the edition is supplied with a complete referenced glossary or word-index, (2) that it has a complete glossary, but without references, and (3) that it has a partial glossary or word-index.

Note 3. Some of the abbreviations given below are used in combination, *e.g.* MtLR = the Lindisfarne and Rushworth MSS of St Matthew; BJPs = the Bosworth and the Junius Psalters; asf. = accusative singular feminine; EK = Early Kentish.

Note 4. If any meanings of adverbs are given, they are *additional* to those which may be inferred from the corresponding adjective.

Note 5. In settling the spelling and alphabetical order of words preference has been given to EWS forms in ie or īe whenever they occur. Where other spellings (i, y; ī, ȳ) have been adopted ' = ie' or ' = īe' has been added in the case of the more important forms.

' ' Quotation marks are used to enclose the English words which should be looked up in the NED in order to find etymological information as to, and examples of the use of, the Anglo-Saxon words to which the articles in this Dictionary relate, see Note 1 above. If they enclose Latin words, they indicate the lemmata of Anglo-Saxon words in glosses or glossaries etc., or the Latin equivalent of such words in the Latin texts from which they are translated. The Latin is especially so given when ·the Ags. word seems to be a blindly mechanical and literal equivalent.

* is prefixed to hypothetical forms. Normalised forms of Ags. words which actually exist are not usually so marked. See also Note 1.

' See Note 1 above.

+ = ge-.

± indicates that the Ags. word to which it is prefixed is found both with and without the prefix ge-.

| = occurs only or mainly in poetical texts. (For references to those texts v. GK.)

a. = accusative.

A = Anglian, or, if followed by numerals, Anglia, Zeitschrift für Englische Philologie, Halle, 1877 etc. AB = Anglia Beiblatt.

AA = Alexander's Letter, in Three English Prose Texts, ed. S. Rypins (EETS), 1924 (1).

Æ = Ælfric. (References followed by numerals in parentheses relate to certain Homilies attributed to Ælfric in HL.) References to books in Ælfric's version of the Heptateuch, in Grein's *Ælfric de vetere et novo Testamento* (Bibl. der Ags. Prosa, vol. 1), or in S. J. Crawford's Heptateuch (EETS), 1929, are given under the abbreviations of their titles (GEN etc.). Words peculiar to Crawford's text are marked C. See also ÆT.

ÆGR = Ælfric's Grammatik und Glossar, ed. J. Zupitza, Berlin, 1880.

ÆH = Ælfric's Homilies, ed. B. Thorpe, London, 1844–6. (Quoted by vol., page and line.)

ÆL = Ælfric's Metrical Lives of Saints, ed. W. W. Skeat (EETS), 1881–1900 (3).

ÆP = Ælfric's Hirtenbriefe (Pastoral Letters), ed. B. Fehr, Hamburg, 1914 (Bibl. der Ags. Prosa, vol. 9).

ÆT = the prefatory matter in Ælfric's Heptateuch (see Æ). Quoted from Crawford by line only up to p. 75, and after that by page and line.

AF = Anglistische Forschungen, ed. J. Hoops, Heidelberg.

ALM = the poem on Alms, in GR.

AN = the poem of Andreas, in GR; or ed. G. P. Krapp, Boston, U.S.A., 1905 (1).

ANDR = the prose legend of St Andrew, in BR.

ANS = Herrig's Archiv für das Studium der neueren Sprachen, Brunswick, 1846 etc.

ANT = Analecta Anglo-saxonica by B. Thorpe, London, 1846 (2).

anv. = anomalous verb.

AO = Alfred's translation of Orosius, ed. H. Sweet (EETS), 1883. (v. also Wfg.)

AP = the poem of the Fate of the Apostles, in GR; or included with Andreas in Krapp's edition (v. AN).

APs = the Arundel Psalter, ed. G. Oess (AF vol. 30), Heidelberg, 1910.

APT = Anglo-Saxon version of Apollonius of Tyre, ed. B. Thorpe, London, 1834.

AS = King Alfred's version of Augustine's Soliloquies, ed. Endter, Hamburg, 1922, or H. L. Hargrove (Yale Studies in Old English), Boston, U.S.A., 1912 (1). References are to Endter. See also SHR.

AZ = the poem of Azarias, in GR.

B = the poem of Beowulf, in GR; also ed. A. J. Wyatt and R. W. Chambers, Cambridge, 1914 (1); or ed. W. J. Sedgefield, Manchester, 1912 (1); or F. Klaeber (Klb.), Boston, U.S.A., 1922 (1).

BAS = The Admonition of St Basil, ed. H. W. Norman, London, 1849.

BB = Bonner Beiträge zur Anglistik, ed. M. Trautmann.

BC = Cartularium Saxonicum, ed. W. de Gray Birch, London, 1883 etc., 3 vols.

Bd = Bede.

BDS = Beiträge zur Geschichte der deutschen Sprache, ed. E. Sievers, Leipzig, 1874 etc.

BF = Byrhtferth's Manual, ed. S. J. Crawford (EETS), 1929. Also in A vol. 8, from which the quotations in NED are made.

BH = the Anglo-Saxon version of Bede's Ecclesiastical History, 2 vols., ed. T. Miller (EETS), 1891–6. (Reference is usually made to the pages in vol. 1 as regards the various readings recorded in vol. 2—not to the pages in the latter vol.) Sch = ed. J. Schipper, Hamburg, 1899.

BK = Texte und Untersuchungen zur AE Literatur, etc., by R. Brotanek, Halle, 1913.

BL = The Blickling Homilies, ed. R. Morris (EETS), 1874–80 (1).

BLPs = Blickling Glosses to the Psalms, at the end of BL.

Bo = King Alfred's translation of Boethius, with the Metres of Boethius, ed. W. J. Sedgefield, Oxford, 1899 (1).

BPs = die AE Glossen im Bosworth-Psalter, ed. U. Lindelöf (Mémoires de la Soc. néo-philologique à Helsingfors, tom. 5), 1909 (3).

BR = An Anglo-Saxon Reader, ed. J. W. Bright, New York, or London, 1923 (1).

Br = the poem of Brunanburh, in GR or †CHR.

BT = An Anglo-Saxon Dictionary, by J. Bosworth and T. N. Toller, Oxford, 1882–98; BTs = the Supplement, 1908–21; BTac = Additions and Corrections at the end of the Supplement.

BTK = C. G. Bouterwek, *de officiis horarum*, in pref. to Caedmon's Biblische Dichtungen, Gütersloh, 1854 (pp. 194–222).

ByH = 12th Century Homilies in MS Bodley 343, ed. A. O. Belfour (EETS vol. 137), 1909.

CAS = Legends of St Andrew and St Veronica, in Cambridge Antiq. Society's Publications, 1851.

CC = The Crawford Charters, ed. A. S. Napier and W. H. Stevenson (Anecdota Oxoniensia), Oxford, 1895.

CHR = Two of the Saxon Chronicles Parallel, ed. J. Earle and C. Plummer, Oxford, 1892 (1). The poetical passages are marked †CHR.

CHRD = the Rule of Chrodegang, ed. A. S. Napier (EETS), 1916.

CM = the tract 'de Consuetudine Mona-
chorum,' in Anglia, vol. 13, pp. 365–
454.

Coll. Monast., v. WW.

Cos = Altwestsächsische Grammatik,
by P. J. Cosijn, Haag, 1888.

cp. = compare.

CP = King Alfred's trans. of Gregory's
Pastoral Care, ed. H. Sweet (EETS),
London, 1871.

Cp = the Corpus Glossary, in OET, or in
WW (cols. 1–54) or (if the numbers
are followed by a letter) in A Latin-
Anglo-Saxon Glossary, ed. J. H.
Hessels, Cambridge, 1890 (1).

CPs = Der Cambridge-Psalter, ed. K.
Wildhagen, Bibl. der Ags. Prosa, vol.
7, Hamburg, 1910. (CHy = Cambridge Hymns in the same vol.) (3).

CR = the poem of Crist, in GR.

CRA = the poem of Men's Crafts, in GR.

CREAT = the poem of the Creation, in
GR.

Ct = Charters, wills and other like documents, as contained in BC, CC, EC,
KC, TC and WC.

d. = dative. dp. = dat. pl. ds. = dat.
singular; etc.

DA = the poem of Daniel, in GR; or ed.
T. W. Hunt (Exodus and Daniel),
Boston, 1885.

DD = the poem 'Be Dōmes Dæge' ('de
die judicii'), ed. J. R. Lumby
(EETS), London, 1876 (1); or in GR
(vol. 2, pp. 250–272).

DEOR = the poem of Deor's Complaint,
in GR and KL.

DEUT = Deuteronomy (see Æ).

DHy = the Durham Hymnarium, ed.
J. Stevenson (Surtees Society, vol.
23), London, 1851. (GL by H. W.
Chapman, Yale Studies, No. 24,
Boston, 1905.)

DOM = the poem 'Be Dōmes Dæge'
from the Exeter Book, in GR (vol.
3, pp. 171–4).

DR = the Durham Ritual, ed. J.
Stevenson (Surtees Society), London,
1840, as re-edited by Uno Lindelöf,
1927. Lines of Anglo-Saxon only
counted. [GL by Lindelöf, Bonn,
1901 (BB vol. 9).]

E = Early.

EC = Land Charters and other Saxonic
Documents, ed. John Earle, Oxford,
1888 (3).

EETS = Early English Text Society's
Publications.

EHR = English Historical Review.

EK = Early Kentish.

EL = the poem of Elene, in GR; or ed.
Kent, Boston, 1889.

Ep = the Epinal Gloss., in OET.

EPs = Eadwine's Canterbury Psalter,
ed. F. Harsley (EETS), London, 1889.
Late text. (EHy = Hymns in the
same vol.)

Erf = the Erfurt Gloss., in OET.

ES = Englische Studien, Heilbronn and
Leipzig, 1876 etc.

Ettm. = L. Ettmüller, Lexicon Anglo-
saxonicum, 1851.

EWS = Early West Saxon.

Ex = the poem of Exodus, in GR or in
Hunt's edition (v. DA). If followed
by two kinds of numerals = Exodus
in Ælfric de vetere et novo Testamento
in the Bibl. der Ags. Prosa, vol. 1,
Cassel, 1872, or in Crawford's
Heptateuch (ExC).

exc. = except.

f. = feminine. fp. = fem. plural.

FAp = the poem 'Fata Apostolorum,'
in GR.

FBO = Das Benediktiner Offizium, ed.
E. Feiler (AF vol. 4), Heidelberg,
1901.

FIN = the poem of Finnsburg, in GR,
and most editions of Beowulf.

FM = The Furnivall Miscellany, Oxford, 1901.

FT = the poem 'A Father's Teachings,'
in GR.

FTP = Falk-Torp, Wortschatz der
Germ. Spracheinheit, Göttingen,
1909.

g. = genitive. gs. = gen. singular. gp. =
gen. pl.; etc.

G = the Anglo-Saxon Gospels, ed. W. W.
Skeat, Cambridge, 1871–87, or by
Bosworth (B) or Kemble (K). See
also LG, NG, RG, WG. (GL to WG
by M. A. Harris, Yale Studies, vol. 6,
Boston, 1899.)

GBG = The meaning of certain terms in
Ags. Charters, by G. B. Grundy,
English Association Essays and
Studies, vol. 8, 1922.

GD = Die Dialoge Gregors den Grossen,
ed. Hans Hecht (Bibl. der Ags. Prosa,
vol. 5), Cassel, 1900–7.

GEN = the poem of Genesis, in GR. If
followed by two kinds of numerals =
Genesis in Ælfric de vetere et novo
Testamento, in the Bibl. der Ags.
Prosa, vol. 1, Cassel, 1872, or in
Crawford's Heptateuch (GENC).

Ger. = German.

GF = Legends of St Swithhun etc., ed. J. Earle, London, 1861 (Gloucester Fragments).

GK = Grein's Sprachschatz der Ags. Dichter, revised by Köhler and Holthausen, Heidelberg, 1912. (A complete referenced glossary to GR.)

GL = Glossary. Used also as a comprehensive sign for all or any of the extant Anglo-Saxon glosses or glossaries: Cp, Ep, Erf, GPH, HGL, KGL, Ln, OEG, WW etc.

GN = The Gnomic Verses, in GR. GNE = those in the Exeter Book and GNC those in the Cotton MS. Separate edition also by B. C. Williams, New York, 1914 (1).

GPH = Prudentius Glosses, in Germania, Vierteljahrsschrift für deutsche Altertumskunde, vol. 11 (ns).

GR = Bibliothek der Angelsächs. Poesie, ed. C. W. M. Grein and revised by R. P. Wülker, Cassel, 1883–98.

GU = the poem of St Guthlac, in GR.

GUTH = the (prose) Life of St Guthlac, ed. C. W. Goodwin, London, 1848 (pp. 8–98), or (pp. 100–176) ed. P. Gonser (AF vol. 27), Heidelberg, 1909.

HELL = the poem of Hell, in GR.

HEPT = Heptateuchus, etc., Anglo-Saxonice, ed. E. Thwaites, Oxford, 1698. See also Æ.

HEX = The Hexameron of St Basil, ed. H. W. Norman, London, 1849, or ed. S. J. Crawford (HEXC), Bibl. der Ags. Prosa, vol. 10, 1921.

HGL = Glosses in (Haupt's) Zeitschrift für deutsches Altertum, vol. 9 (1853).

HL = Homilien und Heiligendleben, ed. B. Assmann, Bibl. der Ags. Prosa, vol. 3, Cassel, 1889. v. also Æ and SHR (3).

HR = Legends of the Holy Rood, ed. R. Morris (EETS), 1871.

HU = the poem 'The Husband's Message,' in GR.

HY = the collection of 'Hymns' at the end of most of the Ags. versions of the Psalms. v. the various Psalters (Ps). [The numbering of verses etc. usually follows that in Wildhagen's Cambridge Psalter (CPs).] †Hy = the 'Hymnen und Gebete,' in GR.

i. = instrumental (case).

IF = Indogermanische Sprachforschungen, 1891 etc.

IM = 'Indicia Monasterialia,' ed. F. Kluge, in Techmer's Internationale Zeitschrift für allgemeine Sprach-wissenschaft, vol. 2, Leipzig, 1885, pp. 118–129.

intr. = intransitive.

JAW = Eigentümlichkeiten des Anglischen Wortschatzes, by R. Jordan (AF vol. 17), Heidelberg, 1906.

JGPh = Journal of (English and) Germanic Philology, Urbana, 1897 etc.

Jn = the Gospel of St John. v. G and NG (JnL = Lindisfarne MS; JnR = Rushworth MS, v. LG, RG).

Jos = Joshua (see Æ).

JPs = der Junius-Psalter, ed. E. Brenner (AF vol. 23), Heidelberg, 1909 (JHy = the Hymns in the same vol.).

JUD = the poem of Judith, in GR, or ed. A. S. Cook, Boston, 1889 (1); or if followed by two kinds of numerals = Judges, in Crawford's Heptateuch.

JUL = the poem of Juliana, in GR.

K = Kentish.

KC = Codex Diplomaticus Aevi Saxonici, ed. J. M. Kemble, 6 vols., London, 1839–48. (3) at end of vol. 3.

KGL = Kentish Glosses to the Proverbs of Solomon (= WW 55–88, or, if quoted by number, in KL).

KL = Angelsächsisches Lesebuch, by F. Kluge, 3rd edition, Halle, 1902 (2).

KLED = F. Kluge's Etymologisches Wörterbuch, or J. F. Davis' translation, London, 1891.

KPs = Psalm 50 (Kentish), in GR, KL or SwtR.

L. = Latin.

LCD = Leechdoms, Wortcunning and Starcraft of the Anglo-Saxons, ed. O. Cockayne, London, 3 vols., Rolls Series, 1864–6 (vol. 2, and pp. 1–80 of vol. 3 are referred to by the folio of the MS, so that the references may also be available for G. Leonhardi's edition of that part of the LCD, in the Bibl. der Ags. Prosa, vol. 6) (3).

LEAS = the poem 'Be manna lease,' in GR.

LEV = Leviticus, in Æ.

LF = An OE Ritual text, ed. B. Fehr, and Keltisches Wortgut im Eng. by M. Förster, in F. Liebermann's Festgabe, Halle, 1921.

LG = the Lindisfarne Gospels, in Skeat's ed. of the Anglo-Saxon Gospels (v. G). (Glossary by A. S. Cook, Halle, 1894.) LRG = Lindisfarne and Rushworth Gospels. v. RG.

Lieb. = F. Liebermann (v. LL).

Lk = the Gospel of St Luke. v. G and

NG (LkL = Lindisfarne MS; LkR = Rushworth MS; v. LG, RG).

LL = the Anglo-Saxon Laws, as contained in Liebermann, Schmid, Thorpe or Wilkins. If followed by numerals not in parentheses, or only partially in parentheses, the reference is to 'Die Gesetze der Angelsachsen,' by F. Liebermann, 3 vols., Halle, 1903–16 (1); if by numerals *entirely* in parentheses, to vol. 2 of 'Ancient Laws and Institutes,' by B. Thorpe, 2 vols., London, 1840 (3).

Ln = the Leiden Glossary, ed. J. H. Hessels, Cambridge, 1906 (1).

Lor = the Lorica Hymn, in Kleinere angelsächsische Denkmäler, by G. Leonhardi (Bibl. der Ags. Prosa, vol. 6), Hamburg, 1905.

LPs = Der Lambeth-Psalter, ed. U. Lindelöf, Acta Soc. Sc. Fennicae, vol. 35, Helsingfors, 1909 (1). (LHy = the Hymns in the same vol.)

LV = Leofric's Vision, ed. A. S. Napier, in the Transactions of the Philological Society for 1907–10, pp. 180–188.

LWS = Late West Saxon.

M = Mercian.

m. = masculine. ms., mp., etc. = masc. sing., masc. plur., etc.

Ma = the poem of the Battle of Maldon, in Gr, also in Br, Kl or Sweet's Anglo-Saxon Reader, Oxford.

Mdf = Altenglisches Flurnamenbuch, by H. Middendorff, Halle, 1902. [See Preface.]

Men = the Menologium, at the end of Chr, or in Hickes' Thesaurus, vol. 1

Met = the Metres of Boethius; v. Bo.

MFB = Max Förster's contribution to A. Brandl's Festschrift (Anglica II, pp. 8–69 in Palaestra 148), Leipzig, 1925. (Quoted by line; v. also RWH.)

MFH = Vercelli-Homilies, etc., in the Festschrift für L. Morsbach (Studien zur Eng. Philologie, vol. 50), Halle, 1913, ed. Max Förster, pp. 20–179; v. also VH.

MH = An Old English Martyrology, ed. G. Herzfeld (EETS), London, 1900. See also Shr.

Mk = the Gospel of St Mark; v. G and NG. (MkL = Lindisfarne MS; MkR = Rushworth MS of St Mark; v. LG, RG.)

MLA = Publications of the Modern Language Association of America, Baltimore.

MLN = Modern Language Notes, Baltimore, 1886 etc.

MLR = Modern Language Review, Cambridge, 1905 etc.

Mod = the poem 'Bi Manna Mōd,' in Gr.

MP = Modern Philology, Chicago.

Mt = the Gospel of St Matthew; v. G and NG. (MtL = Lindisfarne MS; MtR = Rushworth MS of St Matthew; v. LG, RG.)

n. = nominative, *or* neuter, *or* note. (np., nap., etc. = nom. plural, nom. and acc. plur., etc.)

N = Northumbrian.

Nar = Narratiunculae, ed. O. Cockayne, London, 1861.

NC = Contributions to Old English Lexicography by A. Napier, in the Philological Society's Transactions for 1903–1906, London (mostly late texts).

NED = the New English Dictionary, ed. Sir J. A. H. Murray and others, Oxford, 1888–1915. (See Prefaces, and Note 1.)

neg. = negative.

NG = the Northumbrian Gospels, contained in Skeat's edition (v. G, LG, RG).

Nic = the Gospel of Nicodemus, in MLA 13·456–541, MP 1·579–604 and RWH 77–88 (referred to by pages in those texts).

NP = Neophilologus, Groningen, 1915 etc.

NR = The Legend of the Cross (Roodtree), ed. A. S. Napier (EETS), London, 1894.

Num = Numbers (see Æ).

obl. = oblique.

occly. = occasionally.

OEG = Old English Glosses, ed. A. Napier (Anecdota Oxoniensia), Oxford, 1900 (1).

OEH = vol. 1 of Morris, Old English Homilies (pp. 296–304 only) (EETS), 1867.

OET = The Oldest English Texts, ed. H. Sweet (EETS), 1885 (1).

OF. = Old French.

OHG. = Old High German.

ON. = Old Norse.

OP = Oratio Poetica, in DD (Lumby).

OS. = Old Saxon.

p. = page, *or* plural.

Pa = the poem of the Panther, in Gr.

Part = the poem of the Partridge, in Gr.

PH = the poem of the Phoenix, in GR or BR.

pl. = plural.

PPs = the Paris Psalter, ed. B. Thorpe, London, 1835. The prose portion (Psalms 1–50) also ed. Bright and Ramsay, Belles Lettres Series, Boston, 1907, and the remainder (verse portion) in GR.

PR = Proverbs, at end of SOL (Kemble), pp. 258–268.

Ps — any one or more of the Anglo-Saxon Psalters. [NB. In the numbering of the Psalms, the Authorised Version is usually one ahead of the MSS.] v. A, B, C, E, J, L, R, S and VPs; also Hy. PsC = Psalm 100 in GR.

PST = Philological Society's Transactions (v. also LV and NC).

QF = Mone, Quellen u. Forschungen zur Geschichte der teutschen Lit. u. Sprache, Aachen und Leipzig, 1830.

RB = der Benedictinregel, ed. A. Schröer, Bibl. der Ags. Prosa, vol. 2, Cassel, 1885–8 (3).

RBL = the Anglo-Saxon and Latin Rule of St Benet (Interlinear Glosses), ed. H. Logeman (EETS), London, 1888.

RD = The Riddles of the Exeter Book, in GR, or ed. F. Tupper Junr., Boston, 1910 (1).

RG = the Rushworth Gospels, in Skeat's ed. of the Anglo-Saxon Gospels (v. G). Mt (all), Mk 1–2¹⁵ and Jn 18¹⁻³ are in a Mercian dialect, and are usually known as R¹; the rest (R²) is in a Northumbrian dialect (v. also LG). Glossary to R¹ by Ernst Schulte, Bonn, 1904; to R² by U. Lindelöf, Helsingfors, 1897.

RIM = The Rhyming Poem, in GR.

ROOD = the poem 'Dream of the Rood,' in GR.

RPs = der Regius-Psalter, ed. F. Roeder (Studien in Eng. Philologie, vol. 18), Halle, 1904. (RHy = the Hymns in the same vol.)

RSL = Transactions of the Royal Society of Literature, London.

RUIN = the poem of the Ruin, in GR.

RUN = the Rune-poem, in GR.

RWH = Homilies in MS Vesp. D. XIV (12th cent.), ed. R. D. N. Warner (EETS vol. 152), 1917. (pp. 77–88 = NIC, and pp. 134–139 = MFB.)

s. = strong; also = singular. sv. = strong verb. swv. = strong-weak verb.

SAT = the poem 'Christ and Satan,' in GR.

sb. = substantive.

SC = Defensor's Liber Scintillarum, ed. E. Rhodes (EETS), London, 1889 (3). Lines of Ags. only counted.

SCR = Screadunga, by C. G. Bouterwek, Elberfeld, 1858.

SEAF = the poem of the Seafarer, in GR.

SF = Streitberg Festgabe, Leipzig, 1924.

SHR = the Shrine by O. Cockayne, London, 1864–70 [pp. 29–33 and 46–156 = MH; pp. 35–44 = HL pp. 199–207; pp. 163–204 = AS].

SHy = Surtees Hymnarium = DHy.

SkED = An Etymological English Dictionary by W.W. Skeat, Oxford, 1910.

SOL = the poem Solomon and Saturn, in GR (if followed by page and line, or marked SOLK, the reference is to the prose version, ed. J. M. Kemble). Ags. proverbs (PR) are included at pp. 258–268.

SOUL = the poem of the Soul, in GR.

SPs = Psalterium Davidis Latino-Saxonicum, ed. J. Spelman, London, 1640. No Hymns. (Stowe MS, but includes marginal readings from APs, CPs and EPs.)

S²Ps = Psalter Glosses in Salisbury Cathedral Library MS 150 (noted in CPs).

StC = Life of St Christopher, in 3 OE Prose Texts (v. AA).

Swt. = The Student's Dictionary of Anglo-Saxon by H. Sweet, Oxford, 1897.

SwtR = Sweet's Anglo-Saxon Reader, Oxford, 1922.

TC = Diplomatarium Ævi Saxonici, ed. B. Thorpe, London, 1865 (3).

tr. = transitive.

TF = The Capitula of Theodulf, at the end of CHRD.

usu. = usual, usually.

v. = vide, or very.

VH = an art. in A vol. 54 pp. 9–24 on the Homilies in the Vercelli Book; v. also MFH.

v.l. = varia lectio.

VPs = the Vespasian Psalter, in OET (1). [VHy = Hymns at the end of the Psalter.] Glossary also by Conrad Grimm (AF vol. 18), Heidelberg, 1906.

V²Ps = Psalter-Glosses in Cotton Vitellius E 18 (noted in CPs).

W = (I) Wulfstan's Homilies, ed. A. Napier, Berlin, 1883. Glossary by

L. H. Dodd, New York, 1908. (II)
West Saxon.

WA = the poem of the Wanderer, in GR.

WAL = the poem of Waldhere, in GR.

WC = D. Whitelock, Anglo-Saxon Wills, Cambridge, 1930.

WE = Wonders of the East, in 3 OE Prose Texts (v. AA).

Wfg = die Syntax in den Werken Alfreds, by J. E. Wülfing, Bonn, 1894–1901 (copious material, and indexes to words in AO, BH, Bo, CP, AS, PPs, etc.).

WG = West Saxon Gospels (v. G).

WH = the poem of the Whale, in GR.

WID = the poem of Widsith, in GR, or ed. R. W. Chambers, Cambridge, 1912.

WIF = the poem of 'the Wife's Complaint,' in GR.

WNL = Wanley's Catalogue, in vol. 2 of G. Hickes' Thesaurus Antiquae Literaturae Septentrionalis, Oxford, 1705.

WS = West Saxon.

Wt = An Old English Grammar by J. and E. M. Wright, 2nd edition, Oxford, 1914.

WW = Old English Vocabularies, ed. by T. Wright and R. P. Wülker, London, 1884. Cols. 1–54 = Cp; 55–88 = KGL; pp. 89–103 = *Colloq. Monast.* in NED.

Wy = the poem 'Be manna wyrdum,' in GR.

WYN = Wynfrith's Letter, in MLR vol. 18.

ZDA = Zeitschrift für deutsches Altertum, Leipzig and Berlin, 1853 etc.

ZDPh = Zeitschrift für deutsche Philologie, Halle, 1869 etc.

A CONCISE
ANGLO-SAXON DICTIONARY

A

ā I. (āwa, ō) adv. *always, ever, at all, continuously, for ever*, Æ,AO,CP. ā on ēcnisse; ā butan ende *world without end : at any time : in any degree.* [*ON.* ei, ey] **II. f.** = ǣ

ā- (unemphatic verbal prefix); **I.** orig.= *forth, away*, but as a rule only intensive in meaning. **II.**=on- **III.** ym(b)- **IV.**= ā(I.) in pronouns and participles, and gives a sense of indefiniteness. **V.** = ǣ-

āǣ (Bf)=ā

āǣlan=onǣlan; **āǣ ōan**=āīe ōan; **āb**= ōweb

ābacan⁶ *to bake*, ÆH 2·268⁹

ābǣdan *to compel, restrain, ward off : exact, take toll : force out, extract.*

ābǣligan=ābylgan

ābǣran *to disclose, bring to light*, DD 41.

ābǣre (W 274²⁴)=æbǣre

ābǣrnan=onbǣrnan; **abal** (Gen 500) =afol

ābannan⁷ *to summon, convoke, command : announce, proclaim.* ā. ūt *call out, assemble*, Chr. [*' abanne'*]

ābarian *to lay bare, disclose*, Jos,RBL : *strip*, CM.

abbad=abbod

abbod (a, u) m. *' abbot,' BH,Chr*; Æ. [*L.* abbatem]

abboddōm m. *abbatial jurisdiction*, BH.

abbo ōesse f. *abbess*, Chr.

abbodhād m. *abbatial rank, dignity*, LL.

abbodlēast f. *lack of an abbot*, BC 1·155'.

abbodrīce n. *abbey, abbacy, office or jurisdiction of an abbot* (used even of a convent of nuns).

abbot, abbud=abbod

ābēatan⁷ *to beat, strike, break to pieces, make to fall*, Cr. [*' abeat'*]

ābēcēdē f. *ABC, alphabet*, Bf 180, 194.

ābedecian (e ōe-) *to get by asking*, Bo,Chrd.

abedisse=abbodesse; **ābēgan**=ābȳgan

ābelgan³ *to make angry, irritate, offend, Sol*; Æ,AO,CP : *hurt, distress : be angry with.* [*' abelgen'*]

ābeligan=ābylgan

ābēodan² *to order, proclaim, bid, command, direct : summon, call out : announce, relate, declare, present, offer, AO*; Æ. hæl ā. *to wish one good luck, greet, bid farewell to.* [*' abede'*]

ābeofian=ābifian; **ābēogan**=ābūgan

ābeornan³ *to take fire*, PPs 105¹⁶

ābēowan (WW 217⁴⁶)=ābȳwan

āberan⁴ *to bear, carry, Mt : endure, suffer, Bo; Æ,CP : bear (a child),* Æ : *take away, remove : reveal :* (refl.) *restrain oneself : do without*, NC 268. [*' abear'*]

ā-berd, -bered *crafty, cunning*, Lcd,Sc.

āberendlic *bearable*, LL.

ābernan (N)=ābeornan

āberstan³ *to burst out, break out*, Æ,CP : *break away, escape.* ūt ā. *break out.*

ābe ōecian=ābedecian; **ābicgan**=ābycgan

ābīdan¹ *to ' abide,' wait, remain, delay, remain behind, Chr*; AO : *survive : wait for, await, Æ : expect*, Mt 11³.

ābiddan⁵ *to ask for, request, require, demand, pray, pray to, pray for*, Æ : *get by asking, obtain*, Æ,AO,CP : *call out (an army).*

ābies f. *silver fir-tree*, AA 12⁶. [*L.*]

ābifian (eo) *to tremble, quake, shake.*

ābilg ō, ābilh ō=æbylg ō; **ābiran**=āberan

ābirgan (y) *to taste, eat*, Bf.

ābir(g)ing f. *taste* (Bts).

ābisgian (y, -seg-) *to busy, occupy, employ*, CP : *be busy with, engage in, undertake : take up, fill*, GD.

ābisgung (y) f. *occupation : trouble*, CP.

ābītan¹ *to bite in pieces, tear to pieces, devour, gnaw*, Æ,AO : *taste, partake of, consume.* [=on-b.]

ābit(e)rian *to turn bitter*, CP 341²⁴ : *embitter.*

āblācian *to become pale, grow faint : become tarnished*, CP 135².

āblǣcan *to bleach, whiten*, BJPs 50⁹.

āblǣcnes f. *pallor, gloom*, Lcd 1·294 n 6.

āblǣcung f. *pallor*, HGl 518.

āblǣst *inspired, furious : blowing fiercely* (of flame), StC 69⁵.

āblāwan¹ *to blow, blow away, breathe upon* Æ : *puff up, swell*, Lcd 93b. [*' ablow'*]

āblāw-nes, -ung f. *inflation*, Lcd.

āblegned *ulcerated*, Lcd.

āblendan *to blind, put out the eyes of*, Æ, CP : *dazzle, deceive, delude*, Æ. [*' ablend'*]

āblered *bare, uncovered, bald*, ES 8·62. [blere]

āblīcan¹ *to shine, glitter*, Ps.

āblicgan=āblycgan; **āblignes**=æbylgnes

āblindan *to make blind*, Bl 151⁴.

āblindian *to become blind*, Lcd,MH.

āblinnan³ *to cease, leave off, desist*, Æ,AO, CP

āblinnednes (A5·465) =āblinnendnes
āblinnendlīce *indefatigably,* HGL429³².
āblinnendnes f. *cessation,* ÆL23b⁹⁸.
āblisian (Æ)=āblysian
āblissian *to make glad, please,* GD335n.
āblongen=ābolgen, pp. of ābelgan.
āblycgan (i) *to grow pale,* Æ : *make afraid.*
āblynnan=āblinnan
āblysian *to blush,* Ps.
āblysung f. *blushing, shame,* RB133¹¹.
ābodian *to announce, proclaim,* LkR12³.
ābolgennes f. *irritation,* WW230¹⁹. [ābelgan]
āborgian *to be surety for,* LL : (w. æt) *borrow.*
āborian=ābarian
ābracian *to engrave, emboss,* GL.
ābrǣdan I. *to spread out, dilate* : *stretch out,* Æ. II. *bake,* LCD44a.
ābraslian *to crash, crackle,* GD236¹². [brastlian]
ābrēac pret. 3 sg. of ābrūcan.
ābrēat pret. 3 sg. of ābrēotan.
ābrecan⁴ (tr.) *to break, break to pieces, break down, conquer, capture, violate, destroy,* Æ,AO,CP : (intr.) *break out, away, forth,* Æ,AO,CP.
ābrēdan=ābregdan
ābredwian *to lay low, kill,* B2619.
ābrēgan *to alarm, terrify,* BH,GD.
ābregdan³ *to move quickly, draw, unsheath, wrench, pull out,* Mt : *withdraw, take away, draw back, free from,* Æ,AO. ūp ā. *to draw up, raise, lift up,* Æ. : *start up, awake.* ['abraid']
ābrēotan² *to destroy, kill* : *fail, deteriorate.*
ābrēotnes f. *extermination,* OET182.
ābrēoðan² (intr.) *to fail, decay, deteriorate, perish, be destroyed,* Ma; Æ. ābroðen (pp.) *degenerate, reprobate,* ÆGr. (tr. and wk.) *destroy.* [v. 'brethe']
ābrerd-= onbryrd-
ābroðennes f. *baseness, cowardice,* W.
ābrūcan³ *to eat,* A11·1¹⁷.
ābryrd-= onbryrd-
ābrȳtan *to destroy,* CPs36⁹.
ābūfan (= on-) adv. *above,* CHR1090E.
ābūgan² (= on-) *to bow, incline, bend, submit, do reverence,* B,Chr; Æ : *swerve, turn (to or from), deviate,* CP : *withdraw, retire* : *be bent or turned, turn oneself.* ['abow']
ābunden *unimpeded,* WW.
ābūrod *not inhabited,* TC162'.
ābūtan (e³, o³) I. prep. acc. *on, 'about,' around, on the outside, round about,* Chr. II. adv. '*about,' nearly,* Chr. [=onbūtan]
ābycgan *to buy, pay for, requite* : *redeem* : *perform, execute.*

ābyffan *to mutter,* WW447²⁴.
ābȳgan (ē, ē²; =īe²) *to bend, deflect* : *subdue, bring low* : *convert.*
ābȳgendlic v. un-ā
ābyl(i)gan (æ², e²) *to irritate, provoke,* MtR,W.
ābyrg-=ābirg-; ābysg-=ābisg-
ābȳwan (ēo) *to rub off, polish, cleanse, purify.*
ac I. conj. *but* : *but also, moreover, nevertheless, however : because, for* (?). ac gif *unless, except,* BL151'. [*Goth.* ak] II. interrog. particle *why, wherefore, whether* : in direct questions=L. *nonne, numquid.*
āc f. gds. and np. ǣc '*oak*,' Æ,Ct,Lcd;Mdf : *ship of oak,* RUN77 : (w. nap. ācas) name of the rune for a. [*OHG.* eih]
ācǣgan=acīegan
ācǣglod *studded with pegs?* (BTs), AA31².
ācǣnn-=ācenn-; ācǣrran=ācirran
ācalan⁶ *to become frost-bitten,* LCD2b.
acan⁶ *to* '*ache,' suffer pain,* Æ.
acas, acase f. (NG)=æcs
ācbēam m. *oak-tree.* accent m. *accent.* [L.]
ācbearo m. *oak-grove,* KC5·232'.
accutian?=ācunnian
āccynn n. *a kind of oak,* WW430⁶.
ācdrenc m. *oak drink, drink made from acorns?* WW.
ace=ece
ācealdian *to become cold,* CP. ['acold']
ācēapian *to buy off, buy out,* Ct,LL.
ācēlan *to cool off, still, quiet,* Met. ['akele']
ācelma=ǣcelma; ācen=æcen
ācennan *to bring forth, produce, renew,* Æ,Bo,RG : *attribute to.* ['akenne(d)']
ācennedlic '*genuinus,' native,* CHRD,RPs.
ācennednes (WG; Æ), -cennes (NG; AO,CP) f. *birth.* [*'akenn(ed)nes'*]
ācennend m. *parent,* DR197¹¹.
ācennicge f. *mother,* DR.
ācenning f. *birth,* BK16.
ācēocian (tr.) *to choke* : (intr.) *burn out.*
ācēocung f. *rumination,* WW179².
āceorfan³ *to cut off, hew down,* AO,CP. onweg ā. *to cut away.* of ā. *to cut off,* AO.
ācēosan² *to choose,* AO,CP.
acer=æcer; ācerr-=ācirr-
ācīgan (=īe) *to call, summon.*
ācirran (æ, e, y; =ie) (tr.) *to turn, turn away or aside* : (intr.) *turn oneself, go, return.*
-ācirrednes v. onweg-ā.
ācl=ācol; āclǣc=āglǣc
āclǣnsian *to cleanse, purify,* Æ.
āclēaf n. *oak leaf,* LCD.
āclēofan² *to cleave,* EC351¹⁰.
ācleopian *to call out,* WW378⁵.
+āclian† *to frighten, excite.* [ācol]

āclungen *contracted*, WW 239³⁷. [clingan]
ācmelu n. *acorn meal*, LCD.
ācmistel f. *mistletoe*, LCD. ācn-= ēacn-
ācnāwan¹ *to know, recognise, understand*.
ācnyssan *to drive out, expel*, SPs 35¹³.
ācofrian *to recover, Lcd.* ['*acover*']
ācol† *affrighted, dismayed*.
ācōlian *to grow cold*, CP.
ācolitus m. *acolyte*, LL. [*L.*]
ācolmōd† *fearful minded, timid*
+ācolmōdian *to alarm, sadden*, WW 209¹⁶.
ācordian *to make terms, reconcile*, CHR 1120.
ācorenlic *eligible, worthy of choice*, CP 409³⁶.
ācostnian *to try, test, prove*, CM,WW.
ācræftan *to think out, devise*, AO 46²⁹.
ācrammian *to cram*, WW 236¹⁰.
ācrēopian *to creep, crawl*, ExC 16²⁰.
ācrimman³ (y) *to cram, stuff*, WW.
ācrind f. *oak-bark*, LCD.
ācrummen pp. of ācrimman.
acs = æx; ācs-= āsc-; acse = asce
ācstybb m. *oak-stump*, KC (v. MLR 17).
āctān m. *oak-twig*, LCD.
āctrēo n. *oak-tree*, WIF 28, 36.
ācucian (Æ) = ācwician
ācul = ācol; ācum, ācuma (Æ) = ācumba
ācuman⁴ *to come, come forth (from)*, Æ :
bear, bring : endure, withstand, Æ : *get to
or from, reach, Gen.* ['*acome*']
ācum-ba m., -be fn. '*oakum*,' *hards, tow,
Lcd,OEG,WW : ashes of oakum : parings,
clippings.* [cemban]
ācumendlic *tolerable*, Æ : *possible*.
ācumendlicnes f. *possibility*, OEG 3393.
ācunnan (NG) = oncunnan
ācunnian *to try, test, prove : experience*, CP.
ācunnung f. *experience, trial*, GD.
ācusan *to accuse*, MtL 12¹⁰. [*L.*]
ācwacian *to tremble*, GD,PPs.
ācwæncan = ācwencan
ācweccan (tr.) *to move, swing, shake, vibrate,
Ma;* Æ : (intr.) *quiver*, Æ. ['*aquetch*']
ācwelan⁴ *to die, perish*, Æ,AO,CP.
ācwellan *to kill, destroy*, JnL; Æ,AO,CP.
['*aquell*']
ācwellednes (eæ²) f. *slaughter*, EPs 43²².
ācwencan (æ²) *to quench, extinguish, Mt;*
AO. ['*aquench*']
ācweorna m. *squirrel, Gl.* ['*aquerne*']
ācweorran³ *to guzzle, gorge*, EPs 77⁶⁵.
ācwern = ācweorna
ācwerren = ācworren pp. of ācweorran.
ācweðan⁵ *to say, speak out, declare, utter,
express, answer, Gen : reject, banish*, GEN
304. ['*aqueath*']
ācwician (tr.) *to quicken, vivify, Ps :* (intr.)
revive, BH. ['*aquick*']
acwīnan¹ *to dwindle away, disappear, go
out (of fire)*, BH,LPs.

ācwincan³ *to vanish, be extinguished or
eclipsed*, Æ.
ācworren pp. of ācweorran.
ā-cwucian, -cwycian = ācwician
ācwudu m. *an oak wood*, KC 6·218′.
ācwylman (= ie) *to kill, slay*.
ācwylmian (= ie) *to be tormented*, W 220⁵.
ācwyncan = ācwincan
ācynned = ācenned pp. of ācennan.
ācyrr-= ācirr-
ācȳðan *to show, proclaim, reveal, announce,
confirm, prove*.
ād mn. *heap, funeral pile, pyre*, AO : *fire,
flame.* [*OHG.* cit]
ādǣlan *to divide, separate*, BL,BO.
ādēadian *to fail, decay, mortify, become
torpid or callous*, Æ.
ādēafian *to become deaf*, WW 179²⁵.
ādēafung f. *deafening, making deaf, Lcd.*
[v. '*adeave*']
ādel I. = ādl. II. = ādela
ādela m. *mud, dirt, filthy place*, Æ. ['*addle*']
ādelfan³ *to delve, dig, excavate*, Æ,AO,CP.
ādeliht *filthy*, WW.
ādelsēað m. *sewer, sink*, Æ.
ādēman *to judge, try, deprive of or exclude
from by a legal decision : try, afflict*.
ādeorcian *to become dull, obscure, tarnished,
CP : grow dark*, W.
āderian *to hurt*, GD 219¹⁹.
adesa m., adese f. '*adze*,' *hatchet, BH,W.*
ādexe = āðexe
ād-faru f. ds. -fære *way or path to the funeral
pile*, B 3010.
ādfīni n. *limit? ash-heap of a beacon?*
EC 354⁵.
ādfȳr n. *sacrificial fire*, Ex 398.
+ādgian = +ēadgian
ādīdan (GENC 7²², 9¹¹) = ādȳdan
-ādihtian v. fore-ā.
ā-dīlegian, -dīl(i)gian (ȳ) *to destroy, blot out,
annihilate, devastate*, CP.
ādimmian *to become dim or dull, to darken,
obscure, Bo;* CP. [v. '*dim*']
ādl fn., ādle f. *disease, infirmity, sickness,*
AO,CP.
ādlēg m. *flame of the funeral pile*, PH 222.
± ādlian *to be diseased or ill, languish*, Æ :
cause disease, DR : *become ill*, ANS
120·297.
ādlig *sick, diseased*, Æ.
ādliga m. *sick person*. ādliht = ādeliht
ādloma m. *one crippled by fire*, GU 884.
[lama?]
ādlsēoc *in bad health : sick of a contagious
disease?* ES 39·322.
ādl-ōracu f. gs. -ðrace *force of disease*,
GU 935.
ādlung f. *illness*, ÆH 1·122³¹.

ādlwērig *weary from illness*, Gu981.
ādōn (for conj. v. dōn) *to take away, send away* : *cast out, expel, destroy* : (w. preps. tō, on, fram, etc.) *put, place, take, remove, set free*, AO,CP.
adosa = adesa; ādrǣdan = ondrǣdan
ādrǣfan (ē) *to drive away, shut out, expel, NED*; AO,CP. ['adrefe']
ādrǣnct = ādrenced pp. of ādrencan.
ādragan[6] *to draw (sword)*, HL15[356].
ādrēfan = ādrǣfan
adreminte f. *feverfew* (BT).
ādrencan *to submerge, immerse, drown*, Ps; AO. ['adrench']
ādrēogan[2] *to act, do, practise, Æ* : *bear, suffer, endure, An*; CP : *pass time, live, Æ.* ['adree']
ādrēogendlic 'agendus,' 'gerendus,' DHy, RBL.
ādrēohan = ādrēogan
ādrēopan[2] *to drip, drop,* An.
ādrēosan[2] *to fall to pieces, decline, vanish, fail.*
ādrīfan[1] (īe) *to drive, drive away, drive out, pursue, follow up, LL*; Æ,AO,CP : *stake out (a ford)* : *chase (metal), Æ.* ['adrive']
ādrīgan = ādrȳgan
ādrincan[3] *be drowned, extinguished, BH*; AO. ['adrink']
ādrūgian, ādrūwian (Æ,Mt) *to dry up.* ['adroughe']
ādrȳgan (ī) *to dry up* : *dry, wipe dry,* CP.
ādrysnan *to extinguish, repress,* NG.
adsa = adesa; adulsēað = adelsēað
ādumbian *to become dumb, keep silence, Mk*; Æ. [v. 'dumb' vb.]
a-dūn, -dūna, -dūne adv. *down, downward, Æ.* [= ofdūne]
adūne(ā)stīgan *to descend,* CPs.
adūnfeallan *to fall down*, EPs144[14].
adūnweard adv. *downwards, ChrL.* ['a-downward']
ādūstrigan = andūstrian
ādwǣscan (ē) *to put out, quench, extinguish, blot out, destroy, AO* : *suppress,* Æ,CP.
ā-dwellan *to wander, stray,* Æ,LL.
ādwellan, pret. 3 sg. -dwealde *to seduce, lead astray* : *hinder,* Æ.
ādwēscan = ādwǣscan
ādwīnan[1] *to dwindle or waste away,* Bf74[11].
ādȳdan (ī;= īe) *to destroy, mortify, kill,* Æ. ['adeaden']
ādȳfan (= īe) *to overpower with sound,* Sol152[13].
ādylf = ādealf pret. of ādelfan.
ādȳlgian, ādȳlegian = ādīlegian
ādymman = ādimmian
ādysgian *to make foolish,* W185[12].
ǣ- accented verbal prefix, = (1) *without*; (2) ā-.

ǣ I. f. also ǣw f. (and m. or n.? in NG) *law (divine or human), custom, covenant,* AO, CP; WG,NG. butan ǣ *outlaw* : (esp. in pl.) *rite, ceremony : faith, religion, unrihte ǣ false religion.* Crīstes ǣ *gospel : scriptures, revelation : marriage, Æ* : (*lawful*) *wife.* For some comps. v. ǣw-. ['æ']
II. = ēa I. III. interj. *oh! alas!*
ǣa I. = ēa I. II. gp. of ǣ; ǣal- = eal-
ǣalā interj. = ēalā; ǣar = ēar-
āeargian *to become remiss,* AO212[20].
ǣbǣre (ā[1], ē[1]) *manifest, notorious, public, open, evident, clear, LL.* ['eber']
ǣebbian *to ebb away, recede,* Chr.
ǣbbung (= ebb-) f. 'ebbing.' sǣ æ. *gulf, bay,* WW154.
ǣbebod n. *injunction of the law, command,* PPs118[102].
ǣbēc fp. *books of the law,* WW439[15].
ǣbēre = ǣbǣre; ǣbesn = ǣfesn
ǣbilg-, -bili(g)- = ǣbylg-; ǣblǣc- = āblǣc-
ǣblǣce *lustreless, pale, pallid,* Æ.
ǣbod m. *business,* WW114[36] : *statute,* WW114[35].
ǣboda m. *messenger, preacher,* Gu909
ǣbrǣce, -breca = ǣwbrǣce, -breca
ǣbrecð f. *sacrilege,* LPs.
ǣbrucol *sacrilegious,* GPH402.
æbs f? *fir-tree, Æ.* [*L.* abies]
ǣbylg n. = ǣbylgð
ǣbylga m. *anger,* LPs77[49].
±ǣbyl-gan, -i(g)an *to exasperate, offend,* Æ.
ǣbylgnes (ā[1]) f. *anger, offence, Æ.*
ǣbylgð, -bylgðu (ā[1]) f. *anger,* AO.
ǣbylig-=ǣbylig-; ǣ-bylð, -bylygð=ǣbylgð
ǣc I. f. = āc; II. (N) = ēac
ǣcambe f. = ācumbe
ǣcan = īecan; æccyrn = æcern
æce, ǣce = ece, ēce; æced = eced
ǣcelan = ācēlan
æcelma m. *chilblain,* OEG,WW.
æcelmehte (ēcil-) *having chilblains,* OEG 1523.
ǣcen I. *a wood of oaks.* II. *oaken,* WW 270[14]. III. = ēacen pp. of ēacan.
æcer nap. æcras m. *field, cultivated land, Mt*; AO,CP; Mdf : *a certain quantity of land, strip of plough-land (GBG), 'acre,' Æ*; v. LL2·267 : *crop.*
æcerceorl m. *rustic, ploughman, armer,* Chrd,WW.
æceren = æcern
æcerhege m. *hedge of a field,* KC3·33[2].
æcermǣlum *by acres,* KC6·98[5].
æcermann m. *farmer,* WW. ['acreman']
æcern (i[2]) n. *nut, mast of trees, Æ* : 'acorn,' WW.
æcernspranca m. *oak sapling?* ÆGr69[15].

æcersǽd n. *seed enough for an acre?* CHR 1124.

æcertēoðung f. *tithe of the produce of the soil*, W310²⁴.

æcertȳning f. *fencing*, EC377⁹.

æcerweorc n. *field-work*, GPH391.

æces = æx

æcest, æceð pres. 2 and 3 sg. of acan.

ǽcilma = ǽcelma; æcirn = æcern

ǽclǽca = āglǽca; ǽclēaw = ǽglēaw

æcnōsle *degenerate, not noble*, WW.

+ǽcnōsliende *degenerating*, WW218¹².

ǽcræft† m. *knowledge of law or ordinances, religion*.

ǽcræftig *learned in the law*, DA; as sb. = *lawyer, scribe, Pharisee*, MtL.

æcras v. æcer; æcren = æcern

æcs f. *'axe,' pickaxe, hatchet*, CP; *Mt* (æx).

æcst, æcð pres. 2 and 3 sg. of acan.

ǽcumba = ācumba; æcur = æcer

ǽcyrf m. *(wood-)choppings*, BH224¹⁵.

æd (NG) = æt; æd- = ed-

ǽdderseax (WW) = ǽdreseax

ǽddre, ǽdr = ǽdre

ǽdre I. f. *artery, vein, pulse, nerve, sinew*, AO : pl. *veins*, B : *kidneys*, Ps73²¹ : *runlet of water, fountain, spring, stream*. ['*eddre*'] II. adv. *at once, directly, instantly, quickly* : (†) *fully, entirely*. [*OS.* ādro]

ǽdreseax (daer) n. *lancet*, WW410¹⁰.

ǽdrīfan = ādrīfan; ǽdwist = edwist

æfæst = æfest; ǽfǽst = æwfæst

æfdǽll -dell (NG) = ofdǽle

æfdȳne m. *declivity*, GL.

ōfelle *without skin, peeled*, WW190³¹

æfen = efen

ǽfen (ē) nm. *'even,' evening, eventide*, B, *MkL,Gu* (ēfn), *RB* : *eve*, CHR. tō ǽfenes *till evening*.

ǽfencollatio *the 'collatio' read before compline*, CHRD60³⁵.

ǽfendrēam m. *even-song*, RB.

ǽfengebed n. *evening service*, WW129³⁴.

ǽfengereord n. *evening meal, supper* (often used in pl. of one meal).

ǽfengereordian *to sup, give supper to*, CM1030.

ǽfengereordung f. *supper*, NC269.

ǽfengeweorc n. *evening work*, LCD70b.

ǽfengi(e)fl n. *evening repast, supper*, AO,CP.

ǽfen-glōm (*Gu*), -glōma (BF) m., -glōmung (omm-, BH) f. *gloaming, twilight*. [v. '*even*']

ǽfengrom *fierce at eve*, B2074.

æfenian = æfnian

ǽfenlāc n. *evening sacrifice, evening prayer*, PPs140³.

ǽfenlǽcan *to grow towards evening*, Lk24²⁹.

ǽfenlēoht n. *evening light*, B403. [v. '*even*']

ǽfenlēoð† n. *evening song*.

ǽfenlic *of the evening*; adv. -līce.

ǽfenlof n. *lauds (service)*, CM1035.

ǽfenmete m. *supper*, *MtR*; WW. [v. '*even*']

ǽfenoffrung f. *evening sacrifice*, CHRD30²³.

ǽfenrǽding f. *reading (during the evening meal at a monastery), 'collatio,'* CM.

ǽfenrepsung f. *nightfall*, Æ.

ǽfen-rest, -ræst† f. *evening rest*, B.

ǽfensang m. *'evensong,'* Æ,RB.

ǽfensceop m. *evening singer, bard*, RD9⁵. [scop]

ǽfenscīma m. *evening splendour*, GEN2448.

ǽfensprǽc f. *evening talk*, B759.

ǽfensteorra m. *the evening star, Hesperus*, Bo; Æ. ['*evenstar*']

ǽfen-tīd (*Mk*) f., -tima (*GD*) m. *eventide*, Æ. [v. '*even*']

ǽfenðēnung f. *evening service*, TF : *evening repast, supper*, RBL.

ǽfenðēowdōm m. *evening service or office*, WW129³⁴.

ǽfenung = ǽfnung; ǽfer = ǽfre

æferðe f. *name of a plant*, LCD.

æfes- = efes-

æfesa? m., æfese (m.) f. = æfesn

ǽfesian *to shear*, ÆGR157¹⁶.

æfesn, æfesen f. *relish, dainty, special pasturage, pannage; the charge for special pasturage*, LL.

æfesne? = æpsen?

æfest mf. *envy, hatred, malice, spite*, CP; *El,Ps* : *zeal, rivalry*, CHRD. ['*evest*']

ǽfest = æwfæst

æfestful *full of envy*, APT.

±æfest-ian, -igian *to be or become envious*.

æfestig *envious*, CP : *zealous*, CP.

æfestlīce = ofostlīce

æfgǽlō f. *superstition*, OEG.

æfgerēfa (-groefa) '*exactor*,' LkL12⁵⁸.

æfgrynde n. *abyss*, PPs35⁶.

æfhynde = ofhende

æflan (-an?) *to be in a miserable condition*, CR1357 (or æfnan? Gollancz).

æflsc (EC291) = efesc

æflāst m. *a wandering from the way?* Ex473.

±æfnan (e) *to carry out, do, perform, fulfil : cause : endure, suffer* : (+) *hold, sustain*.

æfne = efne

±æfnian *to grow towards evening*, Æ.

æfnung f. *'evening,' sunset*, Æ.

ǽfre adv. *'ever,' at any time*, Sat,Mt : *always, constantly, perpetually*, Æ,Cr,RB, Sat; CP : *henceforth* : ne ǽ.; ǽ. ne (=nǽfre) *never*; ǽ. tō aldre *for ever*. ǽ. ǽlc, W,Chr. ǽ. ǽnig *any at all*, KC.

æfreda m. *what is taken or separated from*, OEG (Napier). [æf; *hreda (hreddan)] : *tow, oakum* (BTs).

æfremmende *pious, religious*, JUL648.

æfse I. = efes; II. = æbs

æfsecgan *to confute*, ES42¹⁶³.

æfst=æfest

æfsweorc n. *pasturage*, WW410¹⁹ (=*æfes-weorc).

æft=eft

æftan adv. *from behind, behind, in the rear*, BR. ['*aft*']

æftanweard adj. *behind, in the rear, following*, RD63⁵.

æftemest adj. *last, hindmost*, Æ,AO.

æfter I. prep. (w. d., i. and—chiefly N.—a.) (local and temporal) '*after*', *along, behind*, B,Chr,G : *through, throughout, during* : (causal) *following, in consequence of, according to, for the purpose of, Æ* : (object) *after, about, in pursuit of, for*, B. II. adv. *after, then, afterwards, thereafter* : *thereupon, later, back* (=*in return*). æ. ðon, ðæm, ðisum; æ. ðæm (ðon, ðan) ðe; *afterwards, thereafter*.

æftera=æfterra

æfterǣ f. *the book Deuteronomy*, ÆT333 (æftre-).

æfterboren adj. '*afterborn*,' *posthumous*, ÆGR.

æftercnēoreso *posterity*, DR61⁹.

æftercweðan⁵ *to speak after, repeat*: *renounce, abjure*, CHR1094. æftercweðendra lof *praise from posterity*.

æftercyning m. *later king*, BH140B²⁴.

æfterealu n. *small beer*, WW129⁴.

æfterfill-, æfterfilig- = æfterfylg-

æfterfolgere m. *follower*, AO142²³.

æfter-folgian, -fylgan (AO) *to follow after, succeed, pursue*.

æfterfylgednes f. *sequel*, ÆL23b³⁶⁵.

æfterfylgend m. *follower, successor*, AO. adv. -līce *in succession*.

æfterfylgendnes f. *succession*, DHy11⁴.

æfterfylgung (eft-, e³) f. *pursuit*, KGL371.

æfterfylig- = æfterfylg-

æfter-genga, -gengea m. *follower, successor* : *descendant*, Æ.

æftergengel m. *successor*, KC5·30.

æftergengnes f. *succession, Æ* : *posterity* : *inferiority*.

æftergyld n. *further payment*, LL.

æfterhǣða m. *autumn drought*, AO102⁷.

æfterhyrigan *to imitate*, BH.

æfterlēan n. *reward, recompense, restitution, retribution*, GEN76.

æfterlic *second*, WW505¹⁹.

æfterra (comp.) *second, following, next, latter, lower*, CP.

æfter-rāp (Æ) -rǣpe m. *crupper*.

æfterrōwan⁷ *to row after*, ES41³²⁵.

æfterryne m. '*occursus*,' CPs18⁷.

æftersang m. (*after-song*), *matins*, CM.

æftersingallic (=-sanglic) *of matins*, CM 476.

æftersingend m. *succentor*, WW129²³.

æftersōna *soon, afterwards, again*, NG.

æftersprǣc f. *after-claim*, LL398,7.

æftersprecan⁵ *to claim*, LL226,9⁴.

æfterspyrian *to track out, search, inquire into, examine*, CP.

æfterweard adj. *after, following, further, behind, in the rear, later, Æ*. on æfterweard-an, -um *at the end*.

æfterweardnes f. *posterity*, WW464¹⁸.

æfterwriten *written afterwards*, LCD69b.

æfter-yld, -yldo f. †*advanced age, old age* : *after age, later time*, BH. [ield(o)]

æfteweard=æfterweard

æftewearde adv. *behind*, Æ(Ex33²³).

æftra=æfterra

æftresta superl. *last*.

æftum adv. *after*, MtR24²¹.

æftyr=æfter

æfðanc, æfðanca (o, u) m. *insult, offence* : *grudge, displeasure, anger*.

æf-weard (CP), -ward (BH) *absent*.

æfweardnes f. *absence*, Bo,GD.

æfwela f. *decrease of wealth*, LCD3·170¹³.

æfwendla (WW223¹) = æfwyrdla

æfwyrdelsa (e²) m. *injury, damage, loss*.

æfwyrdla, m. *injury, damage, loss* : *fine for injury or loss*.

æfwyrð(u)? f. *degradation, disgrace*, RBL.

æfyllende *fulfilling the law, pious*, CR 704.

æfyn=æfen

æfyrmða fp. *sweepings, rubbish*, ÆGR. [feormian]

æg n. (nap. ǣgru) '*egg*,' Ct,G,Lcd,Lk,Met.

ǣg=īeg; ǣgan=āgan

ǣge=ege; ǣgen=āgen

ǣgera (K) dp. of ǣg.

ǣgerfelma f. *egg-skin*, LCD20b.

ǣgergelu n. *yolk of egg*, GL. [ǣg, geolu]

ǣgesetnes f. *law-giving, the (Old) Testament*, BF136⁵.

ǣgflota m. *seafarer, sailor*, AN258. [īeg]

ǣggemang n. *egg-mixture*, WW.

ǣg-hwā mf., -hwæt n. pron. *each one, every one, everything, who or whatever*. ǣghwǣt neut. *anything*.

ǣghwǣr *everywhere, in every direction*, Mk; Æ : *in every case, in every respect* : *anywhere*. ['*aywhere*']

ǣghwǣs (gs. of ǣghwā) *altogether, in every way, entirely, wholly, throughout, in general*.

ǣghwæt v. ǣghwā.

æghwæðer (ægðer, āðer). **I.** pron. adv. *every one, 'either,' both,* AO,KC,Mt (gð) : *each,* An. **II.** conj. æghwæðer (ge)...ge; ægðer...and *both...and; as well...as.*

æg-hwanan, -hwanon(e), -hwannon, -hwanum *from all parts, everywhere, on every side, in every way.*

æg-hwār, -hwēr = æghwær

æghwelc = æghwilc

æghweðer = æghwæðer

æghwider *on every side, in all directions* : *in any direction, anywhere.*

æghwilc adj. *each, every, whosoever, whatsoever, all, every one,* Bo,Met : *any.* ǣ. ānra *each.* ǣ. ōðer *each other,* Ma. æghwilces *in every way.* [v. '*each*']

æg-hwonan, -hwonon (CP), -hwonene = æghwanan

æghwyder = æghwider; æghwylc = æghwilc

ægift f. (m? n?) *restitution, repayment.*

ægilde (y²) adv. *receiving no 'wergild' as compensation,* LL.

ægilt = ægylt; æglæc = āglæc

æglēaw *learned in the law,* An,Lk.

æglēca = āglēca

æglīm m. *white of egg,* WW 164¹². [līm]

ægmang (WW 4²⁹) = æggemang

ægmore f. *root of the eye, socket?* LCD 3·98⁵. [ēage]

ægnan sb. pl. *awns, sweepings, chaff,* GL. [v. egenu]

ægnes = āgnes, v. āgen; ægnian = āgnian

ægru v. æg; ægsa = egesa

ægscill (y) f. *eggshell,* LCD.

ægðer = æghwæðer

ægweard f. *watch on the shore,* B241. [īeg]

ægwern = æghwær

ægwyrt f *dandelion,* LCD 158b.

ægylde = ægilde

ægylt (i²) m. *sin, offence,* WW. [æw, gylt]

ægȳpe (= īe²?) *without skill or cunning* (BTs),PPs 106¹⁰. [gēap]

æhher (MkR 4²⁸) = ēar

æhīw n. *pallor,* OEG 4897.

æhīwe *pallid* : *deformed,* OEG 2⁴⁹⁸.

æhīwnes f. *pallor,* LCD 1·294³.

æhlȳp m. *breach of the peace, assault,* LL. [cp. æthlȳp]

æht = eaht

æht **I.** f. (rare in sg.) *possessions, goods, lands, wealth, cattle,* Mk; AO : *serf* : *ownership, control.* [āgan : '*aught*' sb.] **II.** = ōht

āēhtan *to persecute,* LkL 21¹².

æhtboren *born in bondage,* RB 138²⁰.

æhte = āhte pret. sg. of āgan.

æhteland n. *territory,* BH 358¹⁴.

æhtemann m. *farmer,* Æ : *serf,* LL.

æhteswān m. *swineherd who was a chattel on an estate,* LL 449,7.

æhtgesteald n. *possession,* JUL 115.

æhtgestrēon n. *possessions,* PH 506.

æhtgeweald† mn. *power, control.*

æhtian = eahtian

+æhtle f. *esteem,* B 369.

æhtowe (LkR 2²¹) = eahta

æhtspēd f. *wealth, riches,* LPs 103²⁴.

æhtspēdig *rich,* BL,JUL.

æhtwela† m. *wealth, riches.*

æhtwelig *wealthy, rich,* JUL 18.

ǣ-hwænne, -hwǣr, -hwār = āhwænne, āhwǣr

æhwyrfan = āhwierfan

æhx = æcs; ælg = æg

æl- prefix = **I.** eal(l)-; **II.** el(e)-

æl m. *piercer, 'awl,'* Æ.

æl m. '*eel,*' Lcd,WW ; Mdf.

ælā = ēalā

ælædend m. *legislator,* SPs 9²¹.

ælærend m. *teacher of (God's) law,* EL 506.

ælæte **I.** n. *desert place.* **II.** *desert,* W 47²¹ : *empty,* ERHy 9⁵³. **III.** f. *divorced woman,* LL.

ælæten **I.** = ālæten pp. of ālætan. **II.** = ælæte II.

ælagol *law-giving,* GPH 397³⁶³.

±ælan *to kindle, light, set on fire, burn,* Æ,CP.

ælārēow (-lārua) m. *teacher of the law, Pharisee,* NG.

ælātēow m. *legislator,* CJPs 9²¹.

ælað = ealað; ælbeorht = eallbeorht

ælbitu (GL) = ilfetu

ælc, elc, ealc, ylc (VPs); v. '*EACH*.*' **I.** (pron. subst.) *any, all, every, each (one),* Æ,AO,CP. ælc...ōðrum *the one...the other.* **II.** (adj. pron.) *each,* Lcd : *any,* CP.

ælceald *altogether cold, very cold,* MET 24¹⁹.

ælcor, ælcra = elcor, elcra

ælcræftig *almighty, all-powerful,* MET 20³⁸.

ælcuht (AO), ælcwuht n. *everything.*

æld = æled; æld- = ield-

ældewuta (NG) = ealdwita

ælecung = ōleccung

æled† m. gs. ældes *fire, firebrand.* ǣ. weccan *to kindle a fire,* WH 21. [ON. eldr]

æledfȳr n. *flame of fire,* PH 366?

æledlēoma m. *fire-brand,* B 3125.

ælednes = ālætnes

ælegrædig *greedy,* ÆL 18²¹³. [eall-]

ælegrēne = eallgrēne

ælelendisc = elelendisc

ælemidde f. *exact middle,* Æ.

ælenge **I.** *lengthy, tedious, vexatious.* C.P. ['*elenge*'] **II.** (i²) *weariness.* MET 151⁶.

ælengnes f. *tediousness,* Sc,WW.

ælepe? *'origanum,' wild marjoram,* WW 299¹⁹. [ælene? BTs]

ælepūte f. *'eel-pout,' burbot,* WW.

æleð pres. 3 sg. of alan; ǣleð, ǣlð = ǣled

ælewealdend = eallwealdend

ælf mf. (pl. ielfe, ylfe) *'elf,' sprite, fairy, goblin, incubus, B,Lcd.*

ælfādl f. *nightmare,* LCD 123b.

ælfæle = ealfelo

æl-faru, -fær f. *whole army, host,* Ex 66.

ælfcynn n. *elfin race,* LCD 123a.

ælfen (c¹) f. *nymph, spirit,* WW 352¹⁰.

ælfer = ælfaru

ǣl-flsc, -fix m. *eel,* TC 242¹¹.

ælfltu = ilfetu

æl-fremed, -fremd, (el-) *strange, foreign,* Æ : (+) *estranged,* LPs 57⁴ : (w. fram) *free, separated from,* Æ.

ælfremedung f. *'alienatio,'* RHy 5¹⁴.

ælf-scīene (ī²ȳ²)† *bright as an elf or fairy, beautiful, radiant.*

ælfsiden f. *elvish influencé, nightmare,* LCD 120b.

ælfsogoða m. *hiccough (thought to have been caused by elves),* LCD 124b.

ælfðēodlīce = elðēodiglīce

ælfðone f. *nightshade,* LCD 123b.

ælfylce (= el-) n. *strange land,* EL 36 : *oreign band, enemy,* B 2371

ǣlhyd f. *eel receptacle? eel-skin?* (BTs), LL 455,17

ǣllc *of the law, legal, lawful,* Æ. adv. -līce.

ǣlīf (ā) n. *eternal life,* MFH 150.

ælifn f. *sustenance,* GL? (v. ES 42·166)

ǣling f. *burning, Æ : ardour,* MET.

ǣling- = ǣleng-; æll- = æl-, eal(l)-, el(l)-

ælmes = ælmesse

ælmesæcer m. *ground of which the yield was given as alms, first-fruits,* A 11·3⁶⁹.

ælmesbæð n. *gratuitous bath,* W 171².

ælmesdǣd f. *almsdeed,* Æ.

ælmesdōnd *alms-giver,* CHRD 93²⁸.

ælmesfeoh n. *alms : Peter's pence, Rome-scot,* LL. ['almsfee']

ælmesfull *charitable,* CHR,LL.

ælmesgedāl n. *distribution of alms,* LL,W.

ælmesgeorn *charitable,* Æ.

ælmesgifa (y³) m. *giver of alms,* W 72⁴.

ælmesgifu f. *alms, charity,* W 159²⁰.

ælmeshand *almsgiving, charitableness,* CHRD 12¹⁹.

ælmeshlāf (e¹) m. *dole of bread,* TC 474'.

ælmeslāc *giving of alms,* NC 269.

ælmeslēoht n. *a light in church provided at the expense of a pious layman,* LL (288¹).

ælmeslic *charitable : depending on alms, poor.* -līce, adv. *charitably,* OET (Ct).

ælmeslond (a¹) m. *land granted in frankal-moigne,* (BT)

ælmesmann m. *'almsman,' bedesman, beggar,* Lcd; Æ.

ælmespening m. *alms-penny,* KC (v. MLR 17).

ælmesriht n. *right of receiving alms,* W.

ælmesse f. *'alms,' almsgiving, Da,Mt;* Æ, CP. [*L.* eleēmosyna]

ælmessylen (e³) f. *almsgiving,* GD,LL.

ælmestlīce = ælmeslīce

ælmesweorc n. *almsdeed,* BL 25¹⁷.

ælmidde = ælemidde; ælmiehtig = ælmihtig

œlmihtig (ea², e²) adj. *'almighty,' Ps,TC;* AO,CP : m. *the Almighty, B.*

ælmihtignes f. *omnipotence,* AS 59¹⁹.

ælmyrca m. *one entirely black, Ethiopian,* AN 432.

ælmysse = ælmesse

ǣlnet n. *eel net,* BH 304¹¹.

ǣlpig (CHR 1085) = ānlipig

ælren adj. *of an alder tree,* KC 3·316'. ['aldern']

ælreord = elreord

ælsyndrig *separately,* LkR 2³.

æltǣwe (ēo, ō) *complete, entire, perfect, healthy, sound, true,* Æ,AO,CP : *noted,* Æ. [*Goth.* tēwa] -līce adv.

ælðēod, (ælðīed) = elðēod

æl-walda, -wealda = ealwealda

ælwiht† m. *strange creature, monster* [=*elwiht] : (in pl.) = eallwihta.

æmbern = embren

ǣmelle *insipid,* WW 429³⁰.

ǣmelnes f. *slackness, sloth, Æ : weariness, disgust,* WW.

ǣmen, ǣmenne (AO) *uninhabited, desolate, desert.*

ǣmend = ǣmynd

ǣmenne *solitude,* AS 4¹ (v. Wfg 3).

ǣmerge f. *embers, ashes, dust,* Lcd; Æ. ['ember']

ǣmet- = ǣmett-

ǣmetbed n. *ant-hill,* LCD 121b.

ǣmethwīl (ā¹) f. *leisure,* Æ.

ǣmethyll m. *ant-hill,* CP 191²⁵.

ǣmetian = ǣmtian

ǣmetta m. *leisure, rest,* CP. [mōt]

ǣmette f. *'emmet,' ant,* WW; Æ.

ǣmettig (CP), -m(e)tig (Æ) *'empty,' vacant, Æ,Bl : unoccupied, without employment, Æ : unmarried,* CP.

ǣmettigian = ǣmtian

æmn- = emn-, efen-

ǣmōd (ā) *dismayed, disheartened,* Æ,AO.

ǣmt- = ǣmett-

±ǣmtian *to 'empty,' Æ : to be at leisure, have time for,* Æ,CP.

ǣmtignes f. *emptiness,* GD 35¹⁷.

ǣmūða m. *'cæcum intestinum,'* WW 160¹¹.

ǣmynd (e²) f. *jealousy,* LCD 1·384'.

æmyrce *excellent,* WW 393³⁸.

æmyrie = æmerge; **æmytte** = æmette

æn = ān; +æn- = +en-
+**ænan** (ē)? *to unite oneself to, join with,*
AS 39⁶.

ænbrece = unbrece; **ænd-** = end-

æne (āne) *once, at some time,* Æ,B : *at any
time* : *at once.* ['*ene*']

æned = ened

ænes adv. *once,* GD,LL

ænetre = ānwintre

ænett, ænetnes = ānet; **ænga** = ānga

ængancundes *in a unique way?* (BTs),
Lcd 162b.

ænge, ængel = enge, engel

Ænglisc = Englisc; **ænid** = ened

ænig adj. pron. and sb. '*any,*' *any one,*
Mk,Jn. ænige ðinga *somehow, anyhow.*
adv. *only,* Ps,Rd (v. BTac). [ān]

ænigge = āneage

ænigmon *any one, some one,* NG.

æniht = āwuht; **æninga** = ānunga

ænlænan = onlænan; **ænlefan** = endlufon

ænlēp- = ānlep-

ænlic *one,* '*only,*' *singular, solitary, Ps* :
*unique, glorious, noble, splendid, excellent,
Bo;* Æ,AO. adv. -līce, *WW.*

ænlīpig (Æ) = ānlīpig

ænne (AO,CP) v. ān.

ænote *useless,* LL 254,3³⁴.

ænrædnis = ānrædnes; **ænyge** = āneage

ænytte = ānet; **æpl** = æppel

æpled = æppled

æppel m. (nap. æpplas, rarely ap(p)la,
æppla) *any kind of fruit, fruit in general* :
'*apple,*' *CP,Gen* : *apple of the eye, ball,
anything round, Bo,CP,Sol.*

æppelbære *fruit-bearing,* Gen 1¹¹,HexC 198.

æppelbearu m. *orchard,* PPs 78².

æppelberende *apple-bearing,* DR 98¹⁶.

æppelcynn n. *kind of apple,* Lcd 67a.

æppelcyrnel n. *apple-pip,* WW 440²³.

æppelfæt n. *apple-vessel,* ZDA 31·15⁴⁰¹.

æppelfealu *apple-yellow, bay,* B 2165.

æppelhūs n. *fruit storehouse,* WW.

æppelscealu f. *apple-core,* WW 371¹.

æppelscrēada np. *apple-parings,* WW 118¹.

æppeltrēow n. '*apple-tree,*' *WW.*

æppeltūn m. *fruit garden, orchard,* Æ,CP.

æppelðorn m. *crab-apple tree,* BC 3·93'.

æppelwīn n. *cider,* WW 430⁹.

æppled† *shaped like an apple, round, embossed, El,Jul.* ['*appled*']

æppul- = apul-; **æps** = æsp, æbs.

æpsen *shameless?* OEG 7³⁰¹ and n.

æpsenes f. *shame, disgrace,* Sc 174⁹.

ær I. adv. comp. æror; sup. ærost, ær(e)st
'*ERE,*' *before that, soon, formerly, beforehand, previously, already, lately, till;*
(comp.) *sooner, earlier;* (sup.) *just now,
first of all* : *early, prematurely.* on ær;
ær ðissum *previously, formerly, beforehand,
CP.* tō ær *too soon.* ær oððe æfter *sooner
or later.* hwonne ær *how soon? when?*
hwēne ær *just before.* on ealne ærne
mergen *very early in the morning.* ne ær
ne siððan *neither sooner nor later.* ær and
sið *at all times.* II. conj. '*ere,*' *before that,
until,* Æ,AO,CP. ær ðam (ðe) *before.*
III. prep. (w.d.) *before.* IV. adj. only in
comp. and sup. (ærra, ærest) q.v. V.
f. = ār f. VI. n. = ār n. VII. = ēar II.

ær- = *early, former* (v MP28·157)

æra I. m. *scraper, strigil,* GL. II. = ærra

æræt m. *too early eating,* W.

ærbe- = yrfe-, ierfe-

ærbeðoht *premeditated,* LL 428¹².

ærboren *earlier born, first-born* (or ? two
words), Gen 973.

ærc = earc; **ærce** = arce

ærcwide m. *prophecy?* Mod 4.

ærdæd f. *former deed,* Lk,W.

ærdæg m. (nap. ærdagas) *early morn,
dawn* : in pl. *former days, past times,* AO.

ærdēað m. *premature death,* Ex 539.

ærdian = eardian

ærdon = ærndon? from ærnan (Gr),Ma 191.

ærdung = eardung

ære I. = ȳre. II. in comp. = -*oared.*

ærēafe (= æ²) *detected,* TC 230¹⁶.

æreldo '*anteritus,*' WW 347¹².

æren I. *made of brass, brazen,* Æ,AO,CP :
tinkling; [ār; cp. *Ger.* ehern] II. *oar-
propelled,* GD 347.

ærendbōc f. *message, letter,* Da,WW 511²⁵.

ærenddraca (AO,CP) = ærendraca

ærende n. '*errand,*' *message, BH,Gu;* AO :
mission, An,Chr : *answer, news, tidings,* Æ.

ærendfæst *bound on an errand,* ÆL 26²²¹.

ærendgāst m. *angel,* Gen 2296.

ærendgewrit n. *written message, letter,* Æ,
CP.

±**ærendian** *to go on an errand, carry a
message, send word to,* CP : *intercede,* Æ :
seek for, obtain, BH 2·132⁵ : (+) *speed,
succeed,* W 238⁹. ['*ernde*']

ærendraca m. *messenger, apostle, ambassador, angel,* Æ,AO : *representative, substitute, proxy,* BH 276¹⁹.

ærendscip n. *skiff, small boat,* WW 287²⁸.

ærendsecg m. *messenger,* Gen 658.

ærendsprǣc f. *message,* Rd 61¹⁵.

ærendung f. *errand* : *errand-going* : *intercession,* RB. ['*ernding*']

ærend-wraca (AO), -wreca (CP) = ærendraca

ærendwrit = ærendgewrit

ærenscip = ærendscip; **ærer** = æror

ǣrest I. adv. and superl. adj. *first, at first, before all,* Æ,CP. ðā, ðonne, siððan ǣ. *as soon as.* ǣ. ðinga *first of all.* **II.** = ǣrist

ǣrfǣder m. *forefather,* B2622.

ǣrfǣst = ārfǣst; **ǣrfe** = ierfe, yrfe

ǣrgedōn *done before,* CP.

ǣrgefremed *before committed,* LL(434¹⁴).

ǣrgelēred *previously instructed,* MtL14⁸.

ǣrgenemned, -gesǣd = ǣrnemned

ǣrgestrēon† n. *ancient treasure.*

ǣrgeweorc† n. *work of olden times.*

ǣrgewinn n. *former strife or trouble, old warfare,* CROSS19.

ǣrgewyrht† n. *former work, deed of old.*

ǣrglǣd *bright in armour,* Ex293.

ǣrgōd† *good from old times,* B.

ǣrhwīlum† *erewhile, formerly.*

ǣrian = erian; **ǣrig** (OET) = earh

ǣriht† n. *code of law or faith,* EL.

ǣring f. *day-break, early morn,* JUL,MkL.

ǣrisc = ēarisc

ǣrist I. (ē) mfn. *rising, VPs : resurrection, awakening,* CP,Jn. ['arist'] **II.** = ǣrest

ǣrlēof? 'gratus' OEG56²⁹⁶.

ǣrlēst = ārlēast

ǣrlic (ā) adj.; -līce adv. 'early,' Jn.

ǣrlyft f. *early morning air,* WW415¹³.

ǣrm = earm

ǣrmorgen (a¹, a², e²) m. *dawn, day-break.*

ǣrmorgenlic *of early morning,* DR.

ǣrn (ea) n. *dwelling, house, building, store, closet* (v. GBG).

ǣrn = ǣren

ǣrnan (strictly causative) *to 'run,' ride, gallop,* BH : (+) *to ride, run to, reach, gain by running or riding,* AO.

ǣrndian = ǣrendian

ǣrne-mergen, -merigen (Æ) = ǣrmorgen

ǣrnemergenlic *matutinal,* CM277.

ǣrnemned (ǣ²) *aforementioned,* LL.

ǣrneweg m. *road for riding on, race-course,* BH398³⁰; Bo112²³. [iernan]

ǣrnian = earnian

ǣrning f. 'running,' *riding, racing, Bo,GD : flow of blood,* MtL9²⁰ (iorn-).

ǣrnð = ernð

ǣrnðegen (rend-) m. *house-officer,* GL.

ǣrnung = earnung; **ǣron** = ǣrran

ǣror I. adv. *earlier, before, beforehand, formerly,* B,Rood; Æ,AO : *rather.* **II.** prep. (w. d.) *before.* ['erer']

ǣrost = ǣrest

ǣrra m. ǣrre fn. adj. *earlier, former, preceding, Bo,El;* CP. on ǣrran dǣg *the day before yesterday.* ['ere,' 'erer']

ǣrror = ǣror; **ǣrs** = ears

ǣrsceaft f. *ancient building,* RUIN16.

ǣrschen, ǣrshen = erschen; **ǣrst** = ǣrest

ǣrstǣf = ārstǣf

ǣr-ðam, -ðon, -ðamðe v. ǣr; **ǣrð-** = yrð-

ǣrwacol *early awake,* Æ.

+**ǣrwe** *depraved, wicked,* EPs100⁴.

ǣrwela m. *ancient wealth,* B2747.

ǣrworuld f. *ancient world,* CR937.

ǣrynd = ǣrend; **ǣryr** = ǣror

ǣryst I. = ǣrist. **II.** = ǣrest

ǣs n. *food, meat, carrion : bait.* [OHG. ās]

ǣsc I. m. nap. ascas 'ash'-*tree, Gl,KC*; Mdf: *name of the rune for* ǣ : (†) *spear, lance, B : ship,* Æ. **II.** = ǣcs

ǣscǣre *unshorn, untrimmed,* LL. [scieran]

ǣscan *to demand (legally),* LL177'.

ǣscapo (WW273³⁵) = ǣsceapa

ǣscbedd n. *an ash-plot,* KC5·126'.

ǣscberend† m. *spear-bearer, soldier.*

ǣsce = asce

ǣsce f. *asking, inquiry, search, LL : claim (to insurance money for theft of cattle),* LL175². ['ask' sb.]

ǣsceap (ē¹) n. *remnant, patch,* LkL,WW.

ǣsceda fp. *refuse,* WW148³³.

ǣscegeswāp n. *cinders, ashes,* TC318'.

ǣscen I. fm. *vessel of ash-wood, bucket, pail, bottle, cup.* **II.** adj. *made of ash-wood, ashen,* LCD.

ǣscfealu *ashy-hued,* WW204²³.

ǣscgrǣg *ashy gray,* WW204²⁴.

ǣschere m. *naval force,* MA69.

ǣscholt† n. *spear of ash-wood, spear-shaft, lance* (v. also Mdf).

ǣscian = āscian

ǣscmann m. *ship-man, sailor, pirate,* CHR, WW. [ǣsc]

ǣscplega m. *play of spears, battle,* JUD217.

ǣscrind f. *bark of the ash-tree,* LCD.

ǣscrōf† *brave in battle.*

ǣscsteall? (ǣts-) m. *place of battle,* WALD1²¹.

ǣscstede m. *place of battle,* MOD17; Mdf.

ǣscstederōd f. *cross marking a battlefield?* (BTs), KC3·135'.

ǣscstybb m. *stump of an ash-tree,* BC.

ǣsctīr m. *glory in war,* GEN2069.

ǣscōracu f. *battle,* GEN2153.

ǣscrot-e, -u f. *a plant, ferula? vervain?* LCD.

ǣscwert = ǣscwyrt

ǣscwiga† m. (*spear-)warrior.*

ǣscwyrt f. *verbena, vervain.*

ǣsellend (y²) m. *lawgiver,* Ps.

ǣsil = hǣsel

ǣslītend m. *law-breaker,* LPs.

ǣsmǣl *smallness of the eye,* LCD.

ǣsmogu np. *slough (of snake)* LCD88a. [ā-smūgan]

ǣsne- = esne-; **ǣsp** = ǣspe I.

ǣspe I. f. *aspen-tree, white poplar, GL*; Mdf. ['asp¹'] **II.** = ǣbs

ǣsphangra m. *aspen wood,* KC.

æspreng, æspring(e) = æspryng
æsprind (ps) f. *aspen bark*, *Lcd.* ['*asp*']
æspringnes = āsprungenes
æspryng nf. *spring*, *fountain*, CP. [ēa] :
departure, CREAT 77.
ǣst I. = ǣrest. II. = ēst
ǣstǣnan = āstænan; ǣstan = ēastan
æstel m. *some thin kind of board?* CP 9,
ÆGR 31⁹,WW 327¹ (v. BTac and NED
s.v. '*astel*')
æsul = esol
ǣswǣpa sbpl. *sweepings, rubbish*, OEG.
ǣswic I. m. *offence, stumbling-block, infamy,
seduction, deceit.* II. adj. *apostate*, GD
304²⁸.
ǣswica m. *offender, deceiver, hypocrite,
traitor*, GD.
ǣswice m. *violation of God's laws* (or?
adultery), W 164³.
±ǣswician *to offend, deceive*, Æ : *apostatize,*
WW 342¹² : *desert*, Æ.
ǣswicnes f. *stumbling-block*, LPs 105³⁶ :
reproach, 122⁴.
ǣswicung f. *offence, stumbling-block*, Æ :
deceit, Æ : *sedition*, WW 116²⁶.
ǣswind *idle, slothful*, WW 422¹³. [swīð]
ǣsyllend = ǣsellend
æt I. prep. (w. d. and, more rarely, a)
(local) '*AT*,' *near, by, in, on, upon, with, before, next to, as far as, up to, into, toward,
Chr* : (temporal) *at, at the time of, near,
in, on, to, until* : (causal) *at, to, through* :
(source) *from* : (instrumental) *by.* æt fēawum wordum *in few words*, BH : *in respect to, as to.* II. adv. *at, to, near.* æt
nehstan, æt sīðestan *finally.* æt- in com-
position=*at, to, from.*
ǣt I. (ē) mfn. *eatables, food, meat, flesh,* Æ,
Gu; AO. ǣt and wǣt *food and drink,* Æ :
the act of feeding, eating, PPs; MkL.
['*eat*' sb.] II. pret. 3 sg. of etan.
æt-=oð-; ǣt-=āte-; -ǣta v. self-ǣta.
ǣtǣwian=ætīewan
āetan⁵ *to eat, devour*, AS 18²,38².
ætbēon anv. *to be present*, DHy.
ætberan⁴ *to carry to, bring, produce, show,
Da* : *carry off*, B. ['*atbear*']
ætberstan³ *to break out,or away,escape from,*
Æ. ['*atburst*']
ætbrēdan=ætbregdan
ætbrēdendlic *ablative*, ÆGR 23⁷.
æt-bregdan, -brēdan³ *to take away, carry off,
deprive of, snatch away, draw off, withdraw, Mt*; Æ : *release, rescue, enlarge* :
prevent, ÆL 31¹²⁶. ['*atbraid*']
ætclifian *to adhere*, BJPs 101⁶.
ætclīðan *to adhere*, OET 181.
ætdēman *to refuse, give judgment against*,
EC 202¹⁹.

ætdōn anv. *to take away, deprive*,LL (246¹⁰).
ǣte=āte
ætēaca (eth-) m. *addition*, OEG 53¹⁸.
ætēacnes (BH)=ætȳcnes
ætealdod *too old*, Æ (2¹⁵⁹).
ætēaw-=ætīew-, ætȳw-
ætēcan=ætȳcan; ætegār=ætgār
æteglan *to harm*, PPs 88¹⁹.
ætēode pret. 3 sg. of *ætgān.*
ǣteorian=āteorian
ætēow-=ætīew-, ætȳw-, oðīew-
ǣtercyn=ātorcyn
ǣtere (ē¹) m. '*eater*,' *glutton, KGl*; NG.
ǣtern I. (NG) *viper.* II.=ǣtren
ætēw-=ætīew-, ætȳw-
ætfæstan (=oð-) *to inflict on, afflict with* :
fasten to, drive into, impart to, CP 115¹⁹ :
commit, entrust : *marry to.*
ætfæstnian *to fasten? entrust?* AS 22¹⁰.
ætfaran⁶ *to escape*, SHR 14²³.
ætfeallan⁷ *to fall, fall out* : *fall away, fail, be
reduced, LL*; Æ : *happen.* ['*atfall*']
ætfele m. *adhesion*, PPs 72²³.
ætfeng m. *attaching, distraint* v. LL 2·279.
ætfeohtan² *to grope about*, WY 18
ætfēolan³ (T²) *to stick to* : *adhere, apply
oneself to, continue in*, CP.
ætfeorrian *to take from*, Sc 160⁷ : *remove
oneself from*, CHRD 93³.
ætferian *to carry away, bear off*, CHRD,
LL.
ætfīlan=ætfēolan
ætflēon² *to flee away, escape by flight*, Æ.
['*atflee*']
ætflōwan⁷ *to flow together, accumulate,*
SPs 61¹⁰.
ætfōn⁷ *to seize upon, lay claim to*, LL.
['*atfong*']
ætforan I. prep. w. d. *before, in the presence
of, in front of, close by, JnL*; Æ. ['*atfore*']
II. adv. *beforehand* (time).
ætfyligan, -fylgan *to adhere, cling to*, GD.
æt-gædere (AO), -gæddre (CP), -gædre,
-gæderum adv. *together, united, at the same
time.* [gadrian]
æt-gǣre n., -gār m. *spear, dart, javelin*,
GL.
ætgangan⁷ *to go to, approach*, Az 183.
['*atgo*']
ætgeddre, -gedre=ætgædere
ætgenumen *taken away*, WW 529³⁹.
ǣtgiefa† (eo, i) m. *food-giver, feeder.*
ætgifan⁵ *to render, give*, B 2878.
ætglīdan¹ *to slip away, disappear*, OEG 7¹³².
ætgrǣpe *seizing.* æ. weorðan *seize*, B 1268.
æthabban *to retain*, Æ.
æthealdan⁷ *to keep back*, Sc 109¹⁸.
æthebban⁶ *to take away, take out, hold back,*
Æ : *exalt oneself*, CP 113¹³.

æthindan prep. w. d. *behind, after*, Chr; Æ.
['*athinden*']
æthléapan[7] *to run away, flee, escape*, W162[5].
æthlýp m. *assault*, LL. [cp. æhlýp]
æthrīnan[1] *to touch, move*, Mt; Æ. ['*atrine*']
æthrine m. *touch*, LCD.
æthwā *each, every one*, LL,PA.
æthwāre *somewhat*, HGL421[37].
æt-hwega, -hwæga, -hweg(u) adv. *somewhat, tolerably, a little* : *how*.
æthweorfan[3] *to return, go back*, B2299.
æthwōn adv. *almost, nearly*.
æthýd '*eviscerata*,' *deprived of its sinews*, MtL, WW392' (v. A47·34).
ætiernan[3] *to run away*, Æ. ['*atrin*']
ætīewan (oð-; ē, ēa, ēo, ī, ȳ) pret. sg. -íe(w)de, (tr.) *to show, reveal, display, disclose, manifest*, Mt; CP : (intr.) *show oneself, become visible, appear*, Mt. ['*atew*'] For compounds see ætȳw-.
æting (ē) f. *eating*, Sc170[5] : *pasture?* Mdf.
ætinge (=y²) *speechless*, OEG46[45].
ætis pres. 3 sg. of ætwesan, ætbēon.
ætīw-=ætīew-, ætȳw-
ætlǣdan (=oð-) *to drive away*, Æ. ['*atlead*']
ætlic (ē) adj. *eatable*, WW,LkL.
ætlicgan[5] *to lie idle*, ÆGr2[22]. ['*atlie*']
ætlimpan[3] *to fall away, escape, be lost*, Æ.
ætlūtian *to lurk, hide*, Æ. ['*atlutien*']
ætnēhstan (ȳ) adv. *at last*.
ætnes f. *edibility*, WW226[11].
ætniman[4] *to take away, deprive of*, Ex414.
ætol=etol
æton pret. pl. of etan.
ætor, ǣtorcynn=ātor, ātorcynn
ǣtran=ǣtrian
ætreccan w. d. and a. *to declare forfeit, deprive of*, LCD.
ǣtren *poisoned, poisonous*, MtL (-ern). ['*attern*']
ǣtrenmōd *of venomous spirit, malignant* (or? two words), GNE163.
ǣtrennes f. *poisonous nature*, LCD55a.
±ǣtrian *to poison*, AO : *become poisonous*. ['*atter*']
ǣtrig *poisonous*, Lcd; Æ. ['*attery*']
ætrihte (y) I. adj. *right at, near, present, close at hand*. II. adv. *almost, nearly, immediately*.
ætsacan[6] *to deny*, Lk; Æ : *renounce*, Mk. ['*atsake*']
ætsamne (æ, e, o) adv. *united, together, at once*, AO.
ætscēotan[2] *to escape, disappear*, MFH150.
ætsittan[5] *to sit by, remain, stay*, Chr. ['*atsit*']
ætslāpan[7] *to sleep beside*, LCD83a.
ætslīdan[1] *to slip, glide, fall*, Æ.
ætsomne (Æ)=ætsamne

ætspornan[3] (u) *to strike against, stumble, go wrong*, CP : *rebel* (æt).
ætspornung f. *offence, stumbling-block, misfortune*, CM230.
ætspringan[3] *to rush forth, spurt out*, B1121. ['*atspring*']
ætspringnes, -sprung(en)nes f. *failing*, Ps118[53].
ætspurnan=ætspornan
ætspyrning=ætspornung
ætst=itst pres. 2 sg. of etan.
ætst-=oðst-
ætstæl m. *aid, assistance* (GK);=ætsteall (BT), GU150.
ætstæppan[6] *to step up to*, B745.
ætstandan[6] *to stand still, stand at, near, in or by*, Æ : *remain, stand up* : *check, resist*, Æ : *cease*, Lk; Æ. ['*atstand*']
ætstandend m. *bystander, attendant*, Æ.
ætstandende *standing by*, GD284[21].
ætsteall m. *assistance, meeting with hostile intent* (GK) : *station, camp station* (BT), or ? æscsteall (Sedgef.), WALD 1[21].
ætstentan=ætstyntan
ætstillan *to still*, LCD25b.
ætstrengan *to withhold wrongfully*, LL206'.
ætstyntan *to blunt, dull, weaken*, GL,Hy.
ætswerian[6] *to deny on oath*, LL.
ætswīgan *to keep silence*, GD217[18].
ætswimman[3] *to escape by swimming, swim out*, CHR918.
āettan (āyttan) *to eat up*, LPs79[14].
ǣtter, ǣttor=ātor; ǣttr-=ǣtr-
ætōringan[3] *to take away from, deprive of*, AN,GD.
ætwegan[5] *to bear away, carry off*, B1198.
ǣtwela *abundance of food, feast*, SOUL123.
ætwenian *to wean from*, LL368'.
ætwesan anv. *to be present*, BF,BH276[20].
ætwesende *at hand, imminent*, WW.
ætwindan[3] *to escape*, Æ. ['*atwind*']
ætwist I.† f. *presence*. II.=edwist
ætwītan[6] *to reproach (with), censure, taunt*, B,Met,Ps; CP. ['*atwite*']
ætwrencan *to seize by fraud*, PR34.
ætȳcan *to add to, increase*, BH. [īecan]
ætȳcnes f. *increase*, BH.
ǣtȳnan=ontȳnan; ǣtynge=ǣtinge
ætys=ætis pres. 3 sg. of ætwesan.
æt-ȳwan, -ȳwian=ætīewan
ætȳwednes f. *showing, appearance, manifestation, revelation*, GD.
ætȳwigendlic *demonstrative*, ÆGR.
ætȳwnes f. *showing, manifestation, revelation* : *apparition*, Æ : *Epiphany.*
ætȳwung f. *manifestation, Epiphany*, CM531.
ǣðan I. (±) *to make oath, swear.* +ǣðed *under oath*, LL210,6. [āð] II.=īeðan

æðel=æðele; ǣðel=ēðel
æðelboren of noble birth, distinguished, Æ : free-born, Æ : inborn, natural.
æðelborennes f. nobility of birth or nature, Æ : inborn nature, OEG4518.
æðelcund of noble birth, GD.
æðelcundnes f. nobleness, Bo46¹³.
æðelcyning m. noble king (Christ), Æ.
æðelduguð f. noble retinue, CR1012.
æðele noble, aristocratic, excellent, famous, glorious,Ex,Gen; Æ,AO,CP:splendid,fine, costly, valuable : lusty, young : pleasant, sweet-smelling, Gen : (+) natural, congenial, suitable. ['athel']
æðel-ferðingwyrt, -fyrdingwyrt f. stitchwort (plant), LCD.
+æðeliant to make noble or renowned, Hy. ['i-athele']
æðelic=æðellic; ǣðelic=ēaðelic
æðeling m. man of royal blood, nobleman, chief, prince, Chr; AO (v. LL2·274) : †king, Christ, God, Cr : †man, hero, saint; in pl. men, people, Gen. ['atheling']
æðelinghād n. princely state, LCD3·438⁵.
æðellic noble, excellent. adv. -līce.
æðelnes f. nobility, excellence, BL,MH.
æðelo=æðelu
æðelstenc m. sweet smell, PH195.
æðeltungolt n. noble star.
æðelu fn. nobility, family, descent, origin, B; CP : nature : noble qualities, genius, talents, pre-eminence, Bo : produce, growth. ['athel']
ǣð-=ēð-
ǣðm (ē) m. air, breath, breathing, B; CP : vapour, Sat. : blast, Æ. ['ethem']
ǣðmian to fume, exhale, emit a smell, GL, MH.
ǣðre=ǣdre
ǣðreclic terrible, RPs95⁴.
ǣðret-=ǣðryt-
ǣðrot n. disgust, weariness, GL,RB. [āðrēotan]
ǣðryt I. troublesome, wearisome, disgusting. II. n. weariness, disgust, tediousness, Æ.
ǣðryte=ǣðryt I.
ǣðrytnes f. tedium, v. OEG4582.
±ǣðryttan to weary, Æ,RWH123⁸
ǣðða (Bd, Death-song)=oððe
ǣw I.=ǣ. II.=ǣwe
ǣwǣde without clothes, WW230⁸⁸.
ǣwan to despise, scorn, KPs129.
ǣwbrǣce despising the law, Æ : adulterous, LL.
ǣwbreca (i, y) m. adulterer, LL. ['eaubruche²']
ǣwbryce m. adultery, Æ; LL. ['eaubruche¹']

ǣw-da, -damann m. witness, compurgator, LL.
ǣwe I. fn. married woman, Æ : married people. II. lawful : married : born of the same marriage.
ǣwelm=ǣwielm
ǣwenbrōðor m. brother by the same marriage, WW413²⁹.
ǣwēne doubtful, uncertain, DEUT28⁶⁶.
ǣwerd adj.? religious, or sb.? regular priest, ANS128·298. [cp. ǣweweard]
ǣwerd-=ǣfwyrd-, ǣwierd-
ǣweweard m. priest, BL161'.
ǣwfæst upright, pious, devout, religious, Æ,CP : married, Æ.
ǣwfæsten n. legal or public fast, A11·102.
ǣwfæstlic lawful : religious, CP (æf-). adv. -līce.
ǣwfæstnes f. religion, piety, Æ,BH.
ǣwicnes f. eternity, RPs102¹⁷ (v. p.303).
ǣwielm (e, i, y), -wielme m. source, fount, spring, beginning, AO,CP. [=ēawielm]
+ǣwierdlian (e²) to injure, BH202B²⁰.
ǣwintre=ānwintre; ǣwis-=ǣwisc-
ǣwisc I. nf. offence, shame, disgrace, dishonour, AO. [Goth. aiwisks] II. disgraced, shameless, indecent.
ǣwisc-=ēawisc-
ǣwiscberende shameful, WW264⁴².
ǣwisce=ǣwisc I.
ǣwisc-ferinend (GL), -firina (NG) m. shameless sinner, publican.
ǣwisclic disgraceful, infamous, OEG.
ǣwiscmōdt ashamed, abashed, cowed.
ǣwiscnes (ēa-) f. shameless conduct : openness, WW : reverence, CP34²⁶.
ǣwita m. counsellor, EL455.
ǣwlic legal, lawful. adv. -līce.
±ǣwnian to marry, Æ.
ǣwnung f. wedlock, OEG.
ǣwul basket with a narrow neck for catching fish, WW181¹¹. [?=cawl, BTs]
ǣwumboren lawfully born, LL76'.
ǣwung=ǣwnung; ǣwunge=ēawunge
ǣwyll m. stream, BC1·542.
ǣ-wylm, -wylme=ǣwielm
ǣwyrdla=ǣfwyrdla
ǣwyrp m. what is cast away, RB : an abortion, LL. [āweorpan]
ǣwysc-=ǣwisc-; æx=æcs, eax; æxe= asce
æxfaru f. 'apparatus,' naval expedition? (=æsc-? v. ES37·184), GL.
æxian=ascian; æxl=eaxl; æxs=æcs
āfǣdan=āfēdan
āfǣgan to depict, figure, BH58²⁵. [fāg]
āfǣgrian (æ) to ornament, adorn, BH38B²⁷.
ā-fǣlan, -fællan=āfyllan II.
āfǣman to foam out, PPs118¹³¹.

áfæran *to frighten, PPs,Mk,Chr*; AO,CP. ['*afear,' 'afeared*']

áfæst=ǽwfæst

áfæstan I. *to fast,* LL,W. **II.** *to let out on hire,* MkR12[1].

áfæstlá interj. *certainly! assuredly!* Æ.

áfæstnian (e) *to fix upon, fasten, make firm, confirm,* AO : *enter, inscribe,* Æ : *build.*

áfǣttian *to fatten, anoint,* APs22[5]; LPs 140[5].

áfandelic=áfandodlic

áfandian *to try, test, prove, tempt, Lk,Lcd*; Æ,CP : *find out, experience,* Æ. afandod (and áfanden?) *approved, excellent,* Æ. ['*afond*']

áfand-igendlic, -odlic *proved, approved, laudable.* adv. -odlíce.

áfandung f. *trial, experience,* Æ,GD,WW.

áfangennes f. *reception, assumption,* EHy 15[35].

afara=eafora

áfaran *to go out, depart, march, travel, Da*; Æ,AO. ['*afare*']

áfeallan[7] *to fall down, fall in battle, Lk*; CP : *fall off, decay.* ['*afalle*']

áfeallan=áfyllan

áfēdan *to feed, nourish, bring up, maintain, support,* Æ; AO : *bring forth, produce.* ['*afede*']

áfēgan *to join,* DR (oe).

áfehtan (DR)=áfeohtan

áfellan=áfyllan; **áfelle**=ǽfelle

áfeohtan[3] *to fight, fight against, attack,* AO : *tear out, destroy.*

áfeormian *to cleanse, purge, purify,* Æ,Lcd.

áfeormung f. *scouring, cleansing, purging,* CM,Lcd,Sc.

á-feorran, -feorrian (CP)=áfierran

áfeorðan[2] *to remove, do away, expel, dispel,* Æ : *go away.*

afer=eafor; **áfer**=áfor; **áfēran**=áfǣran

áferclan *to support,* Chrd 90[11].

aferian *to provide horses for team work (as service for a lord),* v. LL445,446 and 3·247.

á-ferian (Gl), -ferran=áfierran

áferscan *to become fresh,* Bo 86[20].

áfersian=áfeorsian

áfestnian (WW49[8])=áfæstnian

afetigan=hafetian

áfierran (eo, i, y) *to remove, withdraw, depart : estrange from, take away, expel, drive away,* CP. [*feorr*]

áfierrednes (y) f. *removal,* NC270.

áfigen *fried,* Gl.

áfilgan=áfylgan

áfindan (=on-) *to find, find out, discover, detect, Jn*; Æ : *experience, feel,* Æ. ['*afind*']

áfir-=áfierr-, áfeor-, áfyr-

áflǣgen pp. of áflēan.

áflǣman=áflīeman

áflēan[6] *to strip off, flay,* GD.

áflēgan (DR)=áflīegan; **áflēman**=áflīeman

áflēon[2], -flēogan *to fly, flee away, Gu* : *fly from, escape.* ['*aflee*']

áflēotan[2] *to skim,* Lcd.

áflian=áflīegan +**aflian**? *to get, obtain?* OEG7[118] (v. BTac).

áflīegan (ī, ē, ȳ) *to put to flight, expel,* Æ. ['*afley*']

áflīegung (ī) f. *driving away,* Lcd 1·338[12].

áflīeman (ȳ) *to put to flight, expel, scatter, disperse, rout, Chr*; CP : *banish.* ['*aflœmo*']

áflīg-=áflīeg-

-**áflīung** v. mete-á.

áflote '*afloat,' KC*4·24[1]. [=on flote]

áflōwan[7] *to flow, flow away from, pass away,* AO,CP.

áflȳg-, áflȳh-=áflīeg-

áflȳgennes f. *attack* (BTs),Lcd 1·336[7].

áflȳman=áflīeman; **áfōgian**=áwōgian

afol n. *power, might,* LL (304 n1).

áfōn (=on-) *to receive, take in, take, Mk, Ps* : *lay hold of, seize, MtR,Jul* : *hold up, support.* ['*afong*']

áfondian=áfandian

áfor *bitter, acid, sour, sharp* : *dire, fierce, severe, harsh, impetuous.* [OHG. eipar]

afora=eafora

áforhtian *to be frightened, take fright, wonder at,* Æ.

á-frēfran, -frēfrian *to comfort, console, make glad,* CP. [*frōfor*]

áfrem-dan, -dian *to alienate,* Æ : *become alienated.*

áfremðan (VPs)=áfremdan

áfremðung f. *alienation,* VHy6[28].

áfrēon *to deliver, free,* DR,LkR.

áfrēoðan[2] *to froth,* Lcd 45 b.

afslōg=ofslōg; **after**=æfter

áfūlian *to become foul, putrefy, rot, be corrupt, defiled.*

afulic *perverse, MtL.* ['*awkly*']

áfullend m. *fuller,* MkR9[3].

áfunde rare wk. pret. 3 sg. of áfindan.

áfundennes f. *invention, device, discovery,* Æ.

áfȳlan *to foul, stain, defile, corrupt, CP*; Æ. ['*afile*']

áfylgan (i[2]) *to pursue,* Gen 14[15].

áfyllan I. (w. g. or d.) *to fill, fill up, replenish, satisfy,* Æ; AO : *complete, fulfil.* ['*afill*'] **II.** (y;=ie) *to cause to fall, fell, beat down, overturn, subvert, demolish, abolish, Lk* : *slay, kill.* ['*afelle*']

áfyndan=áfindan; **áfyr-**=áfierr-, áfeor-

áfȳran *to emasculate.* áfȳred (CP), áfȳrd pp. as sb. *eunuch.*

áfyrhtan *to frighten, terrify,* Æ,AO.

āfȳrida=āfȳred; āfyrran=āfierran
āfyrsian=āfeorsian
āfyrðan (i) to remove, LCD 1·294².
āfȳsan (intr.) to hasten : inspire with longing,
BL : (tr.) urge, impel, excite : drive, drive
away. [fūs]
āga m. proprietor, owner, GD 230¹¹.
āgǣlan to hinder, keep back, preoccupy,
detain, hold back, retard, delay, AO :
neglect, CP : profane.
āgǣlwan (e) to terrify, astonish, AO.
āgalan⁶ to sound forth, sing, chant, B,W.
āgald=āgeald pret. 3 sg. of āgieldan.
āgāllan to become slack, CP 65¹⁸.
āgan I. (conj. Wt 546) to own, possess, have,
obtain, An,Bo,Mt; AO,CP : have control
over, take charge of : give, give up, deliver,
restore : have to pay, 'owe*,' Mt,Lk : have
to do, ANS 123·417. ā. ūt find out, discover. II. pret. 3 sg. of āginnan (onginnan).
āgān (conj. v. gān) to go, go by, pass (of
time), Mk: pass into possession (of inherited property), TC 486' : occur, befall,
Æ : come forth, grow, Ps : approach : lose
strength. of ā. go away. ['ago']
āgangan=āgān
āge f. possessions, property, SAT,BH 196¹⁸.
[ON. eiga]
agēan=ongēan; āgehwǣr=ǣghwǣr
āgeldan I. †to punish. II.=āgieldan
āgelwan=āgǣlwan; āgēman=āgȳman
±āgen I. 'own,' proper, peculiar, Æ,BH,G,
Met,Sat; AO,CP,CHR; proper (gram.),
ÆGR. ā. cyre freewill. āgnes ðonces voluntarily, spontaneously. II. n. property, LL :
own country. III. pp. of āgan.
āgēn=ongēan
āgēnbewendan to return, G.
āgēncuman⁴ to return, Lk 8⁴⁰.
āgend m. owner, possessor, master, lord,
LL. se ā. the Lord, B,Ex.
āgendfrēa I. m. lord, owner. II. f. mistress?
GEN 2237.
āgendfrēo=āgendfrēa
āgendlīce properly, as one's own : imperious-
ly, CP 145⁵ : correctly, v. MLR 17·165.
āgen-friga, -frige=āgendfrēa
āgēngehweorfan³ to return, Lk 2⁴³.
āgēnhwyrfan (y;=ie) to return, Mk 6³¹.
āgēniernan³ to run against, meet, Mk.
āgēnlǣdan to lead back, WW 91⁹.
āgenlic own : owed, due, DR.
āgennama m. proper name, ÆGR 25¹⁶.
āgennes f. property, Æ.
āgēnsendan to send back, Lk.
āgenslaga m. slayer of oneself, suicide, Æ.
āgēnstandan⁶ to press, urge, Lk.
āgenung=āgnung
āgēode=āēode pret. 3 sg. of āgān.

āgeolwian to become yellow, LCD,W.
āgēomrian to mourn, grieve, GD.
āgeornan (=ie) to desire, be eager for, GD
205¹⁹.
āgēotan² to pour out, pour forth, shed, An,
MtL; CP : melt, found (of images) : destroy : deprive (of), JUD 32. ['ageten']
āgētan=āgītan
āgiefan⁵ (eo, i, y) to give, impart, deliver,
give up, yield, relinquish, Mt : restore,
return, repay, pay, AO. eft ā. give back,
return. ['agive']
āgieldan³ (e, i, y) to pay, repay, compensate,
yield, restore, reward, AO : offer oneself,
offer up (as a sacrifice) : perform (an office),
Æ : allow : to punish? PH 408.
āgīemelēasian (i, y) to neglect, despise, CP.
āgīemelēasod neglectful, careless, NC 337.
āgīeta=āgīta; āgifan (AO,CP)=āgiefan
āgiflan to bestow, grant, DR 124¹⁹
āgift=ǣgift; āgildan (CP)=āgieldan
āgilde=ǣgilde
āgiltan=āgyltan
āgīmelēasian (C)=āgīemelēasian
āgimmed set with precious stones, Æ.
āginnan=onginnan
āgīta m. prodigal, spendthrift, CP.
āgitan (y²) to find, find out, RB,W.
āgītan (ē;=ie) to waste, destroy, Chr. ['aget']
āglāchād m. state of misery, RD 54⁵.
āg-lǣc, -lāc† n. trouble, distress, oppression,
misery, grief.
āglǣca† (ē) m. wretch, monster, demon, fierce
enemy.
āglǣccrǣft (āc-) m. evil art, AN 1364.
āglǣcwīf n. female monster, B 1259.
āglǣdan? to cause to slip. v. AB 19·163.
āglēca=āglǣca
āglīdan¹ to glide, slip, stumble, LCD,WW.
agn-=angn-
āgnere m. owner, ÆGR 110¹⁹.
āgnes=āgenes gmn. of āgen adj.
āgnett n. interest, usury, LkL 19²³ (or
? āgnettung, v. ES 42·163).
āgnettan to appropriate, GL.
±āgnian to 'own,' MtL,Rd : claim : appropriate, usurp, Bo; CP : make over (to), Æ :
dedicate, adopt, CP : enslave, Ex.
āgnidan¹ to rub off, WW 386¹⁶.
āgniden I. f. rubbing, GL? (v. A 31·533).
II. used, threadbare, WW 220²⁴.
āgniend (āh) m. owner, possessor, GEN 14²².
±āgniendlic possessive, genitive (case),
ÆGR.
+āgnod own, CP 262²³.
āgnung f. owning, ownership, possession :
claim, declaration or proof of ownership :
(+) acquisition, KC 2·304⁵.
āgotenes f. effusion, shedding, Æ,LCD.

āgrafan[6] *to carve, hew, sculpture,* Æ : *engrave, inscribe,* Æ.
āgrafenlic *sculptured,* ARSPs105[19].
āgrāpian *to grasp tightly,* ÆL8[121].
āgrētan (oe) *to attack,* LkLR9[42].
agrimonia '*agrimony,*' *Lcd.*
āgrīsan[1] (ȳ) *to quake, fear,* LL. ['*agrise*']
āgrōwen *overgrown,* HexC196.
āgrymetian *to rage,* GD.
āgrȳndan *to descend,* Men111.
āgrȳsan=āgrīsan
agu f. *magpie,* WW132[11].
Agus-tus, -tes (AA8[11]) m. *August.*
āgyf-, āgyld-=āgief-, āgield-, ægild-
āgylpan[3] (=ie) *to exult in* (w.d.), Soul165.
āgyltan *to offend, sin, do wrong,* Æ; CP.
  ['*aguilt*']
āgyltend m. *debtor,* EHy13[6].
āgylting f. *guilt, offence,* DR.
āgyltnes f. *guilt,* NC270.
āgȳman (ē;=īe) *to regard,* AS : *heal, cure.*
āgȳmeleāsian=āgīemeleāsian
āgymmed=āgimmed; agynnan=onginnan
āgytan=āgitan
ah (AO,CP)=ac (conj. and adv.)
āh pres. 3 sg. of āgan; āh-=āg-
āhabban *to restrain,* Æ : (refl.) *abstain*
  (fram), BH : *support,* Cp1947.
āhaccian *to pick out,* ÆL23[78].
āhæbban=āhebban
āhældan=āhildan
āhafennes f. *rising, lifting up, elevation,* Ps.
āhalsian *to implore,* RBL15[3].
āhangian *to hang,* LkL23[39].
āhātan *to name,* MtL27[16].
āhātian *to become hot,* WW214[31].
āhealdan[7] (=on-) *to hold, keep,* DR,JnL.
āhealtian *to limp, crawl,* LPs17[46].
āheardian *to be or become hard, grow hard or*
  inured, CP : *endure.*
āheardung f. *hardening,* Lcd.
āhēawan[7] *to cut off, out or down,* Æ,CP :
  cut wood into planks.
āhebban[6] (occl. wk. pret. āhefde and pp.
  āhefed) (often w. ūp) *to lift up, stir up,*
  raise, exalt, erect, Lk; CP : *take away,*
  remove : support, uphold : leaven. ['*aheave*']
āhebbian=āebbian; āhefednes=āhafennes
āhefegian (CP), -hef(i)gian (æ) *to make*
  heavy, oppress : become heavy.
āheld (VPs)=āhild pp. of āhildan.
āhellian? *to cover over, conceal, hide,*
  OEG5410.
āhelpan[3] *to help, support,* DR.
āhēnan *to humble,* LkL : *accuse,* NG.
  [hīenan; hēan]
āheolorian *to weigh, consider,* Gl.
āhēran=āhȳran
āherian *to praise,* DR.

āhērian=āhȳrian
āherstan (BPs101[4])=āhyrstan
āheten pp. of āhatan.
āhicgan=āhycgan; āhīenan v. āhēnan.
āhierdan (i, y) *to make hard, harden,* CP :
  encourage, animate. [heard]
āhierding (y) *hardening,* Sc232[19].
āhīeðan=āhȳðan
āhildan (æ, e, y;=ie) *to bend, incline,* Æ :
  rest, lay down (tr. and intr.) : *turn away,*
  avert : cast down, destroy.
āhildnes '*declinatio,*' RPs72[4].
āhirdan (CP)=āhierdan; āhīðan=āhȳðan
āhladan[6] *to draw out, lead out, draw forth,*
  Æ : *exclude,* Bk18.
āhlǣca=āglǣca
āhlǣnan *to set oneself up,* Mod53.
āhlǣnsian *to become lean,* Æ.
āhlēapan[7] *to leap, spring up,* AO.
āhlēfan (oe) *to pull out,* DR55[10].
āhlēoðrian *to sound, resound,* GD.
āhliehhan[6]† *to laugh at, deride : exult.*
āhlin-ian, -nan=ālynnan
āhlocian *to dig out,* Gl, MtR5[29]. [?=*ālo-
  cian,* cp. lucan (BTs) and v. ES42·165]
āhlōwan *to roar again,* WW492[11].
āhlūttrian *to cleanse, purify,* Gl,Lcd.
āhlyhhan=āhliehhan
āhlȳt(t)rian=āhlūttrian
āhn-=āgn-
āhnēapan[2] *to pluck off,* Gu819.
āhnescian *to become soft or effeminate,* AO :
  weaken. [hnesce]
āhnīgan[1] *to fall down : bow down : empty*
  oneself, DR.
āhogian *to think out, be anxious about,* GD.
āholan=āholian
āholian *to hollow, scoop out,* CP. ūt ā. *to*
  root out, pluck out : engrave, emboss.
āhōn[7] *to hang, suspend, crucify,* MkLR;
  AO,CP. ['*ahang*']
āhopian *to hope for* (tō), Bl17[23].
āhrǣcan *to spit out,* Lcd9a.
āhrǣscian *to shake off?* (BTs),LPs108[13].
āhreddan *to set free, save, rescue, re-capture,*
  AO; Æ. ['*aredde*']
āhredding f. *salvation, deliverance,* EC,
  HL9[281].
āhrēofian *to become leprous,* MH174[12].
āhrēosan[2] *to rush : fall, fall down,* Æ : *be*
  destroyed.
āhrepian *to treat,* FBO80[5].
āhrēran (=on-) *to move, shake, make to*
  tremble, CP.
āhrīnan[1] (=on-) *to touch, handle,* Lk.
  ['*arine*']
āhrisian (y) *to shake, stir up,* CP, Ps : *shake*
  off. ['*arese*']
āhrȳnan=āhrīnan

āhrȳran (=īe) *to cause to fall, destroy*, GL.
āhrysian=āhrisian
ahse=asce; āhsian=āscian
aht, āht=eaht, āwiht; ahta=eahta
āhte, āhton pret. 3 sg. and pl. of āgan.
āhtes (=g. of āht) *of any account or value.*
āhtlīce *stoutly, manfully*, CHR 1071E.
āhwā pron. *any one*, LL.
āhwǣnan *to vex, grieve, afflict*, Lcd; Æ.
['awhene']
āhwǣnne adv. *when, whenever* : *at some
time, any time*, RB : *at all times.*
āhwǣr (ā, ē) *anywhere*, Bo,LL,Ps : *at any
time, ever, in any way.* ['owhere']
āhwǣrgen=āhwergen
āhwǣt n. *anything*, CM 371.
āhwǣðer (āwðer, āðer, āðor) I. pron. *some
one, something; any one* : *anything.* II. adv.
and conj. *either*, AO,CP. āðer...oððe=
either...or, AO. ['OUTHER']
āhwanon=āhwonan; āhwār=āhwǣr
āhwelfan=āhwylfan
āhwēnan=āwēnan
āhweorfan³ (tr.) *to turn, turn away, convert* :
(intr.) *turn aside, turn away*, Gen : *avert.*
['awherf']
āhwēr=āhwǣr; āhwerfan=āhwierfan
āhwergen (æ²) *anywhere* : *in any case.*
āhwettan *to whet, excite, kindle*, AO : *hold
out to, provide* : *reject.*
āhwider *in any direction, from any source*, Æ.
āhwierfan *to turn away, turn from, avert*,
CP.
āhwilc=ǣghwilc; āhwistlian v. āwistlian.
āhwītian *to whiten*, BJPs 50⁹.
āhwonan *from any source, anywhere*, BH,
Bo.
āhwonne=āhwǣnne; āhwyder=āhwider
āhwylfan (e;=ie) *to cover over, submerge,
subvert*, Æ : *roll to*, RWH 78¹⁹. up ā. *pull
up, loosen.*
āhwyrfan=āhwierfan
āhycgan† *to think out, devise.*
āhȳdan *to hide, conceal*, GD,W.
āhyldan=āhildan
āhyldendlic *enclitic*, ÆGR 265¹. [āhildan]
āhyltan *to trip up*, PPs 139⁵.
āhȳran (ē) *to hire*, G.
āhyrd-=āhierd-
āhyrsian=āhrisian
āhyrstan (e²;=ie) *to roast, fry*, LCD 33b;
BPs 101⁴.
āhyspan *to reproach*, LPs 101⁹.
āhȳðan (īe, ī) *to plunder, destroy, devour*,
EL,VPs. [hūð]
āīdan (ȳ)? '*eliminare*' (v. OEG 7¹⁰⁹n; BTs)
ā-īdlian, -īdlan, -īdelian *to be or make useless,
frustrate, empty, annul*, Æ,CP : *profane* :
be free from : *deprive (of).* [īdel]

āīernan³ *to run away, run out, go over* : *pass
by, go*, CHR.
āīeðan (ǣ, ī, ȳ) *to lay low, demolish, destroy,
cast out*, GEN,WW.
al=eall, æl
āl n. *fire, burning*, OEG 4389; 4470. [cp.
ǣlan]
ālādian *to excuse*, Bo 144⁵. ālādiendra
'*excussorum*'(=*excussatorum*,) BJPs 126⁴.
ālǣccan *to catch, take*, CHR 1123.
ālǣdan (tr.) *to lead, lead away, carry off,
withdraw, conduct, bring*, Æ : (intr.) *be
produced, grow, come forth.*
ālǣnan *to lend*, WW : *grant, lease*, Æ.
['alene']
ālǣr=alor
ālǣran *to teach*, PPs 118¹⁰⁸.
ālǣson pret. pl. of ālesan.
ālǣtan⁷ *to let go, give up, leave, lose, resign,
lay aside*, Jn; AO,CP : *let, allow* : *release,
pardon, forgive* : *deliver*, Æ. ['alet']
ālǣtnes (ǣ¹, ē²) f. *desolation* : *loss* : *remission
(of sins).*
alan⁶ *to nourish, produce*, RIM 23. [*Goth.*
alan]
ālangian (impers.) *to affect with longing*,
Soul 154. ['along']
ālatian *to grow sluggish or dull*, GL.
alað=ealað (v. ealu)
ālāðian¹ (GL) *to be or become hateful* : *hate* :
threaten.
alb f. *white garment*, '*alb*,' LL. [*L.*]
ald (EWS,EK,A)=eald; āld=ādl
aldaht=ealdoð
ālecgan *to put, place, lay down, lay aside,
give up, cease from, abandon*, LL; Æ,AO,
CP : *put down, allay, suppress, abolish,
conquer, destroy, overcome, refute*, Æ,LL :
lay upon, inflict : *diminish, lessen, withhold*, Æ. ālecgende word, ālecgendlic
word *deponent verb.* ['allay']
ālēd pp. of (1) ālecgan; (2) ālǣdan (=ālǣd).
ālēfan=ālīefan
ālēfednes f. *infirmity*, ÆL 21⁹⁹.
ālēflan *to injure, maim; enfeeble*, Æ. pp.
ill, Æ. [lēf]
ālenian (K)=ālynnan
ālēodan²† *to spring up, grow.*
ālēofian=ālifian, ālibban
ālēogan² *to lie, deny, deceive, be false to,
leave unfulfilled*, Æ,AO.
ālēon¹ (=on-) *to lend, give up*, DR.
āleonian=ālynnan
ālēoran *to depart, flee away*, RPs 10² : *pass
away*, ARPs 56².
āleoðlan=ālīðian; aler=alor
ālēs-=ālīes-
ālesan⁵ *to pick out, choose*, AS,BH.
ālet (DA 254)=ǣled

ālētan=ālǣtan; **ālēōran**=ālȳōran

alewe, al(u)we f. '*aloe*,' *Jn,Lcd.*

ālēwed ptc. *feeble, weak, ill,* RB51¹⁶. [lēf]

alexandre f. *horse-parsley, Lcd.* ['*alexanders*']

alfæle (AN770)=ealfelo

ālfæt n. *cooking vessel, cauldron,* LL. [ǣlan]

ālgeweorc n. *fire-making, tinder,* GL.

algian=ealgian; **alh**=ealh

ālibban *to live, pass one's life,* AO.

ālicgan⁵ *to be subdued, fail, cease, yield, perish,* AO.

ālīefan (ē, ī, ȳ) *to allow, give leave to, grant,* AO,CP : *hand over, yield up.*

ālīefedlic *lawful, permissible.* adv. -līce (Æ,CP).

ālīesan (ē, ī, ȳ) *to loosen, let loose, free, redeem, release, absolve, Mt*; AO,CP. ['*alese*']

ālīes-ednes (*Mt*), -(e)nes (*Cr,MtLR*) (ē, ȳ) f. *redemption, ransom : remission (of sins),* ERHy9⁷⁷. ['*alese(d)ness*']

ālīesend (ē, ī, ȳ) m. *liberator, deliverer, Redeemer,* CP.

ālīesendlic (ȳ) *loosing, liberating,* BH.

ālīesendnes=ālīesednes

ālīesing, -līesnes=ālīesednes

ālīf=ǣlīf

ālīfan=ālīefan; **ālifian**=ālibban

ālīh (DR) imperat. sg. of ālēon.

ālīhtan I. *to lighten, relieve, alleviate, take off, take away,* CP,LL : '*alight*,' *ÆGr.* II. *to light up,* Æ,*Met* (=onlihtan).

ālimpan³† *to occur, happen.*

ālinnan=ālynnan; **ālīsend**=ālīesend

ālīōlan (eo) *to detach, separate, Gen : set free.* ['*alithe*']

all (strictly Anglian, but found in AO,CP) =eal, eall

almes-=ǣlmes-; **aln-**=ealn-

alo-=ealu-

āloccian *to entice,* AO.

alor, al(e)r m. '*alder*,' *Gl,KC,Lcd*; Mdf.

alorbedd (ælr-) *alder bed,* KC5·153'.

alordrenc m. *drink made of alder sap?* Lcd40a.

alorholt nm. *alder-wood,* WW.

alorrind m. *alder-bark,* Lcd12b.

aloð=ealu; **alr**=alor; **alswā**=ealswā

alter, altar(e), altre m. '*altar*,' *G*; CP. [*L.*]

ālūcan² *to pluck up, pull out, separate, take away,* GD.

ālūtan² (=onl-) *to bend, incline, bend or bow down,* Æ. āloten pp. *submissive.*

aluwe, alwe=alewe; **alwald-**=eal(l)weald-

ālybban=ālibban; **ālȳfan** (Æ)=ālīefan

ālȳfed I.=ālīefed pp. of ālīefan. II.=ālēfed pp. of ālēfian; **ālȳfed-**=ālīefed-

ālȳht-=onlīht-; **ālyhtan**=ālihtan

ālȳman *to come forth,* GL : *show forth.*

ālynnan, -lynian (e, eo, i) *to deliver, let go, release, loosen,* Æ.

ālȳs-=ālīes-

ālȳōran (ē;=īe) *to lather,* LCD. [lēaðor]

am (NG)=eom; **am-**=an-

ām m. *reed or slay of a loom?* RD36⁸ (v. LL3·524 and BTs)

āmǣllian=āmeallian

āmǣnsumian=āmānsumian

āmǣran I. *to extol,* GD206²⁴. II. (usu. ūtāmǣr(i)an) *to exterminate,* BH.

āmǣstan *to feed with mast, fatten, feed up,* CP.

āmagian? (hamacgian) *to revive, be restored to health,* LCD3·184'. (or ? +magian, v. BTac)

āman=onman

āmang prep. w. d. *among, amongst : while, whilst, during.* ā. ðām, ðissum *meanwhile.* [=gemang]

āmanian *to exact, require,* LL202,1.

āmāns-ian, -ung=āmānsum-ian, -ung

āmānsumian *to excommunicate, curse, proscribe, outlaw, BH*; Æ,AO. ['*amanse*']

āmān-sumung, -sumnung f. *excommunication, curse,* Æ. ['*amansing*']

āmarian *to disturb, trouble, confound.* [cp. āmierran]

āmasian *to amaze, confound,* W137²³.

āmāwan⁷ *to cut down,* PPs101⁴.

āmb (LL455,15)=ām; **ambeht**=ambiht

amber (e¹, o¹, æ², o², u²) mfn. *vessel, pail, cask, pitcher, tankard, Gl,MkL : dry or liquid measure* (? *four bushels*), *AO,Ct, WW.* ['*amber*']

ambiht (e¹, o¹, y¹, e²) I. n. *office, service : commission, command, message.* II. m. *attendant, messenger, officer.*

+ambiht-an, -ian (embe-) *to minister, serve,* NG.

ambihtere (embe-) m. *servant,* LkL22²⁶.

ambihthēra (o¹) *obedient servant,* GU571.

ambihthūs n. *workshop,* '*officina*,' CM1087.

ambihtmann m. *manservant,* LL.

ambihtmecg† (o¹, e², y²) m. *servant,* Ps.

ambiht-nes, -sumnes (emb-) f. *service,* NG.

ambihtscealc† m. *functionary, retainer.*

ambihtsecg sm. *minister,* GEN582.

ambihtsmiδ m. *court smith or carpenter,* LL3, 7.

ambihtðegn (omb-)† m. *attendant, servant.*

ambrōsie *ambrosia,* GUTH90³.

ambyht=ambiht

ambyre *unfavourable?* (BTac), AO19¹³.

ambyrian (OEG11¹⁴²)=onbyrgan II.

āmeallian (æ) *to become insipid,* v. OEG61⁴.

āmearcian *to mark out, delineate, define, describe : destine, assign, appoint.*

amel m. *sacred vessel*, WW 348. [*L*.]
āmelcan³ *to milk*, LCD.
āmeldian *to let out, make known, betray*, Æ,AO.
āmeltan³ v. āmolten.
ameos *bishop-weed*, LCD 71b. [*Gk*.]
amerian=hamorian
āmerian *to test, examine* : *purify, refine*, LCD.
āmerran=āmierran
āmetan⁵ *to measure, estimate* : *mete out, assign, grant, bestow*, Æ.
āmētan *to paint, depict*, CP : *adorn*, Æ.
āmetendlic *compendious, measurable, limited*, LPs 38⁶. adv. -līce.
āmethwīl=æmethwīl
āmetsian *to provision*, CHR 1006 E.
āmiddan=onmiddan
āmīdian *to be foolish*, RHy 6⁶.
āmīdlian *to bridle*, BYH 56²⁷,WW 226³⁸.
āmierran (e, i, y) *to hinder, obstruct, prevent, delay*, CP : *mar, injure, disturb, scatter, consume, waste, spoil, destroy*, Lk, Bo; AO,CP : *lose*. [*'amar'*]
āmigdal m. *almond*, LCD. [*Gk*.]
āmōd=æmōd
āmolcen pp. of āmelcan.
āmolsnian *to decay, weaken*, W 147²⁹.
āmolten *molten*, ÆL 5²³⁴.
amore=omer
am-pelle (o², u²) f. *flask, vessel*, Æ. [*L*.]
ampre I. '*varix,' tumour, swelling*, Gl. [*'amper'*] II. f. *dock, sorrel*, LCD.
āmundian *to protect, defend*, Æ.
āmyltan (tr.) *to melt*, Æ.
āmyrgan (LL 318,56A)=āmyrðrian
āmyrgan *to delight, cheer*, SOL 240.
āmyrian=āmerian
āmyrran=(1) āmierran; (2) (LL 348,56G,B) āmyrðran
ā-myrðran, -myrðrian *to murder, kill*, LL; CHR 1049 C. [*'amurder'*]
an I. adv. and prep.=on. II. pres. 1 sg. of unnan.
an- in composition represents (1) and-; (2) un-; (3) in-; (4) on-.
ān I. adj. strong mfn. (asm. ānne, ænne) '*ONE*,' Æ,Chr. in plur. *each, every one, all*. ān and (æfter) ān *one by one*. ānes hwæt *some single thing, a part* : *a, an* : *alone, sole, only*; in this sense it is used also in the weak form (sē āna; hē āna, AO,CP) and with a pl. : *lonely?* AN 258 : *singular, unique* : *single, each, every one, all* (gp. ānra) : *any*. II. adv. (also wk. āna) *alone, only*. on ān *continually, continuously, ever, in one, once for all, immediately*. ðæt ān *only that*. ān and ān *one by one*, Æ.
ana=heonu; āna v. ān.

ānad, ānæd† n. *waste, desert, solitude*. [*Ger*. einöde]
ānægled *nailed down*, AA 6⁶.
anǣl-=onǣl-
anǣðelian=unǣðelian
ananbeam m. *spindle-tree*, LCD 29b.
anawyrm m. *intestinal worm*, LCD 43b.
anbærnes=onbærnes
anbestingan³ *to thrust in, insert*, CP.
anbid (=on-) n. *waiting, expectation, hope*, AO,CP : *interval*, AO.
±an-bidian (on-) (intr.) *to wait, stay* : (tr.) w. g. *wait for, expect*.
anbidstōw (on-) f. *place of meeting*, LL.
±anbidung m. *waiting for, expectation* : *delay*, OEG 3396.
anbiht=ambiht; anbindan=onbindan
anbiscopod=unbiscopod
ānboren† ptc. *only-begotten*.
anbringelle=onbringelle
anbrōce (EL 1029)=unbrǣce?
anbrucol (=on-) *rugged*, GPH 402.
anbryrd-=onbryrd-
ānbūend m. *hermit, anchorite*, GU 59.
anbūgan (AO,CP)=onbūgan
anbyhtscealc=ambihtscealc
ānbȳme *made of one trunk, dug-out (ship)*, WW 181³³.
+anbyrdan (and-) *to strive against, resist, oppose*, LL.
anbyrdnes f. *resistance*, LL 214,14.
anbyrignes (=on-) f. *tasting, taste*, WW.
ān-cenned (æ²), -cend, *only-begotten*, Æ.
ancer=ancor
an-clēow n., -clēowe f. '*ankle*,' Lcd,WW
ancnāwan=oncnāwan
ancor m. '*anchor*,' B,Bo; CP. [*L*. from Gk*.]
ān-cor, -cora m. *anchorite, hermit*, WW; Æ. [*'anchor'*]
ancorbend (oncer-) m. *cable*, B 1918.
āncorlic *like a hermit*, WW 463⁷.
āncorlīf n. *solitary life*, BH.
ancorman m. *man in charge of the anchor*, WW 166⁷.
ancorrāp (o¹, y²) m. *anchor-rope, cable*, WH 14.
ancorsetl (e²) n. *prow of a ship*, WW.
āncorsetl n. *hermitage*, Æ.
āncorsetla m. *hermit*, Æ.
āncorstōw f. *solitary place*, BH 424¹².
ancorstreng (ancer-) m. *cable*, AS 22¹⁹.
ancra (a¹?) m. *anchorite, hermit, monk*, WW; Æ. [*'anchor'*]
ancsum=angsum
ancuman⁴ *to arrive*, GEN 1884.
āncummum *one by one, singly*, NG.
āncyn adj. *only*, A 2·358; LPs 21²¹.

and (e) conj. 'AND' : *but* : *or*, LL 2·13. gelīce and...*like as if*...AO.

and-=an-, on-, ond- (*opposition, negation*; *Ger.* ent-); and occasionally a-.

anda m. *grudge, enmity, envy, anger, vexation, Mt*; Æ : *zeal*, Æ,CP : *injury, mischief* : *fear, horror*, NG. ['*ande*,' '*onde*']

āndæge† *for one day, lasting a day.*

andæt-=andet-

āndaga m. *appointed day*, Æ.

±**āndagian** *to fix a day for appearance* : *adjourn*, EC 163'.

andb-=anb-, onb-

andbīcnian *to make signs to*, WW 378³ (andbēt-).

andbita m. *feast* (*of unleavened bread*), WW.

andclēow=anclēow

andcweðan '*contradicere, frustrari*,' HGL 491.

andcwiss f. *answer*, Gu 992.

andcȳōnes f. *evidence*, BH 158⁵.

andd-=and-, ond-; **ande**=ende

andēages (ǣ) *eye to eye, openly?* B 1935.

andēaw *arrogant, ostentatious*, Sc.

andefn, -efen f. *measure, quantity, amount*, AO : *capacity, nature*, CP.

andel-bær, -bǣre *reversed*, OEG.

andergilde *in repayment, in compensation*, Pr 41.

andet-=andett-

andetla m. *declaration, confession*, LL 18,22.

±**andetnes** (ond- CP) f. *confession*, Æ : *thanksgiving, praise.*

andetta (o¹, æ²) m. *one who confesses*, Bl, LL. a. bēon *to acknowledge.*

±**andettan** *to confess, acknowledge*, Æ,CP : *give thanks or praise* : *promise, vow.* [and, hātan]

andettere m. *one who confesses*, Æ,Chrd.

andettian=andettan

andettung m. *confession, profession*, CP.

andfang n. *acceptance*, WW.

andfangol '*susceptor*,' LPs 45¹².

āndfealdlīce=ānfealdlīce

andfeax *bald*, W 46¹.

andfeng (on-) m. *seizing, receiving, taking*, Æ,RB : *defence* : *defender* : *attack, assault* : *revenue, means*, Lk 14²⁸,Bk 10 : *illegal occupation* (*of land*).

andfenga m. *receiver, defender, undertaker*, Ps.

andfenge I. (anf-, onf-) *acceptable, agreeable, approved, fit, suitable*, Æ,CP : *that can receive* : *taken.* II. m. *undertaker, helper*, PPs.

andfengend m. *helper, defender*, PPs : *receiver.* gafoles a. *tax collector.*

andfengnes f. *acceptance, receiving* : *receptacle* : *acceptableness*, W 253²¹.

andfengstōw f. *receptacle*, Çhrd 109³.

andfex=andfeax; **andgelōman**=andlōman

andget=andgit

andgete *plain, manifest*, Cr 1243. [andgiete]

andgiet (ond-; e, i, y) n., andgiete f. *understanding, intellect, Mt*; Æ,CP : *knowledge, perception*, CP : *sense, meaning*, Æ,CP : *one of the five senses* : *plan, purpose.* ['*angit*']

andgietful (e,i,y) *intelligent, sensible*, RB,W.

andgietfullic (i,y) *intelligible, clear*, ÆGr 4¹¹. adv. -līce, CP.

andgietlēas (i) *foolish, senseless*, Æ.

andgietlēast (i,y) f. *want of understanding*, Æ.

andgietlic (i) *intelligible, clear*, AS 5¹⁶. adv. -līce, WW.

andgiettācen n. *sensible token, sign*, Gen 1539.

andgit=andgiet

andgitol *intelligent, sensible*, RB,WW.

andhēafod n. *heading, unploughed headland of a field*, EC.

andhetan, andhettan=andettan

andhweorfan³ *to move against, blow against*, B 548. [or ? onhweorfan]

andian *to be envious or jealous*, Æ.

andiendlīce *enviously*, Tf 108¹⁸.

andig *envious, jealous*, OEG.

andlāman=andlōman

andlang (o¹, o²) I. adj. *entire, continuous, extended.* andlangne dæg, niht *all day* (*night*) *long*, An,Gu. ['*along*'] II. prep. w. g. '*along*,' *by the side of*, Æ,Chr,KC; AO.

andlangcempa (anl-) *soldier fighting in line*, WW 450¹⁸.

andlanges adv. prep. *along*, Ct.

andlata (Cr 1436)=andwlita

andlēan† n. *retribution, retaliation.*

and-leofen (ie, i, y) f., -leofa m. *nourishment, food* : *money, wages.* [libban]

andlīcnes=onlīcnes

andliefen (AO,CP), andlifen=andleofen

andlōman (ā², u²) m. pl. *utensils, implements, vessels*, Gl.

andlong=andlang; **andlyfen**=andleofen

andmitta=anmitta; **andrǣdlīce**=undrǣdlīce

Andrēasmæsse f. *St Andrew's day* (30 Nov.), ÆGr 43¹¹. [v. '*mass*']

andrecefæt? n. *wine or oil press*, WW 123³⁷.

andribb n. '*pectusculum*,' *breast*, ExC 29²⁶,²⁷

andriesne=ondrysne

an-drysen-, -drysn-=ondrys(e)n-

andsaca† m. *adversary* : *denier, apostate.*

andsacian *to dispute, deny*, CP.

andsæc m. *denial, oath of purgation*, El,LL : *refusal* : *strife, resistance.* ['*andsech*']

andsǣte adj. *hateful, odious, repugnant,*
ÆGr : *hostile.* ['*andsete*']
andslyht† (=ie) m. *blow,* B (hond-).
andspurnan³ (y) *to stumble against,* NG.
andspurnes (y) f. *offence,* MtR.
āndstreces=ānstreces
and-sumnes, -sundnes (=on-) f. *purity,
chastity, virginity.* v. OEG 1696.
±andswarian *to '*answer,*' Lk*; Æ,CP.
andswaru f. '*answer,*' *reply, B,Jn*; CP.
and-swerian (VPs), -sworian=andswarian
andsȳn=ansīen
andtimber (y²)=ontimber
andŏr-=onŏr-
andung f. *jealousy,* LPs 77⁵⁸.
andūstrian *to deny (with oaths),* MtR 26⁷⁴.
andūstrung f. '*abominatio,*' MtR 24¹⁵.
andwǣscan=ādwǣscan
andward-=andweard-
andweal-=onweal-
±andweard *present, actual, existing,* Æ,CP :
opposite to.
±andweardian *to present, bring before one.*
(+andweardian also=andwyrdian.)
andweardlic *present, actual.* adv. -līce.
andweardnes f. *presence,* CP : *present time,*
BH : *dispensation,* W 243²⁵.
andwendednes=onwendednes
andweorc n. *matter, substance, material,* CP :
cause.
andwerd=and-weard, -wyrd
andwīg m. *resistance,* Gu 147.
andwille=ānwille
andwirdan=andwyrdan
andwīs *expert, skilful,* Jul 244.
andwīsnes f. *experience,* WW 20⁵.
andwist f. *support,* An 1542.
andwlata=andwlita
+andwlatod *shameless,* OEG 8³⁶⁵.
andwlita (a, eo) m. *face, forehead, countenance, form, B,MtR*; AO,CP. ['*anleth*']
andwlite n.=andwlita
andwliteful '*vultuosus,*' GPH 393.
andwrāð *hostile, enraged,* Pa 17.
andwreðian (?=āwr-) *to support,* Chrd 62²⁹.
and-wurd, -wyrd=andweard
±and-wyrdan, -wyrdian (e, i) *to answer,*
Æ,AO,Mt; CP. ['*andwurde*']
andwyrde n. *answer,* AO.
andwyrding f. *conspiracy,* WW 373¹¹.
andyde pret. of andōn (ondōn).
andytt-=andett-
āne=(1) ǣne, (2) heonu
ān-ēage, -ē(a)gede (ÆL) '*one-eyed,*' *blind
of one eye.*
ānecge adj. *having one edge,* WW 142³⁷.
+āned v.+ānian.
ānēge, ānēgede=ānēage
ānēhst=ānīhst

ānemnan *to announce, declare, Gu.* ['*aname*']
ānerian *to deliver, rescue,* LPs 24¹⁵; EPs 49²².
ānes=ǣnes; ānescian=āhnescian
ānett mn., ānetnes f. *solitude, seclusion,* CP.
anf-=onf-
ān-feald, -fald, -fealdlic *single, unmixed,
unique, superior,* CP : *simple, modest,
honest, sincere, Mt*; CP : *fixed, invariable:
singular* (gram.), ÆGr. ā. gerecednes *or*
sprǣc *prose.* ['*afald*'] adv. -līce.
ānfealdnes f. *unity, concord,* AO : *simplicity,*
CP.
anfealt f. *anvil,* OEG 11⁶⁷ and n. [cp. anfilte]
anfeng=andfeng
ānfēte *one-footed,* Rd 59¹.
an-fīlt (Æ), -filte (Gl), n. '*anvil.*'
anfindan=onfindan
ānfloga m. *lonely flier,* Seaf 62.
anfōn (AO)=onfōn
anforht *fearful,* Cross 117.
ānforlǣtan⁷ *to let go, lose, relinquish, abandon, surrender,* CP : *omit, neglect.*
ānforlǣtnes f. *loss, desertion,* BL 85' :
intermission.
anforngean *in front of,* RWH 45¹².
anga (o) m. *stimulus, sting, goad,* CP.
ānga† (ǣ, ē) *sole, only : solitary.*
angbrēost n. *tightness of the chest, asthma,*
Lcd.
ange=enge
angeald pret. 3 sg. of angildan.
angēan=ongēan
angel I. m. '*angle,*' *hook, fish-hook, Bo,
MtL* (ongul). II. m.=engel
Angel n. *Anglon, a district in Schleswig,
from which the Angles came,* AO.
Angelcynn n. *the English people : England,*
AO.
āngeld=āngilde
Angelfolc n. *the English people,* BH 472¹⁷.
angelic *like, similar,* Bo 44¹⁸.
angeltwicce fm. *a certain worm used as bait,
earthworm? Lcd,WW.* ['*angletwitch*']
Angelðeod f. *the English people : England.*
Angelwitan (o²) mp. *English councillors,*
LL 236 G 2.
āngenga I. *solitary, isolated,* Æ. II. m.
solitary goer, isolated one, B.
angerǣd=ungerād
āngetrum n. *illustrious company,* Ex 334.
angeweald=onweald
±angian *to be in anguish,* RPs 60³; 142⁴.
angin=anginn; angil=angel I.
angildan=ongieldan
āngilde (e, y) I. n. *single payment or rate of
compensation for damage, LL : the fixed price
at which cattle and other goods were received
as currency, LL.* ['*angild*'] II. adj. *to be
compensated for.* III. adv. *simply, only,* LL.

ãngildes=ãngilde III.

anginn n. *beginning, Æ*; AO,CP : *intention, design, enterprise, undertaking,* CP : *action, onset, attack* : *rising (of sun)* : *tip (of finger),* BF154[6]. ['*angin*']

anginnan (AO)=onginnan

angitan=ongietan; angitful=andgietful

Angle mp. *the Angles or English* (v. Angel).

angmōd *sad, sorrowful,* Æ,RB.

angmōdnes f. *sadness, sorrow,* W188[6].

angnægl m. *corn, 'agnail,'* Lcd30b.

angnere (on-) m. *corner of the eye,* WW 423[34].

angnes f. *anxiety, trouble, pain, fear,* Lcd, Ps.

angol-=angel-

angrisla (y) m. *terror,* BL203[7].

angrislic (y[2]) *grisly, terrible.* adv. -(en)lĭce.

ang-set, -seta m. *eruption, pustule, carbuncle,* WW.

angsum *narrow, hard, difficult.* adv. -sume.

±angsumian *to vex, afflict,* Æ.

angsumlic *troublesome, painful,* RB5[19]. adv. -lĭce, Æ.

angsumnes f. *pain,* Æ : *sorrow, trouble* : *difficulty, perplexity.*

ãngum=ænigum dat. of ænig.

ãngyld, ãngylde=ãngilde

angyn, angytan=anginn, ongietan

anh-=onh-

ãnhaga (o[2])† m. *solitary being, recluse.*

anhende (=on-) *on hand, requiring attention,* AO88[24].

ãnhende *one-handed, lame, weak,* Æ.

ãnhĭwe '*uniformis*,' OEG1046.

anhoga m. *care, anxiety,* Gu970.

ãnhoga=ãnhaga

ãnhorn, ãnhorna m. *unicorn,* Ps.

ãnhrǣdlĭce=ãnrǣdlĭce

ãnhundwintre *a hundred years old,* Gen 47[9].

ãnhȳdig† *resolute, firm, constant, stubborn, brave.*

ãnhyrne I. m. *unicorn.* II.=ãnhyrned

ãnhyrn-ed, -e(n)de *having one horn,* Ps.

-+ãnian *to unite,* BH214[3]. ['*one*' vb.]

ãnĭdan (ē, ȳ;=ĭe) *to restrain, repel* : *force.* ūt a. *expel, drive out.* [nĭed]

ãnig=ænig; ãn-ĭge, -ĭgge=ãnēage

anĭhst (=ĭe) *last, in the last place,* Wid 126.

ãniman[4] (y) *to take,* GD : *take away or from, deprive of,* Mt; CP. ['*anim*']

ãninga=ãnunga

ãniŏrlan *to cast down,* Chr675e.

anl-=andl-, onl-; anlǣc=anlēc

±ãnlǣcan *to unite,* ÆL : *collect,* ÆL.

ãnlaga *acting alone,* WW491[23].

anlang-=andlang-; ãnlāp- (NG)=ãnlĭp-

anlēc (on-) m. *respect, regard,* Æ.

ãnlegere *consorting with one man,* WW 171[15].

ãn-lēp-=ãnlĭ(e)p-

ãnlic '*only,*' *unique,* Lk : *solitary,* Ps : *catholic* : *beautiful.* [cp. ænlic]

+anlĭcian=+onl-

ãn-lĭepig, -lĭpig (Chr), lĭpe (CP), -lĭpie (æn-; ē, ȳ) I. adj. *single, separate, solitary, private, individual, special,* PPs,BH, MtR. ['*anlepi,*' '*onlepy*'] II. adv. *alone, only, severally.*

ãnlĭpnes (on-, ē[2], ȳ[2]) f. *loneliness,* BH128[23].

ãnlĭpum (ē[2]) *singly,* MtR26[22].

ãnlȳp-=ãnlĭ(e)p-

+anmēdan *to encourage,* AO. [mōd]

ãnmēde n. *unanimity, concord,* PPs54[13].

anmēdla m. *pomp, glory* : *pride, presumption, arrogance* : *courage.* [mōd]

anmitta m. *weight, balance, scales,* Gl. [and, mitta]

ãnmōd *of one mind, unanimous,* El; Æ : *steadfast, resolute, eager, bold, brave, fierce, proud,* CP. ['*anmod*'] adv. -lĭce.

ãnmōdnes f. *unity, unanimity,* CP: *steadfastness, resolution,* Lcd3·170[22].

ann pres. 3 sg. of unnan.

anna=heonu; ãnne (AO,CP) v. ãn.

ãnnes f. *oneness, unity,* BH; Æ : *agreement, covenant, Chr* : *solitude, Gu.* ['*annesse*']

ãnnihte adv. *one day old,* Lcd.

anoŏa=anda

ãnpæŏ† m. *narrow path.*

anpolle f. (Æ)=ampella; anr-=onr-

ãnrǣd *of one mind, unanimous* : *constant, firm, persevering, resolute,* Æ. ['*anred*']

ãnrǣdlic *constant, resolute* : *undoubting,* BL13[13]. adv. -lĭce *unanimously* : *resolutely, persistently, constantly, earnestly,* Æ : *definitely, decidedly.*

ãnrǣdnes f. *unanimity, agreement* : *constancy, firmness, diligence,* AO; Æ. ['*arednesse*']

ãnreces (Chr1010cde)=ãnstreces

ãnrēd-=ãnrǣd-; anribb=andribb; ans-= ands-, ons-, uns-

an-scēatan (Cp), -scēotan (Erf)=onscēotan

ãnseld n. *lonely dwelling, hermitage,* Gu 1214.

ãnsetl n. *hermitage,* RB135[9].

ãnsetla m. *anchorite, hermit,* GD,RB.

ansĭen I. (on-; ē, ĭ, ȳ) fn. *countenance, face,* CP,G : *form, figure, presence* : *view, aspect, sight, thing seen,* AO : *surface.* ['*onsene*'] II.† f. *lack, want.*

ansĭene (on-, ȳ[2])† *visible.*

anspel n. *conjecture,* WW382[5].

anspilde *salutary,* Lcd11b.

ãnsprǣce *speaking as one,* PPs40[7].

ānstandende ptc. *standing alone*, RB9⁷. as sb. *hermit*, Æ.

ānstapa m. *lonely wanderer*, PA15.

ānstelede *one-stalked, having one stem*, LCD.

ānstīg f. *narrow path? path up a hill?* (GBG) KC.

ānstonde=ānstandende

ānstrǽc (ǽ?) *resolute, determined*, CP.

ānstreces (ē?) *at one stretch, continuously, continually*, CHR894A.

ansund *sound, whole, entire, perfect, healthy*, Æ (on-) : *solid*, BF80²⁶.

an-sundnes, -sumnes f. *soundness, wholeness, integrity*.

ānswēge *harmonious, accordant*, WW129⁴⁴.

ansȳn=ansīen; ant-=and-, ont-, unt-

Antecrist m. *Antichrist*. [L.]

antefn m. *antiphon, 'anthem,'* BH; Æ.

antefnere (CM), antemnere (ÆP154⁶) m. *book of antiphons*.

āntīd (and-?) f. *similar time?* (*i.e.* the corresponding time of a following day) *appropriate time?* (Klb.) B219.

antifon=antefn

antre f. *radish*, LCD.

ānum *alone, solely*, Æ.

anunder=onunder

anung f. *zeal*, NG.

ānunga (i²) *at once, forthwith* : *quickly, shortly* : *entirely, altogether, throughout, by all means, uninterruptedly*, B : *necessarily, certainly*.

anw-=andw-, onw-, unw-

anwedd n. *security, pledge*, TC201¹⁶.

ānwīg n. *single combat, duel*, Æ,AO.

ānwīglīce *in single combat*, WW512²¹.

ānwiht=āwiht

ānwille I. adj. *wilful, obstinate*, CP, WW; Æ. ['*onwill'*] II. adv. *wilfully, obstinately*.

ānwillīce *obstinately*, CP.

ānwilnes f. *self-will, obstinacy, persistence*, CP. mid ānwilnesse *wantonly, wilfully*.

ānwintre adj. *one year old, yearling*, Ex12⁵.

ānwīte n. *single fine*, LL64,31¹.

anwlōh (DAN585)=onwealg?

ānwuht=āwiht

ānwunung f. *solitary abode*, RB134¹².

ānwylnes=ānwilnes

+anwyrdan *to conspire*, WW209⁴².

+anwyrde *known, acknowledged, confessed*.

anxsum-=angsum-

ānȳdan=ānīdan; anȳhst=anīhst

ānyman=āniman; anȳwan=onȳwan

apa m. '*ape,*' Gl,Lcd.

āpǽcan *to seduce, lead astray*, LL.

āparian *to discover, apprehend*, G,EC164¹⁷.

apelder-=apuldor-

āpinsian *to weigh, estimate, ponder, recount*, CP. [*L.* pensare]

āpinsung f. *weighing*, OEG1757.

apl=appel

āplantian *to plant*, ÆH.

āplatod *beaten into (metal) plates*, OEG. [v. '*plate*']

āpluccian *to pluck, gather*, ÆGR170¹⁴,BF 198²¹.

apostata m. *apostate*, LL(322¹⁴).

apostol (CHR), apostel m. *messenger*, JnL : '*apostle,*' MtR : *disciple*, ÆH1⁵²⁰. [*L.* from Gk.]

apostolhādt m. *apostleship*.

apostolic *apostolic*, BH; Æ. ['*apostly*']

appel, apple=æppel

Aprelis m. *April*, BF,MEN56.

āpriccan *to prick*, W146²¹.

Aprilis (BF84)=Aprelis

aprotane f. *southernwood, wormwood*, LCD 22a. [*L.* abrotonum; from Gk.]

apulder, apuldor fm. *apple-tree*, LCD,WW.

apuldorrind f. *bark of apple-tree*, LCD.

apuldortūn (e³) m. *apple-orchard*, WW.

apuldre, apuldur=apulder

āpullian *to pull*, LCD1·362¹⁰.

āpundrian? *to measure out, requite?* (GK) : *estimate?* (BTac), EL580.

āpyffan *to exhale, breathe out*, GL.

āpyndrian *to weigh*, HGL512⁷⁸ (āwynd-?).

āpȳtan *to put out (eyes)*, NC338.

ār m. I.† *messenger, servant, herald, apostle, angel*. [*Got.* airus] II. f. '*oar,*' Chr,Gn. III. f. *honour, worth, dignity, glory, respect, reverence*, BH,Gen,JnLR,Ph; AO, CP : *grace, favour, prosperity, benefit, help*, B : *mercy, pity. An : landed property, possessions, revenue*, Æ,AO : *ecclesiastical living, benefice : ownership*, LL : *privilege*, LL,76,42². ['*are,*' '*ore*'] IV. n. '*ore,*' *brass, copper*, Æ,BH,CP,G,PS; AO. V.(NG)=ǽr

āracsian=ārasian

ārǽcan wv. *to reach, get at*, Chr : *hold forth, reach out*, Æ : *get (a thing for a person)*, ÆGr. ['*areach*']

ārǽd I. (ē) m. *welfare*, LL184n. II. *prepared, resolute, determined*, WA5; GNE 192?

arǽda (BO46²²)=aroda? v. arod.

ārǽdan¹ (but usu. wk.) *to appoint, prepare : arrange, settle, decide*, BH : *guess, prophesy, interpret, utter*, Lk,Bo,Da,CP : *read, read out, read to (any one)*, CP. ['*aread*']

ārǽdnes (ē²) f. *condition, stipulation*, BH.

ārǽfan *to set free, unwrap*, WW.

ārǽfn-an, -ian *to carry out, accomplish : endure, suffer*, Æ,AO : *keep in mind, ponder*, Æ. [æfnan]

ārǽfniendlic *endurable, possible*, WW.

ārǽman *to raise, elevate (oneself)*, Æ : (†) *rise, stand up*.

āræpsan (*-ræf-) *to intercept*, GL.
ārǣran *to lift up, raise, set up, create, establish, An,Chr,Jn* : *build, erect, Jn* : *rear* (*swine*), LL449 : *spread, disseminate* : *disturb, upset*. ūp ā. *bring up, raise up, exalt, CP.* [*'arear'*]
ārǣrend m. *one who arouses*, DHy18¹⁵.
ārǣrnes f. *raising, elevation*, AO.
ārǣsan *to rush*, ÆH140¹³.
ārāflan *to unravel, disentangle*, CP.
ārāsian *to lay open, search out, test, detect, discover* : *reprove, correct*, CP : *suspect*, BHo256²⁹. ārāsod *skilled*, BF94¹.
ārblǣd n. *oar-blade*, Æ.
arblast m. *cross-bow*, CHR1079D. [*O.Fr.* arbaleste]
arc mf. (also earc, earce) *ark, coffer, chest, box*, Æ. [*L.* arca]
arce I. (æ, e) m. *archiepiscopal pallium*, CHR. II. f. (BF192³³)=arc
arcebiscop (æ¹, e¹, y³, e⁴, eo⁴) m. *'archbishop,' CP,Chr,KC.*
arcebiscopdōm m. *post of archbishop*, CHR 616.
arcebiscophād (eo) m. *post of archbishop*, BH49²³.
arcebiscoprīce n. *'archbishopric,' post of archbishop, Chr.*
arcebiscopstōl m. *archiepiscopal see*, CHR.
arcediacon m. *'archdeacon,' WW.*
arcehād (e) m. *post of archbishop*, ÆH.
arcerīce n. *archbishopric*, CHR1051.
arcestōl (æ¹) m. *archiepiscopal see*, CHR.
ārcræftig *respected, honourable*, DA551.
ārdǣde *merciful*, BL131².
ārdagas mp. *festival days*, WW206³¹.
ardlic=arodlic; **āre** f.=ār III.
āreaflan *to separate, divide*, Ex290.
āreccan *to spread out, put forth, stretch out*: *lift up, erect, build up* : *say, relate, declare, speak out, explain, expound, translate, CP,G* : *astonish* : *adorn? deck?* RIM10. [*'arecche'*]
ārecelēasian *to be negligent, neglect*, A9·102⁶⁸, VH,WYN66.
ared=arod
āre̅d=ārǣd
āreddan=āhreddan
āredian *to make ready, devise, provide, arrange, carry out*, CP : *find, find one's way, reach* : *find out, understand*. [rǣde]
ārefnan=ārǣfnan
ārendan *to tear off*, LCD101a.
ārengan *to make proud, exalt*, A11·117³²? (? arencan, BTs).
āreōdian *to redden, blush*: *put to shame*, RPs69⁴.
āreōsan=āhreōsan; **āre̅ran**=ārǣran
āretan *to cheer, gladden*, Æ. [rot]

arewe=arwe
ārfæst *respected, honest, pious, virtuous, Æ*, CP : *merciful, gracious, compassionate, Æ* : *respectful*.
ārfæstlic *pious*, DR,RWH94¹⁴. adv. -līce.
ārfæstnes f. *virtue, honour, grace, goodness, piety* : *pity, mercy, Æ*.
ārfæt nap. -fatu, n. *brazen vessel, Æ*.
ārfest=ārfæst
ārful *respected, venerable* : *favourable, kind, merciful* : *respectful*. adv. -līce *graciously, Æ*.
arg (NG)=earg; **argang**=earsgang
ārgeblond=ēargebland
argentille f. *argentilla* (*plant*), GL. [*L.*]
ārgeotere m. *brass-founder*, AO54²⁰.
ārgesweorf n. *brass filings*, LCD30b.
ārgeweorc n. *brass-work*, WW398²⁴.
ārgifa m. *giver of benefits*, CRAFT11.
arhlīce=earglīce
ārhwæt *eager for glory*, †CHR937A.
±ārian *to honour, respect, Æ,CP* : *endow* : *regard, care for, favour, be merciful to, spare, pardon, Æ*; CP. [*'are'*]
ārīdan¹ *to ride*, AO118³³.
āriddan=āhreddan
āri(g)end mf. *benefactor, benefactress*, LCD, W257⁴.
āriht *'aright,' properly*, LL.
āriman *to number, count, enumerate*, CP; AO : *relate*. [*'arime'*]
ārinnan³ *to run out, pass away*, SOL479.
ārīsan I. (sv¹) *to 'ARISE,' get up, Æ,CP* : *rise*: *spring from, originate* : *spring up, ascend*. II.=†rīsan I.
ārist=ǣrist
ārlēas *dishonourable, base, impious, wicked, Æ,CP* : *cruel*, JUL4. [*Ger.* ehrlos] adv. -līce Æ.
ārlēasnes f. *wickedness*, BH,Bo.
ārlēast f. *disgraceful deed*, MET.
ārlic I. *honourable* : *fitting, agreeable, proper*, AO : *delicious*. II.=ǣrlic
ārlīce adv. I. *honourably, becomingly, graciously, kindly, pleasantly, mercifully*, CP. II. (RG)=ǣrlīce
ārloc n. *'oarlock,' rowlock*, WW288⁶.
arm=earm
armelu *'harmala,' wild rue*, Lcd.
ārmorgen=ǣrmorgen
arn pret. 3 sg. of iernan. **arn-**=earn-
arod (wk. aroda) *quick, bold, ready*, CP.
ārod pp. of ārian.
arodlic *quick*. adv. -līce *quickly* : *vigorously, Æ,CP*.
arodnes f. *spirit, boldness*, CP41¹⁷.
arodscipe m. *energy, dexterity*, CP.
ārōm? *copperas*, LCD (v. MLR17·165).
aron (NG) used as pres. pl. of wesan.

ārsāpe f. *verdigris*, Lcd 3·14³¹. [sāpe]
ārscamu f. *shame, modesty*, PPs 68¹⁹.
ārsmlŏ m. *coppersmith*, WW 99³.
ārstæft m. (often in pl.) *support, assistance, kindness, benefit, grace.*
art, arŏ (NG)=eart, pres. 2 sg. of wesan.
ārŏegn m. *servant*, BH 378¹¹.
ārŏing n. *a thing of value*, LkR 21¹.
arud=arod
ārung f. *honour, respect, reverence*, AO : *pardon.*
ārunnen=āurnen, pp. of ārinnan.
arwe (rew-, ruw-) f. '*arrow*,' *An,Chr.*
ārwela v. ĕarwela
ār-weorŏ, -weorŏe *honourable, venerable, revering, pious*, CP. adv. -weorŏe.
ārwẹorŏful (u²) *honourable*, Æ.
±ārweorŏian (u², y²) *to honour, reverence, worship, extol.*
ārweorŏlic *venerable, honourable.* adv. -līce *reverentially, solemnly, kindly*, Æ. ['*arworthly*']
ārweorŏnes f. *reverence, honour*, CP.
ārweorŏung (y²) f. *honour*, Ps.
ārwesa *respected*, RB 115²⁰.
+ārwierŏan? (y²) *to honour*, LkL 6³⁴ (BTs).
ārwierŏe=ārweorŏ
ārwiŏŏe f. *oar-thong, rowlock*, Æ.
arwunga, arwunge (A)=earwunga
ārwurŏ, -wyrŏ=ārweorŏ
āryd-dan, -dran, -tran *to strip, plunder*, Gl.
āryderian *to blush, be ashamed*, BRPs 69⁴.
ārȳpan *to tear off, strip*, Rd 76⁷.
ārȳŏ v. ĕarȳŏ.
āsadian *to satiate, surfeit*, MFH 150.
āsæcgan=āsecgan; āsægdnes=onsægednes
āsǣlant *to bind, fetter, ensnare.*
āsǣndan=āsendan
asal, asald (NG)=esol
āsānian *to droop, flag*, Gu 1148, LV 57.
āsāwan⁷ *to sow, sow with*, Æ.
asca (NG) m.=asce; āscacan=āsceacan
āscādan=āscēadan
āscæcan=āsceacan
āscæfen pp. of āsceafan.
āscǣre=ǣscǣre; āscafan=āsceafan
āscamelic *shameful*, HGl 500.
āscamian (ea) *to feel shame*, Ps,Cr. ['*ashame(d)*']
ascas nap. of æsc.
ascbacen (ax-) *baked on ashes*, GD 86³⁰.
asce (æ, cs, x) f. (*burnt*) '*ash*,' *Lcd* : *dust (of the ground)*, MtL.
āsceacan⁶ (a) *to shake off, remove*, Mt : *depart, flee, desert, forsake*, Æ : *shake, brandish*, Ph. ['*ashake*']
āscēadan⁷ (ā) *to separate, hold aloof or asunder, exclude*, CP : *make clear, cleanse, purify.*
āsceafan (a) *to shave off*, Lcd.

āscealian *to peel off*, WW 398¹⁰.
āsceaman *to be ashamed*, WW 229²⁰.
āscearpan=āscirpan
āscellan=āscillan, āscilian
āscĕofan=āscūfan; āsceon-=onscun-
āsceortian=ascortian
āscĕotan² *to shoot, shoot out*, Æ,AO : *drop out, fall*, Æ : *lance* (surgery), ÆL 20⁶³ : *eviscerate*, OEG 46⁴⁷.
āsceppan=āscieppan; āscer-=āscir-
āscian (ācs-, āhs-, āx-) *to* '*ask*,' *inquire, seek for, demand*, CP : *call, summon* : *examine, observe* : (+) *learn by inquiry, discover, hear of*, Chr : (†) *announce.*
āsciendlic (āx-) *interrogative*, ÆGr 260¹⁴.
āscieppan⁶ *to make, create, Ex* : *appoint, determine, assign*, AO. ['*ashape*']
āscihtan (=y²) *to drive away*, RPs 87¹⁹.
āscildan (=ie) *to protect*, DR.
āscilian *to separate, divide*, v. OEG 1367n.; FM 100.
āscīmian *to shine*, Lcd 86b.
āscīnan¹ *to flash or shine forth, beam, radiate, be clear*, GD.
āsciran (e, y;=ie) *to cut off, cut away*, Æ.
āscirian (y;=ie) *to cut off, separate, divide, remove*, Æ : *set free, deprive of* : *arrange, destine.*
āscirigendlic (y²) *disjunctive*, ÆGr 259¹⁴.
āscirpan (e, ea, y;=ie) *to sharpen, make acute*, CP.
āscortian (eo) *to become short, fail*, Æ : *pass away, elapse.*
āscrēadian *to prune, lop*, ÆH 2·74¹².
āscrencan *to displace, trip up, cause to stumble*, CP. ['*aschrench*']
āscrepan⁵ *to scrape, clear away*, Gl,Lcd.
āscrūtnian (ūdn) *to investigate, examine*, Bf.
āscūfan² *to drive out, remove, expel, banish*, Æ : *push (away), give up (to).*
ascun-=onscun-
±āscung f. '*asking*,' *questioning, inquiring, question, Bo,Met*; Æ,CP.
āscyhhan *to scare away, reject*, RPs 50¹³.
āscylfan *to destroy*, GPH 393⁴⁹.
āscylian, āscyllan=āscilian
āscyndan *to separate, part (from)* : *drive away (from)*, Æ : *take away*, RHy 12¹².
āscyr-=āscir-
āscȳran *to make clear*, Æ. [scīr]
āsealcan (Gen 2167)=āseolcan
āsēarian *to wither, dry up, Lcd*; CP. ['*asear*']
āsēcan *to seek out, select* : *search out, examine, explore* : *seek for, require, ask, PPs* : *search through, penetrate.* ['*aseek*']
āsecgan I. *to say out, express, tell, narrate, explain, announce*, AO. II.=onsecgan
āsecgendlic *utterable*, Æ.
āsēdan (oe) *to satiate*, WW 45⁸. [sæd]

äsegendnes f. *an offering*, AA 36¹⁷.
äsellan *to give up, hand over, deliver* : *expel, banish.*
äsencan *to sink, immerse,* OEG 829.
äsendan *to send away, send forth, send, give up, Mt; Æ.* [*'asend'*]
äsengan (JUL 313)=äsecgan
äseolcan³ *to become slack, remiss, relaxed, weak,* Æ,CP.
äsēon I. sv⁵ *to look upon, behold,* HL 16²⁵⁵. **II.** sv¹ *to strain,* LCD.
äseonod *relaxed,* WW 228²⁵. [seonu]
äsēoðan² *to seethe, boil,* CP : *refine, purify : examine.*
äsēowan *to sew,* Cp 421 P (io).
äsetnes f. *institute, law,* LL.
asettan=onsettan
äsettan *to set, put, place* : *store up,* Lk 12¹⁹ (MLR 17) : *fix, establish, appoint, set up or in, erect, build, plant, AO,Mt;* Æ : *apply,* PPs 68²⁸ : *transport oneself over, cross (the sea, etc.)* : *take away,* LL 11,12. sīð *or* sīðas ä. *to perform a journey, travel.* [*' aset'*]
äsēðan *to affirm, confirm,* Æ. [sōð]
äsīcan I. sv¹ *to sigh,* Sc. **II.** (=ȳ) *to wean,* CPs 130².
äsiftan *to sift,* LCD 13b.
äsīgan¹ *to sink, sink down, decline, fall down, Chr;* CP. [*' asye'*]
äsincan³ *to sink down, fall to pieces,* Æ.
äsingan³ *to sing out, sing, deliver (a speech), compose (verse),* BH.
äsittan⁵ *to dwell together, settle, El* : *apprehend, fear : run aground.* ūt a. *starve out.* [*' asit'*]
äslacian *to become slack, decline, diminish,* Æ,CP : *grow tired : make slack, loosen, relax, dissolve.*
äslacigendlic *remissive,* ÆGR 228⁵.
äslæccan *to slacken, loosen,* WW.
äslæcian=äslacian
äslǣpan⁷ (ä) *to slumber, dream : be paralysed,* LCD : *be benumbed,* MFH 91⁶.
äslǣwan *to blunt, make dull,* OEG 18b⁶⁵.
äslāpan=äslǣpan
äslāwian *to become sluggish, be torpid,* CP. [slāw]
äslēan⁶ *to strike, beat, cut,* Æ : *erect : make way : paralyse.* of ä. *strike off, behead, Mt;* AO. [*' aslay'*]
äslēpen=äslēopen pret. opt. 3 pl. of äslūpan.
äslīdan¹ *to slide, slip, fall, Ps;* Æ,CP. [*' aslide'*]
äslīding f. *slipping,* GPH 388⁶².
äslītan¹ (ȳ) *to slit, cleave, cut off, destroy,* CP.
äslūpan² *to slip off, escape, disappear (of), Gen.* [*' aslip'*]
äslȳtan=äslītan

äsmēagan *to consider, examine, investigate, devise, elicit, treat of, think,* Æ : *look for, demand.*
äsmēagung f. *scrutiny, consideration,* APT 3¹⁶.
äsmēan=äsmēagan
±**äsmir-ian,** -wan *to smear, anoint,* LEV 2⁴.
äsmīðian *to do smith's work, fashion, forge, fabricate,* Æ,WW.
äsmorian *to smother, strangle,* AO,CP.
äsmorung f. *choking, suffocation,* LCD 18a.
äsmūgan=äsmēagan
äsnǣsan (ä²) *to spit, impale, stab,* LL 68,36. [*' asnese'*]
asnīðan¹ *to cut off,* LCD.
äsoden (WW 20⁴⁴) pp. of äsēoðan.
äsogen pp. of äsūgan.
äsolcen (pp. of äseolcan) *sluggish, idle, indifferent, dissolute,* Æ.
äsolcennes f. *sleepiness, sloth, laziness, W;* Æ. [*' aswolkeness'*]
äsolian *to become dirty,* A 2·374.
äspanan⁶ *to allure, seduce, persuade, urge, insinuate,* AO.
äspannan⁷ *to unbind, unclasp,* GD 214²⁴.
äsparian *to preserve,* GD 159²⁴.
äspeaft (JnL 9⁶)=äspeoft
äspēdan *to survive, escape,* AN 1628.
äspelian *to be substitute for, represent, take the place of,* LL,RB. ä. of *be exempt from,* CHRD.
äspendan *to spend, expend, distribute, squander, consume, AO;* Æ. [*' aspend'*]
äspeoft pret. 3 sg. *spit out,* JnR 9⁶. [v. speoft]
äsperian=äspyrian
aspide m. *asp, adder, serpent, Ps;* Æ. [*' aspide'*]
äspillan *to destroy,* JnL 12¹⁰.
äspinnan³ *to spin,* WW.
äspirian=äspyrian
äspīwan¹ (ȳ) *to spew up, vomit,* Æ,CP.
äsplǣtan? *to split.* v. ES 49·156.
äspornan *to cast down,* EPs 145⁷. [spurnan]
äsprēadan *to stretch out, extend,* EPs 35¹¹.
äsprecan *to speak out, speak,* PPs.
äsprengan *to cause to spring, fling out,* ÆL 8²¹³.
äsprettan=äspryttan
äsprindlad *ripped up,* LCD 80b.
äspringan³ (y) *to spring up or forth, break forth, spread,* Æ; AO : *arise, originate, be born,* Æ : *dwindle, diminish, fail, cease.* äsprungen *dead.* [*' aspring'*]
äspringung f. *failing,* VPs 141⁴.
äspritan=äspryttan
äsproten pp. of äsprūtan.
ä-sprungennes, -sprungnes f. *failing, exhaustion, death : eclipse.*

āsprūtan² (=ēo) *to sprout forth*, PPs 140⁹.
āspryngan=āspringan
āspryttan¹ (e, i) *to sprout out, bring forth*, Æ.
āspylian *to wash oneself*, Bo 115⁷.
āspyrgend m. *investigator*, VHy 13²⁵.
āspyrging f. '*adinventio*,' WW 513¹⁵.
āspyrian (e, i) *to track, trace out, investigate, study, explore, discover*, BF,SolK.
āspȳwan=āspīwan
assa m. *he-ass*, Æ,Mt,Jn; CP. ['*ass*']
assen f. *she-ass*, WW 108²⁶.
assmyre f. *she-ass*, Gen 32¹⁵.
āst f. *kiln*, WW 185³⁰; A 9·265. ['*oast*']
āstǣgan *to go up, embark*, MkR 6³².
āstǣlan *to lay to one's charge*, LL (264¹⁵).
āstǣnan¹ *to adorn with precious stones*, W.
āstæppan *to imprint (a footstep)*, NC 344¹ (v. MLR 17).
āstærfan (MtR)=āstyrfan
āstandan⁶ *to stand up, stand forth, rise up, arise*, B; Æ : *continue, endure*, Lk; CP. ['*astand*']
āstandennes f. *perseverance*, ÆL 23b²⁷² : *existence, subsistence*.
āstēapan=āstȳpan
āstellan I. *to set forth, set, put, afford, supply, display, appoint*, AO,CP : *set up, establish, confirm, institute, ordain, undertake, start*, AO; Æ : *undergo*, Æ. II. *to fly off, rush.*
āstemnian *to found, build*, BH 4¹⁷.
āstemped *engraved, stamped*, WW 203²⁷.
āstencan *to scatter*, GD 42³³.
āstēop-=āstȳp-
āsteorfan³ *to die*, MH 62²⁷.
āstēp-=āstȳp-; āster-=āstyr-
asterion '*asterion*,' *pellitory*, Lcd 1·164.
āstīflan *to become stiff*, Æ.
āstīfīcian=āstȳfecian
āstīgan¹ *to proceed, go*, Æ : (usu. w. ūp, niðer, *etc.*) *rise, mount, ascend, descend*, Jn; Æ,CP : *be puffed up*, AO 264⁸. ['*astye*']
āstīgend m. *rider*, ARHy 4¹.
āstigian *to ascend, mount*, MkL,WW 93²¹.
āstīgnes (ǣ¹) f. *ascent*, EPs 103⁴.
āstihtan *to determine on, decree*, CHR 998.
āstihting (OEG)=ātyhting
āstillian *to still, quiet*, RWH 75³⁰.
āstingan³ *to bore out, pierce out*, CHR : *stab.*
āstintan=āstyntan; āstirian=āstyrian
āstīðian *to become hard, dry up, wither : grow up? become powerful?* TC 203²⁰.
āstondnes=āstandennes
āstrǣlian *to cast forth, hurl*, RPs 75⁹.
āstreccan *to stretch out, stretch forth, extend, lay low*, Æ : *prostrate oneself, bow down*, CP. ['*astretch*']
āstregdan *to sprinkle*, GD,LL.
āstregdnes? f. *sprinkling*, DR.
āstrenged *(made strong), malleable*, WW.

āstrīenan† (ēo, ȳ) *to beget.*
āstrogden pp. of āstregdan.
āstrowenes f. *length*, HGL 443.
āstrȳnan=āstrīenan
āstundian *to take upon oneself*, Æ.
āstȳfecian *to suppress, eradicate*, CP.
āstyllan=āstellan
āstyltan *to be astonished*, LkLR.
āstyntan (i) *to blunt, repress, restrain, stop, overcome*, Gl. ['*astint*']
āstȳpan (ē, ēa, ēo) *to deprive, bereave*, GD.
āstȳpte *orphans.* [stēop]
āstȳp(ed)nes (ē², ēo²) f. *privation, bereavement*, GD,WW.
āstȳran *to guide, control*, AS 9¹³.
āstyrfan (æ, e;=ie) *to kill, destroy*, Cr,Mt. ['*asterve*']
āstyrian *to stir up, excite, move, move forward, raise*, JnMk; Æ : *be roused, become angry*, Æ. āstyred weorðan *be or become anxious*, Æ. ['*astir*']
-āstyriendlic v. un-ā.
āstyrigend m. *a stirrer-up*, GPH 393⁷⁸.
āstyrred *starry*, Sc.
āstyrung f. *motion*, Lcd.
ā-sūcan², -sūgan *to suck, suck out, drain : consume*, WW 501³³ (ōsogen).
ā-sundran, -sundron=onsundran
āsundrian=āsyndrian
āsūrian *to be or become sour*, Lcd,WW.
āswǣman *to roam, wander about : pine, grieve*, Æ : *be ashamed*, LPs 24²⁰.
āswǣrn-=āswarn-
āswǣtan *to burst out in perspiration*, MH 20¹².
āswāmian *to die away*, Gen 376 : *cease.*
āswāpan⁷ (but pp. āswōpen) *to sweep away, remove, clean*, CP.
āswārcan *to languish*, LPs 38¹².
āswārcnian *to confound*, BSPs 70²⁴.
āswārnian *to be confounded*, Ps.
āswārnung f. *shame, confusion*, LPs 43¹⁶.
āswaðian *to investigate*, OEG 5¹¹.
āsweartian *to turn livid, become ashy or black*, CP.
āswebban† *to lull, soothe, set at rest : put to death, destroy*, Jud. ['*asweve*']
āswefecian *to extirpate*, WW.
āswellan³ *to swell*, CP.
āsweltan³ *to die*, CHR.
āswencan *to afflict*, DR.
āswengan *to swing off, shake off, cast forth.* ā. on *cast upon*, RPs 21¹¹.
āsweorcan³ *to droop*, Jos 2¹¹.
āsweorfan³ *to file off, polish*, GPH.
āswēpa=ǣswēpa
āswerian⁶ *to swear*, PPs 131¹¹.
āswic-=ǣswic-
āswīcan¹ *to desert, abandon, betray, deceive*, Mt : *offend, irritate, provoke.* ['*aswike*']

āswīfan¹ *to wander, stray,* WW.
āswind=æswind
āswindan³ *to become weak, shrink, fade away, perish, decay, dissolve, Bo;* Æ,CP. [' *aswind* ']
āswingan³ *to scourge,* DR42⁶.
āswōgan⁷ *to cover over, choke,* CP411¹⁷.
āsworettan *to sigh, grieve,* GD.
āswornian (NC271)=āswarnian
āswundennes f. *idleness,* BH160²⁵.
āsynderlic *remote,* OEG2514.
±āsynd-ran, -rian (u²) *to separate, divide, disjoin, sever, Soul;* Æ,CP : *distinguish, except.* [' *asunder* ']
āsyndrung f. *division,* WW.
at=æt; ātǣfran (CP467¹⁹)=ātīefran
ātǣsan *to wear out, injure, strike, smite,* Æ : *wound,* CP296¹⁸.
atāwian=ætīewan
āte (ǣ) f. '*oats,*' *Lcd* : *wild oats, tares,* Gl,WW.
āteallan=ātellan; ātēfran=ātīefran
ategār=ætgār; atel=atol
ātellan *to reckon up, count, Bo;* AO. ā. wið balance against : *tell, enumerate,* CP : *explain, interpret.* [' *atell* ']
ātemian *to tame, subdue, render quiet,* CP.
ātendan *to set on fire, kindle, inflame, Chr* : *trouble, perplex,* BF94⁹. [' *atend* ']
ātending f. *incentive,* Sc221¹⁷.
ātēon² *to draw up, out, off or from, remove, pull out, lead out, draw, B,BH;* AO,CP. ūp ā. *draw up, move away : protract,* Æ : *move, journey, roam : deal with, dispose of, apply, use, Mt;* Æ,CP. [' *atee* ']
ātēorian *to fail, become exhausted, weary, cease, Ps;* Æ : *be defective,* ÆGR. [' *atire* ']
ātēori(g)endlic *transitory, perishable,* Æ : *failing : defective,* ÆGR.
ātēorodnes f. *cessation, exhaustion,* Æ (3⁴⁹⁵); BPs118⁵³.
ātēorung f. *failing, weariness,* Æ.
ātēowan=ōðīewan; āter=ātor
āteran⁴ *to tear away,* CP359²⁰.
āteriendlic=āteoriendlic
āterima (ētr-) *oat-bran,* Lcd 3·292'.
ātertānum dp. *with poisoned twigs or poison-stripes?* (or ? -tēarum *with poison-drops*) B1460.
āteshwōn adv. *at all,* CM987. [āwiht]
athēd (GL)=æthȳd
ātīdrian *to grow weak,* GD59²⁶ (ydd).
ātīefran (ǣ, ē, ī, ȳ) *to draw, depict,* CP.
atīewan=ōðīewan; ātīht-=ātyht-
ātillan *to touch, reach,* GenC11⁴.
ātimbr-an, -ian *to erect, build,* AO,CP.
ātimplian *to provide with spikes,* NC271.
ātīwan=ōðīewan
ātland *oat-land,* EC208'.

ātlēag m. *oat-field,* EC448⁹.
atol I. (e², u²) *dire, terrible, ugly, deformed, repulsive, unchaste, B.* [' *atel* '] II.† n. *horror, evil.*
+atolhīwian *to disfigure, make hideous,* WW220³¹.
atolian *to disfigure,* WW220²⁶.
atolic, atollic *dire, terrible, deformed, repulsive,* Æ. adv. -līce.
ātor, āt(to)r, (ǣ) n. *poison, venom, Lcd;* AO, CP : *gall, Gl.* [' *atter* ']
ātorbǣre *poisonous,* ÆH1·72²².
ātorberende *poisonous, venomous,* Lcd,W.
ātorcoppe (ǣ) f. *spider, Lcd;* LPs38¹² (-loppe). [' *attercop* ']
ātorcrǣft (āttor-) m. *art of poisoning,* W.
ātorcyn (ǣ) n. *poison,* Sol219.
ātordrinca m. *poisonous draught,* MH.
ātorgeblǣd n. *swelling caused by poison,* Lcd162b.
ātorlāðe f. *plant used as antidote to poison, betonica?* Lcd,WW. [' *atterlothe* ']
ātorlic *poison-like, bitter,* WW. [' *atterlich* ']
ātorsceaða† m. *poisonous enemy.*
ātorspere n. *poisoned spear,* RD18⁹.
ātorðīgen (ātt-) f. *taking of poison,* Lcd1·4⁵.
ātr=ātor; ātr-=āðr-
ātrahtnian *to treat, discuss,* BF72,142.
ātredan⁵ *to extract, extort,* LL.
ātreddan *to search out, examine,* PPs.
ātrendlian *to roll,* Met5¹⁷. [v. ' *trendle* ']
ātres gs. of ātor.
atrum n. *ink,* A13·28¹⁵. [*L.* atramentum]
ātter, āttor=ātor
attrum=atrum
atul=atol; ātur=ātor
ātwēonian *to cause doubt,* BF182⁸.
ātyddran=ātīdrian
ātȳdran *to beget, create,* EL1279. [tūdor]
ātȳfran=ātīefran
ātyhtan (i) *to entice, allure, incite : be attentive : produce,* RD51³ : *stretch, extend, turn.*
ātyhting (i) f. *intention, aim : instigation,* OEG2³⁰⁴.
ātymbran=ātimbran
ātȳnan I. *to shut off, exclude,* PPs,WW. [tūn] II.=ontȳnan
ātyndan=ātendan; ātȳrian=ātēorian
atȳwan=ōðīewan
āð m. '*oath,*' *(judicial) swearing, B,Chr,Mt;* AO : *fine for an unsuccessful oath,* KC (v. BTac).
āð-=ōð-
aðamans m. *adamant,* CP271². [*L.*]
āðbryce m. *perjury,* W164⁷.
āðecgan *to take food, consume?* Lcd57a : *oppress?* RD1²,⁷(Tupper).
āðegehāt=āðgehāt
āðegen *distended (with food),* WW.

āðencan *to think out, devise, contrive, invent,* AO : *intend,* B.
āðenenes f. *extension,* VHy 7⁴⁸.
ā-ðennan, -ðenian *to stretch out, extend, draw out, expand,* AO : *apply (the mind),* CP : *prostrate.*
āðenung f. *stretching out, distension,* LCD 71b : 'stratum,' ALRPs 131³.
āðēodan=āðīedan
āðēostrian (ē, īe, ī) *to become dark, obscured, eclipsed,* Bo; CP,VPs. ['athester']
āðer=āhwæðer
āðerscan *to thresh out,* ÆL 31¹²¹⁷.
āðēstrian=aðēostrian; āðēwan=āðȳwan
āðexe f. *lizard,* Cp 1182.
āðfultum m. *confirmation (confirmers) of an oath,* LL.
āðgehāt (āðe-) n. *promise on oath, oath,* WW.
āðīddan (=y) *to thrust, push,* OEG 50³.
āðīedan (ēo, ȳ) *to separate,* CP.
āðīerran *to clean,* CP.
āðīestrian (CP)=āðēostrian
āðīndan³ *to swell, puff up, inflate, increase,* CP : *melt, pass away.* (cp. ðindan)
āðīndung f. *swelling,* LCD 93a.
ā-ðīstrian, -ðīsðrigan (CP)=āðēostrian
āðl (BH,VPs)=ādl
āðloga m. *perjurer,* CR 165.
āðol=ādl
āðolian *to hold out, endure, suffer,* Æ.
āðolware mp. *citizens,* GnE 201.
āðor=āhwæðer
āðracian *to dread : frighten.* [=onðracian]
āðræstan *to twist out, wrest out,* GL.
āðrāwan⁷ *to curl, twist, twine,* Æ.
āðrēatian *to dissuade from,* CP 293¹⁰ : *chide, rebuke,* GenC 37¹⁰.
āðrēotan² (pers. and impers.) *to tire of, weary, be tiresome to, displease, disgust,* Æ,AO,CP.
āðrescan=aðerscan
āðrīetan (ȳ) *to weary,* Æ,AO.
āðringan³ *to crowd or press out : rush forth, break out.* ūt ā. *emboss.*
āðrīostrian (MtR 24²⁹)=āðēostrian
āðrīstian *to be bold, presume,* GD 70⁸⁰.
āðrotennes f. *wearisomeness,* WW 409²².
āðrotsum *irksome,* WW 510¹².
āðrōwian *to suffer,* LCD 68b.
āðroxen pp. of āðerscan.
āðrunten (pp. of *āðrintan) *swollen,* RD 38². (or? āðrūten)
āðrūten? (pp. of *āðrūtan) *swollen,* LCD.
āðryccan *to press, oppress,* DR.
ā-ðrysemian, -ðrysman (AO) *to suffocate, smother.* ['athrysm']
āðrytnes (æ¹,e²) f. *weariness,* DHy. [ðrēotan]
āðstæf m. *oath,* CPs 104⁹.

āðswara m.?=āðswaru
āðswaring=āðswerung
āðswaru f. *oath-swearing, oath,* Æ.
āðswerian? *to vow with an oath,* WW 387⁹.
āðswerung f. *oath-swearing,* CHR,RSPs 104⁹.
āðswyrd (æ¹, eo²) n. *oath-swearing,* EJVPs 104⁹; B 2064.
āðum m. *son-in-law, Æ;* AO : *brother-in-law.* ['odam']
āðumswerian mp. *son-in-law and father-in-law,* B 84.
āðundennes f. *swelling, tumour,* LCD : *contumacy,* WW 87¹⁷.
āðwænan *to diminish, soften,* LCD.
āðwēan⁶ *to wash, wash off, cleanse, baptize, anoint,* Æ,CP.
āðwedd n. *promise on oath,* WW 115¹⁶.
āðweran⁴ *to stir up, churn,* LCD.
āðwīnan *to vanish,* NC 338.
āðwītan¹ *to disappoint,* SPs 131¹¹.
āðwyrðe *worthy of credit.* v. LL 2·376.
āðȳan=āðȳwan
āðȳdan=āðīedan
āðylgian *to bear up,* ARSPs.
āðȳn=āðȳwan
āðynnian (i) *to make thin, reduce,* DHy 8¹⁰.
āðȳstrian (Æ)=āðēostrian
āðȳtan I. *to sound, blow (a horn),* DD 109. II. *to expel,* WW 19¹².
āðȳwan (ē) *to drive away,* AO : *press out or into, squeeze out.*
āuht=āwiht; āuðer=āhwæðer
āw=ǣ; āwa=ā
āwacan⁶ (on-) *to awake, Æ : arise, originate, spring forth, be born.* ['awake(n)']
āwacian *to awake,* Æ.
āwācian *to grow weak, decline, fall, belittle, Æ,CP : fall away, lapse, desist from, abstain, Æ : mollify, appease,* MFH 142⁶.
āwacnian=āwæcnian; āwæc-=āwec-
āwǣcan *to weaken,* BHB 250⁴.
āwæc-nian, -nan (on-; a, e) *to awaken, revive, Æ : arise, originate, spring from, AO.* ['awake(n)']
āwǣgan *to deceive : destroy, annul, make nugatory,* Æ.
āwǣlan *to harass, afflict,* NG.
āwǣled pp. of āwilwan.
āwæltan=āwyltan
āwæmmian=āwemman
āwænd-=āwend-, onwend-
āwænian=āwenian
āwærd pp. of āwierdan.
āwærged=āwierged
āwærlan *to avoid,* DR 39¹³.
āwæscan=āwascan; āwǣstan=āwēstan
āwandian *to fear, hesitate,* ÆGR 162².
āwanian *to diminish, lessen,* DR,KC.

āwannian *to become livid or black and blue*, GD 20³² (v. NC 332).

āwansian *to diminish*, KC 4·243⁶.

āwār=āhwǣr

āwārnian *to be confounded*, APs. (=āswarnian)

āwascan⁶ (æ) *to wash, bathe, immerse*, LCD.

āweallan⁷ *to well up, flow out, break forth, issue, swarm*, CP : *be hot, burn*.

āweardian *to guard, defend*, AO 202²⁴ (v.l.).

āweaxan⁶ *to grow, grow up, arise, come forth*, CP.

āweb=ōweb; āwec-=āwæc-

āweccan *to awake, rouse, incite, excite*, Mk, Lk; Æ,CP : *raise up, beget*. ['*awecche*']

āwecenes (æ) f. *incitement*, GD 199⁷.

āwecgan *to undermine, shake, move*, Æ.

āwēdan *to be or become mad, rage*, AO; Æ. ['*awede*'; wōd]

āwefan⁵ *to weave, weave together*, Æ.

āweg (=on-) '*away*,' *forth, out*, Chr,Mt; CP.

āwegan⁵ *to lift up, carry away*, Ex : *weigh, weigh out*, Æ : *estimate, consider : distinguish*. ['*aweigh*']

āwegāworpnes f. *abortion*, LL (154').

āwegcuman⁴ *to escape*, AO 102¹⁰.

āwegēade *went away*, JnL 4⁵⁰ [v. '*away*'; ēode]

āwegflēon² *to fly or flee away*, OEG 2169.

āweggān *to go away*, BH 326¹⁰.

āweggewītan¹ *to depart*, AO 74²⁶.

āweggewītenes f. *departure*, Æ : *aberration (of mind)*, JPs 115¹¹.

āwegweard *coming to a close*, RWH 133³⁷.

āwehtnes f. *arousing*, BH 422²⁰.

awel (o², u²) m. *hook, fork*, GL.

āwellan=āwillan

āwemman (æ²) *to disfigure, corrupt*, BF,HL.

āwemmendnes f. *corruption*, LPs 15¹⁰.

āwēnan *to consider*, RBL 4¹² (āhw-).

āwendan (=on-) *to avert, turn aside, remove, upset*, Ps : *change, exchange, alter, pervert*, Æ; CP : *translate*, Æ,CP : *turn from, go, depart*, Ps; AO : *return : subdue*. ['*awend*']

āwended-=āwendend-

āwendendlic *that can be changed, changeable*, Æ.

āwendendlicnes f. *mutability*, Æ.

āwende(n)dnes f. *change, alteration*, Æ.

āwendennes f. *change*, OEG 191.

āwending f. *subversion, change*, ES 39·322, Sc 188⁴.

āwenian *to disaccustom, wean*, BH,Ps.

āwēodian *to root out, extirpate*, LL,W.

āweorpan³ *to throw, throw away, cast down, cast out, cast aside, degrade, depose*, Mt; Æ, AO,CP. āworpen *divorced, rejected, destroyed, apostate*. of, ūt ā. *to throw out*. ['*awarp*']

āweorpnes=āworpennes

āweorðan³ *to pass away, vanish, become worthless*, Mt : (NG)=+weorðan. ['*aworth*']

āweosung f. '*subsistentia*,' WW 516⁴.

āwer=āhwǣr

āwerdan=āwierdan

āwerde (æ²) m. *worthless fellow*, WW 111²⁹.

āwerg-=āwierg-, āweri-, āwyrig-

āwerian I. *to defend*, AO : *hinder, restrain*, CHR : *protect, cover, surround, enclose : ward off from oneself, spurn from oneself*. II. *to wear, wear out (clothes)*, RB.

āwerpan=āweorpan

āwescnes (VPs)=āwiscnes

āwēstan *to lay waste, destroy*, AO; Æ. ['*awest*']

āwēst(ed)nes f. *desolation, destruction*, LCD.

āwēstend m. *devastator*, W 200¹⁹.

āwexen=āweaxen pp. of āweaxan.

+āwian=+īewan

āwīdlian *to profane, defile*, LL,OEG.

āwierdan (e, y) *to spoil, injure, hurt, corrupt, seduce, destroy, kill*, CP.

āwierding (y) f. *corruption, blemish*, HGL 421⁵⁷.

āwierdnes (y) f. *hurt, harm, destruction*, Æ : *defilement*.

āwierg-an, -ian (æ, e, i, y) I. *to curse, damn, denounce, outlaw*, Æ,Mt,CP,VPs. sē āwier(ge)da *fiend, devil*. ['*awarie*'] II. (i, y) *to strangle, suffocate*, AO; Æ. ['*aworry*']. For compounds see āwyrg-.

āwiht I. n. '*aught*,' *anything, something*, Ps. II. adv. *at all, by any means*. tō āhte *at all*. III. *good, of value*, Æ.

āwildian *to become wild*, Æ,LL.

āwillan (e, y;=ie) *to bring into commotion, boil*, Æ.

āwille (WW)=ānwille II.

awil-wan, -wian (æ;=ie) *to roll (tr.)*.

āwindan³ *to wind, bend, plait : slip from, withdraw, escape*, CP : *become relaxed? cramped?* (BTac), W 148³.

āwindwian (y) *to winnow, blow away, disperse*, Ps.

āwinnan³ *to labour, strive*, JnL : *gain, overcome, endure*, Da. ['*awin*']

āwirgan=āwiergan

āwirgnes=āwyrgednes; āwisc-=āwisc-

āwisnian *to become dry, wither*, LkL.

āwistlian *to hiss*, W 147³¹. [hwistlian]

āwītegian *to prophesy*, VH 9.

āwlacian *to be or become lukewarm*, LCD,RB.

āwlǣtan *to befoul, make loathsome, defile*, Æ.

āwlancian *to exult, to be proud*, OEG 1159.

āwlencan *to make proud, enrich*, DR 59¹.

āwlyspian *to '*lisp*,'* MLN 4·279 (NC 338).

āwo=ā (āwa)

āwoffian *to become proud, insolent* : *rave, be delirious, insane*, Æ.
āwōgian *to woo*, Æ.
āwōh (*crookedly*), *wrongfully, unjustly*, LL.
  [=on wōh]
āwol=āwel; āwolfigan=āwoffian
āwonian (DR)=āwanian; āwor=āfor
āwordennes f. *degeneration*, WW 87²¹.
āworpednes (EPs 21⁷)=āworpennes
āworpenlic *worthy of condemnation*, CP. adv. -līce *vilely*.
āworp(en)nes f. *rejection, what is cast away* : *exposure (of children)* : *a casting out*, BH 482¹¹.
āwrǣnan *to make wanton*, LCD 54b.
āwrǣnsian, *to wax wanton*, A 30·128.
āwrǣstan *to wrest from, extort*, WW 397³⁷.
āwrecan⁵ *to thrust out, drive away* : *strike, pierce* : *utter, sing, relate, recite* : *punish, avenge*, Chr,LL. ['awreak']
āwreccan *to arouse, awake*, Æ.
āwregennes=onwrigenes
āwrēon¹,² (=on-) *to disclose, discover, reveal* : *cover*, NG.
āwreðian *to support, uphold*, CP.
āwrīdian *to originate, spring from*, A 11·2.
āwrigenes=onwrigennes
āwringan³ *to wring, squeeze out*, Æ : *express*, BF 100¹⁰.
āwrit n. *a writing*, DR (io²).
āwrītan *to write, write down, describe, compose*, CP; Æ,AO,CHR : *mark, inscribe, draw, carve, copy*, Æ. ['awrite']
āwrīðan¹ I. *to turn, wind, bind up, bind, wreathe*. II.=onwrīðan
āwrygenes=onwrigenes
āwðer, āwðor=āhwæðer
āwuht=āwiht; āwul=āwel
āwuldrian *to glorify*, DR, JnL.
āwundrian *to wonder, wonder at, admire*, G,GD.
āwunian *to remain, continue*, BH.
āwunigende ptc. *continual*, BL 109².
āwurt-walian, -warian=āwyrtwalian
āwurðan=āweorðan; āwyht=āwiht
āwylian (Æ)=āwilwian
āwyllan=āwillan; āwylm=æwielm
āwyltan (æ;=ie) *to roll, roll away*, Æ : *harass*, DR.
āwyndwian=āwindwian
āwyrcan *to do*, Bo 149¹⁶,LL.
āwyrd- (Æ)=āwierd-; āwyrdla=æfwyrdla
āwyrg-=āwierg-, āwyrig-
āwyrgedlic (NIC 490²⁰) *detestable, shameful, abominable*.
āwyrgednes (o³) f. *wickedness*, Æ : *curse, cursing*. [wearg]
āwyrgendlic (CAS 34²²)=āwyrgedlic
āwyrigende *accursed*, ÆL 18³²⁴.

āwyrigung f. *a curse*, ÆL 15¹¹⁵.
āwyrn (MEN 101)=āhwergen
āwyrpan (=ie) *to recover (from illness)*, ÆL 20⁶⁵ (v.l.), A 41·109⁸⁵.
āwyrtlian=āwyrtwalian
āwyrttrumian *to root out*, MFH 161
āwyrtwalian *to root out*, CP.
āwyrðung f. *stain, aspersion*, HGL 421.
ax-=asc-, ox-; āx-=āsc-; axe=æcs
āȳdan (OEG 8¹⁰⁸)=āīdan; āȳdlian=āīdlian
āȳldan *to delay*, GD 21²². [ieldan]
āyppan '*experiri*' (*aperire?*) DR 70⁵.
āyrnan=āiernan
āȳtan *to drive out*, OEG 4080. [ūt]
āyttan=āettan

B

bā nafn. and am. of bēgen *both*.
bac- v. bæc.
bacan⁶ *to 'bake,'* Æ.
bacas nap. of bæc II.
bacca m. *ridge*, BC (bacce f. Mdf).
bacu nap. of bæc I.
bād I. f. *forced contribution, impost, pledge*, LL : *expectation*. [bīdan] II. (±) pret. 3 sg. of bīdan.
-bādere v. nied-b.
bādian *to take a pledge or fine*, LL.
bæ-=ba-, be-, bea-
bæc I. n. '*back,*' Bo,MtL,Ps; CP. on b. *backwards, behind, 'aback.'* on b. settan, lætan *to neglect*. ofer b. *backwards, back.* under b. *behind, backwards, back.* ofer b. būgan *to turn back, flee.* clæne b. habban *to be straightforward, honest*, LL 128,5. II. mfn. *beck, brook*, KC. [v. ES 29·411,GBG and '*bache*']
+bæc n. *bakemeats*, GEN 40¹⁷ : *baking*, ÆGR 176.
bæcbord n. *left side of a ship, larboard*, AO.
bæce I. *back parts*, WW 160¹⁰. II.=bæc II.
bǣce=bēce
bǣcen-=bēacen-
bæcere I. m. '*baker*,' WW. II.=bæzere
bæcering m. *gridiron*, WW.
bæcern n. *bakery, bakehouse*, Æ.
bæcestre fm. *baker*, Æ. ['*baxter*']
bæceð, bæcð, pres. 3 sg. of bacan.
bæcistre=bæcestre
bæcling(e), bæclinga (on) adv. *backwards, behind*, JnR : *back to back*, RWH 86²⁷. on b. gewend *having one's back turned*, Æ. ['*backlings*']
bæcslitol adj. *backbiting*, W 72¹⁶.
bæcðearm m. *rectum*; pl. *bowels, entrails*, Æ.
+bæcu np. *back parts*, LPs.
bæd I. pret. 3 sg. of biddan. II.=bed

bædan *to defile,* EPs78[1].

bǣdan *to urge on, impel,* CP : *solicit, require* : *afflict, oppress.*

bædd=bedd

bæddæg=bæðdæg

bǣddel m. *effeminate person, hermaphrodite,* WW. [v. '*bad*']

bæddryda=bedrida

bǣdend m. *inciter,* WW.

bǣdewēg n. *drinking vessel,* Gu,BH370[30]. [wǣge]

bǣdling m. *effeminate person,* WW. ['*badling*']

bǣdon pret. pl. of biddan.

bædryda=bedrida; **bædzere**=bæzere

bæfta, bæftan (*Mt*; Æ)=beæftan

bæftansittende *idle,* ÆGR52[2].

-bæftian (ea[1], a[2]) v. hand-b.

bǣg=bēag; **bǣgen**=bēgen; **bǣh**=bēag

bǣl n. *fire, flame, B* : *funeral pyre, bonfire, B.* ['*bale*']

bǣlblys, -blyse, -blǣse† f. '*blaze*' *of a fire, funeral blaze,* Gu.

bælc I.† m. *pride, arrogance.* **II.** m. *covering, cloud?* Ex73.

bælcan *to cry out,* Mod 28.

+bælcan *to root up,* CPs79[14].

bældan=bieldan

bældo (CP), bældu=bieldo

bǣllegsa m. *terror of fire,* Ex121.

bǣlfȳr n. '*bale-fire,' funeral or sacrificial fire, B.*

bælg, bælig (NG)=belg

bǣlstede m. *place of a funeral pile,* B3097.

bǣl-ōracu f. (ds. -ōræce) *violence of fire,* Ph270.

bǣlwudu m. *wood for a funeral pile,* B3112.

bǣlwylm m. *flames of a funeral fire,* Jul336.

bǣm=bām (v. bēgen); **bænd**=bend

+bǣne n. *bones,* GD86[11]n.

bǣnen *made of bone,* Æ,Lcd.

bær I. gsmn. bares '*bare,' uncovered, Bo* : *naked, unclothed, Gen.* **II.** pret. 3 sg. of beran.

bǣr I. f. '*bier,' El*; Æ : *handbarrow, litter, bed, BH, JnR.* [beran] **II.** *a pasture,* KC. **III.**=bār (AB14·233).

+bǣran *to behave, conduct oneself,* CP : *fare,* B2824 : '*exultare,*' PPs. ['*i-bere*']

bærbǣre *barbarous,* EPs113[1].

bǣrdisc m. *tray,* WW. [beran]

bǣre=bere pres. 1 sing. of beran.

bǣre-=bere-

-bǣre suffix (from beran); forms derivatives from substantives, as in cwealmbǣre. [*Ger.* -bar]

bǣre=bǣr

+bǣre n. *manner, behaviour, El* : *gesture, cry* : *action.* ['*i-bere*'; beran]

bærfōt *barefoot,* LL,W.

bærhtm (A)=bearhtm

bærlic I. adj. *of barley,* KC6·79[10]. **II.** *open, clear, public.* adv. -līce.

bǣrmann m. *bearer, porter,* Æ. ['*berman*']

bærn=bereærn

±bærnan (e) *to cause to burn, kindle, burn, consume, Sol*; AO,VPs. [v. '*burn*']

bærnelāc (e) n. *burnt-offering,* PPs.

bærnes=bærnnes

+bærnes f. *bearing, manner,* WW529[13].

bærnett (y[2]) n. *burning, burn, cautery,* Æ : *arson,* LL.

bærning f. *burning* : *burnt offering,* BPs50[18].

bærnīsen n. *branding-iron,* OEG7[118].

bærnnes, bærnes f. *burning,* BH.

bæro=bearu; **bæron** pret. pl. of beran.

bærs m. *a fish, perch,* Gl. [*Ger.* barsch]

+bǣrscipe (LkL)=+bēorscipe

bærst pret. 3 sg. of berstan.

bærstl-=brastl-

bærsynnig (eo[2]) m. *notorious sinner, publican,* NG.

+bǣru v. +bǣre and BTs; **bǣrwe**=bearwe

bæst m? n? *inner bark of trees,* '*bast,*' Æ, OET.

bæsten *made of bast,* Jud15[13].

bæstere=bæzere

bǣtan I. *to bait, hunt, worry,* Æ. [v. '*bait*'] **II.** *to beat against the wind?* (BT) : *make fast?* (Sedgef.=III), Bo144[31]. **III.**(±) *to furnish with a bit or bridle, saddle, curb.*

+bǣte(l) n. *bit, bridle,* pl. *trappings,* BH.

bǣtera, bǣttra=betera

bǣting (ē) f. *beating (against the wind?)* (BTs), *cable* (Sedgef.), Bo144[31].

bæð n. nap. baðu '*bath,'* action of bathing, Lcd : *laver,* AO,Bl : *liquid in which one bathes, medicinal spring, BH,Jul,KC.* ganotes b. *gannet's bath* (*i.e.* the sea), B.

bæð(c)ere=bæzere

Bæðdæg m. *Epiphany (day of Christ's baptism)* DR2[1].

bæðern n. *bath-house,* NC272.

bæðfæt n. *bathing-tub,* LL455,17.

bæðhūs n. *bathing-place,* Æ.

bæðian=baðian

bæðsealf f. *bathing-salve,* Lcd.

bæðstede m., **bæðstōw** f. *bathing-place,* WW.

bæðweg† m. *sea,* An,Ex.

bæzere m. *baptizer, baptist,* G. [*L.* baptista]

bal-=beal-

balc, balca m. *bank, ridge, Bo,WW.* ['*balk*']

ballīce (NG)=bealdlīce

bal-sam, -samum n. '*balsam,' balm, Lcd, WW.*

balsmēðe f. *bergamot,* Lcd3·90'.

balsminte f. *spear-mint, water-mint,* WW
136⁶.

bal-zam n., -zame f., -zamum (AA) n.=
balsam

bām dmfn. of bēgen.

+ban=+bann

bān n. *'bone,' tusk, Æ,Gl,Jn*; AO,CP : *the
bone of a limb.*

+bān *bones,* GD86¹¹.

bana (o) m. *killer, slayer, murderer, B,Chr* :
the devil : f. *murderess,* A10·155. ['*bane*']

bānbeorge f. *leg-armour, greaves,* WW.

bānbryce m. *fracture of a bone,* LCD.

bāncofa† m. *the bodily frame.*

ban-coða m., -coðu f. *baneful disease.*

band pret. 3 sg. of bindan.

bānece *in pain in the thigh,* LCD.

bān-fæt† n. nap. -fatu *body, corpse.*

bānfāg *adorned with bonework* (deer
antlers?), B781.

bangār (o) m. *murdering spear,* B2031.

bāngeberg n.=bānbeorge

bāngebrec n. *fracture of a bone,* AN1439.

bānhelm m. *helmet, shield?* FIN30 (v. also
bārhelm).

bānhring† m. *vertebra, joint.*

bānhūs† n. *body, chest, breast.* bānhūses
weard *the mind,* Ex523.

bānlēas *boneless,* RD46³.

bānloca† m. *joint, limb.*

+bann n. *proclamation, summons, command,* Æ,CP : *indiction (cycle of 15 years).*

±bannan⁷ *to summon, command, proclaim.*
b. ūt *call out,* CHR.

bannend m. *summoner,* GL.

+banngēar (u¹, -ē⁹) n. *indiction, year of the
indiction,* Ct.

bannuc m. *a bit, small piece,* ZDA ; OEG.
[v. LF123 and '*bannock*']

bānrift (y) n. *leggings, leg-armour, greaves,*
GL,WW (-rist).

bānsealf f. *salve for pain in the bones,* LCD
138b.

bānsele m. *(bone-house), body,* DOM102.

bānwærc m. *pain in the bones,* WW200¹².

banweorc n. *homicide, manslaughter,* LL
244'.

bānwyrt f. *violet? small knapweed?* LCD.

bār (æ) m. '*boar,*' ÆGr.

bara, bare wk. forms of bær adj.

barda m. *beaked ship,* WW289¹².

bārhelm m. *helmet with the image of a boar?*
FIN30 (v. also bānhelm).

barian *to lay bare, uncover* : *depopulate,*
W310⁵. [bær I.]

barice=barricge; barm=bearm

barn I. pret. 3 sg. of biernan. II.=bearn

barricge '*braugina,*' '*baruina,*' WW.

bārspere n. *boar-spear,* BF,GL.

bārsprēot m. *boar-spear* (Swt).

barstlung=brastlung

barð m. *barque, 'dromo,'* WW181²⁹.

barða=barda

baru napn. of bær adj.

basilisca (ea¹) m. *basilisk,* EPPs90¹³.

basing m. *cloak,* Æ.

±bāsnian *to await, expect,* AN,GEN.

bāsnung f. *expectation,* DR.

bastard m. *bastard,* CHR1066D. [*OFr.*]

basu (e, ea, eo) gsmn. baswes *purple, scarlet,
crimson.* baswa stān *topaz.*

basuhǣwen *purple,* WW430⁷.

+baswian *to stain red,* ES33·177.

bāt I. fm. '*boat,' ship, vessel, Chr.* II. pret.
3 sg. of bītan.

batian *to heal* : *grow better* : *improve in
health,* CP173²⁰.

bātswegen m. *boatman,* EC254⁵.

batt *bat, cudgel, club,* OEG18b18.

bātwā=būtū

bātweard m. *ship's watchman,* B1900.

bað=bæð

±baðian *to wash, lave, 'bathe'* (tr. and intr.),
give baths (to others), Lcd ; Æ,AO.

baðu v. bæð.

be- prefix. 1. specializes the meaning of a
tr. vb. (as in behōn, besettan). 2. makes
an intr. vb. transitive (beswīcan, beðencan). 3. is privative (bedǣlan, beliðan).
4. does not alter the meaning (becuman).

be prep. w. d. and instr. (of place) '*BY,*'
near, in, on, upon, with, along, at, to : (of
time) *in, about, by, before, while, during* :
*for, because of, in consideration of, by, by
means of, through, in conformity with or
imitation of, in comparison with, Æ,AO* :
about, concerning, in reference to : *on
penalty of.* be āwihte *in any respect.* be
sumum dǣle *partly.* be ānfealdum *single.*
be twīfealdum *twofold.* be eallum *altogether.*
be fullan *in full, fully, perfectly* : *in excess.*
be ðām mǣstan *at the most.* be ðām (ðān)
ðe *because, as, according as, how.* be
norðan, sūðan *to the north, south of...,*
AO. be æftan=beæftan

±bēacen (ē) n. '*beacon,' sign, token, phenomenon, portent, apparition,* JnL :
standard, banner, B : *audible signal,*
CHRD32²⁶.

bēacenfȳr n. *beacon fire, lighthouse,* OET
180⁷ (ǣ).

bēacenstān m. *stone on which to light a
beacon fire,* WW.

bēacn- v. also bīcn-.

+bēacnian *to make signs, indicate,* B,BO.

+bēacnung f. '*categoria,*' WW382³².

bead=bed

bēad I. pret. 3 sg. of bēodan. II. (NG)=bēod

beado=beadu; beadowig=bǣdewēg
beadu† f. gds. beaduwe, beadowe *war, battle, fighting, strife.*
beaducāf *bold in battle,* RD 1¹¹.
beaducrǣft m. *skill in war,* AN 219.
beaducrǣftig† *warlike.*
beaducwealm m. *violent death,* AN 1704.
beadufolm f. *battle-hand,* B 990.
beadugrīma m. *war-mask, helmet,* B 2257.
beaduhrǣgl n. *coat of mail,* B 552.
beadulāc† n. *war-play, battle.*
beadulēoma m. *(battle-light), sword,* B 1523.
beadumǣgen n. *battle-strength, force,* Ex 329.
beadumēce m. *battle-sword,* B 1454.
beadurǣs m. *rush of battle,* MA 111.
beadurinc† m. *warrior, soldier.*
beadurōf† *strong in battle, renowned in war.*
beadurūn f. *secret of a quarrel,* B 501.
beaduscearp *keen in battle (sword),* B 2704.
beaduscrūd n. *coat of mail,* B 453; 2660?
beadusearo n. *war equipment,* Ex 572.
beaduserce f. *coat of mail,* B 2755.
beaduðrēat m. *war-band, army,* EL 31.
beaduwǣpen† n. *weapon of war,* RD.
beaduwang† m. *battlefield,* AN 413.
beaduweorc† n. *warlike operation.*
beaduwrǣd (o²) m. *fighting troop,* LCD 125b.
beæftan I. adv. *after, hereafter, afterwards, behind, AO;* CP (bi-). ['baft'] II. prep. w. d. *after, behind, Chr,Mt.* ['baft']
beǣwnlan *to join in marriage, marry,* CHR 1052 D. [ǣw]
beaftan *to strike (the hands) together? lament?* MtL 11¹⁷. ['beft']
bēag I. (ǣ, ē) m. *ring (as ornament or as money), coil, bracelet, collar, crown, garland, Æ,WW;* CP. ['bee'; būgan] II. pret. 3 sg. of būgan.
bēag-gifa, -gyfa† m. *ring-giver, lord, king, generous chief.*
bēaggifu (bēah-)† f. *ring-giving.*
bēaghord (h)† n. *ring-hoard,* B.
bēaghroden† *diademed, adorned with rings or armlets.*
bēaghyrne (h) f. *corner of the eye,* WW 156⁴¹.
±bēagian (ē) *to crown,* Ps.
bēag-sel n. -sele† m. *hall in which rings are distributed.*
bēagðegu (h) f. *receiving of rings,* B 2176.
bēagwīse n. *round shape,* GD 343¹⁵.
bēagwrīða (h) m. *armlet,* B 2018.
bēah I.=bēag. II. pret. 3 sg. of būgan.
beāh-=bēag-
beāhsian *to ask advice,* BL 199´; 205´.
bealanīð=bealunīð
bealcan, bealcettan *to 'belch', utter, bring up, splutter out, give forth, emit, Mod,Ps;* Æ : *come forth.*

beald (a) *'bold,' brave, confident, strong, Ps;* AO,CP : *presumptuous, impudent,* CP.
bealde adv. *boldly, courageously, confidently : without hesitation, immediately.*
bealdian *to be bold,* B 2177. ['bold']
bealdlīce (a¹) *'boldly,' Jul.*
bealdnes (a) f. *boldness,* MH 6²⁵.
bealdor† m. *lord, master, hero.*
bealdwyrde *bold of speech,* Æ.
beale-=bealu-
bealg, bealh pret. 3 sg. of belgan.
beallucas mp. *'testiculi,' WW.* ['ballock']
bealo, bealo-=bealu, bealu-
bealu I.† gs. b(e)al(u)wes n. *'bale,' harm, injury, destruction, ruin, evil, mischief, Chr,Ps,Sat : wickedness, malice : a noxious thing, Æ.* II. adj. *baleful, deadly, dangerous, wicked, evil.*
bealubend m. *pernicious bond,* W 178².
bealubenn f. *mortal wound,* Ex 238.
bealublonden *pernicious,* GN E 198.
bealuclomm mf. *oppressive bond,* HELL 65.
bealucrǣft m. *magic art,* MET 26⁷⁵.
bealucwealm m. *violent death,* B 2265.
bealudǣd† f. *evil deed, sin.*
bealuful *'baleful,' dire, wicked, cruel, Cr.*
bealufūs *prone to sin,* RIM 50.
bealu-hycgende, -hȳdig *meditating mischief,* B.
bealuinwit n. *deceit, treachery,* PPs 54²⁴.
bealulēas† *harmless, innocent, Chr,Gn.* ['baleless']
bealunīð† m. *malice, wickedness.*
bealuräp m. *oppressive fetter,* CR 365.
bealusearu n. *wicked machination,* JUL 473.
bealusīð† m. *hurt, adversity : death.*
bealusorg f. *dire sorrow,* PH 409.
bealuspell n. *baleful message,* Ex 510.
bealuðonc m. *evil thought,* JUL 469.
bealuwes, bealwes v. bealu.
bēam I. m. *tree, KC,Rd : 'beam,' rafter, piece of wood, Chr,Mt;* CP,Mdf : *cross, gallows, Cr :* (†) *ship, Rd :* column, pillar : *sunbeam, Chr,Ps :* metal girder, AO. II. (NG)=bȳme
bēamere (Mt)=bȳmere
bēamsceadu† f. *shade of a tree.*
bēamtelg m. *ink or dye from wood,* RD 27⁹.
bēamweg m. *road made with logs,* BC 1·417´.
bēamwer m. *wooden weir?* BC 2·242´.
bēan (īe) f. *'bean,' pea, legume, Lcd;* Mdf.
bēan-belgas (LkL), -coddas (Lk) mp. *bean-pods, husks or cods.* [v. 'belly,' 'cod']
bēanbroð v. bēonbroð.
bēancynn n. *a kind of bean,* WW 205³.
bēanen adj. *of beans,* LCD 1·282⁹.
bēanlēag f. *land where beans grow,* KC 5·265. [v. 'bean']

bēanmelu n. *bean-meal*, LCD 31b.
bēansǣd n. *bean-seed*.
bēansc(e)alu f. *bean-pod*, OEG 608.
bēanset n. *bean-plot*, KC 1·315′.
bēar (NG)=bēor
bearce (æ) f. *barking*, GL.
beard m. *'beard,'* *VPs*; Æ.
+bearded *having a beard*, GD 279¹⁴.
beardlēas *beardless, youthful*, ÆGR,GL.
bearg I. (e) m. *'barrow' pig, hog*, *Mt,Rd*.
II. pret. 3 sg. of beorgan.
bearh=bearg I and II; bearht=beorht
bearhtm I. (br-, e, eo, y) m. *brightness,
flash : twinkling (of an eye), instant.* adv.
bearhtme *instantly.* II.=breahtm
bearhtmhwæt *swift as the twinkling of an
eye, momentary*, Az 107 (br-).
bearhtmhwīl f. *moment, twinkling of an eye,
point of time*, GD.
bearm I. (a) m. *lap, bosom, breast, Lk :
middle, inside* : (†) *possession.* II. *emotion,
excitement?* PPs 118. III.=beorma
bearm-clāð, -hrægl n. *apron*, *WW* 127². [v.
'cloth']
bearmtēag *yeast-box*, LL 455,17.
bearn I. (a, eo) n. *child, son, descendant, offspring, issue, B,Mt,TC*; AO,CP. lēoda b.
children of men. mid bearne *pregnant*, LL.
['*bairn*'] II.=barn pret. 3 sg. of biernan.
III. pret. 3 sg. of beiernan. IV.=bereærn
bearnan (N)=biernan
bearncennicge *mother*, DR.
bearn-ēaca (Æ,CP), -ēacen (CP), -ēacnod,
-ēacnigende (Æ) *pregnant.*
bearnende (NG)—biernende ptc. of biernan.
bearngebyrda fp. *child-bearing*, B 946.
bearngestrēon n. *procreation of children*,
RD 21²⁷.
bearnlēas *childless*, Æ.
bearnlēast (ē²) f. *childlessness*, Bo 24¹⁰.
bearnlufe *affection (for a child), adoption*,
BH 454¹¹.
bearn-myrðra m., -myrðre f. *murderer or
murderess of a child*, W.
bearntēam m. *offspring, posterity, AO : procreation of children*, HL. ['*bairnteam*']
bearo=bearu
bears=bærs; bēarscipe=bēorscipe
±bearu gs. bearwes m. *grove, wood, BH*;
CP; Mdf. [berwe]
bearug=bearg
bearunæs m. *woody shore*, RD 58⁵.
bearwe (æ) f. *basket, wheelbarrow*, LL 455,15.
bearwes v. bearu; beasu=basu I.
+bēat n. *scourging*, Æ,H 1·406⁸.
±bēatan⁷ pret. bēot and (rarely) beoft (ES
38·28) *to 'beat,' pound, strike, thrust, dash,
Bo,Bl,Ps : hurt, injure*, DA 265 : *tramp,
tread, B.*

bēatere m. *beater, boxer*, Æ.
bēaw m. *gad-fly*, WW.
bebaðian *to bathe, wash* (tr. intr. and refl.),
Ph. ['*bebathe*']
bebēodan² *to offer, commit, entrust*, CP :
*bid, enjoin, instruct, command, require,
Æ,Lk*; AO,CP : *announce, proclaim.*
['*bibede*']
bebēodend m. *commander, master*, CP.
bebēodendlic *imperative*, ÆGR.
bebeorgan³ *to be on one's guard, defend,
protect, B.* ['*bibergh*']
beber (WW 11¹⁴)=befer
beberan⁴ *to carry to, supply with*, LL 4,18.
bebindan³ *to bind about, bind fast*, Æ.
be-birgan, -birigan=bebyrgan
bebītan (bi-) *to bite*, Cp 251M.
beblāwan *to blow upon*, LCD,LPs.
bebod n. *command, injunction, order, decree,
Mt*; Æ,AO,CP. ðā bebodu *the (ten) com-
mandments.*
beboddæg m. *appointed day*, A 11·102⁶⁷.
bebodian wv.=bebēodan
bebodrǣden f. *command, authority*, LPs
118¹¹⁰.
bebrǣdan *to spread, cover*, MH 44¹⁹.
bebrecan⁴ *to break to pieces*, SOL 295.
bebregdan³ *to pretend*, LkL 20²⁰.
bebrūcan² *to practise*, Æ : *consume (food),*
GD.
bebūgan² *to flow round, surround, enclose* :
turn from, shun, avoid, El : reach, extend.
['*bibugh*']
bebycgan *to sell*, LRG,MH.
bebycgung f. *selling*, WW.
bebyrdan *to fringe, border*, WW 375⁴¹.
be-byrgan (AO) -byrian I. *to raise a mound
to, bury, inter, Æ.* ['*bebury*'] II.=be-
beorgan
be-byrgednes, -byrig(ed)nes f. *burial, bury-
ing.*
bebyrgung f. *burial*, ÆL,GD.
bebyrig-=bebyrg-
bebyrwan (?=-bȳwan, BTs) *to rub over*,
GD 318³.
bec=bæc; bēc v. bōc.
becæflan *to ornament*, WW 137²².
+bēcan *to make over in writing, grant by
charter*, EC 202′.
becarcian *to be anxious (about)*, MFB 99.
becc=bæc II.
becca m. *pick, mattock, WW*; Æ. ['*beck*';
v. also IF 24 and LF 140]
beccen m. *buyer*, WW (KGL) 75³⁶. [=byc-
gend]
bece m.=bæc II.
bēce (oe) f. *'beech' (tree), Gl.* (v. also
bōc.)
becēapian¹ *to sell, Æ : buy, Æ.*

becefed=becæfed, pp. of becæfian.

bēcen I. '*beechen*,' *made of beechwood*, *Lcd*, *WW*. II. (NG)=bēacen

beceorfan³ *to cut, cut off, separate, Æ*. hēafde b. *to behead*.

beceorian *to murmur at, complain of*, CHR, RB.

becēowan² *to gnaw in pieces*, SOUL 111.

becēpan I. *to take notice of*, LPs. II.= becӯpan

beceð pres. 3 sg. of bacan.

becīdan *to complain of*, ÆH 2·470⁶.

becierran (e, y) *to turn, turn round, pass by, avoid, Met*; CP : *wind, twist : pervert, Chr : give up, betray*. ['*bicharre*']

beclǣman *to plaster over, poultice*, LCD.

beclǣnsian *to cleanse*, SPs 18¹⁴.

beclemman *to bind, enclose*, SOL 71.

beclencan *to hold fast*, LPs 104¹⁸.

beclēsung=beclӯsung

beclingan³ *enclose, bind*, EL 696.

beclippan (CP)=beclyppan

beclīsung=beclӯsung

beclypian (eo;=i) *to accuse, challenge, sue at law, LL.* ['*beclepe*']

beclyppan *to clasp, embrace, Mk : encompass, hold, Ps; Æ.* ['*beclip*']

beclypping f. *embrace*, OEG.

beclӯsan *to close, shut up, enclose, confine, imprison, Lk; Æ.* [clūse; '*beclose*']

beclӯsung f. *enclosure, cell*, OEG 1522 : *period, syllogism*, OEG.

bēcn=bēac(e)n; bēcn-=bi(e)cn-

becnāwan⁷ *to know*, RB 38¹⁷.

becnedan⁵ *to knead up*, LCD 93a.

bēcnydlic=bīcnendlic

becnyttan *to knit, tie, bind*, Æ,CP.

becol-a? m., -e? f. *spectre*, WW 530³³.

bēc-rǣde, -rǣding, -trēow=bōc-rǣding, -trēow

becrēopan² *to creep into, crawl*, AO : *be hidden, Æ.*

becst pres. 2 sg. of bacan.

becuman⁴ *to come, approach, arrive, enter, meet with, fall in with, AO,B; Æ,CP : happen, befall, Æ,Bo* : (impers.) *befit*, MkL 14³¹. ['*become*']

bēcun (NG)=bēacen

becwelan⁴ *to die*, LL 400,1.

becweðan⁵ *to say : speak to, address, exhort, A,Ps : admonish, blame :* '*bequeath*,' *leave by will, KC; Æ.*

becweðere m. *interpreter, translator*, EHy 16 (proem.).

becwyddod *bespoken, deposited*, WW 115³⁹.

becwylman? *to torment* (BTs).

becyme m. *event, result*, BH 372¹⁹.

becӯpan (ē;=īe) *to sell*, G,RB.

becyrran=becierran

±bed I. n. *prayer, supplication, Æ,CP : religious ordinance, service, Æ.* II.=bedd. III.=bæd pret. 3 sg. of biddan.

bedǣlan *to deprive, strip, bereave of, rob, Æ : release, free from.* ['*bedeal*']

bēdan=bēodan; +bēdan=+bǣdan

bedbǣr (ē) f. *portable bed*, NG.

+bedbigen f. *payment for prayers*, LL 258,51. [bycgan]

bedbolster m. *bolster, pillow*, WW 124²⁰. ['*bedbolster*']

bedbūr n. *bed-chamber*, HGL 481.

±bedcleofa (e, i, y) m. *bed-chamber*, Ps : *lair*.

bed-cofa m., -cofe f. *bed-chamber*, GL,HL.

bedd n. '*bed*,' *couch, resting-place, Jn,KC*; CP : *garden-bed, plot*, LCD; Mdf.

+bedda mf. *bedfellow, consort, wife, husband, B; Æ.* ['*i-bedde*']

±beddagas mpl. *Rogation days*, ÆH.

beddclāð m. *bed-covering*; pl. *bed-clothes*, HL.

beddclyfa=bedcleofa

+bedde (KC 3·50³)=+bedda

beddgemāna m. *cohabitation*, CP 99²⁵.

beddian *to make a '*bed*,' WW : *provide one with a bed, LL.*

bedding f. '*bedding*,' *bed-covering, LPs, WW; Æ : bed.*

bedd-rēaf, -reda=bed-rēaf, -reda

beddrest† f. *bed*, WW 154¹.

beddstōw f. *bed*, BH 410¹².

-bede v. ēað-b.

be-dēaglian (-dēahl) *to conceal*, GU,KGL.

bedecian *to beg*, Æ,CP.

bedēglian=bedīglian; bedēlan=bedǣlan

bedelfan³ *to dig round, Lk : bury, Rood*; AO. ['*bedelve*']

bedelfung f. *digging round*, WW 149¹¹.

beden pp. of biddan.

be-dēpan (VPs), -deppan=bedīpan, -dyppan

bedfelt mn. *bed-covering*, RB 91¹⁶.

bedgerid n. *food in an ant's nest*, LCD 118a.

+bedgiht f. *evening*, WW 117⁸.

±bedhūs n. *chapel, oratory, Æ.*

+bedian *to pray, worship*, BH 408²⁹.

bedīcian *to surround with a dyke, embank, fortify*, CHR 1016E.

bedidrian=bedydrian

be-dīglian (-dīhl-; ē, ēo, īo;=īe) *to conceal, hide, obscure, keep secret, Æ : be concealed, lie hid.*

bedīgling f. *secret place*, RPs 80⁸.

beding=bedding

bediolan (K)=bedīglian

bedīpan (ē, ȳ) *to dip, immerse : anoint*, CPs 140⁵.

+bedmann m. *worshipper, priest*, Bo,LL.

bedol=bedul

bedōn *to shut*, PPs 147². ['*bedo*']

±**bedrǣden** f. *prayer, intercession*, Æ.
bedragan v. pp. bedrōg.
bedrēaf n. *bed-clothes, bedding*, Ct,RB.
bedreda (i, y) m. (and adj.) *bedridden* (*man*), Æ. [*'bedrid'*]
bedrēf=bedrēaf
bedrēosan[2] *to overcome, deceive?* GEN 528, 823 : *deprive of, bereave, despoil*.
bedrest=beddrest; **bedrida**=bedreda
bedrīfan[1] *to drive, beat, strike, assail*, AO : *follow up, pursue* : *surround, cover*.
bedrincan[3] *to drink up, absorb*, LCD.
bedrīp n. *compulsory service rendered to a landowner at harvest time*, LL. [v. '*bedrip*']
bedrōg *beguiled*, GEN 602.
bedrūgian *to dry up*, LCD 1·336[4].
bedryda=bedreda
bedrȳpan *to moisten*, GPH 391[18].
+**bedscipe**† m. *cohabitation, wedlock*, GEN.
+**bedsealm** m. *precatory psalm*, LCD 51a, 138a.
+**bedstōw** f. *place of prayer, oratory*, BH, BL.
bedstrēaw n. *straw for bedding*, ÆL 31[572].
bedtīd f. *bed-time*, WW 176[2].
+**bedtīd** *time of prayer*, MH 126[18].
bed-ðegn, -ðēn m. *chamber-servant, chamberlain*, WW.
bedu f. *asking, prayer*, CP. [*Goth.* bida]
bedūfan[2] *immerse, submerge, drown*, Æ. [*'bedove'*]
bedul *suppliant*, WW 180[12].
bedwāhrift n. *bed-curtain*, Ct.
bedydrian *to conceal from*, Æ : *deceive*, Æ. [*'bedidder'*]
bedȳfan *to immerse*, GD 73[24]; CPs 68[16].
bedȳglan=bedīglian; **bedȳpan**=bedīpan
be-dyppan (e), *to dip, immerse*, Æ,Mt. [*'bedip'*]
bedyrnan *to conceal*, Æ. [dierne]
beēastan *to the east of*, Chr; AO. [*'beeast'*]
beēastannorðan *to the north-east of*, AO.
beebbian *to leave aground by the ebb tide, strand*, CHR 897A.
beefesian *to cut off the hair*, ÆL 33[84].
beegðan *to harrow*, BYH 74[11].
beerf-=beyrf-; **befædman**=befæðman
befǣlon pret. 3 pl. of befēolan.
befæstan *to fasten, fix, ground, establish, make safe, put in safe keeping*, Æ,CP : *apply, utilize* : *commend, entrust to*, Æ, CP.
befæstnian (ea) *to fix*, Æ : *pledge, betroth*.
befættian *to fatten, anoint*, LPs 140[5].
befæð-man, -mian *to encircle*, Æ.
befaran[6] *to go, go round or among, traverse, encompass, surround*, AO : *come upon, surprise, catch*, LL 230,13[1].

befealdan[7] *to fold, roll up, envelop, clasp, surround, involve, cover*, Æ; CP : *attach*. [*'befold'*]
befealdian (intr.) *to roll up*, MFH 117[11].
befealh pret. of befēolan
befeallan I. (sv[7]) *to fall*, CP,Mt; Æ : *deprive of, bereave of : fall to, be assigned to : 'befall,'* ÆGR. II.=befyllan
befeastnian (NG)=befæstan
befēgan *to join*, ÆL 23[425].
befelgan=befylgan; **befellan**=befyllan
befelōrǣd (HGL 489)=hefeldðrǣd
befeohtan[3] *to take by fighting*, Rd 4[32]. [*'befight'*]
befēolan[3] *to put away, bury : deliver, grant, consign, entrust to*, Ps : *betake oneself to, apply oneself, devote oneself to, persist, persevere*, CP : *importune : put up with, be pleased with*. [*'bifele'*]
befēon *to deprive of property*, OEG 3157.
befer (eo[1], y[1], o[2]) m. *'beaver,'* ÆGr; Mdf.
befēran *to surround*, Æ : *come upon, overtake, pass by : go about : fall among*, NG.
beficlan *to deceive*, LL (320').
befīlan, befilgan=befȳlan, befylgan
beflod (HGL 480) pp. of befēon.
beflēan[6] *to peel, skin, flay*, WW. beflagen flǣsc *entrails*. [*'beflay'*]
beflēogan[2] *to fly upon*, BH. [*'befly'*]
beflēon[2] (w. a.) *to flee from, flee, escape, avoid*, Ps; CP. [*'beflee'*]
beflōwan[7] *to flow round, over*, Wif. [*'beflow'*]
befōn[7] *to surround, clasp, include, envelop, encase, clothe, Bl*; Æ,AO,CP : *comprehend, seize, attach* (at law), *lay hold of, catch, ensnare*, Gen : *contain, receive, conceive : explain*, CP. wordum b. *tell, relate*. on b. *have to do with, engage in*. [*'befong'*]
befor=befer
beforan I. prep. α. (w. d.) (local) *'before,' in front of, in the presence of*, Æ,Bl,G; CP : (temporal) *before, prior to, sooner than*, G. β. (w. a.) *before*, G. II. adv. (local) *before, in front*, B : (temporal) *before, formerly, in former times, earlier, sooner* : *at hand, openly*, An.
beforhtian *to dread*, Æ 23b[525].
befōtian *to cut off one's feet*, Æ 25[117].
befrēogan *to free, liberate*, Ps.
be-frīnan, -frignan[3] *to question, ask, learn*, Æ.
befrīnung f. *inquiry*, OEG 2309.
befrȳnan=befrīnan; **beftan**=beæftan
befullan *entirely, completely, perfectly*, CP 5[20].
befȳlan (ī) *to befoul, defile*, Lcd; Æ. [*'befile'*]
befylgan *to follow after, pursue, persevere with*, LCD.

befyllan I. *to fell, lay low, strike down*, GEN : *take by killing, bereave*, GEN. [feallan] **II.** *to fill up*, BH 64⁵ n (Schipper). [full]

bēg=bēag

bēga gmfn. of bēgen.

begalan⁶ *to sing incantations over, enchant*, Lcd; Æ. ['*bigale*']

begān *to go over, traverse, Æ : get to, come by, fall into : go to, visit, care for, cultivate, Lcd*; AO: *inhabit, occupy, Æ,BH,Lcd: surround, beset, overrun, Chr, Job: practise, do, engage in, perform, attend to, be diligent about, Æ,CP : honour, serve, worship : profess.* on borh b. *pledge oneself*, CP. ūtan b. *besiege*, Chr. ['*bego*']

bēgan=bīegan, bēagian

begang (i¹, o²) mn. *way, course, circuit, extent : district, region : business, undertaking, practice, exercise, service, reverence, worship : cultivation*, GD. [=bīgeng]

beganga=bīgenga; **begangan**=begān

be-gangnes, -geongnes (DR), -gannes (WW), f. '*calendæ*,' *celebration*.

begangol (bigeong-) m.? *cultivator*, LkR : *worship*, DR.

begbēam m. *bramble, thorn-bush*, G,WW.

bēge=bēgen; **bēgea**=bēga

bēgean=bīegan

begēat I. m. *attainment, Æ : acquisitions, property, Æ.* **II.** pret. 3 sg. of begēotan.

begeg-=begeng-; **begēm-**=begīm-

begēmen (KGL)=begīmen

bēgen nm. (but where one thing is m. and the other f. or n., the nom. is bā, bū), nf. bā, nn. bū; gmfn. bēg(e)a, bēgra; dmfn. bǣm, bām; am. bū; af. bā; an. bū *both*, El,G,Lcd. v. also būtū. ['*bo*']

begenga m. *cultivator*, MtR.

bege(n)gnes (i¹) f. *application, study*, GD, WW.

begēomerian *to lament*, W 75¹⁵.

begeondan (AO,CP), begeonde, -geonan prep. w. a. d.; and adv. '*beyond*,' *on the other side, Æ,Chr,Jn.*

begeong-=begang-; **begeotan**=begietan

begēotan² *to pour over or upon, anoint, infuse, flood (with), sprinkle, cover with fluid*, Chr; Æ. ['*bigeten*']

beger n. *berry*, GL.

beget=begeat pret. 3 sg. of begietan.

begeten pp. of (1) begēotan, (2) begietan.

bēgian=bēagian

begiellan³ (i¹, e²) *to scream, screech*, Seaf 24. [v. '*yell*']

begietan⁵ (e, i, y) *to get, find, acquire, attain, receive, take, seize*, AO,CP : *happen : beget.*

begietend (e) m. *one who gets*, WW 214²⁵.

begīman (ȳ;=īe) *to look after, take care of : do service, attend : take heed, observe.*

begīmen f. *attention, observation*, GL,LCD.

begīmend (ȳ) m. *guide, ruler*, SC.

begīming (ȳ) f. *invention, device : observance : care, regard*, OEG.

begīnan¹ *to open the mouth wide, swallow*, GD,RD.

beginnan³ *to 'begin,' Æ*; AO,CP : *attempt, undertake, Æ : attack*, AO.

begīr=beger; **begīrdan**=begyrdan

begitan (AO,CP)=begietan

begleddian *to befoul, pollute, Æ : stain, dye, Æ.*

beglīdan¹ *to leave, desert*, PPs 56¹.

begnagan⁶ *to gnaw*, MH 118¹⁰.

begneorð? *attentive*, BH 370² (?=*becneord, BT).

begnīdan¹ *to rub thoroughly*, LCD 50a.

begnornian *to mourn for*, B 3179.

begong=begang

bēgra gmfn. of bēgen.

begrǣtan=begrētan

begrafan⁶ *to bury*, El 835. ['*begrave*']

begrētan *to lament*, PPs 77⁶³.

begrindan³† *to grind, polish, sharpen*, RD 27⁶ : *deprive of, rob*, GEN 1521.

begrīpan¹ *to grip, seize : chide*, Ps. ['*begripe*']

begriwen ptc. *steeped in, Æ.*

begroren *overwhelmed*, SAT 52.

begrornian=begnornian

begrynian *to ensnare, entrap*, WW 92¹⁰. [grīn]

begyldan *to adorn with gold*, CVPs 44¹⁰.

begylpan (=ie) *to boast, exult*, B 2007?

begȳm-=begīm-

begyrdan *to gird, clothe, Ps; Æ : surround, fortify, BH*; CP. ['*begird*']

begytan=begietan; **bēh**=bēag, bēah

behabban *to include, hold, surround, comprehend, contain*, AO,CP : *detain, withhold.*

behādian *to unfrock (a priest)*, LL.

behæfednes f. *restraint, temperance*, WW 504¹⁰.

behæpsian *to fasten a door*, ÆL 31²¹⁴.

behǣs f. *vow*, CHR 1093. [v. '*behest*']

behættian *to scalp, Æ : make bald*, OEG.

behaldan=behealdan

behamelian *to mutilate*, ÆL 25¹²⁷, MH 216²⁴.

behammen '*clavatus*,' (of shoe) *patched* (BT), *studded with nails* (Napier), GD 37¹³.

behāt n. *promise, vow, Lk; Æ : threat*, LCD. ['*behote*']

behātan⁷ (often w. d. pers.) *to promise, vow, pledge oneself, Æ*; CP : *threaten.* ['*behight*']

behātland n. *promised land*, GD 204¹².

behāwian *to see clearly, take care, consider*, Mt. ['*bihowe*']

behēafdian to 'behead,' Mt; Æ,AO.
behēafdung f. beheading, Æ.
behēafodlic capital (punishment), OEG 4042.
behealdan[7] to hold, have, occupy, possess,
Gen : guard, preserve, CP : contain, belong,
KC : keep, observe, consider, Bl,Ps; AO,
CP : 'behold,' look at, gaze on, observe,
see, Æ,CP : signify, Æ : avail, effect : take
care, beware, be cautious, CP : restrain :
act, behave.
behealdend m. beholder, spectator, BH
26[23].
behealdennes f. observance, DR : continence,
DR.
behealdnes f. regard, observation, Æ.
behēawan[7] to cut, chip, chop, beat, CP : cut
off from, deprive of.
behēdan (KGL)=behȳdan
be-hēfe, -hēf(e)lic suitable, proper, necessary,
G; Æ. ['biheve']
behēfnes f. convenience, utility, GL.
behēfō(u) f. want, need, RWH 134,136
behegian to hedge round, MLR 17·166.
behelan[4] to cover over, hide, AA,BH,BL.
beheldan=behealdan
behelian to cover over, conceal, bury, CP.
behelmian to cover over, SOL 104.
behēofian to lament, LPs,Sc.
be-heonan, -heonon prep. (w. d.) and adv.
on this side of, close by.
be-hēot, -hēt pret. 3 sg. of behātan.
behicgan=behycgan; **behīdan**=behȳdan
behīdiglīce=behȳdiglīce
behienan (CHR)=beheonan
behildan to depart, EPs 138[19].
behindan I. prep. (w. d., a.), adv. 'behind,'
after, Chr,Leas,LG,Met; CP.
be-hinon, -hionan=beheonan
behīring=behȳrung
behīwian to dissimulate, RBL 16[7].
behlæmman=behlemman
behlænan† to surround.
behlēapan[7] to leap upon, settle on, fix upon,
devote oneself to, CP.
behlehhan=behlyhhan
behlemman† to dash together.
behlēotan to assign by lot, MLR 17·166.
behlīdan[1] to close, cover over, Æ,AO.
behliden=beliden pp. of belīðan.
behlīgan[1] to accuse, RWH 4[1].
behlyhhan[6] (e;=ie)† to deride, exult over,
Gu. ['bilaugh']
behlȳðan to rob, deprive of, RD 15[10].
behōf n. behoof, profit : need, OEG 27[34].
behōfian (abs. and w. g.) to have need of,
require, want, BH,Lcd; Æ,CP : (impers.) it
behoves, concerns, belongs, is needful or
necessary, MtL,Jn. ['behove']
behōflic necessary, MkL. ['behovely']

behogadnes f. practice, WW 427[87].
behogian to care for, RB. ['bihogien']
behogod careful, prudent, DR. adv. -līce.
behōn[7] to hang round, CP. ['behung']
behorsian to deprive of horses, CHR.
behrēosan[2] to fall : cover, shelter. pp. behroren
divested of.
behrēowsian to rue, repent of, make amends,
Æ : compassionate, Æ. ['bireusy']
behrēowsung f. repentance, penitence, Æ.
['bireusing']
behrēowsungtīd f. time of repentance,
Septuagesima, Æ.
behrīman to cover with hoar-frost, WIF 48.
behringan to surround, CP.
behrōpan[7] to plague, importune, Lk 18[5].
behrūmian to besmirch, WW.
behrūmig sooty, MH 52[27].
behō f. witness, sign, JUD 174.
behwearf I. (eo) pret. 3 sg. of behweorfan.
II. (EPs)=behwearft
behwearft m. exchange, LPs 43[13].
behweolfan (A)=behwylfan
behweorfan[3] to turn, change, spread about :
see to, arrange, prepare, treat, Æ : bury, Æ.
behwerfan=behwirfan
behwirfan (e, y;=ie) to turn, change, convert, CP : exchange : prepare, instruct,
exercise.
behwon whence, BH.
behwylfan (eo;=ie) to cover, vault over,
Ex,MFH.
behwyrfan (Æ)=behwirfan
behycgan to consider, bear in mind : confide,
trust (on).
behȳdan (ī) to conceal, shelter, Mt; Æ.
['behide']
behȳd(ed)nes f. concealment, LL : secret
place, LPs.
behȳdig careful, watchful, anxious, Æ. adv.
-hȳdiglīce, -hȳdelīce.
behȳdignes f. solicitude, care, anxiety.
v. MP 1·393. [hygdig]
behygd-=behȳd-
behyhtan to trust, W 48[8].
behyldan to flay, skin, AO.
behylian to cover, veil, ÆL 33[237].
behȳpan (ē;=īe) to surround, BH 188[14].
[hȳpe]
behȳpian to heap up, OEG 3322.
behȳran to let on hire, WW.
behȳrung f. letting, loan, WW.
behȳðelīce sumptuously, WW 513[6].
beiernan[3] (i, y) to run up to, over, or into:
incur : occur to.
beigbēam=begbēam; **beinnan**=binnan
beinsiglian to seal up, RHy 6[34].
beirnan=beiernan
beiundane=begeondan; **bel-**=behl-

belācan[7] *to enclose*, RD61[7].
belādian *to excuse, clear*, Æ,AO,CP.
belādiendlic *apologetic, that can be excused*, OEG.
belādigend m. *apologist*, WW332[2].
belādung f. *apology, excuse*, WW.
belǣdan *to lead astray*, RB. [*'belead'*]
belǣfan *to leave, spare* : *be left, remain, survive*, Ps; Æ. [*'beleave'*]
belǣndan=belandian
belǣðan *to make hateful, pervert*, W47[7].
be-lǣwa (Æ), -lǣwend m. *betrayer*.
belǣwan *to betray*, Æ.
belǣwung f. *betrayal, treachery*, Æ.
belāf pret. of belīfan.
belandian *to deprive of lands*, CHR1091.
belcedswēora adj. *having an inflated neck*, RD79[1]. [bælc]
belcentan, belcettan=bealcettan
beld, beldo=bieldo
+**beldan** I. *to cover, bind (a book)?* JnL p188[3]. II.=+bieldan
belē- (NG)=belǣ-
belēan[6] *to censure, reprove* : *charge with* : *dissuade, forbid, prevent*, CP.
belecgan *to cover, invest, surround, afflict, An*; AO : *attribute to, charge with, accuse*. [*'belay'*]
belēfan=belȳfan; **belendan** (CHR1096)= belandian
belene (eo[1], o[2]) f. *henbane*, GL,LCD.
belēogan[2] *to deceive by lying, GD* : (impers.) *be mistaken*. [*'belie'*]
belēoran *to pass by, pass over*, MkL,VPs.
beleorendlic *past*, DR.
belēosan[2]† *to be deprived of, lose*.
belēweda (LL438[5])=belǣwend
belewit=bilewit
belflȳs n. *bell-wether's fleece*, LL451,14.
belg (æ, i, y) m. *bag*, Mt,WW : *purse, leathern bottle, pair of bellows, pod, husk*. [*'belly'*]
+**belg** m. *anger* : *arrogance*, RB69[20].
±**belgan**[3] (intr., refl.) *to be or become angry*, Æ,AO,CP : *offend, provoke*.
belgnes f. *injustice*, MtL20[13] (bælig-).
+**belh**=+belg
belhring m. *bell-ringing*, RB67[20].
belhūs=bellhūs
belibban=belifian
belicgan[5] *to lie round, surround, Gen* : *hedge in, encompass*, Æ; AO. [*'belie'*]
belīfan[1] (ȳ) *to remain over, be left*, Æ. pp. belifen *dead*, AO. [*'belive'*]
belīfend m. *survivor*, OEG.
belīfian *to deprive of life*, Æ; **belig**=belg
belīman *to glue together*, Sc96[19].
belimp n. *event, occurrence, affair*. of belimpe *by chance*.

±**belimpan**[3] *to concern, regard, belong to, conduce to, Bo*; CP : *happen, befall, B*; Æ : *become* : (impers.) *befit*. [*'belimp'*]
belis(t)nian *to castrate*, Æ. belis(t)nod pp. as sbm. *eunuch*. wæs b. '*stupratur*,' HGL507.
belīðan[1]† *to deprive of*. pp. beliden *departed, dead*, AN1087.
bell=belle
bellan[3] *to bellow, bark, grunt, roar*, Rd. [*'bell'*]
belle f. '*bell*,' KC; Æ,CP.
bellhūs n. '*bell-house*,' *belfry*, LL,WW.
belltācen n. *indication (sounding of the hour) by a bell*, HL11[65].
belltīd f. *a canonical hour marked by the ringing of a bell*. (cp. belltācen)
belōcian *to behold*, RPs44[5].
belone=belene
belt m. '*belt*,' *girdle*, WW.
belūcan[2] *to lock, shut up, close, Bl,CP,Mt*; AO : *surround, enclose, embody, VPs* : *stop, impede, block up, choke*, Æ : *preserve, protect* : *shut out, exclude*, Æ: *sum up, define*, RWH137[4]. [*'belouke'*]
belune=belene
belūtian *to lie hid*, GD293[15].
belȳfan (ē;=īe) *to believe*, Æ. pp. belȳfed *having belief*.
belympan=belimpan
belyrtan (N) *to deceive*, MtL2[16]. [*'belirt'*]
belytegian *to allure, seduce*, AO112[26]. [lytig]
bemǣnan *to 'bemoan,' bewail, lament*, Æ.
bemancian *to maim*, LCD3·214[20].
bēmare=bȳmere; **bēme**=bīeme
bemeldian *to disclose, reveal, denounce* (BTs).
bēmere=bȳmere
bemetan[5] *to account, consider*, AO. [*'bemete'*]
bemīðan[1] *to hide, conceal*, CP : *lie hid*.
bemurc(n)ian, *to murmur at*, AO48[17].
bemurnan[3] (also wk.) *to mourn, bewail, deplore, be sorry for* : *care for, take heed for*.
bemūtian *to exchange for*, GU42. [L. mutare]
bemyldan *to bury*, WW. [molde]
ben=benn
bēn I. f. (±) *prayer, request, Lk*; AO, CP : *compulsory service*, LL447 (v. 2·418, Fron.). [*'bene'*] II. pret. 3 sg. of bannan.
bēna m., bēne f. *suitor, petitioner*, AO.
benacian *to lay bare*, Hy. [nacod]
benǣman (ē) *to take away, deprive of, rob of*, Æ,AO. [niman]

benc f. *'bench,' B.*
bencian *to make benches,* LL455,13.
bencsittend† m. *one who sits on a bench.*
bencswēg m. *bench-rejoicing, sound of revelry,* B1161.
bencðel† n. *bench-board, wainscotted space where benches stand, B.* [v. *'theal'*]
bend mfn. (+b. MtL) *bond, chain, fetter, BH,Bl,Mt,Ps;* CP : *band, ribbon, ornament, chaplet, crown, WW.* [*'bend'*]
bēndagas mpl. *days of prayer, Rogation days,* BF166[14].
±bendan *to bend (a bow), Ps : bind, fetter, Chr.* [*'bend'*]
bendfeorm=bēnfeorm
-bene v. ēað-b.
beneah (pret. pres. vb.) pl. benugon, pret. benohte *to have at one's disposal, possess, enjoy : require.*
beneced=benacod pp. of benacian.
benēman=benǣman
benemnan *to name : stipulate, settle, declare, asseverate.*
benēotan[2]† *to deprive of, rob.*
beneoðan (i, y) prep. w. d. *'beneath,' under, below, Æ,Bo,KC,LL.*
bēnfeorm f. *food during (or after) compulsory labour for the lord?* LL452' and 3·252.
bengeat n. *wound-gash,* B1121.
benīdan (ē) *to compel,* A11·110.
beniman[4] *to take, assume, obtain, AO : take away from, deprive of, bereave, rob, BH, Gen,Met;* AO,CP : *contain : catch, apprehend.* [*'benim'*]
beniming f. *deprival,* WW (bi-).
beniðan=beneoðan
bēnlic (oe) *that may be entreated,* DR. adv. -līce *beseechingly,* DR.
benn† f. *wound, mortal injury.* [bana]
+benn n. *edict,* WW398[37]. [=+bann]
bēnn pret. 3 sg. of bannan.
benne f. *reed-grass,* BC (Mdf).
±bennian *to wound,* RD.
benohte v. beneah.
benorðan *in the north, northwards (of), Chr*1087; AO. [*'benorth'*]
benoten pp. of benēotan.
benotian *to use, consume, Chr.* [*'benote'*]
bēnrīp n. *compulsory service rendered to a landowner at harvest time,* LL448. [cp. bedrīp]
±bēnsian *to pray, supplicate,* BH.
benst pres. 2 sg. of bannan.
bēntīd f. *prayer time, Rogation days,* MEN 75.
bēntigðe, bēntīð(ig)e *granting requests, gracious,* LPs : *obtaining requests, successful,* CHR.
benð pres. 3 sg. of bannan.

benugon v. beneah.
bēnyrð f. *ploughing required from a tenant,* LL448,5[2].
benyðan=beneoðan
bēo I. f. nap. bēon; dp. bēo(u)m *'bee,' Lcd, Ps,WW;* Æ. II. pres. 1 sg. of bēon.
bēobrēad n. *honey with the comb, Lk,Met, VPs;* Æ. [*'bee-bread'*]
bēoce=bēce
bēoceorl m. *bee-master, bee-keeper,* LL 448,5.
bēocere m. *bee-keeper,* LL. [MHG. bīkar]
+beod=+bed
bēod m. *table, Mt : bowl, dish.* [*'beod'*]
bēodærn n. *refectory, dining-room,* Æ (-ern). on bēoderne *at table.*
beodan=bidon pret. pl. of bīdan.
±bēodan[2] *to command, decree, summon, Chr;* Æ,AO,CP. b. ūt *call out (an army), banish : declare, inform, announce, proclaim, Gu,LL : threaten : offer, proffer, give, grant, surrender, Æ,Gen;* AO : (refl.) *show oneself, behave : exact, collect.* [*'bid,' 'i-bede'*]
bēodbolle f. *table-bowl,* GL.
bēodclāð m. *table-cloth, carpet,* ÆGR 34[8].
bēoddern=bēodærn
bēoddian *to do joiner's work,* LL455, 13.
bēodend m. *preceptor,* CM967.
bēodendlic=bebēodendlic
bēodern (Æ)=bēodærn
bēodfæt n. *table-vessel, cup,* WW204[25].
bēodfers n. *grace at meal-time,* GD,RB.
bēodgæst m. *table-companion,* AN 1090.
bēodgenēat† m. *table-companion,* B.
bēod(h)rægl n. *table-cloth,* WW126[33].
bēodlāfa fp. *table-leavings,* BL53[13],VH9.
bēodland n. *land from which the table of monasteries, etc., was supplied, glebe-land,* Ct.
bēodrēaf n. *table-cloth,* TC530'.
bēod-scēat n., -scýte m. *table-napkin, towel,* WW449[22].
bēodwyst f. *a table with food on it,* LPs22[5]. [wist]
beofer (o[2])=befer; beofian=bifian
beoft redupl. pret. of bēatan; beoftadon is from a later wk. *beoftian (ANS141·176).
beofung=bifung
bēogang m. *swarm of bees,* WW.
+bēogol (ū, ȳ) *submissive, obedient : forgiving,* Æ. [būgan]
bēohāta m. *chief? prince?* Ex253. [bēot-?]
beolone=belene
bēom I. dp. of bēo I. II.=bēam. III.= bēo pres. 1 sg. of bēon.

bēomōder f. *queen-bee*, OEG.

bēon I. anv. [conj. in full (WS and A) Wt 548] *to* 'BE*,' *exist, become, happen*. b. ymbe *to have to do with*. b. of *to be gone*. (v. also eom, wesan.) II. nap. of bēo I.

bēona gp. of bēo I.

bēonbrēad=bēobrēad

bēonbroð n. *mead?* (or? bēanbroð, ES 38·302).

bēonnon pret. pl. of bannan.

bēor n. *strong drink*, '*beer*,' *mead*, *Lk,WW* (v. A 27·495 and FTP 276).

+bēor m. *pot-companion, guest*, Æ.

beora=bearu; ±beoran=beran

bēorbyden f. *beer-barrel*, LL455,17.

beorc I. (e, i, y) f. '*birch*,' *Gl,Lcd*; Mdf : *name of the rune for* b. II. (±) n. *barking*, ÆGR,LCD.

beorcan³ (tr.) *to* '*bark*,' *ÆGr,CP* : (intr.) *bark at, Lcd*.

beorce=beorc

beorcholt (y) *birch wood*, WW138,361.

beorcragu (e¹) f. *lichen from a birch-tree*, LCD99b.

beorcrind (e¹) f. *birch-bark*, LCD119b.

beord (BH392²⁷)=bord

bēordrǣst(e) f. *dregs of beer*, LCD.

beorg m. *mountain, hill, AO,Lk*; Mdf : *mound*, '*barrow*,' *burial place, Æ,Lcd*.

+beorg n. *protection, defence, refuge, W*. ['*bergh*']

beorgǣlfen f. *oread* (Swt).

±beorgan I. sv³ (w. d.) *to save, deliver, preserve, guard, defend, fortify, spare, An, Ps*; AO,CP : (w. refl. d.) *beware of, avoid, guard against*. ['*bergh*'] II.=birgan

beorg-hlið† (u) n. nap. -hleoðu *mountain-height, mountain-slope*.

+beorglic *fitting, profitable, LL,W* : *safe, prudent, Æ*.

beorgseðel n. *mountain dwelling*, Gu73. [setl]

beorgstede m. *mound*, PH284 (rh).

±beorh (1)=beorg; (2) imperat. of beorgan.

beorhlēode (WW178⁴¹)=burglēode

+beorhnes f. *refuge*, CPs30³.

+beorhstōw f. *place of refuge*, PPs31⁸.

beorht (e, y) I. 'BRIGHT,' *shining, brilliant, light, clear* : *clear-sounding, loud* : *excellent, distinguished, remarkable, beautiful, magnificent, noble, glorious* : *pure, sublime, holy, divine*. II. n. *brightness, gleam, light* : *sight*. ēagan b. *twinkling of an eye*.

beorhtan=bierhtan

beorhtblōwende *bright-blooming*, LCD1·404⁹.

beorhte *brightly, brilliantly, splendidly, B, Met* : *clearly, lucidly, distinctly, CP*.

beorhthwīl (RWH41¹⁸)=bearhtmhwīl

beorhtian (e) *to glisten, shine, BH,Ps* : *to sound clearly, B* : *to make bright, VPs*. ['*bright*']

+beorhtian=+beorhtnian

beorhtlic *brilliant, clear, shining, splendid*. adv. -līce, *Mk*; Æ. ['*brightly*']

beorhtm=bearhtm

beorhtnan *to grow bright*, OEG534.

±beorhtnes (æ) f. '*brightness*,' *clearness, splendour, beauty, JnL,Lk*; CP : *lightning*, LPs109³.

±beorhtnian (e) *to glorify*, NG.

beorhtrodor m. *shining heavens*, Ex94.

beorhtte (=*beorgihte) pl. *mountainous*, AO10²⁵.

beorhtu=bierhtu

beorhtword (y¹) *clear-voiced*, SAT238.

bēorhyrde m. *cellarer, butler*, CRA75.

beorm-=bearm-

beorma m. '*barm*,' *yeast, leaven, Mt*.

+beormad *leavened*, MtR13³³. ['*barm*']

beorn I.† m. *man* : *noble, hero, chief, prince, warrior, B,Ma* : *rich man*, RUN12. ['*berne*'] II.=barn pret. 3 sg. of biernan. III.=bearn

beornan (VPs)=biernan

beorncyning m. *lord of heroes*, B2148.

beorne=byrne

Beornice mp. *Bernicians, inhabitants of part of Northumbria*, BH.

beorning (=ie) f. *incense*, LkL1¹¹.

beornōrēat m. *troop of men*, PA50.

beornwiga m. †*warrior, hero*.

bēorscealc *reveller, feaster*, B1240. [v. A46·233]

±bēorscipe m. *feast, banquet, revel*, Æ,CP.

bēorsele† m. *beer-hall, banqueting hall*.

bēorsetl n. *ale-bench*, JUL687.

beorswinig (NG)=bærsynnig

bēorðegu† f. *beer-drinking*.

-beorðling (ie) v. hyse-b.

±beorðor (e, o, u, y) n. *child-bearing, childbirth* : *what is born, foetus, offspring*.

beorðorcwelm m. *abortion*, WW348²³.

beorðor-ðīnen, -ðīnenu (broðor-) f. *midwife*, GEN38²⁸.

beoruh=beorg; beosmrian=bismerian

bēost m. *beestings, the first milk of a cow after calving, WW* : *swelling (of the ground)?* v. Mdf. ['*beest*']

beosu=basu

±bēot I. n. *boastful speech, boast, threat, Æ, Gen*. on b. *boastfully* : *promise, vow*, AO : *command* : *peril, danger*, DA265. [=behāt; '*beot*,' '*i-beot*'] II. pret. 3 sg. of bēatan.

±bēotian I. *to threaten*, *Jul* : *boast, vow, promise*, AO. ['*beoten*'] II.=bōtian

±bēotlic *arrogant, exulting, boastful, threatening*, Æ. adv. -līce.

bēotmæcg m. *leader,* DA 265.
bēoton pret. pl. of bēatan.
bēotung f. *threatening,* BH,LCD.
bēotword† n. *boast,* B : *threat,* JUL.
bēoðēof m. *bee-thief,* LL 54,9².
bēoum dp. of bēo.
bēow n. *barley,* GL.
bēowan=bȳwan
bēowyrt f. *bee-wort, sweet flag,* LCD.
bepǣcan *to deceive, seduce, Mt;* Æ. ['*bi-peche*']
bepǣcend m. *deceiver,* Æ.
bepǣcestre f. *whore,* ÆGR 175⁹.
bepǣcung f. *deception,* OEG.
beprīwan (ē) *to wink,* Bo,W.
bēr (NG)=bǣr
bera m. '*bear,*' Æ.
beræccan=bereccan
berǣdan *to deprive, take by treachery, rob* : *betray,* Æ : *deliberate on* : *get the better of.*
berǣsan *to rush upon or into,* Æ,CP.
±beran⁴ (eo) *to 'bear,' carry, bring, take away, carry out, extend,* AO,B; Æ,CP : *bring forth, produce, Bl,Mt,Gen;* Æ : *be situated by birth,* LL : *wear, AO* : *endure, support, sustain, LL,Mt;* CP. (with ūp) *set forth, open (a case),* CHR 1052 E. berende *fruitful.* +boren *born.* [v. also '*i-bere*']
berascin n. *bear-skin,* EC 250¹⁷.
+berbed '*vermiculatus,' barbed,* DR 4³.
ber-bēne, -bīne f. *verbena,* LCD.
berc=beorc, berec-
+berd-, +bēre=+byrd-, +bǣre
bere m. *barley,* Æ,JnLR. ['*bear*']
hereæm n. '*barn,' Lh.* [bere, corn]
bereāfere m. *despoiler,* OEG 46³⁶.
bereāflan *to 'bereave,' deprive of, take away, seize, rob, despoil, Bo;* Æ,AO.
bereāfigend m. *despoiler, robber,* APT,GL.
berebrytta m. *barn-keeper,* LL 451,17.
berēcan *to cause to smoke, smoke* (tr.), LCD 1·106¹⁶.
bereccan *to relate* : *excuse or justify oneself,* CP.
berecorn n. *barley-corn,* GL,LL.
berecroft m. *barley-field,* KC 3·260¹ (berc-).
+bered *crushed, kneaded,* WW : *harassed, oppressed,* NG.
berēflan (KGL)=bereāfian
bereflōr m. *barn-floor, threshing-floor, LkL.* [v. '*bear*']
beregafol n. *rent paid in barley,* LL 116,59¹. [cp. gafolbære]
beregræs n. *barley-grass, fodder,* WW 148²⁶.
berehalm m. *barley-haulm, straw,* LCD 157a.
bereland (ber-) *barley-land,* KC 3·367⁹.
beren I. *of barley,* Æ. II.=biren. III.= bereæm
berend m. *bearer, carrier,* GL.

berendan *to peel, take off husk,* LCD.
berende *fruitful,* BH. [beran]
berendlīce *with fecundity,* DR 32⁸.
berendnes f. *fertility,* DR 108¹¹.
berenhulu f. *barley-husk,* Sc 95¹⁹.
berēnian *to bring about,* Ex 147 : *ornament, mount (with silver),* KC 6·101'.
berēocan² *to fumigate,* LL (164⁵).
berēofan²† *to bereave, deprive, rob of.*
berēotan² *to bewail,* HELL 6.
berēowsian=behrēowsian
-berere v. wæter-b.
berern (NG)=bereærn
beresǣd n. *barley,* BH 366²⁷.
beretūn m. *barley-enclosure, threshing-floor, barn, MtL;* Æ. ['*barton*']
berewæstm m. *barley-crop,* LCD 1·402⁶.
berewīc f. *barley-yard, demesne farm, TC.* ['*berewick*']
berg=(1) bearg, (2) beorg
berg-=beri-, birg-, byrg-
berh=bearh pret. 3 sg. of beorgan.
berht, berht-=beorht, beorht-, bierht-
berhtm-=breahtm-
berian I. *to make 'bare,' clear,* B 1239. [bær]
II.=byrgan II.
+berian=+byrian
bericge=barricge
berīdan¹ *to ride round, surround, besiege, LL* : *overtake, seize, occupy,* CHR. ['*beride*']
berie f. '*berry,' Lcd* : *grape,* Æ : *vine,* WE 63²⁰.
berig I. n. *berry,* RPs 77⁴⁷. II.=byrig, ds. of burg.
berigdrence m. *drink made of mulberries,* WW 114²².
berige=berie; berigea=byrga
berind(r)an *to strip off bark, peel,* LCD.
beringan=behringan
berinnan³ *to run upon, run over, wet, bedew, Cr* 1176. ['*berun*']
berīsan¹ *to be fitting,* ByH 78¹³.
berland, bern=bereland, bereærn
bern-=bærn-, biern-
bernan (VPs; v. AB 40·343)=bærnan
bernhus n. *barn,* GD 68²². [=beren-]
berōfen (pret. pl. of *berafan or *berebban) *despoiled,* GEN 2078.
berōwan⁷ *to row round,* CHR 897A.
berst=byrst
+berst n. *bursting,* LCD,W 186⁷.
±berstan³ (intr.; tr. at RD 2⁸) *to break, 'burst,' fail, fall, B,Lcd,LL,Ma;* Æ,AO : *break away from, escape* : *break to pieces, crash, resound.*
berthwīl=bearhtmhwīl; bertūn=beretūn
berð-=beorð-, byrð-
+bēru=+bǣru, +bǣre
berūmod=behrūmod pp. of behrūmian.

berunnen pp. of berinnan.

berwe ds. of bearu.

berwinde f. '*bearbind*,' *navel-wort*, WW 300[19].

berȳfan *to deprive*, MOD 63. [rēaf]

berȳpan (=īe) *despoil of, strip, spoil, rob*, Æ.

besǣgan *to sink*, GPH 388[85].

besǣncan=besencan

besǣtian *to lay wait for*, AO 146[11].

besārgian *to lament, bewail, be sorry for, pity*, Æ. [sārig]

besārgung f. *compassion*, Æ.

besāwan[7] *to sow*, Æ.

bescēad (bi-) n. *distinction*, G.

bescēadan[7] *to separate, discriminate : scatter, sprinkle over*, LCD 20b.

bescead(uw)ian, *to overshadow, Sol*; RWH 138[5], RPs 139[8]. ['*beshade*']

besceafan[6] *to scrape thoroughly*, LCD 143b.

bescēan pret. 3 sg. of bescīnan.

besceatwyrpan '*despondi*,' v. OEG 4555; 2[346]; ES 42·170.

bescēawere m. *observer*, DHy 24[15].

bescēawian *to look round upon, survey, contemplate, consider, watch*, Æ,AO : *look to, care for*. bescēawod *thoughtful, prudent*, LCD 3·436[11].

bescēawiendlic *contemplative*, OEG 991.

bescēawodnes f. *vision, sight*, EPs 9[12].

bescēawung f. *contemplation*, GD,GL.

besceddan=besceadan

bescencan *to give to drink*, GU 596.

bescēofan=bescūfan

besceoren (WW 217[24])=bescoren pp. of bescieran.

bescēotan[2] *to shoot into, plunge into, implant : happen, occur*, AO.

be-sceran, -scerwan=bescieran

bescerian=bescierian

bescieran[4] *to shear, shave, cut hair, give the tonsure*, Æ,AO. ['*beshear*']

bescierednes (y[2]) f. *deprivation*, WW 351[13].

bescierian *to separate from, deprive of*, CHR : *defraud*.

bescīnan[1] *to shine upon, light up, illuminate, Rd*; Æ. ['*beshine*']

bescir-an, -ian=bescier-an, -ian

bescītan[1] *to befoul*, WW 507[28].

bescrēadian *to scrape off, clean off*, ES 42·171.

bescrepan[5] *to scrape*, LCD 101a.

bescrȳdan *to clothe*, RWH 136[32].

bescūfan[2] *to shove, impel, thrust down, hurl, throw*, Æ,AO : *force*, Æ.

bescȳlan (=īe) *to look askance*, Bo 121[30]. [sceol]

bescyldian *to shield, defend*, WYN.

bescyr-=bescier-

besēcan *to beseech, beg urgently*, MFH 151.

besecgan *to announce, introduce* : *defend, excuse oneself* : (w. on) *accuse*, Æ.

beselian=besylian

besellan *to surround, cover (over)* : *hand over*, RPs 105[41].

besema=besma

besencan *to cause to sink, submerge, immerse, drown, Bl,Mt*; AO,CP : *plunge into (fire)*, GD 317. ['*besench*']

besendan *to send*, Æ.

besengan *to singe, burn*, AO.

besēon I. sv[5] (tr., intr. and refl.) *to see, look, look round, behold*, Æ,Mk,Ps; AO : *observe* : *look after, go to see, visit* : *provide for*. b. tō *look upon, have regard to*, CP. ['*besee*'] II. sv[1] *to suffuse*, CR 1088.

besēoðan *to boil down*, LCD.

besēowian (ī, ȳ) *to sew together, sew up, Ep, WW*. ['*besew*']

be-serian, -serwan=besierwan

besettan *to put, place, set near, appoint*, Æ : *own, keep, occupy* : '*beset*,' *cover, surround with, adorn, B*; Æ,CP : *besiege, invest, An* : *institute, set going*.

besibb *related*, RWH 139[4]. (as sb.).

besīdian *to regulate the size of anything*, RB 89[18]. [sīd]

besierwan *to ensnare, surprise, deceive, defraud, oppress*, AO. [searu]

besīgan (on) *to rush*, v. OEG 4126.

besilfran *to silver*, VPs 67[14].

besincan[3] (intr.) *to sink*, AO. ['*besink*']

besingan[3] *to sing of, bewail* : *sing charms, enchant*, Æ.

besirwan (AO,CP)=besierwan

besittan[5] *to sit round, surround, beset, besiege, Chr*; AO : *hold council* : *occupy, possess*. ['*besit*']

besīwian=besēowian

beslǣpan[7] *to sleep*, LL (284[8]).

beslēan[6] *to strike, beat, cut off, take away, deprive by violence*, Æ.

beslēpan *to slip on, cover, put on, clothe*, Bo,Ps.

beslītan[1]† *to slit, tear*, SOUL.

besma m. '*besom*,' *broom, rod*, AO,Mt.

besmēagan *to consider about*, ÆL 23b[633].

+besmed *bellied* (of sails), WW 515[9]. [bōsm]

besming f. *curve, curvature*, WW. [bōsm]

besmirwan (y[2]; =ie[2]) *to* '*besmear*,' WW.

besmītan[1] *to soil, defile, pollute, dishonour, Bl*; Æ,CP. ['*besmit*']

besmitenes f. *soil, stain, defilement, degradation, dirtiness*, Æ.

besmittian *to defile*, RB,MP 1·613.

besmlðian *to work* (*in metal*), *forge, surround with forged work*, B,EETS 46·17.

besmocian *to smoke, envelop with incense*, ANS 84·3.

besmyred=besmirwed pp. of besmirwan.

besnǣdan† to cut, mutilate, DA.

besnīwian to cover with snow, WW. [' be-snow ']

be-snyðian, -snyððan† to rob, deprive of.

besolcen stupefied, dull, inactive, slow, CP.

besorg dear, beloved, Æ.

besorgian to regret : be anxious about, dread, shrink from, Æ.

besorh=besorg

bespǣtan to spit upon, ÆH 2·248′,RWH 137²⁴.

bespanan⁶ to lead astray, entice, incite, urge, persuade, AO.

besparrian to bar, shut, GL.

bespirian=bespyrigan

besprecan⁵ to speak about : speak against, accuse of, Ps : claim at law, LL : complain, AO. [' bespeak ']

besprengan to besprinkle, Lcd : bespatter, CHRD 64³⁶. [' bespreng ']

bespyrigan to track, trace, LL.

besta, beste wk. forms of superl. adj. betst.

bestǣlan (ē) to lay a charge against, convict.

bestǣppan⁶ to tread upon, step, go, enter, Æ.

bestandan⁶ to stand round or about, beset, surround, Æ : attend to, Æ : beset, harass, Jn. [' bestand ']

bestealcian to move stealthily, steal, ' stalk,' ÆL 32⁴⁰. [stealc]

bestefnod ptc. having a fringe, WW 375⁴¹.

bestelan⁴ to move stealthily, steal away, steal upon, AO,LL ; Æ,CP : (†) deprive. [' be-steal ']

bestǣlan=bestǣlan ; bestēman=bestȳman

bestēpan (=īe) to deprive of (children), GD 76¹⁸.

bestingan³ to thrust in, push, Æ.

bestrēdan to bestrew, cover, BHB 154²⁷.

bestrēowian to ' bestrew,' besprinkle, Job.

bestreððan (y²) to bestrew, cover over, RD.

bestrīcan¹ to make a stroke, LCD 186b. [strīca]

bestrīdan¹ to ' bestride,' mount, Æ.

bestrīpan to strip, plunder, Chr. [' bestrip ']

bestrūdan⁷ to spoil, plunder, rob, GEN, WW 424³³.

bestrȳpan=bestrīpan

bestryððan=bestreððan

bestuddian to be careful for, trouble about, RWH 134¹⁰.

bestȳman† (ē;=īe) to bedew, wet, flood. [stēam]

bestyrian to heap up, BH. [' bestir ']

bestyrman to agitate, Bo 9¹¹.

besu=basu

besūpan² to sup up, swallow, LCD 113b.

besūtian to besmirch, GPH 403²⁶.

besūðan in the south, southwards (of).

beswǣlan to burn, singe, scorch, B ; Æ. [v. ' sweal ']

beswǣpan=beswāpan

beswǣtan to sweat, toil, Sc 111¹⁴.

beswāpan⁷ to clothe, cover over, veil, protect, BH ; CP : persuade, BH. [' beswape ']

beswelgan to swallow up, EPs 106²⁷ ; 123³.

beswemman to make to bathe, Bo 115⁸.

beswencan to afflict, CPs 68¹⁸.

besweðian (bi-) to swathe, wrap up, wind round, CR, JnL.

beswic n. treachery, deceit, AO,CP : snare.

beswica (bi-) m. deceiver, BL.

beswīcan¹ to deceive, seduce, betray, circum-vent, frustrate, Bl,Mt; AO,CP : to overcome, supplant, AO. [' beswike ']

beswīcend m. deceiver, seducer, GL.

beswicenes f. deception, MH : surrender, GL.

beswicfalle f. trap, WW 17¹.

beswician to escape, be free from, BH.

beswicol deceitful, CP 238¹⁸. (bi-)

beswicung f. deception, WW.

beswincan³ to toil, exert oneself, make with toil, Jn : till, plough, Æ. beswuncen exhausted, tired out. [' beswink ']

beswingan³ to flog, scourge, beat, strike, Æ; CP. [' beswinge ']

beswylian to drench, flood, ROOD 23. [swilian]

besyftan to sprinkle, ÆL 23¹⁵⁵. [siftan]

besylfran=besilfran

besylian to sully, defile, stain, Æ.

besyr-ewian, -i(a)n=besierwan

bet adv. better, Bo. [' bet ']

-bēta v. dǣd-b.

betācnian to betoken, designate, RWH136²⁰.

betǣcan (w. d.) to make over, give up to impart, deliver, entrust, commend to, Lk. Mt,WW ; AO,CP : betroth : appoint (for), set apart as, dedicate : show, point out, Lk : give orders, RB 130⁴ : pursue, hunt, WW 92²⁸. [' beteach ']

±bētan to amend, repair, restore, cure, CP : make good, make amends, reform, remedy, compensate, atone, pay ' bōt' for an offence, Æ,CP,Lcd,Mt; AO : attend to (fire or light), AO. ðurst b. quench thirst. [bōt; ' beet ' vb.]

betast=betst

betboren of higher birth, LL.

bēte f. ' beet,' beetroot, Lcd. [L. beta]

-bēte v. twi-b.; bētel=(1) bīetl; (2) bītol

beteldan³† to cover, hem in, surround : over-load, oppress.

betellan to speak about, answer, defend one-self (against a charge), exculpate oneself, Chr; Æ. [' betell ']

bētend m. restorer, RUIN 28.

+bētendnes f. amendment, OEG 58⁶.

betēon[1],[2] *to cover, surround, enclose, AO; Æ, CP : dispose of, bestow, bequeath : impeach, accuse.* ['*betee*']

betera '*better*,' *AO,Bl,Bo,Mk.* w. g. *better in respect of....*

-bētere v. dǣd-b.

±**beterian** *to* '*better*,' *improve, CP : trim (lamp), GD.*

±**beterung** f. *improvement, Æ.*

betest=betst; **betīenan** (WW 383[17])=**betȳnan**

betīhtlian *to accuse, LL.*

betillan=betyllan

betimbran *to construct, build, B.* ['*betimber*']

betīnan=betȳnan; **bēting**=bǣting

bētl=bīetl

betlic† *grand, excellent.*

bētnes f. *reparation, atonement, LL* (264[16]).

betoce=betonice

betogenes f. *accusation, LL.*

betolden pp. of beteldan.

betonice f. '*betony*,' *Lcd.*

betost=betst; **betr-**=beter-

betræppan=betreppan

betredan[5] *to tread upon, cover, CPs* 138[10].

betrendan *to roll, ES* 37·180.

betreppan *to entrap, catch, Chr.* ['*betrap*']

be-trymman, -trymian *to enclose, surround, besiege.*

betst I. superl. adj. '*best*,' *first, AO,B,Chr, Cr; CP.* as sb. *people of position, Chr,WW.* **II.** adv. *in the best manner, most, Bo.*

betstboren *best-born, eldest, Æ.*

bett=bet

be-tuh, -tuoxn (CP), **-tux**=betwux

betuldon pret. pl. of beteldan.

+**bētung** f. *repair, maintenance, LL.*

betwēnan=betwēonan

betweoh, betweohs (*Æ*)=betwux

betwēonan, betwēonum I. prep. w. g. d. a. *between, among, amid, in the midst, B,Bl, G,Ps.* **II.** adv. '*between*,' *BH : in the meantime, meanwhile : in turn, by turns, CM* (-twȳn-).

betweox (*LL*), **betweoxn, betwih**(s) (*RG*)= betwux

betwīn-=betwēon-

betwīnforlētnes f. *intermission, DR.*

betwux (*Æ,AO,CP*), **betwuht, betwix, be-twux**(t), *betwisc* prep. w. d. a. *between, among, amongst, amidst : during.* b. ðīsum *meanwhile.* b. ðǣm ðe *whilst.* ['BETWIXT']

betwuxālegednes f. *interjection, ÆGr* 278[2].

betwuxāworpennes f. *interjection, ÆGr* 10[20].

betwuxblinnes (twih) f. *intermission, DR* 12[3].

betwuxfǣc (yx) *internal, OEG* 3861.

betwuxgangende (twih) *separating, VPs* 28[7].

betwuxgesett (eoh, ih, yh) *interposed, Bf* 66[32], BH 288[23].

betwuxlicgan[5] (twih) *to lie between, BH* 72[10].

betwuxsendan *to send between, CM* 104.

betwuxt, -twyh, -twyx(t)=betwux

betȳhtlian=betīhtlian

betyllan *to allure, decoy, BH* 358[4].

betȳnan (ī, īe) *to hedge in, enclose, shut, bury, AO,CP : shut out : end, BH.* [tūn]

betȳnung f. *conclusion, OEG* 3210.

betyran *to pitch, stain a dark colour, Lcd.* [teoru]

betyrnan *to turn round : prostrate oneself, RB.*

beð I.=bið pres. 3 sg. of bēon. **II.**=bæð

beðæncan=beðencan

beðan=beðian

beðearfan *to need, RWH* 6[36].

beðearfende *needy, indigent, KGl* 708.

beðearflic *profitable, ÆL* 23b[242].

beðearfod *needy, ES* 8·474[50].

beðeccan *to cover, protect, cover over, conceal.*

beðen=beðung

beðencan *to consider, remember, take thought for, take care of, care for, Gu :* (refl.) *reflect,* '*bethink*' *oneself, Lk; Æ : trust, confide in, entrust to, AO.*

be-ðenian, -ðennan *to cover, stretch on or upon, spread over, RD.*

beðēodan *to be joined* (to)*, RB* 134[20].

beðerscan *to winnow, thresh, PPs* 43[7].

beðettan *to bathe, foment, Lcd* 3·90[15] (A 30·397).

±**beðian** *to heat, warm, foment, Lcd; Æ : cherish.* ['*beath*']

beðrāwan[7] *to twist, GPH* 391[16].

beðridian (y) *to circumvent, overcome, force, AO.*

beðringan[3]† *to encircle, encompass : beset, oppress, burden.*

beðryccan *to press down, Cr* 1446.

beðrydian, beðryððan=beðridian

beðrȳn *to press, NC* 273.

beððan=beðian

beðuncan (Rd 49[7])=beðencan

beðung f. *bathing, bath, fomentation, cataplasm, Lcd; Æ,CP.* ['*beathing*'; bæð]

be-ðurfan swv. pres., 3 sg. -ðearf, pl. -ðurfon, pret. -ðorfte. (w. g. or a.) *to need, have need of, want, Æ,CP.*

beðwēan[6] *to moisten, wet, LPs* 6[7].

beðwyrian *to deprave, WW* 386[7]. [ðweorh]

beðȳn *to thrust, AO* 158[6].

beufan=bufan; **beūtan**=būtan

bewacian *to watch, guard, Æ.*

bewadian[6] *to emerge, Rd* 88[24].

bewǣfan *to enfold, wrap round, cover over, clothe, Æ,CP.*

bewǣgan *to deceive, frustrate, BVPs.*

bewægnan to offer, proffer, B1193.
bewǣlan to oppress, afflict, AN 1363.
bewǣpnian to disarm, Æ.
bewǣrlan to pass by : be free from, DR.
bewarenian to guard against, be on one's guard, CP.
bewarian to keep watch, guard, preserve, ward off, CP.
bewarnian=bewarenian
bewāwan[7] to blow upon, WA 76. (biwāune= biwāwene)
bewealcan to involve, CHRD 74[33].
beweallan[7] to boil away, LCD.
bewealwian to wallow, Bo 115[9].
beweardian to guard, protect : observe closely.
beweaxan[7] to grow over, cover over, surround, Æ.
beweddendlic relating to marriage, OEG 1122.
beweddian to betroth, marry, Æ : give security. [' bewed']
beweddung f. betrothal, LL442Ha.
bewefan[5] to cover over, LCD 3·146[4].
bewegan[5] to cover, Bo,WY.
bewēled (oe[2], ȳ[2]) poisoned, polluted, GD, JPs,WW; ES38·344. [wōl]
bewellan (=ie) to knead, mix together, GD, WW.
bewendan to turn, turn round, Mk; (refl.) Mt9[22] : turn one's attention, convert, Æ. [' bewend']
bewenian† to entertain, take care of, attend upon, B.
beweorcan=bewyrcan
beweorpan[3] to cast, cast down, plunge, throw, Æ,AO : beat, Æ : surround.
beweorðian to adorn, DD 118.
beweotian=bewitian
bewēpan[7] to weep over, mourn, bewail, Æ. pp. bewōpen tearful, weeping, AO 92[30]. [' beweep']
bewēpendlic lamentable, GL,HL 12[66].
bewēpnian=bewǣpnian
bewerenes f. prohibition, BH 86[13].
bewerian to guard, protect, defend, Æ,AO : check, prevent, forbid, Æ.
bewerigend m. protector, keeper, Æ.
bewerung f. defence, fortification, CM,Sc.
bewestan prep. w. d. or adv. to the west of, Chr; AO. [' bewest']
bewīcian to encamp, CHR 894W.
bewindan[3] to wind round, clasp, entwine, envelop, encircle, surround, B,Mt; AO,CP : brandish (a sword) : turn, wind, revolve. hēafe b. bewail. [' bewind']
bewindla (bi-) m. hedge, border, BC(Mdf).
bewitan swv., pres. 3 sg. -wāt, pret. 3 sg. -wiste to keep, care for, watch over, superintend, administer, lead, guide, Æ,AO.

bewitian (eo) to observe, attend to, care for, administer : perform.
bewlātian to look at, behold, LPs 32[14].
bewlītan[1] to look round, GEN 2925.
bewōpen pp. of bewēpan.
bewrecan[5]† to drive : drive away, banish : drive round, beat round.
bewrencan to deceive, PR 34.
bewrēon[1],[2] to cover, hide, cover over, enwrap, protect, clothe, Sol,Met; CP. [' bewry']
bewreðian to sustain, support, RD 81[21].
bewrigennes f. a covering, WYN 10[13].
bewrītan[1] to record? CREAT 19 : score round, LCD 1·244.
bewrīðan[1]† to bind, wind about, surround, CR.
bewrixl(i)an to change : exchange, sell, PPs.
bewuna adj. indecl. accustomed, wont, AO.
bewyddian=beweddian; bewȳled=bewēled
bewyllan (=ie) to boil away, LCD.
bewylwian (=ie) to roll down, roll together, Sc,WW.
bewȳpð=bewēpð pres. 3 sg. of bewēpan.
bewyrcan to work, construct, surround with, enclose, cover, B; Æ,AO : work in, insert, adorn, Lcd. [' bework']
bewyrpan=beweorpan
beyrfeweardian to disinherit, A 13·321.
beyrnan=beiernan; bezera=bæzere
bi, bī (1)=be (prep.); (2) f.=bēo
bi- v. also be-; bīad=bēod
bibliōðēce f. bibliōðeoco (AO), bibliðēca m. library : bible, Æ. [' bibliotheca' (L.)]
bībrēad=bēobrēad
bicce, bice f. ' bitch,' Lcd,WW.
biccen=byccen
bicgan (Æ)=bycgan; bicge=bicce
±bīcn-an, -ian=bīecnan
+bīcnend (ē), ±bīcni(g)end m. ' index,' indicator, discloser, Sc : forefinger, GL.
bīcnendlic, +bīcni(g)endlic allegorical : (gram.) indicative, ÆGR 124[14].
bīcnol indicating, indicative, GPH 398[193].
±bīcnung (ēa, ē) f. beckoning, nodding : token, symbol, figure, Æ : figurative speech.
bīcwide m. byword, proverb, fable, tale, Æ. [' bequeath']
bīd n. lingering, hesitation, delay, halt, Rd. [' bide']
±bīdan[1] (intr.) to stay, continue, live, remain, delay, AO,G,Ps : (tr. usu. w. g.) wait for, await, expect, B,Bl,Mt; AO,CP : endure, experience, find : attain, obtain : own. [' bide']
biddan[5] to ask, entreat, pray, beseech, A,AO, Bl,G : order, command, require, AO,CP. b. and bēodan, hālsian to beg and pray. [' bid']

+**biddan**[5] (often refl.) *to beg, ask, pray, Bl, Mt*; Æ,CP : *worship*, Æ,AO. ['*i-bid*']

biddend *petitioner*, Sc 32³.

biddere m. *petitioner*, GD,WW.

bidenfæt=bydenfæt

biderīp=bedrīp

bideð (CP) pres. 3 sg. of biddan.

bīdfæst† *firm, forced to stand out.*

bīding f. *abiding place, abode*, Gu 180.

bīdsteall† m. *halt, stand.*

bīe=bēo pres. 1 sg. of bēon.

bīeen—bēacen

bīecn-an, -ian (ē, ī, ȳ) *to make a sign, 'beckon,' wink, nod, Lk*; CP : *signify : summon.* [bēacen] For comps. see bīcn-.

bīegan (ē, ī, ȳ) *to bend, turn, turn back, incline, Bo,Mk* : *depress, abase, humiliate : subject : persuade, convert.* ['*bey*,' būgan]

±**bīeldan** (æ, e, i, y) *to encourage, excite, impel, exhort, confirm, CP,Ma*; Æ,AO. ['*bield*'; beald]

bīeld-o, -u (y) f. *boldness, courage, arrogance, confidence, BH*; CP. ['*bield*']

bīelg=belg; **bīelw-**=bilew-

bīeme (ē, ī, ȳ) f. *trumpet, CP,Mt,WW* : *tablet, billet.* ['*beme*']

bīen=bēan; **bīencoddas**=bēancoddas

+**bīerde**=+byrde

+**bīerhtan** (e, y) *to brighten, be or make bright, illuminate, enlighten, CP* : *make clear : celebrate.* [beorht]

bīerhtu (e, eo, i, y) f. *brightness, effulgence, brilliance, CP.* [beorht]

bīerm=bearm

bīernan³ (ea, eo, i, y) tr. and intr. *to 'burn,' be on fire, give light, Æ,Lk,Ex,Sol,VPs.*

bīersteð, bierst pres. 3 sg. of berstan.

bīerð pres. 3 sg. of beran.

bīesen=bisen; **bīesgian**=bisgian

bīeter-=biter-

bīetl (ē, ī, ȳ) m. '*beetle,' mallet, hammer, CP,Jud.*

bīetr-=biter-

bīeð=bēoð pres. pl. of bēon.

bīfēran *to feed*, Guth 126⁸⁸.

bifian *to tremble, be moved, shake, quake, Bo,Ps*; Æ. ['*bive*']

bifigendlic (byfg-) *terrible*, Chrd 93²⁷.

bifung (y) f. *trembling, shaking*, ÆH.

-**bifung** (eo¹) v. eorð-b.

bīfylce n. *neighbouring people*, BH 196¹. [folc]

big=be; **big-**=be-, bī-, bycg-; **bīg**=bēag

bīgan=bīegan; **bīge**=byge

+**bīgednes** f. *inflection, declension, case*, ÆGr.

bigegnes=begengnes

bīgels m. *arch, vault*, Æ : *curvature*, OEG 2228.

+**bīgendlic** *inflectional*, ÆGr 91⁸.

+**bīgendnes**=+bīgednes

bīgeng f. *practice, exercise, observance, worship, ÆGr* : *cultivation*, Æ. ['*bigeng*']

bīgenga m. *inhabitant : cultivator, Æ* : *worshipper, Æ* : *benefactor.*

bīgenge n. *practice, worship*, Sc,SPs.

bīgengere m. *worker*, WW : *worshipper*, KC.

bīgengestre f. *handmaiden, attendant, worshipper*, Gl.

bīgengnes=begengnes

+**bīgeð**=+bygeð pres. 3 sg. of +bycgan.

bīging (=īe) f. *bending*, WW 216³⁸.

bīgleaf- (eo, i)=bīleof-

bīgnes f. *power of bending, bending, winding, BH,GD.* [bīegan]

+**bīgnes** f. '*confrequentatio*,' EPs 117²⁷.

+**bīgð**=+bigeð

bīgyrdel m. *girdle, belt, purse, Æ,Mt* : *treasury.* ['*bygirdle*']

bīgytan=begietan

bihlanda (MtL 5²⁷)=behindan

bīhst=bȳhst pres. 2 sg. of būgan.

+**bīhð** (Gu 346)=+byht

bil=bill; **bilcettan**=bealcettan

bildan=bieldan

bile m. '*bill,' beak, trunk (of an elephant), WW* : *prow.*

bīle=bȳle; **bīlefa**=bīleofa

bilehwīt=bilewit

bīleofa (i²) m., bīleofen f. *support, sustenance, food, nourishment, Æ,WW* : *money, pay.* ['*bylive*'; libban]

bīlēofian *to support, feed upon*, Guth 34⁷.

bilewet=bilewit

bilewit *innocent, pure, simple, sincere, honest, BH,Mt*; Æ,CP : *calm, gentle, merciful, gracious : plausible.* ['*bilewhit*']. adv. -līce.

bilewitnes f. *mildness, simplicity, innocence, purity*, Æ,CP.

bilgesleht=billgesliht

bilgst, bilhst pres. 2 sg. of belgan.

bilgð pres. 3 sg. of belgan.

bilherge=billere

bilibb-, bilif-=bīleof-; **bilig**=belg

biliw-=bilew-

bill n. '*bill,' chopper, battle-axe, falchion, sword, B,WW.*

billere m. '*bibulta' (plant)*, WW.

billgesliht n. *sword-clash, battle*, †Chr 937.

billhete m. *murderous hate, strife*, An 78.

+**bilod** *having a bill or beak*, HexC 256. [bile]

bil-swæð n. (nap. -swaðu) *sword track, wound*, Ex 329.

bilw-=bilew-; **bīlyht**=bȳliht

bīma (m.?), bīme=bīeme; **bin**=binn

bīnama m. *pronoun*, BF 94¹⁵.

+**bind** n. *binding, fetter* : *costiveness* : *a bind* (measure), TC328′ (v. BTs).

±**bindan** sv³ *to tie,* '*bind,*' *fetter, fasten, restrain,* Æ,Bl,G,WW; AO,CP : *adorn.*

binde f. *head-band?* KC6·133. ['*bind*']

bind-ele, -elle f. *binding,* LL : *bandage,* LCD.

bindere m. '*binder,*' Rd28⁶.

binding f. *binding,* OEG324b.

binn f. '*bin,*' *basket, crib, manger, Bl, LkL,WW.* (*Keltic,* LF124).

binna (LG)=binnan

binnan I. prep. (w. d. a.) *within, in, inside of, into, Jn.* II. adv. *inside, within, less than, during, whilst, LG.* ['*bin*']

binne=(1) binn; (2) binnan (RG)

bint pres. 3 sg. of bindan.

bio-=beo-, bi-; **biosmrung**=bismerung

birce=beorc, beorce; **bird** (LkLR)=bridd

+**bird**=+byrd; **birele**=byrele

biren f. *she-bear,* OET(Ct).

birg=byrg

+**birg** n. *taste,* DR116³.

+**birgan** (e, eo, y) *to taste, eat,* BH,NG.

birging (y) f. *taste,* LCD.

birgnes (eo, y) f. *taste,* BH,WW.

birgð, birhð pres. 3 sg. of beorgan.

birht-=bierht-

birig, birig-=byrig, byrg-

birihte (y) prep. w. d. *near, beside,* AN 850.

birihto=bierhtu; **birle**=byrele

+**birman** (y;=ie) *to ferment, leaven,* LCD 37a. [beorma]

birnan (Æ)=biernan

birst, birsteð pres. 3 sg. of berstan.

birst pres. 2 sg., bir(e)ð pres. 3 sg. of beran.

biryhte=birihte

bisæc n? m? *wallet,* MtR10¹⁰. [LL. bi-saccium]

bisæc *contested, disputed,* LL.

bīsæc f. *visit,* GU188.

bisceop (e², o², u²) m. '*bishop,*' CP : *high-priest, chief priest (Jewish), heathen priest, AO,MkL.*

bisceopcynn (o²) n. *episcopal (high-priestly) stock,* ÆP116¹².

bisceopdōm m. *episcopate, bishopric, Chr* : *excommunication.* ['*bishopdom*']

bisceopealder m. *high-priest,* HL.

bisceopfolgoð m. *episcopate,* GD65³¹.

bisceopgegyrelan mpl. *episcopal robes,* BH90².

bisceophād m. '*bishophood,*' *office of bishop, ordination as bishop, episcopate, bishopric, Ps;* CP.

bisceophādung f. *episcopal ordination,* ÆL 31²⁸⁶.

bisceophām m. *bishop's estate,* EC365¹⁷.

bisceophēafodlīn (o²) n. *head ornament worn by bishops,* WW152²³.

bisceophīred (o) m. *clergy subject to a bishop,* MH,WW.

bisceopian *to confirm, LL.* ['*bishop*']

bisceopland (o) n. *episcopal or diocesan land,* LL173¹⁰.

bisceoplic '*bishoply,*' *episcopal, BH.*

bisceoprīce n. '*bishopric,*' *diocese, province of a bishop, BH* : *episcopal demesne or property,* WC16³.

bisceoprocc (o²) m. *bishop's rochet, dalmatic,* LCD3·202′.

bisceoprōd f. *bishop's cross,* KC4·275¹¹.

bisceopscīr, -scȳr f. *diocese* : *episcopate,* BH.

bisceop-seld, -setl, -seðl n. *bishop's seat or see, bishopric,* BH,CHR.

bisceopseonoð m. *synod of bishops,* A11·8¹.

bisceopstōl m. *episcopal see, bishopric, KC;* CP : *bishop's palace, GD.* ['*bishopstool*']

bisceopsunu m. *godson at a 'bishoping' or confirmation,* CHR,LL.

bisceopðēnung f. *office of a bishop, BH.*

bisceopung f. *confirmation,* Æ,CHRD.

bisceopweorod (o²) n. *bishop's company,* BH309¹¹ (Schipper).

bisceopwīte n. *fine payable to a bishop?* (BTs), *forced entertaining of a bishop?* (Lieb : v. LL2·667).

bisceopwyrt f. *bishop's-wort, betony, vervain, marshmallow,* LCD,WW.

bisceopwyrtil (o²) *vervain,* WW134⁴¹.

biscep=bisceop

bi-sceran, -scerian (i³, y²)=be scioran, -scierian

biscop, bisc(u)p=bisceop

bisegu=bisgu

bisen, bisene (ie, y) fn. *example, pattern, model, JnLR;* Æ,AO,CP : *similitude, parable, parallel* : *rule, command, precept.* ['*bysen*']

bisene (y) *blind,* MtL; NC274; JAW22. ['*bisson*'?]

±**bisenian** (ie, y) *to give, set an example, instruct by example, Bo;* Æ : *follow an example or pattern,* CP : *express figuratively.* ['*bysen*' vb.]

bisenung (y) f. *example, pattern,* Æ.

bises m. *the extra day intercalated in leap year,* MEN32. [L. bissextus]

±**bisgian** *to occupy, employ,* Æ,Bo; CP : *trouble, afflict, Lcd,Met.* ['*busy*']

bisgu, bisigu f. *occupation, labour, Bo;* Æ, CP : *affliction, trouble.* ['*busy*']

bisgung f. *business, occupation, care,* CP.

bisig (y) '*busy,*' *occupied, diligent, Ma,Sol.*

bisignes- f. '*business,*' MtL (Cont. p. xx).

bismær-=bismer-; **bisme**=besma

bismer (y) nmf. *disgrace, scandal, shame, mockery, insult, reproach, scorn, AO,Bl;* CP : *filthiness, defilement, Æ.* tō bismere *ignominiously, shamefully* : *blasphemy* : *infamous deed,* AO. ['*bismer*']

bismerful (y) *infamous, shameful, ignominious, Æ.*

bismerglēow (y) n. *shameful lust,* Æ236²⁴¹.

±**bismerian** (y) *to mock, revile, illtreat, blaspheme, Mk; Æ,AO.* ['*bismer*' vb.]

bismeriend m. *mocker,* KGL298.

bismerlēas (y) *blameless,* CR1326.

bismerlēoð n. *scurrilous song,* GL.

bismerlic *shameful, ignominious, contemptuous,* AO : *ridiculous, frivolous.* adv. -līce.

bismernes f. *pollution* : *insult* : *contemptibleness.*

bismer-spræc, -spæc f. *blasphemy,* G.

±**bismerung** (y) *mockery, scorn* : *blasphemy* : *infamy, disrepute,* AO.

bismerword (æ²) n. *reproach, insult,* LL10¹¹.

bismor, bism(o)r-=bismer, bismer-

bisn-=bisen-

+**bisnere** f. *imitator,* DR45⁷.

bīspell (big-) n. *example, proverb, Æ* : *parable, fable, allegory, story, MtL;* CP. ['*byspel*']

bīspellbōc (big-) f. *book of Proverbs,* ÆT496.

bissextus, gen. -te *the intercalary day of leap year* : *leap year.* [*L.*]

bist pres. 2 sg. of bēon.

bīst=bīdst pres. 2 sg. of bīdan.

bīswæc (e²) *tripping up, treachery,* RPs40¹⁰.

biswic=beswic

bit pres. 3 sg. of biddan.

bīt pres. 3 sg. of (1) bīdan; (2) bītan.

bita m. I. '*bit,*' *morsel, piece, Jn; Æ.* II. *biter, wild beast.*

±**bītan¹** *to* '*bite,*' *tear, B,Rd; Æ : cut, wound :* (+) *dash down,* MkL9¹⁸.

bite m. '*bite,*' *sting, AO,Lcd* : *sword-cut, Ap,B* : *cancer.*

bitela m. '*beetle,*' *Gl.*

biter '*bitter,*' *sharp, cutting, Gu; Æ* : *stinging,* PPs117¹² : *exasperated, angry, embittered* : *painful, disastrous, virulent, cruel, B,Bl.* adv. -līce, *Mt.*

bitere=bitre

±**biterian** *to be or become bitter, CP* : *make bitter.* ['*bitter*' vb.]

biternes f. '*bitterness,*' *grief, Æ,Bl;* CP.

biterwyrde *bitter in speech, Æ.*

biterwyrtdrenc m. *drink of bitter herbs,* WW114¹⁸.

bītl=bīetl

bitmǣlum *piecemeal, bit by bit,* ÆGR239¹⁰.

bitol n. *bridle,* SPs31⁹.

bitor=biter

bitre *bitterly, sharply, painfully, severely* : *very.*

bitres, bittres gsmn. of biter.

bitst pres. 2 sg. of biddan.

bītst pres. 2 sg. of bīdan and bītan.

bitt I. pres. 3 sg. of (1) biddan; (2) beodan. **II.**=bytt

bītt pres. 3 sg. of bītan.

+**bitt** n. *biting, gnashing,* ÆH.

bitter=biter

bittor, bittre=biter, bitre; **bitula**=bitela

bið pres. 3 sg. of bēon.

biwāune v. bewāwan.

bīwist fm. *sustenance, food, provision, necessaries, Æ,Bo.* ['*bewiste*']

bīword (u) n. *proverb, household word* : *adverb,* BF94²⁰.

bīwyrde n. '*byword,*' *proverb,* WW.

bixen=byxen

blāc I. (ǣ) *bright, shining, glittering, flashing, Rd* : *pale, pallid, wan,* AO,CP. ['*bleak,*' but v. FTP286] **II.** pret. 3 sg. of blīcan.

blac=blæc

blāchlēor† *with pale cheeks.*

blācian *to turn pale, Æ.*

blācung f. *a turning pale, pallor, Æ.*

bladesian *to flame, blaze, be hot* : *emit an odour,* OEG554.

bladesnung (at-) f. *odour,* WW405¹.

bladesung (æ¹) f. *shining, lightning,* EPs76¹⁹

blæc (a) **I.** '*black,*' *dark, Æ,B,BH,KC.* **II.** n. *ink,* LL,WW. ['*bleck*']

blæc=blāc

blǣcan *to bleach, whiten* : (+) *disfigure,* CPs79¹⁴. [blāc]

blæcce f. *black matter,* OEG652.

blæce n.? *irritation of the skin, leprosy,* LCD.

blǣcern n. *lamp, candle, light,* CP.

blǣcernleoht (ā) n. *lantern-light,* LV59.

blæcfexede *black-haired,* ÆH1·456¹⁶. [feax]

blæcgymm m. *jet,* BH26¹⁶.

blæchorn (e) n. *ink-horn,* ANS119·125,IM 128¹⁸.

blǣco f. *pallor, WW;* LCD. ['*bleach*']

blǣcpytt m. *bleaching-pit?* EC383'.

blǣcða *leprosy,* WW53²⁸.

blǣcðrustfel n. *leprosy,* Cp103B (? two words).

blæd n. (nap. bladu) '*blade,*' *WW : leaf, Gen.*

blǣd (ē) **I.** m. *blowing, blast,* BH : *inspiration, Ph : breath, spirit, Æ : life, mind : glory, dignity, splendour : prosperity, riches, success.* ['*blead*'; blāwan] **II.**=blēd I.

blǣdāgende *renowned,* B1013.

+**blǣdan** *to puff up, inflate,* APs34²¹

blǣdbylig m. *bellows,* WW241³³.

blǣddæg† m. *day of prosperity.*

blædderwǣrc m. *pain in the bladder,* Lcd.
blǣddre—blǣdre
±**blǣdfæst†** *glorious, prosperous.*
+**blǣdfæstnes** f. *success,* ÆL23b⁴⁹².
blǣdgifa† m. *giver of prosperity,* An.
blǣdhorn m. *trumpet,* Æ.
blǣdnes f. *blossom, fruit,* Bf86². [blēd]
blǣdre (ē) f. *blister, pimple, Æ,Lcd;* AO : *'bladder,' Gl,Lcd.* [blāwan]
blǣdwela m. *abundant riches,* Cr1392.
blǣge f. *gudgeon, bleak, WW.* ['*blay*']
blǣgettan (a) *to cry,* GD278¹².
blǣhǣwen *light blue,* Lev8⁷.
blǣs=blǣst
blǣsbelg (OET28)=blǣstbelg
blǣse (a) f. *firebrand, torch, lamp, Æ,Jn.* ['*blaze*']
blǣsere m. *incendiary,* LL.
blǣshorn m. *trumpet,* LL194,8.
blǣst m. *blowing, 'blast' (of wind), breeze, Ex : flame.*
blǣstan *to blow, belch forth.*
blǣstbelg m. *bellows,* Gl.
blǣstm m? *flame, blaze,* MFH90⁷.
blǣtan *to 'bleat,' ÆGr,Rd.*
blǣtesung=bladesung; **blǣts-**=blēts-
blǣwen (WW163²⁹)=blǣhǣwen
blǣwest, blǣwst pres. 2 sg., blǣw(e)ð pres. 3 sg. of blāwan.
blagettan=blǣgettan
blan pret. 3 sg. of blinnan.
blanca† m. *(white?) horse, B.* ['*blonk*']
±**bland†** n. *blending, mixture, confusion.*
±**blandan⁷** *to blend, mix, mingle, Rd : trouble, disturb, corrupt.* ['*bland*']
blandenfeax† *grizzly-haired, grey-haired, old.* [blandan]
blann pret. 3 sg. of blinnan.
blase, blasere=blǣse, blǣsere
blāstbelg=blǣstbelg; **blaster**=plaster
blāt† *livid, pale, wan, ghastly : low, hoarse (sound)? or pale?* (BTs), An1279. [cp. blēat] adv. **blāte** *lividly, pallidly,* Met.
blates(n)ung=blades(n)ung
blātian *to be livid, pale,* Gen981 (GK).
±**blāwan⁷** (ō) (tr. or intr.) *to 'blow,' breathe, Mt,Lk,Jn; Æ : be blown, sound : inflate :* (+) *kindle, inflame,* WW208¹⁴ : (+) *spit,* MkLR7³³.
blāwend m. *inspirer,* ÆH2·478⁸.
blāwende *blowing hard* (wind), ANS120²⁹⁸.
blāwere m. *'blower,' CP.*
blāwung f. *'blowing,' blast, Æ : inflation.*
bleac=blǣc
blēat *miserable?* Gu963. ['*blete*']. adv. blēate, B2824.
blēað *gentle, shy, cowardly, timid, Rd : slothful, inactive, effeminate,* AO. ['*blethe*']
blec=blǣc; **blēc-**=blǣc-

bled. blēd-=blæd, blēt-
blēd I. (ǣ) f. *shoot, branch, flower, blossom, leaf, foliage, fruit, Mt,Lcd;* CP : *harvest, crops.* ['*blede*'; blōwan] II.=blǣd I.
blēdan *to 'bleed,' let blood,* Sol.
blēdhwæt *growing quickly? profusely?* Rd2⁹.
blēdre=blǣdre
bledu f. *dish, bowl, goblet,* ÆL.
blegen, blegne f. *'blain,' boil, blister, ulcer,* Lcd.
+**blegenod** *blistered, Lcd* 1b, 18b. [v. '*blain*']
blencan *to deceive, cheat, Mod.* ['*blench*']
blēnd (e) pret. 3 sg. of blandan.
blendan I. *to blind, deprive of sight, Bo,Chr : deceive.* ['*blend*'] II. *to mix,* WW425³⁸.
blendian (Chr1086)=blendan I.
blendnes f. *blindness,* DR38⁵.
blent pres. 3 sg. of (1) blendan, (2) blandan.
±**blēo** n. gs. blēos, ds. blēo, gp. blēo(na), dip. blēom, blēo(w)um *colour, Æ,Bo,Met;* CP : *appearance, form, Sol.* ['*blee*']
blēobord n. *coloured board, chess-board,* Wy71.
blēobrygd n? *combination of colours, scintillation,* Ph292. [bregdan]
blēocræft m. *art of embroidery,* WW354⁹.
+**blēod** *beautiful,* Cr909 : *variegated,* KGL (īo).
bleodu=bledu
blēofæstnes f. *delight,* RPs138¹¹.
blēofāg *variegated,* Gl.
bleoh=blēo
blēomete m. *dainty food,* GD99¹⁸.
blēona gp. of blēo.
blēorēad *purple,* WW.
blēostǣning f. *tesselated pavement,* WW444¹⁰.
blēot pret. 3 sg. of blōtan.
blēoum dip. of blēo.
blēow pret. 3 sg. of (1) blāwan, (2) blōwan.
blēowum dip. of blēo.
blere, blerig *bald,* WW.
blese=blǣse
blētan=blǣtan
±**blē** (later e)**tsian** *to consecrate, ordain, Mt, JnL*(oe) : *'bless,' give thanks, adore, extol, Da,Lk,Ps: sign with the cross, Æ: pronounce or make happy, Æ,G,Gen.* [blōd; v. NED]
blētsingbōc f. *blessing-book, benedictional,* EC250'.
blētsingsealm m. *the Benedicite,* RB36¹⁸.
blētst pres. 2 sg. of blōtan.
blētsung f. *consecration, Chr :* '*blessing,' benediction, Chr; Æ : favour (of God), Bl,VPs.*
blēw=blēow pret. 3 sg. of blāwan.
blēwð pres. 3 sg. of blōwan.
blīcan¹ *to glitter, shine, gleam, sparkle, dazzle, Sol235 : appear,* Sol144. ['*blik*']

bliccettan *to glitter, quiver,* GL.

bliccettung f. *glittering, shining,* VPs.

blice m. *exposure,* LL 5,34.

-blicgan=-blycgan

blīcian *to shine,* A 2·357,OEG 1499.

blīcð pres. 3 sg. of blīcan.

blīds=bliss

blin imperat. of blinnan.

blind '*blind*,' *Mk,Mt*; Æ,CP : *dark, obscure, opaque, DD*; Æ : *internal, not showing outwardly* : *unintelligent, Mt* : *not stinging,* WW 322²⁹. adv. -līce *blindly, rashly,* AO.

blindboren *born blind,* JnL 9³².

blindenetele *archangelica (plant),* WW 136, 544.

+blindfellian *to blind, blindfold,* HL 8²⁷⁶.

-blindian v. of-b.

blindnes f. *blindness,* Æ.

blinn n? *cessation,* BH,EL.

±blinnan³ *to cease, leave off, rest from, Mt*; CP : *lose, forfeit, An : be vacant* (bishopric). ['*blin*'; be, linnan]

blinnes f. *cessation, intermission,* LL (156⁵).

blis (CP)=bliss; blisa=blysa

bliscan=blyscan

blisgere m. *incendiary,* LL. [blysige]

bliss f. '*bliss*,' *merriment, happiness, Bl,Ps*; CP : *kindness, friendship, grace, favour, Met* : *cause of happiness, Ps.* [bliðe]

±blissian (intr.) *to be glad, rejoice, exult, CP,Lk*; Æ : (tr.) *make happy, gladden, endow, †Hy* : *applaud,* ANS 109·306. ['*bliss*']

blissig *joyful,* RPs 112⁹.

blissigendlic *exulting,* ÆH 1·354¹¹.

blissung f. *exultation,* EPs 64¹³.

blīð=blīðe

±blīðe I. '*blithe*,' *joyous, cheerful, pleasant, Bl,Cr*; Æ,AO,CP : *gracious, well-disposed, friendly, kind, El* : *agreeable, willing* : *quiet, peaceful, gentle, Ps.* II. adv. *Ps.*

blīðelic *gentle, pleasant, glad, well-wishing.* adv. -līce *Lk*; AO. ['*blithely*']

blīðemōd *glad, cheerful* : *well-wishing, friendly,* BH.

blīðheort *happy, joyful,* AN : *kind, merciful,* GEN.

+blīðian *to make glad,* RPs 91⁴.

blīðnes f. *joy, gladness, pleasure, Lcd*; AO. ['*blitheness*']

blīðs=bliss

blīwum=blēo(w)um, dp. of blēo.

blod=bold

blōd n. '*blood*,' *Æ,Chr,G,Lcd*; AO,CP : *vein.*

blōd-=blōt-

blōd-dolg, -dolh n. *bleeding wound,* LCD.

blōddrync m. *bloodshed,* AO 162³.

blōdegesa m. *bloody horror,* Ex 477.

+blōdegian=blōdgian

blōden *bloody,* WW 217³⁵?

blōdfāg† *blood-stained, bloody.*

blōdgemang n. *a blood-mixture,* WW 220⁷.

blōdgemenged *blood-stained,* W 182¹¹.

blōdgēot=blōdgȳte

blōdgēotend m. *shedder of blood,* LPs 50¹⁶.

blōdgēotende *bloody,* LPs 5⁸.

±blōdgian *to be bloodthirsty,* WW 215⁴³ : *make '*bloody,*' B.*

blōdgyte m. *bloodshed,* AO.

blōdhrǣcung f. *spitting of blood,* WW 113⁶.

blōdhrēow *sanguinary, cruel,* Ps.

blōdig '*bloody*,' *WW*; AO.

blōdigtōð *bloody-toothed,* B 2083.

blōd-lǣs, -lǣswu f. *blood-letting, bleeding,* Lcd. ['*bloodles*']

blōdlǣstīd f. *time for blood-letting,* LCD 55a.

blōdlǣte f. *blood-letting, bleeding,* LCD 6a.

blōdlǣtere m. '*blood-letter*,' *WW*.

blōdlēas *bloodless,* ÆGr 56¹⁴.

blōdrēad *blood-red,* LCD.

blōdrēow=blōdhrēow

blōdryne m. *issue of blood, bloody flux* : *bursting of a blood-vessel,* AO 288²⁷.

blōdscēawung f. *supply of blood?* LCD 83a.

blōdseax (æ, e) n. *lancet,* GL.

blōdseten *something to stop bleeding,* LCD.

blōdsihte f. *flowing of blood,* LCD 64a.

blōdðīgen f. *tasting of blood,* LL.

blōdwīte n. *blood-offering,* LPs 15⁴ (*i.e. penalty for bloodshed?* v. LL 2·25 and 318) : *right to exact such a penalty,* KC 4·216⁵. ['*bloodwite*']

blōdyrnende *having an issue of blood,* BH 78¹⁶ B.

bloedsung (DR 123³)=bletsung

blōma m. *lump of metal, mass, WW.* ['*bloom*']

blon pret. 3 sg. of blinnan.

blonca=blanca; blond-=bland-

blonn pret. 3 sg. of blinnan.

blōsa, blōsma=blōstma

blōstbǣre=blōstmbǣre

blōstm (Æ); blōstma mf. '*blossom*,' *flower, fruit, Bl,Lcd.*

blōstmbǣre (Æ), -bǣrende *flower-bearing.*

blōstmfrēols m. *floral festival,* OEG 4720.

blōstmian *to '*blossom*,' bloom,* BH.

blōstmig (sm-) *flowery,* WW 256³.

±blōt n. *sacrifice,* AO. [blōd]

blōt-=blōd-

blōtan⁷ (and ? wv) *to sacrifice, kill for sacrifice,* AO,CP.

blōtere m. *sacrificer,* GPH 398⁹⁹.

blōtmōnað m. *month of sacrifice* (8 Oct.– 8 Nov.), *November.*

blōtorc m. *sacrificial vessel,* GPH 397.

+blōtsian *to bless*, Percy Soc. vol. 88 p. iii.
blōtspīung f. *spitting of blood*, WW 113⁷.
blōtung f. *sacrifice*, AO 102¹⁶.
±blōwan I. sv⁷ *to 'blow,' flower, flourish, blossom*, Lcd. II.=blāwan
blōwendlic *blooming*, WW 240²⁸.
blunnen pp., blunnon pret. pl. of blinnan.
-blycgan v. ā-b.; blys, blyss=bliss
blysa m. *firebrand, torch*, Æ.
blyscan *'rutilare*,' HGL 434⁷⁵ (v. OEG 1196 and '*blush*').
blyse f.=blysa; blysere=blæsere
blysian *to burn, blaze*, PPs 17⁸.
blysige=blysc; blyssian (Æ)=blissian
blȳðe, blȳðelīce=blīðe, blīðelīce
bō=bā, nafn. of bēgen.
bōc I. fn. ds. and nap. bēc *'beech'-tree*, *WW*; Mdf: *beech-nut*, CHRD 15¹⁰: '*book*,' *writing, Bible, Bl,CP,Jn*; Æ,AO : *deed, charter, conveyance, Mk,TC*. Crīstes b. *gospel*. II. pret. 3 sg. of bacan.
bōcæceras mpl. *freehold lands*, KC.
bōcblæc (e) n. *ink*, W 225¹.
bōcce=bēce
bōc-cest, -cist(e) f. *book-chest*, ApT,RBL.
bōccræft m. *learning, science*, Bo. ['*book-craft*']
bōccræftig *book-learned*, BF 192⁸, JUL 16.
bōcere m. *scholar, scribe, writer*, Æ.
bōcfell n. *parchment, vellum*, LL. ['*book-fell*']
bōcfōdder n. *bookcase*, WW 194¹³.
bōcgesamnung f. *library*, WW 203¹⁵.
bōcgestrēon n. *library*, BH.
bōchaga m. *beech-hedge*, BC 1·515.
bōchord n. *library*, *WW*. ['*bookhoard*']
bōchūs n. *library*, WW 185⁸⁵.
±bōcian *to grant by charter* : *supply with books*.
bōclæden (e²) n. *literary Latin, learned language*, Chr. ['*bocleden*']
bōcland n. *land held by written title*, LL; Æ,AO. v. LL 2·323. ['*bookland*']
bōclār f. '*book-lore*,' *learning*, LL.
bōcleden=bōclæden
bōclic *of or belonging to a book*, Æ : *scientific*, BF 60⁸ : *biblical, scriptural*. b. stæf '*ars liberalis*,' HGL 503.
bōcon pret. pl. of bacan.
bōcrædere m. *reader of books*, WW 439²⁵.
bōcrǣding f. *reading of books*, WW.
bōcread *red colour used in illuminating manuscripts, vermilion*, WW.
bōcrēde f. *reading of books*, A 10·143¹⁰¹.
bōcriht n. *right given by will or charter*, LL 444(1).
bōcstæf m. nap. -stafas *letter, character*, El. ['*bocstaff*'; *Ger*. buchstabe]
bōcstigel f. *beech-wood stile*, BC 1·515.

bōc-tǣcung, -talu f. *teaching or narrative, written in books*, LL.
bōctrēow n. *beech-tree*, ÆGR,WW.
bōcung f. *conveyance by charter or deed*, KC 5·257¹².
bōcweorc n. *study of books*, LL (314¹⁸).
bōcwudu m. *beech-wood*, RD 41¹⁰⁶.
±bod (+exc. N) n. *command, message, precept*, Bo,Hy; Æ : *preaching*. ['*bode*,' '*i-bod*']
boda m. *messenger, herald, apostle, angel*, Æ,CP : *prophet*. ['*bode*']
bodan=botm
bodo pret. of bōgan.
bodeg=bodig
boden pp. of bēodan.
bodere m. *teacher*, NG.
±bodian *to tell, proclaim, announce*, †Hy; AO,CP : *preach, Mt*; Æ,CP : *foretell, El* : *boast*. ['*bode*']
bodiend m. *proclaimer, teacher, preacher*, GL,HL.
bodig n. '*body*,' *trunk, frame, bodily presence*, Æ,BH,Gl,Lcd; CP : *main part*, LCD.
bodigendlic *to be celebrated*, ÆL 7²³².
bodlāc n. *decree, ordinance*, CHR 1129.
±bodscipe† m. *command, message*, GEN.
bodung f. *message, recital, preaching*, Æ : *interpretation* : *assertiveness*, RB 136²².
bodungdæg m. *Annunciation Day*, ÆH 1·200²⁵.
bōg m. *arm, shoulder*, Æ; CP : '*bough*,' *twig, branch, Mt*; CP : *offspring*. [būgan]
boga m. '*bow*' (weapon), Gn; Æ : *arch, arched place, vault*, B : *rainbow*, Æ,Lcd : *folded parchment*. [cp. *Ger*. bogen]
bōga=bōg
bōgan *to boast*, RB.
boganet=bogenett
bogefōdder m. *quiver*, WW 143¹⁹.
bogen I. *name of a plant*, LCD. II. pp. of būgan.
bogenett n. *wicker basket with a narrow neck for catching fish*, WW.
bogetung f. *curve*, WW 355¹⁵.
bōgh=bōg
bōgian I. ±(intr.) *to dwell*, Æ : (tr.) *to inhabit*. II.=bōgan
bogiht *full of bends*, MtL 7¹⁴.
bōgincel n. *small bough*, OEG.
bōgung (bōung) f. *boastfulness, arrogance, display*, Æ.
bōh=bōg
bohscyld m. *curved shield?* (WC 172n), EC 226'.
bohte pret. 3 sg. of bycgan.
bōhtimber n. *building-wood*. [v. AS 1³ and ES 42·172]
bōian=bōgan

bol? m. *bole, trunk,* LCD 143a.

bolca m. *gangway of a ship,* AN,B,GL.

bold (=botl) n. *house, dwelling-place, mansion, hall, castle,* B : *temple.* ['*bold*']

boldāgend† m. *homestead-owner.*

boldgestrēon (botl)† *household goods,* GEN.

boldgetæl *collection of houses* : (*political*) *district, county, province,* GD.

boldgetimbru npl. *houses,* SOL 412.

boldweard (botl-) m. *housekeeper, steward,* ÆGR,WW.

boldwela† (botl-) m. *wealth* : *splendid dwelling, paradise, heaven*:*village,* GEN 1799.

bolgen pp. of belgan.

bolgenmōd† *enraged.*

bolla m., bolle f. '*bowl*,' *cup, pot, beaker, measure,* ÆL,Jn,Lcd.

bolster mn. '*bolster*,' *cushion,* B; CP.

+bolstrian *to support with pillows, prop up,* BF 74[16].

bolt m. '*bolt*' : *cross-bow for throwing bolts or arrows,* WW.

bolttimber n. *building timber, beams.* [v. AS 1[3] and ES 42·172]

bōn I. f. *ornament,* CHR 1063 D. II.=bōgan

bon-, bond-=ban-, band-

bōnda m. *householder, LL* : *freeman, plebeian* : *husband.* ['*bond*']

bōndeland n. *land held by a* bōnda, CHR 777 E. [ON. bōndi]

bōne=bēn

+bōnian *to ornament,* TC. [bōn]

bonn=bann

bor *borer, gimlet,* GL : *lancet, scalpel, graving tool,* GL. [borian]

bora m. *ruler,* SAT 500. [? rǣdbora]

borcen pret. 3 sg. of beorcan.

borcian *to bark,* RD 84[6].

bord n. '*board*,' *plank, Æ* : *table, Ps* : *side of a ship, Gen* : *ship, El,Gn* : *shield, El.* innan, ūtan bordes *at home, abroad,* CP.

borda m. *embroidery, ornament,* GL.

bordclāð m. *table-cloth,* OEG 56[22].

bordgelāc n. *weapon, dart,* CR 769.

bordhæbbende *shield-bearing,* B 2895.

bordhaga m. *cover of shields,* EL 652.

bordhrēoða (ē)† m. *shield-ornament* : *phalanx.*

bordrand m. *shield,* B 2559.

bordrima (e[2]) m. *rim, edge,* Ln.

bordrīðig *a stream running in a channel made of planks?* (BTs),EC 450[11].

bordstæð n. *sea-shore,* AN 442.

bordðaca m. *shield-covering, testudo,* GL : *board for roofing,* WW.

bordweall m. *wall of shields, phalanx* : *buckler, shield* : *side of ship,* RD 34[6].

bordwudu m. *shield,* B 1243

boren (B,Chr,Cp) pp. of beran. ['*y-born*']

borettan *to brandish,* GL.

borg m. *pledge, security, bail, debt, obligation, LL* (v. 2·331; 641); CP : *bondsman* : *debtor.* ['*borrow*' sb.]

borgbryce m. *breach of surety, LL.* ['*borrowbreach*']

borgen pp. of beorgan.

borggelda m. *borrower* : *lender,* CPs 108[11].

borgian *to* '*borrow*,' *Mt,Ps* : *lend* : *be surety for,* OEG 3812.

borgiend m. *lender, usurer,* SPs 108[10].

borg-sorg (burg-) f. *trouble on account of lending or security,* RIM 63.

borgsteall *a steep path up a hill?* BC,KC (v. BTac and Mdf).

borgwedd n. *pledge,* WW 279[16].

borh=borg

borhfæst *fast bound,* HL 203[254].

±borhfæstan *to bind by pledge or surety,* CHR.

borhhand fm. *security, surety* (person), Æ.

borhlēas *without a pledge, without security,* LL 230,5.

borian *to bore, perforate,* GL.

borlīce *very, extremely, fitly, excellently,* BF.

born=barn pret. 3 sg. of biernan.

+borsnung=+brosnung

borsten pp. of berstan.

borðor=beorðor

bōsig m? n? *stall, crib,* LkLR. ['*boosy*']

bōsm (CP), bōsum m. '*bosom*,' *breast, womb, Æ* : *surface, An* : *ship's hold,* Gen.

bōsmig *sinuous,* OEG 8[2].

bōt f. *help, relief, advantage, remedy, An,Da, Lcd*; AO : *compensation for an injury or wrong, LL* (v. 2·336) : (*peace*) *offering, recompense, amends, atonement, reformation, penance, repentance, B,Bl*; CP. tō bōte *to* '*boot*,' *besides, moreover.*

bōtan=bētan

bōtettan *to improve, repair,* W.

bōtian *to get better,* BH,LCD.

±botl (Æ,CP)=bold

bōtlēas *unpardonable, not to be atoned for by* bōt, LL,W.

botm m. '*bottom*,' *ground, foundation, B, Sat,WW* : *abyss,* Gen.

bōtwyrðe *pardonable, that can be atoned for by* bōt, LL,W. [cp. bōtlēas]

bōð=bōgeð pres. 3 sg. of bōgan.

boðen mn? *rosemary* : *darnel, Æ* : *thyme,* GPH 390.

bōung=bōgung

box mn. *box-tree, KC,WW* : '*box*,' *case, M., WW.* [L.]

boxtrēow n. *box-tree,* ÆGR 20[19].

braccas mp. *breeches,* LCD 3·198'. [L.]

bracce (Mdf)=brǣc I.

brachwīl f. *moment,* BF 118[24].

-bracian v. ā-b.

brād I. comp. brādra, brǣdra '*broad*,' *flat, open, extended, spacious, wide, Bl,Gen, Chr,Ps*; Æ,AO,CP : *ample, copious, B,El.* II. n. *breadth,* LV,RIM.

brādæx f. *broad axe,* GL.

brādbrim† n. *wide sea.*

brāde† *far and wide, broadly, widely,* W.

brādelēac n. *leek,* GL.

brādhand f. *palm of the hand,* WW 264³⁴.

brādian *to extend, reach,* AO 234¹⁰ : (+) VPs 47³.

brādlāstæx f. *broad axe,* GL.

brādlinga *flatly, with the hand open,* IM.

brādnes sf. *breadth, greatness, extent, surface,* Æ : *liberality.*

brādpanne=brǣdepanne

brǣc I. *a strip of untilled land?* (BT),KC. II.=pret. 3 sg. of brecan. III. (+) (e) n. *noise, sound,* CP.

brēc I. (±) n. *catarrh, cough.* II. f. *breaking, destruction,* ÆL5²⁹². III.=brēc nap. of brōc I.

brǣcce *breeches,* Cp 1788. [*L.*]

brǣccoðu f. *falling sickness, epilepsy,* WW 112²⁷.

brǣcdrenc (ē) *cough medicine,* WW 351⁸⁸.

+**brǣceo**=brǣc I.

brǣclian *to crackle, make a noise,* GD 236¹².

brǣcon pret. pl. of brecan.

±**brǣcsēoc** *epileptic, lunatic,* BH,LCD.

brǣd I. f. *breadth, width,* AO. [brād] II. f. *flesh,* PH 240. [*OHG.* brāt] III. m. *trick, fraud, deceit, craft, LL,MtL.* [=*brægd; '*braid*'] IV. pret. 3 sg. of brēdan, bregdan. V. pres. 3 sg. and pp. of brǣdan.

brǣd-=brǣgd- (bregd-)

±**brǣdan** (e) I. *to make broad, extend, spread, stretch out, BH*; AO : *be extended, rise, grow.* ['*brede*'; brād] II. *to roast, toast, bake, broil, cook, WW.* ['*brede*']

brǣde m. *roast meat, WW.* ['*brede*']

-**brǣdels** v. ofer-b.

brǣdepanne f. *frying-pan* (v. WW 363N3).

brǣding I. f. *extension,* Bo 46⁶ : *bedding, bed?* DR. II. f. *roast meat,* OEG 3760.

brǣdingpanne=brǣdepanne

brǣdīsen (ē) n. *chisel,* GL,WW.

brǣdra v. brād.

brǣd-u, -o f. *breadth, width, extent, Ps.* ['*brede*']

+**brǣgd**=brād III; **brǣgdan**=bregdan

brǣgdboga m. *deceitful bow,* CR 765.

brǣgden (e) I. (±) *deceitful, crafty,* AO. adv. -līce. [bregdan] II. *fraud,* LL.

brǣgdwīs *crafty,* Gu 58. [bregd]

brǣgen (a, e) n. '*brain,*' Lcd,Ps; Æ,CP.

brǣgenpanne f. *brain-pan, skull,* OEG 2815.

brǣgensēoc *brain-sick, mad,* OEG.

brǣgn=brǣgen

brǣgnloca (hrǣgn-) m. *brain-house, head,* RD 72²¹.

brǣgpanne=brǣgenpanne

brǣhtm (A)=breahtm

brǣmbel, brǣmel=brēmel

brǣme (NG)=brēme; **brǣr**=brēr

brǣs n. '*brass,*' *bronze, WW.*

brǣsen '*brazen,*' *of brass, LPs*; Æ.

brǣsian *to do work in brass, make of brass,* ÆGr 215¹⁷. ['*braze*']

brǣsne=bresne

brǣð m. *odour, scent, stink, exhalation, vapour, AO,WW.* ['*breath*']

brǣw (ēa) m. *eye-brow, eye-lid, BH,Lcd,Ps, WW*; CP. ['*bree*']

bragen=brǣgen

brahton=brohton pret. pl. of bringan.

brand (ō) m. *fire, flame, B*; Æ : '*brand,*' *torch, JnL,Da*; Æ : *sword, weapon, B,TC.*

brandhāt† *burning hot, ardent.*

brandhord (o¹) n? *treasure exciting ardent desires* (BT); *care, anxiety* (GK), RIM 46.

brand-īren, -īsen n. *fire-dog, trivet, grate, WW.* ['*brandise*']

brandōm (o¹) m. '*rubigo,*' WW 44¹⁴.

brandrād (o², e²) f. *fire-dog, trivet, WW.* ['*brandreth*']

brandrida m. *fire-grate,* WW 266²⁶.

brandstæfn (o¹) *high-prowed?* AN 504. [=brant-?]

brang pret. 3 sg. of bringan.

brant† (o) *deep, steep, high, An,El.* ['*brant*']

brasian=brǣsian

+**brastl** (-sl) n. *crackling* (*of flames*), DD,W.

brastlian (-sl) *to roar, rustle, crackle,* Æ. ['*brastle*']

brastlung f. *crackling, rustling, crashing,* Æ.

bratt m. *cloak, MtL5*⁴⁰. ['*bratt*'; v. LF 125]

brēac pret. 3 sg. of brūcan.

brēad n. *bit, crumb, morsel* : '*bread,*' JnL.

+**breadian** (e) *to regenerate, restore,* PH 372, 592.

brēag=brēaw

breahtm I. (bearhtm; æ, e, eo, y) m. *cry, noise, revelry.* II.=bearhtm

breahtmian (earht) *to creak, resound,* GL.

breahtmung f. '*convolatus,*' WW 376³.

breahtumhwæt=bearhtmhwæt

breard=brerd; **brēat-**=brēot-

brēað *brittle,* LCD 1·260⁷.

brēaw=brǣw

brēawern n. *brew-house,* WW 145²⁹.

+**brec**=+brǣc III.

brēc v. brōc; ±**brēc**=±brǣc

±brecan I. sv⁴ to 'break,' shatter, burst, tear, B,Bl,G,Ps : curtail, injure, violate, destroy, oppress, B,Chr,Da,KC; AO,CP : break into, rush into, storm, capture (city), Ma, Chr; CP : press, force : break or crash through, burst forth, spring out, An,Ph : subdue, tame, CP. II. to roar? CR951.

brēchrægl n. breeches, PPs108²⁸.

brecmǣlum=brytmǣlum

±brecnes f. breach, EPs.

-brecð v. ǣ-, eodor-b.

brecða m. broken condition. mōdes b. sorrow of heart, B171.

brecung f. 'breaking,' LkR.

bred n. surface : board, plank, CP : tablet, Æ. ['bred']

brēd=(1) brȳd, (2) brād, (3) brǣd III.

brēdan I. to produce, or cherish, a brood, Æ. ['breed'] II. (±)=bregdan. III. (±)= brǣdan I. and II.

breden (i, y) of boards, wooden, Æ,CHR.

brēdende deceitful, cunning, AO. [bregdan]

brēdettan=brogdettan

+bredian=breadian

brēdi(ng)panne=brǣdepanne

brēdīsern=brǣdīsen

bredweall m. wall of boards, palisade, ES 20·148.

+brēfan to write down shortly, BF72²⁰. [cp. Ger. brief]

brēg (VPs)=brǣw; brega (Æ)=brego

brēgan to alarm, frighten, terrify, Lk; Æ, CP. ['bree'; brōga]

bregd=brǣd III.

+bregd I. n. quick movement, change, Ph57. [v. 'braid'] II.=brǣd III.

bregdan³ (brēd-) to move quickly, pull, shake, swing, throw (wrestling), draw (sword), drag, B,Ma : bend, weave, 'braid,' knit, join together, ÆGr : change colour, vary, be transformed, Ex,Sol,Gu : bind, knot : (intr.) move, be pulled : flash, Æ. up b. bring up (a charge) : (+) scheme, feign, pretend : (+) draw breath, breathe.

bregden=brægden

+bregdnes (ē?) f. quick movement? sudden terror? MFH133¹⁷ (v. BTac).

+bregdstafas mp. learned arts, SOL2.

bregen=brægen

brēgendlic terrible, RPs46³.

brēgh=brǣw

brēgnes f. fear, terror, EPs87¹⁷.

bregot (eo) m. ruler, chief, king, lord. b. engla, mancynnes God.

bregorīce n. kingdom, GEN1633.

bregorōf majestic, mighty, B1925.

bregostōlt m. ruler's seat, throne : rule, dominion.

bregoweardt m. ruler, prince, lord, GEN.

bregu=brego

breht-=breaht-, beorht-, bierht-

brehtnian=bearhtmian

brēman I. (±) to honour, extol : respect, fulfil, CHRD18³⁵ : celebrate, CHRD114¹⁷. [brēme] II. (oe) to rage, NG.

brēmbel (Æ), brēmber=brēmel

brēme (oe, ȳ) I. adj. famous, glorious, noble, PPs; AO. ['breme'] II. adv. An.

brēmel (ǣ) m. brier, 'bramble,' blackberry bush, Æ,Lcd; Mdf. [brōm]

brēmelæppel m. blackberry, Lcd. [v. 'apple']

brēmelberie f. blackberry, Lcd. ['brambleberry']

brēmelbrǣr (ǣ¹) m. bramble-brier, WW 269³⁸.

brēmellēaf n. bramble-leaf, LCD.

brēmelrind f. bramble-bark, LCD.

brēmelðyrne f. bramble-bush, Æ.

brēmen=brēme I.

brēmendlic noted, OEG.

brēmer=brēmel

brēmlas nap. of brēmel.

bremman to rage, roar, JnL, WW. [Ger. brummen]

bremung f. roaring, WW242³⁹.

brencð pres. 3 sg. of brengan.

brene=bryne

breneð=berneð (pres. 3 sg. of bernan) (RUN43)

±brengan to bring, AO,CP : produce, NG.

brengnes f. oblation : (+) food, support, MkL12⁴⁴.

brenting m. ship, B2807. [brant]

breo-, brēo-=bre-, brē-

brēod (NG)=brēad

breodian to cry out, MOD28.

breodwian to strike down, trample? GU258, LCD32¹¹.

breoht-=bearht-, beorht-

brēosa (īo) m. gadfly, WW. ['breeze']

brēost nmf. (usu. in pl.) 'breast,' bosom, B, G,Lcd; AO,CP : stomach, womb : mind, thought, disposition, Gen; CP : 'ubertas,' CPs35⁹.

brēostbān n. 'breast-bone,' WW158.

brēostbeorg=brēostgebeorh

brēostbyden (e²) f. breast, GL.

brēostcearut f. heart-care, anxiety.

brēostcofat m. heart, affections.

brēostgebeorh m. bulwark, WW466¹⁴.

brēostgehygdt, -hȳdt fn. thought.

brēostgeðanct m. mind, thought.

brēostgewǣdut np. corslet, B.

brēostgyrd f. sceptre? OEG3303; 2¹⁸⁸.

brēosthordt n. thought, mind.

brēostlīn n. stomacher, WW407².

brēostlocat m. mind, soul.

brēostnet† n. *coat of mail.*
brēostnyrwet n. *tightness of chest,* LCD 189b.
brēostrocc m. *chest-clothing,* WW151³⁹.
brēostsefa† m. *mind, heart.*
brēosttoga m. *chieftain,* SOL184.
brēostðing n. *region of the heart,* LCD3·146¹⁸.
brēostwærc m. *pain in the chest,* LCD.
brēostweall m. *breastwork, rampart,* WW 490¹³.
brēostweorðung f. *breast-ornament,* B2504.
brēostwylm (e²) m. *breast-fountain, teat,* SPs 21⁸ : *emotion, sorrow,* B.
Breot-=Bryt-
brēotan²† *to break in pieces, hew down, demolish, destroy, kill.*
Breotas=Brittas
Breoten, Breoton=Bryten
breoton=bryten; brēoton pret. pl. of brēatan.
brēoðan² *to decay, waste away,* LCD63a, RPs4¹⁶.
±brēowan² *to 'brew,'* AO.
brēowlāc n. *brewing,* ÆL17¹⁰³.
brēr (ǣ) f. *'brier,' bramble, Lcd,WW.*
brerd (ea, eo, y) m. *brim, margin, border, surface, Jn,WW : shore, bank, Æ.* ['*brerd*']
brerdful *brim-full,* ÆL6²⁸². ['*brerdful*']
brērhlǣw m. *brier-hillock,* EC450⁹.
brērðyrne f. *brier-bush,* KC6·221¹³.
brēsan=brȳsan; bresen=bræsen
bresne (æ)† *mighty, strong.*
Bret=Bryt; bret-, brēt-=bryt-, brȳt-
brēt pres. 3 sg. of brēdan, bregdan.
brēð=brǣð; brēðel=briðel
brēðer ds. of brōðor.
brēw (KGL)=brǣw
bric-, brīc-=bryc-, brȳc-
briceð pres. 3 sg.; bricst pres. 2 sg. of brecan.
brid=bridd; brīd=brȳd
bridd m. *young 'bird,' chicken, Gl,Lk; Æ, CP,Mdf.*
brīdel, brīdels (ȳ) m. *'bridle,' rein, curb, restraint, Run; Æ,CP.*
brīdelshring m. *bridle-ring,* EL1194.
brīdelðwangas mp. *reins,* WW97¹⁰.
briden=breden
brīd-gift, -gifu=brȳd-gift, -gifu
±brīdlian *to 'bridle,' curb, Bo;* CP.
briengan=bringan
brig=brycg; brīg=brīw
brigd n. *change or play of colours,* PA26. [bregdan]
brigdils (GL)=brīdels
briht-=beorht-, bierht-
brim† n. *surf, flood, wave, sea, ocean, water, B : sea-edge, shore.* ['*brim*']

brimceald† *ocean-cold,* PH.
brimclif n. *cliff by the sea,* B222.
brimfaroð n. *sea-shore* (BT), DA322 (or ? 2 words).
brimflōd m. *flood, sea,* Az,WW.
brimfugol m. *sea-bird, gull,* WA47.
brimgiest m. *sailor,* RD4²⁵.
brimhengest† m. *(sea-horse), ship.*
brimhlæst f. *sea-produce, (fish),* GEN200.
brimlād† f. *flood-way, sea-way.*
brimliðend† m. *seafarer, B : pirate,* MA.
brimmann† m. *sailor, pirate,* MA.
brimrād† f. *(sea-road), sea,* AN.
brimsa? *gadfly?* (v. Ln49⁸² and NC354).
brimstæð n. *sea-shore,* AN496.
brimstrēam† m. *current, sea : rapid, river.*
brimðyssa† m. *ship.*
brimwīsa m. *sea-king, captain,* B2930.
brimwudu† m. *(sea-wood), ship.*
brimwylf f. *(she-)wolf of the sea or lake,* B1507.
brimwylm m. *ocean surge, sea-wave,* B1494.
bring m. *offering,* CPs50²⁰.
bringādl f. *epilepsy?* (or? hringādl v. MLR19·201).
±bringan³ (e, ie, y) (and wv) *to 'bring,' lead, bring forth, carry, adduce, produce, present, offer, B,Gen,Jn,Met;* AO,CP.
-bringelle v. on-b.; brīosa=brēosa
brīst, brītst pres. 2 sg., brīt pres. 3 sg. of bregdan.
Brit-, brit-=Bryt-, bryt-
briðel (e) *fragile, weak,* LCD1·384¹⁴ (BTac).
brīw m. *pottage, porridge, ÆGr,Lcd* ['*brew*']
±brīwan *to prepare food, cook, make pottage : make a poultice,* LCD25a.
brīwðicce *as thick as pottage,* LCD190a.
broc I. (±) n. *affliction, misery, care, toil, adversity, Bl,Bo,TC; Æ,AO,CP : disease, sickness, Æ : fragment, G : breach.* ['*broke*'; brecan] II. n. *use, benefit.* III. *a kind of locust?* WW460. ['*brock*'] IV.=brocc
brōc I. f. pl. brēc *breeches, RB,WW : the breech?* Lcd (ES38·345). II. m. *'brook,' torrent, Bo,WW;* Mdf.
brocc m. *badger, Lcd.* ['*brock*']
broccen *of badger's skin,* WW152¹.
brocchol n. *badger's hole,* EC239¹².
broccian *to tremble,* GD156.
brocen pp. of (1) brecan, (2) brūcan.
brocenlīc *fragile,* BYH130²⁹.
±brocian *to crush, hurt, afflict, molest, Æ, AO,CP : blame.* [broc]
broclic *full of hardship,* W248¹.
brōcminte f. *brookmint, horsemint,* LCD, WW.
brōcrið *a tributary stream,* KC5·194'.
brōcsēoc=brǣcsēoc

brocung f. *affliction, sickness,* ÆH 1·472⁷.

brod *shoot, sprout,* LHy 6³.

brōd f. '*brood,*' Æ : *foetus* : *breeding, hatching,* WW 380⁴⁴.

broddetan=brogdettan

broddian=brōdian

brōden pp. of brēdan.

brōdenmǣl† n. *damascened sword.*

brōder=brōðor; **brōdet-**=brogdet-

brōdian *to glitter, shine,* OEG.

brōdig adj. *broody,* BF 78¹⁶.

brōga m. *terror, dread, danger,* CP : *prodigy.*

brogden (*El*) pp. of bregdan. ['*browden*']

brogdenmǣl=brōdenmǣl

brogdettan *to shake, brandish* : *tremble, quake* : *glitter,* HGL 435?

brogdettung f. *trembling, shaking* : *figment, pretence,* CPs 102¹⁴.

±**brogne** *bough, bush, branch,* DR (v. ES 38·340 and JAW).

broht '*viscellum,*' WW 54¹. (?=broð '*juscellum,*' MLR 19·201)

brōht pp., brōhton pret. pl. of bringan.

brōhrēa m. *dire calamity,* GEN 1813. [brōga]

brōm m. '*broom,*' *brushwood,* Lcd; Mdf.

brōmfæsten n. *enclosure of broom,* WW 414⁷.

brōmig *broomy,* BL 207²⁷? (BTs and ac).

bron-=bran-; **brond**=brand, brant

brord m. *prick, point* : *blade* (*e.g.,* of grass or corn) : *herbage,* BH 366²⁶.

±**brosnian** *to crumble, decay, fall to pieces, rot, wither, be corrupted,* AO,CP.

brosniendlic (Æ), +brosnodlic (BL,W) *corruptible, perishable, transitory.*

±**brosnung** f. *decay, corruption, ruin,* Æ.

+**brot** n. *fragment,* G. [breotan]

Broten=Bryten

broten pp. of brēotan.

brotettan *to burst forth, shoot, sprout?* HGL 435, OEG 1218n (or?=brogdettan, BTs)

brōtetung=brogdettung

brōð n. '*broth,*' WW. [brēowan]

brōðar, brōðer=brōðor

brōðhund (WW 329³⁸; 548¹⁹)=roðhund?

brōðor m. ds. brēðer '*brother**,*' Chr,Mt,Lk. nap. (±) brōðor, brōðru, Gen,Jn : *fellowman,* Ps : *co-religionist,* Mt : *monk.*

brōðorbana m. *fratricide* (*person*), GEN 1526.

brōðorcwealm m. *fratricide* (*act*), GEN 1030.

brōðordohter f. *niece,* WW 173³⁰.

brōðorgyld n. *vengeance for brothers?* Ex 199.

brōðorlēas *brotherless,* RD 85¹⁶.

brōðorlic '*brotherly,*' ÆGr.

brōðorlīcnes f. *brotherliness,* BH.

brōðorlufu (-e²) *love,* DR.

brōðorrǣden f. *fellowship, brotherhood,* Æ : *membership of a brotherhood.* ['*brotherred*']

brōðorscipe m. *brotherliness, love,* MtL : (+) *brotherhood, fraternity,* AO. ['*brothership*']

brōðorsibb f. *kinship of brothers* : *brotherly love.*

brōðorslaga m. *brother-slayer,* Æ.

brōðorslege m. *fratricide* (*act*), CP.

brōðorsunu m. *brother's son, nephew,* CHR.

brōðorsybb=brōðorsibb

broðor-ōīnen, -ōīnenu=beorðorōīnen

brōðorwīf n. *brother's wife, sister-in-law,* BH.

brōðorwyrt (e²) f. '*pulegium,*' *penny-royal,* WW 300²⁴.

+**brōð-ru,** -ra mp. *brothers, brethren,* Mt. ['*i-brotheren*']

brōður=brōðor

+**browen** pp. of brēowan.

brū f. nap. brū(w)a, gp. brūna '*brow,*' *eyebrow, eye-lid, eye-lash,* Rd,WW.

±**brūcan²** *to* '*brook,*' *use, enjoy, possess, partake of, spend, B,Wa.* brocen cyrtel *a coat which has been worn,* Æ : *eat,* Æ,JnL : *execute an office,* CP : *cohabit with.*

brūcendlīce *serviceably,* OEG 53¹.

brūcung f. *function, occupation,* BC 1·154¹³.

brūdon, brugdon pret. pl. of brēdan, bregdan.

brūn '*brown,*' *dark, dusky, Ex,Met* : *having metallic lustre, shining* (v. NED).

brūna gp. of brū.

brūn-basu, -b(e)osu *brownish-purple,* OEG.

brūnecg† *with gleaming blade.*

brūneða m. *itch, erysipelas,* LCD 18a.

brūnewyrt=brūnwyrt

brūnfāg *burnished? brown-hued?* B 2615.

brungen pp., brungon pret. pl. of bringan.

brūnian *to become brown,* LCD 106b.

brunna=burna

brūnwann *dusky,* AN 1308.

brūnwyrt f. '*brownwort,*' *water-betony, wood-betony,* Lcd.

bruðon pret. pl. of brēoðan.

brūwa nap. of brū.

±**bryce** (i) **I.** m. '*breach*' ('*bruche*'), *fracture, breaking, infringement, Gu,LL;* Æ : *fragment,* OEG. [brecan] **II.** *fragile, brittle, worthless, fleeting, Bl.* ['*bryche*'] **III.** n. *use, enjoyment, service, exercise, advantage, gain, profit, fruit,* Æ,CP.

brȳce *useful, profitable,* PPs. ['*briche*']

-brycel v. hūs-b.

bryceð pres. 3 sg. of brecan.

brycg f. '*bridge,*' Æ; AO,Mdf.

brycgbōt (i) f. *repairing of bridges,* LL.

brycggeweorc (i¹) n. *work of building or repairing bridges,* Ct,LL.

brycgian *to* '*bridge,*' *make a causeway, pave,* An.

brycgweard (i¹) m. *keeper or defender of a bridge,* Ma 85. ['*bridgeward*'] brycgwyrcende *'pontifex'! DR 194'*.

±brȳc-ian, -sian *to use, enjoy*, DR : *profit, benefit*.

brycŏ pres. 3 sg. of brecan.

brȳcŏ pres. 3 sg. of brūcan.

brȳd I. (ē, i) f. *'bride,' betrothed or newly-married woman, wife, consort*, G,WW; Æ, CP. brȳdes wǣde *wedding garment* : (†) (*young*) *woman*. II.=brygd

bryd-, brȳd-=bred-, brīd-

brȳdbedd n. *bridal bed*, Æ.

brȳdblētsung (ī) f. *marriage blessing*, LL 72,38¹.

brȳdboda m. *paranymph, bridesman*, OEG 18b⁷¹.

brȳdbūr (BL) n., brȳdcofa (HGL) m. *bride-chamber, bed-chamber*.

+bryddan *to frighten, terrify*, SOL 16.

-brȳde v. un-b.

brȳdeala, brȳdealo(ŏ) n. *bride-ale, marriage-feast, Chr.* ['*bridal*']

brȳdelic=brȳdlic

brȳdgifta fpl. *betrothal, espousals*, APT.

brȳdgifu (ī) f. *dowry*, ÆGR 57¹⁴ : (pl.) *espousals*, WW 171⁵.

brȳdguma (Æ,CP), brȳdiguma (Æ) m. '*bridegroom,' Jn :* suitor.

brȳdhlŏp n. *ceremony on conducting a bride to her new home, bridal, wedding, Chr,MtL.* ['*bridelope*']

brȳdhūs n. *bride-chamber*, APs 18⁶.

+brȳdian *to marry*, MH.

brȳdlāc n. *bridal, wedded condition*, Æ : (pl.) *marriage ceremony*, LL; Æ. ['*bridelock*']

brȳdlēoŏ n. *epithalamium*, OEG.

brȳdlic *bridal.* b. gewrit *Song of Solomon*, WW 388²⁰. ['*bridely*']

brȳdloca m. *bride-chamber*, BL.

brȳdlŏp=brȳdhlŏp

brȳdlufe f. *love of a bride*, JUL 114.

brȳdniht f. *wedding-night*, MH 14²⁶.

brȳdrǣst f. *bridal bed*, GD.

brȳdrēaf n. *wedding garment*, MtL 22¹¹.

brȳdsang m. *epithalamium*, WW.

brȳdsceamol? *bridal bed*, DR 110¹ (BTs).

brȳdŏing np. *nuptials, Bl.* ['*brydthing*']

brygc=brycg

brygd I. (bryd) m. *drawing out, unsheathing, brandishing*, LL 356,2. II.=brǣd III.

bryht=beorht; bryhtan=bierhtan

±bryidan *to seize property improperly held by another*, LL. [=*brigdan? BTs]

brym, brymm m. *surf, sea*, AB 35·240.

brȳm-=brēm-

bryne m. *burning, conflagration*, BH : *fire, flame, heat, MtL*; AO : *inflammation, burn, scald, Lcd* : *torch* : *fervour, passion.* ['*brune'*; beornan]

brȳne f. *'brine,' WW*; Æ.

bryneādl f. *fever*, WW 238²⁶.

brynebrōga m. *fire-terror*, Az 161.

brynegield† (i³) m. *burnt-offering*, GEN.

brynehāt *burning hot*, Dom 51.

brynelēoma m. *fire-gleam, flame*, B 2313.

brynenes f. *hard, fiery trial*, HGL 469.

brynetēar m. *hot tear*, CR 152.

bryne-wylm, -welm† m. *wave of fire, flame, burning heat.*

bryngan=bringan

brynig *fiery, burning*, DD 211.

brynstān m. *brimstone*, RWH 143³¹.

bryrd=brerd

bryrdan *to urge on, incite, encourage*, MET 13³. [brord]

bryrdnes f. *incitement, instigation*, BH.

±brȳs-an, -ian (ē; =īe) *to 'bruise,' crush, pound, BH,DD : season*, Sc 20²⁰.

+brȳsednes f. *bruising, crushing*, WW 211²².

brȳsewyrt f .*daisy, soap-wort*, Lcd 1·374. ['*bruisewort*']

brystmian=brytsnian

brȳt pres. 3 sg. of brēotan.

Bryt (e, i) m. *Briton : Breton.*

bryta=brytta

±brȳtan *to crush, pound*:(+)*break up, destroy.*

-brytednes v. for-b.

Bryten (e, eo, i, o) f. *Britain.*

bryten (eo) *spacious, roomy*, SAT 687.

brytencyning m. *powerful king*, WY 75.

brytengrūnd m. *broad earth*, CR 357.

Brytenlond n. *Britain : Wales.*

brytenrīce (eo) n. I. *spacious kingdom*, Az 107. II. *kingdom of Britain.*

Brytonw(e)alda m. *wielder of Britain, Bretwalda, chief king*, CHR,KC.

brytenwongas mp. *spacious plains, the world*, CR 380.

brȳtest pres. 2 sg. of brēotan.

brytian=bryttian

brȳting (ē) f. *breaking (of bread)*, LkL 24³⁵.

Bryt-land, -lond=Brytenlond

brytmǣlum *piecemeal*, OEG 1553n.

brytnere m. *steward*, CP 459¹¹.

±brytnian (i) *to divide, distribute, dispense, administer, BH ; CP.* ['*britten*']

brytnung f. *distribution*, WW 222⁴³.

brȳtofta pl.*espousals,*WW 171⁵. [brȳd, ŏoft]

Bryton=Bryten

±brytsen f. *fragment*, FM,G.

brytsnian *to parcel out, distribute*, OEG 2195 : (+) *enjoy, possess*, ES 8·473³³.

brȳtst pres. 2 sg. of brēotan.

Brytt- v. also Bryt-.

brytta† (e) m. *dispenser, giver, author, governor, prince, lord.* sinces b. *treasure-giver, lord.* [brēotan]

+bryttan=+brȳtan

Bryttas mp. *Britons, BH : Bretons*, CHR.

±**bryttian** (i) *to divide, dispense, distribute,*
CP : *rule over, possess, enjoy the use of.*
Bryttisc (e) *'British,' Chr.*
Bryttwealas, Brytwalas mp. *Britons of
Wales*, CHR.
Brytwylisc *British, Welsh,* CHR.
brȳðen f. *brewing, drink, Gu,Lcd.* [*'bru-
then'*; broð]
brȳwlāc (Æ)=brēowlāc
bū I. n. nap. bȳ *dwelling.* [*Ger.* bau]
II. v. bā, bēgen.
±**būan** anv. (intr.) *to stay, dwell, live,* AO :
lie (of land), WE66¹⁶ : (tr.) *inhabit,
occupy* : *cultivate.* [*Ger.* bauen]
būc, bucc m. *belly, stomach,* Æ : *pitcher,* Æ :
beaver (of helmet)? [*'bouk'*]
bucca m. *'buck,' he-goat, male deer,* Æ,Lcd,
WW ; CP.
budda m. *beetle,* WW543¹⁰.
būde 3 sg., būdon pl. pret. of būan.
budon pret. pl. of bēodan.
būend m. *dweller, inhabitant,* G,LPs.
bufan I. prep. (w. d.) *over, 'above,'* Æ,Chr ;
AO : (w. a.) *on, upon, above,* AO. II. adv.
above, overhead, before, Æ.
bufan-cweden, -nemd, -sprecen *above-mentioned,* GD.
bufon=bufan ; **būg-**=bū-
±**būgan** I. (sv²) *to 'bow,' bow down, turn,
bend, stoop, sink,* Æ,AO,Rood : *submit, give
way,* Æ,B,Chr : *depart, flee, retire,* Æ,AO :
join, go over to, Æ : *convert,* Æ. II.=būan
būgol v. bēogol
būh imperative of būgan.
būlan=būan ; **būl**=būla I.
bula m. *bull, steer,* EC449²².
būl(a) m. *bracelet, necklace, brooch* [bȳl]
bulberende *wearing an ornament,* WW
195³⁷ ; OEG8³¹⁹.
bulentse f. *a plant,* LCD44b.
bulgon pret. pl. of belgan.
bulluc m. *male calf, 'bullock,'* Sc.
bulot, bulut *ragged robin, cuckoo-flower,*
LCD.
būn=būan
bund f? *bundle,* MtL13³⁰.
būnda=bōnda
bunden (B) pp., bundon pret. pl. of bindan.
[*'y-bound'*]
bundenheord *with bounden tresses,* B3151.
+**bundennes** f. *obligation,* LPs.
bundensteina adj. (*ship*) *with an ornamented
prow,* B1911.
bune I.† f. *cup, beaker, drinking vessel.* II.
reed, cane? WW198¹². [*'bun'*]
+**būnes** f. *dwelling,* NC292.
būr n. *'bower,' apartment, chamber, Gen,
WW* : *storehouse, cottage, dwelling,* B,KC ;
Æ. [būan]

±**būr** (usu.+ ; but būr at LL92,6³) m. *free-
holder of the lowest class, peasant, farmer.*
[*'gebur'*]
būrbyrde (æ²) *of peasant birth,* Ct.
būrcniht n. *chamberlain, eunuch,* HL.
būrcot n. *bed-chamber,* CP.
burg (burh) f. (gds. and nap. byrig) *a
dwelling or dwellings within a fortified
enclosure, fort, castle, Chr,WW* ; CP :
'borough,' walled town, AO,Mt ; Æ. [v.
GBG and Mdf]
burg- v. also burh- and beorg-.
burgāgend m. *city-owner,* EL1175.
burgat=burggeat
burgbryce m. *breaking into a (fortified)
dwelling,* LL : *penalty for that offence,*
LL.
burgen=byrgen
būrgerihta np. *peasant's rights or dues,*
LL446,4.
būrgeteld† n. *pavilion, tent,* JUD.
burgfæsten n. *fortress,* GEN1680.
burgfolc n. *townspeople,* B2220.
burggeat n. *castle gate, city gate.*
burghege m. *fence of a 'burg,'* Ct.
burg-hlið† n. nap. -hleoðu *fortress-height
(or?=beorg-hlið).
burglagu f. *civil law,* GPH388.
burg-lēod, -lēoda m. *citizen,* AO.
burglocat m. *fortified enclosure, walled town.*
burglond n. *native city,* CR51.
burgon pret. pl. of beorgan.
burgrǣced n. *fortress,* RUIN22.
burgrūn f. *sorceress* ; pl. *fates, furies,* GL.
burg-sæl† n. nap. -salu *city-hall, house.*
burgsǣta (ē²) m. *town-dweller, citizen,* WW.
burgscipe m. *borough,* WW497¹⁹.
burgsele m. *castle-hall, house,* RIM30.
burgsittende† mpl. *city-dwellers.*
burgsorg=borgsorg
burgsteall m. *citadel? city?* WW205³⁶. (or?
borg-)
burgstede† m. *city, castle.*
burgstrǣt *town road,* BC3·15¹¹.
burgtūn m. *city,* Wif31. [*'borough-town'*]
burgðelu f. *castle floor,* Fin30 (burh-). [v.
'theal']
burg-waran, -waru fp., -ware (AO,CP),
-waras mp. *inhabitants of a 'burg,'
burghers, citizens.*
burgweall m. *city-wall,* Æ.
burgweg m. *road, street,* Æ.
burgwīgend m. *warrior,* EL34.
burh=burg
burhbiscop m. *bishop of a city,* HR15¹⁶.
burhbōt f. *liability for repair of the walls of a
town or fortress,* LL.
burhealdor m. *burgomaster, mayor,* Æ.
burhgeard m. *castle yard,* EC328'.

burhgemet n. *measure used in a town*, LL 477,6.

burhgemōt n. *town's meeting*, LL.

burhgerēfa m. *chief magistrate of a town, provost, mayor*, WW. ['*borough-reeve*']

burhgerihta np. *town due*, TC432, 433.

burhgeðingð f. *town council (as judicial body)*, LL228,1².

burhmann m. *citizen*, WW. ['*borough-man*']

burhrǣdden f. *citizenship*, WW441¹⁰.

burhrest f. *chamber-couch*, IM125⁸⁶. [?= *būrrest, ES38·347]

burhriht n. *town right, town law*, LL477,6.

burh-rūn, -rūne f. *fury, sorceress*, WW245¹⁶.

±burhscipe m. *township, civil district*, Gl, LL. ['*boroughship*']

burhscīr f. *city limits, city, township*, Æ.

burhsprǣc f. *courtly speech*, GL.

burhstaðol m. *foundation of the wall of a 'burg,'* LCD1·328'.

burhðegn m. *living in a 'burg'*; or?= būrðegn

burhwarumann m. *burgess*, BH40³¹.

burhwealda m. *burgess*, BH40³¹B.

burhweard† m. *city defender*.

burhwela m. *treasure of a city*, B3100.

burhwelle f. *spring in a 'burg'?* KC3·394'.

burhwerod n. *townsfolk*, KC,WW.

burhwita m. *town councillor*, CC.

būrland n. *land occupied by peasants*, EC 384', (+) BC201¹⁴.

burn f., burna (CP) m., burne f. *brook, stream, Jn* (v. GBG and Mdf) : *spring or well water, Cp,WW*. ['*burn*']

burnon pret. pl. of biernan.

burnsele m. *bath-house*, RUIN22.

burnstōw f? *bathing-place*, KC.

būrrēaf n. *tapestry (for a būr)*, TC530'.

būrscipe=burhscipe

burse f. *bag, pouch*, LCD.

burston pret. pl. of berstan.

būr-ðegn, -ðēn m. *page, chamberlain*, CC,MA.

burðre f. *birth, issue*, BL105²⁰.

buruh=burg

būst pres. 2 sg. of būan.

būt m. *a vessel*, LL455' (?=būc; BTs).

būta=(1) būtan, (2) būtū

būtan (o²) I. prep. w. d. and (rarely) a. *out of, outside of, off, round about, Æ* : *except, without, all but, but only, Chr* : *besides, in addition to* : *in spite of*. II. conj. (w. ind.) *except, except that, but, only*. b. ðæt *except that* : (w. subj.) *unless, save that* : (w. subst.) *except, but, besides, if only, provided that, AO*. III. adv. *without, outside, Chr*. ['BOUT', 'BUT']

būte=(1) būtan, (2) būtū

butere f. '*butter*,' *Lcd*; Æ : *milk for butter-making*, LCD (v. A52·186). [*L.*]

buter-flēoge, -flēge f. '*butterfly*,' WW.

butergeðwēor n. *butter-curd, butter*, WW98³.

+buterian *to butter*, LCD121a.

buter-ic, -uc=butruc

buterstoppa m. *butter-vessel*, WW280²⁵.

būton=būtan; butre=butere

butruc m. (*leather*) *bottle*, Æ.

butsecarl m. *boatman, mariner, Chr*. ['*buscarl*']

buttorflēoge=buterflēoge

buttuc m. *end, small piece of land*, KC4·19'.

būtū (būtwu, būta, būte) *both* (neuter). v. also bēgen.

butueoh (CHR) v. betwux.

būtun=būtan; buturuc=butruc

būtwū=būtū; būwan=būan

bȳ=bū; bȳan (N)=būan

byccen (i) *of a goat, goat's*, CHRD48²⁶.

bȳcera m.=bēocere

±bycgan (i) *to 'buy,' pay for, acquire, Mt, Jn* : *redeem, ransom* : *procure, get done* : *sell*, LL.

bycgend v. beccen; bȳcn-=bēacn-, bīecn-

byd-, bȳd-=bed-, bid-, bīd-

bydel m. '*beadle,' apparitor, warrant officer, Lk*; Æ : *herald, forerunner, Æ* : *preacher, Æ*. [bēodan]

bydelæcer m. *land of a 'bydel,'* KC6·152'.

byden f. *measure, bushel* : *bucket, barrel, vat, tub*. [*Low L.* butina; *Ger.* bütte]

bydenbotm m. *bottom of a vessel*, WW123⁴.

bydenfæt n. *bushel, barrel*, BL.

bȳdla m. *worshipper*, NG.

bȳencg (DR)=bȳing; bȳend=būend

byf-=bif-, beof-

-bȳffan v. ā-b.

byg-, bȳg-=big-, bē-, bī, bīg-

bȳgan=bīegan

byge (ȳ?; i) m. *curve, bend, corner, angle, cone (of a helmet)*, AO,CP : *traffic, commerce*, LL128,5.

bȳgel, bȳgle=bēogol

bygen f. *purchase*, LL(328¹¹).

bygendlic *easily bent, flexible*, BH.

bygeð pres. 3 sg. of bycgan.

bȳgeð pres. 3 sg. of būgan.

+bygu f. *a bend*, KC. [=byge]

byht m. I. (±) *bend, angle, corner, Ct* : *bay, 'bight.'* [būgan] II.† n? *dwelling*. [būan]

+byhte=byht I. +byhð=byht II.

bȳhð pres. 3 sg. of būgan.

bȳing=bū I.

bȳl m? bȳle f? '*boil,' carbuncle*, WW.

bylcettan=bealcettan

±byld=bieldo

bylda m. *builder? householder?* CRA75. [bold]

byldan I. *to build, construct*, KC. II.= bieldan

byldu, byldo=bieldo; bȳle=bȳl
byledbrēost (=bylged-?) *puff-breasted*, RD
81¹.
bylewit=bilewit; bylg=belg
bylgan *to 'bellow,'* MH.
+bylgan *to anger, provoke*, GD.
bylgð pres. 3 sg. of belgan.
bylig=belg, bylg
bȳliht (īly-) *ulcerous*, LCD 63b.
bylwet, byl(y)wit=bilewit
bȳme (Æ)=bīeme
bȳmere (WW), bȳmesangere (ē, ēa; =īe) m.
trumpeter, Æ. ['*bemer*']
bȳmian (=īe) *to blow the trumpet*, Ps,WW :
trumpet forth, BF 172²⁸. ['*beme*']
bynd=bind
byndele, byndelle=bindele
bȳne *cultivated, inhabited, occupied*, AO.
[būan]
+bȳran *to colonize*, WW 210¹⁴.
byrc, byrce=beorc, beorce
byrcð pres. 3 sg. of beorcan.
byrd I. (i) f. *birth* (pl. w. sg. meaning),
ApT 11²⁰. II. f. *burden*, GD 215¹.
+byrd I. fn.; +byrdo, -u f. *birth, Cr* : *descent, parentage, race, BH* : *offspring*, BL :
nature, quality, rank, Æ,AO : *fate*.
['*birde*'; beran] II. *burdened*, MtR 11²⁸.
III.=+byrded
+byrdan *to beard, fringe, embroider*, GL.
-byrdan v. an-b-, +ed-b.
+byrdboda m. *herald of a birth*, OP 17.
+byrddæg m. *birthday*, Mt 14⁶.
byrde *of high rank, well-born, noble, rich*,
AO.
+byrde I. *innate, natural*, Bo,EL. II.=
+byrd I.
+byrdelīce *energetically, zealously*, CP 160¹⁹.
byrden=byrðen
byrdicge f. *embroideress*, WW 262¹⁸.
byrdinenu=byrððinenu
byrding f. *embroidering*, WW 294¹⁰.
-byrding v. hyse-b.
byrdistre *embroiderer* (v. ANS 123·418).
+byrdlic *harmonious*, AS 5¹³.
byrdling *tortoise*, OEG 23²¹.
-byrdling v. in-, frum-b.
byrdscype m. *child-bearing*, CR 182.
+byrd-tīd (G) f., -tīma (W) m. *time of birth*.
+byrdu=+byrd I.
+byrdwiglere m. *birth-diviner, astrologer*,
WW 108¹⁴.
+byrdwītega m. *astrologer*, WW 189¹.
byre I.† m. (nap. byras, byre) *child, son,
descendant* : *young man, youth*. [beran]
II. m. *mound*. III. (±) m. *time, opportunity*, Æ : *occurrence*, AS 62? IV. m.
strong wind, storm, GPH 400.
bȳre n. *stall, shed, hut*, Gl. ['*byre*']

+byredlic *suitable, fitting, convenient, congenial*, DR. adv. -līce.
byrele (i) mf. *cup-bearer, butler, steward, B*,
Gen. ['*birle*']
byrelian *to give to drink, serve with drink*,
Gu. ['*birle*' vb.]
+byrelic=+byredlic
byren I. (and byrene) f. *she-bear*, MH,WW.
[bera] II.=beren
-bȳren v. nēahge-b.
byres f. *borer, graving tool, awl, chisel*, GL.
[borian]
byreð I.=bierð pres. 3 sg. of beran. II.=
pres. 3 sg. of byrian I.
byrg gds. and nap. of burg.
byrg- v. also byrig-, birg-.
+byrg, bēon on gebyrge (w. d.) *to help,
protect*. [beorgan]
byrga m. *security, surety, bail, one who gives
bail*, GL. [*Ger.* bürge]
±byrgan I. (i) *to raise a mound, hide, 'bury,'*
inter, Hy; AO. II.=birgan. III.=beorgan
+byrgednes f. *burial*, BH (Sch.) 546³.
byrgels (e, i) m. *tomb, Æ,Ct*. ['*buriels*']
byrgelslēoð (e¹) n. *epitaph*, HGL 427.
byrgelssang m. *dirge*, OEG : *epitaph*, HGL
427.
byrgen (i, u) f. *burying-place, grave, sepulchre, El,Mt; Æ,AO,CP* : *burial*. ['*burian*';
beorgan]
+byrgen I. f. *caul? grave?* (BTs), LCD 185a.
II. '*tinipa,*' WW 277².
byrgend m. *grave-digger*, PPs 78³.
byrgenlēoð n. *epitaph*, BH 94¹².
byrgensang m. *dirge*, OEG.
byrgenstōw f. *burying-place*, W.
byrgere m. *corpse-bearer*, WW. ['*burier*']
byrgian=byrgan
byrging I. f. *burial*, A 11·173. II.=birging
byrglēoð n. *dirge, epitaph*, GL.
byrht, byrht-=beorht, beorht-, bierht-
byrhtm=breahtm
±byrian I. (impers.) *to happen, pertain to,
belong to, befit, Æ,Chr,Mk,MtR*; AO,CP.
['*bir*'; '*i-bure*'] II.=byrgan
byric=beorc
byrig v.=burg, and gds. of burg.
byrig-=byrg-, burh-
byrigberge f. *mulberry*, LCD 86a.
byrignes I. f. *burial, BH* : *grave*, BYH
124. ['*buriness*'] II.=birgnes
-bȳrild v. nēah-geb.; byris=byres
byrisang (i) m. *dirge*, HGL 488⁵⁷.
byrl-=byrel-
byrla m. *trunk* (*of body*), LCD 58b.
+byrman (i; =ie) *to ferment, leaven* : *swell
up, be proud*. [beorma]
+byrmed n. *leavened bread*, Ex 12¹⁵,¹⁹.
byrnan (Æ)=biernan

byrne I. f. *corslet*, WW; CP. ['*burne*']
II.=burne, burn. III.=bryne
byrnete f. *barnacle*, NC275.
byrn-ham, -hama† m. *corslet*.
+**byrnod** *corsleted*, ÆGr256¹⁶. ['*i-burned*']
byrnsweord n. *flaming sword*, BL109³⁴.
byrnwiga† m. *corsleted warrior*, AA.
byrn-wīgend, -wīggend† m. *corsleted warrior*.
byrs, byrse=byres
byrst I. (e) m. *loss, calamity, injury, damage, defect*, Æ. [berstan] II. n. (*land-*)*slip*, KC3·52⁹ (v. also KC5·112¹⁹ and Mdf).
III. f. '*bristle*,' *Ep,Lcd,WW*; Æ. ['*birse*,' '*brust*'] IV. pres. 3 sg. of berstan. V. pres. 2 sg. of beran.
+**byrst** *furnished with bristles*, OEG23³.
byrstende '*rugiens*'? DR122⁷.
byrstful *disastrous*, CHR1116.
byrstig *broken, rugged*, OEG,RWH141³⁸. [berstan]
+**byrtīd**=+byrdtīd
byrð pres. 3 sg. of beran.
byrðen f. '*burden*,' *load, weight*, *Bl,G,WW*; Æ,CP : *charge, duty*.
+**byrðen** f. *what is born, a child*, W251ᴅ¹⁴.
byrðenmǣlum *a heap at a time*, ÆH 1·526'.
byrðenmǣte (ē³) *burdensome*, KGL1011
byrðenstān m. *millstone*, MtL18⁶.
byrðenstrang *strong at carrying burdens*, ÆH1·208¹³.
byrðere=byrðre
byrðestre (e) f. *female carrier*, HGL498¹⁸.
byrðling (e) m. *carrier*, OEG4922.
byrðor=beorðor
byrðre I. m. *bearer, supporter*, ÆH. [beran]
II. f. *child-bearer, mother*, W251¹³.
+**byrðtid**=+byrdtīd
byrðōīnenu f. *midwife*, GPH392.
bysceop=bisceop; **byseg-**=bysg-
bysen=bisen; **bysig-**, bysg-=bisg-
bysmer, bysmor=bismer; bysmr-=bismr-
bysn=bisen
byst=bist pres. 2 sg. of bēon.
bÿsting (=īe) f. '*beestings*,' WW129². [bēost]
byt I.=bit pres. 3 sg. of biddan. II.=bytt
bÿt pres. 3 sg. of (1) bēodan, (2) bēatan.
bÿtel, bÿtl=bīetl; **byter**=biter
bytla†=bylda
bytlan, ±bytlian *to build, erect*, Æ,CP. [botl]
+**bytlu** np. *building, dwelling*, Æ.
±**bytlung** f. *building*, Æ.
bytme f? *keel* : *head of a dale*, Ct.
bytming f. *hold, keel of ship*, ÆH1·536.
bytne=bytme
bÿtst pres. 2 sg. of bēatan and bēodan.

bytt I. f. *bottle, flagon*, *Mt,WW*; Æ : *cask*. ['*bit*'] II. *small piece of land*, KC3·85¹¹.
III. pres. 3 sg. of biddan.
bytte=bytt I.
byttehlid n. *butt-lid*, WW213²³.
byttfylling f. *filling of casks*, LL178,8¹.
byð=bið pres. 3 sg. of bēon.
bÿð pres. 3 sg. of būan.
byðme=bytme
bÿwan (ēo;=īe) *to rub, brighten, furbish up, adorn*, B,WW.
byxen (i) *made of boxwood*, WW. [box]

C

cæb-, cæc-=cæf-, cēac-
cæcepol *taxgatherer*, WW111⁹. (hæce-)
cæderbēam=cederbēam; **cæf**=ceaf
cæfertūn=cafortūn
cæfester (cæb-) n. *halter*, GL. [*L.* capistrum]
-cæflan v. be-, ofer-, ymb-c.
cæfing f. *hair-ornament*, GL.
cæfl m. *halter, muzzle*, WW.
cǣg, cǣge f., cǣga m. '*key*' (lit. and fig.), *Ex,G,LL,MH,Rd* : *solution, explanation*, CP.
cǣgbora m. *key-bearer, jailor*, GL,MH.
cǣghiorde m. *keeper of keys, steward*, WW.
cǣgloca m. *locked depository*, LL362,76¹.
-cǣglod v. ā-c.
cæh-=ceah-; **cœl-**=cel-, ceal-, ciel
cælð pres. 3 sg. of calan.
cæm-; **cæn-**=cem-; **cen-**, cyn-
cǣpehūs=cīepehūs
cæppe f. '*cap*,' WW : *cope, hood*. [*Lat.*]
cæpse f. *box*, NC276. [*L.* capsa]
cær-=car-, cear-, cer-, cier-
cærse (e) f. '*cress*,' *water-cress*, Lcd; Mdf.
cærsiht *full of cress*, KC3·121¹⁸.
cærte=carte
cǣs=cēas pret. 3 sg. of cēosan.
cǣse=cÿse; **cǣstel**=castel
cǣster (NG)=ceaster
cāf *quick, active, prompt*, Æ : *strenuous, strong* : *bold, brave*. adv. cāfe, El. ['*cofe*']
cāflic *bold*. adv. -līce *promptly, vigorously* : *boldly*, ÆL. ['*cofly*']
caflwyrt=cawlwyrt
cāfnes f. *energy*, ÆH2·282⁴.
cafortūn (æ, ea¹, e²) m. *vestibule, court, courtyard*, Æ : *hall, residence*, Æ.
cāfscipe m. *alacrity, boldness*, RB,W.
+**cafstrian** *to bridle, curb*, CP218²². [cæfester]
cahhetan=ceahhetan; **cāl**=cawl, cawel
calan⁶ *to grow cool or cold*, BH,Bo.

calc I. m. *shoe, sandal*, Mk6⁹. [*L.*] II.= cealc

calcatrippe=coltetræppe

calcrond *shod (of horses)*, GnE143.

cald (A)=ceald

cālend m. *the beginning of a month*, AO : *month, Men* : (†) *span of life*. [' *calends* ']

cālendcwīde m. *tale of days*, Sol479.

calf (A)=cealf

calfur (VPs) nap. of cealf.

calic m. '*chalice*,' *Lcd,Lk,Mt,Ps*. [*L.*]

-calla (ZDA 10·345) v. hilde-c.

calu (cal(e)w- in obl. cases) '*callow*,' *bare, bald, Rd,Pr*.

calwer (*Gl*)=cealer

calwer-clīm, -clympe *curds?* WW.

cāma m. *muzzle, collar, bit*, PPs31¹¹. [*L.*]

camb (o) m. '*comb*,' *crest, Ep,WW* : *honey-comb*, LPs.

cambiht *combed, crested*, WW.

cambol=cumbol

camel m. '*camel*,' *Mt,Mk*.

cammoc (u²) nm? '*cammock*,' *rest-harrow*, *Lcd,WW*.

±camp (o) I. mn. *combat, battle, struggle, warfare, B,Rd*. [' *camp* '] II. *field, plain?* EC183². [*L.* campus]

campdōm m. *military service, warfare*, Æ.

campealdor m. *commander*, OEG4433.

campgeféra m. *fellow-soldier*, Gl.

camphād m. *warfare*, BH.

±campian (o) *to strive, fight*, *Gu*; Æ. [' *camp* ']

camplic *military*, Æ,Chrd.

campræden f. *war, warfare*, An 4.

campstede† m. *battlefield*.

campung f. *fighting, warfare*, Bl,Gl.

campwǣpen (o¹) n. *weapon*, Rd 21⁹.

campweorod (e², ea², e³) n. *army, host*, BH.

campwīg (o¹) n. *battle, combat*. Jud333

campwīsa m. *director of public games*, HGl 405.

campwudu m. *shield?* El51.

can pres. 1 and 3 sg. of cunnan.

cān m. *germ, sprout?* PPs79¹⁰. [*OS.* cīnan]

±cane n. *jeering, scorn, derision*, Gl.

canceler m. *chancellor*, Chr1093. [*Low L.* cancellarium]

cancer m. *cancer*, Æ. [*L.*]

cancerādl f. *cancer*, Lcd41a.

cancerwund f. *cancerous wound*, Lcd.

cancet(t)an, *to cry out, mock, deride*, Gl, LL.

cancetung f. *boisterous laughter*, WW382³⁶.

cancor=cancer

candel (o¹, o²) fn. *lamp, lantern*, '*candle*,' *Gl*; Æ. [*L.* candela]

candelbora m. *acolyte* (Swt).

candelbryd (?=bred; BTs) *flat candlestick*, IM120.

candellēoht n. '*candle-light*,' *RB*.

Candelmæsse f. '*Candlemas*,' *the feast of the Purification*, *Chr*.

Candelmæsseæfen n. *Candlemas eve*, LL.

Candelmæssedæg m. *Candlemas day*, NC 276.

candelsnȳtels m. *candle-snuffers*, WW126²⁸. [v. '*snitels*']

candelstæf m. *candlestick, Mt,WW*. [' *candlestaff* ']

candelsticca m. '*candlestick*,' *EC*250'.

candeltrēow n. *candelabrum*, MtR5¹⁵.

candeltwist m. *pair of snuffers*, Gl.

candelwēoce f. '*candle-wick*,' *torch, WW*.

candelwyrt f. *candlewort*, WW137⁹.

cann I. f. *cognizance, averment, asseveration, clearance*, LL. II. (±) pres. 3 sg. of cunnan.

canne f. '*can*,' *cup, WW*.

cannon sbp. *reed, cane*, AA30¹⁹. [*L.* canna]

canon m. *canon, rule*. canones bēc *canonical books*. [*L.* canon]

canonbōc *a book of canons*, LL (316¹⁴).

canonic I. m. *canon*, LL. II. *canonical*, Æ.

canoniclic (e³) *canonical* (BT).

cans=canst pres. 2 sg. of cunnan.

cantel m? n? *buttress, support*, Bf142²³.

cantelcāp m. *cope*, Chr1070e.

cantercæppe f. *cope (vestment)*, Ct.

cantere m. *singer*, CM904.

canterstæf m. *chanter's staff*, EC250¹⁵.

cantic (Æ), canticsang (CPs), m. *canticle, song*. [*L.*]

-cāp v. cantel-c.

capellan m. *chaplain*, EC,Chr (late). [*L.*]

capian *to look*. ūp c. *to look up, lie on its back (of the moon)*, Lcd3·266²³. capiende ' *supinus*,' GPH393a.

capitel=capitol

capitelhūs n. *chapter-house*, IM122⁴.

capit-ol, -ul, -ula m. *chapter (cathedral or monastic)* : *chapter (division of a book), lesson, LL* : *anthem*. [' *chapitle* ']

capitolmæsse f. *early mass, first mass*, WW 101¹⁶.

+capitulod *divided into chapters*, LL (204²).

cappa=cæppe

capun m. '*capon*,' *WW*. [*L.* capōnem]

carbunculus m. *carbuncle*, CP. [*L.*]

carc-ern (AO,CP), -ærn n. *prison, jail*. [*L.* carcer]

carcernȳstru f. *prison darkness*, LL.

carcernweard m. *jailor*, MH24¹⁵,¹⁹.

-carcian v. be-c.

cārclife=gārclife; care-=car-

carful (ea) *anxious, sad, Gu,Soul* : '*careful*,' *attentive, painstaking, Ps,WW* : *troublesome*. adv. -līce, *LL*.

carfulnes f. *care, anxiety* : '*carefulness*,' Æ, *Lcd*.

cargealdor (ea¹) n. *sorrowful song*, JUL618.
cargēst (ea¹) m. *sad spirit, devil*, GU365.
carian *to* ' *care' for, be anxious, grieve*, B,Cr; Æ.
caricum dp. of sb. *with dried figs*, ÆL23b⁶⁸¹. [*L.* carica]
carig (ea, e)† *sorrowful, anxious*, Cr,Soul : *grievous, DD.* ['*chary*']
carl m. *man*, LCD. [*ON.* karl]
carlēas '*careless*,' *free from care*, Ex,RB.
carlēasnes, carlēast f. *freedom from care, security*, WW. ['*carelessness*']
carlfugol (ea¹, e³) m. *male bird, cock*, RWH 148⁴.
carlīce (ea) *wretchedly*, PPs85⁶.
carlmann m. *male, man*, CHR1086.
carr m. *stone, rock*, NG. [*Keltic*]
carseld (ea) n. *home of care*, SEAF5.
carsīð (ea) *painful journey*, B2396.
carsorg f. *sad anxiety*, GEN1114.
carte (æ) f. *paper for writing on, Æ* : *document, deed* : *letter*, RWH87³⁴. [*L.* charta]
caru (ea) f. '*care*,' *concern, anxiety, sorrow*, B,Lk,Ps; AO.
carwylm (æ², e²)† m. *welling sorrow.*
casebill n. *club*, GPH394 (v. A31·66).
cāserdom m. *imperial sway*, DR,LL.
Cāsere (Cāser, JnL) m. *Cæsar, emperor, Bo*; Æ,AO. ['*Kaser*']
cāsering f. *coin with Cæsar's head on it, drachma, didrachma*, NG.
cāserlic *imperial*, WW427⁴⁰.
cāsern f. *empress*, AO266¹⁴.
cassuc m. *hassock, sedge*, LCD.
cassuclēaf np. *hassock or sedge leaves*, LCD 170a.
castel I. m. '*castle*,' *fort, Chr* : *walled enclosure?* Ct (v. GBG). II. n. *town, village*, Mt,Mk,Lk.
castelmann m. *townsman*, CHR.
castelweall (æ¹) m. *city wall, rampart*, RWH134²⁷.
castelweorc n. *castle-building*, CHR1137.
castenere m. *cabinet, chest*, TC531⁷.
casul m. *over-garment,* '*birrus,' cloak*, WW 196³⁹. ['*casule*']
cāsus m. (*grammatical*) *case*, ÆGR.
catt m., catte f. '*cat*,' *Gl*; Mdf.
caul [S6N1]=cawl I. and II.
caulic *a medicine*, LCD102b.
cawellēaf n. *cabbage-leaf*, LCD166b.
cawelsǣd n. *cabbage-seed*, LCD187a.
cawelstela m. *cabbage-stalk*, LCD3·102⁷.
cawelstoc (cāl-) m. *cabbage-stalk*, LCD1·378⁸.
cawelwurm m. *caterpillar*, WW121²⁹. [v. '*cawel*']
cawl I. (e, ea, eo) m. *basket*, AO,Gl. ['*cawl*'] II. (ā?) m. '*cole*' ('*caul*,' '*cawel*'), *kale, cabbage*, Lcd.

cēac sm. *basin, pitcher, jug*, Æ,CP : *kettle, cauldron* (*for hot-water ordeal*), LL24; 104; 116.
cēacādl (ēo) f. *jaw-ache*, LCD109a,113a.
cēacbān n. '*cheek-bone*,' *jaw*, WW.
cēacbora m. *yoke for buckets*, GL.
cēace (ē, ei, ēo) f. '*cheek*,' *jaw, jawbone, G, Lcd,VPs,WW.*
ceacga m. *broom, furze*, BC,KC.
ceacl=ceafl
ceaf (e) n., nap. ceafu '*chaff*,' Æ,Mt,Lk, WW; CP.
ceaf-=caf-, ceaf-, cief-
ceafflnc m. *chaffinch*, ANS76·206.
ceafl m. *jaw, cheek, jaw-bone, cheek-bone, Æ,Whale.* ['*jowl*']
ceaflādl (cealf-) f. *disease of the jaws*, LCD90b.
ceafor (e) m. *cock-*' *chafer,' beetle*, Ps,WW; Æ.
ceahhe f. *daw*, KC3·48'.
ceahhetan *to laugh loudly*, BH428¹.
ceahhetung f. *laughter, jesting, Æ.*
cealc (a) m. '*chalk,' lime, plaster*, AO; Mdf : *chalkstone, pebble*, Ep,WW.
+**cealcian** (æ) *to whiten*, MtL23²⁷.
cealcpyt m. *chalk-pit*, KC5·346. [v. '*chalk*']
cealcsēað m. *chalk-pit*, KC.
cealcstān m. *limestone, chalk*, GL,LCD.
ceald (a) I. adj. '*cold*' ('*cheald*'), *cool*, A, Mt,Jn; AO,CP. adv. cealde. II. n. *coldness, cold.*
cealdheort (a) *cruel*, AN138.
cealdian *to become cold, Rim.* ['*cold*']
cealdnes f. *coldness, cold*, ÆL23b¹⁷⁵.
cealer m. '*galmaria,' pressed curds, jelly of curds or whey, Gl.* ['*culver*']
cealerbrīw m. *pottage of curds*, LCD.
cealf I. (æ, e) nm. (nap. cealfru) '*calf*,' Æ, G,Gl. II.=ceafl
+**cealfe** *great with calf*, GENC33¹³.
cealfādl=ceaflādl
cealflan *to calve, Æ.*
cealffloca m. *calf-pen*, KC1·312⁶.
cealfre=cealre, cealer
cealfwyrt (a) '*eruca*,' WW136¹⁷.
ceallian *to* '*call,' shout*, Ma91. [*ON.* kalla]
cealre=cealer and das. of cealer.
cēap (ē, ȳ) m. *cattle*, CP : *purchase, traffic, bargain, gain, B*; CP : *payment, value, price, LL* : *goods, possessions, property, Chr*; AO : *market, Æ.* dēop c. *high price.* būtan cēape *gratis.* ['*cheap*']
cēapcniht m. *bought servant, slave*, GL.
cēapdæg m. *market-day*, WW.
cēapēadig? *rich, wealthy*, GNE108.
cēapealeðel n. *alehouse*, LL(410¹⁸)? (v. BTs).
cēapgyld n. *purchase money, market price* : *compensation*, v. LL2·338.

±cēapian *to bargain, trade, Mt* : *buy, Jn,Cr*;
AO : *endeavour to bribe, DA* 739. ['*cheap*']
cēapland *purchased land,* TC 580¹³.
cēapman m. '*chapman,' trader, BH,LL.*
cēapsceamul m. *seat of custom or toll, treasury,* G.
cēapscip n. *trading vessel,* AO 116⁴.
cēapsetl (ē¹) n. *toll-booth,* G.
cēapstōw f. *market-place, market,* CP.
cēapstrǣt (ē, ȳ) f. *market-place,* ÆGR.
cēapung f. *traffic, trade,* LL. ['*cheaping*']
cēapunggemōt n. *market,* WW 450¹.
cear=car
cearcetung f. *gnashing, grinding,* W 200¹⁸.
cearcian *to creak, gnash, Æ.* ['*chark*']
cearde=cierde pret. 3 sg. of cierran.
+cearfan (NG)=+ceorfan
cearm m. *noise,* W 186¹⁸.
cear-rige, -ruce *a vehicle?* GL.
ceart I. *wild common land,* KC. II.=crǣt
cearwund *badly wounded?* LL 6,63 and 3·12
(or ? scearw- BTs).
cēas I.=cēast. II. pret. 3 sg. of cēosan.
-cēasega v. wæl-c.
cēaslunger *contentious,* CHRD 19¹².
cēast (ǣ, ē) f. *strife, quarrelling, contention,* WW : *reproof.*
ceastel=castel
ceaster (æ, e) f. *castle, fort, town,* CP :
†*heaven, hell.*
ceasteræsc m. *black hellebore,* LCD.
ceasterbūend m. *citizen,* B 768.
ceastergewar-=ceasterwar-
ceasterherpað *high road?* (BTs),KC 5·217¹.
ceasterhlid n. *city gate,* CR 314.
ceasterhof n. *house in a city,* AN 1239.
ceaster-lēod f. np. -lēode *citizens,* NC 276.
ceasternisc (æ) *urban, municipal,* TC 244¹³.
ceaster-sǣtan, -sǣte mp. *citizens,* TC.
±ceaster-waran mp., -ware, -waru f.
burghers, citizens.
ceasterweall (e¹) m. *city wall,* MH 150⁹.
ceasterwīc f. *village,* BL 69³⁵.
ceasterwyrt f. *black hellebore,* LCD.
cēastful *contentious,* Sc 105⁵.
ceastre=ceaster
cēaw pret. 3 sg. of cēowan.
ceawl (*MtL*)=cawl I.
cēce (*VPs*)=cēace
cēcel (coecil) *a little cake, Ep.* ['*kechel*']
cecil '*suffocacium,*' WW 49²⁸.
cecin '*tabetum,' a board,* WW 279¹.
cēde (VPs)=cīegde pret. 3 sg. of cīegan.
cedelc f. *the herb mercury, Lcd,WW.* ['*ked-lock*']
ceder nmf. *cedar,* BLPs. [*L.* cedrus]
ceder-bēam mn., -trēow (ȳ) n. *cedar-tree,* Ps.
cedor-=ceder-

cēdrisc *of cedar,* DR 65¹⁵.
cef (Æ)=ceaf; cef-=ceaf-, cif-
cēgan (VHy), cēgian=cīegan
cehhettung=ceahhetung
ceīce (MtLR); ceig- (N)=cēace; cīg-
ceir *cry, clamour,* DR.
cel=cawl
cēlan (ǣ) *to cool, become cold, be cold, MH,*
VPs (oe) : (+) *quench (thirst), refresh.*
['*keel*']
celc (1) (VPs)=calic. (2)=cealc
celde f. *copious spring?* KC 3·429¹³.
celdre=ceoldre; cele=(1) ceole; (2) ciele
celen-dre f., -der n. '*coliander,' coriander,* Lcd.
cele-ðonie, -ðenie, cileðonie f. *celandine, swallow-wort,* LCD.
celf (A)=cealf; celic=calic
+celfe (GEN 33¹³)=+cealfe
cēling f. *cooling, Æ* : *cool place, Æ.*
celis '*peditis,' foot-covering,* A 37·45.
celiwearte=cielewearte
cell m. *(monastic) cell,* CHR 1129.
cellender n., cellendre f.=celendre
cellod (ē?)† part. *round? hollow? embossed? beaked?* FIN 29 (or ? celced=cealced); MA 283.
celmertmonn m. *hireling,* NG (v. ES 42·172).
±cēlnes f. *coolness, cool air, breeze,* CP.
[cōl]
celod v. cellod.
celras=cealras, nap. of cealer.
±cemban (æ) *to comb, Æ.* ['*kemb*']
cemes f. *shirt,* GD. [*L.* camisia]
cempa (æ) m. *warrior, champion, Gl,Ma;*
Æ,AO,CP. [camp; '*kemp*']
cempestre f. *female warrior,* OEG.
cēn† m. *pine-torch, pine : name of the rune for* c. [*Ger.* kien]
cendlic=cynlic
cēne *bold, brave, fierce, CP,Ex,Lcd,Ma,Ps;*
Æ,AO : *powerful, Ps : learned, clever, Met* 10⁵¹. ['*keen*'] *also adv.*
cenep m. *moustache,* CHR : *bit (of a bridle),* WW 486¹⁶. [*ON.* kanpr]
cenlic=cynlic
cēnlīce *boldly, Æ.* ['*keenly*']
±cennan *to conceive, bring·forth, Æ* : *beget, create, produce, Mt,VPs;* CP : *nominate, choose out, Æ* : *assign, attribute, give* : *declare, show oneself, clear oneself, make a declaration in court* (v. LL 2·32; 279, '*cennan,' 'Anefang'), B,LL,Ps.* ['*ken*']
cennend m. *parent,* BL.
cennendlic *genital,* GD.
cennes f. *produce, what is produced,* EHy 6²² : *childbirth : birthday.*
+cennes f. *summons,* BH 436¹⁵ (cæne-).

cennestre f. *mother*, Æ.
cenning f. *procreation*, CP : *parturition, birth*, Æ : *declaration in court* (v. cennan).
cenningstān (y¹) m. *testing-stone*, LL 192,4.
cenningstow f. *birthplace*, Æ.
cenningtīd f. *time of bringing forth*, Æ.
cennystre=cennestre
Cent, Centescīr f. *Kent*. [*L.* Cantia]
centaur m. *centaur*, WW.
centaurie f. *centaury* (plant), LCD.
Centingas mp. *Kentish men*, CHR.
Centisc *Kentish*, CHR.
Cent-land, -lond (AO) n. *Kent*.
Centrīce n. *kingdom of Kent*.
centur m. *centurion*, G.
Centware mp. *inhabitants of Kent*, CHR.
cēnðu f. *boldness*, B 2696.
cēo f. *chough, jay, jackdaw*, ÆGR.
cēoce (*WW*)=cēace; -cēocian v. ā-c.
ceod? ceode? *bag, pouch*, CP,LL.
ceodor-=ceder-; ceofl, ceol (NG)=cawl I.
cēol m. *ship*, AN,B,CHR.
ceolas mp. *cold winds, cold*, Az 103. [ciele?]
ceolbor-=cilfor-
ceoldre I. f. *milk-pail*, WW 33¹⁷. II.=cealre
ceole (e) f. *throat : gorge, chasm : beak of ship*, GL. [*Ger.* kehle]
ceolor m. *throat*, GL : *channel*, Ct.
cēol-ōel n., -ðelu? f. *deck of a ship*, HU 8.
ceolwærc m. *pain in the throat*, LCD 113a.
ceorcing f. *complaining*, GPH 398.
±ceorfan³ *to cut, cut down, slay*, Mk,Æ; LkL : '*carve*,' *cut out, engrave : tear*.
ceorfæx f. *axe*, AO 160¹⁵.
ceorflngīsen n. *branding iron*, SC 43².
ceorfsæx n. *surgeon's knife, scalpel*, Æ.
±ceorian *to murmur, complain*, Æ,AO.
ceorig *querulous, complaining*, OEG.
ceorl m. '*churl*,' *layman, peasant, husband-man*, CP : *freeman of the lowest class*, LL; AO,CP : *man : husband*, Jn,WW; CP : †*hero, noble man*.
ceorlǣs (=ceorllēas) *unmarried* (of women), LL 360,73 B.
ceorlboren *low-born, not noble*, LL.
ceorlfolc n. *common people*, ÆGR.
±ceorlian *to marry* (of the woman), LL,Mt; Æ. ['*churl*']
ceorlic=ceorllic
ceorlisc (ie) *of a* '*ceorl*,' '*churlish*,' *common, rustic*, LL,WW. adv. -lisce.
ceorllic *common, belonging to the people generally*. adv. -līce *commonly, vulgarly, popularly*.
ceorlman m. *freeman*, LL 73; 463.
ceorlstrang *strong as a man*, WW 108¹⁸.
ceorm=cirm
ceorran I. (sv³) *to creak*, LCD 160a. II. (+) =cierran

ceorung f. *murmuring*, Æ.
±cēosan² *to '*choose**' ('*i-cheose*,' '*y-core*'), seek out, select, AO*; Æ : *decide, test : accept, approve*, B,Gen.
ceosel (i, y) m. *gravel, sand, shingle*, Ep,Mt; Æ. ['*chesil*']
ceoselbǣre *gravelly, shingly*, A 13·32.
ceoselstān m. *sand-stone, gravel*, WW.
ceoslen (OEG 7¹⁶¹), ceoslig (4⁴⁰) *gravelly*.
ceosol I. m? n? *gullet, maw*, GL. II.=ceosel
±cēowan² *to '*chew*,' gnaw*, Æ,Soul : *eat, consume*, Æ.
ceowl (NG)=cawl
cēowung (ī, ȳ) f. '*chewing*,' WW.
cēp=cēap; cēp-, cēpe-=cēap-, cȳp-
cēpan I. *to seize*, Æ : *seek after, desire*, Æ : *await*, Æ : *receive*, RBL : '*keep*,' *guard, observe, attend, watch, look out for, take heed*, Æ,Chr,Lcd,Ps : *take*, Æ : *avail oneself of, betake oneself to, take to, bear : meditate : regulate by*. II.=cȳpan
cēpnian *to await eagerly*, NC 276.
cer=cierr
ceren I. (æ, y) n? *new wine, sweet wine*, GL, LCD. [*L.* carenum] II.=cyrn
cer-felle, -fille f. '*chervil*,' Lcd,WW. [*L.* cerefolium]
cerge=carig; cerlic=cirlic
cerm=cirm; cerr=cierr
cers-=cærs-; cert-=cyrt-
certare *charioteer*, ÆL 18²⁹⁵.
ceruphīn *cherubim*, EL 750.
ces-=ceos-; cēs-=cīs-, cȳs-
cēs=cēas pret. 3 sg. of cēosan.
Cēsar (AO)=Cāsere
cester=ceaster; cestian=cystian
cēte=cȳte; cetel, cetil=citel
cēðan=cȳðan; cewl (NG)=cawl
chor, chora m. *dance, choir* (*singers*), CP : *church-choir* (*place*). [*L.* chorus]
chorglēo n. *dance*, LPs.
cīan sbpl. *gills*, GL. [*Ger.* kieme]
cicel=cycel
cicen (y) n. '*chicken*,' Mt,WW.
cicene (Æ)=cycene
cicropisc *cyclopean?* WW 217¹³.
+cīd n. *strife, altercation*, CP,DR,GD : *reproof*, RB.
±cīdan (w. d. or wið) *contend, quarrel*, Æ, WW : *complain*, Æ : '*chide*,' *blame*, Mk; Æ,CP.
cīdde (1) pret. 3 sg. of cīdan. (2)=cȳðde pret. 3 sg. of cȳðan.
cīdere m. *a chider*, CHRD 41³⁰.
cīdung (ȳ) f. *chiding, rebuke*, AO,EPs.
ciefes=cifes
±cīegan (ē, ī, ȳ) (tr.) *to call, name*, Æ : *call upon, invoke, summon, convene*, CP : (intr.) *call out*. For comps. v. cīg-.

ciele (e, i, y) m. *coolness, cold, 'chill,' frost,* *Bl,CP,VPs*; AO. [ceald]

cielegicel† (y¹) m. *icicle.*

cielewearte (e¹, y¹) f. *goose-skin,* WW.

cielf=cealf

cielle (i, y) f. *fire-pan, lamp,* BH,GD. [*OHG.* kella]

cīepa (e, i, y) m. *merchant, trader,* Æ,CHRD.

cīepe=cīpe

cīepehūs (ǣ¹) n. *storehouse,* WW 186¹¹.

cīepemann (CP), cīepmann (LL) m. *merchant.*

cīepeðing (ē, ȳ) np. *merchandise,* BH,GL.

cīeping (ē, ī, ȳ) f. *marketing, trading,* CP : *market-place, market* : *merchandise* : *market dues,* WW 145²⁸.

cīeplic (ȳ) *for sale, vendible,* Sc 98¹⁷.

cierice=cirice; **cierlisc**=ceorlisc

cierm=cirm

cierr (e, i, y) m. *turn, change, time, occasion,* Æ,CP,Lk,Lcd : *affair, business.* æt sumum cierre *at some time, once.* ['*chare*']

±**cierran** (eo, i, y) (tr. and intr.) *turn, change,* *Ps,Sat* : (intr.) *turn oneself, go, come, proceed, turn back, return, Mt*; Æ : *regard* : *translate* : *persuade, convert, be converted, agree to,* CP : *submit,* CHR,W : *make to submit, reduce.* ['*chare*,' '*i-cherre*']

+**cierrednes** (y) *conversion,* Æ : *entrance, admission,* RB.

±**cierring** (e, y) f. *turning,* LPs 9⁴ : *conversion,* NC 341.

cīest, cīesð pres. 3 sg. of cēosan.

cifes (ie, e, y) f. *concubine, harlot,* AO. [*Ger.* kebse]

cifesboren adj. *bastard,* OEG 5042.

cifesdōm m. *fornication,* OEG 5042.

cifesgemāna m. *fornication,* LL (Wilk.) 84¹.

cifeshād (y) m. *fornication,* WW.

cīgan=cīegan

+**cīgednes** f. *calling, summons* : *name* (cīed-), OEG 1503.

+**cīgendlic** *calling, vocative,* ÆGR 23².

cīgere (ei) *one who calls,* DR 194¹.

+**cīgnes** f. *calling, invocation, entreaty* : *name,* A 10·143⁷⁹.

±**cīgung** f. *calling, invocation,* GD 289, NC 292.

cild (y) (nap. cild, cild-ra, -ru; gp. -ra) n. '*child**,' *infant,* Ct,G,Lcd,WW; Æ,AO, CP : *a youth of gentle birth,* KC.

Cildamæssedæg m. *Childermas, Innocents' Day* (Dec. 28).

cildatrog=cildtrog

cildclāðas mp. *swaddling-clothes,* Gl. [v. '*cloth*']

cildcradol m. *cradle,* Æ.

cildfaru f. *carrying of children,* GEN 45¹⁹.

cildfēdende *nursing,* MtR 24¹⁹.

cild-fōstre, -fēstre f. *nurse, LL.* [v. '*foster*']

cildgeogoð f. *childhood,* ÆL 30³²⁰.

cildgeong *youthful, infant,* LCD,RB.

cildhād m. '*childhood,' MkL.*

cildhama m. *womb,* GL : *after-birth,* WW.

cildisc '*childish,' Gen.*

cildiugoð=cildgeogoð

cildlic *childish, young, BH*; Æ. ['*childly*']

cildru v. cild.

cildsung f. *childishness,* LL (314').

cildtrog (cilt-, cilda-) m. *cradle,* GL.

cile (AO)=ciele

cilforlamb (eo¹) n. *ewe-lamb,* Æ,WW. ['*chilverlamb*']

cilic m. *sack-cloth of hair,* NG. [*L.* cilicium]

cille=cielle, cyll; **cim-**=cym-

cimbal(a) m. '*cymbal,' Lcd,VPs.* [*L.*]

cimbalglīwere m. *cymbal-player,* GD 61²⁰.

cimbing f. *commissure, joining,* WW 15⁵: 206¹². [v. '*chime*']

cimbīren n. *edge-iron?* (*joining-iron, clamp?* BTs), LL 455,15.

cimbstān m. *base, pedestal,* Sc 226². [v. '*chimb*']

cin=(1) cinn; (2) cynn, n.; **cin-**=cyn

cīnan¹ *to gape, yawn, crack,* GL,LCD. ['*chine*']

cinbān n. *chin-bone, jaw-bone,* Æ.

cinberg f. *defence of the chin or cheek, cheek-guard,* Ex 175. [beorg]

cincung f. *boisterous laughter,* WW 171³⁹.

cind=cynd

cine I. f. *sheet of parchment* (*folded*), '*diploma,'* Æ. II. f. *chink, fissure, depth, cavern,* Æ,Bo,WW. ['*chine*']

cine-=cyn(e)-

cineht (io) *chinky, cracked,* WW 43³⁷.

cing, cining=cyning

cinn (1) n. '*chin,' WW.* (2)=cynn n.

cinnan *to gape, yawn?* RIM 52.

cintōð m. *front tooth, grinder,* GL.

cinu=cine II.

cio-=ceo-; **cīo**=cēo

cip=cipp; **cīp-**=cēap-, cīep, cȳp-

cīpe (īe) f. *onion,* GL,LCD. [*L.* cepa]

cīpelēac n. *leek,* WW 380²⁹.

cipersealf (y) f. *henna-ointment,* WW 205¹¹. [*L.* cypros]

cipp (y) m. *log, trunk,* WW : *coulter, plough-share,* WW : *weaver's beam,* LL 455,15¹.

cir=cierr; **cir-**=ciric-

circian *to roar,* LCD 1·390¹¹ (v. A 31·56).

circolwyrde m. *computer, mathematician,* BF 66⁹.

circul m. *circle* : *cycle, zodiac,* LCD. [*L.* circulum]

circulādl f. *the shingles,* LCD.

cirebald (AN 171)=cynebeald?

ciricǣw nf. *marriage to the church* (as when one takes orders), LL.
ciricbelle f. '*church-bell*,' Lcd.
ciricbōc f. '*church-book*,' *manual of the church services*, W.
ciricbōt f. *repair of churches*, LL.
ciric-brǣc f., -bryce m. *sacrilege, Æ.*
ciric-dor n., -duru *church-door*, LL.
ciric̣e (ie, y) f. '*church*,' *religious community, Æ,BH,CP,G,LL,OET* : *church (building), temple, AO,Bl,Chr,Ct*; CP : *congregation (non-Christian), Ps.*
ciricend m. *an ecclesiastic*, MtLp8[10].
ciricfrið mn. *right of sanctuary* : *penalty for breach of the right.* v. LL2·537.
ciricfultum m. *support from the church*, LL.
ciricgang (y) m. *going to church*, LL473,7 : *churching, purification (of the B.V.M.)*, CM484.
ciricgemāna (y) m. *church-membership*, W103[23].
ciricgeorn *zealous in church-going*, LL,W.
ciricgeriht (y) n. *church-due*, LL(328[1]).
ciricgrið (y) n. *church-peace, right of sanctuary*, LL : *penalty for breach of the right*, LL263,3; v. 2·537. ['*church-grith*']
cirichād m. *an order of the church*, LL.
cirichālgung f. *consecration of a church*, CHR.
cirichata m. *church-tormentor, persecutor*, W.
ciricland (y) n. *land of the church*, GD.
ciriclic (circ-) *ecclesiastical, BH,Chr,Wnl.* ['*churchly*']
ciricmǣrsung (y) f. *dedication of a church*, W277[10].
ciricmangung f. *simony*, LL.
ciriomitta m. *church measure (of ale)*, TC 144'.
ciricnēod f. *requirements of the church*, LL.
ciricnytt f. *church service*, CRA91.
ciricragu f. *church-lichen or moss*, LCD51b.
ciricrēn (y[1]) n. *sacrilege*, LL254K. [rān]
ciricsang m. *hymn* : *church-singing*, BH.
ciricsangere m. *church-singer*, BH466[17].
ciricsceat m. '*church-scot*,' *church-due at Martinmas, BH,W.*
ciricsceatweorc n. *work connected with the grain given as church-scot*, KC.
ciricsōcn (y[1]) f. *church-privilege, sanctuary*, LL : *territory of a church* : *attendance at church.* ['*churchsoken*']
cirictīd (y[1]) f. *service-time*, LL(314[20]).
cirictūn m. *churchyard*, LL(250[7]).
ciricðēn m. *minister of a church*, LL.
ciricðēnung (y) f. *church-duty or service*, LL.
ciricðing n. *object belonging to a church*, LL381,27.
ciricðingere m. *priest*, WW155[29] (yrc).
ciricwæcce f. *vigil*, LL.

ciricwǣd f. *vestment*, LL258,51.
ciricwāg m. *wall of a church*, LL.
ciricwaru f. *congregation*, LL400'; 2·539.
ciricweard (e[2], y[2]) m. *church-keeper, warden, sexton, Æ.* ['*churchward*']
cirisbēam m. *cherry-tree*, GL. [*L.* cerasum]
cirlic I. (e, y) *charlock*, LCD. II.=ciriclic
cirlisc=ceorlisc
cirm (e, eo, y;=ie) m. *cry, shout, outcry, uproar, Gl,MtR.* ['*chirm*']
cirman (e, y;=ie) *to cry, cry out, call, shriek, Gu,Jud.* ['*chirm*']
cirnel (GL)=cyrnel
cirps (y) *curly, Æ.* ['*crisp*']
±**cirpsian** (y) *to crisp, curl*, CHRD,GL.
cirr=cierr
cīs (=īe) *fastidious*, LCD,CHRD23[9]. [cēosan]
cīse=cȳse
cisel, cisil=ceosel
ciseræppel m. *dried fig*, WW367[2]. [=ciris-?, cherry (BTs)]
ciser-bēam, cisir-=cirisbēam
cīsnes f. *fastidiousness*, LCD65a,RB63[12].
cist (e, y) I. f. '*chest*,' *casket, Gl,JnR* : *coffin, BH,Lk* : *rush basket, WW* : *horn (as receptacle?)*, WW. II.=cyst I.
cīst pres. 3 sg. of cēosan.
ciste=cist I.
cistel I. '*cistella*'? Ct (v. GBG). II.=cystel
cistenbēam m. *chestnut-tree*, GL. [*L.* castanea]
cīstmēlum *earnestly*, OEG4[32]. [cēast]
citel (e, y) m. '*kettle*,' *cauldron, Ep,Lcd.*
citelflōde (y[1]) f. *bubbling spring*, BC2·371[9].
citelhrūm (e[1]) m. *kettle-soot*, LCD50a.
citelian *to tickle* (Lttm., Leo).
citelung f. *tickling*, WW278[6]. ['*kittling*']
citelwylle (y[1]) *bubbling spring*, BC2·270[4].
citere, citre (y) f. *cithara*, CJVPs.
cið m. *seed, germ, shoot, Æ* : *mote, CP.* ['*chithe*']
ciðfæst *well-rooted*, ÆH1·304'.
cīwung=cēowung; **clā**=clēa, clāwu
clābre (GL)=clǣfre; **clac**=clǣc-, cleac-
clacu f. *injury*, W86[10] (v. FTP55).
+**clāded** (MkL5[15]) pp. of +claðian.
cladersticca m. *rattle-stick*, GL.
clǣclēas *harmless*, WW419[1] : *uninjured.* [clacu]
clǣdur (ea) *rattle*, GL. [clader]
clǣferwyrt f. *clover*, LCD.
clǣfre f. '*clover*,' *trefoil, Lcd,WW*; Mdf.
clǣg m. '*clay*,' WW.
clǣig '*clayey*,' Ct.
±**clǣman** *to smear, caulk, plaster, anoint, Æ,Lcd.* ['*cleam*']
clǣming f. *blotting, smearing*, ÆGR256[4].
clǣmman (e) *to press*, GD.
clǣmnes f. *torture*, BH290[2].

clǣne (ā, ē) **I.** '*clean*,' *CP,Ct,LL* : *pure, chaste, innocent, Æ,Bl* : *unencumbered, unfettered* : *hallowed* : *clear, open, El,Lcd,Ps.* on clǣnum felda *in the open field* (*of battle*), CP 227²⁵ : *honourable, true* : *acute, sagacious, intellectual.* **II.** adv. *clean, clearly, fully, purely, entirely, Æ,Ct*; AO, CP.

clǣngeorn *yearning after purity, celibate* : *cleanly*, CHRD 19¹⁹,²⁰.

clǣnheort *pure in heart, Æ.*

clǣnlic ('*cleanly*'), *pure, Bo,Met* : *excellent.* adv. -līce (*Bf*)=clǣne II.

clǣnnes f. (*moral*) '*cleanness*,' *purity, chastity, BH*; *Æ,CP.*

clǣnsere (e) m. *priest*, CP 139¹⁵; W 72⁶.

±**clǣnsian** (āsn-) *to* '*cleanse*' ('*yclense*'), *purify, chasten, Æ,CP* : *clear out, purge, Lcd* : (w. a. and g.) *justify, clear oneself, LL.*

clǣnsnian=clǣnsian

±**clǣnsung** f. '*cleansing*,' *purifying, chastening, castigation, expiation, Mk*; *Æ* : *purity, chastity.*

clǣnsungdæg m. *day for purging*, LCD 1·330⁸.

clǣnsungdrenc (sn) m. *purgative*, MH 72²⁷.

clæppan (a¹) *to clap, beat, throb*, LCD 3·88⁵.

clæppettan *to palpitate*, LCD,WW.

clæppetung f. *clapping* : *pulsation, pulse, Æ.*

clǣsn-=clǣns-; **clǣð**=clāð

clǣweða=cleweða

clāf pret. 3 sg. of clīfan.

clǣfre (GL)=clǣfre

clām I. m. *paste, mortar, mud, clay, Æ,Lcd* : *poultice.* ['*cloam*'] **II.**=clēam dp. of clēa.

clamb pret. 3 sg. of climban.

clamm m. *band, bond, fetter, chain, An,Bl, Rd* : *grip, grasp.* ['*clam*']

clān-=clǣn-

clang pret. 3 sg. of clingan.

clap-=clæp-

+**clāsnian** (JVPs)=clǣnsian

clātacrop=clāte

clāte f. *bur, burdock, clivers, Gl,Lcd.* ['*clote*']

clatrung f. *clattering, noise*, WW 377²⁷.

clāð m. '*cloth*,' *Mt* : '*clothes*,' *covering, sail, Bo,Cp,Ps,Chr,Jn,Lcd*; AO,CP. under Crīstes clāðum *in baptismal garments*, CHR 688 E.

clāðflyhte m. *patch*, MtR 9¹⁶.

+**clāðian** (clǣðan) *to* '*clothe*,' LG.

clāðwēoce f. *wick of cloth*, GPH 391.

clauster=clūstor

clāwan⁷ *to claw*, ÆGR,WW.

clāwian *to scratch*, '*claw*,' *ÆGr* 170¹¹n.

clawu (ā?) f. nap. clawe '*claw*,' *Æ,Gl,Ph* : *hoof, Æ* : *hook* : (pl.) *pincers? Æ.*

clāwung f. *griping pain*, LCD.

clea-=clǣ-, cleo-

clēa=clawu

cleac f. *stepping-stone*, KC 4·36. [*Keltic*]

cleacian *to hurry*, ÆL 23⁴⁹³.

clēaf pret. 3 sg. of clēofan.

clēm-, clēn-=clǣm-, clǣn-

-**clencan** v. be-c.

clengan *to adhere*, RD 29⁸.

cleo-; clēo-=cli-; clīe-, clū-

clēo=clēa, clawu

cleofa (ea, i, y) m. *cave, den, BH* : *cell, chamber, cellar, Æ,Ps.* ['*cleve*']

clēofan² *to* '*cleave*,' *split, separate, A,Bo,Ct.*

cleoflan=clifian; **cleofu**=nap. of clif

clēofung f. '*cleaving*,' WW.

clēone=clēowene, ds. of clēowen, clīewen.

cleop-=clip-

clep-=clæp-, clip-; **clerc**=cleric

cler-ic (-ec, -oc; clerus, PPs 67¹³) m. '*clerk*' *in holy orders, WW* : *clerk in minor orders, LL* : *educated person, Chr.* [L. clericus]

clerichād m. *condition of a* (*secular*) *clerk, clerical order, priesthood*, CHR,RB.

cleweða (æ¹) m. *itch*, CP 71¹⁹. [clāwan]

clib-=clif-

clibbor *clinging*, MEN 245. [clifian]

+**clibs** (e; cleps; clæsp, y) *clamour*, CP.

clid-ren, -rin f. *clatter*, Ep,Erf 928.

cliepian=clipian

clīewen, cliewen? (ēo, īo, ī, ȳ) n. *sphere, ball, skein, Æ,CP,Ph,WW* : *ball of thread or yarn, KC* : *mass, group.* ['*clew*']

clif n. (nap. cleofu, clifu) '*cliff*,' *rock, promontory, steep slope, An,B,Ct; Æ,CP.*

clifa=cleofa; **clifæhtig**=clifihtig

clifan¹ *to* '*cleave**,' *adhere, Æ,CP.*

clife f. '*clivers*' ('*cleavers*'), *burdock, Lcd, WW.*

clifeht=clifiht

clifer m. nap. clifras *claw, GPH*; Æ. ['*cliver*']

cliferfēte *cloven-footed*, ÆL 25⁷⁹.

clif-hlēp, -hlȳp m. *a cliff-leap, plunge to ruin?* (BTs),GL.

+**clifian** (eo, y) *to adhere, Æ,CP.*

clifig, clif-iht, -ihtig *steep*, GL.

clifr- v. clifer.

clifrian *to scarify, scratch, Æ*,CHRD.

clifrung f. *clawing, talon*, GPH 398.

clifstān m. *rock*, WW 371²³.

clifwyrt f. *cliff-wort, water-wort, foxglove*, WW 134³ and N.

+**cliht** pp. of +*cliccan, clyccan.

-**clīm** v. calwer-c.

climban³ (y) *to* '*climb*,' Sol.

climpre=clympre

clincig *rough*, DHy 104¹⁸.

clingan³ *to stick together, An* : *shrink, wither, pine, Æ,Sol.* ['*cling*']

clipian (e, eo, y) (tr. and intr.) *to speak, cry out, call, DR,Chr,Mt,Jn,Ps;* CP : (±) *summon, invoke,* Æ : (w. d.) *cry to, implore.* ['*clepe,*' '*yclept*']

clipigendlic (y) *vocalic,* ÆGR 5 : *vocative* (gram.), ÆGR 23.

clipol *sounding, vocal,* BF 94²⁹ : *vocalic, vowel,* BF 100¹⁶.

clipung (e, eo, y) f. *cry, crying, clamour, MtR* : (±) *prayer,* Ps : *call, claim,* CHR 1129. ðā clypunga *kalends.* ['*cleping*']

clipur m. *bell-clapper,* WNL 109b¹⁶,²⁰.

cliroc=cleric; +**clistre**=+clystre

clite f. *coltsfoot,* LCD 146a.

cliða (eo, y) m. *poultice,* Æ,LCD.

-**cliðan** v. æt-c.

cliðe f. *burdock,* GL. [v. '*clithe,*' '*clithers*']

cliðwyrt f. '*rubea minor,*' '*clivers,*' *Lcd* 173b.

clīwe, clīwen=clīewen

cloccettan *to palpitate,* LCD 82b.

cloccian *to cluck, make a noise,* BF 78¹⁷.

clodhamer m. *fieldfare,* WW 287¹⁷.

clof-=cluf-

+**clofa** m. *counterpart (of a document),* CC 80. [clēofan]

clofe f. *buckle,* GL.

clofen pp. of clēofan.

clomm I. m.=clamm. II. pret. 3 sg. of climban.

clop m? *rock?* v. Mdf.

clott *lump, mass,* HGl 488. ['*clot*']

clucge f. *bell,* BH 340⁶.

clūd m. *mass of stone, rock,* Æ,AO : *hill,* ES 38·13. ['*cloud*']

clūdig *rocky, hilly, AO.* ['*cloudy*']

clufeht(e) (i²) *bulbous,* Lcd. [v. '*cloved*']

clufon pret. pl. of clēofan.

clufðung, clufðunge f. *crowfoot : a vegetable poison.* v. OEG 896.

clufu f. *clove (of garlic, etc.), bulb, tuber,* LCD. [clēofan]

clufwyrt f. '*batrachion,*' *buttercup,* Lcd. ['*clovewort*']

clugge=clucge

clumben pp. of climban.

clum(m)ian *to murmur, mumble, mutter,* W.

clungen pp. of clingan.

clūs, clūse f. *bar, bolt : enclosure : cell, prison.* [*L.* clausum]

cluster=clyster; **clūster**=clūstor

clūstor n. *lock, bar, barrier : enclosure, cloister, cell, prison.* [*L.* claustrum]

clūstorcleofa m. *prison-cell,* AN 1023.

clūstorloc n. *prison,* GL.

clūt m. '*clout,*' *patch, cloth,* Ep : *piece of metal, plate,* Æ.

+**clūtod** '*clouted,*' *patched,* Æ.

±**clyccan** *to clutch, clench, IM,Sc.* ['*clitch*']

clyf=clif; **clyf-**=clif-, cleof-

+**clyft** adj. *cleft,* GPH 393. [clēofan]

clymmian *to climb, ascend,* SOL 414.

-**clympe** v. calwer-c.

clympre m. *lump of metal,* LCD,RD,WW. ['*clumper*']

clyne n. *lump of metal,* GL.

clynian I. *to roll up, enfold,* GPH. II.= clynnan

clynnan (intr.) *to resound, ring,* EL 51 : (tr.) *knock,* NG.

clyp-=clip-

clypnes f. *embrace,* BH 238³.

clypp m., *clypping* f. *embracing,* GD.

±**clyppan** *to embrace, clasp,* Æ,LG : *surround, enclose, VPs : grip, Gen : prize, honour, cherish, CP.* ['*clip*']

-**clȳsan** v. be-c. [clūse]; +**clysp**=+clibs

clyster, +clystre n. '*cluster,*' *bunch, branch,* Æ,Cp,WW.

clȳsung f. *enclosure, apartment,* Æ : *closing, period, conclusion of a sentence, clause.*

clyða=cliða; **clȳwen**=clīewen

cnæht (*NG*)=cniht

cnæpling m. *youth,* Æ. [cnapa]

cnæpp (e) m. *top, summit,* Æ,Lk : *fibula, button,* WW. ['*knap*']

+**cnǣwe** (w. g.) *conscious of, acknowledging,* Æ : *known, notorious, manifest,* Æ.

cnǣwð pres. 3 sg. of cnāwan.

cnafa, cnapa m. *child, youth, Æ,Sc : servant, Æ,Mt,Ps.* ['*knape,*' '*knave*']

±**cnāwan⁷** (usu. +) *to* '*know*' ('*y-know*'), *perceive, Æ,B,Bl,Jul,OEG : acknowledge : declare :* (+) *ascertain.*

+**cnāwe**=+cnǣwe

cnāwelǣcing f. *acknowledgement,* KC 4·193¹².

cnāwlǣc (ē²) *acknowledgement,* CHR 963 (ES 42·176).

+**cnāwnes** f. *acknowledgement,* EC 265².

cnēa gp. of cnēo(w).

cnearr m. *small ship, galley (of the ships of the Northmen),* †CHR. [*ON.* knorr]

±**cnēatian** *to argue, dispute,* GL.

cnēatung f. *inquisition, investigation,* OEG : *dispute, debate,* Sc.

cnedan⁵ *to* '*knead**,' *Lcd,LkL.*

cneht (VPs)=cniht; **cnēo**=cnēow

cnēodan, cneoht=cnōdan, cniht

+**cnēord** *eager, zealous, diligent,* Æ,BH.

±**cnēordlǣcan** *to be diligent, study,* Æ.

cnēordlic *diligent, earnest, zealous,* Æ. adv. -lice.

±**cnēordnes** f. *zeal, diligence, study,* GL.

cnēordnes (Æ)=+cnēorenes

+**cnēor-(e)nes,** -ednes f. *generation, race,* GL.

cnēores=cnēoriss

cnēorift n? *napkin* (BTs), *kneehose?* (Kluge), GL.

cnēorisbōc f. *Genesis*, WW 414[29].
cnēorisn (BL), cneor(n)is(s) f. *generation, posterity, family, tribe, nation, race.*
cneorŏlǣcan=cneordlǣcan
cnēow I. (cnēo) n. '*KNEE*,' *AO* : *step in a pedigree, generation, LL*; Æ. II. pret. 3 sg. of cnāwan.
cnēowbīgung f. *kneeling, genuflection*, CM.
cnēow-ede, -ade *having big knees*, WW.
cnēowgebed n. *prayer on one's knees*, Æ.
cnēowholen m. '*knee-holly*,' *butcher's broom, Lcd*.
cnēowian I. (±) *to kneel*, Æ2[154]. ['*knee*'] II. *to know carnally*, ÆL 12[7].
cnēowlian *to* '*kneel*,' *LL*.
cnēowmǣg m. (nap. -mǣgas, -māgas) *kinsman, relation, ancestor*.
cnēowrīm† n. *progeny, family*, GEN.
cnēowsibb f. *generation, race* (BDS 8·527).
cnēowung f. *kneeling, genuflection*, CM.
cnēowwærc m. *pain in the knees*, LCD.
cnēowwyrst f. *knee-joint*, WW.
cnepp=cnæpp; cnēw=cnēow
cnīdan[1] *to beat*, MtR 21[35].
cnieht=cniht
cnīf m. '*knife*,' *WW*.
cniht (e, eo, ie, y) m. *boy, youth, AO,Bl,LL* : *servant, attendant, retainer, disciple, warrior, Chr,Mt,Met* : *boyhood, ÆGr* : *junior member of a guild* (BTac),Ct. ['*knight*']
cnihtcild (eo[1]) n. *male child, boy*, BH 284[30], MH 12[9].
cnihtgebeorðor n. *child-birth, child-bearing*, BL 3[12].
cnihtgeong *youthful*, EL 640.
cnihthād m. *puberty, youth, boyhood*, Æ, Bo; AO : (*male*) *virginity*. ['*knighthood*']
cnihtiugoð f. *youth*, BF 12[3].
cnihtlēas *without an attendant*, ÆL 23[395].
cnihtlic *boyish, childish, Guth*. ['*knightly*']
cnihtðēawas mp. *boyish ways*, GD 111[9].
cnihtwesende† *when a boy, as a youth*, B.
cnihtwīse f. *boyishness*, GUTH 12[13].
cnissan=cnyssan
cnītian *to dispute*, Sc 51[12].
cnittan=cnyttan; cnocian=cnucian
±cnōdan (ēo) *to attribute to, assign to, load with*, CP.
cnoll m. '*knoll*,' *Ps*; Mdf : *summit*, Æ, Bo.
cnop '*ballationes*,' *knob*, WW 8[28]; 357[32].
-cnoppa v. wull-c.
+cnos n. *collision*, WW 376[2]. [cnyssan]
cnōsl n. *stock, progeny, kin, family* : *native country*.
cnossian *to strike, hit upon*, SEAF 8.
cnotmǣlum '*strictim*,' A 13·35[201].
cnotta m. '*knot*,' *fastening*, Æ : *knotty point, puzzle*, Æ.

±cnucian (o) *to* '*knock*' (*door*), Æ,G : *beat, pound, IM,Lcd*.
cnūlan, cnūwian *to pound*, LCD.
+cnyce n. *bond*, DR 59,66.
±cnyccan pret. 3 sg. cnycte, cnyhte *to tie*.
+cnycled *bent, crooked*, WW 458[33].
cnyht=cniht; cnyhte v. cnyccan.
cnyll m. *sound or signal of a bell, RB,WW*. ['*knell*']
±cnyllan *to toll a bell, RB* : *strike, knock, LkR,MtL*; LV 28. ['*knell*']
cnyllsian (LkL)=cnyllan; cnyrd-=cneord-
±cnyssan *to press, toss, strike, hew to pieces, dash, crash* (*together*), *beat*, Æ,AO,CP : *overcome, overwhelm, oppress*, CP.
cnyssung f. *striking, stroke*, ÆGR.
±cnyttan *to fasten, tie, bind, 'knit'* ('*i-knit*,' *Mt,WW*), *Æ,Lcd*; CP : *add, append*, BF 32[30]. [cnotta]
cnyttels m. *string, sinew*, OEG 2935.
coc=cocc
cōc m. '*cook*,' *Æ,Ps*; CP. [*L*. coquus]
cocc m. *cock, male bird, Æ,CP,Lcd,Mt*; Mdf.
coccel m. '*cockle*,' *darnel, tares, Bf,Mt*.
cocer (o[2], u[2]) m. *quiver, case, sheath, Æ* : *spear*, Ps.
cōcerpanne f. *cooking-pan, frying-pan*, PRPs.
+cōcnian (cōca-) *to season food*, WW 504[12].
cōcnung f. *seasoning*, LCD,WW.
cocor=cocer
cōcormete m. *seasoned food*, WW 281[6].
+cōcsian *to cook, roast*, RPs 101[4].
cōcunung=cōcnung; cocur (Æ)=cocer
codd m. '*cod*,' *husk, Lcd* : *bag, Mt* : *scrotum*.
coddæppel m. *quince*, WW 411[15].
codic (coydic) '*lapsana*,' *charlock?* A 37·47.
cofa m. *closet, chamber* : *ark* : *cave, den*. ['*cove*']
cofgodas mp. *household gods*, GL.
cofincel n. *little chamber*, WW.
-cofrian v. ā-c.
cohhetan *to make a noise, cough?* JUD 270.
col n. (nap. colu, cola) '*coal*,' *live coal, Æ,CP,Lcd,VPs*.
cōl I. '*cool*,' *cold, B,Bo,Lcd* : *tranquil, calm*. II. pret. 3 sg. of calan.
cōlcwyld f. '*frigida pestis*,' *ague?* WW 243[11].
-cole v. ōden-, wīn-c.
cōlian *to* '*cool*,' *grow cold, be cold, An,Gu,Lcd*.
coliandre f. *coriander*, LCD.
coll-, cōll-=col-, cōl-; -colla v. morgen-c.
collecta f. *collect*, ÆP,CM.
+collenferhtan *to make empty*, LPs 136[7].
collen-ferhð, -fyrhð, -ferðt *proud, elated, bold*. [*cwellan* (*to swell*)?]
collon-croh, -crog m. *water-lily, nymphæa*, LCD,WW.

colmāse f. '*coal-mouse*,' *tit-mouse*, *WW*.
cōlnes f. '*coolness*,' *Ps*.
colpytt m. (*char-*)*coal pit*, Ct.
colsweart *coal-black*, NC277.
colt m. '*colt*,' *Æ*.
coltetræppe f. *a plant*, '*caltrop*,' *WW*.
coltgræg f? *colt's-foot*, WW136¹⁸.
coltræppe=coltetræppe
col-ŏrǣd, -ŏrēd m. *plumb-line*, GL.
columne f. *column*, AA6.
cōm pret. 3 sg. of cuman.
coman (AO70²⁴)=cuman
comb, combol=camb, cumbol
comēta m. *comet*, †CHR975. [*L*.]
commuc=cammoc
communia *psalm sung at Eucharist*, ÆP 168¹⁶.
cōmon pret. pl. of cuman.
comp=camp
con (v. '*con**')=can pres. 1, 3 sg. of cunnan.
condel=candel
conn=cann pres. 1, 3 sg. of cunnan.
consolde f. *comfrey*, LCD125b. [*L*.]
const=canst pres. 2 sg. of cunnan.
consul m. *consul*, AO. [*L*.]
coorte f. *cohort*, AO240, 242. [*L*.]
cop=copp
cōp m? '*ependytes*,' *cope, vestment*, GL.
+cōp *proper, fitting*, CP.
copel *unsteady, rocking?* (BTs),BC3·624.
cōpenere m. *lover*, CP405¹⁴.
coper, copor n. '*copper*,' *Lcd,WW*. [*L*. cuprum]
copian *to plunder, steal*, WW379¹⁷.
+cōplic *proper, fitting*, GD. adv. -līce, Bo.
copp I. m. *top, summit*, HGl. ['*cop*'] II. m. *cup*, NG. ['*cop*']
-coppe v. ātor-c.
copped *polled, lopped, pollard*, Ct. ['*copped*']
cops (*WW*)=cosp
+cor n. *decision*, OET436¹⁵,¹⁶. [cēosan]
corcīŏ m. *increase? choice growth?* LCD 3·212⁹ (v. A31·56).
+corded *having a cord?* WW187.
cordewānere m. '*cordwainer*,' *shoemaker*, EC257'. [*OFr*.]
±coren (pp. of cēosan) *chosen, elect, choice, fit, Æ : precious, dear.*
corenbēg m. *crown*, A11·172. [*L*. corona]
+corenlic *elegant*, WW393³⁷. adv. -līce, WW396²⁶.
±corennes f. *choice, election* : (+) *goodness.*
±corenscipe m. *election, excellence*, DR.
corfen pp. of ceorfan.
corflian *to mince*, IM,LCD. [ceorfan]
corn n. '*CORN*,' *grain*, Chr,CP; Æ,AO : *seed, berry*, CP,Jn,Lcd; Æ : *a corn-like pimple, corn*, LCD.
cornæsceda fp. *chaff*, WW118¹.

cornappla np. *pomegranates*, OEG.
corn-bǣre (Æ), -berende *corn-bearing.*
corngebrot n. *corn dropped in carrying to barn*, LL451,17.
corngesǣlig *rich in corn*, LCD3·188¹¹.
corngesceot n. *payment in corn*, Ct.
cornhūs n. *granary*, WW185²⁸
cornhwicce (æ², y²) f. *corn-bin*, Æ.
cornlād f. *leading of corn*, LL453,21⁴.
cornsǣd n. *a grain of corn*, GD253¹.
corntēoŏung f. *tithe of corn*, W.
corntrēow n. *cornel-tree*, WW.
corntrog m. *corn-bin*, WW107¹.
cornuc, cornuch (WW25)=cranoc
cornwurma m. *scarlet dye*, GL.
corōna m. *crown*, NC277. [*L*.]
+corōnian *to crown*, PPs5¹³.
corsnǣd f. *piece of consecrated bread which an accused person swallowed as a test of innocence*, LL.
corŏor†, corŏer† fn. *troop, band, multitude, throng, retinue* : *pomp.*
corwurma=cornwurma; cos=coss
cosp m. *fetter, bond*, Bo. ['*cops*']
+cospende, +cosped *fettered*, LPs.
coss m. '*kiss*,' *embrace*, Æ,Lk,WW.
cossetung f. *kissing*, NG.
cossian *to* '*kiss*,' ÆGr,BH,G.
cost I. m. *option, choice, possibility* : *manner, way*, DR : *condition*. ŏæs costes ŏe *on condition that*. ['*cost*'; v. NC341] II. (±) †*tried, chosen, excellent.* [cēosan] III. m? *costmary, tansy*, Lcd. ['*cost*']
costere I. m? *spade, shovel*, WW106¹⁸. II. m. *tempter*, Æ.
±costian (w. g. or a., also intr.) *to tempt, try, prove, examine*, AO,CP. [*Ger*. kosten]
costigend m. *tempter*, BL.
costn-=cost-
+costnes f. *proving, temptation, trial*, BH 218¹⁰.
costnungstōw f. *place of temptation*, DEUT 6¹⁶.
±costung, costnung f. *temptation, testing, trial, tribulation*, Mt; Æ,CP. ['*costnung*']
cot (AO) n. (nap. cotu); cote (LL?) f. '*cot*,' *cottage, bed-chamber, den*, AO,Lk,Mt; Mdf. [v. also '*cote*']
cotlīf n. *hamlet, village, manor*, Chr : *dwelling*. ['*cotlif*']
cotsetla (cote-) m. *cottager*, LL. ['*cotsetla*']
cotstōw f. *site of cottages*, KC.
cott=cot
cottuc, cotuc m. *mallow*, GL.
coŏa m., coŏe f.=coŏu
coŏig *diseased*, CHRD62⁸.
coŏlīce *ill, miserably*, MET25³⁶.
cōŏon (AO)=cūŏon pret. pl. of cunnan.

coðu f. *disease, sickness*, Æ,*Chr,Lcd*.
['*cothe*']
+**cow** n. *thing to be chewed, food*, NC292.
cowen pp. of cēowan.
crā n? *croaking*, WW208¹⁰.
crabba m. '*crab*,' *WW* : *Cancer* (*sign of the zodiac*), *Lcd*.
cracelung? '*crepacula*,' OEG56²⁴⁹.
crācettan (ǣ) *to croak*, GD119²⁵. [crā]
crācetung (ǣ) f. *croaking*, GUTH48⁴.
cracian *to resound*, '*crack*,' *Ps*.
cradol, cradel m. '*cradle*,' *cot, WW*.
cradolcild n. *child in the cradle, infant*, W158¹⁴.
crǣ=crāwe
crǣcet-=crācet-
crǣf-=craf-
crǣft m. *physical strength, might, courage*, A,*AO,Sol* : *science, skill, art, ability, talent, virtue, excellence, Bo*; Æ,CP : *trade, handicraft, calling, BH,CP,RB*; Æ : *work or product of art, Hex* : *trick, fraud, deceit*, BL : *machine, instrument*. in pl. *great numbers, hosts?* DA393 (v. MP26·434). ['*craft*']
crǣfta=cræftiga
±**crǣftan** *to exercise a craft, build* : *bring about, contrive*, Æ.
cræftelīce=cræftlīce
+**cræftgian** *to strengthen, render powerful*, AO.
cræftglēaw *skilful, wise*, †CHR975.
cræf-t(i)ca, -t(e)ga=cræftiga
cræftig *strong, powerful, AO* : *skilful, cunning, ingenious, Bl* : *learned, instructive*, BF132⁸ : *knowing a craft, scientific*, RB. ['*crafty*']
cræftiga m. *craftsman, artificer, workman*, Æ,CP : *architect*, BH.
cræftiglīce *skilfully*, WW.
cræftlēas *artless, unskilful*, RBL52¹.
cræftlic *artificial*, BF112²⁵ : *skilful*. adv. -līce.
cræftsprǣc f. *scientific language*, ÆGR18¹⁵.
cræftwyrc n. *skilled workmanship*, Sc109⁵.
cræt n. nap. cr(e)atu *cart,waggon,chariot*,Æ.
crætehors n. *cart-horse*, WW108²⁴.
crætwǣn m. *chariot*, AO.
crætwīsa m. *charioteer*, ÆL18²⁹⁵.
crǣwð pres. 3 sg. of crāwan.
crafian (æ) *to* '*crave*,' *ask, implore, demand, Chr,LL* : *summon, Lcd*.
crafing (æ) f. *claim, demand*, TC645⁴.
±**crammian** *to* '*cram*,' *stuff*, ÆGr.
crammingpohha m. '*viscarium*,' CHRD68⁹.
crampul m. *crane-pool*, Ct(Swt). [=cran, pōl]
cran m. '*crane*,' *WW*.
crancstæf m. *weaving implement, crank*, LL455,15 and 3·254.

crang pret. 3 sg. of cringan.
cranic m. *record, chronicle*, Æ. [*L.*]
cranicwrītere m. *chronicler*, OEG7²⁴.
cranoc m. '*crane*,' *WW* (corn-).
crat (WW140³¹)=cræt; **cratu** v. cræt.
crāwa m., crāwe f. '*crow*,' *raven, Gl,Ps*.
±**crāwan⁷** *to* '*crow*,' *Mt*; CP.
crāwan-lēac (crāw-) n. *crow-garlic*, WW.
crēac-=crēc-
crēad pret. 3 sg. of crūdan.
creaft-=cræft-
crēap pret. 3 sg. of crēopan.
crēas *fine, elegant*, NC277 : *dainty*, BDS 48·460.
crēaslic *dainty, rich*. v. NC277.
crēasnes f. *elegance* : *presumption, elation*, OEG1108.
creat=cræt
Crēcas (ēa, v. AB40·342) mp. *the* '*Greeks*,' *AO,BH*.
Crēce=Crēcas
Crēcisc *Grecian, Greek*, AO.
crēda m. *creed, belief, confession of faith*, Æ. [*L.* credo]
credic? *a bowl*, OEG29³.
creft (AS)=cræft
crencestre f. *female weaver, spinster*, KC 6·131'. [cranc]
±**crēopan** (occly. refl.) *to creep, crawl*, Æ, *Bo*; AO,CP.
creopel=crypel
crēopere m. *cripple*, ÆL,GF. ['*creeper*']
crēopung f. '*creeping*,' *Gl*.
crēow pret. 3 sg. of crāwan.
crepel=crypel
cressa m. (GL), cresse f.=cærse
cribb (y) f. '*crib*,' *stall, Cr*1426 : *couch*, CHRD31³.
cricc=crycc
crīde pret. 3 sg. of crīgan.
crīgan? *to bubble up*. v. OEG7¹⁰¹.
±**crimman³** *to cram, put in, insert*, LCD, WW.
crinc '*cothurnus*,' ZDA33·250².
crincan=cringan
cring (gr-) *downfall, slaughter*, EL115.
±**cringan³**† *to yield, fall* (*in battle*), *die*.
cringwracu (gr-) f. *torment*, JUL265.
cripel=crypel; **crippan**=cryppan
cripð pres. 3 sg. of crēopan.
crisma m. *chrism, holy oil*, LL : *chrisome-cloth*, BH : *anointing*, CHR.
crismal m? n? *chrismale*, W36¹⁷.
crismhālgung f. *consecration of the chrism*, WNL121b'.
crismlīsing (ȳ²) f. *chrism-loosing, loosing of the chrismale, confirmation*, CHR.
crisp (*BH*)=cirps ['*crisp*']
Crīst m. *Anointed One, Christ*, Æ,CP.

cristalla m. *crystal,* Æ.

cristallisc *of crystal,* AA7[6].

cristelmæl=cristesmæl

cristelmælbēam m. *tree surmounted by a cross? upright shaft of a cross?* EC385′.

cristen '*Christian,*' *AO,BH*; Æ. ða cristnan=*the English as opposed to the Danes,* CHR894.

cristen m., **crist(e)na** m. '*Christian,*' *Ao.*

cristendōm m. '*Christendom,*' *the church, Christianity, AO,Jud*; Æ.

cristenlic *Christian,* DR91′.

cristenmann m. *a Christian,* MH170[25].

cristennes f. *Christianity : Christian baptism,* LL412,1; 413,13a.

Cristes-mæl (CHR), **-mēl** mn. (*Christ's mark*), *the cross.* wyrcan C. *to make the sign of the cross.*

Cristesmæsse f. *Christmas,* CHR1021D.

cristlic *Christian,* LL(Thorpe)1·318[11]n4.

cristna=cristen

cristnere m. *one who performs the rite of* cristnung, MH92[1].

cristnes=cristennes

±cristnian *to anoint with chrism* (*as a catechumen*), '*christen,*' *baptize,* BH.

cristnung f. *christening, anointing with chrism or holy oil,* W33[16].

criō=crigeð (v. crigan)?

crocc f., **crocca** m. '*crock,*' *pot, vessel,* Lcd.

crocchwer? m. *earthen pot,* OEG4672.

croced=croged

+crōcod *crooked, bent,* NC292.

crocsceard n. *potsherd,* Æ.

crocwyrhta m. *potter,* ÆCR.

+crod v. hlōð-gec.; lind-gec.

croden pp. of crūdan.

croft m. '*croft,*' *small field,* KC; GL.

crog, croh m. *saffron,* Lcd. [v. '*crocus*']

crōg m. *crock, pitcher, vessel,* Gl. ['*croh*']

crōgcynn n. *kind of vessel, wine-jar,* WW 210[39].

+crōged (ōc) *saffron-hued,* OEG5204n.

crōh I. m. *shoot, twig, tendril.* II. (WW431′) =crōg ['*croh*']

crohha=crocca; **croma**=cruma

crompeht '*placenta,*' *a flat cake, crumpet,* WW241[34](A40·352); A37·48.

crong=crang pret. 3 sg. of cringan.

crop=cropp

cropen pp. of crēopan.

crop-lēac, -lēc n. *garlic* Lcd,WW.

cropp, croppa m. *cluster, bunch : sprout, flower, berry, ear of corn,* Ep,LkL,WW : '*crop*' (*of a bird*), Æ : *kidney : pebble.*

croppiht *clustered,* Lcd38b.

crūc m. *cross,* Lcd; LV74. ['*crouch*']

crūce f. *pot, pitcher,* Gl. ['*crouke*']

crucethūs n. *torture-chamber,* CHR1137.

crūdan[2]† *to press, hasten, drive.*

cruft m? crufte f. *crypt,* GL. [*L.*]

cruma (o) m. '*crumb,*' *fragment,* Mt,WW.

crumb, crump *crooked, bent, stooping,* Gl. ['*crump*']

crumen (crumm-) pp. of crimman.

cruncon pret. pl. of crincan.

crundel mn. *ravine, chalk-pit, quarry,* Ct (v. GBG and Mdf).

crungen pp. of cringan.

crupon pret. pl. of crēopan.

crūse f? *cruse,* A37·50.

crūs(e)ne f. *fur coat,* GL. [cp. *Ger.* kürschner]

crybb=cribb

crycc (i) f. '*crutch,*' *staff,* BH; Æ.

cryccen *made of clay,* GPH398.

crȳdeð pres. 3 sg. of crūdan.

crymbing f. *curvature, bend, inclination,* WW382[2]. [crumb]

+crymian, +crymman (tr.) *to crumble,* LCD3·290[28].

+crympan *to curl,* WW378[26].

crypel I. (eo) m. '*cripple,*' LkL. II. (o[2]) *crippled,* HL179[322]. III. (e, i) m. *narrow passage, burrow, drain,* OEG; v. Mdf.

crypelgeat n. *small opening in a wall or fence?* BC2·399[1].

crypelnes f. *paralysis,* Lk.

crȳpeð, crȳpð pres. 3 sg. of crēopan.

±cryppan *to crook* (*finger*), *close* (*hand*), *bend,* IM.

cryps=cirps; **crysm-**=crism-

crȳt=crȳdeð pres. 3 sg. of crūdan.

cū f gs cū(e), cȳ, cūs; ds, çȳ; nap. cȳ, cȳe; gp. cū(n)a, cȳna; dp. cūm; '*cow,*' Æ,G, VPs; Mdf.

cūbutere f. *butter,* LCD. [cū]

cūbȳre m. *cow-byre, cow-shed,* Ct.

cuc=cwic

cūcealf (æ) n. *calf,* Erf, LL. ['*cowcalf*']

cuceler, cuce(le)re=cucler(e)

cucelere '*capo,*' WW380[25].

cucler, cuculer, cuclere m. *spoon, spoonful,* LCD. [cp. *L.* cochlear]

cuclermæl n. *spoonful,* LCD.

cucu (Æ,AO,CP) v. cwic.

cucurbite f. *gourd,* LCD92a. [*L.*]

cudele f. *cuttlefish,* WW181[7].

cudu (Æ)=cwudu

cūeage f. *eye of a cow,* LL116Bn.

cueðan=cweðan

cufel f. '*cowl,*' *hood,* BC (at NED2 p. ix).

cūfel=cȳfl

cufle, cuffie=cufel

cugle, cug(e)le, cuhle f. *cap,* '*cowl,*' *hood, head-covering,* RB, WW (v. '*cowl*').

cūhorn m. *cow's horn,* LL116.

cūhyrde m. '*cowherd,*' LL.

cūle=cugle

culfer, cul(e)fre f. 'culver,' pigeon, dove, Gen,VPs,WW.

culmille f. small centaury, Lcd 22a.

culpan as. of *culpa? m. or *culpe? f. fault, sin, Cr 177.

culpian to humble oneself, cringe, Bo 71²⁴.

culter m. 'coulter,' WW : dagger, knife, WW. [L. culter]

culufre=culfre; cūm v. cū.

cuma mf. stranger, guest, Æ,AO,CP. cumena hūs, inn, wīcung inn, guest-chamber.

cuman⁴ to 'come*,' approach, get to, attain, Æ,AO,CP. c. ūp land, be born : (±) go, depart, Æ,AO : come to oneself, recover : become : happen (also c. forð) : put : (+) come together, arrive, assemble, Æ : (†) w. inf. of verbs of motion, forming a sort of periphrastic conjugation for such verbs. cōm gangan he came. cōm swimman he swam, etc.

cumb I. m. valley, BC; Mdf. ['coomb'] II. m. liquid measure, BC. ['coomb']

cumbelgehnād (Br 49)=cumbolgehnāst

cumbl=(1) cumbol; (2) cumul

cumbol† n. sign, standard, banner.

cumbolgebrec (KPs 11), -gehnāst, Br 49 (v.l.), n. crash of banners, battle.

cumbolhaga m. compact rank, phalanx, Jul 395.

cumbolhete m. warlike hate, Jul 637.

cumbolwīga† m. warrior, Jud.

cumbor, cumbul=cumbol

cumen pp. of cuman.

cumendre f. godmother, sponsor. [=cu-medre, *cumædre. v. A 37·52]

cūmeoluc f. cow's milk, Lcd 15a.

Cumere? -eras? np. Cumbrians, ÆL 21⁴⁵¹.

cumfeorm f. entertainment for travellers, Ct. [cuma, feorm]

cū-micge (Lcd 137a) f. -migoða (Lcd 37a) m. cow's urine.

cuml=cumbl

cumlīðe hospitable, Æ,W. [cuma]

cumlīðian to be a guest, RBL 11¹.

cumlīðnes f. hospitality, Æ : sojourn as guest, RB.

cummāse f. a kind of bird, 'parra,' WW 260¹⁹.

cumpæder m. godfather, Chr 894A. [L. compater]

cumul, cuml n. swelling, Lcd.

cūna v. cū; cund=cynd

-cund adjectival suffix denoting derivation, origin or likeness. (-kind) as in deofol-cund, god-cund.

cuneglæsse f. hound's-tongue, Lcd 41b. [L. cynoglossum]

cunel(l)e, cunille f. wild thyme. [Ger. quendel]

cuning=cyning

±cunnan pres. 1 and 3 sg. can(n), pl. cunnon; pret. cūðe, pp. cūð swv. to be or become acquainted with, be thoroughly conversant with, know, AO,B,Lcd,Mt; CP : know how to, have power to, be able to, can, Æ,CP : express (thanks), Chr 1092 : have carnal knowledge, Cr 198. ['can*,' 'con*']

cunnere m. tempter, NG.

±cunnian (w. g. or a.) to search into, try, test, seek for, explore, investigate, B,Bo,Cr, Sol; Æ,CP : experience : have experience of, to make trial of : know. ['cun']

cunnung f. knowledge : trial, probation, experience : contact, carnal knowledge, DR 110¹ (A 45·187).

cuopel f? small boat, MtL. ['coble']

cuppe f. 'cup,' Lcd,WW; Æ.

curfon pret. pl. of ceorfan.

curmealle (e, i) f. centaury, Lcd.

curnstān=cweornstān

curon pret. pl. of cēosan.

curs m. imprecatory prayer, malediction, 'curse,' Ct,LL,Sc. [v. MP 24·215]

cursian I. to 'curse,' Ps. II. to plait? MkR 15¹⁷.

cursumbor incense, MtL 2¹¹.

cursung f. 'cursing,' damnation, LkL : place of torment, MtL.

cūs v. cū.

cūsc chaste, modest, virtuous, Gen 618. [Ger. keusch]

cūscote (eo, u) f. 'cushat' dove, wood-pigeon, Gl.

cūself f. cow's fat, suet, GPH 392. [sealf]

cū-sloppe, -slyppe f. 'cowslip,' Lcd,WW.

cūsnes=cīsnes

cūtægl m. tail of a cow, LL 169,59B.

±cūð known, plain, manifest, certain, Rd; Æ,AO,CP : well known, usual, Da,Ps : noted, excellent, famous, Ex : intimate, familiar, friendly, related. ['couth']

cūða m. acquaintance, relative, CP.

cūðe I. clearly, plainly, Ps. ['couth'] II. pret. 3 sg. of cunnan.

cūðelic=cūðlic

±cūðian to become known, take knowledge of, regard, JVPs 143³.

cūðlic=cūðlīce

±cūðlǣcan to make known : make friends with, ÆL.

cūðlic known, certain, evident. adv. -līce clearly, evidently, certainly, openly, BH, Jul; Æ,CP : familiarly, kindly, affably, An,BH; Æ : therefore, to be sure, hence. ['couthly']

cūðnes f. acquaintance, knowledge, HL.

cūðnoma m. *surname*, NG.
cūðon pret. pl. of cunnan.
cūwearm *warm from the cow (milk)*, LCD 126a.
cuwon pret. pl. of cēowan.
cwacian *to 'quake,' tremble, chatter (of teeth)*, Æ,AO,Cr,LkL,VPs.
cwacung f. *'quaking,' trembling*, Æ,VPs; AO.
cwæc-=cwac-
cwǣdon pret. pl. of cweðan.
cwæl pret. 3 sg., cwǣlon pret. pl., of cwelan.
cwæl-=cwal-, cwiel-, cwil-
cwǣman=cwēman; **cwǣn**=cwēn
cwærtern=cweartern
cwǣð pret. 3 sg. of cweðan.
cwal-=cweal-
cwalstōw (LL556,10²)=cwealmstōw
cwalu f. *killing, murder, violent death, destruction*, Æ,CP. [cwelan]
cwānian† (tr. and intr.) *to lament, bewail, deplore, mourn*. [*Goth.* kwainon]
cwānig *sad, sorrowful*, EL377.
cwānung f. *lamentation*, NC279.
cwartern=cweartern
cwatern *the number four at dice*, GL. [*L.*]
cwēad n. *dung, dirt, filth*, LCD. [*Ger.* kot]
cweaht pp. of cweccan.
cweald pp. of cwellan.
cwealm (e) mn. *death, murder, slaughter : torment, pain : plague, pestilence*, ÆH; AO. ['*qualm*'; cwelan]
+cwealmbǣran (c, y) *to torture*, LPs.
cwealmbǣre *deadly, murderous, bloodthirsty*, Æ.
cwealmbǣrnes (e) f. *mortality, destruction, ruin*, Æ.
cwealmbealu n. *death*, B1940.
cwealmberendlic (y¹) *pestilent, deadly*, NC279.
cwealmcuma m. *death-bringer*, B792.
cwealmdrēor m. *blood shed in death*, GEN985.
+cwealmful (y¹) *pernicious*, HGL428.
cwealmlic *deadly*, WYN281b (MLR17·166).
cwealmnes f. *pain, torment*, BH40³³.
cwealmstede m. *death-place*, GL.
cwealmstōw f. *place of execution*, Æ,Cp. [v. '*qualm*']
cwealmþrēa m. *deadly terror*, GEN2507.
cwearn=cweornstān
cweartern (a, æ, e) n. *prison*, Æ.
cwearternlic *of a prison*, GPH400.
cwearte(r)nweard? *jailor*, GPH399.
±cweccan *to shake, swing, move, vibrate*, Mt,VPs; Æ : *shake off, give up*, CHRD99³⁴. ['*quetch*'; cwacian]
cweccung f. *moving, shaking, wagging*, LPs 43¹⁵.

cwecesand m. *quicksand*, WW357⁶.
+cwed n. *declaration*, WW423²².
cweddian=cwiddian; **cwedel**=cwedol
cweden pp. of cweðan.
+cwedfæsten f. *appointed fast*, A11·99; ES 43·162.
cwedol *talkative, eloquent*, LCD.
+cwedrǣden (i, y) f. *agreement*, AO : *conspiracy*.
+cwedrǣdnes (y) f. *agreement, covenant*, NC292.
+cwedstōw f. *appointed place, place of meeting*, GD183⁷.
cwehte pret. sg. of cweccan.
cwelan⁴ *to die*, LCD; Æ,CP. ['*quele*']
cweldeht *corrupted, mortified*, LCD47b. [=*cwildeht]
cwelderǣde (æ¹)? *evening rider? bat*, SHR 29⁸. [*ON.* kveld]
±cwellan *to kill, murder, execute*, Æ, CP; AO. ['*quell*']
cwellend m. *killer, slayer*, GPH400.
cwellere m. *murderer, executioner*, BH,Mk; Æ. ['*queller*']
cwelm=cwealm (but v. MFH106), cwielm
cwelmere, cwelre=cwellere
±cwēman (w. d.) *to gratify, please, satisfy, propitiate*, Æ,AO,CP,Sol : *comply with, be obedient to, serve*. ['*queme,' 'i-queme*']
±cwēme *pleasant, agreeable, acceptable*, NG, WG. ['*i-queme*']
cwēme-, cwēmed=cwēm
±cwēming f. *pleasing, satisfaction, complaisance*, CP.
±cwēmlic *pleasing, satisfying, suitable*. adv. **-līce** *graciously, kindly, humbly, satisfactorily*.
±cwēmnes f. *pleasure, satisfaction, mitigation*.
+cwēmsum *pleasing*, OEG5000.
cwēn (ǣ) f. *woman*, Sc; Æ : *wife, consort*, AO,Gen : '*queen,' empress, royal princess*, Æ,AO,Chr,VPs : *Virgin Mary*, Bl,Cr. [*Goth.* kwēns]
-cwencan v. ā-c.
cwene f. *woman*, Rd,W : *female serf, 'quean,' prostitute*, AO. [*Goth.* kwinō]
cwenfugol *hen-bird*, RWH148⁵.
cwēnhirde m. *eunuch*, MtL19¹².
cwēnlic *queenly*, B1940.
cweodu=cwudu
cweorn f. *'quern,' hand-mill, mill*, Æ,MtL; CP.
cweornbill *'lapidaria,' a stone chisel for dressing querns* (BT),WW438¹⁸.
cweornburna m. *mill-stream*, Ct.
cweorne=cweorn
cweornstān m. *mill-stone*, MtL. ['*quernstone*']

cweorntēð mp. *molars, grinders*, GL.

-cweorra v. mete-c.; -cweorran v. ā-c.

cweorð *name of the rune for* cw(q).

cwern (NG)=cweorn; cwertern=cweartern

±cweðan⁵ *to say, speak, name, call, proclaim, summon, declare, BH,Bl,VPs*; Æ, AO,CP : (+) *order, give orders : propose,* AO 68¹⁶ : ±c. (tō) *agree, settle, resolve, Chr :* (+) *consider, regard,* ÆL 1¹¹⁷. c. on hwone *assign to one.* cwyst ðū lā *sayest thou?* '*numquid.*' cweðe gē *think you?* ['*quethe*']

cwic [cuc, cucu (this last form is archaic, and has an occasional asm. cucone, cucune)] 'QUICK,' *living, alive, CP*; AO : as sb. *living thing*, PPs 103²⁴.

cwicǣht f. *live-stock*, LL 60,18¹.

cwicbēam m. *aspen, juniper, Gl,Lcd.* ['*quick-beam*']

cwicbēamen *of aspen*, LcD 3·14²⁵.

cwicbēamrind f. *aspen bark*, LcD.

cwiccliende *moving rapidly? tottering?* OEG 2234.

cwice fm. '*couch*' ('*quitch*')-*grass, Gl,Lcd.*

cwicfȳr n. *sulphur*, LkR 17²⁹.

cwichege *a quick hedge*, KC 3·380¹¹.

cwichrērende *living and moving*, CREAT 5.

±cwician *to quicken, create, JnL : come to life, come to one's self,* Æ,Lcd. ['*quick*']

cwiclāc n. *a living sacrifice*, NG.

cwiclic *living, vital*, DR. adv. -līce *vigorously, keenly*, Ps. ['*quickly*']

cwiclifigende† *living.*

cwicrind=cwicbēamrind

cwicseolfor n. '*quicksilver,*' *Lcd*; WW.

cwicsūsl nf. *hell-torment, punishment, torture,* Æ.

cwicsūslen *purgatorial*, ApT 26.

cwictrēow n. *aspen*, WW.

cwicu=cwic

+cwicung f. *restoration to life*, GD 218¹⁷.

cwicwelle *living (of water)*, JnR.

cwid-=cwed-, cwud-

cwidbōc f. *Book of Proverbs, CP : book of homilies*, MFH 136,152.

cwiddian (e, y) *to talk, speak, say, discuss, report : make a claim against*, LL 400,3¹.

cwiddung (y) f. *speech, saying, report,* Æ.

cwide (y) m. +cwide n. *speech, saying, word, sentence, phrase, proverb, argument, proposal, discourse, homily, Bo;* Æ,CP : *opinion : testament, will, enactment, agreement, decree, decision, judgment, TC;* Æ. ['*quide*'; cweðan]

cwidegiedd (i) n. *speech, song*, WA 55.

cwidelēas (y) *speechless,* Æ : *intestate,* EC 212¹⁷.

±cwielman (æ, e, i, y) *to torment, afflict, mortify, destroy, kill, Bl,VPs;* AO,CP. ['*quelm*'] For compounds v. cwylm-.

cwiferlīce *zealously, RB* 122². ['*quiverly*']

cwild (y;=ie) mfn. *destruction, death, pestilence, murrain.* [cwelan] For compounds v. also cwyld-.

cwildbǣre (æ, y) *deadly, dangerous, pestiferous,* Sc : *stormy.* adv. -bǣrlīce.

cwildberendlic (y) *deadly*, NC 279.

cwild(e)flōd nm. *deluge*, CJVPs 28¹⁰, 31⁶.

±cwildful (y) *deadly*, OEG.

cwildrōf *deadly, savage*, Ex 166.

cwildseten (u, y) f. *first hours of night*, GL.

cwildtīd (u) m. *evening*, WW 211⁴². [*ON.* kveld]

cwilman=cwielman

cwilð pres. 3 sg. of cwelan.

-cwīnan v. ā-c.; -cwincan v. ā-c.

cwine=cwene

+cwis conspiracy, OEG 4955.

-cwisse v. un-c.

cwist pres. 2 sg. of cweðan.

cwið I. (also cwiða) m. *belly, womb*, LcD. [*Goth.* kwiðus] II. pres. 3 sg. of cweðan.

cwīðan *to bewail : accuse*, LL.

cwīðe=cwide

cwīðenlic *natural*, WW 412³⁰.

cwīðnes f. *complaint, lament*, GD.

cwīðst pres. 2 sg. of cweðan.

cwīðung (qu-) f. *complaint*, WW 488³⁷.

cwolen pp. of cwelan.

-cwolstan v. for-c.

cwōm pret. 3 sg. of cuman.

cwuc, cwucu=cwic

cwudu (eo, i) n. *what is chewed, cud,* Æ : *resin of trees.* hwīt c. *chewing gum, mastic.*

cwyc=cwic; cwyd-=cwed-, cwid-, cwidd-

cwydele f. *pustule, tumour, boil*, WW 112, 161.

cwyl-=cwild-; cwyld=cwild

cwylla m. *well, spring*, KC 2·265³⁰. [*Ger.* quelle]

cwylm=cwealm; cwylman=cwielman

+cwylmful *pernicious*, HGL 428.

cwylmian (intr.) *to suffer :* (tr.) *torment, kill, crucify,* Æ. [cwealm]

cwylming f. *suffering, tribulation,* Æ : (metaph.) *cross : death.*

cwylttīd (WW 117⁸)=cwildtīd

cwylð pres. 3 sg. of cwelan.

cwyne=cwene; cwyrn=cweorn

±cwȳsan *to squeeze, dash against, bruise,* Æ.

cwyst pres. 2 sg. of cweðan.

cwyð pres. 3 sg. of cweðan.

cwȳðan, cwyðe=cwīðan, cwide

cȳ v. cū.

cycel (i) m. *small cake*, Lcd 159b. ['*kichel*']

cycen=cicen, cycene

cycene f. '*kitchen,*' Æ,WW. [*L.* coquina]

cycenðēnung f. *service in the kitchen*, NC 279.

cycgel m. '*cudgel*,' BDS,CP.

+cȳd(d) (*Chr,HR*)=+cȳðed pp. of +cȳðan. ['*ykid*']

cȳdung=cīdung

cȳe I. v. cū. II.=cēo

cȳf f. *tub, vat, cask, bushel*, Æ. ['*keeve*']

cyfes=cifes

cȳfl m. *tub, bucket*, BC.

cȳgan, cȳgling=cīegan, cȳðling +cygd=+cīd; +cȳgednes=+cīgednes

cylcan '*ructare*,' OEG 20².

cyld=(1) cild; (2) ceald

cyle=ciele

cylen f. '*kiln*,' *oven, Cp,WW*. [*L.* culina]

cyleðenie=celeðonie; cylew=cylu

cylin=cylen

cyll f. *skin, leather bottle, flagon, vessel, censer*, Æ,AO,CP. [*L.* culeus]

cylle I. m.=cyll. II.=cielle

cyllfylling f. *act of filling a bottle*, GD 250²⁷.

cyln=cylen

cylu *spotted, speckled*, WW 163²⁹.

cym imperat. of cuman.

cymbala=cimbala

cyme (i) m. *coming, arrival, advent, approach, Bo,MtR*; AO,CP : *event : result*, BH 372ᴮ¹⁹. ['*come*']

cȳme (ī) *comely, lovely, glorious*, PPs.

cymed n. *germander*, LCD.

cymen I. mn. '*cumin*,' *CP,Mt*. [*L.*] II. pp. of cuman. III. (and cymin)=cinimin

cȳmlic† '*comely*,' *lovely, splendid, Ps*. adv. -līce, B.

cȳmnes f. *fastidiousness, daintiness*, GL.

cymst pres. 2 sg., cym(e)ð 3 sg. of cuman.

cyn=(1) cynn; (2) cinn

cȳna gp. of cū.

cyncan as. of sb. *small bundle, bunch?* (BTs),LCD 2·58²².

±cynd (usu.+) nf. *origin, generation, birth : race, species, Bl,Bo,El : place by nature : nature,' kind*' ('*i-cunde*'),*property,quality : character, Bo : offspring : gender, Ph : 'genitalia*,' Æ.

+cyndbōc f. *Book of Genesis*, ÆT 77⁴⁶.

+cynde *natural, native, innate, B,Bo,Gen, WW*; Æ,AO,CP : *proper,fitting, Met : lawful, rightful, Chr,Met*. ['*kind,*' '*i-cunde*']

±cyndelic '*kindly*,' *natural, innate, Bl,Bo, Lcd : generative, of generation*, LL7,64 : *proper, suitable, Bo : lawful, BH*. adv. -līce, Bo.

+cyndlim n. *womb*, Lk : pl. '*genitalia*.'

+cyndnes f. *nation : produce, increase*, RHy 6²².

+cynd-o, -u f.=cynd

cyne=cine II. ; cȳne=cēne

cynebænd m. *diadem*, NC 279.

cynebeald† *royally bold, very brave*, B.

cynebearn (a³) n. *royal child, Christ*, CHR, LCD.

cyneboren *royally born*, Æ.

cynebōt f. *king's compensation*, LL 462',463'.

cynebotl n. *palace*, Æ,WW.

cynecynn n. *royal race, pedigree or family*, Æ,AO.

cynedōm (cyning-, *Da*) m. *royal dignity, kingly rule, government, Chr,Gl*; AO : *royal ordinance or law* : '*kingdom*' ('*kindom*'), *royal possessions*.

cyneg=cyning

cyne-geard, -gerd=cynegyrd

cynegewǣdu np. *royal robes*, BH 32²⁵.

cynegierela (e³) m. *royal robe*, MET 25²³.

cynegild n. *king's compensation*, LL 462.

cynegōd† *noble, well-born, excellent*.

cynegold† n. *regal gold, crown*.

cyne-gyrd, -ge(a)rd f. *sceptre*, Æ,GL.

cynehād m. *kingly state or dignity*, CP.

cynehām m. *royal manor*, EC.

cyne-helm, -healm m. *diadem, royal crown*, Æ : *royal power*.

±cynehelmian *to crown*, MFB,Sc.

cynehlāford m. *liege lord, king*, Æ.

cynehof n. *king's palace*, GPH 391.

cynelic I. *kingly, royal*, CP : *public*. adv. -līce. II.=cynlic

cynelicnes f. *kingliness*, BH 194³⁴.

cynemann m. *royal personage*, NG.

cynerēaf n. *royal robe*, VH 10.

cyneren=cynren

cynerīce (cyning-) n. *rule, sovereignty, Chr, Ct*; CP : *region, nation*, AO. ['*kinrick,*' '*kingrick*']

cyneriht n. *royal prerogative*, EC 202¹⁸.

cynerōf† *noble, renowned*.

cynescipe m. *royalty, majesty, kingly power* : Æ.

cynesetl (æ³) n. *throne, capital city*, Æ,AO.

cynestōl m. *throne, royal dwelling, city*, Æ, AO,CP.

cynestrǣt f. *public road*, WW 71⁶.

cyneðrymlic *very glorious*, NC 279.

cyneðrymm† m. *royal glory, majesty, power : kingly host*, DA 706.

cynewāðen *of royal purple*, TC 538¹⁰. [?=cynewǣden]

cynewīse f. *state, commonwealth*, BH.

cynewiððe f. *royal diadem*, GL.

cyneword n. *fitting word*, RD 44¹⁶. [cynn]

cynewyrðe (u) *noble, kingly*, BF 74¹², MFH 157.

cyning m. '*king,*' *ruler, Bo,Bl,Chr,Ct*; Æ, AO,CP : *God, Christ, Bl,Ct* : (†) *Satan*.

cyning-=cyne-

cyningǣðe *man entitled to take oath as a king's thane*, LL112,54BH.

cyningeswyrt f. *marjoram*, WW301[17].

cyningfeorm f. *king's sustenance, provision for the king's household*, KC2·111'.

cyninggenīðla m. *great feud*, EL610.

cyninggereordu np. *royal banquet*, WW 411[28].

cynlic I. *fitting, proper, convenient, becoming, sufficient*. adv. -līce. II.=cynelic

cynn I. (i) n. *kind, sort, rank, quality : family, generation, offspring, pedigree, 'kin,' race, people, Æ,CP,Chr : gender, sex, Æ : propriety, etiquette*. II. adj. *becoming, proper, suitable*, CP.

+**cynn**=+cynd; **cynn-**=cenn-, cyn-

cynnig *noble, of good family*, OEG.

cynnreccenes f. *genealogy*, NG.

cynren (y²), cynrēd (EPs) n. *kindred, family, generation, posterity, stock*, CP : *kind, species*.

cynresu *a generation*, Mt (pref.).

cȳo, cyp=cēo, cipp; **cȳp-**=cīep-

cȳpa m. I. (also cȳpe) f. *vessel, basket, Lk, OEG*. ['*kipe*'] II. (ē, ī) m. *chapman, trader, merchant, Æ.*

±**cȳpan** (ī;=īe) *to traffic, buy, sell, barter*. [Ger. *kaufen*]

+**cȳpe** adj. *for sale*, ÆH.

cȳpe-=cēap-, cīepe-

cȳpedæg m. *market day*, OEG.

cȳpend m. *one who sells, merchant*, Mt.

cypera m. *spawning salmon*, MET19[12] : '*esox*,' *pike?* A38·516.

cyperen (Æ)=cypren; **cypp**=cipp

cypersealf (i) f. *henna-ointment*, WW205[11] [L. cyperos].

cypren *made of copper, copper*, AO. [copor]

cypresse f. *cypress*, LCD3·118'. [L.]

cypsan=cyspan; **cyr-**=cer-, cier-, cir-

cyre m. *choice, free-will*, Æ. ['*cure*']

cyreāð m. *oath sworn by an accused man and by other chosen persons*. v. LL2·293.

cyrelīf n. *state of dependence on a lord whom a person has chosen? : person in such a state* (v. BTs and NC279).

cyren=(1) ceren, (2) cyrn

cyrf m. *cutting, cutting off, Æ : what is cut off*. ['*kerf*']

cyrfæt=cyrfet

cyrfel m. *little stake, peg*, WW126[18].

cyrfet m. *gourd*, LCD. [Ger. *kürbis*]

cyrfð pres. 3 sg. of ceorfan.

ðyric-=ciric-

cyrige v. wæl-c.

cyrin, cyrn (e) f. '*churn*,' *WW*.

cyrnel (i) mn. (nap. cyrnlu) *seed, 'kernel,' pip, Æ,Lcd : (enlarged) gland, swelling*, Lcd. [corn]

+**cyrnod**, +cyrnlod *granulated, rough*, OEG.

cyrps=cirps

cyrriol *the Kyrie Eleison*, BF126³.

cyrs-=cærs-, cris-

cyrstrēow n. *cherry-tree*, WW 138. [ciris; L.]

+**cyrtan** *to shorten*, GPH400.

cyrtel m. *(man's) tunic, coat, Æ,AO : (woman's) gown, Ct.* ['*kirtle*']

cyrten I. *fair, comely, Æ : intelligent*. adv. -līce (and cyrtelīce) *elegantly, neatly, fairly, well, exactly*. II. *ornament?* WW216⁷.

cyrtenes (e¹) f. *elegance, beauty*, OEG.

±**cyrtenlǣcan** (e¹) *to beautify, make elegant, Æ : (+) make sweet*, OEG.

cyrð pres. 3 sg. of cyrran.

cys-=cyse-, ceos-

cȳse (ȳ, ē;=īe) m. '*cheese*,' WW.

cȳsefæt n. *cheese vat*, WW379[27] (v. LL 3·255).

cȳsehwǣg n. *whey*, LCD119b.

cȳsfæt (LL455,17)=cȳsefæt

cȳsgerunn n. *curd-like mass*, WW98³ (v. A51·158).

cysirbēam=cirisbēam

cȳslybb n. *rennet, Cp,Lcd*. ['*cheeselip*']

±**cyspan** *to fetter, bind, Æ*. [cosp]

±**cyssan** *to 'kiss,' Æ,BH,Mt*. [coss]

cȳssticce n. *piece of cheese*, CHRD15.

cyst I. fm. *free-will, choice, election* : (w. gp.) *the best of anything, the choicest, Æ : picked host : moral excellence, virtue, goodness*, CP, Æ : *generosity, munificence*, CP. [cēosan] II.=cist I.

cȳst pres. 3 sg. of cēosan.

cystan *to spend, lay out, get the value of*, CHR1124.

cystbēam=cistenbēam

cystel, cysten (=cist-) f. *chestnut-tree*, LCD, WW.

cystelīce=cystiglīce

cystian (e) *to put in a coffin*, W. [cist]

cystig *charitable, liberal, generous, CP; Æ : virtuous, good.* ['*custi*'] adv. -līce.

cystignes, cystines f. *liberality, bounty, goodness, Æ : abundance.*

cystlēas *worthless, bad*, GEN1004.

cystlic=cystig; **cystnes**=cystignes

cȳsð=cīesð pres. 3 sg. of cēosan.

cȳswucu f. *the last week in which cheese was allowed to be eaten before Lent*, Mt(B)5⁴³ n.

cȳswyrhte f. *(female) cheese-maker*, LL 451,16.

cȳta m. '*kite*,' *bittern*, Cp.

cȳte (ē) f. *cottage, hut, cabin, Æ : cell, cubicle, Æ.*

cytel=citel; **cytere**=citere

cytwer m. *weir for catching fish*, KC3·450.

cȳð=(1) cȳðð, (2) cīð

±**cȳðan** *to proclaim, utter, make known, show forth, tell, relate,* Cp,Cr,HR,Jn; CP : *prove, show, testify, confess,* Mt,VPs : *become known : exercise, perform, practise,* B : (+) *confirm,* LL : (+) *make celebrated.* wundor c. *perform a miracle.* ['*kithe*'; '*y-kid*']

+**cȳðednes** f. *testimony,* LPs 121⁴.

cȳðere m. *witness, martyr,* Æ.

cȳðig *known* : (+) *knowing, aware of,* DR.

cȳðing f. *statement, narration,* GD 86¹⁴.

±**cȳðlǣcan** *to become known,* GL.

cȳðing=cȳðing

±**cȳðnes** f. *testimony : testament* (often of Old and New Test.), Æ : *knowledge, acquaintance.*

cȳðð, cȳððu f. *kinship, relationship :* '*kith,*' *kinsfolk, fellow-countrymen, neighbours,* Lk : *acquaintance, friendship :* (±) *native land, home,* Bo; AO,CP : *knowledge, familiarity,* Æ,BH.

cywes-=cyfes-

cȳwð pres. 3 sg. of cēowan.

cȳwung=cēowung

D

dā f. '*doe*' (*female deer*), ÆGr; WW 320³⁵.

dǣd I. (ē) f. (nap. dǣda, dǣde) '*deed,*' *action, transaction, event,* Æ,B,Bl,VPs. II.=dēad

dǣdbana m. *murderer,* LL 266,23.

dǣdbēta m. *a penitent,* Æ.

dǣdbētan *to atone for, make amends, be penitent, repent,* Æ. [dǣdbōt]

dǣdbētere m. *a penitent,* CHRD 80²⁴.

dǣdbōt f. *amends, atonement, repentance, penitence,* Mt; AO. ['*deedbote*']

dǣdbōtlihting f. *mitigation of penance,* LL (288').

dǣdbōtnes f. *penitence,* Sc 41⁴.

dǣdcēne *bold in deed,* B 1645.

dǣdfrom *energetic,* PPs 109⁸.

dǣdfruma† m. *doer of deeds (good or bad), worker.*

dǣdhata m. *ravager,* B 275.

dǣdhwæt† *energetic, bold.*

dǣdlata m. *sluggard,* OET 152⁸.

dǣdlēan n. *recompense,* Ex 263.

dǣdlic *active,* ÆGr.

dǣdon=dydon pret. pl. of dōn.

dǣdrōf† *bold in deeds, valiant.*

dǣdscūa (CR 257)=dēaðscūa?

dǣdweorc n. *mighty work,* Ex 575.

dæf-=daf-

±**dæftan** *to put in order, arrange,* Æ,CP.

+**dæfte** *mild, gentle, meek,* Mt. ['*daft*']

+**dæftelīce,** +dæftlīce *fitly, in season, in moderation, gently,* CP.

+**dæftu** f. *gentleness,* GD 202¹².

dæg m. gs. dæges; nap. dagas '*day*,*' *lifetime,* Æ,Mt,Mk; AO,CP : *Last Day, Bl* : *name of the rune for* d. andlangne d. *all day long.* dæges, *or on* d. *by day.* tō d., tō dæge *to-day.* d. ǣr *the day before.* sume dæge *one day.* ofer midne d. *afternoon.* on his dæge *in his time.* dæges and nihtes *by day and by night.* lange on d. *far on, late in the day.* emnihtes d. *equinox.* ealle dagas *always,* Mt.

dægcandel (o²)† f. *sun.*

dægcūð *open, clear as the day,* DD 40.

dǣge f. (*female*) *bread maker,* WW 277². ['*dey*']

dæge-=dæg-

dægehwelc *daily,* DR 90'.

dægenlic *of this day,* A 17·121.

dæges adv. v. dæg.

dæges-ēage, -ēge n. '*daisy,*' *Lcd,WW.*

+**dægeð** pres. 3 sg. *dares? braves?* W 220²⁸.

dægfæsten n. *a day's fast,* LCD,LL.

dægfeorm f. *day's provision,* EC 226².

dæghlūttre adv. *clearly, as day,* GU 665.

dæghryne=dægryne

dæghwām (ǣ²) adv. *daily,* GU,LCD.

dæghwāmlic (ǣ²) *of day, daily,* Æ. adv. -līce, Æ,AO.

dæghwīl f. (pl.) *days, lifetime,* B 2726.

dæghwonlīce=dæghwāmlīce

dæglang (o²) *lasting a day,* SOL 501.

dæglanges adv. *during a day,* Æ.

dæglic=dæghwāmlic

dægmǣl nm. *horologe, dial,* BF,LCD.

dægmǣlspīlu f. *gnomon of a dial,* WW 126³¹.

dægmēlscēawere m. *astrologer,* WW.

dægmete m. *breakfast, dinner,* WW 267¹³.

dǣgol=dīegol

dæg-rēd (or ? dægred) (Æ,CP), -rǣd n. *day-break, dawn,* Lk. ['*dayred*']

dægrēdlēoma m. *light of dawn,* NC 280.

dægrēdlic *belonging to morning, early,* WW.

dægrēdoffrung f. *morning sacrifice,* ExC 29⁴¹.

dægrēdsang m. *matins,* RB,CM.

dægrēdwōma† m. *dawn.*

dægrīm† n. *number of days.*

dægrima m. *dawn, daybreak, morning,* Æ. ['*dayrim*']

dægryne *daily, of a day,* WW 224²⁹.

dægsang m. *daily service,* W 290²².

dægsceald m? (*shield by day?*) *sun,* Ex 79.

dægsteorra m. '*daystar,*' *morning star,* Æ, Lcd.

dægswǣsendo np. *a day's food,* LL (220 n3).

dægtīd f. *day-time, time, period.* on dægtīdum *at times,* RD.

dægtīma m. *day-time, day*, LPs 120⁶.
dægðerlic *of the day, of to-day, daily, present,* Æ.
dægðern f. *interval of a day,* LCD.
dægðerne adj. *for use by day, every-day,* CM.
dægwæccan fp. *day-watches,* WW 110²⁴.
dægweard m. *day-watchman,* WW 110²⁵.
dægweorc n. *work of a day, fixed or stated service, Ex* : *day-time.* ['*daywork*']
dægweorðung f. *feast-day,* EL 1234.
dægwilla *wished for day,* GEN 2776.
dægwine n? *day's pay,* GL.
dægwist f. *food, meal,* Æ,RB.
dægwōma (EX,GU)=dægrēdwōma
dæl I. nap. dalu n. '*dale,' valley, gorge, abyss, AO* : *hole pit, Gl* (v.GBG). **II.** pret. 3 sg. of delan.
dæl (ā) m. (p. dæl-as, -e) *portion, part, share, lot, Cp,Bl,Bo,G,VPs*; AO,CP : *division, separation, Æ* : *quantity, amount, Lcd* : *region, district,* AO : *part of speech, word,* ÆGR. d. wintra *a good number of years.* be dæle *in part, partly.* be healfum dæle *by half.* be ænigum dæle *at all, to any extent.* be ðæm dæle *to that extent.* cyðan be dæle *to make a partial or 'ex parte' statement.* sume dæle, be sumum dæle *partly.* ['*deal*']
±**dælan** *to divide, part, separate, share, Da;* Æ,CP : *bestow, distribute, dispense, spend, hand over to, An,Mk* : *take part in, share with, Gen* : *be divided* : *diffuse* : *utter.* †hilde, earfoðe dælan *to fight, contend, Ma.* ['*deal*']
+**dæledlīce** *separately,* WW 487¹⁹.
dælend m. *divider,* Lk 12⁴.
dælere m. *divider, distributor, WW* : *agent, negotiator, Æ* : *almsgiver,* Æ. ['*dealer*']
dæling f. *dividing, sharing,* HGL 423.
+**dælland**=+dælland
dællēas *deficient, unskilled, WW* : *destitute of, without,* W.
dælmælum adv. *by parts or pieces,* ÆGR, LCD.
dæl-neom-, -nym-=**dælnim-**
dælnes f. *breaking (of bread),* LkL p11¹¹.
dælnimend m. *sharer, participator, VPs;* Æ : *participle,* ÆGR. [v. '*deal*']
dælnimendnes f. *participation,* BJPs 121³.
dælnimung f. *participation, portion, share,* Ps,RBL.
dælnumelnes=dælnimendnes
dæm-, dæn-=**dēm-, den-;** **dæp**=dēop
dære v. daru; **dæred** (S²Ps 62⁷)=dægrēd; **dærne**=dierne
dærst, dærste, dræst (e¹) f. *leaven,* NG,DR : (pl.) *dregs, refuse, Lcd,Ps.* ['*drast*']
+**dærsted** *leavened, fermented,* NG.

dæð, dæwig=dēað, dēawig
+**dafen** I. n. *what is fitting,* GD 84⁶. **II.** *becoming, suitable, fit, proper.*
+**dafenian** (often impers.) *to beseem, befit, be right,* Æ.
+**dafenlic** *fit, becoming, proper, suitable, right.* adv. -līce.
±**dafenlicnes** f. *fit time, opportunity,* Æ.
+**daflic**=+dafenlic; **dafn-**=dafen-
+**dafniendlic**=+dafenlic
dāg m? (dāh) '*dough,' Lcd* : *mass of metal.*
dagas, dages v. dæg.
dagian *to dawn, be day, BH*; Æ. ['*daw*']
dagung f. *daybreak, dawn, BH.* on dagunge *at daybreak.* ['*dawing*']
dāh, dāl=dāg, dæl
+**dāl** n. *division, separation, sharing, giving out, CP* : *distinction, difference* : *destruction* : *share, lot,* GD 311¹¹.
+**dālan** (VH 10)=+dælan
dalc m. *bracelet, brooch,* GL.
dalf (NG)=dealf pret. 3 sg. of delfan.
dalisc (? for *dedalisc) '*dedaleus,'* WW 221³.
+**dālland** n. *land under joint ownership, common land divided into strips.* v. LL 2·443.
dālmæd f. *meadow-land held in common and apportioned between the holders,* KC 3·260³.
dalmatice? f. *dalmatic (vestment),* GD 329²⁴.
dalu v. dæl; **dara**ð, **dareð**=daroð
darian *to lurk, be hidden,* ÆL 23³²².
daroð† m. *dart, spear, javelin.* daroða lāf *those left by spears, survivors of a battle.*
daroðhæbbende *spear-bearing,* JUL 68.
daroðlācende† (eð) mp. *spear-warriors.*
daroðsceaft (deoreð-) m. *javelin-shaft,* GEN 1984.
daru f. gds. dære *injury, hurt, damage, calamity,* Æ.
datārum m. (indecl.) *date,* BF 46.
dað '*bloma,' mass of metal,* WW 141³⁶.
Davīdlic (DHy).
Davītic adj. *of David,* LCD 3·428¹⁷.
dēacon=dīacon
dēad (±) '*dead,' Æ,B,Mt;* AO,CP : *torpid, dull* : *still, standing (of water).* d. blōd *congealed blood.*
dēad-=dēað-
dēadboren *still-born,* LCD 1·206⁶.
±**dēadian** *to die, JnL.* ['*dead*']
dēadlic *subject to death, mortal, perishable, Æ* : *causing death, 'deadly,' fatal, AO* : *about to die.* adv. -līce.
dēadrægel n. *shroud,* WW 37⁶. [hrægl]
dēadspring m. *ulcer,* LCD.
dēadwylle *barren,* AO 26¹⁶.
dēat I. '*deaf,' Mt,Jul;* VPs : *empty, barren,* CP 411²⁰. **II.** pret. 3 sg. of dūfan.

-dēafian v. ā-d.; dēaflīc=dēfelic
dēafu f. deafness, LCD.
deag=dæg
dēag I. hue, tinge, Æ,WW : 'dye,' WW.
II. pres. 3 sg. of dugan.
dēagel=dī(e)gol
dēaggede gouty, WW 161³¹. [dēaw]
±dēagian to 'dye,' OEG.
dēagol=dīegol
dēagung f. 'dyeing,' colouring, Æ.
dēagwyrmede gouty, WW 161³¹. [dēaw]
dēah=dēag I. and II.
dēahl, deal=dīegol, deall
dealf pret. 3 sg. of delfan.
deall† proud, exulting, bold, renowned.
dēap-=dēop-
dear pres. 3 sg. of *durran.
dearc, dearcð=deorc, daroð
dearf I. pret. 3 sg. of deorfan. II. bold,
NG.
dearflic bold, presumptuous, NG.
dearfscipe m. boldness, presumption, NG.
dearn-unga, -unge (e², i²) secretly, privately,
insidiously, Æ,AO,CP.
dearoð=daroð
dearr pres. 3 sg. of *durran.
dearste (VPs)=dærste
dēað (ēo) m. 'death,' dying, An,Bo,G; CP :
cause of death, Bl : in pl. 'manes,' ghosts.
dēað-=dēad- (v. ES 39·324).
dēaðbǣre deadly, CP.
dēaðbǣrlic (dēad-) deadly, Mk 16¹⁸.
dēaðbǣrnes (ē²) f. deadliness, destructive-
ness, LkL,OEG.
dēaðbēacnigende boding death, DD,W.
dēaðbēam m. death-bringing tree, GEN 638.
dēaðbedd† n. bed of death, grave, B.
['death-bed']
dēaðberende fatal, deadly, CP.
dēaðcwalu† f. deadly throe, agony, EL: death
by violence, B.
dēaðcwealm m. death by violence, B 1670.
dēaðcwylmende killed, LPs 78¹¹.
dēaðdæg† m. 'death-day,' OET; VH.
dēaðdenu† f. valley of death.
dēaðdrepe m. death-blow, Ex 495.
dēaðfǣge doomed to death, B 850.
dēaðfiren f. deadly sin, CR 1207.
dēaðgedāl n. separation of body and soul by
death, GU 936.
dēaðgodas mp. infernal deities, WW 447¹⁹.
+dēaðian to kill, DR 48⁷.
dēaðlēg m. deadly flame, GR 983.
dēaðlic 'deathly,' mortal, Bl : deadly : dead.
dēaðlicnes f. mortal state : deadliness,
liability to death, BL.
dēaðmægen n. deadly band, GU 867.
dēaðrǣced (=e²) n. sepulchre, PH 48.
dēaðrǣs m. sudden death, AN 997.

dēaðrēaf n. clothing taken from the dead,
spoils, WW 397²².
dēaðrēow murderous, fierce, AN 1316.
dēað-scūa, -scufa m. death-shadow, spirit of
death, devil.
dēaðscyld f. crime worthy of death, LL 130'.
dēaðscyldig (LL), dēadsynnig (NG) condemned to death.
dēaðsele† m. death-hall, hell.
dēaðslege m. death-stroke, RD 6¹⁴.
dēaðspere n. deadly spear, RD 4⁵³.
dēaðstede m. place of death, Ex 589.
dēaðsynnignes f. guiltiness of death, DR
42'.
dēaððēnung f. exequies, last offices to the
dead, funeral, NC,WW.
dēaðwang m. plain of death, AN 1005.
dēaðwēge n. deadly cup, GU 964. [wǣge]
dēaðwērig dead, B 2125.
dēaðwīc n. dwelling of death, B 1275.
dēaðwyrd f. fate, death, WW 408²³.
dēaw mn. 'dew,' Æ,Cp,VPs.
+dēaw dewy, bedewed, LCD 10a, 35a.
dēawdrīas m. fall of dew? DA 277. [drēosan]
dēawig (ǣ, ē) 'dewy,' Ex : moist, Lcd.
dēawigendlic? dewy, HGL 408.
dēawigfeðera† dewy-feathered.
dēawung f. dew, EHy 7⁶⁴.
dēawwyrm m. 'dew-worm,' ring-worm,
tetter, Lcd.
decan m. one who has charge of ten monks,
RB 125n.
±dēcan to smear, plaster, Æ, Lcd. ['deche']
decanhād m. office of a 'decan,' RBL 54³.
decanon=decan
December m. g. -bris December, MEN.
declīnian to decline, ÆGR 88,100.
declīnigendlic subject to inflection, ÆGR 88.
declīnung f. declension, BF 94¹⁶.
dēd I. (A)=dǣd. II.=dēad
dēde (KGL)=dyde pret. 3 sg. of dōn.
+dēfe (doefe once, in NG) befitting, suitable,
proper : meek, gentle, kindly, good. also
adv.
+dēf-elic, -edlic fit, becoming, proper. adv.
-līce, BH.
defen-=dafen-; dēflic=dēfelic
+dēfnes f. mildness, gentleness, LPs 89¹⁰.
+deftlīce=+dæftlīce; deg=dæg
dēg (NG)=dēag pres. 3 sg. of dugan.
dēg-=dēag-, dīeg-, dīg-; degn=ðegn
dehter ds. of dohtor.
dehtnung (KGL)=dihtnung; del=dæl
dela nap. of delu.
dēlan=dǣlan
+delf† n. digging, excavation, Æ,AO : what is
dug, trench, quarry, canal, Mdf.
delfan³ to 'delve,' dig, dig out, burrow, Æ,
Bo,G,VPs; AO : bury.

delfere m. *digger*, Bo 140[13].
delfîn *dolphin*, WW 293[13]. [*L.*]
delfîsen n. *spade*, WW.
delfung f. *digging*, WW 149[10].
+delgian=+telgian
dell nm. *dell, hollow, dale*, BH; Mdf.
delu f. *teat, nipple*, CP 405[1]. [*OHG.* tili]
dem=demm
dēma m. *judge, ruler*, Æ,CP.
±dēman *to judge, determine, decide, decree, sentence, condemn, BH,Cra,El,G,VPs*; CP : *assign* : '*deem*' ('*i-deme*'), *consider, think, estimate, compute, Æ,BH,Cp* : (†) *praise, glorify* : (†) *tell, declare, FAp*.
dēmedlic *that may be judged*, GD 336[20].
dēmend† m. *judge, arbiter*.
dēmere m. *judge, MtL* (oe). ['*deemer*']
demm m. *damage, injury, loss, misfortune*, AO,CP.
-demman v. for-d.
dēmon *demon, devil*, DR.
den=denn, denu; dēn=dōn pp. of dōn.
Denalagu, f. *the '* *Dane law,' law for the part of England occupied by the Danes*, LL.
den-bǣr f., -berende n. *swine-pasture*, Mdf.
dene=denu
Dene mp. *the 'Danes,' Chr*; AO.
deneland (æ) *valley*, LPs 59[8].
Denemearc (æ[1], a[2], e[3]), Denmearce f. *Denmark*.
dengan (ncg) *to beat, strike*, CHRD 60[30].
denge=dyncge
Denisc '*Danish,' Chr*. wk. nap. ðā Deniscan *the Danes*.
denn n. '*den,' lair, cave, B,WW*; Æ : *swine-pasture*. v. Mdf.
dennian *to stream?* BR 12 (v. ANS 118·385).
denstōw f. *place of pasture*, BC 3·144[21]
denu f. I. *valley, dale, Æ,Lk,VPs*; Mdf. ['*dean*'] II. (MFH 108)=denn
dēof=dēaf pret. 3 sg. of dūfan.
dēofel-, dēofl-=dēofol-
deofenian=dafenian
dēofol mn. gs. dēofles, nap. dēoflu, dēofol *a 'devil,' demon, false god, B,Cr,G,VPs*; AO : *the devil, Cp,G,Jul,Sol,VHy*; Æ: *diabolical person, JnLR*. [*L.* diabolus]
dēofolcrǣft m. *witchcraft*, AO,BH.
dēofolcund *fiendish*, JUD 61.
dēofolcynn n. *species of devil*, RWH 105[21].
dēofoldǣd f. *fiendish deed*, DA 18.
dēofol-gield (AO,CP), -gild, -geld (AO,VHy), -gyld (Æ) n. *devil-worship, idolatry* : *idol, image of the devil*, Æ.
dēofolgielda (y[3]) m. *devil-worshipper, idolater*, ÆH 1·70'.
dēofolgieldhūs n. *idol-temple*, AO 284[9].
dēofolgītsung (dīwl-) f. *unrighteous mammon*, LkL 16[11].

dēofollic *devilish, diabolical, of the devil*, Æ. ['*devilly*'] adv. -līce.
dēofolscīn n. *evil spirit, demon, Sc*. ['*devil-shine*']
dēofolscīpe m. *idolatry*, NC 286.
dēofolsēoc *possessed by devils, lunatic*, Æ.
dēofolsēocnes f. *demoniacal possession*, G.
dēofolwītga m. *wizard, magician*, DA 128.
dēoful=dēofol
dēog pret. 3 sg. of dēagan (MLR 24·62).
dēohl, dēogol=dīegol
±dēon *to suck*, LG (JAW 19).
dēop I. '*DEEP,' profound* : *awful, mysterious, CP* : (†) *heinous* : *serious, solemn, earnest*. d. cēap *high price, great price*. II. n. *deepness, depth, abyss, Ex,Mt* : *the '* *deep,' sea, Lk*.
dēope adv. *deeply, thoroughly, entirely, earnestly, solemnly, Ps*. ['*deep*']
dēophycgende† dēophȳdig† *deeply meditating, pensive*.
±dēopian (ēa) *to get deep*, DR 81[24],LCD 125b.
dēoplic *deep, profound, thorough, fundamental, Æ,CP* : *grievous*. adv. -līce '*deeply,' Bo,WW* : *ingeniously*, BF 64, 70.
dēopnes f. *depth, abyss, LPs,Nic* : *profundity, mystery, Hy*; Æ : *subtlety, cunning, W*. ['*deepness*']
dēopþancol *contemplative, very thoughtful*, BF 164[28]; W 248[7]. adv. -līce.
dēor I. n. *animal, beast* (usu. *wild*), *Lk,Met, WW*; Æ,CP : '*deer,' reindeer*, AO. II. *brave, bold, An,Sal,Seaf,Sol* : *ferocious, B* : *grievous, severe, violent, Da,Sol*. ['*dear*'] III.=dēore
±dēoran (ȳ)† *to hold dear, glorify, endear*.
dēorboren *of noble birth*, LL 104,34[1].
deorc '*dark,' obscure, gloomy, B,Ps* : *sad, cheerless, Wa* : *sinister, wicked, Lk,Sat*. adv. deorce.
deorcegrǣg *dark grey*, WW.
deorcful *dark, gloomy, Sc*. ['*darkful*']
deorcian *to grow dim*, LPs.
deorclīce '*darkly,' horribly, foully*, GPH 391[22].
deorcnes f. '*darkness,' Sc* 228[3].
deorcung f. *gloaming, twilight, WW*; Æ. [v. '*dark*' vb.]
dēorcynn n. *race of animals*, Bo.
dēore I. '*dear,' beloved, G,Jul* : *precious, costly, valuable, AO,Bo* : *noble, excellent, Ps,Rd*. II. adv. *dearly, at great cost, Met, WW*. III. adv. *fiercely, cruelly*. [dēor II.]
dēoren *of a wild animal*, GL.
deoreðsceaft=daroðsceaft
±deorf n. *labour, WW* 91 : *difficulty, hardship, trouble, danger*, Æ. ['*derf*']

dēorfald m. *enclosure for wild beasts*, WW 201³⁴.

±deorfan⁰ *to exert oneself, labour*, Æ : *be in peril, perish, be wrecked*, AO. ['*derve*']

dēorfellen *made of hides*, WW328¹⁸.

+deorflēas *free from trouble*, GL.

+deorfnes f. *trouble, tribulation*, LPs45².

dēorfrið n. *preservation of game*, Chr 1086. [v. '*frith*']

+deorfsum (y¹) *troublesome, grievous*, CHR 1103; 1005.

dēorgēat n. *gate for animals*, Ct.

dēorhege m. *deer-fence*, LL.

deorian (CHR)=derian

dēorlic *brave, renowned*, B585.

dēorlīce '*dearly*,' *preciously, richly*, El : *sincerely, acceptably*, AS4¹⁹ (or ? dēoplīce).

dēorling (ī, ȳ) m. '*darling*,' *favourite, minion*, Æ,Bo,CP : *household god.*

dēormōd† *courageous, bold.*

dēornett n. *hunting-net*, WW183¹².

deornunga=dearnunga

deorsterlīce=dyrstiglīce

dēortūn m. *park*, GL.

dēor-wierðe (CP), -wurðe (Æ), -wyrðe *precious, dear, costly*, Bl,Bo. ['*dearworth*']

dēorwyrðlic (eo², u²) *precious, valuable.* adv. -līce *splendidly*, Æ : *as a thing of value*, Æ.

dēorwyrðnes (u²) f. *treasure*, Bo : *honour, veneration*, RWH139¹⁸ ['*dearworthness*']

dēoð (NG)=dēað; dēpan=dȳpan

dēpe=dēop; deppan=dyppan; dēr=dēor

Dēra, Dēre mp. *Deirans, inhabitants of Deira.*

+derednes f. *injury*, LCD 1·322¹.

derian (w. d.) *to damage, injure, hurt*, Bo, Chr; Æ,AO,CP. ['*dere*']

deriendlic *mischievous, noxious, hurtful*, Æ.

dērling (NG)=dēorling

derne=dierne

dernunga (NG)=dearnunga

derodine m. *scarlet dye*, CP83²⁵.

derste (VPs)=dærste

derung f. *injury*, GD.

desig=dysig; dēst v. dōn.

dēð I. 3 p. sg. pres. of dōn. II. '*manipulus*,' *sheaf?* EPs125⁶.

+dēðan (=īe) *to kill*, NG : *mortify*, DR.

dēðing f. *putting to death*, DR72¹³.

deððan? *to suck*, LkR11²⁷.

dēwig=dēawig

dīacon (ǣ) m. '*deacon*,' *minister, Levite*, Æ,BH,Jn. [L. diaconus]

dīacongegyrela m. *deacon's robe*, BH90².

dīaconhād m. *office of a deacon*, ÆH.

dīaconrocc m. *dalmatic*, CM723.

dīaconðēnung f. *office of a deacon*, BH 272¹⁷.

dīan (A)=dēon

dīc mf. '*dike*,' *trench, ditch, moat*, AO,BH, Chr,Ct; Æ; Mdf : *an earthwork with a trench.*

+dīcan=+dīcian

dīcere m. *digger*, WW149¹⁶. ['*diker*']

±dīcian *to make a dike or bank*, BH. ['*dike*']

dīcsceard n. *breach of a dike*, LL455,13. [v. '*shard*']

dīcung f. *construction of a dike*, WW. ['*diking*']

dīcwalu f. *bank of a ditch?* KC5·334'.

dide, didon=dyde, dydon (v. dōn).

dīegan *to die*, NR38.

dīegel=dīegol

±dīeglan, -lian *to hide, cover, conceal, hide oneself*, CP.

dīegle=dīegol

dīegol (ǣ, ē, ēa, ēo, ī, ȳ) I.adj. *secret, hidden, obscure, unknown, deep*, B,DD. ['*dighel*'] II. n. *concealment, obscurity, secrecy, mystery* : *hidden place, grave.*

dīegolful (ē¹) *mysterious*, RD80¹⁴.

±dīegollīce (ē, ēa, ēo, ī, ȳ) *secretly*, AO,CP : *softly (of the voice)*, ÆP28.

dīegolnes f. (ē, ī, īo, ȳ) *privacy, secrecy, solitude*, CP : *secret, secret thought, mystery*, Æ,AO,CP : *hiding-place, recess*, Æ.

dīelf=dealf pret. 3 sg. of delfan.

dīelgian=dīlegian

dīend m. *suckling*, NG. [dēon]

dīere (ȳ) '*dear*,' *beloved*, Lk : *precious, costly*, AO : *noble, excellent.*

±diernan (e, y) *to keep secret, hide, restrain, repress*, Æ,AO : *hide oneself*. ['*dern*']

dierne (æ, e, y) I. *hidden, secret, obscure, remote*, B,El,Lk,Ps; CP : *deceitful, evil, magical*, B,CP,Gen. ['*dern*'] For comps. v. dyrne-. II. (y) n. *secret*, GnE. ['*dern*']

dīerra comp. of dīere, dēore.

dīgan=dēagian

+dīgan (ē, ȳ;=īe) *to endure, survive, overcome* : *escape* : *profit*, LCD.

dīgel=dīegol (wk. dīgla, dīgle).

dīgl-, dīhl-=dīegl-, dīegol-

digner=dīnor

dīgol, dīgul=dīegol

dihnian=dihtian

diht n. *arrangement, disposal, deliberation, purpose*, Æ : *administration, office* : *direction, command, prescription*, Æ : *conduct*, Æ : (+) *piece of writing, composition, literary work.*

±dihtan, dihtian *to arrange, dispose, appoint, direct, dictate, impose*, Æ,G : *compose, write*, Æ : *make, do.* ['*dight*']

dihtere m. *informant, expositor*, WW : *steward*, Æ (=dihtnere) : *one who dictates*, Guth. ['*dighter*'] dihtfæstendæg m. *appointed fast*, Swt (? for riht-).

dihtig=dyhtig

dihtnere m. *manager, steward*, ÆH2·344⁵.

dihtnian=dihtian

±diht-nung, -ung f. *ordering, disposition.*

dile m. '*dill*,' *anise, Gl,Mt,Lcd*; CP.

±dīlegian *to destroy, blot out, CP* : *perish,* LL. ['*dilghe*']

dīlemengan v. for-d.

dilfō pres. 3 sg. of delfan.

dīlgian (CP)=dīlegian

dīlignes f. *annihilation, destruction*, GL.

dill, dim=dile, dimm

dimhīw *of dark colour*, DD106.

dim-hof n., -hofe f. *place of concealment*, Æ.

dimhūs n. *prison*, OEG.

dimlic (y) *dim, obscure, secret, hidden*, Æ.

dimm '*dim*,' *dark, gloomy, obscure, Bo,Gen, Sat* : *blurred, faint, MH* : *wicked* : *wretched, grievous.*

dimmian *to be or become dim*, LCD.

dimnes (y) f. '*dimness*,' *darkness, obscurity, gloom, Lcd,VPs*; Æ : *evil* : *obscuration, moral obliquity*, LL476,14 : *a dark place.*

dimscūa m. *darkness, sin?* AN141.

dincge=dyncge; dīner=dīnor

ding I. v. dung I. II.=dung II.

dinglung f. *manuring*, WW104⁸. [v. '*dung*']

dinig? (A8·450)=dung

dīnor m. *a piece of money*,ÆGR.[*L.*denarius]

dīo-=dēo-; dīowl- (NG)=dēofol-

dippan=dyppan

dirige *dirge*, '*vigilia*,' CM433,444.

dīrling (CP)=dēorling

dirn-=diern-, dyrn-; dis-=dys-

disc m. '*dish*,' *plate, bowl, Gl,Mt.*

discberend m. *dish-bearer, seneschal*, WW.

discipul m. '*disciple*,' *scholar, BH,MtL.*

discipula *female disciple*, BH236³⁴.

discipulhād m. '*disciplehood*,' *BH*362.

disc-ōegn, -ōen m. *dish-servant, waiter, seneschal, steward*, Æ.

disg, disig=dysig

dism (ōism) m. '*vapor*,' '*fumus*,' ES41·324.

disma m., disme f. *musk*, OEG46⁴ (A30·123) : '*cassia*,' Ps44⁹ (y).

distæf m. '*distaff*,' *WW*; Æ.

dīō-=dēō-

dīwl-=dēofol; dob-=dof-, dop-

dix (LL455)=disc

dōc m. *bastard son*, WW.

docce f. '*dock*,' *sorrel, Lcd.*

docga m. '*dog*,' *GPH*.

dōcincel n. *bastard*, GL.

dōefe v. +dēfe.

doeg, doema (NG)=dæg, dēma

dōere m. *doer, worker*, DR198⁶.

doeō-=dēaō-

dofen pp. of dūfan.

dofian (dobian) *to be doting*, GL.

dofung f. *stupidity, frenzy, madness*, GL (?+at OEG418).

dōger=dōgor; dogga=docga

dogian *to endure?* RD1⁹.

dōgor mn. (ds. dōgor(e)) *day*, AO,CP.

dōgor-gerīm, -rīm† n. *series of days, time, allotted time of life.*

dōh=dāg; dohtar, dohter=dohtor

dohte pret. 3 sg. of dugan.

dohtig *competent, good, valiant*, '*doughty*,' *Chr.* [dugan]

dohtor f. gs. dohtor, ds. dohtor, dehter, nap. ±doh-tor, -tra, -tru '*daughter*,' *Mt*; Æ,AO,CP : *female descendant, Jn.*

dohtorsunu m. *daughter's son, grandson*, CHR982c.

dohx=dox

dol I. adj. *foolish, silly, Seaf*; CP : *presumptuous.* [v. '*dull*'] II. n. *folly*, CP.

dolc=dalc; dolcswaōu=dolgswaōu

dolfen pp. of delfan.

dolg (dolh) nm. *wound, scar, cut, sore* : *boil, tumour*, Æ.

dolgbenn f. *wound*, AN1399.

dolgbōt f. *fine or compensation for wounding*, LL62,23².

±dolgian *to wound*, RD.

dolgilp m. *idle boasting*, B509.

dolgrūne f. *pellitory*, LCD25a.

dolgsealf f. *poultice for a wound*, LCD.

dolgslege† m. *wounding blow*, AN.

dolgswæō n., dolgswaōu f. *scar*, Æ.

dolh=dolg

dolhdrenc m. *drink for a wound, antidote*,LCD.

dolhsmeltas mp. *linen bandages*, WW107³³.

dolhwund *wounded*, JUD107.

dol-lic *audacious, rash, foolhardy, foolish.* adv. -līce, CP : *bewildered*, BF144¹.

dolmanus=dulmunus

dolsceaōa m. *fell destroyer*, B479.

dolscipe m. *folly, error*, CP387³⁴.

dolsmeltas=dolhsmeltas

dolsprēc f. *silly talk*, CP385⁶.

dolwillen I. *rash, bold*, JUL451. II. n. *rashness, madness*, JUL202.

dolwīte n. *pain of a wound?* (BTs), *punishment of the wicked, pains of hell?* (Tupper), RD27¹⁷.

dōm m. '*doom*,' *judgment, ordeal, sentence, BH,JnL*; Æ,CP : *decree, law, ordinance, custom, Æ,VPs* : *justice, equity, Mt,VPs* : *opinion, advice* : *choice, option, free-will* : *condition* : *authority, supremacy, majesty, power, might, Jn*; AO : *reputation, dignity, glory, honour, splendour*, AO : *court, tribunal, assembly* : *meaning, interpretation.*

-**dōm** masc. abstract suffix=*state, condition, power, etc.*, as in frēodōm.

dōmærn n. *judgment-hall, tribunal*, Æ.

dōmbōc f. *code of laws, statute-book, manual of justice*, Æ,LL. ['*doombook*']

dōmdæg m. '*doomsday,' judgment-day, Mt.*

dōmēadig† *mighty, renowned.*

dōmere m. *judge, Bo,LL;* CP. ['*doomer*']

dōmern (Æ)=dōmærn

dōmfæst† *just, renowned, mighty.*

dōmfæstnes f. *righteous judgment,* LPs 100[1].

dōmgeorn† *ambitious : righteous.*

dōmhūs n. *law-court, tribunal,* GL.

dōmhwæt adj. *eager for renown? strenuous in judgment?* CR 428.

dōmian† *to glorify, magnify,* DA.

dōmisc adj. *of the day of judgment,* SOL 148'.

dōmlēas† *inglorious, powerless.*

dōmlic *famous, glorious, praiseworthy : judicial,* Æ : *canonical,* CM 268. adv. -līce.

domne mf. *lord,* CHR : *nun, abbess.* [*L.*]

dōmsetl n. *judgment-seat, tribunal,* Æ.

dōmsettend m. *jurisconsult,* WW 429[6].

dōmstōw f. *tribunal,* W 148[31].

dōmweorðung† f. *honour, glory.*

±**dōn** anv. pres. ptc. dō(e)nde, pres. 2 sing. dēst, 3 dēð, pret. sg. dyde, pl. dydon (æ,i), pp. dōn *to* 'DO*' ('*i-do*'), *make, act, perform:cause* (often followed by the inf. with a passive sense—as in hig dydon rīcu settan *they caused kingdoms to be founded,* i.e. *they founded kingdoms*—or by ðæt) : *add (to) : put, place, take (from, to or away) : give, bestow, confer : consider, esteem : observe, keep:* to avoid repetition of another verb, Æ : (+) *arrive at,* CHR : (+) *halt, encamp, cast anchor,* CHR : (+) *reduce,* CHR. d. tō hīerran hāde *promote, advance to a higher position.* d. tō nāhte *annul, make of none effect.* d. tō witanne *cause to know.* betre, furðor, d. *prefer.* +d. forð *manifest, show forth.* d. ūp *put ashore.* +d. ūp *exhume.*

dōnlic *active,* RBL.

dop-ened, -ænid f. *diver, water-fowl, moorhen, coot,* GL.

dopfugel m. *water-fowl, moorhen,* GL.

-**doppa** v. dūfe-d.; -**doppe** v. fugol-d.

doppettan *to plunge in, immerse,* Æ.

dor n. (nap. doru, dor) *door, gate : pass, Lcd, Ps.* [v. '*door*']

dora m. *humble-bee, Ep,Lcd,WW;* Æ. ['*dor*']

dorfen pp. of deorfan.

dorste (Æ,AO,CP) pret. 3 sg. of *durran.

dorweard m. *doorkeeper,* DR,MkRL.

dott m. *head of a boil, Lcd.* ['*dot*']

-**dōung** v. on-d.

dox *dark-haired, dusky, A,WW.* ['*dusk*']

doxian *to turn dark, VH* (v. ES 43·330). ['*dusk*']

draca m. *dragon, sea-monster, B,MH,Ps : serpent, Pa,Ps : the devil : standard representing a dragon or serpent,* GPH 392. ['*drake*']

drā-centse, -cente, -conze f. *dragon-wort,* LCD. [*L.* dracontea]

dræce (N)=draca

drǣdan[7] *to dread, fear,* Sc 67[1].

drǣf=drāf; **drǣf-**=drēf-

±**drǣfan** *to drive, drive out,* CHR.

drǣfend I. m. *hunter,* CRA 38. II.=drēfend

+**dræg**† n. *concourse, assembly : tumult.*

dræge f. *drag-net,* WW. [drāgan]

drægeð pres. 3 sg. of dragan.

drægnett n. *drag-net, WW.* ['*draynet*']

dræhð, drægð pres. 3 sg. of dragan.

drǣn, drænc=drān, drinc

dræp pret. 3 sg. of drepan.

dræst=dærst

dræstig *full of dregs, rubbishy, WW.* [dærste; '*drasty*']

drǣt pres. 3 sg. of drǣdan.

drāf I. f. *action of driving, Bl : expulsion,* LL : '*drove,' herd, Chr;* Æ : *company, band, W;* Æ : *road along which cattle are driven,* KC 5·217[6]. [drīfan] II. pret. 3 sg. of drīfan.

dragan[6] *to drag, 'draw*,' JnL,CP : go : protract,* CHRD 57[7].

drāgense=drācentse

drān (ǣ) f. '*drone,' WW;* Æ.

dranc pret. 3 sg. of drincan.

drapa—dropa; **drēa**—drȳ

drēag, drēah pret. 3 sg. of drēogan.

+**dreag**=+dræg

drēahnian (ē) *to '*drain,' strain out, Lcd,Mt.*

dreaht pp. of dreccan.

drēam m. *joy, gladness, delight, ecstasy, mirth, rejoicing, Ct,Chr,Sat;* AO : *melody, music, song, singing,* Æ. ['*dream*']

drēamcræft m. *art of music,* Bo 38[7],MH 212[30].

drēamere m. *musician,* Bo 38[7].

drēam-hæbbende (GEN 81), **-healdende** (B 1227) *happy, joyful.*

drēamlēas† *joyless, sad.*

drēamlic *joyous, musical,* GL.

drēamnes f. *singing,* LPs 136[3].

drēap pret. 3 sg. of drēopan.

drēap- (VPs)=drēop-

drēariend *inrushing tide?* WW 225[12].

drēarung=drēorung

drēas pret. 3 sg. of drēosan.

±**dreccan** *to vex, irritate, trouble, torment, oppress, afflict, Æ,Gen,OET.* ['*dretch*']

±**drec(c)ednes** (Æ), **dreccung** (*Sc*) f. *tribulation, affliction.* ['*dretching*']

drēd=dræd pret. 3 sg. of drædan.

±**drēfan** to stir up, excite, disturb, trouble, vex, afflict, B,Jn; Æ,CP. [drōf; 'dreve']

+**drēfedlic** oppressive, AO 38¹⁴.

±**drēfednes** (æ) f. tribulation, trouble, distress, scandal, disorder.

±**drēfend** (æ) m. disturber, LPs,RB.

dreflian to 'drivel,' WW.

+**drēfnes** f. confusion : tempest, OEG.

drēfre m. disturber, RB121¹². [drōf]

drēfung f. disturbance, WW109².

drēge, drēgan=drȳge, drȳgan

drēhnian (Mt)=drēahnian

dreht pp. of dreccan.

+**drehtnes** f. contrition, BH424¹³.

drēm-=drȳm-

drenc m. 'drink,' drinking, draught, Æ,Lcd, WW; CP : drowning. ['drench,' 'drunk']

drencan to give to drink, to ply with drink, make drunk, Ps; CP : soak, saturate : submerge, drown, Æ. ['drench']

drenccuppe f. drinking-cup, WW329¹⁹.

drence-=drenc-, drinc-, drync-

drencflōd† m. flood, deluge.

drenchorn m. drinking-horn, Ct. ['drench']

drenchūs n. drinking-house, WW186²⁵.

dreng m. youth, warrior, Ma149. ['dreng'; ON.]

drēocræft (Bl)=drȳcræft

dreofon=drifon pret. pl. of drīfan.

+**drēog** I. n. a dressing for keeping (shoes) in good condition, Æ : usefulness? gravity? RB123⁶. tō +d. gān to ease oneself, RB 32²². II. fit, sober, serious : tame, gentle (horse), GD78¹².

±**drēogan²** to lead a (certain) life, do, work, perform, fulfil, take part in, conduct, Gu,Ps; AO. wīde d. wander : be busy, employed : experience, suffer, endure, sustain, tolerate, Ex; CP : to enjoy. ['dree,' 'i-dree']

+**drēoglǣcan** to put in order, regulate, arrange, attend to, Æ.

+**drēoglīce** (h) discreetly, carefully : meekly, modestly, humbly.

drēoh=drēog

±**drēopan²** to drop, drip, PPs. ['dreep']

drēopian (ēa) to drop, drip, trickle, Ps.

drēopung (ēa) f. dropping, VV²Ps.

drēor† m. blood. [drēosan]

dreord pret. 3 sg. of drǣdan.

drēorfāh bespattered with gore, B485.

drēorgian=drēorigian

drēorig adj. †bloody, blood-stained, B : cruel, grievous, Gu : sad, sorrowful, Æ : headlong? ['dreary'] adv. -līce sorrowfully, Æ. ['drearily']

drēorigferð sorrowful, CR1109.

drēorighlēor sad of countenance, WA83.

drēorigian to be 'dreary,' sad, Ruin; Æ.

drēorigmōd sad in mind, Gen2804. ['drearymood']

drēorignes f. sadness, sorrow, GD; Æ. ['dreariness']

drēorlic, drēorlic=drēorig

drēorsele m. dreary hall, WIF50.

drēorung† (ēa) f. falling, distilling, dropping. [drēosan]

±**drēosan²** to fall, perish : become weak, fail.

drēosendlic perishable, ByH130⁸.

drep=ðrep?

+**drep** m. stroke, blow, AN1446.

±**drepan⁵** to strike, kill, overcome, B. ['drepe']

drepe† (y) m. stroke, blow, violent death.

+**drettan** to consume, PPs70¹².

drī-=drȳ-

±**drif** f. fever, MkR1³¹; ANS84·324.

+**drīf** I. n. a drive, a tract through which something moves rapidly (BTs), SoLK186. II. what is driven, stubble, EPs82¹⁴.

±**drīfan¹** to 'drive*,' force, hunt, follow up, pursue, Æ,AO,CP : drive away, expel, BH, Gen,Met,Mk,Ps : practise, carry on, RB; Æ : rush against, impel, drive forwards or backwards, Cr,KC : undergo.

drīg(i)ō, **drīhō** pres. 3 sg. of drēogan.

+**drīhō** f. sobriety, gravity, LL (314,318).

drīm=drēam

±**drinc** (y) 'drink,' beverage, Bo,Chr,G : draught, Cp,Mt : drinking, carousal. [v. also 'drunk']

drinc- v. also drync-, drenc-.

drinca (m.), drince (f.)=drinc

+**drinca** m. cup-bearer, RWH39².

±**drincan¹** to drink, Æ,Lk; AO,CP : be entertained, LL3,3 : to swallow up, engulf, Æ. pp. druncen refreshed, elate (with drink), drunk.

drincere m. 'drinker,' drunkard, MtL.

drīorig=drēorig

drisne (y) f. 'capillamenta'? v. A41·108.

+**drītan¹** 'cacare,' Lcd1·364⁹. ['drite']

drīting f. 'egestio' (sc. ventris), WW; A8·449. [v. 'drite']

±**drōf** dirty, muddy, swampy, turbid, troubled, Lcd. ['drof'; drēfan]

drōfe grievously, severely, LCD3·286¹¹.

+**drōfednes**=+drēfednes

drōfig troubled, BAS44¹⁶.

drōflic troublesome, tormenting, DOM19.

drōg pret. 3 sg. of dragan.

droge f? excrement, LCD118b.

drogen pp. of drēogan.

drōgon pret. pl. of dragan.

drōh pret. 3 sg. of dragan.

drohnian=drohtnian

droht I. m? n? condition of life. II. (ō?) pull, draught, WW486²⁷.

drohtað m. *mode of living, conduct : environment, society : condition, employment.*

drohtian (CP), drohtnian (Æ) *to conduct oneself, behave, associate with, lead a life, live, continue.* [drēogan]

droht-(n)oð, -nung=droht-að, -ung

±drohtnung f. *condition, way of life, reputation, conduct*, Æ,CP.

dronc=dranc pret. 3 sg. of drincan.

dropa m. *a 'drop,' Az,Lcd,Lk,VPs*; AO, CP : *gout?* Lcd : *humour, choler.*

+dropa m. *a kind of date*, OEG 474.

dropen I. pp. of drēopan. II. (B 2891)= drepen pp. of drepan.

drop-fāg, -fāh I. *spotted, speckled*, LCD. II. *starling*, GL.

dropian *to 'drop,' drip, trickle, Ps.*

dropmǣlum *drop by drop, Æ.* ['dropmeal']

droppetan, -ian *to drop, drip, distil*, Ps.

droppetung, drop(p)ung (Ps) f. *'dropping,' dripping, falling, Æ.*

droren pp. of drēosan.

+drorenlic *perishable*, NC 293.

drōs, drōsna (Æ) m., drōsne (VPs) f. *sediment, lees, dregs, dirt, ear-wax, WW.* [drēosan; 'dros,' 'drosen']

drūgað=drūgoð

±drūgian *to dry up, wither*, LRG,Ps. [drȳge]

drugon pret. pl. of drēogan.

drūgoð f., drūgoða m. *'drought,' dryness, WW* : *dry ground, desert*, LPs. [drȳge]

drūgung=drūgoð

druh m. *dust?* SOUL 17.

druncen I. n *drunkenness, LG,LL.* ['drunken'] II. pp. of drincan. III. adj. *'drunken,' drunk, Sc;* AO.

druncenes=druncennes

druncengeorn *drunken*, HL,RB.

druncenhād m. *drunkenness*, CHR 1070.

druncenig *drunken*, LkL 12⁴⁵.

druncenlǣwe *'inebrians,'* CPs 22⁵.

druncennes f. *'drunkenness,' AO,Lk;* Æ.

druncenscipe m. *drunkenness*, HL 12n³⁴.

druncenwillen *drunken*, CP 401²⁹.

druncmennen n. *drunken maidservant?* RD 13¹.

±druncnian *to be drunk, Æ* : *get drunk* : *furnish with drink*, EPs 22⁵ : *sink, drown, MtL.* ['drunken']

druncning f. *drinking*, LPs 22⁵.

druncon pret. pl. of drincan.

drupian=dropian

drupon pret. pl. of drēopan.

drūpung f. *drooping, torpor, dejection*, WYN 59.

druron pret. pl. of drēosan.

drūsian† *to droop, become sluggish, stagnant, turbid.* [drēosan]

drūt f. *beloved one*, DD 291.

drūw-=drūg-

drȳ (ē, ī) m. *magician, sorcerer*, Æ,AO : *sorcery.* [Kelt. drūi]

+drycned *dried up, emaciated*, AO 102¹⁰.

drȳcrǣft (ēo) m. *witchcraft, magic, sorcery*, Æ,AO : *magician's apparatus*, ÆH 2·418⁸.

drȳcræftig *skilled in magic*, Bo 116³,Ex 7¹¹.

drȳcræftiga m. *sorcerer*, GD 27¹⁵.

drȳecge=drȳicge

drȳfan=(1) drīfan; (2) drēfan

±drȳgan (ī) *to 'dry,' dry up, rub dry, Bo,Jn;* CP.

drȳge (ī) *'dry,' A,Bo,Mt : parched, wiᵗhered, Lk.* *on* drȳgum *on dry land.* *tō* drȳgum *to the dregs.*

drȳgnes (ī) f. *dryness*, Ps.

drȳgscēod *dry-shod*, W 293¹⁷.

drȳhst pres. 2 sg. of drēogan.

dryht (i) I.† f. (±) *multitude, army, company, body of retainers, nation, people, Ex* : pl. *men.* ['dright']; drēogan] II. (+) f. *fortune, fate*, OEG.

+dryhta m. *fellow-soldier* (BT).

dryhtbealo=dryhtenbealu

dryhtbearn n. *princely youth*, B 2035.

dryhtcwēn f. *noble queen*, WID 98.

dryhtdōm m. *noble judgment*, VPs 9¹⁷.

dryht-ealdorman (CHRD), -ealdor (WW) m. *'paranymphus,' bridesman.*

dryhten (i) m. *ruler, king, lord, prince, Æ,B : the Lord, God, Christ*, CP. ['drihtin']

dryhtenbēag (drihtin-) m. *payment* (to a lord) *for killing a freeman*, LL 3,6.

dryhtenbealu† n. *great misfortune.*

dryhtendōm m. *lordship, majesty*, AN 1001.

dryhtenhold (i) *loyal*, GEN 2282.

dryhtenlic *lordly : divine, of the Lord, Æ.* adv. -līce.

dryhtenweard m. *lord, king*, DA 535.

dryhtfolc† n. *people, troop, Ex.* ['drightfolk']

dryhtgesīð m. *retainer, warrior*, FIN 44.

dryhtgestrēon n. *princely treasure*, RD 18³.

dryhtguma m. †*warrior, retainer, follower, man : bridesman.*

dryhtin-=dryhten-

dryhtlēoð n. *national song, hymn*, EL 342.

dryhtlic (i) *lordly, noble, B,Gen.* d. gebed *the Lord's Prayer.* ['drightlike'] adv. -līce.

dryhtmann m. *bridesman*, GL.

dryhtmāðm m. *princely treasure*, B 2483.

dryhtnē m. *warrior's corpse*, Ex 163.

dryhtscipe† m. *lordship, rulership, dignity : virtue, valour, heroic deeds.*

dryhtsele† m. *princely hall*, B.

dryhtsibb† f. *peace, high alliance*, B.

dryhtwēmend, -wēmere (i) m. *bridesman*, OEG 1774.

dryhtwerast† mp. *men, chieftains*, GEN.

dryhtwuniende *living among the people*, CRA 7.

dryhtwurŏ (i) *divine*, ÆL.

dryhtwurŏa (i) m. *theologian*, ÆL.

drȳhŏ pres. 3 sg. of drēogan.

drȳicge f. *witch*, MH 28³ (-egge), NC 282.

drȳlic *magic, magical*, NAR 50¹³.

drȳman (ē;=īe) *to sing aloud, rejoice, LPs.* ['*dream*']

drȳmann m. *sorcerer, magician*, Æ.

±drȳme (ē), +drȳmed *melodious, harmonious, cheerful*, Æ,GL.

drync m. *drink, potion, draught, drinking*, *Cp*; AO,CP. ['*drunk*'] (v. also drinc.)

drync- v. also drenc-, drinc-.

dryncehorn (i) *drinking-horn*, TC 555⁶.

dryncelēan (i) n. *scot-ale, the ale given by a seller to a buyer on concluding a bargain* (BT). v. LL 2·56.

dryncfæt n. *drinking vessel*, AA 7⁶.

dryncgemett (i) n. *a measure of drink*, CHRD 15²⁴.

+dryncnes f. *immersion, baptism*, ÆL 23b, 723.

dryncwīrig *drunk*, WW 437²¹. [wērig]

±drȳpan (=īe) *to let drop, cause to fall in drops*, Æ,AO : *moisten*, Æ. ['*dripe*']

drype=drepe

dryppan? *to drip* (v. NED '*drip*,' BTs and FTp 214).

dryret† m. *ceasing, decline : fall, deposit.* [drēosan]

dryslic *terrible*, WW 191²⁸.

drysmiant† *to become obscure, gloomy.*

±drysnan *to extinguish*, NG. [drosn]

+drysnian *to vanish, disappear*, LkL 24³¹.

dubbian *to '*dub*,' strike, knight (by striking with a sword)*, *Chr* 1085 E.

dūce f. '*duck*,' *Ct.*

±dūfan² *to duck, '*dive*,' Rd*; Æ : (+) *sink, be drowned*, AO,CP.

dūfedoppa m. *pelican, LPs.* ['*divedap*']

dugan pres. 1, 3 dēag, dēah, pl. dugon, pret. dohte swv. (usu. impers.) *to avail, be worth, be capable of, competent, or good for anything*, *Chr,MtL : thrive, be strong : be good, virtuous, kind*, *B,Fa,Sat.* ['*dow*']

dug-aŏ, -eŏ, -oŏ=duguŏ

duguŏ fm. *body of noble retainers, people, men, nobles, the nobility*, *An,Ex*; AO : *host, multitude, army : the heavenly host : strength, power : excellence, worth*, *Hy*; Æ, AO : *magnificence, valour, glory, majesty : assistance, gift : benefit, profit, wealth, prosperity, salvation*, *Cr* : *what is fit or seemly, decorum.* ['*douth*']

duguŏgifu (a², e²) f. *munificence*, GL.

duguŏlic *authoritative, chief, noble*, OEG. adv. -līce.

duguŏmiht f. *supreme power*, LCD.

duguŏnæmere m. '*municeps*,' OEG 7¹².

duhte=dohte (v. dugan).

dulfon pret. pl. of delfan.

dulhrune=dolgrune

dulmunus? m. *a kind of warship*, AO 46,80.

dumb '*dumb*,' *silent*, *An,Mt*; Æ,CP.

-dumbian v. ā.-d.

dumbnes f. *dumbness*, NC 282.

dun=dunn

dūn fm. nap. dūna, dūne '*down*,' *moor, height, hill, mountain*, *Bl,Chr,Mt*; Æ; Mdf. of dūne *down, downwards.*

dūn-ælf, -elf, -ylf f. *mountain elf*, BF,GL.

dūne *down, downwards*, LkL 4³¹. [dūn]

dūnelfen f. *mountain elf*, WW 189⁹.

dūnestīgende *descending*, VPs 87⁵.

dunfealu *dun-coloured*, WW.

dung I. f. ds. dyng, ding *prison*, AN 1272. II. f. '*dung*,' *WW*.

dungrǣg *dark, dusky*, WW 246⁴. [dunn]

dunh-=dimh-

dūnhunig n. *downland honey*, LCD 132a.

duniendlic (dunond-) *falling down, tottering*, LPs 108¹⁰ (BTs).

dūnland n. *downland, open country*, ÆT, LCD.

dūnlendisc *mountainous*, ÆGR 11¹⁵.

dūnlic *of a mountain, mountain-dwelling*, WW 376⁶.

dunn '*dun*,' *dingy brown, dark-coloured*, *Ct,WW.*

dunnian *to obscure, darken*, Bo. ['*dun*']

dunondlic v. duniendlic.

Dūnsǣte mp. *inhabitants of the mountains of Wales*, LL.

dūn-scræf† n. nap. -scrafu *hill-cave.*

dure=duru

durfon pret. pl. of deorfan.

durhere (durere) m. *folding door*, GL.

durran* (+in NG) swv. pres.1, 3 sg. dear(r), 2 dearst, pl. durron, subj. durre, dyrre, pret. sg. dorste (u, y), pl. dorston *to '*dare**,' *venture, presume*, Æ,AO,BH,Bo,Met.

durstodl n. *door-post*, WW.

duru (dure) f. gs. dura, ds. and nap. dura, duru '*door*,' *gate, wicket*, *B,Bl,G,VPs*; CP, CHR.

duruhaldend (e²) *doorkeeper*, JnL 18¹⁷.

durustod (WW)=durstodl

duruŏegn m. *doorkeeper*, AN 1092.

duruŏīnen f. *female doorkeeper*, Jn 18¹⁶,¹⁷.

duruweard m. *doorkeeper*, Æ,JnL (dur-weard). ['*doorward*']

dūst (u) n. '*dust*,' *Æ,Lcd,MH,Mt*; AO,CP.

dūstdrenc m. *drink made from the pulverized seeds of herbs*, LCD 114a.

dūstig *dusty*, OEG 15; 3⁹.

dūstscēawung f. *(viewing of dust), visit to a grave*, BL 113²⁹.

dūstswerm m. *dust-like swarm*, OEG 23⁵².

dūsŏ=dūst

dūŏhamor (ȳ¹, o², e³) m. *papyrus, sedge*, WW 135³⁵, 492⁴⁰.

dwæl-=dwel-; +dwǣrian=+ŏwǣrian

±dwǣs I. *dull, foolish, stupid.* II. m. *clumsy impostor*, ÆL 23⁶⁹⁶.

±dwǣscan *to put out, extinguish, destroy*, GD,LCD.

dwǣsian *to become stupid*, Æ (6¹⁴⁶).

dwǣslic *foolish*, W. adv. -līce, LL.

+dwǣsmann m. *fool*, ÆL 17¹⁰¹.

dwǣsnes f. *stupidity, foolishness*, Æ.

dwal-=dwol-

dwān pret. 3 sg. of dwīnan.

dwealde pret. 3 sg. of dwellan.

dwel-=dwol-

±dwellan *to go astray : lead astray, deceive*, Æ.

dwellan pret. sg. dwealde, pp. dweald *to lead astray, hinder, prevent, deceive*, Æ,Bo, Rd : *to be led astray, wander, err*, Æ,Mt. ['*dwele*,' '*dwell*']

dwelsian *to wander*, LPs 118¹¹⁰.

+dweola (*BH*), +dweolsa=+dwola

dweoligan=dwellan

dweorg (e, i) m. '*dwarf*,' *Gl*. [*Ger.* zwerg]

dweorge-dwosle, -d(w)os(t)le f. *pennyroyal, flea-bane*, GL,LCD.

dweorh=dweorg

±dwild (y;=ie) n. *wandering*, BF 172⁸ : *error, heresy*, *Chr*. ['*dwild*']

+dwildæfterfolgung (dwel-) f. *heresy*, A 8·450; 13·318.

+dwildlic (y) *deceptive?* W 196²⁰.

+dwildman m. *heretic*, CHRD,NC.

-dwilman v. for-d.

±dwimor (e²) n. *phantom, ghost, illusion, error*, Æ.

+dwimorlic *illusory, unreal.* adv. -līce, Æ.

dwīnan¹ *to waste away, languish, disappear*, Lcd,WW. ['*dwine*']

+dwol *heretical*, GD.

±dwola m. *error, heresy*, BH,MtLR : *madman, deceiver, heretic*, Æ,Bl : '*nenia*,' MtL p 8⁹. ['*dwale*,' '*dwele*']

+dwolbiscop m. *heretical bishop*, GD.

±dwolcræft m. *occult art, magic*, AN,BL.

dwolema=dwolma

+dwolen† *perverse, wrong, erroneous*, GL.

+dwolenlic *foolish*, CHRD 115⁵.

+dwolfær n. *a going astray*, RHy 6³⁶.

+dwolgod m. *false god, idol, image*, W 106³⁰.

+dwolhring m. *erroneous cycle*, BH 470²¹.

±dwolian *to be led astray, err, wander*, BH; CP. ['*dwele*']

dwollic *foolish : erroneous, heretical*, Æ. adv. (±) -līce.

±dwolma m. *chaos*, WW 378¹⁶.

±dwolman m. *one who is in error, heretic*, Æ,AO,CP.

+dwolmist m. *mist of error*, Bo,MET.

dwolscipe m. *error*, BF 130¹⁸.

+dwolsprǣc f. *heretical talk*, ÆL 23³⁶⁹.

+dwolsum *misleading, erroneous*, ÆT 80¹.

dwolŏing n. *imposture, idol : sorcery*, LCD.

dwolung f. *foolishness, insanity*, WW 390³¹.

dwomer=dwimor

dworgedwostle=dweorgedwosle

dwyld=dwild

dwy-mer, -mor=dwimor

dwyrgedwysle=dweorgedwosle

dybbian *to pay attention to*, OEG 645.

dȳdan (=īe) *to kill*, LL 132,1. [dēad]

dyde pret. 3 sg., dydon pret. pl. of dōn.

dyder-=dydr-

dydrian *to deceive, delude*, Bo 100⁵.

dydrin m? *yolk*, LCD. [*Ger.* dotter]

dydrung f. *delusion, illusion*, Æ.

±dȳfan (=ī) *to dip, immerse*, BH,RD. ['*dive*']

dȳfing f. *immersion*, W 36⁹.

dȳfst pres. 2 sg. of dūfan.

dȳgel-, dȳgl-, dȳhl-=dīegol-, dīeg(o)l-

dyht, dyhtan=diht, dihtan

dyhtig (o) '*doughty*,' *strong*, B,Chr,Gen. [dugan]

dyl-=dil-; +dȳlegian=+dīlegian

dylmengon (=dilemengum? dat. of sb.) *dissimulation*, CHRD 45¹⁰.[cp. fordilemengan]

dylsta m. *festering matter, filth, mucus* LCD.

dylstiht *mucous*, LCD 26a.

dym-, dyn-=dim-, din-; ±dyn=dyne

dyncge f. *dung, manure, litter : manured land, fallow land*, OEG. [dung]

±dyne m. '*din*,' *noise*, Sat,Sol.

+dyngan (AO), dyngian (*WW*) *to* '*dung*.'

dynian *to make a* '*din*,' *sound, resound*, B; Æ.

dȳnige f. *a plant*, LCD 113b. [dūn]

dynn, dynnan=dyne, dynian

dynt m. '*dint*,' *blow, stroke, bruise, stripe*, CP,JnL : *thud*, Bo 117³⁰.

dȳp=dēop

dȳpan (ē;=īe) I. (±) *to dip : baptize*, MtR : (+) *anoint*, EPs 140⁵. ['*depe*'] II. *to make greater*, LL 388¹. ['*deep*']

dȳpe=dēop

dyple *double*, BF 186¹⁵.

dyppan (e, i) *to* '*dip*,' *immerse*, Lcd,Mk : *baptize*, MtR.

dȳr=dēor; dyre ds. of duru.

dȳre adj.=dīere

+dyre n. *door-post, door*, Æ.

±**dyrfan** (=ie) *to afflict, injure : imperil, endanger.* v. ES39·342. [deorfan]
dyrfing (=ie) f. *affliction,* GPH395.
dyrfō pres. 3 sg. of deorfan.
dyrn-=diern-, dern-
dyrneforlegen *adulterous,* LL(144').
dyrneforlegernes f. *fornication,* BH280³.
dyrne(ge)legerscipe (e¹) m. *adultery, fornication,* JnLR8³.
dyrnegeligre I. (ie, e) n. *adultery,* AO,CP.
 II. m. *fornicator,* DR107¹.
dyrneleger (e¹) *adulterous,* NG.
dyrnelegere (e¹) I. *licentiously,* NG. II. (RWH78⁴)=dyrnegeligre I.
dyrngewrit n. *apocryphal book,* WW347³⁸.
dyrnhǣmende (i) *fornicating, adulterous,* WW383⁴⁰.
dyrnlic *secret,* LL. adv. -līce, LCD3·424'.
dyrnlicgan⁵ *to fornicate,* CPs108³⁹.
dyrnmaga m. *president at mysteries,* GPH 397.
dyrnunga=dearnunga; **dyrodine**=derodine
dȳrra=dīerra; **dyrre** v. *durran.
+**dȳrsian** *to praise, glorify, hold dear, prize,* JUD300. [diēre]
+**dyrst** f. *tribulation,* HELL108.
dyrste=dorste pret. 3 sg. of *durran.
+**dyrstelīce**=dyrstiglīce
±**dyrstig** *venturesome, presumptuous, daring, bold,* CP. adv. -līce. [*durran]
+**dyrstigian** *to dare, presume,* BH468¹⁹.
±**dyrstignes** f. *boldness, insolence, daring, presumption, arrogance, rashness,* Æ,CP.
dyrstingpanne=hyrstingpanne
±**dyrstlǣcan** *to presume, dare,* Æ.
dyrstlǣcung f. *courage, boldness,* GD71¹⁹.
+**dyrstlic**=+dyrstig
±**dyrstnes**=dyrstignes
dyru ds., dyrum dp. of duru.
dȳr-wurðe, -wyrðe=dēorwierðe
dys-=dis-; **dyseg**=dysig, dysg-
dyselic (Æ)=dyslic
±**dysgian** *to act foolishly, make mistakes,* Bo; Æ : *blaspheme,* G. ['*dizzy*']
dysgung f. *folly, madness,* LCD53b.
dysian=dysgian
dysig (e, i) I. *foolish, ignorant, stupid,* Bl, Mt,VHy; Æ,CP. ['*dizzy*'] II. n. *foolishness, error,* AO,CP. III. m. *fool,* VPs91⁶.
dysigan=dysgian
dysigcræftig? (i¹, ea³) *skilled in foolish arts,* ANS128·300 (BTac).
dysigdōm m. *folly, ignorance,* CM,Sc.
dysiglic *foolish,* VH10. adv. -līce, VH10.
dysignes f. *folly, madness, blasphemy,* BH, Mk; Æ,AO : *foolish practice,* NC300²⁵. ['*dizziness*']
dysigu=dysig II.
dyslic *foolish, stupid,* Æ,CP. adv. -līce.

dȳstig *dusty,* WW517²³. [dūst]
dyttan *to shut to, close, stop,* Lk,PPs. ['*dit*']
dȳō f. *fuel, tinder,* OEG2⁴³; cp. 1655n.
dȳō-homar, -homer=dūðhamor

E

ē ds. of ēa.
ēa I. f. (usu. indecl. in sg., but with occl. gs. ēas; ds. īe, ē, ǣ, ēæ; nap. ēa, ēan; gp. ēa; dp. ēa(u)m, ēan) *water, stream, river,* Æ, Chr,Ps; AO. ['*ea*'; '*æ*'] II. interj. v. ēalā.
ēac I. adv. *also, and, likewise, moreover,* B, Ep,Mt; AO,CP. ge...ge ēac *both...and also.* nē...nē ēac...*neither...nor even....* ēac swā, ēac swilce *also, likewise, moreover, as if.* ēac gelīce *likewise.* ēac hwæðre *however, nevertheless.* ēac ðon *besides.* ['*eke*'] II. prep. w. d. *together with, in addition to, besides.*
ēaca m. *addition, increase, reinforcement, advantage, profit, usury, excess,* Chr,Sol; Æ,AO,CP. tō ēacan (w. d.) *in addition to, besides, moreover,* Bo. ['*eke*']
ēacan *to increase,* Bo,LL.
ēacen *increased, augmented : richly endowed, strong, great, vast, vigorous : pregnant.*
ēacencræftig *huge,* B2280.
ēacerse f. *water-cress,* Lcd35b. [ēa; v. '*cress*']
ēacian *to increase,* CP163,231.
±**ēacnian** *to add, increase, be enlarged : become pregnant, conceive, bring forth,* Æ,CP.
ēacniendlic adj. *to be increased,* OEG1078.
±**ēacnung** f. *increase,* GL : *conception, bringing forth,* Æ.
ēad† n. *riches, prosperity, good fortune, happiness.*
ead-=ed-; **ēad-**=eað-
ēaden† (pp. of *ēadan) *granted (by Fate,* [ēad]
eadesa=adesa
ēadfruma† m. *giver of prosperity.*
ēadga wk. form of ēadig.
ēadgian=ēadigian
ēadgiefa† m. *giver of prosperity.*
ēadgiefu† f. *gift of prosperity.*
ēadhrēðig† *happy, blessed, triumphant.*
ēadig *wealthy, prosperous,* Cr : *fortunate, happy, blessed, perfect,* Gu,VPs; Æ,CP. ['*eadi*']
±**ēadigan** *to count fortunate, call blessed,* HL : *enrich, make happy.*
ēadiglic *prosperous, rich, happy, blessed.* adv. -līce, B. ['*eadily*']
ēadignes f. *happiness, prosperity,* Æ.

eadlēan=edlēan

ēadlufu f. *blessed love*, JUL 104.

ēadmēd, ēadmōd=ēaðmōd

ēadmētto=ēaðmēttu

ēadnes f. *inner peace, ease, joy, prosperity, Run* : *gentleness*. ['*eadness*'; ēað]

ēadocce f. *water-lily*, WW 116[16]. ['*edocce*']

eador=(1) geador, (2) eodor

ēadorgeard m. *enclosure of veins, body ?*(GK), AN 1183 (or ? ealdor-).

eaduse (A 10·143[90])=adesa

ēadwela† m. *prosperity, riches, happiness.*

ēæ v. ēa, eǣ-=ea-; eafera=eafora

ēaflsc† m. *river-fish.*

eafor I. mn? *the obligation due from a tenant to the king to convey goods and messengers?* KC (v. IF 48·262). II. (afer) *draught-horse,* v. LL 498f and 2·57. III.=eofor

eafora† m. *posterity, son, child; successor, heir.* [cp. Goth. afar]

eafoð† n. *power, strength, might,* B.

eafra=eafora; eaftra=æfterra

ēagbrǣw m. *eyelid,* Lcd 1·352. ['*eyebree*']

ēagduru f. *window,* MH.

ēage (ē) n. '*eye,*' G,Lcd,RB,VPs; AO,CP : *aperture, hole,* Lk.

ēagēce m. *eye-ache,* LCD.

ēagflēah m. *albugo, a white spot in the eye,* WW.

ēaggebyrd f. *nature of the eye,* PH 301.

ēaggemearc (ēah-) n. *limit of view, horizon,* DD 148.

ēaghring (ēah-, ēh-) m. *eye-socket, pupil,* Æ.

eaghoyri=eagōyrel

ēaghyll m. *eyebrow?* WW 415[22].

ēaghyrne (hēah-) m. *corner of the eye,* WW 156[41].

ēagmist (ēah-) m. *dimness of the eyes,* LCD 11a.

ēagor=ēgor; eagospind=hagospind

ēagsealf f. '*eye-salve,*' WW.

ēagsēoung f. *eye-disease, cataract,* WW 414[12].

ēagsȳne *visible to the eye,* AN. adv. -sȳnes, Æ.

ēagōyrel n. *eye-hole, window,* BH. ['*eye-thurl*']

ēag-wǣrc (y²), -wrǣc m. *pain of the eyes,* LCD.

ēagwund f. *wound in the eye,* LL 20,47.

ēagwyrt f. *eye-wort, eye-bright,* LCD 117a.

ēah-=ēag-, ēa-

eaht (a, æ, e) f. *assembly, council.* e. besittan *to hold a council : esteem, estimation, estimated value.*

ēaht=ǣht

eahta (a, æ, e) '*eight,*' B,Chr,Men; CP.

eahtafeald *eightfold,* Æ.

eahtahyrnede *eight-cornered,* ÆH 2·496'.

eahtan† I. *to persecute, pursue.* II. *to estimate, appreciate.*

eahtanihte *eight days' old* (*moon*), LCD 3·178[14].

eahtatēoða '*eighteenth,*' AO.

eahta-tīene, -tȳne '*eighteen,*' Lk (eht-).

eahtatig *eighty,* AO.

eahtatȳnewintre *eighteen years old,* ÆL 33[36]

eahtawintre *of eight years old,* Æ.

eahtend m. *persecutor,* PPs 118[150].

-eahtendlic v. unge-e.

eahtēoða—(1) cahtatēoða, (2) eahtoða

eahtere (e¹, æ¹) m. *appraiser, censor,* LCD.

eahteða (AO)=eahtoða

±eahtian (æ, e) *to estimate, esteem,* CP : *consult about, consider, deliberate : watch over,* Æ : *speak of with praise.* [Ger. achten]

ēahtnes=ēhtnes

eahtoða '*eighth,*' Men; CHR.

eahtung f. *estimation, valuation,* CP : (+) *deliberation, counsel,* PPs.

eal=eall, æl (LL); eala=ealu

ēalā interj. *alas! oh! lo!* Æ,AO,CP. [ēa II.]

ēalād f. *watery way,* AN 441.

ēaland n. *island,* CHR : *maritime land, sea-board,* B 2334.

ealað v. ealu.

ealbeorht=eallbeorht; ēalc=ǣlc

eald (a) comp. ieldra, yldra; sup. ieldest, yldest '*OLD*,' *aged, ancient, antique, primeval, Æ,CP*; AO : '*elder,*' *experienced, tried : honoured, eminent, great.* ða ieldstan men *the chief men.*

ealda m. *old man,* RHy 6[25] : *chief, elder : the Devil,* Leas. ['*old*']

ealdbacen *stale,* ÆP 31[7].

eald-cȳðð (AO), -cȳððu f. *old home, former dwelling-place : old acquaintance,* Æ.

ealddagas (æa¹) mp. *former times,* AO.

ealddōm m. *age,* AO 76[2].

ealde=ielde

ealdefæder m. *grandfather,* CHR.

ealdemōdor f. *grandmother,* Ct.

ealder=ealdor

ealdfæder m. *forefather,* Æ,B. ['*eldfather*']

ealdfēond (ī)† m. *old foe, hereditary foe, the devil.*

ealdgecynd† n. *original nature,* MET.

ealdgefā m. *ancient foe,* AO 118[34].

ealdgeféra m. *old comrade,* AO 152[24].

ealdgemǣre *ancient boundary,* BC 3·546'.

ealdgenēat m. *old comrade,* MA 310.

ealdgenīðla† m. *old foe, Satan.*

ealdgeriht (a¹) n. *ancient right,* TC 70[22].

ealdgesegen f. *ancient tradition,* B 869.

ealdgesīð† m. *old comrade.*

ealdgestrēon n. *ancient treasure,* AO.

ealdgeweorc† n. *old-standing work, the world*, MET.

ealdgewinn n. *old-time conflict*, B 1781.

ealdgewinna m. *old enemy*, B 1776.

ealdgewyrht† n. *former deeds : deserts of former deeds?* B 2657.

ealdhettende mp. *old foes*, JUD 321.

ealdhlāford m. *hereditary lord*, AO,CP.

ealdhrīðer? n. *an old ox*, LL.

±ealdian (a) *to grow old*, *Jn,VPs*; Æ. ['*eld*,' '*old*']

ealdland n. *land which has been long untilled?* (BTs), *ancestral property?* (Earle), EC 327[14].

ealdlandrǣden f. *established law of landed property*, LL 448,4[6] (or ? two words, BT).

ealdlic *old, venerable*, Æ.

ealdnes f. *old age*, Æ. ['*eldness*,' '*oldness*']

ealdor (a[1], e[2]) I. m. *elder, parent*, BH,Gen. pl. *ancestors : civil or religious authority, chief, leader, master, lord, prince, king, G*; Æ : *source : primitive*, ÆGR. [eald; '*alder*'] II. n.(f?) (†) *life, vital part* : (†) *age, old age : eternity*. on ealdre tō ealdre *for ever, always.* āwa tō ealdre, tō wīdan ealdre *for ever and ever.* [*Ger.* alter]

ealdorapostol (a) m. *chief apostle*, NC,BH 314[7].

ealdorbana (a[1]) m. *life-destroyer*, GEN 1033.

ealdorbealu† n. *life-bale, death.*

ealdorbiscop m. *archbishop*, Æ : *high-priest*, Æ.

ealdor-bold, -botl n. *palace, mansion*, BH.

ealdorburg f. *metropolis*, BH,GL.

ealdorcearu (a[1]) f. *great sorrow*, B 906.

ealdordæg† m. *day of life*, B.

ealdordēma† (a[1]) m. *chief judge, prince*, GEN.

ealdordēofol m. *chief of the devils*, NC 282.

ealdordōm (a[1]) m. *power, lordship, rule, dominion, authority, magistracy*, PPs; Æ, AO,CP : *superiority, preeminence : beginning?* JUL 190. ['*alderdom*']

ealdordōmlic *preeminent*, EPs 50[14] (cp. ealdorlic).

ealdordōmlicnes f. *authority, control*, RBL 68[12].

ealdordōmscipe? m. *office of alderman*, CHR 983 c.

ealdorduguð† f. *nobility, flower of the chiefs.*

ealdorfrēa (a[1]) m. *lord, chief*, DA 46.

ealdorgeard m. *enclosure of life, body*, AN 1183? (or? ēador-).

ealdorgedāl† n. *death.*

ealdorgesceaft f. *state of life*, RD 40[23].

ealdorgewinna† m. *deadly enemy.*

ealdorlang *life-long, eternal*, †CHR 937A.

ealdorlēas I. *lifeless, dead*, B 15. II. *deprived of parents, orphaned : without a chief.*

ealdorlegu† f. *destiny : death*, GU.

ealdorlic '*principalis*,' *chief, princely, excellent : authentic.* adv. -līce.

ealdorlicnes f. *authority*, CP.

ealdormann (o[3]) [v. LL 2·359] m. '*alderman*,' *ruler, prince, chief, nobleman of the highest rank, high civil or religious officer, chief officer of a shire, Chr*; Æ,AO,CP : as trans. of foreign titles, *JnL,Mt.*

ealdorneru† f. *life's preservation, safety, refuge*, GEN.

ealdorsācerd m. *high-priest*, AN,G.

ealdorscipe m. *seniority, headship, supremacy, sovereignty*, Æ.

ealdorstōl m. *throne*, RIM 23.

ealdorðegn m. *chief attendant, retainer, distinguished courtier, chieftain : chief apostle*, MFH,VH.

ealdorwisa (a[1]) m. *chief*, GEN 1237.

ealdoð (ald-aht, -ot) *vessel*, GL.

ealdriht n. *old right*, LL 11,12.

Eald-Seaxe, -Seaxan mp. *Old-Saxons, Continental Saxons*, AO.

ealdspell n. *old saying, old story*, Bo.

ealdsprǣc f. *proverb, by-word*, PPs 43[15].

ealdung f. *process of growing old, age*, Æ,AO.

ealdur=ealdor

ealdwerig (=-wearg) *accursed from old times*, Ex 50.

ealdwīf n. *old woman*, GEN 18[13].

ealdwita m. *venerable man, priest, sage* : BH,LL.

ealdwrītere m. *writer on ancient history*, OEG 5449.

ēales v. ealh.

ealfara m. *pack-horse*, AA 13[7] and n.

ealfela† *very much.*

ealfelo *baleful, dire*, AN 771 (ælfæle); RD 24[9].

ealgearo† *all ready, prepared.*

±ealgian *to protect, defend*, Æ.

ealgodwebb n. '*holosericus*,' *all-silk cloth*, WW 395[15].

ealgodwebben *all-silk*, WW 501[2].

ealh† (a) m., gs. ēales *temple.*

ealhstede† m. *temple*, DA.

ēalifer f. *liver-wort?* Lcd. ['*eileber*'?]

ēalīðend m. *seafaring man*, AN 251.

eall I. adj. (has no weak form) '*ALL**,' *every, entire, whole, universal*, Æ,*Chr.* pl. *all men*, Æ. II. adv. *fully, wholly, entirely, quite*, Cr,GD,Gen. e. swā *quite as, just as.* e. swā micle swā *as much as.* mid ealle, mid eallum *altogether, entirely*, CP. ealra swīðost *especially, most of all.* ealne weg (also contr. ealneg) *always.* ofer e. (neut.) *everywhere, into all parts.* III. n. *all, everything*, Æ.

ealla=gealla

eallbeorht† (æl-) *all-bright, resplendent, Sat.* [v. '*all*']

eallcræftig† (æl-) *all-powerful.*

eallencten m. *season of Lent,* RB66⁵.

eallenga=eallunga

ealles, ealle adv. (g. of eall) *entirely, wholly, fully, quite.* e. for swīðe *altogether, utterly.*

eallgelēaflic *universally believed, catholic,* BH (Sch) 648³.

eallgōd *all-good,* ÆT 65.

eallgrēne *all-green, green, An : young, fresh,* RV²Ps 127³. [v. '*all*']

eallgylden (æl-) *all-golden,* B,CP 169²¹.

eallhālgung f. *consecration,* A 41·106.

eallhālig '*all-holy,*' Met; PPs 131⁸.

eallhwīt *entirely of white,* Ct.

eallic *universal, catholic,* GD.

eallinga=eallunga

eallīren *entirely of iron,* B 2338.

eallīsig *all-icy, very cold,* Bo,Met.

eallmægen† n. *utmost effort,* Met.

eallmǣst (al-, æl-) adv. *nearly all, ' almost,' for the most part,* Æ,Chr.

eallmiht f. *omnipotence,* PPs 135¹².

eallmihtig=ælmihtig

eallnacod *entirely naked,* Gen 871.

eallneg=ealneg

eallnīwe *quite new,* Æ. [v. '*all*']

eallnunge=eallunga

ealloffrung f. *holocaust,* WW 130¹² (eal-).

eallreord=elreord

eallrihte adv. *just, exactly,* RB 131¹³.

eallseolcen *entirely made of silk,* Gl.

eallswā *just as, even as, ' as,' as if, so as, likewise,* Æ,Mt.

eallswilc *just such,* Æ,Chr.

ealltela adv. *quite well,* Gen 1905.

eallunga adv. *altogether, entirely, utterly, quite, indeed,* Æ,Bo,Mt; CP. [' *allinge* ']

eallwealda† I. *all-ruling, almighty.* II. m. *God, the Almighty.*

eallwealdend (alw-) m. *ruler of all,* Hu; ÆL. [' *all-wielding* ']

eallwealdende (alw-) ' *all-wielding,' all-ruling,* Æ.

eallwihta† (æl-) fp. *all creatures,* W.

eallwriten adj. *holograph,* WW 463²⁸.

eallwundor n. *marvel,* Ex 578.

ealm-=eallm-; ealmihtig=ælmihtig

ealneg (AO,CP), ealneweg, ealnuweg, ealnig, ealning(a) *always, quite, perpetually.*

ealnunga=eallunga; ealo=ealu

ealoffrung f. *holocaust,* WW 130¹².

ēalond=ēaland; ealoð (AO) v. ealu.

ealsealf f.' *ambrosia,' an aromatic plant* (BT).

ealswā=eallswā; ealtēawe=æltēawe

ealu (ealo) m? n? gds. ealoð (AO), ealað; gp. ealeða ' *ale,' beer,* Æ,Lcd. [v. A 27·495]

ealubenc† f. ' *ale-bench,' B.*

ealuclyfa m. *beer-cellar,* OEG 4⁴².

ealufæt n. *ale-vat,* Lcd 53b.

ealugafol n. *tax or tribute paid in ale,* LL 448.

ealugāl *drunk with ale,* Gen 2408.

ealugālnes f. *drunkenness,* MFH 94¹.

ealugeweorc (o²) n. *brewing,* AO 222⁷.

ealuhūs (a²) n. *alehouse,* LL 228,1².

ealumalt (alo-) n. *malt for brewing,* Lcd 157a.

ealuscerwen f. (*ale-deprival), deprival of joy, distress, mortal panic?* B 770.

ealuscop m. *singer in alehouses,* LL.

ealusele m. *alehouse,* AB 34·10.

ealuwǣge† n. *ale-flagon, ale-can, B.* [v. ' *ale* ']

ealuwosa (o²) m. *ale-tippler,* Wy 49.

ealw-=eallw-; eam (VPs)=eom (v. wesan).

ēam I. m. *uncle* (usu. maternal; paternal uncle=fædera), Æ,B; AO. [' *eme* '] II. dp. of ēa.

+ēane *yeaning,* Gen 33¹³.

±ēanian *to bring forth young* (usu. lambs), LPs 77⁷¹. [' *ean* ']

ēaðfer m. *river-bank,* Met 19²².

eapel, eapl=æppel; eappul-=æppel-

ear ' *occa,' harrow?* OEG 2359 (v. A 36·72).

ēar I. n. ' *ear' (of corn),* Cp,Mt; AO. II. (ǣ)† m. *wave, sea, ocean.* III.† m. *earth :* name of the rune for ēa. IV.=ǣr. V.=ēare

ēar- v. ār-

ēaracu f. *river bed,* KC 5·122¹⁵.

earan-=earon; earb-=earf-

ēarblǣd (ē¹) n. *stalk, blade (of corn), straw.*

earc, earce (a, æ, e) f. *chest, coffer, Rd :* ' *ark,' Mt,Ps;* CP. [L.]

ēarclǣnsend m. *little finger,* WW 265¹.

earcnanstān=eorcnanstān

ēarcoðu f. ' *parotis,' a tumour near the ears,* WW 113³¹.

eard m. *native place, country, region, dwelling-place, estate, cultivated ground, B,Ps;* Æ,AO,CP : *earth, land : condition, fate,* †Hy. [''ērd']

eardbegenga m. *inhabitant,* LPs.

eardbegengnes f. *habitation,* RLPs.

eardeswrǣcca (LPs 118¹⁹)=eardwrecca

eardfæst *settled, abiding,* AO.

eardgeard† m. *place of habitation, world.*

eardgyfu f. *gift from one's homeland,* PPs 71¹⁰.

±eardian tr. and intr. *to inhabit, dwell, abide, live, AO,B,G;* Æ,CP. [' *erde* ']

eardiend m. *dweller,* GD.

eardiendlic *habitable,* BH 366¹⁰.

eardland n. *native land,* PPs 134¹².

eardlufe f. *dear home?* B 693.

eardrīce n. *habitation,* Gu 825.

eardstapa m. *wanderer*, WA6.

eardstede m. *habitation*, PH195.

±**eardung** f. *living : abode, tabernacle*, Ps. ['*erding*']

eardungburg f. *city of habitation*, Ex1¹¹.

eardunghūs n. *tabernacle, habitation*, GD.

eardungstōw f. *tabernacle, habitation*, Mt; CP. ['*erdingstow*']

eardweall m. *land-rampart, bulwark*, B 1224?

eardwīc† n. *dwelling*.

eardwrecca m. *exile*, LL51n5.

eardwunung f. *dwelling in one's own country*, W120¹³.

ēare n. '*ear*,' *Mt,Rd,VPs*; Æ,CP.

ēarede *having a handle*, WW122⁸⁹.

ēarefinger m. *little finger*, ÆGr; WW. ['*earfinger*']

ēarelipprica=ēarliprica

earendel (eo) m. *dayspring, dawn, ray of light*, BL,CR.

earfað-=earfoð-

earfe, earbe f? *tare*, LCD. [*L.* ervum]

earfed-=(1) earfoð-; (2) yrfe-

earfeð=earfoð

ēarfinger=ēarefinger; **earfod-**=earfoð-

earfoðcierre (að-) *hard to convert*, MH112²⁰.

earfoðcynn n. *depraved race*, PPs77¹⁰.

earfoðdǣde *difficult*, CP147¹².

earfoðdæg m. *day of tribulation*, PPs76².

earfoðe I. n. *hardship, labour, trouble, difficulty, suffering, torment, torture*, AO,CP. [*Ger.* arbeit] II. adj. *hard, difficult, troublesome*, Æ,Bo. ['*arveth*'] III. adv. *with difficulty*.

earfoðfēre *difficult to pass through*, AS44²⁵.

earfoðfynde *hard to find*, ÆL23⁸². [cp. ēaðfynde]

earfoðhāwe *difficult to be seen*, MET.

earfoðhwīl f. *hard time*, SEAF3.

earfoðhylde *dissatisfied*, ÆH1·400¹.

±**earfoðian** *to trouble*, Ps.

earfoðlǣre *hard to teach*, GD110¹⁹ : *undisciplined*, CHRD18⁶.

earfoðlǣte *hard to discharge*, WW113²⁰.

earfoðlic *difficult, full of hardship*, Æ. ['*arvethlich*'] adv. -līce *with difficulty, painfully, reluctantly, hardly, scarcely*, Mt. ['*arvethliche*']

earfoðlicnes (Æ)=earfoðnes

earfoðmæcg† m. *sufferer*.

earfoðnes f. *difficulty, hardship, trouble, affliction, pain, misfortune*, Æ. ['*arvethness*']

earfoðrecce *hard to relate*, W22¹⁴.

earfoðrihte *hard to correct, incorrigible*, CHRD42¹.

earfoðrīme *hard to enumerate*, Bo1⁷.

earfoðsǣlig *unhappy, unfortunate*, CRA8.

earfoðsīð† m. *troublesome journey : misfortune*.

earfoðtǣcne *difficult to be shown*, MET20¹⁴⁷.

earfoððrāg f. *sorrowful time*, B283.

earfoðwylde *hard to subdue*, LCD3·436¹².

earg (earh) *slothful, sluggish*, Gn : *cowardly*, BH; AO : *craven, vile, wretched, useless*, MtL. ['*argh*'] adv. earge.

eargēat=earngēat

ēargebland† (ār-) n. *wave-blend, surge*.

ēargespeca m. *whisperer, privy councillor*, WW351². [=-spreca]

±**eargian** (i, y) *to shun, fear, turn coward*, Æ : *terrify*.

earglic *slothful, shameful, bad*, Æ. adv. -līce. *timidly, fearfully?* Gen20⁴ : *basely*, Chr1086. ['*arghly*']

eargnes (arog-) f. *licentiousness*, MkR8³⁸.

ēargrund m. *bottom of the sea*, Az40.

eargscipe m. *idleness, cowardice : profligacy*.

earh I. f. '*arrow*,' *An,LL*. II.=earg

earhfaru f.† *flight, or shooting, of arrows*.

ēarhring m. '*ear-ring*,' Æ; WW.

ēarisc (ǣ, ēo) f. *rush, reed, flag*, GL,LCD. [ēa]

ēarīð m. *water-stream*, GUTH20⁵.

ēarlæppa m. *external ear*, WW157. ['*earlap*']

ēarliprica m. *flap of the ear, external ear*, NG.

ēarlocc m. *lock of hair over the ear*, WW152³⁰.

earm (a) I. m. '*arm*' (of the body, sea, etc.), *AO,LkL* : *foreleg*, Æ : *power*, Jn. II. *poor, wretched, pitiful, destitute, miserable*, Chr, Mk; Æ,CP. ['*arm*']

earm-bēag, -bēah m. *bracelet*, B,GL.

earmcearig† *full of sorrows*.

earme adv. *miserably, badly*, GEN.

earmella m. *sleeve*, RB136²³.

earmful *wretched, miserable*, LCD3·440' : *poor in spirit, humble*, VH10.

earmgegirela m. *bracelet*, WW386¹³.

earmheort *humble, poor in spirit*, CP209² : *tender-hearted, merciful*.

earmhrēad f. *arm-ornament*, B1194.

earmian *to pity, commiserate*, CHR,HL.

earming m. *poor wretch*, Æ. ['*arming*']

earmlic *miserable, pitiable, mean*, Met. adv. -līce, BH. ['*armlich(e)*']

earmscanca m. *arm-bone*, LL82,55.

earmsceapen *unfortunate, miserable*.

earmslīfe f. *sleeve*, RBL93⁹.

earmstoc n. *sleeve*, IM128¹¹⁰.

earmstrang *strong of arm, muscular*, WW158⁷.

earmswīð *strong of arm, muscular*, WW435³³.

earmðu f. *misery, poverty*, Bo. ['*armthe*']

earn I. m. *eagle*, El,Mt; Æ. ['*erne*'] II.=ǣrn. III.=arn (v. iernan).

earnan (VPs)=ǣrnan

earncynn n. *eagle tribe*, Lev 11[13].

earn-gēap (v. AB 19·164), -gēat, -gēot f. *vulture*, Gl.

±earnian (a) (w. g. a.) *to 'earn,' merit, win*, Ct : *labour for*, Bo,Gu.

earningland n. *land earned or made freehold* (=bōcland; BT), Ct.

earnung f. *merit, reward, consideration, pay*, Æ : *labour*, Bo 52[20].

earo=gearo

earon (VPs)=sindon pres. 3 pl. of eom (v. wesan).

ēaron=gēarum dp. of gēar.

earp *dark, dusky*, Rd 4[42]. [*ON.* jarpr]

earpa=hearpa

ēarplætt m. *box or blow on the ear*, ÆH 2·248'.

±ēarplætt(ig)an *to box the ears, buffet*, ÆH, RWH 137[25].

ēar-prēon, -ring m. *ear-ring*, Æ.

earre (N)=ierre

ears (æ) m. *fundament, buttocks*, WW. ['*arse*']

ēarscripel (ēo[1], y[2]) m. *little finger*, Gl.

ēarsealf f. *ear-salve*, Lcd.

earsendu np. *buttocks*, WW.

earsgang (ars-) m. *privy*, Lcd,OEG : *excrement*, Lcd : '*anus*' (BT).

ēarslege m. *a blow that strikes off an ear*, LL 20,46.

earsling *backwards*, Ps. ['*arselings*']

earslȳra? m? *buttocks, breech*, Æ. [līra]

earsode '*tergosus,*' WW. ['*arsed*']

ēarspinl f. *ear-ring*, KGl 960.

earsðerl n. '*anus*,' WW 160[1].

eart 2 sg. of eom pres. of wesan.

earð I.=eorð, yrð. II.=eart

ēarðan=ǣr ðam (v. ǣr II.).

earðe (N)=eorðe

ēarðyrel n. '*fistula, arteria*,' *ear-passage?* (BT),WW 238[29]. [or=ears-ðyrel, -ðerl?]

earu=gearu; earun (VPs)=earon

ēarwærc n. *ear-ache*, Lcd 14b.

ēarwela (ā[1]) m. *watery realm*, An 855.

earwian (APs 225[5])=gearwian

ēarwicga (ēo) m. '*earwig*,' Lcd,WW.

earwunga *gratuitously* : *without a cause*, PPs.

ēarȳð (ā[1]) f. *wave of the sea*, An 535.

ēas v. ēa.

ēase '*caucale*' (*caucalia?*), *lipped vessel, beaker*, WW 202[1] (v. IF 48·266).

ēaspring=ǣspryng

ēast I. adj. comp. ēast(er)ra, sup. ēastmest, ēastemest *east, easterly*. II. adv. *eastwards, in an easterly direction, in or from the east*, BH,Gen,Met. ['*east*']

ēastæð (e[2]) n. *river-bank, sea-shore*, Ma 63.

ēastan, ēastane *from the east, easterly*, AO. ['*east*']

ēastannorðan *from the north-east*, WW.

ēastannorðanwind m. *north-east wind*, WW 364[5].

ēastansūðan *from the south-east*, WW 3[4].

ēastansūðanwind m. *south-east wind*, WW 144[3].

ēastanwind (e[2]) m. '*east wind*,' WW 143[36].

ēastcyning m. *eastern king*, AO 148[35].

ēastdǣl m. *eastern quarter, the East*, Æ,AO.

ēaste f. *the East*, OEG 1894.

ēastemest (AO) v. ēast.

ēastende m. '*east-end*,' *east quarter*, Chr; AO,LV.

ēastene=ēastane

Eastengle mpl. *the East-Anglians* : *East Anglia*.

Easterǣfen m. *Easter-eve*, BH,Chr.

Easterdæg m. *Easter-day, Easter Sunday, day of the Passover*, Æ. on ōðran Easterdæge *on Easter Monday*, Chr 1053 c.

Easterfæsten n. *Easter-fast, Lent*, BH,Chr.

Easterfeorm f. *feast of Easter*, LL 450,452'.

Easterfrēolsdæg m. *the feast day of the Passover*, Jn 13[1].

Eastergewuna m. *Easter custom*, ÆL 23b[643].

Easterlic *belonging to Easter, Paschal*, Lk. ['*Easterly*']

Eastermōnað m. *Easter-month, April*, Men, MH.

Easterne *east, 'eastern,' oriental*, Æ,Gen, WW.

Easterniht f. *Easter-eve*, Hell 15; MP 1·611'.

ēasterra v. ēast.

Eastersunnandæg (tor) m. *Easter Sunday*, W 222[21].

Eastersymbel (tro) n. *Passover*, Jn 19[42] (mg).

Eastertīd f. *Easter-tide, Paschal season*, Æ.

Easterðēnung f. *Passover*, Mt 26[19]. [v. '*theine*']

Easterwucu f. *Easter-week*, Guth. [v. '*week*']

ēasteð=ēastæð

ēasteweard (e[2]) *east, eastward*, Mt.

ēastfolc n. *eastern nation*, WW 396[30].

ēastgārsecg m. *eastern ocean*, AO 132[29].

ēastgemǣre n. *eastern confines*, AO 132[29].

ēasthealf f. *east side*, Chr 894 A.

ēastland n. *eastern land, the East*, Æ : *Esthonia*, AO. ['*Eastland*']

ēastlang *to the east, eastwards, extending east*, Chr 893 A.

ēastlēode mp. *Orientals*, BH 254[33].

ēastmest v. ēast.

ēastnorð *north-easterly*, AO 16.

ēastnorðerne *north-east*, ApT 11[2].

ēastnorðwind m. *north-east wind*, GL.
ēastor-=ēaster-
ēastportic n. *eastern porch*, ÆH 2·578¹².
ēastra v. ēast.
Ēastre (usu. in pl. Ēastron, -an; gs. -es in N) f. '*Easter*,' *BH,WW* : *Passover, Bl, Mk* : *spring*.
ēastrēam m. *stream, river*, DA 385.
+ēastrian *to elapse (during Easter)*, W 208²⁴.
ēastrīce n. *eastern kingdom, eastern country, empire* : *the East*, Æ,AO : *East Anglia*.
ēastrihte (y²) *due east, eastwards*, AO 17¹⁴.
ēastrihtes (ēst-) *due east*, KC 3·449'.
Ēastro, Ēastru, np.=Ēastre; Ēastro-=Ēaster-
ēastrodor m. *eastern sky*, PPs 102¹².
Ēastron dp. of Ēaster.
ēastsǣ f. *east sea*, BH.
East-Seaxan, -Seaxe mpl. *East-Saxons, people of Essex* : *Essex*.
ēaststæð n. *east bank of a stream*, Ct.
ēastsūð *south-eastwards*, AO. be ēastsūðan *to the south-east*.
ēastsūðdǣl m. *south-east part*, BH 264²².
ēastsūðlang *from east to south*, AO 22¹⁷.
ēastðēod f. *an eastern people*, AA 4¹⁷.
ēast-weard, -werd *east*, '*eastward*,' *Ct,Mt*.
ēastweardes *eastwards*, ÆL.
ēastweg† m. *path in or from the east*.
eata (N)=eta imperat. of etan.
eatan=etan; eatol=atol
ēað (ē, ȳ)=(1) ēaðe, (2) īeð
ēað-bede, -bēne *easy to be entreated*, Ps.
ēaðbe-gēate, -gēte *easy to get*, LCD.
ēaðbylgnes f. *irritability*, NC 288.
ēaðbylige (y¹, e²) *easily irritated*, VH 10, W 253¹¹.
ēaðcnǣwe *easy to recognise*, ÆGR 147⁸.
ēaðdǣde (ȳ) *easy to do*, LCD,W.
ēaðe (ē, ēo) I. *easy, B* : *smooth, agreeable, kindly* : *easily moved*. II. adv. *easily, lightly, soon, Met*; AO,CP : *willingly, readily, An*. ē. mæg *perhaps, lest*. ['*eath*'] III. n. *an easy thing*, W 185¹.
ēaðelic (ǣ) *easy, possible, Mt* : *insignificant, scanty, slight, BH*; Æ. ['*eathly*'] adv. -līce (*Lk*).
ēaðelicnes (ēð-) f. *easiness*, WW 400³⁹.
ēaðfēre *easy for travelling over*, WW 146²⁹.
ēaðfynde (ē, ȳ)† *easy to find*.
ēaðgeorn (ēð-) *easily pleased*, WW 218¹⁶.
ēaðgesȳne (e¹, y¹, ē³)† *easily seen, visible, Cr*. [v. '*eathe*']
ēað-gēte, -gēate *easy to obtain, prepared, ready*, Æ. [v. '*eathe*']
ēaðhrēðig=ēadhrēðig
ēaðhylde *contented, satisfied*, RB.
ēað-lǣce (ā²), -lǣcne *easy to cure*, LCD.

ēaðlǣre (ēad-) *capable of being taught, instructed*, Jn 6⁴⁵ : *easily taught*, CHRD 96¹³.
±ēað-mēdan, -mēttan, -mēdian *to humble, humble oneself, prostrate oneself, adore* : *lower*.
ēaðmēde=(1) ēaðmōd, (2) ēaðmēdu
ēaðmēdlīce (ēad-) *humbly*, CHR 1070.
ēaðmēdu, -mēdo (CHR) f. *gentleness, humility, Ps* : *obedience, submission, reverence* : *good-will, kindness, affability*. ['*edmede*']
ēaðmēdum *humbly, kindly*, AN.
ēaðmelte=ēaðmylte
ēað-mēttu, -mētto np. *humility, weakness, impotency*, AO.
ēað-mōd (CP), -mēde *humble-minded, gentle, obedient, Mt,Ps* : *benevolent, friendly, affectionate, gracious*. ['*edmede*']
ēaðmōdheort *humble-minded*, Az 152.
±ēaðmōdian *to humble or submit oneself, obey* : (+) *condescend* : (+) *adore, worship*.
ēaðmōdig=ēaðmōd
ēaðmōdlic *humble, respectful*, CP. adv. *humbly, meekly*, CP : *kindly*.
ēaðmōdnes (ēad-) f. *humility, meekness, Bo*; AO : *kindness, condescension*. ['*edmodness*']
ēaðmylte *easily digested*, LCD.
ēaðnes f. *easiness, lightness, facility, ease* : *gentleness*.
ēaðrǣde (ēð-) *easy to guess*, ES 36·326.
ēaðwylte (ēð-) *easily turned*, OEG 1151.
ēaum dp. of ēa.
ēaw=(1) ēa; (2) ēow V.; (3) ǣ(w)
ēawan=īewan
ēawdnes f. '*ostensio*,' *disclosure*, LL 412,3.
ēawenga (AO)=ēawunga
ēawesc-=ēawisc-; ēawfǣst=ǣwfǣst
ēawian=īewan
ēawisc- v. also ǣwisc- (but see SF 395).
ēawisclic *manifest, open*, DR. adv. -līce, BH.
ēawlā=ēalā; ēawu=ēowu
ēawunga (CP,Æ), ēawunge (LG) adv. *openly, plainly, publicly*. [īewan]
ēawyrt f. *river-wort, burdock*, LCD.
eax (æ) I. f. *axis, axle, axle-tree, Bo,Gl*. ['*ax*'] II.=ǣcs
eaxlgespann n. *place where the two beams of a cross intersect*, ROOD 9.
eaxl, eaxel (æ) f. *shoulder*, Æ.
eaxlclāð m. *scapular*, LEV 8⁷.
eaxle=eaxl
eaxlgestealla† m. *shoulder-companion, comrade, counsellor* : *competitor?* HGL(BTs).
eb-=ef-, eof-; ēb-=ǣb-
ebba (æ) m. '*ebb*,' *low tide*, Ma.
±ebbian *to* '*ebb*,' *Gen*.
ebind (Ln 33⁶)=+bind

ebol- (N)=yfel-
Ebrēisc (e, i) *Hebrew, Bf,Jn.* [*'Hebreish'*]
ēc=ēac
ēca wk. m. form of ēce adj.
ēcambe=ācumbe; ēcan=īecan
ēccelic=ēcelic
ece (æ) m. *'ache,' pain, BH,Lcd;* Æ. [acan]
ēce *perpetual, eternal, everlasting, Ct,VPs;*
Æ,CP : *durable,* ÆP 126²⁶. adv. *eternally,*
ever, evermore. [*'eche'*]
eced (æ) mn. *acid, vinegar,* Æ. [*L.* acētum]
eced-drenc (Lcd), -drinca (VH) m. *acid*
drink, vinegar.
ecedfæt n. *vinegar-vessel,* Gl.
ecedwīn (æ) n. *wine mingled with myrrh,*
MkL 15²³.
ēcelic *eternal, everlasting.* adv. -līce, VPs.
[*'echliche'*]
ēcen=ēacen; ecer=æcer
ēcere gfs. of ēce adj.
ecg f. *'edge,' point, B,Lk;* Æ,CP; Mdf : (†)
weapon, sword, battle-axe, B.
±ecgan *to sharpen : harrow, Cp.* [*'edge'*]
ecgbana† (o²) m. *slayer with the sword,* B.
ecgheard *hard of edge,* An 1183.
ecghete† m. *sword-hatred, war.*
ecghwæs? *keen-edged,* B 1459,2778 (Trautmann).
ecglāst mf. *sword's edge,* Sol 150¹⁹,²¹.
ecgplega m. *battle,* Jud 246.
ecgðracu f. *hot contest,* B 596.
ecgung f. *harrowing,* WW 104¹².
ecgwæl n. *sword-slaughter,* Gen 2089.
ēcilm- (M)=æcelm-
ecīinga (=ecgl-) *on the edge,* IM.
eclypsis n. *eclipse,* AA 42¹³. [*L.*]
ēcnes f. *eternity, VPs.* ā on ēcnesse *for ever*
and ever. [*'echeness'*]
ēcre dfs. of ēce.
ēcsōð, ēcsōðlīce (NG) *verily.*
ed- prefix, denotes *repetition, turning.*
ēd-=ēað-
+edbyrdan *to regenerate,* Soul 100.
edcēlnes f. *refreshment,* VPs 65¹¹ (oe).
+edcennan *to regenerate, create,* ÆH.
edcenning f. *regeneration,* ÆH.
+edcīegan (ē²) *to recall,* LPs 101²⁵.
edcierr (e, i, y) m. *return,* CP.
+edcucoda (ea¹) m. *man restored to life,* Æ.
edcwic *regenerate, restored to life,* CM 499.
±edcwician (cwyc-, cuc-) *to re-quicken,*
revive, Æ.
edcwide (eð-) m. *relation, narrative,* WW
43.
edcynn-=edcenn-; edcyrr=edcierr
ēde=ēowde; eder=eodor; edesc=edisc
+edfrēolsian *to re-grant by charter,* EC 197n.
edgeong† *becoming or being young again.*
edgift f. *restitution,* TC 202'.

edgrōwung f. *growing again,* WW 149²¹.
edgung=edgeong
edgyldan² (=ie) *to remunerate,* Sc 162¹¹.
edgyldend m. *remunerator,* Sc 127¹⁷.
+edhīwian *to re-shape, conform, reform,*
Sc 58.
edhwierfan (æ) *to return, retrace one's steps,*
RHy,RPs.
edhwyrft† m. *change, going back (to a former*
state of things), reverse.
+edhyrtan *to refresh, recruit,* GPH 390.
edisc (e²) m. *enclosed pasture, park, Ct,Gl,*
Ps; Mdf. [v. *'eddish'*]
edischenn (e²) f. *quail, VPs;* ExC 16¹³. [v.
'eddish']
ediscweard m. *park-keeper, gardener,* Gl.
ediung=edgeong
±edlǣcan *to repeat, renew,* ÆL.
edlǣcung f. *repetition,* LL (416').
edlǣht pp. of edlǣcan.
edlǣs-=edles-
+edlǣstan *to repeat,* ANS 84·6.
edlēan n. *reward, retribution, recompense,*
requital, Bo; Æ,CP. [*'edlen'*]
+edlēanend m. *rewarder,* OET 420²⁸.
±edlēanian (ēæ) *to reward, recompense,* Ps.
edlēaniend m. *rewarder,* GD.
±edlēanung f. *recompense, remuneration,*
retribution, Gl.
edlēc-=edlǣc-
±edlesende *relative, reciprocal,* ÆGr.
edlesendlic *relative, reciprocal.* adv. -līce, Æ.
edlesung (æ², y²) f. *relation, relating,* ÆGr.
edmǣle (ē) n. *religious festival,* WW 45⁹.
edmǣltid f *festinal time,* TC 158²⁰.
ēdmōd=ēaðmōd; ednēow-=ednīw-
ednīwan adv. *anew, again,* OEG.
ednīwe I. *renewed, new,* Æ. II. adv. *anew,*
again, Æ.
±ednīwian (ēo) *to renew, restore, reform,* Æ.
ednīwigend m. *restorer,* A 11·115⁹.
ednīwinga (ēo², u³) *anew, again,* AA 26³.
±ednīwung f. *renewal, reparation, renova-*
tion, Æ,CP.
ēdo (NG)=ēowde; edor=eodor
ēdr-=ǣdr-; edrec=edroc
edreccan *to chew, ruminate,* WW 533³⁸.
[=eodorcan]
edric=edroc; edrine=edryne
edring f. *refuge?* (GK),Soul 107. [or? ieðr-]
edroc m. *gullet,* Gl : *rumination,* Gl.
edryne m. *return, meeting,* ERPs 18⁷.
edsceaft f. *new creation, regeneration : new*
creature, Bo.
edsihð (etsith) f. *looking again, respect,*
WW 43³³.
+edstalian *to restore,* CM 366¹⁵.
±edstaðelian *to re-establish, restore,* Æ.
±edstaðeligend m. *restorer,* Æ.

±**edstaðelung** f. *re-establishment, renewal,* Æ.

edstaðol-=edstaðel-

edðingung f. *reconciliation,* WW 172⁴⁰.

+**edðrāwen** *twisted back,* OEG 1062.

ēdulfstæf=ēðelstæf

ed-walle, -welle=edwielle

edwendan *to return,* RPs 77³⁹.

ed-wend(en)† f. *change, reversal, end,* B.

edwīd=edwīt

edwielle (a, e, i) f. *eddy, vortex, whirlpool,* GL.

edwihte? *something, anything,* GEN 1954.

edwille=edwielle

ed-winde, -wind f. '*vortex,*' *whirlpool,* GL.

edwist f. *being, substance,* Æ : *sustenance, food.*

+**edwistian** *to feed, support,* LPs 22² : *make to share?* 140⁴.

edwistlic *existing, substantive,* ÆGR 201⁸.

edwīt n. *reproach, shame, disgrace, scorn, abuse,* Ps; AO,CP. ['*edwit*']

edwītan¹ *to reproach,* VPs. ['*edwite*']

edwītful *disgraceful,* GL. adv. -līce.

edwītian=edwītan

edwītlīf n. *life of dishonour,* B 2891.

edwītscipe m. *disgrace, shame,* WALD 1¹⁴.

edwītsprǣc† f. *scorn,* AN,PPs.

edwītspreca m. *scoffer,* GU 418.

edwītstæf† m. *reproach, disgrace,* PPs.

edwylm m. *whirlpool of fire,* WHALE 73.

±**edwyrpan** (=ie) *to amend, recover, revive.*

edwyrping f. *recovery,* ÆH 2·26²⁹.

+**edyppol** adj. *that is to be reviewed,* GPH 396.

efe-=efen-

efen (æfen, efn, emn) **I.** adj. '*even,*' *equal, like, level, AO* : *just, true, Æ* : *calm, harmonious, equable, CP.* on efen v. onemn. **II.** adv. *evenly, Æ,Ps* : *equally, Bo* : *exactly, just as, B,Cr* : *quite, fully, CP,Gen* : *namely, Gu,Met.*

efen- often=L. con-

ēfen n.=ǣfen

efenǣðele (emn-) *equally noble,* Bo.

efenāmetan=efenmetan

efenapostol (efn(e)-) m. *fellow-apostle,* DR.

efenbehēfe (efn-) *equally useful or needful,* MET 12⁷.

efenbeorht† *equally bright,* MET.

efenbisceop (-cop) m. *co-bishop,* BH 112²⁷.

efenblissian *to rejoice equally,* BH,GD.

efenblīðe *rejoicing with another,* MH 28⁸.

efenboren *of equal birth,* LL (256 n 5).

efenbrād *as broad as long,* ES 8·477.

efenbyrde *of equal birth,* ÆL 33³.

efenceasterwaran mp. *fellow-citizens,* BH 62²⁰; GD 205¹.

efencempa m. *fellow-soldier,* Æ.

efencrīsten (em-) *fellow-Christian,* LL. ['*even-Christian*']

efencuman⁴ *to come together, agree,* BH.

efendȳre *equally dear,* LL.

efenēadig *equally blessed,* †Hy 8²¹.

efeneald *contemporary, coeval,* Æ,Wid. ['*evenold*']

efeneardigende *dwelling together,* CR 237.

efenēce† (efn-) *co-eternal,* CR. adv. B.

efenedwistlic *consubstantial,* ÆH.

efenēhð f. *neighbourhood? neighbouring district?* CHR 894A (v. BTs).

efenesne (efne-) m. *fellow-servant,* DR,MtL.

efenetan *to eat as much as,* RD 41⁶³.

efenēðe *just as easy,* MET 20¹⁶⁷ (efn-).

efenfela (eo³) num. adj. *just so many, as many,* AO (em-).

efenfrē-fran, -frian '*consolari,*' EPs 125¹.

efengedǣlan (efn-) *to share alike,* EX 95.

efengefēon⁵ *to rejoice together, sympathise,* BH.

efengelic *like, co-equal,* G.

efengelīca m. *equal, fellow,* W.

efengemæcca (efn-) m. *companion, fellow, consort,* CP.

efengemyndig *commemorative,* BL 101¹.

efengespittan '*conspuere,*' MkL 14⁶⁵.

efengōd (emn-) *equally good,* Bo.

efenhāda m. *an equal in rank, co-bishop,* GD 43²².

ēfenhālig *equally holy,* BL 45¹⁸.

efenhēafda m. *fellow, comrade,* NC 283.

efenheafodling m. *mate, fellow,* GUTH 14³.

efenhēah *equally high,* SOL 85'.

efenhēap m. *band of comrades,* WW 375²⁰.

efenhemman? *to fetter,* EPs 145⁷.

efenheort(e)? -nes? *harmony,* DR (æfne-).

efenherenes f. *praising together,* CPs 32¹.

efenherian *to praise together,* VPs 116¹.

efen-hlēoðor (PH 621) n., -hlēoðrung (WW 213³⁷) f. *harmony, union of sounds or voices.*

efenhlēoðrian *to sing together,* NC 283.

efenhlȳte (ē³) *equal in rank,* BH.

efen-hlytta, -hlēta m. *sharer, partner,* ÆH.

efenīeðe (ē) *just as easy,* MET 20¹⁶⁷.

±**efenlǣcan** *to be like* : *make like, match, imitate,* Æ. ['*evenleche*']

efenlǣcend m. *imitator,* ÆH.

efenlǣceres m. *imitator,* OEG 1957.

+**efenlǣcestre** f. *female imitator,* Sc 71¹¹.

±**efenlǣcung** f. *copying, imitation,* Æ.

efenlang (em-) *equally long* : prep. (w. d.) -lange *along.*

efenlāste f. *the herb mercury,* Lcd. ['*evenlesten*']

efenlēof (em-) *equally dear,* AO.

efenleornere m. *fellow-disciple,* OEG 56²⁶⁴.

±**efenlic** *even, equal, comparable to, of like age, Cr.* ['*evenly*'] adv.-līce *equally, evenly, alike : patiently.*

efenlīca (efn-) m. *equal,* MET 20¹⁹.

+**efenlician** *to make equal, liken,* BH 372³¹ : *adjust* : (±) *conform to,* AV²Ps 25³.

efenlicnes f. *evenness, equality,* CP,Ps. (ēm-). ['*evenliness*']

efenling (efn-) m. *consort, fellow,* EPs 44⁸. ['*evenling*']

efenmǣre (efn-) *equally famous,* MET 10³².

efenmæsseprēost m. *fellow-priest,* GD 283³.

efenmedome (efn-) *equally worthy,* MH 134⁹.

efenmetan⁵ *to assemble together,* EPs 61⁹ : *compare,* VPs 48²¹.

efenmicel *equally great : just as much as,* LCD.

efenmid adj. *middle,* PPs 73¹².

efenmihtig *equally mighty,* W 16⁷.

efenmōdlīce *with equanimity,* OEG 2978.

efennēah adv. *equally near,* Bo,MET.

efenneahtlic *equinoctial,* A 52·190.

efennēhð=efenēhð

efennes f. *equity, justice,* Ps : *comparison.* [v. '*even*']

efen-niht f., -nihte? n. *equinox* (23 Sep.).

efenrēðe (emn-) *equally fierce,* AO 68⁶.

efenrīce *equally powerful,* BH 416⁹.

efensācerd m. *fellow-priest,* A 11·7⁴.

efensāre (emn-) *equally bitterly,* CP 413²⁹.

efensārgian *to sorrow with, commiserate,* Æ.

efensārgung f. *sympathy,* GD 180⁸.

efensārig adj. (w. d.) *equally sorry (with),* AO : *compassionate,* GD.

efenscearp *equally sharp,* PPs 63³.

efenscolere (emn-) m. *fellow-pupil,* AO 132¹.

efenscyldig *equally guilty,* LL 364,76².

efensorgian (efn-) *to be sorry for,* GD 345¹⁸.

efenspēdiglic *consubstantial,* BH 312.

efensprǣc (efne-) *confabulation,* LkL p 11¹¹.

efenstālian *to prepare, make ready, execute,* WW 208²⁶. [=*efenstaðelian]

efensung=efesung

efenswīðe (efn-) *just as much,* CP.

efentēam (efne-) m. *conspiracy,* JnL 9²².

efenðegn (efne-) m. *fellow-servant,* NG.

ēfenðēnung f. *supper* (BT).

efen-ðēow, -ðēowa m. *fellow-servant,* Æ,CP. -ðēowen f. *fellow-servant (female),* HL 18²⁵⁶.

efenðrōwian *to compassionate, sympathise,* CP (efn-), Æ (em-).

efenðrōwung f. *compassion,* Sc 147,148.

efenðwǣre *agreeing,* CM 32.

efenunwemme *equally inviolate,* LL 250,14.

efenwǣge f. *counterpoise,* GL.

efenweaxan *to grow together,* LCD.

efenwel *as well,* LL (324¹). e. and *equally as well as,* AS 61¹¹ (æmn-).

efenweorð *of equal rank : very worthy equivalent.*

efenwerod n. *band of comrades,* WW 381¹⁶.

efenwesende *contemporaneous, co-existent,* CR 350.

efenwiht n. *equal, fellow, associate,* CHR,W.

efenwrītan (emn-) '*conscribere,*' EPs 149⁹.

efenwyrcend (æ) m. *cooperator,* BH 464²⁵.

efenwyrhta (em-) m. *fellow-worker,* Æ.

efenwyrðe=efenweorð

efenyrfeweard m. *co-heir,* WW; BH. [v '*even*']

efeostlīce (CHR 1114 E)=ofostlīce

efer, eferfearn=eofor, eoforfearn ; **ēfer** v. ȳfre.

ēfern (N)=æfen

efes, efesc f. '*eaves*' (*of a house*), LPs *brim, brink, edge, border* (*of a forest*), *side,* Chr.

efesdrypa=yfesdrype

±**efesian** *to clip, shear, cut,* ÆGr. ['*evese*']

efest (VPs)=æfest, ofost

±**efestan** *to hasten, hurry,* Æ. [=ofestan]

efestlīce *hurriedly,* NG.

efestung f. *hastening,* GD,VPs.

efesung f. *shearing, shaving, tonsure,* Cp, WW. ['*eavesing*']

efeta (WW) m., efete (Æ) f. '*eft,*' *newt, lizard,* Æ.

efgǣlð (OEG 8¹⁶⁸)=æfgǣlð; **efn**=efen

±**efnan** I. *to make even, level,* Rd 28⁸ : *liken, compare,* MtL. ['*even*'] II.=æfnan

efne I. adv. '*even,*' *evenly,* Bo,Ps : *quite, fully,* CP,Gen : *equally, exactly, indeed, precisely, just, only, simply, merely,* B,Cr : *alike, likewise : just now : namely,* Gu,Met. e. swā *even so, even as, just as if, when.* e. swā ðēah *even though.* e. tō *next to.* II. (æ,eo) interj. *behold! truly! indeed!* Æ. [efen] III. f? *alum,* WW. IV.? (æ) n. *material,* DR 116'.

efne-=efen-

efnenū interj. *behold now,* CLPs 7¹⁵.

efnes *quite, exactly,* DD,W.

±**efnettan** (emn-) *to equal, emulate : make even, adjust :* (+) *compare.*

efnian=efnan I.

efning m. *partner,* BHCA 194⁴.

ēfod (RPs 49⁹)=ēowd

efol-=eoful-; **efor**=eofor; **ēfre**=ǣfre

efsian=efesian

efst-=efest-

eft adv. *again, anew, a second time,* Æ,VPs; CP : *then, thereupon, afterwards, hereafter, thereafter,* Chr; Æ : *back,* CHR : *likewise, moreover,* Mt. ['*eft*']

eftācenned *born again,* DR.

eftācenn(edn)es f. *regeneration,* DR,MtR.

eftǣrist (ē) *resurrection,* NG.

eftārīsan[1] *to rise again*, VPs.
eftbētung f. *making whole*, NG.
eftboren *born again*, JnLR3[5].
eftbōt f. *restoration to health*, NG.
eftcerran=eftcyrran
eftcneoreso *regeneration*, DR108'.
eftcuman[4] *to come back*, BH,Bo.
eftcyme† m. *return*.
eftcymeð pres. 3 sg. of eftcuman.
eftcynnes (=cen-) f. *regeneration*, NG.
eftcyrran (=ie) *to turn back, return*, Æ.
eftdrægend (? -ðræcend) 'recalcitrans' LkLp3[6].
eftedwītan[6] *to reprove*, MtL21[42].
efter=æfter
eftern? *evening*, LkL24[29].
eftflōwan[7] *to flow back*, HGL418; 462.
eftflōwung f. *redundance*, HGL418[45].
eftforgifnes f. 'remissio,' 'reconciliatio,' NG,DR.
+eftgadrian *to repeat*, GD277[1].
eftgeafung f. *remuneration*, DR59[1].
eftgecīgan *to recall*, BH250[21].
eftgecyrran=eftcyrran
eftgemyndgian *to remember*, DR.
eftgemyndig *remembering*, NG,DR.
eftgian *to repeat*, CP421[10,11] : (+) *restore, strengthen*.
efthweorfan[3] *to turn back, return*, BH.
efthwyrfan (i[2]) *to return*, EPs108[14], V[2]Hy 6[15] : *recur*, ÆL23B[613].
eftlēan n. *recompense*, Cʀ1100.
eftlēaniend m. *rewarder*, DR89'.
eftlīsing (ē) f. *redemption*, NG.
eftlōcung f. 'respectus,' *regard*, DR86'.
eftmyndig *remembering*, NG.
eftnīwung f. *restoration*, DR.
eftonfōnd? *receiver*, MtLp16[8].
eftryne m. 'occursus,' *return*, VPs18[7].
eftscēogian *to put one's shoes on again*, CM687.
eftsel(e)nes f. *requital*, NG,DR.
eftsittan[5] 'residere,' ÆGʀ157[5].
eftslōt† m. *journey back, return*, B.
eftslōgende *turning back, retreating*, WW 491[19].
eftsōna *a second time*, Mk : *repeatedly* : *soon after, again, likewise*, Mt. ['eftsoon']
eftspellung f. *recapitulation*, WW491[24].
efttōselenes=eftselenes
eftðingung f. *reconciliation*, DR88[5].
eftwyrd f. *judgment day, resurrection day?* (or? adj. *future*, GK),Ex539.
eftyrn=eftryne
efulsung=yfelsung; ēg=īeg
ēg-=æg-, ēag-, īeg-; eg v. eg-lā-eg.
-ēgan v. on-ē.
egcgung (WW104[12])=ecgung
egde (OET,Ep)=egðe

ege (æ) m. 'awe,' *fear, terror, dread*, Chr,Ps, MtL; Æ,AO,CP : *overawing influence*, Æ : *cause of fear*, VPs.
egean (WW459[15])=ecgan
egeful 'awful,' *inspiring or feeling awe*, Æ,Bo. adv. -līce.
egelāf? f. *survivors of a battle*, Ex370 (or ? ēgorlāf, GK).
egelēas *fearless*, CP. ['aweless'] adv. -līce, CP.
egelēasnes f. *boldness*, Bʟ85'.
egelic *terrible*, SPs75[7].
egenu f. *chaff, husk*, WW412[3].
egesa m. *awe, fear, horror, peril* : *monstrous thing, monster* : *horrible deed*, W281[4]. [ege]
egesful=egeful
egesfullic *terrible*, BH. adv. -līce.
egesfulnes f. *fearfulness, fear*, JPs,LL.
egesgrīma m. *terror-mask, ghost*, Gʟ,MH 54[1].
±egesian[1] *to frighten*, AO,CP : *threaten*, OEG2481.
egesig (eisig) *terrible*, Sat36.
egeslic *awful, dreadful, terrible, threatening*, CP. adv. -līce *sternly*, GD59[20].
egesung f. *threatening, terror*, Cʜʀᴅ,RBL.
egeswīn n. *a kind of fish*. v. NC284.
egeðe=egðe
egeðgetigu npl. *harrowing implements*, LL 455,17.
egewylm m. *terrible wave*, PPs106[24].
+eggian *to egg on, incite*, MkL15[11].
ēghw-=æghw-
egide I.=ecgede pret. 3 sg. of ecgan.
II.=egðe
egile=egle
Egipte (y) mp. *Egyptians*, ÆT.
Egiptisc (y) *Egyptian*, ÆT.
egis-=eges-; egiðe=egðe
egl fn? *mote, beard, awn, ear (of barley)*, Lk : *claw, talon*. ['ail']
eg-lā-eg 'euge!' BRPs69[4].
±eglan tr. (Jud,Lcd) and impers. (Chr,LL) *to trouble, plague, molest, afflict*, Æ,CP. ['ail']
egle I. *hideous, loathsome, troublesome, grievous, painful*, Rᴅ. ['ail'] II.=egl
eglian=eglan
-ēgnan v. on-ē.
ēgnes f. *fear*, EPs88[41].
egnwirht 'merx,' EPs126[3] (=gēnwyrht? BT; āgenwyrht? ES38·1).
ēgo (NG)=ēage
ēgor n? *flood, high tide*, WW386[29]; 474[4].
ēgorhere† m. *flood, deluge*, Gᴇɴ.
ēgorstrēam† (ēa), m. *sea, ocean*.
egs-=eges-; ēgs-=ēges-, īegs-
+egðan *to harrow*, Bғ30[17].
egðe f. *harrow, rake*, Gʟ.

egðere m. *harrower*, GL.

egðwirf n. *a young ass used for harrowing?* (BTac),BC3·367'.

Egypt-=Egipt-

eh=eoh; ēh-=ēag-, īeg-, īg-

eher (NG)=ēar; ehhēoloðe=hēahhēoloðe

ehsl=eaxl; eht=æht, eaht

ōht? (æ) f. *pursuit*, B2957? [=ōht]

ehta=eahta

±ēhtan *to attack, persecute, pursue, harass,* Æ,AO,CP : (+) *acquire, purchase,* Æ. [ōht]

ehtefeald=eahtafeald

ēhtend m. *pursuer, persecutor,* AO.

ēhtere m. *persecutor,* Æ,CP.

ēhtian=ēhtan

ēhtnes f. *persecution,* Æ,AO,CP.

ēhtre=ēhtere

ēhtung f. *persecution,* AO274¹⁰.

ehtuwe (RD37⁴)=eahta

ēig=īeg; eige=ege; eis-=eges-

el-, ele- (prefix) *foreign, strange.*

ēl=(1) īl, (2) æl; elan=eglan

elboga (Æ)=elnboga

ēlc (NG)=ǣlc; elch=eolh

elcian *to put off, delay,* Æ.

elciend m. *procrastinator,* ÆL12¹⁶⁶.

elcor adv. *else, elsewhere, otherwise, except, besides,* BH. ['*elchur*']

elcora, elcra, elcran (æ¹) adv. *else, otherwise.*

elcung f. *delay,* Æ.

elcur=elcor; eld=ield; eldor=ealdor

ele mn. *oil,* Lcd,Mt; Æ,AO,CP. ['*ele*'; L.]

ele-=el-

elebacen *cooked in oil,* ÆT.

elebēam m. *olive-tree,* Æ : *elder? privet? elm-tree?* (GBG),EC379'.

elebēamen *of the olive-tree,* WW128⁷.

elebēamstybb m. *stump of an elder,* EC190'.

elebearu m. *olive-grove,* NG.

eleberge f. *olive,* GD,Ps.

eleboga (*WW*)=elnboga

elebytt f. *oil-vessel, chrismatory,* WW432²⁵.

electre=elehtre

eledrōsna pl. *dregs of oil,* Lcd1·310'.

elefæt n. *oil-vessel, ampulla,* WW. ['*elvat*']

elegrēofa m. *oil-vessel?* OEG (v. BTs).

elehorn m. *oil-flask,* WW434⁷.

elehtre f. *lupine,* Lcd. [L. *electrum*]

elelēaf n. *olive-leaf?* Lcd102b.

elelēast f. *lack of oil,* GD44²¹.

elelendisc *strange, foreign,* Gl,Ps. *as sb. stranger, exile.* [ellende]

elene=eolone; elesdrōsna=eledrōsna

elesealf f. *oil-salve, nard,* HGl405.

eleseocche f. *oil-strainer,* WW154¹².

elestybb=ellenstybb

eletredde f. *oil-press,* GD.

eletrēow n. *olive,* GD, Ps.

eletrēowen *of olive-trees,* Swt.

eletwig n. *oleaster,* WW460²⁸.

ēleð m. *allodium, freehold,* Gu38. [=ēðel]

elewana m. *lack of oil,* GD44⁹.

elfen=ælfen

elfetu=ilfetu; elfremed=ælfremed

elh=eolh

elhygd f. *distraction, ecstasy,* GD,Lcd.

ell m. *the letter* l, ÆGR200.

ell-=el-

ellærn (*Cp*), ellarn=ellen II. and III.

ellandt n. *foreign country,* B. ['*eilland*']

elle I. (pl. of *el) *the others,* MtR22⁶. [v elra] II.=ealle. III.=ellen II.

elletne (*An*)=endleofan

ellen I. nm. (always n. in †) *zeal, strength, courage,* B,Bo,Gu : *strife, contention,* WW424¹². on e. *boldly.* ['*elne*'] II. n. '*elder*'-*tree,* Gl,Lcd; Mdf. III. adj. *of elder-wood,* Lcd.

ellenahse f. *elder ash,* Lcd121b. [=asce]

ellencræft m. *might, power,* PPs98⁵.

ellendǣdt f. *heroic deed.*

ellende I. adj. *foreign, strange, exiled.* II. n. *foreign parts.*

ellenga=eallunga

ellengǣst m. *powerful demon,* B86.

ellengrāfa m. *elder-grove,* BC2·469²⁷.

ellenheardt *mighty, brave, bold.*

ellenhete m. *jealousy,* A11·98²⁶.

ellenlǣca m. *champion, combatant,* WW.

ellenlēaf n. *elder-leaf,* Lcd122a.

ellenlēas *wanting in courage,* Jul. ['*ellenlaes*']

ellenlic *brave,* Æ. adv. -līce.

ellenmǣrðut † *fame of courage,* B.

ellenrind f. *elder-bark,* Lcd.

ellenrōft *courageous, powerful,* Æ.

ellensēoc *mortally wounded,* B2787.

ellensprǣc f. *strong speech,* Gu1128.

ellen-stubb, -stybb m. *elder-stump,* Ct.

ellentān m. *elder-twig,* Lcd116b.

ellentrēow n. *elder-tree,* KC3·379¹⁵.

ellenðrīste *heroically bold,* Jud133.

ellenweorct n. *heroic deed: good work,* VH11.

ellenwōd I. f. *zeal,* PPs68⁹. II. *furious,* Jul140 : *zealous, earnest,* OEG364.

ellenwōdian *to emulate,* Cps,WW.

ellenwōdnes f. *zeal,* BH,EPs.

ellenwyrtf.*elderwort,dwarf-elder,*Lcd,WW.

ellenwyrttruma m. *root of elder,* Lcd101a.

elleoht n. *elision of the letter* l, OEG5471.

ellern=ellen II.

elles adv. *in another manner, otherwise,* Mt; Æ,CP : '*else,*' *besides,* Bl,Seaf; Æ,CP : *elsewhere,* OEG2²⁵². e. hwǣr, hwergen, hwider *elsewhere.* e. hwæt *anything else, otherwise.*

ellicor (Chrd 80²²)=elcor

ellnung=elnung

ellor† *elsewhere, elsewhither, to some other place.* e. londes *in another land.*

ellorfūs† *ready to depart.*

ellorgāst† (ǣ) m. *alien spirit,* B.

ellorsīð m. *death,* B2451.

ellreord, ellreordig=elreord

ellðēod=elðēod

elm m. '*elm,' elm-tree,* Lcd. [*L.* ulmus]

elm-=ælm-; **elmboga**=elnboga

elmrind f. *elm-bark,* Lcd.

eln f. *fore-arm,* '*ell*' (a foot and a half to two feet), *Mt,WW*; Æ,AO,CP.

elnboga m. '*elbow,' WW*(ele-); CP.

elne, elnes ds. and gs: of ellen.

elngemet n. *ell-measure,* Gen 1309.

±elnian *to emulate, be zealous* : *strengthen, comfort oneself* : *gain strength,* Lcd.

elnung f. *comfort, consolation,* ÆL23⁵²⁵ : *emulation, zeal,* Æ.

elone=eolone; **elotr,** eloðr (Gl)=elehtre

elpan- (VPs), elpen-=elpend-

elpend (y¹) m. *elephant,* AO.

elpendbǣnen (elpan-, ylpen-) *of ivory,* Ps 40⁹.

elpendbān n. *ivory,* AA6¹⁸,Gl.

elpendtōð m. *ivory,* WW397²⁷.

elpent=elpend

elra comp. adj. *other,* B753. [*el; Goth.* aljis]

el-reord (BH), -reordig (AA) *of strange speech, barbarous.*

elreordignes f. *barbarism,* Gl(Swt).

-els masc. suffix for inanimate things, as in rēcels, wǣfels.

eltst (Æ)=ieldest superl. of eald.

elðēod f. *strange people, foreign nation,* (in pl.) *foreigners, enemies* : (pl.) *all people, all nations,* Cr 1084,1337 : *exile,* AO.

elðēod(g)ian *to live abroad, wander as a pilgrim* : (+) *make strange, disturb,* Sc 106¹⁹.

elðēodgung=elðēodung

elðēodig (æ¹) *foreign, strange, barbarous, hostile, Bo,Met* (æl-); AO,CP : *exiled.* wk. form mp. el-ðēodian, -ðēodigan *strangers, foreigners, pilgrims, proselytes.* ['*altheodi*']

elðēodige (īo) *abroad,* LkR15¹³.

elðēodiglic (æ¹) *foreign, strange, born abroad.* adv. -līce.

elðēodignes (æ¹) f. *foreign travel or residence, pilgrimage, exile,* AO,CP,Chr.

elðēodisc *foreign, strange,* Mt27⁷.

elðēodung f. *residence or travel abroad,* BH 332¹⁸.

elðīd-, elðīed-, elðīod-=elðēod-

eluhtre=elehtre; **elwiht**=ælwiht

em m? *the letter* m.

em-=ef(e)n-, emn-, ym-, ymb-, ymbe-

ēm-=ǣm-

emb, embe=ymb, ymbe

embeht (NG)=ambiht

embehtian=ambihtan; **embiht**=ambiht

embren (æ¹, i²) n. *bucket, pail,* Gl. [*Ger.* eimer]

emdenes, emdemes=endemes

emel=ymel; **emer**=omer

emleoht n. *elision of* m *before vowels in scanning verse,* OEG5473.

emn, emne=ef(e)n, efne

emnet n. *plain,* AO186²². [efen]

emtwā (on) *into two equal parts, in half,* Æ.

-en suffix **I.** *diminutive* (neut.) as in mægden (from mægð). **II.** *to form feminines* (a) *with mutation* (gyden, *from* god). (b) *without mutation* (ðēowen *from* ðēow). **III.** *adjectival, with mutation, denoting material.*

ēn-=ān-, ǣn-; **end** conj.=and

+endadung f. *finishing,* DR105¹⁴.

ende m. '*end,' conclusion, Ct,Met,Mt,Ps* : *boundary, border, limit, Ps*; Æ,AO,CP : *quarter, direction* : *part, portion, division, Chr*; AO : *district, region, AO* : *species, kind, class* : *death.* æt (ðǣm) e. *finally.*

ende-berd-, -bird-, -bred-=endebyrd-

endebyrd f. *order,* Met13⁴.

±endebyrdan *to arrange, ordain, dispose,* Æ.

endebyrdend m. *one who orders or arranges,* OEG.

endebyrdes† *in an orderly manner, regularly, properly,* Met.

endebyrdian=endebyrdan

endebyrdlic *ordinal,* ÆGr282¹⁴. adv. (±) -līce *in an orderly manner, in order, in succession,* Æ,CP.

endebyrdnes f. *order, succession, series, arrangement, method, rule,* Æ,CP : *grade, degree, rank, condition,* Æ,CP.

endedæg† m. *last day, day of death.*

endedēað m. *death as the end of life,* Cr 1653?

endedōgor† mn. *last day, death-day.*

endefæstend m. *finisher,* DR27¹⁵.

endefurh f. *end-furrow,* KC3·384¹⁶.

endelāf f. *last remnant, last,* B2813.

endelēan† n. *final retribution.*

ende-lēas, -lēaslic (Æ) '*endless,' boundless, eternal, Bo.* adv. -līce, Æ.

endelēasnes f. *infinity, eternity,* ÆGr116¹⁰.

endelīf n. *life's end, death,* EL585.

endemann m. *man of the world's (supposed) final age,* Æ.

endemes (Æ,CP), endemest adv. *equally, likewise, at the same time, together, unanimously* : *fully, entirely* : *in procession.*

endemest (ænde-) *last,* MFH157.

endemestnes? f. *extremity*, RBL33¹⁵ (?= endenēhstnes, BTs).

ende-nēhst, -nēxt (ī, ȳ) *extreme, final, last*, Æ.

enderīm m. *number*, SAT 12.

endesǣta m. *border-watchman*, B 241.

endespǣc f. *epilogue*, CM 1166.

endestæf† m. *end, conclusion*.

endetīma m. *end of life, last hour*, LL.

endeōrǣst (ænde-) f. *end, destruction*, GD 337⁹.

±**endian** *to 'end,' finish*, G; Æ : *abolish, destroy*, Ps; AO,CP : *to come to an end, die, Gu*; AO. [v. also *'yend'*]

end-lefte (AA 16′,31′), -lifta=endlyfta

endleofan (e², i², u², y²; o³) num. *'eleven,'* Æ,BH.

endlifangilde *entitled to eleven-fold compensation*, LL 3,1; 470,7.

endlyfenfeald *eleven-fold*, ByH 36¹⁴.

end-lyfta, -leofta, -leofeða *'eleventh,'* Bl,Mt.

endlyfte *in the eleventh place, eleventhly*, LL 182,11.

+**endodlic** *finite*, Bo 44²¹.

±**endung** f. *'ending,' end*, Mt; CP : (+) *death*. [*'yend'*]

endwerc n. *pain in the buttocks*, LCD 174a. [wærc]

ened (æ¹, i²) mf. *drake, duck*, Gl. [*'ende'*]

enelēac=ynnelēac

ēnetere=ānwintre; **ēnga**=ānga

enge I. (a, æ) *narrow, close, straitened, constrained : vexed, troubled, anxious : oppressive, severe, painful, cruel*. **II.** (a, o) adv. *sadly, anxiously*

+**enged** *troubled, anxious*, WW 357⁷.

engel (æ) m. *'angel,' messenger*, Mt; Æ,CP. [*L.* angelus]

Engel=Angel

engelcund *angelic*, GU 72.

engelcynn† n. *race or order of angels*.

engellic *angelic, of angels*, ÆH.

engetrēow=hengetrēow

Englaland n. *country of the Angles, 'England,'* BH.

Englan, Engle mp. *the Angles* (as opposed to the Saxons) : *the English generally*. [Angel]

englelic=engellic

Englisc *'English,'* Ct,LL; CP. on E. *in (the) English (language)*, ÆGr,BH,Mt.

Engliscman m. *'Englishman,'* LL.

engu† f. *narrowness, confinement*.

enid=ened; **ēnig**=ǣnig; **ēnitre**=ānwintre

enlefan=endlufon; **ēnlīpig**=ānlīpig

enne-lēac, -lēc=ynnelēac; **eno**=heonu

ent m. *giant*, Æ,AO (v. AB 40·21ff).

entcynn n. *race of giants*, NUM 13³⁴.

entisc *of a giant*, B 2979.

entse=yndse

enu=heonu

ēnwintre=ānwintre

eobor, eobot=eofor, eofot; **ēoc**=gēoc

ēode (B,G,Gl) I. pret. 3 sg. of gān. [*'yode'*] II.=ēowde

eodor† m. *hedge, boundary : limit, region, zone : enclosure, fold, dwelling, house : prince, lord*.

eodor-brecð f., -brice m. *breach of an enclosure, house-breaking*, LL.

eodorcan *to chew, ruminate*, BH 346². [=edrocian]

eodorgong (eder-) m. *begging?* (GK) : *robbery?* (Liebermann), CR 1676. (v. also BTac.)

eodorwīr m. *wire fence*, RD 18².

eodur=eodor; **eofel**=yfel

eofer=eofor; **eofera**=eafora

eofermodig=ofermodig

eofet=eofot; **eofne**=efne

eofole f? *danewort, endive?* LCD.

eofon=heofon

eofor (e¹, ea¹, e²) m. *boar, wild boar*, Lcd,Ps : *boar-image on a helmet*. [*'ever'*]

eofora=eafora

eoforcumbol n. *boar-image on a helmet? boar-shaped ensign?* EL 76; 259.

eoforfearn (e¹) n. *a kind of fern, polypody*, Lcd,WW. [*'everfern'*]

eoforhēafodsegn (ea¹) n. *banner with a boar's head design?* B 2152 (? two words, Klb. p. 196).

eoforlīc m. *boar-image (on a helmet)*, B 303.

eoforspere (u²) n. *boar-spear*, OEG 7⁵⁶.

eoforsprēot n. *boar-spear*, GL.

eoforswīn n. *boar*, LCD 98b.

eoforðring m. *(boar-throng), the constellation Orion*, Cp 1464 (ebur-).

eoforðrote f. *carline thistle*, LCD.

±**eofot** n. *crime, sin, guilt*, LL.

eofoð=eafoð; **eoful-** (A)=yfel-

eofur (VPs)=eofor; **eofut** (NG)=eofot

ēogor=ēgor; **eogoð**=geoguð

eoh† nm., gs. ēos *war-horse, charger : name of the rune for* e. [*Goth.* aihwa]

ēoh† [=īw] m. *'yew'-tree*, WW : *name of the rune for* ēo.

eola, eolc=eolh; **eoldran**=ieldran

eolene=eolone

ēoles gs. of eolh.

eolet n. *voyage?* (Cosijn), B 224.

eolh m. [g. ēoles] *elk*, GL : *name of a rune*, RUN 15. [*OHG.* elho]

eolh-sand (-sang, HGL 431) n. *amber*, GL.

eolhsecg (colhx-, eolx-, ilug-) m. *'papyrus,' reed, sedge*, GL.

eolhstede (AN)=ealhstede

eolone f. *elecampane*, GL,LCD.

eoloð=ealað (v. ealu).

eolxsecg=eolhsecg

eom I. v. wesan. II.=heom, him dp. of hē, hēo, hit.

eond=geond

eonde?=ende (but v. JAW 31).

eonu=heonu

eor-; ēor-=ear-, ier-; ēar-

eorcnanstān (AA), eorc(l)anstān† m. *precious stone.* [*Goth.* -airkns]

ēored (o²) nf. *troop, band, legion, company* : *chariot?* AA 13⁵. [eoh, rād]

ēoredcist (o², ie³, e³, y³)† f. *troop, company.*

ēoredgeatwe fpl. *military apparel,* B 2866.

ēoredgerīd n. *troop of horsemen,* WW 229¹.

ēoredhēap m. *troop, host,* DD 113.

ēoredmæcg m. *horseman,* RD 23³.

ēoredmann m. *trooper, horseman,* BH,WW.

ēoredmenigu f. *legion,* GD 73,74.

ēoredōrēat m. *troop, host,* RD 4⁴⁹.

ēored-weorod, -wered n. *band, company,* GD 71⁶.

eorl m. *brave man, warrior, leader, chief, B, Cr,Gen,Rd* : *man* : '*earl,' nobleman* (origly. a Danish title=the native 'ealdorman'), *Ct,LL,Ma.*

eorlcund *noble,* LL.

eorldōm m. *earldom, rank of an earl,* CHR.

eorlgebyrd† f. *noble birth,* MET.

eorlgestrēon† n. *treasure, wealth.*

eorlgewǣde n. *armour,* B 1442.

eorlic (1)=ierlic; (2) eorllic

eorlisc *of noble rank,* LL 173.

eorllic *chivalrous, manly,* B,WW 416³³.

eorlmægen† n. *band of noble warriors.*

eorlriht n. *earl's right,* LL 458,5.

eorlscipe† m. *manliness, courage.*

eorlweorod n. *host of noble warriors,* B 2893.

eormencynn (y¹)† n. *mankind.*

eormengrund n. *wide world,* B 859.

eormenlāf f. *huge legacy,* B 2234.

eormenstrȳnd f. *race, generation,* SOL 329.

eormenðēod (y¹) f. *mighty people,* MEN 139.

eorn-=georn-

eornes f. *anger,* BL 123⁸ ; HL.

eornest=eornost

eornost f. *earnestness, zeal,* Æ,CP : *seriousness, W* : *battle.* on eornost(e) *in earnest, earnestly, truly.* ['*earnest*']

eornoste (e²) I. '*earnest,' zealous, serious,* Æ. II. adv. *courageously* : *fiercely.*

eornostlīce I. adv. '*earnestly,' strictly, truly, in truth, indeed, Mt,LL.* II. conj. *therefore, but.*

eornust=eornost; ēorod=ēored

eorp=earp; eorre (AA 37¹⁶)=ierre

eorð=eorðe, heorð

eorð-æppel m. nap. -æppla '*earth-apple,' cucumber, Æ* : '*mandragora,' WW.*

eorðærn† (e²) n. *earth-house, grave,* WW.

eorðbeofung (i²) f. *earthquake,* AO.

eorðberge f. *strawberry,* WW 242⁶. [berie]

eorðbīgenga m. *earth-dweller,* BH 268³¹.

eorðbīgennes f. *agriculture,* WW 144²¹.

eorðbrycg f. *bridge of poles covered with earth,* BC 3·223²¹.

eorð-būend†, -būg(ig)end m. *earth-dweller, man,* Æ.

eorðburh=eorðbyrig

eorðbyfung=eorðbeofung

eorðbyrgen f. *grave,* NC 284.

eorðbyrig f. *earthwork, mound, embankment, road,* Ct,GL.

eorðcafer m. *cockchafer,* WW 122¹⁶. [ceafor]

eorð-cenned, -cend *earth-born,* Ps.

eorðcræft m. *geometry,* OEG 3119.

eorðcry(p)pel m. *paralytic, palsied man,* NG.

eorðcund, eorðcundlic (CP) *earthly, mortal.*

eorðcyning m. *earthly king, king of the country.*

eorðcynn n. *human race,* Ex 370.

eorðdenu f. *valley,* NC 284.

eorðdraca m. *dragon that lives in the earth, B.* [v. '*earth*']

eorðdyne m. *earthquake,* Chr 1060. ['*earthdin*']

eorðe f. *ground, soil, Æ,B,LkL* ; AO,CP : '*earth,' mould, Gu* : *world, Æ,B,Mt* : *country, land, district, Jn.*

eorðen adj. *of or in the earth,* OEG 3312?

eorðern=eorðærn

eorðfæst '*earthfast,' firm in the earth, Æ.*

eorðfæt n. *earthly vessel, body,* SOUL 8.

eorðg(e)alla, m. *earth-gall, lesser centaury, Lcd* ; GL. [v. '*earth*']

eorðge-byrst, -berst n. *landslip,* Ct.

eorðgemǣre n. *boundary of the earth,* PPs 21²⁵.

eorðgemet n. *geometry,* GL.

eorðgesceaft f. *earthly creature,* MET 20¹⁹⁴.

eorðgræf n. *hole in the earth,* RD 59⁹.

eorðgrāp f. *earth's embrace,* RUIN 6.

eorðhele m. *a covering of the ground,* Ex 16¹⁴.

eorðhrērnes f. *earthquake,* BL,NG.

eorðhūs n. *cave-dwelling, den,* ÆL.

eorðīfig (ea¹, ȳ²) n. *ground-ivy, Lcd, WW* : '*terebinthus,' DR 68'.* [v. '*earth*']

eorðlic '*earthly,' worldly, Bl,Mt* ; Æ. adv. -līce.

eorðling=yrðling

eorðmægen n. *earthly power,* RIM 69.

eorð-mata [-maða?] m. '*vermis,' worm,* GL.

eorðmistel m. *basil (plant),* LCD 33a.

eorðnafela (a³, o³) m. *asparagus,* LCD.

eorðnutu f. '*earth-nut,' pig-nut,* Ct. [hnutu]

eorðreced n. *cave-dwelling,* B 2719.

eorðrest f. *bed laid on the ground*, WW 362¹¹.
eorðrīce n. *earthly kingdom*, CP : *earth*, LCD.
eorðrima m. *a plant*, LCD 120a.
eorðscræf n. ds. -scrafe *cave-dwelling, cavern*, CP : *sepulchre*.
eorðselet m. *cave-dwelling*.
eorðslihtes *close to the ground*, NUM 22⁴.
eorðstede m. *earth*, PPs 73⁷.
eorðstirung=eorðstyrung
eorð-styren (GD), -styrennes (NG), -styrung (Æ) f. *earthquake*.
eorðtilia m. *'earth-tiller,' husbandman, farmer*, Æ(*Gen*); W 305³¹. [—yrðtilia]
eorðtilð f. *'earth-tilth,' agriculture*, WW.
eorðtūdor n. *human race*, PPs 117²².
eorðtyrewe f. *earth-tar, bitumen*, AO 74¹⁷.
eorðu (N)=eorðe
eorðwæstm f. *fruit of the earth*, BH,LL.
eorð-waran (CP), -ware mpl., -waru fpl. *earth-dwellers*, AO. ['*earthware*']
eorðweall m. *earth-wall, mound*, B,BH.
eorðweard m. *region of earth*, B 2334.
eorðwegt m. *earth*, EL,Ps.
eorðwela m. *wealth : fertility*, AO.
eorðweorc n. *work on the land*, Ex 1¹⁴.
eorðwerod n. *inhabitants of earth*, W 25²¹; 203⁵.
eorð-westm, -ȳfig=eorð-wæstm, -ífig
ēorwicga=ēarwicga
ēos gs. of eoh.
eosel, eosol=esol
eosen=iesen
ēost-=ēast-; eosul=esol
eotan (VI's)—etan; Eotas=Eotenas
eotent m. *giant, monster, enemy.* [v. '*eten*']
Eotenas mpl. *Jutes*, B.
eotend—etend
eotenisc *gigantic*, B. ['*etenish*']
Eotolware mp. *Italians*, BH 108¹¹.
ēoton=ǣton pret. pl. of etan.
eotonisc=eotenisc
eotonweard f. *watch against monsters?* B 668.
ēoðe (N)=ēaðe
ēow I. dat. of gē pers. pron. *to you*, 'YOU.'
II. interj. *wo! alas!* III.=gīw. IV.=īw. V. m. *sheep.*
ēowā=ēow II.; ēowan=īewan
ēowberge=īwberge; ēowcīg=ēowocig
ēowd f. *sheepfold*, Æ : *flock, herd*, Æ.
ēowde fn. *flock (of sheep), herd*, An,Ps. ['*eowde*']
ēowdescēap n. *sheep of the flock*, PPs 64¹⁴.
ēowe I. gs. of ēowu. II.=ēowu
ēowed, ēowede=ēowd, ēowde
ēowende (dat.) '*testiculus*,' LL 64,25¹.
ēower I. gp. of gē pers. pron. (2nd pers.). II. possess. pron. YOUR, *yours*.

ēowerlendisc *of your land, 'vestras,'* ÆGR 94¹.
ēowestre (ē¹, ēa¹, i²) mf. *sheepfold*, GD.
ēowian=īewan
ēowic acc. pl. of ðū (v. gē).
ēowistre=ēowestre
ēowocig '*yolky,' greasy with yolk, as unwashed wool*, Lcd 16a (v. NED).
ēowod, ēowode=ēowd, ēowde
ēowohumele f. *female hop-plant*, LCD.
ēowomeoluc f. *ewe's milk*, LCD 70a.
ēowu f. *'ewe,'* Æ,KC,LL.
ēowunga=ēawunga
epactas sbp. *epacts*, LCD.
epistol, epistola m. *letter*, AA.
epl, eppel=æppel; eppan=yppan
er-=ǣr-, ear-, ier-, yr-
ēr=(1) ǣr, (2) ȳr, (3) ēar I.
erce=arce; ercna(n)stān (NG)=eorcnanstān
eretic *heretic*, BH 312¹⁹. [*L.*]
erian, erigean *to plough*, Æ,Bo,Lk; CP. ['*ear*']
erinaces pl. *hedgehogs*, PPs 103¹⁷.
eringland n. *arable land*, KC 6·200⁷.
eriung f. *ploughing*, WW 104⁶.
ernð (æ) f. *crop of corn*, BHc 44²³.
ersc m? *stubble-field*, EC 282'; 290'.
erscgrāfa *a copse near a stubble-field?* KC 374'.
erschen f. *quail*, Æ,WW.
ēsa v. ōs.
ēsceap=ǣsceap; esl=eaxl
esne m. *labourer, slave, servant, retainer : youth, man*, CP. [*Goth*. asneis]
esnecund *of a labourer*, WW 212⁴⁴.
esnemon (æ¹) m. *hireling*, JnR 10¹³.
esnewyrhta m. *mercenary, hireling*, GD,LL.
esnlīce *like a man, manfully*, Æ,CP.
esol mf. *ass*, CP. [*L.* asellus]
esole f. *she-ass*, BL.
ess m. *name of the letter* s, ÆGR.
essian *to waste away*, RPs 118¹³⁹.
ēst mf. *favour, grace, bounty, kindness, love*, An,B : *pleasure*, Lk : *harmony, consent* : (usu. in pl.) *delicacies*, WW; Æ. ['*este*']
ēstan (w. d.) *to live luxuriously*, W 190¹⁷.
ēstan=ēastan
ēste *gracious, liberal*, B,Gen. ['*este*']
ēstelic *kind, gracious*, EPs 68¹⁷ : *devout*, DR : *delicate, dainty (of food)*, MFH 157. adv. -līce, CP : *courteously*, An 292 : *luxuriously*, WW. [v. '*este*']
ēstful *gracious, devoted, devout*, Æ : *fond of luxuries*, WW 218¹⁸,¹⁹. ['*estful*'] adv. -līce.
ēstfulnes f. *devotion, zeal*, CP : *daintiness*, WW : *luxury, lechery.* [v. '*este*']
ēstgeorn *delicate, fond of luxuries*, WW 218¹⁸.

ēstig *gracious, liberal*, PA 16.

ēstines f. *benignity*, EPs 64¹².

ēstlic=ēstelic

ēstmete m. *dainty (food), delicacy, luxury,* ÆGr. [v. '*este*']

-estre=f. agent, as in wītegestre, *prophetess.*

ēstum† *freely, willingly, gladly.*

esul=esol

esulcweorn f. *mill-stone turned by an ass,* CP 31¹⁷.

ēswic=ǣswic

et I.=æt prep. II. pres. 3 sg. of etan.

et-=æt-, ed-; ēt (NG)=æt

±etan⁵ (ea, eo) *to 'eat,'* Æ,AO,Jn : *devour, consume,* Jn; CP : (tr.) *feed* : (reflex.) *provision oneself* : (+) *eat together.* [v. also '*yeten*']

etelond n. *pasture land,* KC 2·95¹⁴.

etemest=ytemest; eten=eoten

etend I. m. *eater, glutton.* II. *voracious, gluttonous,* WW 396,523 (eot-).

etenlǣs f. *pasture,* LL 452,20.

eting f. *eating,* Sc 170⁵.

etol (ettul) *voracious,* ÆGr 69⁷,WW 226¹.

etolnes (ettul-) f. *greediness, gluttony,* Sc 55⁶.

etonisc (B)=eotenisc; etsomne=ætsamne

etst=itst pres. 2 sg. of etan.

ettan *to graze, pasture land,* AO 18²⁵.

ettul=etol

ēð I. comp. adv. *more easily.* II.=ȳð

eð-=æð-, ed-

ēð-=ǣð-, ēað-, īeð-

eðcwide (GL)=edcwide

ēðel (oe, N) mn. gs. ēðles *country, native land, ancestral home,* Lk,Met; CP : *name of the rune for* œ. †hwǣles ē. *the sea,* Chr 975A. ['*ethel*']

ēðelboda m. *land's apostle, native preacher,* Gu 976.

ēðelcyning m. *king of the land,* Cr 997.

ēðeldrēam m. *domestic joy,* Gen 1607.

ēðeleard m. *native dwelling,* Gen 1945.

ēðelfæsten n. *fortress,* Rd 72²².

ēðelland† n. *fatherland, country.*

ēðellēas† *homeless, exiled.*

ēðelmearc† f. *boundary of one's country, territory,* Gen.

ēðelrīce† n. *native country.*

ēðelriht† n. *hereditary right.*

ēðel-seld†, -setl† n. *settlement,* Gen.

ēðelstæf (ul, yl) m. *heir, successor,* Gen 2223.

ēðelstaðol m. *settlement,* Gen 94.

ēðelstōl† m. *hereditary seat, habitation* : *royal city, chief city.*

ēðelstōw† f. *dwelling-place,* Gen.

ēðelturf† f. (ds. -tyrf) *fatherland.*

ēðelðrymm m. *glory of one's own land,* Gen 1634.

ēðelweard† m. *lord of the realm, man.*

ēðelwynn† f. *joy of ownership,* B.

ēðgung f. *breath, breathing, inspiration* : *hard breathing,* RB 68³.

±ēðian *to breathe,* GD : *smell.* ['*ethe*']

ēðmian=ǣðmian

ēðr (N)=ǣdr, ǣdre; ēðr-=īeðr-

eðða (MtR)=oððe

ēðung I. f. *laying waste, destroying,* Gl. [ēðe, īðan] II.=ēðgung

ēðwilte *easily turned,* OEG 1151.

ēuwā interj. *woe!* Gl.

evangelista m. *evangelist,* VH 11.

ēw-=ǣw-, ēaw-, ēow-, īew-; ēwe=ēowu

ex, exe f. *brain,* Lcd (v. A 30·129).

ex=eax; exen v. oxa.

exlistealla (HGl 405)=eaxlgestealla

exorcista m. *exorcist,* ÆL 31¹⁴¹.

---

fā v. fāh I.

faca gp. of fæc.

fācen n. nap. fācnu *deceit, fraud, treachery, sin, evil, crime,* Mt,LL; Æ,AO : *blemish, fault (in an object),* LL 114,56; 398,9. ['*faken*']

fācendǣd f. *sin, crime,* PPs 118⁵³.

fācen-ful, -fullic *deceitful, crafty.* adv. -līce.

fācengecwis f. *conspiracy,* WW.

fācenlēas *guileless,* VH 11 : *pure,* NG.

fācenlic *deceitful,* RB 95¹²,¹⁵. adv. -līce, Æ. ['*fakenliche*']

fācensearu† n. *treachery.*

fācenstafas mp. *treachery, deceit,* B 1018.

fācentācen n. *deceitful token,* Cr 1566.

facg m. *plaice? loach?* WW 180³².

fācian *to try to obtain, get,* AO 152⁷ : *get to, reach,* BC 2·305'.

fācn=fācen; fācne=fǣcne

fācnesful=fācenful

facum dp. of fæc.

±fadian *to arrange, dispose, guide,* LL; Æ. ['*fade*'? v. IF 48·257]

fadiend m. *manager,* OEG 56³⁰⁸.

±fadung f. *arrangement, order, disposition, dispensation, rule,* Æ : *interpretation, version,* Bf 238¹⁶.

fadur (A)=fæder

fæc (e) n. *space of time, while, division, interval,* Lk; Æ,CP : *period of five years, lustrum,* WW 431¹⁶. ['*fec*']

fǣcan *to wish to go,* LL 128B².

fæccan=feccan

fæcele (e¹) f. *torch,* WW. [Ger. fackel]

fæcenlīce=fācenlīce

fǣcful *broad, spacious,* Sc 185¹⁵.

fæcile (Gl)=fæcele

fǣcne I. *deceitful, treacherous,* Ps : *vile, worthless.* II. adv. *deceitfully, maliciously, disgracefully* : (†) *exceedingly.* ['*faken*']

fǣcnig *crafty,* RPs 72¹⁸.

+**fǣd** I. *orderly, well-conducted,* LL : *calm, composed,* W 51²⁴. II. n? *discretion,* LL (244¹⁵). [fadian]

fǣd-=fēd-

fǣder (e¹) m. usu. indecl. in sg. '*father,*' Æ, VPs; AO,CP : *male ancestor,* LkL,Mt : the Father, God, Jn,Mt,VPs : (in pl.) *parents,* Æ. eald f. *grandfather.* ðridda, fēower-ða f. etc. *great-grandfather, great-great-grandfather, etc.*

fǣdera (e¹) m. *paternal uncle,* AO. ⌊cp. Ger. vetter]

+**fǣdera** m. *male sponsor, godfather,* Æ. [Ger. gevatter]

fǣderæðelo† npl. *patrimony* : *paternal kinship.*

+**fǣdere** f. *female sponsor, godmother,* LL.

fǣderen *paternal,* ÆT,Sc.

+**fǣderen** *born of the same father,* AO 114¹⁴.

fǣderenbrōðor m. *brother (from the same father),* PPs 68⁸.

fǣd(e)rencnōsl n. *father's kin,* LL 54,9.

fǣderencynn n. *father's kin,* CHR.

fǣderenfeoh=fæderfeoh

fǣderenhealf f. *father's side,* CHR 887A.

fǣderenmǣg m. *paternal kinsman,* CHR 887 E.

fǣderenmǣgð f. *paternal kindred,* LL 392,3.

fǣderēðel m. *fatherland,* AO.

fǣderfeoh n. *dowry paid by the father of the bride,* LL.

fǣdergeard m. *father's dwelling,* GEN 1053.

fǣdergestrēon n. *patrimony,* GL.

fǣderhīwisc n? '*paterfamilias,*' NG.

fǣderingmǣg=fæderenmæg

fǣderland n. *paternal land, inheritance,* CHR 1101.

fǣderlēas *fatherless,* W.

fǣderlic '*fatherly,*' *paternal, ancestral,* El. adv. -līce.

fǣdern-=fæderen-

fǣderslaga m. *parricide,* WW.

fǣderswica m. *traitor to one's father,* ÆL 19²²⁴.

+**fǣdlic** *fit, suitable, proper.* adv. -līce *orderly, quietly* : *craftily?* CPs 82⁴. [fadian]

fǣdm=fæðm; **fǣdr-**=fæder-

+**fǣdred** (AO)=+fæderen

fǣfne (LkR 1²⁹)=fæmne

+**fǣge** *popular with, acceptable to,* B 915. [OHG. gifag]

fǣgan *to paint,* GL.

fǣge '*fey,*' *doomed (to death), fated, destined,* An,B,Ma : *dead* : *unhappy, accursed,* Cr : *feeble, cowardly,* Gu.

±**fǣgen** (w. g.) '*fain,*' *glad, joyful, rejoicing,* B,Bo; AO,CP.

fǣgenian=fægnian

fǣgennes f. *joy,* NC 285.

fǣger I. '*fair,*' *lovely, beautiful,* B,Bo,Gen; AO,CP : *pleasant, agreeable, Ex* : *attractive, Gen;* Æ. II. n. *beauty, Bo* : *beautiful object.*

fǣger-=fægr-

fǣgerlīce *splendidly,* LkL 16¹⁹.

fǣgernes f. '*fairness,*' *beauty,* LPs,Sc; Æ.

fǣgerwyrde *smooth-speaking,* FT 12.

fǣgn=fægen

fǣgnes (LPs 44¹⁵)=fāgnes

+**fǣgnian** (a) (w. g. etc.) *to rejoice, be glad, exult, Bo,Met* : *fawn,* Æ : *applaud.* ['*fain*']

±**fǣgnung** f. *rejoicing,* Æ, ELSPs.

+**fǣgon** pret. pl. of +fēon.

fǣgre (e) *fairly, elegantly, beautifully,* Æ, Gen : *pleasantly, softly, gently, kindly, Gen,Men* : *well, justly* : *early,* LkR 24¹. ['*fair*']

±**fǣgrian** *to become beautiful,* Seaf : *adorn, decorate.* ['*fair*']

fǣgð? f. *imminent death,* AN 284(GK).

fǣhan=fǣgan; **fǣht**=feoht

fǣhð f. *hostility, enmity, violence, revenge, vendetta,* AO. [fāh; cp. Ger. fehde]

fǣhðbōt f. *payment for engaging in a feud,* LL 266,25; 286,5²ᵈ.

fǣhðe, fǣhðo, fǣhðu=fǣhð

fǣl-=feal-, fel-, fiel-, fyl-

fǣlǣcan=fālǣcan

fǣle† I. *faithful, trusty, good,* Ps : *dear, beloved.* ['*fele*'] II. adv. *truly, well, pleasantly.*

±**fǣlsian** *to cleanse, purify* : *expiate,* WW : (+) *pass through.*

fǣman *to* '*foam,*' MkL. [fām]

fǣmhādlic=fǣmnhādlic; **fǣmig**=fāmig

fǣmnanhād=fǣmnhād

fǣmne (ē) f. *maid, virgin, bride,* Æ : (+) *woman* : *virago.*

fǣmne(n)dlic=fǣmnhādlic

fǣmnhād m. *virginity, maidenhood,* AO.

fǣmnhādesmon m. *virgin,* RB 136²⁴.

fǣmnhādlic (OEG), fǣmn(en)lic *maidenly, virginal.*

fǣn=fen

fǣr n. nap. faru (±) *way, journey, passage, expedition, Bf,Ex,Lk.* mannes f. *highway,* ÆL 25⁴⁴¹ : *movement,* MET 31⁴ : *proceedings, life,* Æ : *movable possessions, means of subsistence,* HL : *ark, ship.* ['*fare*']

fǣr (ē) I. m. *calamity, sudden danger, peril, B,Ex* : *sudden attack* : *terrible sight,* BL 199²⁴. ['*fear*'] II.=fēfer. III.=fǣger

fǣr-=fer-, fear-, feor-, fier-, for-

fǣr- prefix=(1) *sudden, fearful;* (2) fēr-

fǣrærning f. *quick riding,* GD 14²⁴.

fǣran (ē) *to frighten, Æ*; CP: *raven*, MtL 7¹⁵.
['*fear*']
fǣrben-a, -u m. *peasant, small-holder?*
(Lieb.), LL 383,50 : '*epibata*,' Erf 1112.
fǣrbifongen *beset by dangers*, B 2009.
fǣrblǣd (ē¹) m. *sudden blast (of wind)*,
Jul 649.
fǣrbryne m. *scorching heat*, Ex 72.
fǣrclamm (ē) m. *sudden seizure*, Ex 119.
fǣrcoðu f. *apoplexy*, Lcd.
fǣrcwealm m. *sudden pestilence*, LL,W.
fǣrcyle m. *intense cold*, Gen 43.
fǣrdēað m. *sudden death*, MH,WW 351¹⁹.
fǣrdryre m. *sudden fall*, Cra 48.
fǣredlic (Æ)=fǣrlic; **fǣreht**=fǣrriht
fǣreld (a¹) nm. *way, journey, track, passage,
expedition*, Æ,AO,CP : *retinue, company*,
AO : *course of life, conduct*, Æ : *movement,
progress, power of locomotion*, Æ : *vehicle*,
OEG : *the Passover*, Æ.
fǣreldfrēols m. *Passover-feast*, Jos 5¹⁰.
fǣrelt (AO,CP)=fǣreld
fǣrennes=fǣrnes
fǣreð pres. 3 sg. of faran.
fǣrfyll (on) *headlong*, WW 426⁸.
fǣrgripe† m. *sudden grip*, B.
fǣrgryre† m. *awful horror*.
fǣrhaga m. *hedge of terrors*, Gu 933.
fǣring (ē) f. **I.†** *journey, wandering*. **II.**
accusation, WW 27⁸. **III.** *ecstasy*, WW
398¹⁶.
fǣringa (ē) *suddenly, unexpectedly, quickly,
forthwith, by chance*, Lk; Æ,CP. ['*feringe*']
fǣrlic *sudden, unexpected*, AO,WW; Æ,CP,
rapid. adv. -lice, Lk. ['*ferly*']
fǣrnes f. *passage, traffic*, BH,MtR.
fǣrnið m. *hostile attack*, B 476.
fǣrrǣs m. *sudden rush*, LkL 8³³.
fǣrrǣsende (ē¹) *rushing headlong*, DR 125¹⁶.
fǣrriht n. *passage-money*, ÆL 23b³⁵².
fǣrsceatt m. *passage-money, fare*, Andr.
fǣrsceaða m. *enemy*, Ma 142.
fǣrscyte m. *sudden shot*, Cr 766.
fǣrsearo n. *sudden artifice*, Cr 770.
fǣrsēað m. *deep pit*, WW 193⁶.
fǣrslide m. *sudden fall*, PPs 114⁸.
fǣrspell† n. *dreadful tidings*.
fǣrspryng m. *sudden eruption*, Lcd 134a.
fǣrst pres. 2 sg. of faran.
fǣrsteorfa m. *murrain*, Lcd 177a.
fǣrstice m. *sudden stitch (pain)*, Lcd 3·52¹¹.
fǣrstylt m? *amazement*, LkL 5²⁶.
fǣrswige (ē) f. *amazement*, MkL 5⁴².
fǣrswile m. *sudden swelling*, Lcd 27b.
fǣrð **I.**=ferð. **II.**=pres. 3 sg. of faran.
fǣrunga, fǣrunge (Æ)=fǣringa
fǣruntrymnes f. *sudden sickness*, Lcd 107b.
fǣrweg m. *cart road*, Ct.
fǣrwundor n. *terrible wonder*, Ex 279.

fæs (a, ea) n. *fringe, border*, MtL. ['*fas*']
fǣsceaftnes=fēasceaftnes
fǣsl† n? *seed, offspring, progeny*, Gen.
fǣsnian=fæstnian
fǣst **I.** '*fast*,' *fixed, firm, secure*, Bo,Lcd;
CP : *constant, steadfast, BH : stiff, heavy,
dense, Lcd : obstinate, bound, costive, Lcd*;
Æ : *enclosed, closed, watertight*, CP : *strong,
fortified, BH*; Æ,AO : *reputable? standard?*
(BTs), AO 286⁴. **II.** (Gu 192)=fæsten
±**fǣstan** **I.** *to fasten, make firm, ratify,
establish*, LkL : *entrust, commit*. ['*fast*'] **II.**
*to '*fast*' ('i-fast'), abstain from food*, Bf,
Bl,Lcd; CP : *atone for (by fasting)*, Da
592.
fǣste (e) '*fast*,' *firmly, securely*, BH,Bo; Æ :
straitly, strictly : heavily (sleep) : speedily.
fǣsten n. **I.** *fastness, stronghold, fortress*,
AO,CP : *cloister*, Æ : *enclosure, prison :
fastener*. **II.** (±) *fast (abstinence from food)*
Bl,LL,Mt,VPs; CP : *firmament, sky*.
['*fasten*']
fǣstenbryce m. *breach of fast*, LL,W.
fǣstendæg m. *fast-day*, Ct; RB,W. [v.
'*fasten*']
fǣstendic m. *fort-ditch, moat*, KC 1·257'.
fǣstengangol=fæstgangol
fǣstengeat n. *castle-gate*, Jud 162.
fǣstengeweorc n. *liability for repair of the
defences of a town*, KC.
fǣstenlic (ern) *quadragesimal, Lenten*, DR.
fǣstentid f. *fast*, LL. [v. '*fasten*']
fǣstenwuce f. *week of fasting*, ÆL 23b¹¹¹.
fǣstermōdor=fōstormōdor
fǣstern n. *fast : Quadragesima*, LG.
[=fæsten II.]
fǣstern-=fæsten-
fǣstgangol (o², e³) *steady, faithful*, Cra
80.
fǣsthafol *retentive, tenacious*, Æ : *sparing,
miserly*, CP.
fǣsthafolnes f. *economy*, CP 453²⁸ : *stinginess*, DD.
fǣstheald *firmly fixed*, ÆL 23⁴²³.
fǣsthydig† *constant, steadfast*.
±**fǣstian** (ea) *to commend, entrust, commit*,
LkL.
fǣsting f. *commendation, trust, guardianship*, GD 239¹⁵,LL 58,7 : *quartering (of the
king's servants)*, KC 2·60'.
fǣstingan=fæstnian
fǣstingmann m. *a kind of retainer*, EC.
fǣstland (o²) n. *land easily defended*, AA
25⁸.
fǣstlic *firm, fixed, steadfast, resolute*. adv.
-lice *certainly*, AS 32²¹ : (+) *fixedly, steadily,
constantly*, Bo : *unceasingly*, Æ,Bl : *verily,
but*, NG : *strictly*, Chrd. ['*fastly*']
fǣstmōd *constant in mind*, AO 288¹⁷.

fæstnes f. *firmness, massiveness, stability,* Bo : '*fastness*,' *stronghold,* Æ : *firmament,* Æ.

fæstnian *to* '*fasten*,' *fix, secure, bind,* An, Ps : *confirm, ratify, conclude* (*peace*), Ct, Ma : *betroth* : *bestow upon, secure for,* VH 11.

±**fæstnung** f. *fastening, bond* : *strengthening, stability* : *security, safety* : *protection, shelter* : *confirmation, ratification, pledge, engagement* : *exhortation,* MkL p 25.

fæstrǣd *firm, constant, steadfast,* B,Bo; Æ, CP. ['*fastrede*']

fæstrǣdlic *constant, steadfast,* Bo 20²¹. adv. -līce.

fæstrǣdnes f. *constancy, fortitude,* Bo.

fæststeall *standing firmly,* PPs 121².

fæsõ=fæst

fæt n. nap. fatu *vat, vessel, jar, cup,* Æ,B, JnL,WW; AO,CP : *casket, El* 1026 : *division,* Bf 4²⁶. ['*fat*']

fǣt I.† n. *plate, beaten out metal* (*especially gold*), *gold ornament.* II.=fǣtt I.

±**fǣtan** *to cram, put* (*in*), *load,* CP : *adorn.*

fǣted I.† *ornamented with gold.* [pp. of fǣtan] II.=fǣtt

fǣtedhlēor *with cheek ornaments,* B 1026.

fǣtedsinc n. *beaten gold,* An 478.

fǣtels, fǣtel m. *vessel, AO,Lcd*; Æ : *pouch, bag, sack,* Æ,CP. ['*fetles*']

fǣtelsian *to put into a vessel,* Lcd 1·328¹⁷.

fǣtelsod=fetelsod

fætfyllere (a¹, e²) m. *cupbearer,* GD,TC,WW.

fǣtgold n. *beaten gold,* B 1921.

fǣthengest m. *riding-horse,* Rd 23¹⁴.

fǣtian=fetian

fǣtnes f. '*fatness*,' Ps; Æ,CP : *the richest part of anything,* Ps.

+**fǣtnian**=+fǣttian

fǣtt I. (ē) '*fat*,' *fatted,* Æ,AO,Lk,Ps,Rd. II. =fǣted

fǣttian (+) *to become fat,* Ps : (+) *anoint,* Ps : *fatten.* ['*fat*']

+**fǣttig** *fat, rich,* CPs 19⁴.

fǣõe=fēõe

fæõel *play-actor?* v. OEG 39².

fæõer=feõer

fæõm (e) m. *outstretched or encircling arms, embrace, grasp, An,Rd* : *protection* : *interior, bosom, lap, breast, womb* : '*fathom*,' *cubit,* Æ,Cp,WW; Æ : *power,* B,Cr : *expanse, surface.*

fæõman, fæõmian *to surround, envelop, clasp, embrace, An,B.* ['*fathom*']

fæõmlic *embracing, enclosing, sinuous,* WW 486⁴.

-**fæõmnes** v. on-f.

fæõmrīm n. *fathom, cubit,* Ph 29.

fæx=feax

fāg I. *variegated, spotted, dappled, stained, dyed,* B,Gl,Lcd : *shining, gleaming, Ps.* ['*faw*'] II.=fāh I.

fāg-=fāh-; **fāge** f. (WW 94)=facg

fagen, fagen-=fægen, fægn-

fāgettan *to change colour,* Lcd 3·240²³. mid wordum f. *speak evasively.*

fāgetung f. *change* (*of colour*), ÆH 2·538'.

±**fāgian** *to change in colour, vary, be variegated,* RB 137⁸.

fāgnes f. *scab, ulcer, eruption,* Æ : *variety of colour, brilliancy,* HL,OEG.

fagnian=fægnian

fāgung f. *variety* (esp. *of colour*), DR,GD.

fāgwyrm m. *basilisk,* VPs 90¹³.

fāh I. nap. fā *hostile, B* : (±) *proscribed, outlawed, guilty, criminal, B.* ['*foe*'; fēogan] II. (±) m. '*foe,*' *enemy, party to a bloodfeud, LL*; Æ,AO. III.=fāg I.

fahame '*polentum,*' WW 40²⁸.

fāhmann m. '*foeman,*' *object of a bloodfeud, LL* 50,5.

fahnian=fægnian

fala I. (WW 52¹¹) ? ð. of *fealh tube? pipe? plank?* (BTs) (ES 38·337). II.=fela

fālǣcan *to be at enmity with, show hostility to, LL* 160,20⁷.

fal-d, -æd, -od, -ud m. '*fold,*' *stall, stable, cattle-pen, Gl,Jn,LL.*

fald- (N)=feald-

faldgang m. *going to the* (*sheep-*)*fold,* W 170²⁰ᴇ.

faldhrīõer n. *stalled ox,* MFH 158.

faldian *to make a fold, hurdle off sheep, LL* 454,9. ['*fold*']

falew-=feal(e)w-

fall- (VPs; NG)=feall-; **falod**=fald

fals I. '*false,*' *WW*; LL,W 272⁴. II. n. *falsehood, fraud, counterfeit.* [L.]

falõing *mass, load,* WW 33⁸.

falu=fealu; **falud**=fald

fām n. '*foam,*' BH,Ep; Æ : *sea,* Rd.

fāmblæd=fāmig; -**fāmblǣwende** v. lig-f.

fāmgian *to foam, boil,* Ex 481.

fāmig (ǣ) '*foamy,*' Rd.

fāmigbord *with foaming banks* (*of a stream*), Met 26²⁶.

fāmigbōsm *with foamy bosom,* Ex 493.

fāmigheals† *foamy-necked.*

fana m. *banner, standard,* Met; OEG : *plant, iris? Lcd.* ['*fane*']

+**fāna** gp. of +fā.

fanbyrde *standard-bearing,* v. OEG 1744.

fand pret. 3 sg. of findan.

fandere m. *trier, tester,* Sc 206⁴.

±**fandian** (often w. g., but also d. and a), *to try, attempt, tempt, test, examine, explore, search out, experience, visit, AO,B,Gen, Mk,Run*; CP. ['*fand,*' '*fond*'; findan]

fandung f. *investigation, trial, temptation, test, proof, A ,Gen*; Æ,CP. ['*fanding*']
fane (1) (NG, o¹)=fann. (2)=fanu
fang m. *plunder, booty, Chr* 1016. ['*fang*']
fangen pp. of fōn.
+**fangian** *to join, fasten,* Bo 96¹⁴.
fann f. *winnowing,* '*fan,*' *Cp,Lk,LL.* [*L.* vannus]
fannian *to* '*fan,*' *winnow, Sc* 186¹⁷.
fant (o) m. *fount,* '*font,*' *LL* : *baptismal water,* HL 15²⁹³.
fantbæð n. *baptismal water, laver of baptism,* ÆL,W.
fantblētsung f. *consecration of a font,* ÆP 188¹².
fantfæt n. *baptismal font,* ÆH 2·268'.
fanthālgung (o¹) f. *consecration of a font,* W 36².
fanthālig *holy from connection with the font,* Lcd 140b.
fantwæter (o¹) n. '*font-water,*' *water used at baptism, laver of baptism, Lcd*; Æ.
fanu=fana
fāra gp. of fāh I.
+**fara** m. *travelling companion, comrade,* BH,Rd.
±**faran**⁶ *to set forth, go, travel, wander, proceed, Bl,Chr,Gen,JnL*; AO,CP : *be, happen, exist, act, Bo* : '*fare*' ('*i-fare*'), *get on, undergo, suffer,* Æ : (+) *die,* AO,CP : (+) *attack, overcome, capture, obtain,* AO.
faraÞ=faroÞ-; **fareld**=færeld
fareð=faroð-
Fariseisc *of or belonging to the Pharisees,* OEG,WG.
farm=feorm
farnian *to prosper,* DR 176¹³.
faroÞ† m. *shore : stream.*
faroÞhengest (ea¹) m. *sea-horse, ship,* El 226.
faroÞlācende† *swimming, sailing.* as sb. *sailors.*
faroÞrīdende *sailing,* An 440.
faroÞstrǣt f. *path of the sea,* An 311,900.
faru f. *way, going, journey, course,* Æ : *expedition, march* : *procession, retinue, companions* : *life, proceedings, adventures,* Æ : *movable possessions.*
fas-=fæs-; **fatian** (NG)=fetian
fatu v. fæt.
faðe, faðu f. *father's sister, paternal aunt,* Æ.
faðusunu m. *father's sister's son,* Chr 1119.
faul m? *evil spirit,* Lcd 43a.
fēa I. (±) m. *joy,* AO,CP. **II.** n.=feoh. **III.** (fēawa) adj. nap. fēawe, superl. fēawost, fēast '*few,*' *B,BH,Chr,Mt,VPs.* fēawum sīðum *seldom.* adv. *even a little, at all.*
feadur (A)=fæder;±**fēagan**(NG,Ps)=±fēon
feah=feoh

±**feaht** I. pret. 3 sg. of feohtan. **II.**=feoht
feal-=fel-
+**feald** n. *region, abode?* Wald 2¹⁰.
±**fealdan**⁷ *to* '*fold,*' *wrap up, furl, entangle,* Æ,Bo,Rd : *roll about,* MkR 9²⁰.
fealdestōl=fyldstōl
feale, fealewes v. fealu.
fealewian=fealwian; **fealfor**=felofor
fealg pret. 3 sg. of fēolan.
fealga v. fealh.
fealgian *to fallow,* LL 454,9 (v. A 36·71).
fealh I. f. nap. fealga, *fallow land.* **II.** (e) f. '*felloe,*' *felly (of a wheel), Bo,WW.* **III.** pret. 3 sg. of fēolan. **IV.** v. fala.
+**fēalic** *joyous, pleasant.* adv. -līce, W 284¹⁶.
feall=fiell
feallan⁷ (±) *to* '*fall*' ('*i-falle,*' '*y-falle*'), *Bl, Ps* : *fall headlong, fail, decay, die, B,Ps*; AO,CP : *inflict (on), attack : flow,* AO 19¹⁸ : (+) *overthrow,* DR 115⁶ (æ).
fealle f. *snare, trap,* OEG 4979. ['*fall*']
feallen(d)lic *unstable, perishable, transient,* Bl,W.
fealletan (a¹) *to fall down,* '*concīdere,*' (mistaken for *concīdere*), MkLR 5⁵.
-**feallung** v. feax-f.
+**fealnis** (æ) f. *ruin,* LkL 2³⁴.
fealo=(1) fealu; (2) fela
fēalōg w. g. *destitute,* Gu 217.
fealohilte *yellow-hilted,* Ma 166.
fealu I. (feale) adj. gsm. feal(e)wes, fealuwes '*fallow,*' *yellow, tawny, dun-coloured, grey, dusky, dark, B,Rd*; Æ. **II.** n. *fallow ground,* EC 179'.
fealu-=felo-
fealuwian=fealwian; **fealwes** v. fealu.
fealwian *to become* '*fallow,*' *fade, wither, Sol* : *grow yellow, ripen.*
fēanes f. '*fewness,*' *paucity,* BH,Ps. [=fēawnes]
+**fēanes** f. *joy,* Guth 134,VH 12.
fear=fearr; **fēar**=fearh
fēara gen. of fēa.
fearh (æ, e) m. gs. fēares *little pig, hog, Ep, WW.* ['*farrow*']
fearhhama m. *hide of pig,* WW 161⁵ (IF 48·254).
fearhrȳðer (e¹) n. *bull,* Bl. [fearr]
+**fearhsugu** f. *sow in farrow,* WW.
fearlic *of a bull,* OEG 11¹⁸⁷
fēarlic=færlic
fearm m. *freight, cargo,* Gen 1394.
fearn n. '*fern,*' *Bo,Cp*; Æ; Mdf.
fearnbed n. *fern-bed,* BC,WW.
fearnbracu f. *fern-brake,* KC 5·173¹⁸.
fearnedisc n. *fern-pasture,* BC 1·519².
fearnhege m. *hedge with ferns,* KC 3·54'.
fearnig *fern-covered,* Ct.
fearnlǣs n. *fern-pasture,* KC 2·59¹⁹.

fearoð-=faroð-
fearr I. m. *beast of burden, ox, bull,* Æ,AO.
  II.=feorr
feas (VPs)=fæs
fēasceaft† *destitute, miserable, helpless, poor.*
fēasceaftig *destitute, poor,* SEAF 26.
fēasceaftnes (ǣ¹) f. *poverty,* OEG 1171.
feast-=fæst-
featu (VPs)=fatu nap. of fæt.
fēaw-=fēa-; **fēawa**=fēa
fēawlic *few,* EPs 104¹².
fēawnes f. *fewness, paucity,* LPs 101²⁴.
feax (æ, e) n. *hair, head of hair,* B,BH,Lcd;
  Æ,CP. ['*fax*']
feaxclāð n. *cap,* WW 411¹⁷.
+**feaxe** *furnished with hair,* BH 96¹¹.
feaxēacan m. pl. *forelocks,* WW 343³³.
feaxede *hairy, bushy* : *long-haired (of a
  comet),* Chr 892. ['*faxed*']
+**feaxen** (WE 61¹⁴?)=+feaxe
feaxfang n. *seizing or dragging by the hair,*
  LL 5,33.
feaxfeallung f. *shedding of hair, mange,*
  WW 113³⁰.
feaxhār *hoary, grey-haired,* RD 73¹.
feaxnǣdel f. *crisping-pin,* WW 108².
feaxnes (æ, e) f. *head of hair,* WW.
feaxnett n. *hair-net,* WW.
+**feaxod**=+feaxe
feaxprēon m. *hair-pin,* WW 107³⁸.
feaxscēara (e¹) fp. *scissors for hair-cutting?
  curling-tongs?* WW 241⁴¹.
feaxwund f. *wound under the hair,* LL 20,45.
feb-=fef-; **fec**=fæc
±**feccan** (æ) *to 'fetch,' bring, bring to, draw,*
  Æ,Mt : *seek* : *gain, take.* [=fetian]
fecele=fæcele; **fecgan**=feccan
±**fēdan** *to 'feed,' nourish, sustain, foster,
  bring up,* Bl,Mt,Ps; Æ,CP : *bear, bring
  forth, produce.* pp. +fēd, OEG. [fōda]
fēdednes=fēdnes
fēdelfugol (oe¹) m. *fatted bird,* MtR 22⁴.
fēd-els, -esl m. *feeding, keep* : *fatted animal
  (bird?),* WW; Cp. ['*feddle*']
fēdelsswīn *fattened pig,* NC 343.
feder, federa=fæder, fædera
fēding f. '*feeding,*' CP.
fēdnes (ǣ) f. *nourishment,* BH 88⁶.
fedra=fædera
fēfer mn. gs. fēfres '*fever,*' Lk,G; CP.
fēferādl f. '*fever,*' AO.
fēfercyn n. *a kind of fever,* LCD 5b.
fēferfūge f. *feverfew,* LCD,GL. [*L.* febrifugia]
fēferian *to be feverish, suffer from fever,*
  LCD.
fēferig (o²) *feverish,* LCD 1·334'.
fēfersēoc *feverish,* WW 405³⁴.
fēfor, fēfur=fēfer
fēfr-=fēfer-

+**fēg** n. *joining, joint,* Æ : *composition* :
  diagram, BF 10³. [*Ger.* gefüge]
fēgan I. (±) *to join, unite, fix, adapt,* Lcd,
  Rd; Æ,CP : *compose, confine.* ['*fay*'] **II.**
  (WW 469⁸)=fǣgan?
+**fēgednes** f. *conjunction, connection* : *bond,
  fetter,* DHy 5⁶ : *figure,* ÆGR 105²⁰.
feger, fegere=fǣger, fǣgre
±**fēging** f. *conjunction, composition,* ÆGR
  10⁸.
+**fēgnes** f. *association, companionship* : *conjunction,* BF 94²³.
feh=feoh
+**feh**=+feah pret. 3 sg. of +fēon.
feht *sheepskin with the fleece on it?* TC 119²¹;
  v. ES 37·177.
+**feht**=+feoht; **fehtan** (N)=feohtan
fēhð pres. 3 sg. of fōn.
fel=fell; **fēl**=fēol
fela (ea, eo) **I.** sbn. and adj. (w. g., or in
  agmt.: rarely inflected) *many, much,* Chr.
  II. adv. *very much, many.* ['FELE']
felaǣte '*mordax,*' QEG 23¹⁵.
felafācne *very treacherous,* GnE 148.
felafeald *manifold, many times over,* Ps.
  ['*felefold*']
felafealdnes (fele-) f. *multitude,* EPs 5¹¹.
felafrēcne *very fierce, bold,* RUN 2.
felagēomor *very sad, sorrowful,* B 2950.
felageong *very young,* FT 53.
felageonge *much-travelled,* CREAT 3. [gan-
  gan]
felahrōr *full of exploits,* B 27.
felaīdelsprǣce *emptily chattering,* CP 174²⁵.
felalēof *very dear,* WIF 26.
felameahtig† *most mighty.*
felamōdig† *very bold,* B.
±**fēlan I.** (w. g.) *to touch, 'feel'* ('*y-fele*'),
  AO : *perceive,* Rd. **II.** (VPs)=fēolan
felaspecol *talkative,* LCD,Ps.
fela-specolnes, -sprecolnes f. *talkativeness,*
  BH,Sc.
felasprǣc (eo) f. *much speaking, loquacity,*
  MtR 6⁷.
felasprǣce *talkative,* CP 281¹⁴.
felasynnig *very guilty,* B 1379.
felawlonc *very stately,* RD 13⁷.
felawyrde *talkative,* W 40¹⁸.
felawyrdnes f. *talkativeness,* GD 208⁴.
felcyrf m. *foreskin* (BT).
feld m. ds. felda, felde *open or cultivated
  land, plain,* Bf,Met,RBL; AO,CP; Mdf :
  battlefield. on clǣnum felda *in the open
  field (of battle),* CP 227²⁵. ['*field*']
feldælbin (WW 352¹⁰)=feldelfen
feldbēo f. *humble-bee,* WW.
feldbisceopwyrt f. *field-bishopwort,* ANS
  84·325.
feldcirice f. *country church,* LL 264,5¹; 282,3².

felde=fylde pret. 3 sg. of fyllan.

feldefare? f. *fieldfare?* WW287¹⁷ (-ware).

feldelfen f. *wood-nymph,* WW189⁶. [v. *'elven'*]

feldgangende† *roaming over the land,* Sol.

feldhriðer n. *field-ox,* NC285 (cp. feldoxa).

feldhūs† n. *tent,* Ex.

feldlǣs (ē²) n. *pasture in open country,* KC.

feldland n. *'field-land,' meadow-land, plain,* Æ.

feldlic *rural,* ÆGR : *growing wild,* ÆH.

feldmǣdere f. *field-madder, rosemary, Lcd;* WW300¹⁰. [v. *'field'*]

feldminte f. *field-mint, wild mint,* WW.

feld-more, -meru f. *parsnip,* Lcd.

feldoxa f. *field-ox* (i.e. an ox out to grass, not a stalled ox), ÆH2·576'.

feldrude f. *wild rue,* Lcd3·325.

feldsæten f. *field,* LPs77¹². [seten]

feldswamm m. *fungus, toadstool,* WW404²⁶.

feldwēsten n. *desert,* Deut1¹.

feldwōp m. *plantain,* Gl (?=*feldhoppe, ANS119·435; FM200) : *peewit?* (BTs).

feldwyrt f. *gentian,* Lcd.

+**fēle** *sensitive,* Lcd.

fele-=**felo-**

felefeald=felafeald

fēleleas *insensible, dead,* Wy40.

felg(e) f. *'felloe,' rim of a wheel,* Bo. [fēolan]

felge-role, -roðe *'polipodium,'* A24·432 (v. MLN23·186).

felh=fealh pret. 3 sg. of fēolan.

felhð (KGl)=fylgð pres. 3 sg. of fylgan.

feligean=fylgan

fell I. n. *'fell,' skin, hide, B,Jul,Lcd;* Æ,AO, CP : *garment of skin,* Chrd64³³. [*L.* pellis] **II.** m.=fiell

fell-=**fyll-**

fellen (i¹) *made of skins,* Æ.

fellerēad (ēo³; =*pællerēad? ES43·31) *purple,* NG.

fellstycce n. *piece of skin,* Lcd1·330⁵.

fēllun=fēollon pret. pl. of feallan.

-felma v. æger-f.; **felmen-**=fylmen-

±**fēlnes** f. *sensation, feeling,* Æ.

felo-=**fela-**

felofe(o)rð (eo¹, e², u², ea³) *stomach, maw* (*of an animal*), Lcd,Gl.

felofor (ea¹, eo¹, u², e³) m. *bittern,* Gl.

fēlon (A)=fulgon pret. pl. of fēolan.

+**fēlsian**=+fælsian

felst pres. 2 sg. of feallan.

felt m? n? *'felt,'* WW.

felt-ere, -erre *a plant,* Lcd.

feltūn m. *privy, dunghill,* CP. [=feld-]

feltūngrēp f. *dunghill,* NC285.

feltwurma m. *wild marjoram,* Lcd.

feltwyrt f. *mullein (plant),* ÆGr, Lcd.

felð=fielð pres. 3 sg. of feallan; **fēlð**=fylð

felða (Cp128s) rare gp. of feld.

felu-=felo-; **fēm-,** fēmn- (VPs)=fǣmn-

fen=fenn

fenampre (o²) f. *a marsh plant,* Lcd38b.

fencerse f. *water-cress, Lcd.* [v. *'fen'*]

fenester n? m? *window,* GD220. [*L.*]

fenfearn n. *marsh-fern, 'salvia,' water-fern,* WW135⁴.

fenfisc m. *fen-fish,* Lcd95b (n.).

fenfreoðo f. *fen-refuge,* B851.

fenfugol m. *moor-fowl,* Lcd95b?

±**feng** m. *grip, grasp, embrace : capture : prey, booty.* [fôn]

fēng pret. 3 sg. of fôn.

fengel† m. *lord, prince, king,* B.

fengelād n. *marsh-path, fen,* B1359.

fengnes f. *'susceptio,'* CPs82² (? for and-f.).

fengnett n. (*catching-*)*net,* PPs140¹².

fengon pret. pl. of fôn.

fengtōð (æ) m. *canine tooth,* LL81n16.

fenhleoðu np. *fen-coverts,* B820. [hlið]

fenhop n. *fen-hollow,* B764.

fenix m. *the bird 'phœnix,'* ÆGr,Ph : *date-palm.*

fenland n. *fen-land, marsh,* Æ,AO.

fenlic *marshy,* Æ,Guth. [*'fenlich'*]

fenminte f. *water-mint,* Lcd14b.

fenn nm. *mud, mire, dirt, CP,WW* : *'fen,' marsh, moor, B,Bo;* AO : *the fen country,* Chr905.

fenn-=fen-

fennig I. *marshy, WW* : *muddy, dirty, CP.* [*'fenny'*] **II.**=fynig

fennðæc n. *covering of thatch from a fen,* OET (Bd²).

fenol=finul; **fenompre**=fenampre

fenȳce f. *snail?* OET,WW : *tortoise?* Rd41⁷¹.

fēo=feoh; also ds. of feoh.

fēode pret. 3 sg. of fēogan.

+**fēogan** (fîa, N; fēon) *to hate, persecute,* LG. [*'ivee'*]

feogað *hatred,* MtR.

fēogȳtsung (BH130³⁴)=fēohgītsung

feoh n. gs. fēos, ds. fēo *cattle, herd, LL,Sol;* AO : *movable goods, property, Bo,Ps;* AO : *money, riches, treasure, B,BH,Mt,OET;* Æ,CP. wið licgendum fēo *for ready money,* ÆL9⁵⁴ : *name of the rune for f.* [*'fee'*]

feohbehāt n. *promise of money,* Chr865e.

feohbīgenga m. *cattle-keeper,* AA28².

feohbōt f. *money compensation,* LL46n5; 258,51.

feohfang n. *offence of taking a bribe,* LL318,15¹.

feohgafol n. *usury,* Chrd76³².

feohgehāt n. *promise of money,* Chr865a.

feohgeorn *covetous, greedy,* LL,RWH.

feohgerêfa m. *steward*, LkLR 12⁴².
feohgesceot n. *payment of money*, Bᴋ28, 29.
feohgesteald n. *possession of riches*, Jᴜʟ685.
feohgestrêon n. *treasure, possessions, riches*, Cʜʀᴅ,W.
feoh-gîdsere, -gîetsere (CP)=feohgîtsere
feohgîfre *avaricious*, Wᴀ68.
feohgift† f. *bounty-giving, largess*.
feohgîtsere m. *miser*, Bo,Mᴇᴛ.
feohgîtsung f. *avarice*, CP 1496.
feohgôd n. *property (in cattle)*, LL60n1.
feohgyrnes (=eo²) f. *greed*, LL 396,4.
feohhûs n. *treasure-house*, WW.
feohlǽnung f. *lending of money*, WW 115⁴⁵.
feohland n. *pasture*, PPs.
feohlêas *without money : not to be bought off, past compensation*, B 2441.
feohlêasnes f. *want of money*, Swt.
feohsceatt n. *money-payment*, Dᴀ744.
feohspêda fp. *riches*, GD 273².
feohspilling f. *waste of money*, Cʜʀ1096.
feohstrang *well off*, Gʟ.
±feoht (i, o, y) n. *action of fighting*, B,Ps : '*fight,*' *battle*, AO : *strife*, Mod.
±feohtan³ (e) *to fight, combat, strive*, Chr, Lk,Rd,LL; Æ,AO,CP. : (+) *gain by fighting, win*. on f. *attack, fight against*.
+feohtdæg m. *day of battle*, PPs 139⁷.
feohte f.=feoht
feohtehorn (y¹) m. *battle-horn*, PPs 74⁹.
feohtend m. *fighter*, OEG 3805.
feohtere m. *fighter*, ES 39³²⁶.
feohtgegyrela m. '*falarica,*' WW 399³⁰.
feohtlâc n. *fighting*, LL. ['*fightlac*']
feohtling (y¹) m. *fighter*, GD 110¹³; MP 1·610.
+feohtsumnes f. *joyfulness*, NC 292. [+feon]
feohtwîte (i¹, y¹, ȳ²) n. *penalty for fighting*, LL.
feohwîte n. *fine for coining false money*, LL 319 col. 2.
fêol pret. 3 sg. of feallan.
fêol (ê, î) f. '*file,*' Cp,Rd; ÆL.
feola=fela
fêolaga m. *partner*, '*fellow,*' Chr 1016 D. [ON. fêlagi]
fêolagscipe m. *fellowship*, TC.
±fêolan³ (ê) *to cleave, be joined to, adhere : enter, penetrate, pass into, through or over, betake oneself to*, Cʜʀ : *undergo : persevere in*. [Goth. filhan]
fêold pret. 3 sg. of fealdan.
feolde=folde
fêoldon pret. pl. of fealdan.
fêolheard *hard as a file? hard enough to resist the file? file-hardened?* Mᴀ108 (or ?=*felaheard).
fêolian *to file*, ÆL 32²⁰³.

fêoll pret. 3 sg., fêollon pret. pl. of feallan.
feologan *to become discoloured?* Lᴄᴅ 125b.
feolu=fela; feolu-fer, -ferð, -for=felofor
feon=fenn
fêon I. (±, usu. +) sv⁵ w. in or g. *to be glad, rejoice, exult*, CP. II. (êa) *to gain*, MtL 16²⁶. III.=fêogan
fêond (îe, ȳ) m. ds. fiend, fêonde, nap. fiend, fêond *adversary, foe, enemy*, B,Bf,Mt; AO,CP [f.=*female enemy*] : '*fiend,*' *devil*, Gu; CP : *the Devil*, Lcd,Hy. [pres. ptc. of fêogan]
fêondǽt m. *eating things sacrificed to idols*, PPs 105²⁴.
fêondgrâp f. *grip of a foe*, B 636.
fêondgyld n. *idolatry, idol*, GD,PPs : *demoniacal possession?* MtL 4²⁴.
fêondlic *hateful, hostile, fiendish*, WW; Æ. adv. -lîce, Jul. ['*fiendly*']
fêondrǽden f. *enmity*, Æ.
fêondrǽs m. *hostile attack*, Gᴇɴ900.
fêondsceaða† m. *enemy, robber*.
fêondscipe m. *hostility, hatred*, AO,CP.
fêondsêoc *devil-possessed, demoniac*, BH 184⁵.
fêondulf m. *public enemy, criminal, malefactor*, GPH 396. [fêond, wulf]
fêong=fêoung; feonn=fenn
feor=feorr; fêor=feorh, fêower
fêora gp. of feorh.
+fêora=+fêra
feorbûend *dwelling far off*, B 254.
feor-cumen, -cund=feorran-cumen, -cund
feorcȳðð f. *distant land*, B 1838.
feord, feord-=fierd, fierd-, fyrd-
fêores gs. of feorh; feorg=feorh
feorh (e) mn. gs. fêores, nap. feorh *life, principle of life, soul, spirit*, AO,CP. tô wîdan fêore *for eternity, for ever*. f. gesellan, âgiefan *to die* : *living being, person*.
feorhâdl f. *fatal disease*, Æ.
feorhbana† m. *man-slayer*, Gʟ.
feorhbealu† n. *deadly evil, violent death*, B.
feorhbenn f. *deadly wound*, B 2740.
feorhberend† m. *living being*.
feorhbold n. *body*, Rᴏᴏᴅ73.
feorhbona=feorhbana
feorhbora m. *life-bearer*, Rᴅ92².
feorhcwalu† (e) f. *slaughter, death*, Gʟ.
feorhcwealm† m. *slaughter, death*, Gᴇɴ.
feorhcynn† n. *race of mortals*, B.
feorhdagas mp. *days of life*, Gᴇɴ2358.
feorhdolg n. *deadly wound*, Cʀ1455.
feorhêacen *living*, Gᴇɴ204.
feorhfægen *gan of life, glad to preserve one's life*, ÆL 23³⁰⁹.
feorhgebeorh n. *refuge*, Ex 369.
feorhgedâl† n. *death*.

feorhgener n. *preservation of life*, LL
204,7³.

feorhgenīðla† m. *mortal foe*, B.

feorhgiefa† m. *giver of life.*

feorhgiefu f. *gift of life*, RIM 6?

feorh-gōme? f. *means of subsistence*, or
-gōma? m. *jaw.* CR 1547.

feorhhord† n. *breast, soul, spirit.*

feorhhūs n. *soul-house, body*, MA 297.

feorhhyrde m. *life's guardian, protector*,
BH.

feorhlāst m. *step taken to preserve life, flight?*
step stained by one's life-blood? (BTs),
track of vanishing life? (Klb), B 846.

feorhlēan n. *revenge for bloodshed? gift for
life saved?* (BTs), Ex 150.

feorhlegu† f. *death*, B, EL.

feorhlic (fera-, ferh-) *vital*, HGL 453.

feorhlīf n. *life*, PPs 142².

feorhloca m. *breast*, GU 625.

feorhlyre m. *loss of life*, LL 466,3.

feorhneru f. *preservation of life, refuge, salvation : nourishment of life, food.*

feorhrǣd m. *salvation*, AN 1656.

feorhscyldig *guilty of death*, LL.

feorhsēoc *mortally wounded*, B 820.

feorhsweng m. *fatal blow*, B 2489.

feorhðearf f. *urgent need*, PPs 69¹.

feorhwund f. *deadly wound*, B 2385.

feorland (o²) n. *distant land*, PA 10.

feorlen=fyrlen

feorlic *far off, alien, strange*, RWH
137'.

feorm (a, æ, o, y) f. *food, provision, sustenance : entertainment, meal, feast, supper*,
ÆE, AO, CP : *goods, possessions : stores : rent
in kind*, EC : *profit, benefit*, CP : *tilling*,
LL 454,8.

feorma=forma

feormehām m. *farm*, CHR 1087.

feormend I. m. *entertainer*, WY 30. II.
cleanser, polisher, furbisher, B 2256.

feormendlēas *wanting a burnisher*, B 2761.

feormere m. *purveyor*, KC 4·278²¹.

feormfultum m. *help in food*, LL 356,69¹.

±feormian I. *to entertain, receive as guest* :
*cherish, support, sustain, feed : consume :
benefit, profit* : (+) *harbour (stolen goods)*,
LL 108,4⁶. II. *to scour, cleanse, furbish*,
Lk. ['*farm*']

feormung f. I. *harbouring*, LL. II. *fur-
bishing, cleansing*, LL.

feornes f. *distance*, BH 72¹⁰.

feorr I. comp. fi(e)rra, fyrra; sup. fierresta
'*far,*' *remote, distant*, Wif; CP. II. adv.
comp. fierr, firr, fyr(r); sup. fi(e)rrest,
fyrrest '*far,*' *far away, distant, remote*, BH,
CR, RBL, VPs; CP : *far back (in time)* :
further, besides, moreover.

feorran I. adv. *from afar, from a remote time
or place*, B, El, Gen : *far off, at a distance*,
Bo; ÆE, CP. ['*ferren*'] II. (æ, y) *to remove,
avert, turn aside, withdraw*, B : *proscribe.*
['*far*']

feorrancumen *come from afar, strange*, LL.

feorrancund (B), feorrcund (LL) *come from
afar, foreign born.*

feorrane, feorren(e)=feorran I.

feorrian (ea) *to keep apart*, ÆE : (±) *depart*,
NG.

feorrung f. *removal, departure*, GD 49¹⁶.

feorsian (y) *to go beyond* : *put far from,
expel* : *depart, remove, separate*, Ps.
['*ferse*']

feorsibb *distantly related*, LL 346,51.

feorsn=fiersn

feor-stuðu, -studu (e¹) f. *support*, WW.

feorting f. '*pedatio,*' WW 162⁴².

feorð=ferhð

fēorða (ēa, N) '*fourth,*' Lk, MkL; AO, CP.
fēorðe healf *three and a half.*

feorðandǣl *fourth part*, ÆE.

feorðe *fourthly*, LL 158,15.

feorðēod *a far country*, WYN 186.

fēorð-ling, -ung m. *fourth part* : '*farthing,*'
MkL, LkL; ÆE. ['*ferling*']

fēorum dp. of feorh.

feorweg† m. *remote part.*

feorwit=fyrwit

fēos gs. of feoh.

feostnode (CHR 963 E)=fæstnode pret. 3 sg.
of fæstnian.

feot-=fet-

fēoð pres. 3 sg. of fēogan.

fēoðer-, fēoðor-=fēower-, fiðer-

fēoung f. *hatred*, CP. [fēogan]

feow-, fēower- v. also fiðer-.

fēower, fēowere [indecl. before a sb. but
when alone, usu. g. fēow(e)ra, d. fēo-
werum] '*four,*' Cr; ÆE, AO, CP : *four times.*

fēowerdōgor mn. and adj. *four days*, JnR
11³⁹.

fēowerecg(ed)e *four-cornered, square*, LCD.

fēowerfeald *four-fold*, Lk 19⁸.

fēowerfealdlīce *quadruply*, BL.

fēowerfēte *four-footed*, AO; ÆE. ['*four-foot*']

fēower-fōte (BH), -fōtede (HL) *four-footed.*

fēowergild n. *four-fold compensation*, LL
228'.

fēowerhwēolod (fȳr-) *four-wheeled*, RHy 4¹⁹
(v. ES 38·15).

fēowernihte *four days old*, BH 392¹².

fēowerscȳte *four-cornered, square*, AO.
[scēat]

fēowertēme (fēoður-) *four-teamed*, VHy 6³⁴.

fēower-tēoða, -tēogða '*fourteenth,*' BH,
MH; AO.

fēowertīene (ē³, ȳ³) '*fourteen,*' MtL; AO.

fēowertīeneniht (ȳ) *fortnight, LL.* [v. *'fourteen'*]

fēowertīenewintre (ȳ) *fourteen years old,* LL.

fēowertig *'forty,'* MtL; AO.

fēowertigfeald *forty-fold,* Æ,WW.

fēowertiggēare adj. *of forty years,* ÆL 3⁴⁶⁹.

fēowertiglic *quadragesimal,* BH.

fēowertigoða *'fortieth,'* Æ (-tēoða; in error).

fēowertȳne=fēowertīene

fēowerða (*Mt*)=fēorða

fēowerwintre *four years old,* ÆGr 287¹⁹.

fēowr-=fēower-, fēor-

fēowra v. fēower.

±**fēowung** f. *rejoicing, joy,* OEG 1118. [+fēon]

fēowur-=fēower-; **fer**=fær

fer-=fær-, fear-, fier-, feor-, for-, fyr-

fēr=(1) fær I.; (2) fēfer; **fēr-**=fǣr-, fȳr-

+**fēra** (fera in A only) m. *associate, comrade, fellow-disciple,* Æ,G,OET; AO,CP : *wife* : *man, servant,* v. LL 2·427f. [*'fere,' 'y-fere'*]

fēran *to go, come, depart, set out, march, travel,* B,JnL (oe); CP : *behave, act* : (+) *accomplish, attain, obtain* : (+) *fare, speed, undergo, suffer* : *bring,* MkR 1³². [*'fere'*]

fērbedd n. *portable bed, litter,* WW 154⁴.

fērblǣd=fǣrblǣd

fercian (ē?) *to convey, bring, Chr* : *support,* ÆL 23⁵⁹⁷ : *stuff up (with lies),* ÆL 23⁷¹³ : *proceed,* Bf 68²⁹. [*'ferk, firk'*]

fercung f. *sustenance, provision, food,* Æ (9¹⁷²), CHRD.

ferdwyrt ? *a plant* (or ?=feld-), LCD 57b.

fēre *able to go, fit for (military) service,* CHR.

+**fēre** I. n. *company, community.* II. m. *companion.* III. *accessible,* PH 4. [faran]

+**fēred** *associated,* WW 216¹³.

ferele f. *rod,* GD. [*L.* ferula]

fērend† m. *sailor,* WH : *messenger,* JUL.

fērende *mobile,* GD.

fēresceat m. *passage-money,* WW 34³.

feresōca? *'sibba,'* WW 277²³.

fēreð pres. 3 sg. of (1) faran, (2) ferian.

fēreð pres. 3 sg. of fēran.

fergan=ferian

fergenberig (N)=firgenbeorg

ferht I. (=eo) *honest,* GL. II.=ferhð

ferhtlic (=eo) *just, honest,* PPs 95¹⁰.

ferhð I.† (ferð) mn. *mind, intellect, soul, spirit* : *life* : *person,* SEAF 26. wīdan f. *eternally, for ever.* II.=fyrhð

ferhðbana m. *murderer,* Ex 399.

ferhðcearig *of anxious mind,* GEN 2217.

ferhð-cleofa, -cofa† m. *breast.*

ferhðfrec *bold, brave,* B 1146.

ferhðfriðende (rð) *sustaining life,* RD 39³.

ferhðgenīðla m. *mortal enemy,* B 2881.

ferhðgewit (rð) n. *understanding,* CR 1184.

ferhðglēaw† *wise, prudent.*

ferhðgrim (rð)† *savage,* JUL,WA.

ferhðloca† m. *breast, body.*

ferhðlufu (y) f. *heartfelt love,* AN 83.

ferhðsefa† (i, y) m. *mind, thought,* EL.

ferhðwērig† *soul-weary, sad.*

±**ferian** *to carry, convey, bring, An,B,El;* Æ : (with refl. a.) *betake oneself to, be versed in* : *depart, go, Ma.* [*'ferry'*]

feri(g)end m. *leader, bringer,* SOL 80.

fering f. *vehicle,* GD.

+**fērlǣcan** (ē²) *to associate, unite,* Æ.

+**fērlic** *associated.* adv. -līce *sociably, together;* -līðlīce GD 313²⁴.

±**fērnes** f. *passage, transition, passing away,* BL 163¹³ (v. BTs).

+**fērrǣden** (usu. +) f. *companionship, fellowship,* Æ,AO,CP : *friendship* : *society, fraternity, congregation,* Æ.

fers nm. *verse,* Æ : *sentence,* Æ. [*L.*]

fersc *'fresh' (not salt),* AO : *not salted,* KC. -ferscan v. ā-f.

fersceta m. *freshet,* A 20·382.

±**fērscipe** m. *fraternity, community, retinue* : *order, clan* : *society, fellowship, companionship,* CP : *wedlock,* OEG 2544.

+**fērscipian** *to accompany,* DR.

fersian *to versify,* ÆGr 218³.

ferð=ferhð

ferðan=furðum

ferðe m. *skin, hide?* LCD 8b.

ferwett-=fyrwit-

fēsan, fēsian=fȳsan, fȳsian

fest=fæst; **fēst**=fȳst; **fēster-**=fōstor-

fēstermenn mp. *bondsmen,* BC,LL.

fēstrian=fōstrian

fet pres. 3 sg. of fetian.

fēt I. pres. 3 sg. of fēdan. II. ds. and nap. of fōt.

+**fetan**⁴ *to fall,* MtR 13⁷,⁸. (v. FTP 225).

fetel, fetels m. *belt, Bo,Met.* [*'fettle'*]

fetelhilt n. *belted or ringed sword-hilt,* B 1563.

fētels=fǣtels

±**fetelsod** *provided with a sheath?* BC 3·215².

feter=fetor

+**feterian**† *to fetter, bind.*

±**fetian** (æ) *to bring near, fetch, obtain, AO, B,Gen,Sol* : *bring on, induce, Pr* : *marry.* [*'fet,' 'y-fet'*]

fetor (eo¹, e²) f. *'fetter,' shackle, Cp,MkL, Ps* : *check, restrain, Wa.*

fetorwrāsen f. *fetter, chain,* AN 1109.

+**fetran,** +fetrian=+feterian

fētt I. pres. 3 sg. of fēdan. II.=fǣtt

fettan=fetian

fette pret. 3 sg. of fetian.

fēð=fēhð pres. 3 sg. of fōn.

fēða m. *foot-man, foot-soldier, AO* : *band of foot-soldiers, troop,* Æ.

fēðan to go on foot? Æ (116⁴⁴⁹).
fēðe n. power of locomotion, walking, gait, pace, Æ,AO.
fēðecempa† m. foot-soldier, B.
fēðegang m. journey on foot, GEN 2513.
fēðegeorn anxious to go, RD 32⁹.
fēðegest† m. guest coming on foot, traveller.
fēðehere m. infantry, AO.
fēðehwearf m. band of footmen, GU 162.
fēðelāst† m. step, track, course.
fēðelēas† footless, crippled.
fēðemann m. pedestrian, LRG,WW 481³ : foot-soldier, WW 399²⁷.
fēðemund f. fore-paw, RD 16¹⁷.
feðer (æ) f. nap. feð(e)ra, feð(e)re 'feather,' Lcd,Ph; pl. wings, Bo,Mt,OET; CP : pen, Lk; CP.
feðer-=fēower-, fiðer-; **feðeran**=fiðerian
feðerbǣre having feathers, winged, GPH 390.
feðerbedd n. 'feather-bed,' WW 124¹⁹.
feðerberend m. feathered creature, WW 465²⁰. [v. 'feather']
feðercræft m. embroidery, WW 491³.
feðergearwe fp. feathers of the arrow, B 3119.
feðergeweorc n. feather-embroidery, WW 459²⁷.
feðerhama m. wings, plumage, Cp,Gen. ['featherham']
fēðespēdig speedy of foot, CRA 53.
fēðewīg† m. battle on foot, affray.
feðm=fæðm
feðorbyrste split into four, LCD 148a.
feðra, feðre v. feðer.
fēðre loaded, A2·373.
feðrian to become fledged, OEG 26²⁷.
+fēðrian to load, AS 1¹⁰. [fōðor]
feðriht feathered, MtLp 7¹⁷.
fēðu (WW 110²⁹)=fēða
fēðung f. walking, motion, ÆH 2·134.
fex=feax
fīag- (N)=fēog-; **fibulae** (GL)=fīfele
+fīc n. deceit, EL,RB [v. 'fickle']
fīc m. fig, fig-tree, MtR : (fig-disease), venereal ulcer, hemorrhoids, LCD. ['fike'; L. ficus]
fīcādl f. fig-disease (v. fīc), LCD.
fīcæppel m. fig, Æ,GL.
fīcbēam m. fig-tree, Æ,CP.
fician to flatter, AB 34·10.
fīclēaf n. fig-leaf, GEN 3⁷.
ficol 'fickle,' cunning, tricky, KGl; W.
fictrēow n. fig-tree, G.
ficung f. fraud, trickery, LL 242,24; 254, 28².
ficwyrm m. intestinal worm, LCD 122a.
ficwyrt f. fig-wort, WW 134³².
fieftiene=fiftiene
fieht pres. 3 sg. of feohtan.

±**fiell** (æ, e, ea, y) mn. fall, destruction, AO, CP : death, slaughter : precipice : case, inflection, ÆGR 91¹⁴. [feallan] For comps. v. fyll-.
fielt pres. 3 sg. of fealdan.
fielð pres. 3 sg. of feallan.
fiend=fēond, also ds. of fēond.
+**fiend** (ȳ) mp. foes, enemies, Lk; AO. ['i-feond']
fiendwīc n. enemy's camp, LPs 77²⁸.
fier v. feorr II.; **fier-**=fēower-
fierd (æ, e, eo, y) f. national levy or army, Chr : military expedition, campaign, Ma, PPs; AO : camp. ['ferd'] For comps. v. fyrd-.
fieren-=firen-; **fierfēte**=fēowerfēte
-fierme (eo) v. or-f.
fierra, fierrest, fierresta v. feorr II.
fiersn (e, eo, y) f. heel, GEN,WW. [Ger. ferse]
fierst=first
fīf usu. indecl. before sb.; but when alone, has na. fife, g. fīfa, d. fīfum 'five,' Bf,G, Gen.
fīfalde f. butterfly, GL. [Ger. falter]
fīfbēc fp. Pentateuch, WW 470⁸.
fīfe v. fīf.
fīfecgede having five angles, ÆGR 289¹⁵.
fīfel n. (huge) sea-monster, giant, WALD 2¹⁰.
fīfelcynn n. race of sea-monsters, B 104.
fīfeldōr n. door of sea-monsters, river Eider, WID 43.
fīfele f. buckle, WW 403⁷. [L. 'fibula']
fīfelstrēam m. ocean, sea, MET 26²⁶.
fīfelwǣg m. ocean, sea, EL 237.
fiffalde=fīfalde
fīfeald 'five-fold,' ÆGr : five each, CM 840.
fiffētede five-footed (verse), OEG 130.
fiffingre f. 'potentilla,' 'primula,' cinquefoil, oxlip? Lcd. ['fivefinger']
fīflēre five-storied, Æ. [flōr]
fīfgēar n. period of five years, lustrum, WW 431¹⁶.
fīfhund(red) num. five hundred, EL,GL.
fīflæppede having five lobes, LCD 59b.
fīf-lēaf n., -lēafe f. 'potentilla,' cinquefoil, Lcd. ['fiveleaf']
fīfmægen n. magic power, SOL 136. [fīfel]
fīfnihte five days old, ANS 129·22.
fīfta 'fifth,' Æ,Chr,Lcd; AO,CP.
fīftafæder v. fæder.
fīfte fifthly, LL 158,16.
fīfteg=fīftig; **fīftegða**=fīftēoða
fīftēne=fīftiene
fīfteogoða (i²) 'fiftieth,' ÆGr; CP.
fīf-tēoða (ȳ¹), tēða, -tegða 'fifteenth,' BH, Lcd.

fíftíene (ȳ¹, ē², ȳ²) (often w. g.) *'fifteen,'* B,Bf,Gu; AO.

fíftíenehte *fifteen days old,* LCD 3·180.

fíftíenewintre (e²) *fifteen years old,* BL 213¹.

fíftig num. *'fifty,'* ÆB : sb. *a set of fifty,* Mk.

Fíftigdæg m. *Pentecost,* MkL p 5¹⁰.

fíftі(g)esman m. *captain of fifty,* Ex 18²¹, DEUT 1¹⁵.

fíftigeða, fíftigoða=fífteogoða

fíftigfeald *'fifty-fold,' containing fifty,* Æ.

fíftigwintre *fifty years old,* Jn 8⁵⁷.

fíftȳne (Æ)=fíftíene

fífwintre *five years old,* ÆGR 287¹⁴.

-fígen v. ā-f.

+fígo ? np. *a disease, 'cimosis'* (? +fligo, v. BTac), LCD 1a, 14a.

fíhl, fihle m? *cloth, rag,* NG. [?=fliht]

fíht I. pres. 3 sg. of feohtan. **II.**=feht

fíht-=fyht-; **fíhtan**=fȳhtan

+fíhð pres. 3 sg. of +fēon.

fíl (GL)=fēol

+fílan=+fȳlan; +fílce=+fylce

fíld sb. *curdled milk,* LCD 53b (LF130).

fíldcumb m. *milk-pail,* LCD 122b.

fílde *field-like, of the nature of a plain,* AO 74¹².

+fílde n. *field, plain,* AO 12¹⁰. [feld]

fíleðe n. *hay,* PPs 36².

fílgð, filhð pres. 3 sg. of fēolan.

fíli-=fylg-

fíliende ptc. *rubbing,* WW 407³⁶.

fílíðe=fileðe

fílíðlēag m. *meadow,* Ct.

fíll=fyll

fílle f. *thyme,* LCD,OEG 56³⁸. [=cerfille?]

fíllen I.=fellen **II.** (?) f. *a dropping,* LCD 18a (fyln).

fílmen (y) n. *'film,' membrane, thin skin,* Lcd; Æ : *foreskin,* Æ.

fílst-=fylst-

fílð pres. 3 sg. of feallan.

fín f. *heap, pile.* v. OEG 2456.

fín-=fyn-

fína m. *woodpecker,* WW 49².

fínc m. *'finch,'* Ep,WW.

fínd=fiend

fíndan³ (but occl. wk. pret. funde) (±) *to 'find'* ('y-find,' 'y-found'), *meet with,* B, BH,Gen,Jul,LG,Met : *discover, obtain by search or study, recover,* Cr,MtL,Ps : *provide : consider, devise, arrange, dispose, decide,* AO,CP : *show, inform.* f. æt *obtain from.*

fíndend m. *finder,* GPH 391.

+fíndig (y) *capable,* ÆGR 69⁴.

fínding f. *invention, initiative,* CM 1082.

fínel=finol

fínger m. *'finger,'* Bf,MtL,VPs; Æ,CP.

fínger-æppla, -appla npl. *finger-shaped fruits, dates,* ÆL,OEG.

fíngerdocca? m? *finger-muscle,* GL.

fíngerlíc *belonging to a finger or ring,* WW 291²⁶.

fíngerlíð n. *finger-joint,* NC 343.

fíngermǣl n. *finger's length,* NR 22⁸.

fínn m. *'fin,' Æ.*

fínol (e¹, u², y²) m. *'fennel,' Ep,WW.* [L. foenuculum]

fínolsǣd n. *fennel-seed,* LCD 157a.

fínst=findest pres. 2 sg. of findan.

fínt pres. 3 sg. of findan.

fíntа† m. *tail : consequence, result.*

fínu(g)l m., finu(g)le f.=finol

fío=fēo; **fír**=fȳr

fíras† mp. *men, human beings.*

fírd=fierd; **fírd-**=fierd-, fyrd-

fíren f. *transgression, sin, crime : outrage, violence : torment, suffering.*

fírenbealu n. *transgression,* CR 1276.

fírencræft m. *wickedness,* JUL 14.

fírendǣd† f. *wicked deed, crime.*

fírenearfeðe n. *sinful woe,* GEN 709.

fírenfremmende *sinful,* CR 1118.

fírenful (y) *sinful, wicked,* Æ.

fírengeorn *sinful,* CR 1606.

fírenhicga (y¹, y²) m. *adulterer,* GPH 389.

fírenhicge (fyrn-) f. *adulteress,* OEG.

fírenhicgend (fyrn-) *adulteress, harlot,* OEG.

±fírenian (y) *to sin : commit adultery : revile.*

fírenleahter (y¹) m. *great sin,* ÆH 2·420¹⁶.

fírenlíc (y) *wicked.* adv. *-líce vehemently, rashly,* WALD 1²⁰ : *sinfully.*

fírenligerian *to commit fornication,* RSPs 105³⁹.

fírenlust m. *lust, sinful desire, luxury, wantonness,* AO,CP.

fírenlustful *wanton, luxurious,* A 12·502¹⁰.

fírenlustgeorn *wanton,* W 253⁵.

fírensynn f. *great sin,* JUL 347.

fírensynnig *sinful,* CR 1379.

fírentācnian (y) *to commit misdeeds,* RHy 6²¹.

fírenðearf (y) f. *dire distress,* B 14.

fírenðēof (i², ēa³) m. *robber,* DR.

fírenum *excessively, very, intensely : malignantly.* [dp. of firen]

fírenweorc† n. *evil deed, sin,* CR.

fírenwyrcende† *sinning, sinful,* PPs.

fírenwyrhta (y)† m. *evil-doer,* PPs.

fírfoda=fȳrfoda

fírgenbēam (y) m. *mountain tree,* B 1414. [Goth. fairguni]

fírgenbeorg (fergenberig) *mountain,* RUNE-CASKET (v. FM 368).

fírgenbucca m. *ibex,* LCD.

fīrgendstrēam=firgenstrēam

fīrgen-gāt f. nap. -gǣt *ibex*, GL.

fīrgenholt n. *mountain-wood*, B 1393.

fīrgenstrēam† m. *mountain-stream, woodland-stream*.

fīrgin-=firgen-; **fīrh**=fyrh

fīrht=friht; **fīrhð**=ferhð

fīrigendstrēam=firgenstrēam

fīringgāt=firgengāt; **fīrmdig**=frymdig

fīrmettan *to ask, beg*, AO 186⁶.

fīrn-=firen-, fyrn-

fīrr, firra, firre, firrest v. feorr.

fīrst I. (e, ie, y) mn. *period, space of time, time, respite, truce*, B,*Chr*; CP. [*'frist'*] **II.** (ie) f. *ceiling, (inner) roof, WW : ridgepole.* [*'first'*] **III.**=fyrst

fīrsthrōf n. *ceiling, ridge-pole*, OEG 2812.

fīrst-mearc, -gemearc fm. *period of time, appointed time, interval, respite*.

fīrð-=fyrð-; **fīrwet**=fyrwit

fīsc m. *'fish,' VPs*; Æ,AO,CP; Mdf.

fīsc-að, -(n)oð m. *fishing*, AO : *fishpond : a catch of fish : fishing rights*. [v. NC 286]

fīscbrȳne m. *fish-brine, WW* 128³⁹. [v. *'fish'*]

fīsccynn n. *fish tribe*, ÆT.

fīscdēah f. *fish-dye, purple*, OEG 5193.

fīscere m. *'fisher,' fisherman, AO,Mt : kingfisher (bird)*.

fīscfell (NG)=fiscpōl

fīscflōdu? m. *fish-flood, sea*, OET 127⁴.

fīschūs n. *place where fish is sold*, WW 184⁴⁰.

fīscian *to 'fish,' Bo*.

fīsclacu f. *fishpond or stream*, BC 2·374¹⁶.

fīscmere m. *fishpond*, WW 484¹¹.

fīscnað=fiscað

fīscnett n. *fishing-net*, MET 176¹¹.

fīscnoð, fiscoð=fiscað

fīscpōl m. *fishpond, JnL,WW*. [*'fishpool'*]

fīscōrūt m. *small fish*, MtL 15³⁴.

fīscwelle m. *fishpond*, A 13·321.

fīscwer m. *'fish-weir,' fish-trap, LL* 454,9 : *fishing-ground*, Lk.

fīscwylle *full of fish*, BH. [weallan]

fīsting f. *'fesiculatio,' WW*. [*'fisting'*]

fītelfōta *white-footed* (BTs),WW 161²⁰.

fīstersticca m. *tent-nail*, WW 187⁵.

fītt I. f? *struggle, contest, fight*, Gen 2072. [*'fit'*] **II.** f. *'fit,' song, poem, Bo*; GL (FTp 226).

fiðele f. *fiddle* (BT).

fiðelere m. *'fiddler,' WW* 311²³.

fiðelestre f. *female fiddler*, WW 311²⁴.

fiðer-=fēower-, feðer-

fiðerbǣre *feathered*, OEG.

fiðercian *to flutter*, GD 100¹⁹. [fiðere]

fiðerdǣled *quadripartite, quartered*, OEG.

fiðere (y) n. nap. fið(e)ru, fiðera(s) *wing*, Æ,CP.

fiðerfeald *four-fold*, EHy 4¹⁹.

fiðerflēdende (y¹) *flowing in four streams*, GPH 390.

fiðerflōwende *flowing in four streams*, OEG 48².

fiðerfōtnīeten (e¹) m. *four-footed animal*, AA 23²⁰.

fiðerhama (y¹) m. *wing-covering*, ÆL 34⁷⁴.

+**fiðerhamod** *covered with feathers*, ÆH 1·466²⁷.

fiðerhīwe *'quadriformis,'* OEG 177.

+**fið(e)rian** *to provide with feathers or wings, Bo*; PPs. [*'feather'*]

fiðerlēas *without wings*, Wy 22.

fiðerrīca (y¹) m. *tetrarch*, ÆH.

fiðerrīce (y²) n. *tetrarchy*, CHR 12 c.

fiðerscēatas mp. *four quarters?* SOL 32.

fiðersleht m. *flapping of wings, joy?* OEG 4892.

fiðertēme (eo¹, u²) *with four horses abreast, VHy* 5³⁴. [v. *'team'*]

fiðertōdǣled=fiðerdǣled; **fiðru** v. fiðere.

fīxa, fīxas, fīxum=fisca, fiscas, fiscum, gp., nap. and dp. of fisc.

fīxen=fyxen

fīxian, fīxoð, fīxnoð=fiscian, fiscað

flā f. *arrow, AO*. [*'flo'*;=flān]

flacg *cataplasm, plaster*, WW 380²⁸.

flacor† *flying (of arrows)*. [cp. *Ger.* flackern]

flǣ-=flea-, fleo-

flǣ-=flēa-, flēo-, flīe-

flǣre f. *earlap*, WW 157¹².

flǣsc (DD 51)=fleax

flǣsc (ē) n. *'flesh,' Æ,Cp,Lk,VP*; CP : *body (as opposed to soul), B,Jn : carnal nature, Mt : living creatures, Lk,Ps*.

flǣscǣt m. *animal food*, RB.

flǣscbana m. *murderer, executioner*, GD.

flǣscbesmitennes f. *defilement of the flesh*, Sc 69¹¹.

flǣsccofa m. *body*, LPs 118¹²⁰.

flǣsc(c)wellere m. *executioner*, WW 382²⁹.

flǣsccȳping f. *meat-market*, WW 145²⁶.

flǣsceht *fleshy*, LCD 83a.

flǣscen *of flesh, like flesh*, GPH; Æ. [*'fleshen'*]

flǣscennes (BF 142¹²)=flǣscnes

flǣscgebyrd f. *incarnation*, OEG 429.

flǣschama (o²)† m. *body, carcase*.

+**flǣschamod** *incarnate*, Æ.

flǣschord n. *body*, SOUL 103.

flǣschūs n. *'flesh-house,' place where meat is sold, WW*.

flǣsclic *'fleshly,' corporeal, carnal, Æ,BH, Bl,Bo*.

flǣsclicnes f. *incarnate condition, Æ*. [*'fleshliness'*]

flǣscmangere m. *butcher, WW*. [*'fleshmonger'*]

flǣscmaðu f. *maggot*, WW 122¹³.

flǣsc-mete m. nap. -mettas *flesh, animal food, LL*; Æ,CP. ['*fleshmeat*']

±**flǣscnes** f. *incarnation*, CHR.

+**flǣscod** *incarnate*, Æ.

flǣscsand *portion of meat*, CHRD 14'.

flǣscstrǣt f. *meat-market*, Æ.

flǣsctǣwere m. *torturer of the flesh, executioner*, WW 189¹⁹.

flǣsctōð m. *one of the teeth*, WW 415²⁴.

flǣscōðenung f. *allowance of food*, CHRD 15¹¹.

flǣscwyrm m. *maggot*, Lcd. ['*fleshworm*']

flǣslic=flǣsclic

flǣðecomb m. *weaver's comb*, WW.

flœx (MtR)=fleax

flagen pp. of flēan.

flāh I. n. *wickedness, treachery*, RIM 47.
II.† adj. *wily, deceitful, hostile*. [*ON.* flār]

flān mf. *barb, arrow, javelin, dart, B,Ma*; Æ,AO,CP. ['*flane*']

flānbogaf m. *bow*, B.

flanc m. *flank*, OEG 50³⁵.

flāngeweorcf n. *shooting-gear, arrows.*

flānhred? *arrow-swift? arrow-equipped? (of death)*, RIM 72.

flāniht (e) *relating to darts*, WW 425³⁴.

flānðracuf f. *onset, attack.*

flasce (x) f. '*flask,' bottle, GD,WW.*

flāt pres. 3 sg. of flītan.

flaxe=flasce

flaxfōtef *web-footed*, HEXC 251. [=flox-]

flēa I. mf. '*flea,' Ep,Lcd.* **II.** (LCD)=flēah n.

flēag pret. 3 sg. of flēogan.

flēah I. n. *albugo, a white spot in the eye*, CP 69. **II.** m.=flēa I. **III.** pret. 3 sg. of flēogan. **IV.** pret. 3 sg. of flēon.

flēam m. *flight, B*; Æ,AO. on f. gebrengan *to put to flight*. on f. weorðan *to flee*. ['*fleme*']

flēamdōm m. *flight*, NC 287.

flēamlāst m. *apostasy*, WW 500³.

flēan⁶ *to* '*flay,' Cp.*

±**fleard** n. *nonsense, vanity, folly, deception, fraud, superstition, LL*; OEG. ['*flerd*']

fleardere m. *trifler*, CHRD 20¹².

fleardian *to be foolish, err, go astray*, CHRD, LL.

flēat I. pret. 3 sg. of flēotan. **II.**=flēot

fleaðe, fleaðorwyrt f. *water-lily*, LCD.

flēawyrt f. *fleabane*, WW. ['*fleawort*']

fleax (æ, e) n. '*flax,' linen, CP*; Æ.

fleax- v. flex-.

flecta=fleohta; **fled**=flett

-fled v. ofer-f.

flēde adj. *in flood, full, overflowing*, AO. [flōd]

flēding f. *flowing*, ÆH 2·180².

flēg- (N)=flēog-

flēge *little ship*, JnL 6²²(oe).

flehta, flehtra=fleohta; **flēm-**=flīem-

flene=flyne; **flēo**=flēa

+**flenod** *describes some attribute of a cloak*, WW 187¹⁴.

±**flēogan²** (intr., cp. flēon) *to* '*fly,' B,El, Jud,Jul*; Æ,CP : *flee, take to flight, Ma.*

flēoge (ē, ȳ) f. *any winged insect,* '*fly,' Æ, MtL*; CP.

flēogenda m. *bird*, CPs.

flēogende '*flying,' winged, ÆGr* 44⁹.

flēogendlic *flying, winged, ÆGr* 55².

flēogryft n. *fly-curtain*, WW 373²¹.

flēohcynn m. *a kind of flies*, PPs 104²⁷.

flēohnet n. '*fly-net,' curtain*, Jud.

fleohta (flecta) m. *hurdle*, Cp 600. [*Ger.* flechte]

±**flēon²** *to fly from,* '*flee**,' *avoid, escape, An, B,G,Met,VPs*; AO,CP : *put to flight,* Æ : *fly* (intr.), Æ.

flēos (VPs)=flīes; **fleos-**=fles-

flēot (ēa) m. **I.** *water, sea, estuary, river, AO.* **II.** *raft, ship, Hy.* ['*fleet*']

flēotan² *to float, drift, flow, swim, sail, Æ,B, CP :* (tr.) *skim*, LCD. ['*fleet*']

flēote=flīete

flēotende *floating*, GEN 1447. ['*fleeting*']

flēotig *fleet, swift*, RD 52⁴.

flēotwyrt f. *seaweed*, LCD 101a.

fleoðe (ea) f. *water-lily*, LCD.

flēow pret. 3 sg. of flōwan.

flēowð=flēwð pres. 3 sg. of flōwan.

-**flēre** v. ðri-, fīf-f.

flēring f. *story (of a building)*, Æ. [flōr]

flēs=flīes; **flēsc**=flǣsc

fleswian (eo) *to whisper? pull a wry face?* BH 122¹⁷ (JAW 30). [or ? flēswian *dissemble*, ES 44·470]

flet=flett; **flēt**, flēte=flīete

fletrǣst f. *couch*, B 1241.

fletsittendf m. *sitter in hall, courtier, guest.*

flett n. *floor, ground, B,LL :* *dwelling, hall, mansion, B,LL*. ['*flet*']

flettgefeoht n. *fighting in a house*, LL 18,39.

flettgestealdf n. *household goods*, GEN.

flettpǣð m. *floor of a house*, GEN 2729.

fletwerod n. *hall-troop, body-guard*, B 476.

fleðecamb=flǣðecomb

flēwsa m. *flowing, flux, issue (bodily disorder)*, LCD. [flōwan]

flēwð pres. 3 sg. of flōwan.

flex=fleax

flexǣcer (y³) m. *flax land*, KC 5·389¹⁸.

flexgescot n. *contribution of flax*, W 171²⁷.

flexhamm m. *flax field*, KC 5·374'.

flexlīne f. *flax-winder, reel? flax line? thread?* LL 455,15.

flicce n. '*flitch' of bacon, ham, Gl,KC.*

flicorian (e²) *to move the wings, flutter*, Æ. ['*flicker*'] flīe=flēah I.

flīehð pres. 3 sg. of flēon.

flīema (ē, ī, ȳ) m. *fugitive, exile, outlaw, Æ, Gen*; AO. Godes f. *excommunicate person,* LL 352,66. ['*fleme*']

±flīeman (ǣ, ē, ȳ) *to put to flight, drive away, banish, Gen*; CP. ['*fleme*'; flēam]

flīeman-feorm, -feorming f. *offence of, or penalty for, sheltering fugitives from justice,* LL 102,30; 2·302.

+flīeme (ē) adj. *fugitive,* DR 147⁸.

flīeming (flȳmig) sb. *fugitive,* OEG 2965.

flīes (ē, ēo, ī, ȳ) n. '*fleece,*' *wool, fur, sealskin, LL,Ps.*

flīet (WW 489³)=flēot; flīetan=flītan

flīete (ē, ēo, ȳ) f. I. *cream, curds.* II. *punt, boat, raft,* WW.

flīg=flēah I.; flīg-=flēog-, flȳg-

flīgel m? n? '*flail,*' *A* 9·264.

fliht=flyht; fliht-, flihte-=flyhte-

flīhð pres. 3 sg. of flēon.

flīma=flīema

flint m. '*flint,*' *rock, Æ,Cr,Ep,WW.*

flinten *of flint,* W 252¹.

flintgrǣg *grey like flint,* RD 4¹⁹.

flīo=flēah I.; flīs=flīes

±flit (usu. +) n. *strife, Ps* : *dispute, contention* : '*scandalum*'; tō +flītes *emulously.* ['*flite*']

±flītan¹ *to strive, quarrel, dispute, contend, B,BH*; Æ,CP. ['*flite*']

flitcræft m. *dialectics, logic,* OEG.

flitcræftlic *logical,* HGL 481.

flītere m. *disputer, chider, brawler, schismatic, Gl.* ['*fliter*']

±flit-ful (OEG), -fullic (CHR) *contentious.*

+flitfulnes f. *litigiousness,* A 11·102⁸⁴.

±flitgeorn I. (±) m. *contentious person,* BF, LCD. II. (+) *contentious,* RB 130²⁰.

+flitglīw n. *mockery,* WW.

+flitlīce *emulously,* BH 406¹⁷.

±flitmǣlum *contentiously, emulously,* OEG, RBL.

-flitme? v. un-f.

flīusum (OET)=flēosum dp. of flēos.

flōc n. *flat fish, flounder,* WW.

flōcan *to clap, applaud,* RD 21³⁴.

flocc m. '*flock,*' *company, troop, Æ,Chr.*

floccmǣlum *in troops, AO.* ['*flockmeal*']

flocgian *to spring forth,* GPH 399.

flocrād f. *invading band, troop,* CHR.

flōd mn. *mass of water,* '*flood,*' *wave, Æ,Gen, Chr,Mt,VPs;* AO,CP : *flow (of tide as opposed to ebb), tide, flux, current, stream,* AO : *the Flood, Deluge, B,Lk;* Æ.

flōdblāc *pale as water? pale through fear of drowning,* Ex 497.

flōde f. *channel, gutter,* GL : *flood?* (Earle), EC 120³¹.

flōdegsa m. *flood-terror,* Ex 446.

flōden *of a river,* WW 240.

flōdhamm m. *piece of land surrounded by water?* KC 1·289¹⁶.

flōdlic *of or belonging to a stream,* ÆGR 54⁹.

flōdweard f. *sea-wall,* Ex 493.

flōdweg† m. *watery way, sea.*

flōdwudu m. *ship,* CR 854.

flōdwylm† m. *flowing stream, raging billows.* [weallan]

flōdȳð f. *wave of the sea,* B 542.

+flog n. *infectious disease,* LCD 3·34⁹.

flogen I. pp. of flēon. II. pp. of flēogan.

flogettan *to fluctuate : flutter,* Sc,GD 100¹⁹.

flogoða m. *liquor,* GPH 402.

flōh f. *chip,* WW 416⁴.

flohtenfōte *web-footed,* LCD 33b.

flōr fm. ds. flōra, flōre '*floor,*' *pavement, ground, B,Bo,Lk;* Æ : *bottom (of a lake, etc.), Sat.*

flōrisc *flowery,* CM 44.

flōrstān m. *paving-stone, tessella,* WW 150²⁷.

flot n. *deep water, sea.* on flot(e) '*afloat,*' *Chr,Ma.*

flota m. (*floater*), *boat, ship, vessel : fleet, Chr : crew : sailor :* (†) *pirate.* ['*flote*']

+flota m. *floater (whale),* WH 7.

floten pp. of flēotan.

floterian *to flutter, fly, flicker, Æ : float, be carried or tossed by waves, Æ.*

flothere m. *piratical fleet,* B 2915.

flotian *to* '*float,*' *Chr.* [flēotan]

flotlic *nautical, naval,* WW 205²⁷.

flotmann m. *sailor, pirate, ÆL,W.*

flotorian=floterian

flotscip n. *ship, bark,* WW.

flotsmeru n. *floating grease, fat,* LL 453,4.

flotweg m. *ocean,* HU 41.

flōwan⁷ *to* '*flow,*' *stream, issue, Bf,Sol,VPs;* AO,CP : *become liquid, melt, VPs : abound, PPs :* (+) *overflow, AO.*

flōw(ed)nes f. *flow, flux, overflow, torrent,* CP.

flōwende '*flowing,*' *Ma* 65.

flōwendlic *flowing,* LPs 147¹⁸.

flōwing f. '*flowing,*' *flux, MtL.*

flugl- (OET 26)=fugl-

flugol *fleet, swift : fleeting,* Sc.

flugon I. pret. pl. of flēogan. II. pret. pl. of flēon. III.=fulgon pret. pl. of fēolan.

flustrian *to plait, weave,* WW 485¹ (IF 48·254).

fluton pret. pl. of flēotan.

flycerian=flicorian

-flycge v. unfl-.

flycticlāð (GL)=flyhteclāð

flyge† (i) m. *flight.*

flȳge=flēoge

flygepīl n. *flying dart,* Mod 27. [v. '*pile*']

flygerēow *wild in flight*, Gu 321.

flygul=flugol

flȳhst pres. 2 sg. of flēon.

flyht (i) m. *flying, 'flight,'* Æ,OET. on flyhte *on the wing.*

flyhte m. *patch*, MkLR 2²¹.

flyhteclāð (i) m. *patch*, Cp. [v. '*cloth*']

flyhthwæt† *swift of flight*, Ph.

flȳhð pres. 3 sg. of flēon.

flȳm-=flīem-

flyne (e) f. *batter*, Lcd.

flȳs (Æ)=flīes; **flyt, flȳt-**=flit, flīt-

flȳt pres. 3 sg. of flēotan.

flȳte=flēot(e), flīete

flȳtme f. *fleam (blood-letting instrument)*, Gl. [*L.* phlebotomum]

flyð=flyht

±**fnæd** n. nap. fnadu *fringe, border, hem*, Æ.

fnǣran, fnǣrettan *to breathe heavily, snort, fume*. v. NC 356.

fnæs I. n. dp. fnasum *fringe*, WW 425²⁷. II. pret. 3 sg. of fnesan.

fnǣst m. *blowing, blast, breath, Lcd: voice*, LF 56³. ['*fnast*']

fnǣstian *to breathe hard, Lcd.* [v. '*fnast*']

fnēosung f. *sneezing*, WW. [v. '*fnese*']

fnēsan⁵ *to pant, gasp*, GD : (+) sneeze, Lcd.

fnora m. *sneezing*, Æ,Gl.

fō pres. 1 sg. of fōn.

foca m. *cake (baked on the hearth)*, ÆL 18¹⁶⁴.

fōd-=fōdd-

fōda m. '*food,' nourishment*, Æ,CD : *fuel*, Sc.

fōdder (o², u²) I. n. gs. fōd(d)res '*fodder,' food*, Æ,LL ; *darnel, tares*, MtL 13 (fōter). II. n. *case, sheath*, Gl,MH. III. *hatchet?* WW.

fōdderbrytta m. *distributor of food, herdsman*, WW 111³⁹.

fōddergifu (u²) *food*, PPs.

fōdderhec *rack for food or fodder*, LL 455,17.

fōddornoð m. *sustenance*, GD 193¹⁷.

fōddorðegu† f. *feeding, repast, food.*

fōddurwela m. *wealth of food, provisions*, Rd 33¹⁰.

fōdnoð m. *substance, food*, TC.

fōdrað (OET 180²⁰)?=fōdnoð

fōdrere m. *forager*, AO 156³⁵.

foe- (N)=fe-, fē-

+**fōg** I. n. *joining, joint.* II. n. *suitability*, Lcd 10b. III. *suitable*, Lcd 89b.

+**fōgstān** (fōh) m. *hewn stone*, CP 253¹⁹.

fōh imperat. of fōn.

foht=feoht

fohten pp. of feohtan.

fol (wk. adj.)=full

+**fol** adj. *with foal*, Gen 32¹⁵.

fol-=ful-

fola m. '*foal,' colt*, Bl,MkL ; Æ.

folc n. '*folk,' people, nation, tribe*, Æ,B, Chr; AO,CP : *a collection or class of persons, laity*, Bl,Bo : *troop, army.*

folcāgende† *ruling.*

folcbealo n. *great tribulation*, Men 125.

folcbearn† n. *man*, Gen.

folccū (folcū) f. *people's cow*, PPs 67²⁷.

folccūð *noted : public*, BH.

folccwēn f. *queen of a nation*, B 641.

folccwide n. *popular saying*, NC 287.

folccyning† m. *king of a nation.*

folcdryht† f. *multitude of people.*

folcegetrum=folcgetrum

folcegsa m. *general terror*, PPs 88³³.

folcfrēa m. *lord of the people*, Gen 1852.

folcfrig *having full rights of citizenship*, LL 13,8; 344,45. [v. '*folk*']

folcgedrēfnes f. *tribulation*, NC 287.

folcgefeoht n. *pitched battle*, AO.

folcgemōt n. *meeting of the people of a town or district*, LL. ['*folkmoot*']

folcgerēfa m. *public officer*, WW.

folcgeriht=folcriht

folcgesīð† m. *prince, noble, chief, officer.*

folcgestealla† m. *companion in war*, Gen.

folcgestrēon n. *public treasure*, Gen 1981.

folcgetæl n. *number of fighting men*, Ex 229.

folcgetrum† n. *army, host*, Gen.

folcgewinn n. *fighting, war*, Met 1¹⁰.

folcherepað m. *highway*, KC.

folcisc *of the people, popular, secular, common*, LL.

folclǣsung=folclēasung

folclagu f. *law of the people, public law*, LL.

folcland n. *land held by freemen according to tribal rules of family inheritance*, LL (v. 2·403 and NED). ['*folkland*']

folclār f. *homily*, GD.

folclēasung f. *slander*, LL. [v. '*folk*']

folclic *public*, Æ : *common, popular : secular : populous*, OEG.

folcmægen† n. *public force, army, tribe.*

folcmægð† f. *tribe, nation*, Gen.

folcmǣlum=floccmǣlum

folcmǣre *celebrated*, Gen 1801.

folcmōt=folcgemōt

folcnēd f. *people's need*, PPs 77¹⁶.

folcrǣd† m. *public benefit.*

folcrǣden f. *decree of the people*, Cra 42.

folcriht I. n. *right of the people, common law*, LL. ['*folkright*'] II. adj. *according to common law*, LL 30¹³.

folcsǣl n. *house*, Rd 2⁵.

folcscearu† f. *people, nation, province : people's land*, B 73 (Earle).

folcsceaða m. *villain*, An 1595.

folcscipe m. *nation, people*, Rd 33¹⁰.

folcslite n. *sedition*, WW 116²⁶.

folcsōð n. *simple truth?* ÆL 23⁶⁶.

folcstede† m. *dwelling-place, B* : *battlefield.* [v. *'folk'*]

folcstōw f. *country place,* BH 160¹⁶.

folcswēot m? *troop, multitude,* Ex 577.

folctalu f. *genealogy,* Ex 379.

folctoga† m. *chieftain, commander.*

folctruma m. *host,* LPs.

folcū=folccū

folcweleg *populous,* WW 476¹⁶.

folcwer† m. *man,* GEN.

folcwiga m. *warrior,* RD 15²³.

folcwita m. *public councillor, senator,* CRA 77.

folcwōh n. *deception of the public,* ÆL 23²⁶¹.

foldærn† n. *earth-house, grave.*

foldāgend m. *earth-possessor, earth-dweller,* PH 5. (MS folcāgend)

foldbold n. *house, castle,* B 773.

foldbūend m. *earth-dweller, man, inhabitant of a country,* CP.

folde (eo) f. *earth, ground, soil, terra firma,* B,Jud : *land, country, region,* Gen : *world.* [*'fold'*]

foldgræf† n. *earth-grave.*

foldgrǣg *grey as the earth?* GnC 31.

foldhrērende *walking on the earth,* PA 5.

foldræst f. *rest in the earth,* CR 1029.

foldwæstm m. *fruits of the earth,* PH 654.

foldweg† m. *way, path, road* : *earth.*

foldwela m. *earthly riches,* RIM 68.

foldwong† m. *plain, earth.*

folen, folgen pp. of fēolan.

folgað (AO)=folgoð

folgere m. *'follower,' attendant, disciple,* Bo, WW ; Æ,CP : *successor,* AO 150²⁷ : *freeman who is not a householder.*

±folgian (often w. d.) *to 'follow,'* Jn,Lk : *accompany,* Chr,Ps : *follow after, B* : (+) *attain,* CP 383²⁷ : *obey, serve, observe, El.* (v. also fylgan.)

folgoð m. *body of retainers, following, retinue* : *pursuit, employment, service, dignity, office, rule,* Æ,AO,CP : *jurisdiction, district* : *condition of life, destiny.*

folm†, folme f. folma m. *palm, hand.* [fēlan]

fon=fann; **fon-**=fan-

fōn⁷ (±) *to take, grasp, seize, catch, B, BH,Gen,Ma* ; AO,CP : *capture, make prisoner, Chr* : *receive, accept, assume, undertake, B,Sol* ; CP : *meet with, encounter.* f. *on take up, begin, resume, take to,* Æ,Bo,Chr : *attack,* CHR 1085E. f. *tō rīce ascend the throne, Chr* ; AO. f. *tōgædre join together, join issue, engage in battle.* him tōgēanes feng *clutched at him, B.* him on fultum feng *helped them,* JUD 300. hlyst +f. *listen.* [*'fang,' 'i-fang'*]

fond=fand pret. 3 sg. of findan.

fong-=fang-; **fonn**=fann; **font**=fant

fonu=fanu

for I. prep. (with d., inst. and a.) (local) *before, in the sight of, in or into the presence of, as far as,* IM 119¹³ : (temporal) *during, before,* Æ : (causal) *'FOR,' on account of, for the sake of, through, because of, owing to, from, by reason of,* Æ : *as to* : *in order to* : *in place of, instead of, equivalent to, at the price of,* Æ : *in preference to, Rood* : *in spite of, Chr.* for worulde *as regards this world,* Æ. for Dryhtne *by God.* **II.** conj. *for, because.* for hwȳ, for hwām, for hwon *wherefore?* for ðām, for ðon, for ðȳ (*'forthen'*) *therefore, BH* : *because, since.* for ðām ðe (ðȳ), for ðȳ ðe *because, AO.* for ðȳ ðæt, for ðām ðæt *in order that.* **III.** adv. *too, very,* Æ. for ān *only.*

for- I. denotes *loss or destruction* (as in fordōn, forgiefan), or is *intensitive or pejorative,* as in forbærnan, forrotian. It is not connected with the preposition 'for.' [Ger. ver-] **II.** occly.=fore-

fōr I. f. *going, course, journey, expedition, BH* ; AO : *way, manner of life.* [*'fore'*] **II.** m. *pig, hog,* OEG. **III.** pret. 3 sg. of faran.

fora (N)=foran; **fora-**=fore-; **forad**=forod

foran I. prep. (w. d.) *before, opposite.* **II.** adv. *before, in front, forward, Rd* ; Æ, AO,CP : *to the front, Da.* foran ongean *opposite.* fōran tō *opposite* : *beforehand.* [*'forne'*]

foranbodig n. *thorax, chest,* WW 158⁴¹.

forandæg *early part of the day,* Æ(NC).

forane *opposite* : *beforehand.*

foranhēafod n. *forehead,* Æ.

foranlencten m. *early spring,* LCD 96a.

forann, iht f. *early part of the night, dusk, evening,* Æ.

forannihtsang m. *compline,* BTK 194,218.

forað=foreað

forbærnan *to cause to burn, burn up, consume by fire, be consumed,* Æ,Chr ; AO. [*'forburn'*]

forbærnednes f. *burning,* LCD.

forbearan=forberan

forbearnan=forbærnan

forbed n. *portable bed, litter,* ZDA 31.

forbēgan=forbīgan

forbelgan³ *to be enraged,* BL.

forbēn f. *prayer,* DHy 138¹³.

forbēodan *to 'forbid,' prohibit, Chr,G* ; Æ : *restrain, Ps* : *refuse, Lk* : *repeal, annul,* LL 42,49.

forbēodendlic *dehortative, dissuasive,* ÆGR 225¹¹.

forbeornan³ (e, y) *to burn, be consumed by fire, AO,B.* [*'forburn'*]

forberan I. (sv⁴) *to 'forbear,' abstain from, refrain,* CP : *suffer, endure, tolerate, humour, CP,B,BH,Mt* : *restrain.* II.=foreberan

forberendlīce *tolerably,* Sc 137⁶.

forbernan=forbærnan

forberstan³ *to break, burst asunder, vanish, fail,* LL : *let go by default,* EC 201'. ['*forburst*']

forbētan=forebētan

forbīgan (ē, ȳ) *to bend down, bow down, depreciate, abase, humiliate, degrade.*

forbīgels m. *arch, arched roof,* WW 126³.

forbindan³ *to bind (up), muzzle,* CP 105⁷. ['*forbind*']

forbisen=forebysen

forbītan¹ *to bite through,* HL 18³⁹¹.

forblāwan⁷ *to blow,* AO : *blow out, inflate,* Lcd. ['*forblow*']

forblindian *to blind,* MkR 6⁵².

fŏrbōc f. *itinerary,* OEG 2023.

forbod n. *prohibition,* LL; CP. ['*forbode*']

forboda=foreboda

forbrecan⁵ (æ²) *to break in pieces, bruise, violate, crush, destroy,* Jn; AO,CP. **forbrocen** *broken down, decrepit.* ['*forbreak*']

for-brēdan³, -bregdan *to tear, pull, snatch away : draw over, cover : change, transform,* Bo. ['*forbraid*']

forbrītan *to break in pieces, crush, bruise.*

forbrȳt-ednes (ESPs), -ennes (V²Ps) f. *contrition.*

forbrytian, forbryttan=forbrītan

forbūgan² *to bend from, refrain from, avoid, decline, Æ,Ma;* CP : *flee from, escape,* CP : *hold down* ['*forbow*']

forbȳgan=forbīgan

for-byrd, fore- f. *abstention,* AO 30³⁵ : *longsuffering,* CP 41¹⁷.

forbyrdian *to wait for,* EPs 32²⁰.

forbyrdig *forbearing,* NC 287.

forbyrnan (Æ)=forbeornan

force f. forca m. '*fork,*' Æ,WW.

forcēap *forestalling (in trade),* LL 234,2¹⁰. [=*forecēap]

forcel m. *pitchfork,* NC 287.

forceorfan³ *to carve out, cut down, cut off, cut through, divide, Æ,Chr;* AO,CP. ['*forcarve*']

forcēowan² *to bite off,* Bo 36²³.

forcierran (e², y²) *to turn aside, prevent, avert, avoid,* CP : *turn oneself away, escape : pervert.*

forcierrednes (e², y²) f. *perversity,* GD 119¹⁵ : *turning aside,* BPs 125¹.

forcierring (e, y) f. *turning aside,* CVPs 125¹.

forcilled *chilled,* LCD.

forcippian (y) *to cut off,* RHy 2¹². [v. '*chip*']

forclǣman *to stop up,* GL.

forclas pl. of forcel.

forclingan³ *to wither, shrink up,* CAS 36¹⁹, Cp. ['*forcling*']

forclyccan *to stop, close (ears),* RPs 57⁵.

forclȳsan *to close up,* LCD 3·92'.

forcnīdan=forgnīdan

forcostian *to tempt,* ByH 98³².

forcrafian *to require,* RBL 82⁵.

forcuman⁴ *to come before, prevent, surprise : harass, wear out, destroy : reject,* LG : *overcome, conquer, obtain : surpass.*

forcunnian *to tempt, try,* G.

for-cūð (Æ) *bad, wicked, infamous, foul, despicable, despised, Æ,Bo;* AO,CP. adv. -cūðe. ['*forcouth*']

forcūð-lic, -līce=for-cūð, -cūðe

forcweðan⁵ *to speak ill of, abuse, revile,* CP : *reprove : refuse, reject,* CP : *boast, promise great things,* GNE 49.

forcwolstan³? *to swallow,* LCD 18a.

forcwȳsan *to shake violently,* SPs 109⁷.

forcyppian=forcippian

forcyrran (Æ)=forcierran

forcȳðan *to reprove, rebuke : refute?* SOL.

ford m. ds. forda '*ford,*' Æ,AO; Mdf.

fordǣlan *to spend,* Lk(B) 8⁴³.

fordēad *dead,* MtL 28⁴.

fordelfan³ *to delve, dig up,* EC 120²⁸.

fordēman *to condemn, sentence, doom,* Mt; Æ : *prejudice,* EC 145' : *decide,* Sc 125⁵. ['*fordeem*']

fordēmedlic *to be condemned,* GD 208⁹.

fordēmednes f. *condemnation, proscription,* BH 34⁵.

fordēmend m. *accuser,* JnL p 5⁹.

fordēming f. *plunder, spoliation,* OEG 3149.

fordemman *to dam up, block up,* EPs 57⁵.

fordettan (KGL)=fordyttan

fordīcigan *to shut out by a ditch, block up,* CP.

fordilemengan *to gloss over,* CHRD 18⁹.

for-dīligian, -dīlegian, -dīligian *to blot out, destroy, abolish,* BH. ['*fordilghe*']

fordimmian *to obscure, darken,* Sc. ['*fordim*']

fordittan=fordyttan

fordōn anv. *to undo, bring to nought, ruin, destroy,* BH,MtL; Æ,AO : *abolish,* Chr : *kill,* LL : *corrupt, seduce, defile.* pp. fordōn *corrupt, wicked, abandoned.* ['*fordo*']

fordrǣfan *to drive, compel,* LL 24,62.

fordrencan (æ) *to make drunk, intoxicate,* Æ. ['*fordrench*']

fordrīfan¹ *to drive, sweep away : drive on, impel, compel,* AO : *drive away, expel,* Chr; Æ : *overtax.* ['*fordrive*']

fordrifnes f. *objection, opposition,* MkL Pref 2¹⁵.

fordrincan³ *to make drunk, be drunk,* CP.

fordrūgian *to become dry, wither,* Met; ÆL ['*fordry*']

fordruncen pp. *drunk, CP.* ['*fordrunken*']
fordruncnian (fore-) *to be made drunk,* LL.
fordrūwian=fordrūgian
forduttan (VPs)=fordyttan
fordwer m. *weir at a ford,* KC.
fordwilman *to confound,* Bo 14⁵.
fordwīnan *to vanish, ÆL.* ['*fordwine*']
fordyslic *very foolish,* Bo 42¹⁰.
fordyttan (e, i, u) *to obstruct, block up, close, Cp,VPs; Æ.* ['*fordit*']
fore I. prep. w. d. a. (local) *before, in the sight of, in presence of, B* : (causal) *because of, for the sake of, through, on account of, by reason of, from, BH* : (temporal) *before, Cr : for, instead of.* II. adv. *before, beforehand, formerly, once, Ps.* ['*fore*']
fore-=for-
foreādihtian *to arrange, order beforehand,* CP 9⁹.
forealdian *to grow old, decay, BH; Æ,CP.* ['*forold*']
foreāstreccan *to lay low, overthrow,* EPs 105²⁶.
foreāð m. *preliminary oath, LL* (v. 2·546). ['*foreoath*']
for-ēaðe (Æ), -ēaðelīce *very easily.*
forebē(a)cen n. *sign, portent, prodigy, Æ.*
forebegān *to intercept,* CHR 1009 E.
foreberan *to prefer,* BH 294⁷.
forebētan *to make legal amends* (*vicariously*), LL.
forebirig=forebyrig ds. of foreburh.
forebiscop m. *high-priest,* MtL 1¹⁸ (mg).
forebisegian *to preoccupy,* OEG 1236.
foreblǣsting (ē) f. *shoot, branch,* EPs 79¹².
fōrebōc (HGL 454)=fōrbōc
forebod n. *prophecy, preaching,* NG.
foreboda m. *forerunner, messenger, crier,* ANS 84¹⁴.
forebodere m. *herald, crier,* DR 48,194.
forebodian *to announce, declare,* ASPs.
forebodung f. *prophecy,* NG.
forebrǣdan *to prolong,* EPs 119⁵ : *overshadow,* MkL 9⁷.
forebrēost n. *chest,* WW.
foreburh f. *outwork : outer court, vestibule,* Æ.
forebyrd=forbyrd
forebysen f. *example,* CHR(Thorpe) 67'.
foreceorfan³ '*praecidere,*' ÆGR 172⁴.
foreceorfend m. *front tooth,* WW 264¹¹.
forecēosan *to choose in preference,* BCJRPs 131¹³,¹⁴.
foreclipian (y) '*proclamare,*' BHy 3⁴; ANS 122·265.
forecnēo(w)ris(n) f. *progeny,* ERPs.
forecnyll m. *first ringing* (*of a bell*), RBL 82¹¹.

forecostigan *to profane,* EPs 88³².
forecostung f. *profanation,* EPs 88³⁵.
forecuman⁴ *to come before, prevent, BH* : *overcome? Ps : come out, come upon,* NG. ['*forecome*']
forecweden *aforesaid,* GD 12,344.
forecweðan⁵ *to preach, predict,* G,DR.
forecwide m. *prophecy : introduction, heading* (*of chapter*), NG.
forecyme m. *proceeding forth,* MtL p4³.
fore-cynren, -cynrēd n. *progeny,* RPs, WW.
forecȳðan *to make known* (*beforehand*), *tell forth,* EPs,TC : *prophesy,* GD 339²¹.
fored=forod
foreduru f. -dyre, -dere n. *vestibule,* GL.
foredyrstig? *presumptuous,* LL 409,22.
forefǣger *very fair,* ES 8·479⁸⁹.
fore-feng, -fong=forfang
forefēran *to go before,* BL,LkLR.
forefex (=ea²) n. *forelock,* OEG 5326; 2⁴⁵³.
foreflēon *to flee,* MkL 14⁵².
forefōn⁷ *to prevent, anticipate,* CPs,DR.
foregān anv., foregangan⁷ *to go before, precede, BH,VPs : go in front of, project : excel.* ['*forego*']
forege-=for(e)-
foregearwung f. *preparation, parasceve,* G.
foregebiddan⁵ *to intercede,* RB 62⁸.
foregeblind *blinded,* MkL 6⁵³.
foregecēosan *to choose beforehand,* Æ.
foregegān=forgangan
foregehāt n. *vow,* ÆL 23b⁵⁴³.
foregehātan *to promise : invite,* NG.
foregelēoran *to pass away,* LkL.
foregenga m. *forerunner : predecessor, ancestor, CP : attendant,* JUD 127.
foregengel (for-) m. *predecessor,* CHR 963 E.
foregescēaw-=forescēaw-
foregesecgan *to predestine,* MtL p 1⁹.
foregesettan=foresettan
foregeswuteliende '*indagande,*' OEG 1504.
foregetēon² *to point out,* HGL 411.
foregeðingian=foreðingian
foregeðistrod *darkened,* MkL 6⁵².
foregidd n. *proverb,* JnR 16²⁹.
foregielpan³ *to boast greatly,* AO 4¹⁸,BF 188¹³.
foregīmnes (ē³) f. *observation,* LkL 17²⁰.
foregīsl m. *preliminary hostage,* CHR 878.
foreglēaw *foreseeing, provident, wise, prudent, Æ.* adv. -līce.
foregyrnan *to show before,* Sc 203¹⁷.
forehālig *very holy,* ANS 84·3.
forehrādian *to hasten before,* CHRD 26¹⁸.
forehūs n. *porch,* LV 33.
foreiernan (for-) *to run before, outrun,* JnL 20⁴. ['*forerun*']
fore-iernend, -iernere m. *forerunner,* WW.

forelād-tēow, -twa m. *chief, leader*, LkLR 22²⁶.

forelǣdan *to lead forth*, MtL 15¹⁴.

forelǣrend m. *teacher*, BL 149¹³.

forelār f. *preaching*, MtL p 16⁵.

forelcian *to delay*, RWH 142³⁴.

foreldan=forieldan

forelegnis=forlegis

forelēoran *to go before, pass by*, NG.

forelēornes (EPs 100³)=forlēornes

forelocc m. *'forelock,'* OEG.

forelōcian *'prospicere,'* EPs 101²⁰ : *'re-spicere,'* EPs 101¹⁸.

foremǣre *illustrious, renowned, famous*, Æ.

foremǣrlic *eminent*, Bo 75²⁴.

foremǣrnes f. *eminence, fame*, Bo.

foremanian *to forewarn*, BH 412³⁰.

foremanig *very many*, MtL p 18¹².

foremeahtig=foremihtig

foremearcod *before-mentioned*, CM 378.

foremearcung (e²) f. *title, chapter*, NG.

foremihtig (ea) *most mighty*. adv. -līce.

foremunt m. *promontory*, WW 464¹⁷.

forenama m. *'pronomen,'* RBL 11¹³.

forene=forane

forenemnan *to mention beforehand*, VH 12.

forenyme m. *taking before*, WW 42⁷.

forerīm m. *prologue*, Mt(K) pref. 1¹.

forerynel m. *forerunner, herald, morning star*, Æ,CP.

foresacan⁶ *to forbid*, MtL 3¹⁴.

foresǣd *aforesaid*, Æ. *['foresaid']*

fore-sǣgdnes, -saga f. *preface*, NG.

foresǣndan=foresendan

forescēawere (for-) m. *'provisor,'* ES 39·327.

forescēawian *to 'foreshow,' foresee*, Æ : *pre-ordain, decree, appoint*, Æ : *provide, furnish with*, Æ.

forescēawodlīce *with forethought, thoughtfully*, CM 76.

forescēawung f. *contemplation, foresight, providence*, Sc; Æ. *['foreshowing']*

forescēotan (Bo 124¹¹)=forscēotan

forescieldnes f. *protection*, EPs 120⁵.

forescynian *to shun*, NG.

forescyttels m. *bolt, bar*, CR 312.

forescȳwa m. *shadow*, DR 13¹⁴.

forescȳwung f. *overshadowing*, DR 28⁶.

foresēcan *to appeal (for justice)*, LL 152,3 and nn.

foresecgan *to mention before*, Æ : *proclaim, preach : foretell*, BH. *['foresay']*

foreseld n. *first seat*, MtL 23⁶.

foresellan *to spend, advance (money)*, LL (or ? 2 words).

foresendan *to send before*, ÆGr; CM 448. [v. *'fore'*]

foresēon⁵ *to 'foresee,'* Ps : *provide*, BH : *provide for*, BH.

foresēond m. *provider*, BH 338¹⁰.

foresēones f. *care, foresight, providence*, BH.

fore-setnes, -sete(d)nes f. *proposition, purpose*, BF 2⁸ : *preposition*, ÆGR 267¹⁵.

foresettan *to place before, shut in*, VPs : *propose : prefer : precede*. *['foreset']*

foresingend m. *precentor*, WW 129²¹.

foresittan⁵ *to preside over*, BH.

fore-smēagan, -smēan *to think beforehand*, G,GL.

foresnotor *very wise*, B 3163.

fore-spǣc, -speca=fore-sprǣc, -spreca.

fore-sprǣc (CP), -sprēc, -spǣc (WW) f. *advocacy, defence, excuse : agreement, arrangement : preamble, preface, prologue*, Æ,CP : *promise*. *['forespeech']*

forespreca m. *intercessor, advocate, mediator : sponsor*, LL 442,1.

foresprecan⁵ I. *to speak or answer for, be surety for, intercede for*, CP : *say before*. **foresprecen** *above-mentioned, aforesaid*, Bo. *['forespoken']* **II.**=forsprecan

forestǣppan⁶ (e³) *to precede, go before, anticipate*, Æ : *excel : forestall, prevent*.

forestǣppend m. *precursor*, Lk 22²⁶.

forestǣppung f. *anticipation*, BF 172¹⁷.

forestandan⁶ *to preside, lead : excel*, WW 464¹⁵ : *prevail against*, MtL 16¹⁸.

forestapul *going before*, GPH 396.

foresteall (for-) m. *intervention, hindrance (of justice) : ambush, assault, offence of waylaying on the highway*, Æ,LL : *fine for such an offence : resistance, opposition*. *['forestall']*

forestemman *to prevent, hinder*, NG.

forestēora m. *look-out man, pilot*, WW 464⁸.

foresteppan⁶=forestǣppan

forestīgan¹ *to excel*, ÆGR 154¹¹n.

forestige m. *vestibule*, OEG 4688 and n.

forestihtian *to fore-ordain*, Æ.

forestihtung f. *predestination*, Æ.

foreswerian⁶ *to swear before*, NUM 11,14.

foretācn n. *'fore-token,' prognostic, prodigy, sign, wonder*, Bo; CP.

foretācnian *to foreshow*, BH 216¹⁷.

foreteohhian *to fore-ordain*, WW 219³¹.

foreteohhung f. *predestination*, Bo.

foretēon *to fore-ordain, frame beforehand, arrange*, BH,PPs.

foretēð mp. *front teeth*, WW. *['foretooth']*

foretīge m. *forecourt, porch*, Mt 11¹⁶.

foretrymman *to testify*, JnL 13²¹.

foretȳned *shut in*, BH 386².

foreðanc m. *forethought, providence, consideration, deliberation*, CP.

foreðancful *prudent*, AS 14⁵.

foreðanclic *thoughtful, careful, prudent*, CP. adv. -līce.

foreðancol (u³) *prudent*, CP305².
foreðancolnes f. *prudence*, PPs48³.
foreðencan *to premeditate, consider, be mindful, CP.* ['*forethink*']
foreðēon *to surpass, excel*, RB131¹⁹.
foreðingere m. *intercessor, mediator, Æ.*
foreðingian *to plead for, intercede, defend*, Bo,LL.
foreðinglend m. *intercessor*, WNL294³⁰,³².
fore-ðingrǣden (WNL), -ðingung (Æ) f. *intercession.*
foreðonc=foreðanc; **forewall**=foreweall
foreward=foreweard
forewarnian *to take warning beforehand* : *forewarn*, NC288.
foreweall m. *rampart, bulwark, Ex.* ['*forewall*']
foreweard (a², e²) **I.** fn. *condition, bargain, agreement, treaty, assurance, Chr.* ['*foreward*'] **II.** m. *outpost, scout.* **III.** adj. '*forward*,' *inclined to the front, Æ* : *fore, early, former, BH; Æ.* f. gēar *new year.* **IV.** adv. (-wearde at AS55¹⁴) *in front, CP* : *towards the future, Gen.* on f. *at the beginning*, BF174 : *above all*, BYH40⁵. fram foreweardum *once more*, RB.
foreweardnes (e³) f. *beginning*, BF198².
foreweorðan³ *to predestinate*, MkLp1¹⁶
fore-wesan anv. pret. 3 sg. -wæs *to be over, rule over*, BH.
forewīs *foreknowing*, HL18³⁶³.
forewitan swv. *to foreknow, Bo.* ['*forewit*']
forewītegian *to prophesy*, ÆH.
forewītegung f. *prophecy*, ÆL,OEG.
forewitig *knowing*, LCD3·436 : *foreknowing, Æ* : *prophetic*, OEG.
forewitol *foreknowing*, CHR1067D.
forewittlendlic *prescient*, OEG1502.
foreword n. *stipulation, condition*, KC, LL.
forewost=forwost.
forewrēgan=forwrēgan
forewriten *above or before-written*, CM.
forewritennes f. *proscription, exile*, WW 466⁵.
forewyrcend m. *servant*, ÆL2¹⁵⁶.
forewyrd f. *agreement, condition*, GL.
±**forewyrdan** (æ³) *to agree*, KC3·274¹².
forfang (forefeng) n. *capture, (legal) seizure, recovery of cattle or other property, LL* : *reward for rescuing property, LL* (v. 388–391 and 2·279). ['*forfang*']
forfangfeoh n. *reward for rescuing cattle or other property*, LL390,3².
forfaran⁶ *to pass away, perish, Chr* : *lose* : *destroy, ruin, cause to perish, LL* : *intercept, obstruct.*
forfeallan *to overwhelm*, AA35⁴.
forfeng **I.** pret. 3 sg. of forfōn. **II.**=forfang

forfēran *to depart, die, Chr; Æ.* ['*forfere*']
forferian *to let die*, LL58,17.
forflēon² *to flee from, escape, avoid, evade, Æ.*
forflȳgan *to put to flight*, ZDA31·16⁴¹⁸.
forfōn⁷ *to seize* : *anticipate, forestall* : *surprise* : *prevent* : *forfeit.*
forfyllan *to stop up, obstruct*, WW463¹⁰.
forg-=foreg-
forgǣgan *to transgress, trespass, prevaricate, Æ* : *pass by, omit, neglect*, OEG,W.
forgǣgednes f. *transgression, trespass, Æ.*
forgǣgend m. *transgressor*, CHRD41³¹.
forgǣgung f. *fault, excess*, Sc115⁹.
forgǣlan *to avoid*, LkL.
for-gān, -gangan **I.** *to go or pass over, by or away, Æ,MtL* : '*forgo*,' *abstain from, neglect, lose, Æ*; CP,Æ. **II.**=foregān
forgeare *very certainly*, ÆL23⁵⁵⁶.
forgedōn=fordōn
forgeearnung f. *merit*, DHy132¹.
forgefenes=forgiefnes
forgēgan=forgǣgan
forgeldan=forgieldan
forgēm-=forgiem-
forgenge *hard to carry out?* (BTs), TC159².
forgeorne *very earnestly, very attentively*, BL.
forgeot-=forgit-, ofergit-
forget=forgiet pres. 3 sg. of forgietan.
forgief- v. also forgif-
forgiefan⁵ (i, y) *to give, grant, allow, BH,Bl*; CP : '*forgive*,' *overlook, Gen,Lk,Mt*; AO, CP : *give up, leave off, CP* : *give in marriage.*
forgiefen (e², ea², i²) *indulgent, AO* : *mild, tolerable*, NG.
for-giefnes (e, i, y) f. *pardon, '*forgiveness*,' remission, Bl; CP* : *indulgence, permission, BH* : *gift?* CR425.
forgieldan³ (e, i, y) *to pay for, CP* : *requite, reward, Bl; AO,CP* : *indemnify, make good* : *pay double (as penalty), LL* : *give* : *give up, forfeit*, VH12. ['*foryield*']
forgielpan³ *to boast in public, trumpet forth*, W234¹⁶.
forgīeman (ē, i, ȳ) *to neglect, pass by, transgress, B.* ['*foryeme*']
forgīemelēasian (ī, ȳ) *to neglect, abandon, give up, omit*, CP.
forgietan⁵ (i, y) w. a. or g. *to '*forget,*' Bf, Bo,G,Ps*; AO,CP. For comps. v. forgit-.
forgif- v. also forgief-.
forgifendlic (y²) *dative*, ÆGR22¹⁶.
forgifenlic *excusable, tolerable, Mt.* ['*forgivelich*']
forgifestre f. *female giver*, DHy49⁶.
forgifu f. '*gratia*,' DHy78⁷ (? 2 words).
forgifung f. *gift*, WW115¹².
forgildan=forgieldan
forgīm-=forgīem-

forgit-=forgiet-, ofergi(e)t-
forgitel (eo², y², o³, u³) *forgetful, Æ.* ['*for-getel*']
forgitelnes (y²) f. *forgetfulness, oblivion, LPs.* ['*forgetelness*']
forgiten pp. *forgetting, forgetful, Æ,Bl.*
forgiting f. *forgetfulness,* CM 1065.
forglendrian *to devour, swallow up,* W.
forgnagan⁶ *to eat up, Æ.* ['*forgnaw*']
forgnīdan¹ *to grind together, dash down, crush, break, LPs.* ['*forgnide*']
forgniden *contrite,* SPs 50¹⁸.
forgnidennes f. *tribulation,* APs 146³,LPs 13³.
forgnȳdan=forgnīdan
forgrindan³ I. *to grind down, ruin, destroy, consume.* II. (=y²) *to send to the bottom, destroy,* A 11·2⁴⁰. [grund]
forgrindet n. *grinding, pounding,* Cp. 776 c.
forgrīpan¹ *to seize, assail, attack, overwhelm.*
forgrīwan *to sink (in vice),* NC (BTs).
forgrōwen *grown up? overgrown?* Rim 46. [v. '*forgrow*']
forgumian (LL 474,2)=forgīman
forgyf-=forgief-, forgif-
forgyldan=forgieldan
forgyltan *to sin, be or become guilty,* W. forgylt *condemned, guilty.*
forgȳm-=forgīem-
forgyrd=forðgyrd
forgyrdan *to enclose, encircle,* Chr 189 n 4.
forgyt-=forgiet-, forgit-
for-habban, pret. 3 sg. -hæfde *to hold in, restrain, retain, keep back : draw back, refrain from, avoid, Æ.* forhæted *continent, abstemious, celibate,* CP.
forhæbbend m. *abstinent, continent person,* OEG 1254.
forhæfd=forhēafod
forhæf(e)(d)nes f. *temperance, continence, self-restraint, abstinence, BH; Æ,CP : parsimony,* OEG 3748. ['*forhevedness*']
forhæfendlīce *continently,* Chrd 42²⁹.
forhǣlan *to injure?* WW 464⁴.
forhǣtan *to overheat,* Lcd 91b.
forhǣðed *burnt up,* WW 234¹.
forhātan⁷ *to renounce, forswear, Æ.* se forhātena *the devil,* Gen 609. ['*forhight*']
forheafdnes (AS 23⁷)=forhǣfednes
forhēafod n. '*forehead,' brow, skull, WW; Æ.* [=fore-]
forhealdan⁷ *to forsake, fall away from, rebel against, B : let go,* LL 360,11 : *defile, pollute,* Bl : *withhold,* LL 130,6¹ : *misuse, abuse, Bo.* ['*forhold*']
forhealdnes f. *unchastity,* NC 288.
forheard *very hard,* MA 156.
forheardian *to grow hard,* LVPs 89⁶.

forhēawan⁷ *to hew in pieces, cut down, kill, Ma.* ['*forhew*']
forhefednes=forhæfednes
forhegan (Kgl)=forhogian
forhelan⁴ *to cover over, conceal, hide, protect, Æ,Bo; CP.* sacne f. *conceal a guilty man.* ['*forhele*']
forhelian *to hide,* OEG 5410n : *cover, clothe,* Chrd 108¹³.
forhergend m. *ravager,* Gl.
for-hergian, -herigean, -heregian *to plunder, harry, ravage, devastate, destroy,* AO,CP. [*Ger.* verheeren]
for-hergung, -her(g)iung f. *harassing, devastation,* AO 74⁸⁶.
forhicgan=forhycgan
forhīenan *to cast down, defeat, humiliate, outrage, oppress, waste,* AO. [*Ger.* verhöhnen]
forhigan=forhycgan
for-hoged-, -hogd-=forhogod-
forhogian *to neglect, disregard, despise, BH; Æ,CP.* ['*forhow*']
forhogiend m. *despiser,* Chrd,GD.
forhogi(g)endlic *contemptible,* Sc.
forhogod pp. of forhycgan.
forhogodlic *contemptuous,* Bl 77²³. adv. -līce.
forhogodnes f. *contempt,* BHb 342¹⁰.
forhogung f. *contempt,* BPs,CM.
forhohnes=forhogodnes
forhradian *to hasten,* CP : *prevent, anticipate, frustrate, Æ,CP.*
forhraðe *very speedily, quickly, soon, Æ.*
forhrēred *annulled,* WW.
forht *afraid, timid, cowardly,* AO,CP: *frightful, terrible.* adv. forhte *despairingly.*
forhtful *fainthearted, timorous,* WW 93⁹.
±forhtian (tr. and intr.) *to be afraid, surprised, fear, dread, Æ.*
forhtiendlic *timorous,* WW 442⁵ : *dreadful,* GD.
forhtige *humbly, submissively,* RB 70⁵.
forhtigend *timid,* W : *dreadful,* W.
forhtlic *fearful, afraid : dreadful.* adv. -līce.
forhtmōd *timorous, timid, Æ.*
forhtnes f. *fear, terror, Æ.*
forhtung f. *fear, ÆH.*
forhugian=forhogian
forhwǣn, forhwan=forhwon
forhwega (æ²) *somewhere, somewhere about, Æ,AO.*
forhweorfan³ *to come to an end, be destroyed,* W 183⁴.
forhwerf-=forhwierf-
for-hwī, -hwig=forhwȳ
forhwierfan (e, i, y) *to change, transform : remove, transfer : pervert,* CP.

forhwierfedlic (y²) *perverse*, BL 31⁴.

forhwierfednes (y²) f. *perversity*, NC 288.

forhwon *wherefore, why, for what reason*, BH.

forhwȳ (ī²) *why, wherefore*, Ps. ['*forwhy*']

forhwyrf-=forhwierf-

forhycgan *to disdain, despise, reject*, CP.

forhȳdan *to hide*, Ps; CP. ['*forhide*']

forhygdelic *despised*, LPs 118¹⁴¹.

forhylman *to refuse obedience to*, AN 735.

forhȳnan=forhīenan

forhyrdan (i) *to harden*, EPPs 94⁸. [heard]

forieldan *to put off, delay*, CP.

foriernan=foreiernan

forierð (y) *a head-land* (v. heafodlond) *in the case of land with furrows at right angles to those of the adjacent land* (BTs), KC 5·153²¹.

forinlīce *thoroughly, exceedingly*, Bo 94⁶.

forinweardlīce *thoroughly, genuinely*, Bo 137¹⁵.

forlācan⁷† *to mislead, seduce, deceive, betray*.

forlǣdan *to mislead, seduce*, Æ,AO,CP : *bring out* (=forð-), Æ. [*Ger.* verleiten]

forlǣran *to teach wrongly, lead astray, seduce, pervert, An,CP*; Æ. ['*forlere*']

forlǣtan⁷ *to let go, relinquish, surrender, lose, leave, abandon, neglect, An,Bl*; Æ,CP : *remit, pardon, excuse* : *loose, release* : *let, permit, allow, BH* : *grant, give*. ūp, in f. *to direct upwards, within*. ān(n)e f.=ān-forlǣtan. ['*forlet*']

for-lǣtennes (Æ), -lǣt(ed)nes f. *leaving, departure, absence* : *loss, perdition* : *intermission, cessation, end* : *remission* : *divorce*.

forlǣting f. *leaving, intermission*.

forlǣtu sbpl. *losses, sufferings*, VH 12.

forlǣðan *to loathe*, W 165³.

forlēan *to blame much*, A 12·517.

forlecgan *to cover up*, LCD 25a.

forlegen pp. of forlicgan.

forlegenes=forlegnes

forlegenlic *mean-looking, ugly* (Swt).

for-legis, -leges f. *prostitute, adulteress*, CP.

for-legis-, -legor-=forliger-

forlegnes f. *fornication*, BH,CP.

forlegnis f. *prostitute*, CP.

forlēogan² *to lie, perjure oneself, slander*, Æ.

forlēoran (EPs 143¹⁴)=forelēoran

forlēornes f. *transgression*, EPs 100³ (cp. ofer-l.).

forleornung f. *deception*, BL 183³⁴.

forleorte redupl. pret. sg. of forlǣtan.

forlēosan² *to lose, abandon, let go, B* ; Æ,AO, CP : *destroy, ruin*, Gen. ['*forlese*']

forlēt-=forlǣt-

forlettan (fore-) *to prevent*, MkL 10¹⁴.

forlicgan⁵ *to commit adultery or fornication*, AO,LL;Æ,CP:*fail,lapse, be neglected*, LL 178,7:*screen* (*a thief*), LL 274,12. ['*forlie*'] pp. forlegen used as sb. *adulterer, fornicator*.

forlicgend m. *fornicator*, Sc,WW.

forliden I. *much-travelled*, CAS 9·11. II. pp. of forlīðan.

forlidennes=forliðennes

forligan=forlicgan

for-ligenes, -lignes=forlegnes

forliger I. n. *adultery, fornication, wantonness, immorality*, Æ. II. m. *whoremonger, adulterer*, Æ : f. *fornicatress, adulteress*. III. adj. *adulterous*.

forligerbed n. *bed of fornication*, ÆH.

forligere=forliger I.

forligeren adj. *fornicating*, OEG 8²³².

forligerhūs n. *house of ill fame*, OEG.

forligerlic *unchaste, impure*, OEG. adv. -līce.

forligerwīf (e², o³) n. *prostitute*, MH 140¹⁹.

forliges=forlegis

forliggang m. *adultery, fornication*, WW 499¹².

forligrian *to commit fornication*, ERSPs 72²⁶.

forlīr=forliger II.

forlīsgleng *harlot's dress*, OEG 8³⁶¹ (= forlegis-).

forlīðan¹ *to suffer shipwreck*, OEG.

forlīðennes f. *shipwreck*, OEG.

for-long, -longe adv. *long ago*, NG.

forlor m. *loss, destruction*, AO,CP. tō forlore gedōn *to destroy*, CP.

forlorenes f. *state of being forlorn, perdition, destruction, VPs*. ['*forlornness*']

for-lorian, -losian *to lose*, NG.

forlustlīce *very willingly*, Bo 51¹⁸.

forlytel *very little*, Bo.

form=feorm; **form-** (NG)=frum-

forma (eo) *first, earliest, B,Bo,Mt*; CP. ['*forme*'] on forman *at first*.

for-mǣl, -māl fn. *negotiation, agreement, treaty*, LL. [mǣl II.]

formǣr-=foremǣr-

formanig (ǣ², o², e³) *very many*, MA,RB.

formelle f. *bench*, ANS 84·9. [*L.* formella]

formeltan³ (y) *to melt away, dissolve, liquefy, burn up, AO* ; Æ. ['*formelt*']

formengan *to associate*, CP 395⁴.

formesta=fyrmesta wk. superl. of forma.

förmete m. *food for a journey*, Æ.

formicel (y²) *very great*, CP,LL.

formogod *corrupted*, ÆL 23³⁷⁵.

formolsnian *to rot away, crumble, decay*, Æ.

formolsnung f. *corruption*, OEG 1251.

formycel=formicel; **formyltan**=formeltan

formyrðrian to murder, LL,W.
forn I. f? m? trout, WW 180³⁹. II.=foran
fornæman to be worn out, afflicted (with grief), GD 245³.
forne=foran adv.; **forne** f.=forn
fornēah very nearly, almost, about, Æ,AO, CP.
for-nēan (Æ), -nēh, -nēon=fornēah
fornerwian (=ie²) to check the growth or fecundity of, LCD 3·164'.
Fornētes folm a plant, LCD (v. BTs).
fornēðan to expose to danger, sacrifice, AO 222¹.
forniman⁴ to take away, deprive of, plunder waste, devastate, destroy, consume, B,Lcd; Æ,AO : annul : disfigure : overcome. ['fornim']
fornȳdan (=īe) to coerce, compel, W 158¹⁰.
fornyman=forniman
fornytlīce very usefully, GD 174²⁰.
forod (a², e²) broken down, worn out, useless, void, abortive, Æ,AO,CP.
foroft very often, Æ.
forpǣran to turn away, lose, spoil, pervert, destroy, Æ,CP.
forpyndan to do away, remove, CR 97.
forracu f. itinerary, OEG 7¹²¹.
forradian=forhradian
forrǣda? m. traitor, plotter, MP 1·592.
forrǣdan to plot against, betray, W : condemn : injure. ['forrede']
forraðe (Æ)=forhraðe
forrepen taken, JnLp 5⁸. [hrepian]
forrīdan¹ to intercept by riding before, CHR 894 A.
forridel m. fore-rider, forerunner, messenger, Æ. ['forridel']
forrotednes (a³, o³) f. corrupt matter, rottenness, Æ.
forrotian to rot away, decay, CP, WW : putrefy, Æ. ['forrot']
forrynel=forerynel
forsacan⁶ to object to, reject, oppose, deny, refuse, AO,Cp,LL : give up, renounce, AO, CP. ['forsake']
forsacennes f. denial, RWH 102¹⁰.
forsacung f. denial, RWH 144²⁵.
forsǣcan=forsēcan
forsǣtian to lay wait for, beset, surround, AO 146¹⁰.
forsǣtnian=forsetnian
forsǣwestre=forsewestre
forsawen=forsewen
forsc=frosc
forscād-=forscēad-
forscæncednes (LPs 40¹⁰)=forscrencednes
forscamian to make ashamed (impers. w. a.), CP,Sc : be ashamed. ['forshame']
forscamung f. modesty, GPH 390.

forscapung f. mishap, mischance, AO 40, 50.
forscēadan⁷ to scatter, disperse, CP : damn, condemn? GU 449 (GK).
forsceamian=forscamian
forsceap n. evil deed? GEN 898.
forscēaw-=forescēaw-
forscending f. confusion, LkR 21²⁵.
forsceorfan³ to gnaw off, bite, eat up, AO 226⁹.
forscēotan to anticipate, forestall, prevent, Bo.
forsceppan=forscieppan
forsceta flood-gate, BLPs 41⁸. [=forsscēta]
forscieppan⁶ to change, transform, Æ. ['forshape']
forscip n. 'foreship,' prow, WW. [=fore-]
forscired the dead? VH 12.
forscrencan (æ²) to supplant, overcome, vanquish, cast down, Æ : dry up, OEG 4926.
forscrencednes (scænc-) f. supplanting, deceit, LPs 40¹⁰.
forscrencend m. supplanter, ÆH 1·198'.
forscrīfan¹ to decree, GL : proscribe, condemn, doom, Æ : (†) bewitch.
forscrincan³ (intr.) to shrink, dry up, wither away, Æ,Mt. ['forshrink']
forscūfan² to cast down (pride), EX 204.
forscyldig wicked, Æ (58¹⁷⁰).
forscyldigian to condemn. pp. guilty, Æ.
forscyppan=forscieppan
forscyrian to separate, MFH 159.
forscyttan to exclude, prevent, obviate, Æ. ['forshut']
forsēarian to sear, dry up, wither, Æ,CP.
forseawennes=forsewennes
forsēcan I. to afflict, attack. II.=foresēcan
forsecgan to accuse falsely, slander, accuse, Æ : to speak about, discourse on.
forsegen-=forsewen-
forsēgon=forsāwon pret. pl. of forsēon.
forsellan to sell, ÆP 202⁷ : give up, lose, LL.
forsencan to reject, CP 345¹³.
forsendan to send away, banish, send to destruction, AO.
forsēon⁵ to overlook, neglect, scorn, despise, reject, renounce, Bl; Æ,AO,CP : refrain from. ['forsee']
forsēones=foresēones.
forsēoðan² to wither, consume, ÆH 1·84¹⁵.
forsērian (AS 10³?)=forsēarian
forsetnian (æ) to beset, ERPs 21¹⁷.
forsettan I. to hedge in, obstruct, BH : oppress. ['forset'] II.=foresettan
forsettednes=foresetnes
forsewen I. f. contempt, LPs 122⁴. II. pp. of forsēon.
forsewenlic despicable, ignominious, wretched, of poor appearance. adv. -līce, Æ.

forsewennes f. *contempt*, Æ,AO.

forsewestre (æ²) f. *female despiser*, OEG 4430.

forsingian=forsyngian

forsittan⁵ *to neglect, delay, LL* : *block, obstruct, besiege*, AO : *injure* : *absent oneself* (*from*). ['*forsit*']

forsīð=forðsīð

forsīðian *to perish*, B1550.

for-slǣwan, -slāwian *to be slow, unwilling, delay, put off, Bo*; CP. ['*forslow*']

forslēan⁶ *to cut through, strike, break, kill, destroy*, AO.

forslegenlic *mean, ignominious*, MH156²⁰.

forsliet m. *slaughter*, WW28¹⁶. [slieht]

forslītan *to consume, devour*, PPs77⁴⁶.

forsmorian *to smother, choke, stifle*, Æ.

forsorgian *to despond*, W69¹⁶.

forsōð *indeed, verily, Bo*. ['*forsooth*']

forspǣc=foresprǣc

forspanan⁶ *to mislead, lead astray, seduce, entice, Æ*; CP. ['*forspan*']

forspaning f. *allurement*, OEG.

forspeca=forespreca

forspecan=forsprecan

forspēdian *to speed, prosper*, SPs (? forswefian).

forspendan *to spend, give out, squander, consume*, AO. ['*forspend*']

forspennen (OEG612)=forspenning

forspennend m. *procurer*, ÆGR36¹¹.

forspenn-ende, -endlic *seductive, voluptuous, defiling*, OEG.

forspennestre f. *procuress*, ÆGR36¹².

forspenning f. *enticement, seduction, evil attraction*, ÆL.

forspild m. *destruction*, CP294¹⁹.

forspildan *to waste, lose, disperse, bring to nothing, destroy, ruin, kill, CP*. ['*forspill*']

forspillan (*AO*)=forspildan

forspill(le)dnes f. *waste, destruction, perdition*, Æ.

forspillian *to wanton*, OEG.

forsprec-=foresprec-; **forspyll-**=forspill-

for-sprecan, -specan⁵ *to speak in vain* : *state amiss* : *deny* : *denounce* : *lose* (*a case*).

forspyrcan (=ie) *to dry up*, PPs101³.

forst (frost) m. '*frost*,' *Gl,Ph,Rd*. [frēosan]

forstæppan=forestæppan

forstal (*LL*)=foresteall

forstalian (refl.) *to steal away*, LL.

forstandan⁶ *to defend, help, protect, LL* : *withstand, prevent, hinder, resist, oppose, Met* : *benefit, avail*, CP : *understand, Bo*; CP : *signify, be equal to*, EC,LL. ['*forstand*']

forsteall=foresteall

forstelan⁴ *to steal away, steal, rob, deprive, MtR,LL; Æ*. ['*forsteal*']

forstig *frosty*, ÆL23b⁵⁷⁵. [v. fyrstig]

forstlic *glacial, frozen*, WW175¹⁶.

forstoppian *to stop up, close*, LCD15b.

forstrang *very strong*, RD51⁴.

forstregdan³ *to destroy*, JPs105²³.

forstrogdnes f. '*precipitatio*,' NC289 (v. BTs).

forstyltan *to be amazed*, MkLR.

forstyntan *to blunt, break, crush*, WW375⁶ : *check, impair*, WYN132.

forsūcan² *to suck up*, OEG3343.

forsūgan² *to suck in*, LCD.

for-sugian (Æ,AO), -suwian (Æ)=forswigian

forsuwung f. *silence*, OEG2085.

forswǣlan *to burn, burn up, inflame, consume, Æ*. ['*forsweal*']

forswæð (DHy38¹⁶)=fōtswæð

forswāpan⁷† *to sweep away, drive off*.

forswarung f. *perjury*, CHRD40³⁴.

forswefian (-sweb-) *to prosper*, EPs88²³ (forð-), 117²⁵.

forswelan⁴ *to burn, burn up*, PH532.

forswelgan³ *to swallow up, devour, consume, absorb, B*; Æ,CP. ['*forswallow*']

forsweltan³ *to die, disappear, Bo*; WW. ['*forswelt*']

forsweogian=forswigian

forsweolgan=forswelgan

forsweorcan³ *to grow dark, obscure*, B,W.

forsweorfan³ *to polish, cleanse*, WW227¹⁷ : *grind away, demolish*, WW218²³.

forsweotole *very clearly*, AS2¹⁷.

forswerian⁶ (refl. and intr.) *to swear falsely, Æ,LL* : *make useless by a spell, B*. ['*forswear*']

forswigian *to conceal by silence, suppress, pass over, Æ,CP* : *be silent*.

forswīð *very great*, CREAT26.

forswīðan, forswīðian *to crush, press upon, overcome, repress*, CP.

forswīðe adv. *very much, utterly, Bo*.

forsworcenlic *dark, obscure*, DHy24¹⁰.

forsworcennes f. *darkening, darkness, Æ*, W.

forsworen (pp. of forswerian) '*forsworn,*' *perjured, Æ,Chr,WW*.

forsworennes f. *perjury, Æ*. ['*forsworenness*']

for-swugian (CP), -sygian=forswigian

forsyngian (i) *to sin greatly, LL*. ['*forsin*'] pp. as sb. forsyngod m. *sinner*.

fortācen=foretācn

fortendan *to burn away, sear*, AO46¹⁴.

fortēon² *to mislead, seduce, Cr* : *draw over, cover, obscure*. ['*fortee*']

fortiht=fortyht-

for-timbran, -timbrian *to close up, obstruct*, CVPs62¹².

fortog n. *gripes*, Lcd 109[6].
fortogen *pulled together*, WW 106[14].
fortogenes f. *griping, spasm*, Lcd 89a.
fortogian *to contract*, Lcd 3·120[8].
fortredan[5] *to tread down, trample on*, Æ; CP. ['*fortread*']
fortreddan *to tread down*, BH 44[23].
fortreding f. *treading down, crushing*, Sc 95[10].
fortrendan *to block (by rolling a stone)*, v. OEG 114.
fortrūgadnes, fortrūwednes=fortrūwodnes
fortrūwian *to be presumptuous, over-confident, rash*, CP.
fortrūwodnes f. *presumption*, CP.
fortrūwung f. *presumption*, Bo,CP.
fortrymman *to testify, confirm*, NG.
fortyhtan *to seduce*, EL 208.
fortyhtigend m. *polluter, defiler*, OEG 3337.
fortyllan *to seduce*, CR 270.
fortymbrian=fortimbrian
fortynan *to shut in, enclose, block up*, CP.
forð I. adv. '*forth*,' *forwards, onwards, further*, Æ : *hence, thence* : *away*, Æ : *continually, still, continuously, henceforth, thenceforward, simultaneously*. f. mid ealle *forthwith*. and swā f. *and so forth*, ÆGr. swā f. swā *so far as*, LL. f. on *continually*. fram orde oð ende f. *from the beginning to the end*. f. ðæt *until*. II. prep. *during*, Bo.
forð- (N)=furð-
forðācīgan *to call forth*, BH 444[24].
forðādīgian *to bring to nothing, blot out*, MFH 160.
forðǣm, torðam, torðan (CP), forðon (AO, CP) I. conj. *for (the reason) that, owing to (the fact) that, for, because, on that account, therefore, seeing that*. for ðǣm ðe, etc. with same signification. II. adv. *for that cause, consequently, therefore*.
forðāgoten *poured forth*, ÆL 23b[798].
forðahting (=eaht-) f. *exhortation*, CM 447.
forðancful *very thankful*, ES 18·336; 43·162.
forðātēon[2] *to bring forth, produce*, Æ. pp. forðātogen.
forðāurnen ptc. *elapsed*, BH 280[21].
forðbǣre *productive*, GEN 132.
forðbecuman[4] *to come forth*, BH,PPs.
forðberan[4] *to bring forth, produce, BH*; Æ. ['*forthbear*']
forðbesēon[5] *to look forth*, LPs 101[20].
forðbi, forðbie prep. *by, past*, CP 197[13].
forðbigferende *passing by*, NC 343.
forðblǣstan *to blow forth, burst out*, WW 393[33],WYN 24.
forðblāwan *to blow or belch forth*, WW 397[10].
forðboren *of noble birth*, LL.

forð-brengan, -bringan *to bring forth, produce, Bl,Lk* : *bring to pass, accomplish* : *bring forward* : *adduce, quote*, Æ. ['*forthbring*']
forðbylding f. *emboldening, encouragement*, CHR 999 E.
forðclypian *to call forth, Gal* (Lye). ['*forthclepe*']
forðcuman[4] *to come forth, proceed, arrive at, succeed* : *come to pass, come true* : *be born*.
forðcyme m. *coming forth, birth, Æ*. ['*forthcome*']
forðcȳðan *to announce, declare*, CVPs 118[26].
forðdǣd f. *advantage, Æ*.
forðdōn *to put forth, BH*. ['*forthdo*']
forðeahtung (a[2]) f. *exhortation*, A 13·447.
forðearle *very much, greatly, strictly, Æ*.
forðearlīce *absolutely, entirely*, RB 11[19].
forðeccan *to shield, protect*, APs 18[6].
forðelgian (KGL)=forðyld(g)ian
forðencan I. (æ) *to mistrust, despise, despair, Ps*. pp. forðōht *despaired of*; as sb. *poor wretch, Æ*. ['*forthink*'] II.=foreðencan
forðēofian (īo) *to steal*, MkL 10[19].
forðēon I. *to crush, oppress*, ROOD 54. II.=foreðēon
forðēostrian (īe) *to darken*, LPs 104[28].
forðerscan[3] *to beat down*, GD 57[4].
forðfæder m. *forefather, ancestor, Æ*. ['*forthfather*']
forðfæderen *paternal*, CHRD 96[6].
forðfaran[6] *to depart, die, Bo,Chr*; Æ. ['*forthfare*']
±**forðfēran** *to depart, die, Æ*.
forðfērednes f. *death*, BHcs 290[29].
forðfēring f. *death*, Sc 65[3].
forðflōwan *to flow*, BH 418[21].
forðfolgian *to follow*, CM 1052.
forðfōr I. f. *departure, death, BH*. ['*forthfore*'] II. pret. 3 sg. of forðfaran.
forðforlǣtenes f. *licence*, Bo 12[2].
forðframian *to grow to maturity*, WW 465[10].
forðfromung f. *departure*, CVPs 104[38].
forðfyligan *to follow, fall out, happen*, CM 1109.
forðgān anv., pret. 3 sg. -ēode *to go forth, advance, proceed, pass by, go away, go on, precede, succeed, Chr,Mk*. ['*forthgo*']
forðgang m. *going forth, progress, advance, success* : *privy, drain* : *purging, evacuation*, ÆL 16[207].
forðgangan[7] *to go forth, Ma*. ['*forthgang*']
forðgecīgan *to call forth*, REPs 67[7] : *exhort*, BH 54[15].
forðgeclipian (y) *to call forth, provoke*, Sc, EPs.

forðgefaran=forðfaran
forðgeféran=forðféran
forðgegyrdu *ornaments of a* forðgyrd, WW 195²⁹.
forðgelǽstan=forðlǽstan
forðgelang *dependent*, LL (280¹²).
forðgeléoran *to pass away, die*, BH.
forðgeléorednes f. *departure, death*, GD 282¹¹.
forðgelócian (BPs 101²⁰)=forðlócian
forðgenge *increasing, thriving, effective, successful*, Æ,CP.
forðgeong=forðgang
forðgeorn *eager to advance*, MA 281.
forðgéotan² *to pour forth*, BH. ['*forthyete*']
forðgerīmed *in unbroken succession*, B 59.
forðgesceaft† f. *creature, created being or thing, world : future destiny.*
forðgestrangian '*confortare*,' LPs 68⁵.
forðgesȳne *visible, conspicuous*, CRA 1.
forðgewītan¹ *to go forth, pass, proceed, go by : depart, die.* forðgewiten tīd, tīma *past tense*, ÆGR.
forðgewītenes f. *departure*, LPs 104³⁸.
forðgyrd m. *fore-girdle, martingale*, WW.
forðheald *bent forward, stooping : inclined, steep*, RB 5²⁰.
forðhealdan⁷ *to hold to, follow out, keep up, observe*, Æ.
forðheold I.=forðheald. II. pret. 3 sg. of forðhealdan.
forðherge m. *van (of an army)*, Ex 225.
forðhlīfian *to be prominent*, BH 322²⁴.
forðhnīgan¹ *to fall down, fall forward*, VH 13.
forðhréosan *to rush forth*, Sc 101¹³.
forðī=forðȳ
±forðlan *to put forth, contribute : further, advance : carry out, accomplish*, Chr. ['*forth*']
forðlg=forðȳ
forðlndan³ *to swell up*, LCD 127a.
forðlngian *to arrange for a man's wergild*, LL (Wilk.) 39³⁴.
forðlǽdan *to lead forth, bring forth*, Sat; Æ. ['*forthlead*']
forðlǽdnes f. *bringing forth*, BH 76¹⁵.
forðlǽstan *to persevere in, accomplish*, BH 352¹⁴.
forðlǽtan⁷ *to send forth, emit*, BL.
forðléoran *to proceed*, BH 312²⁷.
forðlic *forward, advanced*, CHR 1066 D: *thoroughly*, RWH 138¹⁶. adv. -līce.
forðlīfian=forðhlīfian
forðlócian *to look forth*, BL.
forðlūtan *to lean forward, fall down*, VPs: *be prone (to)*, CHRD 54³¹.

forðmǽre *very glorious*, CREAT 69.
forðman m. *man of rank*, NC 289.
forðmest *foremost*, MtL. ['*forthmost*']
forðolian *to go without, lack*, WA 38.
forðon I. *forthwith*, MH. ['*forthon*'] II.= forðæm
forðoncol=foreðancol; forðor=furðor
forðrǽcan (tr.) *to protrude*, ÆL 25¹³⁵.
forðrǽsan *to rush forth, rise up : jut out, protrude*, RPs 72⁷. [rǽsan]
forðrǽstan (ē) *to crush, afflict, oppress*, VPs: *suppress, stifle : destroy*, CPs 104¹⁶. ['*forthrast*']
forðrǽst(ed)nes (ē) f. *tribulation*, VPs.
forðres-=forðrys-
forðriccednes=forðryccednes
forðriht adj. *direct, plain*, WW. ['*forthright*' adj.]
forðrihte adv. *straightway, at once : unmistakeably, plainly : straight on*, ZDA 9·406. ['*forthright*' adv.] -rihtes *without a break*, RBL 48⁶.
forðringan *to rescue from, defend against*, B 1084 : *elbow out, displace*, RB 115⁷.
forðroccetan *to belch forth*, APs 18³.
forðryccan *to press, squeeze, crush, oppress, suppress.*
forðryccednes (i) f. *pressure, oppression*, G, Ps.
forðrycnes f. *extortion, oppression, tribulation*, LL; MFH 159 (fore-).
forðryne m. *onward course*, GEN 215.
for-ðrysman, -ðrysmian *to choke, suffocate, strangle : becloud*, WW 246⁶. [ðrosm]
forðscacan⁶ *to pass away*, RPs 143⁴.
forðscencan *to pour forth, give to drink*, WW 464⁹.
forðscype m. *progress*, BHc 92¹⁴.
forðsetennes f. '*propositio*,' MtR 12⁴.
forðsīð m. *going forth, decease*, Chr; Æ,CP. ['*forthsithe*']
forðsnoter (tt)† *very wise*, EL.
forðspell n. *declaration*, MOD 47.
forðspōwnes f. *prosperity*, BH 106²⁵.
forð-stæppan, -steppan⁶ *to issue forth, proceed, pass by*, ÆL,BF 184,198.
forðstæpping f. *advance*, DHy 80¹⁴.
forðstefn m. *prow*, LCD 3·180⁴.
forðswefian=forswefian
forðsyllan *to give out, pay out*, LL 175,3.
forðtēge (KGL)=forðtīge
forðtēon² *to draw forth, bring forth*, GEN 1¹².
forðtīge (e², y²) m. *vestibule*, OEG 3828.
forððegn m. *chief noble*, ÆL 6¹²⁵.
forððéon *to profit*, GD 200¹¹.
forðum=furðum
forðung f. *furtherance*, LCD 3·198' (v. ANS 125·49).

forðweard (e²) I. *inclined forwards or to-wards* : *advanced, progressing, growing, ready* : *enduring, everlasting, continual* : *future.* adv. *continually, PPs* : *prospec-tively, ÆGr* : *from now on* : *forwards, on-wards,* W 17⁸. ['*forthward*'] II. m. *look-out man, pilot,* GEN 1436.

forðweardes (e²) *forwards,* HL 16²⁰³.

forðweardnes f. *progress,* GD 117¹⁹.

forðweaxan *to break forth, burst forth,* GD. ['*forthwax*']

forðweg† m. *journey, departure.* in (on) forðwege *away.*

forðwerd=forðweard

forðwīf n. *matron,* WW 309⁴⁴.

forðwyrft *tortured, mutilated,* v. OEG 5028.

forðȳ I. conj. *for that, because, therefore, Jn.* ['*forthy*'] II. adv. *for that, therefore, con-sequently.*

for-ðyldian, -ðyld(i)gian, -ðyl(de)gian *to bear, support, endure, wait patiently,* Æ.

forðylm-an, -ian *to shut in, enclose, envelop, obscure, cover over, overwhelm* : *choke, suffocate, consume.*

forðyppan *to make manifest,* CVPs.

forðyrnan³ *to run before, precede* : *continue,* Æ.

forðyrrian *to dry up,* LCD 82b.

forðysmed *obscured,* WW 246⁶.

forðȳðe=forðȳ; forud=forod

for-ūtan, -ūton adv.; prep. w. d. *except, without,* Chr 1122. ['*forout*']

forwærnan=forwiernan

forwærnian (WW 442¹⁸)=forweornian

forwana m. *abundance?* CP 465¹⁶.

forwandian *to hesitate, be reluctant,* CP : *be ashamed* : *reverence.*

forwandung f. *shame,* VPs 68²⁸.

forwarð=forwearð pret. 3 sg. of forweor-ðan.

forweallan *to boil away,* LCD 95a.

forweard I. (NG) *beginning, front* : *heading, title, chapter.* II. adv. *continually, always,* GEN 788. [?=forðweard; or foreweard, JGPh 12·257]

forweardmercung f. *heading,* JnL p 3¹.

forweaxan⁷ *to progress, grow too much, be-come overgrown,* CP; AO. ['*forwax*']

forweddod *pledged,* WW 115⁴⁴. [wedd]

forwegan⁵ *to kill,* MA 228.

forwel adv. *very, very well,* Æ.

forwened '*insolens,*' GL. [wenian]

forwēned '*suspectus,*' BDS 30·12¹⁰⁶. [wē-nan]

forwenednes f. '*insolentia,*' ANS 79·89.

forweoren=forworen

forweornan=forwiernan

forweornian *to dry up, wither, fade, grow old, rot, decay,* Æ.

forweorpan *to throw, cast out, cast down, drive off, reject, throw away, squander,* B. ['*forwerpe*']

forweorpnes f. *migration,* MtL 1¹⁷.

forweorðan³ (y) *to perish, pass away, vanish, Mt;* AO,CP,Æ : *deteriorate, sicken.* f. on mōde *be grieved.* ['*forworth*']

forweorðenes=forwordenes

forweorðfullic *excellent,* Bo 65¹⁵.

forweosnian=forwisnian

forwercan=forwyrcan; forwerd=foreweard

forwered=forwerod

forweren (WW 217¹⁵)=forworen

forwerennes (RPs 70¹⁸)=forwerodnes

forwerod *worn out, very old,* Æ. [werian]

forwerodnes (e³) f. *old age,* SPs 70¹⁹.

forwest=forewost

forwiernan (e, eo, i, y) *to hinder, prohibit, prevent, repel, refuse, repudiate, deny, with-hold, oppose,* AO,B; CP. ['*forwarn*']

forwiernedlīce (e²) *continently,* W 284⁸.

forwiernednes (y²) f. *restraint, self-denial, continence,* BH 160¹⁰,MFH 118.

for-wird, -wirn-=for-wyrd, -wiern-

forwisnian (eo) *to dry up, decay, rot.*

forwitan=forewitan

forwitolnes f. *intelligence, diligence,* RBL 58¹⁰. [=fore-]

forwlencan *to fill with pride, puff up,* CP. ['*forwlench*']

forword I. n. *iota,* MtL 5¹⁸. II.=foreword

forwordenes f. *destruction, failure,* CHR 1105.

forwordenlic *perishable,* W 263¹³: *perishing,* ByH 130²⁹.

forworen (pp. of *forweosan) *decrepit, de-cayed,* OEG 2109.

forwost (e²) m. *chief, captain,* NG.

forwracned *banished,* RB 82².

forwrecan⁵ *to drive forth, carry away* : *expel, banish.*

forwrēgan *to accuse, calumniate, Chr.* ['*forwray*']

forwrēon¹ *to cover over,* LkR 23⁴⁵.

forwrītan¹ *to cut in two,* B 2705.

forwrīðan¹ *to bind up,* LCD 122a.

forwundian *to wound, Chr.* ['*forwound*']

forwundorlic *very wonderful,* GD. adv. -līce.

forwurðan=forweorðan

forwynsumian *to enjoy thoroughly,* VH 13.

forwyrcan I. (e) *to do wrong, sin,* Æ,CP. forworht mann *criminal,* CP : *ruin, undo, destroy, Cr* ; Æ,AO,CP : *condemn, convict, curse* : *forfeit.* ['*forwork*'] II. *to barricade, obstruct, close up.*

forwyrd fn. *destruction, ruin, fall, death,* Æ,CP. [forweorðan]

forwyrdan *to destroy,* GD 201¹⁵.

forwyrdendlic *perishable,* Sc 43¹¹ (wyrð-).

forwyrht f. *misdeed*, LL : *ruin*, MFH 160.

forwyrhta m. *agent, deputy* : *evil-doer, malefactor, ruined person.* [fore-]

forwyrn- (Æ)=forwiern-

forwyrpnes f. *casting out*, LPs 21⁷.

foryld=foreald; **foryldan**=forieldan

foryldu f. *extreme old age*, RB 114¹¹.

foryrman *to reduce to poverty, bring low*, BH,W. [earm]

foryrð=forierð

fōster=fōstor

fōstor m. *sustenance, maintenance, food, nourishment, Lcd*; Æ. ['*foster*']

fōstorbearn n. *foster-child*, GL.

fōstorbrōðor m. '*foster-brother*,' WW.

fōstorcild (e²) n. *foster-child*, ÆL.

fōstorfæder m. '*foster-father*,' *Cp,MH*.

fōstorland (e²) n. *land granted for the support of the recipients*, TC. [v. '*fosterland*']

fōstorlēan n. *payment for maintenance*, LL 442,2; MEN 152.

fōstorling m. *foster-child, nursling, pupil*, WW. ['*fosterling*']

fōstormann (ē) m. *bondsman, security*, LL 668,18.

fōstormōdor f. '*foster-mother*,' *MH*.

fōstornōð m. *pasture, sustenance*, EPs 22².

fōstorsweostor f. *foster-sister* (BT).

fōstrað (e²) m. *food* : *manna*, JnL 6⁴⁹.

-fōstre v. cild-f.

fōstrian (ē) *to* '*foster*,' *nourish, Sc*; MFB 205.

fōstring m. *foster-child, disciple*, NG.

fōstur=fōstor

fōt m. ds. fēt, fōte, nap. fēt, fōtas '*FOOT*' (*as limb and as measure*), *B,LL,NG*: Æ,AO,CP.

fōtādl fn. *gout in the feet* : '*morbus regius*,' OEG (v. BTs).

fōtādlig *having gout in the feet*, ÆH 2·26¹⁹.

fōtbred n. *foot-board, stirrup*, WW 107⁶.

fōtclāð m. *joining, patch*, MtL 9¹⁶.

±fōtcopsian, +fōtcypsan *to fetter*, Pss.

fōt-cosp, -cops m. *foot-fetter*, *VPs,WW*; Æ. [v. '*cops*']

fōtcoðu f. *gout in the feet*, OEG : '*morbus regius*' (v. fōtādl).

fōtece m. *gout in the feet*, LCD.

fōter=fōdder I.

fōtfeter f. *fetter of the feet*, WW 116⁸.

fōtgangende *going on foot*, OEG 5254.

fōtgemearc n. *space of a foot*, B 3043.

fōtgemet n. *foot-fetter*, EPs 104¹⁸.

fōtgewæde fn? *covering for the feet*, RB 88¹⁴.

+fōtian *to hasten up*, MkL 15⁴⁴.

fōt-lāst (Æ), -læst mf. *footprint, spoor* : *foot*.

fōtlīc *on foot*, ÆH 2·468²¹ : *pedestrian*, GPH 403.

fōtmæl n. *foot-measure, foot*, WE 55¹.

fōtmǣlum adv. *step by step, by degrees*, CM 883.

fōtrāp m. *the loose part of the sheet by which a sail is trimmed to the wind*, '*propes*,' WW 167¹¹.

fōtsceamol (e², e³, u³) m. *footstool*, Æ.

fōtsceanca m. *foreleg*, *Lcd* 1·362'. [v. '*shank*']

fōtsetl n. *footstool*, CHR 1053 C.

fōtsīd *reaching to the feet*, NC 289.

fōtspor n. *footprints, spoor*, LCD.

fōtspure n. *foot-rest, foot-support*, CHR 1070 E.

fōtstān m. *base, pedestal*, WW 191³⁵.

fōtstapol m. *footstep*, LPs 17³⁷.

fōtswæð n. (nap. -swaðu), fōtswaðu f. *footprint, footstep* : *foot*, Æ.

fōtswyle (i) m. *swelling of the foot*, LCD.

fōtðwēal n. *washing of the feet*, W,WW.

fōtwærc n. *pain in the foot, gout*, LCD 1·342¹⁰.

fōt-welm, -wylm, -wolma m. *instep*, Æ (v. IF 48·254).

fōð ind. pres. pl. of fōn.

fōð-or I. (-er, -ur) n. *load, cartload, Chr* : *food, fodder*. ['*fother*'] II. *covering, case, basket*, GL.

fōðorn m. *lancet?* LCD 19b (v. BTac).

fōwer=fēower

fox m. '*fox*,' *Lk,VPs*.

foxesclāte f. *burdock*, LCD 54a.

foxesclīfe f. *foxglove? greater burdock?* WW 135n1.

foxesfōt m. *fox-foot, xiphion*, LCD.

foxesglōfa m. *foxglove*, WW 296²⁵.

foxhol n. *fox-hole*, KC.

foxhyll m. *fox-hill*, SR 57'.

foxung f. *foxlike wile, craftiness*, ÆL 16¹⁶².

fra=fram; **fraced**, fraceð, fracod=fracoð

fracoð I. adj. *vile, bad, wicked, criminal, impious, filthy, abominable*, BH : *useless, worthless*. ['*fraked*'] II. n. *insult, contumely, disgrace* : *wickedness*.

fracoðdǣd (-od) f. *misdeed*, W 188¹⁵.

fracoðe adv. *shamefully*, PPs.

fracoðlic *base, ignominious, shameful, lewd*, Æ,CP. adv. -līce, CP.

fracoð(līc)nes f. *vileness, coarseness, obscenity*, Æ.

fracoðscipe (-od) *scandalous conduct*, RB 141⁵.

fracoðword n. *insulting word*, GD 152⁷.

fracud, fracuð=fracoð; **frǣ-**=frēa-

fræc=frec; frēc-=frēc- (v. ES 39·327 ff. as to these four forms).

fræcūð (GL)=fracoð

fræfel n? and adj. *cunning*, GL.

fræfelian *to be cunning*, GL.

fræfellīce (e¹) *shamelessly*, AO : *carefully* : *astutely*.

fræfelnes f. *sharpness, shrewdness*, OEG.

+**frǣge** (ē) I.† n. *hearsay, report, knowledge.* mine +f. *as I have heard say.* II. adj. *well-known, celebrated, reputable,* CP : *notorious, disreputable.* [fricgan]

frǣgn I. pret. 3 sg. of frignan. II. fregen II.

frǣgning f. *questioning,* GD 323²³.

frǣm-=frem-

frǣng=frægn

±**frǣpgian** (NG) *to accuse,* MtL : *reverence,* LG.

frǣt I.† *perverse, proud, obstinate : shameful.* II. pret. 3 sg. of fretan.

frǣtegung (Æ)=frætwung

frǣtenes f. *ornament,* WW 524⁵.

frǣtew-=frætw-

frǣtgenga (ē¹) m. *apostasy,* GL.

frǣtig *perverse, proud,* JUL 284.

frǣtlæppa m. *dew-lap,* WW 179³.

frǣton pres. pl. of fretan.

frǣtwa, frætwe fp. *treasures, ornaments, trappings, armour* : m. *adorner,* CR 556. [+tāwe]

frǣtwǣdnes=frætwednes

±**frǣtwan,** frǣt(te)wian *to ornament, adorn,* AO : *clothe, cover over,* CP 83¹⁰.

frǣtwednes (æ², o²) f. *adorning, decoration, ornament,* BH.

frǣtwian v. frætwan.

±**frǣtwung** f. *adorning, ornament,* Æ.

fragendlic=framigendlic

+**frāgian** *to learn by inquiry,* MtL 2¹⁶.

fram (o) I. prep. w.d. (instr.) (local) 'FROM,' *by,* Æ,*Chr* : (temporal) *from, since* : (agent) *by* : *as a result of* : (with verbs of saying and hearing) *of, about, concerning.* f. gān *to depart.* comps. v. fram-, from-. II. adv. *from, forth, out, away.* III. adj. (eo) *strenuous, active, bold, strong.* [*Ger.* fromm]

framācyrran=framcyrran (In this and the following words fram- may often be taken as a separate preposition).

framādōn anv. *to take from, do away, cut off, cut out,* LCD,LPs.

framādrȳfan¹ *to drive away, expel,* WW 98¹⁹.

framāhyldan *to turn from,* LCD 1·328¹⁰.

framānȳdan *to drive away,* LCD 1·226¹³.

framāscæcan⁶ *to shake off,* GD,Sc.

framāstyrian *to remove,* RPs 65²⁰.

framātēon² *to draw away from,* Ps.

framāteran⁴ '*diripere,*' ÆGR 168¹⁰.

framāwendan *to turn from or away,* Sc 169².

framāweorpan³ *to cast away,* ÆGR.

frambige m. *backsliding, apostasy, default,* KC,W.

frambringan³ *to take away,* LCD.

framcyme (o) m. *issue, posterity,* GEN 1765.

framcynn† (o) n. *issue, posterity : origin.*

framcyrran (e) *to turn from, avert : take from.*

framdōn anv. *to put off, stop, interrupt,* Sc 131⁸.

frameald *very old,* KC 3·60¹⁷.

fram-fær, -færeld mn. *departure,* Æ.

framfaru (o) f. *excess,* DR 178⁸.

framfundung f. *departure,* BH.

framgewītan¹ *to apostatize,* Sc 83².

framian *to avail, benefit,* RB.

framierning (o¹, e²) f. *outflowing,* DR 8¹.

framigendlic *effective, beneficial,* LCD.

framlād (o) f. *departure,* GEN 2098.

framlēce *turned from,* GPH 401.

framlic *strong, daring,* BH 30²⁸. adv. -līce *boldly, strongly, strenuously, quickly.*

framlōcian (o) *to look back,* CP 403⁶.

framnes (o) f. *vigour, excellence,* AA 10¹⁷.

framrinc (o) *chief, prince,* RHy 4¹.

framscipe (o) I. m. *exercise, action : progress, success,* BH 92¹⁴. II. m. *fraternity,* BH 160⁶.

framsīð (o) m. *departure,* GD.

framslitnes (o) f. *desolation,* NG.

framswengan *to swing away, shake off,* WW 524³⁰.

framung=fremung

framweard (o) *about to depart, departing, doomed to die,* Bo,*Seaf*; CP : *with his back turned,* LCD 126a. ['*fromward*']

framweardes (o) adv. *away from,* Lcd. ['*fromwards*']

framwesende *absent,* DR 178′.

frān pret. 3 sg. of frīnan.

franca m. *lance, javelin,* ÆL.

±**frāsian** *to ask, inquire, find out by inquiry* : *tempt, try.*

frāsung f. *questioning, temptation,* GU 160, Mt p 19.

fratwian=frætwian

frēa† I. m. gs. frēan *ruler, lord, king, master : the Lord, Christ, God* : *husband.* [*Goth.* frauja] II. (VPs)=frēo I.

frēa- intensitive prefix (=*L.* prae-).

frēabeorht *glorious,* BL.

frēabeorhtian (ǣ) *to proclaim,* CPs 41⁹.

frēabodian *to proclaim, declare,* LPs 118¹⁷².

frēabregd? *mighty device,* MLR 22·3.

frēadrēman *to exult,* LPs.

frēadrihten† m. *lord and master.*

frēafætt (ǣ¹) *very fat,* WW 532²⁴.

frēaglēaw *very wise,* DAN 88.

frēahrǣd (ǣ¹, -hrǣð) *very quick,* GL.

frēamǣre (ǣ¹) *very celebrated,* PA,WW.

frēamicel (ǣ¹) *preeminent,* WW 530¹³.

frēamiht *great strength,* RPs 42².

freamsum=fremsum

frēan=frēon

frēaofestlice (ǣ¹) *very quickly,* WW 530¹³.

frēareccere m. *prince,* LRPs 118¹⁶¹.

frēas pret. 3 sg. of frēosan.

frēasian=frāsian

frēatorht *very bright, radiant,* GL.
frēaðancian *to exult,* RPs 52⁷.
frēawine† m. *lord and friend,* B.
frēawlitig *very beautiful,* NC 290.
frēawrāsn f. *splendid chain,* B 1451.
frēbran=frēfran
frec (æ, i) *greedy,* MtL; Æ : *eager, bold, daring,* Met : *dangerous* (v. ES 39·327 ff.). ['*freck'*]
freca† m. *warrior, hero.*
frēced-=frēcen-; **frēcelnes**=frēcennes
frēcelsod *exposed to danger,* WW 465²⁵.
frēcendlic, frēcenlic (CP) *dangerous, mischievous, perilous, terrible.* adv. -līce, AO.
frēcennes f. *harm, danger,* CP.
frecful (æ) *greedy,* OEG 2445.
frecian *to be greedy,* WW (BTs).
freclīce *greedily,* GD 31¹.
frecmāse f. *titmouse,* WW.
frēcn-=frēcen-
frēcne (ǣ) I. *dangerous, perilous,* CP : *terrible : savage, wicked : daring, bold.* [v. ES 39·328 f.] II. n. *peril.* III. adv. *dangerously : fiercely, severely : boldly, audaciously.*
frecnes f. *greediness,* GL.
±**frecnian** *to make bold,* DA 184 : *endanger, imperil,* ÆL 30·436.
frecwāsend m. *gluttony,* A 6·100.
+**frēdan** *to feel, perceive,* Æ,Bo; CP. ['*frede'*; frōd]
+**frēdendlic** *perceptible,* ÆGr 4⁶.
+**frēdmǣlum** *little by little,* OEG 3245.
+**frēdnes** f. *feeling, perception,* Bo.
+**frēdra** *more acute,* CP 123¹⁹.
frefellīce=fræfellīce
frēfer (CHRD), frēfernes (LkL) f. *consolation.*
frefllīce=fræfellice
±**frēfran** *to cheer, console,* BH; CP. ['*frover'*]
frēfrend (ie²) mf. *comforter, consoler : the Comforter* (*Holy Ghost*), BL.
frēfrian (Jn; Æ)=frēfran
frēfriend=frēfrend
frēfrung f. *consolation,* GEN 37³⁵, LPs 93¹⁹.
+**frēge**=+fræge
fregen, fregn I.=frægn pret. 3 sg. of frignan. II. n. *question,* AN 255.
fregensyllic *very strange,* WNL 223a²⁴.
fregnan=frignan
fregnðearle *inquiringly,* ÆL 23⁵⁶⁶.
fregnung f. *questioning,* MkL p 4¹⁹.
freht=friht
frem=fram adj.
fremde *foreign, alien, strange,* JnL,LL; AO,CP : *unfriendly, Sol* (-ede) : *estranged from, devoid of, remote from.* ['*fremd'*]
±**fremdian** *to estrange,* RB : *curse, anathematize, excommunicate.*

freme I.† *vigorous, flourishing,* B,Gen. ['*frim'*; fram] II.=fremu
fremede=fremde
fremedlǣcan *to alienate,* RPs 57⁴.
fremedlīce *perfectly,* Sc 129³.
±**fremednes** f. *fulfilment, effect,* Æ.
fremful *useful, profitable, beneficial,* Lcd : *well-disposed,* WE 67³. ['*fremeful'*] adv. -līce *efficaciously.*
fremfullic=fremful
fremfulnes f. *utility, profit,* RB 83¹⁶.
±**fremian** *to avail, benefit, do good,* Æ,Mt. ['*freme'*]
fremigendlic *profitable,* LcD,OEG.
fremlic (eo, o) *profitable,* BH 30²⁸.
fremman *to further, advance, support,* An, B : *frame, make, do, accomplish, perfect, perpetrate, commit, afford,* B,Gen; CP. ['*freme'*]
±**fremming** f. *purpose, effect, performance, progress,* Æ.
fremnes=fremednes
fremsum *beneficent, benign, kind, gracious,* Æ,CP. adv. -sume.
fremsumlic *benignant, kind,* GD 280. adv. -līce, CP.
fremsumnes f. *benefit, benignity, kindness, liberality.*
fremð- (NG)=fremd-
+**fremðian** (MkL 14⁷¹)=fremdian
fremðlic=frymðlic
fremu f. *advantage, gain, benefit,* Bo,Ep, Lcd; CP. ['*freme'*]
fremung (eo, o) f. *advantage, profit, good,* LL.
frence f. *a coarse cloak,* WW 212²⁶.
Frencisc '*French,*' Chr.
frēnd=frēond
frendian (WW 484³¹)=fremdian
freng=frægn pret. 3 sg. of frignan.
frēo I. nap. often frīge '*free,*' Bo,Ex,G; Æ, CP : (†) *glad, joyful :* (†) *noble, illustrious,* Gen. [frēo- v. also frīg-, frīð-] II.† f. *woman, lady.* III. m.=frēa. IV. imperat. of frēogan. V. f? *freedom, immunity* (Swt).
frēobearn† n. *child of gentle birth,* WW.
frēoborh=frið̄borh
frēobrōðor m. *own brother,* Ex 338.
frēoburh f. *city,* B 694.
frēod I.† f. *peace, friendship : good-will, affection.* II. pp. of frēogan. III.=frēot
frēode pret. 3 sg. of frēogan.
frēodohtor f. *freeborn daughter,* W 193⁶.
frēodōm m. '*freedom,*' *state of free-will, charter, emancipation, deliverance,* Bf,Bo; AO,CP.
frēodryhten†=frēadrihten
frēodscipe (ES 39·340)=frēondscipe?

±**frēogan** to 'free' ('y-free'), liberate, manumit, Æ,Chr; AO : love, embrace, caress, think of lovingly, honour.

+**frēoge**=+frǣge; **frēoh**=frēo

+**frēogend** (ī) m. liberator, CPs.

frēolāc n. free-will offering, oblation, LPs 50²¹.

frēolǣta m. freedman, WW.

±**frēolic** free, freeborn : glorious, stately, magnificent, noble, B,Rd : beautiful, charming. ['freely'] adv. -līce 'freely,' readily, Bo,VPs : as a festival, ÆP196¹².

frēols I. mn. freedom, immunity, privilege : feast-day, festival. [origl. frīheals] II. adj. free, festive.

frēolsǣfen m. eve of a feast, LL383,56.

frēolsbōc f. charter of freedom, Ct.

frēolsbryce (i) m. breach of festival, LL,W.

frēolsdæg m. feast-day, festival-day, Æ.

frēolsdōm=frēodōm

frēols-end, -iend m. liberator, EPs.

frēolsgefa m. emancipator, LL13,8.

frēolsgēr (=ēa²) n. year of jubilee, WW420³¹.

±**frēolsian** (ī, ȳ) to deliver, liberate, BL, EPs : to keep a feast or holy day, celebrate, Æ. ['frels']

frēolslic festive, festival, CM350. adv. freely : solemnly.

frēolsmann m. freedman, KC3·295⁶.

frēolsniht f. eve of a festival, NC290.

frēolsstōw f. festival-place, LL338,38.

frēolstīd f. festival, feast-day, Æ.

frēolsung f. celebration of a feast, LL.

freom=fram III.; **freom**-=fram-, frem-

frēomǣg† m. free kinsman, GEN.

frēomann m. 'free-man,' freeborn man, Gen, LL.

frēonama m. surname, BH.

frēond m. ds. frīend, nap. frīend, frēond, frēondas 'friend,' relative, B,Chr,El,Gen; AO,CP : lover.

frēondheald amiable, LCD3·192¹⁵.

frēondhealdlic related, akin, WW217²⁹.

frēondlār f. friendly counsel, B2377.

frēondlaðu f. friendly invitation, B1192.

frēondlēas 'friendless,' JnL : orphan. f. mann outlaw, LL.

frēondlēast f. want of friends, LL336,35.

frēondlic 'friendly,' well-disposed, kindly, BH; W. adv. -līce, CP.

frēondlīðe kind to one's friends, ES39·340.

frēondlufu f. friendship, love, GEN1834.

frēondmyne f. amorous intention, GEN1831.

frēondrǣden f. friendship, Bo; Æ : conjugal love. ['friendrede']

frēondscipe m. 'friendship,' B,Lcd; AO, CP : conjugal love.

frēondspēd f. abundance of friends, GEN 2330.

frēondspēdig rich in friends, LL(286¹³).

frēone asm. of frēo adj.

frēonoma=frēonama

frēorig† freezing, frozen, cold, chilly : blanched with fear, sad, mournful. [frēosan]

frēorig-ferð, -mōd† sad, GU.

frēoriht n. rights of freemen, LL,W.

±**frēosan²** to 'freeze,' Æ,Bl,Gn.

frēosceat m. freehold property, RB138²¹.

frēot m. freedom, LL. frēotes ðolian to be reduced to slavery.

frēotgifa m. liberator, WW.

frēot-gifu, -gift f. emancipation, WW.

frēotmann m. freedman, BK,TC,W.

freoð-=frið-; -**frēoðan** v. ā-f.

freoðo-, freoðu-=friðo-, friðu-

frēowīf (ī¹) n. free-woman, LL7,73.

frēowine=frēawine; **Fresan**=Frisan

Fresilc (y) in the Frisian manner, Frisian, CHR. [Frisan]

±**fretan⁵** to devour, eat, consume, Æ,B, Chr,LG; CP : break, Ex147. ['fret,' 'y-fret']

fretgenga=frætgenga

frettan to feed upon, consume, CHR,PPs. [fretan]

frettol greedy, gluttonous, WW171³⁴.

fretw-=frætw-

freðo=friðo

frī=frēo I.; **frīa**=frēa

frīand (A)=frēond

frīborh (v. LL2·81)=friðborh

fric (NG)=frec

fricca, friccea m. herald, crier, CP (? v. ES 39·336).

fricgan⁵† to ask, inquire into, investigate : (+) learn, find out by inquiry.

frician to dance, Mt. ['frike']

frician† w. g. to seek, desire.

friclo f. appetite, LCD73a.

frico f. 'usura,' MtL25²⁷ (v. ES39·328f.).

fricolo (OP21)=friclo

frictrung (OET26)=frihtrung

frīdhengest v. frīðhengest.

frīenan=frīnan, frignan

frīend v. frēond.

+**frīend** (ȳ) pl. friends, AO,Lk. ['i-freond']

frīg=frēo; **Frīgdæg**=Frīgedæg

frīge I.† fp. love. II. v. frēo.

frīgea m. lord, master, LL (=frēa).

Frīgeǣfen m. Thursday evening, Æ.

Frīgedæg m. 'Friday,' LL,Ma; Æ.

frigenes=frignes

Frīgeniht f. Thursday night, LL,W305²⁴.

frigest, frigeð pres. 2, 3 sg. of frican.

±**frignan³**, frīnan² ask, inquire, B,BH,Cp, Ps; AO,CP : †learn by inquiry. ['frayne']

±**frignes** f. interrogation, question, BH.

frīgnes f. *freedom*, CHR 796.

frignung f. *question*, GD 137²⁹.

frigst, frihst pres. 2 sg. of fricgan.

friht (e, y) n. *divination*, DR,LL.

frihtere m. *diviner, soothsayer*, NAR 37².

frihtrian *to divine*, KL.

frihtrung f. *soothsaying, divination*, WW.

frimdig=frymdig; frīnan=frignan

frīnd=frīend; frīo=frēo

frīs (ȳ) *crisped, curled*, GnE 96.

Frisan (e) mp. *Frisians*, AO.

frisca=frysca

fristmearc (GL)=firstmearc

frit, friteð, fritt pres. 3 sg. of fretan.

frið (y) mn. *peace, tranquillity, security, refuge, AO,Chr,MtL*; CP, Æ. f. niman *to make peace* : *privilege of special protection, and penalty for the breach of it*, LL 10,5 : *restoration of rights (to an outlaw)*, LL 316,13. ['*frith*']

frīð *stately, beautiful*, RD 10⁹.

friða (eo) m. *protector*, PPs 70³.

friðāð m. *oath of peace*, CHR 1012 E.

friðbēna m. *suppliant, refugee*, LL.

friðborh m. *surety for peace*, LL.

friðbræc f. *breach of the peace*, LL.

friðburg f. *town with which there is peace, city of refuge*, LL 222,2¹.

friðcandel f. *the sun*, GEN 2539.

friðeleas=friðlēas

friðgeard m. *enclosed space, asylum, sanctuary*, LL : *court of peace (heaven)*, CR.

friðgedāl n. *death*, GEN 1142. [ferhð?]

friðgegilda m. *member of a peace-guild*, LL 173 Pro.

friðgeorn *peaceable*, MtL 5⁹.

friðgewrit m. *peace agreement*, LL 144.

friðgild n. *peace-guild*, LL 181. [v. '*frith*']

friðgīsl m. *peace-hostage*, LL 378,9¹.

friðhengest (frīd-) m. *stately horse?* (*ON.* frīðr), *or horse of peace?* (frið-h.), RD 23⁴.

friðherpað m. *king's highway*, KC 5·214′.

friðhūs n. *sanctuary*, WW 186²³.

friðian (eo) *to give '* frið' *to, make peace with, be at peace with* : (±) *cherish, protect, guard, defend, keep, AO,Chr*; CP : *observe*. ['*frith*']

friðiend m. *helper, defender*, PPs,W 239⁷.

friðland n. *friendly territory*, CHR.

friðlēas *peaceless, outlawed*, LL 318.

friðlic *mild, lenient*, LL.

friðmāl n. *article of peace*, LL 220 Pro.

friðmann m. *man under special peace-protection*, LL 222.

friðo=friðu

friðobēacen (eo¹) n. *sign of peace*, GEN 1045.

friðoscealc (eo¹)† m. *angel*, GEN.

friðosibb f. *peace-bringer*, B 2017.

friðospēd (eo¹)† f. *abundant peace*.

friðotācn n. *sign of peace*, GEN 2369.

friðoðēawas (eo¹) mp. *peaceful state*, GEN 79.

friðowær (eo¹)† f. *treaty of peace*.

friðowang (eo¹) m. *peaceful plain*, B 2959.

friðowaru (eo¹)† f. *protection*.

friðo-webba (eo¹) m., -webbet f. *peacemaker*.

friðscip n. *ship for defence*, LL 441 (? read fyrdscip).

friðsōcn f. *sanctuary, asylum*, LL.

friðsplott m. *peace-spot, asylum*, LL (248⁵).

friðstōl m. *sanctuary, asylum,refuge, LL,Ps*. ['*frithstool*']

friðstōw f. *refuge, sanctuary*, CP.

friðsum *pacific, peaceful* : (+) *safe, fortified*.

friðsumian *to make peaceful, reconcile*, NC 290.

friðu (eo) fm. *peace, safety, protection, AO, Chr,MtL* : *refuge, asylum*. [v. '*frith*']

friðu-=friðo-; frocga=frogga

frōd† *wise : old*. [*ON.* frōðr]

frōdian *to be wise*, RIM 32.

frōfer=frōfor; frōferian=frēfran

±frōfor fmn. (e², u²) gs. frōfre *consolation, joy, refuge, Æ*; CP : *compensation, help, benefit*. ['*frover*']

frōforbōc (e²) f. *book of consolation*, Bo 50⁶.

frōforgāst (frōfre-) m. *consoling spirit, Holy Ghost, Comforter, BH,Jn*; Æ. [v. '*frover*']

frōforlic (e²) *kind, helpful*, W. adv. -līce, W 295³.

frōfornes f. *consolation*, LkL 6²⁴ (oe).

frōforword n. *word of consolation*, GD 344²⁸.

frōfrian=frēfran

frogga m. '*frog*,' Æ,WW.

froht (NG)=forht

from=fram; from- also=frem-, frum-

froren pp. of frēosan.

frosc m. *frog*, Æ (frox); GL. ['*frosh*']

frost=forst

frōwe f. *woman*, DD 291. [*Ger.* frau]

frox (Æ)=frosc

frugnen pp., frugnon pret. pl. of frignan.

frum I. *primal, original, first*. II.=fram

fruma m. *beginning, origin, cause, B,Mt; AO,CP* : *creation*, CHR 33 : *originator, inventor, founder, creator* : *first-born*, CPs 135¹⁰ : (†) *prince, king, chief, ruler*. on fruman *at first*. wæstma fruman *first-fruits*. ['*frume*']

frumācennes f. *nativity*, JnLp 5¹⁹.

frumbearn† n. *first-born child*.

frumbyrd f. *birth*, TC 369⁹.

frumbyrdling n. *youth*, WW 171²³. ['*frumberdling*']

frumcenned *first-begotten, first-born, Æ,AO* : *original, primitive*, ÆGr.

frumcennende *primitive*, OEG 1775.

frumcnēow n. *primal generation*, Ex 371.

frumcyn† n. *ancestry, origin, descent, lineage* : *race, tribe.*

frumcynnend=frumcenned

frumcyrr m. *first time*, LL 164,25².

frumdysig n. *first offence, beginning of sin*, CHRD 18¹⁶.

frum-gār†, -gāra† m. *leader, patriarch, chieftain, noble.* [cp. *L.* primi-pilus]

frumgesceap n. *creation of the world*, CR 840.

frumgeweorc n. *original construction*, A 11·174⁶.

frumgewrit n. *deed, document*, W 252¹².

frumgifu f. *prerogative, privilege*, GL.

frumgripa m. *firstling*, W 113⁶.

frumgyld n. *first instalment*, LL 190.

frumhēowung (=ī²) f. *original formation*, WW 467²⁷.

frumhrægl n. *first garment* (sc. *of fig-leaves*), GEN 943.

frumildo f. *early age*, WW 341²². [ieldo]

frumlēoht n. *dawn*, AF 4·56.

frumlic *original, primitive*, GL. adv. -līce, GL.

frumlīda m. *chief sailor.* v. OEG 32.

frumlȳhtan *to dawn*, BL 207³⁵.

frummeoluc f. *'nectar' (new milk?* BTs), WW 456¹⁸.

frummynetslæge m. *first coinage*, ÆL 23⁴⁷⁹.

frumrǣd m. *primary ordinance*, LL 246.

frumrǣden f. *space of time*, AN 147.

frumrinc=framrinc

frumrīpa m. *first-fruits*, LL 40,38.

frumsceaft m. *first creation, origin, primeval condition, B,BH* : *creature* : *home.* [*'frumschaft'*]

frumsceapen *first created, first*, Æ.

frumsceatt m. *first-fruits*, ELPs.

frumscepend m. *creator*, DR 16¹⁰.

frumscyld f. *original sin*, SOL 445.

frumsetnes f. *authority*, DR 123⁸.

frumsetnung f. *foundation, creation*, JNR 17²⁴.

frumslǣp m. *first sleep*, Æ,AO.

frumspellung f. *first relation, original story*, OEG 1153; 2³¹.

frumsprǣc f. *opening words*, ÆL 23¹²⁰ : †*promise.*

frumstaðol m. *first state*, RD 61³.

frumstemn m. *prow*, WW 288²¹.

frumstōl m. *first or principal seat, paternal home*, LL.

frumtalu f. *first statement in an action?* (Lieb), *of a witness?* (BT), LL 385 and 3·226.

frumtīd f. *beginning*, GD 212⁵.

frumtyhtle f. *first accusation, first charge*, LL 336,35. [tēon II.]

frumð=frymð

frumwæstm mf. *first-fruits*, Æ.

frumweorc n. *primeval work, creation*, AN 805.

frumwīfung f. *first marriage*, W 304²⁷.

frumwylm (e²) m. *new-born zeal*, RB 135⁵ : *first inflammation*, LCD 30b.

frumwyrhta m. *creator*, DR 37⁴.

frunen pp., frun(n)on pret. pl. of frīnan.

frungon=frugnon pret. pl. of frignan.

fruron pret. pl. of frēosan.

frȳ=frēo; **fryccea**=fricca

fryht=friht

fryht- (N)=forht-, fyrht-

frylsian (Bo)=freolsian

frym-=frum-, fyrm-

frymdig (i) *curious, inquisitive*, Æ : *desirous.* f. bēon *to entreat.*

frymetling f. *young cow*, LL 451,13.

frymð I. mf. *origin, beginning, foundation*, *Bo*; Æ,AO : *creature*, (in pl.) *created things*, *El.* [*'frumth'*] II.=fyrmð

frymð-lic, -elic *primeval, primitive, first* : *chief.* adv. -līce, OEG 5211.

frymðu, frymðo (*MtL*)=frymð

frymðylde *of early age?* v. OEG 2381.

frȳnd (Æ) nap. of frēond.

+**frȳnd**=+frīend

frȳs=frīs

Frysan=Frisan

frysca I. (i) m. *kite, bittern*, GL. II. *'pusio'?* GL (v. A 19·495).

frȳsð pres. 3 sg. of frēosan.

fryt pres. 3 sg. of fretan.

fryð=frið; **fryð-** also=fyrð-

fugel m. gs. fugles *'fowl,' bird*, B,*Mt*; CP.

fugelbona m. *fowler*, CRA 80.

fugelcynn n. *bird-tribe*, Æ. [*'fowlkin'*]

fugeldæg (u²) m. *day on which poultry might be eaten*, TC 460²⁰.

fugeldoppe f? *water-fowl*, WW 131²⁰.

fugelere (AO)=fuglere

fugeleswȳse f. *larkspur*, WW 298²⁴.

fugelhwata m. *augur*, WW 140⁵.

fugellīm m. *bird-lime*, OEG 3105.

fugelnett n. *bird-net*, WW 277¹⁵.

fugelnoð, fugeloð *bird-catching, fowling*, Æ.

fugeltimber n. *young bird*, PH 236.

fugeltrēo n. *prop (of a snare for birds)*, WW 349¹⁹.

fugelweohlere m. *augur*, WW 108¹². [wiglere]

fugelwylle (o²) *swarming with birds*, BH 30¹⁰ [weallan]

fuglere m. *'fowler,' AO.*

fuglesbēan f. *vetch*, GL.

fuglian *to catch birds*, ÆGR. [*'fowl'*]

fuglung f. *bird-catching*, WW 268,352.

fugol-, fugul-=fugel-; **fuhl-**=fugl-

fūht *damp, moist*, LCD,CHRD 64³⁶. [*Ger.* feucht]

fūhtian *to be moist*, NC 290.

fuhton pret. pl. of feohtan.

ful I. n. *beaker, cup*, Æ. II.=full

fūl I. '*foul*,' *unclean, impure, vile, corrupt, rotten*, Æ,*Bl,Cp,Cr,Gl*; CP : *guilty*, LL. f. bēam *black alder*, LCD 29b. II. n. *filth, foulness, impurity, crime, offence*, *El,OET*. ['*foul*']

fulbeorht *very bright, resplendent*, CP 87²³.

fulbrecan⁴ *to violate*, LL 280,2².

fulaon anv. *to complete, perform*, RB 70²¹ : *arrange*, ÆL 33¹⁴²⁵.

fūle adv. *foully*, Æ.

fulēode pret. 3 sg. of fullgān.

fūletrēo n. *black alder*, Cp 430 A.

fulfæstnian *to ratify fully*, CHR 675 E.

fulfaran⁶ *to travel*, LL 383,56.

fulfealdan⁷ '*explicare*,' ÆGR 138⁹.

fulgeare *quite well*, ÆL 3⁴⁵⁶. [gearwe]

fulgōd *very good*, ÆL 6¹²⁴.

fulgon pret. pl. of fēolan.

fulhār *entirely grey, very hoary*, WW 380¹³.

fulhealden *contented*, WW 211³⁰.

fulht-=fulwiht-

fūlian *to be or become* '*foul*,' *decay, rot*, AO, *Ps,Sc*.

full I. adj. (w. g.) 'FULL,' *filled, complete, perfect, entire, utter*, Æ,AO,CP : *swelling, plump*, LCD. be fullan *fully, perfectly, completely*. II. adv. *very, fully, entirely, completely, thoroughly, Bo,Chr,Met,Ps*. f. nēah *almost, very nearly*. ['*full*' adv.] III.=ful

full- v. also ful-.

fulla I. m. *fulness*, ÆL 13¹⁰⁴. II. m. *assembly?* Ct (Swt).

fullǣst (ā, ē; fylst) m. *help, support*, *Ex, Met*. ['*filst*']

±fullǣstan (ē) w. d. *to help, support*, AO, Lk. ['*filst*']

fullæðele *very noble*, Bo 24⁷.

+fullan=+fyllan

fullberstan³ *to burst completely*, W 267¹⁸.

fullbētan *to make full amends*, ÆGR,RB.

fullblīðe *very glad*, JUD 16²³.

fullboren *fully born*, CP 367¹⁸ : *of noble birth*.

fullbryce m. *complete breach of the peace*, LL : *violation of the rights of a clerical offender*, LL.

fullclǣne *very pure*, AS 30².

fullcuman⁴ *to attain*, RWH 136¹.

fullcūð *well-known, notorious, famous*, HL 201²¹¹.

-fulle v. sin-f.

fullendian *to complete*, BH. ['*fullend*']

fullere m. '*fuller*,' *bleacher, Mk*.

fullest=fullǣst

fullflēon² *to take to flight, escape completely*, ÆGR 179¹⁶.

fullforðian *to fulfil*, NC 291, RWH 138²⁵.

fullfrem-ed, -edlic *perfect*, CP. adv. -līce *fully, perfectly, completely*, *Bl*. ['*fullfremed(ly)*']

fullfremednes f. *perfection, BH*; CP. ['*fullfremedness*']

±full-fremman, -fremian *to fulfil, perfect, practise, complete*, *Bo*; CP. ['*fullfreme*']

fullfylgan *to follow, obey*, W 95¹⁹ : *pursue*, EPs 7⁶.

fullfyllan *to* '*fulfil*,' *ÆGr* 153¹.

full-gān pret. 3 sg. -ēode anv., -gangan⁷ *to accomplish, fulfil, perform, carry out*, Æ : *follow, imitate, obey* : *help*, AO.

fullgearwian *to finish, complete*, GD 126² : *prepare fully*, CP.

fullgedrifen (w. g.) *full (of wild beasts)*, SOL 150²³.

fullgeorne *very eagerly*, CP 255²².

fullgewēpned *fully armed*, CHR 1083.

fullgrōwan⁷ *to grow to perfection*, CP 67²³.

fullhāl *thoroughly well*, GD 248¹.

fullhealden *contented*, WW 211³⁰.

±fullian I. *to complete, fill up, perfect*. II. (*Jn*)=fulwian

fullic *full* : *universal, catholic*, CHy 15. adv. -līce *entirely*, '*fully*,' *perfectly, completely*, *Bf,BH*; Æ.

fūllic *foul, unclean, objectionable, shameful, base*, LCD,W. adv. -līce.

fulligan=fulwian

fullmægen n. *great power*, W 186¹⁴.

fullmannod *fully peopled*, Bo 40¹⁷.

full-medeme *excellent, perfect*, GD. adv. -medomlīce, GD 320²¹, 331¹³.

fullnes f. *fulness*, DR 11¹³.

fūllnes=fūlnes

fulloc *final or definite agreement?* LL 385.

fulloft adv. *very often*, CP.

fullraðe adv. *very quickly*, AO.

fullricene *very quickly, immediately*, PPs 140².

fullrīpod *mature*, RB 139⁹.

fullslēan *to kill outright*, ÆP 138⁴.

fullsumnes f. *abundance*, EPs 48⁷.

fullðungen (ful-) *full-grown*, RB 133¹.

fullðungennes f. *full development*, MFH 160.

fulluht=fulwiht

fullunga adv. *fully*, N

fullwearm *fully warm*, CP 447⁵.

fullweaxan *to grow to maturity*, CP 383³⁰, BYH 6¹¹.

fullwelig *very rich,* Bo 24⁷.

fullwēpnod *fully armed*, CHR 1070 E.

fullwer m. *complete* '*wer*,' *full atonement*, RD 24¹⁴?

fullwērig *very tired*, MFH 160.

fullwyrcan *to complete, fulfil*, ÆL.

fulnēah I. adj. *very near.* II. adv. *very nearly, almost,* CP.

fūlnes f. *foulness, filthy smell,* BH,GL.

fūlon rare pret. pl. of fēolan.

fūlstincende *foul-stinking,* GD,LCD.

fultēam (Erf.)=fultum

fultem- (CP), fultom-=fultum-

fultrūwian *to confide in,* Bo 60²³.

fultum (ēa) m. *help, support, protection, B, Gl*; Æ,AO,CP:*forces,army,* AO. ['*fultum*'] +**fultuma** m. *helper,* SPs 18¹⁶.

±**fultum-an,** -ian *to help, support, assist,* Æ,CP : (†) *be propitious to, overlook.*

±**fultum(i)end** m. *helper, fellow-worker,* Æ, CP.

fultumlēas *without help,* AO 56²¹.

fulwa m. *fuller,* MH 26²⁶.

fulwere m. *baptizer, baptist,* MH 14,102.

±**fulwian** *to baptize, BH,Jn,MH*; AO,CP. ['*full*']

fulwiht, fulluht (*Mt*) mfn. *baptism, Christianity, Mt*; AO,CP. ['*fullought*']

±**fulwiht-an,** -ian *to baptize,* CHR,NG.

fulwihtbæð n. *baptismal bath, font,* Æ (fulluht-).

fulwihtbēna m. *applicant for baptism,* WW 207¹⁶.

fulwihtele m. *baptismal oil,* LL (258¹⁵).

fulwihtere m. *baptizer : the Baptist,* Æ,G.

fulwihtfæder m. *baptismal father, godfather, baptizer,* BL 205¹⁷.

fulwihthād m. *baptismal order or vow,* BL 109²⁶.

fulwihtnama m. *baptismal name, Christian name.*

+**fulwihtnian** (fulhtn-) *to baptize,* NC 291.

fulwihtstōw f. *baptistry,* BL 140²⁰.

fulwihttīd f. *time of baptism,* MEN 11.

fulwihtðēaw m. *rite of baptism,* MET 1³³.

fulwihtðēnung (-uht) f. *baptismal service,* W 38⁹.

fulwihtwæter n. *laver of baptism,* NC 291.

fulwihtwere m. *baptist,* BL 161⁶.

fulwuht=fulwiht

funde wk. pret. 3 sg., funden pp. of findan. **-fundelnes,** -fundennes v. on-f.

fundian I. (w. of, tō) *to tend to, wish for, strive after, go, set out, go forward, hasten,* Æ,B,Cr,Gen,Gu; CP : *spread?* LCD 125b. ['*found*'] II.=fandian

fundon pret. pl. of findan.

fundung f. *departure, Chr* 1106; ByH 12²⁰. ['*founding*']

funta? funte? *spring? brook?* KC (v. ES 54·102) or ?=finta (IF 48·255).

fūra v. furh.

furh f. gs. fūre, ds. fyrh, furh, gp. fūra '*furrow,*' *trench, BC,Bo*; Æ.

furhwudu m. *pine,* Cp 420 P.

±**fūrian** *to furrow,* OEG.

furlang n. *length of furrow,* '*furlong,*' *BH, Lk* : *land the breadth of a furrow,* KC.

furðan, furðon=furðum

furðor adv. (of place and time) '*further,*' *more distant, forwards, later,* Æ,Bf,Chr; CP : *more : superior,* CP 117². f. dōn *to promote,* CP.

furðorlucor (e²) cp. adv. *more perfectly,* MFB 133 and n 30.

furðra cp. adj. '*further,*' *greater, superior, Jn.*

furðum (-an, -on) adv. *even, exactly, quite, already, just as, at first, Bl,Mt*; AO,CP : *further, previously.* sȳððan f. *just as soon as.* ['*forthen*']

furðumlic *luxurious, indulging,* AO 50³⁰.

furður=furðor; **furuh**=furh

fūs *striving forward, eager for, ready for, inclined to, willing, prompt, B*; Æ : *expectant, brave, noble : ready to depart, dying.* ['*fous*']

fūslēoð† n. *death-song, dirge.*

fūslic *ready to start : excellent.* adv. -līce *readily, gladly.*

fūsnes f. *quickness,* EHy 6²⁵.

fustra (OEG 1428). ?=fȳrstān (BTs).

fȳf-=fīf-; **fyhfang**=feohfang

fyht-=feoht-

fȳhtan (ī) *to moisten,* OEG. [fūht]

fyl=fiell, fyll

±**fȳlan** *to befoul, defile, pollute,* Æ.

+**fylce** n. *band of men, army, host,* CP. [folc]

±**fylcian** *to marshal troops,* CHR 1066 C,D. [folc]

fyld m. *fold, crease,* OEG.

fyld(e)stōl m. *folding-stool, ZDA* 31·10. ['*faldstool*']

fylen=fellen?

±**fylgan** w. d. or a. *to '*follow,*' pursue, LG*; Æ,CP : *persecute : follow out, observe, obey* : *obtain : attend to : practise, Bl.*

fylgend m. *follower, observer,* BH 472⁷.

fylgestre f. *female follower,* OEG 1228.

fylgian=fylgan

fylging f. I. *following,* DR. II. (æ) *fallowland.* [fealh]

fylian, fyligan=fylgan

fyligendlic *that can or ought to be imitated,* CM 803.

fylignes f. *following, practice,* BH 160²³.

fyll=(1) fyllu; (2) fiell

±**fyllan** I. *to '*fill,*' fill up, replenish, satisfy, An,Gen*; Æ : *complete, fulfil, Az.* ['*full*'] II.± (æ, e;=ie) wv. *to cause to fall, strike down,* '*fell*' ('*y-fell*'), *cut down, AO,Bl,Ps, Rd* : *throw down, defeat, destroy, kill, BH, Cr,Ps* : *tumble : cause to stumble, MtR.* +**fylled** (wdg.) *bereft.*

fyllað n. *filling, filling up,* GEN 1513.

+**fyllednes** (i) f. *fulness, completion, fulfilment,* Æ.

fyllen (=i) f. *a dropping,* LCD 18a.

-**fyllen** (fylen) v. mönað-f.

fyllend=fylgend

+**fyllendlic** *filling, expletive,* ÆGR 261[5] : *capable of completion,* WW 209³⁸.

fyllesēoc (=ie) *epileptic,* LCD,WW 112²⁷.

fyllesēocnes f. *epilepsy,* LCD 1·164⁹.

fylleðflöd m. *high tide,* GL.

fyllewærc (e¹;=ie) n. *epilepsy,* LCD 65a.

±**fylling** f. *filling,* GD : *completion,* LRSPs.

+**fyllingtid** f. *compline,* WW 207⁴⁴n.

±**fyllnes** f. *fulness, plenitude, satiety* : *supplement* : *completion, fulfilment.*

fyllo, fyllu f. *fulness (of food), 'fill,' feast, satiety,* AO,B; CP : *impregnation.*

fylmen=filmen

fylnes I. (±) f. *fall, stumbling-block, offence, ruin,* NG. **II.**=fyllnes

fȳlnes=fūlnes

fylst I. m. *help, aid, Mt;* Æ,AO. **II.** pres. 2 sg. of feallan. **III.** pres. 2 sg. of fyllan.

+**fylsta** m. *helper,* Æ.

±**fylstan** (w. d.) *to aid, support, help, protect,* Æ,AO. [=fullæstan]

±**fylstend** m. *helper,* Æ,BRPs.

fylt pres. 3 sg. of fealdan.

fylð I. pres. 3 sg. of fyllan. **II.** pres. 3 sg. of feallan.

fȳlð I. f. *'filth,' uncleanness, impurity, Mt,Sc, W.* [fūl]

fylwērig *faint to death,* B 963. [fiell]

fyn-=fin-; **fȳnd**=fēond; +**fȳnd**=+fiend

fyndele m. *invention, devising, Sc.* ['findal']

fyne m? n? *moisture, mould,* WW 183¹⁹.

fynegian *to become mouldy,* LL. ['finew']

fynig (i) *mouldy, musty, Jos.* ['fenny']

fyniht *fenny, marshy,* LCD 92a.

fyr v. feorr.

fȳr (ī) n. *'fire,' Ex,G,VPs;* Æ,AO,CP : *a fire, Gen.*

fȳran I.=fēran. **II.** (±) *to cut a furrow,* OEG 2492n : *castrate,* LCD 3·184¹⁹.

fȳras=fīras

fȳrbǣre *fire-bearing, fiery,* OEG.

fȳrbæð† n. *fire-bath, hell-fire,* CR.

fȳrbend m. *bar forged in the fire,* B 722.

fȳrbēta m. *fireman, stoker,* WW.

fȳrbryne m. *conflagration,* AO 252²⁰.

fyrclian (ȳ?) *to flash, flicker,* CHR 1106.

fȳrclomm m. *band forged in the fire,* SAT 39.

fȳrcrūce f. *crucible, kettle,* GL.

fȳrcynn n. *fire,* AO 252²⁰ c.

fyrd=fierd

fyrdcræft (i) m. *warring host,* NUM 22⁴.

fyrdend *enrolled for military service,* ÆL 25³⁶³.

fyrdesne m. *warrior,* BH 148⁸.

fyrdfæreld n. fyrdfaru f. *going to war, military service,* LL. [v. 'ferd']

fyrdför f. *military service,* KC.

fyrdgeatewe fp. *war-gear,* RUN 27.

fyrdgemaca m. *fellow-soldier,* Æ.

fyrdgestealla† m. *comrade in arms.*

fyrdgetrum† n. *band of warriors,* EX.

fyrdhama (o²) m. *corslet,* B 1504.

fyrdhrægl n. *corslet,* B 1527.

fyrdhwæt† *warlike, brave.*

fyrdian (ie) *to go on an expedition,* CHR.

fyrding (e) f. *soldiering : army, expedition, militia,* LL ; Æ : *camp : fine for evading military service,* LL : *march, progression,* BF 46²⁸. ['ferding']

fyrdlāf f. *remnant of an army,* ÆL 25³⁷⁷.

fyrdlēas (ie) *without an army,* CHR 894A.

fyrdlēoð† n. *war-song,* B.

fyrdlic *martial,* Æ.

fyrdmann m. *warrior,* Bo 40¹⁸.

fyrdnoð (e) m. *liability to military service,* BC 3·71⁷.

fȳrdraca m. *fire-spewing dragon,* B 2689. ['firedrake']

fyrdrian *to serve in the army,* ÆL 28¹¹.

fyrdrinc† (e) m. *warrior, soldier.*

fyrdsceorp n. *armour,* RD 15¹³.

fyrdscip n. *battle-ship,* LL.

fyrdsearu† n. *accoutrements,* B.

fyrdsōcn f. *military service,* Ct.

fyrdstemn m. *body of soldiers who serve for a fixed term, army-corps,* CHR 921.

fyrdstrǣt f. *military road,* KC.

fyrdtīber n. *military sacrifice?* (Swt) WW 418²²; A 15·187.

fyrdtruma m. *martial band, army,* ÆH 1·442'.

fyrdung=fyrding

fyrdwǣn (i) m. *military carriage?* EC 250'.

fyrdweard f. *military watch,* LL 444,1.

fyrdwerod n. *host, army,* WW 399³⁰.

fyrdwīc n. *camp,* Æ.

fyrdwīsa m. *chieftain,* CRA 77.

fyrdwīse f. *military style,* AA 14⁵.

fyrdwīte n. *fine for evading military service,* LL.

fyrdwyrðe *distinguished in war,* B 1316.

-**fȳrede** v. twi-, ðri-f.

fyren=firen

fȳren *of fire, fiery, Bl,MH;* AO,CP : *on fire, burning, flaming.* ['firen']

fȳrenful *fiery,* LPs,W.

fyrengāt (WW 423¹¹)=firgengāt

fȳrentācen n. *fiery sign,* MFH 131¹².

fȳrentācnian *to pollute with sin.* RHy 6²¹.

fȳrenðecele f. *firebrand,* BH 476¹⁵.

fyres=fyrs

fyrest=fyrst, fyrmest superl. adj.

fyrewyt=fyrwit

fȳrfeaxen *fiery-haired*, WW 425,519.

fȳrfōda (ī) m. *fuel, twigs for burning*, OEG 7⁸⁸.

fȳrgearwung f. *cooking*, WW 401⁹.

fȳrgebeorh *fire-screen*, LL 455,17.

fȳrgebræc n. *crackling of fire*, GEN 2560.

fyrgen=firgen

fȳrgnāst m. *spark of fire*, AN 1548. [*ON.* gneisti]

fyrh I. f. *fir*, KC 6·102'. II. v. furh.

fȳrhāt *hot as fire, burning, ardent*, El. ['*firehot*']

fȳrheard *hardened by fire*, B 305.

±**fyrht** I. *afraid, timid.* [forht] II.=friht

±**fyrht-an**, -ian (fryht-, N) *to fear, tremble, DR : frighten, terrify, BH.* ['*fright*,' vb.]

fyrhtnes f. *fear*, AO,MtL.

±**fyrhto**, fyrhtu (fryht-, N) f. '*fright*,' *fear, dread, trembling*, Ps,VHy; Æ,AO,CP : *horrible sight*, NR 26⁶,⁹. [forht]

fyrhŏ=ferhŏ

±**fyr(h)ŏ**, fyrhŏe nf. *wooded country*, Ct. ['*frith*']

fȳrhūs n. '*caminatum*,' *house or room with a fireplace in it?* WW; CHRD 45⁶. ['*fire-house*']

fȳrhwēolod v. fēowerhwēolod.

fyrian (B 378)=ferian

fȳrian I. *to supply with firing*, LL. ['*fire*' vb.] II. (±) *to cut a furrow.* [furh]

fyrlen I. (eo, e) *far off, distant, remote*, Æ. II. n. *distance*, Æ.

fȳrlēoht n. *gleam of fire*, B 1516. ['*firelight*']

fȳrlēoma m. *gleam of fire*, SAT 128.

fȳrlīce=fǣrlīce

fȳrlocа m. *fiery prison*, SAT 58.

fyrm I. (=ie) *cleansing*, LL 454⁸. II.=feorm

fyrm-=frym-

fyrmǣl m. *mark burnt in by fire*, AN 1136.

fyrmest (o) superl. of forma I. '*foremost*,' *first*, LCD; Æ,CP : *most prominent, chief, best*, El,Mt. II. adv. *first of all, in the first place, at first, most, especially, very well, best*.

fyrmŏ (=ie) f. I. *harbouring, entertainment*, LL. II. *cleansing, washing*.

fyrn I. (i) adj. *former, ancient*, Rd. II. adv. (±) *formerly, of old, long ago, once, Gu*; ÆL. ['*fern*']

fyrn-=firen-

±**fyrndagas** mp. *days of yore, An*; ÆL. [v. '*fern*'] frōd fyrndagum *old, aged*.

fyrngēar n. *former year(s), Gn,Ps : preceding year*, LCD 3·228. ['*fernyear*']

fyrn-geflit† n. nap. -geflitu *former quarrel, old strife*.

fyrngeflita m. *old-standing enemy*, PA 34.

fyrngemynd n. *ancient history*, EL 327.

fyrngesceap n. *ancient decree*, PH 360.

fyrngesetu np. *former seat, habitation*, PH 263.

fyrngestrēon n. *ancient treasure*, SOL 32.

fyrngeweorc† n. *former, ancient work*, PH.

fyrngewinn n. *primeval struggle*, B 1689.

fyrngewrit† n. *old writings, scripture*, EL.

fyrngewyrht n. *former work, fate*, GU 944.

fyrngidd n. *ancient prophecy*, EL 542.

fyrnmann m. *man of old times*, B 2761.

+**fyrnnes** f. *antiquity*, CHRD 25,26.

fyrnsǣgen f. *old saying, ancient tradition*, AN 1491.

fyrnsceaŏa m. *old fiend, devil*, AN 1348.

fyrnstrēamas mp. *ocean*, WH 7.

fyrnsynn (JUL 347)=firensynn

fyrnweorc† n. *work of old, creation*.

fyrnwita (eo²)† m. *sage, counsellor*.

fȳr-panne, -ponne f. '*fire-pan*,' *brazier*, WW.

fyrr v. feorr.

fȳrrace (fērrece) f. *fire-rake*, WW 273⁶.

fyrran=feorran

fyrs I. m. '*furze*,' *gorse, bramble, Bo,WW.* II. n.=fers

fȳrscofl f. '*fire-shovel*,' WW 358¹⁶.

fyrsgāra m. *furzy corner*, KC 4·8'.

fyrsian=feorsian

fyrsīg (=īeg) f. *furzy island*, KC 5·300¹⁷.

fyrslēah m. *furzy lea*, KC 5·232'.

fyrsmeortende v. smeortan; **fyrsn**=fiersn

fȳrspearca m. *fire-spark*, WW 100².

fyrspenn m. *a pen of furze*, EC 266'.

fyrst I. '*first*,' *Chr,Ex : foremost, principal, chief*, LL. II. adv. *in the first place, firstly, at first, originally*, Ct. III. (Æ)=first I. and II.

+**fyrst** n. *frost*, LL 454,11.

fyrst-=first-

fȳrstān m. '*firestone*,' *stone used for striking fire, flint*, WW.

fyrstig '*frosty*,' BH 216²⁷. [v. forstig]

fȳrsweart *black with smoke*, CR 984.

fȳrtang f. '(*fire-*)*tongs*,' LL 453,15. [v. '*fire*']

fȳrtorr m. *beacon, lighthouse*, WW.

fyrŏ=fyrhŏ; **fȳrŏ-**=fēorŏ-

fȳrŏolle f. *furnace*, EPs 20⁹ : *stage on which martyrs were burned*, OEG.

±**fyrŏran** (GL,AO), fyrŏian (Bo; Æ) *to 'further,' urge on, advance, promote, benefit*, BC.

fyrŏriend m. *promoter*, BC.

+**fyrŏring** f. *removal*, CHRD 79¹⁵.

fyrŏringnes f., fyrŏrung (Lcd; W) f. *furtherance, promotion.* ['*furthering*']

fyrwit (e²) I. n. *curiosity, yearning*, Æ. II. adj. *curious, inquisitive*.

fyrwitful (æ¹, e²) *curious, anxious*, LkL 12²⁶.

fyrwitgeorn *curious, anxious, inquisitive*.

fyrwitgeornes (e², e³, y³) f. *curiosity*, BL 69²² : *fornication?* MFH 146¹¹.

fyrwitgeornlïce (e²) *studiously*, GD 174²⁸.
fyrwitnes f. *curiosity*, Æ.
fȳrwylm m. *wave of fire*, B 2672.
±fȳsan *to send forth, impel, stimulate* : *drive away, put to flight, banish* : (usu. reflex.) *hasten, prepare oneself, An,Gen.* ['*fuse*']
fȳsian (ē) *to drive away, LL,W.* ['*feeze*']
fȳst (ē) f. '*fist*,' *Æ,Gl*; CP.
fȳstgebēat n. *blow with the fist*, CP 315.
+fȳstlian *to strike with the fist*, Sc 7¹⁴.
fȳstslægen *struck with the fist*, WW 396³³.
fyðer-=fiðer-, fēower-
fyðera, fyðeras, fyð(e)ru, nap. of fiðere.
fyðerling=fēorðling
fyx=fisc
fyxe f. *she-fox, vixen*, KC 2·29'.
fyxen (i) adj. *of a fox*, Lcd.
fyxenhȳd (i) f. *she-fox's skin*, Lcd 1·342¹¹.

G

gā imperat. and pres. 1 sg. ind. of gān.
gab- (GL)=gaf-
gabote (u²) f. *side-dish*, EGL. [*L.* gabata]
gād I.† n. *lack, want, need, desire.* [*Goth.* gaidw] II. f. '*goad,' point, arrow-head, spear-head, Cp,Sol.*
±gada m. *comrade, companion*, ÆL. [*Ger.* gatte]
+gadere *together*, ÆL 30³⁸⁵.
+gaderednes f. *gathering, abscess*, Lcd.
gaderian (Æ)=gadrian
±gaderscipe (æ) m. *matrimony*, OEG.
gadertang (æ, ea) *continuous, united*, KC.
gadertangnes (æ) f. *continuation*, Sc 52¹.
±gaderung (æ) f. *gathering together* : '*gathering,' Bf,Lcd* : *union, connection*, BH : *assembly, Jn* : *text*, Mtp 8¹⁷.
±gaderwist (o²) f. *companionship*, WW 174⁴⁵.
+gaderwyrhtan np. *assembled workmen*, ÆL 6·186.
gadinca m. *wether sheep*, WW.
gād-īren (LL 455,15), -īsen n. *goad.*
gador=geador; gador-=gader-, gadr-
±gadrian (æ) *to* 'GATHER,' *unite* : *agree*, (refl.) *assemble, Chr* : *collect, store up*, Æ, CP : *pluck (flowers, etc.)* : *compile* : *associate (with)* : *concentrate (thoughts)*, Bo. [geador]
gadrigendlic *collective*, ÆGR 229⁴.
gǣ=geā; gǣc=gēac
gæd n. *society, fellowship*, SOL 449.
gǣd=gād I.
gǣdeling† m. *kinsman, fellow, companion in arms, comrade, B,Da.* ['*gadling*']
gæder-, gædr-=gader-, gadr-

gæf=geaf pret. 3 sg. of giefan.
gæfe=giefu
gǣfel (MtL)=gafol
gǣfon=gēafon pret. pl. of giefan.
-gǣgan v. for-, ofer-g.
gægl-=gagol-
gǣl-=geal-
gǣlan *to hinder, impede, keep in suspense*, CP : (intr.) *linger, delay* : *dupe*, KGL. [gāl]
gæleð pres. 3 sg. of galan.
gǣling f. *delay*, CP 39¹.
gǣlnes=gālnes
gǣlsa (ē) m., gæls (OEG 611) f. *pride, wantonness, luxury*, Æ,W : (*worldly*) *care*, MtL 13²² : *a greedy person*, Lcd. [gāl]
gǣlslic '*luxuriosus*,' NC 291.
gælð pres. 3 sg. of galan.
-gǣlwan v. ā-g.
gæmnian=gamenian; gǣn-=gēan-
-gǣnan v. tō-g.; +gǣnge=+genge
gǣp=gēap; gær-=gear-, grǣ-
gǣr=gēar
gǣred *wedge-shaped*, BC 3·251'. [gār]
-gǣrede v. twi-, ðri-g.
gærs (græs) n. '*grass,*' *blade (of grass), herb, young corn, hay, plant, An,Cp,CP,G;* Æ : *pasture, Ct.* v. also græs, grǣs-
gærsama=gærsuma
gærsbedd n. (*grass-bed*), *grave*, PPs 102¹⁵.
gærscið m. *blade of grass*, AO 38¹¹.
gærsgrēne *grass-green*, WW 199²⁴.
gærs-hoppa m., -hoppe (e¹) f. '*grasshopper,*' *locust, MtR* (græs-), *Ps,VPs.*
gærsstapa=gærstapa
gærsswȳn n. *pasturage-swine*, LL 445,2.
gærstapa m. *grasshopper, locust*, Æ,AO.
gærstūn m. *grass-enclosure, meadow*, LL. ['*garston*']
gærstūndīc m. *meadow-dike*, Ct.
gærsum mn., gærsuma f. *jewel, costly gift, treasure, riches, Chr.* ['*gersum*']
gærswyrt f. '*herba,' grass*, APs 36².
gærsyrð f. *pasturage in return for ploughing-labour*, LL 447,4,1c. ['*grassearth*']
gǣsne (ē, ēa) w. g. or on. *deprived of, wanting, destitute, barren, sterile, An,Cr,Jul* : *dead.* ['*geason*']
gǣst=giest
gǣst I. m.=gāst. II. pres. 2 sg. of gān.
gǣstan *to frighten, Jul* 17. ['*gast*']
gǣsð=gāst
gǣt=geat; gǣt nap. of gāt.
gǣtan=gēatan
gǣten *of or belonging to a goat*, Lcd,WW 152¹.
gǣð pres. 3 sg. of gān.
gaf=geaf pret. 3 sg. of giefan.
gafel=gafol

gafeluc m. *spear, javelin, OEG,WW*; ÆL. ['*gavelock*']

gaffetung f. *scoffing, mocking,* Æ.

gafol (æ, ea¹; e, u²) **I.** n. gs. gafles *tribute, tax, duty, due, debt, AO,Gl,MtL* : *interest, usury, profit, rent, Gl,Mt*; Æ (v. A36·60, 377 and LF168). ['*gavel*'] **II.** f. *fork, Æ, LL,WW*; OET463 (v. A36·60). ['*yelve*']

gafolbere m. *barley paid as rent,* TC145².

gafolfisc m. *fish paid as rent,* TC307′.

gafolfrēo (e²) *tax-free,* KC4·191,215.

gafolgerēfa (æ¹, e²) m. *taxgatherer,* MtR.

gafolgielda (i³, y³) m. *tributary, tenant, debtor, AO.*

gafolgyld n. '*fiscus*,' *revenue?* GPH395.

gafolgyldere m. *tributary, debtor,* Æ.

gafolheord f. *taxable swarm (of bees),* LL 448,5.

gafolhwītel m. *tribute-blanket, a legal tender instead of coin for the rent of a hide of land,* LL108,44¹.

±**gafolian** (e²) *to rent (land), Ct* : *confiscate, seize as tribute,* WW. ['*gavel*']

gafolland n. *leased land, land let for rent or services,* LL126,2.

gafollic *fiscal,* OEG6²⁰.

gafolmǣd f. *meadow which was mown as part of the rent,* TC145³.

gafolmanung (ea¹, o³) f. *place of tribute or custom,* MkR2¹⁴.

gafolpenig m. *tribute-penny,* LL446.

gafolrǣden f. *tribute, rent,* LL.

gafolrand (e²) m. *compasses,* WW.

gafolswān m. *swine-herd who paid rent in kind for permission to depasture his stock,* LL448,6.

gafoltīning f. *fencing-wood given as part of the rent,* TC145⁸.

gafolwydu (y³=u) m. *firewood supplied as part of the rent,* TC145⁶.

gafolyrð f. *ploughing, etc. done by a gebūr as part of his rent,* LL447; 3·249.

±**gafsprǣc** f. *foolish speech, scurrility,* ÆL.

gaful=gafol

gagātes, gagātstān (WW148⁵) m. *agate, jet, BH.* ['*gagate*']

gagel m? '*gale,*' *bog-myrtle,* Lcd; Mdf.

gagelcroppan mpl. *tufts of gale,* Lcd 33a.

gagelle, gagolle f.=gagel

gagol=(1) gāl; (2) gagel

gagolbǣrnes (gægl-) f. *wantonness,* CP,WW.

gagolisc (æ, e, ea) *light, wanton,* BH400¹³, MHc156¹⁸.

gāl I. n. *lust, luxury, wantonness, folly, levity.* **II.** adj. *gay, light, wanton, Bo,BH* : *proud, wicked.* ['*gole*']

±**galan⁶** *to sing, call, cry, scream, B,Met* : *sing charms, practise incantation.* ['*gale*']

galder-=galdor-

galdor (ea) n. *sound, song,incantation, spell, enchantment,* Æ.

galdorcræft m. *occult art, incantation, magic,* Bl,LL.

galdorcræftiga m. *wizard,* LL38,30,VH14.

galdorcwide m. *incantation,* RD49⁷.

galdorgalend (e²) m. *enchanter,* WW448²².

galdorgalere m. *wizard,* WW346¹⁵.

galdorlēoð n. *incantation,* WW509¹⁷.

galdorsang m. *incantation,* W253¹⁰.

galdorword n. *magic word,* RIM24.

galdre m. *wizard, magician,* Æ.

galdricge f. *enchantress,* GL.

galdru nap. of galdor.

galere m. *wizard, snake-charmer,* WW.

gālferhð *wanton, licentious,* JUD62.

gālfrēols m. *revel,* '*lupercalia*,' OEG.

gālful *wanton, lustful, luxurious.* adv. -līce.

galg-=gealg-

gālian *to be wanton,* Sc87¹⁰.

Galilēisc *Galilean,* G.

galla (VPs; DR)=gealla

gallac=galloc

Galleas, Gallias mp. *Gauls, Franks, French.*

galled=gealled

gāllic *wanton, lustful, BH,Bo*; Æ. ['*golelich*'] adv. -līce, CHRD108¹⁸.

Gallie=Galleas

Gallisc *Gaulish, French,* AO.

galloc (u²) m. *comfrey, gall-apple,* GL, LCD.

gālmōd *wanton, licentious,* JUD256.

gālnes f. *frivolity, wantonness, lust, Sc*; Æ. ['*goleness*']

gālscipe m. *excess, luxury, lasciviousness, wantonness,* Æ : *pride.* ['*goleship*']

gālsere m. *licentious person,* W72⁶.

gālsmǣre *frivolous, facetious, jocose,* RB 30⁸. [v. '*smere*']

galung f. *incantation,* OEG4940. [galan]

Galwalas mp. *Gauls, Frenchmen* : *France,* CHR.

gambe=gombe

gamel=gamol; **gamelic**=gamenlic

gamen (o) n. *sport, joy, mirth, pastime,* '*game,*' *amusement, B,Met*; Æ,CP.

gamenian *to pun, play, joke,Æ,Sc.* ['*game*']

gamenlic *belonging to games, theatrical, Gl* : *ridiculous.* adv. -līce *artfully,* Æ. ['*gamely*']

gamenung f. *jesting, pastime,* BAS,LPs.

gamenwāð (o¹) f. *merry journey,* B854.

gamenwudu (o¹)† m. *harp,* B.

gamnian=gamenian

gamol† *old, aged, hoary, ancient.* [ge-, mǣl]

gamolfeax† *grey-haired.*

gamolferhð *old, aged,* GEN2867.

gamolian (o¹, e²) *to grow old,* GNE11.

gān pret. 3 sg. of gīnan.

±**gān** pret. 3 sg. ēode, anv. *to* 'GO*' ('*i-go*'),
*come, move, proceed, advance, traverse,
walk,* Æ; CP : *depart, go away* : *happen,
turn out, take place* : (+) *get, gain,
conquer, occupy, overrun,* AO : (+) *observe,
practise, exercise, effect.*
gandra m. '*gander,*' *ÆGr*; Ct.
ganet=ganot
gang I. (eo, o, iong) m. *going, journey,
progress, track, footprint,* B,Lcd,LG,RB;
Æ : *flow, stream, way, passage, course,
path, bed,* AO,Bl,LG : *drain, privy,* Æ :
(in pl.) *steps, platform, stage,* GPH 394 :
legal process, LL 396,2. ['*gang,*' '*gong,*'
'*yong*'] **II.** imperat. and pret. sg. of gangan.
+**gang** n. *hap, occurrence,* WW 394⁹ :
passage (lapse) of time, GD 179¹⁰.
±**gangan**⁷ (B,Bl) pret. geng (eo, a)=gān
gangdæg m. *one of the three processional
days before Ascension day, Rogation day,
Chr.* ['*gangdays*']
gangehere=ganghere
gangelwǽfre=gangewifre
gangende *alive,* W : *going on foot,* Æ,AO.
gangern n. *privy,* WW 184¹⁵. [ærn]
gangewifre (eo¹, o¹; æ²; æ³) f. (*a weaver as
he goes*), *spider,* Lcd,Ps.
ganggeteld n. *portable tent,* WW 187³.
ganghere m. *army of foot-soldiers,* AO 154²⁴.
gang-pytt (*Scr* 21⁷) m., -setl n., -stōl m.,
-tūn m. (Æ) *privy.* [v. '*gong*']
gangweg m. *thoroughfare,* WW. ['*gangway*']
Gangwuce f. *Rogation week, the week of Holy
Thursday, Mk.* ['*gangweek*']
gānian *to yawn, gape, open,* Gl,Ps. ['*gane*']
ganot m. '*gannet,*' *sea-bird, water-fowl,* B,
Chr. ganotes bæð *the sea.*
ganra=gandra
gānung f. *yawning,* WW 162³⁷ : *gaping (in
scorn),* WW 476⁹. ['*ganing*']
-**gapian** v. ofer-g.
gār† I. m. '*spear,*' *dart, javelin,* B,PPs.
['*gare*'] II. *tempest? piercing cold? sharp
þain?* Gen 316. III.=gāra (Mdf).
gāra m. *corner, point of land, cape, promontory,* AO. [gār; '*gore*']
gārǽcer m. *a pointed strip of land,* KC 5·153'.
gārbēam m. *spear-shaft,* Ex 246.
gārberend† m. *warrior.*
gārcēne *bold in fight,* B 1958.
gārclife f. *agrimony,* Lcd.
gārcwealm m. *death by the spear,* B 2043.
gare=gearo; **gāre**=gār
gārfaru† f. *warlike expedition.*
gārgetrum *armed company,* CR 673.
gārgewinn† n. *fight with spears, battle.*
gārhēap m. *band of warriors,* Ex 321.
gārholt n. *shafted spear,* B 1835.

gārlēac n. '*garlic,*' Lcd; Æ.
gārmitting f. *battle,* †Chr 937.
gārnīð m. *conflict, war,* GnE 128.
gārrǽs m. *battle,* Ma 32.
gārsecg m. *ocean, sea,* AO.
gārtorn m. *fighting rage,* Sol 145.
gār-ðracu f. ds. -ðræce *battle,* El 1186.
gārðrīst *bold, daring,* El 204.
garuwe=gearwe
gār-wiga, -wīgend m. *spearman, warrior,* B.
gārwudu m. *spear-shaft, lance,* Ex 325.
gāsrīc m. *savage animal,* OET 127.
gast=giest
gāst (ǽ) m. *breath,* Ps,VPs : *soul, spirit, life,
Gen,Ex,Mt;* CP : *good or bad spirit, angel,
demon,* BH,Mt; Æ : *Holy Ghost,* A,Jn,
VPs : *man, human being, Gu.* ['*ghost*']
gāstan *to meditate?* AS 2²⁰ (or ? geāscian).
gāstberend (æ)† m. *living soul, man.*
gāstbona m. *soul-slayer, the Devil,* B 177.
gāstbrūcende *practising in the spirit,* Æ.
gāstcofa m. *breast,* Leas 13.
gāstcund (ǽ) *spiritual,* Gu 743.
gāstcwalu (ǽ) f. *torment, pains of hell,* Gu
651.
gāstcyning m. *soul's king, God,* Gen 2883.
gāstedom (ǽ) *spirituality,* MFH 112⁸.
gāstgedāl† n. *death.*
gāstgehygd† n. *thought.*
gāstgemynd (ǽ) n. *thought,* Gu 574.
gāstgenīðla (ǽ) m. *devil,* Jul 245.
gāstgerȳne† n. *spiritual mystery* : *thought,
consideration.*
gāstgewinn (ǽ) n. *pains of hell,* Gu 561.
gāstgifu f. *special gift of the Holy Spirit* (e.g.
gift of tongues), WW 200⁸.
gāsthālig† *holy in spirit, holy.*
gāstlēas *lifeless, dead,* El. ['*ghostless*']
gāstlic *spiritual, holy,* Æ,Bf; CP : *clerical
(not lay),* BH; Æ,CP : *ghastly, spectral,
Nic.* adv. -līce *spiritually,* Æ. ['*ghostly*']
gāstlufu (ǽ)† f. *spiritual love,* Az.
gāstsunu† m. *spiritual son.* Godes g.
Christ.
gat=geat
gāt f. gs. gǽte, gāte, nap. gǽt, gēt *she-'goat,*
Cr,Ep,Lcd,Rd.
gātahierde=gāthyrde
gātahūs n. *goat-house,* WW 185⁸.
gātbucca m. *he-goat,* WW. ['*goat-buck*']
gātehǽr n. *goat's hair,* ÆT 79⁸²,⁸⁷.
gātetrēow n. *cornel tree?* Lcd 32b.
gāthyrde (io) m. '*goat-herd,*' LL,WW.
gatu v. geat.
gāð pres. pl. of gān.
ge conj. *and, also,* Cr,Lcd. ge...ge *both..
and,* B,Chr : *not only...but also; whether..
or.* ǽg(hwæ)ðer ge...ge *both...and; eithe
...or.* ['*ye*']

ge- prefix (indicated by the sign + in this Dict.), original meaning *together*; but it has usually lost all collective or intensive force.

gē I. (īe) pron. 2 pers. pl., dp. ēow, ap. ēow(ic) '*ye*,*' you, B,G,Mt. **II.**=gēa

gēa adv. '*yea,*' *yes, Æ,B,BH,G,WW*.

geabul=gafol

gēac m. *cuckoo, Cp, Gu.* [v. '*gowk,*' '*yeke*']

gēacessūre f. *wood-sorrel,* GL.

geador† *unitedly, together.*

geadrung=gaderung

geaduling=gædeling

geaf pret. 3 sg. of giefan.

geaf-=gif-; **geafl**=gafol

geaflas† *jaws,* WW.

geafol=gafol

gēafon pret. pl. of giefan.

geafu=giefu

gēagl I. mn. *jaws, throat, gullet,* LCD. **II.**=gāl

geaglisc=gagolisc

gēaglswile m. *swelling of the jaws,* LCD.

geagn-=gegn-; **gēahl**=gēagl

gēahð=gēað

geal pret. 3 sg. of giellan.

gealādl f. *gall-disease, jaundice,* LCD 40b.

gēalāgē (gēa lā gēa, AS) *yea, amen,* RHy.

geald pret. 3 sg. of gieldan.

geald-=gald-

gealg (-lh) *sad, Æ,WW*.

gealga I. (a) m. '*gallows,*' *cross, B,Jul,WW*; CP. **II.** m. *melancholy,* WW 445,499.

gealgian=geealgian

gealgmōd† *sad, gloomy, angry.*

gealgtrēow (a) n. '*gallows-tree,*' *gallows, cross, B,DR.*

gealh=gealg; **gēalhswile**=gēaglswile

gealla (a, e) m. **I.** '*gall,*' *bile, Mt,VPs,WW*; Æ,CP. **II.** *a galled place on the skin, Lcd.* ['*gall*'] (I. and II. possibly the same word, v. NED.)

geallādl f. '*melancholia,*' v. OEG 7²²³.

geallede '*galled*' (*of horses*), *Lcd.*

gealp pret. 3 sg. of gielpan.

gealpettan (a) *to boast, live gluttonously?* NC 291,MFH 144.

gealpettung (æ) f. *boastfulness,* NC 291.

gēamrung (VPs)=gēomrung

gēamung=gēmung

gēan, gēana=gēn, gēna

gēan-, see also gegn-

geanbōc? f. *duplicate charter, counterpart,* Ct.

gēancyme (ē) m. *meeting,* EPs 63³,ARSHy.

gēancyrr m. (-cyrnes? f. RPs 18⁷) *meeting, SPs 18⁷ : return.* ['*gainchare*']

gēandele? (ē) *sleep,* HGL 416.

gēandȳne *arduous,* LL (134⁶).

gēanfær n. *going again, return,* CHR 1119.

gēangang (ǣ) *return?* LL 8,84.

gēangewrit (ē) '*rescriptio,*' OEG 862.

gēanhweorfan³ *to return,* HGL.

gēanhworfennes f. *return,* HGL 470.

gēanhwurf m. *return,* OEG 559.

gēanhwyrft (ǣ) m. *turning again,* LPs 125¹.

gēannes f. *meeting,* OEG 4610.

gēanoð? *complaint,* OEG xiv. [*Goth.* gaunōðus]

gēanryne m. *meeting,* ERLPs 58⁶.

geantalu f. *rejoinder, contradiction,* Ct (v. talu, LL 3·226).

gēanðingian *to reply,* GEN 1009.

geanul '*obvius,*' GPH 399.

gēap I. (ǣ, ē) *open, wide, extensive, broad, spacious, lofty, steep, deep* : *bent, crooked* : *deceitful, cunning, Æ,Shr* : *intelligent, shrewd, Lcd.* ['*yepe*'] **II.** pret. 3 sg. of gēopan.

gēaplic *deceitful, cunning, Æ.* adv. -līce, *Æ, Bf,KGl.* ['*yeply*']

gēapneb adj. (*epithet of corslet*) *meshed,* WALD 2¹⁹ (?=*gēapweb *wide-meshed*).

gēapnes f. *astuteness,* WW 192¹.

gēapscipe m. *cleverness, cunning, craft, deceit, trickery, artifice, Æ.* ['*yepship*']

gēapweb v. gēapneb.

gear pret. 3 sg. of georran.

gēar (ē, ǣ) nm. '*YEAR,*' *Æ,AO,CP* (as to epacts v. *Bf* 60). tō gēare *in this year* : *yearly tribute* : *name of the rune for* **g.**

geara=gearwe; **geara-**=gearo-

gēara *of '*yore,*' formerly, in former times, once, long since, B,BH,Met,RG,WW*; AO, CP. gēara gēo=gēogēara (gp. of gēar).

gearbōt f. *penance lasting a year,* LL (278¹¹).

±gearcian *to prepare, procure, supply, Æ* (*Gen*). ['*yark*']

gearcung f. *preparation, Æ.*

±gearcungdæg m. *preparation-day, day before the Sabbath, G.*

gēarcyning m. *consul,* WW 375².

geard I. m. '*yard,*' *fence, enclosure, court, residence, dwelling, land, B,Gen,Gu*; Mdf. in geardum *at home, in the world* : *hedge,* GD,MtR. **II.**=gierd

gēardagas† mp. *days of yore,* W : *lifetime.*

geardsteall m. *cattle-yard,* KC 3·391⁸ (v. BTs).

geardung f. *habitation,* APs 77⁶⁰.

gēare=gearwe I. and II.

geare-=gear-, gearo-; **gēare**=gēara

gēarfæc n. *space of a year,* W 72¹.

gearfoð=earfoð

gēargemearc n. *space of a year,* GU 1215.

gēargemynd n. *yearly commemoration,* NC 292. ['*year's mind*']

gēargeriht n. *yearly due,* W 113⁹.

gēargerím (ǣ) n. *numbering by years,* v. ES 39·342.

gēargetæl (æ[1], a[3], e[3]) n. *number of years*, LCD,LL.

gēarhwamlīce *yearly*, EC 226[6].

gēarlanges *for a year*, Æ.

gēarlēac=gārlēac

gēarlīc '*yearly,*' *of the year, annual, Bas,Cp, LL*; Æ. adv. -lice, WW; CP.

gearlīce=gearolīce

gēarmǣlum *year by year*, MET 1[5].

gēarmarcet n. *annual fair*, TC 372[15].

gearn (e) n. '*yarn,*' *spun wool, Gl.*

gearnful (NG)=geornful

gearnung=geornung

gearnwinde f. *yarn-winder, reel, Cp,WW*; LL 455,15. ['*yarn-wind*']

gearo (gearu) I. (wk gearwa) gsmn. -(o)wes; asm. gearone; napn. gearu *prepared, ready, equipped, finished, An,B,Bl,Bo,Cr*; CHR. ['*yare*'] II. (e[1], a[2], e[2])=gearwe adv. (*B, Cr,G,Met.*).

gēaro=gēara

gearobrygd m. *quick movement, deft playing (of an instrument)*, CRA 50.

gearofolm *with ready hand*, B 2085.

gearolīce *readily, fully, clearly, El.* ['*yarely*']

gearor comp. of gearo adj. and gearwe adv.

gearo-snotor, -snottor† *very skilful.*

gearoðoncol *ready-witted*, JUD 342.

gearowes gsmn. of gearo.

gearowita m. *intellect, understanding,* Bo.

gearowitol (rw-) *sagacious*, OEG 56[108] : *austere*, LkL 19[21].

gearowitolnes (a[2]) f. *sagacity*, W 53[16].

gearowyrde *fluent of speech, BH.* [v. '*yare*']

gearowyrdig *ready of speech*, MOD 51.

gēarrīm n. *number of years*, AO.

gēartorht *perennially bright*, GEN 1561.

gēarðēnung f. *annual service*, LL 382,38.

gearu=gearo

gearugangende *going swiftly*, RD 41[17].

gēarwǣstm *yearly fruit*, EC 168′.

gearwan=gierwan

gearwanlēaf=geormanlēaf

gearwe I. (gearo) adv. comp. gear(w)or; sup. gear(w)ost *well, effectually, sufficiently, thoroughly, entirely,* Æ,AO,CP : *quickly : near.* ['*yare*'] II.† f. (usu. pl.) *clothing, equipment, ornament, trappings, harness, armour.* III. (a, æ) f. '*yarrow,*' *Cp,Lcd,WW.*

±gearwian (æ, e, i, ie, y) *to equip, prepare, facilitate, do, make ready, Bo,G*; Æ,CP : *construct, erect, make : procure, supply : clothe, adorn : grant*, DR 18[11]. ['*yare*']

±gearwung f. *preparation : working : parasceve.*

gearwungdæg (eo[1]) m. *parasceve*, JnR.

+gearwungnes f. *preparation*, LPs (but v. BTs).

gēasceaft v. gēosceaft.

gēasne (*Jul*)=gǣsne

geaspis *jasper*, ZDA 34·239.

geat n. (æ, e) nap. gatu (geatu VPs) '*gate,*' *door, opening, Æ,BH,Bl,Ct,G,Ps*; AO,CP; Mdf.

gēat pret. 3 sg. of gēotan.

gēatan (ǣ, ē, ēo) *to say* '*yea,*' *consent, grant confirm, Chr.* ['*yate*']

geatolic† *adorned, magnificent, stately.*

geatwa=geatwe

geatwan *to equip*, RD 29[6].

geatwe fp. *arms, equipments, trappings, ornaments*, BL,CHR. [=getāwa]

geatweard m. *gate-keeper, door-keeper, porter, Jn.* ['*gateward*']

gēaðt f. *foolishness, mockery.* [gēac]

gebellic (OET,Cp 881)=gafollic

gēc (OET)=gēoc; gecel, gecile (GL)=gicel

gecs-=geocs-

ged=gæd, gidd; gedd=gidd

gederian=(1) gaderian; (2) derian

gee=gēa

gef=(1) geaf pret. 3 sg. of giefan; (2) (N) gif

gef-=gief-

gēgan *to cry out*, BHT 88, WW 355[13] (v. JAW 17).

geglisc=gagolisc

gegn=gēn; gegn- see also gēan-.

gegncwide† m. *reply, answer, retort* : (in pl.) *conversation.*

+gegnian *to meet*, DR 45[11]. ['*yain*']

gegninga=gegnunga

gegnpæð m. *opposing path*, RD 16[26].

gegnslege m. *battle*, AN 1358.

gegnum† adv. *away, forwards, straight on, thither.*

gegnunga adv. *immediately, directly : certainly, plainly, precisely : completely, fully.*

gegoð=geoguð; geher (NG)=ēar

Gehhol=Geohol, Gēol

gehðu† (eo, i) f. *care, anxiety, grief.*

-gelan v. tō-g.

geld=gield; geld-=gild-, gyld-

-geldan v. ā-g.

gelde *sterile*, WW 226[22]; 394[26]. ['*yeld*']

gell-=geall-, giell-

gellet n? *bowl*, LCD 122a.

gelm=gilm; gelo=geolu

gelostr=geolster; gelp=gielp

gēlsa=gǣlsa; gelt (KGL)=gylt

gēm-=gīem-; gēmer-=gēomr-

gemstān (ES 7·134)=gimmstān

gēmung (ēa, ī, ȳ;=ie) f. *marriage*, MtR,DR.

gēmungian *to marry*, DR 109[17].

gēmunglic *nuptial*, MtR,DR.

gēn I. (īe) (A, rare in prose) adv. *yet, now, still, again : further, besides, also, moreover : hitherto.* II. adj. *direct*, AA 8[10]. III.=gēgan, gōian

gēn-=gēan-, gegn-; gēna=gēn I.
gend=geond
gende=gengde pret. 3 sg. of gengan.
gēnde=v. gēn III.
geng I.=geong. II.=gang. III. pret. 3 sg.
of gangan.
+genga m. *fellow-traveller, companion*, W.
gengan, pret. gengde *to go*, Æ. [gong]
±genge I. *prevailing, effectual, appropriate*,
BH,Gu : *seasonable* : *agreeable*. ['genge']
II. n. *troop, Chr*; FBO,W. ['ging'] III. f.
privy, Æ,WW. ['gong']
-gengel v. æfter-, for(e)-g.
genigend=giniend pres. ptc. of ginian.
gēnlād *estuary*, KC 1·238⁶.
gēno, gēnu=gēn
gēo (iu) adv. *once, formerly, of old, before,
already, earlier*, CP (gīo).
geoc (iu) n. *'yoke,'* Bo,CP,Gl,Mt; Æ, AO :
yoke of oxen, etc., LL,WW : *a measure of
land*, Ct,WW : *consort*, NG.
gēoc† (ēoc) f. *help, support, rescue* : *safety* :
consolation.
geocboga (iuc-) m. *yoke-bow, yoke*, WW.
gēocend† m. *preserver, Saviour*.
±geocian (iuc-) *to 'yoke,' join together*, Æ,
WW.
gēocian (w. g. or d.) *to preserve, rescue, save*,
Æ.
geocled n. geocleta (ioc-) m. *a measure of
land*, Ct, OET (v. LL 2·527). ['yoklet']
gēocor† *harsh, terrible* : *bitter, sad*. adv.
gēocre DA 211.
geocsa (i) m. *sob*, Met : *hiccough*, G,Lcd.
[=gesca; 'yex']
geocsian (i) *to sob*, Bo. ['yex']
geocstecca m. *yoke-stick* (BTs), WW 35,459.
[sticca]
geocsung f. *sobbing*, WW 179,423. ['yex-
ing']
geoctēma (ioc-) m. *animal yoked with another*, WW 106³⁶.
geocða=gicða
gēodǣd (iū-)† f. *deed of old, former deed*.
gēodæg (iū) m. *day of old*, BF,Bo.
geof=gif; geof-=gief-, gif-
geofen=geofon
geofena gp. of geofu=giefu
geofola m. *morsel, bit of food*, WW. [=giefla]
geofon (i, y)† n. *ocean, sea, flood*.
geofonflōd m. *ocean flood*, Az 125.
geofonhūs n. *ship*, GEN 1321.
geogað=geoguð
gēo-gēara, -gēare adv. *of old*, BH.
gēog(e)lere m. *magician*, W 98⁹; HGL. [Ger.
gaukler]
geoguð (o²) f. *'youth,'* Bl,Cp,G; Æ, AO :
young people, B,CP : *junior warriors* (*as
opposed to* duguð) : *young of cattle*.

geoguðcnōsl n. *young offspring*, RD 16¹⁰.
geoguðfeorh† n. *time of youth*.
geoguð-hād (Bl,Sc) m., -hādnes f. *state of
youth* : *adolescence*. ['youthhood']
geoguðlic *youthful*, BH. ['youthly']
geoguðlust m. *youthful lust*, BL 59⁹.
geoguðmyrð f. *joy of youth* (GK), *tenderness
of youth?* (BTs),RD 39².
Geohol, Geohhol=Gēol; Geoh(h)el-=Gēol-
geohsa=geocsa
geoht (iuht) n. *yoke, pair*, v. OEG 7¹³⁵.
gāohwīlum *of old*, Bo 8⁷.
geohðu=gehðu
Gēol n., Gēola m. '*Yule'-tide, Christmas*,
BH,KC,LL,MH. ǣrra Gēola *December*.
æftera Gēola *January*.
geolca=geoloca; geold=gield
Gēoldæg (Geoh(h)el-) m. *Yule-day, day at
Yuletide*, MA.
geole=geolwe
gēolēan (iū-) n. *reward for past deed*, WAL 2⁷.
geoleca=geoloca; geolerēad=geolurēad
geolhstor=geolster
Gēolmōnað (Iūl-) m. *December*, MEN (CHR
p 280).
geolo=geolu
geoloca, geol(e)ca m. '*yolk*,' Æ,Lcd,Met.
[geolu]
geolorand† m. *buckler covered with yellow
linden-bark*.
geol-ster, -stor mn. *matter, pus, poison,
poisonous humour, disease*, OEG.
geolstrig *secreting poison, purulent*, OEG.
geolu gmn. geolwes '*yellow*,' B,Gl,Lcd.
geolwe ādl *jaundice*.
geoluhwīt *pale yellow*, WW. [v. 'yellow']
geolurēad *reddish yellow*, WW 375¹⁸. [v.
'yellow']
geolwe *yellowish*, LCD.
±geolwian *to become yellow*, OEG, Sc. [v.
'yellowed']
gēomann (īu)† m. *man of past times*.
gēomēowle (īo)† f. *aged wife?* B.
gēomer-=gēomor-, gēomr-
gēomor (īo¹, u²) *troubled, sad, miserable*, B,
Hu. ['yomer'] adv. -more.
gēomorfrōd *very old*, GEN 2224.
gēomorgidd† n. *dirge, elegy*.
gēomorlic *sad, painful, miserable*, B; AO.
adv. -līce, Sol. ['yomerly']
gēomormōd *sorrowful*, Æ.
gēomornes f. *tribulation*, LPs 118¹⁴³.
gēomorung=gēomrung
gēomrian *to be sad, complain, lament,
bewail, mourn*, B,Bl,DHy; Æ,AO,CP.
['yomer']
gēomrung (e, ea) f. *groaning, moaning,
grief*, Æ.
geon adj. pron. '*yon*,' CP.

geon-=geond-; **gēona** (NG)=gēna, gēn
geonað pres. 3 sg. of geonian.
geond (e, i, ie, y) **I.** prep. (w. a. and, rarely,
d.) *throughout, through, over, Bo,G : up to,
as far as, during.* geond...innan *throughout.* ['*yond*'] **II.** adv. *yonder, thither, BH,
RG.*
geondan prep. (w. a.) *beyond,* CHR 1052.
geondblāwan[7] (i[1]) *to inspire, illuminate,* GL.
geondbrǣdan *to cover entirely,* B 1239 : *enlarge, extend,* VH 14.
geonddrencan (i) *to drink excessively, get
drunk,* CHRD,KGL 58[40].
geondeardian *to inhabit,* RPs 32[8].
geondfaran[7] *to traverse, pervade,* BF,GD.
geondfēolan[3] (only in pp. geondfolen) *to fill
completely,* GEN 43.
geondfēran *to traverse : surpass,* ÆL 23b[333].
geondflōwan[7] *to flow over or through,* HELL
105.
geondflōwende *ebbing and flowing,* OEG
2363.
geondfolen v. geondfēolan.
geondgangan[7] *to traverse, go round,* RB,
VPs.
geondgēotan[2] (tr. and intr.) *to pour, pour
upon, suffuse, spread, soak,* Æ.
geondhweorfan[3]† *to pass over, pass through.*
geondhyrdan *to harden thoroughly,* SOL 150[28].
geondlācan[7] *to traverse, flow over,* PH 70.
geondleccan *to water, irrigate,* LPs 103[13],
CHRD 108.
geond-leccung (gynd-) f. *moistening, watering,* Sc 27[7].
geondlīhtan (ȳ[2]) *to illuminate, enlighten,* CP.
geondlīhtend (ēo) m. *illuminator,* DHy 128[5].
geondmengan *to confuse, bewilder,* SOL 59.
geondrēcan *to fill with smoke,* LCD 124a.
geondsāwan[7] *to strew, scatter,* DA 278.
geondscēawian *to look upon,* GUTH,WA :
consider, have regard to, LPs 118[6].
geondscīnan[1] *to shine upon, illuminate,* CP.
geondscrīðan[1] *to pass through, traverse,
stride to and fro,* BF,W 250[3] : *ramble (of
the mind),* MFH 147.
geondscrīðing f. *course, passage,* OEG 263.
geond-sēcan pret. 3 sg. -sōhte *to search
thoroughly,* CP : *pervade.*
geondsendan *to overspread,* GEN.
geondsēon[5] *to examine,* B 3087.
geondsmēagan *to investigate, discuss,* BH,
GL.
geondspǣtan *to squirt through,* LCD 78a.
geondsprengan *to besprinkle,* GUTH,RBL.
geondspringan[3] *to penetrate, be diffused,*
OEG 2840.
geondsprūtan[2] *to pervade,* CR 42.
gēond-strēdan, -stregdan *to scatter, suffuse,
besprinkle,* Æ.

geondstrēdnes f. *dispersion,* APs 146[2].
geondstyrian *to stir up, agitate,* MET 6[15].
geondðencan† *to reflect upon, consider.*
geondwadan[6] (i[1]) *to know thoroughly, be
versed in,* CP 9[10].
geondwlītan[1]† *to look over, contemplate,
examine, scan.*
geondyrnan[3] (=ie[2]) *to run over,* ÆGR 277[3].
geong I. (e, i, u) '*young,' youthful,* Æ,AO,
CP : *recent, new, fresh :* comp. gingra
'*younger,' LL,Ps :* superl. gingest '*young-
est,' AO : last, B,CP.* **II.** (LG)=gang.
['*yong*'] **III.**=geng pret. 3 sg. of gangan.
gēong=gōung
geonga (iu-) m. *young man,* Lk,WW.
geongan (LG)=gangan. ['*yong*']
geongerdōm=geongordōm
geongewifre=gangewifre
geonglǣcan (gyng-, iung-) *to pass one's
youth, grow up,* HGL 508; OEG 4361.
geonglic *young, youthful,* Æ. ['*youngly*']
geonglicnes f. *youth,* Sc 124[3].
geongling (iu-) m. *a youth, GD ;* ÆGR 3[1].
['*youngling*']
geongordōm, geongorscipe m. *discipleship,
allegiance,* GEN. [OS. jungardōm ; jun-
garskepi]
geongra (i) m. *youth : disciple, follower,
dependant, servant, vassal, BH,Gen ;* AO,
CP : *assistant, deputy,* Æ. ['*younger*']
geongre (i) f. *female attendant, assistant,*
JUD 132 : *deputy,* BH 340[17].
geonian=ginian
geonlic (MFH 103[20])=geonglic
geonofer adv. *thither.*
geonsīð m. *departure hence, death,* MFH 163.
geonung=ginung
gēopan[2] *to take in,* RD 24[9].
geormanlēaf n. *mallow,* LCD.
geormenletic *mallow,* WW 135[27]. [?=-lēaf]
georn I. (usu. w. g.) *desirous, eager, earnest,
diligent, studious, AO,Bl,Gu ;* CP. ['*yern*']
II.=gearn pret. 3 sg. of +iernan.
geornan (M)=giernan
georne adv. *eagerly, zealously, earnestly,
gladly, B,Bo,Chr ;* Æ,AO,CP : *well, carefully, completely, exactly,* Æ : *quickly, W.*
['*yerne*']
geornes=geornnes
georneste (WW 499[1])=eornoste
georn-ful, -fullic *desirous, eager, zealous,
diligent, Bo,G ;* AO,CP. ['*yearnfull*'] adv.
-līce, Æ.
geornfulnes f. *eagerness, zeal, diligence, Bo,
RB ;* Æ,AO,CP : *desire.* ['*yearnfulness*']
geornian=giernan
geornlic adj. *desirable,* AO. adv. -līce
*zealously, earnestly, diligently, carefully,
Cp BH,G ;* Æ,CP. ['*yernly*']

geornnes (i, ie, y) *desire, endeavour* : *zeal, industry* : *importunity*, NG.

geornung (i, ie, y) f. *'yearning,' desire*, CP, Sc : *diligence*.

geornust-=eornost-

georowyrde (BH)=gearowyrdig

georran=gyrran; **georst**=gorst

georst-=gierst-

georstu interj. *O!* VPs. [hīeran]

gēosceaft m. *destiny, fate*, B1234.

gēosceaftgāst m. *doomed spirit*, B1266.

geostra, geostran (ie, ei, y) *'yester'(-day, -night)*, Æ,B,G,Ps.

gēot=gīet.

gēotan I. (sv²) *to pour, pour forth, shed, Æ, BH,CP,Cr,Lcd*; AO,CP : *gush, flow, flood, overwhelm, El,Gu* : (±) *found, cast, Æ,Ps.* *['yet']* **II.**=gēatan

gēotend m. *artery*, WW352²⁵.

geotendǣder f. *artery*, LCD.

gēotenlic *molten, fluid*, GPH394.

gēotere m. *founder (of metal)*, AO54. *['yeter']*

-gēoting v. in-, on-g.

gēotton pret. pl. of gēotan II.

geoðu=geohðu=gehðu; **gēow**=gīw

gēower (GPH395)=ēower

gēowian=+ēowan=+īewan

gēowine (īu) m. *departed friend*, SEAF92.

geox-=geocs-; **gēp**=gēap

ger-=gær-, gearw-, gier-; **gēr**=gēar

gerd(A)=gierd; **gerd-**=gyrd-

gerew-, gerw-=gearw-, gierw-

gernwinde=gearnwinde

gērscipe m. *jest?* RIM11.

gēs v. gūs.

gesca, gescea (eo, i) m. *hiccough, sobbing*, GL,LCD.

gēse (ī, ȳ) adv. *'yes,' Æ,Bo,CP,G.*

gesen *entrails, intestines*, WW231³⁹.

gēsine, gēsne=gǣsne

gest, gēst=giest, gāst; **gest-**=giest-

gēstende (OEG2499)=ȳstende; **get**=geat

gēt I.=gǣt, nap. of gāt. **II.**=gēat pret. 3 sg. of gēotan. **III.** (VPs), gēta=gīet(a)

gētan I. *to destroy, kill*, B2940 (? for gītan or grētan). **II.**=gēatan

gētenwyrde *consenting, agreeing*, Ct (Swt). [gēatan]

gi- (NG, etc.)=ge-; **gib**=gif

giccan *to 'itch,'* Lcd.

gicce (y) *'itch,'* Ln33³.

giccig *purulent, itchy*, HGL453.

gicel(a) (y) m. *icicle, ice, DD,WW.* *['ickle']*

gicelgebland n. *frost*, RHy7⁷⁰.

gicelig *glacial, icy*, OEG.

gicelstān (y¹) m. *hailstone*, BL261,LRPs 147¹⁷.

gicenes (y) f. *itching, itch*, GL.

gicer (y) n. *acre*, OET114⁹².

gicða (ie, io, y) m. *scab, itch, itching, Æ,CP* : *hiccough? Lcd* (v. BTs). *['yekth']*

gid-=gyd-; **gīd-**=git-; **gidd-**=giedd-

gīe=gē; **giecða** (CP)=gicða?

giedd (e, i, y) n. *song, poem, B* : *saying, proverb, riddle* : *speech, story, tale, narrative* : *account, reckoning, reason*, VH14. *['yed']*

±gieddian (i, y) *to speak formally, discuss* : *speak with alliteration, recite, sing, Bo*; AO. *['yed']*

gieddung (e, i, y) f. *utterance, saying, prophecy, song, poetry, poetical recitation, metre, LG*; Æ. *['yedding']*

gief (rare EWS)=gif; **gief-**=gif-, geof-

giefa (eo, i, y) m. *donor*, CP.

giefan⁵ (e, ea, eo, i, ia, io, y) w. d. and a. *to 'GIVE*,' bestow, allot, grant, Æ*; AO,CP : *commit, devote, entrust, Da* : *give in marriage, Chr.*

giefend (e) m. *giver*, DR.

gīefernes (CP)=gīfernes

giefl (i, y)† n. *morsel, food* (v. also geofola).

giefnes (e) f. *grace, pardon*, DR,†Hy.

giefu (e, eo, i, y) f. *giving, gift, B,Bo,Mt*; AO,CP. *tō giefe, giefes gratis, freely* : *favour, grace, Bl,Lk* : *liberality* : *sacrifice* : *name of the rune for g.* *['give']*

gield (eo, i) n. *service, offering, worship, sacrifice, Jul* : *money-payment, tax, tribute, compensation, substitute, LG,LL* : (±) *guild, brotherhood, Ct* : *idol, god.* *['yield']*

gield- v. also gild-.

±gieldan³ (e, i, y) *to 'yield*,' pay, AO,LG* : CP : *pay for, Æ,LL* : *reward, requite, render, B,Bl,CP,Gen,Ps* : *worship, serve, sacrifice to, CP* : *punish.*

-gieldere (y) v. gafol-g.

gieldra=ieldra comp. of eald.

-giella (e, i) v. stān-g.

giellan³ (e, i, y) *to 'yell,' sound, shout, An, Fin,Rd.*

giellende *'yelling,' Ex,Lcd,Wid.*

gielp (e, i, y) mn. *boasting, pride, arrogance* : *fame, glory, Æ,B,BH,Bo*; AO,CP. *['yelp']*

gielpan³ (i, y) *to boast, exult, B,Bo,Da,W*; AO,CP : *praise, CP.* *['yelp']*

gielpcwide† m. *boastful speech.*

gielpen (i) *boastful,* SOL207.

gielpgeorn (i, y) *eager for glory*, BH92⁴ : *arrogant*, W.

gielpgeornes (i) f. *desire for glory, pride, arrogance*, W.

gielphlǣden (i) *boastful*, B868.

gielping (y) f. *glory, boasting*, Sc144¹¹. *['yelping']*

gielplic (i) *vainglorious, boastful* : *ostentatious, showy.* adv. -līce.

gielpna (i) m. *boaster*, CP.

gielpnes (e) f. *boastfulness*, LPs.

gielpplega (y) m. *war*, Ex 240.

gielpsceaða† (e¹, a²) m. *boastful enemy*.

gielpsprǣc f. *boastful speech*, B 981.

gielpword (y) n. *boast*, AO.

gielt=gylt; **giem**=gimm

gīeman (ē, ī, ȳ) (w. g. or a.) *to care for, heal, CP : correct, reprove : take notice of, take heed to, regard, observe, Æ,Bl,Bo,Cr*; AO, CP : *take charge of, control, Æ(Gen)*. ['yeme']

gīeme f. *care, AO,CP*. ['yeme']

gīemelēas (ē, ȳ) *careless, negligent, CP : neglected, uncared for, stray : incurable*, MtL p 20¹¹. ['yemeles']

gīemelēasian *to neglect, despise*, BH 362¹³.

gīemelēaslic *careless*, CP. adv. -līce, *Lcd*. ['yemelesliche']

gīemelēasnes (ē, ȳ) f. *negligence*, BH 242²⁸.

gīeme-lēast, -līest f. *carelessness, neglect, CP : presumption*, RB 77⁵. ['yemelest']

gīemen (ē, ī, ȳ) f. *care, oversight, heed, diligence, rule*, AO,CP.

gīemend (ȳ) m. *governor*, Sc 117⁷ : *keeper : observer*.

gīem(e)nes (ē) f. *care, anxiety*, DR,NG.

gīeming f. *care, anxiety*, CP : *custody : rule*.

gīen, gīena=gēn, gēna; **giend**=geond

gieng=geong

gierd (ea, i, y) f. 'yard,' *rod, staff, twig, Æ, G,Lcd*; CP : *measure of length, LL* : g. landes *an area of land about one-fourth of a hide*, EC,KC,LL.

gierdweg (y) m. *road fenced on either side? road made with faggots?* (BTs),KC.

gierdwīte (y) n. *affliction caused by (Moses') rod*, Ex 15.

gierede pret. 3 sg. of gierwan.

±**gierela** (e, i, y) m. *dress, apparel, adornment*, AO,CP : *banner*, WW 435¹⁵. [gearwian]

±**gier(e)lian** (e) *to clothe*, G,Ps.

+**gierelic** (e) adj. *of clothes*, WW 503¹⁸.

gierian=gearwian

+**giering** f. *direction*, RPs 138³.

gierman (y) *to cry, mourn, LPs* 37⁹. ['yarm']

±**giernan** (eo, y) (w. g.) *to* 'YEARN' *for, strive, be eager, desire, entreat, seek for, beg, demand, AO,CP*. [georn]

giernendlic (y) *desirable*, Sc 111¹³, (+) EPs 18¹¹.

giernes=geornnes

gierning (CP)=geornung; **gierran**=gyrran

gierst-=giestr-

±**gierwan** (e, ea, y) *to prepare*, AO : *cook, CP : deck, dress, clothe, adorn : direct*, CP.

giest (æ, e, i, y) m. 'guest,' *B,Gen,RB : stranger, MtL,Rd*.

giestærn (e, y) n. *guest-chamber* : *inn* : *shelter*.

giesterdæg (e, io) 'yesterday,' *JnRL* 4⁵².

giesternlic (eo, y) *of yesterday*.

giesthof (æ) n. *guest-house*, Cr 821.

giesthūs (a, æ, e, y) n. 'guest-house,' *ApT, Mk* ; CP.

giestian (y) *to lodge, be a guest*, Sc 153'.

giestig (e) adj. *being a stranger*, MtL 25³⁸.

giesting (e) f. *exile*, GL.

giestlic (a¹) *hospitable*, Gen 209.

giestlīðe (i¹) *hospitable*, MH 168²⁴,WW 97¹⁵.

giestlīðian (æ¹) *to be hospitable*, Nar 38¹⁸n.

giestlīðnes (æ, e, i, y) f. *hospitality, shelter*, BH.

giestmægen (i) n. *band of guests*, Gen 2494.

giestning (e) f. *hospitality, lodging*, NC 296.

giestran (e¹,o²)adv.*yesterday,Rd*. ['yestern']

giestranǣfen m. *yesterday evening*, DD. adv. -ǣfene, *Æ,GD*. ['yesterneve']

giestrandæg (eo, y) m. 'yesterday,' *Æ,G, PPs*.

giestranniht (y) f. 'yesternight,' *B* 1334.

giestsele (e, y) †m. *guest-hall*.

gīet I. (ē, ī, ȳ) adv. 'YET' : *still* : *besides* : *hitherto* : *hereafter* : *even* : *even now*. ðā g. *yet, still, further, also*. nū g. *until now* : *hitherto, formerly* : *any longer* **II.** pres. 3 sg. of gēotan.

gīeta=gīet

gīetan (i) *to get*, RBL 56¹⁵.

gīetsere, gīetsian=gītsere, gītsian

gif I. (e, ie, y) conj. (w. ind. or subj.) 'IF,' *Chr*; CP : *whether, though, B*. **II.** n. *gift, grace*, An 575,BH 34¹⁷.

gifa, gifan=giefa, giefan

gifect (Gl)=gefeoht; **gifel**=giefl

gifen I. pp. of giefan. **II.**=geofon

gifer m. *glutton*, Soul 118.

gīfere=gīfre

gīferlīce *greedily*, BH,OEG. ['yeverly']

gīfernes f. *greediness, gluttony, avarice, Bo, Bl ; Æ,CP*. ['yeverness']

gifeðe I. *granted by fate, given*. **II.** n. *fate, lot*, B 3085.

gifæst *endowed, talented* : (w. g.) *capable of*.

gifheall f. *hall in which gifts were made*, B 838.

gifian (ea, eo) *to present, endow : glorify*, DR 78¹⁴ : (+) 'prestolari,' DR 20⁸.

gifig *rich*, A 11·171.

gifl=giefl

gifnes† f. *grace, favour*.

gifol (e) *liberal, generous, bountiful*, CP : *gracious*, WW 66¹.

gifola m. *giver*, AS 2⁸.

gifolnes (io) f. *liberality*, CP 321²².

gifre *useful*, Rd 27²⁸ ; 50³.

gīfre *greedy, rapacious, ravenous*, B,Bo ; CP : *desirous of*. ['yever']

gifsceatt m. *present*, B378.

gifstōl† m. *gift-seat, throne.*

gift (y) nf. *'gift,' portion, marriage gift (by the bridegroom), dowry* : (pl.) *nuptials, marriage, Æ.* [giefan]

giftbūr m. *bride-chamber*, BF6²⁰,EPs18⁵.

giftelic=giftlic

giftfeorm f. *marriage-feast*, NC297.

gifthūs (y) n. *house at which a wedding is being celebrated*, Mt22¹⁰.

giftian (y) *to give in marriage (of the woman)*, G.

giftlēoð n. *epithalamium*, WW165³³.

giftlic *nuptial, belonging to a wedding, Æ.*

gifu (Æ)=giefu; **giful**=gifol

gifung (y) f. *consent*, BH86²⁵.

gīg (Cp142G)=gīw

gīgant m. *giant*, B,BL. [*L.* gigantem]

gīgantmæcg m. *son of a giant*, GEN1268.

gigoð=geoguð; **gihsa**=geocsa

gihða=gicða; **gihðu**=gehðu

gild=gield; **gild-**=gyld-

±**gilda** m. *member of a brotherhood of related persons*, v. LL2·378; 445.

gildan=(1) gieldan; (2) gyldan

gilddagas mp. *guild-days, festival-days*, WW107²².

gilde v. twi-g.

+**gilde** n. *membership of a guild*, TC.

+**gildheall** (y) f. *guild-hall*, KC4·277′

gildlic adj. *of a guild, festival*, A41·106.

gildrǣden (y) f. *guild-membership*, Ct.

±**gildscipe** m. *guild, brotherhood*, Ct,LL. ['*guildship*']

gildsester (y) m. *measure of bulk belonging to a corporate body*, TC606,611.

gillan=giellan

gillister n. gillistre f. *phlegm, pus, matter*, LCD. [=geolster]

gilm, gilma (e) m. *handful*, Lcd,OEG : *sheaf, Æ.* ['*yelm*']

gilp I. *dust, powder*, WW521¹⁸. **II.**=gielp

gilt=gylt

gilte (y) f. *young sow*, WW119²⁵. ['*yelt*']

gim=gimm; **gīm-**=gīem-

gimbǣre *gem-bearing, set with gems*, OEG.

gimcynn n. *precious stone, gem*, AA,BO.

gimfæst (B1272)=ginfæst

gimm (y) m. (occl. nap. gimme) *precious stone, 'gem,' jewel, Æ,Bl,VPs*; CP : (†) *sun, star.* [*L.* gemma]

±**gimmian** *to adorn with gems*, ÆGR.

gimmisc *jewelled*, AA7⁶.

gimreced n. *bejewelled hall, palace*, MET8²⁵.

gimrodor? m. *draconite (precious stone)*, OEG (v. BTac).

gimstān m. *stone capable of being made into a gem, jewel, Æ*; AO. ['*gemstone*']

gīmung=gēmung

gimwyrhta (y) m. *jeweller*, ÆH1·64⁹.

gin I. n. *yawning deep*, Ex430. **II.** adj.= ginn

gīn, gīna=gēn, gēna

gīnan I. *to yawn.* **II.** *to drive back*, ÆL25⁶³⁶.

gind=geond

ginfæst† *ample, liberal.* [ginn]

ginfæsten n. *great fastness, stronghold?* Ex 524.

ging, gingest v. geong.

gingi-ber, -fer(e) f. '*ginger,*' Lcd.

gingra I. (Æ) v. geong. **II.**=geongra

gingre=geongre

ginian (eo, y) *to 'yawn,' gape*, *AO,CP,GD, Gl,Lcd,Ps* : *utter a sound*, WW. [gīnan]

giniend (e, eo, y) '*yawning,*' *AO,BH,GD.*

ginn† *spacious, wide, ample.*

ginnan=onginnan

ginnes f. *gap, interval*, Cp373ı.

ginnfæst=ginfæst

ginnwīsed (y) *very wise*, Gu839? (or? ginn-wīse *of noble manners*, BTs).

ginung (e, eo, y) f. *opening of the mouth, howling, biting*, Gl. ['*yawning*']

gīo=gēo; **giofol**=gifol

giohðhād=geoguðhād; **gīow**=gīw

giowian (RG)=giwian

gip-=gyp-

gir-=gearw-, geor-, gier-, gyr-

gird=gierd; **giren** (VPs)=grīn

girsandæg (VH15)=gierstandæg

girstbītung=gristbītung

girwan=gearwian

+**gīscan** *to close, bolt, bar*, GL.

giscian *to sob*, Bo8⁸. [=geocsian]

gīse=gēse

gīsl, gīsel m. *hostage*, AO. ['*yisel*']

gīsldu (-ðu) f. *the giving of hostages*, WW 459⁷.

gīslhād m. *state of being a hostage*, Cp99o.

gīslian *to give hostages*, CHR.

gist I. m. '*yeast,*' *froth*, Lcd. **II.**=giest

gist-=giest-; **gīst**=ȳst

gistran=geostran; **gīstung**=gītsung

git dual of pron. 2 pers. (ðu); g. incer; d. inc; a. inc(it) *you two, B,Bl,G.* git Johannis *thou and John.* ['*yit*']

gīt, gīta=gīet, gīeta; **gitrife**=giðrife

gītsere m. *miser, Æ,*CP.

gītsian (ȳ) *to be greedy, long for, covet, B,Bo, CP,G*; Æ : (+) *obtain with greed*, CP364²². ['*yisse*']

gītsiendlic *insatiable*, RPs100⁵.

gītsiendnes f. *avarice*, W188n.

gītsung (ȳ) f. *avarice, greediness, covetousness, desire*, CP.

giðcorn n. *a plant, spurge-laurel?* LCD,WW.

giðrife (y) f. *cockle*, LCD,WW.

giðu=gehðu

gīu (Æ)=gēo; giu-=geo-
Gīūlī (Bᴦ24)=Iūla, Gēola
Gīuling, Giūluling *July*, Cp70ǫ (A20·137).
gīw (ēo) m. *griffin, vulture*, WW258⁷.
±giwian (ī? v. A16·98) *to ask*, NG.
giwung f. *petition*, DR,NG.
glād pret. 3 sg. of glīdan.
glad- v. glæd.
gladian (ea) (†) *to gleam, glisten* : (±) intr.
be glad, rejoice, JnL,Lcd : (±) tr. *gladden,
rejoice, gratify, appease*, Æ,VPs. ['*glad*']
gladine=glædene
gladung f. *rejoicing*, RB : *gladdening*, W :
appeasing, LPs. ['*gladding*']
glæd I. (glad- in obl. cases) (†) *bright,
shining, brilliant, gleaming*, Gen,Ph,Sol :
cheerful, '*glad*,' *joyous*, B,CP,Chr,Cr,G,
Ps; Æ : *pleasant, kind, gracious*, Æ,B. II.
n. *joy, gladness*, Wy68. ['*glad*']
glædene (a, e) f. *iris, gladiolus*, Gl; Lᴄᴅ.
['*gladdon*']
glǣdestede=glēdstede
glædine (Gʟ)=glædene
glædlic *bright, shining*, Wid : *kindly,
pleasant, agreeable*, Ps. adv. -līce '*gladly*,'
joyfully, kindly, willingly, BH,Chr.
glædman '*hilaris*,' WW171⁴⁰ : *kind, gracious*, B367.
glædmōd *cheerful, joyous* : *kind, gracious*.
glædmōdnes f. *kindness, bounty*, CP391⁶.
glædnes (e¹) f. '*gladness*,' *joy*, BH; Æ,DR
(+) : *good-nature*, WW74²².
glædscipe m. *gladness, joy*, JnR,Lcd.
['*gladship*']
glǣdstede=glēdstede
glǣm† m. *a brilliant light*, Gu : '*gleam*,'
brilliance, brightness, splendour, beauty,
Gen,Jul.
glæng=gleng
glæppe (a) f. *buck-bean*, Ct,Lᴄᴅ.
glær m. *amber, resin*, WW.
glǣren *vitreous, glassy* (Sievers234a).
[glæs]
glæs I. n. nap. glasu, and (once) glæsas
(GPH397) '*glass*,' Bo,Cr; Æ. II. *a glass
vessel*, BH,Lᴄᴅ.
glæsen *of glass, glassy*, Bl. ['*glassen*']
glæsenēage *grey-eyed*, WW416¹.
glæsfæt n. *glass* (*vessel*), BH398ʙ,ᴏ³,GD
10¹⁶.
glæsful m. *a 'glassful*,' BH398т³.
glæsgegot? *poured or molten glass*, WE63⁹.
glæshlūtor† *clear, transparent*.
glæterian *to glitter*, OEG,WW.
glæterung f. *shining*, RPs48¹⁵.
glǣtlic=glædlic; glǣw=glēaw
glappe=glæppe
glasu v. glæs; glāw=glēaw
glēam m? n? *revelry, joy*, Gᴇɴ12.

glēaw (ā, ǣ, ē) *penetrating, keen, prudent,
wise, skilful*, G,Gl,VPs; Æ,AO,CP : (†)
good. ['*glew*'] adv. -e.
glēawferhð† *prudent*.
glēawhycgende (Jᴜʟ), glēawhȳdig† *thoughtful, wise, prudent*.
glēawlic (ǣ, ēo) *wise, prudent, skilful, diligent*. adv. -līce.
glēawmōd *wise, sagacious*, CP.
glēawnes (ǣ) f. *wisdom, prudence, skill,
penetration*, Æ : *diligence* : *sign, token*, Bᴦ.
glēawscipe m. *wisdom, thoughtfulness, diligence* : *proof, indication, test*, Bᴦ156²⁴.
glēd (oe) f. *glowing coal, ember, fire, flame*,
LG,Ps; Æ. [glōwan; '*gleed*']
+glēdan *to make hot, kindle*, PPs77²³.
gleddian *to sprinkle, throw over*, Lᴄᴅ3·292¹⁴.
glēde f. *glowing coal*, LPs17⁹.
glēdegesa m. *fiery terror*, B2650.
gledene=glædene
glēdfæt n. *chafing-dish*, Lᴄᴅ123b : *censer*,
WW.
gledine=glædene
glednes (KGʟ)=glædnes
glēdscofl (oe) f. *fire-shovel*, Cp7ᴜ.
glēdstede† m. *altar*, Gᴇɴ.
glemm m? *blemish, spot*, W67⁸.
glencan=glengan
glendran *to devour, swallow*, MtR.
+glendrian *to precipitate*, LkL4²⁹.
gleng mf. (nap. gleng(e)as, glenge, glenga)
ornament, honour, splendour, CP.
±glengan (æ) *to adorn, decorate*, ÆL : *trim
(lamp)* : (+) *set in order, compose*.
+glengendlīce *elegantly*, OEG1202.
glengful *decked out, adorned*, GPH395.
glengista? (meaning doubtful) AA1²⁰ (v.
BTs and ac).
glenglic *magnificent, brilliant*, WW467²⁵.
glengnes f. *adornment*, MFH123¹⁵.
glentrian=glendran
glēo=glīw; glēof=glēow II.
gleomu f. *splendour*, Rᴜɪɴ34?
glēow I.=glīw. II. pret. 3 sg. of glōwan.
glēow-=glēaw-, glīw-
glēsan *to gloss*, ÆGʀ293¹³. [L. glossa]
glēsing f. *glossing, explanation*, ÆGʀ293¹⁴.
glēw=glēaw
glīa (OEG3173)=glīga gp. of glīg.
glid *slippery*, CPs34⁶.
glida (io) m. *kite, vulture*, Æ,Cp. ['*glede*']
±glīdan¹ *to 'glide,' slip, slide*, An,B; Æ,AO,
CP : *glide away, vanish*.
glidder *slippery*, VHy : *lustful*. ['*glidder*']
gliddrian *to slip, be unstable*, OEG4104.
glider (W239¹⁴)=glidder
gliderung (y) f. *phantom*, WW401⁴⁰.
glīg=glīw
glind m. *hedge, fence*, BC1·296'.

glioda (Cp)=glida

glisian *to glitter*, WW. ['*glise*']

glisnian (y) *to* '*glisten*,' *gleam*, Shr, Run.

glīt pres. 3 sg. of glīdan.

glitenian *to glitter*, *shine* : *be distinguished*, Bf44⁶.

glitenung f. *coruscation*, *gleam*, SPs143⁸.

glitin-, glitn-=gliten-

glīw (ēo, īg, īo, īu, ēow) n. '*glee*,' *pleasure*, *mirth*, *play*, *sport*, Bas,Gl,Ph : *music*, Gn, Ps : *mockery*.

glīwbeam (īg) m. *musical instrument*, *harp*, *timbrel*, LRSPs149³.

glīwbydenestre (ȳ) f. *female musician*, LPs 67²⁶.

glīwcræft m. *music*, *minstrelsy*, GD62¹³.

glīwcynn? (ȳ) *a kind of music?* (BTs), LPs146¹⁰.

glīwdrēam (ēo) m. *music*, *mirth*, B3021.

glīwere m. *buffoon*, *parasite*, OEG.

glīwgamen (īg) n. *revelry*, W46¹⁶.

glīwgeorn (īg) *fond of sport*, LL.

glīwhlēoðriendlic *musical*, WW446³⁶.

glīwian (ēo) *to make merry*, *jest*, *play* (*music*), *sing*, BH,LL : *adorn*, Rd27¹³. ['*glew*']

glīwiend m. *performer*, *player*, SPs67²⁶.

glīwingman m. *debauchee?* OEG50⁹.

glīwlic *mimic*, *jesting*, GPH396.

glīwmǣden (īe) n. *female musician*, ERPs 67²⁸.

glīwman (ēo, īg) m. '*gleeman*,' *minstrel*, *player*, *jester*, B; CP,WW : *parasite*, HGL.

glīwre=glīwere

glīwstæf m. *melody*, *joy*, Wa52.

glīwstōl m. *seat of joy*, Rd88⁸.

glīwung f. *boisterous laughter*, *mockery*, OEG1472.

glīwword (ēow) n. *song*, *poem*, Met7².

glōf, glōfe f. '*glove*,' *pouch*, B,Guth; LF60. foxes g. *foxglove*.

+glōfed *gloved*, AS43⁴.

glōfung f. *supplying with gloves*, LL450,10.

glōfwyrt f. *glovewort*, *dog's tongue*, *lily of the valley*, Lcd.

glōm m? *gloaming*, *twilight*, Creat71.

glōmung f. '*gloaming*,' *twilight*, DHy,WW.

gloria m. *doxology*, RB.

glōwan⁷ *to* '*glow*,' Æ,OEG.

glōwende '*glowing*,' *burning*, Lcd80b.

gly-=gli-

gnād pret. 3 sg. of gnīdan.

gnǣgen=gnagen pp. of gnagan.

gnæt m. '*gnat*,' *midge*, AO,Lcd,Mt.

gnagan⁶ *to* '*gnaw*,' Æ,Ct,DD.

-gnāst v. fȳr-g.

gnēad-=gnēað-

gnēað *niggardly*, B,BH : *frugal*, *sparing*, Shr. [v. '*gnede*']

gnēaðlicnes f. *frugality*, OEG2437.

gnēaðnes (ē) f. *frugality* : *scarcity*, MH.

gnēðe *scanty*, *sparing*, WW. ['*gnede*'] adv. -līce, GD. ['*gnedely*']

gnēðelicnes=gnēaðlicnes

gnīdan¹ *to rub*, *grind together*, *crumble*, Lk; Æ,AO. ['*gnide*']

gnidil m. *rubber*, *pestle*, Cp440p.

gnīding f. *rubbing*, Lcd11b.

gnīt pres. 3 sg. of gnīdan.

gnōgon pret. pl. of gnagan.

gnorn† I. *sad*, *sorrowful*, *troubled*, *depressed*. II. m. *sadness*, *sorrow*, *trouble*.

gnornan=gnornian

gnorncearig *sad*, *troubled*, Jul529.

gnorngan=gnornian

gnornhoft† n. *prison*, *cell*, An.

gnornian *to be sad*, *murmur*, *complain*, *mourn*, *lament*, *grieve*, CP.

gnornscendende *hastening away in sadness*, PPs89¹⁰. [*scyndan*]

gnornsorg† f. *sadness*, *sorrow*.

gnornung (e) f. *sadness*, *sorrow*, *lamentation*, *discontent*, Æ,AO,CP.

gnornword n. *lamentation*, Gen767.

gnuddian *to rub*, OEG56³³.

gnyran=gnyrran

gnyrn† f. *sadness*, *mourning*, *calamity* : *wrong*, *insult*, *fault*, *blemish*. [gnorn]

gnyrnwracu f. *revenge*, *enmity*, El359.

gnyrran *to grind the teeth*, W138²⁹ : *creak*, Lcd. [v. '*gnar*']

+gnysan=cnyssan; **gnȳðe**=gnēað

gōað 3 p. sg. pres. of gōian.

gōc=gēoc

God m. np. -as, -u *a* 'god,' *image of a god*, Æ; AO : *God*, *the* (*Christian*) *Deity*, Æ; CP : *godlike person*, Bo.

gōd I. comp. bet(e)ra, bettra, superl. bet(e)st 'good' (*of persons or things*), *virtuous* : *desirable*, *favourable*, *salutary*, *pleasant* : *valid*, *efficient*, *suitable* : *considerable*, *sufficiently great*. II. n. *good thing*, *advantage*, *benefit*, *gift*, B,Bl,Mt; Æ, AO,CP : '*good*,' *goodness*, *welfare*, CP : *virtue*, *ability*, *doughtiness* : *goods*, *property*, *wealth*, CP.

godæppel m. *quince*, WW364¹⁶. [=coddæppel]

godbearn n. *divine child*, *Son of God* : *godchild*, W. ['*godbairn*']

godborg m? *solemn pledge* (*given in church?*), LL18·33; 66,33 and v. 2·232,1d.

godbōt f. *atonement*, LL258,51.

godcund *religious*, *sacred*, *divine*, *spiritual*, *heaven-sent*, Gen,Chr; Æ,CP. ['*godcund*']

godcundlic *divine*, *of or from God*, *spiritual*, *celestial*, Æ,CP. adv. -līce *divinely*, Æ : *canonically*.

godcundmæht n? *divine majesty*, MtL.

godcundnes f. *divine nature, divinity, God-head, Æ,Lcd* : *divine service* : *oblation*, LL. ['*godcundness*']

godcundspēd f. *divine nature, godhead*, VH 14.

gōddǣd f. *good work, Cr* : *benefit, PPs.* ['*good deed*']

goddohtor f. '*goddaughter,' Ct.*

gōddōnd† m. (nap. gōddēnd), *benefactor.*

goddrēam† m. *joy of heaven*, Gu.

godē-=god-

godfæder m. *God the Father* : '*godfather,' Ct,LL.*

godfrecnes (BH 70¹²)=godwrecnes

gōdfremmend m. *doer of good?* B 299.

godfyrht (e, i) *godfearing, An,Chr.* ['*god-fright*']

godgeld=godgield

godgesprǣce (BH)=godsprǣce

godgield (e², i², y²) n. *heathen god, idol* : *heathen rite*, AO.

godgildlic *of idol-worship*, WW 466¹⁶.

godgim m. *heavenly jewel?* El 1114.

godhād m. *divine nature*, CP 261¹⁷.

±gōdian *to improve, get better, Chr,Lcd* : *make better* : *endow, enrich, KC*; Æ. ['*good*']

Goding m. *Son of God*, LkR 4¹.

gōdlār f. *good teaching*, LL 304B.

gōdlēas *bad, evil*, BH. ['*goodless*']

godlic *godlike, divine*, WW 220,221.

gōdlic '*goodly,' excellent, Gen* : *comely, fair*, GPH 394.

gōdlīf n. *good life*, CHR 1095.

godmægen n. *divine power, divinity*, AA 37,42.

godmōdor f. '*godmother,' Shr.*

gōdnes f. '*goodness,' virtue, Bo* : *good-will, beneficence, kindliness, Bo,Æ* : *good thing.*

godsǣd n. (*God's seed), divine progeny?* DA 90.

gōdscipe m. *kindness, DR.* ['*goodship*']

godscyld f. *sin against God, impiety*, JUL 204.

godscyldig *impious*, Gu 834.

godsibb m. *sponsor*, W. ['*gossip*']

godsibbrǣden f. *sponsorial obligations*, W 228³.

gōdspēdig† *rich, happy.*

godspel n. '*gospel,' glad tidings, Mt* : *one of the four gospels, An*; Æ,CP : *the gospel (for the day), Mt.*

godspelbodung f. *gospel-preaching, new dis-pensation*, ÆL,ÆT.

godspellbōc f. *book containing the four gospels*, LL. ['*gospel-book*']

godspellere m. '*gospeller,' evangelist, Bl*; Æ,CP.

godspellian *to preach the gospel, evangelize, Ps*; Æ,CP. ['*gospel*']

godspell-ic (Æ), -isc *evangelical.*

godspelltraht m. *gospel commentary, homily,* Æ.

godsprǣce (ē) n. *oracle*, BH.

godsunu m. '*godson,' BH,Chr,Ma.*

godðrymm m. *divine majesty*, GD.

godðrymnes f. *divine glory*, AS 9²?

godwebb I. n. *fine cloth, purple, CP* : *fine clothes* : *curtain* : *flag.* II.=godwebben

godwebbcyn? (gode-) n. *purple (cloth)*, SOL 152′.

godwebben *of purple*, BL 95¹⁹, LF 47¹⁵ : *of silk or cotton*, HGL.

godwebgyrla m. *cloth of purple*, W 197¹.

godwebwyrhta m. *weaver of purple*, AA 8¹⁸.

gōdwillende *well-pleased*, EHy 16⁶.

godwrǣc (e²) *wicked*, BL.

godwrǣclic *impious, sacrilegious*, GD 232¹³.

godwrece=godwrǣc

godwrecnes f. (-wyrc- WYN 45) *wickedness, impiety*, BHB 70¹².

goffian *to be vain*, BYH 80¹¹.

gofol=gafol

gōlan *to lament, groan*, BH 88(v.also gēgan).

gōl pret. 3 sg. of galan.

gold n. '*gold,' Æ,OET*; CP.

goldǣht f. *wealth in gold*, B 2748.

goldbeorht *bright with gold*, RUIN 34.

goldblēoh *golden-hued*, WW 140²⁴.

goldblōma m. *golden bloom?* (v. BTs), W 251¹¹; BL 105¹⁸.

goldburg† f. *city in which gold is given? rich city?* AN,GEN.

golde f. '*solsequia,' marigold*, WW 301⁶. ['*gold*']

golde-=gold-

golden pp. of gieldan.

goldfæt† n. *golden vessel.*

goldfǣted *plated or adorned with gold*, LL 460,10H.

goldfāg *variegated or shining with gold.*

goldfell n. *gold plate*, WW 358¹⁵.

goldfellen *of gilded leather*, ÆL 31²⁵².

goldfinc m. '*goldfinch,' WW.*

goldfinger m. *ring-finger*, LL.

goldfrætwe fp. *gold ornaments*, CR,W.

goldfyld *covered with gold*, WW 518⁴.

goldfyll? *gold leaf, gold foil*, ES 8·478 (v. BTs).

goldgearwe fp. *gold ornaments*, NC 298.

goldgewefen *woven with gold*, OEG 4297.

goldgeweorc n. *golden object*, MH 222.

goldgiefa† (i, y) m. *gold-giver, prince, lord.*

goldhilted *golden hilted*, RD 56¹⁴.

goldhladen *adorned with gold*, FIN 13.

goldhoma m. *gold-adorned coat of mail*, EL 992.

goldhord nm. *treasure of gold, treasury, El, VPs*; Æ,AO. ['*goldhoard*'] goldhordhūs n. *privy*, WW 184¹⁴.

goldhordian *to collect treasure, hoard*, Sc 173¹².

goldhroden† *ornamented with gold*. [hrēodan]

goldhwæt *greedy for gold*, B 3074?

goldlæfer f. *gold plate*, HGL 431.

goldlēaf n. *gold leaf or plate*, W 263⁶. [=læfer]

goldmæstling (e) n. *brass*, WW. [v. '*gold*']

goldmāōm m. *treasure*, B 2414.

goldmestling=goldmæstling

goldōra m. *gold ore*, OEG 1810.

goldsele† m. *hall in which gold is distributed*.

goldsmiō m. '*goldsmith*,' Æ.

goldsmiōu f. *goldsmith's art*, WY 73.

goldspēdig *rich in gold*, JUL 39.

goldtorht *bright like gold*, CREAT 78.

goldōēof m. *stealer of gold*, LL 54,9².

goldōræd m. *gold thread*, WW 196¹⁵.

goldweard m. *keeper of gold (dragon)*, B 3081.

goldwecg m. *a lump of gold*, OEG 451.

goldwine† m. *liberal prince, lord, king*.

goldwlanc† *brave with gold, richly adorned*.

goldwlencu f. *gold ornament*, BL 195.

goldwyrt f. *heliotrope, marigold*, OEG 26²⁶.

golfetung (LPs 78⁴)=gaffetung

gōlon pret. pl. of galan.

golpen pp. of gielpan.

gom-=gam-

gōma m. (sg. or pl. used indifferently) *inside of mouth or throat, palate, jaws*, Lcd, Rd,VPs; Æ. ['*gum*']

gombe (a)† f. *tribute*.

gomor *Hebrew measure, omer*, Æ. ['*gomer*']

gon-=gan-, gond-=gand-, gcond-

gōp m. *slave, servant*, RD 50³. [or ?=gēap]

gor n. *dung, dirt, filth*, Æ,Cp,Rd. ['*gore*']

gōr=gār III.

gorettan *to gaze, stare about*, OEG 5³ : *pour forth, emit*, GPH 398.

gorettung f. *gazing*, OEG 5³n.

gorian *to gaze, stare about*, OEG 7⁶.

gors (Cp?), gorstm. '*gorse*,' *furze, MH,MrR: juniper*, Lcd : '*rhamnus*,' S²Ps 57¹⁰.

gorstbēam m. *furze bush*, Mk 12²⁶.

gōs f. nap. gēs '*goose*,' LL,Rd,WW; Æ.

gōs-fugol m. nap. -fuglas *goose*, Ct.

gōshafoc (u³) m. '*goshawk*,' WW.

gost=gorst; gōst=gāst

+got n. *shedding (of tears)*, BH 376¹².

Gota sg. -an pl. '*Goth*,' BH.

goten pp. of gēotan.

-gotennes v. tō-g.

Got-isc (GD), -onisc (OEG) adj. *of the Goths*.

gōtwoōe f. *goatweed*, LCD. [gāt]

gōung (ēo) f. *groaning*, BH 76¹⁵. [gōian]

grād m. (Æ), grāde f. *step, grade, rank*. [L.]

grǣd m. *grass*, WW.

grǣda=grēada

grǣdan I. *to cry, call out*, Lcd : *crow*, CP,Rd. ['*grede*'] II. ds. of wk. adj. *grassy*, ÆL 18²⁴⁵.

grǣde I. *grassy*, Æ. II.=grǣd

grǣde-, grǣdi-=grǣdig-

grǣdig (ē) '*greedy*,' *hungry, covetous, Æ,B, Bl,Sol : eager*, CP. adv. -līce, Æ,Bas.

grǣdignes f. *greediness, avarice*, Æ.

grǣdum adv. *greedily*, GU 710.

græf I. (a) n. *cave*, '*grave*,' *trench, Seaf; Mdf*. [grafan] II. n? *style for writing*, WW. [L. graphium]

grōōfa m. græfe f. *bush, bramble, grove, thicket*, WW ; Mdf : *brush-wood (for burning), fuel*, Chr. ['*greave*']

græfen pp. of grafan.

græfhūs n. *grave*, SAT 708.

græfsex n. *graving tool*, WW. [seax]

græft mfn. *graven image, carved object, sculpture*, Æ.

græftgeweorc n. *graven image*, DEUT 5⁸.

græfō pres. 3 sg. of grafan.

grǣg '*grey*,' *Æ,Ep,Gen,Met,WW*.

grǣggōs f. *grey (wild) goose*, GL.

grǣghǣwe *grey*, WW 402⁴⁰.

grǣghama *grey-coated*, FIN 6.

grǣgmǣl *grey-coloured*, B 2682.

grǣgōs=grǣggōs

grǣm-, grǣn-=grem-, gren-; grǣp=grēp

+grǣppian *to seize*, MtL 14³¹.

grǣs n. (nap. grasu) '*grass*,' Cp,CP. [v. also gærs]

grǣsgrēne (e¹, oe²) '*grass-green*,' Ep.

grōshoppa v. gærshoppa.

grǣsmolde f. *greensward*, B 1881.

grǣswang† m. *greensward*, VH 14.

grǣt I.=pres. 3 sg. of (1) grǣdan, (2) grētan. II.=grēat

grētan=grētan; graf=græf

grāf nm. '*grove*,' BC ; Mdf.

grāfa m. *grove*, KC.

grafan⁶ *to dig, dig up, Met,Rd,Rim* : '*grave*,' *engrave, carve, chisel*, PPs.

grafere m. '*sculptor*,' *graver*, WW 164¹⁴.

grafet n. *trench*, EC 354; 355.

gram (o) adj. *angry, cruel, fierce, B,G; AO* : *oppressive, hostile* : (as sb.) *enemy*. ['*grame*']

grama I. m. *rage, anger, Æ* : *trouble*, Lcd. ['*grame*'] II. *devil, demon*, ÆL.

gramatisccrǣft=grammaticcrǣft

grambǣre *passionate*, CP 289⁵.

grame adv. *angrily, fiercely, cruelly*.

gramfærnes f. *wrath*, LL (226²⁵). [=*grambærnes]

gramhegdig=gramhȳdig

gramheort† *hostile-minded*, VH 14.

gramhycgende *hostile*, PPs 68²⁵.

gramhȳdig† *hostile, malignant*, VH 14.

gramian *to anger, enrage*, W 199². gramigende *raging*, GPH 402.

gramlic *wrathful, fierce, cruel, severe*, Æ. adv. -lice, Ps. ['gramely']

grammatic *grammatical*, ÆL 35¹⁴.

grammaticcræft m. *art of grammar*, BH 258¹⁵.

grammaticere m. *grammarian*, Bf 158¹⁷.

grammatisc=grammatic

grammōd *cruel*, Bl 223³³.

gramword n. *evil speech*, PPs 74⁵.

grand pret. 3 sg. of grindan.

grandorlēas (o) *guileless*, Jul 271.

grānian² *to 'groan,' lament*, Bl,Ps.

granu f. *moustache*, Cp 335 m (v. BTs).

grānung f. *'groaning,' lamentation*, Æ.

grāp I. f.† *grasp, grip*. [grīpan] II. pret. 3 sg. of grīpan.

±grāpian *to feel for, lay hold,of, seize, touch*, Æ,B,Bl,Rd,VPs : *attain, reach*, Bf 144¹. ['grope']

grāpigendlic *tangible*, ÆH 1·230.

grāpung f. *sense of feeling, touch*, Æ. ['groping']

grāscinnen *made of grey skins or grey fur*, Chr 1075 d. [ON. grāskinn]

grasian *to 'graze,'* Lcd.

grasu v. græs.

gratan (Lcd 3·292²⁴)=grotan

graðul *gradual, antiphon*, CM 1020.

grēada m. *lap, bosom*, CP,Lk. ['greade']

grēat (æ) comp. grīetra *'great,' tall, thick, stout, massive*, A,Æ,Bo,Chr,WW : *coarse*, BC,Lcd.

grēatewyrt f. *meadow saffron*, WW 298⁷.

grēatian² *to become enlarged*, CP. ['great']

grēatnes (ē) f. *'greatness,'* RB 88¹⁵.

Grēcas mpl. *Greeks* (v. AB 40·342).

Grēcisc *Greek, Grecian*, Æ.

grēd=grǣd; gref-, grēf-=græf-, grǣf-

grēg-=grǣg-; grem-=grim-

gremet-=grymet-

±gremian *to enrage, provoke, irritate*, AO; Æ,CP : *revile*, Mk. ['greme']

gremman=gremian

gremung (æ) f. *provocation*, LPs 94⁹.

grēne 'green,' Ct,Gl,Lcd : *young, immature*, Lcd : *raw : growing, living*, LkL (oe) : *as* sb., Lcd.

grēnhǣwen *green-coloured*, WW 379²⁴.

grēnian *to become 'green,' flourish*, Met.

grēnnes f. *greenness*, BH; CP : (in pl.) *green things, plants*, Bf 82⁴.

grennian *to 'grin,' gnash the teeth*, Jul,Sc.

grennung (æ) f. *grinning*, Cp 174 r.

grēofa m. *pot, pan*, WW. [Ger. griebe]

grēop=grēp

grēosn (īo) *gravel, pebble*, KGl 76³. [Ger. greiss]

grēot n. *'grit,' sand, earth*, An,B,Gen; Æ.

grēotan² *to cry, lament*, B,Sol. [v. 'greet']

grēothord n. *body*, Gu 1240.

grēow pret. 3 sg. of grōwan.

grēp, grēpe f. *ditch, furrow, drain : privy*, ES 9·505 ; Gl. [v. 'grip']

gres-=græs-; grēt-=grēat-

grētan I. (±) *to 'greet,' salute, accost, speak to, challenge*, B,Gl,Mk,Jul : (±) *to seek out, approach, visit*, AO,B,Gen,LG : *illtreat, attack*, AO : *touch, take hold of, handle, deal with*, ÆGr : *have an effect upon*, ZDA 34·232 : *cohabit with*. hearpan grētan *play the harp*, Cra. II.† (ǣ) *to weep, bemoan, lament, deplore*, B,Cp,Cr. [v. 'greet']

grēting f. *'greeting,' BH,LkL* (oe) : *present*.

grētinghūs n. *audience chamber*, WW 184³.

grētingword n. *word of greeting*, ÆGr 209¹⁴.

+grētlic *commendatory*, RBL 103⁶.

gretta=grytta

greðe *'sodalis'?* OEG 29².

grēwð pres. 3 sg. of grōwan.

griellan=grillan

grīetra v. grēat.

grīghund m. *'greyhound,'* WW 276³.

grillan (ie, y) *to provoke, offend*, CP : *gnash the teeth*, Gl. ['grill']

grim (CP)=grimm

grīma† m. *mask, helmet*, El : *ghost*, Rd.

grimena *'bruchus,' caterpillar?* EPs 104³⁴.

grimet-=grymet-

grimful *fierce, violent*, ES 39·348.

grīmhelm† m. *helmet (with visor)*.

grīming *spectre*, WW 446²⁶.

grimlic *fierce, blood-thirsty, cruel, terrible, severe*, Æ,AO,B. adv. -lice. ['grimly']

grimm *fierce, savage*, B,Bl,Ma : *dire, severe, bitter, painful*, BH,Bl,Chr. ['grim']

grimman³† *to rage : hasten on*, B 306.

grimmān n. *terrible sin*, BHB 50⁸.

grīmme *savagely, cruelly, severely*, AO,Gen. ['grim']

grimnes f. *ferocity, cruelty*, Bl,Gu,WW : *severity*. ['grimness']

grimsian *to rage*, BH.

grimsung f. *harshness, severity*, CP 125¹⁴.

grin *'ilium,' region of the groin*, LL.

±grīn (ī, ȳ; also short?) nf. *snare, gin*, PPs, VPs; Æ,CP : *halter, noose*, Mt. ['grin']

+grind† n. *impact, crash*.

±grindan³ (y) *to rub together, grate, scrape*, Rd : *gnash*, Ps : *'grind,' sharpen*, Æ,Mt, pp. WW.

grinde f. *shingle*, BC (v. Mdf).

grindel m. nap. grindlas *bar, bolt*. pl. *grating, hurdle*, Gen 384 (v. BT).

grindere m. *grinder*, Lcd 3·178¹.

grinde-tōð, grindig- m. *grinding tooth, molar*, WW 440[26].

grindle f. *herring*, WW 356[12].

gring=cring

+**grīnian** *to ensnare*, KGl. ['*grin*']

grint pres. 3 sg. of grindan.

grinu '*avidius*' (said of some colour), WW 163[19],356[25].

grīosn=grēosn

gripa m. *handful, sheaf*, Lcd.

±**grīpan** intr. (w. d. g. on or tō) *to seek to get hold of, assail, attack*, B,Bl,Gen; CP : tr. (w. g.) *seize, snatch, take, apprehend*, Sol,WW. ['*gripe*']

gripe m. '*grip*,' *grasp, seizure, attack*, B, WW; Æ. gūðbilla g. *shield* : *handful*, Lcd,Ps.

grīpend m. *seizer, robber*, WW 516[13].

+**gripennes** f. *seizing, snare, captivity*, EPs 34[8].

±**grippan** (io) *to seize, obtain*, DR, LG.

gripu f. *kettle, caldron*, Sol 46.

gripul '*capax*,' WW 198[39]. ['*gripple*']

-**grīsan** (ȳ) v. ā-g.

grislic '*grisly*,' *horrible*, HL 15[182]. adv. RWH 84.

grīst n. *action of grinding*, WW. ['*grist*']

gristan? *to gnash, grind*, HGL 513 (cp. OEG 4605 and n).

gristbāt-=gristbit-

gristbite m. *gnashing*, W 188[5].

gristbitian *to gnash the teeth, rage*, Æ,BH, Mk,WW; Æ. ['*gristbite*']

gristbitung f. *gnashing of teeth*, Bl,Mt. ['*gristbiting*']

gristle f. '*gristle*,' Gl,WW.

gristlung (y) f. *gnashing*, Lk 13[28].

grīstra m. *baker*, WW.

gritta=grytta

grið n. *truce*, (*temporary*) *peace*, Ma : *protection of the person, asylum, sanctuary, guarantee of safety*, LL. ['*grith*']

griðbryce m. *breach of* '*grið*,' LL : *penalty for such a breach*, LL. ['*grithbreach*']

±**griðian** *to make a truce or peace*, Chr : *protect*, LL. ['*grith*']

griðlagu f. *law of temporary or local peace*, LL 470,9.

griðlēas *unprotected*, W 158[7].

groe-=grē-

grōf pret. 3 sg. of grafan.

grom=gram; **gron-**=gran-

grond pret. 3 sg. of grindan.

gronwisc (=a) '*acus*,' Cp 160 A (v. AB 9·35).

grōp f. *ditch*, Ln 150.

gropa m. *a liquid measure*, WW 204[3].

grōpian=grāpian; **-groren** v. be-g.

grorn I. m. *sorrow, sadness*, Rim 89. II. adj. *sad, agitated*, OET 127[6]. adv. -e.

grornhof n. *sad home, hell*, Jul 324.

grornian *to mourn, complain*, Cr,Ps.

grorntorn *sadness*, Rim 66?

grornung f. *complaint*, NG.

grost *cartilage*, Ln 57.

grot I. n. *particle, Bo*; AO : *meal*. ['*grot*'] II. sbpl. (grotan) '*groats*,' *coarse meal*, Lcd.

grotig *earthy*, GPH 396.

±**grōwan**[7] *to* 'GROW,' *increase, flourish* : *germinate*, CP : *become ?* WW 441[28] (v. NP 15·272).

grōwende '*growing*,' Gen,KGl.

grōwnes f. *growth*, BH : *prosperity*, HL 124[257].

grummon pret. pl. of grimman.

gruncian *to desire*, GPH 396.

grund m. 'GROUND,' *bottom* : *foundation* : *abyss, hell* : *plain, country, land, earth* : *sea, water*.

grundbedd n. *ground, soil*, Rd 81[24].

grundbūend† m. *earth-dweller*.

grunddēope *depths of the sea*, APs 64[8].

grunden pp. of grindan.

grundeswelge (i[3], u[3], v[3]) f. '*groundsel*,' Gl, Lcd.

grundfūs *hastening to hell*, Mod 49.

grundhyrde m. *keeper of the abyss*, B 2136.

grundinga=grundlinga

grundlēas *bottomless, unfathomable, Bo* : *boundless, vast*. ['*groundless*']

grundlēaslic *boundless, vast*, CP 417[10].

grundling m. *groundling* (*fish*), BC 3·525.

grundlinga (u[2]) adv. *from the foundation, completely*, Æ : *to the ground, prone, prostrate*, Æ.

grundon pret. pl. of grindan.

grundscēat† m. *region*, Cr.

grundsele m. *abysmal dwelling*, B 2139.

grundsopa '*cartilago*,' Gl (v. BTs).

grundstān m. *foundation-stone*, WW. ['*groundstone*']

+**grundstaðelian** *to establish firmly*, ÆL 8[21].

grundwæg m. *earth*, An 582.

grundwang† m. (*ground-plain*), *the earth*, B : *bottom* (*of a lake*).

grundweall m. *foundation*, Æ,Lk. ['*groundwall*']

+**grundweallian** *to establish, found*, EPs 23[2].

grundwela m. *earthly riches*, Gen 957.

grundwiergen (y) f. *water-wolf*, B 1518.

grunian, grunnian, *to grunt* (OEG) : *chew the cud?* Sc 54'.

grunnettan *to* '*grunt*,' Cp.

grun(n)ung f. *grunting, bellowing*, OEG.

grut m. *gulf, chasm, abyss* : *stone, rock*, OEG 1814.

grūt f. (ds. grȳt, grūt) *groats, coarse meal,* Cp,Ct,Lcd : *grains, the spent grain after brewing,* Lcd. ['*grout*']
grutt, grutte=grut; gryllan=grillan
grym=grim(m)
grymet-(t)an, -tian (e, i) *to grunt, roar, rage,* Æ.
grymet(t)ung f. *grunting, roaring, bellowing,* Æ.
grymm=grimm
grymman I. *to mourn, wail,* LPs 37⁹ (gyrm-). ['*yarm*'] II.=gremian
gryn=gyrn; grȳn=grīn
+grynd n. *plot of ground,* TC 231²².
gryndan I. *to set, sink (of the sun),* WW. ['*grind*'; grund] II. (+) *to found (of a house),* MtL 7²⁵ (wry-). III.=grindan
grynde n. *abyss,* Sat 331.
grynel (WW 291³)=cyrnel
grȳnian=grīnian
grynsmið m. *worker of ill,* An 919.
grȳpe (=ī) f. *ditch, drain,* OEG. [v. '*grip*']
gryre† m. *horror, terror* : *fierceness, violence,* DD 8 : *horrible thing.*
gryrebrōga† m. *terror, horror.*
gryrefæst *terribly firm,* El 76a.
gryrefāh† adj. (used as sb.) *spotted horror,* B.
gryregæst (æ)? m. *terrible stranger,* B 2560.
gryregeatwe fp. *war-gear,* B 324.
gryrehwīl f. *terrible time,* An 468.
gryrelēoð† n. *terrible song.*
gryrelic† *terrible, horrible,* B.
gryremiht f. *terrible power,* W 195²⁰.
gryresīð m. *dangerous expedition,* B 1462.
gryrran *to gnash,* DD 195.
grys-, grȳs-=gris-, grīs-
grȳt I. pres. 3 sg. of grēotan. II. v. grūt.
grȳtan *to flourish,* WW 240²⁹. [grēat]
grȳto f. *greatness,* AA 12⁷. [grēat]
grytt n. *dust, meal,* GL.
grytta, gryttan f. pl. *coarse meal, bran, chaff,* Ep,Lcd,WW. ['*grit*']
grytte f. *spider,* JLVPs 89⁹.
grȳttra (A 4·151)=*grietra cp. of grēat. ['*greater*']
gryð-=grið-; gū=gēo
guldon pret. pl. of gieldan.
gullisc? (an attribute of silver), Sol 150⁹.
gullon pret. pl. of giellan.
gulpon pret. pl. of gielpan.
guma† m. *man, lord, hero,* B. ['*gome*']
gumcynn† sn. *human race, men, nation.*
gumcyst† f. *excellence, bravery, virtue, liberality.* adv. -um *excellently.*
gumdrēam m. *enjoyment of life,* B 2469.
gumdryhten m. *lord,* B 1642.
gumfēða m. *troop,* B 1401.

gumfrēa m. *king,* Da 651.
-gumian v. ofer-g.
gummann m. *man,* B 1028.
gumrīce† n. *kingdom, earth.*
gumrinc† m. *man, warrior.*
gumstōl m. *ruler's seat, throne,* B 1952.
gumðegen m. *man,* Cra 83.
gumðēod f. *folk, people,* Gen 226.
gund m. *matter, pus,* Lcd. ['*gound*']
gundeswilge (Ep,Erf,Ln)=grundeswelge
gundig *goundy, mattery,* Erf.
gung=geong; gung-=ging-
gungon pret. pl. of gangan.
gunnon (BH) pret. pl. of ginnan.
gupan '*clunibus, renibus, coxe,*' WW 205⁴¹ (v. A 31·522).
gurron pret. pl. of gyrran.
guton pret. pl. of gēotan.
guttas mp. '*guts,*' *entrails,* HGl 408.
gūð† f. *combat, battle, war.*
gūðbeorn m. *fighting-hero,* B 314.
gūðbill† n. *battle-bill, sword.*
gūðbord† n. *war-shield,* Gen.
gūðbyrne f. *corslet, coat of mail,* B 321.
gūðcearu f. *war-trouble,* B 1258.
gūðcræft m. *war-craft,* B 127.
gūðcwēn† f. *warrior queen,* El.
gūðcyning† m. *warrior king,* B.
gūðcyst f. *troop, warrior band?* (Kluge) : *bravery?* (BT),Ex 343.
gūðdēað m. *death in battle,* B 2249.
gūðfana m. *gonfanon, war-banner, ensign, standard,* Æ,AO.
gūð-flā? f., -flān? mf. *battle-arrow,* Gen 2063.
gūðfloga m. *winged fighter,* B 2528.
gūðfona=gūðfana
gūðfrēa m. *warlike prince,* An 1335.
gūðfrec *bold in battle* (GK), *greedy for destruction* (BTs),An 1119.
gūðfreca† m. *warrior.*
gūðfremmend† m. *warrior.*
gūðfugol m. *bird of war, eagle,* Rd 25⁵.
gūðgeatwe† fp. *armour,* B.
gūðgelæca m. *warrior,* El 43.
gūðgemōt† n. *battle, combat.*
gūðgetāwe=gūðgeatwe
gūðgeðingu† np. *battle, contest,* An.
gūðgewæde† n. *war-dress, armour,* B.
gūðgeweorc† n. *warlike deed,* B.
gūðgewinn† n. *battle.*
gūðhafoc m. *war-hawk, eagle,* †Chr 937a.
gūðheard *bold in battle,* El 204.
gūðhelm m. *helmet,* B 2487.
gūðhere m. *warlike host, army,* Gen 1967.
gūðhorn m. *war-horn, trumpet,* B 1432.
gūðhrēð m. *martial glory,* B 819.
gūðhwæt *fierce in battle,* Ap 57.
gūðlēoð n. *war-song,* B 1522.

gūð-mæcga, -maga m. *warrior*, SOL90.
gūðmōdig? *of warlike mind*, B306.
Gūðmyrce pl. *Ethiopians*, EX69.
gūðplega† m. *attack, battle*.
gūðrǣs† m. *battle-rush, onslaught*, B.
gūðrēaf n. *armour*, JUL387.
gūðrēow *fierce in battle*, B58. [hrēow]
gūðrinc† m. *warrior, hero*.
gūðrōf† *brave in battle*.
gūðscearu f. *slaughter in battle*, B1213.
gūðsceaða m. *ravaging invader*, B2318.
gūðsceorp n. *armour*, JUD329.
gūðscrūd n. *armour*, EL258.
gūðsearo† n. *armour*.
gūðsele m. *hall of warriors*, B443.
gūðspell n. *tidings of a war*, GEN2097.
gūðsweord n. *sword*, B2154.
gūðöracu† f. *hostile attack*, GEN.
gūðörēat m. *warlike troop*, EX193.
gūðweard† m. *war-lord, king*.
gūðweorc n. *warlike deed*, AN1068.
gūðwērig *wounded*, B1586.
gūðwiga m. *warrior*, B2112.
gūðwine† m. *battle-friend, weapon*, B.
gūðwudu m. *spear*, FIN6.
gy-=ge-, gi-; gyc-=gic-; gyd=gid(d)
gyden (AO), gydenu f. (occl. gs. gydenan)
goddess. [god]
gydenlic *'vestalis'* (=dealis? A31·63), WW
524³³.
gydig (i) *possessed (by a spirit), insane*,
OEG5009. ['*giddy*']
gyf=gif; gyf-=geof-, gief-, gif-
gȳf-=gīf-
gyhða (Æ)=gicða; gyhðu—gehðu
gyld=gield; gyld-=gild-, gylt-
+gyld=gylden
±gyldan I. *to gild*, Ps,WW. ['*gilded*'] II.
(AO)=gieldan
±gylden *golden*, B,Dan; Æ,AO,CP. ['*gild-
en*']
gyldenbēag (i) m. *crown*, LEV8⁹.
gyldenbend *golden band*, LEVC8⁹.
gyldenfeax *golden-haired*, WW348³⁵.
gyldenhilte *golden-hilted*, BC3·74'.
gyldenhīwe *golden-hued*, OEG43⁵.
gyldenmūða *golden-mouthed* (*Chrysostom*),
GD94²⁴; ZDA31·7.
gyldenwecg (gylding-) m. *gold mine*, WW
241¹⁷.
gylece (IM127¹⁴)?=pylece
gylian, gyllan *to yell, shout*. gyliende
'*garrulus*,' OEG56¹³⁸.
gylm=gilm; gylp=gielp
gylt (e, i, ie) m. '*guilt,*' *sin, offence, crime,
fault*, Bf,Bl,Chr,Mt,Ps; AO,CP.
±gyltan *to commit sin, be guilty*, CP,Mt,RB,
VPs. ['*guilt*,' '*guilting*']
gyltend m. *sinner, debtor*, CP.

gyltig *offending*, '*guilty,*' *Mt*.
gylting (u¹) f. *sin*, DR.
gyltlic *sinful*, Mt26⁶⁵. adv. -līce *faultily*, Sc
35³.
gyltwīte n. (gyld-) *fine for unpaid tax*, KC
2·406 : *for a crime*, 6·240.
gylung? '*garrulitas,*' OEG56¹⁴¹.
gym=gimm; gym-=gim-
gȳm-=gīem-; gymian=gymmian
gymm=gimm
±gymmian *to cut the flesh*, OEG3799.
gyn-=geon-, gin-; gȳn-=gīn-
-gȳpe (=īe?) v. ǣ-g.
gypigend (=i) *yawning*, GPH398.
gypung (=i) f. *gaping, open mouth*, GPH
402.
gyr I. m. *filth, mud, marsh*. II. *fir tree*, WW
269¹⁴.
gyr-=geor-, gier-; gyra=gyr I.
±gyrdan (pret. gyrde), *to '*gird*'* (*sword*),
Gen,PPs : *encircle, surround*, JnL : (+)
invest with attributes, PPs.
gyrdel (e) m. '*girdle,*' *belt, zone*, Lcd,Mt;
Æ : *purse*.
gyrdelbred n. *writing-tablet*, WW277¹³.
gyrdelhring n. *girdle, buckle*, WW432.
gyrdels, gyrder=gyrdel; gyrdil-=gyrdel-
gȳren=grīn
gyrman=grymman
gyrn† mn. *sorrow, misfortune*.
gyrnstafas mp. *injury, affliction*, JUL245.
gyrnwracu† f. *revenge for injury*.
gyrran³ [=gierran, georran] *to sound, chatter*,
Æ : *grunt : to creak,grate*,An,OEG. ['*yerr*']
gyrretan *to roar (of lions)*, LPs.
gyrsandæg (MFH97)=gierstandæg
gyrst *gnashing of teeth, anger*, HGl513.
[v. '*grist*' and OEG4605n]
gyrstandæg (Æ)=gierstandæg
gyrtrēow n. *fir-tree*, WW138¹¹.
gyru I. (?) *muddy*, KC3·412. II. f.=gyr
gyrwan=gierwian
gyrwefenn n. *marsh*, ÆGR60¹⁰.
gȳse=gēse; gȳsel=gīsl
gyst=(1) giest, (2) gist
gyst-=giest-
gysternlicdæg=gierstandæg
gyt=git pron.
gȳt I. pres. 3 sg. of gēotan. II.=giet
gȳt-=gīet-, gīt-
gyte, gytt (NG) m. *pouring forth, shedding*,
Æ : *flood*, Æ. [gēotan]
gytesǣl m. (dp. gytesālum) *joy at wine-
pouring, carousal*, JUD22.
gytestrēam m. *running stream*, WW.
gytfeorm f. *ploughing-feast*, LL452,21⁴.
gyð-=gi ð-; gȳu=gēo

H

h is often wrongly prefixed to words, or (conversely) dropped, as in Cockney English.

hā m. *oar-thole, rowlock.* æt hā *for each oar,* or *each oarsman,* CHR 1040 c. [*Icel.* hār]

habban anv. ptc. pres. hæbbende; pres. 1 sg. hæbbe, 2. hæfst, 3. hæfð, pl. hæbbað, habbað; pret. 3 sg. hæfde; subj. hæbbe; imperat. hafa; pp. (±)hæf(e)d *to* 'HAVE*,' AO,CP : *possess, own, hold,* AO,CP : *keep, retain* : *entertain, cherish* : *look after, carry on* : *esteem, consider,* AO,CP : *be subject to, experience* : *get, obtain,* Chr : *assert* : used as auxiliary to indicate past tense, *have,* Æ,Chr. h. for *consider* : (+) *hold, keep from, restrain, preserve,* Æ,CP. yfle +h. *afflict, torment.*

haca m. *hook, door-fastening,* Cp311 P (v. BTs).

-haccian v. tō-h.

hacele (æ) f. *cloak, coat, vestment, cassock,* '*pallium,*' AO,WW; Æ. ['*hackle*']

hacod (æ, e) m. *pike, mullet,* Cp,Ep,WW. ['*haked*']

hacole, hacule=hacele

hād m. (rare gs. hāda) *person, individual, character, individuality,* Æ,BH,Mt : *degree, rank, order, office* (*especially holy office*), Æ,BH,CP : *condition, state, nature, character, form, manner,* B,Sol : *sex,* BH, Chr : *race, family, tribe* : *choir.* ['*had*']

-hād masc. suffix; usu. denotes state or condition, as cildhād, mægðhād. [*Eng.* -hood]

+hada m. *brother monk,* LL.

hādārung f. *respect of persons,* LL474,18.

hādbōt f. *compensation for injury or insult to a priest,* LL. ['*hadbot*']

hādbreca m. *injurer of one in* (*holy*) *orders,* LL.

hād-bryce, -brice m. *injury of one in* (*holy*) *orders,* LL.

hādelīce adv. *as to persons,* DHy 29⁶.

hādesmann m. *member of a particular order,* CHR 995 F.

hādgrið n. *privilege* (*as regards peace*) *of holy orders,* LL471,19.

±hādian *to ordain, consecrate,* BH,Chr; Æ. ['*hade*']

hādnotu f. *office of a priest,* LL458H.

hādor I. n. *clearness, brightness,* B414 (or ? hador,=heaðor). **II.†** (ǣ) *bright, clear, fresh* : *distinct, loud.* [*Ger.* heiter] adv. hādre.

hādswǣpa m. *bridesman,* WW174³⁵.

hādswǣpe (ā) f. *bridesmaid,* WW.

hādung f. *consecration, ordination, LL.* [v. '*hade*'] hādunge underfōn *to take the veil.*

hādungdæg (i²) m. *ordination day,* ÆL 33⁵⁹.

hæb, hæb- (GL)=hæf, hæf-

hæbb-=habb-, hebb-

hæbbednes f. *continence,* BF124²⁵.

hæbbendlic '*habilis,*' ÆGR54⁵.

-hæbbere v. sulh-h.

hæbbung (e²) f. *constraint,* WW372,503.

hæc-=hac-

hæc(c) I. fm. *grating,* '*hatch,*' *half-gate, Ct.* **II.**=hæcce I.

+hæcca *sausage,* WW411²⁰. [haccian]

hæcce I. fn. *crozier.* **II.** (e) *fence,* BC 3·147′. **III.**=hæc

hæccelēas *without a fence? or hatch?* EC389′.

hæcgeat (e²) n. *hatch-gate,* KC5·376¹⁴.

hæcine (a) f. *a thin vinous drink,* '*posca,*' WW129³ (v. A8·451 and Ducange, s.v.).

hæcwer m. *hatch-weir, a weir in which fish were caught,* KC3·450.

hædor=hādor

hædre† *straitly, anxiously,* SOL.

hædre=hādre

hæf I.† n. (heaf-, haf- in obl. cases) *sea, ocean,* WW. **II.** m. *leaven,* OEG.

hæfd=hēafod

hæfde pret. sg. of habban.

hæfe I. m. *leaven,* Sc. [*Ger.* hefe] **II.**= hefe I.

hæfed=hēafod

-hæfednes v. be-, for-h.

hæfegītsung? f. *covetousness,* EPs 118³⁶.

hæfen I. f. *the having, owning* : *property, possessions,* Æ. [*Ger.* habe] **II.** f. '*haven,*' *port, Chr.* **III.**=hefen. **IV.** pp. of hebban.

hæfen-=hafen-; **hæfenblǣte**=hæferblǣte

hæfene=hæfen II.

hæfer (e) m. *he-goat,* WW.

hæferbīte m. *forceps,* WW198¹⁶. [v. hæfern]

hæferblǣte f? *bittern? snipe?* WW116⁴¹; 361¹⁷.

hæfergāt=hæfer

hæfern m. *crab,* WW.

hæfig=hefig; **hæfne**=hæfen

hæfreblēte=hæferblǣte; **hæfst** v. habban.

±hæft I. m. *bond, fetter* : *captive, slave, servant* : *bondage, imprisonment, affliction,* Æ : (±) *seizing, thing seized,* CLPs123⁶. **II.** adj. *captive.* **III.** n. '*haft,*' *handle,* Lcd, WW; Æ. **IV.** pp. of hæftan.

±hæftan *to bind, fetter* : *arrest, detain, imprison* : *condemn,* DR197¹³. [*Ger.* heften]

hæfte=hæft II.

hæfteclomm m. *fetter,* †CHR942A.

+hæftednes f. *captivity* : *snare,* Ps.

hæftedōm m. *slavery, captivity,* MET25⁶⁵.

hæften f. *confinement,* CHR1095.

+hæftend m. *prisoner,* MFH136.

hæftenēod=hæftnīed

hæftincel (e²) n. *slave*, WW.

hæfting f. *fastening, lock*, Nic502²⁵.

hæftlic *captious*, OEG3208.

hæftling m. *prisoner, captive*, Æ.

hæftmēce m. *hilted sword*, B1457.

±**hæftnes** (RWH22²⁰, v. also MFH165)= hæftednes

hæftneð=hæftnoð

±**hæftnian** *to take prisoner : seize, detain.*

hæftnīed (ē, ȳ) f. *custody, imprisonment, bondage.* Æ,AO.

±**hæftnīedan** *to take captive*, GD135¹⁵.

hæftnīedling (ē², y²) m. *captive*, ÆL.

hæftnīednes (ē², ȳ²) f. *captivity*, GD346²², NC299.

hæftnoð (e²) m. *confinement, imprisonment*, CHR.

hæftnung f. *confinement, captivity*, Æ,CHR.

hæftnȳd (Æ)=hæftnīed

hæftung f. *fetter*, MFH166.

hæftworld f. *world under bondage*, BL9⁴.

hæfð pres. 3 sg. of habban.

hæfuc=hafoc; **hæg-**=hago-, hagu-, hege- +hæg n. *enclosure, meadow*, OEG; Mdf.

+**hǣgan?** *to vex, harass?* Ex169 (GK). or ?=+hnǣgan (BTs).

hæghāl *safe and sound*, DR.

hægsugga m. *hedge-sparrow*, ZDA33·241.

hæg-tes(se), -tis f. *fury, witch, pythoness*, Æ,GL.

hægðorn (Æ)=haguðorn

hægweard m. *keeper of cattle in a common field*, LL452,20.

hæh-=hēah-; **hæhtis**=hægtes

hǣl I. n. *omen*, B204,WW36². II.=hǣlu. III. adj.=hāl

hæl-; **hǣl-**=hel-; hāl-, hēl-

hǣlan I. (±) *to 'heal,' cure, save*, Lcd,Mt,Ps; Æ,CP : *greet, salute*, GD36²⁷. +hǣl! *Hosanna!* [hāl] II. *to castrate*, LcD3·186²²: (+) ÆP106⁶.

+**hǣld**=+hield

hæleᵗ m. *man, hero.*

hǣle n.=hǣlu

±**hǣle** *safe*, SPs7¹¹.

+**hǣled**=hāl

+**hǣlednes** f. *healing*, GD247¹¹.

hǣlend (ē) m. *Saviour, Christ*, Æ,G. ['heal-end']

hǣlendlic *wholesome, salutary*, OEG153⁸.

hǣlet-=hālet-

hæleðᵗ m. (nap. hæleðas, hæleð) *man, hero, fighter*, B. ['heleth']

hæleðhelm=heoloðhelm

hælf-ter, f. -tre, m. *'halter,'* WW.

hǣlgere (a²) m. *sanctifier*, DR.

hǣlhiht=healhiht

hǣlig *unstable, inconstant*, Bo115³.

hǣling f. *'healing,'* Nic.

hælm=healm

hǣlnes f. *salvation, safety*, CP : *sanctuary.* ['healness']

hǣlnesgrið n. *peace-privileges attaching to a sanctuary*, LL471,19.

hǣlotīd f. *prosperous time*, CHR1065D.

hǣls-=hāls-

hǣlð, hǣlðo f. *'health,'* Æ : *salvation*, Lcd; Æ : *healing*, Æ.

hǣlu f. *health*, Cr,Lcd : *prosperity*, MtL : *safety, salvation*, KC,Lk; Æ,CP : *healing, cure.* ['heal']

hǣlubearnᵗ n. *Saviour, Christ*, CR.

hǣlwyrt f. *'pulegium,' pennyroyal*, WW300²⁴.

hǣlynd=hǣlend

hǣmæht (MkR1²²)=hēahmiht

±**hǣman** *to have intercourse with, cohabit with*, Æ,CP : *marry*, MtR.

hǣmed (ē) n. (nap. hǣmedru) *cohabitation*, Æ,CP : *marriage : adultery, fornication*, WW420¹⁰.

hǣmedceorl m. *married man*, LL.

hǣmedgemāna m. *matrimony*, WW441²⁴.

hǣmedlāc n. *coition*, RD43³.

hǣmedrīm m. *'lenocinium,'* OEG5046. [=-drēam]

hǣmedru v. hǣmed.

hǣmedscipe m. *cohabitation, wedlock*, OEG.

hǣmedðing n. *coition, cohabitation*, ÆL : *marriage.*

hǣmedwīf n. *married woman*, WW450²⁴.

hǣmend m. *fornicator*, WW420¹³.

hǣmere m. *consort, bedfellow*, Æ.

hǣmet, hǣmeð=hǣmed; **hæn**=henn

hǣnan I. *to stone*, Jn; Æ. ['heno'] II.= hīenan

hænep (e) m. *'hemp,'* Lcd,WW.

hænfugel=hennfugol; **hænn**=henn

hǣnðu=hīenðo

+**hæp**, +hæplic (GL) *fit, convenient.*

+**hæplicnes** (e) f. *convenience, opportunity*, OET122⁶.

hæppan? *to go by chance*, ÆL31⁴⁷⁷.

hæpse f. *'hasp,' fastening*, Æ.

hæpsian *to 'hasp,' fasten*, Æ.

hæpte (pret. 3 sg.) *jumped*, ÆL31⁴⁷⁷.

hǣr (ā, ē) n. *'hair,'* Lcd,Mk; Æ : *a hair*, Æ, Cp,Mk.

hær-=har-, hear-, her(e)-; **hǣr-**=hēr-

hǣre (ē) f. *sackcloth of hair*, Mt,VPs; Æ. ['haire']

+**hǣre** *hairy*, AA33³.

hǣren *of hair*, Bl,Lcd. ['hairen']

hærenfagol sb. *hedgehog*, SPs103¹⁹ (v. BTs).

hærfest (e) m. *autumn, 'harvest'-time*, Bf, Ct,WW; AO : *August*, A10·185. h. hand-ful *handful of corn* (*a due belonging to the husbandman on an estate*), LL450.

hærfestlic *autumnal* : *of harvest,* Æ (108¹⁹⁸).

Hærfestmōnað m. '*harvest-month,' September,* ÆGr 43⁸.

hærfest-tīd (BH) f., -tīma (BF) m. *autumn, harvest-time.*

hærfestwǣta m. *autumn rain,* AO 102⁷.

hǣrgripa (ē) m. *seizing by the hair,* LL 611.

hǣriht *hairy,* WW 513⁸.

hǣring (ē) m. '*herring,' Gl,WW* ; Æ.

hǣringtīma m. *herring season,* Ct.

hǣrloccas mp. *locks of hair, HGl.* ['*hairlock*']

hærmberg (N)=hearmbeorg

hærn I. f. *wave, tide* : (†) *sea, ocean.* II. *brain,* CHR 1137.

hǣrnǣdl f. *curling-pin,* OEG 1200.

hærnflota m. *ship,* Gu 1307.

hærsceard n. *hare-lip,* LCD.

hǣrsyfe (ē) n. '*hair-sieve,' A* 9·264.

hǣs f. '*hest,' bidding, behest, command, Æ, Gen.* [hātan]

hæsel m. '*hazel' shrub, Gl,Lcd* ; Æ; Mdf.

hæselhnutu (a¹) f. '*hazel-nut,' Gl,WW.*

hæselræw f. *a row of hazels,* EC 445¹⁹.

hæselwrīd m. *hazel-thicket,* KC 2·250'.

hǣsere m. *master, lord,* LkLR.

hæsl=hæsel

hæslen *of hazel,* Lcd. ['*hazelen*']

hæsp=hæpse ; **hæssuc**=hassuc

hǣst† I. *violent, vehement.* adv. hæst-e, -līce. II. (ē) f. *violence, strife.*

hǣswalwe (WW 7²⁸)=sǣswealwe?

hæt m. *head-covering, 'hat,' Cp,AO* ; Æ.

hǣt pres. 3 sg. of hātan.

±hǣtan (ā) tr. *to 'heat*,' Lcd,Shr* : intr. *become hot, Gl.*

hǣtcole=hǣðcole

hǣte f. *heat,* Æ,AO. [hāt]

hæteru np. *garments,* ÆH. ['*hater*']

hǣting f. *heating,* WW 281⁸.

hǣto=hǣtu ; **hǣts** (ÆL 18³⁵⁰)=hægtes

hǣtst pres. 2 sg. of hātan.

hætt=hæt ; **hǣtte**=hātte, v. hātan.

hættan=hettan

hættian I. (e) *to scalp,* LL 334,30⁵. II.= hatian

hǣtu (o², e²) f. '*heat,' warmth, Bl,Lcd,Mt, VPs;* Æ : *fervour, ardour, VHy.*

hǣð I. mn. '*heath,' untilled land, waste, Ex;* Mdf : *heather, Gl,Lcd.* II. f. (WW 317²⁴)= hǣða

hǣða m. *heat, hot weather* ÆL 14¹⁶⁸.

hǣðberie f. *whortleberry,* LCD.

hǣðcole f. *name of a plant,* WW.

hǣðen I. (ē) '*heathen,' heathenish, pagan,* Æ,Bl,Ct ; AO,CP. II. m. *gentile, heathen man (especially of the Danes),* Æ,Mk.

hǣðena m. *heathen,* LkR 21²⁵.

hǣðencyning m. *heathen king,* DA 54.

hǣðencynn n. *heathen race,* GEN 2546.

hǣðendōm m. '*heathendom,' false religion, LL.*

hǣðenfeoh n. *heathen sacrifice?* JUL 53.

hǣðenfolc n. *heathen people,* W 223¹².

hǣðengield (i³, y³) n. *idolatry,* Æ : *idol,* Æ.

hǣðengilda (y³) m. *idolater,* Æ.

hǣðenhere m. *Danish army,* CHR.

hǣðenisc '*heathenish,' pagan, AO.*

hǣðennes f. *heathenism, paganism, BH* : *heathen country,* OET 175⁷. ['*heathenesse*']

hǣðenscipe (ē) m. *paganism, idolatry, Æ, Chr.* ['*heathenship*']

hǣðenstyrc m. *heathen calf (the golden calf of the Israelites),* PPs 105¹⁷.

hǣðfeld m. *heath-land,* Bo,Ct.

hǣðiht *heathy,* KC.

hǣðin-=hǣðen-

hǣðstapa† m. *heath-stalker, wolf, stag.* [stæppan]

hǣðung f. *heating, parching,* ÆH 1·286. [=hǣtung]

hǣwe *iron-coloured, bluish, grey,* GL.

hǣwen (ē) *blue, purple, azure, green, Gl.* ['*haw*']

hǣwengrēne *cerulean,* WW 379²³.

hǣwenhydele f. *a plant,* LCD.

hafa, imperat. of habban ; hafast, hafað= hæfst, hæfð pres. 2 and 3 sg. of habban.

-hafa v. wan-h ; **hafala**=hafela

hafastu=hafast ðu

hafecere=hafocere

hafela† (ea¹, o², u²) m. *head,* LCD.

hafelēst=hafenlēast

hafen pp. of hebban.

hafenian† *to hold, grasp.* [hebban]

hafenlēas *destitute, needy, poor,* Æ,WW. ['*haveless*'; hæfen]

hafenlēast f. *want, poverty,* ÆH.

hāfern=hæfern

hafetian (i²) *to clap, flap,* Æ.

hafoc (ea) m. '*hawk,' Gl,Wy.*

hafoccynn n. *hawk-tribe,* Æ.

hafocere m. '*hawker,' LL;* WW 235⁹,ÆP 140²⁴.

hafocfugel m. *hawk,* LL (162¹⁹).

hafocung f. *hawking,* BC 1·280'.

hafocwyrt f. *a plant,* LCD.

hafola=hafela ; **-hafol(nes)** v. wan-h.

hafuc=hafoc

hafudland (WW 147¹⁸)=hēafodland

haga I. m. *hedge, enclosure, curtilage, WW;* Mdf : *fortified enclosure, B* : *homestead, house,* KC 4·86' : *game-enclosure?* GBG. ['*haw*'] II. m. '*haw,' WW* 204²⁰ : *trifle,* WW 138³⁹ ; 269⁵.

hagal=hagol

hagaðorn=haguðorn ; **hage-**=hago-

+**hagian** (impers.) *to please, suit.* gif him (hine) tō ðǣm +hagige *if he can afford it.*

hago- v. also *hæg-.*

hagol (æ[1], e[1], a[2], e[2]) mn. '*hail,' Æ,Gen,Met, Ph,VPs : hail-shower, hailstorm, Bo : name of the rune for* h.

hagolfaru (hægl-) f. *hailstorm,* WA105.

hagolian (a[2]) *to 'hail,' AO*104[20].

hagolscūr (æ[1], e[2]) m. *hail-shower, An;* MEN 35. [v. '*hail'*]

hagolstān m. '*hailstone,' Æ.*

hagorūn (ea) f. *spell,* NAR50[14].

hagospind (ea) n. *cheek,* GL,LCD. [haga]

hagosteald I. (hæg-, heh-) *unmarried, independent : military* (of young men). II. m. *unmarried man attached to a court, bachelor, young man, young warrior, liege man.* [*Ger.* hagestolz] III. n. *celibacy,* RD21[31]. IV. (heh-) *virgin,* LL,NG.

hagostealdhād (hægst-) m. *unmarried state,* NG.

hagostealdlic (heh-) *virgin,* DR66[1].

hagostealdman (hægst-) m. *bachelor, warrior,* GL,RD.

hagostealdnes (heh-) f. *virginity,* Jnp13.

hagu-=hago-

haguðorn (æ[1]) m. '*hawthorn,' whitethorn, Gl,Mt,Lcd.*

ha ha interj. '*ha! ha!' ÆGr.*

hal=heal; **hal-**=heal(h)-; **hāl-**=hæl-

±**hāl** '*hale,' 'whole'* ('*y-hole'), entire, uninjured, healthy, well, sound, safe, genuine, straightforward, Lcd,Mt;* Æ,CP. wes ðu h., h. westu, h. bēo ðu *hail!*

hala I. m. *after-birth,* LCD. [helan (IF 48·256)] II. (+) (o) m. *counsellor, confidant, supporter,* ÆL23[290],WW110[21].

hālbǣre *wholesome, salutary,* Sc32[78].

halc (OET489)=healh

hald-=heald-

hāleg, hāleg-=hālig, hālg-

±**hālettan** (ǣ) *to greet, hail, salute,* GD.

hālettend m. *middle finger (used in saluting),* WW.

hālettung f. *greeting, salutation,* BL.

hālfæst *pious? healthy?* RB72[6].

hālga I. wk. form of adj. hālig. II. m. *saint, Æ,Ct.* ['*hallow'*]

hālgawaras=hāligwaras

±**hālgian** *to 'hallow,' sanctify, Æ,Jn : consecrate, dedicate, ordain, BH,Bl,Chr;* Æ : *reverence,* †*Hy,Mt* : *keep holy, Bl.*

+**hālgigend** m. *sanctifier,* DHy64[2].

±**hālgung** (ǣ) f. '*hallowing,' consecration, BH : sanctuary,* EPs73[7].

hālgungbōc f. *benedictional,* NC299.

hālgungram m. *consecrated ram,* Ex29[22].

hāli-=hālig-

hālig '*holy,' consecrated, sacred, Bf,Lk : venerated, Æ,G,VPs : godly, saintly, CP, MkL* : *ecclesiastical* : *pacific, tame,* GEN 201. as sb. *what is holy, MtL.*

±**hāligan** I. *to heal up, get well, CP* : *save* : *be saved.* II.=hālgian

hāligdæg m. *holy day, Sabbath, MkL,LL.* ['*holiday'*]

hāligdōm m. *holiness, righteousness, sanctity, Æ; CP* : *holy place, sanctuary, chapel, Æ* : *relics, holy things, LL* : *holy office, CP*51[1] : *sacrament* : *holy doctrines, CP* 383[7]. ['*halidom'*]

hāligdōmhūs m. '*sacrarium,' CM818.

hāligern n. *holy place, sanctuary* : *sacrament.*

hāliglīce *holily,* CHRD117[4].

Hāligmōnað m. (*holy month*), *September,* MH.

hālignes f. '*holiness,' sanctity, religion, Bl, Ps; Æ* : *holy place, sanctuary, CP,W* : *holy thing, relic* : *sacred rites,* BH136[24].

hāligportic m. *sanctuary,* CJVPs.

hālig-rift, -ryft, -reft n. *veil, Æ.*

hāligwæcca m. *vigil-keeper,* LL(224').

hāligwæter n. '*holy water,' BH.*

hālig-waras, -ware mp. *saints,* N.

hāligweorc n. *sanctuary,* APs73[7].

halm=healm

hālnes f. '*wholeness,' ANS.*

hālor† n? *salvation,* JUL. [hǣl]

hālp=healp pret. 3 sg. of helpan.

hals-=heals-

hāls f. *salvation,* CR587?

hālsere (ǣ) m. *soothsayer, augur, Cp.*

halsgang (WW190[32])=healsgund

±**halsian** (ǣ, ea) *to adjure, Mt* : (+) *take oath, swear, Nic* : *call upon, VPs* : *convoke* : *implore, entreat, CP,OET* : *augur, WW* : *exorcise, LL.* [v. '*halse'* and healsian]

hālsi(g)end m. *exorcist, soothsayer, augur, Æ.*

halstān=healstān

hālsung f. *exorcism, LL, OET* : *augury, divination* : *entreaty,Bl,VPs.* [v.'*halsing'*]

hālsunggebed n. *prayer in a church service,* RBL39[6].

hālsungtīma m. *time of supplication,* CHRD 30[2].

hālswurðung f. *thanksgiving for safety,* Ex581. [hāls]

halt=healt; **halð**=heald II.

hālwenda m. *Saviour, Æ* : *safety* RBL12[13].

hālwende *healing, healthful, salutary, Æ, CP* : *sanctifying, Æ.*

hālwendlic *salutary, wholesome.* adv. -līce, Æ,CP.

hālwendnes f. *salubrity,* BH28[30] : *salvation,* LPs.

hālwynde=hālwende

ham I. m? *under-garment* ('*subucula*,' OEG), *WW*. ['*hame*'] II.=hamm

hām I. m. ds. hām *village, hamlet, manor, estate, Æ,BH,Chr,LG* : '*home,*' *dwelling, house, BH,Ct,G,LL* : *region, country,* AO. II. adv. '*home,*' *homewards, Chr,Jn*; Æ. III. '*cauterium,*' A 30·258; 33·390.

hama m. *covering, dress, garment* : *womb,* '*puerperium,*' v. OEG : *slough of a snake,* NC 299.

hāma m. *cricket,* WW.

hamacgian=āmagian? (or +m.)

hāmcūð *familiar,* MtKp 11[1].

hāmcyme m. *home-coming, return,* Æ. ['*homecome*']

hamel? *rugged,* KC.

hamela=hamola

hamele f. *rowlock* (only in phr. æt ǣlcre hamelan *for every oar,* i.e. *rower,* CHR 1039 E). [*ON*. hamla; v. also hā]

hamelian *to hamstring, mutilate, Chr.* ['*hamble*']

hamer=hamor; **-hamer** v. clod-h.

±**hāmettan** *to domicile,* Ct,LL : *bring debtors back to their home,* CHRD 116[1].

hāmfǣrelt n. *going home,* AO 146[21].

hāmfǣst *resident, settled in or owning a house,* Æ.

hāmfaru f. *attack of an enemy in his house, housebreaking* : *fine for housebreaking.* [v. LL 2·504]

hāmhenn f. *domestic fowl,* LCD 92a.

+**hāmian** *to establish in a home,* JnL p 188[7].

hamland (o[1]) n. *enclosed pasture,* EC 208[11]. [hamm]

hāmlēas *homeless,* RD 40[9].

hamm I. m. *piece of pasture-land, enclosure, dwelling, Ct;* ÆL; Mdf. ['*ham*'] II. f. '*ham*' (*part of leg*), *Lcd,WW;* Æ.

+**hammen** *patched?* (of shoes), GD 37[13].

-hamod v. +fiðer-h.

hamola (o[1]) *man with cropped hair.* tō hamolan *besciran to shave the hair off* (*as insult*), LL 68,35[3].

hamor (o[1], e[2]) m. '*hammer,*' *Jul,WW.*

hamorian (amer-) *to beat out, forge,* GPH 396.

hamorsecg m. *hammer-sedge,* LCD.

hamorwyrt f. *black hellebore, wall-pellitory, Lcd* 1·374; WW 300[22]. ['*hammerwort*']

hāmscīr f. *aedileship,* GL.

-hāmscyld v. riht-h.

hāmsittende *living at home,* LL.

hāmsīð m. *return home,* HL 10[273].

hāmsīðian *to return home,* WW 118[18].

hāmsōcn f. *offence of attacking a man in his own house, LL* : *the franchise of holding pleas of this offence and receiving the penal-*

ties for it : *the penalty itself, Ct.* ['*hamesucken*']

hāmsteall m. *homestead, Ct.* ['*homestall*']

hāmstede m. '*homestead,*' *Ct.*

hamule (CHR 1039 E)=hamele

hamur=hamor

hāmweard *homewards, towards home, on the way home, Chr;* Æ,AO. ['*homeward*']

hāmweardes adv. '*homewards,*' *Chr.*

hāmweorðung f. *ornament of a home,* B 2998.

hāmwerd (Æ)=hāmweard

hāmwerod (eo[2], u[3]) n. *household,* BH 191[22].

hāmwyrt f. *house-leek, Lcd.* ['*homewort*']

hān I. f. (*boundary-*)*stone, BC.* ['*hone*'] II.?=hā

hana m. *cock,* Æ. [*Ger.* hahn]

hanasang m. *cock-crow,* MH 4[16].

hancrēd (ǣ) m. *cock-crow,* Æ. [crāwan]

hancrēdtīd (o[1]) f. *time of cock-crow,* WW 413[35].

hand I. (o) f. (gds. handa) '*hand*,*' *Jn,VPs, WW;* Æ,AO,CP : *side* (*in defining position*), *Æ* : *power, control, possession, charge, Ps,RB* : *agency, Ps,VPs* : *person regarded as holder or receiver of something.* brād h. *palm.* on h. gān *to yield.* swīðre, winstre h. *right, left, hand.* on gehwæðere h. *on both sides.* on h. āgiefan, tō handa lǣtan *to hand over* (*to*). on handa sellan, *to give a pledge, promise, bargain.* tō handa *healdan hold* (*land*) *of another.* wel on h. *favourably.* II. adv. *exactly,* RBL.

handæx f. '*dextralis,*' *a kind of axe,* WW 221[22].

handbæftian (ea[2], a[3]) *to lament,* NG.

handbana† m. *slayer by hand,* B.

handbelle f. '*hand-bell,*' *Ct.*

handbōc f. '*handbook,*' *manual, Bf,LL,WW.*

handbona=handbana

handbred n. *palm of the hand, breadth of the hand, span,* WW 158[11]; ÆL. ['*handbrede*']

handclāð n. *towel,* Æ. ['*handcloth*']

handcops m. *handcuff, manacle, CPs,WW.* [v. '*cops*']

handcræft m. *manual skill, power of the hand, handicraft,* Æ,LL. ['*handcraft*']

handcwyrn f. *hand-mill,* ANS,JUD 16[21]. [cweorn]

handdǣda m. *doer with his own hand,* LL.

handele=handle

+**handfæstan** *to betroth,* RWH 135[14].

handfæstnung (e[2]) f. *joining hands in confirmation of a pledge,* WW.

handfang-=infang-

handful nf. '*handful,*' *Ep,LPs.*

handgang m. *submission, surrender,* GL.

handgemaca m. *companion,* ÆL 23[421].

handgemōt† n. *battle,* B

handgesceaft f. *handiwork,* GEN455.
handgesella (o¹) m. *companion,* B1481.
handgesteallа† m. *companion,* B.
handgeswing n. *blow, stroke,* EL115.
handgeweald n. *power, possession,* PPs 105³⁰.
handgeweorc n. '*handiwork,*' *creation, Æ, Ps.*
handgewinn n. *manual labour, work,* BH, HL : (†) *struggle, contest.*
handgewrit n. *handwriting, autograph, holograph, agreement, deed.*
handgewriðen *hand-woven,* B1937. [wrīðan]
handgift f. *wedding present,* †Hy10¹⁸.
handgong=handgang
handgripe m. '*hand-grip,*' B965?
handgrið n. *security, peace, protection given by the king's hand,* LL (v. 2·494). ['*handgrith*']
handhabbend *red-handed (thief),* LL172,6. ['*handhabbend*']
handhæf n. *burden,* LkL11⁴⁶.
handhamur m. '*hand-hammer,*' WW448².
handhrægl n. *napkin, towel,* WW127¹.
handhrine m. *touch,* AN1022.
handhwīl f. *instant, Æ.* ['*handwhile*']
handle f. '*handle,*' Cp,WW.
handlēan† n. *requital, recompense.*
handleng(u) f. *a hand's length,* IM124⁷⁴.
±handlian *to '*handle,*' feel, Æ,Lcd* : *deal with, discuss,* Bf56,72.
handlīn n. *hand-cloth, napkin* : *maniple,* WW124³⁴.
handlinga adv. *by hand,* ÆL11²⁴⁷ : *hand to hand, at close quarters, Æ.* ['*handlings*']
handlocen† *joined together by hand,* B.
handlung f. '*handling,*' Æ.
handmægen† n. *bodily strength.*
handmitta=anmitta
handnægl m. *finger-nail,* LCD125a.
handplega† m. *fight, battle.*
handprēost m. *domestic chaplain, Æ.*
handrǣs m. *onrush, attack,* B2072.
handrōf *famed for strength,* EX247.
handscalu=handscolu
handscolu† f. *retinue,* B.
handscyldig *condemned to lose a hand,* LL 471,13¹.
handseald *given personally (by the king),* LL 637,12.
handseax (e²) n. *dirk, dagger, Æ,*BH.
handselen '*mancipatio,*' WW449²⁹.
handseten f. *signature, ratification,* Ct.
handsex=handseax; handslyht=andslyht
handsmæll m. *blow with the hand,* '*alapa,*' JnLR19³.
handspitel m. *hand-shovel, spade,* WW241⁴⁵.
handsporu f. *claw, finger,* B986.

handstoc n. *cuff, sleeve,* v. ES38·352.
handswyle m. *swelling on the hand,* WW 205¹⁰.
handtam *submissive to handling,* ÆL8⁸⁶. [v. '*hand-tame*']
handðegn m. *retainer, servant,* BH.
handðwēal n. *washing of the hands,* WW 146⁹.
handweorc n. *handiwork,* Rd,LL. ['*handwork*']
handworht *made with hands,* Mk14⁵⁸.
handwundor n. *marvel of handiwork,* B 2768.
handwyrm (o) m. *a kind of insect,* Cp,WW. ['*handworm*']
handwyrst f. *wrist,* WW. ['*handwrist*']
-hanga v. līc-h.
+hange (o) *disposed, inclined to,* RIM42.
+hangelle f. *a hanging object,* '*mentula*'? RD 45⁶.
hangen pp. of hōn.
hangian (±) (intr.) *to* '*hang**,' *be hanged, Æ, B,El,G;* CP : *depend, rest on, Æ* : (tr.) *hang, suspend, Æ,Chr,G,Lcd.*
hangra m. '*hanger,*' *wooded slope,* KC; Mdf.
hangrǣd? (ES39·348)=hancrēd
hangwīte? n. *penalty for miscarriage of justice,* EC. [v. '*hangwite*']
hār I. '*hoar,*' *An* : *hoary, grey, old, B,Ct, Jud,Met,Wa.* II.=hǣr
hara m. '*hare,*' *Ep; Æ.*
haranhige *hare's foot (plant),* LCD.
haransprecel *viper's bugloss,* LCD57b,WW 299⁶.
hāranwyrt=hārewyrt
harasteorra m. *dogstar,* WW198³⁴.
hara ð, harad m. *wood* (only in place-names, FTP76)
hard—heard; hārehūne=hārhūne
hāre-wyrt, hāran- (LCD) f. *a plant,* '*colocasia,*' WW135⁵.
hārhūne f. *horehound,* LCD.
hārian *to become hoary or grey, Æ,Shr.* ['*hoar*']
hārnes f. *hoariness,* WW. ['*hoarness*']
hārung f. *hoariness, old age,* ÆGR295¹⁴.
hārwelle, hārwenge (Æ) *hoary, grey-haired.*
hārwengnes f. *hoariness, old age,* WW198³¹.
hās '*hoarse,*' *ÆGr,WW.*
hāsæta m. *oarsman, rower,* CHR1052E. [hā]
hasewa=haswa wk. form of hasu.
hāshrīman (ȳ²) *to sound harshly,* GUTH 128¹²⁷.
hāsian *to be or become* '*hoarse,*' *ÆGr*190¹⁰.
haslhnutu (WW)=hæselhnutu
hāsnes f. '*hoarseness,*' *WW; Æ.*
hassuc m. *coarse grass,* KC. ['*hassock*']
hāsswēge *sounding hoarsely,* GPH391.
hasu† (ea) *dusky, grey, ashen.*

hasufāg *grey, ashen*, RD 12¹.

hasupād *grey-coated*, †CHR 937.

haswigfeðre *grey-feathered*, PH 153.

hāt I. '*hot*,' *flaming, Gu,Lcd*; Æ,AO,CP : *fervent, excited, Bl* : *intense, violent, An, Gu,Ph* : *inspiring? attractive?* SEAF 64. II. n. *heat, fire.* III. (±) n. *promise, vow, LkL*; CP.

+hata m. *enemy, opponent*, WW 393³⁰.

±hātan⁷ *active pret.* hē(h)t, hē(h)ton; *passive pret.* (origly. pres.) hātte (*CP,Mt*) *to command, direct, bid, order, Æ,Ct* : *summon, Dan* : *vow, promise, Jul* : (w. nom.=voc.) *name, call, AO*; CP : *be called, CP,Gen,Mt*; Æ. ['*hight*']

hāte adv. *hotly, fervidly, Æ.* ['*hot*']

hātheort (y²) I. n. *anger, rage.* II. (±) *wrathful, furious, passionate, Æ,CP* : *ardent, whole-hearted.* adv. -līce.

+hātheortan=hāthiertan

hātheorte f.=hātheort I.

hātheortnes f. *rage, mania, Æ,CP* : *zeal.*

±hāthiertan (eo, i, y) *to be or become angry,* CP : *enrage.*

hāthige m. *anger,* PPs 89⁷. [hyge]

hāthort (KGL)=hātheort

±hat-ian, -igan *to* '*hate*,' *treat as an enemy, CP*; Æ.

hātian *to be or get* '*hot*,' *VPs.*

hatigend m. *enemy,* ÆGR 205⁸.

hātigende *becoming hot,* LCD.

hatigendlic *hateful,* ÆL 3⁶⁰⁵.

+hātland n. *promised land,* BH 346⁸.

hātlīce *ardently,* Sc.

hātnes f. *heat,* ES 58·478.

hatol *hostile, bitter, Æ,WW* (*KGl*) : *odious.* ['*hatel*'; cp. hetol]

hātte v. hātan.

hattefagol sb. *hedgehog,* APs 103⁸ (cp. hæren-f.).

hatung f. *hatred, LPs*; Æ. ['*hating*']

hātung f. *heating, inflammation,* LCD.

hātwende *hot, burning,* Ex 74.

+haðerian=heaðorian

haðoliða m. *elbow,* LCD 99a (v. AB 29·253).

-hāwe v. earfoð-h.

hāwere m. *spectator,* CP 229¹⁷.

±hāwian *to gaze on, view, look at, observe, notice, Æ,CP.*

hāwung f. *observation,* AS.

hē m., hēo f., hit n. (pers. pron.) 'HE*,' *she, it*; pl. *they* : (reflex. pron.) *himself, herself, itself.*

hēa I. np. and nsm. (wk.) of hēah adj. II.=hēah adv. III.=hīe, hī, nap. of hē.

hēa-=hēah-; heador=heaðor

hēador, hēadēor=hēahdēor

hēaf m. *lamentation, wailing,* AO. [=hēof]

hēafd-=hēafod-

hēafdian *to behead,* ÆL,MH.

+hēafdod *having a head,* WW 152⁴⁵

hēafed=hēafod; heafela=hafela

hēaflan (Æ)=hēofian

hēaflic *sad, grievous,* BL 123⁶.

heafo (B 2478) nap. of hæf.

heafoc=hafoc

hēafod n. gs. hēafdes '*head*,' *Æ,JnR,VPs* : *top, OET* : *source, origin* : *chief, leader, CP, Chr* : *capital* (*city*), *AO.* hēafdes ðolian *to forfeit life.*

hēafodæcer (afu) m. '*a strip of land an acre in extent, lying at the head of a field*' (BTs), KC,WW 147¹⁹.

hēafodædre f. *cephalic vein,* LCD 95b.

hēafodbæð n. *a wash for the head,* LCD 57b.

hēafodbald (=ea³) *impudent,* WW 401¹⁹.

hēafodbān n. *skull,* LCD.

hēafodbēag m. *crown,* Bo 112²³.

hēafodbend m. *diadem, crown* : *head-bond, fetter about the head, Æ.*

hēafodbeorg I. f. *helmet,* B 1030. II. m. *prominent hill?* KC.

hēafodbeorht *with a splendid, shining head,* RD 20².

hēafodbiscop m. *high-priest,* ÆH 2·420³¹.

hēafodbolla m. *skull,* NC 300.

hēafodbolster n. *pillow,* LCD,WW.

hēafodbotl n. *ancestral seat,* Ct.

hēafodburh f. *chief city, Æ,AO.*

hēafodclāð n. *head-cloth, head-dress, WW*; ÆL. ['*headcloth*']

hēafodcwide m. *important saying,* LL : *chapter,* DR.

hēafodcyrice f. *cathedral,* LL 282 n19.

hēafodece m. '*headache*,' *Lcd* 7b; Æ.

hēafodfrætennes (e³) f. *hairpin, ornament for the hair,* WW.

hēafod-gemæcca, -gemaca (CP) m. *mate, companion, fellow-servant.*

hēafodgerīm n. *number by heads, greatest number,* JUD 309.

hēafodgetel n. *cardinal number,* ÆGR 283⁸.

hēafodgewæde n. *face-covering, veil, Æ,W.*

hēafodgilt m. *deadly sin,* W : *capital offence,* LL 380,2.

hēafodgimm† m. *head's gem, eye,* AN.

hēafodgold n. *crown,* PPs,W.

hēafodhær n. *hair of the head,* WW.

hēafodhebba m. *beginning, starter,* BF 62¹² : *prime mover,* ÆL 23³⁶⁵.

hēafodhrægl (u²) n. *an article of clothing or bedding,* RBL 93³, Sc 74².

hēafodhrīefðo f. *scurfiness of the head,* LCD 85b.

hēafodiht (e³) *with a head or tuft,* LCD 86a.

hēafodleahter m. *capital crime, deadly sin,* Æ.

hēafodlēas '*headless,*' *WW*; Æ.

hēafodlic *capital, deadly* (crime), *Bl* : *at the top*, WW : *principal*, AO. ['*headly*']

hēafodling (u²) m. *equal, fellow-servant, MtL.* ['*headling*']

hēafodloca m. *skull*, LCD.

hēafodlond n. *strip of land in a field, left for turning a plough, Ct*; WW. ['*headland*']

hēafod-mǣg†, -māga (AN) m. *near blood-relation.*

hēafodmǣgen n. *cardinal virtue*, ÆL 16³¹².

hēafodmann m. '*head-man*,' *captain, WW; Æ.*

hēafodmynster n. *church, cathedral*, LL.

hēafodpanne f. *skull, Mt.* ['*headpan*']

hēafodport m. *chief town*, CHR 1086.

hēafodrīce n. *empire*, AO 58³¹.

hēafodsār m. *pain in the head*, LCD.

hēafodsealf f. *head-salve*, LCD 130b.

hēafodsegn m? n? *banner*, B 2152 (v. eofor-h.).

hēafodsīen (ȳ³)† f. (*eyesight*), *eye*, GEN,WY.

hēafodslǣge (u²) m. *head of a pillar, architrave?* (BTs),WW 376¹⁵.

hēafodsmæl '*capitium*,' *part of a woman's dress*, WW 276¹⁸, 369¹⁹.

hēafodstede m. *chief place*, AO : *high place, sacred place*, LL 470,3⁵.

hēafodstocc m. *stake on which the head of a beheaded criminal was fixed*, Æ,KC.

hēafodstōl m. *capital*, AO 124,144.

hēafodstōw f. *place for the head*, BH 324³.

hēafodswīma m. *dizziness*, GEN 1568.

hēafodsȳn=hēafodsīen

hēafodsynn (ǣ¹) f. *deadly sin*, W 290²⁵.

hēafodþwēal n. *washing of the head*, WW 146⁸.

hēafodwǣrc m. *pain in the head*, Lcd ; WW. ['*headwark*']

hēafodweard I. f. *watch over the head, death-watch*, B 2909 : *body-guard*, LL 444,1. ['*headward*'] **II.** m. *chief protector, leader.* **III.** f. *chapter.*

hēafodweg m. *head-road* (v. BTs), Ct.

hēafodwind m. *chief wind* (*E, S, W or N wind*), LCD 3·274.

hēafodwīsa m. *chief, director*, GEN 1619.

hēafodwōō f. *voice*, RD 9³.

hēafodwund f. *wound in the head*, LL 20, 44.

hēafodwylm m. *tears*, EL 1133 : *burning pain in the head*, LCD 9b.

hēafodwyrhta m. *chief workman*, ÆH 2·530.

heafola=hafela ; **hēafre**=hēahfore

hēafsang m. *dirge*, WW 430²². [hēofan]

heafu (B 1862) nap. of hæf.

heafuc (VPs)=hafoc ; **hēafud**=hēafod

hēag=hēah ; **heaga-**=hago-

hēage (Æ)=hēah adv.

heago-=hago-, hagu- ; **hēagum** v. hēah.

---

hēah I. (ē) gsm. hēas, asm. hēan(n)e, gp. hēar(r)a, dp. hēagum, hēam, comp. hīerra (ē, ēah, īe, ȳ) ; sup. hīehst (ēa, ē, ȳ) '*HIGH*,' *tall, lofty, Æ* : *high-class, exalted, sublime, illustrious, important, CP* : *proud, haughty* : *deep* : *right* (*hand*). **II.** adv. '*high*,' *aloft, ÆGr.*

hēahaltāre m. *high altar*, W.

hēahbeorg m. *mountain*, PPs 94⁴.

hēahbiscop m. *archbishop, pontiff, LL* : (*Jewish*) *high-priest*, HL 104³⁰. [v. '*high*']

hēahbliss f. *exultation*, PPs 118¹¹¹.

hēahboda m. *archangel*, CR 295.

hēahburg f. *chief city* : (†) *town on a height.*

hēahcāsere m. *emperor*, †Hy 7⁶⁰.

hēahcleofa m. *principal chamber*, AA 6¹⁵

hēah-clif n. nap. -cleofu *high cliff*, CR,W.

hēahcræft m. *high skill*, RD 36⁴.

hēahcræftiga m. *architect*, BH.

hēahcyning† m. *high king, B* : *God.* [v. '*high*']

hēahdēor n. *stag, deer*, CHR.

hēahdēorhund (hēador-) m. *deer-hound*, LL,TC.

hēahdēorhunta m. *stag-hunter*, Ct.

hēahdīacon m. *archdeacon*, BL,MH.

hēah-eald* superl. -yldest (CM 36) *excellent, distinguished.*

hēah-ealdor, -ealdormann m. *ruler, patrician.*

hēahengel m. *archangel, Bf; Æ.* [v. '*high*']

hēahfæder m. *God* : *patriarch, Bl* ; Æ,CP : (*church*) *father.* [v. '*high*']

hēahfæst *permanent, immutable*, WID 143.

hēahfæsten n. *fortified town, city*, DR,WW.

hēahflōd m. *deep water*, GEN : *high tide*, WW.

hēahfore f. '*heifer*,' Æ,BH,WW.

hēahfrēa† m. *high lord*, CR.

hēahfrēols m. *great festival*, LL 344,17.

hēahfrēolsdæg m. *great feast-day*, LL 252,25.

hēahfrēolstīd f. *great festival*, LL 252,22².

hēahfru (WW)=hēahfore

hēahfȳr n. *towering flame*, WH 22.

hēahgǣst m. *Holy Ghost*, CR 358.

hēahgealdor n. *charm*, PPs 57⁴.

hēahgerēfa m. *high sheriff, chief officer, pro-consul, prefect*, Æ.

hēahgesamnung f. *chief synagogue*, Mk 5²².

hēahgesceaft f. *noble creature*, GEN 4.

hēahgesceap n. *fate*, B 3084.

hēahgestrēon† n. *rich treasure.*

hēahgetimbrad *high-built*, SAT 29.

hēahgetimbru† npl. *lofty edifice.*

hēahgeðring n. *whelming flood*, RD 4²⁷.

hēahgeðungen=hēahðungen

hēahgeweorc† n. *excellent work.*

hēahgnornung f. *deep grief*, PPs 101¹⁸.

hēahgod m. *Most High, God, PPs* 56². ['*high God*']

hēahgræft *carved in bas-relief,* WW348⁹.
hēahhād m. *holy orders,* LL(334⁶).
hēahhæf? n. *deep sea,* Hu25 (Sedgefield).
hēahhelm *loftily crested,* ZDA33·238.
hēahheolode (ēh-) f. *elecampane,* Lcd28b.
hēahheort *proud,* Da540.
hēahhliō† n. *high hill.*
hēahhlūtor *very pure,* BH348b¹⁹.
hēahhwīolod (ē¹) *having high wheels,* WW 140³².
hēahhylte n. *a high-placed shrubbery,* Ct.
hēahhyrde m. *head abbot,* OEG910.
hēahhyrne=ēaghyrne
hēahlǣce (ē²) m. *learned physician,* MH.
hēahland n. *mountainous country,* Ex385.
hēahlārēow m. *head teacher,* WW.
hēahlēce=hēahlǣce
hēahleornere n. *high teacher, master,* OEG 910.
hēahlic=hēalic
hēahlufe f. *great love,* B1954.
hēahmǣgen n. *great force : power, virtue,* ÆL.
hēahmǣsse f. *high mass,* Chr.
hēahmǣssedǣg m. *high mass day,* NC300.
hēahmiht f. *high authority, great might,* PPs150²,VH15 : *the Almighty,* VH15.
hēahmōd† *high spirited, exultant : proud, haughty.*
hēahmōdnes f. *pride,* CP301¹.
hēahmōr m. *high moor,* BHb364⁴.
hēahnama m. *most exalted name,* †Hy7¹⁸.
hēahnes (Æ)=hēanes; **hēahra** v. hēah.
hēahreced† n. *high building, temple.*
hēahrodor m. *high heaven,* Gen151,ByH 124²⁸.
hēahrūn f. *pythoness,* WW493³⁸.
hēahsācerd m. *high or chief priest,* G,HL.
hēahsǣ f. *high sea, the deep,* Met166³. [v. 'sea']
hēahsǣl† f. *great happiness,* PPs.
hēahsǣōēof? m. *chief pirate,* WW.
hēahsangere m. *chief singer,* BH314³.
hēahsceaða m. *chief pirate,* OEG8²²⁸.
hēahscēawere (ē¹) m. '*pontifex,*' DR21¹.
hēahscīreman (ē¹) m. '*procurator,*' DR193⁶.
hēahseld n.† *throne : rostrum,* WW.
hēahsele m. *high hall,* B647.
hēahsetl (ē) n. *exalted seat, throne, judgment-seat,* Æ,JnL. [v. 'settle']
hēahsittende *sitting on high,* A8·368.
hēahsomnung (MkL; ē¹)=hēahgesamnung
hēahstēap *very high,* Gen2839.
hēahstede m. *high place,* B285.
hēahstefn† *having a high prow.*
hēahstrǣt m. *highway,* Ct. ['high street']
hēahstrengōu f. *strength,* PPs107⁷.
hēahsunne (ē¹) adj. mp. *very sinful,* MkR2¹⁵.
hēahsynn f. *deadly sin, crime,* DR,LL.

hēahtīd f. *holy day,* LL. ['high tide']
hēahtimber m. *lofty building,* Cra45.
hēahtorr m. *high mountain,* OEG2035.
hēahtrēow f. *solemn compact,* Ex388.
hēahðearf f. *great need,* PPs117.
hēahðegen m. *chief officer, captain,* Æ : *apostle,* Æ : *angel.*
hēahðegnung f. *important function,* Ex96.
hēahðēod (ē¹) f. *great people,* Guth.
hēahðrēa m. *great affliction,* Gen2545.
hēah-ðrymm m., -ðrymnes† f. *great glory.*
hēahðu†=hīehðu
hēahðungen *of high rank, illustrious,* AO.
hēahweg m. *highway,* EC130' (hēi-).
hēahwēofod n. *high altar,* WW186²¹.
hēahweorc=hēahgeweorc
hēahwita m. *high councillor,* Chr1009.
hēahyldest v. hēaheald.

heal=(1) healh; (2)=heall
hēal (Bl)=hāl; **hēal-**=hēl-
hēala m. *hydrocele,* CP65⁵.
healærn n. *hall-building,* B78.
healc=healoc
heald I. n. *keeping, custody, guard, protection,* Chr1036, KC : *observance, observation, watch : protector, guardian.* ['hold'; =hield] **II.** *sloping, inclined, bent.*
±healdan⁷ (a) (tr. and intr.) *to* 'hold*' ('i-hald'), contain, hold fast, grasp, retain, possess, inhabit,Æ,Chr; CP: curb, restrain, compel, control, rule, reign,* Chr,CP : *keep, guard, preserve, foster, cherish, defend, Æ, Bl,Mt,Ps;* AO : *withhold, detain, lock up : maintain, uphold, support, Æ,LL : regard, observe, fulfil, do, practise,* Bl; Æ : *satisfy, pay: take care,* CP : *celebrate, hold (festival) : hold out* (intr.), *last : proceed, go : treat, behave to, bear oneself : keep in mind.* ongēan h. *resist.* tō handa h. *hold (land, etc.) of another.*
+healddagas mp. *kalends,* WW176²⁷.
+healde *contented? careful?* v. MFH162.
+healden f. *observance,* BHb468⁶.
healdend m. *protector, guardian, ruler, king, lord, God: economical person,* Lcd3·192²³.
+healdendgeorn (a¹) *continent,* DR45¹⁰?
+healdfæst *safe,* Lcd.
healdiend m. *preserver,* CEPs114⁶.
healding (a) f. *keeping, observance,* VPs118⁹.
±healdnes f. *keeping, observance,* BH : *guard, watch,* APs38² : *office of a bishop,* WW400⁹.
healdsum (hal-) *careful,* ANS129·25.
+healdsum *provident, economical, frugal,* CP : *virtuous, chaste, continent,* ÆL : *safe.*
±healdsumnes f. *keeping, observance, devotion,* Æ : *custody, preservation : restraint, abstinence : continence, chastity.*
hēalēce (Gl)=hēahlǣce

healede I. *suffering from hydrocele, ruptured,* CP72⁴. II.=hēlede

healf (a) I. adj. *'half,' Bf,Ct,Jud,Lcd;* Æ, AO. ðridde h., etc.=*two and a half, etc.* [*Ger.* drittehalb] II. f. *half, Æ,G,Chr* : *side, Gl,Mt,Ct;* Æ,AO : *part,* CP.

healfbrocen *half-broken,* BH436⁶.

healfclǣmed *half-plastered,* HL17²⁶⁷.

healfclungen (a¹) *half-congealed,* Cp265s.

healfclypigende adj. *semi-vowel,* ÆGR.

healf-cwic, -cucu *half-dead,* AO,CP.

healfdēad *half-dead,* LCD.

healfeald (a¹) *half-grown,* LCD92a.

healffers *hemistich,* ZDA31·10.

healffēðe *lame,* GPH396.

healffrēo *half-free,* W171⁴E.

healfgemet *'diametra,'* ZDA31·10.

healfhār *somewhat hoary,* A8·449.

healfhēafod n. *front of the head,* ÆGR74⁵.

healfhrūh *half-rough,* WW152¹⁴.

healfhunding m. *cynocephalus,* AA33¹⁴, WE54¹¹.

healfhwīt *somewhat white,* WW163⁷.

healfhȳd *half a hide (of land),* LL460,7¹.

healfmann m. *'half-man,'* ÆGr27.

healfmarc *half a mark* (v. marc), Ct,LL.

healfnacod *half-naked,* AA15³.

healfpenigwurð n. *halfpenny-worth,* LL,W.

healfrēad *reddish,* WW149³⁵.

healfrūh *half-rough,* WW152²⁴.

healfscyldig *partially guilty,* ZDA31·23.

healfsester m. *half a 'sester' (measure of bulk),* WW444⁴. [*L.* sextarius]

healfsinewealt *semicircular,* WW179²⁸.

healfslǣpende *half-asleep,* LV3; MH138¹.

healfsoden *half-cooked,* LCD,LL.

healfter=hælfter

healftryndel n. *hemisphere,* WW140⁷.

healfunga *to a certain extent, partially, imperfectly,* Æ,CP. [*'halfing'*]

healfweg m. *half-way,* KC.

healfwudu m. *field-balm,* LCD44b.

healgamen n. *social enjoyment,* B1066.

healgian=halgian

healh m. (? n. at LHy6³¹) (nap. halas) *corner, nook, secret place, CP,Guth,WW* : *small hollow in a hill-side or slope,* Ct, (GBG). [*'hale'*]

healhālgung (æa¹) f. *'ceremonia,'* WW180¹⁵.

healhihte *having many angles,* OEG121.

hēalic (ē) *high, elevated, exalted, lofty, sublime,* Æ; CP : *deep, profound, intense,* Æ, CP : *lordly, noble, great, illustrious, distinguished, notable, excellent,* Æ; CP : *proud, haughty* : *egregious, heinous,* W. adv. -līce *highly, aloft,* Æ : *in or to high position or rank, loftily,* BH : *intensely, very,* Bl. [*'highly'*]

hēalicnes f. *sublimity, majesty,* Æ.

heall I. f. *'hall,' dwelling, house, B,Mt;* Æ, CP : *palace, temple, law-court.* II.=healh. III. *rock,* OEG4111.

heallic *palatial,* WW499²⁹.

heallrēaf n. *wall-tapestry,* TC530'.

heallreced n. *hall-building,* B68 (heal-).

heallsittend† m. *sitter-in-hall,* B (heal-).

heallðegn† m. *hall-officer,* B (heal-).

heallwāhrift n. *wall-tapestry,* TC530'.

heallwudu m. *woodwork of hall,* B (heal-).

healm I. (a, æ) m. *'haulm,' stalk, straw, stubble, Lcd,MtL,VPs* : *'culmen,' thatched roof? harvest-land?* (v. LL116,61; 3·79 and BTs). II.=helm

healmstrēaw n. *stubble,* SPs82¹⁴.

healoc. healc m. *cavity, sinuosity,* LCD.

healp pret. 3 sg. of helpan.

heals (a) m. *neck, Gen* : *prow of a ship.* [*'halse'*]

hēals-=hāls-

healsbēag† m. *collar, necklace,* B.

healsbeorg f. *neck-armour,* OEG.

healsbōc f. *phylactery,* G. [hāls]

healsbrynige *corslet,* v. OEG2⁴¹⁸.

healsed (a¹; o²) mn. *head-cloth,* NG : *neck of a tunic,* WW514¹.

healseta m. *the neck of a tunic,* MH200¹.

healsfæst, *arrogant,* GEN2238.

healsfang n. *fine prescribed in substitution for capital and other punishments, preferential share of the 'wergeld,'* LL (v. 2·489 and BTs). [*'halsfang'*]

healsgang m. *neck-tumour,* WW190³².

healsgebedda f. *beloved bedfellow, wife,* B63

healsgund (a¹) m. *neck-tumour,* LCD,WW.

healsian *to entreat earnestly, beseech, implore, CP;* AO. [v. also hālsian]

healsi(g)endlic (ā) *that may be intreated,* APs89¹³ : *imploring,* GD17²³. adv. -līce *importunately.*

healsleðer n. *reins,* OET522.

healsmǣgeð f. *beloved maid,* GEN2155.

healsmyne m. *necklace,* Æ : *neck-ornament.* [mene]

healsōme f. *neck-tumour,* LCD132b.

healsrefeðer (a¹) f. *feathers of a pillow, down,* RD41⁸⁰. [cp.OHG. halsare *'cervical'*]

heals-scod, -ed=healsed

healstān (a, e) m. *small cake,* WW.

healswǣrc m. *pain in the neck,* LCD113a.

healswriða m. *necklace,* RD5⁴.

healswyrt (a) f. *a plant, daffodil? Lcd,WW;* OEG. [*'halswort'*]

healt (eo) *'halt,' limping, lame, AO.*

healt-=heald-

healtian (a) *to 'halt,' limp, CP,VPs;* Æ : *hesitate,* ÆL18⁹⁸ : *fall away,* BH.

heal̃ōegn† m. *hall-officer*, B.

healwudu m. *woodwork of hall*, B1317.

hēam v. hēah.

hēam-ol, -ul *miserly*, Cp.

hēamolscipe m. *miserliness*, NC300.

hēan I. *lowly, despised, poor, mean, bare, abject,B,VPs*; Æ,AO. [*'hean'*] adv. hēane. II. v. hēah. III. (±) *to raise, exalt, extol, BH*. [=*hīen, hȳn; 'high'*]

hēanes f. *'highness,' Bf* (hēah-),*CP* : *something high, high place, height, Mt*(hēah-), *VPs*. on hēanissum *in the highest, 'in excelsis,'* Æ : *excellence, sublimity,* CP : *high rank* : *deep place*, LkL5⁴.

hēanhād m. *difficulty*, WW345²⁹, 488⁴.

hēanlic *abject, poor*, AO. adv. -līce.

hēanmōd† *downcast, depressed, sad*.

hēannes I. (ē) f. *treading down*, NG. II.= hēanes

hēanspēdig *poor*, CRA26.

hēap mf. (*of things*) *'heap,' Cp,CP* : *host, crowd, assembly, company, troop, band, B, Bl*; Æ,CP. on hēape *together*.

±hēapian *to 'heap' up, collect, bring together, accumulate, Lk*.

hēapmǣlum adv. *by companies, in troops, flocks, Æ,CP; AO.* [*'heapmeal'*]

hēapum adv. *in heaps, in troops*.

hēapung f. *heap, BH*. [*'heaping'*]

hear- (N)=heor-

hēara=hēahra (v. hēah).

heard I. (a) *'hard,' harsh, severe, stern, cruel* (*things and persons*), *B,Bl,Cr,Mt,Lcd* : *strong, intense, vigorous, violent, B,Bl* : *hardy, bold, B; AO* : *resistant*, BF158². II. n. *hard object*.

heardcwide m. *harsh speech, abuse* (or ? hearmcwide), CR1444.

hearde adv. *'hard,' hardly, firmly, very severely, strictly, vehemently, Æ : exceedingly, greatly, Æ : painfully, grievously*.

heardecg I.† *sharp of edge*. II. f. *sword*, EL758.

heard(ha)ra m. *a fish, mullet?* GL.

heardhēaw *chisel*, Cp408C.

heardheort *hard-hearted*, Æ : *stubborn*, Æ.

heardheortnes f. *hard-heartedness*, Æ,CP.

heardhicgende† *brave*, B.

±heardian *to be or become hard, Lcd* : *harden, Lcd*. [*'hard'*]

hearding† m. *bold man, hero*.

heardlic *stern, severe, harsh, terrible* : *bold, warlike* : *excessive*. adv. -līce *harshly, resolutely, severely, sternly* : *stoutly, bravely, Æ : excessively* : *hardly* (*'paulatim,' 'tractim'*), ES42·174.

heardlicnes f. *austerity*, GUTH70¹⁵.

heardmōd *brave, bold, over-confident, Æ* : *obstinate*, ÆL36³²⁶.

heardmōdnes f. *obstinacy*, ÆH1·252¹⁸.

heardnebba m. *raven*, ÆH2·144¹⁵.

heardnes f. *'hardness,' Ep,Mt,Lcd,RB*.

heardra (OEG)=heardhara

heardrǣd *firm, constant*, GEN2348.

heardsǣlig *unfortunate, unhappy*, Bo.

heardsǣlnes f. *calamity*, AO104¹⁷.

heardsǣlð f. *hard lot, calamity, unhappiness*, AO : *misconduct, wickedness*, CP.

heardung f. *hardening*, LCD.

heardwendlīce *strictly*, BH365¹⁵.

hearg, hearga (æ, e) m. *temple, altar, sanctuary, idol*, AO,CP : *grove*, Az110.

heargeard (herh-) m. *dwelling in the woods*, WIF15.

hearglic (h) *idolatrous*, WW236².

heargtræf (æ¹) n. *idol-temple*, B175.

heargweard m. *temple-warden, priest* (herig-), AN1126.

hearh=hearg

hearm (e) I. m. *damage, 'harm,' injury, evil, affliction, B,Chr,Gen*; Æ,CP : *grief, pain, Gen* : *insult, calumny*. II. adj. *harmful, malignant, evil*.

hēarm=hrēam

hearma m. *mouse? weasel?* OET (*'mygale,'* Ep,Erf; *'netila,'* Cp). [*OHG*. harmo]

hearmascinnen *made of ermine*, CHR1075D.

hearmberg (æ) m. *mound of calamity*, FM 373, RUNE CASKET.

hearmcwalu f. *great suffering*, CR1609.

hearmcweodelian (VPs)=hearmcwidolian

hearmcweðan⁵ *to speak evil of, revile*, NG.

hearmcweðend (e¹) m. *slanderer*, JPs71⁴.

hearmcwiddian (y²) *to calumniate*, Bo,LPs 118²².

hearmcwide† m. *calumny, blasphemy* : *heavy sentence, curse*.

hearmcwidol *evil-speaking, slanderous*, Æ.

hearmcwidolian (eo², e³) *to speak evil, slander*, ARSPs118¹²².

hearmcwidolnes f. *slander*, EPs118¹³⁴.

hearmdæg m. *day of grief*, B3153.

hearmedwīt n. *grievous reproach*, PPs68²¹.

hearmful *hurtful, noxious*, OEG46¹³.

-hearmgeorn v. un-h.

hearmheortnes f. *complaint*, WW511¹⁶.

hearmian *to 'harm,' injure, Æ,Rood*.

hearmlēoð† n. *elegy, lamentation*.

hearmlic *harmful, grievous*, Æ.

hearmloca† m. *prison* : *hell*.

hearmplega m. *fight, strife*, GEN1898.

hearmscaða m. *terrible enemy*, B766.

hearmscearu† f. *affliction, punishment, penalty*, GEN. [sceran]

hearmslege m. *grievous blow*, CR1435.

hearmsprǣc f. *calumny*, WW198³.

hearmstæf† m. *harm, sorrow, tribulation*.

hearmtān m. *shoot of sorrow*, GEN992.

hearpe (æ) f. '*harp*,' Æ,*VPs*; CP.

hearpenægel m. *plectrum*, ApT 17⁷.

hearpere (a) m. '*harper*,' *Bo,Ln*; Æ,CP.

hearpestre f. (*female*) *harper*, WW 190⁶.

hearpestreng m. '*harp-string*,' *ApT* 17⁸.

hearpian *to* '*harp*,' *Bo*; Æ.

hearpnægel (WW)=hearpenægel

hearpsang m. *psalm*, WW 129⁴⁰.

hearpslege m. *plectrum* (*instrument for striking the harp*), OEG : *harp-playing*.

hearpswēg m. *sound of the harp*, BLPs 150³.

hearpung f. '*harping*,' *Bo*.

hearra I.† (æ, e, ie, eo) m. *lord, master, Chr, Gen.* ['*her*'] **II.**=heorr

hēarra=hēahra (v. hēah).

hearstepanne=hierstepanne

hēarsum=hiersum

heart (NG)=heord, heorot

-hearwa v. Sigel-h.; **hēas** v. hēah.

heascan=hyscan; **heasu**=hasu

heaðo-=heaðu- (=*war*)

heaðor n. *restraint, confinement*, RD.

±**heaðorian** (e²) *to shut in, restrain, control*.

hēaðrym=hēahðrymm

heaðubyrne† f. *war-corslet*.

heaðudēor† *bold, brave*, B.

heaðufremmende *fighting*, El 130.

heaðufȳr† n. *cruel fire*, B.

heaðugeong *young in war*, Fin 2.

heaðuglemm m. *wound got in battle*, RD 57³.

heaðugrim† *fierce*.

heaðulāc† n. *battle-play, battle*, B.

heaðulind f. *linden-wood shield*, †Chr 937.

hēaðuliðende† m. *seafaring warrior*, B.

heaðumære *famed in battle*, B 2802.

heaðurǣs† m. *onrush, attack*, B.

heaðurēaf n. *war-gear*, B 401.

heaðurinc† m. *warrior*.

heaðurōf† *famed in war, brave*.

heaðusceard? *dinted in war*, B 2830? (or ? heaðuscearp *battle-sharp*).

heaðusēoc *wounded*, B 2754.

heaðusigel m. *sun*, RD 72¹⁶.

heaðustēap† *towering in battle*, B.

heaðuswāt† m. *blood of battle*, B.

heaðusweng m. *battle-stroke*, B 2581.

heaðutorht *clear as a battle-cry*, B 2553.

heaðuwǣd f. *armour*, B 39.

heaðuweorc n. *battle-deed*, B 2892.

heaðuwērig *weary from fighting*, Wald 2¹⁷.

heaðuwylm† (æ³, e³) m. *fierce flame*.

hēaum=hēagum dp. of hēah.

+**hēaw** n. *gnashing, grinding*, HL,Sat.

hēaw-=hǣw- (hēawi, Cp 303c=hēawen).

±**hēawan**⁷ *to* 'hew*,' *hack, strike, cleave, cut, cut down, kill* : *make by hewing*, LL. æftan h. *to slander*, W 160⁴.

heawen (K)=heofon

-hēawere v. hrīðer-, wudu-h.

-hebba v. hēafod-h.

±**hebban**⁶ (æ) pres. 3 sg. hōf, pl. hōfon, pp. hafen (hæfen) (wk. forms in LWS, pret. hefde, pp. hefod) *to* '*heave**,' *raise, lift, lift up, exalt*, Æ,B,Bl,Ps; CP : intr. *rise*, W 100³.

hebbe=hæbbe (v. habban).

-hebbe, -hebbing v. ūp-h.

hebbendlic *exalted*, DR 181¹⁴.

hebeld=hefeld; **heben**=heofon

heber=hæfer; **hebuc**=hafoc

hecc=hæc; **heced**=hacod

hēcen (y²) n. *kid*, Bf 134¹⁷,ES 35·332.

heog, hecge f. *enclosure, hedge.*

hecga-spind, -swind=hagospind

±**hēdan** I. (w. g.) *to* '*heed*,' *observe*, B,LL; Æ : *care for, guard, protect, take charge of*, LL : *obtain, receive, take*, Æ. **II.**=hȳdan

hēddern (ȳ) n. *storehouse, storeroom*, BH,Gl.

hēde pret. 3 sg. of hēgan.

hedeclāð m. *a coarse, thick, upper garment like a chasuble*, Lcd 1·346¹⁷.

heden m. *robe, hood, chasuble*, LL.

hedendlic *captious*, OEG 3208. adv. -līce, WW 199¹.

hef-=heof-

hefaldian=hefeldian

hefde I. (VPs)=hæfde pret. 3 sg. of habban. **II.** v. hebban.

hefe I. (æ) m. *weight, burden*, Æ : '*mina, talentum*,' GPH 396. **II.**=hæfe

+**hefed** *weighed down*, WW 251¹⁶.

hefeg=hefig

hefeld n. *thread* (*for weaving*), Gl. [v. '*heald*']

±**hefeldian** (a²) *to fix the weft, begin the web*, Gl.

hefeldðrǣd m. *thread* (*for weaving*), Gl,Lcd. [v. '*heald*']

hefelgyrd (e³) f. *weaver's shuttle*, Gl.

hefe-lic, -līce=hefig-lic, -līce

hefen I. (æ) f. *burden*, RB 49¹³. **II.**=heofon

hefetīme=hefigtīme

hefeð pres. 3 sg. of hebban.

hefgian=hefigian

hefig (æ) '*heavy*,' *Met,Mt* : *important, grave, severe, serious*, Bf,Bl,Mt,Chr : *oppressive, grievous*, Ps,LL : *slow, dull*. [hebban] adv. hefige, Ps.

±**hefigian** *to make heavy*, VPs : *weigh down, oppress, afflict, grieve*, BH,CP,Mt : *aggravate, increase* : *become heavy, depressed, weakened*, CP,Gu. ['*heavy*']

hefiglic *heavy, weighty, serious, severe, burdensome, grievous, sad*, Æ. adv. -līce, *violently, intensely*, CP,Lk : *sorrowfully*, Gen : *sluggishly*, Mt. ['*heavily*']

hefigmōd *oppressive*, ERPs 54⁴ : *heavy-hearted*, NC 300.

hefignes (æ) f. '*heaviness,' weight, burden, affliction*, MtL; CP : *dulness, torpor, Bo.*

hefigtӯme (i³) *heavy, grievous, severe, troublesome, oppressive*, Æ. [tēam]

hefigtӯmnes f. *trouble*, Æ.

hefod wk. pp., hefð pres. 3 sg. of hebban.

hefon=heofon; **heft-**=hæft-

hefug=hefigu pl. of hefig, CP 285¹.

heg-=hege-; **hēg**=hīeg

±hēgan† *to perform, achieve* : *hold (a meeting)*, An : *exalt, worship*, Da 207⁷.

hegdig=hygdig

hege (ea) m. '*hedge,' fence*, Æ,Ct,Gl. ['*hay*']

hegeclife f. *hedge-clivers*, Lcd 20a.

hegegian=hegian

hegehymele f. *hop-plant*, WW 302⁵.

hegel (VPs)=hægl, hagol

hegerǣw (e³) f. '*hedgerow,' KC.*

hegerife f. *cleavers, goose grass*, Lcd. ['*hairif*']

hegesāhl m. *hedge-stake*, GD 24²⁸. [sagol]

hegessugge *hedge-sparrow*, WW 131³⁴. [sucga; '*haysugge*']

hege-steall m. -stōw f. *place with a hedge*, KC.

hegewege m. *road between hedges*, KC.

hegge f. (BC,Chr)=hege

±hegian *to fence in, hedge, enclose*, Sc. grep h. *to cut a grip*, LL 455,13. ['*hay*']

hēgnes=hēanes

hegstæf m. *bar to stop an opening in a fence* (BTs),WW 205³¹.

hegstald-=hægsteald-

hēh (VPs, N), hēh-=hēah, hēah-

+hēhan (VHy)=hēan III.

hē hē indicates laughter, ÆGr. ['*he*']

hēhst pres. 2 sg. of hōn.

hehstald=hagosteald

hēht pret. 3 sg. of hātan.

hēhðu=hīehðu; **+heige** (KGL 83⁴⁰)=+hæg

hēlsta=hēhsta (v. hēah).

hēiweg=hēahweg

hel=hell, helle-

hēla (ǣ) m. '*heel,' Gl,JnL,Lcd,OET,WW.*

hēla-=hāle-

hēlade (ēa¹) *having large heels*, WW.

±helan⁴ *to conceal, cover, hide*, AO,VPs, Æ (pp.); CP. ['*hele*']

hēlan I. (oe) *to calumniate*, MtR 5⁴⁴. **II.**=hǣlan I.

held=hield

helde I. f. *tansy*, Lcd,WW; Æ. ['*helde*'] **II.**=hyldo

hele f. *subterfuge*, LL (320¹⁷). or ?=hāl (BTs). ['*hele*']

hele-=helle-, ele-

hēlend=hǣlend

helerung=heolorung; **heleð**=hæleð

helf-=healf-, hielf-

helfan *to halve*, Cp 303b? (herbid).

helgod=hellgod; **helhrūne**=hellerūne

±helian *to conceal, cover, hide*, Æ,LL. ['*hele*']

hēlic, hēlīce=hēahlic, hēalīce

hell (y) f. *Hades*, Æ,VPs : '*hell,' place of torment, Gehenna*, Bo,RB; Æ,AO,CP. [helan]

hell- v. also helle-.

hellbend mf. *bond of hell*, B 3072.

hellcniht m. *devil, demon*, ÆL 3³⁷².

hellcræft m. *hellish power*, An 1104.

hellcund *of hell*, W 254¹⁵.

hellcwalu f. *pains of hell*, Cb 1190.

helldor† n. *gate of hell*, Gu. [v. '*hell*']

helle m. *hell*, WW.

hellebealu n. *hell-bale*, Cr 1427.

hellebrōga m. *terror of hell*, LPs,VH.

hellebryne m. *hell-fire*, Jud,W.

hellecǣgan pl. *keys of hell*, MFH 128.

helleceafl m. *jaws of hell*, An 1702.

hellecinn n. *hellish race*, Cr 1620.

helleclamm m. *hell-bond*, Gen 373.

helledēofol† mn. *devil.*

helle-dor n., -duru f. *gate of hell.*

helleflōr m. *floor of hell, courts of hell*, Sat 70.

hellefӯr n. *hell-fire*, GD.

hellegāst† (ǣ³) m. *spirit of hell*, B.

hellegeat n. *gate of hell*, ÆH 1·288, MP 1·610.

hellegrund† m. *abyss of hell*, VH.

hellegrut n. *pit of hell*, OEG 689.

hellegryre m. *horror of hell*, Sat 433.

hellehæft(a), -hæftling† m. *prisoner of hell, devil.*

hellehēaf m. *wailings or howlings of hell*, Gen 38.

hellehinca m. *hell-limper, devil*, An 1173. [cp. Ger. hinken]

hellehund m. *hell-hound*, KC 3·350¹⁸.

hellehūs n. *hell-house*, Gu 649.

hellelic=hellic

helleloc n. *hell-prison*, GD 325³⁰.

hellemægen n. *troop of hell*, MFH 166,VH.

hellemere m. *Stygian lake*, WW.

helleniÞ m. *torments of hell*, Gen 775.

hellerūne f. *pythoness, sorceress*, Æ : *demon*, B 163.

hellescealc m. *devil*, Sat 133.

hellesceaða=hellsceaða

hellesēað m. *pit of hell.*

hellestōw f. *infernal region*, GD 332⁹.

hellesūsl n. *hell-torment*, Æ.

helletintreg *hell-torment*, MFH 128¹⁹,VH.

helletintrega m. *hell-torment*, VH 16.

helleðegn (hel-)† m. *devil.*

hellewīte n. *hell-pains, torment*, Æ,CP.

hellewītebrōga m. *horror of hell-torment,* W 151²⁴.
hellfiren f. *hellish crime,* PART 6.
hellfūs† *bound for hell.*
hellgeðwing n. *confinement in hell,* GEN 696.
hellgod n. *god of the lower world,* Bo,WW.
hellheort *terrified,* NC 301.
hellheoðo f. *vault of hell, hell,* SAT 700 (or ? two words).
hellic *of hell, hellish,* Æ. ['*hellick*']
hellsceaða m. *hell-foe, devil : grave.*
hell-træf, nap. -trafu n. *devil's temple,* AN 1693.
helltrega m. *hell-torture,* GEN 73.
hell-waran, -ware mp., -waru fp. *dwellers in hell,* Æ. [v. '*hell*']
hellwendlic (helw-) *infernal,* WW 437³¹.
hellwerod n. *host of hell,* W 25²¹.
hellwiht (hel-) fn. *devil,* W 186².
helm I. m. *protection, defence, covering, crown,* Æ,Rd : *summit, top (of trees),* Æ, Bo,WW; CP : *helmet,* Cp,WW : (†) *protector, lord.* ['*helm*'] II. (WW 279¹⁴)=elm
helma m. '*helm,*' *rudder,* Bo,Cp,WW; Æ.
helm-bǣre, -berende *leafy,* WW. [v. '*helm*']
helmberend m.† *helmeted warrior,* B.
±**helmian** (y) *to cover, crown,* An : *provide with a helmet,* ÆGr. ['*helm*'; '*i-helmed*']
-**helmig** v. lēaf-h.
helmiht *leafy,* WW 395⁵; 493²⁸.
helmweard (holm-) m. *pilot,* AN 359.
hēlo=hǣlu; **helor**=heolor
help (y) fm. '*help,*' *succour, aid,* AO,B,Bl.
±**helpan**³ (w. g. or d.) *to* '*help*,' *support, succour,* Æ,ĊP,Ct,G,LL,Ps : *benefit, do good to,* Lcd(intr.),LL : *cure, amend,* Mk.
helpe f.=help
helpend m. *helper, Bl.* ['*helpend*']
helpendlic adj. *to be liberated,* GPH 402.
helpendrāp m. *helping-rope,* WW 463³⁵.
helrūn=hellerune
helrūna m. *hellish monster,* B 163.
helrȳnegu f. *sorceress, witch,* WW 472¹¹.
hēlspure f. *heel,* VPs.
helt I.=hilt. II. pres. 3 sg. of heldan.
III. (KGL)=hielt pres. 3 sg. of healdan.
helto-=hielto-
helðegn=helleðegn; **helur**=heolor
helustr (Ep,Erf)=heolstor
hem m. '*hem,*' *border,* WW 125¹³.
+**hēme?** *customary,* AS 33¹³n.
hemed (BC 2·522′) v. hemman.
hēmed, hēmeð=hǣmed
hemeðe n. *under-garment,* OEG 3725. [*Ger.* hemd]
hemlic (Æ)=hymlic
hemman? *to stop up, close* (GK),PPs 106⁴². [*MHG.* hemmen]

hemming (i) m. *shoe of undressed leather,* WW 468³¹. ['*hemming*']
hen=henn; **hēn**=hēan; **hēn-**=hīen-
hēnan=hīenan
+**hendan** *to hold,* PPs 138⁸ : *seize, catch,* LPs 58¹³. [hand]
+**hende** *near, at hand,* Æ,Mk : *convenient,* AO. adv. *near, at home,* Æ : *closely, in detail,* BF 72²². ['*hend*']
-**hendig** v. list-h.
+**hendnes** f. *neighbourhood, proximity,* Æ.
henep=hænep
heng pret. 3 sg. of hōn.
hengeclif n. *overhanging cliff,* WW 180⁴.
hengen f. *hanging,* Æ : *cross,* Æ : *rack, torture,* Æ : *imprisonment.*
hengenwītnung f. *imprisonment,* LL 471,16.
hengest, hengst m. *stallion, steed, horse, gelding,* Ct,WW; Æ. ['*hengest*']
hengetrēow (enge-) n. *gallows,* GPH 395.
hengwīte n. *fine for not detaining an offender,* LL 496,4.
henn (æ) f. '*hen,*' Bf,Mt,Lcd.
henna m. *fowl,* LL (220¹³).
henneæg n. *hen's egg,* LCD.
hennebelle (æ) f. *henbane,* Lcd,WW. ['*henbell*']
hennebroð n. *chicken broth,* LCD.
hennfugol m. *hen,* Ct.
hēnnis (LG)=hīennes
hentan *to pursue, attack,* LL; Æ : (±) *appropriate, seize, Chr.* ['*hent,*' '*i-hente*']
hēnð=hīenð; **henu**=heonu
hēo I. nasf. and nap. of pron. 3 pers. '*she,*' *they.* II.†=hīw
heodæg adv. *to-day,* GEN 661. [*Ger.* heute]
hēof I. m. *wailing, mourning, grief,* Æ,AO. II. str. pret. 3 sg. of hēofan.
hēofan⁷? (pret. hēof, hōf, hēofon) *to lament,* CP.
heofan, heofen=heofon
hēofendlic *dismal, mournful,* WW. adv. -līce.
hēof-ian, -igian *to lament,* Æ.
heofig-=hefig-
hēofigendlic *lamenting,* A 10·146; 188.
hēofod=hēafod; **heofog** (BL)=hefig
heofon (e¹, a², e², u²) mf. (often in pl.) *sky, firmament,* Æ,Bo,Chr,Met,VPs : '*heaven,*' Æ,G : *the power of heaven,* Mt,Lk.
hēofon I. f. *lamentation?* Ex 46. II. str. pret. pl. of hēofan.
heofonbēacen n. *sign in the sky,* Ex 107.
heofonbeorht† *heavenly bright.*
heofonbig(g)ende *chaste,* DHy. [*ON.* byggja]
heofonbȳme f. *heavenly trumpet,* CR 949.
heofoncandel† f. *sun, moon, stars.*
heofoncenned *heaven-born,* DHy 108⁴.

heofoncolu npl. *heat of the sun*, Ex71.
heofoncund *celestial, heavenly*, CP.
heofoncundlic *heavenly*, W.
heofoncyning m. *king of heaven, Christ, Bl* 201. [*'heavenking'*]
heofondēma m. *heavenly ruler*, Sat658.
hēofondlīce=hēofendlīce
heofondrēam† m. *joy of heaven*.
heofonduguð f. *heavenly host*, Cr1655.
heofone (Æ,W)=heofon
heofonengel m.† *angel of heaven*, Cr.
heofonflēogende *flying*, JPs103¹².
heofonflōd m. *torrent (of rain)*, -waru fp. BH236¹⁷.
heofonfugol† m. *fowl of the air*, Gen.
heofonfȳr n. *fire from heaven, lightning*, W 262¹⁵.
heofonhæbbend m. *possessor of heaven*, WW385²¹.
heofonhālig *holy and heavenly*, An728.
heofonhām† m. *heavenly home*, PPs.
heofonhēah *reaching to heaven*, Da553. [*'heavenhigh'*]
heofonheall f. *heavenly hall*, LL (382¹⁰). [v. *'heaven'*]
heofonhlāf m. *bread of heaven, manna*, PPs 104³⁵.
heofonhrōf m. †*vault of heaven, heaven, Ph*: *roof, ceiling.* WW432⁸? [v. *'heaven'*]
heofonhwealf† f. *vault of heaven*, An.
heofonhyrst f. *ornament of the heavens*, Gen2189.
heofonisc (e²) *heavenly*, AO1⁶.
heofonlēoht n. *heavenly light*, An976.
heofonlēoma m. *heavenly light*, An840.
heofonlic *'heavenly,' celestial, Bl,Lk*; CP : *chaste*, ÆGr66³,WW203²¹. adv. -līce, ÆGr239⁷,WW375²².
heofonmægen† n. *heavenly force*.
heofonrīce n. *kingdom of heaven, Bl,Cr*; AO. [*'heavenric'*]
heofonsetl n. *throne of heaven*, DD277.
heofonsteorra† m. *star of heaven*.
heofonstōl m. *throne of heaven*, Gen8.
heofontimber n. *heavenly structure*, Gen 146.
heofontorht† *very bright, glorious*.
heofontungol† n. *heavenly luminary*, VH 16.
heofonðrēat m. *heavenly company*, Sat222.
heofonðrymm m. *heavenly glory*, Æ.
heofon-ware, -waran mp., -waru fp. *inhabitants of heaven*, Æ. [*'heavenware'*]
heofonwealdend (e²) *the God (ruler) of heaven*, OEG23¹⁰.
heofonweard† m. *heaven's keeper, God*, Gen.
heofonwerod n. *heavenly host*, W.
heofonwlitig *divinely fair*, NC301.
heofonwolcen† n. *cloud of heaven*, VH16.
heofonwōma† m. *terrible noise from heaven*.

heofonwuldor n. *heavenly glory*, †Hy6¹².
hēofsīð m. *lamentable state*, Rim43? [hēof]
heofun=heofon
hēofung f. *lamentation, mourning*, Æ.
hēofungdæg m. *day of mourning*, Æ.
hēofungtīd f. *time of mourning*, Æ.
heolan=helan
heolca m. *hoar-frost*, LPs118⁸³.
heold pret. 3 sg. of healdan.
heoldan=healdan
heolfor† n. *gore, blood*, An,B.
heolfrig† *gory, bloody*, Jud.
heolor (e¹, e², u²) f. *scales, balance*, Gl.
heolorbledu (e¹, u²) f. *scale of a balance*, WW427³⁵.
heolorian *to weigh, ponder*, Gl.
heolorung (e¹, e²) f. *'momentum,' the turning of a scale*, WW450¹².
heoloðcynn n. *denizens of hell*, Cr1542.
-heoloðe v. hēah-h, hind-h.
heoloðhelm† (æ) m. *helmet which makes the wearer invisible*.
heolp=healp; **heolr-**=heolor-
heolstor (e²) **I.** m. *darkness, concealment, cover, hiding-place, retreat.* [helan] **II.** adj. *dark, shadowy*, Æ.
heolstorcofa m. *dark chamber, grave*, Ph49.
heolstorhof n. *hell*, El764.
heolstorloca† m. *prison, cell*, An.
heolstor-sceado (Gen103) f., -scuwa (An 1255) m. *concealing shade, darkness*.
heolstrig *shadowy, obscure*, WW.
heolstrung ? f. *darkness*, DR182¹⁷.
heolt=healt
heom dp. of hē, hēo, hit.
heona (LkL) heonan VPs; heonane (Gen)= heonon(e)
heono (NG)=heonu
heonon(e) (a²) *hence, from here, away, Mt : from now.* h. forð *henceforth.* [*'hen'*]
heononsīð m. *departure, death*, Dom86.
heononweard *transient*, Bl,Gen.
heonu (an(n)a, āne, eno, (he)ono) *if, but, therefore, moreover, whether*, ANS91·205 : *lo! behold!* NG.
heonun (Mt)=heonon
hēop (LPs67¹⁴)=hēap
hēopa m. *bramble*, LkL20³⁷.
hēopbrēmel (ȳ²) m. *dog-rose, bramble*, Lcd. [v. *'hip'*]
hēope f. *'hip,' seed-vessel of wild-rose, Cp, Lcd,WW*; Æ : *bush, brier*.
heor=heorr
heora gp. of hē, hēo, hit.
hēoran=hīeran
±heorcnian (e, y) tr. and intr. *to 'hearken,' listen, Æ,Guth.*
heorcnung f. *'hearkening,' listening, power of hearing*, Æ.

heord I. (e, io) f. *'herd,' flock, Æ,LL,Mt, WW; CP : keeping, care, custody,* CP. **II.** *sycamore,* LkR19⁴. [heorot-?] **III.=** hīred. **IV.** (+) (S²Ps38²)=+heordung
heorde I. f. *'hards' (of flax), tow, Cp,WW.* **II.** (VPs)=hierde. **III.=**heord
±**heordnes** f. *custody, keeping, watch,* GD, Ps.
±**heordrǣden** (y¹) f. *custody, care, keeping, watch, ward, ÆL : keeping-place,* LPs78¹.
+**heordung** f. *guard, watch,* ERPs38².
hēore I.† (ȳ;=īe) *pleasant, secure, B : gentle, mild, pure, Gen.* ['*here*'] **II.=**hīere
heorl=eorl; **heoro=**heoru; **hēorod=**hīered
heorot (u²) m. *'hart,' stag, Bo* (heort), *VPs.*
heorotberge f. *buckthorn-berry,* WW.
heorotbrem(b)el m. *buckthorn, Lcd.* [v. '*hart*']
heorotbrembellēaf n. *leaf of the buckthorn,* Lcd119b.
heorotbrēr f. *buckthorn,* LkR17⁶(heart-).
heorotclǣfre f. *'hart-clover,' hemp agrimony, Lcd.*
heorotcrop m. *cluster of hartwort flowers,* Lcd.
heorotsmeoru n. *hart's grease,* Lcd45a.
heorotsol n. *stag's wallowing-place,* KC.
heorr mf. *hinge, B,Bo,Cp,LPs : cardinal point, Lcd.* ['*harre*']
heorra=(1) hearra; (2) heorr
heort I. (±) *high-minded, stout-hearted,* ÆL. **II.=**heorot
heortan=hiertan
heortancnys f. '*(com)pulsus cordis'?* v. ZDA31·13n.
heortbucc m. *roebuck,* WW119¹².
heortcoða m. *heart disease,* WW199³⁵.
heortcoðu f. *heart disease,* Lcd65b.
heorte f. '*HEART' (organ) : breast, soul, spirit: will, desire : courage : mind, intellect : affections.*
heortece m. *'heartache,' Lcd.*
heorten (y) *of a hart,* Lcd1·216¹⁵.
heortgesida pl. *entrails,* Lev3³.
heortgryre m. *terror of heart,* W86¹⁵.
heorthama m. *pericardium, internal fat, Æ.*
heorthogu f. *heart-care,* W177⁷.
heortlēas *dispirited,* DD124,W137²².
+**heortlīce** adv. *cheeringly,* GD317¹⁶.
heortlufu f. *hearty love,* †Hy9²⁹.
heortsārnes f. *grief,* GenC6⁶.
heortscræf n. *heart,* DD39.
heortsēoc *ill from heart disease* (Swt).
heortwærc m. *pain at the heart,* Lcd.
heorð (e) m. *'hearth,' fire, Gl,Az : house, home, Æ,LL.*
heorð-=eorð-
heorða m. *deer- (or goat-?) skin,* WW337³.
[hyrð]

heorðbacen *baked on the hearth,* WW. [v. '*hearth*']
heorðcneoht m. *attendant,* CP361¹⁸.
heorðe=heorde
heorðfæst *having a settled home,* LL322'.
heorðgenēat† m. *retainer,* B.
heorðpening m. *'hearth-penny,' tax (for the Church), Peter's penny,* LL (v. 2·506).
heorðswǣpe f. *bridesmaid,* Cp701p.
heorðwerod† n. *body of retainers.*
heoru† m. *sword,* B.
heorublāc *mortally wounded,* B2488? (or ?hildeblāc)
heorucumbul n. *standard,* El107.
heorudolg n. *deadly wound,* An944.
heorudrēor† m. *sword-blood, gore, B.*
heorudrēorig† *blood-stained : deathly sick,* Ph217.
heorudrync m. *sword-drink, blood shed by the sword,* B2358.
heorufæðm m. *deadly grasp,* Ex504.
heoruflā f. *arrow,* LPs56⁵.
heorugīfre† *fierce, greedy for slaughter.*
heorugrǣdig† *bloodthirsty,* An.
heorugrimm† *savage, fierce.*
heoruhōciht *savagely barbed,* B1438.
heorung=herung
heoruscearp *very sharp,* Rd6⁸.
heorusceorp n. *war equipments,* Hell73.
heoruserce f. *coat of mail,* B2539.
heoruswealwe f. *falcon, hawk,* Wy186.
heorusweng† m. *sword-stroke.*
heorut=heorot
heoruwǣpen n. *sword,* Jud263.
heoruweallende *gushing with destruction,* B2781.
heoruwearg m. *bloodthirsty wolf,* B1267.
heoruword n. *hostile speech,* FT84.
heoruwulf m. *warrior,* Ex181.
hēow I. pret. 3 sg. of hēawan. **II.=**hīw
hēow-=hīw-; **hēowan=**hēofan
heplic=hæplic; **her-=**hear-, hier-, here-
hēr I. adv. *'here,' in this place, Æ,G,VPs : in this world, Bl,LL : at this point of time, at this date, now, Chr,Ct : towards this place, hither, B.* **II.=**hǣr
hēr-=hǣr-, hier-, hȳr-
hēræfter (ȳ) adv. *'hereafter,' later on, A,BH.*
hērbeforan adv. *before, previously,* W52¹¹; FM361²³.
hērbeufan (u², iu²) adv. *here above, previously, Ct;* CP. [v. '*here*']
hērbūende† mp. *dwellers on this earth.*
herbyrg=herebeorg; **hercnian=**heorcnian
hērcyme m. *coming here, advent,* Cr250.
herd=heord; **herd-, hērd-=**hierd-, hīerd-
here (obl. cases usu. have herg-, herig-) m. *predatory band, troop, army, host, multitude, Chr,Mt; AO,CP* ('se h.' almost

always=*the Danish army* in CHR) : *battle, war, devastation.* [' *here*']

hēre I. f. *dignity, importance?* MET10⁵⁴? (Sedgef. reads 'here'). II. (VPs)=hǣre

here-bēacen, -bēacn n. *military ensign, standard* : *beacon, lighthouse.*

here-beorg, -byrg f. *lodgings, quarters,* NC 346. [*Ger.* herberge]

herebeorgian (y³) *to take up one's quarters, lodge,* CHR1048F : RWH137⁹. [*Ger.* herbergen]

hereblēað *cowardly,* Ex453.

herebrōga m. *dread of war,* B462.

herebӯme f. *trumpet, sackbut,* Ex,OEG.

herebyrgian=herebeorgian

herebyrne f. *corslet,* B1443. [v. '*here*']

herecirm m. *war cry,* GU872.

herecist=herecyst

herecombol n. *standard,* EL25?

herecyst† f. *warlike band,* Ex.

+heredlic (LPs105²)=+hierendlic

herefeld† m. *battlefield, field.*

herefeoh n. *booty,* AO118⁵.

herefēða m. *war-troop,* CR1013.

hereflӯma (ē, ī) m. *deserter,* BR23.

herefolc† n. *army,* JUD.

herefong m. *osprey,* WW.

herefugol m. *bird of prey,* Ex161.

hereg-=herg-, herig-

heregang m. *invasion,* W312¹ : *devastation,* BH306B⁷. [v. '*here*']

heregeatland n. *heriot-land,* EC220. [v. '*heriot*']

here-geatu fn. gp. -geat(w)e, -geat(w)a, -geatu *war-gear, military equipment,* Bo, Ma : '*heriot,*' Ct,LL (v. 2·500).

heregild (e, eo, y) n. *war-tax, Danegeld,* Chr,Ct. ['*heregeld*']

heregrīma† m. *helmet,* B.

herehand f. *violence of war,* BH356²².

herehlōð f. *war-host, troop,* GU1042.

herehūð (ӯ³) f. *booty, prey, plunder,* Æ, AO.

herelāf f. *remains of a host,* Æ : *spoil,* Æ.

herelic *martial,* WW374²⁶.

herelof mn. *fame, glory,* OEG : *trophy,* OEG.

heremæcg m. *warrior,* GEN2483.

heremægen† n. *warlike force, multitude.*

heremann m. *soldier,* LkL7⁸.

hēremann=hīeremann

heremeðel n. *national assembly,* EL550.

±herenes (æ) f. *praise,* BH,PPs.

herenett n. *corslet,* B1553.

hereniþ m. *warfare,* B2474.

herenuma m. *prisoner,* LL(238¹¹).

herepāð† f. *corslet, coat of mail.*

her(e)-pað, -pæð m. *military road, highway,* v. CC46 and Mdf.

hererǣs m. *hostile raid,* W271².

hererǣswa m. *commander,* EL995.

hererēaf f. *war spoil, plunder, booty,* Æ.

hererinc† m. *warrior.*

heresceaft m. *spear,* B335.

heresceorp n. *war-dress,* FIN45.

heresīð† m. *warlike expedition.*

herespēd f. *success in war,* B64.

hērespel n. *glorious discourse,* CREAT37.

herestrǣl m. *arrow,* B1435.

herestrǣt f. *highway, main road,* CP375⁹ and N (LL556,10²).

hereswēg m. *martial sound,* RUIN23.

heresyrce f. *corslet,* B1511.

heretēam m. *plunder, devastation,* GEN : *predatory excursion,* LL.

heretēma† (ӯ³) m. *general, king, ruler.*

here-toga, -toha m. *commander, general, chieftain, Æ,BH* ; AO,CP. ['*heretoga*']

hereð m. *booty,* GD224²⁶. [hergað]

hereðrēat m. *war-band, troop,* Ex,WW.

hereðrym m. *phalanx,* WW411³⁴.

herewǣd f. *mail, armour,* B1897.

herewǣpen n. *weapon,* PPs34³.

herewæsma m. *prowess,* B677.

herewǣða† m. *warrior,* JUD.

hereweg m. *highway,* WW146³³.

hereweorc n. *war-work,* EL656.

herewian=hierwan

herewīc n. *dwellings, camp,* BL.

herewīsa† m. *captain, general.*

herewōp m. *the cry of an army,* Ex460.

hereword n. *praise, renown,* CHR1009F.

herewōsa† m. *warrior.*

herewulf m. *warrior,* GEN2015.

herewurd (HGL423)=hereword

herfest=hærfest; herg=hearg

herg-=hereg-, heri(g)-

hergað (here-, o²) m. *harrying, devastation* : *booty,* GD.

hergere m. *one who praises,* DR. ['*heryer*']

±hergian *to ravage, plunder, lay waste,* '*harry,*' AO,Chr; Æ,CP : *seize, take, capture.* ['*harrow*'; here]

hergiend m. *plunderer,* GL.

hergoð=hergað

hergung (AO), hergiung f. '*harrying,*' *ravaging, raid, invasion, attack, BH,Chr* : *plunder, booty* : '*harrowing,*' Æ.

herh=hearg

herian I. (æ) *to extol, praise, commend,* Æ,AO,BH,Bl,CP,VPs. ['*hery*'] II.= hierwan. III.=hergian. IV.=erian

herig=hearg; v. also here.

herigend m. *flatterer,* Sc205¹⁵.

±herigendlic *laudable, commendable,* Æ : *praising* : *excellent.* adv. -lice.

herigendsang m. *song of praise,* WW335¹⁷.

hering=herung; hēring=hīering

hērinne adv. '*herein*,' Æ.
herlic I. (æ) *noble*, MET. II.=herelic
hērnes=hīernes
hērof adv. '*hereof*,' *of this*, A.
hēron adv. *herein*, Ct; LL. ['*hereon*']
hērongean adv. *contrariwise*, W52⁸.
hērongemong *at this point, in this connection, meanwhile*, CP : *among others* CP.
her-pað, -poð=herepað
hērra=hēarra, hīerra (v. hēah).
hērrihte (ǣ) *at this point*, AS.
herst-=hierst-; hērsum=hīersum
hērtō *thus far*, OEG56⁸⁰.
hērtōēacan *besides*, W.
herð=heorð
herðan pl. '*testiculi*,' LL84,65.
herðbelig m. '*scrotum*,' WW.
herðland (NC357)=yrðland
herung (eo) f. *praise*, Æ,CP. ['*herying*']
herutbeg (OEG54²)=heorotberge
herw-=hierw-
herwið adv. '*herewith*,' EC236.
hes-=hys-; hēst=hǣst
hēt pret. 3 sg. of hātan.
hetan *to attack*, ÆL35²⁸⁰.
hete (ea) m. '*hate*,' *envy, malice, hostility, persecution, punishment*, B,BH,VPs; Æ, AO,CP.
hetegrim† *fierce, cruel*, AN.
hetel=hetol
hetelic *hostile, malignant, horrible, violent, excessive*, AO,B. ['*hatelich*'] adv. -līce, Æ. ['*hately*']
hetend=hettend
hetenlð† m. *hostility, spite, wickedness*.
heterōf *full of hate*, AN1422.
heterūn f. *charm which produces hate*, RD34⁷.
hetesprǣc f. *defiant speech*, GEN263.
hetesweng m. *hostile blow*, B2225.
heteðanc† m. *hostile design*.
heteðoncol *hostile*, JUL105.
hetol *hating, hostile, evil*, Æ,WW : *savage : violent, severe*, RB67¹⁶. [v. '*hatel*']
hetolnes (e²) f. *violence, fierceness*, OEG11¹⁵².
hēton pret. pl. of hātan.
hētt (AO)=hǣt pres. 3 sg. of hātan.
hettan (æ) *to chase, persecute*, OEG8³⁸⁸.
hettend† m. *enemy, antagonist*.
hettende pres. part. of hatian.
hēðen=hǣðen; hēwen=hǣwen
hī=hēo, hīe
hīce *name of a bird*, '*parruca*,' WW38².
hīcemāse f. *blue titmouse*, WW132²⁴.
hīcgan=hycgan
hīcol m. *woodpecker*, BC1·47²⁵ (Mdf).
hīd I. fn. a '*hide*' *of land* (about 120 acres, but amount varied greatly), Chr,Ct,LL, v. ECpp457–461 and LL2·513. [hīwan]
II.=hȳd

hīdan=hȳdan
hider adv. '*hither*,' *to this side, on this side*, Æ,Cp,VPs. comp. hideror *nearer*. h. and ðider (Cp,CP), hidres ðidres (Bo), *hither and thither*.
hidercyme m. *advent, arrival, BH.* ['*hithercome*']
hidere *hither*, WW522³.
hidergeond adv. *thither, yonder*, Mt26³⁶.
hiderryne adj. (i¹, i³) *of our country*, OET 115¹³¹.
hidertōcyme=hidercyme
hiderweard adj. and adv. '*hitherward*,' *towards this place*, Chr.
hīdgild I. n. *tax paid on each hide of land*, Ct. ['*hidegeld*'] II.=hȳdgild
hīdir-=hider-
hīdmǣlum adv. *by hides*, KC6·98⁴.
hidres v. hider.
hīe I. nap. of hē, hēo, hit. ['HI*, *hy*']
II.=hēo nasf. of hē. ['HI, *hy*']
hieder=hider
hieftnīed (EPs123⁶)=hæftnīed
hīeg (ē, ī, ȳ) n. '*hay*,' *cut grass*, G,Lcd,VPs. [hēawan]
hīeghūs (ē, ī) n. *hay store*, WW. ['*hayhouse*']
hīegian (CP)=hīgian
hīegsīðe (ē) m. *hay-scythe*, GD37¹³.
hīehra, hīehst ['*highest*'] v. hēah.
hīehð(u) (ē, ēa, ȳ) f. (often indecl.) '*height*,' *highest point, summit*, Gen,Sc : *the heavens, heaven*, Cr,El,Gu,Sc : *glory*. [hēah]
±hield (æ, e, eo, i, y) f. (usu. +) *keeping, custody, guard, protection*, CP : *loyalty, fidelity*, Chr,LL : *observance, observation, watching : secret place : protector, guardian*. ['*held(e)*']
±hieldan (e, y) intr. *to lean, incline, slope*, Bo : tr. *force downwards, bow or bend down*, B,Lk. ['*hield*']
hielde (e, y) f. *slope, declivity*, KC,WW. ['*hield*']
-hielde (y) v. earfoð-h.
+hieldelic (y) *safe*, GD348¹⁰.
+hieldnes (y) f. *observance*, PPs18¹⁰.
hielfe (e, y) n. *handle*, CP,WW. ['*helve*']
hielfling (e) m. *mite, farthing*, LkL12⁶. [healf]
hiellan *to make a noise*, EPs82³.
hielpeð pres. 3 sg. of helpan.
hielt pres. 3 sg. of healdan.
-hieltan (y) v. ā-h. [healt]
hielto (e, y) f. *lameness*, MH116¹⁰.
±hīenan (ǣ, ē, ȳ) *to fell, prostrate : overcome : weaken, crush, afflict, injure, oppress : abase, humble, insult*, B,LkL : *accuse, condemn*, CP. ['*hean*']
hiene as. of hē (CP). ['*hin*']

+**hīene** (ē) *ready to fall, frail,* DR189¹⁶.
hīenend (e¹) m. *accuser,* JnLp5⁹.
hīennes (ē, ȳ) f. *crushing, destruction,* BH, LkR.
hīenð, hīenðo (ǣ, ē, ȳ) f. *humiliation, affliction, oppression, annoyance,* CP : *loss, damage, harm* : *act of hanging,* DHy 59⁷.
hīera gp. of hē, hēo, hit. ['HER*']
hīera=hīerra v. hēah.
±**hīeran** (ē, ēo, ī, ȳ) tr. and intr. *to* 'HEAR' ('*y-here*'), *listen* (*to*), Æ : (w. d.) *obey, follow,* Æ; CP : *accede to, grant* : *be subject to, belong to, serve,* AO : (+) *judge.*
±**hīerdan** (i, y) *to harden, make hard* : *strengthen, fortify, confirm, encourage,* CP. [heard]
hierde (eo, i, y) m. (f. at ÆGR57¹⁶) *shepherd, herdsman,* CP,G; AO : *guardian, keeper,* B,Bl,Gen,Met,WW : *pastor,* Bl. ['herd']
hierdebelig (e) m. *shepherd's bag,* Bl31¹⁷. [v. 'belly']
hierdebōc f. *pastoral book* (translation of the *Cura Pastoralis* of Pope Gregory), CP.
hierdecnapa (y) m. *shepherd boy,* ÆL23⁴¹⁸.
hierdelēas (i, y) *without a shepherd or pastor,* Æ. ['herdless']
hierdelic (y) *pastoral,* CP.
hierdeman (y) m. *shepherd,* Æ. ['herdman']
hierdenn (y) f. *hardening,* SOL150'.
hierdewyrt (i) f. *name of a plant,* LCD.
±**hierdnes** (eo, i, y) f. *custody, watch, guard.*
hierdung (y) f. *strengthening, restoring,* WW 150³⁴.
hiere gds. of hēo. ['HER*']
hīered=hīred
hīereman (ē, ī, ȳ) m. *retainer, servant, subject, hearer, parishioner,* Mk; CP. ['hireman']
+**hīerend** m. *hearer,* CP.
+**hīerendlic** (e¹, y¹) *audible,* LPs142⁸,ÆGR 152⁶.
+**hīering** (ē) f. *hearing, hearsay,* LPs111⁷.
hīeringman (ē, ȳ) m. *subject,* RWH96⁵ : *hireling,* 126³⁵.
hīernes (ē, ȳ) f. (+) *hearing, report* : (±) *obedience, subjection, allegiance,* CP : *jurisdiction, district.*
hīerra=hearra
hīerra v. hēah.
±**hīerstan** (e, i, y) *to fry, roast, scorch, pain,* CP. [cp. *OHG.* giharsten]
hierste (e, y) f. *frying-pan* : *gridiron,* WW 214⁴⁰.
hierstepanne (ea, y) f. *frying-pan,* CP.
hiersting (y) f. *frying, burning,* CP : *frying-pan?* ÆGR175³.
hierstinghlāf (e) m. *crust,* WW372¹⁸.

±**hīersum** (ē, ēa, ī, ȳ) w. d. *obedient, docile,* BH,Gu. ['hearsum']
±**hīersumian** (ēa, ī, ȳ) w. d. *to obey, serve,* BH,Mt; AO : (+) *reduce, subject, conquer,* CHR. ['hearsum']
hīersumlic (ȳ) *willing,* GD152¹.
±**hīersumnes** (ī, ȳ) f. *obedience, submission,* BH; CP : *service* : *humility.* ['hersumnesse']
±**hiertan** (e, eo, y) *to cheer, encourage,* CP; Æ : *be renewed, refreshed* : *revive* : *cherish.* ['heart'; heort]
hierting (y) f. *soothing,* OEG17¹⁰.
±**hierwan** (e, i, y) *to abuse, blaspheme, condemn, illtreat* : *to deride, despise.*
hierwend (i) m. *blasphemer,* LEV24¹⁴.
hierwendlic *contemptible.* adv. -līce (e) *with contempt.*
hierwing (y) f. *blasphemy,* Sc137¹².
hierwnes (i, y) f. *contempt, reproach* : *blasphemy,* W70¹².
hīew=hīw
hīewestān m. *hewn stone,* AO212¹⁰.
hīewet (ȳ) n. *cutting,* CP,WW. [hēawan]
hīewian=hīwian
hīewð (CP) pres. 3 sg. of hēawan.
hīf- (v. OEG3913)=hīw-
hīg=hīe I.; **hīg**=hīeg
hīgan=hīwan; **hige**=hyge
hīgendlīce *quickly, immediately,* RWH25¹³. [hīgian]
higera m., higere f. *jay, magpie, jackdaw, woodpecker.* [*Ger.* häher]
higgan=hycgan
hīgian *to* 'hie,' *strive, hasten,* Bl,Bo,CP.
hīgid=hīd
hīglā 'heu!' RPs119⁵.
hīglēast=hygelēast; **hīgna** v. hīwan.
hīgo (N)=hīwan; **higora, higra**=higera
hīgre=higere; **hīgscipe**=hīwscipe
hīgð f. *exertion, effort,* ZDA. ['hight']
hīgung f. *effort,* GD254³⁴.
hihsan=hyscan; **hiht**=hyht
hihting f. *exultation, gladness,* WW233⁴².
hīhðo=hīehðu; **hilc**=hylc
hīlā=hīglā
hild I.† f. *war, combat.* II.=hield
hildbedd n. *deathbed,* AN1094.
hildebill† n. *sword,* B.
hildeblāc? *deadly pale, mortally wounded,* B2488 (or ?heorublāc).
hildebord† n. *buckler,* B.
hildecalla m. *war-herald,* Ex252.
hildecorðor n. *warlike band,* AP41.
hildecyst f. *valour,* B2598.
hildedēoful n. *demon,* PPs95⁵.
hildedēor *war-fierce, brave,* Æ.
hildefreca† m. *warrior.*
hildegeatwe† fp. *war-harness,* B.

hildegesa m. *terror of battle*, EL113.

hildegicel m. *battle-icicle (blood dripping from a sword)*, B1606.

hildegiest m. *enemy*, RD54⁹.

hildegrāp† f. *hostile grip*, B.

hildeheard *bold in battle*, AP21.

hildehlem† m. *crash of battle*, B.

hildelēoma† m. *Gleam of battle (name of a sword)*, B.

hildelēoð n. *war-song*, JUD211.

hildemēce m. *sword*, B2202.

hildemecg m. *warrior*, B799.

hildenǣdre† f. *war-snake, arrow*.

hildepīl† m. *dart, javelin*, Rd. [v. '*pile*']

hilderǣs m. *charge, attack*, B300.

hilderand m. *shield*, B1242.

hilderinc† m. *warrior, hero*.

hildesǣd *battle-worn*, B2723.

hildesceorp n. *armour*, B2155.

hildescūr m. *shower of darts*, GU1116.

hildeserce f. *corslet*, EL234.

hildesetl m. *saddle*, B1039.

hildespell n. *warlike speech*, EX573.

hildestrengo f. *vigour for battle*, B2113.

hildeswāt m. *vapour of battle?* B2558.

hildeswēg m. *sound of battle*, GEN1991.

hildetorht *shining in battle*, MET25⁹.

hildetux m. *tusk (as weapon)*, B1511.

hildeðremma m. *warrior*, JUL64.

hildeðrymm (AN1034) m., hildeðrўð (RD 20⁴) f. *warlike strength, valour*.

hildewǣpen m. *weapon of war*, B39.

hildewīsa m. *commander*, B1064.

hildewŏma† m. *crash of battle*.

hildewrǣsn f. *fetter for captives*, SOL292.

hildewulf m. *hero*, GEN2051.

hildfreca—hildefreca

hildfrom *valiant in war*, AN1204.

hildfruma† m. *battle-chief, prince, emperor*.

hildlata m. *laggard in battle, coward*, B2846.

hildstapa m. *warrior*, AN1260.

hildŏracu f. *onset of battle*, GEN2157.

hileð=hilð; hilhāma=hyllehāma

hilk=hyll, hell

+hilmed (y) *helmeted*, WW413²⁷ : *covered with foliage*, WW405,526.

hilpestu=hilpest ðu (pres. 2 sg. of helpan and pron. 2 pers. sing.).

hilpeð, hilpð pres. 3 sg. of helpan.

hilt I.=hielt pres. 3 sg. of healdan. II. mn. =hilte

±hilte fn. *handle, 'hilt' (of sword)*, B,WW; (pl.=sg.) Æ,B,Sol.

hilt(e)cumbor n. *banner with a staff*, B1022 (or ?hilde-).

hilted *'hilted,' with a hilt*, B.

hilting m. *sword*, OEG758.

hiltlēas *having no hilt*, WW142³⁴.

hiltsweord (y) n. *hilted sword*, BO111¹⁶.

±hiltu np. of hilte.

hilð pres. 3 sg. of helan.

him ds. of hē, dp. of hē, hēo, hit. ['HIM']

himming (CP1557)=hemming

hīna v. hīwan.

hinan=heonon; hīnan=hīenan

-hinca v. helle-h.

hind (y) f. '*hind*' *(female deer)*, Chr,WW.

hindan *from behind, behind, in the rear*, Æ,AO. æt h. *behind*, Æ. [*Ger.* hinten]

hindanweard adv. *hindwards, at the end*, PH298.

hindberge f. *raspberry*, Cp,Ep,Lcd : *strawberry?* WW409¹². ['*hindberry*']

hindbrēr m. *raspberry bush*, LCD146b (hinde-).

hindcealf mn. *fawn*, WW. ['*hindcalf*']

hindema† superl. adj. *hindmost, last*.

hinder adj. *after (thought), sad, sinister (thought)?* MFH,RWH143¹³. adv. *behind, back, after, in the farthest part, down*. on h. *backwards*, Æ.

hindergēap *wily, cunning, deceitful*, WW. ['*hinderyeap*']

hindergenga m. *one who walks backwards*, OEG26²³ : *apostate*, OEG5¹⁶.

hinderhōc m. *trick*, MOD34.

hinderling I. m. *mean wretch, sneak*, LL 665'. II. adv. in phr. 'on hinderling' *backwards*, PPs. ['*hinderling*']

hindernes f. *wickedness, guile*, NC301; MFH 166.

hinderscipe m. *wickedness*, DHy,OEG.

hinderðēostru np. *nether darkness*, PPs85¹².

hinderweard *slow, sluggish*, PH314.

hindeweard *reversed, wrong end first, from behind*, CP.

hindfalod n. *hind-fold*, KC6·112³¹.

hind-hæleðe, -heoloð(e) f. '*ambrosia,' water agrimony*, WW. [v. '*hindheal*']

±hindrian *to 'hinder,' check, repress*, Chr, LL.

hindsīð (BL)=hinsīð

hine I. as. of hē. II.=heonon

hīne=hīwene

hinfūs† *ready to depart or die*.

hingang† m. *departure, death*, OET149. [v. '*yong*']

hingrian (Bl; Æ)=hyngrian

hinn-=hin-; hinon=heonon

hinsīð† m. *departure, death*. [heonon]

hinsīðgryre m. *fear of death*, SAT456.

hīo v. he; hio-=heo-

hionne? f. '*dura mater*,' LL5,36.

hior=heorr; hiored=hīred

hioro-=heoru-

hīowesclīce=hīwisclīce; hip-=hyp-

hipsful (OEG11¹⁸⁰)=hyspful

hīr=hўr; hīr-, hir-=hier-, hēor-, hīer-

hīra gp. of hē, hēo, hit; **hīrd-**=hīred-
hīre gds. of hēo. ['HER*']
hīred (ēo, īe, ȳ) m. *household, family, retinue, AO,Bo,Mt,WW : brotherhood, company, Æ,Ct.* ['hird']
hīredcniht m. *domestic, member of a household, Æ.*
hīredcūð *domestic, familiar,* So 203¹³.
hīredgerēfa m. *'ex-consul,'* WW 110⁶.
hīredlic *pertaining to a household or court, domestic, familiar.*
hīredlōf (=lēof) *friendly,* A 13·445.
hīredman m. *retainer, follower, Æ,Ma.* ['hirdman']
hīredprēost (ȳ) m. *chaplain,* TC 571² : *regular priest,* EC 255.
hīredwīfman m. *female member of a household,* TC 531⁶.
hīredwist f. *familiarity,* Sc 203¹².
hīru=hūru
his gs. of hē. ['HIS']
hīs (BH)=īs; **hisc-**=hysc-
hislic *suitable,* GD 183⁵.
hispan=hyspan; **hiss**=hos; **hisse**=hyse
hit v. hē. ['IT']
hittan (y) *to fall in with, meet with, 'hit' upon,* Chr 1066. [ON. hitta]
hīð-=hȳð-; **hīðer**=hider
hiu (NG)=hēo
hīw I. (ēo, īe, īo, ȳ) n. *appearance, form, species, kind, Æ,Bl,Cr,G,WW : apparition,* WW 236⁸ : 'hue,' colour, Bf,Bl : beauty : *figure of speech.* II. (io) f. *fortune,* AA 11².
hīwan mp. (gen. hīwna, hī(g)na) *members of a family, household or religious house, Chr, G; Æ.* ['hind,' 'hewe']
hīwbeorht† *radiant, beautiful.*
hīwcund (hīl-) *familiar, domestic,* GL.
hīwcūð (īe) *domestic, familiar, well-known,* Æ,CP.
hīwcūðlic *domestic, familiar.* adv. -līce.
+**hīwcūðlician** *to make known or familiar to,* NC 294.
hīwcūðnes f. *familiarity,* GD 71²⁴; 140⁷.
hīwcūðrǣdnes f. *familiarity,* WW 191²⁴.
hīwen n. *household, Æ.* ['hewen']
+**hīwendlic** *allegorical,* WW 354⁴.
hīwere m. *dissembler, hypocrite, Æ.*
hīwfæger *comely of form,* MFH 167.
hīwfæst *comely, fair,* OEG.
hīwgedāl n. *divorce,* G.
±**hīwian** I. *to form, fashion, WW : colour : dissimulate, feign, pretend, Æ : figure, signify, Æ : (+) transform, transfigure.* ['hue,' 'hued'] II. *to marry,* CP 318¹.
hīwisc n. *household, Æ : hide (of land v. hīd).* adv. -līce *familiarly.*
+**hīwlǣcan** *to form, shape, fashion,* NC 294 : *colour,* LCD 1·262¹⁴.

hīwlēas *shapeless, WW : colourless,* Lcd 11. ['hueless']
hīwlic I. *comely,* LCD,OEG : *figurative,* HGL. II. *matronly?* WW 442².
hīwna v. hīwan.
hīwnes f. *hue, colour, appearance,* WE 65¹⁴.
+**hīwodlīce** *in form,* ÆGR 250,251.
hīwrǣden f. *family, household, religious house, Æ.*
hīwscipe m. *family, household : hide (of land),* CC 127.
hīwð pres. 3 sg. of hēawan.
hīwung I. (ēo, ȳ) f. (±) *appearance, likeness, form, figure : portrayal,* ByH 102³³ : *pretence, hypocrisy, Æ : irony,* WW 416³² . II. f. *marriage,* AO 64²⁴.
hlacerian *to deride, mock,* LPs 24³.
hlacerung f. *unseemly behaviour, or words, mockery,* LPs 43¹⁴.
±**hladan**⁶ (æ, ea) *to 'lade,' draw, or take in water, Æ,JnR : heap up, lay on, build, load, burden, B,Gen,Rd;* CP.
hladung f. *drawing ('haustus'),* DHy 58⁶.
hlǣ=hlǣw
hlǣd n. *heap? burden?* CP 21¹⁶⁰. ['lade']
hlǣdder (Bl), hlǣddre=hlǣder
hlǣddisc m. *loaded dish?* WW 126³⁹.
hlǣdel m. *'ladle,'* LL,ZDA.
hlǣden I. m. *bucket,* WW 123⁵. II. pp. of hladan.
hlǣder f. *'ladder,' steps, Æ,Bf,LL;* CP.
hlǣderstæf f. *rung of a ladder,* ByH 80³⁰.
hlǣderwyrt f. *ladder-wort, Jacob's ladder,* LCD.
hlǣdhweogl n. *water-wheel, wheel for drawing up water,* WW 347⁷.
hlǣdrede *having steps,* BC 3·492'.
hlǣdst=hlǣtst pres. 2 sg. of hladan.
hlǣdtrendel m. *wheel for drawing water,* OEG 502.
hlǣfde *'sparsio panis,'* WW 277⁶.
hlǣfdige (ā, ē) f. *mistress (over servants), LL,VPs,WW : chatelaine, 'lady,' queen, Chr,Ct : the Virgin Mary, Cr.* sēo ealde h. *the queen dowager,* CHR 1051 C.
hlǣfl=læfel
+**hlǣg** n. *derision, scorn,* DOM 15.
hlǣgulian (Cp 317)=hlagolian
hlǣhan (N,VPs)=hliehhan
hlǣhter=hleahtor
hlǣnan I. *to cause to lean,* JUL 63. II.= lǣnan
-hlǣnan v. ā-hl.
hlǣne *'lean,' Æ;* AO.
±**hlǣnian** *to become lean, CP : make lean, starve, CP.* ['lean']
hlǣnnes f. *'leanness,' Æ,OEG.*
±**hlǣnsian** *to make lean, weaken,* OEG. ['lense']

hlǣpewince (WW)=lēapewince
hlæst n. *burden, load, freight, B,Rd.* holmes h. *finny tribe.* ['*last*']
+hlæstan (e) *to load, burden, BH* : *adorn,* JUD 36. [v. '*last*' vb.]
hlæsting f. *toll on loading a ship,* TC 359, 411.
hlæstscip n. *trading-vessel,* Cp 147 H.
hlæt=læt
hlætst pres. 2 sg. of hladan.
hlǣw† (ā) mn. *mound, cairn, hill, mountain, B* : *grave-yard, barrow, Met* : *hollow mound, cave.* ['*low*']
hlāf m. '*loaf,*' *cake, bread, food, Bf,NG*; Æ, AO,CP : *sacramental bread,* ÆP 108²³.
hlāfæta m. ('*loaf-eater*'), *dependant, LL* 4,25.
hlāfbrytta m. *slave in charge of the bread-store?* EC 255.
hlāfdie (VPs)=hlǣfdige
hlāfgang m. *attendance at, or participation in, a meal,* RB : *partaking of the Eucharist,* LL 473,27.
hlāf-gebrecu f. (PPs), -gebroc (MH) n. *bit of bread.*
hlāfhwǣte m. *bread-wheat,* TC 144'.
hlāflēast f. *want of bread,* CAS 34²⁰.
hlāfmæsse f. '*Lammas*' (*August* 1), *AO*; Æ.
hlāfmæssedæg m. *Lammas-day.*
hlāfmæssetīd f. *Lammas-tide,* LCD 6a.
hlāfofn m. *baker's oven,* WW 411⁸.
hlāford m. '*lord,*' *master, ruler, AO,B,Bf, Chr,G*; Æ,CP : *husband, Ct* : *the Lord, God,* Æ. [hlāf, weard]
hlāforddōm m. *lordship, authority, CP* : *patronage.* ['*lorddom*']
hlāfordgift m? n? *grant* (*or appointment*) *by a lord,* HGL 412 (v. BTs).
hlāfordhold *loyal to a lord,* Bo 42⁹⁴.
hlāfordhyldo f. *loyalty,* AO.
hlāfording m. *lord, master,* W 298⁷.
hlāfordlēas *without a lord, leaderless, B.* ['*lordless*']
hlāfordlic '*lordly,*' *noble,* OEG 187¹.
hlāfordscipe m. '*lordship,*' *authority, rule, CP* : '*dominatio*' (*title of an order of angels*), ÆH 1·342'.
hlāfordsearu fn. *high treason, LL.*
hlāfordsōcn f. *act of seeking the protection of a lord, LL.*
hlāfordswica m. *traitor, Lcd*; Æ. ['*lord-swike*']
hlāfordswice m. *high treason, treachery,* W 160.
hlāford-swicung (MFH 167; W 225²³), -syr-wung (LL 16 n 5) f. *betrayal of one's lord.*
hlāfordðrimm m. *dominion, power,* NC 302.
hlāfræce f. *oven-rake,* OEG 53⁴³ (hlāb-).

hlāfsēnung f. *blessing of bread* (*on Lammas-day*), MH 136¹.
hlāfurd=hlāford
hlāfweard m. *steward,* PPs 104¹⁷ (v. GK 884 s.v. healf-).
hlagol *inclined to laugh,* W 40⁸.
hlagolian (æ) *to sound,* Cp 317.
hlāmmæsse=hlāfmæsse
hlanc '*lank,*' *lean, thin, Jud,PPs.*
hland (o) n. *urine, Lcd.* ['*lant*']
hlaðian=laðian; hlāw=hlǣw
hleadan=hladan; hleahter=hleahtor
hleahterful *scornful,* GUTH.
hleahterlic *ridiculous,* Sc 38⁷.
hleahtor (e) m. '*laughter,*' *jubilation, B,Bl, CP,Sc* : *derision.*
hleahtorbǣre *causing laughter,* RB 18⁸.
hleahtorsmið m. *laughter-maker,* Ex 43.
hleahtrian (e) *to deride,* LPs 21⁸.
hlēapan⁷ *to* '*leap,*' *run, go, jump, dance, spring, Æ,B,BH,Chr,CP* : (+) *leap upon, mount* (*a horse*).
hlēapere m. *runner, courier, Chr* : *wanderer* : *horseman* : '*leaper,*' *dancer, WW* : *itinerant monk,* RB 135²⁰.
hlēapestre f. *female dancer,* WW 311³³.
hlēapettan v. *to leap up,* BH 390⁹.
hlēapewince f. '*lapwing,*' *WW.*
hlēapung f. *dancing, Æ.* ['*leaping*']
hlēat pret. 3 sg. of hlēotan.
hlec *leaky, CP,OEG.* [v. '*leak*']
hlecan⁵ *to cohere,* CP 361²⁰.
hlēda, hlēde (ȳ) m. *seat,* ÆGR 34³.
hlēf=hlǣw; -hlēfan (oc) v. ā-hl.
hlēga (LkL 6¹⁶)=lǣwa; hlēnhan=hliehhan
hlēg(i)ende (æ¹, u²) *deep-sounding,* WW 9⁹⁷, 358¹⁹.
hleht-=hleaht-
hlem m. *sound,* CP 253¹⁷.
hlemman *to cause to sound, clash,* WH 61.
hlēnan=lǣnan
+hlencan *to twist, bend?* LCD.
hlence f. *coat of mail,* Ex 218.
hlennan=hlynnan
hlenortēar m. *hyssop,* LPs 50⁸.
hlēo† m? n? (hlēow), gs. hlēowes (no pl.) *covering, refuge, defence, shelter, protection, Cr,PPs* : *protector, lord.* ['*lee*']
hlēo-=hlēow-
hlēobord n. *book-cover,* RD 27¹².
hlēoburh† f. *protecting city, B.*
hlēod=hlōd
+hleodu pl. of +hlid.
hlēohrǣscnes f. '*supplantatio*'? LPs 40¹⁰.
hlēolēas† *without shelter, comfortless.*
hleomoc m. hleomoce f. *speedwell, Lcd.* [v. '*brooklime*']
hlēon=hlēowan; hleon-=hlin-
hlēonaÐ m. *shelter,* GU 222.

hlēonian *to cherish*, WW377³².
hlēop pret. 3 sg. of hlēapan.
hlēor n. *cheek*, Lcd,WW : *face, countenance*,
Ep,Gu. ['leer']
hlēoran (ÆL)=lēoran
hlēorbān n. (*cheek-bone*), *temple*, LPs131⁵.
hlēorberg? f. *cheek-guard, helmet*, B304?
hlēorbolster m. *pillow*, B688.
hlēordropa m. *tear*, Gu1315.
hlēorsceamu f. *confusion of face*, PPs68⁸.
hlēorslæge m. *a blow on the cheek*, CP
261⁶.
hlēortorht *beautiful*, Rd69⁶.
hlēosceorp n. *sheltering robe*, Rd10⁵.
hlēotan¹ *to cast lots*, Æ,AO : (±) *get by lot,
obtain.*
hlēoð=(1) hlēowð; (2) pres. pl. of hlēowan.
hlēoð-=hlōð-
hlēoðor n. *noise, sound, voice, song : hearing.*
+hlēoðor *harmonious*, BH60¹⁸.
hlēoðorcwide† m. *speaking, words, discourse,
song, prophecy.*
hlēoðorcyme m. *coming with trumpet-sound*,
Da710.
hlēoðorstede m. *place of conference*, Gen
2399.
hlēoðrere (ō) m. *rhetorician*, OET180⁴.
hlēoðrian *to sound, speak, sing, cry aloud,
resound, proclaim*, Æ.
hlēoðrung f. *sound*, MFH130 : *harmony,
hymn*, Bf198⁵ : *reproof*, SPs37¹¹.
hleoðu v. hlið.
hlēow=hlēo
±hlēow I. (ī) *sheltered, warm, sunny*, Lcd,
Nar. adv. hlēowe. [v. 'lew'] II.=+hlōw
±hlēowan (ī, ȳ) *to warm, make warm,
cherish*, Bl : *become warm or hot.* ['lew']
hlēowdryhten m. *protector, patron*, Wid94.
hlēowfæst *protecting, consoling*, Cr,RB.
hlēowfeðre fp. *sheltering wings*, Gen2740.
hlēowlora m. *one who has lost a protector*,
Gen1953.
hlēowmǣg† m. *kinsman who is bound to
afford protection.*
hlēownes f. *warmth*, A8·451.
hlēowon pret. pl. of hlōwan.
hlēowsian *to shelter, protect*, WW235²⁹.
hlēowstede m. *sunny place*, WW336³⁰.
hlēowstōl m. *shelter, asylum*, Gen2011.
hlēowð (ī, ȳ) f. *shelter, covering, warmth*, Æ,
Hex. ['lewth']
±hlēowung (ē, ī, ȳ) f. *shelter, protection,
favour*, CM,WW.
hlestan=hlæstan, hlystan
hlet (KGl) pres. 3 sg. of hladan.
hlēt (VPs; MkR)=hlīet
+hlēða† m. *companion, denizen.* [hlōð]
hlēðrian=hlēoðrian; hlēw=hlǣw
hlēw-=hlēow-

hlēwesa (EPs139¹³)=lēwsa
hlēwð pres. 3 sg. of hlōwan.
hlid I. n. 'lid,' *covering, door, gate, opening*,
Æ. II.=hlið
+hlid† n. (nap. hlidu, hleodu) *covering,
vault, roof.*
hlīdan¹ *to come forth, spring up*, PPs79¹¹?
hlidfæst *closed by a lid*, TC516⁴.
hlidgeat n. *swing-gate, folding-door*, BC,
EC; Æ; Mdf. ['lidgate']
+hlidod (eo) *having a lid*, BH320¹⁰.
['lidded']
hliehhan⁶ (e, i, y) *to laugh*, Æ,CP : (±) *laugh
at, deride*, Æ,MtL : *rejoice.*
hlīep (ȳ) mf., hlīepe f. 'leap,' *bound, spring,
sudden movement*, Cr,Lcd : *thing to leap
from*, AO : *place to leap over?* v. CC54 :
waterfall, Ct.
hlīepen pres. pl. of hlēapan.
hlīepgeat (ȳ) n. *a low gate*, KC. ['leapgate']
hlīet (ē, ȳ) m. *lot, share : chance, fortune*,
CP.
hlīfend (hlīb-) *threatening*, Cp223m.
hlīfian *to rise high, tower, overhang*, B,GD.
hlīgan¹ᵛ *to attribute* (to), CP,Da.
hlīgsa (CP)=hlīsa
hlihan, hlihcan, hlihhan=hliehhan
hlimman³† (y) *to sound, resound, roar, rage.*
hlimme† f. *stream, torrent*, PPs.
hlin I. (=y) m. *maple-tree*, Rd56⁹. [Ger.
lehne] II.=hlynn
hlinbedd n. *sick-bed, couch*, B3034.
hlinc m. *ridge, bank, rising ground, hill*, EC,
Ph; v. GBG and Mdf. ['link']
hlincrǣw f. *bank forming a boundary*, EC,
KC.
hlinduru† f. *latticed door.*
±hlinian (eo, y) *to 'lean,'* B; Æ : *recline, lie
down, rest*, Jn,MkL; CP.
hliniend m. *one who reclines*, HGl414.
hlinræced† n. *prison*, An,Jul.
hlinscū(w)a† m. *darkness of confinement.*
hlinsian=hlynsian
±hlinung f. *'leaning,'* Lk : *seat, couch.*
hlīosa=hlīsa
hlīpð pres. 3 sg. of hlēapan.
hlīra=līra
hlīsa (īo, ȳ) m. *sound : rumour, fame, glory*,
CP.
hlīsbǣre *renowned*, OEG.
hlīsēadig *renowned, famed*, Bo.
hlīsēadignes f. *renown*, Bo75²⁸.
hlīsful *of good repute, famous*, Æ. adv. -līce,
Æ,AO.
hlīsig *renowned*, OEG8²⁵⁰.
hlīstan=hlystan; hlīt=hlyt
hliþ I.† n. (nap. hleoðu) *cliff, precipice,
slope, hill-side, hill*, An,B; Mdf. ['lith']
II.=hlid

hlīw=hlēow
hlīwe f. *shelter*, KC.
hloccetung f. *sighing*, HGL421[7].
hlōd pret. 3 sg. of hladan; hlodd=hlot
hlōgon pret. pl., hlōh pret. 3 sg. of hliehhan.
hlom (WW117[25]), hlond=hland
hlōse f. *pigsty*, LL454,10; NC302; Mdf.
hlosnere m. *listener*, OEG2333 : *disciple*, BF56[11].
hlosnian *to listen* : *wait*, Æ : *be on the look out for, spy*, Æ. hlosniende '*attonitus*,' WW.
hlōsstede m. *site of a pigsty*, KC.
hlot, hlott n. '*lot*,' *part, portion, share*, BC,LkL : (+) *selection by lot, choice, decision*, Æ,AO. hl. sendan, weorpan *to cast lots*, Bl,Mt.
hloten pp. of hleotan.
+hlotland n. *allotted land, inheritance*, Jos 24[30].
hlōð f. *troop, crowd, band*, AO : *booty, spoil* : *complicity with a band of robbers*, LL 94,14.
hlōðbōt f. *penalty imposed on a member of a gang of malefactors*, LL64,29.
hlōðere m. *robber*, WW506[36]. [hlōð]
hlōðgecrod n. *mass of troops*, RD4[63].
hlōðian (ēo) *to spoil, plunder*, BH.
hlōðsliht m. *murder by a member of a gang of malefactors*, LL18,29.
+hlōw n. *lowing, bellowing, bleating*, Æ.
hlōwan[7] *to '*low*,' roar, bellow*, Æ,El.
hlōwung f. *lowing, bleating, bellowing*, WW 102[7]; 195[13].
hlūd adj. comp. hlūdre, hluddre '*loud*,' *noisy, sounding, sonorous*, Bl,CP; Æ.
hlūdclipol *loud, noisy*, RBL35[11] (hlūt-).
hluddre v. hlūd.
hlūde adv. *loudly, aloud*, Bl; Æ,CP. ['*loud*']
hlūdnes f. '*loudness*,' *clamour*, Bf176[23].
hlūdstefne *loud-sounding*, WW416[18].
hlūdswēge adv. *loudly*, Æ.
hlummon pret. pl. of hlimman.
hlupon pret. pl. of hlēapan.
hluton pret. pl. of hlēotan.
hlūtor, hlūttor (e[2]) gsm. hlūtres *pure, clear, bright, sincere*, Æ,CP. [*Ger.* lauter] adv. -līce.
hlūtorlicnes=hlūtornes
hlūtornes f. *clearness, brightness, simplicity, purity*, Æ.
hlūtre I. adv. *clearly, brightly* : *untroubled*, PPs104[3]. II. ds. of hlūtor.
hlūtter, hlūttor=hlūtor
±hlūttrian *to clear, purify, make bright* : *to become clear*.
hlyd=hlid
±hlȳd fm. *noise, sound* : *tumult, disturbance, dissension*. [hlūd]

hlȳda=hlēda
Hlȳda m. *March, Lcd*. ['*Lide*'; hlūd]
hlȳdan *to make a noise, sound, clamour, vociferate*, Æ,CP. [hlūd]
hlȳde I. f. *torrent*, BC (Mdf). II. (LL455')= hlēde?
hlȳdig *garrulous*, OEG1418. [hlūd]
hlȳding f. *noise, cry*, MtL25[6] (lȳ-).
hlyhhan=hliehhan
hlymman=hlimman; hlyn=hlynn
hlynian=(1) hlynnan; (2) hlinian
±hlynn I. m. *sound, noise, din, tumult*, AO. II. f. *torrent*, JnR. ['*linn*']
hlynnan (e) *to make a noise, resound, shout, roar*.
hlynrian *to thunder*, WW519[34].
hlynsian† (i) *to resound*.
hlȳp=hlīep
hlȳrian (=īe) *to blow out (the cheeks)*, LPs 80[4]. [hlēor]
hlȳsa (Æ)=hlīsa
hlȳsfullīce=hlīsfullīce
hlysnan *to '*listen*,' MtL; Cp.
hlysnere m. *hearer*, DR29[4] (ly-).
±hlyst f. *sense of hearing*, Æ,Lcd : *listening*. ['*list*']
±hlystan (e, i) *to listen, hear*, CP,LL; Æ : *attend to, obey*, Lk. ['*list*']
+hlyste *audible*, CHRD22[36].
hlystend, hlystere m. *listener*, Æ.
+hlystful *attentive, gracious*, LPs89[13].
hlysting f. *act of listening*, RWH136[23].
hlyte m. *lot, portion*, WW40[13].
+hlyta m. *companion*, CPs44[9]. [hlot]
hlȳtere m. *priest*, NC302. (v. BTs)
hlytm̄ m. *casting of lots*, B3120?
hlytman *to decide by lot*, MFH167.
hlytta m. *diviner, soothsayer*, AO184[26] : (+) *partner, fellow*, RPs44[8]. [hlot]
+hlytto (e) *fellowship, lot*, DR.
hlȳttor (HGL418)=hlūttor, hlūtor
hlȳttrian *to purify*, ÆGR222[7].
hlȳttrung f. *cleaning, refining*, WW179[36].
-hlȳðan (=īe) v. be-hl.; hlȳðre=lȳðre
hlȳw-=hlēow-; hlȳwing=hlēowung
hnacod=nacod
hnǣcan *to check, destroy, kill*, Æ. [=nǣcan]
±hnǣgan I. *to bow down, bend, humble, curb, vanquish*. [hnīgan] II. *to '*neigh*,' ÆGr*. III.=nǣgan
hnǣgung f. '*neighing*,' ÆGr,Cp.
hnæpp m. *bowl*, EC,OEG,WW. ['*nap*']
hnæpp-=hnapp-
hnæppan *to strike*, Bo130[19,20].
hnæsce=hnesce
+hnǣsc, +hnāst† n. *collision, conflict, battle*. [hnītan]
+hnǣstan (nǣst-) *to contend with*, RD 28[10].

hnāg, hnāh I. *bent down, abject, poor, humble, lowly* : *niggardly*. II. pret. 3 sg. of hnīgan.

hnappian (æ, e, ea) *to doze, slumber, sleep*, CP,Mt,Sc,VPs; Æ. ['*nap*']

hnappung (æ, ea) f. *napping, slumbering*, VPs; CP.

hnāt pret. 3 sg. of hnītan.

hneap- (VPs)=hnap-

-hnēapan v. ā-hn.

hnēaw *mean, niggardly, stingy, miserly*, CP. [*Ger.* genau] adv. -līce.

hnēawnes f. *meanness*, CP.

hnecca m. '*neck*,' Æ,CP.

hnēgan=(1) nǣgan; (2) hnǣgan

hneofule f.=hnifol

hneoton pret. pl. of hnītan.

hnep (GD 186²⁷)=hnæpp

hneppian (KGL)=hnappian

hnescan=hnescian

hnesce I. (æ, i, y) *soft, tender, mild*, CP : *weak, delicate*, Æ : *slack, negligent*, CP : *effeminate, wanton*, Æ. ['NESH'] II. n. *soft object*. III. adv. *softly*, ÆL37³⁰¹.

±**hnescian** *to make soft, soften*, Æ,EPs : *become soft, give way, waver*, CP,Lcd; ÆL. ['*nesh*']

hnesclic *soft, luxurious, effeminate*, AO. adv. -līce *softly, gently, tenderly*, CP. ['*neshly*']

hnescnes f. *softness, weakness, effeminacy*, CP,Lcd,MtL; Æ : *soft part of anything*. ['*neshness*']

hnett (MtL 4¹⁸)=nett

hnexian (Æ)=hnescian

hnifol m. *brow, forehead*, Lcd,WW.

hnifol-crumb, -crump *inclined, prone*, WW.

hnīgan¹ *to bow oneself, bend, bow down* : *fall, decline, sink*. [*Ger.* neigen]

±**hnīgan** *to bow down* (*the head*), Lcd 7a, LL.

hnīgian=hnygelan

hnipend *bending, lowly*, HGL436.

hnipian *to bow down*, Met,OEG; Æ : *bow the head, look gloomy*, CP. ['*nipe*']

hnippan? *to bow down*, OEG 1579n.

hnisce (MkR 13²⁸)=hnesce

hnītan *to thrust, gore, butt*, Æ : *knock, come into collision with, encounter*.

hnītol *addicted to butting* (*of an ox*), Æ,LL.

hnitu f. *louse-egg*, '*nit*,' Ep,Lcd; Æ.

hnoc m. *wether sheep*, WW120³⁴.

hnoll m. *top, crown of the head*, Æ,VPs. ['*noll*']

hnoppian *to pluck*, WW480²⁷.

hnor? *sneezing* Ln65. [*hnēosan]

hnossian *to strike*, RD6⁷.

hnot *bare, bald,* '*close-cropped*,' ÆGr. ['*not*']

hnutbēam m. *nut tree*, Lcd; WW. [v. '*nut*']

hnutcyrnel mn. *kernel of a nut*, Lcd.

hnutu f. gs. and nap. hnyte '*nut*,' Erf,Lcd, MtR; Mdf.

+**hnycned** *wrinkled?* Lcd 97a.

hnydele=hydele

hnygelan (i) pl. *clippings*, WW.

hnȳlung f. *reclining*, WW153²⁴.

+**hnyscan** *to crush*, MtR21⁴⁴. [hnesce]

hnysce=hnesce

+**hnyst** *contrite*, PsC127.

hnyte gs. and nap. of hnutu.

hō I.=hōh. II. pres. 1 sg. of hōn.

hōbanca m. *couch*, WW280¹². [hōh]

hōc m. '*hook*,' BH,WW : *angle*, Mt,Nar.

hoc(c) m. *mallow*, Cp,Lcd. ['*hock*']

hōced *curved*, KC. ['*hooked*']

hocer=hocor; **hocg**=hogg

hōciht(e) *with many bends?* KC3·365', 6·227⁹.

hōcīsern n. *small sickle*, WW235¹.

hoclēaf n. *mallow*, Lcd.

hocor n. *insult, derision*, W164¹⁷. ['*hoker*']

hocorwyrde *derisive, scornful*, W164¹³. [v. '*hoker*']

hōd m. '*hood*,' Ep,WW.

hof n. *enclosure, court, dwelling, building, house, hall* : *temple, sanctuary*. [*Ger.* hof]

hōf I. m. '*hoof*,' Run,WW; Æ. II. pret. 3 sg. of hebban.

hofding m. *chief, leader*, CHR1076. [*ON.* höfðingi]

hōfe f. '*hove*,' *alehoof* (*plant*), Lcd,WW.

hofer (o²) m. *hump*, ÆL : *swelling*, GL.

hofer-ede, -od *humpbacked*, CP,Lcd,WW. ['*hovered*']

hoferiend, +hoferod (ÆL)=hoferede

-hōflan v. be-h.

hōflic *pertaining to a court*, OEG 2996.

+**hōfod** *hoofed*, ÆL25⁴⁴.

hōfon pret. pl. of hebban.

hofor=hofer

hōf-rec, -ræc n. *hoof-track, bridle-track*, Lcd.

hofrede *bedridden*, WW162⁸.

hōfring m. *print of a horse's hoof* (=hr.), OEG 18.

hofweard m. *ædile*, WW111²⁰.

hog-=hoh-

hoga I. *careful, prudent,* DR,MtL. ['*howe*'] II. m. *fear, care* : *attempt, struggle*, OEG 8²⁸³.

hoga-=hog-, hoh-; **hogade**=hogode

hogascipe (o²) m. *prudence*, DR,LkL.

hogde pret. of hycgan or hogian.

hogelēas *free from care*, RWH79³³.

hogg m. *hog*, NC302 (v. LF132).

±**hogian** (LWS *for* hycgan *q.v.*) *to care for, think about, reflect, busy oneself with*, G; Æ : *intend*, B : *strive, wish for*. ['*how*,' '*howe*']

hogu f. *care*, Æ. ['*how*,' '*howe*']

hogung f. *endeavour*, DHy8¹².
hōh m., gs. hōs, nap. hōas, hōs, dp. hōum *hough, heel*, Æ,Jn,Ps. on h. *behind : point of land*, Ct,Gl,Nar; Mdf. [' ho,' ' hoe '; v. also ' hough ']
hoh-fæst, hog(a)- (NG) *cautious, wise*.
hōhfōt m. *heel*, LPs55⁷.
hohful (hoga-, N) *careful, thoughtful*, Æ : *full of care, anxious, pensive, sad*, Ct,Sc : *persistent*, ÆL31¹⁰⁸⁴. [' howful ']
hohfulnes f. *care, trouble*, RBL, W.
hōh-hwyrflng, -hwerfing f. *heel-turning, circle?* v. OEG18n.
hōhing f. *hanging*, WNL294a¹².
hohlīce (hog-) *prudently*, LkL16⁹.
hohmōd *sad, sorrowful*, W72⁸.
hōhscanca m. *leg, shank*, LCD14a.
hōhsinu f. *sinew of the heel*, Æ,Lcd. [' hough-sinew ']
-hōhsnian v. on-h.
hōhspor n. *heel*, WW160²⁶.
hol I. *hollow, concave*, LCD : *depressed, lying in a hollow*, CP,Ct,MH. [' holl '] II. n. *hollow place, cave, hole, den*, Ct,Lk,Met,Ps, WW; Æ,AO : *perforation, aperture*, Cp. [' hole,' ' holl ']
hōl n. *calumny, slander*, ÆL,W.
-hola v. oter-h.
+hola=+hala
hole n? holca? m. *hole, cavity*, Lcd. [' holk ']
hold I. *gracious, friendly, kind, favourable*, AO,B; Æ : *true, faithful, loyal*, Æ,LL; CP : *devout : acceptable, pleasant*. [' hold '] adv. holde, Ps. [' holde '] II. n. *dead body, carcase*, Mt; Æ. [' hold '] III. m. *holder of allodial land, ranking below a* jarl *(Danish title)*, LL : *notable, chief*, MkR6²¹. [ON. holdr]
holdāð m. *oath of allegiance*, CHR1085.
holdelīce=holdlīce
holdhlāford m. *gracious lord, liege lord*, CHR 1014E.
holdian *to cut up, disembowel*, ÆL23⁷³. [hold II.]
holdingstōw f. *slaughterhouse*, KC.
holdlic *faithful, friendly*, OEG50²⁹. adv. -līce *graciously*, Æ,WW : *faithfully, loyally : devoutly*. [' holdely ']
holdrǣden f. *faithful service*, ÆH2·150³⁰.
holdscipe m. *loyalty, allegiance*, CHR.
holecerse a *plant*, LCD29b.
holegn=holen I.
holen I. m. ' *holly*,' WW; Æ; Mdf. adj. *of holly*. II. pp. of helan.
hōlenga=hōlinga
holenlēaf n. *holly leaf*, LCD127a.
holenrind f. *holly bark*, LCD29b.
holenstybb m. *holly-stump*, KC3·338'.
holh (CP), holg n. gs. hōles *hole*, ' *hollow*.'

hollan *to hollow out, scoop out*, Æ : *to become hollow, be perforated*, Æ. [' hole ']
hōllan *to oppress*, LPs. [' hole ']
+hollan *to obtain*, CP209¹⁹.
holing f. *hollow place*, GD113¹¹.
hōlinga (o², u²) adv. *in vain, without reason*, BH,LL.
holl=hol II.
hollēac n. a *kind of onion*, WW270²⁹. [' holleke ']
holm m. †*wave, sea, ocean, water*, B : (in prose, esp. in place-names) *island* (esp. in a river or creek), Chr. [' holm ']
holmærn n. *ship*, GEN1422.
holmclift n. *sea-cliff, rocky shore*, B.
holmeg adj. *of the sea*, Ex118.
holmmǣgen n. *force of the waves*, RD3⁹.
holm-ōracu† f., gs. -ōrǣce *restless sea*.
holmweall m. *wall of sea water*, Ex467.
holmweard (AN359)=helmweard
holmweg m. *sea-path*, AN382.
holmwylm m. *billows*, B2411.
holnes f. *hollow place*, GDo99²².
holoc=holc
hōlonga=hōlinga
holpen pp. of helpan.
holrian=heolorian
holstæf m. ' *apex*,' *tittle*, MtR5¹⁸.
holt nm. *forest, wood, grove, thicket*, Æ,B; CP; Mdf : *wood, timber*, Jul. [' holt ']
holt-hana, -ana m. *woodcock*, WW344³⁰.
hōltihte f. *calumny*, WW116²⁵,198³.
holtwudu† m. *forest, grove*, Ph : *wood (timber)*. [v. ' holt ']
hōlunga=hōlinga; hom=ham
nōm=om; **nōman**=ōman
hōn I. (sv⁷) pret. heng, pp. hangen *to hang, suspend, crucify*, Æ : *put on (clothes)*, Bo 42¹⁵n. II. pl. *tendrils of a vine?* A4·143.
hon-=han-; **hona**=(1) heonu; (2) hana
hōnende *having heels*, WW161²⁶. [hōh]
+honge=+hange
hongen pp. of hōn.
hop n. *privet?* OEG36¹⁴ (but v. BTs) : *enclosed land in a marsh*, KC6·243¹⁴.
hōp m. *hoop?* NR22; v. NC303.
-hop v. fen-, mōr-h.
hopa m. ' *hope*,' Æ. [usu. tōhopa]
hōpgehnāst n. *dashing of waves*, RD4²⁷.
±hopian *to* ' *hope*,' *expect, look for*, Æ,Bf; CP : *put trust in*, Æ,Bo,Bl.
hōpig *eddying, surging*, PPs68².
+hopp n. *small bag, seed-pod*, WW405³.
hoppāda m. *upper garment, cope*, WW188¹⁴.
hoppe f. a *kind of ornament*, AO : *dog-collar*, LL194,8.
hoppestre f. *female dancer*, Æ. [' hoppestere ']
hoppetan *to hop, leap for joy : to throb*.

hoppian *to 'hop,' leap, dance, Æ : limp,* ÆL21⁴¹⁷.

hopscÿte f. *sheet, counterpane,* Æ(9³⁰⁷).

hopsteort *train of a dress,* WW438¹⁶ (v. BTs).

hōr n. *adultery* (Swt).

hora-=horu-; horas v. horh.

hōrcwene f. *whore, adulteress,* LL.

hord nm. *'hoard,' treasure,* B,Chr,Cr,Gen, MtR,WW.

hordærn=hordern

hordburg f. *treasure-city,* B,BC,GEN.

hord-cleofa, -clyfa m. *treasure-chest, treasury, secret chamber,* Æ.

hordcofa m. *treasure-chamber, closet :* (†) *breast, heart, thoughts.*

hordere m. *treasurer, chamberlain, steward,* Æ,KC. *['hoarder']*

hordern n. *treasury, storehouse,* B,LL.

horderwÿce f. *office of treasurer,* CHR1137.

hordfæt n. *treasure-receptacle,* Æ.

hord-geat n., gs. -gates *door of a treasure-chamber,* RD43¹¹.

hordgestrēon† n. *hoarded treasure.*

hordian *to 'hoard,'* Æ.

hordloca m. *treasure-chest, coffer :* (†) *secret thoughts, mind.*

hordmægen n. *riches,* DA675.

hordmāðm† m. *hoarded treasure,* B.

hordweard m. *guardian of treasure : king : heir, first-born.*

hordwela m. *hoarded wealth,* B2344.

hordweorðung f. *honouring by gifts,* B952.

hordwynn f. *delightful treasure,* B2270.

hordwyrðe *worth hoarding,* B2245?

hōre f. *whore, prostitute,* OEG.

horeht=horwiht

+hor(g)ian *to defile,* BK : *spit upon,* NG.

horh (horg) mn., gs. hor(w)es, instr. horu, nap. horas *phlegm, mucus,* Æ,El,Ep,Lcd : *dirt, defilement, uncleanness;* Mdf. *['hore']*

horheht=horwiht

+horian (N)=+horgian

horig *foul, filthy,* Æ,ApT,LL. *['hory']*

hōring m. *adulterer, fornicator,* W309²¹.

horn m. *'HORN' (musical instrument, drinking-horn, cupping-horn), beast's horn,* AO : *projection, pinnacle.*

hornbære *horned,* ÆGR27¹⁶.

hornblāwere m. *'horn-blower,' trumpeter,* Gl.

hornboga† m. *bow tipped with horn? curved like a horn?*

hornbora m. *horn-bearer, trumpeter,* WW.

hornede *having horns,* AA19¹⁸.

hornfisc m. *garfish,* AN370.

hornfōted *hoofed,* WW213²².

horngēap† *broad between the gables,* ES 64·207.

horngestrēon n. *wealth of pinnacles (on a house)?* [or ?=hordgestrēon], RUIN23.

+hornian *to insult,* MkL12⁴. [?=+horgian]

hornlēas *without horns,* ES39·349.

hornpic m. *pinnacle,* MtL. [v. *'pike'*]

hornreced n. *hall with gables,* B704.

hornsæl n.=hornsele

hornscēað f. *pinnacle,* MtL4⁵.

hornscip n. *beaked ship,* AN274.

hornsele m. *house with gables,* GEN1821.

hornungsunu m. *bastard,* WW456¹⁰.

horo-=horu-

horpytt m. *mud-hole,* EC445¹⁵.

hors n. *' horse,' OET,WW,VPs;* Æ,AO,CP.

horsbær f. *horse-litter,* BH; ÆL. *['horsebier']*

horsc I. *sharp, active, ready, daring : quick-witted, wise, prudent.* II. *foul,* KC3·456¹⁶.

horscamb m. *'horse-comb,' curry-comb, strigil,* WW.

horschwæl (=*horshwæl) m. *'walrus,' AO* 17³⁶. [v. *'horse'*]

horsclic *squalid, foul,* OEG1789. [horh]

horsclice *briskly, readily, promptly : prudently, wisely,* GL.

horscniht m. *groom, esquire,* Æ(8²⁴²).

horscræt n. *'biga,' chariot,* WW194²⁶.

horselene f. *elecampane,* WW. *['horseheal']*

horsern n. *stable,* WW.

horsgærstūn m. *meadow in which horses are kept,* KC3·414'. [v. *'horse'*]

horshelene=horselene

horshere m. *mounted force* (BTs).

horshierde (i², y²) m. *ostler, groom,* GL.

±horsian *to provide with horses,* AO,Chr. *['horse,' 'y-horsed']*

horslīce=horsclice

horsminte *wild mint,* LCD187b.

horspæð m. *horse-track,* KC5·157'.

hors-ðegn, -ðēn m. *ostler, groom, equerry : muleteer.*

horswǣn m. *chariot,* WW140⁴.

horswealh m. *groom, equerry,* LL22; 132.

horsweard f. *care of horses,* LL445,2.

horsweg m. *bridle-road,* KC. *['horseway']*

hortan sbpl. *'whortle'-berries,* v. OEG2⁴³³.

horu=horh

horusēað m. *sink, pit,* Bo112¹⁵.

horuweg (o²) m. *dirty road?* KC5·173¹⁷.

horweht=horwiht; horwes v. horh.

horwig=orweg

+horwigian=+horgian

horwiht (e²) *mucose, defiled, filthy,* GUTH 36⁹.

horwyll m. *muddy stream,* EC445¹⁹.

horxlic=horsclic

hos *shoot, tendril,* GL.

hōs I. f. *escort, company,* B924. II. v. hōh.

hosa m., hose f. *'hose,'* WW.

hosebend m. *hose-band, garter,* OEG4822.
hosp m. *reproach, insult,* Æ : *blasphemy,* Æ.
hospcwlde m. *insulting speech,* EL523.
hospettan *to ridicule,* Cp697s.
hosplic *insulting,* ÆH2·232³¹.
hospsprǣc f. *jeer, taunt,* ÆH2·514¹¹.
hospul *despised,* RPs88³⁵.
hospword n. *abusive language, contemptuous expression,* Æ.
hoss=hos; hosse=hyse
hōstig (ÆL35¹⁹²)=ōstig
hosu f. *hose,* RB : *pod, husk,* Cp1867.
hotor=otor
hoðma† m. *darkness, the grave.*
hr-=r-
hrā=hrǣw
hraca? m. (*Lcd*)=hrace
hrāca (ǣ) m. *clearing of the throat : mucus.*
hracca (e, ea) '*occiput,*' WW463²¹.
hrace, hracu (æ) f. *throat,* Æ,*VPs* : *gorge,* KC3·440'. ['*rake*']
hrad- v. hræd-; hrade=hraðe
±hradian (ea, ð) *to be quick, hasten, come quickly : do quickly or diligently : put briefly,* BF52⁸ : *further, prosper,* ÆL20⁷⁸.
hradung (æ) f. *quickness, despatch, diligence.*
hræ-=hra-, hre-, hrea-
hrǣ-=hrǣw; hrǣ-=hrēa-, hrēo-, rǣ-
hrǣcan tr. and intr. *to* '*reach,*' *bring up (blood or phlegm),* CP,*Lcd*; Æ.
+hrǣcan=+reccan
hrǣcea m. *clearing of the throat,* LCD9a. [=hrāca]
hrǣcetan *to eructate,* LCD84a.
hrǣcetung f. *eructation,* LCD69b.
hrǣcgebrǣc n. *sore throat,* WW.
hrǣcing=rǣcing
hrǣctan=hrǣcetan
hrǣctunge f. *uvula,* LCD17a.
hrǣcung f. *clearing of the throat, Lcd* : *phlegm,* WW162³⁴. ['*reaching*']
hræd (e) (hrad- occly. in obl. cases) *quick, nimble, ready, active, alert, prompt,* Bo,CP, Gl,*Mt.* ['*rad*']
hrædbita m. *blackbeetle,* WW (hrǣð-).
hrædfērnes f. *swiftness,* Bo72¹⁷.
hrædhȳdig *hasty* (Swt).
hrædhȳdignes f. *haste, precipitation,* CP.
hræding f. *haste.* on hrædinge *quickly,* Æ, W.
hrædlic (ð) *quick, sudden, premature,* Æ, AO,CP. adv. -līce *hastily, soon, forthwith,* B,Bo,DR; Æ,CP. ['*radly,*' '*rathely*']
hrædlicnes (e) f. *suddenness,* GUTH : *earliness,* EPs118¹⁴⁷.
hrædmōd *hasty,* ÆL16³⁴².
Hrǣdmōnað=Hrēðmōnað
hrædnes f. (eð) *quickness, promptitude : brevity.*

hrædrīpe (ræd-) *ripening early,* WW.
hrædtǣfle *quick at throwing dice?* CRA73 (v. ES43·339).
hrædung=hradung
hrædwǣn m. *swift chariot,* MET24⁴¹.
hrædwilnes f. *haste, precipitation,* CP.
hrædwyrde *hasty of speech,* WA66.
hræfn Ī. hræfen (e) m. *raven,* Æ,B,G,Gl, Ma,VPs : *sign of the raven (the Danish banner).* II.=hæfern
hræfncynn (e) n. *raven-species,* Æ.
hræfnesfōt m. *ravensfoot, cinquefoil, Gl, Lcd.*
hræfneslēac *orchid,* LCD.
-hrǣgan v. ofer-hr.
hrǣge=rǣge; hrǣgel=hrægl
hrǣgelgefrætwodnes f. *fine clothing,* LL (396²⁷).
hrǣgelðegn m. *keeper of the robes.*
hrægl n. (e) *dress, clothing, Gl,Jn*; AO : *vestment, CP* : *cloth, sheet* : *armour* : *sail,* BF14⁷. ['*rail*']
hrægleyst f. *clothes-box, trunk,* Ct.
hrǣglgewǣde n. *dress,* WW430³³.
hrǣglhūs f. *vestry,* RB.
hrǣglscēara fp. *tailors' shears,* WW241⁴⁰ (rægl-).
hrǣgltalu f. *clothing store,* KC,RB (v. BTs).
hrǣglung f. *clothing,* WW151⁵.
hrǣglweard m. *keeper of vestments or robes,* WW279¹⁹.
hrægnloca=brægnloca
hræmn, hrǣm=hræfn; hræn=hærn
hrǣron pret. pl. of hreran.
hrǣs v. hrǣw and rǣs.
hrǣscetung=rǣscetung
-hrǣsclan v. ā-hr.
hrætelwyrt f. *rattlewort,* WW301³.
hræð=hræd. ['*rathe*']
hrǣw I. (ā, ēa) nm. gs. hrǣs *living body* : *corpse, carcase, carrion.* II.=hrēaw I.
hrǣwīc (hrēa-) n. *place of corpses,* B1214.
hrāfyll m. *slaughter,* B277.
hrāgīfre *deadly,* WW408¹⁰.
hrāgra m. *heron,* GL.
hrālic=hrāwlic
hramgealla=ramgealla; hrāmig=hrēmig
hramma m. *cramp, spasm,* LCD,WW.
hram-sa (o) m., -se f. *onion, garlic,* Gl,Lcd, WW. ['*rams,*' '*ramson*']
hramsacrop m. *head of wild garlic,* GL.
hran (o) m. *whale,* GL.
hrān I. m. *reindeer,* AO. II. pret. 3 sg. of hrīnan.
hrand I.=rand. II. pret. 3 sg. of hrindan.
hrandsparwa (o¹) m. *sparrow,* MtL10²⁹.
hranfix (o) m. *whale,* AA33⁷,B540.
hrānhund? m. *deerhound?* v. LL2·117.

hranmere (o) m. *sea*, MET5[10].
hranrād† f. *(whale's-road)*, *sea*.
hratele f. '*bobonica*' *(plant)*, WW296[2].
['*rattle*']
hratian *to rush, hasten*, OET (=hradian?).
hraðe (æ, e) I. *quick, Bo,Chr,PPs*. II. adv.
comp. hraðor, superl. hraðost *hastily,
quickly, promptly, readily, immediately,
soon, Æ,B,Bo,Cr,G,Ps*; CP : *too soon, Bo*.
swā h. swā *as soon as, Æ*. ['*rathe*,' '*rather*,'
'*rathest*']
hraðer=hreðer; hraðian=hradian
hrāw=hrǣw
hrāwērig *weary in body*, PH554.
hrāwlic *funereal*, WW406[1].
hrēa I. f. *indigestion?* LCD94b. [hrēaw I.]
II.=hrēaw I. and II.
hrēac m. '*rick*,' *heap, stack*, TC,WW.
hrēaccopp m. *top of a rick*, LL453,21[4].
hrēacmete m. *food given to the labourers on
completing a rick*, LL452'.
hrēad-=hrēod-
-hrēad v. earm-hr. [hrēoðan]
hrēaf=rēaf
hrēam m. *noise, outcry, alarm, Æ,CP* : *cry,
lamentation, sorrow, B,Cr*. ['*ream*']
hrēamig=hrēmig
hrēanes=hrēohnes
hrēas pret. 3 sg. of hrēosan.
hrēat pret. 3 sg. of hrūtan.
hreaðemūs (a²) f. *bat*, AA,LCD.
hreaðian (VPs)=hradian
hrēaw I. '*raw*,' *uncooked, Æ,Lcd*. II.=
hrǣw nm. III. pret. 3 sg. of hrēowan.
hrēaw-=hrēow-
hrēawan *to be raw*, WW215[43] (rēaw-).
hrēawīc=hrǣwīc
hrēawnes I. f. *rawness*, OEG3283. II.=
hrēownes
+hrec=+rec; hrēc-=hrǣc-
hrecca=hracca
hred (KGL)=hrǣd; -hreda v. æfreda.
hreddan *to free from, recover, rescue, save,
Cr; Æ* : *take away*. ['*redd*']
hreddere m. *defender*, CHRD94[4].
hreddung (æ) f. *salvation, liberation, Æ*.
Hredmōnað=Hrēðmōnað
±hrēfan *to roof, Æ*. [hrōf]
hrefn=(1) hræfn; (2) hæfern
hrefnan=ræfnan
hrefncynn=hræfncynn
hregresi? *groin*, MLN11·333; ZDA33·244.
hrēh=hrēoh; hrem=hræfn I.
hrēman I.† *to boast*. [Ger. rühmen] II.=
hrīeman
hrēmig (ēa)† *boasting, vaunting, exulting*:
clamorous, loud.
hremm=hræfn I.
±hremman *to hinder, cumber, Æ*.

hremming f. *hindrance, obstacle*, GL,LCD.
hremn=hræfn I.
hrenian *to smell of, be redolent of*, Sc106[5].
hrēo=hrēoh, hrēow; hrēocan=rēocan
hrēodn. '*reed*,' *rush, Æ,BH,Gl,LG*; CP; Mdf.
hrēodan² *to adorn* (only in pp. ±hroden).
hrēodbedd n. '*reed-bed*,' *Æ*.
hrēodcynn n. *kind of reed*, NC303.
hrēod-ig (-iht, -ihtig (e²) *reedy*, KC,WW.
hrēodpīpere m. *flute-player*, WW190[7].
hrēodwæter n. *reedy marsh*, AA30[19].
hrēof *rough, scabby, leprous, Wh*; CP. as
sb.=*leper*. ['*reof*']
-hrēoflan v. ā-hr.
hrēofl I. f. *scabbiness, leprosy*, CP. II. adj.
leprous.
hrēofla m. *roughness of the skin, leprosy,
Æ* : *leper, Æ*. [hrēof]
hrēof-lic, -lig (Æ) *leprous, suffering from
skin-disease*.
hrēofnes f. *leprosy*, NUM12[10].
hrēofol, hrēoful=hrēofl I.
hrēog=hrēoh
hrēogan *to become stormy*, AA34[19].
hrēoh (ē) I. adj. *rough, fierce, wild, angry,
Met; Æ,AO,CP* : *disturbed, troubled, sad*
(v. hrēow) : *stormy, tempestuous, B,Bo,
Chr*. ['*reh*'] II. n. *stormy weather, tempest*.
hrēohful *stormy*, ES39·349.
hrēohlic *stormy, tempestuous*, W136[27].
hrēohmōd† *savage, ferocious* : *sad, troubled*.
hrēohnes (ēa) f. *rough weather, storm, Æ*.
hrēol sb. '*reel*,' LL,WW; Æ.
hrēon-=rēon-
hrēones=(1) hrēohnes; (2) hrēownes
hrēop pret. 3 sg. of hrōpan.
hreopian=hrepian
hrēorig adj. *in ruins*, RUIN3. [hrēosan]
±hrēosan² *to fall, sink, fall down, go to ruin,
Æ,B,Cr,VPs*; AO,CP : *rush* : *rush upon,
attack*. ['*reose*']
hrēosendlic *perishable* : *ready to fall*, OEG.
hrēosian=hrēowsian
hrēosð (KGL) pres. 3 sg. of hrēosan.
-hrēoða (ē, ēa) v. bord-, scild-hr.
hrēoung (īu) f. *hardness of breathing*, LCD,
WW.
±hrēow I. f. *sorrow, regret, penitence, repentance, penance, B,Bl,CP,Cr*. ['*rue*'] II.
sorrowful, repentant, BH352[5]. III. adj.=
hrēoh? IV. *raw*, Ex12[9]. ['*row*']
±hrēowan² (often impersonal w. d. pers.)
*to affect one with regret or contrition, Bo,
CP,Gen,LL* : *distress, grieve, Cr,Gen* :
(intr.) *be penitent, repent*, MkL. ['*rue*,'
'*i-rew*']
hrēowcearig† *troubled, sad.*
hrēowende (ǣ) *penitent*, LkL. ['*rueing*']
hrēowesung=hrēowsung

hrēowian *to repent*, MkL1¹⁵.

hrēowig *sorrowful, sad*, GEN799.

hrēowigmōd† *sad, sorrowful.*

hrēowlic (ī, ȳ) *grievous, pitiful, sad, wretched, cruel, Chr,Ps.* adv. -līce, *AO,Chr.* ['*ruly*']

hrēownes (ēa) f. *penitence, contrition, repentance, Gl,LL*; CP. ['*rueness*,' '*rewniss*']

hrēowon=rēowon pret. pl. of rōwan.

hrēowsende=hrēosende, v. hrēosan

±hrēowsian (ȳ) *to feel sorrow or penitence, AO,Mt*; CP : *do penance*, HL149¹²⁶. ['*reusie*']

hrēowsung f. *repentance, penitence, sorrow, CP,Lk*; Æ. ['*reusing*']

hrēpan *to cry out*, WW375¹⁰.

±hrepian (eo), hreppan *to touch, treat (of), Mt*; Æ : *attack*, BK6. ['*repe*']

hrepsung (ÆL)=repsung

hrepung f. *sense of touch, touch*, Æ.

±hrēran (tr.) *to move, shake, agitate.* [hrōr; Ger. rühren]

hrēre *lightly boiled*, Lcd. ['*rear*']

hrērednes (ȳ) f. *haste*, LPs51⁶.

hrēremus f. *bat, WW.* ['*rearmouse*'; hrēran]

hrēr(e)nes (ȳ) f. *disturbance, commotion, tempest.*

hresl=hrisil

+hresp n. *stripping, spoliation*, NC294.

+hrespan *to strip, spoil*, PPs43¹².

hrēst=hrȳst pres. 3 sg. of hrēosan.

hreð=hræd

hrēð† mn. *victory, glory.*

hrēða m. *covering of goat-skin, mantle*, GL.

hrēðan *to exult, rejoice*, Ex573.

hrēðe=hraðe; hrēðe=rēðe

hrēðēadig† *glorious, victorious.*

Hrēðemōnað=Hrēðmōnað

hreðer† (a, æ) m. *breast, bosom: heart, mind, thought : womb.*

hreðerbealo n. *heart-sorrow*, B1343.

hreðercofa m. *breast*, CR1323.

hreðerglēaw *wise, prudent*, Ex13.

hreðerloca† m. *breast.*

-hrēðig v. ēad-, sige-, will-hr.

hrēðlēas *inglorious*, Gu878.

Hrēðmōnað m. *month of March*, MH.

hrēðnes=rēðnes; hreðor=hreðer

hrēðsigor m. *glorious victory*, B2583.

hricg=hrycg

hrīcian *to cut, cut to pieces*, ÆL23⁷³.

hricsc *rick, wrench, sprain*, LCD27a.

hriddel n. '*riddle*,' *sieve*, LL455,17.

hridder(n), hrider n. *sieve* Æ,GL; GD. ['*ridder*']

hrīdrian *to sift, winnow*, Lk. ['*ridder*']

±hrīeman (ē, ī, ȳ) *to cry out : shout, rave*, Æ,CP : *bewail, lament*, JnL. ['*reme*']

+hrīered *destroyed*, WW496¹⁸.

hrīewð pres. 3 sg. of hrēowan.

±hrif n. *belly, womb*, Æ,AO.

hrif (AA8¹)=rīf

+hrifian *to bring forth*, LPs7¹⁵.

+hrifnian (ī?) *to tear off? become rapacious?* AO142²⁶.

hriftēung f. *pain in the bowels*, WW112²³.

hrīfðo f. *scurfiness*, LCD90b. [hrēof]

hrifwerc m. *pain in the bowels*, WW112²³.

hrifwund *wounded in the belly*, LL6,61.

hrig=hrycg

hrīm m. '*rime*,' *hoar-frost, Cp,Ph*; Æ.

hrīman=hrīeman

-hrīman v. be-hr.

hrīmceald *icy cold*, WA4.

hrīmforst m. *hoar-frost*, LPs77⁴⁷ (rīm-).

hrīmgicel m. *icicle*, SEAF17.

hrīmig *rimy, frosty*, BL.

hrīmigheard *frozen hard*, RD88⁷.

hrimpan (rim-) pp. (h)rumpen *to twist, coil*, WW366⁴⁰.

+hrin n. *morsel*, EPs147¹⁷.

+hrīn (NG)=+rīn=+rēn

±hrīnan¹ (w. a. g. or d.) *to touch, lay hold of, reach, seize, strike, B,Ps* : *have connection with*, DR106'. ['*rine*']

hrincg=hring; hrind=rind

hrindan³ *to thrust, push*, RD55⁴.

±hrine m. *sense of touch : touch : contact*, AA41²⁷.

±hrinenes f. *touch, contact*, BH.

hring I. m. RING, *link of chain, fetter, festoon, CP : anything circular, circle, circular group, Ph : border, horizon, Gen : (†) (pl.) rings of gold (as ornaments and as money) : (†) corslet : circuit (of a year), cycle, course : orb, globe.* II.† m. *(only in wōpes hr.) sound? flood? (of tears, v. BTs).*

hringādl (?br-) f. *a disease, ringworm?* MLR19·201.

hringan *to '*ring**,' sound, clash, B,Sol : announce by bells, RB.*

hringbān n. *ring-shaped bone*, WW157. ['*ringbone*']

hringboga m. *coiled serpent*, B2561.

hringe f. *ring*, Æ,GL.

hringed† *made of rings*, B.

hringedstefna† m. *ring-prowed ship*, B.

hring-fāg, -fāh *ring-spotted, variegated*, GEN37³.

hringfinger m. '*ring-finger*,' Lcd,WW.

hringgeat n? *ring-gate*, RUIN4.

hringgewindla m. *sphere*, WW426²⁵.

hringīren n. *ring-mail*, B322.

hringloca m. *coat of ring-mail*, MA145.

hringmǣl *sword with ring-like patterns*, B.

hringmǣled *adorned with rings (of a sword)*, GEN1992.

hringmere n. *bath*, RUIN455.

hringnaca m. *ring-prowed ship*, B1863.

hringnett n. *ring-mail*, B1889.

hringpytt m. *round pit*, KC.

hringsele† m. *hall in which rings are bestowed*, B.

hringsetl n. *circus*, OEG.

hringsittend m. *spectator, onlooker*, OEG65.

hringðegu† f. *receiving of rings*.

hringweorðung f. *ring-ornament, costly ring, rings*, B3017.

hringwīsan adv. *ringwise, in rings*, AA23¹⁴.

hringwyll m. *circular well*, KC.

hrīning f. *touch*, JnL. [v. '*rine*']

+hriorde (w)=+reorde; hrīp-=rīp-

hrīs I. n. *twig, branch*. II. *covered with brushwood?* KC.

hrisc=risc; hrīscan=hrȳscan

hrīseht *bushy, bristly*, WW513⁸.

hrisel=rysel

hrīsel, hrīs(i)l f? *shuttle : bone of the lower arm, radius*. [hrisian]

hrisian (y) (tr. and intr.) *to shake, move, be shaken, clatter, An,B,Ps,VPs* : (+) *to shake together*, WW370,485. ['*rese*']

hrīsig (rȳsig) *bushy*, OEG8³³⁷.

hrīst pres. 3 sg. of hrēosan.

hrīstle f. *rattle*, WW391¹⁸.

hrīstlende *noisy, creaky*, WW504⁸.

hrīstung f. *quivering, rattling noise*, LCD 97a.

hrið (u) m. *fever*, LCD80a.

hrīð I. f. *snow-storm, tempest*, WA102. II.= hrīðer

hrīðādl f. *fever*, LCD80a.

hrīðer (ȳ) n. *neat cattle, ox, bull, cow, heifer, Bl,Ct,Lcd,WW*. ['*rother*']

hrīðeren *of cattle*, Lcd. ['*rotheren*']

hrīðerfrēols (ȳ) m. *sacrifice of a bull*, OEG 4719.

hrīðerhēawere (ȳ) m. *butcher*, WW129¹⁶.

hrīðerheord (ȳ) *herd of cattle*, Æ. [v. '*rother*']

hrīðerhyrde (ȳ) m. *herdsman*, ÆH1·322'.

hrīðfald m. *cattle-pen*, WW195³⁴.

hrīðheorde (ie)=hrīðerhyrde

hrīðian *to shake, be feverish, have a fever*, Æ.

hrīðig (ȳ) *storm-beaten? ruined?* WA77.

hrīðing f. *fever*, LCD96b.

hrīung=hrēoung; hrīw-=hrēow-

hrīwð pres. 3 sg. of hrēowan.

hrōc m. '*rook*,' ÆL,Cp.

hrōd=rōd

hroden I. (±) *covered, adorned, ornamented* (pp. of hrēodan). II.=roden

hroder=rodor

hrōf m. '*roof*,' *ceiling, Æ,B,Cr,G*; AO,CP : *top, summit, Bo,Cr,Mk : heaven, sky, Cr*.

hrōffæst *with a firm roof*, MET7⁶.

hrōflēas (rōf-) *roofless*, WW186³⁰.

hrōfsele m. *roofed hall*, B1515.

hrōfstān m. *roof stone*, ÆH1·508'.

hrōftīgel f. *roofing tile*, WW.

hrōftimber n. *material for roofing*, OEG 2256.

hrōfwyrhta m. *roof-maker, builder*, WW.

hrog *mucus from the nose, phlegm*, WW 290³²

hromsa=hramsa; hron=hran; hrop=rop

hrōp m. *clamour, lamentation, Bl*. ['*rope*']

hrōpan⁷† *to shout, proclaim : cry out, scream, howl, Gu,Ps*. ['*rope*']

-hrops v. ofer-hr.

hropwyrc=ropwærc

hrōr *stirring, busy, active : strong, brave*.

+hror n. *calamity, plague, ruin*, BH284⁴. [hrēosan]

±hroren pp. of hrēosan.

+hrorenes f. *downfall, ruin*, LPs31⁴.

+hrorenlic *perishable, transitory, unstable*, NC294; MFH147.

hrōse=rōse

hrōst m. *perch, 'roost,'* LL454,11.

hrōstbēag m. *woodwork (of a roof)*, RUIN32.

hrot m. *scum*, LCD84a.

hrōðer=hrōðor

hrōðgirela m. *crown*, RPs20⁴.

hroðhund (A8·450)=roðhund

hrōðor† m. *solace, joy, pleasure : benefit*.

hrūm m. *soot*, MH,WW.

-hrūmian v. be-hr.

hrūmig *sooty*, WW362¹².

hrumpen v. hrimpan.

hrung f. *cross-bar, spoke*, Rd23¹⁰. ['*rung*']

hruron pret. pl. of hrēosan.

hrurul *deciduous*, BDS30·11⁶³.

hrūse† f. *earth, soil, ground*.

hrūt *dark-coloured?* (BTs),WW361¹³.

hrūtan⁵ *to make a noise, whiz, snore, Æ,Cp*. ['*rout*']

hruð=hrið; hrūðer (KC)=hrīðer

+hrūxl n. *noise, tumult*, v. ES39·344.

hrūxlian (rūx-) *to make a noise*, MtR9²³.

hryc=hrycg

hrycg (i) m. *back, spine, Æ,CP,Lcd*; AO : '*ridge*,' *elevated surface, B,Ct,Lk,Ps*; Mdf.

hrycgbān n. *back-bone, spine, Ps*. ['*ridge-bone*']

hrycgbrǣdan (hrig-) pl. *flesh on each side of the spine*, LCD3·118'.

hrycghǣr n. *hair on an animal's back*, LCD 1·360¹⁹.

hrycghrægl (i) n. *mantle*, TC529¹⁰.

hrycg-mearg (i, -mearð) n. *spinal marrow*, WW292⁷.

hrycgme(a)rglið n. *spine*, WW265²³.

hrycgrib (i) n. *rib*, WW.

hrycg-rible, -riple *flesh on each side of the spine*, WW.

hrycgweg m. '*ridge-way*,' *road on a ridge, Ct.*
hrycigan *to plough over again,* GPH 398.
hryding f. *clearing, cleared land,* WW 147¹².
hrȳfing f. *scab,*·LCD 32b. [hrēof]
hryg=hrycg
hrȳman=hrīeman
hrympel? *wrinkle,* WW 531⁴ (hryp-). [v. '*rimple*']
+hryne=+ryne
hryre I. m. *fall, descent, ruin, destruction, decay, Æ,B,Bo;* AO,CP. ['*rure*'] II. *perishable, Æ.*
hrȳre-=hrēr-, hrēre-
hrȳsc *a blow,* LCD 2b.
hrȳscan *to make a noise, creak,* v. ES 39·344.
hrysel=rysel; hrysian, hryssan=hrisian
hryst=hyrst
hrȳst pres. 3 sg. of hrēosan.
hrystan=hyrstan
hrȳte (y?) '*balidinus*,' WW 163¹⁸ (cp. hrūt).
hrȳðer=hrīðer; hrȳðig=hrīðig
hryðða=ryðða; hrȳwlic=hrēowlic
hrȳwsian=hrēowsian
hrȳwð pres. 3 sg. of hrēowsian.
hū adv. 'HOW,' *Æ,CP.* hū gerādes; hū meta *how.* hū gēares *at what time of year.* hū nyta *wherefore.* hū ne dōð...? *do not...?* hū nys...? *is not...?* : (with comparatives) *the* : (±) *in some way or other, Shr.* hū ne nū '*nonne.*'
hūcs, hūcx=hūsc
hūdenian *to shake,* CP 461¹⁶.
hūf=ūf I. and II.
hūfe *covering for the head, Cp,WW.* ['*houve*']
hunan *to put a covering on the head,* LEV 8¹³.
+hugod *minded,* GEN 725.
hū-hwega, -hugu *somewhere about.* h. swā *about.*
hui! huig! interj.
huilpe=hwilpe
hulc m. I. '*hulk*,' *ship, LL,WW;* Æ. II. *hut, Æ,LL,WW.*
hulfestre f. *plover,* WW 287¹⁴.
hūlic pron. *of what sort,* AO.
hulpon pret. pl. of helpan.
hulu f. *husk, pod, WW.* ['*hull*']
hūluco (AO)=hūlic; huma=uma
humele=hymele; hūmen (VHy)=ȳmen
hūmeta adv. *in what way, how, Æ.*
hun?=hunu
huncettan *to limp, halt,* RPs 17⁴⁶.
hund I. n. *hundred, AO,Bf,G;* Æ : (in comp.) *decade.* ['*hund*'] II. m. *hound, dog, Bo, CP,Jud;* Æ,AO : *sea-beast* (v. sǣhund), OEG.
hundæhtatig (*VPs*)=hundeahtatig
hundællef- (-ændlæf-)=hundendlufon-

hundeahtatig num. '*eighty*,' AO.
hundeahtatigoða *eightieth,* GEN 5²⁵.
hundeahtatigwintere *eighty years old, Æ.*
hunden *of dogs, canine,* BLRPs 77⁴⁵.
hundend-lufontig, -leftig (æ²) *hundred and ten, Ct.*
hund-endlufontigoða, -ælleftiogoða *hundred and tenth,* CP 465²³.
hundesbēo (WW 380²¹)=hundespēo
hundescwelcan pl. *colocynth berries,* WW 364³¹.
hundesflēoge f. *dog's parasite,* AO,GL.
hundeshēafod n. *snapdragon,* LCD 2·395.
hundeslūs f. *dog's parasite,* WW 319⁴.
hundes-micge, -tunge f. *cynoglossum* (*plant*), LCD 3·333.
hundes-pēo (CPs), -pīe (VPs 104³¹) f. *dog's parasite.*
hundeswyrm m. *dog's worm, parasite,* WW 122²⁵.
hund-feald, -fealdlic *hundred-fold, Æ.* ['*hundfold*']
hundfrēa m. *centurion,* MtL 22¹⁹ mg.
hundlic *of or like dogs, canine, Æ.*
hundnigontēoða *ninetieth, Æ.*
hundnigontig *ninety, Mt.* [v. '*hund*']
hundnigontiggēare *ninety years* (*old*), GEN 5⁹.
hundnigontigoða *ninetieth, Æ,CP.*
hundnigontigwintre *ninety years old,* GEN 17¹⁷.
hund-red, -rað n. '*hundred*' (*number*), *Bf, G,Ps,WW;* Æ : *hundred* (*political district*), *hundred-court, assembly of the men of a hundred, LL.* hundredes ealdor, mann *head of the hundred court, centurion.*
hundredgemōt n. *hundred-moot,* LL.
hundredmann m. *centurion, Æ* : *captain of a hundred,* Ex 18²¹,DEUT 1¹⁵.
hundredpenig m. *contribution levied by the sheriff or lord of the hundred for the support of his office,* TC 432,433.
hundredseten f. *rules of the hundred,* LL.
hundredsōcn f. *attendance at the hundred-moot* : *fine for non-attendance,* Ct.
hundreð (*MkR*)=hundred
hundseofontig num. *seventy, Mt;* Æ. [v. '*hund*']
hundseofontigfeald *seventy-fold,* ÆH.
hundseofontiggēare *seventy years* (*old*), GEN 5¹².
hundseofontigoða *seventieth,* CP (io², io⁴).
hundseofontigseofonfeald *seventy-seven-fold,* GEN 4²⁴.
hundseofontigwintre *seventy years old,* GEN 5³¹.
hundtēontig *hundred, Æ,Gen,Shr.* [v. '*hund*']
hundtēontig-feald, -fealdlic *hundred-fold.* adv. -līce, W 237⁹.

hundtēontiggēare *a hundred years old,* Æ.

hundtēontigoða *hundredth,* ÆGr,RB.

hundtēontigwintre *a hundred years old,* NC 303.

hundtwelftig *hundred and twenty,* AO.

hundtwelftigwintre *aged a hundred and twenty,* DeutC31².

hundtwentig *hundred and twenty,* ÆT.

hundtwentigwintre *aged a hundred and twenty,* Deut31².

hundwealh (æ²) m. *attendant on dogs,* WW 111²⁵.

hundwelle *a hundred-fold,* MtL13⁸. [= -wille]

hundwintre *aged a hundred years,* Æ (Gen).

hūne f. *horehound,* Lcd.

hū ne nū '*nonne,*' RPs52⁵; Hy6⁶.

hunger=hungor

hungerbiten *starving,* Chr1096.

hungergēar mn. *famine-year,* Æ,Gen41⁵⁰.

hungerlǣwe *famishing, starving,* LHy3⁵.

hungerlic *hungry, famishing,* WW.

hungor m. '*hunger,*' *desire,* An,Cr,VPs, WW; CP : *famine,* Æ,Mt,Chr.

hungrig '*hungry,*' *famishing, Gu,MtL*; Æ, AO : *meagre,* OEG.

hungur=hungor

hunig n. '*honey,*' *AO,VPs*; Æ,CP.

hunigæppel m. *pastille of honey? Ep,WW.*

hunigbǣre *honeyed,* OEG.

hunigbin f. *vessel for honey,* LL455,17.

hunigcamb f. '*honey-comb,*' Sc50⁹.

hunigflōwende *flowing with honey,* Gu1250.

huniggafol n. *rent paid in honey,* LL448,4⁵.

hunigsūge f. *honeysuckle? clover? privet? Cp,WW.* ['honeysuck']

hunigswēte '*honey-sweet,*' *mellifluous,* Æ.

hunigtēar m. *honey which drips from the comb,* Gl,Lcd.

hunigtēar-en, -lic *nectar-like,* Gl.

huni-sūge, -sūce=hunigsūge

hūnsporu mf. '*dolon,*' *pike? Cp356D.

hunta m. *huntsman,* Æ,AO : *a kind of spider,* Lcd54a. ['hunt']

huntað=huntoð

huntaðfaru f. *hunting expedition,* LL252,22.

±huntian, huntgan *to* '*hunt*' (intr.), Lcd, WW; (tr.) Æ.

hunticge f. *huntress,* A6·188.

huntigspere n. *hunting-spear,* WW142¹².

huntigystre=hunticge

huntoð, huntnoð, huntnold, huntnað m. *hunting, what is caught by hunting, game, prey.* Æ,Ct,Lcd; AO. ['hunteth']

huntung f. '*hunting,*' WW : *a hunt, chase, DR* : *what is hunted, game,* ES37·188.

hūnðyrlu np. *holes in the upper part of a mast,* WW288¹⁵.

hunu? *a disease,* WW502³¹.

hūon=hwōn; hupbān, huppbān=hypbān -hupian v. on-h.

hupseax=hypeseax

hurnitu=hyrnetu

hūru adv. *at least, at all events, however, nevertheless, yet, even, only, LL*; Æ : *about, not less than, AO* : *surely, truly, certainly, indeed, especially,* CP. h. swīðost *most particularly.* ['hure']

hūruðinga *at least, especially,* Æ.

hūs n. '*house,*' *B,G,RB*; Æ,AO,CP : *temple, tabernacle, G,Ps* : *dwelling-place, El,Ph* : *inn* : *household, JnL* : *family, race, Ps.* ±hūsa m. *member of a household,* G.

hūsǣrn n. *dwelling-house,* Chrd102¹.

hūsbonda (ō²?) m. *householder, master of a house, Mt,Chr.* ['husband']

hūsbonde f. *mistress of a house,* Ex3²².

hūsbryce (e², i²) m. *housebreaking, burglary, LL.* ['housebreach']

hūsbrycel *burglarious,* WW205²⁸.

hūsbryne m. *burning of a house,* Ct.

hūsbunda=hūsbonda

hūsc n. *mockery, derision, scorn, insult. Gen,WW.* ['hux']

hūscarl m. *member of the king's body-guard, Chr,KC.* ['house carl'; *ON.*]

hūsclic *shameful, ignominious, outrageous,* Æ. adv. -līce.

hūscword n. *insulting speech, An.* [v. '*hux*']

+hūsed *furnished with a house,* WW121³².

hūsel n. '*housel,*' *Eucharist,* Æ,BH : *the Host, LL* : *a sacrifice, MtL12⁷.

hūselbearn (-ul) n. *communicant,* Gu531.

hūselbox *housel-box,* ÆP178⁶.

hūseldisc m. *housel-dish, paten,* Gl,Lcd.

hūsel-fæt n. nap. -fatu *sacrificial or sacramental vessel,* BH,LL.

hūselgang m. *going to, partaking of the Eucharist,* Æ,LL.

hūselgenga m. *communicant,* v. LL2·263.

hūselhālgung f. *attendance at the Eucharist, communicating,* Æ : *Holy Communion,* W34⁵.

hūsellāf f. *remains of the Eucharist,* ÆP27¹⁰.

hūselportic (u²) m. *sacristy,* BH94¹⁰.

hūselðēn m. *acolyte,* LL.

hūsfæst adj. *occupying a house,* Ct.

hūshefen m. *ceiling,* WW432⁸. [heofon]

hūshlāford m. *master of the house,* Æ.

hūshlēow n. *housing, shelter,* LL(282′); W74⁴.

±hūsian *to* '*house,*' *receive into one's house, LL.*

hūsincel n. *habitation,* DR,BJVPs.

±hūslian *to administer the sacrament, A* (pp.),*LL.* ['housel']

hūslung f. *administration of the sacrament,* Æ. ['houseling'] hūslwer (sel) m. *communicant*, Gu768.

hūsrǣden f. *household, family*, LPs.

±hūsscipe m. *house* (e.g. *of Israel*), *race*, Ps.

hūsstede m. *site of a house*, LCD.

hūsting n. *tribunal, court* (*esp. in London*), Chr. ['*husting*']

hūsul, hūsul=hūs(e)l

hūswist f. *home*, LPs5⁸.

hūð I. f. *plunder, booty, prey*, Æ. II. f., hūðe f.=hȳð

hūx=hūsc

hwā mf., hwæt n. pron. (interrog.) '*who*,' *Æ,B,Met* : '*what*,' *Æ,Bo,Ps*; AO,CP : (indef.) *any one, some one, anything, something*, *Æ,AO,CP* : *each*. swā hwā swā *whosoever*. swā hwæt swā *whatsoever*. tō hwǣm *wherefore*.

+hwā *each one, every one, any one, whoever*.

hwæcce v. hwicce.

+hwǣde *slight, scanty, small, young*, Æ.

hwæder (CP)=hwider

+hwǣdnes f. *smallness, fewness, insignificance*.

hwǣg (ē) n? '*whey*,' *Cp,LL*.

hwæl I. (usu. hwal- in obl. cases) m. '*whale*,' *walrus, Æ,AO,Bf*. II. pret. 3 sg. of hwelan. III.=hwall. IV. (Ex 161)=wæl n?

hwælc (N)=hwilc

hwælen *like a whale*, Sol263.

hwælhunta m. *whale-fisher, whaler*, Æ,AO.

hwælhuntað m. *whale-fishery, whaling*, AO.

hwælmere† m. *sea*, An,Rd.

hwælweg (wæl-) m. *sea*, Seaf63.

hwæm=hwemm

hwǣm (*LkL,VPs*) ds. of hwā, hwæt. ['*whom*']

+hwǣmlic *each, every*, LkL9²³.

-hwǣnan v. ā-hw.

hwæne (*G*)=hwone, asm. of hwā.

hwǣne=hwēne

hwænne (*G, Ps*), hwæne ('*when*')=hwonne

hwær=hwer

hwǣr (ā) adv. and conj. '*where*,' *whither, somewhere, anywhere, everywhere*, CP. wel h. *nearly everywhere*. swā hw. swā *wheresoever, wherever*. elles hw. *elsewhere*. hwǣr...hwǣr *here...there*.

+hwǣr *everywhere, in all directions*, Æ : *on every occasion, always, Æ,B* : *somewhere*. ['*y-where*']

hwærf=hwearf; hwærfan=hwierfan

hwærflung=hwyrflung

hwǣr-hwega, -h(w)ugu *somewhere*.

hwæs I. *sharp, piercing*, Cr1444. II. gs. of hwā, hwæt (*CP,G,WW*). ['*whose*']

hwǣst m. *blowing*, v. OEG2452n.

hwǣstrian (ā) *to murmur, mutter*, NG.

hwǣstrung (ā) f. *murmur, whispering, muttering*.

hwæt I. (neut. of hwā, which see) adv. *why, wherefore* : *indeed, surely, truly, for*. interj. '*what*!' *lo!* (calls attention to a following statement) *ah! behold!* Æ. II. adj. (obl. cases have hwat-) *sharp, brisk, quick, active* : *bold, brave, B,Cra*; AO. ['*what*'] III. (CP) pres. 3 sg. of hwettan.

+hwæt (*Cr*) neut. of +hwā. ['*i-hwat*']

hwǣte (ē) m. '*wheat*,' *corn*, *G,VPs*; CP. [hwīt]

hwǣtēadig *very brave*, El1195?

hwǣtecorn n. *corn of wheat*, Lcd13a. ['*wheatcorn*']

hwǣtecroft m. *wheat-field*, BC3·135'.

hwǣtecynn n. *wheat*, PPs147³.

hwǣtegryttan pl. *wheaten groats*, WW141²⁰.

hwǣtehealm m. *wheat-straw*, Lcd49a.

hwǣteland m. '*wheat-land*,' KC3·159²¹.

hwǣtemelu n. '*wheat-meal*,' Lcd126a.

hwǣten '*wheaten*,' *G,Lcd,OET*; Æ.

hwǣtesmedma m. *wheat-meal*, Lcd.

hwǣtewæstm m. *corn, wheat*, CPs77²⁵.

hwæthwara=hwæthwugu

hwæt-hwugu, -hwigu, -hugu, -hwega, -hwegu, -hwygu adj. sb. pron. and adv. *somewhat, slightly, a little, something*.

hwæt-hwugununges (CP), -hweganunges, -huguningas adv. *somewhat*.

hwǣtlīce adv. *quickly, promptly*, Ps. ['*whatliche*']

hwǣtmōd† *bold, courageous*.

±hwætnes f. *quickness, activity*, Bf,Bo.

hwætrēd (=rǣd) *firm, determined*, Ruin20.

hwætscipe m. *activity, vigour, boldness, bravery*, AO,CP.

hwæðer (e) adj. pron. conj. (with subj.) and adv. '*whether*,' *Æ,G* : *which of two*, '*whether*,' *Æ,AO,G*. swā hw. swā *whichever*. hwæðer...ðe *whether...or* : *each of two, both* : *one of two, either*, CP.

+hwæðer *both, either, each*.

hwæðere, hwæð(ð)re I. adv. *however, yet, nevertheless, still*, B,Lcd; Æ,AO,CP. ['*whether*'] II.=hwæðer adv.

+hwæðere *nevertheless*, Run10.

hwæðreðēah (RPs72¹⁸)=ðēahhwæðre

hwal- v. hwæl; hwalf=hwealf I.

hwall (=æ) *forward, bold*, WW. [hwelan]

hwām (*B,Bl,G*) ds. of hwā, hwæt. ['*whom*']

hwamm (o) m. *corner, angle, prominence*, Æ,CP : *porch*.

hwamstān (o¹) m. *corner-stone*, MtL21⁴².

hwan=hwon instr. of hwæt.

hwān=hwām; hwanan=hwanon

hwane (*Bl*)=hwone asm. of hwā.

hwanne (*Bl*)=hwonne

hwanon, hwanone adv. *whence*, Æ,B,Bo, LG,Mt. ['*when*']

+hwanon adv. *from every quarter*, Æ.

hwanonhwegu adv. *from anywhere*, Ep 1095.

hwār (G), hwāra (AO)=hwǣr

hwarne (*not*) *at all*, MtL 8³⁰.

hwāst-=hwǣst-

hwasta? m. *eunuch*, Mt,WW.

hwat- v. hwæt.

hwat-a I. m. *augur, soothsayer*, Æ. II. (æ), -an fpl. *augury, divination*, Æ,Lev. ['whate']

hwatend '*iris Illyrica*' (*plant*), WW.

hwatu f. *omen*, W.

hwatung f. *augury, divination*, LL.

hwaðer-=hweðer-

hwēal (WW 162²⁵)=ðwēal

hwealī I. *concave, hollow, arched, vaulted*. II. f. *vault, arch*. [cp. *Ger.* gewölbe]

hwealhafoc=wealhhafoc

hwealp=hwelp

hwearf I.† m. *crowd, troop, concourse, Gu.* ['wharf'; hweorfan] II. (a, e, eo) m. *exchange : what is exchanged :* (+) *vicissitude : error*, MtR 27⁶⁴ : *going, distance*, LkLR 24¹³. III. pret. 3 sg. of hweorfan. IV. m. '*wharf,*' *embankment, Ct.*

hwearfan=hwierfan

hwearflan (e, eo) *to turn, roll or toss about, revolve*, GD; Æ : *wave : change*, CP : *wander, move, pass by*, AO. ['wharve']

hwearflic (e³) *changing, transitory*, Bo 25¹⁰n : *quick, agile*, FIN 35? adv. -līce *in turn*.

+hwearfnes f. *conversion*, CP 447¹³.

hwearft m. *revolution, circuit, circle : lapse* (*of time*).

hwearftlian (y) *to revolve, turn round*, Æ : *wander, be tossed about*, OEG.

hwearfung f. *revolution : change, vicissitude : exchange.*

hwebbung=webbung; hweder=hwider

+hwēdnes (KGL)=+hwǣdnes

hwēg=hwǣg; hwega *about, somewhat.*

hwegl=hwēol

hwelan⁴ *to roar, rage*, AN 495.

hwelc (AO,CP)=hwilc

±hwelian, hwellan? *to suppurate, cause to suppurate, develop weals, come to a head*, CP,Lcd,Sc. ['wheal']

hwelp(a) (ea, y) m. '*whelp,*' *the young of an animal, cub*, Lcd,LG,Sc,VPs,WW; AO.

hwelung f. *din*, WW 423²⁰.

hwem=hwemm

hwemdragen *sloping, slanting*, BL 207¹⁷.

hwemm (æ) m. *corner, angle*, Æ. [hwamm]

±hwemman *to bend, turn, incline*, CHR 1052.

hwēne (ǣ) adv. *somewhat, a little*, Æ,AO,CP. [instr. of hwōn]

hweogl=hwēol

hwēol, hweogol, hweohl n. '*wheel,*' Bo,Lcd, MH,OEG : (*as instrument of torture*) ÆL, Bo : *circle*, Bo,DHy,MH.

hwēolfāg *having a circular border or decoration*, WW 375³².

hwēolgodweb n. *robe with a circular border?* WW 382³⁵ (hwegl-).

hwēollāst m. *orbit*, DHy 93¹⁷.

hwēolrād f. *rut, orbit*, Cp 233o.

hwēolrīðig n. *a brook that turns a wheel*, KC 3·289,381.

hwēolweg m. *cart-road*, KC 3·386⁴.

hwēop pret. 3 sg. of hwōpan.

+hweorf I. n. *a turning*, LCD 91a. II. *converted*, MtR 18³ (+werf) : *active?* CRA 68.

hweorfa m. *joint : whorl of a spindle, Lcd.* ['wharve']

±hweorfan³ (o, u) *to turn*, Bo : *change, CP : turn out*, Bo : *move, go, come : wander about, roam, go about*, GD : *turn back, return, turn from, depart : die : be converted.* feohtan mid hweorfendum sigum *to fight with varying success*, AO. ['wharve']

hweorfbān (u, y) n. *joint, kneecap*, LCD, WW.

hweorflan=hwearfian

hwēos pret. 3 sg. of hwōsan.

hweoða=hwiða

hweowl, hweowol=hwēol

hwer (æ, y) m. *pot, bowl, kettle, caldron*, Æ.

+hwēr=+hwǣr

hwerb (WW 53¹³)=hweorfa

hwerbān=hweorfbān

hwerf=hwearf

hwerf-=hwearf-, hweorf-, hwierf-

hwergen adv. only in phr. elles hwergen *elsewhere*, B 2590.

hwerhwette f. *cucumber*, LCD,WW.

hwēst v. hwōsan; hwēt=wǣt

hwēte (KGL)=hwǣte

hwete- (Cp), hwet-stān (AO) m. '*whetstone.*'

±hwettan *to* '*whet,*' *sharpen, incite, encourage*, B,Bl,CP.

-hwette v. hwer-h.; hweðer=hwæðer

hweðre=hwæðere; hwī=hwȳ

hwicce f. *locker, chest, trunk*, OEG 18b¹¹. ['whitch']

hwicung f. *squeaking* (*of mice*), GD 185⁴ (c).

hwider (æ) adv. '*whither*,*,' Æ,Bl,Bo;LG; AO,CP. swā hw. swā *wherever, whithersoever.*

+hwider *in every direction, everywhere, anywhere, whithersoever.*

hwiderhwega *somewhither*, LCD 68a.

hwiderryne adj. *directed whither*, Ln 43³³.

hwidre *whither*, Bo 78¹.

hwīe=hwȳ

+**hwielfan** (e, y) *to arch, bend over, IM.*
['*whelve*']
±**hwierfan** (æ, e, ea, i, y) *to turn, revolve, change, transfer, convert, return, Bo,CP;* AO : *wander, move, go, depart,* AO : *exchange, barter* : (+) *overturn, destroy.* ['*wharve*'] For comps. see hwyrf-.
-**hwierfere** v. pening-hw.
hwig=hwȳ
hwīl f. '*while,*' *time, Bl,Bo,Gen,LG;* Æ,CP : *a long time* : *hour, NG.* nū hwīle *just now, a while ago.* ealle hwīle *all the while.* ōðre hwīle...ōðre hwīle *at one time...at another time, Hy.* adv. hwīle *once, Deor.* ðā hwīle (ðe) *while, whilst, meanwhile, Bl,RB.*
hwilc (e, y) interrog. pron. and adj. WHICH*, *what, CP* : (indef.) *whosoever, whichever* : *any (one), some (one).* swā hw. swā *whosoever, whatever, Chr.*
+**hwilc** *each, any, every (one), all, some, many, whoever, whatever.* anra +hw. *each one.*
hwilchwega=hwilchwugu
hwilc-hwene, -hwone, -hwegno pron. *some, some one, something, NG.*
hwilc-hwugu, -hugu (e²) (hwilc is declined) pron. *any, some, some one, AO,CP* : *not much, little* : *anything, something, NG.*
±**hwilcnes** f. *quality, Æ.*
hwīle v. hwīl.
hwīlen *passing, transitory,* WH87 : *temporal,* GD 181¹². ['*whilend*']
hwīlend-e (*Sc*; '*whilend*'), -lic (CP)=hwīlwend-e, -lic
hwīleð pres. 3 sg. of hwelan.
hwīlfœco n. *a ʒpaoo of timo,* OEC 1178.
hwīlhwega adv. *for some time.*
hwīlon (Æ)=hwīlum
hwīlpe f. *curlew?* SEAF21. [*Du.* wilp]
hwīlsticce n. *interval, short space of time, odd moment,* GD 254²⁴,WW420²⁸.
hwīltīdum adv. *sometimes, at times,* Æ,CP. hwīltīdum...hwīltīdum *at some times...at others.*
hwīlōrāg f. *period of time,* GD 243¹⁹.
hwīlum adv. (dp. of hwīl) '*whilom,*' *sometimes, once, Met;* Æ,CP. hwīlum... hwīlum *now...now, at one time...at another, MH.*
hwīlwende *transitory, temporary* : *temporal, Æ.*
hwīlwendlic *transitory, temporary, temporal, G;* Æ. adv. -līce, Æ. ['*whilwendlic*']
hwimpel=wimpel
hwīnan¹ *to hiss, whizz, whistle, Wid.* ['*whine*']
hwinsian *to whine,* NC 303.
hwinsung f. *whining,* NC 303.
hwirfan=hwierfan

hwirfð pres. 3 sg. of hweorfan.
hwīrlic (HGL 434)=hwearflic
hwiscettung f. *squeaking (of mice),* GD 185⁴ (o).
hwisprian *to* '*whisper,*' *murmur, NG.*
hwisprung f. '*whispering,*' *murmuring, JnR* 7¹².
hwistle f. *reed,* '*whistle,*' *pipe, LG,WW.*
hwistlere m. '*whistler,*' *piper, G.*
hwistlian *to* '*whistle,*' *hiss, Gl,Lcd.*
hwistlung f. '*whistling,*' *hissing, piping, music, CP,Gu,LG,WW.*
hwīt I. '*WHITE*' : *bright, radiant, glistening, flashing, clear, fair.* **II.** n. *whiteness* : *white food* : *white of egg, Æ,Lcd.*
±**hwītan** *to whiten* : *brighten, polish, LPs,* WW.
hwītcorn n. *manna,* JnL 6³¹mg.
hwīt-cwidu, -cudu m. *mastic,* LCD.
hwīte *white,* LCD.
hwīteclæfre f. *white clover,* LCD.
hwītegōs *white goose,* WW 259,351.
hwītehlāf m. *white bread,* TC 474'.
hwītel (ȳ) m. *blanket, cloak, Æ,BH.* ['*whittle*']
hwītelēac n. *white leek,* WW 353⁸.
hwītfōt *white-footed,* GL.
hwītian *to whiten, become white, be white, Æ.*
hwītingmelu n. *whiting-powder, Lcd* 119b. [v. '*whiting*']
hwītingtrēow n. '*whitten*' *tree, WW* 139¹.
hwītlēac n. *onion,* WW 353⁸.
hwītling m. *a kind of fish, whiting?* NC 303.
hwīt-loo, *loccede fair-haired, blonde, Rn.*
hwītnes f. '*whiteness,*' *Bl;* Æ.
hwiða m., hwiðu (eo) f? *air, breeze, Æ,* CP.
hwol? '*infigens,*' OEG 37⁶.
hwomm=hwamm
hwon form of instr. case of hwā, only found in adverbial phrases like 'tō hwon, for hwon' *why, LG* : 'bi hwon' *how, Gu.* ['*whon*']
hwōn I. adj. *little, few.* **II.** n. *a little, trifle, Lcd,LG* : *somewhat* : *a little while.* ['*whon*'] **III.** adv. *somewhat.*
hwonan=hwanon
hwone (CP) asm. of hwā.
hwōnlic *little, small, Æ.* adv. -līce, *moderately, slightly, little, Æ* : *cursorily,* BF 30¹².
hwōnlotum (=-hlot-) adv. *in small quantities,* GL.
hwonne (a, æ, e) adv. '*when,*' *then, at some time* : *at any time, Bl,Gu,Ps;* CP : *as long as, until.* nū hw. *just now.*
hwonon=hwanon
hwōpan⁷† *to threaten,* EX.

hworfan=hweorfan
hwōsan 3 pers. pres. hwēst; pret. hwēos _to cough,_ Æ,LCD 96b.
hwōsta m. _cough, WW._ ['_hoast?_']
hwoðerian (a¹) _to foam, surge? roar?_ ÆH 2·388¹⁹. [hwiða]
hwoðrung f. _a harsh sound,_ OEG 26¹⁴.
hwu (LWS)=hū; hwugu=hwega
hwugudǣl m. _small part,_ HL 18³⁴⁶.
hwurf-=hwearf-, hweorf-, hwierf-, hwyrf-
hwurfon pret. pl. of hweorfan.
hwurful _fickle,_ CP 245⁷. [hweorfan]
hwurfulnes f. _inconstancy, mutability,_ CP.
hwȳ (inst. of hwæt) adv. and conj. '_why._' tō hwȳ _wherefore._
hwyder (Æ)=hwider; hwylc=hwilc
hwylca (=e) m. _pustule, tumour, boil, WW_ 161¹⁷. ['_whelk_']
hwylfan=hwielfan
hwȳlon=hwīlum; hwylp=hwelp
hwyr=hwer; hwyrf-=hweorf-, hwierf-
+hwyrfe(d)nes f. _inclination,_ Æ : _conversion,_ BH.
hwyrfel m. _circuit, exterior, higher part?_ BL 125²¹ : (meaning doubtful), EC 328'.
hwyrfepōl m. _whirlpool, eddy,_ WW 383³⁴.
hwyrflede _round,_ v. OEG 23⁴².
hwyrfling m. _orb,_ OEG 1992.
hwyrflung (æ) f. _change, turning, revolution,_ BF,DR : _wandering, error,_ MtL 24²⁴.
hwyrfnes f. _dizziness, giddiness,_ LCD.
±hwyrft m. _turning, circuit, revolution, motion, course, orbit_ : _way out, outlet._ +hw. gēares _anniversary._
hwyrftlian=hwearftlian
+hwyrftnes f. _return,_ Ps.
hwyrftweg m. _escape,_ RD 4⁶.
hwystl-=wistl-; hwȳtel=hwītel
hȳ=hīe; +hȳan=hēan III.
±hycgan (i) _to think, consider, meditate, study_ : _understand_ : _resolve upon, determine, purpose_ : _remember_ : _hope._ h. fram be averse to (v. also hogian).
+hycglic _considerable,_ GD 328¹⁶.
hȳd I. '_hide,_' _skin, Chr,LL;_ Æ,AO,CP. hȳde ðolian _to undergo a flogging._ II.=hīd +hȳd I. _furnished with a skin,_ NAR 50⁵. II. pp. of hēan. III.=+hygd
±hȳdan I. _to_ '_hide_' ('_i-hede_'), _conceal, preserve, CP_ : (refl. and intr.) _hide oneself, CP,Ps_ : _sheath (a sword), bury (a corpse),_ Æ. II. _to fasten with a rope of hide_ (BTs), WH 13. III.=hēdan
hȳddern=hēddern; -hydele v. hǣwen-h.
+hȳdelicnes=+hyðelicnes
hȳdels m. _hiding-place, cave, MkR,LL._ ['_hidels_']
hyder=hider
hȳdesacc m. _leather sack or bag,_ ANS 151·80.

hȳdgild (y²) n. _fine to save one's skin_ (_i.e. instead of flogging_), _LL._ ['_hidegild_']
hȳdig I. _leathern,_ WW 125³⁵. II.=hygdig
+hȳdnes I. f. _comfort,_ CP 210o : _security,_ CP 387. II.=+hȳðnes
hȳdscip=hȳðscip
hȳf f. '_hive,_' _Cp,Lcd,WW._
hȳg=hīeg
+hygd (i), hygd (PPs 120⁴,VH) fn. _mind, thought_ : _reflection, forethought._
hygdig (e¹) _heedful, thoughtful,, careful_ : _chaste, modest._ adv. -līce _chastely._
hygdignes f. _chastity, modesty,_ DR.
hyge (i)† m. _thought, mind, heart, disposition, intention, Seaf,Da_ : _courage_ : _pride,_ GEN 354. ['_high_']
hygebend mf. _heart-strings,_ B 1878.
hygeblind _mentally blind,_ JUL 61.
hygeblīðe† _blithe of heart, glad, joyful._
hygeclǣne _pure in heart,_ PPs 104³.
hygecræft† m. _power of mind, wisdom._
hygecræftig† _wise, prudent._
hȳgedriht f. _band of household retainers?_ RIM 21. [hīw]
hygefæst _wise,_ RD 43¹⁴.
hygefrōd _wise,_ GEN 1953.
hygefrōfor† f. _consolation._
hygegǣlsa _hesitating, slow, sluggish,_ PH 314. [gǣlan]
hygegāl _loose, wanton,_ RD 13¹².
hygegār m. _wile,_ MOD 34.
hygegēomor† _sad in mind._
hygeglēaw† _prudent in mind._
hygegrim _savage, cruel,_ JUL 595.
hygelēas (e, i) _thoughtless, foolish, rash,_ Æ : _unbridled, extravagant._
hygelēaslic (i) _unbridled,_ OEG 3170. adv. -līce _thoughtlessly._
hygelēast f. _heedlessness, folly,_ Æ.
hygemǣðum (i) _reverently,_ B 2909.
hygemēðe _sad. saddening,_ B 2442.
hygerōf† _stout-hearted, brave,_ GEN.
hygerūn f. _secret,_ EL 1099.
hygesceaft f. _mind, heart,_ GEN 288.
hygesnottor† _sagacious, wise._
hygesorg† f. _heart-sorrow, anxiety._
hygestrang (i) _brave,_ MEN 42.
hygetēona† m. _injury, insult,_ GEN.
hygetrēow f. _fidelity,_ GEN 2367.
hygeðanc† m. _thought._
hygeðancol† _thoughtful, wise._
hygeðihtig (i¹) _courageous,_ B 746.
hygeðrymm (i¹) m. _courage,_ B 339.
hygeðrȳð (i) f. _pride, insolence,_ GEN 2238.
hygewælm m. _mental agitation, anger,_ GEN 980.
hygewlanc† _haughty, proud,_ RD.
hyggean=hycgan; hȳglā (LPs)=hīglā
hyhsan=hyscan; hȳhst v. hēah.

hyht (e, i) mf. (±) *hope, trust, Bl,Ps; Æ,CP :
joy, exultation* : (±) *desire, expectation* : (+)
comfort. ['*hight*']
±hyhtan (i) *to hope, trust, Ps : rejoice, exult,
be glad* : *soften* (*hardship*), GUTH 86[8].
['*hight*']
+hyhtendlic *to be hoped for,* GD 269[13].
hyhtful (e, i) *hopeful* : *full of joy, mirthful,
pleasant, glad.*
hyhtgiefu f. *pleasing gift,* RIM 21.
hyhtgifa m. *giver of joy,* EL 852.
hyhting (i[1]) f. *exultation,* WW 233[42].
hyhtlēas (i[1]) *unbelieving,* GEN 2387.
hyhtlic† *hopeful, joyful, pleasant.* adv. -lice.
hyhtplega† m. *joyous play, sport.*
hyhtwilla m. *hoped-for joy,* SAT 159.
hyhtwynn f. *joy of hope, joy,* JUD 121.
hyhðo=hiehðu; hyl=hyll
hylc (i) m. *bend, turn,* GL: *unevenness,* WW.
+hylced *bent, curved, bandy,* GPH 398.
hyld (*Gen*)=hield
hyldan I. *to flay, skin,* Æ,WW. ['*hild*';
hold II.] II. (+)=ieldan
hyldāð m. *oath of allegiance,* LL 396B.
hylde=hielde
hyldemǣg† m. *near kinsman,* GEN.
hyldere m. *flayer, butcher,* GL. [hold II.]
+hyldig *patient,* SPs 7[12].
hylding (=ie) f. *curve, inclination,* WW
382[2]. [heald]
hyldo f. *favour, grace, kindness, protection* :
allegiance, loyalty, reverence, AO,CP.
[=hield]
hyldrǣden (e[1]) f. *fidelity,* TC 610'.
hyldu (Æ)=hyldo
hylest pres. 2 sg. of helan.
hylfe (Æ)=hielfe; -hylian v. be-h.
hyll I. mf. '*hill,*' Æ; Mdf. II.=hell
hyllehāma (i) m. '*cicada,*' *cricket, grasshopper,* GL.
hyllic (i) *hilly,* BC 3·577.
+hylman=helmian; -hylman v. for-, ofer-h.
hylp=help
hylpð pres. 3 sg. of helpan.
hylsten *baked* (*on the hearth*), WW 393[31].
hylsung (o[2]) f. '*tympanum,*' EPs 150[4] (v.
ES 53·359).
hylt=hielt pres. 3 sg. of healdan.
hylt-=hilt-
-hylte v. hēah-h.
hylto=hielto
hylu f. *a hollow,* KC 3·407.
hylwyrt f. '*hillwort,*' *pulegium,* WW.
hym=him; hymblice (GL)=hymlic
Hymbre sbpl. *Northumbrians,* OET 571.
hymele f. *hop plant,* WW; Mdf. [L.]
hymelic=hymlic; hymen=ymen
hym-līc (e) m., -līce f. '*hemlock,*' *Gl,Lcd,
WW.*

hȳn=hēan; hȳnan (Æ)=hīenan
hynd=hind
-hynde v. six-, twelf-, twi-h.; of-hende.
hynden f. *community of 100 men,* LL.
hyndenmann m. *chief man in the community
of 100 men,* LL 175; 178.
hyne=hine as. of hē.
±hyngran, hyngrian (i) *to be hungry,
' hunger,'* (impers.) Æ,JnL; (intr.) Cr,Lk :
(trans.) *hunger for,* Mt 5[6].
hyngrig=hungrig
hȳnnes (=īe) f. *persecution, destruction,*
BH 34[5]. [hēan]
hynnilǣc (Ep)=ynnilēac
hȳnð, hȳnðu=hīenðo
hyp-=hype-
+hȳpan (Æ)=+hēapian
hype m. '*hip*' *Bl,WW;* Æ,CP.
hȳpe (=īe) f. *heap,* Æ.
hypebān n. *hip-bone,* WW 159[25].
hypebānece m. *sciatica,* LCD.
hȳpel (=īe) m. *heap, mound,* GL.
hypeseax (hup-)† n. *short sword, dagger,* GL.
+hypsan (LPs 9[25])=hyspan
hypwærc (i[1], e[2]) n. *pain in the hips,* WW
113[15].
hȳr (ī) f. '*hire,*' *wages,* Æ,LL : *interest,
usury,* Æ.
hyra gp. of hē, hēo, hit.
hȳra (ē) m. *follower, mercenary* : *servant,
hireling,* CP 88[15] : *dependant,* BH 104[19].
hyran *to spit,* MkR 14[65]. [cp. +horian]
±hȳran=(1) hīeran; (2) hȳrian
hyrcnian=heorcnian
hyrd I. f. *door,* GEN 2695 (GK). [cp. *Ger.*
hürde] II. *parchment?* GUTH 213[10].
hyrd-, heord-=hierd-
hyrdel m. '*hurdle,*' *frame,* Æ,WW.
hyre gds. of hēo; hȳre=hēore
+hȳre-=+hīere-
hȳreborg (īe) m. *interest,* WW 515[1].
hȳred=hīred; hȳrefter=hēræfter
hȳre-geoc, -geoht=hȳrgeoht
hȳregilda m. *mercenary, hireling,* WW 111[11].
hȳremann=hīeremann
hyrfan (TC 611[5])=yrfan
hȳrgeoht n. *hired yoke of oxen,* LL 24,60.
hyrian *to imitate,* Bo.
hȳrian *to* '*hire*' ('*i-hire*'), Æ,Mt,WW (pp.).
hȳrigmann m. *hireling.* [=hīeremann]
hyring (e[1]) f. *imitation,* RB 128[14].
hȳrling m. '*hireling,*' *Mk* 1[20].
hȳrmann=hȳrigmann
hyrnan *to jut out like a horn,* Ct.
hyrne f. *angle, corner, CP,Mt;* Mdf. ['*hern*']
±hyrned *horned, beaked,* Lcd; Æ. ['*i-
horned*']
hyrnednebba† *horny-billed, horn-beaked,*
BR,JUD. [horn]

hyrnen I. *of horn,* LRPs 97[6]. II. *angular,*
OEG 7[20].
hyrnes=hīernes
+hyrnes (VH 16)=+herenes
hyrnet, hyrenetu f. '*hornet,*' *Gl,WW* : *gadfly,*
WW 121[12].
hyrnful *angular, with many angles,* OEG 121.
hyrnig *angular,* OEG 121.
hyrnstān m. *corner-stone, keystone,* ÆH
1·106.
hȳroxa m. *hired ox,* LL 116 B.
hyrra (KGL)=heorra, heorr
hȳrra I. v. hēah. II.=hȳra
hyrsian *to go on horseback?* BHB 194[35].
hyrst† I. f. (±) *ornament, decoration, jewel,*
treasure : *accoutrements, trappings, armour.* [*Ger.* rüstung] II. m. *hillock, height,
wood, wooded eminence, Rd,Ct.* ['*hurst*']
hyrst-=hierst-
±hyrstan I. *to decorate, adorn, ornament,
equip.* [*Ger.* rüsten] II. (+) *to murmur,*
LkLR 15[2]. III.=hierstan
hȳrsum=hīersum ; hyrtan=hiertan
hyrten=heorten
hyrð f. *skin, hide,* ES 41·323.
hyrðil (*Cp*)=hyrdel ; hȳru=hūru
+hȳrung f. *hiring,* WW 213[12].
hyrw-=hierw-
hys=his
±hyscan (ea, i) (tr.) *to jeer at, reproach, Ps* :
(intr.) *to rail, W.* ['*heascen*']
hyscend (i) m. *reviler,* GPH 398.
hyscild (WW 170[12])=hysecild
hyse† nap. hyssas m. *son, youth, young
man, warrior,* GL : *shoot, scion,* HGL 419[69].
hysebeorðor n. *the bearing of male offspring,*
GL : *boy, young man,* AN.
hyse-berðling, -byrding m. *the bearing of
male offspring,* GL.
hyseberðre f. *woman who bears a son,* DHy
50[17].
hysecild n. *male child,* Æ,AO.
hyserinc m. *young man,* GD 338[22].
hysewīse adv. *like young men,* WW 417[35].
hysope=ysope
hyspan (e, i) pret. hyspde and hyspte *to
mock, scorn, deride, revile, reproach,* AO.
[hosp]
hyspend m. *calumniator,* RPs 71[4].
+hyspendlic *abominable,* LPs 13[1].
hyspful *contumelious,* OEG 11[180].
hysp-nes (EPs), -ung (Bo) f. *contumely.*
hysse=hyse
hyt I. f. *heat,* B 2649. [*ON.* hita ; or ? read
hāt] II.=hit pron.
hȳt pres. 3 sg. of hȳdan.
hyttan=hittan
hȳð I. f. *landing-place, harbour, creek, port,
Cp,Guth,Met,Ps* ; Æ,CP. ['*hithe*'] II.=hȳðð

hȳðan (ī) *plunder, ravage,* BH,GD. [hūð]
+hȳðe *appropriate, convenient,* Æ.
±hȳðegian *to facilitate,* GPH,Sc.
hȳðegung f. *advantage,* Sc 12[6].
±hȳðelic *suitable, proper, convenient, ad-
vantageous.* adv. -līce.
+hȳðelicnes f. '*opportunitas,*' NC 345.
hȳðgild n. *harbour festival, sacrifice or
service,* OEG.
hȳðlic *belonging to a harbour,* WW.
+hȳðlic=+hȳðelic
+hȳðnes f. *advantage,* ÆL 23b[252] : *occasion,*
EPs 9[22].
hȳðscip (ī) n. *a light, piratical vessel,* GL.
hȳðð, hȳððo f. *gain, advantage,* Æ.
+hȳððo n. *subsistence,* ÆL 23b[492].
hȳðweard m. *warden of a harbour,* B 1915.
hȳw=hīw ; +hȳwan=+īewan
hyxan=hyscan

I

la (Æ)=gēa ; lacessūre=gēacessūre
lacinctus, īacintus m. *jacinth,* CP. [*L.*
hyacinthus]
lagul=gēagl ; lara=gearo
larwan=gierwan ; lb-=īf-
ic pron. (1st pers.) '*I,*' *Cp,Jn.* [*Ger.* ich]
ican, īcean=īecan ; lce=ȳce
icend m. '*auctor,*' ÆGr 48[12]. [īecan]
icestre f. '*auctrix,*' ÆGr 48[12].
icge *only in phr.* '*icge gold,*' *treasure-gold?
rich gold?* B 1108 (v. Klb p 168 and
BTs).
idæges adv. *on the same day,* Æ.
idel (ȳ) I. (*often* īdl- *in obl. cases*) *worthless,
useless, vain,* Æ,CP,Gen,Mt,VPs : *empty,
desolate, bare, void, destitute, devoid (of),*
Æ,B,VPs ; CP : '*idle,*' *unemployed, Mt.*
on ī. adv. *in vain,* Æ. II. n. *emptiness,
frivolity, idleness, Lcd,LL,Sol* : *inattention,
carelessness.*
idelgeorn *slothful, idle,* Bo : *useless, W.*
idelgielp (e[3], i[3]) n. *empty boasting, vainglory,*
CP,DHy,WW.
idelgild n. *vain worship, idolatry,* Æ.
idelgildoffrung f. *offering to an idol,* Æ.
idelhende *empty-handed, empty,* Æ,CP.
idelinga (a[2]) '*frivola,*' GPH 389.
idellic *vain, idle.* adv. -līce, VPs. ['*idly*']
idelnes f. *frivolity, vanity, emptiness, falseness, VPs* ; CP : '*idleness,*' *vain existence,
LL* : *superstition.* in (on) īdelnisse *in vain.*
-īdelsprǣce v. fela-ī.
ides *virgin* : (†) *woman, wife, lady, queen.*
idig *busy? active?* (BT) : *greedy for? desirous
of?* (GK), PH 407?
idl- v. idel.

±**īdlian** *to become empty or useless* : *profane,* BH362¹¹.

īdol n. *idol,* LL. [*L.*]

īe v. ēa.

±**īecan** (ǣ, ē, ī, ȳ) pret. īecte, īhte *to increase, enlarge, add to, augment, prolong,* An,Lcd,Lk; AO,CP : *fulfil, carry out,* RSL11·486. ['*eche*'; ēac]

īecinctus=īacinctus

īecessūre=gēacessūre; **īedel-**=īdel-

īeg (īg) f. *island.* [ēa]

īegbūend (ī) m. *islander,* CP.

īegclif (ēg-) n. *sea-cliff,* B2893.

īegland (ē, ī) n. '*island,*' BH,Bo,Chr,Wh.

īegstrēam (ē¹)† m. *current, river, sea.*

īehtan=ēhtan; **īelc-**=īlc-; **īeld**=īeldo

±**īeldan** (i, y) *to delay, put off, prolong, hesitate, tarry,* CP : *connive at, dissimulate.* ['*eld*'; eald]

īeldcian (CP)=elcian

īeldet† (e, ea, i, y) mp. *men.*

īelden (æ) n. *delay,* BH400²⁰.

īeldendlic (e) *dilatory,* WW441².

īeldest (æ, e, y) superl. of eald '*eldest,*' *chief,* Æ,Mt,CP.

īeldesta (y¹) m. *chief,* Ex17⁵.

īeldful (i, y) *dilatory, delaying,* OEG.

īeldian (y) *to put off, delay,* Æ.

īelding f. *delay, tarrying,* CP : *dissimulation.*

īeldo (æ, e, i, y) f. *age,* Æ,Gu,Lcd : *period* : *old age, old people,* Æ,Bl ; CP : *an age of the world,* Æ,Gu. ['*eld*'; eald]

īeldra (y) (comp. of eald) used as sbpl. *parents, ancestors,* Bl,El,Ct. ['*elder*']

īeldrafæder (æld-) m. *grandfather,* WW7³⁴.

īeldu=īeldo, **īelf**=ælf

īemung (WW277²²)=gēmung; **īerd**=gierd

īerf- v. also yrf-.

īerfa m. *heir,* OET446⁸ (erba).

īerfe (æ, e, i, y) n. *heritage, bequest, property,* CP : *cattle.* [*Ger.* erbe]

īerfian (i, y) *to inherit, possess* : (+) *to stock with cattle,* TC158¹⁰.

īergan *to dishearten, dismay,* Jos,W. [earg]

īergð(u) f. *remissness, sloth, cowardice,* AO. [earg]

īerlic (i, y) *angry, vehement,* ApT.

±**īerman** *to harass, vex, afflict,* CP. [earm]

īerming (eo, e, y) m. *person of no account, poor wretch,* AO,CP.

īermð, iermðu (e, ea, eo, y) f. *misery, distress, poverty,* B,Bo,Ps : *disease* : *crime* : *reproach,* CPs118¹³⁴. ['*ermth*'; earm]

īernan³ (æ, i, y; rinnan) pret. 3 sg. arn, orn, pl. urnon; pp. urnen (±) *to* '*run*,' *move rapidly, hasten, flow, spread,* Æ,AO, CP,Lcd,VPs : *pursue,* Bo,Ps : *cause to move rapidly, turn, grind,* AO,BH : (+) *get to, attain, meet with* : (+) *occur* (*to one's*

mind), GD : (+) *coagulate,* Lcd : (+) *grow up.* [v. also '*ern*']

īernes (eo, y) f. *anger,* BL123⁸,HL.

īerning (e) f. *discharge, flow,* NG.

īerre I. (i, y) *wandering, erring, perverse, depraved,* Ps,Sol : *angry, fierce,* Æ,Bl,Chr, CP,G; AO. **II.** n. *anger,* Bl,CP,El,Lk. ['*irre*']

īerremōd (y) *wrathful, wild,* B726.

īerrenga (eo¹, y¹, i², u²) adv. *angrily, fiercely,* CP.

īerreðweorh (y) *very angry,* Sat399?

īerscipe (y) m. *anger,* LPs9²⁵.

±**īersian** (i, io, y) *to be angry with, rage* : *enrage, irritate,* CP.

īersigendlic (y) *passionate, emotional,* Æ.

īersung (i, y) f. *anger,* CP.

ierð-=eorð-, yrð-

īesca (Ep,Erf)=geocsa

īesend, iesende *entrails,* WW. [=gesen]

īeteð pres. 3 sg. of etan.

īeð adv. comp. (=ēað) *easily,* An,Met; AO, CP. ['*eath*'] For comps. v. also ēað-.

+**īeðan I.** (ē) *to alleviate,* Gu1179 : *be merciful,* GD. **II.** (ǣ, ē, ȳ) *to lay waste, ravage, devastate, destroy,* Æ.

īeðe I. *easy, good-natured, pleasant,* AO. **II.** (ē)† *barren, waste, desolate.*

īeðegean=ȳðgian

īeðelic *easy,* CP : *moderate sized,* GD. adv. -līce *easily,* AO,CP.

īeðnes f. *ease, pleasure,* CP425¹¹.

+**īeðrian** (ē) *to make or become easier,* GD, Lcd.

īeðrung? f. *amelioration, a making easier?* (BTs), Soul107 (MS edring q.v.).

īeðtogen (ȳ) *easily brought about,* ÆL23³¹⁷.

±**īewan** (ēa, ēo, ȳ) *to show, display, reveal, disclose, point out,* CP. [ēage; cp. ēowan]

īfe? *a kind of plant,* WW301¹² (iue).

īfegn (Cp)=īfig

īfig n. '*ivy,*' Gl,Lcd,Shr.

īfigbearo *ivy-grove,* CC50.

īfig-crop, -croppa m. *cluster of ivy berries,* Lcd,WW. [v. '*ivy*']

īfiglēaf n. '*ivy-leaf,*' Lcd117b.

īfigrind f. *ivy-bark,* Lcd121b.

īfig-tearo, -tara n. *ivy-tar, resin from tar,* Lcd.

īfigtwig n. *ivy-twig,* Lcd117a.

īfiht *ivy-covered,* KC.

īg=īc; **Īg**=īeg; **īgbūend**=īegbuend

īgdæges=īdæges; **īgel**=īl; **īgg**=īeg

īggað, iggoð, īg(e)oð m. '*ait,*' *eyot, small island,* Æ,Chr. [īeg]

īgil, igl (Æ)=īl

īgland=īegland

īgoð, īgð=īggað; **īh**=īc

īhte pret. 3 sg. of īecan.

Īl (igil) m. *hedgehog, porcupine,* CP,Shr, WW. ['*il'*]
īland=īegland
±īlca (y) pron. (usu. wk) *the same, An,Bo, Chr,Ct*; CP. ['*ilk'*]
īlce adv. v. swā; īld-=ield-
īle (y) m. *sole of the foot,* Æ : *callosity, corn,* Æ. [cp. *Ger.* eilen]
īlfetu, ilfe(t)te (y;=ie) f. *swan,* GL; Mdf.
īll n.=ile; īllca=ilca
īlleracu f. *surfeit,* WW378¹⁵.
+īllerocad *surfeited,* CVPs77⁶⁵.
īlnetu (WW367²⁷)=ilfetu
īlugsecg v. eolhsecg; īmb- v. ymb-
īmberdling, imbyrdling=inbyrdling
impa? m., impe? f. *graft, shoot, scion,* CP 381¹⁷. ['*imp'*]
impian *to* '*imp*,' *implant, graft,* LL454,12. (+) *busy oneself with,* CP132²⁵.
in I. prep. with a. and d. (instr.) (local) '*IN*,' *into, upon, on, at, to, among* : (temporal) *in, at, about, towards, during* : (purpose) *in, to, for.* II. sb. and adv.=inn
in- (v. BH xxxiii ff.)=on-, inn-
ināberan⁴ (inn-) *to bring in,* Æ.
inādl f. *internal disease,* LCD.
inǣlan (VPs)=onǣlan; ināgān=ingān
ināgēode=inēode pret. 3 sg. of ingān.
ināsendan *to send in,* Mk2⁴.
ināwritting f. *inscription,* LkL20²⁴.
inbærnednes (e²), inbærnes f. *burning, incense, frankincense.* [=onb-]
inbecweðan⁵ *to inculcate,* WW429³⁶.
inbelǣdan *to lead in,* LHy.
inbelūcan² *to shut,* BL217²⁶.
inbend mf. *internal bond,* GU928.
inber-=on-, in-byr-
inberan *to carry in,* LL386,1.
inbernes (VPs)=inbærnes
inbeslēan *to hack into* (*any one*), LL86,74.
inbestingan *to penetrate,* LL7,64².
inbetȳnednes f. *life of a recluse,* GD212⁵.
inbewindan³ *to enfold, enwrap,* LkL (inn-).
inbirdling=inbyrdling
inblāwan⁷ *to inspire, breathe upon,* JnR : *inflate, puff up,* EC. ['*inblow'*]
inboden *proclaimed.* [onbēodan]
inbolgen *exasperated,* DR. [=onb-]
inboren ptc. *indigenous, native,* SR; GPH390. ['*inborn'*]
inborh m. *bail, security in cases of theft,* LL. ['*inborgh'*]
inbrēdan³ *to burst in upon,* GPH393.
in-brengan, -bringan *to bring in, present,* Mk. ['*inbring'*]
inbryne (byr) m. *conflagration,* DR64⁶.
inbryrd-=onbryrd-
±inbūan *to inhabit,* MtL23²¹.
inbūend m. *inhabitant,* WW210¹³.

in-burg, -burh f. *hall,* WW.
inbyrde (e²) *born on the estate,* TC.
inbyrdling (e²) m. *slave born in a master's house,* Æ : *native,* OEG.
inbyrne (DR)=inbryne
inbyrð pres. 3 sg. of inberan.
inc (*Mt,Mk*) da. of git, dual pers. pron. ['*inc'*]
inca m. *question, scruple, suspicion, doubt* : *occasion,* RB : *grievance, quarrel, grudge,* BH. incan witan *to have a grudge.*
incaðeode=ingeðēode; ince=ynce
incēgan (=īe) *to call upon,* DR119³.
incēgung (=īe) f. *invocation,* DR.
incempa m. *soldier of the same company,* WW207⁶.
incer (y) I. gen. of git, dual pers. pron. II. adj. pron. *of or belonging to both of you,* MH,Mt. ['*inker'*]
+incfullian *to offend, scandalize,* MtR. [inca]
incga=inca
incit acc. of git, dual personal pronoun.
incleofe (i, y) f. *chamber, closet* : *cave, den.*
incniht m. *household servant,* Æ.
incofa m. *inner chamber,* ÆL : *heart,* MET 22¹⁸.
incoðu f. *internal disease,* Æ.
incuman⁴ *to come in, go into, enter,* Æ. ['*income'*]
incund *interior, internal, inward, secret,* Æ,CP. adv. -līce, Æ.
incundnes f. *inward conviction, sincerity,* W105³⁰ : *inward part, recess,* DHy.
incūð *strange, extraordinary.* adv. -līce, ÆT1104.
incyme m. *entrance,* LV32.
indǣlan *to infuse,* DR.
indēpan (=īe) *to dip in,* LkL16²⁴.
indīegelnes f. *hiding-place,* RPs17¹².
Indisc *Indian,* Æ.
indrencan *to steep, saturate* : *fill to overflowing,* VPs22⁵. [=ondrencan]
indrīfan¹ *to ejaculate, utter,* SAT80.
indrihten=indryhten
indrincan³ *to imbibe, drink.* indruncen *plied with drink.*
indryhten *distinguished, noble, excellent,* WW.
indryhto† f. *honour, glory.*
ineardian *to dwell in, inhabit,* VPs.
inēddisc n. *household stuff, furniture,* WW 147³². [yddisc]
inelfe=innelfe; inerfe=innierfe
inēðung f. *inspiration, breathing,* APs17¹⁶. [ēðgung]
infær n. *ingress, entrance, entry, admission,* Æ,WW. ['*infare'*]
infæreld n. *in-coming, entrance, admission,* Æ : *interior* : *vestibule.*

infangene-ðēof, infangen-ðēf sb. *right of judging thieves caught within the limits of one's jurisdiction, and of taking the fines for the crime, Ct*; v. LL2·523. ['*infangthief*']

infaran⁶ I. *to enter, Æ,Jn.* ['*infare*'] II.= innefaran

infaru f. *incursion, inroad,* CHR1048.

infeallan⁷ *to fall in,* VPs.

infeccan *to fetch in,* BL175¹.

infēran *to enter in, Æ.*

inflht n. *brawl in a house,* LL597′.

infindan³ *to find, discover,* NG.

inflǣscnes f. *incarnation,* EC161²³.

inflēde† *full of water.*

inflēon² *to fly from,* RIM44.

infōster n. *bringing up, rearing,* LL396′.

infrōd† *very aged, experienced,* B.

ing I. *name of the rune for* ng. II.=ging, geong. III.=inn

-ing suffix, as in earming, lytling (originally patronymic).

in-gān anv. pret. -ēode *to go in, enter,* BH, Mt. ['*ingo*']

ingang (eo²) m. *ingress, entrance, access, beginning,* BH,Ps (inn-) : *entrance-fee.* ['*ingang*']

ingangan⁷ *to go in, enter, Æ.*

ingebed n. *earnest prayer,* PPs87².

ingeberigan (NG)=onbyrgan

ingebringan³ *to bring in,* LL150′.

inge-cīgan, -cēgan '*invocare*,' VPs; CPs 90¹⁵.

ingedōn anv. *to put in,* BH434²⁰.

ingedrincan (GPH391)=indrincan

ingefeallan⁷ '*incidere*,' Ps.

ingefeoht n *internal war,* BH.

ingefolc n. *native race,* Ex142.

ingehrif (-gerif) n. *womb,* LPs21⁸.

inge-hygd, -hȳd (Æ), -hīd f. *consciousness, mind, conscience, sense, understanding : meaning, intention, purpose, design.*

ingehygdnes f. *intention,* LPs48⁵.

ingelǣdan=inlǣdan

ingelaðian *to invite,* Lk14.

ingemang v. ongemang prep.

ingemynd† fn. *recollection, memory, mind.*

ingemynde *well-remembered,* EL896.

ingenga m. *visitor, intruder,* B1776.

ingeongan (*LG*; v. '*yong*')=ingangan

ingēotan² *to pour in, fill,* GUTH.

ingēoting (yn-? =ymb-) f. *inpouring,* OEG.

ingerec n. *broil,* BH. [=ungerec]

ingerif=ingehrif

ingeseted *placed in, inserted,* WW427¹⁷.

ingesteald *household goods,* B1155.

ingeswel n. *internal swelling,* WW113⁵.

ingeðanc mn. *thought, mind, conscience, intention,* Æ,CP.

ingeðēod† f. *nation,* Ex,PPs.

ingeðōht *conscience,* GD72¹².

ingeweaxen *implanted,* WW427⁸.

ingewinn n. *civil war,* AO88²⁹.

ingewitnes f. *consciousness, conscience,* BH.

ingong (CP)=ingang

ingyte m. *pouring in, infusion, inspiration,* CM424. [gēotan]

inhǣtan *to inflame,* GD29⁹.

inheald *in bas-relief, embossed,* WW423²⁸.

inhebban (CR313)=onhebban

inheldan=onhieldan

inheord f. *herd kept by the lord on his lands,* LL449,7.

inhīred m. *family, household, Æ.*

in-hīwan, -hīgan sbpl. *members of a household or community, servants.*

inhold *loyal in heart,* LCD3·442′.

inhȳrnes f. *possession,* EC364′.

inilfe=innylfe; **ininnan**=oninnan

inlād f. *right of water-passage inland,* KC 4·209⁵ : *entrance-fee,* Jn p188⁹.

inlǣdan '*inducere*,' *to introduce,* NG.

inlænd-=inlend-

±inlagian *to reverse sentence of outlawry,* Chr,LL. ['*inlaw*']

inland n. *land in the lord's own occupation, domain, demesne,* EC,LL. ['*inland*']

inlaðian *to invite,* G.

inlaðigend m. *inviter,* Sc170¹².

inlec=inlic; **inlēgan** (VPs)=onlīegan

inlēhtan=inlīhtan

inlenda m. *native,* GL.

in-lende, -lendisc (LCD) *native, indigenous.*

inlēohtan=inlīhtan

inlic *internal, interior, inward,* BH ; *native,* adv. -līce *inwardly : thoroughly, sincerely, heartily,* BH,Bo. ['*inly*']

inlīchomung f. *incarnation,* DR.

inlīgian=onlīgian

±inlīhtan *to illuminate, enlighten.*

inlīhtend m. *illuminator,* DR2⁶.

inlīhtian (NG)=inlihtan

inlīhtnes f. *illumination,* VPs.

inliðewāc=unleoðuwāc

inlīxan *to become light, dawn,* LkL23⁵⁴.

inlocast superl. adv.=inlīcost

inlȳhtan=inlīhtan

inmearg n. *marrow,* GPH397.

inmēde *close to one's heart, important in one's estimation,* RB; BK15.

inn I. n. *dwelling, apartment, lodging, chamber, house,* Æ,Mt; AO : *quartering oneself (of soldiers).* ['*inn*'] II. adv. '*in*,' *into, inwards, within, inside of, Æ,AO,B, BL,G : inwardly.* inn on *into.* inn tō is used with words of granting to indicate the grantee, CC125 (ES57·4).

inn-=in-; **inna** (LkL)=innoð

innan I. prep. (w. a. g. d.) *from within* :
within, in, into, CP. **II.** adv. *within, in-side, in, AO.* ['INNE']
innanbordes adv. *at home, CP.*
innanburhware sbpl. *residents within the walls of a town,* TC510'.
innancund *inner, inward, internal,* LCD : *thorough, hearty,* PPs 118², ¹⁰.
innane=innan II.
innanearm m. *inner side of arm,* LCD 87b.
innantīdernes (īe, ȳ) f. *internal weakness,* LCD.
innanweard=inweard
innanwund f. *internal wound,* LCD 3b.
innað=innoð
innāwritting (*LkL*)=onwriting
inne adv. *in, inside, within, in-doors, A, AO,BH,Chr,Ct,Lcd.* ['*inne*']
inne-=inn-, in-
innecund adj. *inward,* CP 139.
inne-faran, -foran *bowels,* LCD.
innefeoh n. *household goods,* LL5,28; v. 3·9.
innelfe=innylfe
innemest (superl. of inne) adj. '*inmost,' Sc* : *most intimate, deep or close, CP.* adv.
innera, in(n)ra (compar. of inne) '*inner,' interior, GF,WW* : *mental, spiritual, BH, LL,Sc.*
inneð=innoð
inne-weard, -werd=inweard
innheardmann m. *one of the household troops,* MtL 8⁹. [inhīred]
innhere m. *native army,* CHR 1006 E.
innian *to go in, Bo* : (±) *put up, lodge, Chr* 1048 : (+) *include* : (+) *fill, restore, make good, Æ.* ['*inn*']
innierfe (e²) n. *household stuff, furniture, goods,* Bo 31¹⁹.
innifli (Cp 1151)=innylfe
±**innīwian** *to renew,* DR.
innon=innan
innor (*ÆGr*) compar. of inne. ['*inner*']
innoð mf. *inside, entrails, stomach, womb, breast, heart, BH,Bo,G; Æ,CP.*
innoðmægen (e³) n. *strength,* EHy 5¹⁶.
innoðtȳdernes f. *weakness of the bowels,* LCD 105a.
innoðwund f. *internal wound,* LCD 88b.
innra=innera
innung f. *dwelling* : *contents, takings, re-venue, Bo,KC.* ['*inning*']
innweardlīce=inweardlīce
innweorud n. *retainers, household,* WID 111.
innylfe (e, i) n. *bowels, womb,* LCD.
inorf n. *household goods, furniture,* LCD,WW.
inra (*Æ*)=innera
inrǣcan '*ingesserunt,*' WW 420¹⁸ (v. A 31·532).
inrǣsan *to rush upon,* MtL.

inrēcels n. *incense,* LkR 1⁹.
insǣglung=inseglung
insǣte adj. *dependent,* WW 185⁹.
insætnes=insetnes
inscēawere m. *inspector,* DR 194.
inscēawung f. *inspection, view,* NG.
insceðende=unscæððende
in-seg(e)l (æ) n. *seal, signet, Ct,WW.* ['*inseil*'; *L.*]
±**inseglian** (æ) *to seal, LL; ÆL.* ['*inseil*']
inseglung (æ²) f. *sealing, seal, Æ.*
insendan *to send in, put in,* VPs.
inseten f. *an institution,* DR.
insetnes f. *regulation,* DR.
insettan *to institute,* BH, JnL.
insigle n. *seal, signet,* DR,TC. [insegel]
insiht f. *narrative,* JnL.
insittende *sitting within,* RD 47⁷.
insmoh m. *slough,* MH 162¹¹.
insōcn f. *brawl in a house,* LL 597,80¹².
insomnian *to gather in,* BH 274¹.
inspīderwiht '*spider,' Lcd* 167b (very doubt-ful, v. BTac).
inspinn n. *spindle,* WW.
instæpe I. m. *entrance,* ÆH 1·84. **II.**= instæpes
instæpes (e²) adv. *forthwith, directly,* BL.
instæppan (*Æ*)=insteppan
instandan⁶ (o²) *to be present,* DR.
instandendlic (o²) *required for present use,* MtR 6¹¹.
instede (y) *immediately,* NG.
in-stepe, -stepes=instæpes
insteppan⁶ (æ) *to go in, enter, Æ.*
instice m. *internal stitching pain,* LCD.
instīgan¹ *to climb in,* GD 24.
instihtian *to appoint, arrange,* LkL p 2⁶.
insting=onsting; **instyde**=instede
inswān m. *lord's swineherd,* LL 447.
inswōgan⁷ *to invade,* BH 278⁸.
inswōgennes (ēo²) f. *onrush,* BH 110³³.
intiga (KGL)=intinga; **intimb-**=ontimb-
intinga m. *matter, business, Æ* : *cause : fault.* butan intingan *in vain, emptily.*
intō prep. w. d. (instr.), a. 'INTO,' *to, against, in, Æ,Chr.*
intrahtnung f. *interpretation,* MtL p 2⁷.
intrepettan *to trip, dance,* Ln 37¹⁹⁷.
inðanc (ByH 132¹⁴)=ingeðanc
inðer adv. *apart,* MtR 17¹.
inðicce *crass, thick,* MtL 13¹⁵.
inðīnen f. *female servant,* GPH 401.
inðing (N)=intinga; **inðwēan**=onðwēan
in-wærc, -wræc m. *internal pain,* GD,LL.
inwǣte f. *internal humour,* LCD 97a.
inwaru f. *services due to the lord on his* '*inland,*' Ct.
inweard I. (innan-, inne-) adj. *internal, inward, inner, intrinsic, deep, sincere,*

earnest, _Æ,B,Bo,Cr._ as sbn. _inward parts,_
_Æ,WW._ **II.** adv. _within_ : _mentally,_
spiritually, LkL. [‘_inward_’]
inweardlic (e, o, u) _internal, Lcd_ : _inner,_
RWH 136¹⁷ : _earnest, sincere,_ W. adv. _-līce_
‘_inwardly,_’ Æ : _deeply, thoroughly, heartily,_
Æ,Met.
inwendan _to change,_ VPs.
inweorc n. _indoor work,_ LL454,11.
inwerd-=inweard-; **inwid**=inwit
inwidda m. _adversary, evil one,_ Jud 28.
inwise f. _condiment,_ Lcd 69a.
inwit I. n. _evil, deceit._ **II.** adj. _wicked,_
deceitful.
inwitfeng m. _spiteful clutch,_ B 1447.
inwitflān m. _treacherous shaft,_ Mod 37.
inwitful _wicked, crafty,_ Ps,WW.
inwitgæst m. _evil guest,_ B 2670.
inwitgecynd n. _evil nature,_ Sol 329.
inwitgyren f. _treacherous snare,_ PPs 139⁵.
inwithlemm (id) m. _treacherous wound,_
Rood 47.
inwithrōf m. _unfriendly roof,_ B 3123.
inwitnet n. _net of malice,_ B 2167.
inwitnīð† m. _cunning hostility._
inwitrūn f. _evil, crafty counsel,_ Jul 610.
inwitscear m. _murderous attack,_ B 2478.
inwitsearo n. _artful intrigue,_ B 1101.
inwitsorh† f. _sorrow._
inwitspell n. _tale of woe,_ Gen 2024.
inwitstæf† m. _wickedness, evil,_ PPs.
inwitðanc† m. _evil thought, hostile intent._
inwitwrāsn† f. _hostile fetter,_ An.
inwræc=inwærc
inwrītere m. _writer, secretary,_ ZDA31·23.
inwritting f. _inscription,_ MtK p 4⁵. [=onwr-]
inwudu m. _private woodland,_ BC 3·189².
inwund f. _internal wound,_ Lcd 70a.
inwunenes f. _persistence,_ WW 426⁵.
inwunung f. _residence in,_ NC 304.
inwyrm m. _intestinal worm,_ Lcd.
io-=geo-; **īo** (=īu)=gēo; **ioc**=geoc
iom=eom; **iong** (N)=geong, gang
ionna (N) adv. _within._
ionnað=innoð
ior m. _name of a river-fish_ (_eel?_) : _name of_
the rune for **io,** Run 28.
iorning=ærning
iornð=iernð pres. 3 sg. of iernan.
iorsian (KGL)=iersian
Iotas mpl. _the Jutes,_ Chr.
iow m.=īw; **iowan**=īewan
ippingīren=yppingīren; **īren**=īsen
irfe=ierfe; **irgian**=eargian
Iringes weg m. _Milky Way,_ WW 53²³.
irm-=ierm-; **irn-**=iern-, eorn-
irre=ierre; **irs-**=iers-
irsen-=īsen-; **irðling**=yrðling
is pres. 3 sg. of eom, anv.

īs n. ‘_ice,_’ B,BH,Met,PPs : (pl.) _pieces of_
ice, BH : _name of the rune for_ ī.
īsærn (Gl)=īsearn
īsceald† _icy cold,_ Met,Seaf. [‘_icecold_’]
īse (N)=gese
īsearn (æ, e) m. _halcyon, kingfisher,_ Gl.
īsen I. (īsern, īren) n. ‘_iron,_’ Æ,CP : _iron_
instrument : _fetter_ : (†) _iron weapon, sword_ :
ordeal of red-hot iron, LL 230,6. **II.** adj. _of_
iron, ‘_iron,_’ Æ,CP. **III.** (WW)=īsearn
īsenbend† (īr-) mf. _iron bond, fetter._
īsenbyrne (īsern-) f. _iron corslet,_ B 671.
īsend=iesend; **īsenesmið**=īsensmið
īsenfetor (īsern-) f. _iron fetter,_ Gl.
īsengelōma (īr-) m. _iron instrument, weapon,_
AA 13¹⁶.
īsengræf m. _iron-mine,_ KC 5·234′.
īsengrǣg (grēi) ‘_iron-grey,_’ WW.
īsenheard (īr-) ‘_iron-hard,_’ B 112.
īsenhearde f. (‘_iron-hard_’), _black centaury,_
vervain, knapweed, Lcd.
īsenhelm (irsen-) m. _iron helmet,_ WW 142².
īsenhere (-ern) m. _iron-clad army,_ Ex
348.
īsenhyrst adj. _with iron fittings,_ KC.
īsenordāl (ȳ) n. _ordeal by iron,_ LL.
īsenōre (īsern-) f. _iron mine,_ WW 237²⁰.
īsen-panna m., -**panne** f. _frying-pan,_ Gl.
īsenscofl f. _iron shovel,_ Gl (īsernscobl).
īsenscūr f. _shower of arrows,_ B 3116 (-ern).
īsensmið m. _blacksmith,_ WW.
īsenswāt? m. _dross of iron?_ (v. BT s.v.
swāt). Lcd 108a.
īsentange f. _snuffers,_ WW 327¹⁴.
īsenōrēat m. _iron-clad troop,_ B 330 (īr-).
īsenwyrhta m. _blacksmith,_ WW 310³³.
īsern (Lcd)=iesend
īsern (1)=īsen; (2)=īsearn
īsgebind n. _fetters of ice,_ B 1113.
īsgeblǣd (ȳ) n. _ice-blister, chilblain?_ Lcd.
īsig ‘_icy,_’ Met : _covered with ice,_ B 33.
īsigfeðera _with frosted wings,_ Seaf 24.
īsiht _icy,_ Æl 23b⁵⁷².
īsīðes adv. _immediately,_ LL (338¹¹).
īsmere m. _icy lake,_ Met 28⁶².
±īsnian _to cover with iron._ pp. īsnod _iron-_
clad, WW 236¹⁹.
ītest, itst pres. 2 sg., iteð, itt pres. 3 sg. of
etan.
īð=īeð; **īu-,** iū=geo-, gēo; **īuc**=geoc
Iūdēas sbmp. _the Jews,_ G.
Iūdēisc _Jewish,_ G.
iugian=geocian; **īuih** (NG)=ēowic, ēow
Iūla (Men 221)=Gēola
Iutan=Iotas
īuwian (AS 7¹⁶ and n.)=īewan
īw (ēow) m. ‘_yew,_’ _yew-tree,_ Cp,KC,Rd; Æ;
Mdf.
īwberge (ēow) f. _yew-berry,_ Lcd. [v. ‘_yew_’]

K

Words beginning with **k** will be found under **c**.

L

lā interj. *lo! behold! oh! ah!* Æ. lā lēof *O Lord! O sir!* : *indeed, verily,* Æ. hwæt lā *what!* wā lā wā! *alas!*

label=(*lafel), læfel; **laber** (*Lcd*)=læfer

lāc nf. *play, sport* : (†) *strife, battle* : *sacrifice, offering,* Æ,CP : *gift, present, Mt*; Æ : *booty, B* : (†) *message.* ['*lake*']

+lac† n. *tumult, commotion.* sweorda +l. *battle* : *crowd, host,* CR896.

lācan⁷ pret. 3 sg. leolc *to move up and down, leap, jump, swing, fly, Jul* : *play (instrument)* : *play upon, delude,* AO,Bo : (†) *fight, contend, B.* ['*lake*']

lācdǣd f. *munificence,* OEG3833.

lacen? *a cloak,* WW377²². [*Ger.* laken?]

lācfæsten *the offering of a fast,* BL37¹⁸.

lācgeofa m. *generous giver,* PPs67¹⁸.

+lācian *to present, bestow* : *accompany with gifts.*

lāclic *sacrificial,* ÆPD116⁸.

±lācnian (ǣ, ē) *to heal, cure, treat, look after,* Æ,BH,LkL; AO,CP : *foment, dress (a wound).* ['*lechne*']

lācnigendlic *surgical,* HGL478.

lācnimende only in bēon l. '*munerari*,' BHy 3¹⁹.

lācnung (ǣ) f. *healing, cure,* Æ : *medicament, remedy, Lcd*; RB. ['*lechning*']

lācsang m. *offertory hymn,* WW130².

lac-tuc(e), m. -tuca f. *lettuce,* Æ,LCD. [*L.*]

lacu f. *stream, EC* : *pool, pond, Chr*656E. ['*lake*']

lād I. f. *course, journey, An,B* : (±) *way, street, water-way* : *leading, carrying, LL* : *maintenance, support.* ['*load*,' '*lode*'] **II.** f. *clearing from blame or accusation, purgation, exculpation,* CP.

ladan (NG)=hladan

±lādian *to exculpate oneself* : *let off, excuse,* Æ,AO,CP.

lādiendlic *excusable,* WW233³¹.

lādmann m. *leader, guide,* Æ. ['*lodeman*']

lād-rinc? -rincman m. *conductor, escort, LL* 3,7 (v. 2·441 and 3·6).

ladsar=laser

lādscipe m. *leadership,* WW481⁶.

lādtēow, lādðēow=lāttēow

lādung f. *exculpation, excuse, defence, apology,* Æ,CP.

lǣc=(1) lēac; (2) lāc; **lǣca**=lǣce

-lǣca v. āg-, ellen-l. etc.

+lǣca m. *a rival,* GPH391.

lǣcan *to spring up, rise, flare up,* SAT716.

+lǣcan *to emulate,* GPH391 : *join with, make common cause with?* CPs140⁴. [lāc]

±lǣccan *to seize, grasp, comprehend,* Æ : *capture, catch, Chr,G,LL* : *take, receive,* Æ. ['*latch*,' '*i-lecche*']

lǣccung (e) f. *reproach,* EPs88³⁵.

lǣce (ē, ȳ) m. *physician, doctor, BH,LkL*; Æ,CP : '*leech*,' WW; Æ.

lǣcebōc f. *book of prescriptions,* LCD.

lǣcecræft m. '*leech-craft*,' *art of healing, Bo,Lcd*; Æ : *remedy, prescription,* Æ.

lǣcecræftig *skilled in medicine,* LCD186b.

lǣcecynn n. *race of physicians,* RD6¹⁰.

lǣcecyst f. *medicine chest,* GD344¹⁷.

lǣcedōm (ē) m. *medicament, medicine, BH, WW* : *healing, salvation,* CP. ['*leechdom*']

lǣcedōmlic *salutary,* A5·458.

lǣcedōmnes f. *cataplasm,* WW.

lǣcefeoh n. *doctor's fee,* LL(148¹⁹).

lǣcefinger m. ('*leech-finger*'), *fourth finger, Lcd,WW*.

lǣcegeatwa? (-getea) fp. *medical apparatus,* v. NC304.

lǣcehūs n. *hostelry, hospital,* Lk10³⁴.

lǣceīren n. *surgeon's knife, lancet,* GD32.

lǣcesealf f. *medicinal ointment,* WW514²¹.

lǣceseax n. *lancet,* CP187⁹.

lǣcewyrt f. *medicinal herb, drug,* Æ : *ribwort* : *medical treatment.*

lǣcnian=lācnian

lǣdan (±) *to* '*LEAD*,' *guide, conduct, carry, lift, take, bring,* Æ,Chr; CP : (±) *produce, bring forth* : *pass, lead (life)* : *to mark or beat the bounds of land,* EC155⁸ : *do* : *place, lay,* Æ : *sprout forth, grow, spread.* wīf l. *take a wife, marry.*

lǣde (BH400²)=lǣwede

lǣden I. (ē, ēo) n. '*Latin*,' *Bf,BH,CP,LG* : *any foreign language, Lcd.* ['*leden*'] **II.** (ē, ȳ) adj. *Latin.*

lǣdenbōc (ē, ȳ) f. *Latin book,* Æ.

lǣdend I. m. *bringer,* CR. **II.** m. *excuser, apologist,* PPs140⁵. [*lǣdan]

+lǣdendlic *ductile, malleable,* LRPs97⁵.

lǣdengereord n. *Latin language,* LCD3·440'.

lǣdengeðēode n. *Latin language,* CP7.

lǣdenisc *Latin,* BH.

lǣdenlār f. *knowledge of Latin,* W124¹².

Lǣdenlic *Latin,* NC304.

+lǣdenlic (EPs97)=+lǣdendlic

lǣdennama m. *Latin noun,* ÆGR292¹⁸.

lǣdensprǣc (ē) f. *Latin language,* Æ,CP.

lǣdenstæfum (ē) adv. *in Latin,* Jn19²⁰.

lǣdenware mpl. *Latin people, Romans,* CP

lǣdenword (ē) n. *Latin word,* ÆGR122⁶.

lǣdere m. *leader,* S²Hy6¹³.

lǣdnes f. *bringing forth,* BHo76¹⁵.

lǣdtēow=lāttēow

lāf=(1) lāf; (2) lēaf
±**lǣfan** (ē) **I.** *to 'leave' ('yleft'), bequeath, B,Jn*; Æ,CP : *spare, leave behind, have left, G : remain,* Æ. [lāf] **II.**=līefan
lǣfel (e) m. *spoon, basin, vessel, bowl, cup.* [*Ger.* löffel; *L.* labellum]
lǣfend (WW 168¹⁷)=lǣwend
lǣfer f. *rush, reed, iris, gladiolus, Lcd,WW*; Æ : *metal plate,* Æ. ['*laver*'; '*levers*']
lǣferbed n. *reed-bed,* WW 138²⁹.
lāfnes=lēafnes
lǣg pret. 3 sg. of licgan.
lǣg=(1) lēag; (2) līeg
lǣgde=legde pret. sg. of lecgan.
lāgon pret. pl. of licgan.
lǣgt=līget
lǣht pp., lǣhte pret. sg. of læccan.
lǣl (ē) f., lǣla m. *rod, whip, switch : bruise, weal, stripe,* Ex.
lǣlan? *to be bruised,* An 1445 (GK read lǣla m.).
lǣlian I. *to become black and blue,* WW 431³⁰. **II.** (ē) *to level, aim at,* Lcd.
lǣmen (ē) *of clay, earthen,* Æ. [lām]
lǣmian=lēmian
lǣn (ā) **I.** nf. *loan, borrowing, lease, grant, gift, present, benefit,* Æ,CP. [lēon] **II.**=lǣnland
lǣn-=lēn-
±**lǣnan** (ē) *to 'lend,'* Æ,WW; CP : *give, grant, lease, Gen*; Æ.
lǣndagas† mpl. *loan-days, transitory days, days of a man's life,* B.
lǣnde-, lǣnden-=lenden-
lǣne (ē) *lent, temporary, inconstant, transitory,* CP ; *perishable, frail, poor : weak, sinful,* CP. [lēn]
lǣnelic *passing, transitory,* Bl 73⁹.
lǣnend m. *lender,* WW. ['*lenend*']
lǣnendlic (W)=lǣnelic
lǣnere m. '*lender,*' WW 189²¹.
lǣng=leng; **lǣngten-**=lencten-
lǣnian=lēanian
lǣnland n. *leased land,* v. LL 2·323.
lǣnlic (LL)=lǣnelic; **-lǣnung** v. fēoh-l.
lǣpeldre f. *dish,* ÆH,WW. [lapian]
lǣpewince (e) f. *lapwing,* Gl.
lǣppa (a) m. *lappet, piece, section, lobe, portion, district,* CP,Lcd; Æ. ['*lap*']
lǣppede v. fif-l.
+**lǣr** *empty : empty-handed.* [*Ger.* leer]
+**lǣran** (ē) *to teach, instruct, guide,* BH,LL : *enjoin, advise, persuade, urge, preach :* (+) *convert :* (+) †*recall,* ES 37·197. 1. forð *hand down (to others),* CP. hence *clerical (as opposed to* lǣwed), *spiritual (as opposed to temporal),* Æ,CP. ['*lere,*' '*ylere(d)*']
-lǣre=lǣr

+**lǣrednes** f. *learning, skill,* Æ,BH.
lǣrend m. *misleader, instigator,* HL 154⁷¹.
lǣrest=lǣst
lǣrestre f. *instructress,* Æ.
lǣrgedēfe *adapted for instruction?* FT 61.
lǣrig m. *border? cover? (of a shield),* v. A 37·55 and LF 171.
-lǣrigian v. ymb-l.
lǣringmǣden n. *female pupil,* ApT 20¹³.
lǣringmann m. *disciple,* RB 20⁶.
lǣrnes f. *emptiness,* Lcd 22b. ['*leerness*']
lǣs pret. 3 sg. of lesan.
lǣs I. (ē) adv. and sbn. *less, lest,* Æ,AO,CP. ðȳ lǣs (ðe) conj. w. subj. *lest.* **II.** f. gs. lǣswe *pasture,* JnL,WW; Æ; Mdf. ['*lease,*' '*leasow*'] **III.** f. *(blood-)letting,* Lcd.
lǣsboren *of lower birth,* LL (246′).
lǣsest (MtR)=lǣst I.; **lǣsian**=lǣswian
lǣson pret. pl. of lesan.
lǣssa (ē) adj. (comp. of lȳtel) '*less,*' *smaller, fewer,* Æ,Bo,Chr : *inferior, MtL,MtR.* sb. Æ,Bf. adv. BH.
lǣst f. *fault, sin,* NC 305. [*ON.*]
lǣst I. superl. of lȳtel '*least,*' G,Gu,Lcd; CP; AO. ðe lǣste *lest,* CM. **II.** f. *performance, fulfilment,* Ex 308. **III.**=lāst
±**lǣstan** (ē) *to follow, help, serve,* B,Bl,Met, OET; AO : *perform, do, carry out, accomplish, B,Bo,Gen*; AO : *endure, last, continue, Cr,Met*; Æ : *furnish, pay, grant,* W. ['*last,*' '*ylast*']
lǣste f. '*last*' *(for the foot),* WW.
lǣstend m. *doer, performer,* BH.
+**lǣstfullian** *to testify,* LPs 80⁹.
lǣstwyrhta (eo²) m. *shoemaker,* WW.
lǣswe v. lǣs II.
±**lǣswian** tr. and intr. *to depasture, graze, feed,* Æ,LkL. ['*leasow*']
lǣt I. (lat- in obl. cases) comp. lǣtra; sup. lǣtest, lǣtemest *slow,* B,Bl,CP,Lcd; Æ : *slack, lax, negligent :* '*late,*' *An,Lk.* **II.** m. *man of the class between the slave and the ceorl,* LL (v. 2·564). ['*laet*']
lǣt pres. 3 sg. of lǣdan.
+**lǣt**=+lǣte II.
±**lǣtan⁷** pret. 3 sg. lēt, leort *to allow to remain, leave behind, depart from, 'let' alone, Bl,CP : leave undone, BH : bequeath, EC : allow, Bl,LL : cause to do, BH : regard as, consider, BH,Chr,CP : suppose : conduct oneself : behave towards, treat : allow to escape, emit, let out, set free,* Æ,Lcd : '*let*' *(on lease), BC : assert, pretend, Lk : allot, assign.* 1. from *refrain from.* 1. ūt *to put to sea.* +l. nēah land *approach the shore?* (ES 37·191). on bæc l. *leave behind.* 1. for *to take (one) for.* on trēowe +l. *to entrust,* WW 239⁷.
lǣtania=lētanīa

lætbyrd f. *slow birth*, LCD 185a.
+lǣte I. n. *manners, bearing*, NC 295. [*ON*.
læti] II. n. *junction of roads*, Æ,CHRD.
lætemest I. adv. *lastly, finally*, NG. II. v.
læt. ['*latemost*']
læthȳdig *slow-minded, dull*, CRA 10.
lætlīce adv. *slowly*, *Gu*. ['*lately*']
lætmest=lætemest
lætnes f. *slowness*, ÆL 23b⁶⁴⁷ : *sloth*, GD
174²³.
lætra (*Æ,LL*) v. læt. ['*latter*']
lætrǣde *slow, deliberate*, CP 149¹⁴. ['*lat-
rede*']
lætsum *backward*, *Chr*. ['*latesome*']
lætt f. (pl. latta) *beam*, '*lath*,' WW.
lǣttēow=lāttēow
lǣttewestre f. *guide*, Æ 23b⁵⁰⁸. [lāttēow]
lætting=letting; -lǣttu v. un-l.
lǣð n. *a division of a county containing
several hundreds*, '*lathe*,' BC 3·162 : *landed
property? (meadow) land?* LL 400,3².
lǣð-=lāð-
lǣðan *to abuse, revile, hate* : *cause to shun*,
RB 11¹⁸. [lāð]
lǣðð, lǣððo (CP) f. *wrong, injury* : *hatred,
malice*, *Bl*. ['*leth*'; lāð]
lǣuw=lēow
lǣw (ē) f. *injury*, W 165⁹.
lǣwa (ē) m. *betrayer, traitor*, *Lk*; Æ. [v.
'*lewe*']
±lǣwan *to betray*, BL,Ps. [*Goth*. lēwjan]
-lǣwe v. druncen-, hunger-l.
lǣwede *lay, laic, unlearned*. as sb. *layman*,
BH; Æ,CP. ['*lewd*']
lǣwel=lǣfel
lǣwend m. *betrayer, traitor*, GL.
lǣwerce=lāwerce; lǣwil=lǣfel
lǣx=leax
lāf f. *what is left, remnant, legacy, relic,
remains, rest, Bl,Chr*; Æ : *relict, widow*,
Æ,AO. tō lāfe *alone*. tō lāfe bēon *to
remain over*, *Bl*. wǣpna, daroða l. *survivors of battle*. hamora lāfa *results of
forging, swords*. ['*lave*'; līfan]
lāferce=lāwerce
±lafian *to pour water on, wash*, '*lave*,' *bathe*,
B,Lcd : *ladle out*, *Lcd*.
lafor m. *leopard*, AA 22³.
lag-=lah-; -laga v. lund-l.
laga m. *law*, LL,WW.
lage-=lagu-
lagen pp. of lēan II.
±lagian *to ordain*, *W*. ['*law*,' '*i-lahen*']
lago-=lagu-; -lagol v. ǣ-l.
lāgon=lǣgon pret. pl. of licgan.
lagu I. f. (old neut. pl. lagu; CHR 1052 D)
'*law*,' *ordinance, rule, regulation*, Æ; *Chr,
LL,RB,W* : *right, legal privilege*, LL : *district governed by the same laws*. II. m.

water, flood, sea, ocean, Gen,Mt : *name of
the rune for* l. ['*lay*']
+lagu np. *extent, surface (of sea)*, SEAF 64?
[*OS*. gilagu]
lagucrǣftig *skilled in seafaring*, B 209.
lagufæsten† n. *sea, ocean*.
lagufæðm m. *enveloping waves*, RD 61⁷.
laguflōd m. *wave, stream, waters, flood, sea,
ocean*.
lagulād† f. *water-way, sea*.
lagumearg m. *sea-horse, ship*, GU 1306.
lagusīð† m. *sea-journey*, GEN.
lagustrǣt f. *sea-path*, B 239.
lagustrēam† m. *water, sea, ocean*.
laguswimmend m. *swimming in the sea
(fish)*, SOL 289.
lāh pret. 3 sg. of lēon.
lah-=lag-
lahbreca m. *law-breaker, impious man*, Sc
9¹⁰. [lagu]
lahbrecende *impious, profane*, Sc 9⁹.
lahbryce m. *breach of the law*, LL.
lah-cēap, -cōp m. *money paid (by an outlaw)
for restitution of legal rights*, LL.
lahlic *lawful, legal*, Sc 46². adv. -līce.
lahmann m. *an official declarer of the law*,
LL 376. ['*lawman*']
lahriht n. *legal right*, LL.
lah-slitt fn., -slite m. *fine for breach of the
(Danish) law*, LL.
lahwita m. *lawyer*, LL (308¹³).
lām n. '*loom*,' *clay, earth*, Æ,WW; Mdf.
lama (o) wk. adj. and sbm. *crippled*, '*lame*,'
paralytic, weak, Æ,BH,Cp,El,Mt,WW.
lamb (e, o) pl. lamb(e)ru, lambor (A) n.
'*lamb*,' *Æ,G,Gl,Gu,VPs*.
lambyrd f. *imperfect birth*, LCD 185a.
lāmfæt n.† *vessel of clay (the body)*.
lamp I. pret. 3 sg. of limpan. II. (KGL)=
lamb
lamprede f. *lamprey*, WW 94¹⁷. [*L*.]
lāmpytt m. '*loampit*,' KC 3·252²⁴.
lāmsceall *tile*, APs 21¹⁶.
lāmsēað m. *loampit*, EC 448¹³.
lāmwyrhta m. *potter*, G.
lān=lǣn
lanan obl. cases of lanu.
land (o) n. *earth*, '*land*,' *soil, B,BH,Gen,Sc,
WW*; Mdf : *territory, realm, province,
district, Cp,Chr,Bl,VPs* : *landed property*,
Æ,Bl : *country (not town)*, *Æ,BH* : *ridge in
a ploughed field*.
+landa (o) m. *compatriot, kinsman*, WW
211²⁰.
landādl=hlandādl?
landælf f. *land-elf*, WW 516²⁷.
landāgend m. *native*, BH.
landāgende *owning land*, LL.
landār f. *landed property*, Æ.

landbegenga (i²) m. *husbandman, peasant, native*, CP.
landbegengnes (o¹) f. *habitation*, BPs 119⁵.
landbīgong (o¹) m. *dwelling in a country*, BPs 118⁵⁴.
landbōc f. '*land-book,' written grant of land*, Ct,WW.
landbrǣce m. *first ploughing (after land has lain fallow)*, WW 105¹¹.
landbūend I. mf. *inhabitant, native : husbandman.* **II.** f. *colony*, WE 51¹.
landbūende *dwelling on the land*, CREAT 80.
landbūnes f. *colony, settlement*, WE 51¹².
land-cēap, -cōp m. *fine paid to the lord on the alienation of land, BC.* ['*landcheap*']
landcofa m. *land, district*, LPs 59⁸.
landefn(e) n. *measure or proportion of land*, CHR 1085.
landesmann (Æ,Chr)=landmann
landfæsten (o¹) n. *natural fortress*, AO 80¹⁴.
landfeoh n. *recognitory rent for land*, KC.
landfolc n. '*land-folk,' natives, Æ.*
landfruma m. *ruler, prince*, B 31.
landfyrd f. *army*, BH,CHR.
landfyrding f. *military operations on land*, CHR 999.
landgafol n. *land-tax, tribute*, LL. ['*landgavel*']
landgehwerf (=ea³) n. *exchange of land*, TC 191⁶.
landgemaca m. *neighbour*, OEG.
landge-mǣre, -mirce n. *boundary, limit, frontier*, AO.
landgesceaft f. *earthly creature*, DA 360.
landgeweorc n. *fortified place*, B 938.
landgewyrpe n. *heap of earth?* KC.
landhæbbende *owning or ruling land*, DR, LL.
landhæfen f. *real property*, LL 22,32.
landhere m. *native force : land force (opposed to naval force).*
landhlāford m. *lord of a country, lord of a manor, 'landlord,'* EC,LL.
landhredding f. *redemption of land*, CC 9¹¹⁸.
landlagu f. *local law*, LL. ['*landlaw*']
landlēas *not owning land*, LL. ['*landless*']
land-lēod m., nap. -lēode, -lēoda, -lēodan *inhabitant of a country, native*, AO.
landlyre m. *loss of territory*, CHR 1105.
landmann m. *inhabitant of a country, native, Ex,LL.* ['*landmann*']
landmearc m. *boundary*, Jul,KC. ['*landmark*']
landmearca m. *land, country*, LPs 59⁸.
+**landod** *having landed property*, LL 182,11.
landopenung f. *first ploughing of land*, WW 147⁹.
landrǣden v. ealdlandrǣden.
landrest f. *grave*, AN 782.

landrīca m. *landed proprietor*, LL.
landrīce n. *territory*, AO,WW.
landriht n. '*land-right,' right to own or occupy land or connected with its occupation, B,Ex,Gen : that which is due from land or estates.*
landscearu (a²) f. *tract of land, province, country*, CP : *boundary, landmark*. [v. CC 48]
landscipe m. *region*, GEN 376.
landscoru=landscearu
landsēta m. *settler*, WW 111¹⁵. [sǣta]
landseten f. *occupation of land*, Ct : *occupied land, estate*, LL.
landseðla m. *occupier of land*, TC 593⁶.
landsidu m. *custom of a country*, CP.
landsittende *occupying land*, CHR 1085.
landsōcn† f. *search for land to settle on.*
landspēd f. *landed property*, KC 3·349'.
landspēdig *rich in land*, ÆGR.
landsplott m. *plot of land*, KC,LPs.
landstede (o) m. *region*, WIF 16.
landstycce m. *small plot of ground*, GD,LL.
landwaru f. *inhabitants, population*, B 2321.
landweard m. *coast-warden*, B 1890.
landwela m. *earthly possessions*, PH 505.
lane=lanu
lang (o) comp. lengra, superl. lengest '*long,' tall*, ÆGr,AO,BH,G,Lcd,Ma; CP : *lasting.*
+**lang** (usu. w. æt or on) *dependent on, attainable from, present in, belonging to, Æ,AO,Gu.* [v. '*along*']
Langafrīgedæg m. *Good Friday*, LL.
langað=langoð
langbolster mn. *feather-bed*, WW 276³⁶.
lange (o) adv. comp. leng, lenge, superl. lengest '*long,' a long time, far*, B,BH,Bl, Bo.
langfǣre *lasting, protracted*, Æ.
langfērnes f. *length, long duration*, Sc 29¹.
langfirst m. *long space of time*, GU 920.
langgestrēon n. *old store of wealth*, B 2240.
langian I. (o) (impers. with acc. of pers.) *to 'long' for, yearn after, grieve for, be pained, AO : lengthen, grow longer, Lcd : summon.* **II.** *to belong*, KC 4·215⁴.
+**langian** *to send for, summon, call, Æ : apprehend, seize*, LL 202,6².
langieldo f. *advanced age* (Swt).
langlīce adv. *for a long time, long, at length, Æ.*
langlīfe *long-lived*, Æ.
langmōd *constant, patient*, Ps. adv. -līce.
langmōdig *long-suffering*, EPs 7¹².
langmōdnes f. *long-suffering*, Sc 10¹⁷.
langnes f. *length, Æ.* ['*longness*']
langoð† m. *longing, discontent.*
langsceaft *having a long shaft*, AA 23¹⁰.
langscip n. *man of war*, CHR 897 A.

langstrang 'longanimis,' LPs 102⁸.

langsum (o¹) long, lasting, tedious, protracted, B,Lcd; Æ. ['longsome']

langsumlic (o) tedious, ÆH 1·362'. adv.-līce long, AO 58¹⁷ : patiently, ÆL 23b³⁹¹.

langsumnes f. length, Ps; Æ : patience, NC 305. ['longsomeness']

langswēored (ȳ²) long-necked, HEXC 253, 279.

langtwidig lasting, assured, B 1708.

langung (o) f. 'longing,' Bl : weariness, sadness, dejection, Æ : delay, CP. [langian]

langunghwīl f. time of weariness, AN 125.

langweb n. warp (in weaving), WW 187¹².

langwege (o¹, oe²) 'peregre,' MkL 13³⁴.

langwyrpe oblong, NC 305³⁴⁷.

lānland=lǣnland

lann (o)† f. chain, fetter.

lanu (o) f. 'lane,' street, Bl.

lapian to 'lap' up, drink, Lcd; Æ.

lappa (GL)=læppa

lār f. 'lore,' learning, science, art of teaching, preaching, doctrine, Bl; Æ,CP : study : precept, exhortation, advice, instigation, JnL; AO : history, story : cunning, GEN 2693.

lārbōc f. book containing instruction (used of St Paul's Epistles, and Bede's works), Æ.

lārbodung f. teaching, preaching, CHRD 50¹⁰.

lārbysn f. example, WW 163⁴³.

lārcniht (e²) m. disciple, LkL p 2².

lārcrǣft m. knowledge, SOL 3 : erudition, CHRD 66³⁶.

lārcwide† m. teaching, precept.

lārdōm m. teaching, instruction, LL 258,51.

lār-ēow, -ow, -uw(a) m. teacher, master, preacher, BH,JnL,WW; Æ,AO,CP. ['larew']

lārēowdōm m. function of teacher, instruction, CP : ecclesiastical authority, Æ,CP.

lārēowlic like a teacher, OEG,RB.

lārēowsetl n. teacher's seat, pulpit, OEG,Mt.

lārēwes=lārēowes gs. of lārēow.

lārfæsten n. prescribed fast, A 11·99.

lārhlystend m. catechumen, OEG 2881.

lārhūs n. school, HGL 405.

lārlēast (ē, ȳ) f. want of instruction, ignorance, LL,W.

lārlic of or conducive to learning, instructive, Æ : learned : doctrinal : persuasive. betwux lārlicum gefylcum amongst soldiers in training, Æ.

lārsmið† m. (nap. -smeoðas) teacher, counsellor.

lārspell n. homily, treatise, Æ. ['lorespell']

lārsum teachable, NC 305.

lārswice m. trickery, W 309¹⁴.

lār-ðēaw, -ðēow (Jn 1³⁸; 'lorthew')= lārēow

lārðegn m. teacher, NC 305.

lāruw(a) (LG)=lāreow

lārwita m. learned man, LL (308¹³).

lāser (o²) m? weed, tare, BF 30¹⁶,GL.

lāst (ǣ, ē, ēa) m. sole of foot : spoor, footprint, track, trace, B,Bl; Æ,CP : gait, step. on lāst(e) behind, after, in pursuit of. on l. lecgan to follow. lāstas lecgan to go. ['last']

±lāst (ǣ, ē) n. accomplishment, observance, RB 5⁵ : duty, due, obligation, vow.

+lāstful helpful, serviceable, LL; AO. ['lastfull']

lāstweard m. successor, heir, follower : pursuer.

lāstword n. fame after death, SEAF 73.

lasur=laser; lat- v. læt-; lāt=lād

lata m. slow person, BL 163⁸.

late adv. comp. lator, sup. latest ' late,' Chr, Jul : slowly, Lcd : at last, AO : lately, RB. [læt]

latemest=lætemest II.; lātēow=lāttēow

±latian to be slow, indolent : linger, delay, hesitate, Æ.

lator, adv. comp., latost (æ), superl. slower, later, Bf; AO,CP. ['latter,' 'last']

latt=lætt

lattēh f. guiding rein, WW 120⁹. [lād]

lāttēow, lāttēowa (ǣ) m. leader, guide, general, Bo,VPs (lad-); AO,CP. ['lattew']

lāttēowdōm m. leadership, guidance, instruction, CP.

lātðēow, lātuw=lāttēow

latu f. delay : (+) hindrance, DR 96⁵?

latung f. delay, hindrance, OEG 7¹²⁹.

lāð I. (±) hated, hateful, hostile, malignant, evil, AO,B : loathsome, noxious, unpleasant, Chr,Ep; CP. ['loath'] II. n. pain, harm, injury, misfortune, AO : insult, annoyance, harmful thing, BH,Lcd; CP. ['loath']

lāðbite m. wound, B 1122.

lāðe adv. inimically, in detestation, BH,PPs.

lāðēow=lāttēow

lāðettan (ǣ) to hate, loathe : make hateful or repulsive, Æ.

lāðgenīðla† m. persecutor, foe.

lāðgetēona† m. enemy, B.

lāðgewinna m. enemy, RD 16²⁹.

laðian to invite, summon, call upon, ask, Æ, CP. [Ger. laden]

lāðian to hate, be hated, AO; Æ. ['loathe']

lāðlēas inoffensive, innocent, WW. ['loathless']

lāðlic 'loathly,' hateful, horrible, repulsive, unpleasant, BH; Æ. adv. -līce, Met.

lāðscipe m. misfortune, GEN 2048.

lāðsearu n? hateful contrivance, DA 436.

lāðsīð m. painful journey, death, Ex 44.

lāðspel n. sad tidings, AO.

lāððēow=lāttēow

±laðung f. *calling, invitation, CP*: *assembly, congregation, church*, Æ. [*'lathing'*]
lāðwende† *hateful, hostile, bad.*
lāðwendemōd *hostile-minded*, GEN 448.
lāðwendnes f. *hostility*, LCD.
lāðweorc n. *evil deed*, PPs 105²⁶.
laur m. *laurel, bay, laver*, LCD.
laurbēam (lawer-) m. *laurel*, WE,WW.
laurberige f. *laurel-berry*, LCD.
+laured *laurel-flavoured*, LCD 84a.
laurice (*Cp*)=lāwerce
laurisc *of laurel*, AA 6²⁰.
laurtrēow n. *laurel-tree*, LCD.
lauwer, lawer=laur
lāwerce (ǣ) f. *'lark,'* *WW*; Mdf.
lawernbēam m. *laurel*, WE 6¹².
lēa I. (VPs)=lēo. II. gdas. of lēah.
lēac I. (ǣ, ē, ēo) n. *'leek,'* *onion, garlic, garden-herb, Lcd*; Æ. II. pret. 3 sg. of lūcan.
lēac-=lēah-
lēacblǣd n. *leek leaf*, NC 305.
lēaccærse (e²) f. *cress, nasturtium, Erf*; LCD. [v. *'cress'*]
lēac-trog, -troc *a bunch of berries*, GL.
lēactūn (lēah-, lēh-) m. *kitchen-garden, garden of herbs*, LkL,WW. [*'leighton'*]
lēactūnweard (ē¹) m. *gardener*, WW 127¹⁴. [*'leightonward'*]
lēacweard (ē¹, o²) m. *gardener*, G,WW.
lēad (ē) n. *'lead,'* *BH*; Æ,CP : *leaden vessel, cauldron*, LL.
lēaden (ē) *'leaden,'* Æ,LL.
lēadgedelf n. *lead-mine*, KC 3·401⁷.
lēadgewiht n. *lead-weight, a scale of weight*, v. CC 77.
lēadgota m. *plumber*, LL 455,16.
lēadstæf m. *loaded stick*, WW 441²⁰.
lēaf (ī) I. (±) f. *'leave'* (*'y-leave'*), *permission, privilege, BH,Chr,Sc*; Æ,CP. II. (ēo) n. *'leaf,'* *shoot*, pl. *foliage, MtL,VPs*; Æ : *sheet of paper, BH.* III. (+) *leafy*, WW 411¹².
±lēafa m. *belief, faith*, Æ,Bo,Mt; AO : *creed.* [*'leve,'* *'yleve'*]
±lēafe (ǣ) f. *leave, permission, licence*, Æ.
±lēafful *believing*, JnR : *orthodox* (*Christian*) : *faithful, trustworthy, MtL.* [*'leafful'*] adv. -līce.
+lēaffulnes f. *faith, trust, faithfulness*, Æ.
lēafhelmig *leafy at the top*, GPH 390.
±lēafhlystend (e) m. *catechumen*, OEG.
+lēaflēas *unbelieving*, Æ.
+lēaflēasnes f. *unbelief*, W 294².
+lēaf-lēast, -lȳst f. *unbelief*, Æ.
lēaflēoht *easy to believe?* RB 5¹⁹.
+lēaflic *credible, faithful*, Æ : *catholic*, WW 201²⁶. adv. -līce.
lēafnes (ē, ȳ) f. *leave, permission*, BH.

+lēafnesword n. *password*, B 245.
lēafscead n. *leafy shade*, PH 205.
lēafsele m. *booth*, ByH 118¹⁵.
+lēafsum (ǣ) *believing, faithful* : *credible.*
lēafwyrm (i²) m. *caterpillar*, ASPs 77⁵¹.
lēag I. (ē) f. *'lye,'* *alkalized water, Ep,Lcd.* II.=lēah I. III. pret. 3 sg. of lēogan and lēon.
lēah I. lēage (CHR) m. *piece of ground, 'lea,' meadow, BC*; v. GBG and Mdf. II.=lēag I. and III.
leahte pret. 3 sg. of leccan.
leahter=leahtor
leahtor (e¹) m. *vice, sin, offence, crime, fault*, Æ,CP : *reproach* : *disease, injury*, LCD.
leahtor-=hleahtor-
leahtorcwide m. *opprobrious speech*, JUL 199.
leahtorful (e¹, e²) *vicious, seductive*, Æ.
leahtorlēas (e²) *faultless, blameless*, EL, LL.
leahtorlic *vicious, faulty*, GUTH 101¹¹. adv. līce *foully, wickedly*, Æ.
-leahtorwyrðe v. un-l.
leahtras nap. of leahtor.
±leahtrian (e) *to accuse, revile, reprove, blame*, Æ; AO,CP : *corrupt.* [*'lehtrie'*]
leahtric m. *lettuce*, LCD,WW. [*L.* lactuca]
lēahtrog=lēactrog
lēahtrung (ē) f. *derogation*, WW 150¹.
lēahtūn=lēactūn
lēan I. n. *reward, gift, loan, compensation, remuneration, retribution, B,Mt*; Æ. [*'lean'*] II. sv⁰ (pret. 3 sg. lōg, lōh) and wv. *to blame, reproach*, AO,CP.
lēangyfa m. *rewarder*, LCD 3·436'.
±lēanian (ǣ) *to reward, recompense, repay, requite*, Æ,CP. [*Ger.* lohnen]
lēap m. *basket*, W : *basket for catching or keeping fish*, WW : *measure* : *trunk (body)*, JUD 111. [*'leap'*]
lēas I. adj. (w. g.) *without, free from, devoid of, bereft of* : (±) *false, faithless* : *untruthful, deceitful, WW*; Æ : *lax* : *vain, worthless.* II. n. *falsehood, lying*, Bo; CP : *untruth, mistake.* [*'lease'*]
lēasbrēd (-bregd) I. *lying, false, deceitful*, Æ. II. m. *cheating, trickery*, LL,W.
lēasbrēda m. *trickster*, ES 43·306.
lēasbrēdende *wily, deceitful*, ÆGR 286⁶.
lēasbrēdnes (ǣ²) f. *deception, falsehood*, ÆL.
lēasbregd=lēasbrēd
lēascræft m. *false art*, BL 25¹².
lēase *falsely*, BH 122¹⁷.
lēasere m. *liar, hypocrite, MtL* : *buffoon, mime, jester, fool.* [*'leaser'*]
lēasest (*MtL*)=lǣst I.
lēasettan *to pretend*, Æ,RB.
lēas-ferhð, -fyrhð *false*, NC 305.

lēasferðnes f. *levity, folly,* CP313¹⁰.
lēasfyrhte=lēasferhð
lēasgewita m. *a false witness,* ÆH 1·46'.
lēasgewitnes f. *false witness,* Æ.
lēasgielp m. *vainglory,* CP367²⁴.
lēasian *to lie, Ps.* ['*lease*']
lēaslic *false, deceitful, sham, empty,* Æ,CP.
    adv. -līce, Æ,CP.
lēaslīccettan *to dissemble,* WW388³³.
lēaslīcettung f. *dissimulation,* GUTH12¹⁸.
lēasmōdnes f. *instability,* CP308⁶.
lēasnes f. *lying : levity,* BH322²³.
lēasōleccan *to blandish, flatter,* GD34²⁷.
lēasōlecung f. *empty flattery,* WW430²¹.
lēassagol (u³) *lying, false,* Æ.
lēasscēawere m. *spy,* B253.
lēasspell n. *lie, fiction, fable,* BH,WW.
lēasspellung f. *empty or false talk,* AO.
lēassponung f. *allurement,* WW452³.
lēast=lāst; lēast-=læst-
lēastyhtan *to cajole,* WW431⁴.
lēastyhtung f. *cajolery,* WW430²¹.
lēasuht (=wiht?) *enticer, seducer,* OEG4014.
lēasung f. '*leasing,*' *lying, false witness, deceit, hypocrisy, artifice, JnL : a lie, Ps : empty talk, frivolity, laxity.* **II.** f. *indemnity?* WW.
lēasungspell n. *idle tale,* AO40⁶.
lēaswyrcend m. *deceiver,* ÆH 1·102.
lēat pret. 3 sg. of lūtan.
leatian=latian; +leaðian=+laðian
lēaðor n. *soap, soda, Lcd,WW.* ['*lather*']
lēaðorwyrt (lēoðo-) f. *soap-wort?* LCD 16a.
lēawede=lǣwede
lēawfinger (=ǣ¹) m. *index-finger, forefinger,* PPs72¹¹.
leax (æ, e) m. *salmon, Cp,Met,WW;* ÆL. ['*lax*']
leb-=lef-, læf-; lec=hlec
+lec pret. 3 sg. of +lacan.
lēc **I.** m. *look, regard,* Æ; A11·118⁵⁰. **II.**= lēac I. and II.
+lecc-=+læcc-
leccan pret. 3 sg. leahte, le(o)hte *to water, irrigate, wet, moisten, slake,* CP. [cp. Ger. lechzen]
leccing f. *irrigation, watering, WW (KGl).* ['*leaching*']
lēce=lǣce; lēcetere (KGL65²⁹)=līcettere
lecg f. *part of a weapon?* (BT) *sheath?* (WC), TC527⁹.
±lecgan *to* '*lay,*' *put, place, deposit, set,* Æ, G,Gen,Lcd,Rd;* CP : *dispose, arrange : attach, W : bury, Jn,Chr : put before, submit, Æ : betake oneself, go : lay (egg), Lcd : prostrate, cast down, lay low, kill, Bo,Lk,LL.* l. on (w. d.) *put upon, charge with, Chr,Gu;* CP. lāstas l. *go, journey, Gen.* on lāst l. *follow.* [causative of licgan]

lēclwyrt (Cp)=lǣcewyrt
lēcnian (NG)=lācnian
lectric=leahtric; lēctūn-=lēactūn-
lecða m. *ship's bottom or hold,* Ep,WW46¹⁴.
+led '*catasta,*' WW (v. BTs).
lēd=lēad; lēdan=lǣdan
lēde=legde pret. 3 sg. of lecgan.
lēden=lǣden. lēaden
lēf **I.** (ī) *feeble, infirm, weak, injured.* **II.**=lēaf
lēf-=lēaf-; lēfan=(1) līefan; (2) lǣfan
+lēfed *weak, sickly, aged,* BH,W.
lefel, lefil=læfel
+lēfenscipe m. *justification,* JnL15²².
lēfmon m. *sick person,* GnE45.
lēfung f. *paralysis,* ÆH 2·486¹⁸.
leg (=læg) pret. 3 sg. of licgan.
lēg=(1) līeg; (2) lēah; lēg-=līg-, lēog-
lēga (A)=lǣwa
legde pret. 3 sg. of lecgan.
+lege f? *lair, bed,* Mdf (or ?+legu (BTs)).
lēgelēoht n. *light (of flame),* MFH168.
legen pp. of licgan.
leger n. *lying, illness, AO,B;* Æ : '*lair,*' *couch, bed, Wif : grave, LL;* Æ. clǣne legere *consecrated grave.* on life ge on legere *in life and in death,* LL. [licgan]
lēgeræsc (RWH 79,81)=ligetræsc
legerbǣre *sick, ill,* TC611²⁰.
legerbedd n. *bed, sick bed, Æ : grave.*
+leger-ed, -od *confined to bed,* Æ.
legerfæst *sick, ill,* RB64⁷.
+legergield n. '*lupercalia,*' WW437¹⁴.
legerstōw f. *burial place,* ÆH.
legertēam m. *cohabitation, marriage,* MH 174⁹.
legerwīte fm. *fine for unlawful cohabitation,* LL. ['*lairwite*']
lēges=lēages gs. of lēah.
legeð pres. 3 sg. of lecgan.
legie f. *legion,* AO. [*L.*]
+legu v. +lege.
-legu v. ealdor-l.; leh-=leah-
lēh=lēah; lēh-=lēac-; lēhnan=lȳgnian
lēht=lēoht; lēhtan (Nar)=līhtan
lehte pret. 3 sg. of leccan.
lehtor=leahtor; lēl (KGL)=lǣl
leloðre f. *silverweed?* GL.
lemb=lamb
lēmen (KGL82⁴⁰)=lǣmen
±lemian (æ) *to subdue,* CP303¹¹ : *lame, disable,* B905.
lempedu f. *lamprey,* WW438¹⁷. ['*limpet*'; L. lampreda]
lemphealt *limping, Gl,WW.* ['*limphalt*']
lempit f. *dish, basin,* OET108'.
lēnan (KGL)=lǣnan
lencten (æ) **I.** m. *springtime, Lcd,LL;* Æ : *the fast of Lent, W.* **II.** adj. *pertaining to Lent, Bf,RB.* ['*lenten*']

lenctenādl f. *spring fever, tertian ague, dysentery,* BH,LCD.
lenctenbere m. *Lent barley,* ANS84³²⁶.
lenctenbryce m. *breach of the Lenten fast,* LL344,47.
lenctendæg m. *day of Lent,* CHRD,W117¹⁵.
lenctenerðe f. *land ploughed in spring,* WW 105⁷. [eorðe]
lenctenfæsten n. *Lent,* CHRD,RB.
lenctenhǣto f. *heat of spring,* AO102⁶.
lenctenlīc *of spring, vernal,* Æ : lenten, Æ.
lenctenlifen f. *Lenten fare,* CHRD15³.
lenctenmōnað m. *a spring month,* ExC34¹⁸.
lenctensufel (længt-) n. *Lent food,* LL450,9.
lenctentīd f. *spring, Lent,* Æ.
lenctentīma m. *spring,* OEG3837 : *Lent,* Æ.
lenctenwuce f. *a week in Lent,* Jn5⁸ (rubric).
lenctin-=lencten-
+lend I. *furnished with land (by the lord),* LL448'. II.=+lynd
+lenda m. *one rich in land,* OEG3154.
lendan *to land, arrive, Chr;* Æ,AO,CP : *go :* (+) *endow with land,* Æ. ['*lend*'; land]
lende-=lenden-
lendenādl f. *disease of the loins,* LCD87a.
lendenbān n. *loin-bone,* WW159¹³. [v. '*lend*']
lenden-brǣde, -brēde f. *loin,* LCD,LL.
lendenece m. *pain in the loins,* LCD24a.
lendensēoc *diseased in the loins,* LCD.
lendensīd *reaching to the loins,* NC306.
lendenu (æ) np. *loins, Mt,WW;* Æ. ['*lend*']
lendenwyrc m. *a disease of the kidneys,* WW 113¹². [wærc]
-lendisc v. dūn-, up-, ūre-, ut-l.
lēne=lǣne
leng I. (æ) f. *length, height,* Æ. II. adv. (comp. of lange) *longer,* Æ,Lk. ['*leng*']
lengan I. (±) *to lengthen, prolong, protract, delay, Da : extend, reach, attain : belong.* on hornum gelengdum '*tubis ductilibus*,' CVPs97⁶. ['*leng*'] II. (+) *to call for,* DHy90³.
lengcten-=lencten-
-lenge (æ) I. adj. (±) *belonging, related : near (of time),* B83. II. v. lange. III.=lengu
+lenge *belonging to, related to,* Æ : *addicted to.*
lengest (*Chr,Mk*) superl. of lang(e). ['*lengest*']
lengfære *more durable,* ANS119·435.
englan (impers. w. a.) *to long,* SOL270.
lenglīfra comp. of langlīfe.
engo=lengu
engra (*BH*) comp. of lang. ['*lenger*']
engten=lencten
engtogra comp. adj. *more prolix,* Sc161¹⁸.
engðu f. '*length.*' on lengðe *at length, finally,* AO144¹.

lengu f. *length, Bo,BH : height, Sol.* ['*lengh*']
lent f. *lentil,* GL. [*L.* lentem]
lenten=lencten
lēo mf. gdas. lēon, also ds. lēone, lēonan, asf. lēo, and dp. lēonum '*lion,*' *lioness, AO,Lcd,VPs,WW;* Æ. [*L.*]
lēoc (WW283²¹)=lēac
lēod I. m. *man,* LL14,25 : '*wergeld*' *for manslaughter,* LL (=lēodgeld) : (+) *fellow-countryman, compatriot :* (†) *chief, prince, king, B.* ['*lede*'] II. f. (usu. in pl. lēode) *people, nation, An,B,Bl,Lk;* Æ,AO. ['*lede*']
lēoda I.=+lēod I. II. (LWS)=lēode
lēodan²† *to spring up, grow : spring from.*
lēodbealu† n. *calamity to a people,* B.
lēodbisceop m. *suffragan bishop, provincial, Chr;* Æ. [v. '*lede*']
lēodburg† f. *town,* B,GEN.
lēodbygen f. *sale of one's compatriots, slave-traffic,* LL20,11Ld (v. 2·133).
lēodcyning m. *king, ruler,* B54.
lēode fp. *men, people, country, B,Lk;* AO (v. lēod).
lēoden (LCD)=lǣden
lēodfruma† m. *prince, patriarch, chief.*
lēodgeard† m. *country,* GEN.
lēodgebyrga† m. *lord, protector, prince, king.*
lēodgeld n. '*wergeld*' *for manslaughter,* LL.
lēodgeðincð f. *order, rank,* LL.
lēodgewinn n. *strife,* JUL201.
lēodgota=lēadgota
lēodgryre m. *general terror,* SOL278.
lēodhata m. *persecutor, tyrant,* GD.
lēodhete† m. *popular hatred, hostility,* AN.
lēodhryre m. *fall of a prince (or nation?),* B2030,2391.
lēodhwæt *very valiant,* EL11.
-lēodisc v. ðider-l.
lēodmǣg† m. *relative, comrade.*
lēodmægen† n. *might of the people, host.*
lēodmearc† m. *domain, country,* AN.
lēodrǣden f. *country, region,* GD204²⁸.
lēodriht n. *law of the land,* AN,KC.
lēodrūne f. *pythoness, sorceress,* LCD52b.
lēodscearu† f. *tribe, nation,* Ex337.
lēodsceaða† m. *public enemy.*
lēodscipe m. *nation, people,* Æ : *country, region.*
lēodstefn m. *assembly,* PPs82⁷.
lēodðēaw m. *popular usage,* AA,GEN.
lēodweard† f. *government.*
lēodweras† mp. *men, human beings.*
lēodwerod n. *host of people,* Ex77.
lēodwita m. *wise man, elder, chief,* LL456.
lēodwynn f. *home joy,* †Hy4⁸⁹.
lēodwyrhta=lēoðwyrhta
lēof I. (±) adj. *dear, valued, beloved, pleasant, agreeable, Æ,B,Chr,CP,HGl,LL.* ['*yleof*'] II. m. *beloved one, friend :* (in addressing

persons) *sir! sire! Æ,EC* : *impure companion*, GPH 394. [*'lief'*]
leofen=lifen; **leoflan** (*Bl*)=libban
lēoffæst *dear, precious*, ÆP 172¹³.
lēoflan *to be or become dear*, Gu 110.
lēoflic *dear, lovable, pleasant, beautiful, delightful, B,Cr* : *precious, valued.* adv. -līce *lovingly, kindly, gladly, willingly, BH.* [*'liefly'*]
lēofspell n. *good news*, EL 1017.
lēof-tǣl, -tǣle *kind, lovable, loving, dear, grateful, agreeable*, CP.
lēofwende *kind, loving, gracious, acceptable, estimable, agreeable.*
lēofwendum *ardently*, CR 471.
±**lēogan²** *to 'lie,' Bl,WW* : *deceive, belie, betray, Æ,CP* : *be in error*, ÆGR. l. on *to charge falsely.*
lēogere (e¹, o²) m. *'liar,' false witness, W, MtL; Æ* : *hypocrite*, MkL 7⁶.
lēoht (ē, ĭ) I. *'LIGHT,' not heavy, AO*; CP : *slight, easy, trifling, inconsiderable, CP* : *quick, agile* : *gentle.* II. n. *'LIGHT,' daylight, Æ* : *power of vision* : *luminary.* III. *luminous, bright, 'light,' clear, resplendent, renowned, beautiful, BH,Lcd,VPs*; AO,CP.
lēohtan=līhtan
lēohtbǣre *brilliant, luminous*, CRA,LCD.
lēohtbēamede *bright-shining*, ÆH 1·610.
lēohtberend m. *light-bearer, Lucifer*, Æ.
lēohtberende *light-bearing, luminous*, Æ (GEN).
lēohtbora m. *light-bearer*, LV 36.
lēohtbrǣdnes f. *levity, frivolity, wantonness.*
leohte=lehte pret. 3 sg. of leccan.
lēohte I. adv. *lightly, easily, comfortably, BH.* [*'light'*] II. adv. *brightly, clearly, brilliantly, Bl,Cr.* [*'light'*]
lēoht-fæt, n. nap. -fatu *lantern, torch, lamp, light*, Æ,CP.
lēohtfætels m. *lamp*, LPs 17²⁹.
lēohtfruma† m. *source of light.*
lēoht-gesceot, -gescot n. *payment for providing lights in church*, LL.
lēohtian I. *to be lightened, relieved.* II. *to become light, dawn*, CM 474 : *give light, illuminate.*
lēohting=līhting
lēohtīsern (ē¹) n. *candlestick*, NG.
lēohtlēas *dark*, Æ. [*'lightless'*]
lēohtlic I. *light, of little weight or importance*, Æ,CP. adv. -līce *lightly, slightly, BH, Lcd* : *inconsiderately* : *easily, quickly* : *gently, softly, slowly, CP*; Æ. [*'lightly'*] II. *bright, radiant, Rd.*
lēohtmōd *easy-going*, GNE 86.
lēohtmōdnes f. *inconstancy, frivolity*, CP.
lēohtsāwend *author of light*, GPH 389².
lēohtscēawigend *light-seeing*, WW 434²⁰.

lēohtsceot=lēohtgesceot
lēohtwyrhta=lēoðwyrhta
leolc pret. 3 sg. of lācan.
±**lēoma** m. *ray of light, beam, radiance, gleam, glare, B; Æ* : *lightning.* [*'leam'*]
+**lēomod** *having rays of light*, Lcd 3·272⁴. [v. *'leam'*]
leomu nap. of lim.
±**lēon** I. (sv¹) *to lend, give, grant*, B,LkL. [*Ger.* leihen] II. gdas. of lēo.
lēona mf. *lion, lioness*, Æ.
lēones? *league*, WE 51.
lēonesēað m. *lions' den*, GD 150⁹.
lēonflǣsc n. *lion's flesh*, Lcd 1·364'. [v. *'lion'*]
lēonfōt m. *lion's foot (plant)*, LCD,WW.
lēonhwelp m. *lion's cub*, WW 434⁶.
±**lēoran** (wv., but rare pp. loren) *to go, depart, vanish, die* (A; v. JAW 44).
±**lēorednes** f. *departure, transmigration* : *death*, ÆL : *anniversary of a death*, MH : *vision.*
lēorende, +lēorendlic *transitory*, DR.
lēorendnes=lēorednes
lēorian=lēoran
leornan=leornian
leornere m. *'learner,' disciple*, Æ,CP : *scholar, BH* : *reader.*
leornes f. *learning*, BHo,CA 162²⁰.
lēornes=lēorednes
±**leornian** *to 'learn,' read, study, think about, Æ,Bf,BH,Bl,MkR*; AO,CP.
leorningcild n., leorningcniht (Æ,CP) m. *student, disciple.*
leorningende *teachable*, W 172²².
leornung f., ds. leornunga *'learning,' reading, study, meditation, CP*; AO : *discipleship*, WW 223²⁶.
leornungcræft m. *learning*, EL 380.
leornungmann m. *learner, disciple* (used even of women), Æ.
leornungscōl f. *school*, GD 14⁶.
leort pret. 3 sg. of lǣtan.
-lēosan v. be-l., for-l.
leoð=leoðu v. lið; leoð-=lið-
lēoð n. *song, lay, poem, B,WW*; Æ,AO. [*'leoth'*]
lēoðcræft m. *poetic art* : *poem, poetry*, Æ.
lēoðcræftig *skilled in song*, DEOR 40.
lēoðcwide m. *lay, poem*, AO 120².
leoðe-=leoðu-
lēoðgidding f. *lay, song, poem*, AN 1481.
leoðian†=liðian
lēoðlic *versified*, ÆH,BF 42¹⁴.
leoðo-=leoðu-
lēoðorūn f. *wise counsel given in song*, EL 522.
lēoðowyrt=lēaðorwyrt?

lēoðr-=hlēoðr-
lēoðsang m. *song, poem, poetry,* BH.
leoðu I. f. *retinue, following?* RIM 14 (GK).
II. v. lið.
leoðubend† mf. *chain, fetter, bond.*
leoðubīge (i¹, e²) *flexible, yielding,* Æ.
['*litheby*']
leoðubīgnes (i¹, o²) f. *flexibility of limbs,*
GUTH 90²¹.
leoðucǣga m. *limbs serving as a key,* CR 334.
lēoðucræft† m. *skill of hand,* B,CRA.
leoðucræftig *agile,* PH 268.
leoðufæst *able, skilful,* CRA 95.
leoðulic *appertaining to the limbs, bodily,*
AN 1630.
leoðusār n. *pain in the limbs,* WW 213⁸.
leoðusyrce† f. *corslet,* B.
leoðuwāc (i) *with supple limbs, flexible,
pliant,* CRA 84. ['*leathwake*']
+**leoðuwācian** (i) *to mitigate, soften,* Æ.
leoðuwācunga (liðe-)? '*compeditorum,*' EPs
78¹¹.
±**leoðuwǣcan** (i) *to be or become calm or
pliant : appease, mitigate : revive : soften :
adapt?* ÆL 31⁴⁸².
lēoðweorc n. *poetry,* WW 188³⁰.
lēoðwīse f. *verse, poetry,* Æ,BF.
lēoðword n. *a word in a poem,* AN 1490.
lēoðwrenc m. *trick in a poem? spurious
passage?* BF 186²⁷.
lēoðwyrhta m. *poet,* ÆGR.
lēow (ǣu) n. *ham, thigh,* KC.
-lēow (ē, ā) v. mund-l.
leowe f. *league (distance),* WW 147²².
lēower pl. of lēow.
leowð (ÆGR 129 J)=hlēuwð
lepewince=læpewince
leppan *to feed (hawks),* WY 89 (v. ES 37·195).
lēran (KGL)=læran
lere (KGL 83¹⁹)=lyre; **lēreow-**=lārēow-
+**les**=+lise
lēs-=līes-
lesan⁵ *to collect, pick, select, gather, glean,* Æ.
['*lease*']
lesca m. *groin,* HGL,OET.
-lesende, -lesendlic, -lesung v. ed-l.
lēst=lāst; **lesu**=lysu; **lēsw-**=lǣsw-
lēt I. pret. 3 sg. of lǣtan. **II.**=lǣt
pres. 3 sg. of lǣdan. **III.**=lēat pret. of
lūtan.
lētan=lǣtan
lētanīa m. '*litany,*' MH; BH,WW. [*L.*
litania]
letig (KGL)=lytig
±**lettan** (æ) *to 'let,' hinder, delay, impede,
oppress,* Æ,Bo,Gu (w. g.), W; AO,CP.
lettend m. *hinderer,* ES 39·349.
letting (æ) f. '*letting,' hindrance, delay,* Chr,
RB; CP.

lēð=lǣð; **-leðer** v. heals-, weald-l.
leðera=liðera
leðercodd m. *leather bag,* WW 117³. [v.
'*leather*']
leðeren=leðren
leðerhelm m. *leathern helmet,* WW 142¹.
leðerhosu f. *leathern gaiter,* WW.
leðern=leðren
leðerwyrhta m. *tanner, currier,* GL.
lēðr-=lȳðr-
leðren (i) '*leathern,*' WW.
lēud=(1) lēod; (2) lǣwede
lēw f.=lǣw
+**lēwed** *weak, ill?* Æ (*Ex* 22¹⁰, cp. limlǣweo;
or ? read +lēfed).
lēwend=lǣwend; **lēwer**=lēower
lēwsa (=ǣ) m. *weakness,* EPs 87⁹.
lex=leax; **lēxnian** (WW 241²¹)=lācnian
lib-, libb-=lif-, lyb-
libban (y) pret. 3 sg. lif(e)de *to 'LIVE,' experience, be, exist,* Æ; AO,CP.
libr-=lifer-
līc n. *body,* B,Cr : *corpse,* AO,B; Æ,CP.
['*lich*']
+**līc I.** adj. (w. d.) *like : 'alike' ('ylike'),
similar, equal,* B,BH,Jul,LL; Æ,CP
suitable : likely, Mt. +līcost *double, twin.*
II. n. *something like another thing :
similitude.*
+**līca,** +līce wk. forms used as sb. *an equal,*
Æ,CP. adv. ±līce (usu. +; and +līc in
NG) *as, like, equally, similarly,* AO,Bl.
+līce and *like as if.*
līcam-=līcham-
līcbeorg f. *coffin, sarcophagus,* Cp 45 s.
| **līobisnung** f. *imitation,* DR 76¹
līcburg f. *cemetery,* Cp 433 c.
līccere, līccetere=līcettere
līccettan (Æ)=līcettan
līccian *to 'lick,'* Æ,Ps : *lap, lick up,* Lcd.
līccung f. *licking,* ÆH 1·330²³.
līcema=līchama; **līcendlic**=līciendlic
līcettan *to feign, dissimulate,* CP : *flatter,* BH.
līcettere (ē) m. *deceiver, hypocrite,* CP.
līcettung, līcetung f. *feigning, deceit, hypocrisy, flattery.*
līcewyrðe=līcwyrðe
līcfæt† n. *body,* GU.
±**līcgan**⁵ *to 'LIE*,' be situated, be at rest,
remain, be,* Æ,AO,CP : *lie down, lie low,
yield, subside, fall, lie prostrate, fail, lie
dead,* Æ,AO,Chr : *lead, extend to,* Æ;
AO : *flow, go, run,* AO : *belong to : lie
along, border?* AN 334. l. for *take the part
of,* LL 152,3. l. mid *cohabit with.* l. on
cnēowum *to kneel.* wið licgendum fēo *for
ready money.*
līchama m. *body, corpse,* Bo,Mt : Æ,CP :
trunk, CR 628. ['*licham*']

+līchamian *to clothe with flesh*, RWH 136³³.
+līchamod *incarnate*, BL33¹⁵.
līchamlēas *incorporeal*, ÆT.
līchamlic (o²) *bodily, carnal, physical, material, Bo,Lk*; Æ. adv. -līce *bodily, personally, in the flesh, BH*; Æ. ['*lichamly*']
-līchamung v. in-l.; līchom-=līcham-
līchanga m. *gibbet?* KC5·321' (BTac).
līchord† n. *interior of the body*, Gu.
līchrægel n. *winding-sheet*, MH76²⁶.
līchryre m. *bodily decay, death*, GEN 1099.
līchryst=līcrest; līchwamlic=līchamlic
līcian I. (±) (w. d. or impers.) *to please, Æ, AO,Bl,Bo*; CP : *be sufficient*. ['*like,*' '*ylike*'] II. (+) *to be or make like : seem likely*, AO.
līciendlic *agreeable, pleasant*, PPs. adv. -līce.
+līclǣtan⁷ *to liken, compare*, MkLR4³⁰.
līclēoð n. *dirge*, OEG.
līclic *relating to the dead, funeral*, GPH 401.
+līclic *fitting, proper*, LCD. adv. -līce *equally*.
līcmann m. *bearer, pall-bearer*, Æ.
līcnes (±) f. '*likeness*' ('*i-likeness*'), *similarity : figure, stature, image, Æ,MtL* : (+) *parable*.
līcpytt m. *grave*, ÆGR66¹⁰? (or ? dīc, pytt).
līcrest f. *sepulchre, tomb, Lcd*; Æ : *hearse*, ÆL26¹⁸¹ : *cemetery*, OEG4347. [v. '*lich*']
līcs-=līx-
līcsang m. *dirge*, OEG.
līcsār† n. *wound*, B,CR.
līcstōw f. *place of burial*, GD340³⁵.
līcsyrce f. *corslet*, B550.
līctūn m. *burial-ground*, LL.
līcðēnung f. *obsequies, funeral*, Æ : *laying out (of corpse)*, ÆL31¹⁴²⁹.
līcðēote f. *pore*, WW159¹³.
līcðrōwere m. *leper*, Æ.
līcðrūh f. *sepulchre*, GD225.
līcum-=līcham-
±līcung f. *pleasure*, CP. ['*liking*']
līcwīglung f. *necromancy*, LL(248³).
līcwund f. *wound*, Ex239.
±līcwyrðe (e, eo, o, u) *pleasing, acceptable, Bo*; CP : *estimable, praiseworthy : accepted, recognised, sterling*. ['*likeworth*']
līcwyrðlīce *pleasingly*, ÆL23b⁵⁷.
līcwyrðnes f. *good pleasure*, LPs88¹⁸.
līd† n. *ship, vessel*. [līðan]
līda m. *sailor*, GnE 104.
Līda=Līða; līden pp. of līðan.
līdeð pres. 3 sg. of lēodan.
līdmann† m. *seafarer, sailor, pirate*.
līdrin=leðren
līdweard m. *ship-master*, AN244.
līdwērig *weary of sea-voyages*, AN482.

±līefan I. (ē, ī, ȳ) *to allow, grant, concede, Mt,CP*. ['*leve*'; lēaf] II. (ē, ēo, ī, ȳ) tr. and intr. *to believe, trust, confide in, Bl,Bo, Met,MH*. ['*leve,*' '*yleve*'] III. (+) *to be dear to*, CR1645.
+līefed (ȳ) *believing, faithful, pious*, Æ.
+līefedlic (ȳ) *permissible*, LL(436').
+līefedlīce (ȳ) *trustfully, credulously*, AO.
+līefen (ē) *excused*, LkR14¹⁹.
+līefenscipe m. *justification*, JnLR15²².
līeffæstan=līffæstan
līeg (æ, ē, ī) mn. *fire, flame, lightning, B,Bl*; CP. ['*leye*']
līeg- v. līg-
līeget=līget
līegeð I.=legeð pres. 3 sg. of lecgan. II. pres. 3 sg. of licgan.
līeht-=lēoht-, līht-
līehð pres. 3 sg. of lēogan.
±līesan (ē, ȳ) *to loosen, release, redeem, deliver, liberate, Cr,LkR*. ['*leese*']
līesing I. (ī, ȳ) m. *freedman*, LL. II. (ē) f. *deliverance, release, LkL*. ['*leesing*']
+līesnes (ē) f. *redemption*, DR12¹⁷.
līeð-=līð-; līexan=līxan
līf I. n. '*life,*' *existence, Æ,B,Chr,JnL : lifetime, RB*. on līfe, tō līfe, līfes *alive, Æ, BH : way of life* (e.g. *monastic*), *BH,Chr, Lk,W*; CP : *place where the life is according to rule, monastery*, CHR. II.=lēf. III.= lēaf I.
līf-=līef-
līfbrycgung f. *way of life*, DR7¹⁵.
līfbysig *struggling for life*, B966.
līfcearu† f. *care about life*, GEN.
līfdæg m. nap. lifdagas (usu. in plur.) '*life-day,*' *lifetime, B,Cr*.
lifde, lifede pret. sg. of libban.
līfen (eo) f. *sustenance*, AN,GL.
lifer I. f. '*liver,*' *Bo,WW*; Æ. II. f. *a weight*, WW432²⁸. [L. *libra?*]
liferādl f. *liver complaint*, LCD,WW.
liferbȳl m. *protuberance of the liver*, LCD 76b.
liferhol n. *hollow in the liver*, LCD76b.
liferlæppa m. *lobe of the liver*, WW.
lifersēoc *ill in the liver*, LCD.
lifersēocnes f. *disease of the liver*, LCD.
liferwærc m. *pain in the liver*, LCD60a.
liferwyrt n. *liverwort*, ANS84·326.
lifesn (BH362¹⁶)=lybesn
līffadung f. *regulation of life*, LL82²² (Wilk.).
līffæc n. *lifetime, life*, LL,W.
±līffæst *living, quickened, full of life, vigorous : life-giving : settled*.
±līffæstan (īe, ȳ) *to quicken, endow with life*, Æ,CP.
+līffæstnian *to quicken*, RPs142¹¹.
liffet-=lyffet-

līffrēa† m. *Lord of life, God.*
līffruma† m. *source of life (God).*
līfgan=libban
līfgedāl n. *death,* GD.
līfgesceaft† f. *life's conditions or record,* B.
līfgetwinnan mp. *twins,* Sol 141.
līflan (*LG,Nar*) ['*ylife*']=libban
līflende (y) *that lives or has life, BH* : *when alive, BH,VPs* : as sb. *the 'living,' VHy.*
līflād f. *course of life, conduct, RB.* ['*livelihood*']
līflǣst=līflēast
līflēas *not endowed with life, 'lifeless,' inanimate, Æ* : *dead, Æ.*
līflēast f. *loss of life, death, Æ.*
līflic *living, Æ* : '*lively*' : *long-lived* : *necessary to life, vital, DHy,Hex.* adv. -līce *vitally, so as to impart life, Æ.*
līflyre m. *loss of life,* LL466,2.
līfneru f. *food, sustenance,* An 1091.
līfnes (BHca 362¹⁶)=lybesn
līfre gs. of lifer I.
līfre-=lifer-
līfrig *clotted,* A 30·132.
līft=lyft
līfweard m. *guardian of life,* El 1036.
līfweg m. *way of life, way in life,* W.
līfwela† m. *riches.*
līfwelle *living (water),* JnL4¹⁰.
līfwraðu† f. *protection of life,* B.
līfwynn† f. *enjoyment of life.*
līg (Æ)=līeg; līg-=lyg-
līgbǣre, līgberende *flaming,* Gl.
līgberend m. *flame-bearer,* WW 239²⁴.
līgbryne (ē)† m. *burning, fire.*
līgbysig (ē) *busy with fire,* Rd 31¹.
līgcwalu f. *fiery torment,* El 296.
līgdraca (ē)† m. *fiery dragon,* B.
līgegesa m. *flaming terror,* B 2780.
līgen I. (ē) *flaming, fiery, Æ.* II. pp. of lēon.
līgenword=lygeword
+līg-ere n. -ernes f. *concubinage, fornication, adultery,* AO.
līget nm., līgetu (ē) f. *lightning, flash of lightning, BH,Bl,Mt; Æ,AO.* ['*lait*'; līeg]
līgetræsc (ē) m. *lightning, flash of light, coruscation,* Lk 10¹⁸. [līget]
līgetsleht (ē¹, æ³) m. *lightning-stroke, thunderbolt,* GD,MH.
līgetung f. *lightning,* EHy 6⁴¹.
līgeð pres. 3 sg. of licgan.
līg-fǣmende, -fāmblāwende *vomiting fire,* BH 432⁷.
līgfȳr n. *fire,* Ex 77.
līgge=līege ds. of līeg; līgit=līget
līglic (ē) *fiery,* Guth 131¹⁹⁶.
līg-locc, -locced *having flaming locks,* WW.
līgnan (=īe)† *to deny.*
līgræsc (ē¹, e²)=līgetræsc

līg-ræscetung, -ræscung (ȳ¹) f. *lightning,* LPs.
līgspīwel *vomiting flame,* GPII,W.
līgð pres. 3 sg. of licgan.
līg-ōracu† f. gds. -ōræce *fiery onset, violence of flames,* Ph.
līgȳð f. *wave of fire,* B 2672.
līh imperat. sg. of lēon.
līht=lēoht
līhtan (ē, ēo, ȳ) I. (±) *to make 'light,' easy, relieve, alleviate, Lcd; CP* : *dismount, 'alight,' BH.* II. (=īe; ȳ) *to lighten, illuminate, give light, shine, Æ,Jn* : *grow light, dawn, Da* : '*light,*' *kindle.*
līhtian=līhtan
līhting I. f. *relief, alleviation, release,* LL. ['*lighting*'] II. (ēo) f. *shining, illumination, light, Æ* : *dawn* : *lightning.* ['*lighting*']
līhtingnes f. *lightness of taxation,* LL (306²¹).
līhtnes f. *brightness,* W 230¹². ['*lightness*']
līhð pres. 3 sg. of lēogan.
līlie f. '*lily,' Bl,Lcd; Æ.* [L. lilium]
lim (y) n. nap. leomu '*limb,' member, Æ, B,Bl;* AO,CP : *branch, B* : *agent, offspring? Bl 33* : *bone?* CPs 6³.
līm m. *anything sticky, 'lime,' mortar, cement, gluten, Æ,Ep,WW* : *bird-lime, snare,* Bf 144⁶.
+līman *to cement, join, stick together,* ÆGr.
līmfīn f. *lime-heap,* BC 1·518'.
limgelecg n. *shape,* WW.
limgesīhō f. *body,* RHy 11⁴⁰.
limhāl *sound of limb,* Gu 661.
+līmian=+līman
līming f. *smearing, plastering,* WW. ['*liming*']
limlǣw f. *injury to limbs, mutilation,* LL (278n4).
limlǣweo *maimed,* LL 132,10.
limlēas *without limbs,* Æ 2·270²².
limmǣlum adv. *limb by limb,* WW. ['*limb-meal*']
limlama *crippled,* W 4¹².
limnacod *stark naked,* Gen 1566.
+limp n. *occurrence* : *misfortune, accident,* CP.
±limpan³ *to happen, occur, exist, B,Bo,Chr, Met; Æ,AO,CP* : *belong to, suit, befit, Ct* : *concern, CP.* ['*limp,' 'i-limp*']
±limpful *fitting, convenient,* AS 1²¹.
limplǣcan *to unite, connect,* OEG 80.
+limplic *fitting, suitable, ÆL* : *happening* : '*accidentia,' ÆGr.* adv. -līce (±).
+limplīcnes f. *opportunity,* VPs 9¹⁰.
limrǣden f. *form? disposition of the limbs?* v. OEG 2530.
limsēoc† *lame, paralytic.*
limwǣde n. *clothing,* PPs 103².
limwǣstm m. *stature,* Sat 130.

līmwērig *weary of limb*, Rood 63.
līn n. *flax, linen, cloth, napkin, towel*, Ct,Gl, JnR,MtR; CP. ['*line*']
līnacer m. *flax-field*, EC239¹⁰.
lind I. f. *lime-tree, linden, Ct, Gl*; Æ; Mdf : (†) *shield* (*of wood*). ['*lind*'] II.=lynd
lindcroda m. *crash of shields, battle*, Gen 1998.
linde=lind I.
linden *made of ' linden'-wood, GnE.*
lindgecrod n. *shield-bearing troop*, An 1222.
lindgelāc n. *battle*, Ap76.
lindgestealla† m. *companion in war.*
lindhæbbende† m. *shield-bearer, warrior.*
lindplega† m. *shield-play, battle.*
lindrycg m. *ridge where limes grow*, EC 447²³.
lindwered n. *troop armed with shields*, El 142.
lindwīga m. *warrior*, B2603.
lind-wīgend†, -wīggend† m. *shielded warrior.*
līne f. *line, cable, rope*, Sol,WW : *series, row* : *rule, direction.*
līnece (WW286²¹)=līnete
līnen adj. '*linen,' made of flax*, CP,Ep; Æ.
līnenhrægl n. *linen cloth*, NG.
līnenweard *clad in linen*, ÆP84¹⁹, RWH 66⁵.
līnete (-ece) f. *linnet*, WW286²¹.
līnetwig(l)e f. *linnet*, Cp,Erf,WW. ['*lintwhite*']
-ling suffix (1) for forming personal nouns (dēorling, ræpling). (2) for forming advbs. (hinderling).
līnhǣwen *flax-coloured*, Lcd.
līnland n. *land in flax*, KC3·19⁴.
līnlēag m. *flax ground*, EC166².
linnan³ (w. instr. or g.) *to cease from, desist, lose, yield up* (*life*), B. ['*lin*']
līnsǣd (e²) n. '*linseed,' Lcd,LL.*
līnwǣd f. *linen cloth or garment*, NG.
līnwyrt f. *flax*, Lcd.
līo (WW438²²)=lēo
lippa m., lippe? f. (LL2·136) '*lip,' Lcd,RB, WW.*
līra m. *any fleshy part of the body, muscle, calf of the leg*, Lcd,WW. ['*lire*']
+līre=+ligere
līreht *fleshy*, Lcd91a.
līs=liss; **līs-**=līes-; **līsan** (Gl)=lesan
+līse (e) nap. +leosu n. *reading, study*, BH.
+līsian *to slip, glide*, CP437.
-līsnian, -listnian v. be-l.
liss (līðs) f. *grace, favour, love, kindness, mercy*, Æ : *joy, peace, rest*, Ph,W : *remission, forgiveness*, †Hy10⁵⁴ : *alleviation*, Æ : *saving* (*of life*). ['*liss*'; līðe]
lissan *to subdue*, Sol294. ['*lisse*']

list mf. *art, cleverness, cunning, experience, skill, craft*, Cr,Gen. listum *cunningly, skilfully.* ['*list*']
listan=lystan
līste f. '*list,' fringe, border, Ep.*
listelīce adv. *carefully*, Lcd11a.
listhendig *skilful*, Cra95. **listum** v. list.
listwrenc m. *deception*, W81; 128n⁹.
lisð pres. 3 sg. of lesan.
līt *colour, dye*, RWH141¹⁰.
līt=lȳt
lītan *to bend, incline*, Met26¹¹⁹.
līte-, lītel=lytig-, lȳtel; **lītig**=lytig
lītigere m. *dyer*, RWH141⁹.
lītl-=lȳtl-; **lītsmann**=liðsmann
lið I. nm. nap. leoðu, liðu *limb, member*, BH,Cr; Æ,AO,CP : *joint*, Lcd : *tip* (*of finger*), Lk. ['*lith*'] II. n. *fleet.* [ON. lið]
līð I. n. *cider, native wine, fermented drink*, CP : *beaker, cup.* II. *mercy*, VH16. III. pres. 3 sg. of licgan. IV.=līðe adj. V.=līhð
Līða m. *name of months June* (ǣrra L.) *and July* (æftera L.), Men,MH.
līðādl f. *gout*, Lcd,WW.
līðan¹ I. (±) *to go, travel, sail*, B,BH : (+) *arrive*, WW. ['*lithe*'] II. *to be bereft of*, GnE26? III. (*CP*)=liðigian
līðe I. adj. *gentle, soft, calm, mild*, ApT,B, Mt; Æ,AO,CP : *gracious, kind, agreeable, sweet*, Bo,Gen; Æ. ['*lithe*'] II. adv.
līðe-=leoðu-; **līðeg**=liðig
līðelic *gentle, soft, mild*, CP. adv. -līce, CP. ['*lithely*']
+līðen (y) *having travelled much*, Cas26¹³. [liðan]
līðercian *to smooth down, flatter*, Gl.
līðere f., liðera m. *sling, slinging pouch*, BH, Cp; Æ. ['*lither*'; leðer]
līðeren=leðren
līðerlic *of a sling*, WW247⁴.
līðgeat=hlidgeat
līðian (*CP*; Æ)=liðigian
±līðian (eo) *to unloose, release*, GD.
līðig *lithe, flexible, bending, yielding*, Æ,W. ['*lithy*']
līðigian (±) *to soften, calm, mitigate, assuage, appease*, CP; Æ : *be mild.* ['*lithe*']
liðincel n. *little joint*, WW.
līðlic=liðelic; **līðmann**=lidmann
līðnes f. *mildness, softness, gentleness, kindness*, Æ,CP.
līðo-=leoðu-; **liðre**=liðere
līðre=lȳðre; **liðrin**=leðren; **līðs**=liss
līðsēaw n. *synovia*, Lcd.
liðsmann m. *seafarer, pirate*, Chr.
liðu v. lið.
līðule m? *synovia*, Lcd. [lið, ele]
līðung f. *alleviation, relief*, Lcd1·112² : '*venia,' 'miseratio,'* OEG8³⁹⁸.

līðwǣge n. *drinking-cup*, B1982.
līðwǣrc m. *pain in the limbs*, LCD49b.
līðwyrde *mild of speech*, NC348.
līðwyrt f. *dwarf elder*, LCD,WW.
līxan (=īe) *to shine, flash, glitter, gleam*.
līxende *splendidly*, LkL16¹⁹.
līxung f. *brilliance, brightness*, DR.
-lō pl. -lōn v. mæst-, sceaft-l.
lob (GL)=lof
lobbe f. *spider*, LPs. ['*lob*']
loc I. n. '*lock*,' *bolt, bar, Æ,BH*; AO : *enclosure, fold, prison, stronghold*, CP : *bargain, agreement, settlement, conclusion* : *clause*, OEG7¹⁹⁵. [lūcan] II.=locc I.
lōc, lōca interj. '*look*,' *see, look you*. l. hū *however* : *whatever, Gen*16⁶. l. hwænne, hwonne *whenever*. spel l. hwænne mann wille *a discourse for any occasion you please, Æ*. l. hwǣr *wherever*. l. hwǣðer *whichever*. l. hwā, l. hwæt, *whoever, whatever*. l. hwylc *whichever*. l. nu *observe, note, behold, ÆGr*.
loca I. m. *enclosure, stronghold*. II. m. *lock (of wool)*, GL.
lōca-hū v. lōc interj.
locbore f. *one who wears long hair, free woman*, LL7,73.
locc I. m. '*lock*' (*of hair*), *hair, curl, Bl,CP, Ep*; Æ. II.=loc I.
loccetan (MtL)?=rocettan (JAW77).
±loccian *to attract, entice, soothe*, CP
loccod *hairy, shaggy*, OEG56¹³.
locen I. pp. of lūcan. II. (SAT300?)=loc
locer=locor
locfeax n. *hair*, WW379⁴².
locgewind n. *hair*, WW199⁷.
lōc-hū, -hwænne etc. v. lōc hū, lōc hwænne, etc.
lochyrdel m. *hurdle for sheepfolds*, LL454,9.
lōcian (±) *to see, behold, look, gaze, Bl,G, Met*; AO : *observe, notice, take heed, CP*; Æ : *belong, pertain, Æ*. l. tō *regard with favour, CP*.
locor m. *plane (tool)*, GL.
locstān m. *stone closing an entrance*, ÆL 23³⁴⁵.
-lōcung v. ðurh-l.
loddere m. *beggar, Æ*; Mdf. [lȳðre]
+lodr f. *backbone, spine*, LCD65a.
lodrung f. *rubbish, nonsense*, WW478⁸.
+lodwyrt f. *silverweed*, LCD,WW.
loerge (Ep) np. of lorg.
lof I. n. (m. B1536) *praise, glory, repute, Cp*; Æ,CP : *song of praise, hymn*. ['*lof*'] II. n. *protection, help?* Æ.
lōf '*redimicula*,' OEG5241=glōf (?), v. ES 37·186, or ?*fillet, band*, at AN991 (BTs).
lofbǣre *praising, giving praise*, VHy.
lofdǣd f. *praiseworthy deed*, B24.

lofgeorn *eager for praise*, ÆL16³⁰² : *lavish? ostentatious?* RB54⁹; 55³.
lofherung f. *praising*, LPs55¹².
lofian *to praise, exalt, Gen,PPs*; CP : (±) *appraise, value*. ['*love*']
loflāc n. *offering in honour of any one*, W 107⁶.
loflǣcan *to praise*, LPs118¹⁷⁵.
loflic *laudable*, HGL498. adv. -līce *gloriously*, BL165¹⁶.
lofmægen n. *praise*, PPs105².
lofsang m. *song of praise, canticle, hymn, psalm, BH*; Æ : *lauds*. ['*lofsong*']
lofsealm m. *the 148th Psalm, lauds*, RB36¹⁹.
lofsingende *singing hymns of praise*, OEG 4912.
lofsum *praiseworthy*, GEN468.
lofte (on) adv. phr. *in the air, aloft, Hex, MLN*. ['*loft*']
lofung f. *praising, laudation* : *appraising, Æ*.
lōg pret. 3 sg. of lēan.
-loga v. āð-, trēow-, wed-, word-l. [leogan]
+logendlic adj. *to be kept in order*, RBL63⁵.
lōges v. lōh; logeðer=logðer
±lōgian *to lodge, place, put by, Æ* : *put in order, arrange, collect, settle, Æ* : *discourse, Æ* : *divide, portion out*. +l. ūp *lay by, deposit*. +lōgod *interpolated*, BF70²². +lōgod sprǣc (*well*)-*ordered speech, style*.
logðer (o²) *cunning, artful*, WW.
+lōgung f. *order*, CM599.
lōh I. n., gs. lōges *place, stead* (only in phr. on his lōh), CHR779E. II. pret. 3 sg. of lēan II.
lōhsceaft m. *bolt, bar? stick with a strap to it?* (BT3), AS1².
loma=lama
±lōma m. *tool, utensil, article of furniture, BH*; GL. ['*loom*']
lomb, lomber=lamb
±lōme (1) adj. *frequent*, ÆL31¹⁰¹⁹; (2) adv. *often, frequently, Gen*. oft (and) +l. *constantly, diligently*. ['*ylome*']
+lōmed=+lēomod; lōmelic=lōmlic
±lōmlǣcan *to frequent, Æ* : *be frequent*.
+lōmlǣcende *frequent, Æ* : *frequentative* (vb), ÆGR213⁷.
+lōmlǣcing f. *frequency, frequenting, ÆGR* 213⁷.
+lōmlǣcnes f. *a numerous assembly*, Ps.
+lōmlic *repeated, frequent, numerous*, AO, CP. adv. -līce.
+lōmlīcian *to become frequent*, BL109².
+lōmlicnes f. *repetition*, BF174²¹ : *a numerous assembly*, CPs117²⁷.
lomp pret. 3 sg. of limpan.
+lomrǣde *frequent*, TC.
lond=land
londādl f. *strangury?* LCD108a. [hland]

lone=lane; long=lang
Longbeard-an, -as sbmpl. *Lombards*, AO.
lonn, lonu=lann, lanu
loppe f. *spider, Bo,WW*. ['*lop*']
loppestre f. '*lobster,' WW*; Æ : *locust*, MkL.
lopust, lopystre=loppestre
lor n. (in phr. tō lore, tō lose) *loss, destruction, Bl*; CP. ['*lore*']
-lora v. hlēow-l.
loren pp. (str.) of lēoran.
lorg, lorh fm. *pole, distaff, weaver's beam*, GL,WYN 168.
los=lor ['*loss*']; losewist=loswist
losian (u) wv. (±) *to be lost, fail, perish, Bo, CP*; Æ : (±) *escape, get away* : '*lose,' LkL* 15⁴ : *destroy, LkL* 17²⁷.
losigendlic *ready to perish*, ÆH.
losing, loswist f. *loss, destruction*, NG.
lot n. *fraud, guile*, ÆL,CP.
loten pp. of lūtan.
lotwrenc m. *deception, deceit, cunning, artifice, trick*, Æ,AO,CP.
lotwrencceast f. *cunning*, Mk 12¹⁵.
loða m. *upper garment, mantle, cloak*, CP.
lox m. *lynx*, BH,WW. [*Ger.* luchs]
luba-, lube-=lufe-
lūcan² I. (±) (tr.) *to lock, close, enclose, fasten, shut up, An* : (intr.) *close up, form one mass, Ph* : *interlock, intertwine, twist, wind*, CP : *conclude*. ['*louk*'] II. *pluck out, pull up, Met*. ['*louk*'²]
-lucor v. MFB n30.
ludgæt n. *side-gate, postern gate*, GL.
ludon pret. pl. of lēodan.
lufelic=luflic
lufen f. *hope?* (BT; GK), DA 73,B 2886.
lufestice f. *lovage (plant)*, LCD. [*L.* levisticum]
lufestre f. *female lover*, OEG.
luffendlic=lufiendlic
luffeorm f. *hospitality*, AB 34·10.
±lufian *to* '*love,' cherish, show love to*, Æ, *Chr,JnL,VPs*; CP : *fondle, caress* : *delight in, approve, practise*.
lufiend m. *lover*, Æ.
lufiende *affectionate*, ÆGr. ['*loving*']
lufi(g)endlic *lovely, beautiful*, Æ : *lovable*, Æ.
luflic *amiable, loving, Lcd* : *lovable*, Ps. adv. -līce *kindly, CP* : *willingly, gladly*, BH. ['*lovely*']
lufræden f. *love*, LPs. ['*lovered*']
lufsum *loving, lovable, pleasant, Cr*. ['*lovesome*']
lufsumlic *gracious*, BH 248¹⁷. adv. -līce.
lufsumnes f. *pleasantness, kindness, WW* 218³⁴. ['*lovesomeness*']
luftācen n. '*love-token,' B* 1863.
luf-tȳme (Æ), -tēme (RB) *pleasant, sweet, grateful, benevolent*.

luftȳmlic *pleasant*, OEG 56²⁵⁴.
lufu f. '*LOVE,' strong liking, affection, favour*, Æ; AO,CP : *desire* : *kind action* : *love (of God), JnR* : *amicable settlement, LL* 392'.
lufung f. *action of loving*, GD 73¹⁴.
lufwende *lovable, pleasant*, BF,LCD.
lufwendlic *friendly*, KGL 73³⁴. adv. -līce *gently*, KGL 80²¹.
lugon pret. pl. of lēogan.
luh n. *loch, pond*, NG; Mdf. [*Keltic*]
+lumpenlic *occasional*, A 10·143 : *suitable*, A 10·141. [limpan]
lumpon pret. pl. of limpan.
luncian? *to limp* LPs 17⁴⁶. [cp. *Norw*. lunke?]
lundlaga m. *kidney*, Æ,LCD,WW.
lungen f. '*lung,' Lcd,WW*.
lungenādl f. *lung-disease*, LCD.
lungenǣder f. *vein of the lungs*, LCD 40b.
lungensealf f. *lung-salve*, LCD 141a.
lungenwyrt f. '*lung-wort,' Lcd*.
-lunger v. cēas-l.
lungre† adv. *soon, forthwith, suddenly, quickly*.
lunnon pret. pl. of linnan.
lūs f. nap. lȳs '*louse,' Æ,Cp,Hex*.
lusian (GPH)=losian
lust I. m. *desire, appetite*, Æ,BH,JnL : *pleasure, Bo,Lk* (pl.) : *sensuous appetite, lust, Jul,Lcd,WW*. II. adj. *willing*, W 246¹⁰.
lustbǣre I. *desirable, pleasant, agreeable, cheerful, joyous*, Æ,AO : *desirous*, ÆL 4¹¹⁶. II. adv. *gladly, willingly*.
lustbǣrlic *pleasant*, AO. adv. -līce.
lustbǣrnes f. *enjoyment, pleasure, desire*, CP.
lustful *wishful, desirous, AO* 100²⁷ : (+) *desirable*, WW 220⁵. ['*lustful*']
±lustfullian *to rejoice, enjoy*, Æ : *desire*, BF 4¹⁸ : *be pleasing to*, CP 70²⁴.
±lustfullice *gladly, heartily, Bl*. ['*lustfully*']
±lustfullung f. *desire, pleasure, delight*, Æ.
±lustfulnes f. *desire, pleasure*, BH; CP. ['*lustfulness*']
lustgeornnes f. *concupiscence*, G.
lustgryn f. *snare of pleasure*, SOUL 23.
+lustian *to delight in*, Sc.
lustlice *willingly, gladly, Bl*; Æ,AO.
lustmoce f. *lady's-smock (plant)*, LCD.
lustsumlic *pleasant*, AO. adv. -līce *willingly*.
lustum adv. *with pleasure, gladly*, CR,PPs.
lūsðorn m. *spindle-tree*, EC 445'.
±lūtan² *to bend, stoop, decline*, Æ,AO. +loten dæg *after part of day* : *bow, make obeisance, fall down, Bl,VPs* : (+) *lay down*, MtL 8²⁰ : *entreat*. ['*lout*']

±lūtian *to lie hid, hide, lurk, Æ,VHy*; AO, CP. ['*lout'*[2]]
lûtter, lūttor=hlūttor, hlūtor
lūðer-=lȳðer-
lybb n. *drug, poison, charm,* LCD,GL.
lybban=libban
lybbestre f. *sorceress,* WW200[25].
lybcorn n. *a medicinal seed, wild saffron?* GL.
lybcræft m. *skill in the use of drugs, magic, witchcraft,* BL.
lybesn (i) f. *charm, amulet, knot,* BH,GL.
lyblāc nm. *occult art, use of drugs for magic, witchcraft,* LCD,LL.
lyblǣca m. *wizard, sorcerer,* GL.
lybsin, lybsn=lybesn
lȳc-=lǣc-, līc-; lycce=lyge II.
lȳcð pres. 3 sg. of lūcan.
lȳden (LWS)=lǣden; lȳf=līf
lȳf-=lēaf-, lēf-, līef-, lif-
lyfde, lyfede pret. 3 sg. of libban.
lyfesn=lybesn
lyffetere m. *flatterer,* Æ,GL.
lyffet-tan, -tian *to flatter,* Æ.
lyffetung f. *adulation, flattery,* Æ.
lyflan=lifian, libban
lyft fmn. *air, sky, clouds, atmosphere, B, Lcd*; Æ,AO,CP. on lyfte *on high, aloft.* ['*lift*'; Ger. luft]
lyftādl f. *paralysis, palsy,* BH,LCD.
lyftedor m. *clouds,* Ex251.
lyften *of the air, aerial,* ÆH,HEX.
lyftfæt n. *vessel in the air (moon),* RD30[3].
lyftflēogend m. *flier in the air, bird,* SOL289.
lyftfloga m. *flier in the air, dragon,* B2315.
lyftgelāc† n. *flight through the air,* AN.
lyftgeswenced *driven by the wind,* B1913.
lyfthelm† m. *air, mist, cloud.*
lyftlācende† *sporting in the air, flying.*
lyftlic (u[1]) *aerial,* ByH118[2].
lyftsceaða m. *aerial robber (raven),* WY39.
lyftwundor n. *aerial wonder,* Ex90.
lyftwynn† f. *pleasure in flying.*
lyge I. (i) m. '*lie,' falsehood,* BH,Sat. II. *lying, false* (MtR26[60]; =*lygge, JAW25). III. '*sicalia,' secale? corn? rye?* WW301[2].
lygen (i) f. *lie, falsehood,* GEN,PR.
lygenian=lygnian
lygesearu† n. *lying wile, trick.*
lygespell (i) n. *falsehood,* WW449[2].
lygesynnig (i) *lying, false,* EL899.
lygetorn (i) *feigned anger or grief,* B1943.
lygeword (i)† n. *lying word, lie.*
lygewyrhta (i) m. *liar,* LEAS.
lygnes (i) f. *falseness: false things,* WW239[9].
±lygnian (i) *to give one the lie, convict of falsehood,* Æ. +lygnod *perjured,* Æ.
lȳht-=līht-
lyhð pres. 3 sg. of lēan.

lȳhð pres. 3 sg. of lēogan; lym=lim
lȳman *to shine,* GD171[5].
lymp-=limp-
±lynde, lyndo (i) f. *fat, grease,* LCD.
+lyndu np. *joints of the spine,* WW159[22].
-lynian v. ā-l., tō-l.
lynibor n. *borer, gimlet,* WW273[13].
lynis m. '*linch'-pin, Ep,WW.*
lypenwyrhta m. *tanner,* WW.
lyre (e) m. *loss, destruction, damage, hurt, WW; Æ.* ['*lure*'; lēosan]
lyrewrenc m. *hurtful intrigue,* MFH169.
-lyrtan v. be-l.; lȳs v. lūs; lȳs-=līes-
lysferht=leasferhð
lysnan, lysnere=hlysnan, hlysnere
lȳssa (KGL)=lǣssa; lyssen=lyswen
±lystan impers. w. a. (d.) of pers. and g. of thing or inf. *to please, cause pleasure or desire, provoke longing, Æ,Bl,Bo,Met;* AO, CP. +lysted *desirous of.* ['*list*'; lust]
lystere (OEG4674)=?lyftere, lyffetere
+lystfullīce=lustfullīce
lysu I. *base, false, evil,* AN1222. II. n. *evil deed,* LL.
lyswen I. *purulent, corrupt,* LCD. II. n. *pus, matter,* LCD.
lȳt adv., adj. and indecl. sb. *little, few, B, DD,Gen,Run;* Æ,AO. ['*lite*']
lȳtan=lūtan; lyteg=lytig
lȳtel I. adj. 'LITTLE,' *not large, Æ,AO* : *unimportant, mean* : *short (distance, time), B* : *not much, Mt,Ps.* II. adv. *little, slightly, Ps.* III. sb. *AO,Lcd,Ps.*
lȳtelhȳdig *pusillanimous,* CRA10.
lyte-lic, -līce=lytig-lic, -līce
lȳtelmōd *pusillanimous,* CP.
lȳtelne=lȳtesne
lȳtelnes f. *smallness,* ÆGr228[14]. ['*littleness*']
lȳtesnā (JUL), lȳtes(t)ne (BH) adv. *nearly, almost.*
lȳthwōn adv. and sb. (w. g.) *little, but little, very few,* Æ,CP.
lytig (e) *crafty, cunning,* AO : *prudent,* KGL.
lytigian *to feign, act crookedly,* MA86.
lytiglic *deceitful, crafty.* adv. -līce, CP.
lytignes f. *cunning,* CP237[22].
lȳtle f. *female slave,* Æ(9[401]).
±lȳtlian *to lessen, decrease, diminish, Bo, JnL;* CP : *shorten, curtail, abrogate ⁄ fall out of use,* LL267,37 : *belittle.* ['*little*']
lȳtling m. *little one, infant, child,* Æ,CP : *unimportant person,* CHRD2[4].
lȳtlum adv. (d. of lȳtel) *little by little, gradually, Æ;* CP. ['*litlum*']
lȳtlung (ī) f. *diminution* : (+) *insufficiency, want,* Sc57[1] (cp. EHy5[12]).
lyttl-=lȳtl-

lyttuccas mpl. *particles, small pieces*, GPH 400.
lyð=lið; **lýða**=līða; +**lyðen**=+liðen
lýðerful *evil, vile*, W 40⁵.
lýðerlic *bad, sordid, mean, vile*, AO. adv. -līce (ū¹), *WW* 178²⁷. ['*litherly*']
lýðernes (ū¹) f. *wickedness*, HL 18⁸.
lýðran (ē;=īe) *to anoint, smear*, '*lather*,' *JnL,Lcd.* [lēaðor]
lyðre=liðere
lýðre I. (ē, ī) adj. *bad, wicked, base, mean, corrupt, wretched*, Æ,*AO,Lk,WW*. ['*lither*'] adv. SAT 62. **II.** comp. of liðe.
lýðwyrt=liðwyrt; **lýxan**=līxan

M

mā I. (ǣ) adv. [comp. of micle] *more, rather, longer, hereafter, further*, Æ,*CP*. ðe mā ðe *more than.* **II.** sb. (indecl.) *more*, Æ. **III.** adj. *more*, Æ. ['*MO*'] **IV.**=man I.
mabuldor=mapulder; **maca**=+mæcca
macalic *convenient*, MkR 6²¹.
macian *to* '*make*,' *form, construct, do, A,Æ* : *prepare, arrange, cause*, Æ,*Gen,Mt* : *use*, Æ : *behave, fare*, Æ,*Bo*; *CP* : *compare* : *transform*, ÆP 204¹¹. macian ūp *to put up*, Æ.
mācræftig (=mægencr-)† *mighty.*
macung f. *making, doing*, CHR 1101.
+**mād** *silly, mad*, WW.
mādm=māðm
mādmōd n. *foolishness*, MOD 25.
mǣ (*VPs*)=mā
±**mǣc** *well-suited, companionable* : *similar, equal.*
mǣcan=mecgan, mengan
+**mǣcca** (a, e) mf. *mate, equal, one of a pair, comrade, companion*, *ÆGr,MtR* : (±) *husband, wife*, Æ,*Bl,Ct,Mt* : pl. *pair*, CHRD 48²⁶. ['*match*']
mǣcefisc=mēcefisc
mǣcg† m. *man, disciple* : *son.*
mǣcga m. *man*, Wy 52.
mǣcian=mecgan, mengan
+**mǣclic** *conjugal*, Sc.
+**mǣcnes** f. *cohabitation*, BH.
+**mǣcscipe** m. *cohabitation*, CR 199.
mǣd (ē) f. ds. (EWS) mēda; nap. mǣd(w)a, mǣdwe '*mead*,' '*meadow*,' *pasture*, BC, OEG; Æ,AO; Mdf.
+**mǣdan** *to make mad or foolish.* pp. +mǣd(ed), *Cp,Rd,WW.*
mǣddre f. '*madder*,' *Lcd*; Æ.
mǣden (Æ,AO,CP)=mægden
mǣdencild n. *female child, girl, AO*; Æ. ['*maiden-child*']
mǣdenhēap m. *band of virgins*, DD 289.

mǣdenlic *maidenly, virgin*, Æ.
mǣdere=mæddre
mǣderecīo m. *sprig of madder*, LCD.
+**mǣdla** m. *madness*, LCD 122b.
mǣdlacu f. *meadow-stream*, KC.
mǣdland m. *meadow-land*, KC.
mǣdmǣwect (=-wett) *mowing of a meadow*, LL 448,5².
Mǣdmōnað (e¹) *July*, MEN (Hickes).
mǣdrǣden f. *mowing, tract of mown grass*, KC 6·153¹⁰.
mǣdsplott m. *plot of meadow-land*, KC 4·72⁷.
mǣdwa m., mǣdwe f.=mǣd
mǣdweland=mǣdland
mǣg I. pres. 3 sg. of magan. **II.** (Sc 4¹⁹; 12¹⁷)=mægen
±**mǣg** (ē) **I.** m. nap. māgas (v. LL 2·651) *male kinsman, parent, son, brother, nephew, cousin, B,Ep*; Æ,AO,CP : *compatriot*, A 46·76. ['*may*'] **II.**† f. *female relation, wife, woman, maiden*, Rd 10⁹. ['*may*']
mǣgbana m. *destroyer of kinsfolk*, W 242⁵.
mǣgbōt f. *compensation paid to the relatives of a murdered man*, LL.
mǣgburg f. *family, tribe, race, people, nation* : *genealogy.*
mǣgcild n. *young kinsman*, Ct,LCD.
mǣgcnafa m. *youthful kinsman*, BC 2·329'.
mǣgcūð *related*, OEG.
mǣgcwalm (ē) m. *murder of a relation*, Cp 179P.
mǣgden (ǣd) n. *maiden, virgin, LL*; Æ : *girl, Mt* : *maid, servant, Bl.*
mǣgden- see also mǣden-.
mǣgdenǣw f. *marriage with a virgin*, LL (1·332').
mǣgdenhād m. '*maidenhood*,' *Cr*; CP.
mǣgdenmann m. '*maid*,' *virgin*, AO,*Lcd.* ['*maidenman*']
mǣge=māge
mǣgen I. (e) n. *bodily strength, might*, '*main*' *force, power, vigour, valour, B*; Æ,CP : *virtue, efficacy, efficiency, Lcd* : *good deed* : *picked men of a nation, host, troop, army, An,Chr*; AO : *miracle.* [magan] **II.** subj. pl. of magan.
mǣgenāgende *mighty*, B 2837.
mǣgenbyrðen† f. *huge burden, B.* [v. '*main*']
mǣgencorðor n. *strong troop*, GEN 1986.
mǣgencræft† m. *main force, great strength, might.*
mǣgencyning† m. *mighty king, Cr.* [v. '*main*']
mǣgendǣd f. *mighty deed*, CRA 12.
mǣgenēaca m. *succour*, Az 138.
mǣgenēacen† *mighty, vigorous.*
mǣgenearfeðe† n. *great misery or trial.*

mægenellen n. *mighty valour*, B659.
mægenfæst *vigorous, strong, steadfast*, Æ.
mægenfolc n. *mighty company*, Cr877. [v. 'main']
mægenfultum m. *mighty help*, B1455.
mægenhēap m. *powerful band*, Ex197.
mægenheard *very strong*, Run5.
mægenian (gn-) *to gain strength* : (+) *establish, confirm*, BH306¹⁸.
mægenig? (mēn-) *strong*, Ex6¹(BTs).
mægenlēas *powerless, feeble, helpless*, WW; Æ. ['*mainless*'] adv. -līce.
mægenlēast f. *weakness, feebleness*, Æ : *inability*, RB.
mægenrǣs m. *mighty onslaught*, B1519. [v. '*main*']
mægenrōf† *powerful*, Ex,Rd.
mægenscype m. *might, power*, Da20.
mægensibb f. *great love*, VH16.
mægenspēd† f. *power, virtue*.
mægenstān m. *huge stone*, Met5¹⁶. [v. '*main*']
mægenstrang† *of great virtue or strength*.
mægenstreng-o, -ðu f. *great might*.
mægenðegen m. *mighty minister*, Gu1099.
mægenðīse f. *violence, force*, Rd28¹⁰.
mægenðrēat† m. *mighty host*.
mægenðrymm m. *power, might, majesty, greatness, glory*, Mt; Æ,CP : *virtue*, Bf : *heavenly host* : (†) *Christ* : (†) *heaven*. [v. '*main*']
mægenðrymnes f. *great glory, majesty*, Æ.
mægenweorc† n. *mighty work*, PPs.
mægenwīsa m. *general*, Ex553.
mægenwudu m. *strong spear*, B236.
mœgonwundor n. *striking wonder*, Cr927.
mæger *meagre, lean*, Guth,Lcd.
mægerian *to macerate, make lean*, WW. [*Ger.* magern]
mægester=magister
mægeð, mǣgeð=mægð, mǣgð
mǣggemōt n. *meeting of kinsmen*, AO248¹⁸.
mǣggewrit n. *genealogy, pedigree*.
mǣggieldan³? *to contribute towards the fine for manslaughter by a kinsman*, LL122,74².
mǣghǣmed n. *incest*, BH280¹.
mǣghand (mēg-, mēi-) f. *natural heir, relative*, Ct.
mǣgister=magister
mǣglagu f. *law as to relatives*, LL266,25.
mǣglēas *without relatives*, LL.
mǣglēast (RWH29⁷)=mægenlēast
mǣglic *belonging to a kinsman*, ÆH.
mǣglufu f. *love*, Jul70.
mǣgmorðor n. *murder of a relative*, Gl.
mǣgmyrðra m. *murderer of a relative, parricide*, OEG,GD239⁴.
mægn=mægen; mægnan=mengan
mægon=magon pres. pl. of magan

mǣgracu f. *generation, genealogy*, Æ.
mǣgrǣden f. *relationship*, AO.
mǣgrǣs m. *attack on relatives*, W164⁴.
mǣgscīr [mēg-] f. *division of a people containing the kinsmen of a particular family* (BT), DR193¹⁰.
mǣgsibb f. *relationship* : *affection of relatives*.
mǣgsibbung f. *reconciliation, peace-making*, JGPh1·63.
mǣgsiblīc *related*, WW375¹⁷.
mǣgslaga m. *slayer of a relative, parricide, fratricide*, Æ.
mǣgsliht m. *murder of a relative*, W130².
mǣgster=magister
mǣgð† f. gp. mǣgða, dp. mǣgðum, otherwise uninflected *maiden, virgin, girl, woman, wife*. [*Goth.* magaðs]
±mǣgð I. (ȳ) f. *family group, clan, tribe, generation, stock, race, people*, Æ,AO : *province, country*, Æ. II. *longing, ambition*, Gl,Lcd : *greed*, Bo.
mǣgða m. *mayweed*, Lcd,WW.
mǣgðblǣd (geð) n. *pudendum muliebre* GPH400⁸.
mǣgðbōt f. *fine for assault on an unmarried woman?* LL7,74.
mǣgðhād m. *virginity, chastity, purity*, MH; Æ,CP : *band of young persons* : *relationship*, Æ. ['*maidhood*']
mǣgðhādlic *maidenly*, OEG1469
mǣgðlagu=mæglagu
mǣgðlēas *not of noble birth*, WW219⁸.
mǣgðmann m. *maiden, virgin*, LL8,82.
mǣgðmorðor (ē¹) nm. *murder of kin*, OEG 2⁴¹²
mǣgðmyrðra m. *murderer of kin*, OEG2³³⁵.
mǣgðrǣden f. *friendship, relationship*, OEG.
mǣgðsibb (y²) f. *kindred*, HGL523.
mǣgwine† m. *friendly relative, clansman*.
mǣgwlite (ā, ē) m. *aspect, species, form*.
mǣgwlitian (ē¹) *to fashion*, MtL17².
mǣgwlitlīce (ē¹) *figuratively*, MkL p4¹⁰.
mǣht=meaht, miht
mǣhð (AS38¹¹)=mǣgð II.
mǣl I. (ā, ē) n. *mark, sign, ornament* : *cross, crucifix* : *armour, harness, sword* : *measure*, Lcd : (†) *time, point of time, occasion, season* : *time for eating, 'meal,' meals*, CP; Æ. II. f. (†) *talk, conversation* : *contest, battle*. [mæðel] III.=mál
+mǣl *stained, dyed*, An1333.
+mǣlan *to mark, stain*, Jul591.
±mǣlan† *to speak, talk*, Gen,Ps. ['*mele*,' '*i-mele*'; mæðlan]
mǣlcearu f. *trouble of the time*, B189.
mǣld-=meld-
mǣldæg† m. *appointed time, day*, Gen.

mǣldropa m. *phlegm, saliva, mucus,* WW 240⁹.

mǣldropiende *running with mucus,* WW 161³³.

mǣle I. m. (ē) *cup, bowl, bucket, Ep,Lcd.* [*'meal'*] II. *marked,* KC.

mǣlgesceaft f. *fate,* B2737.

mǣlsceafa (æ?) m. *canker, caterpillar, WW.* [*'malshave'*]

mǣltan (VPs)=meltan

mǣl-tang m., -tange f. *pair of compasses,* WW.

mǣl-tīd f., -tīma m. *meal-time,* NC348.

mǣn=menn nap. of man.

mǣn-=man-, men-

±**mǣnan** I. (ē) *to ' mean,' signify, intend, Æ, Bo,Sol*; CP : *consider.* II. *to tell : mention, relate, declare, communicate to, speak of, B : speak (a language).* III. *to complain of, lament, bewail, sorrow, grieve, Bo; Æ,AO,* CP.

mǣne I. (±, usu.+) *common, public, general, universal, Mt*; AO : *owned in common, WW : catholic : lower (clergy) : mutual.* habban +m. *to have or hold in common.* [*'i-mene'*] II. (+) n. *fellowship, intercourse.* III. *false, mean, wicked.* [mān] IV. (+) *subdued, overpowered,* GEN,GNE. [=*+mægne, ES43·308]

±**mǣnelic** (usu. +) *common, ordinary : mutual : public, general, universal, Æ.* adv. -līce.

+**mǣnelicnes** f. *generality,* OEG.

mǣnibrǣde *relating to many things,* WW 115⁸.

mǣnlic=mǣnelic

+**mǣnnes** f. *community, fellowship, intercourse, union, Shr : sharing : land held in common,* BC1·597'. [v. *'i-mene'*]

+**mǣnscipe** m. *community, fellowship : union,* W248²³ : *common ownership,* RB 103²⁰.

±**mǣnsumian** *to impart : partake of, participate in, have fellowship with : live with, marry : communicate : administer Eucharist, Æ.*

+**mǣnsumnes** f. *fellowship, participation (in Eucharist),* BH.

mǣnsumung f. *fellowship, participation, ÆH : (+) administration of the Eucharist,* CM,RBL.

mǣnu=menigu

+**mǣnung** f. *marriage,* HL.

mǣrāc f. *boundary-oak,* KC3·379'.

mǣran (ā) I. (±) *to declare, proclaim, celebrate, glorify, honour.* II. (+) *to determine, fix limits,* WID42.

mǣrapeldre f. *apple-tree on a boundary,* KC3·390⁵.

mǣrbrōc m. *boundary-brook,* KC.

mǣrc (1)=mearc; (2)=mearg

mǣrcnoll m. *boundary-knoll,* EC445.

mǣrcumb m. *border valley,* KC.

mǣrdīc f. *boundary-dike,* KC.

mǣre=(1) mare; (2) mere I.

mǣre I. (ē) *famous, great, excellent, sublime, splendid, Æ,B,Ep*; AO,CP. [*'mere'*] II. *pure, sterling (of money).* [v. *'mere'* adj.] III. (±, usu. +) *boundary, border, Mk,VPs*; AO; Mdf : *balk of a plough-land,* GBG : *end.* IV. *declaration,* TC646,648 (v. A 46·214). [*'mere'* sb.]

mǣrelsrāp m. *ship's rope, cable,* WW.

mǣretorht=meretorht

mǣrflōde *border channel,* EC370⁵.

mǣrford *border ford,* KC5·126'.

mǣrfurh *border furrow,* KC.

mǣrgeard *border fence,* KC3·462³.

mǣrgen=morgen

mǣrh (*Cp,Ep*), mærh-=mearg, mearh-

+**mǣrhaga** (ē) m. *boundary-hedge,* EC388¹⁰.

mǣr-hege m. *boundary-hedge,* EC447.

mǣrhlinc *border ridge,* KC.

mǣrhlīsa m. *notoriety,* WW382¹⁰.

mǣrian *to be distinguished,* DHy.

+**mǣrian**=+mǣrsian II.

mǣringcwudu n. *mastic of sweet basil?* LCD131a.

+**mǣrlacu** f. *boundary-stream,* EC387'.

mǣrlic (ȳ) *great, splendid, glorious, famous,* Æ,AO,CP. adv. -līce, Æ.

mǣrnes f. *greatness, honour, fame,* LPs, WW.

mǣr-pōl, -pul m. *boundary-pool,* EC445⁸, KC5·198'.

mǣrpytt m. *pit on a boundary,* KC.

mǣrsc=mersc

mǣrsere (ē) m. *herald,* DR56¹⁷.

±**mǣrsian** (ē) I. *to make or become famous, proclaim, declare, announce,* Æ,CP : *celebrate: glorify, honour, exalt, praise, Æ : spread (fame) : enlarge.* II. *to mark out, bound, limit.*

mǣrsīc *border rivulet,* KC6·60¹⁷.

mǣrstān m. *boundary-stone,* BC3·154. [*'merestone'*]

mǣrsung (ē) f. *fame, report, renown : celebration, festival, Æ : exalting, magnifying : (±) magnificence, celebrity.*

mǣrsungtīma m. *time of glorifying,* ÆH 2·360²⁵.

+**mǣrtrēow** *boundary-tree,* KC3·342'.

mǣrð=mearð

mǣrð f. *glory, fame : famous exploit, Æ,* AO,CP.

±**mǣr-ðorn**, -ðyrne *boundary-hawthorn,* KC.

mǣrðu=mærð

mæru=mearu

+mǣrung? *ending*, RHy5¹⁰.

mærw-=mearu-

±mǣrweg m. *boundary-road*, Ct.

mǣrweorc m. *noble work*, PPs110⁴.

+mǣrwyll m. *boundary-stream*, KC3·193⁹.

mæscre (ǣ?) f. *mesh*, WW450¹⁰.

mæsen *brazen* (Earle): *of maple* (BT), EC 250.

mæslere m. *sacristan*, GD228¹⁵.

mæsling, mæslen (*MkL*)=mæstling

mæssanhacele=mæssehacele

mæsse (e) f. '*mass*,' *Eucharist, celebration of Eucharist, Æ,BH,Ct*; CP : *special mass-day, festival of the church*. [*L*. missa]

mæsseǣfen m. *eve of a festival*, CHR,LL.

mæsse-bōc f. nap. -bēc '*mass-book*,' *missal*, LL.

mæssecrēda m. *creed said at mass, Nicene creed*, LL. ['*mass-creed*']

mæssedæg m. '*mass-day*,' *festival*, Bl.

mæssegierela m. *mass-vestment, surplice*, CP87¹⁹.

mæssehacele f. *mass-vestment, cope, chasuble*, LV40,WW327²².

mæssehrægl n. *vestment, surplice*, CP.

mæsselāc n. *mass-offering, host*, WW.

mæsseniht f. *eve of a festival*, CHR,W.

mæsseprēost m. '*mass-priest*,' *clergyman, high-priest*, Æ,AO; CP. [v. also '*priest*']

mæsseprēosthād m. *office or orders of a mass-priest*, BH.

mæsseprēostscīr f. *district for which a mass-priest officiated*, LL.

mæsserbana m. *murderer of a priest*, W 165²⁸.

mæssere m. *priest who celebrates mass*, Az. ['*masser*']

mæsserēaf n. *mass-vestments*, Æ.

mæssesang m. *office of mass*, BH,LL.

mæssesteall m. *seat in a church choir* (Napier), *place from which the priest said mass?* (BTs), v. NC307,348.

mæssetīd f. *time of saying mass*, LL(140²⁰).

mæsseðegn m. *mass-priest*, LL460,5.

mæsseðēnung f. *service of the mass, celebration of mass*, A11·8¹⁵, ByH76¹⁵.

mæsseūhta m. *hour, or service, of matins on a feast-day*, NC307.

mæssewīn (e) n. *wine used at mass*, WW.

mæssian (±) *to celebrate '*mass*,'* Æ : (+) *attend mass*.

mæssung f. *office of mass*, CHRD35¹³.

mæst I. m. (*ship's*) '*mast*,' *B*; Æ,AO. II. m. '*mast*,' *food of swine, acorns, beech-nuts*, *Bl*.

mǣst (ā, ē) I. adj. (superl. of micel), *AO, Chr,Bo,Mt*. ['*most*'] II. adv. *mostly, for the most part, in the greatest degree, chiefly,*

especially, very much. eal m., m. eal *almost, nearly*. m. ǣlc *nearly every one*, Æ,AO, CP. **III.** n. *most*.

±mǣstan *to feed with '*mast*,' fatten*, BC; *anoint*, RPs22⁵,Æ,CP.

mæstcyst f. *mast-socket*, WW.

mæstelberg m. *fattened hog*, MtL6⁷. [bearg]

mæsten n. *mast, pasture for swine*, Ct,LL.

mæstenrǣden f. *right of feeding swine in mast-pastures*, KC3·451¹⁰.

mæstentrēow n. *tree yielding mast*, WW 137²³.

mæstland f. *land yielding mast*, TC140².

mǣstlīcost adv. (superl.) *particularly*, CM 1169.

mæstling I. n. *brass*, WW : *brazen vessel*, Mk. ['*maslin*'] II. *fatling*, OEG61²⁹.

mæstlingsmið m. *brass-worker*, WW539⁶.

mæstlōn sbpl. *pulleys at the top of a mast*, WW199³⁰.

mæstrǣden=mæstenrǣden

mæstrāp m. *mast-rope*, Ex82.

mæsttwist m. *rope supporting a mast*, WW.

mǣt I. pret. 3 sg. of metan. II.=mete m.

±mǣtan *to dream* (impers.), Æ; (trans.) Lcd. ['*mete*']

mǣte=mete

mǣte (ē) *mean, moderate, poor, inferior, small, bad*. also adv.

+mǣte *suitable*, RB; ÆL. ['*meet*']

mætfæst-=metfæst-

+mætgian (ÆL)=+metgian

mǣting f. *dream*, Lcd. ['*meting*']

mǣton pret. pl. of metan.

mǣð I. f. *measure, degree, proportion, rate*, Æ; AO : *honour, respect, reverence*, LL : *what is meet, right, fitness, ability, virtue, goodness*, Æ,CP : *lot, state, rank*, Æ. ['*methe*'] II. n. *cutting of grass*, BC. ['*math*']

mǣð-=mǣgð-

±mǣðegian *to honour, respect, spare*, W; ÆT. ['*methe*']

mǣðel (e) n. *council, meeting, popular assembly* : (†) *speech, interview*.

mǣðelcwide† (e) m. *discourse*.

mǣðelern n. *council-house, prætorium*, WW.

mǣðelfrið (ðl) mn. *security* ('frið') *enjoyed by public assemblies*, LL3,1 (v. 2·464 and 3·4).

mǣðel-hēgende†, -hergende *holding conclave, deliberating*.

mǣðelstede† (e) m. *place of assembly : battle-field*.

mǣðelword (e) n. *address, speech*, B236.

mǣð(e)re m. *mower*, WW235,237.

mǣðful *humane*, ÆGr. ['*metheful*']

mæðian=mæðegian; mæðl=mæðel
mæðlan (Cr)=maðelian
mæðlēas rapacious, Æ. ['metheless']
mæðlic moderate, proportioned, befitting, Ct,
LL. adv. -līce humanely, courteously,
ÆGr. ['methely']
mæōmēd f. pay for haymaking, LL452'.
mæðre=mæðere
±mæðrian to honour, LL.
mæðung f. measuring, adjudication, CHRD
35¹⁸.
mǣw (ea, e) m. 'mew,' sea-gull, An,Cp,Shr.
mǣwpul (ā) m. sea-gulls' pool, Ct.
māfealdra comp. of manigfeald.
maffian to go astray, wax wanton, CHRD
74²,77².
mag-=mæg-
maga I. m. 'maw,' stomach, Cp,Lcd,WW;
Æ,CP. II. powerful, strong : able, competent, having means.
māga I.† m. son, descendant, young man,
man. II. gp. of mæg.
magan swv. pres. 1, 3 sg. mæg; 2, meaht,
miht; pl. magon; pret. 3 sg. meahte to be
able, Bo,G,WW : have permission or power
(I 'may*,' I can), DD,G : to be strong,
competent, avail, prevail, Æ,B,BH,Gl,
VPs; CP. mæg wið avails against, cures,
LCD.
māgas v. mǣg; magaðe=mageðe
magaðiht strong of stomach, LCD 3·68¹⁷.
magdalatrēow n. almond-tree, WW 139¹¹.
[L. amygdala]
mage f. (WW 159¹⁴)=maga
māge (ā) f. female relative, B; Æ. ['mowe']
māgeēct ptc. augmented, WW. [īecan]
mageðe (æ¹, o²) f. camomile, mayweed, Lcd,
WW. ['maythe']
magian to prevail, ERPs12⁵; NC348 : (+)
recover (health), LCD 3·184²¹? (BTac; or
?āmagian).
magister (æ) m. leader, chief, 'master,'
teacher, Æ,Bo; AO,CP. [L. magister]
magisterdōm (mægster-) m. office of a master
or teacher, Sc120⁹. ['masterdom']
+māglic=+mālic
mago† (magu) m. gs. maga, nap. mæcgas
male kinsman, son, descendant : young
man, servant : man, warrior.
magodryht f. band of warriors, B67.
magogeoguð f. youth, CRI1429.
magorǣdend m. counsellor of men, AN
1463.
magorǣswa† m. chief, prince.
magorinc† m. youth, man, warrior.
magotimber† n. child, son, GEN : increase
of family, progeny, GnE.
magotūdor† n. descendant, offspring.
magoðe, magðe=mageðe

magoðegn† m. vassal, retainer, warrior, man,
servant, minister.
magu=mago; māgwlite=mǣgwlite
±māh bad, wanton, shameless, importunate.
mahan=magon pres. pl. of magan.
+māhlic importunate : wanton, shameless :
wicked. adv. -līce impudently.
+māhlicnes f. importunity, CP : wantonness,
shamelessness : time of need, SPs9²².
+māhnes f. importunity, persistence : shamelessness : boldness : contumacy, WYN57.
maht (VPs)=miht
Māius 'May,' Bf.
māl I. n. suit, cause, case, action, terms,
agreement, covenanted pay, Chr. hē scy-
lode ix scypa of māle he paid nine ships
out of commission, CHR1049c. ['mail']
II. n. spot, mark, blemish, Æ. III.=mǣl n.
māl-=mǣl-, māhl-
malscrung f. enchantment, charm, Cp,Lcd.
['maskering']
mālswyrd (u²) n. sword with inlaid ornament, TC560'. [mǣl]
malt (Gl)=mealt; malwe (WW)=mealwe
mamme f. teat, GPH401⁷⁷. [L. mamma]
mamor, mam(e)ra m. lethargy, heavy sleep,
GL.
mamrian to think out, design, PPs63⁵.
man I. pron. indef. one, people, they, B,Mt;
Æ. ['man'] II.=mann. III. pres. 3 sg.
of munan.
mān I. n. evil deed, crime, wickedness,
guilt, sin, B,Ps; Æ : false oath, ÆP
216¹⁴. II. adj. bad, criminal, false, Ps;
AO. ['man']
+man (o) having a mane, WW492²⁰.
man-=mann-
+māna m. community, company, Æ : common property : communion, companionship, intercourse, Bo,BH; CP : cohabitation, LG. tō +mānan in common, CP.
['mone,' 'ymone']
manað pres. 3 sg. of manian.
mānāð m. false oath, perjury, LL; HL.
['manath']
mānāðswaru f. perjury, LL.
mānbealu n. crime, cruelty, DA45.
manbōt (o¹) f. fine paid to the lord of a man
slain, LL (v. 2·576). ['manbote']
mānbryne m. fatal, destructive fire, CHR
962A.
mancgere=mangere
-mancian v. be-m.
man-cus, -cas, -cos, -cs m. gp. mancessa
(CP) a 'mancus,' thirty silver pence, one-
eighth of a pound, Æ,BC.
mancwealm m. mortality, pestilence, destruction, Chr; AO. ['manqualm']
mancwealmnes f. manslaughter, NG.

mancwyld (o) f. *mortality, pestilence*, BH 190[8].

mancynn n. *mankind, Æ,B,Bl : inhabitants, people, men*, CP. ['*mankin*']

mancyst f. *human virtue*, MFH169.

mand (o) f. *basket, Cp,MtL,WW.* ['*maund*']

māndǣd f. *sin, crime, Ph*; Æ,AO,CP. [v. '*man*']

māndǣda m. *evil-doer*, NC329.

māndǣde *evil-doing, wicked*, LL,W.

māndeorf *bold in evil?* ÆPD120[31].

mandrēam† m. *revelry, festivity*.

māndrinc m. *poison*, RD24[13].

mandryhten† m. *lord, master*, B.

+**māne** *having a mane*, WE57[16].

maneg=manig

mānfǣhðu f. *wickedness*, GEN1378.

manfaru f. *host, troop*, GU257.

mānfeld m. *field of crime*, AO108[20].

mānfolm f. *evil-doer*, PPs143[8].

mānfordǣdla m. *evil-doer*, B563.

mānforwyrht n. *evil deed, sin*, CR1095.

mānfrēa† m. *lord of evil, Devil*.

mānfremmende† *sinning, vicious*.

mānful *wicked, evil, infamous, degraded*, Æ: *fearful, dire*.

mānfullic *infamous, evil, sinful*, Æ. adv. -lice, Æ.

mānfulnes f. *wickedness*, Æ.

manfultum (o[1]) m. *military force*, AO216[8].

+**mang** I. n. *mixture, union : troop, crowd, multitude, Jud : congregation, assembly : business : cohabitation*. in +m. *during*. on +m. *in the midst of*. ['*ymong*'] II. prep. (w. d. or a.) *among*, AO,G; Æ,CP. ['*ymong*']

māngenga m. *evil-doer*, BH36[5].

māngenīðla m. *evil persecutor*, AN918.

+**mang(en)nes** f. *mingling, mixture*, OEG.

mangere m. *trader, merchant, broker*, Æ.

māngewyrhta m. *sinner*, PPs77[38].

±**mangian** *to gain by trading*, Æ,CP.

mangung f. *trade, business*, Æ.

mangunghūs n. *house of merchandise*, Jn2[16].

mānhūs n. *home of wickedness, hell*, EX535.

±**manian** I. (o) *to remind;· admonish, warn, exhort, instigate*, Æ,CP : *instruct, advise*, Æ : *claim, demand, ask*. II. (+) *to be restored to health?* GD338[30].

mānīdel *vain and bad (words)*, PPs143.

maniend m. *admonisher*, CP407[13] : *collector : creditor*.

manif-=manigf-

manig (æ[1], e[1], o[1], e[2]) nap. manega '*many,*' *many a, much*, Æ,AO,B,BH,Ps; CP.

manigean=manian; **manigeo**=menigu

manigfeald (æ, e, o[1]) '*manifold,*' *various, varied, complicated*, Æ,WW; CP : *numerous, abundant : plural*, ÆGr. adv. -fealde.

±**manigfeald(l)an** (æ[1], a[3], y[3]) *to multiply, abound, increase, extend*, OEG; CP : *reward*. ['*manifold*']

manigfealdlic *manifold*. adv. -lice *in various ways*, LG,VPs; CP : (gram.) *in the plural number*. ['*manifoldly*']

manigfealdnes f. *multiplicity, abundance, complexity*, LG,WW. ['*manifoldness*']

manigsīðes (mani-) adv. *often*, W144[11].

manig-tēaw (æ[1]), -tīwe, -tȳwe *skilful, dexterous*, Æ.

manigtēawnes (mænitȳw-) f. *skill, dexterity*, OEG.

manlēas (o) *uninhabited*, WW. ['*manless*']

mānlic *infamous, nefarious*, Æ. adv. -lice *falsely, wickedly*.

manlīca m. *effigy, image, statue*, GEN,BL.

manlīce adv. *manfully, nobly*, B. ['*manly*']

manlufu f. *love for men*, GU324.

manm-=mannm-

mann (o) m., nap. men(n) *person (male or fem.)*, Æ,Bl,Lcd,G,VHy; AO,CP : *man : mankind, Mk,VPs : brave man, hero : vassal, servant : name of the rune for* m. *used indefinitely, like Mod. Eng. 'one,'* v. man I.

mann-, see also man-.

manna I. m. *man*, Æ. II. n. '*manna*' *(food)*, Æ,CP. [L.]

mannbǣre *producing men*, ÆH1·450.

mannēaca (mon-) m. *progeny*, AO158[20].

mannhata (o[1]) m. *man-hater*, BYH38[32].

mannian *to 'man,' garrison*, CHR1087E.

mannmǣgen (o) n. *troop, force, cohort*, JnL18[3].

mannmenigu (o) f. *multitude*, AO.

mannmyrring f. *destruction of men*, CHR1096.

mannmyrðra m. *a homicide*, LL.

mannsylen (i[2]) f. *traffic in men, sale of men unlawfully as slaves*, LL,W. [selen]

manrǣden f. *dependence, homage, service, tribute, due*, Æ. ['*manred*']

manrīm† n. *number of men*.

mānsceatt m. *usury*, PPs71[14].

mānsceaða† m. *enemy, sinner*.

mānscild f. *crime, fault, sin*, †Hy8[23].

manscipe m. *humanity, courtesy*, BC. ['*manship*']

mānscyldig† *criminal, guilty*.

mansillen=mannsylen

manslæht=manslieht

manslaga m. *man-slayer, murderer*, Æ.

mānslagu f. *cruel blow*, AN1218.

manslēan *to kill, murder*, RB16[18] (or ? two words).

manslege m. *manslaughter, homicide*, BL, LL.

manslieht (e[2], i[2]) m. *manslaughter, murder*, CP. ['*manslaught*']

manslot *share in ownership of land? measure of land?* v. NC307. [*ON.* mannshlutr]

-mānsumian, -mānsumung v. ā-m.

manswǣs *meek,* RPs24⁹.

mānswara (o²) m. *perjurer, Bl.* ['*man-swear*']

mānswaru f. *perjury,* LL,WW. [swerian]

mānswerian⁶ *to forswear, perjure oneself, LL.* ['*manswear*']

mānswica m. *deceiver, traitor* (mann-? v. LL2·142).

mansylen (i²) f. *traffic in men, act of selling men as slaves.* [sellan]

manðēaw† m. *habit, custom* (?sometimes mānðēaw *sinful custom*).

manðēof m. *man-stealer,* v. L2·542.

manðrymm m. *troop of men,* MFH97¹¹.

manðwǣre (o) *gentle, kind, humane, mild, meek,* ÆL,CP. [*OHG.* mandwāri]

+manðwǣrian *to humanize,* CP362²¹.

manðwǣrnes (o¹, y²) f. *gentleness, courtesy, weakness,* ÆL,CP.

manu f. '*mane,' Erf*1182; WE54¹³.

manung f. *admonition,* CP : *claim : place of toll : district for purposes of tribute or taxation : residents in a taxing district.*

mānwamm (o²) m. *guilty stain,* CR1280.

mānweorc I. n. *crime, sin.* **II.** adj. *sinful,* EL.

manweorod (o) m. *collection of men, troop, congregation, assembly,* AO.

manweorðung f. *adoration of human beings,* LL (248³).

manwīse† (o) f. *manner or custom of men.*

mānword n. *wicked word,* PPs58¹².

mānwrǣce *wicked,* WW426¹⁹.

mānwyrhta† m. *evil-doer, sinner,* PPs.

manwyrð n. *value or price of a man,* LL.

mapulder (o²) m. *maple tree,* Ct,Lcd.

mapuldern *made of maple,* Ct,WW.

mapul-dre, -dor, -dur f., -trē(ow) m. (Mdf)= mapulder

māra m., **māre** fn. (compar. of micel) *greater, 'more,' stronger, mightier, Æ,Bl, CP,LL.* adv. *in addition, Mt.*

māran=mǣran

mārbēam (VPs)=mōrbēam

marc n. *a denomination of weight* (usu. half a pound), *mark* (money of account), CHR, Ct.

marcian=mearcian

mare (e) f. *nightmare, monster, Ep,Lcd.* ['*mare*']

māre v. māra; **mārels**=mǣrelsrāp

marenis=mearuwnes; **margen-**=morgen-

+mārian *to increase,* Sc40¹⁶.

market n. *market,* TC422²⁰ (v.l.). [*L.* mercatum]

marma m. *marble,* Lcd1·154¹⁴. [*L.* marmor]

marman-stān (marmel-, marm(or)-) m. *marble, piece of marble, Æ,Bl.* ['*marm-stone*']

marmstāngedelf n. *quarrying of marble,* ÆH1·560³².

-marod v. ā-m.

martir, martyr(e) m. '*martyr,' BH,Men;* Æ,AO. [*L.*]

martirlogium m. *martyrology,* IM122⁴⁵.

martr-=martyr-

martyrcynn m. *race of martyrs,* ÆL23⁸⁵.

martyrdōm m. '*martyrdom,' BH;* Æ,CP.

martyrhād m. *martyrdom,* BH,GD.

+mar-tyrian, -trian *to* '*martyr,' torture, AO, BH.*

martyrracu f. *martyrology,* ÆL23³³⁴.

martyrung f. *passion (of Christ),* AO254²⁴. ['*martyring*']

mārðu=mǣrð

masc=max

māse f. *name of a small bird,* GL. [*Ger.* meise]

-masian v. ā-m.

massere m. *merchant : moneylender,* Bk 10.

māst=mǣst; **matt,** matte (*CP*)=meatte

mattuc (æ¹, ea¹, e¹, eo¹, o²) m. '*mattock,' AO,Gl,LL;* Æ : *fork, trident.*

māð pret. 3 sg. of mīðan.

maða m. *maggot, worm, grub, WW.* ['*mathe*']

maðal-=maðel-

+maðel n. *speech, talking,* NIC507²⁰. [=mæðel?]

maðelere m. *speaker, haranguer, WW.* ⌊v. '*mathele*']

maðelian† (æ¹, e¹, a², o²) *to harangue, make a speech, speak, An,B,Cp,Cr.* ['*mell,' 'mathele*']

maðelig *talkative, noisy,* KGL75²³.

maðelung f. *loquacity, OEG.* [v. '*mathele*']

māðm=māðum

māðm- see also māððum.

māðmǣht† f. *valuable thing, treasure,* B.

māðmcleofa (mād-) m. *treasure-chamber,* Æ (9²⁷⁷).

māðmcyst f. *treasure-chest,* Mt27⁶.

māðmgestrēon n. *treasure,* B,MFH.

māðmhord n. *treasure-hoard,* Ex368.

māðmhūs n. *treasure-house, treasury,* AO, CP.

māðmhyrde m. *treasurer,* Bo64¹³.

maðolian=maðelian

māððum=māðum, māðm

māððum-fæt n., pl. -fatu *precious vessel,* Æ.

māððumgesteald n. *treasure,* Jul36.

māððumgifu f. *gift of treasure,* B1301.

mǎððumgyfa m. _giver of treasure, prince, king_, WA92.
mǎððumsele m. _hall of treasure_, SOL189.
mǎððumsigle n. _costly ornament_, B2757.
mǎððumsweord n. _costly sword_, B1023.
mǎððumwela m. _valuables_, B2750.
maðu f.=maða
mǎðum m., gs. mǎðmes _treasure, object of value, jewel, ornament, gift, Gn,Met_; CP. ['_madme_']
mǎðum-=mǎðm-, mǎððum-
mǎwan[7] _to_ '_mow_,' _AO,BH._
mǎwpul=mǣwpul
max n. _net_, WW. ['_mask_']
mǎxwyrt f. _mash-wort (malt soaked in boiling water)_, LCD. [v. FTP322]
me I. das. of pers. pron. ic _me_. **II.** (RB35[9]; 127[13])=menn
meagol (e[1]) _mighty, strong, firm, emphatic, impressive._ [magan]
meagollíce adv. _earnestly_, BL.
meagolmód _earnest, strenuous_, A11·97[3].
meagolmódnes f. _earnestness_, BL.
meagolnes f. _earnestness, strength of will_, BL,HL.
meaht I.=miht. **II.** pres. 2 sg. of magan.
meahte pret. 3 sg. of magan.
mealc pret. of melcan.
mealclíðe?=meolclíðe; **mealehūs**=meluhūs
mealewe=mealwe; **mealm**=mealmstān
-meallian v. ā-m.
mealmeht _sandy? chalky?_ KC3·394[13]. [v. '_malm_']
mealmstān m. _soft stone, sandstone? limestone?_ AO212[28]. [v. '_malm_']
mealt I. n. _steeped grain_, '_malt_,' _Ct,Ep_ [meltan] **II.** _sour_, LCD3·6[17]? **III.** pret. 3 sg. of meltan.
mealtealoð n. _malt-ale_, ANS84[325].
mealtgescot n. _payment in malt_, W171[2].
mealthūs n. '_malt-house_,' WW.
mealtwyrt (u[2]) f. '_malt-wort_,' WW.
mealu=melu
mealwe f. '_mallow_,' _Lcd,WW._ [L. malva]
mear=mearh
mearc (æ, e) f. (±) '_mark_,' _sign, line of division, Æ,MkL,RB_ : _standard, ÆGr_ : (±) _boundary, limit, term, border, BC,Gen_; CP; Mdf : _defined area, district, province_, AO. tō ðæs +mearces ðe _in the direction that._
mearca m. _space marked out_, GD197[4].
mearcdíc (e) f. _boundary-ditch_, BC1·295[7].
mearcere (æ) m. _writer, notary_, OEG.
mearcford _boundary-ford_, EC382[1].
mearcgemot _court for settling boundaries of properties?_ v. LL2·143.
mearcgrǣfa m. _boundary-thicket_, KC3·135'.
mearchlinc m. _boundary-ridge_, KC6·33[22].

mearchof n. _dwelling_, Ex61.
±mearcian _to_ '_mark_,' _stain, brand, seal, BC, LL,MtL,Ph_; Æ : _mark a boundary, measure, define, describe, designate, Æ, Gen_ : _mark out, design, Bo_ : _create_ : _note, observe._ +mearcod _baptized_, BF124[14].
mearc-īsern, -īsen n. _branding-iron_, GL,MH.
mearcland n. _border-land, march, moor_ : (†) _province, country, district_ : _sea-coast_, RD4[23].
mearcpæð† m. _road, path_, AN,EL.
mearcstapa† m. _march-haunter_, B.
mearcstede m. _border-land, desolate district_, SOL217.
mearcðrēat m. _army, troop_, Ex173.
mearcung (æ, e) f. _marking, branding_ : _mark, characteristic_ : (±) _description, arrangement_ : _constellation_ : _title, chapter_, NG.
mearcweard m. _wolf_, Ex168.
mearcweg m. _border-road_, BC,KC.
mearcwill m. _boundary-spring_, EC293'.
meard=(1) meord, mēd; (2) mearð
mēares v. mearh I
mearg (æ, e) nm. **I.** '_marrow_,' _pith_, Lcd. **II.** _sausage_, GL. [=mærg] **III.**=mearh I.
mēargealla (e[1], e[2]) m. _gentian_, LCD. [mearh] +**meargian** _to be rich, marrowy_, LPs65[15].
mearglic (e) _marrowy, fat_, VPs.
mearh I.† m. gs. mēares _horse, steed._ **II.**=mearg
mearhæccel n. _sausage-meat_, WW411[20].
mearhcofa m. _bone_, PPs101[3].
mearhgehæc n. _sausage-meat_, WW427[30].
mearmstān=marmanstān
mearn pret. 3 sg. of murnan.
+**mearr I.** n. _stumbling-block, obstruction, error_, CP : _emptiness, vanity_, RPs88[48]. **II.** _wicked, fraudulent_, LL140,1[5].
mearrian _to err_, Bo55[23].
mearð (æ, e) m. _marten_, Ep,AO. ['_mart_']
mearu (æ, e, y), mear(u)w- in obl. cases _tender, soft_, Lcd,MtR : _callow_, OEG : _delicate_, RB : _frail_, GD119[17]. ['_meruw_']
mearulic (merwe, mærw-) _frivolous, delicate, luxurious_, GD. adv. -líce _weakly._
mearuwnes f. _tenderness, frailty_, CP211[18].
mēast=mǣst
meatte (a) f. '_mat_,' _mattress_, Gl. [L.]
mēaw=mǣw
mec as. of ic pers. pron.
+**mec**=+mæc
mēce m. _sword, blade_, GL. [Goth. mēkeis]
mēcefisc (ǣ) m. _mullet_, ÆGR308[5].
mecg=mæcg
mecgan _to mix, stir_, LCD.
mech=me
mechanisc _mechanical_, ÆL5[251]. [L.]
mēd I. f. '_meed_,' _reward, pay, price, compensation, bribe, ÆEL_ (gs. mēdes), _B,BH, Bl_; CP. **II.**=mǣd

med- in comp. principally indicates mediocrity, but often comes to have a distinct negative value; see, *e.g.*, medtrum, medwīs. [midde]

mēda v. mǣd; **-mēdan** v. on-m.

medder=mēder; **mēdder-**, mēddr-=mēdr-

meddrosna fp. *dregs of mead,* LCD 48a.

+mēde I. n. *consent, good-will, pleasure,* Ct : *covenant.* **II.** *agreeable, pleasant : suitable.*

medel=mæðel

medema (eo¹) m. *treadle,* WW.

medeme (eo¹) *middling, average, mean, little: sufficient, considerable, respectable, proper, fit, worthy, trustworthy, perfect,* CP.

±medemian (eo¹) *to mete out, allot, assign, place : moderate : (+) humble : respect, honour,* Æ : (+) *condescend,* Æ : (+) *advance, promote, deem worthy,* Æ.

medemlic *moderate, mediocre : intermediate : simple : worthy.* adv. **-līce** *slightly, moderately, incompletely : suitably, worthily, kindly.*

medemlicnes f. *mediocrity,* OEG.

medemmicel (Æ)=medmicel

medemnes f. *dignity, worth,* Æ,CP : *benignity, condescension,* BL.

medemung f. *measuring, measure,* Ct,LL.

mēden=mægden

mēder ds. and LWS gs. of mōdor.

mēderce=mȳderce; **medere**=mæddre

mēderen, mēdern=mēdren

mēderwyrhta=mēterwyrhta

medewyrt=meduwyrt

mēdgilda (ǣ) m. *pensioner, hireling,* Æ.

mēdian *to reward,* GD 237²³.

mēdl-=mǣðl-; **-mēdla** v. an-, ofer-m.

medlen=midlen

medm-=medem-

medmicel I. *moderate-sized, short, small, limited, unimportant, slight, mean, poor.* **II.** n. *a little.*

medmicelnes f. *smallness (of mind),* SPs 54⁸.

medmicle comp. medmāre, adv. *humbly, meanly, slightly.*

medo=medu; **medom-**=medem-

+mēdred=+mēdren I.

mēdren I. *maternal, of a mother.* **II.** n. *the mother's side (by descent),* LL 156,11.

+mēdren *born of the same mother,* AO 114¹³.

mēdrencynn n. *mother's kindred,* CR 246.

mēdrengecynd n. *mother's nature,* W 17⁷.

mēdrenmǣg m. *maternal kinsman,* LL.

mēdrenmǣgð f. *maternal kindred,* LL 392,3.

medrīce *of low rank,* WW 115²⁶.

mēdsceatt m. *payment, fee, reward, bribe, gift,* Æ,CP.

medsēlð (ǣ) f. *ill-fortune,* AO 164²⁸.

medspēdig *poor,* CRA 9.

medstrang *of middle rank,* BL 185¹⁶.

medtrum *weak, infirm, sickly, ill,* CP : *of lower rank.* [cp. medmicel]

medtrumnes (met-; y²) f. *weakness, infirmity, sickness, illness, disease,* AO,CP.

medu (eo) mn. gs. med(e)wes '*mead*' (*drink*), *B,Rd*; AO.

+mēdu=+mēde

meduærn (o²) n. *mead-hall, banqueting-house,* B 69.

medubenc† f. *bench in a mead-hall,* B.

meduburg† *mead-city, rejoicing city.*

medudrēam† m. *mead-joy, jollity,* B.

medudrenc (eo¹) m. *mead,* W 245⁴.

medudrinc (o²) m. *mead-drinking,* SEAF 22.

meduful† n. *mead-cup,* B,WY.

medugāl† *mead-excited, drunk.*

meduheall† f. *mead-hall.*

medum-=medem-

medurǣden (eo¹) f. *strong drink?* (ḂT), *dealing out of mead?* (GK), GNE 88.

meduscenc (eo¹) m. *mead-cup,* B 1980.

meduscerwen (ea¹) f. *deprival of (mead-) joy, distress, mortal panic?* AN 1526.

meduseld n. *mead-hall,* B 3065.

medusetl n. (eo¹, o²) *mead-seat,* B 5.

medustīg f. *path to the mead-hall,* B 924.

meduwērig† *overpowered with mead, drunk.*

meduwong (eo¹, o²) m. *field (where the mead-hall stood),* B 1643.

meduwyrt (eo¹, e²) f. *meadow-sweet,* Lcd : '*rubia,' madder,* OEG 56⁴⁰. ['*meadwort*']

medwīs *dull, stupid, foolish,* CP. [cp. medmicel]

mēdwyrhta m. *a hireling,* Sc 123¹².

meg=mæg

mēg=(1) mǣw; (2) mǣg

mēg-=mǣg-; **megol**=meago

meh=mec, me, as. of ic

meht=meaht, miht; **mēl,** mēig=mǣg

meige (KGL 81³²)=mǣge pres. 3 sg. subj. of magan.

meiðhād (KGL 56⁷)=mægðhād

mēl=mǣl n.

mela=melu

±melcan³ (i) *to milk,* ÆGR,LCD.

melcingfæt=meolcfæt

meld f. *proclamation,* DA 648.

melda m. *reporter, informer, betrayer,* Æ.

meldan (Rd)=meldian

melde f. *orache (plant),* Lcd. ['*milds*']

meldfeoh n. *informer's reward,* LL 96,17.

±meldian *to announce, declare, tell, proclaim, reveal,* Ps; Æ : *inform against, accuse.* ['*meld*']

meldung f. *betrayal,* BH 240⁴.

mēle=mǣle

meledēaw mn. *honey-dew, nectar,* Ph,WW (mild-). ['*mildew*']

melewes=melwes gs. of melu.

-melle, -melnes v. æ-m.
melo=melu; melsc=milisc
±meltan I. (y) (sv³) *to consume by fire,*
'melt,' *burn up,* B,MH,Ps,WW; Æ :
dissolve, digest. II.=mieltan
meltestre=myltestre
meltung f. *digestion,* LCD.
melu (ea, eo) n., gs. mel(u)wes '*meal,' flour,*
Lcd; Æ.
melugescot n. *payment in meal,* W171.
meluhūdern n. *meal-house,* LL455,17.
meluhūs (ea¹, e²) n. *meal-house,* WW
185²⁷.
meluw (LWS)=melu
men v. mann; mēnan=mǣnan
mend-=mynd-; +mēne-=+mǣne-
mene (y) m. *necklace, collar, ornament, jewel,*
Æ. [v. KLED s.v. mähne]
menegian=myndgian; menego=menigu
menen=mennen
menescilling m. *moon-shaped ornament,*
coin worn as ornament, GL.
±mengan (æ) tr. and intr. *to mix, combine,*
unite, Lk,Sat,WW; CP:(±) *associate with,*
consort, cohabit with, BH,Ps : disturb, B :
(†) *converse.* ['*meng*']
+mengedlic *mixed, confused,* Cp1542. adv.
-līce? GL.
+mengednes, +meng(d)nes f. *mingling,*
mixture, connection, Æ,BH : *sexual inter-*
course, CP.
mengeo, mengo, mengu=menigu
mengung f. *mixture, composition, ZDA : fel-*
lowship, GD : (+) *confusion.* ['*menging*']
meni (LWS)=manig; menian=mynian
menig (LWS)=manig; mēnig v. mægenig.
mawilō]
menigdu f. *band of people,* WW448²⁷.
menigu (a¹, æ¹, eo³) f. usu. indecl. in sg. *com-*
pany, multitude, host, Æ,AO,CP. [manig]
menio, meniu (LWS)=menigu
menisc=mennisc
menn v. mann.
mennen, mennenu (æ¹, i¹) nf. *handmaiden,*
slave, GD,LL.
mennesc=mennisc
mennisc I. adj. *human, natural, Bo,CP*; Æ.
II. n. *mankind, folk, race, people, Bl*; Æ,
CP. ['*mannish*']
mennisclic *human,* Æ,CP : *humane,* Bo,
RB. adv. -līce, Æ.
mennisc-licnes (EHy15³⁵), -nes f. *state of*
man, human nature, incarnation, BH;
Æ : *humaneness, humanity.* ['*mannish-*
ness']
menniscu f. *humanity, human state,* CP39²⁴.
mentel (æ) m., gs. mentles *mantle, cloak,*
CP. [*L.* mantellum]
mentelprēon m. *mantle-pin, brooch,* TC533'.
menung=(*mynung), mynegung

mēo mf? gs. and nap. mēon *shoe-sole, sock?*
sandal? RB,WW.
meocs=meox
+meodnes f. *dignity,* DR192'. [=medem-
nes]
meodo, meodu=medu; meodom-=medem-
meodoma=medema; mēodren=mēdren
meodum-=medem-
meolc I. *giving milk, milch.* II. (i) f.
'*milk,' BH*; Æ,AO.
meolcdēond (i; -tēond) m. *suckling.* JVPs
8³.
meolcen (i¹, y¹) adj. *of milk,* LCD
meolcfæt n. *milk-pail,* WW123²⁸.
meolchwīt '*milk-white,' GPH.*
meolcian (i, y) *to 'milk,' Lcd,Shr :* (±) *give*
milk, suckle, Bl.
meolclīðe (ea) *soft as milk,* CM49.
meolcsūcend m. *suckling,* WW.
meolo (*Bo*)=melu; meoloc (CP)=meolc
meolu=melu; meoluc=meolc
mēon v. mēo.
mēoning m. *garter,* WW234²² (wēon-).
meord f. *reward, pay,* BH GD. ⌜*Goth.*
mizdō]
meoring f. *danger?* Ex62?
meorð=meord
mēos I. m. *moss, BH.* ['*mese*'] II. adj.
mossy.
mēose=mēse; meotod, meotud=metod
meottoc (*Cp*)=mattuc
+meotu=+metu nap. of +met.
meotud-=metod-
meoðon (BH)=miðon pret. pl. of mīðan.
mēowle† f. *maiden, virgin : woman.* ⌜*Goth.*
mawilō]
meox (e, i, y) n. *filth, dirt, dung,* Æ,Bo,Lk.
['*mix*']
meoxbearwe f. *dung-barrow,* WW336⁸.
meoxen=mixen
meoxforce (y¹) f. *dung-fork,* WW106³⁹.
meoxscofl (e¹) f. *dung-shovel,* LL455,17.
meoxwilie (cs) f. *dung-basket,* LPs80⁷.
mēr-=mǣr-
mera m. *incubus,* GL.
merc (A)=mearc; merce=merece
+merce=+mierce; mercels=mircels
Mercisc=Miercisc
mercong (NG)=mearcung
mere I. m. (†) *sea, ocean, An :* *lake, pond,*
pool, cistern, B,Ep,Jn; CP; Mdf. ['*mere*']
II.=mare. III.=miere
mēre (VPs)=mǣre I.
merebāt m. *sea-boat, vessel,* AN246.
merecandel f. *sun,* MET13⁵⁷.
merece m. *smallage, wild celery,* Æ,Gl,Lcd.
merecīest f. *sea-chest, ark,* GEN1317.
meredēað† m. *death at sea,* EX.
meredēor n. *sea-animal,* B558.

merefara m. *sailor*, B502.
merefaroð† m. *surging of the waves*.
merefix m. *sea-fish*, B549.
mereflōd† m. *sea, body of water, deluge*.
mere-grot (Æ) n., -grota (BH) m. *pearl*.
  [v. '*margarite*']
meregrund† m. *lake-bottom, depths of the sea*.
merehengest† m. *sea-horse, ship*.
merehrægl n. *sail*, B1905.
merehūs† n. *sea-house, the ark*, GEN.
merehwearf m. *sea-shore*, Ex516.
mērehwīt *pure white, sterling (of silver)*.
  [mǣre II.]
merelād f. *sea-way*, HU27.
merelīðende† m. *seafaring (man), sailor*.
mere-menn(en), -menin n. *mermaid, siren*,
  Cp,WW. ['*mermin*']
mere-næddra m., -næddre, -nædre f.
  '*murena*,' *sea-adder, lamprey*, GL.
meresmylte *quiet as the sea, calm*, MET21¹².
meresteall m. *stagnant water*, MFH169.
merestrǣt† f. *sea-path*.
merestrēam† m. *sea-water*.
merestrengo f. *strength in swimming*, B523.
mereswīn n. *porpoise, dolphin*, Cp,Lcd.
  ['*mereswine*']
meretorht (æ)† *(rising) bright from the sea*.
meretorr m. *towering wall of the (Red) sea*,
  Ex484.
mereðyssa† m. *ship*, AN.
mereweard m. *sea-warden*, WH53.
merewērig *sea-weary*, SEAF12.
merewīf n. *water-witch*, B1519.
merg (Cp195M)=mearg
merg-=mearg-, meri-, morg-, myrg-
merian *to purify, cleanse*, Sol : test. ['*mere*']
merice (GL)=merce; **merien**=morgen
merig=(1) myrge; (2) mearg
merig-=myrg-; **merigen** (Æ,AO)=morgen
merisc=mersc
merne=mergenne ds. of mergen.
merr-=mierr-; **mērs-**=mǣrs-
mersc (æ) m. '*marsh*,' *swamp*, Gl; CP.
merschōfe m. *marsh-hove*, Lcd35b.
merschop n. *high ground in fenny country*,
  BC2·526.
merscland n. '*marsh-land*,' Chr1098.
merscmealwe f. '*marsh-mallow*,' Lcd.
merscmeargealla m. *gentiana pneumo-
  nanthe*, Lcd.
merscmylen f. *mill in a fen*, KC6·100¹².
merscware pl. *inhabitants of marshes*. (1)
  Romney marsh, CHR796. (2) *the fens?*
  CHR838.
mertze f. *merchandise*, WW32²⁵ : *trading
  dues*, 145²⁸. [L. mercem]
merð=mearð
merðern *made of skins of martens*, CHR
  1075D.

mērðu (N)=mǣrð; **meru** (MtR)=mearu
meruw-, merwe-=mearu(w)-
mēs (K)=mȳs, v. mus.
mesa fpl. *dung*, Lcd37a (v. NP15·272).
mēsan *to eat*, RD41⁵². [mōs]
mēse (ēo, ī, ȳ) f. *table, Æ : what is placed on
  a table*, GL. [L.]
mēshrǣgel (ȳ¹) n. *napkin*, RBL93¹⁰.
mess-=mæss-
mēsta (KGL)=mǣsta superl. of micel.
±**met** (usu. +) *measure (vessel or amount)*,
  Æ : *act of measuring, appointed share,
  quantity, Mt : space, distance, LL : boundary, limit, Bo,Met : manner, degree, way :
  ability, adequacy, capacity : rule, law :
  mood* (gram.) : *metre : moderation, MtR.*
  ealle +mete *in all respects.* on +m. *in vain*,
  RPs88⁴⁸. nānum +m. *by no means, on no
  account.* ['*met*,' '*i-met*']
+**met**† *fit, proper, apt, meet.* adv. -mēte.
+**mēt**=+mōt; -**mēt** v. wēa-m.
meta (Sc153)=mete; **metærn**=meteærn
±**metan**⁵ *to measure, 'mete' out* ('*ymete*'),
  *mark off, Æ,Ex,Mt,VPs : compare, Bo;
  CP : estimate, Bl : pass over, traverse, B.*
±**mētan** I. *to 'meet,' find, find out, fall in
  with, encounter, Bo,Bl; Æ,AO,CP : obtain,
  CP.* II. *to paint, design, ÆGr.* ['*mete*']
metbælg m. *wallet*, LkR22³⁵. [v. '*belly*']
met-cund, -cundlic *metrical*, GL.
mete (æ) m. nap. mettas '*meat*,' *food, BH,
  CP,Lk,Sc*; Æ,AO.
mēte=mǣte
meteærn n. *refectory*, GD,WW.
meteāflīung f. *atrophy*, WW.
meteclȳfa m. *food-store, pantry*, OEG56²⁷⁰.
metecorn n. *allowance of corn to dependants*,
  TC. ['*metecorn*']
metecū f. *cow for killing*, LL450',451.
metecweorra m. *surfeit, indigestion*, Lcd
  3·60⁴.
+**mētednes** f. *finding, discovery*, LPs27⁴.
metefæt [met-] n. *dish*, GPH403.
metefætels m. *cupboard for food*, WW107⁵.
  ['*metefetill*']
meteg-=metg-
metegafol n. *payment in food*, LL448,4⁵.
metegearwa fp. *preparations of food*, Lcd
  78b.
metegyrd=metgeard
metelǣst=metelīest
metelāf f. *leavings of a meal*, Æ,LL.
metelēas *without food*, Æ.
mete-līest (AO), -lē(a)st, -līst, -lȳst f. *lack
  of food, starvation*.
metend m. *measurer*, WW398²⁸ : *God*, GEN
  1809.
+**mētend** '*inventor*,' GPH391.

metenēad f. *requisites in the way of food*, LL 383'? (v. 2·145).

mēter n. *'metre,' versification, Bf,BH.* [*L.*]

meterǣdere m. *reader at meal-times*, NC 309.

mētercrǣft m. *art of versifying*, BH 258[15].

mētercund *relating to metre*, WW.

mētere m. *painter*, Ct,WW.

mēterfers n. *hexameter verse*, BH.

mētergeweorc n. *verse*, BH 484[9].

mēterlic *metrical*, OEG 124.

metern=meteærn

mēterwyrhta m. *metrician, poet*, WW.

metesōcn f. *craving, appetite*, LCD 65a.

metesticca m. *spoon*, WW 126[35].

meteswamm m. *edible mushroom*, WW.

metetīd f. *meal-time*, GD 277[24].

meteðearfende† *needing food, destitute*, AN.

meteðegn m. *seneschal, steward*, Ex 131.

meteðiht *well-nourished*, LCD 3·68[17].

meteðing n. *operation connected with cooking*, CHRD 19[19].

meteūtsiht f. *dysentery*, WW.

+**metfæst** *moderate, reasonable, modest, meek*.

+**metfæstan** (æ[1], e[2]) *to compare*, LPs 48[21].

+**metfæstlic** *moderate : modest, gentle.* adv. -līce *modestly, humbly, meekly.*

+**metfæstnes** f. *moderation, modesty, sobriety*, BH.

metfæt=metefæt

+**metfæt** n. *a measure (vessel)*, Æ,WW.

+**metfest**-=metfæst-

metgeard f. *measuring-stick, rod, pole, perch*, WW 147[20].

±**metgian** *to moderate, control, govern*, Æ, CP : *weigh in mind, consider : assign due measure to : prepare : regulate.*

+**metgiend** m. *ruler, governor*, AS 11[2].

±**metgung** f. *moderation, temperance*, AO, CP : *reflection, meditation : rule, regulation.*

metgyrd=metgeard

metian I. *to provision*, CHR 1013. II.= metgian

mēting I. (±) f. *meeting (friendly or hostile)*, Æ,AO : *assembly, congregation*, Ps,RB : *finding, discovery : agreement*, GD. II. *painting, picture*, Æ.

+**metlǣcan** *to moderate*, CP 101[12].

+**metlic** *measurable : fitting, suitable : moderate*, CP : *mild, discreet*, CP. adv. -līce.

+**metlicung** f. *adjustment, regulation*, LCD 60b,86a.

+**metnes** f. *moderation*, RWH 7[19].

+**mētnes** (MH 136[23])=+mētednes

metod† m. *fate : Creator, God, Christ.*

+**metodlīce** *inevitably*, ByH 40[25].

metodsceaft† f. *decree of fate, doom, death.* gewītan m. sēon, tō metodsceafte *to die*, B.

metodwang (meotud-) m. *battlefield*, AN 11.

metrāp m. *measuring-rope, sounding-line*, Cp 178B.

mētsceat=mēdsceatt

metscipe m. *feeding, meal*, LL 178,8[1]. [*'meteship'*]

metseax n. *meat-knife*, AO 244[18].

±**metsian** *to supply with food*, Æ.

metsung f. *feeding, provisioning*, CHR.

+**metta** m. *sharer in food, guest*, Æ. [*'mette'*]

mettac=mattuc; **mettas** v. mete.

mette-=mete-

mētte pret. 3 sg. of mētan.

metten f. *one of the Fates*, Bo 102[22].

mettian=mētan I.; +**metting**=+mēting -**mētto** v. wēa-m.; **mettoc** (*Ep*)=mattuc

mettrum=medtrum; **metud** (N)=metod

mēðe (†) *tired, worn out, dejected, sad : troublesome.* [*Ger.* müde]

meðel=mæðel; **meðema**=medema

+**mēðgian** *to exhaust, tire out*, GU 950.

mēðian *to grow weary*, LCD 57a.

mēðig *tired, weary*, AO 86,134.

meðl=mæðl, mæðel; **meðl-**=mæðl-, maðel-

mēðnes f. *fatigue*, OET (Bd[2]).

+**mēðrian** *to honour*, LL (1·384[4]).

mēw=mǣw; **mexscofl**=meoxscofl

miccl-=micel-, micl-

micel (y) adj. comp. māra, superl. mǣst(a) *great, intense, much, many*, Æ,BC,Bo,Chr, *Lcd,MH* ; AO,CP : (of time) *long : loud.* sb. with gen. *much*, AO,CP. adv. *greatly, much*, CP,Gen. [*'mickle'*]

micelǣte (y) *greedy*, SHR 16[20].

micoldōond (i[2]) *doing great things*, DR 15[7].

micelhēafdede *big-headed*, WW 380[12].

micelian=miclian

micellic *great, splendid, magnificent.* adv. -līce *grandly : very, exceedingly.*

micelmōd *magnanimous*, PPs 144[3].

micelnes (y) f. *greatness, size*, Æ,CP : *mass : quantity : multitude, abundance : magnificence : great deed.*

micelsprecende *boasting*, LPs 11[4].

micelu (y) f. *largeness, size*, LCD.

micg=mycg

micga m., **micge** f. *urine*, Lcd. [*'mig'*]

micgern (y) *internal fat, suet*, WW. [*'midgern'*]

micgða=migoða; **micl-**=micel-

micle, micles, miclum adv. (obl. cases of micel) *much, very, greatly.*

±**miclian** (y) *to become great, increase*, AN ; AO : *make great, make larger, magnify, extol*, Bl. [*'mickle'*]

±**miclung** (y) f. *the doing of great things, great deeds, greatness*, Ps.

micul=micel

mid I. prep. w. d. inst. (WS) and a. (A only) *with, in conjunction with, in company with, together with, Æ,Chr : into the presence of : through, by means of, by : among, in : at* (time) : *in the sight of, opinion of, Æ.* m. ealle, eallum *altogether, completely, entirely, Æ, Chr.* m. ðām *with that, thereupon.* m. ðām ðe *when.* m. ðām ðæt *through that, on that account, because, when.* m. ðȳ (ðe) *when, while.* **II.** adv. *at the same time, together, simultaneously, likewise,* Lcd. ['MID'] **III.**=midd

midd superl. mid(e)mest *mid, middle, midway, BH,CP,Lcd.* tō middes adv. *in the midst.* ['mid']

middæg m. '*mid-day,*' *noon,* Lcd : *one of the canonical hours, sext, WW.* fram middæge oð nōn *from noon to 3 p.m., Æ.*

middæglic adj. *mid-day, meridian,* BH,Ps.

middægsang m. *mid-day service, sext,* RB, LL.

middægtīd f. *noon,* WW 450[5].

middægðēnung f. *dinner,* NC 309.

middan (on) v. onmiddan.

middandæglic=middæglic

middan(g)eard m. *the globe, world, earth, B, Jn;* Æ,AO,CP : *mankind.* ['middenerd']

middan(g)earden *worldly,* Sc 16[16].

middangeardlic *earthly,* BH 118[19].

middansumer m. *midsummer* (24 *June*).

middanwinter m. *midwinter, Christmas.*

midde I. adj. *mid, middle.* **II.** f. *middle, centre* (only in phr. on middan).

middel I. n. '*middle,*' *centre, El,Mk,Ps, WW : waist, Bl.* **II.** adj. (superl. midlest) *middle, intermediate, BH,LL.*

middelǣdr f. *median vein,* Lcd.

middeldæg m. *mid-day, noon,* Lcd.

middeldǣl m. *middle,* AO 10[6].

middelfinger m. *middle finger,* LL,WW.

middel-flēra m., -flēre f. *partition, septum,* WW.

middelfōt m. *instep,* WW 160[25].

middelgemǣru npl. *central region,* Sol 255.

middelgesculdru npl. *part of the body between the shoulders,* WW 159[17].

middelhrycg m. *middle ridge,* Ct.

middelniht† f. *midnight.*

middelrīce n. *the middle kingdom,* Chr 887A.

midden-=middan-

midde-niht, -neaht, middernæht (*LkL*) f. '*midnight.*' [v. ES 39·350]

middesumer=middansumer

middeweard I. adv. *in the middle of, through the midst.* **II.** adj. *middle, AO.* **III.** sb. *middle, LPs.* ['midward']

middewinter=middanwinter

middun- (N)=middan-

mideard=middangeard

midel=middel; **midemest** v. midd.

midfæsten m. *mid-Lent,* Chr 1047.

mid-feorh, -feorwe (CP), -ferh(ð) mn. *youth, middle age* ('*juventus*' GL).

midfyrhtnes f. *middle age* Bl 163.

midgearwung f. *preparation,* MkL p 5[10].

midgeslō n. *companion,* OEG 680? (v. BTs).

midhelp [mið-] f. *help, assistance,* DR 29[18].

midhilte f. *middle of the hilt,* WW 199[21].

midhlȳt m. *fellowship,* Tf 103[7].

midhrif nm. '*midriff,*' *diaphragm,* Lcd : *bowels.*

midhriōre (y²) n. *diaphragm, Cp,WW.* ['midred']

-midian v. ā-.

midl n. *bit (of a bridle), Æ : oar-thong,* WW.

midle=middele, ds. of middel.

+midleahtrian *to reproach,* Sc 200[6].

midlen I. (e) n. *middle, centre, midst.* **II.** adj. *midmost,* ÆGr 14[21].

midlencten n. *mid-Lent,* Chr.

midlest superl. of middel.

midlhring m. *ring of a bit,* WW 456[14].

+midlian *to halve, divide,* CPs 54[27].

±midlian *to bridle, curb, CP : muzzle,* W 191.

midligend m. *mediator,* BH 206[26].

midlung f. *middle, midst.* adv. -lunga *to a moderate extent.*

midmest v. midd; **midmycel**=medmicel

midnedæg m. *mid-day,* Æ,MH.

midnes f. *middle, midst,* HL.

midniht f. *midnight,* Æ.

midor compar. of midd, adj.

midrād f. *riding in company,* LL 175,4.

midrece=mȳderce; **midrif**=midhrif

midsingend m. *one who sings with another,* WW 129[25].

±midsīō(eg)ian *to accompany, associate with,* GL.

midspecend m. *interlocutor, advocate,* MP 1·592[6].

midsp(r)eca m. *advocate,* ÆH : '*liberator,*' *excuser,* Chrd 62[26].

midsprecende *speaking for,* Nic.

midstrēam m. *mid-stream,* KC 5·380.

midsumer (o³) m. '*midsummer,*' *Bf,BH.*

Midsumermōnað *June,* Men (Hickes).

midswēgan *'concinere,'* EPs 57[3].

midðām, midðy=mid ðam, mid ðȳ

midðeahtian *to consent,* RHy 6[27].

midðolian *to sympathise,* Sc.

midðrōwung f. *compassion,* Sc.

midweg m. '*midway,*' *CP*; GD 314[11].

midwinter m. '*midwinter,*' *Christmas, Chr, Lcd.*

Midwintermōnað *December,* Men (Hickes).

midwist f. *presence, society : cooperation, participation,* LL 378[6].

midwunung f. *living in company, fellowship*, Æ.

midwyrhta m. *cooperator*, CP.

midyrfenuma m. *coheir*, Sc 148⁴.

mieht=miht

±**mieltan** (i, y) (tr. and intr.) *to 'melt,' El, Lcd*; Æ: *digest, CP*: *refine, purge*: *exhaust*, MH 54³.

Mierce, Miercan pl. *Mercians*: *Mercia*, CHR (lit. *borderers*; cp. mearc).

+**mierce** (e) n. *boundary, limit*, AA 3³ : *sign, token*, MkL 16¹⁷.

Miercisc (e) *Mercian*, LL 464,1.

miere (e, i, y) f. *'mare,' BH,WW.* [mearh]

mierra (e) m. *deceiver*, MtL 27⁶³.

±**mierran** (e, i, y) *to 'mar,' disturb, confuse, CP*: *scatter, squander, waste*: *upset, hinder, obstruct*, Æ; AO : *err, MtL.*

mierrelse (y) f. *cause of offence*, JUL 338.

mierrend (y) *prodigal, wasteful*, NC 311.

mierring (e, i, y) f. *hindering*: *squandering, waste*, CP.

±**mīgan**¹ *to make water*, LCD,ÆGR.

migeða=migoða; **migga** (Æ)=micga

miggung, mīging f. *making water*, WW.

migol *diuretic*, LCD.

migoða m. *urine*, LCD.

miht (a, æ, ea, e, ie, y) **I.** f. *'might,' bodily strength*: *power, authority, ability, BH,Bl, Lcd*; Æ : *virtue, Lcd*: *mighty work, miracle*, G. pl. *Gods*, OEG : *angels*, Æ. **II.** adj. †*mighty, powerful*: *possible*.

mihte pret. sg. of magan.

mihtelēas=mihtlēas

mihtelic, mihtlic *possible*. adv. -līce *mightily, powerfully, by might, miraculously*, Æ,BH. [*'mightly'*]

mihtesetl n. *seat of power*, EETS 34·301.

mihtful *powerful*, HL 15¹³⁷.

mihtig (æ, ea) *'mighty,' important, BH,CP, VPs* : *able, effective, Lcd* : *possible*. adv. -līce, Bo. [*'mightly'*]

mihtlēas *powerless, weak, exhausted*, Æ.

mihtloc (ea¹) *belt of might*, CREAT 88.

mihtmōd n. *violent temper, passion*, Ex 149.

mihtu=miht ðu

mīl I. f. *'mile,' Bl,WW*; AO. [*L.*] **II.** n. *millet, WW.* [*'mile'*]

milc (VPs)=meolc; **milcan**=melcan

milde I. adj. *'mild,' merciful, kind, generous, gentle, meek, B,Bl,Gu,LL*; AO,CP. **II.** adv. *mercifully, graciously*, Cr.

mildēaw=meledēaw

mildelic *propitious*. adv. *graciously, affably, kindly, AO*; Æ. [*'mildly'*]

+**mildgian** *to mitigate, make mild or calm*, Ps. [mildian]

mild-heort, -heortlic *merciful, clement, compassionate, MtL* (milt-); Æ,AO. [*'mild-heart'*] adv. -līce, Æ,CP.

mildheortnes f. *loving-kindness, mercy, pity, LL*; Æ,AO. [*'mildheartness'*]

mildian *to become mild*, GPH 399.

mildnes f. *mildness, mercy*, NC 309.

milds=milts

mīlgemæt m. *mile-measure, milestone?* KC 3·252²¹.

mīlgemearc n. *measure by miles*, B 1362.

mīlgetæl n. *mile*, WE 51,59.

milisc (e, y) *sweet, mild, mulled*, GL,LCD.

mīlite *soldiers*, NC 309.

mīlitisc *military*, GD. [*L.* miles]

mīlpæð† m. *distance reckoned by miles? road with milestones on it?* EL,EX,RUN.

+**milscad** *honeyed, mixed with honey*, WW.

milscapuldor f. *sweet apple tree*, GL.

milt m. (LCD 87a)=milte; **milt**-=mild-, milte-

milt-coðe, -coðu f. *disease of the spleen*, LCD.

milte mf. *'milt,' spleen, Gl,Lcd*; Æ.

miltesēoc *splenetic*, LCD,WW.

miltestre=myltestre

miltewærc m. *pain in the spleen*, LCD.

milts f. *mercy, compassion, benevolence, kindness, favour, B,VPs*; CP : (†) *joy*. [*'milce'*]

±**miltsian** (w. d.) *to compassionate, pity, show mercy, Bo,Mt,Ps*; Æ,CP : *soften, make merciful*. [*'milce,' 'i-milce'*]

±**miltsi(g)end** m. *pitier*, Æ,Ps.

miltsigendlic *pardonable, venial*, GPH.

miltsung f. (±) *mercy, sympathy, pity, indulgence, pardon*, Æ,CP : *moderation, reduction (of punishment)*, LL 468,10.

miltwræc=miltewærc; **milz**=milts

mīma m. *'mime,' MH.*

+**mimor** (w. d.) *well-known*. adv. -līce *by heart*.

min† ? *evil, harmful*. [v. BTs, and NED s.v. '*min*']

mīn I. pron. *my, 'mine,' Æ,B,G.* mīnes ðances *by my will*. **II.** gs. of ic *of me*.

mind I. *diadem*, DR 92⁵ (v. LF 160). **II.**= mynd

mindōm? m. *state of exile*, PPs 54⁷.

mine=myne; **minet**-=mynet-

minlic *petty* (Swt).

mīnlīce adv. *in my manner*, WW 449¹⁶.

minnæn *'manipulos,' sheaves?* EPs 128⁷; *'magnalia,'* 105²¹.

minne I. nap. of min? **II.**=myne

minnen=menen

±**minsian** *to diminish*, W.

minsung f. *parsimony*, OEG 3748.

mint? (MtR), minte f. *'mint,' G*; CP; Mdf. [*L.*]

minthamm m. *field of mint*, KC 5·374'.

mio-=meo-
mircapuldur (Cp)=milscapuldor?
Mirce, Mircan=Mierce
mirce I. (y;=ie) adj. *murky, dark, black,
uncanny, evil, B,Ph.* II. adv.? An1315.
III. n. *murkiness, darkness, Da*448.
['*murk*']
mircels (e, y;=ie) mf. *sign, token, seal,
signet* : *mark, marked place,* ÆL : *trophy,*
Gu429. [mearc]
mire=miere; mîre=mînre gdfs. of mîn.
mirg-, mîrig-=myrg-
mirgŏ, mirhŏ=myrgŏ; mirr-=mierr-
misbegān anv. *to disfigure,* MtL6¹⁶.
misbēodan² (w. d.) *to ill-use, injure, do
wrong to, LL,W.* ['*misbede*']
misboren *abortive, Lcd* : *degenerate.* ['*mis-
born*']
misbrŏden *drawn aside,* WW224²¹.
misbyrd f. *abortion,* Gl.
misbyrdo f. *malformation,* Lcd.
misbysnian *to set a bad example,* ÆH2·50⁴.
miscalfian *to cast a calf,* WW456¹².
miscenning f. *a mistake or variation in
pleading before a court* : *a fine exacted for
this, EC,LL* (v. 2·148). ['*miskenning*']
miscian *to mix, apportion,* Bo,Lcd. [*L.*]
miscrōcettan *to croak or shriek horribly,*
Guth36¹. [crācettan]
miscwēman *to displease,* ÆL23²⁸⁷.
miscweŏan⁵ *to speak ill, curse,* NG : *speak
incorrectly.*
miscyrran (=ie) *to pervert,* Met2⁸.
misdǣd f. '*misdeed,' evil deed, sin, CP;* Æ.
misdōn anv. *to do evil, transgress, do amiss,
err, JnL,LL,W.* ['*misdo*']
mîse=mēse
misefesian *to cut the hair amiss,* LL(254¹³).
misendebyrdan (i⁴) *to arrange amiss,* LL382.
misenlic, misendlic=missenlic
misfadian *to order amiss,* LL.
misfadung f. *misconduct, irregularity,* RB,
WW.
misfaran⁶ *to go wrong, transgress, CP* : *fare
ill, Æ,W.* ['*misfare*']
misfēdan (oe) *to nourish ill,* EVPs.
misfeng m. *misdeed, sin,* NC309.
misfēran *to do wrong, err, Æ.* ['*misfere*']
misfōn⁷ *to make a mistake, be deceived* : *fail
to get.*
misgedwield n. *error, perversion,* Jul326.
misgehygd fn. *evil thought,* An772.
misgelimp n. *misfortune,* W211³⁰.
misgemynd f. *evil memory,* Sol495.
mis(ge)widere m. *bad weather, storm,* Lcd,
VH.
misgrētan *to greet amiss, insult,* Ct.
misgȳman *to neglect,* LL. ['*misyeme*']
mishæbbende *being ill,* MtL8¹⁶.

mishealdan⁷ *not to keep, to neglect,* Æ (9¹³⁰).
mishealdsumnes f. *carelessness,* LL(196³).
mishērnes (=îe²) f. *act of disobedience,* W.
mis-hweorfed, -hwyrfed, -hworfen *perverted, inverted,* Bo,Gl.
mishȳran (=îe²) *to hear amiss, not to listen
to, disobey, RB,W.* ['*mishear*']
mislǣdan *to '*mislead,' Æ.*
mislǣran *to teach amiss, give bad advice to,
ÆL5·119.* ['*mislear*']
mislǣr f. *ill teaching, evil suggestion,* Sc.
mislēc-=mislîc-
mislic *unlike, various, manifold, Bl,Bo;* Æ,
CP : *wandering, erratic.* ['*mislich*'] adv.
-lîce *in various ways, diversely, aimlessly,
Bo,Chr.* ['*misliche*']
mislîcian (w. d.) *to displease, disquiet, Æ,
CP.* ['*mislike*']
mislîcnes f. *variety, diversity, Æ.*
mislîcum *variously,* AS54⁴.
mislimp n. *misfortune,* VHy,WW.
mislimpan³ impers. w. d. *to go wrong, turn
out badly,* AO.
mislybban (=i²) *to lead a bad life, Æ.* ['*mis-
live*']
mismacian *to mar,* ByH64³.
mismicel *of varying sizes?* Ex373.
misrǣcan *to abuse,* ÆH2·590'.
misrǣd m. *misguidance, Æ* : *misconduct, Æ.*
misrǣdan *to advise wrongly, RB* : *read
wrongly,* ApT3¹¹.
miss n. *absence, loss,* ÆL23²⁷¹.
miss-=mis-
missan (w. g.) *to '*miss' (a mark), B* : (w. d.)
escape the notice of a person.
missare=missere
misscrence *distorted, shrivelled,* Guth.
misscrȳdan *to clothe amiss,* ÆH1·530'.
misse-=mis-
missenlic *various, manifold, different, diverse,* AO. adv. -lîce, CP.
missenlicnes f. *variety, diversity* : '*qualitas'?*
GD46⁹.
misseret n. *half-year, year.*
misspōwan⁷ *to fare badly,* AO82³⁴.
missprecan⁵ *to grumble, murmur,* JnL6⁴¹,⁴³.
mist m. '*mist,' Æ,Bo,Met,WW* : *dimness
(of eyesight), Lcd.*
mist-=mis-
mistǣcan *to teach amiss, Æ.* ['*misteach*']
mistel m. *mistletoe, Cp,Ep* : *basil, Lcd.*
['*missel*']
mistellām n. *birdlime,* WW279¹⁵.
misteltān (i²) m. '*mistletoe,' WW.*
mistglōm m? *misty gloom,* WH47.
misthelm m. *covering of mist,* Jul470.
misthliŏt n. *misty cliff, cloud-capped slope.*
mistian *to be or grow misty, ÆGr.* ['*mist*']
mistîd f. *evil time,* FM360¹².

mistīdan (impers.) *to miscarry, fail,* LL 348'.
['*mistide*']

mistig '*misty,*' *B.*

mistihtan (=y²) *to lead astray, dissuade,* Æ.

mistihtendlic *dehortative,* ÆGR 225¹².

mistil-=mistel-

mistīmian [impers. w. d.] *to happen amiss, Bas.* ['*mistime*']

mistlic=mislic

mistran *to grow dim,* DEUT 34⁷.

mistrīwan *to mistrust,* DR 39¹⁶.

mistūcian *to ill-treat,* CHR 1083,GD 15.

misðēon³ *to mis-thrive, degenerate,* CHRD,GL.

misðyncan (impers.) *to be mistaken,* APT 14²⁵.

misweaxan⁶ *to grow improperly,* ÆH 2·74¹².

miswendan *to pervert, abuse,* Æ : *be perverted, err,* Æ.

miswende *erring, ill-behaving,* Æ.

miswenian *to misuse, abuse,* Sc 224¹⁰ (?= miswerian, MLN 25·80).

misweorc n. *misdeed,* JnR 3¹⁹.

misweorðan³ *to turn out amiss,* W 240⁴.

miswidere=misgewidere

miswissian *to mislead,* LL 130; 381.

miswrītan¹ *to write incorrectly,* ÆGr. ['*miswrite*']

miswurðlan (=eo²) *to dishonour, ill-treat,* LL 381,25.

miswyssigan=miswissian

mīte f. '*mite*' (*small insect*), WW 122⁶ (v. BTs).

mitta m., mitte f. *a measure, bushel, Ct, WW;* Æ,CP. ['*mit*'; metan]

±mittan *to meet, meet with, find.*

mitte=mitta

±mitting f. *meeting, convention,* AO.

mittȳ=mid ðȳ; mið (*LkL*)=mid

mīðan¹ *to hide, conceal* (tr. and intr.), *keep to oneself, dissemble, BH,Bo,WW*; CP : *conceal oneself, remain concealed, Lcd* : (†) *avoid, shun, refrain from.* ['*mithe*']

mīðgian *to conceal,* GD 122³.

mīðl=mīdl; mix=meox

mixen (y) f. *dung-heap, dung,* Æ,LkL. ['*mixen*']

mixendynge (y¹) f. *dung,* LL 454,9.

mixenplante f. *nightshade (plant),* LCD.

mixlan=miscian

mōd n. (±) *heart, mind, spirit,* '*mood,*' *temper, B,BH,Bl;* Æ,AO,CP : *courage, B;* AO : *arrogance, pride,* AO : *power, violence.* +mōd *of one mind, harmonious, peaceful,* CP.

mōdblind† *blind, undiscerning.*

mōdblissiende *exulting,* PPs 67¹⁷.

mōdbysgung f. *anxiety,* DOM 84.

mōdcearig *sorrowful of heart,* WA 2.

mōdcearu† f. *sorrow, grief.*

mōdcræft† m. *intelligence.*

mōdcræftig *intelligent,* CRA 62.

mōddor=mōdor

mōddren *of mothers,* APT 4¹².

mōddri(g)e=mōdrige; mōde-=mōdig-

mōdearfoð n. *grief of mind,* †Hy 4⁸⁷.

mōdeg=mōdig; mōder=mōdor

mōdercynd=mēdrengecynd

mōderge=mōdrige

mōdful *proud, haughty,* LCD 3·188'.

mōdgehygd† n. *thought.*

mōdgemynd† n. *mind, thought.*

mōdgēomor† *sad, dejected.*

mōdgeðanc m. *thought, understanding, mind.*

mōdgeðōht m. *thought, understanding, mind.*

mōdgeðyldig *patient,* AN 983.

mōdgewinna m. *care,* GEN 2797.

mōdgian=mōdigian

mōdgidanc (N)=mōdgeðanc

mōdglæd *joyous,* GU 1311.

mōdglēaw *wise,* SOL 180.

mōdhæp? *brave,* EX 242 (GK).

mōdhete m. *hatred,* GEN 1756.

mōdhord n. *secret thoughts,* AN 172.

mōdhwæt† *brave, bold.*

mōdig (CP), mōdi *spirited, daring, bold, brave, high-souled, magnanimous, B;* Æ : *impetuous, headstrong,* Æ; CP : *arrogant, proud,* Æ,CP. ['*moody*']

mōdigan, mōdigian *to grow proud or overbearing, be high-minded, glory, exult, show bravery,* Æ : *take offence through pride,* Æ.

mōdiglic (mōde-) *high-souled, lofty, proud : brave, bold : splendid, magnificent.* adv. -līce, *Ma* (mōde-). ['*moodily*']

mōdignes f. *greatness of soul : pride, arrogance, haughtiness,* Æ. ['*moodiness*']

mōdilic=mōdiglic

mōdlēas *spiritless,* KGL 66⁴⁰ : *senseless,* CHRD.

mōdlēast f. *want of courage, despondency,* Æ.

mōdlēof *dear, precious,* FT 28.

mōdlufu† f. *heart's affection, love.*

mōdnes (RWH 2³⁶)=mōdignes

+mōdod *disposed,* ÆH 1·524¹⁸.

mōdor (e²) f., ds. mēder '*mother,*' *WW;* (*of animals*), *LL;* AO,CP.

mōdorcild (mōð-) n. *a child of one's (own) mother,* PPs 68⁸.

mōdorcynn n. *maternal descent,* CHR 1067 D.

mōdorhealf f. *mother's side,* CHR 1076 D.

mōdorhrif n. *womb,* PPs.

mōdorlēas (e²) *motherless,* W 228²².

mōdorlic (e²) *maternal,* ÆGr. ['*motherly*'] adv. -līce.

mōdorlufu f. *love for a mother,* NC 309.

mōdorslaga m. *matricide,* WW 335⁶.

mōdrige, mōdrie f. *mother's sister, maternal aunt*, Æ,AO : *cousin*. [mōdor]

mōdrōt *valiant*, AN 1493.

mōdsefa† m. *heart, mind, spirit, soul : thought, imagination, purpose, character.*

mōdsēoc *sick at heart*, GEN 1235.

mōdsēocnes f. *disease of the heart*, WW 199³⁵.

mōdsnotor† *wise.*

mōdsorg† f. *heart-sorrow.*

mōdstaðol m. *principle, character*, LL (318 n1).

mōd-staðolnes, -staðolfæstnes f. *firmness of mind*, W 53¹⁰.

+**mōdsum** *accordant, in agreement*, CP 360¹³.

+**mōdsumian** *to agree*, CP.

+**mōdsumnes** f. *agreement, concord*, CP.

mōdswīð *resolute*, PsC 89.

mōd-ðracu f. gs. -ðræce *courage*, B 385.

mōdðrēa m. *anguish*, RD 4⁵⁰.

mōdðwǣre *meek*, LPs 24⁹.

mōdðwǣrnes f. *patience, meekness*, W.

mōdur=mōdor

mōdwǣg m. *proud wave*, Ex 499.

mōdwelig *gifted, talented, wise*, CP 9¹².

mōdwlanc† *stout-hearted : haughty.*

mōdwyn f. *heart's joy, property*, RD 87⁷.

moetan (Cp)=mētan

mohða, mohðe (N)=moððe

molcen n. *coagulated or curdled milk*, LCD, WW. [*Ger.* molke]

+**molcen** *milked*, LCD 34a.

molda? m. v. molde II.

moldærn (e²)† n. *grave.*

moldcorn n. *granular tuber of saxifraga granulata, and the plant itself*, LCD.

molde I. f. *sand, 'mould,' dust, soil*, Cp,BH, GK; Æ : *land, country : world*. **II**? f. *top of the head*, Lcd 3·42 (or molda.?). ['*mould*']

moldern=moldærn

moldgewind n. *top of the head*, NC 310.

moldgræf† n. *grave.*

moldhrērende *moving upon earth*, CREAT 27.

moldhȳpe f. *heap of dust*, ÆH 1·492'.

moldstōw f. *site, sepulchre*, GPH 391.

moldweg† m. *earth.*

moldwyrm m. *earth-worm*, SOUL 72.

molegn n. *curds*, GL.

molegnstycce n. *piece of curd*, GL.

moling=molegn

molsn n? *decay*, NC 310.

±**molsnian** *to moulder, decay*, Æ.

molten pp. of meltan.

momra=mamera, mamor; **mon**=man

mōna m. '*moon*,' Bo,Lcd; Æ,AO,CP.

mōnanǣfen m. *Sunday evening*, LL.

mōnandæg m. '*Monday*,' Bf,Jn.

mōnanniht f. *Monday eve, i.e. Sunday evening*, LL.

mōnað m. nap. mōn(e)ðas, mōnað '*month*,' BH,Bo,Lk,Lcd; AO,CP. [mōna]

mōnaðādl f. *morbus menstrualis*, BH.

mōnaðādlig *menstruous*, BH 78⁵.

mōnaðblōd n. '*menstruum*,' WW.

mōnaðbōt f. *penance for a month*, LL (278¹¹).

mōnaðfylen f. *time of full moon*, OEG.

mōnaðgecynd f. '*menstruum*,' LCD.

mōnaðlic *monthly, lunar*, GL : as sb.= mōnaðādl, LCD.

mōnaðsēoc I. *menstruous*, Æ. **II.**=mōnsēoc

mōnaðsēocnes (o²) f. *lunacy*, LCD 1·170⁴.

moncus=mancus; **mond**=mand

mōndæg=mōnandæg; **mōne** f.=mōna

mōnelic *lunar*, Æ,LCD.

+**mong**=+mang; **monig**=manig

mōnlic=mōnelic; **monn**=mann

mōnoð=mōnað

mōnsēoc '*moonsick*,' *lunatic, epileptic*, MtR.

mont=munt; **mōnð**=mōnað

monuc=munuc

mōr m. '*moor*,' *morass, swamp*, B; Mdf : *hill, mountain*, AO.

morað (ō?) n. *sweet boiled wine with herbs*, GL,LCD. [*L.* moratum]

mōrbēam (ā, ū) m. *mulberry tree, bramble*, VPs. [v. '*more*']

mōrberie f. *mulberry* (*fruit*), ÆL 25⁵⁷⁶.

more f. *carrot, parsnip*, Lcd,WW. ['*more*']

moreð=morað

mōrfæsten n. *moor-fastness*, CHR.

mōrflēoge f. '*cariscus*,' *a kind of fly*, NC 310.

morgen (a, e) m. ds. morgenne '*morn*,' *morning, forenoon*, B,MtL,VPs : *sunrise*, B : *morrow*, Æ,B; CP. on mor(gen)ne (1) *in the morning*, (2) *to-morrow.*

morgenceald *chill at morn*, B 3022.

morgencolla m. *morning terror*, JUD 245.

morgendæg (e¹) m. *morrow*, BL,GUTH.

morgendlic=morgenlic

morgendrenc m. *morning drink*, LCD.

morgengebedtīd f. *morning prayer*, GUTH 40²⁵.

morgengifu f. *gift by a husband to his wife the morning after the wedding*, BC,WW. ['*moryeve*']

morgenlēoht n. *dawn, morning*, B.

morgenlic *matutinal, morning : of the morrow*. morgenlica dæg *to-morrow.*

morgenlong *lasting a morning*, B 2895.

morgenmæsse f. *morning mass, first mass*, ANS 84·2.

morgenmete m. *morning meal*, SOL 192¹⁹.

morgenrēn m. *morning rain*, Az 82.

morgensēoc *sad at morn*, AN 241.

morgenspǣc f. *regular meeting of a guild on the morrow after the guild-feast*, TC. ['*mornspeech*']

morgenspell n. *news published at morn*, EL 970.

morgensteorra m. *morning star*, Bo. ['*morn-star*']

morgenswēg m. *cry at morn*, B129.

morgentīd (a¹, e¹) f. *morning*, CHR,Ps.

morgentīdlic *matutinal*, BPs129⁶.

morgentorht *bright at morn*, AN241.

morgenwacian *to rise early*, WW.

morgenwlǣtung f. *morning sickness*, LCD 169b.

mōrhǣð f. *mountain-heath*, PPs82¹⁰.

mōrheald *heathy, marshy?* Ex61.

mōrhop n. *moor-swamp*, B450.

mōrig *marshy*, GEN41².

mōrlǣs *marshy pasture*, KC3·408²².

mōrland n. '*moor-land,*' *mountain-waste*, LkL.

morne ds., **mornes** gs. of morgen.

morod, moroð=morað

mōrsceaða m. *robber*, NG.

mōrsecg mn. *sedge*, LCD3·140'.

mōrseohtre f. *marshy ditch*, CHRD96²⁸.

mōrslǣd n. *marshy valley*, KC.

mōrstapa m. *traverser of moors*, RUN2.

mortere m. *a mortar*, LCD,WW. [L. mortarium]

morð nm. *death, destruction, homicide,* '*murder,*' AO; Æ : *deadly sin.* ['*murth*']

morð-=morðor-

morðcrundel mn. *barrow raised over a dead body? deadly pool? corpse-pit?* KC3·23'.

morðdǣd f. *murder, deadly sin, crime*, Æ.

morðor nm., gs. morðres (mp. morðras) *deed of violence,* '*murder,*' *homicide, man-slaughter, B,Bl* : *mortal sin, crime* : *injury, punishment, torment, misery.*

morðorbealu† n. *violent death, murder.*

morðorbed n. *bed of death (by violence)*, B 2436.

morðorcofa m. *prison*, AN1006.

morðorcræft m. *murderous crime*, AN177.

morðorcwalu f. *murder*, NC310.

morðorcwealm m. *murder, death*, GNE 152.

morðorhete m. *blood-feud*, B1105.

morðorhof n. *place of torment*, EL1303.

morðorhūs n. *house of torment*, CR1625.

morðorhycgende *with murderous thoughts*, WIF20.

morðorlēan n. *retribution for sin*, CR1612.

morðorscyldig *guilty*, AN1601.

morðorslaga m. *homicide, murderer*, NG.

morðorslagu f. *homicide, murder*, NG.

morðorslege m. *homicide, murder*, LL (148¹⁴).

morð(or)sliht (e²) m. *slaughter, murder.*

morð(or)wyrhta m. *murderer*, W.

morðslaga (Æ)=morðorslaga

morðsliht=morðorsliht; **morður**=morðor

morðweorc n. *deadly work, act which causes death, murder*, LL.

morðwyrhta=morðorwyrhta

moru f. *parsnip, carrot* (=more).

mōrwyrt f. *moor-wort*, LCD48b.

mōs n. I. *bog, marsh, BC.* ['*moss*'] II. n. *food, victuals.* [*Ger.* mus]

mōst, mōste v. *mōtan.

mot n. '*mote,*' *speck, atom, Mt,WW.*

mōt I. (±, usu. +) n. '*moot*' ('*gemot*'), *society, assembly, court, council, synod, Chr,MtL;* Mdf. +m. wyrcan *to take counsel* : *litigation, Bo* : (+) *conflict, encounter.* II. f. *toll, tribute*, MkL. [*Ger.* maut] III. pres. sg. of *mōtan.

±mōtærn (e²) n. *courthouse*, AO.

mōtan* swv. pres. 1, 3 sg. mōt, pres. 2 sg. mōst, pres. pl. mōton, pret. mōste (*may*). *to be allowed, be able to, have opportunity to, be compelled to, must, B,Gen;* AO,CP. mōste ic *would that I might!* ['*mote*']

+mōtan=mētan

mōtbell f. *bell for summoning a moot*, LL. [v. '*moot*']

±mōtbeorh m. *hill of meeting*, BC.

mōtere m. *public speaker*, WW. ['*mooter*']

mōtern=mōtærn

mōtgerēfa m. *moot-reeve, chairman of a moot*, EC342'.

±mōthūs n. *moot-hall, place of assembly*, WW; W. ['*moothouse*']

±mōtian *to speak to or about, converse with, address, harangue, Æ* : *argue, plead, discuss, dispute, Hex.* ['*moot*']

mōtlǣðu sbpl. *courts, assemblies?* TC433²² (v. BTs).

+mōtlēah m. *meadow of meeting*, BC.

+mōtmann m. *orator, counsellor*, WW164³⁵; 310²⁹.

+mōtstede m. *place of meeting*, SOUL152.

±mōtstōw f. *place of meeting, forum*, EPs, GL.

mōtung f. *conversation, discussion*, OEG. ['*mooting*']

mōtweorð (u²) *qualified to attend the moot*, EC343'.

mōðfreten *moth-eaten*, ÆL23⁴³⁷.

mōðor=mōdor

mōððe f. '*moth,*' *Lk,MtL* (mohðe).

mucgwyrt f. *artemisia,* '*mugwort,*' *Lcd, WW.*

mucxle=muscelle; **mūdrica**=mȳderce

mūga m. '*mow,*' *heap of corn,* Æ.

mugan*=magan; **mugwyrt**=mucgwyrt

mūha (Cp)=muga

mūl m. '*mule,*' *Ps*; ÆL. [L. mulus]

mūlhyrde m. *mule-keeper*, ÆGR35⁵.

multon pret. pl. of meltan.

+mun (w. g.) *mindful, remembering*, AO 48[11].

±munan (usu. +) pres. 1, 3 sg. man (mon), 2 manst, pl. munon, pret. munde swv. *to think about, be mindful of, remember, mention*, *Bl,Jul,Lk*; *Æ,AO,CP* : *consider*. ['*i-mune*']

mund f. I.† *hand :palm (of the hand, as a measure)* : *trust, security, protection, guardianship, Æ : protector, guardian : the king's peace : fine for breach of the laws of protection or guardianship of the king's peace*, v. LL2·555; 641. [cp. *Ger.* vormund] II. m. *money paid by bridegroom to bride's father, bridegroom's gift to bride*, CR93. III.=mynd

mundbeorg m. *protecting hill*, PPs124².

mundberd=mundbyrd

mundbora m. *protector, preserver, guardian, advocate, Æ : prefect.*

mundbryce (i²) m. *breach of the laws of protection or guardianship*, LL : *fine for the breach of such laws.*

mundbyrd f. *protection, patronage, help : fine for a breach of the peace*, LL.

±mundbyrdan *to protect*, Bo,VH.

mundbyrdnes f. *protection : security, independence : protector, guardian, advocate.*

mundbyre=mundbyrde (ds. of mundbyrd).

mundcræft m. *protecting power*, LCD 1·384[13].

munde v. munan; +munde=+mynde

mundgripe† m. *hand-grasp*, B.

mundheals f. *protection?* CR445.

±mundian *to protect, watch over, act as guardian of, Æ.*

mundiend m. *protector*, TC525⁸.

mund-lēow, -lēu, -lāu f. *wash-hand basin*, WW. [*ON.* munnlaug]

mundrōf *strong with the hands*, RD84³.

mundwist f. *guardianship, protection*, NC 310.

munec=munuc

munetere=mynetere

mungung=mynegung

+muning f. *remembrance*, CM378.

munt m. *mountain, hill*, Æ,AO,CP. [*L.*]

muntælfen f. *mountain nymph*, WW189⁴. [v. '*elven*']

muntclȳse f. *mountain prison*, W84H.

muntland n. *hill-country*, Lk1³⁹.

munuc (e²) m. '*monk*,' *BH,RB* : (used also of women, A27·255). [*L.* monachus]

munucbehāt n. *monastic vow*, HL18⁸¹,⁹⁵.

munuccild n. *child intended for monastic life*, Æ,BF102¹⁶.

munuccnapa m. *young monk*, GD.

munucgegyrela m. *monastic garb*, BH34²⁷.

munuchād m. *monastic orders, the monastic life*, Æ,BH; CP. ['*monkhood*']

munuchēap m. *company of monks*, BF150¹⁹.

munucian (e²) *to make a monk of*, LL. ['*monk*']

munuclic *monkish, monastic, BH*; Æ. adv. -līce. ['*monkly*']

munuclīf n. *monastic life, Æ : cloister, monastery*, Æ,AO.

munucrēaf n. *monk's garb*, GD27¹⁷.

munucregol m. *monastic rule, mode of life, Æ : a body of monks under a certain rule*, TC544¹².

munucscrūd n. *monk's garb*, ÆP142⁵.

munucstōw f. *place of monks*, BH236²⁵.

munucðēaw m. *monastic rule*, ANS84·7.

munucwīse f. *fashion of a monk*, ÆL 6·247.

mūr m. *wall*, CR1143. [*L.* murus]

mūr-bēam, -berie=mōr-bēam, -berie

murc *dismal, wretched*, PPs145⁶. [myrce]

murcian *to complain, repine, grieve*, CP.

murcnere m. *complainer*, RB21⁵.

murcnian=murcian

murcung f. *complaint, sorrow*, CP.

murge=myrge

murnan³ (and wv.) *to care, be anxious or fearful about, An,Bo,Wald : hesitate : 'mourn,' sorrow, bemoan, Wy : long after*, An37.

murnung f. *complaint, grief*, Bo18¹⁹ (v.l. murcnung), LCD,VH.

murra, murre=myrra, myrre

mūs f. gs. mūs, mūse, nap. mȳs '*mouse*,' *Bo*; Æ; Mdf : *muscle (of the arm)*, WW158⁶.

mus-celle, -cule f. *shell-fish, 'mussel,' Gl.* [*L.*]

muscflēote f? *a small fly found in wine* (mustflēoge? BT), WW121²².

muscle=muscelle

mūsepise f. *mouse-pea, vetch*, WW148³⁵.

mūsfealle (a²) f. *mouse-trap*, WW.

mūsfealu *mouse-coloured*, WW448⁹.

mūshafoc n. *mouse-hawk, buzzard*, WW.

musle=muscelle; musscel (GL)=muscelle

must m. '*must,' new wine, Bo*; Æ. [*L.*]

-mūtian v. be-m.

mūtung f. '*mutuum,' loan*, WW449³⁰.

mūð m. '*mouth,' opening, door, gate, Æ,BH, CP,Mt.*

mūða m. *mouth (of a river), estuary*, AO, CHR : (†) *entrance to a house, door.*

mūðādl f. *mouth-disease*, WW.

mūðberstung f. *eruption of the mouth*, WW.

mūðbona m. *devourer*, B2079.

mūðcoðu f. *mouth-disease*, WW.

mūðettan *to blab out, let out*, Æ(6¹⁶⁰).

mūðfrēo *free to speak*, PPs11⁴.

mūðhæl f. *wholesome speech*, Ex552.

mūðhrōf m. *palate*, OEG332.

mūðlēas *mouthless*, RD61⁹.

mūðsīr *pain in the mouth*, LL.
mūðsealf f. *mouth-salve*, LCD 18ᵇ
mūwa (*WW* 348⁶)=mūga
muxle=muscelle
myce? (ES 43·309), mycel (LW͞S)=mīcel
mycg (i) m. *'midge,'* *Cp,Lcd,WW*.
mycgern=micgern
mycgnet (i) n. *mosquito-net*, WW 183¹³.
mycl-=micl-; myd-=mid-
mydd n. *bushel*, AO 190¹². [*L*. modius]
mȳderce f. *money storing-place, chest*, ÆGR
(IF 48·267).
mygg (GL)=mycg; mȳgð=mǣgð
myhtig=mihtig
mȳhð pres. 3 sg. of mīgan.
myl n. *dust*, JAW 32; ES 41·163. [*Ger.*
müll]
mylc=meolc
myldan=miltan; -myldan v. be-m.
myle-=mylen-
mylen mf. *'mill,'* *KC,LL,RB*; Mdf.
mylendīc f. *mill-dike*, Ct.
mylenfeld m. *mill-field*, KC 5·381′.
mylengafol n. *mill-tax, mill-rent?* NC 310.
mylengear m. *mill-yair*, Ct (v. A 46·228
and BTs).
mylenhwēol n. *'mill-wheel,'* Lcd.
mylenpull m. *mill-pool*, Ct.
mylenscearp *sharpened on a grindstone*, BR
24.
mylenstān m. *grindstone, WW.* [*'mill-
stone'*]
mylen-steall, -stede m. *mill*, KC.
mylenstīg f. *path to a mill*, KC 3·389⁸.
mylentroh n. *mill-trough, mill-conduit*, WW.
mylonwaru f. *mill weir*, KC 3·454⁷.
mylenweg *road to a mill*, KC 6·31′.
myle(n)wer m. *'mill-weir,' mill-dam*, KC
4·92′.
mylenwyrd, myleweard m. *tenant of a
(manorial) mill, miller*, WW. [*'millward'*]
mylestrēam m. *'mill-stream,'* BC 2·377.
mylier (EC 179¹)=myle(n)wer?
mylisc, mylsc=milisc
mylma m. *retreat?* GPH 398¹⁵⁰.
myln=mylen
myltan=(1) meltan; (2) mieltan
myltenhūs n. *brothel*, ES 9·39.
myltestre (e, i) f. *prostitute*, Æ. [*L.*
meretricem]
myltestrehūs n. *brothel*, WW 186².
myltestrern? (=ærn) *brothel*, v. OEG 8²²⁵.
mymerian *to remember*, W 74¹⁵.
+mynan=+munan
±mynd (usu. +) fn. *memory, remembrance,
Æ,BH,Met : memorial, record, Æ : act of
commemoration, Bl,MH : thought, purpose,
Bl : consciousness, mind. intellect.* on
+m. niman *to recollect.* [*'mind'*]

+myndblīðe (i¹) *memorial*, EP 101¹³; 134¹³.
+mynddæg f. *anniversary, BH.* [v. *'mind'*]
+mynde I. *mindful*, EL 1064. II. *river-
mouth*, BH 398¹⁷ (v. JAW 31).
+mynde-=myndig-
+myndewyrðe *worth mentioning or remembering*, BH 486¹².
+myndful (e¹) *of good memory*, LCD 3·186.
±myndgian *to remember, be mindful of* :
(w. g.) *remind, W; CP : intend : com-
memorate, mention, PPs : exhort, impel,
warn* : *demand payment*, LL 206,1².
+myndgod *aforesaid.* [*ming'*]
myndgiend m. *one who reminds*, B 1105.
±myndgung f. *admonition, CP : remembrance, memorandum*, LL 453²¹ (myng-) :
memorial, AO 98²⁵.
±myndig *mindful, recollecting, Mk : memorable* : *thoughtful, wise*, HELL 77. se
+myndiga *the aforesaid.* [*'mindy'*]
+myn-diglic, -delic *memorable* : *hortatory.*
adv. -līce *by heart*, Æ : *thoughtfully*,
MFB 103.
+myndiglicnes f. *remembrance*, SPs 101¹³.
±myndlēas *foolish, senseless*, Æ. [*'mind-
less'*]
+myndlȳst f. *madness*, ZDA 31·22.
+myndstōw f. *monument, tomb*, G,RPs.
+myndwyrðe=+myndewyrðe
myne I.† m. *memory, remembrance : feeling,
affection, love, favour : purpose, desire,
wish, B : memorial.* m. witan *to love.*
[*'min'*] II. m. *minnow*, WW. III.=mene
+myne I. *mindful*, MtR 5²³. II. pres. subj.
of +munan.
mynecen, mynecenu f. *female monk, nun*,
WW; Æ. [*'minchen'*; munuc]
mynegian=myndgian
mynegiendlic *hortatory*, CM 30.
±mynegung f. *warning, admonition, exhortation*, Æ : *claim.* (=+myndgung)
mynelic *desirable*, WID 4.
mynescilling=menescilling
mynet n. *coin, money, Cp,Lcd,MtR.* [*'mint';
L.* moneta]
mynetcȳpa m. *money-changer*, ÆH 1·412.
mynetere m. *'minter,' coiner*, Æ : *money-
changer, Mt; Æ.*
±mynetian *to coin*, LL 158,14; BC 3·75.
mynetīsen n. *coinage? die for stamping
coin?* (BTs), ÆL 23⁴⁴⁷.
mynetslege m. *minting, coinage*, ÆL 23⁴⁷⁵.
mynetsmiððe f. *mint*, LL 158,14¹.
myng-=myneg-, myndg-
mynian (e) *to intend, be impelled : direct
oneself towards an object*, AS 1⁹.
mynig-=myneg-; mynīt=mynet
mynle f. *desire*, MET 26⁶⁷.
mynnan=mynian

mynster (æ²) n. *monastery, nunnery, BH* : *mother-church, 'minster,' cathedral, LL.* [*L.* monasterium]

mynsterbōc f? *minster-book,* NC310.

mynsterclǣnsung f. *purification of a minster,* LL.

mynsterclūse f. *monastic enclosure, stall, cell, monastery,* CM22.

mynsterfæder m. *abbot,* GD293¹.

mynsterfǣmne f. *nun,* BH20¹⁹.

mynstergang m. *act of joining an order of monks,* LL(146').

mynstergēat n. *monastery gate,* GD145².

mynsterhām m. *monastery,* LL,TC.

mynsterhata m. *persecutor of monasteries,* W165²⁸.

mynsterland n. *land owned by a monastery,* KC3·60'.

mynsterlic *monastic,* Æ. adv. -līce.

mynsterlīf n. *monastic life,* Æ : *monastery.*

mynstermann m. *monk,* Æ,Bf.

mynstermunuc m. *monk who lives in a monastery (i.e. not an anchorite),* ÆH.

mynsterprafost m. *provost of a monastery,* TC434⁴.

mynsterprēost m. *priest of a church or minster,* LL(254⁸).

mynsterscīr f. *control of a monastery,* BH458¹¹.

mynsterstede m. *monastic buildings,* GD182¹⁹.

mynsterstōw f. *place of a minster, town,* BH160¹⁶.

mynstertimbrung f. *building of a monastery,* GD147¹¹.

mynsterðēaw m. *monastic custom,* BH452¹².

mynsterðegnung f. *monastic service,* RB85¹⁷.

mynsterwīse f. *monastic custom,* GF110²⁷.

+mynt n. *intention,* RWH135¹⁵.

±myntan *to intend, determine, resolve,* Æ, B,Bo : *destine : think,* Jud : *bring forth,* Sc215¹ : *give up to,* LL400,3. ['*mint,*' '*i-munte*']

myranhēafod n. *mare's head* (a nick-name), Chr1010e.

Myrce, Myrcan=Mierce; **myrce**=mirce

myre (Æ,AO)=miere

myrenæddra=merenæddra

myrgan *to be* '*merry,*' *rejoice,* PPs.

myrge adj. (e, i, u) *pleasing, agreeable,* Æ,Bo,Met : *pleasant, sweet,* DHy. ['*merry*'] adv. myrge (AS,W), myriglīce *pleasantly, melodiously,* GD286¹. ['*merry*']

myrgelēoð n. *epitaph?* BHb94¹².

myrgen I. f. *joy, pleasure,* Met (Introd.) 5. **II.**=morgen

myrgnes f. *melody,* WW33³¹.

myrgð (e, i), **myrhð** f. '*mirth,*' *joy, pleasure, sweetness (of sound),* Æ,Bo.

myrig-=myrg-; **myrlic**=mærlic

myrr-=mierr-

myrra m., **myrre** f. (u) '*myrrh,*' Æ,MtR,VPs.

myrrelse f. *offence, scandal, stumbling-block,* Jul338.

myrten I. n. *flesh of an animal which has died of itself, carrion,* LL. **II.** adj. *dead* (of animals which have not been killed), LL.

myrð=myrgð, v. also myrðu.

myrðra m. *homicide, murderer,* LL,W. -myrðran, -myrðrian v. ā-, for-, of-m.

myrðrung f. *parricide, murder,* WW467²¹.

myrðu (=ie) f. *mischief, trouble,* B810.

myrw-=mearuw- (v. mearu); **mȳs** v. mūs.

±myscan *to injure, afflict,* PPs : *offend,* OEG17⁴⁷.

mysci sbpl. *flies,* PPs104²⁷.

mȳse=mēse; **mytting**=mitting

+mȳðe n. (usu. pl.) *mouth, confluence, junction of two streams,* BH,Ct.

myx=meox; **myx-**=mix-

N

nā (ō) adv. conj. *not,* '*no,*' *not at all, not even, never, by no means,* Bl,Cr,Met,VPs; Æ,AO,CP. nā ðæt ān *not only.* nā…nā *neither…nor.* ne nā *nor.* nā mā *no more,* ÆGr,Bl. ['*no mo*'] nā māre sb. *nothing more,* Bo,Mk. ['*no more*']

nab-=naf-

nabban anv. pres. 1 sg. næbbe, 2 næfst, 3 nafað, næfð, pl. nabbað, næbbað; pret. næfde (v. habban) *not to have, to lack, be without,* Bo(+næfd), Jn; AO,CP. [v. '*have*']

naca† m. *vessel, boat, ship.* [*Ger.* nachen]

naced=nacod; **naclan**=nacodian

nacod, nacud (æ) (+) **I.** adj. '*naked,*' *nude, bare,* Æ,CP : *empty : not fully clothed.* **II.** f. *nakedness.*

+nac(od)ian *to lay bare, strip,* BH,MkL.

næ adv.=ne

næbbað, næbbe v. nabban.

nǣbre=nǣfre

nǣcad (Cp499e '*exserta*')=nacod

±nǣcan (Æ)=hnǣcan

nǣced=nacod

nǣcednes f. *nakedness,* Æ.

nǣcedu f. *nakedness,* MFH169.

nǣct=niht; **nǣdder-**=nǣder-

nǣddre (CP)=nǣdre

nǣddrewinde f. *adder-wort,* WW287¹⁶.

nǣderbita m. *ichneumon,* WW.

nǣdercynn n. *snake-tribe,* Lcd: *a kind of snake,* AA.

nǣderfāh *spotted like a snake,* HL15¹⁸³.

nǣdl (ē) f. '*needle,*' G,Soul; Æ.

nǣdre (ē) f. '*adder,*' *snake, serpent, viper,* Mt; AO,CP.

nǣdrewyrt (der) f. *adder-wort,* LCD,WW.

nǣfde pret. 3 sg. of nabban.

nǣfebor *auger,* A9·263³. [nafu]

nǣfig (NG)=næftig; **nǣfne**=nefne

nǣfre (ē) adv. '*never,*' B,Bl,Bo,Chr,G,LL; CP. [ne, æfre]

nǣfst v. nabban.

nǣft f. *need, want, poverty,* Sc157³,⁷.

nǣftcyrrend *not returning,* CP77³⁹. [ne eft]

nǣftig *poor,* Sc190¹.

±**nǣgan** I.† (ē) (often followed by wordum) *to approach, accost, speak to : attack.* II.= hnǣgan

nǣgel=nægl; **nǣgen**=ne mægen

nǣgl m. '*NAIL,*' *peg, AO;* Æ : *finger-nail, toe-nail, claw,* Æ : *plectrum,* WY84 : *spear,* WW377¹⁵ : (in comp.) *handle.*

nǣgledbord† *with nailed sides.*

nǣgledcnearr m. *nail-fastened vessel,* †CHR 937.

nǣgledcræt n. *iron chariot* (Swt).

nǣgledsinc n. *studded vessel,* B2023.

±**nǣglian** '*to nail,*' *fasten with nails,* MtLR; Æ.

nǣglsex n. *knife for cutting the nails,* WW. [seax; v. '*nail*']

nǣh=nēah; **nǣhsta**=nīehsta

nǣht (NG,VPs)=niht; **nǣht**=nāht

nǣlēacan (S²Ps54²²)=nēalǣcan

nǣllæs=nealles; **nǣm**=neom

nǣm f. *taking, receiving,* NC311.

+**nǣman** *to take away,* GUTH14¹¹.

nǣmel *receptive,* NC311. ['*nimble*']

nǣming f. *bargain, contract,* WW180¹⁷.

nǣmne=nemne

+**nǣmnian** (LL455')=nemnian

nǣmniendlic=nemniendlic

nǣnig pron. *no one, none, not any, no* (used as sb. w. gen. and as adj.). **nǣnige ðinga** adv. *not at all, in no wise.* [ne, ǣnig]

nǣnig-wuht, -uht *in no wise, nothing,* ANDR119⁶.

nǣniht (NG)=nānwiht

nǣnne v. nān.

nǣp m. *turnip, rape,* Cp,Lcd. ['*neep*']

nǣpsǣd n. *rape seed,* LCD.

nǣpte=nefte

nǣre, **nǣron** (Æ,AO,CP)=ne wǣre, ne wǣron

nǣrende ptc. *not being.* [ne, wesan]

nǣrra=nēara

nǣs I. (AO,CP)=ne wæs. II. adv. *not, not at all,* CP. [=nalæs] III.=næss. IV. pret. 3 sg. of nesan.

nǣsc *fawn-skin,* GL,LCD.

nǣse (NG)=nese

nǣsgristle f. *nose-gristle,* GL.

nǣs-hliŏ n. dp. -hleoðum *declivity, slope* (*of a headland*), B1428.

nǣss (e), nǣssa m. '*ness,*' *cliff, headland, cape, An,B,Chr,Ct :* (†) *earth, ground.*

nǣstan=hnǣstan

nǣster '*caucale*' (=caucalia?), *lipped vessel,* WW202¹ (v. A49·378 and IF48·266).

nǣsŏyrl n. *nostril,* Æ,LCD.

±**nǣtan** *to annoy, afflict, press upon, subdue, injure, destroy,* CP.

nǣting f. *blaming,* CP353¹¹.

nǣŏl=nǣdl

nafa I. m.=nafu. II.=ne hafa imperat. of nabban

nafaŏ pres. 3 sg. of nabban.

nafela m. '*navel,*' AO,Gl,Lcd; Æ.

nafeŏa m. *nave* (*of a wheel*), WW106²⁷.

nafogār m. '*auger,*' Gl,WW.

nafu f. *nave* (*of a wheel*), Bo,WW

nafula=nafela

nafulsceaft f. *navel,* LCD3·124'.

+**nāg** *striking, pressing?* RIM57?

nāgan* pres. 3 sg. nāh; pret. nāhte, nāhton *not to owe, not to be bound, not to be allowed, to have no right to, not to own, not to have, to lose, to be unable to,* AO. **nāhte** *ought not.* [ne, āgan]

nāht (ǣ, āu, āw, ō) I. n. '*NAUGHT,*' *nothing,* CP : *wickedness, evil-doing,* CP. instr. nāhte w. comparatives=*nothing.* II. *useless, bad, poor,* Æ. III. adv. *not, not at all, Æ, CP.* [nā, wiht]

nāhte v. nāgan.

nāhtfremmend m. *evil-doer,* PPs58².

nāhtgītsung (āu¹) f. *wicked avarice,* CP333⁵.

nāhtlic *worthless, of no avail,* CHR979 E. adv. -līce (ō¹) *wickedly, badly.* VPs.36⁸,⁹. ['*noughtly*']

nāhtnes f. *worthlessness,* CHR449a.

nāhtscipe f. *worthlessness,* CHR449E.

nāh-wǣr, -wǣrn (o¹) adv. '*nowhere,*' *in no case, never, not at all, Æ,Bf,Bl,GD.*

nāhwǣŏer *neither,* Bo,Bl; CP. ['*nauther*']

nāhwār=nāhwǣr

nāhwider '*no-whither,*' *nowhere,* Bo,RB.

nāhwonan adv. *from nowhere,* Bo89².

nalæs, nalas, nales (AO,CP), nalles (CP), nals=nealles

nalde (N,VPs)=nolde pret. of *nyllan.

nam I. pret. 3 sg. of niman. II. (N)=ne eom

nām f. (*legal*) *seizure,* LL.

nama (o) m. '*NAME,*' Æ; AO,CP : *reputation :* *noun,* ÆGR.

nambōc (o) f. *register of names,* WW342¹¹.

nambred (o) n. *register of names* (*on a tablet*), WW499⁴⁰.

namcūŏ *well-known,* LL : *celebrated,* HL; (nome-), Æ. ['*namecouth*']

namcūðlīce adv. *by name, individually,* Æ.
namcyging (=ie²) f. *naming,* CHRD 9²⁹.
±namian *to 'name,' Gen : mention,* Æ : *call, Scr : nominate, appoint,* Æ,LL.
nammǣlum adv. *by name,* LF 55¹⁴, OEG.
+namn adj. *of the same name,* RD 53³ ; 54¹³?
namnian *to address, invoke,* ÆT 683.
nāmon pret. pl. of niman.
nāmrǣden f. *learning,* WW 431⁸.
nān as. nǣnne, nǣnne I. pron. and adj. 'NONE,' *not one, no.* nāne ðinga *on no account.* II. sb. w. g. *none, no one, nothing.* [nē, ān]
nān-wiht, -(w)uht I. n. (often w. g.) *nothing, naught,* AO,CP. II. adv. *not at all, in no wise.*
nāp pret. 3 sg. of nīpan.
nard m. *spikenard, unguent,* LCD. [*L.* nardus]
nart (*JnL*)=neart; naru=nearu
nas=næs=ne wæs
nāst (=ne wāst) v. nytan.
nasðyrl=næsðyrl; nasu=nosu
nāt (*Bo,Jn*)=ne wāt, v. nytan.
nāteshwōn (Æ), nāteðæshwōn adv. *not, not at all, by no means.*
nāthwā adj. pron. *some one* (=*L.* nescio quis).
nāthwǣr adv. *somewhere or other,* RD.
nāthwæt pron. *something or other,* RD.
nāt-hwilc, -hwylc adj. pron. (indef.)† (*I know not which), some one or other.*
nātōhwōn, nātōðæshwōn=nāteshwōn
nāðēlǣs (AO)=nāðȳlǣs
nāðer (Æ,AO,CP), nāðor (Æ)=nāhwæðer
nāðinc n. *nothing,* HL 18⁴⁸.
nāðȳlǣs (ō¹, ē²) *nevertheless,* AO.
nāuht=nāht
nāwa adv. *never,* LCD 94b. [ne, āwa]
nāwer=nāhwǣr
nāwĕrn [=nāhwǣrn] adv. *nowhere,* WW.
nāwht, nāwiht=nāht; nāwðer=nāhwæðer
nāwuht (*CP*)=nāwiht, nāht
ne I. adv. *not, no,* Æ,CP. II. conj. *neither, nor,* Æ,CP.
nēa-=nēah-
nēad=nīed; nēad- v. also nīed, nȳd-.
nēadclamm n. *necessity, extremity,* LPs 106²⁸.
nēadcofa m. *prison,* AN 1311.
nēadgafol n. *tax, tribute,* LL.
nēadgewuna m. *enforced custom,* WW 221⁸.
nēadgylda m. *debtor,* WW 221¹⁰.
nēadhād m. *compulsion, force,* WW 480²¹.
nēadhǣs f. *order which one must obey,* LL 12.
±nēadian I. *to compel, force, constrain, urge, impel,* Æ. II. v. nēodian.
nēadignes f. *obligation,* OEG 2106.

nēadinga (AO), nēadlunga=nēadunga
nēadnēod f. *unavoidable necessity,* CHRD 61⁹.
nēadprin? n. *necessary equipment,* ÆP 13⁷ (or ?=nēadðing).
nēadðing n. *necessary thing,* RB 57; ÆP 13⁷?
nēadung f. *compulsion,* Æ.
nēadunga, nēadunge adv. *forcibly,* Æ.
nēadwīs *needful, fitting, due,* Æ. adv. *of necessity,* Æ.
nēadwīsnes f. *necessity,* OEG 2396.
nēadwīte n. *inevitable punishment,* MFH 170.
nēadwraca m. *avenger by necessity,* TC 611'.
nēah I. (ē, ī) [comp. nēara, superl. nīehsta q.v.] adj. 'NEAR' ['NAR'], 'NIGH,' *close, AO,CP : late.* II. adv. 'NEAR,' 'NIGH,' *AO : about, almost, nearly, lately, CP.* nēar *next, at length, finally.* III. prep. w. d. *near, close to : according to,* AO.
+nēah I.† *sufficiency, abundance.* II. (ē) *closely, seriously,* BL 101³². III. pres. 3 sg. of +nugan.
nēahbūend m. *neighbour,* RD 26².
nēahceaster f. *nearest town,* BH 52²⁷ (nēh-).
nēahcyrice f. *neighbouring church,* GD.
nēahdǣl m. *neighbourhood,* GD 71³⁰.
nēahdūn f. *neighbouring hill,* AA 20¹⁷.
nēahēa f. *neighbouring river,* AA 33⁷.
nēahēaland n. *neighbouring island,* MH 84¹⁷.
nēahfæder m. *'vicinus pater,'* GD 179⁷.
nēah-feald, -fealdlic (GD) *intimate.*
nēahfrēond (ē¹) m. *near friend, near kinsman,* GUTH 56²².
nēahgangol (w. d.) *placed near,* ÆL 23¹³¹.
nēahgebūr (ē) m. *'neighbour,'* Bf,CP,HL, Lk.
nēahgebȳren (nēhhe-) f. *neighbour,* Lk 15⁹.
nēahgebȳrild (nēhe-) m. *neighbour,* LkL 15⁹.
nēahgehūsa (ē) m. *neighbour,* JVPs.
±neah-he, -hi(g)e (usu. +) *sufficiently : abundantly : often, frequently : earnestly.*
nēahhebūr=nēahgebūr
+neahhelīce (nehl-) *sufficiently, frequently, usually,* LL,GUTH.
nēahhergung f. *warring close at hand,* HL 200¹⁷⁴.
neah-hie, -hige=neahhe
+neahian *to draw near to,* LPs 90¹⁰.
nēahlǣcan=nēalǣcan
nēahland n. *neighbourhood,* GD 69²⁸.
nēah-mǣg m. nap. -māgas *near relation,* LL.
nēahmǣgð f. *neighbouring tribe,* BH.
nēahmann (ē¹) m. *neighbour,* BH.
nēahmunt m. *neighbouring mountain,* AA, GD.
nēahnes (ē¹) f. *nearness, neighbourhood,* BH.

nēahnun(n)mynster *neighbouring convent,* BH254[10].

nēahsibb I. adj. *related,* LL. **II.** f. *affinity, near relationship,* W.

nēahsta=nīehsta

nēahstōw f. *neighbourhood, place near,* Bo, MH.

neaht (*Met*)=niht

nēahtīd f. *approaching time,* BH290[29].

nēahtūn (ē) m. *neighbouring town or village,* HL199[157].

nēahðēod f. *neighbouring nation,* AO46,96.

nēahwæter n. *neighbouring piece of water,* AA34[2].

+**nēahwian** (ē) *to draw near, approach, cleave to,* NG.

nēahwudu m. *neighbouring wood,* GD229[20].

±**nēalǣcan** (w. d.) *to come or draw near, approach, BH,Bl,LG*; Æ,AO,CP : *be near,* GD85[9] : *be like : cling to,* CPs136[6]. ['*nehleche*'; nēah, lǣcan]

nēalǣcung f. *approach, access,* Æ,RB. ['*nehleching*']

nēalic (ē) *near, neighbouring.* adv. -līce *nearly, about,* Bl; CP. ['*nighly*']

nealles adv. *not, not at all, by no means,* CP.

neam=neom; **nēam-**=nēahm-

nēan adv. *from near by : close at hand, near : nearly, about.*

+**nēan**=+nēahwian; **neap**=hnæpp

nēar comp. of nēah, adv. *near, nearer,* AO.

+**near**=+ner

nēara, nēarra (AO), comp. of nēah, adj. *later, latter, nearer.*

neara=nearo-; **nearo** (AO)=nearu

noarobrogd f. *crafty trick,* JUL302.

nearocræft m. *skill in enclosing?* B2243.

nearofāh *intensely hostile,* B2317.

nearogrāp f. *close grasp,* RD81[6].

nearolic *oppressive, straitened,* EL913. adv. -līce '*narrowly,' closely, briefly, accurately,* Æ,CP : *strictly, stringently, oppressively : evilly.*

nearonēd f. *urgent need,* AN102.

nearones f. *strait,* AO : *small space : scantiness : oppression : distress, anxiety, trouble.*

nearosearu† (u[2]) f. *dark cunning.*

nearosorg (u[2]) f. *crushing distress,* EL1261.

nearoðanc (u[2]) m. *wickedness,* OEG.

nearoðancnes f. *wickedness,* LPs27[4].

nearoðearf f. *dire need,* CR69.

nearowrenc (u[2]) m. *evil trick,* MOD44.

neart *art not,* Bo. ['*nart*'; ne eart]

nearu I.† f? n? gs. nearu, near(o)we *strait, danger, distress, difficulty.* n. ðrōwian *to be in straits : confinement, imprisonment : prison, hiding-place.* **II.** adj. '*narrow,*' *constricted, limited, petty, AO,B,Bo,G : causing*

or accompanied by difficulty, hardship, oppressive, Bl,Rd : strict, severe, CP.

nearu-=nearo-

nearwe adv. *narrowly, closely, strictly, B,* Met : *carefully, exactly, El*; CP : *oppressively, forcibly : artfully : anxiously.* ['*narrow*']

nearwelīce=nearolīce

nearwian (±) *to force in, cramp, confine, afflict : crowd : become smaller, shrink.*

nearxnewang=neorxnawang

nēasian (VPs)=nēosian

nēat n. *animal, beast, ox, CP,VPs*; pl. *cattle, Met,VPs.* ['*neat*']

+**nēat** m. *companion, follower* (*esp. in war*), *Chr,WW : dependant, vassal, tenant who works for a lord,* v. LL2·427. [v. '*geneat*']

nēaten=nīeten

±**nēatland** n. *land of a dependant or vassal,* LL196,1[1].

+**nēatmann**=+nēat

+**nēatriht** n. *regulations as to the tenure of '*geneatland,*' LL445,2.

+**neatscolu** f. *band of comrades,* JUL684.

nēawest (AO,CP), nēawist (Æ) fm. *neighbourhood, nearness, presence : society, cohabitation.* [nēah, wesan]

nēawung f. *nearness,* MtL13[28].

neb(b) n. *bill, beak, beak-shaped thing, Cp, Ph : nose, LL : face, countenance, complexion, Æ,CP.* n. wið n. *face to face,* RWH138[38]. ['*neb*']

nebb-=neb-

nebbian *to retort upon, rebuke, confront,* ÆH1·256.

noboorn n. *pimple,* LCD1·118'.

nebgebrǣc n. *nasal mucus,* WW.

nebsealf f. *antimony, face-powder,* OEG.

nebwlātful *barefaced, shameless,* OEG2[317].

nebwlātung f. *impudence,* OEG4306.

neb-wlite, -wlitu m. *face, countenance,* Æ.

nechebūr=nēahgebūr; **necti-**=nihte-

ned=net(t); **nēd**=(1) nīed; (2) nēod

nēd- (A)=nēad-, nīed-, nȳd-; **nēdl**=nǣdl

nēdre (VPs), nēddre=nǣdre

nefa m. (±) *nephew,* Æ,AO : *stepson : grandson : second cousin.*

nefene f. *granddaughter : niece,* WW173[31].

nefne=nemne; **nēfre**=nǣfre adv.

nefte f. *cat's mint,* LCD,WW. [*L. nepeta*]

nēfugol m. *bird of prey,* GEN2158. [cp. nēobedd]

nēgan=nǣgan; **negled-**=nægled-

nēh=nēah; +**nehe**, +nehh(ig)e=+neahhe

nēhst, nēhsta=nīehst, nīehsta

neht=niht

neirxnawong (N)=neorxnawong

nēista=nīehsta

nele (AO,CP)=nelle (Æ) pres. 1, 3 sing.,
nelt=pres. 2 sg. of nellan. [v. 'will']
nellan=*nyllan
nem-nan, -nian (±) to name, call, Bl,Bo,
Lcd,MkL; Æ,AO,CP : enumerate : address, speak to : nominate : invoke :
mention, relate, Bo; Æ. ['nemn']
nemne (A;=WS nymðe) conj. and prep.
unless, except, save, only.
nemnian=nemnan
nemni(g)endlic naming, nominative, ÆGR
22¹⁰.
nemning (æ) f. name, ÆL23⁸⁶⁴.
nemðe=nymðe
nenā (WW252¹)=ne nā v. nā.
nēnig (KGL)=nænig
nēobedd† n. corpse-bed, bed of death, GEN,
PH. [cp. Goth. naus]
nēod I. f. (ē, īe, ȳ) desire, longing : zeal,
earnestness : pleasure, delight. [FTP299]
II.=nīed
nēode adv. (instr. of nēod) eagerly, zealously,
diligently.
nēodfracu f. yearning, greed, MET31¹⁵ (v.
ES39·335).
nēodfrēond m. kinsman, friend, HL18¹⁵⁰.
[nīed]
nēodful I. zealous, earnest, JUL720. II.=
nīedful
nēodhūs (NC312)=nīedhūs
±nēodian (=ēa; impers. w. g.) to be necessary, require, be required, RB. ['need']
nēodlaðu f. wish, B1320.
nēodlīce adv. eagerly, carefully, zealously,
diligently, Æ : (†) greatly, PPs.
nēodlof n. zealous praise, PPs148¹².
nēodspearuwa m. (restless?) sparrow, PPs
123⁶.
nēodðearflic necessary, GD148⁶.
nēodweorðung f. zealous honouring, PPs
142¹¹.
neofa=nefa; nēol=neowol
nēo-lǣcan (VPs), -lēcan (MtL)=nēalǣcan
neom=ne eom (am not).
neoman=niman
nēomian to sound sweetly? WYRD84.
nēon=nīwan
+nēopan²? to engulf, overwhelm, Ex475.
nēor adv.=nēar
+neorð contented, Cp544. [from Nerthus?
IF48]
neorxnawang m. Paradise, Æ,CP; v. A
53·337 and IF48·267.
neorxnawanglic adj. of Paradise, GD179¹.
nēosan, nēosian (Æ) to search out, find out,
inspect : (±) visit, go to : attack, visit with
affliction.
nēoslð m. death, MOD55.
neosu=nosu

±nēosung f. access : visitation, visit, Æ.
nēotan² (usu. w. g.) to use, have the use of,
enjoy, employ. [Ger. geniessen]
nēoten=nīeten
neoð-an, -ane (i) adv. below, down, beneath,
from beneath, Æ,Bl,Bo (-on). ['nethen']
neoðanweard (io) adj. lower, WW26⁶.
neoðe-=niðe-; neoðon=neoðan
neoðor, neoðor-=niðor, niðer-
neoðoweard=niðeweard; neoðra=niðera
nēow-=nīw-; neowel=neowol
nēowērno (WW454²⁸)=nāwērn
neowol (i) precipitous : headlong : prone,
prostrate, Æ,Bo : obscure, deep down,
abysmal. ['nuel']
neowollic (i¹, e²) profound, deep, ÆL7⁶⁶.
neowolnes (i¹) f. depth, abyss, chasm, Æ.
nēp only in phr. forðganges n. without power
of advancing? Ex469.
nēpflōd m. 'neap'-tide, ebb, low tide, Gl,MH.
nepte=nefte
±ner (ea) n. refuge, protection, ÆL,AO.
nēr=nēar
+ner-ednes (BH), -renes (GD) f. deliverance.
nergend m. saviour, preserver (Christ,
God).
nergendlic that should be preserved? (BTs).
±nerian to save, rescue, liberate, Æ,AO,CP :
preserve, defend, protect. [Ger. nähren]
neriend, nerigend=nergend
nērra=nēar(r)a
+nerstede m. refuge, sanctuary, WW186²³.
nerung f. guard, protection, OEG5395.
nerw-=nearw-, nirew-; nerx-=neorx-
±nesan⁵ (usu. +) to escape from, survive, be
saved.
nese (æ) adv. no, Æ,CP. [ne, sī]
ness=næss
nest I. n. 'nest,' MtL,Ph; Æ : young bird,
brood. II. n. food, provisions, victuals.
nēst, nēsta (VPs)=nīehst, nīehsta
nestan to spin, NG.
nestig=nihstig
nestlian to make a nest, LPs103¹⁶. ['nestle']
nestpohha m. wallet, MtL10¹⁰.
net=nett; net-=nyt-
neta m. caul, WW266²⁰.
netan=nytan
netel, netele f. 'nettle,' Lcd.
nēten (Bo,VPs)=nīeten
netenes=nytennes; nētl (Cp)=nǣdl
netle (Cp)=netele
neton=nyton
netrāp m. snare, gin, WW.
nett (y) n. 'net,' Bo,LG,WW : netting, net-
work, Ex,WW : spider's web, PPs. [Goth.
nati]
nette (y) f. the net-like caul, WW.

nettgern n. *knitting yarn*, EC377¹⁴. [gearn]

+nettian *to ensnare*, OEG4596.

±nēðan *to venture on, dare, risk*, AO. [nōð]

+nēðedlic=+nīededlic

+neðerian=+niðerian

nēðing f. *boldness, daring*, Gu: *risk*, AO.

nēðl (A)=nǣdl

neurisn f. *aneurism*, Lcd.

newesēoða (i¹) m. *pit of the stomach? bowels?* Gl,Lcd.

nēwest=nēawest

next (LWS)=nīehst; **nī-**=nīg-, nīw-

nic, nicc adv. *not I* (=no). [ne, ic]

niccan *to say 'no,' refuse*, KC6·201⁶.

nicor (e²) m. nap. nicras *water-sprite, sea-monster, B,Bl : hippopotamus, walrus, Nar.* ['*nicker*']

nicorhūs n. *sea-monster's dwelling*, B1411.

nīd=nīed; **nīd-**=nēad-, nīed-, nȳd-

nīed I. (ē, ēa, ēo, ī, ȳ; see NED) fn. '*NEED*,' *necessity, compulsion, duty, AO*; CP : *errand, business, Æ : emergency, Æ : hardship, distress, difficulty, trouble, pain, AO : force, violence : what is necessary : inevitableness : fetter*, Deor5 : *name of the rune for* n. **II.**=nēod

nīed- v. also nēad-, nȳd-.

nīedan (ē, ī, ȳ) *to compel, force, urge, press, Æ,Bo,Bl,LG,VHy*; AO,CP. ['*need*']

nīedbād (ē, ȳ) f. *toll, exaction, blackmail : bodily torment*, ES49·350.

nīedbādere (ē) m. *toll-collector*, TC29¹⁰.

nīedbehǣfdlic *necessary*, BH396²⁴.

nīedbehǣfednes (ē¹) f. *necessity*, Æ.

nīedbehǣfnes (ȳ¹) f. *requisite*, ÆL30⁸.

nīedbehēfe (y¹) *needful, necessary*, Æ.

nīedbe-hof (Æ), -hoflic (BH) (ȳ) *necessary*.

nīedbeðearf (y³) *necessary*, CP7⁷.

nīede, nīedes (ēa, ēo, ī, ȳ) adv. (instr. and gs. of nīed) *of need, needs, necessarily, compulsorily*, CP.

+nīededlic (ē) *compulsory*, BH62²³(v.l.).

nīedenga, nīedunga adv. *necessarily, by force, forcibly*, CP.

nīedfaru f. *compulsory journey, death*, OET149.

nīedful (ēo) *needful*, CM377.

nīedhǣmed (ē, ȳ) n. *rape*, LL.

nīedhīernes (ē¹, ē²) f. *slavery*, DR6⁵.

nīedhūs (ēo) *needed room*, Chrd21¹⁸.

nīedling m. *slave*, AO : *captive*, GD : *sailor*, BH.

nīedmicel (ē) *urgent*, Bl233¹¹? (MS med-).

nīednǣm f. *seizure*, BH,LL.

nīedscyld f. *moral necessity*, CP57⁶.

nīedsibb (ēa) f. *relationship*, OEG,WW.

nīedðearf I. f. *need, necessity, compulsion, force*, CP : *distress : want, thing needed.* **II.** adj. *necessary.*

nīedðearflic (ē, ēa, ȳ) *necessary, useful.* adv. -līce, ÆGr,GD.

nīedðearfnes (ēa, ē, ȳ) f. *need, necessity : compulsion : trouble : time of need*, EPs9²².

nīedðēow (ē, ȳ) m. *slave*, LL,W.

nīedðrafung f. *reproof*, CP297²².

nīedwǣdla m. *poor wretch*, Gen929.

nīehst (ē) **I.** adv. (superl. of nēah) *most nearly, in closest proximity : last (in time), Bl,Gen.* **II.** adj. *latest, last, Æ : nearest,* '*NEXT*,' *CP,Chr.* æt nīehstan *at last, next.*

nīehsta mf. *closest friend, CP :* (±) *neighbour, MkL,VPs : next of kin*, LL. ['*next*']

nieht (CP)=niht

±nier-wan, -wian (i, y) *to confine, repress : beset, rebuke, chasten.* [v. '*narrow*']

nīeten (ē, ēo, ī, ȳ) n. *small animal, beast, cattle, Bo,Lcd,VPs*; AO,CP. ['*neten*'; nēat]

nīetencynn n. *kind of animal*, Æ.

nīetenlic (ē, ȳ) *animal, brutish*, Bo35²⁸. adv. -līce *like an animal*, W55¹⁶.

nīetennes (ȳ) f. *brutishness*, Æ.

nieðemest=niðemest; **nieðer**=niðer

niewe=nīwe

nīfara (nīw-) m. *newcomer, stranger*, PPs 38¹⁵.

nifol *dark, gloomy.* [=neowol]

nift f. *niece, BH,Ep,TC : granddaughter : step-daughter.* ['*nift*']

nīg-=nīw-; **nigan**=nigon; **nige-**=nigo-

nīgecyrred *newly converted*, OEG3447.

nīgefara=nīfara

nīgehalgod *newly consecrated (of a king), newly crowned*, ÆL18³²⁶.

nīgehwyrfed *newly converted*, ÆL5¹²⁶.

nigend(e) (KC)=nigoða

nīghworfen *newly converted*, ÆH2·130'.

nigon (e²) '*nine*,' *Bf,Bl,Chr,Ct,G*; AO,CP.

nigonfeald '*nine-fold*,' *ÆGr.*

nigongylde *entitled to nine-fold compensation*, LL470,7.

nigonnihte *nine days old*, ANS129·22.

nigontēoða '*nineteenth*,' *Chr,MH :* '*nineteth*,' OEG2521 (nigen-).

nigontīene (ȳ³) '*nineteen*,' *Bf,Men.*

nigontig '*ninety*,' *Lk*; CP.

nigontȳnlic *containing the number nineteen*, BH470²⁰.

nigonwintre *nine years old*, AO186¹⁰.

nigoða (y) '*ninth*,' *Bl,KC,LG,MH : ninth part, Bl.*

nigoðe *ninthly*, LL181,9.

nīgslȳcod ptc. *freshly smoothed, glossy, MH 206²⁷.* [v. '*slick*']

nigun=nigon; **nīh** (KGL55²⁵)=nēah

nihold (Gl), nihol=neowol

nīhst, nīhsta=nīehst, nīehsta

nihstig *fasting*, Lcd. [ne, wist]

niht (æ, e, ea, ie, y) f. (gs. also nihtes) 'NIGHT' (often used in enumerations where mod. Eng. uses days), *darkness*, AO,CP.
niht-=nyht-
nihtbealu n. *destruction by night*, B193.
nihtbutorflēoge f. *beetle or moth which flies by night*, WW121¹³; A8·450.
nihtēage *that can see at night*, WW.
nihteald *that happened yesterday*, LL.
nihtegale (a, æ, e) f. *nightingale, Cp : nightjar*. ['*nightgale*']
nihtēge=nihtēage
nihtegesa m. *nocturnal terror*, PPs90⁵.
nihtelic=nihtlic
nihterne adv. *by night : during a night*, LCD.
nihternnes f. *night season*, LCD3·288'.
nihtes (æ) adv. (gs. of niht) *by night*, Æ.
nihtfeormung f. *shelter at night*, GEN2433.
nihtgenga† m. *night-goer, goblin*.
nihtgenge f. *night-prowler, hyæna*, WW.
nihtgerīm† n. *number of nights*.
nihtgild n. *night sacrifice or service*, GL.
nihtglōm m? *gloom of night*, GU916.
nihthelm† m. *shades of night*.
niht-hræfn, -hrefn, -hremn m. *night-raven, night-jar*, GL,PS.
nihthrōc m. *night-raven*, LPs101⁷.
nihthwīl f. *space of a night*, W147⁹.
+nihtian *to become night, grow dark*, NC295.
nihtlang *lasting through the night*, Æ. adv. -langes, Æ.
nihtlic *nocturnal, of the night, at night*, Æ, CP.
nihtnihstig (ea¹, e²) *having fasted for a night*, LCD.
nihtremn=nihthræfn
nihtrest f. *couch*, GEN2863.
nihtrīm=nihtgerīm
nihtsang m. *compline : book of service for compline*, Ct.
nihtscada *night-shade (plant)*, WW135³ (v. MP24·217).
niht-scūa† m., gs. -scū(w)an *shades of night*.
nihtslæp m. *night's sleep*, ÆL23⁴⁴².
nihtsum=nyhtsum
nihtwacu f. *night-watch, Seaf 7*. ['*nightwake*']
nihtwæcce f. '*night-watch,' vigil, Lk*.
nihtwaru f. *clothing for night*, RB90⁴.
nihtweard m. *guardian at night*, Ex116.
nihtweorc n. *deed done at night*, B827.
nihð (MP1·613) pres. 3 sg. of nēahwian.
nihwyrfed (OEG3138)=nīgehwyrfed
nīlæred *newly initiated*, OEG3138.
nile=nyle, pres. 1 sg. of *nyllan.
±niman⁴ (eo, io, y) *to take, assume, undertake, accept, receive, get, obtain : hold, seize, catch, grasp, pluck up, carry off : occupy :*

adopt, appropriate : bear, carry, bring : betake oneself, go : contain : experience : suffer, tolerate : give : (+) grasp, comprehend : (+) take to wife. friÐ +n. *make peace*. hē hine genam *he collected himself, reflected*. sige n. *gain victory*. on n. *take effect*, LCD. se nimenda dæl *the participle*, BF94²². ['NIM*']
-nimend, -nimendnes v. dæl-n.
niming f. *action of taking, LkL*. ['*nimming*']
nimðe=nymðe; nīol=neowol
nīow-=nēow-
nip? sb. *rope*, GPH399⁴⁵¹.
+nip *darkness, mist, cloud, obscurity*, Æ.
±nīpan¹† *to grow dark, obscure*.
+nipful *dark, gloomy*, ES39·347.
nirewett (nirw-) n. *narrowness : narrow place, defile, pass*, AO : *hardness of breathing*.
nirwan=nierwan
nirwð (=ie) f. *prison house*, WW399⁵.
nis (Æ,Bo,VPs)=ne is (*is not*). ['*nis*']
nisēoða=newesēoða
nīsoden ptc. *newly-boiled*, OEG326 (=nīw-).
nistan (VPs), nistian (SPs) *to build nests*. ['*nest*']
nistig=nihstig
nist-lan (PPs), -lian (EPs) (y) *to build nests*. ['*nestle*']
nit-=nyt-; nīten=nīeten
niton (Bo,RG)=nyton; v. nytan. ['*niten*']
nið n. *abyss*, SAT634?
nīð m. *strife, enmity, attack, war : evil, hatred, spite, Bl,Cr,VPs*; AO,CP : *oppression, affliction, trouble, grief*, AO. ['*nith*']
nīðan=neoðan
nīðan *to envy, hate*, GD117⁵.
nīðas=niððas
nīðcwalu f. *violent death, destruction*, CR 1258.
nīðcwealm m. *violent death*, PPs77⁵⁰.
nīðdraca m. *hostile dragon*, B2273.
nīðemest (Bo,Bl) v. niðera.
nīðer (eo, io, y) adv. *below, beneath, down, downwards, B,Bo*; AO,CP. ['*nether*']
nīðera (eo, y) (comp.) adj. niðemest, nyðemest (superl.; positive not found) *lower, under, lowest, Bl,Bo,VPs,WW*; CP. ['*nether*']
nīðerāscūfan (ēo⁴) *to push down*, Æ.
nīðerāstīgan¹ *to descend*, Æ,CP.
nīðerbogen ptc. *bent down*, KC4·72¹.
nīðerdæl m. *lower part*, PPs138¹³. [v. '*nether*']
nīðere adv. *below, down, low down*, Bo,Cr. ['*nether*']
nīðerecg f. *lower edge*, KC.
nīðerflōr f. *lower story*, GD170¹⁷.

niðergān (y¹) *to descend,* Æ.
niðergang (y) m. *descent,* Lcd 3·246⁶. [v.
'*nether*']
niðerheald *bent downwards,* MET 31²³.
niðerhrēosende (y) *falling down,* Æ.
niðerhryre (y¹) m. *downfall,* Sc 229¹².
±**niðerian** (e, y) *to depress, abase, bring low,
oppress,* Jud,Lk,VPs; AO,CP : *accuse* :
condemn. +nyðred *ignominious,* ÆL
23b¹⁴. ['*nither*']
+**niðerigendlic** (y) *deserving condemnation,*
Sc 162¹⁸.
niðerlecgung (y) f. *deposition, entombment,*
CM 421.
niðerlic *low, low lying, inferior, lowly,*
CP.
niðernes (y) f. *deepness, bottom,* BH 212²¹.
niðeronwend *downwards,* GD.
niðerra=niðera
niðerscēotende (y) *rushing downwards,*
OEG.
niðerscyfe m. *rushing downwards, descent,*
HGL 468.
niðersige (y¹) m. *going down,* LPs.
niðerstīgan=niðerāstīgan
niðerstīge (y¹) m. *descent,* RB. [v. '*nether*']
niðerstīgende *descending,* RB. [v. '*nether*']
niðertorfian *to throw down,* GPH 390.
±**niðerung** (y) f. *humiliation, abasement,
downthrow, condemnation,* BH,LG,OEG;
Æ. ['*nither*']
niðerweard adj. *directed downwards.* adv.
-weardes, Æ,OEG,RG. ['*netherward(s)*']
niðeweard *situated beneath, low, nethermost,*
Æ,Ph. ['*netheward*']
niðful *envious, quarrelsome, ill-disposed,
evil,* Æ. ['*nithfull*']
niðfullīce *maliciously,* ÆH 1·46'.
niðgæst† (y²) m. *hostile alien, fell demon.*
niðgetēon n. *attack,* GEN 2068.
niðgeweorc n. *evil deed,* B 683.
niðgrama m. *anger, malice,* W 180⁹.
niðgrim† *fierce, hostile,* B,PPs.
niðgripe m. *fierce grasp,* B 976? [or ? nȳd-]
niðheard† (and EPs 27⁴) *bold, brave in
battle.*
niðhell f. *hateful hell,* HL 15¹⁵⁰.
niðhete† m. *hostility, evil intent* : *affliction,
torment* : *foe,* AN 833?
niðhycgende† *evil-scheming.*
niðhȳdig (ē²) *valorous,* B 3165.
niðig *envious, malicious,* OEG p 224n.
niðing m. *wretch, villain, coward, outlaw,*
Chr,LL. ['*nithing*']
+**niðla**† m. *enemy* : *enmity, fierceness*
(?+niðle).
niðlīce adv. *abjectly,* OEG 744.
niðloca m. *place of torment,* HELL 64.
niðor=niðer

niðplega m. *battle, fight,* AN 414.
niðr-=niðer-
niðsceaða m. *foe, persecutor,* RD 16²⁴.
niðscipe m. *wickedness,* LPs 7¹⁰.
niðsele m. *hall of conflict,* B 1513.
niðsynn f. *grievous sin,* SAT 180.
niððas† mpl. *men.*
niðweorc n. *battle,* †CHR 973.
niðwracu† f. *severe punishment.*
niðwundor n. *dire wonder, portent,* B 1365.
nīwan (ēo) adv. *newly, lately,* Æ,AO.
nīwanācenned *new-born,* MH 170¹².
nīwancumen (WW)=nīwcumen
nīwane=nīwan
nīwbacen (nīg-) *newly baked,* Jos 9¹².
nīwcend *new-born,* BH 144²³ (nīc-).
nīwcīlct *newly whitewashed,* AO 286³⁰.
nīwcumen (nī(g)-) *new-comer, neophyte,* RB.
nīwe (ēo, īe) I. (nīg-, nī-, in compounds)
adj. '*NEW*,' *fresh, recent, novel, unheard of,
untried, inexperienced,* Æ,AO; CP. nīwan
stefne again. II. adv. (Bl)=nīwan. ['*new*']
nīwel=neowol
nīwerne (ȳ) *tender,* ÆH 1·566⁵.
nīwesēoða=newesēoða
nīwian *to renew, restore,* Chr,El,Lcd. ['*new*']
nīwiht=nāht
nīwlic (ȳ) *fresh.* adv. -līce *lately, recently,*
Æ,AO,Ps. ['*newly*']
nīwlinga (ēo) *anew,* GD 266²⁸.
nīwnes (ēo, īo) f. '*newness*,' *novelty,* BH,
Lcd.
nīwol=neowol
nīwtyrwed *newly tarred,* B 295.
nīwung f. *rudiment,* OEG 914.
nīwunga (eo) adv. *newly, anew,* AN,NG.
nixtnig (RB 138³)=nihstig
nō (CP)=nā
noctern m? n? *nocturn* (religious service),
CM 220⁵⁶¹. [L.]
+**nōg,** +nōh I. adj. '*enough,*' *sufficient,
abundant,* AN,Bo,RB; CP : *much, many.*
II. adv. *sufficiently,* Bo : *fully, quite,
abundantly,* Bo.
+**nōgian** *to be abundant,* NC 345.
nōh-=nāh-
nolde (Æ) v. *nyllan* and '*will.*'
nom pret. 3 sg. of *niman.*
nom-, nome-=nam-
non m. *title of senior monks,* RB.
nōn fn (m. RB 73¹⁴) *the ninth hour* (=3 p.m.),
B,BH,Lcd : *nones* (service held at the ninth
hour), RB,WW. tō nōnes *till three o'clock.*
['*noon*'; L. nona (hora)]
nōnbelle f. *noon-bell,* LL (436').
nōngereord n. *meal after nones, dinner,* RB
74⁸.
nōnhring m. *ringing of the noon-bell,* TF
114¹⁴.

nōnmete m. *afternoon meal, Sol,WW.*
['*noonmeat*']
nonne=nunne
nōnsang m. *service at 3 p.m., nones,* ÆP.
nōntīd f. *ninth hour, Æ,Bl.* ['*noontide*']
nōntīma m. *ninth hour,* BTK216³¹.
norð I. adj. comp. norð(er)ra, superl.
norðmest *northern,* AO. II. adv. comp.
norðor *northwards, Chr,Met : in the north,*
'*north,*' *AO,B,Bl.*
norðan adv. *from the north,* AO. be...
norðan prep. (w. d.) *north of,* AO.
norðanēastan adv. *from the north-east,*
north-easterly, AO.
norðanēastanwind m. *north-east wind,* WW.
Norð(an)hymbre mp. *Northumbrians, Chr :*
Northumbria. ['*Northumber*']
norðanweard *northward,* BL,CHR.
norðanwestan adv. *from the north-west,*
north-westerly, AO.
norðanwestanwind m. *north-west wind,* WW
8¹⁰.
norðanwind m. *north wind,* Bo,WW.
norðdǣl m. *north quarter, northern part,*
north, Æ,AO,Chr. ['*northdeal*']
norðduru f. *north door,* BL203.
norðēast m. (and adv.) '*north-east,*' *BC,*
Chr.
norðēastende m. *north-east end,* AO14¹⁴.
norðēasthyrne f. *north-east corner,* LV71.
norðēastlang *extending north-eastwards,* AO.
norðēastrodor m. *north-east quarter,* BH
424²⁰.
norðefes f. *northern border,* KC5·221².
norðemest=norðmest
norðende m. *northern quarter,* CHR,MET.
norðerne '*northern,*' *Northumbrian, Scan-*
dinavian, Æ,Chr,Met.
norðerra (*BC,Chr*) comp. adj. v. norð.
['*norther*']
norðeweard adj. *northward, north,* AO.
norðfolc n. *northern folk : people of Nor-*
folk.
norðgemǣre n. *northern limit,* AO10'.
norðheald *inclined northwards,* BC2·246'.
norðhealf f. *north side, north, AO,Bl.*
['*northhalf*']
norðhere m. *army from the north,* CHR910A.
norðhylde f. *north slope,* KC3·418'.
Norðhymbre=(1) Norðanhymbre; (2)
Norðhymbrisc
Norðhymbrisc *Northumbrian,* Æ (SR15⁵⁸).
norðhyrne f. *north corner,* KC3·449²⁰.
norðland n. *northern land or shore, AO,Chr.*
['*northland*']
norðlang *north-along,* KC.
norðlanu f. *north lane,* Ct.
norðlēode mp. *northern folk, Angles,* LL.
norðlic *northern,* WW361¹.

Norðmann m. *dweller in the north, Scandi-*
navian, Æ,AO,Chr. ['*Northman*']
norðmest (*AO,Met*) superl. of norð adj. and
adv. ['*northmost*']
norðor (*AO*) v. norð. ['*norther*']
norðportic m. *north porch,* BH106².
norðra v. norð.
norðrihte (y; AO17), -rihtes (KC3·450⁵)
direct northwards, due north.
norðrodor m. *northern sky,* GU1253.
norðryhte=norðrihte
norðsǣ f. *northern sea, Bristol Channel,*
Chr : Baltic, ' North Sea,*'* Æ.
norðscēata m. *northern point, promontory,*
AO28³.
norðsciphere m. *Danish fleet,* CHR980C.
norððēod f. *northern people,* BH50¹².
norððunor m. *thunder from the north,* ES
39·351.
Norð-wēalas, -wālas mp. *North Welsh* (*i.e.*
not Cornish) : *Wales.*
Norðwēalcynn n. *inhabitants of* (*North*)
Wales, CHR.
norðweard adj. and adv. *north,* '*northward,*'
Chr; AO.
norðweardes adv. '*northwards,*' *Chr.*
norðweg m. *a way leading northwards,* Ex
68 : *Norway.*
norðwest adv. '*north-west,*' *AO,BC.*
norðwestende m. *north-west end,* AO.
norðwestgemǣre m. *north-west boundary,*
AO8³¹.
norðwind m. *north wind,* WW378⁸.
nōse† f. *ness, promontory,* B.
nosgrisele (WW427)=nosugrisle
nosle (*WW*153)=nostle
nostle f. *fillet, band, CP,WW.* ['*nostel*']
nos-ðirl, -ðyr(e)l, -terl (*WW*) n. '*nostril,*'
Æ,Lcd.
nosu f. gds. nosa, nose '*nose,*' *Æ,Chr,*
CP.
nosugrisle f. *nose-gristle,* WW290³⁰
nōt m. *mark, note,* BF182²⁴. [*L.* nota]
nōtere m. *scribe, writer,* OEG2846. [*L.*]
nōteðǣshwōn=nāteshwōn
notgeorn *industrious,* W72⁹. [nēotan]
±notian I. *to enjoy : use, employ,* Bo,RB,
WW; Æ,CP : *discharge an office.* ['*note*']
II. (+) *note,* Mt p12².
notu f. *enjoyment, use, advantage, utility,*
AO,RB : employment, office, discharge of a
duty, Æ,RB; CP. ['*note*'; nēotan]
notwierðe (u²) *useful,* ANS129·18.
notwrītere m. *one who makes notes, scribe,*
WW451³⁵.
nōð† f. *daring, boldness : booty, plunder*
(GK), WH28?
nōðer (*CP*)=nāhwæðer. ['*nother*']
nōwend m. *shipmaster, sailor,* OEG.

nōwēr=nāhwǣr

nōwiht (*CP,VPs*) (u², y²)=nāht. ['*nought*']

nōwðer (*BC*)=nāhwæðer. ['*nouther*']

nū I. adv. '*now,*' *at present, at this time, immediately,* Æ,*AO,Bl,VPs*; CP : *very recently, Bf,Bo* : *introducing commands, requests* (*Bl,Cr,Ps*) *and arguments* (*Æ,Bo, CP*). nū gēn *still.* nū ȝīet *as yet, still.* nū ðā *now, already,* Æ ('*nowthe*'). II. conj. *now that, inasmuch as, because, since, when, Bl,Bo,VPs*; AO,CP. III. interj. *lo! behold! come!* Æ. nū lā *now.*

+nugan* swv. impers. pres. 3 sg. +neah *to suffice, not to lack.*

nūhwīlum *now-a-days,* Bo 123⁶.

numen I. pp. of niman. II. '*vulsio,*' MkL p2¹⁷ (v. A16·74).

numol (æ¹, e², u²) '*capax,*' *holding much, quick at learning,* ÆGr,*WW* : '*mordax,*' *biting,* CHRD 74²⁰. ['*nimble*']

nūna adv. *now,* WW254²⁴.

nunfǣmne f. *nun,* GD 50,340. [v. '*nun*']

nunhīred m. *nunnery,* TC232⁶.

nunlīf n. *life of a nun,* GD199¹⁶.

nun(nan)mynster n. *convent, nunnery,* Ct, GD.

nunne f. '*nun,*' Æ,*BH* : *pagan priestess, vestal,* AO.

nunscrūd n. *nun's dress,* TC538¹².

nusēoða=neweseoða; nūðā v. nū.

nuton (DR)=nyton (v. nytan).

nybōe (VHy)=nymðe

+nycled (GL)=+cnycled

nȳd I.=nīed. II.=nēod

nȳd-=nēad-, nīed-

nȳdbebod n. *command,* CREAT72.

nȳdboda m. *messenger of evil?* Ex474.

nȳdbrice (ē) m. *requirement, need,* ÆH 2·144'.

nȳdbysgu f. *toil, trouble,* RIM44.

nȳdbysig *distressed,* JUL423.

nȳdcleofa† m. *prison,* EL,JUL.

nȳdcosting f. *affliction,* GU1126.

nȳddǣda m. *one who acts under compulsion,* LL36,26.

+nȳdenlic *compulsory,* BH62²³B.

nȳdfara m. *fugitive, exile,* Ex208.

nȳdgedāl† n. *forced dissolution, death,* GU.

nȳdgenga m. *wretched wanderer,* DA633.

nȳdgestealla m. *comrade in need,* B882.

nȳdgewald m. *tyranny,* CT1451.

nȳdgild n. *exaction, tribute,* W162¹¹.

nȳdgrāp f. (RIM73), nȳdgripe m. (B976) *coercive grip.*

nȳdhǣmedre m. *adulterer,* OEG.

nȳdhǣmestre (ē) f. *mistress? concubine? adulteress?* OEG4451.

nȳdhelp mf. *help in trouble,* LL(278²).

nȳdlic (ēo) *necessary,* Sc.

±nȳd-mǣg m., -māge f. *blood-relation, cousin,* LL.

nȳdmǣgen (ē¹) n. *force,* DR117¹³.

nȳdnǣman *to force, ravish,* LL.

nȳdnes f. *necessity,* LL(158¹⁰).

nȳdnima (ē) m. *one who takes by force,* NG.

nȳdniman³ (ēa) *to take by force, abduct,* LL360,73,2.

nȳdnimend (ē¹) f. *rapine,* MtR23²⁵.

nȳdnimu (ē) f. *rapine, forcible seizure,* DR.

nȳdnimung f. *rapine, abduction,* WW116²⁹.

nȳdriht n. *duty, office : due, tribute,* LL.

nȳdðēowetling m. *bond-slave,* TC628¹³.

nȳdðēowigan *to reduce to servitude, exact service from* (*an ecclesiastical establishment*), LL381,21.

nȳdwracu† f. *violence, distress.*

nȳdwrǣclīce *violently,* ÆL23b⁴⁰⁴.

nȳdwyrhta m. *involuntary agent,* LL.

+nyhe=+neahhe

nȳhst=nīehst; nyht=niht

+nyht fn. *abundance, fulness, sufficiency,* CP. [+nugan]

+nyhtful *abundant, plentiful,* WW40³⁴.

+nyhtlīce *abundantly,* WW3².

±nyhtsum *abundant, abounding* : (+) *satisfied, contented.* adv. -līce, VPs.

+nyhtsumian *to suffice, abound,* Æ.

+nyhtsumnes f. *abundance, plenty,* VPs.

+nyhtsumung (-ihð-) f. *abundance,* RPs 77²⁵.

+nyhð (W1)6²¹)=+nyht?

nyllan* anv. pret. nolde *to be unwilling,* Æ, *CP*; AO : *refuse, prevent,* PPs5³. ['NILL*'; ne, willan]

nyman=niman; -nyme v. fore-n.

nymne=nemne

nymðe (e, i) conj. *unless, except : nor,* EPs 130¹.

+nyp=+nip

nypel m. *trunk* (*of an elephant*), Æ (4²⁸⁶).

nȳr=nēar=nēah adv.

nyrgend=nergend; nyrðra=norðerra

±nyrwan, nyrwian=nierwan

nyrwett=nirewett; nys=nis=ne is

nysse, nyste (*Bo,Bl,VPs*)=ne wisse, ne wiste v. nytan. ['*nist*']

nystlan=nistlan; nyt=(1) nytt; (2) nett

+nȳt pres. 3 sg. of +nīedan.

nytan (e, i) anv. pres. 1, 3 sg. nāt, 2 nāst, pl. nyton, pret. nyste, nysse *not to know, to be ignorant,* Æ,AO,CP. [ne, witan]

nyten *ignorant,* ÆH1·62¹⁴. [ne, witan]

nȳten (*Lcd*)=nīeten

nytende adv. *ignorantly,* Æ.

nytennes=nytennes

nytenlic *ignorant,* ÆH2·134².

nytennes (e, i) f. *ignorance, laziness, ignominy,* Æ : *unknown state,* ÆL33²⁶⁰.

nytlic *useful, profitable,* AA,LCD. [*Ger.* nützlich] adv. -līce.

nytlicnes f. *utility,* LCD 1·314⁸.

nytnes f. *use, benefit, convenience,* BH,GD.

nyton v. nytan.

nytt I. f. *use, utility, advantage,* AO,CP : *duty, office, employment,* B : *supervision, care,* GD 180²⁸. **II.** adj. *useful, beneficial, helpful, profitable,* AO,CP. [nēotan]

nytte=nette

±**nyttian** *to enjoy, use,* Lcd : *eat.* ['*nutte*']

nyttnes=nytnes

nytto=nytt I.

nyttol *useful,* LCD 32b.

nyttung (i) f. *profit, advantage,* WW 116³⁷.

nytu (*MtR* 7¹⁶)=hnutu

nytun=nyton=ne witon

nytweorð-=nytwierð-

nyt-wierðe (CP), -wirðe, -wyrðe (Æ) *useful, profitable.*

nytwierðlic *useful, profitable.* adv. -līce, CP.

nytwierðnes (eo, y) f. *utility,* WW.

nytwurð-, nytwyrð-=nytwierð-

nyðan=neoðan

nyðe-, nyðer-=niðer-, niðr-; **nȳw-**=nīw-

nywel, nywol=neowol; **nȳxt**=nīehst

nyxtnig (LCD)=nihstig

O

o=on; **ō** (N)=ā; **ob,** ob- (K)=of, of-

obet (*Cp,Ep*)=ofet; **obst** (Cp 217 E)=ofost

oc=ac

ōc pret. 3 sg. of acan.

ōcon pret. pl. of acan.

ōcusta m. *armpit,* GL.

ōden (o?) f. *threshing-floor,* AS,Sc.

ōdencole *hollow serving as a threshing-floor,* EC 121².

+**ōdon**=+ēodon; **oe-**=a-, e-, ē-

oeg (N)=woeg=weg

ōeg-hwēr, -hwelc (Cp)=æg-hwær, -hwilc

oeht- (N)=ēht-; **oembeht** (Cp)=ambiht

oemseten (=ymb-) f. *shoot, slip?* (Swt), *row (of vines)?* (BT), Cp 534A.

oexen=exen v. oxa.

of I. prep. w. d. 'OF,' *from, out of,* Æ,AO, etc. : *among, concerning, about, AO* : *by,* Chr : *derived from, made of, belonging to,* Æ,AO,CP. **II.** adv. '*off,' away, absent,* Bl, Chr,LL,Mt.

of-=æf-

ofācēapian *to buy off,* LL 122,74.

ofāceorfan³ *to cut or prune off,* AO,CP.

ofāscian *to find out by asking, be informed, hear of, learn,* Æ.

ofādōn anv. *to pull out, tear out,* LL 86,70⁷⁴ : *leave out, except,* LL 182,10.

ofādrincan³ *to drain,* Æ : *quench,* AO.

ofādrygan *to dry off, wipe off,* CP 71¹¹

ofæt=ofet

ofǣte? f. *food,* HEX 194.

ofāhēawan⁷ *to cut off,* ÆL 29²⁹³.

ofāniman *to take away,* GUTH 19²⁶.

ofāsceacan⁶ *to shake off,* CM 993 : *excuse.*

ofāsciran (e, y) *to cut off,* LL 68,35⁵.

ofāsēoðan² *to purge, purify,* BH 288⁹.

ofāslēan⁶ *to smite off,* CHR.

ofāsnīdan *to cut off,* LCD.

ofātēon² *to pull out, withdraw,* CP.

ofāweorpan *to cast aside, throw off* (or ? two words), VH 17.

ofāxian (Æ)=ofācsian

ofbēatan⁷ *to beat to death, kill,* AO.

ofblindian *to blind,* JnLR 12⁴⁰.

ofcalan⁶ *to chill, make or grow cold,* Æ,W.

ofclipian *to obtain by calling, call for,* Æ.

ofcuman⁴ *to spring from, be derived from,* Æ.

ofcyrf m. *a section, cutting,* Æ : *amputation,* Æ.

ofdæl *inclined* (*downwards*), Bo 53¹⁴.

ofdæle (e²) n. *decline, declivity, descent, abyss.* CP.

ofdōn anv. *to put out, put off, take off* (*clothes*).

ofdrǣdan⁷ (but wk. pp. ofdrædd) *to fear, be afraid, terrified,* Æ,CP.

ofdrincan *to intoxicate,* LL.

ofdruncnian *to get drunk* (*on*), CHRD 74⁷.

ofdūne adv. *down,* AO,CP.

ofdūneheald adv. *directed downwards* (Swt).

ofdūneonwend *downwards,* GD 24²⁸.

ofdūnesettan *to set down,* VHy.

ofdūnestīgan¹ *to descend,* VPs.

ofdūneweard(es) adv. *downwards,* GD.

ofdūnrihte *downwards,* MFH 170.

ofe-=ufe-

ofearmian *to be pitiful,* RSPs 36²²,76⁹.

ofearmung f. *compassion,* BLPs 102⁴.

ofēhtan *to persecute,* RPs 43¹⁷.

ofelēte=oflǣte

ofen m., gs. ofnes *furnace, MH,MtLR* : '*oven,'* Æ.

ofenan=ufenan

ofenbacen *baked in an oven,* Æ.

ofen-raca m., -racu f. *oven-rake,* WW.

ofer I. prep. [w. d. (rest) and a. (motion)] '*OVER,' beyond, above, upon, in, across, past,* Æ,AO,CP. ofer bæc *backwards, back : throughout : against, in contravention of, contrary to, beyond,* AO,CHR : (*time*) *after, through, during, at the end of, AO,* Chr : *more than : in addition to, besides, beyond.* **II.** adv. *above, on high : to or on the other side, AO : from side to side, across, AO : beyond, above* (*quantity*).

ōfer (o²) m. (gs. ōfres) *border, margin, edge* : *brink, river-bank, sea-shore, Æ,B,Lcd*; AO. [' *over* '; v. Mdf]

oferæt m. *gluttony, feasting, excess, CP*; Æ : *feast.* [' *overeat* ']

oferæte *gluttonous,* RB17¹⁵.

oferāhebban=oferhebban

oferāwrit-=oferwrit-

oferbæcgetēung f. *tetanus,* WW112²⁰.

oferbebēodan² *to rule,* WW178³⁷.

oferbecuman⁴ *to supervene,* CM133,1060.

ofer-bēon anv. pres. 3 pl. -sind *to be over, command,* CM112; WW178³⁷.

oferbīdan¹ *to outlast, outlive, TC.* [' *overbide* ']

oferbiternes (y³) f. *excessive bitterness, SPs.* [' *overbitterness* ']

oferblica m. *surface,* OET181⁴⁴.

oferblīðe *too light-hearted, CP.*

oferbrǣdan *to spread over, suffuse, be spread over, overshadow, cover over, CP*; Æ. [' *overbrede* ']

oferbrǣdels m. *outside, surface, covering* : *coverlet, veil, garment, Æ,CP* : *cerecloth,* MFH153.

oferbrāw m. *eye-brow,* LCD3·188⁵. [brǣw]

oferbrecan⁴ *to transgress, violate,* AO.

oferbrēdan=oferbregdan

oferbrēdels (KGL)=oferbrǣdels

oferbregdan³ *to draw over, cover, overspread* : *be covered over, show a film over.*

oferbrū f. *eye-brow,* GL.

oferbrycgian (i³) *to span as by a bridge, Æ.* [' *overbridge* ']

ofercǣfed *overlaid with ornament,* GPH394.

oferceald *excessively cold,* Run11. [' *overcold* ']

ofercīdan *to chide sharply,* EPs,LL.

ofercīdung f. *chiding, reproof,* EPs149⁷.

ofercierr (e) m. *passing over,* MtL1¹¹.

ofercierran (e) *to cross over,* LkL16²⁶.

oferclif n. *steep place, overhanging cliff,* WW480².

oferclimban³ *to climb over,* AO134¹³. [' *overclimb* ']

oferclipian *to cry out,* LkL23¹⁸.

ofercostung f. *great tribulation,* JnL16³³.

ofercræft m. *fraud,* LL(166²⁰).

ofercuman⁴ *to overcome, subdue, compel, conquer, AO,B,Lcd,WW*; CP : *obtain, attain, reach, overtake, BH,Cp,Jud,WW.* [' *overcome* ']

ofercwealm *great mortality,* A3·113.

ofercyme m. *arrival,* BH436²⁸.

ofercymend (mm) m. *assailant,* LkL.

ofercȳðan *to outdo by preponderance of oaths,* v. LL2·689.

oferdōn anv. *to* ' *overdo,*' *do to excess, Æ.* oferdōne ðing *excesses, Æ.*

oferdrenc (Æ)=oferdrync

oferdrencan *to make drunk,* AO,CP : *give copiously to drink,* GEN43³⁴.

oferdrīfan¹ *to overcome, defeat, dispense, Æ, DR* : *confute, Æ* : *cover* (*by drifting sand*), AO40¹ : *outvote,* LL. [' *overdrive* ']

oferdrinc=oferdrync

oferdrincan³ *to drink too much, get drunk, CP,LL.* [' *overdrink* ']

oferdrincere m. *drunkard,* HL12⁹⁵,¹²⁴.

oferdruncen I. n. *drunkenness,* LL. II. ptc. *drunk.*

oferdruncennes f. *drunkenness,* Æ,CP.

oferdrync m. *over-drinking, drunkenness, CP* : *revelry, feasting.* [' *overdrink* ']

oferdyre n. *lintel,* WW280¹⁶.

ofere *over, across,* v. LV8 : *from above,* RPs.

oferēaca m. *surplus, overplus, remainder, addition, increase, Æ.*

ofereald (y) *very old,* RB61¹².

oferealdormann m. *chief officer,* BH264¹ (v.l.).

ofereall *anywhere,* BF138²¹.

oferēca=oferēaca

ofereldu (HL11⁶⁰N)=oferyldu

oferēt=oferæt

ofer-etol (CP), -eotol, -ettol *gluttonous.*

oferetolnes f. *gluttony,* CP317¹⁸.

oferfær n. *passing over,* NG.

oferfæreld n. *passage, journey over or across,* Æ,AO.

oferfæt *too fat,* WW. [' *overfat* ']

oferfæðman† *to envelop, overshadow.*

oferfaran⁶ (intr.) *to pass, cross, go over, Ps* : (tr.) *traverse, go through, penetrate, Gen,W*; Æ,AO : *come across, meet with, overtake* : *pass through, withstand, overcome.* [' *overfare* ']

oferfeallan⁷ *to attack,* BL203.

oferfeng I. m. *fibula, buckle, clasp,* GL. II. pret. 3 sg. of oferfōn.

oferfeohtan³ *to conquer,* Æ,CP.

oferfēran *to traverse, cross, pass along, over, by, or through, Æ,AO* : *come upon, meet with.*

oferferian *to carry over, transport,* OEG3680.

oferfērnes f. *fordable place,* BH58¹.

oferfēðre *overloaded,* v. ES43·312.

oferfil=oferfyll

oferflēdan *to overflow, flood,* LCD3·252'.

oferflēde *in flood,* LCD3·252'.

oferflēon² *to fly over, Æ* : *flee from, yield to,* B2525.

oferflēwednes=oferflōwednes

oferflītan¹ *to overcome, beat, confute,* AO.

oferflōwan *to flow over, run over,* ' *overflow,*' *AO,Lk.*

ofer-flōwed(līc)nes, -flōwen(d)nes (Æ) f. *excess, superfluity.*

ofer-flōwend (*RB*), -flōwe(n)dlic *super-fluous* : *excessive*, VH 17. [' *overflowing* ']
adv -līce.
oferflōwnes f. *superfluity*, CP.
oferfōn⁷ *to seize, take prisoner*, AO.
oferfrēcednes f. *oppression*, V²Ps 31⁷.
oferfroren *frozen over*, AO.
oferfull *too full*, LPs. [' *overfull* ']
oferfunden *tested*, AO 296⁹.
oferfundennes f. *trial, experiment*, OEG 543.
oferfylgan *to pursue, attack*, CP.
ofer-fyll, -fyllo, -fyllu f. *surfeit, gluttony, excess*, Bo,Lcd; Æ,CP : *overplus, resulting liquor*, Lcd 47a. [' *overfyll* ']
oferfyllan *to cram*, RB,WW.
oferfylnes f. *surfeit, excess*, GD 339³.
oferfyrr f. *excessive distance*, AO 24²¹. [feorr]
ofergǣgan *to transgress*, Æ.
ofergǣgednes f. *transgression*, Æ.
ofergǣgend m. *transgressor*, ÆL 30⁴¹¹.
ofer-gān anv., -gangan⁷ *to pass over, beyond, across, traverse, cross*, Æ,Lcd,VPs; AO, CP : *transgress, overstep*, Met, MtL, Ps : *overrun, overcome, overspread, conquer*, Chr,Ex,Lcd,Rd; Æ : *come upon, overtake, seize, attack*, Æ,An : *pass off, pass away, end*, AO,CP : *overreach*, Chrd 110³⁴. [' *overgo*,' ' *overgang* ']
ofergapian *to be forgetful of, neglect*, RB 112².
ofergēare *old*, Lcd 19a.
ofergeatu f. *oblivion*, PPs 128⁶.
ofergeatul=ofergitol
ofergedrync n. *excess in drinking*, Bl 99²¹.
ofergedyre=oferdyre
ofergemet I. n. *excess*, AS,CP. II. *excessive*, VH 17 (or ? two words).
ofergēmnes f. *watching for*, NG. [gīeman]
ofergenga m. *traveller*, Lcd.
ofergenihtsumian *to superabound*, Sc 131¹⁵.
ofergeong (=gang) m. *going across*, MtK p 12¹³.
ofergeot-=ofergi(e)t-
ofergēotan² *to pour upon, suffuse, flood, overwhelm*, Æ.
ofergeotende *forgetful*, BH 114²². [ofergietan]
ofer-geotol, -geottol=ofergitol
ofergesāwan=ofersāwan
ofergesettan *to set over*, CP,VPs.
ofergestondan⁶ (=a⁴) *to stand over*, BH.
ofergetilian *to overcome*, ÆL 23b¹⁸⁵.
ofergetimbran *to erect*, Bl 205.
ofergetol-=ofergitol-
ofergeðyld *intolerable state*, Sol 84²⁴.
ofergeweorc n. *superstructure : sepulchre*, Æ.
ofergewrit n. *superscription, inscription*, G, WW.
ofergietan⁵ *to forget, disregard, neglect*, CP.
ofergīfre *gluttonous*, CP 177,308.

ofergildan=ofergyldan
ofergīman *to neglect, disregard*, RB,Sat.
ofergitan=ofergietan
ofer-gitol, -gittol (ea, eo, y) *forgetful*, Ps.
ofergitolian (e, eo) *to forget*, JVPs.
ofergitolnes (e, eo, y) f. *forgetfulness*, Bl,Ps.
oferglenged (æ³) *over-adorned*, ÆPd 134¹¹.
oferglēsan (oe) *to write glosses over*, Jn p 188⁷.
oferglīdan¹ *to glide over, traverse, pass over, overshadow*, Æ.
ofergrǣdig *too covetous*, W. [' *overgreedy* ']
ofergrōwan⁷ *to overgrow*, CP 336⁸.
ofergumian *to neglect, disregard*, RB 113².
ofergyld *gilt*, Æ.
ofergyldan (i) *to encase, overlay or adorn with gold*, Æ,CP.
ofergylden *overlaid with gold*, LL 460,10.
ofergȳman=ofergīman
ofergyrd ptc. *girt*, GPH 394.
ofergytan=ofergietan
ofergytnes f. *oblivion, forgetfulness*, LkR, PPs.
oferhacele f. *hood*, LL (140²²).
oferhangen *covered*, GD 202¹⁹.
oferhāt *over-hot*, Lcd 4a.
oferhēafod adv. *in each case*, ÆH 1·30⁴.
oferhēah *very tall, lofty*, Run 26. [' *over-high* ']
oferhealdan *to overcome, overtake*, VH : ' *supertenere*,' LL (198¹¹)?
oferhealfhēafod n. *crown of the head*, WW 156¹¹.
oferheargian=oferhergan
oferhebban⁶ *to pass over, omit, neglect*, AO, LL; CP. [' *overheave* ']
oferhebbendlic *highly exalted*, DR.
oferhelian *to cover over, conceal*, Sc; CP. [' *overhele* ']
oferheling f. *covering*, Sc. [v. ' *overhele* ']
oferhelmian *to overshadow*, B 1364.
oferheortnes f. *vehemence of feeling*, AO 166²⁰.
oferhergean *to overrun, ravage*, AO,Chr.
oferhīd-=oferhygd-
oferhīeran (ēo, ȳ) *to* ' *overhear*,' *hear*, AO : *disobey, disregard, neglect*, AO.
oferhīernes (ē, ī, ȳ) f. *neglect, disobedience* : *fine for transgression of law or legal orders* (=' *superauditio* '), LL.
oferhigd=oferhygd
oferhige? m. *pride*, PPs 87⁷. [hyge]
oferhigendlīce *daringly, presumptuously*, ByH 102¹⁶.
oferhigian *to delude, turn the head of*, B 2766.
oferhīran (AO)=oferhīeran
oferhīwian *to transfigure : paint over*, NG.
oferhlæstan *to overload*, AO.
oferhlēapan⁷ *to jump over, surmount, overcome*, BH : *pass over*, Lcd. [' *overleap* ']

oferhlēapend m. *over-leaper*, WW 190².

oferhlēoōrian *to surpass in loudness*, AA, Sol 152¹².

oferhlēoōur *failing to hear*, PPs 93⁹.

oferhlīfan¹ (OEG), oferhlīfian (Æ,CP) *to tower over, overtop, excel, exceed, surpass*.

oferhlīfung f. *loftiness, sublimity*, Gl.

ofer-hlūd, -hlȳde *clamorous, noisy*, WW. ['*overloud*'] adv. -hlūde.

oferhlȳp m. *a jump, leap (over something)*, Bf 72,112.

oferhlyttrian *to clarify, strain*, ÆGr 222⁸.

oferhoga m. *despiser, proud man*, W.

oferhogian *to despise*, Bl,Bo. ['*overhow*']

oferhogiend m. *despiser*, RB 48⁶.

oferhogodnes f. *pride, disdain*, GD 144³.

oferholt n. *phalanx of shields*, Ex 157.

oferhrǣgan (w. d.) *to tower above?* Sol 35.

oferhrēfan *to roof over, cover*, Bl,Lcd.

oferhrēred *overthrown*, WW.

oferhrops *greediness*, WW 102¹⁹.

oferhrȳfan=oferhrēfan

oferhrȳred=oferhrēred

oferhycgean *to despise*, AO,CP.

oferhȳd=oferhygd

oferhygd (i) I. fn. *pride, conceit, arrogance*, CP : *highmindedness*, AS. II. adj. *haughty, proud*.

oferhygdgian *to be proud*, CVPs 9²³.

oferhygdig I. n. *pride*, MFH,PPs. II. adj. *haughty, proud*, Æ.

ofer-hygd(ig)līce, -hīdlīce *arrogantly*, GD.

oferhygdnes f. *excessive pride, arrogance*, VH 18.

oferhygdu f.=oferhygd I.

oferhylmend m. *dissembler*, PPs 118¹¹⁹.

oferhȳran=oferhīeran

oferhȳre *heedless, neglectful*, LL (244').

oferhyrned *having horns above*, Run 2.

oferhȳrnes f. *heedlessness, neglect, disobedience*, LL.

+oferian *to elevate*, HGl 428 (=uferian).

oferīdyllīce *vainly, emptily*, CPs 30⁷.

ofering f. *superabundance*, Bo.

oferlād f. '*translatio*,' *solemn removal of the body or relics of a saint to a shrine*, DR 62⁹.

oferlǣdan *to oppress*, Bl : *translate*. ['*overlead*']

oferlǣfan *to leave over* : *be left over, remain*, LkLR. ['*overleave*']

oferlagu f. *cloak*, Gl.

oferlecgan *to place over*, CM 899 : *overburden, surfeit*, HL 11⁹⁹; 12⁷³.

oferlēof *very dear*, Run 23.

oferlēoran *to pass over, or by* : *transgress, prevaricate*.

oferlēornes f. *transgression*, CPs 100³.

oferlibban *to survive*. ÆGr,TC. ['*overlive*']

oferlīce *excessively*, W. [v. '*overly*']

oferlifa (y³) m. *excess*, NC 348.

oferlīfian=oferhlīfian

oferlīhtan *to light upon*, ÆL 23b⁵⁵⁸ : *excel in brightness*.

oferlīōan¹ *to pass over, sail over*, Guth,MH.

oferlufu f. *too great love*, W. ['*overlove*']

oferlyfa=oferlifa

oferlyftlic *above the air*, NC 314.

ofermǣcga m. *very illustrious being*, Gu 664.

ofermǣgen† n. *overpowering might*.

ofermǣstan *to over-fatten*, BH (Wheloc 228').

ofermǣte *excessive, immoderate*, AO,CP. ['*overmete*']

ofermǣtlic *vast*, AO 52¹⁰.

ofermǣto=ofermētto

ofermagan swv. *to prevail*, Sc 97¹⁹.

ofermāðum m. *costly treasure*, B 2993.

ofermearcung (e³) f. *superscription*, MkL p5¹.

ofermēde I. n. *pride*, CP. II. adj. *proud, arrogant*. [mōd]

ofermēdla m. *haughtiness, pride*, LL.

ofermēdu (CP)=ofermētto

ofermete m. *gorging, gluttony*, CP.

ofermētto f. (often in pl.) *pride*, Æ,AO, CP.

ofermicel *over-much, excessive*, AO,RB. ['*overmickle*']

ofermicelnes f. *excess*, Sc 50¹³.

ofermōd I. n. *pride, insolence*, Gen,Ma. ['*overmod*'] II. adj. *proud, overbearing, insolent*, Bl; Æ,CP.

ofer-mōdgian (CP), -mōdig(i)an *to be proud, arrogant*.

ofermōdgung f. *pride*, CP 109¹¹.

ofermōdig *proud, arrogant*, Lcd; AO. adv. -līce. [v. '*overmod*']

ofermōdignes f. *pride, haughtiness, arrogance*, Mk. [v. '*overmod*']

ofermōdlic *proud, haughty, insolent*, CP. adv. -līce.

ofermōdnes=ofermōdignes

ofernēod I. (ī³) f. *extreme need*, LL,W. II. *very necessary*, CM.

oferniman⁴ (y) *to take away, carry off, seize, ravish* : *come over*, BH 410b¹².

ofernōn fn. *afternoon (after 3.0 p.m.)*, WW 175⁴⁷.

oferorn=oferarn pret. 3 sg. of oferyrnan.

oferprūt I. '*over-proud*,' *presumptuous, arrogant=haughty*, Sc. II. f. *excessive pride*, W 81'.

oferrǣdan *to read over*, Æ : *consider, infer*. ['*overread*']

oferranc *too luxurious*, W 46¹. ['*overrank*']

oferreccan *to confute, convince, convict*, CP.

oferrencu f. *extravagance*, W 46².

oferrīcsian *to rule over*, CP 119¹⁹.

oferrīdan¹ *to ride across*, BH 196⁸. [' *over-ride'*]

oferrōwan⁷ *to row over*, Æ.

ofersǣlic *on the other side of the sea*, BH 246³.

ofersǣlig *excessively happy*, DD 246.

ofersǣlð f. *excessive pleasure*, MET 5²⁷.

ofersǣwisc *from across the sea, foreign*, LCD, MH.

ofersāwan⁷ *to sow* (*over*), *Mt* 13²⁵. [' *over-sow'*]

oferscēadan⁷ *to scatter over, sprinkle over*, LCD 67b.

ofer-sceadian (CP), -sceadewian *to over-shadow*.

ofersceatt m. *usury, interest*, MtR 25²⁷.

oferscēawian *to superintend*, LL.

oferscēawigend m. *overseer, bishop*, LL.

oferscīnan¹ *to illuminate*, BF,BL : *excel* (*in brightness*), ByH 112′.

oferscūwian *to overshadow*, MtR 17⁵.

ofersēam m. *bag*, LkL 12³³.

ofersēcan *to overtax*, B 2686.

ofersegl m. *top-sail*, WW 7⁴.

oferseglian *to sail across*, *Mt*. [' *oversail'*]

ofersēgon=ofersāwon pret. pl. of ofersēon.

ofersendan *to transmit*, ÆGR 172¹³.

ofersēocnes f. *great illness*, LL.

oferseolfrian (y) *to cover over with silver*, AO.

ofersēon⁵ *to see over, overlook, survey, ob-serve, see*, Bo : *despise, neglect*, W. [' *over-see'*]

ofersettan *to set over*, VPs : *overcome*, GD 347³⁰.

ofersittan⁵ *occupy, possess*, Bo,VPs : *forbear, desist, refrain from*, Æ,B. [' *oversit'*]

oferslǣge=oferslege

oferslǣp m. *too much sleep*, LCD 1·342¹³.

oferslēan⁶ *to subdue, overcome*, RB 32¹⁵.

oferslege n. *lintel*, Æ,BF.

oferslop n. *loose upper garment, surplice, stole*, Lcd,LkL. [' *overslop'*]

oferslype m. *over-garment, surplice*, Æ.

ofersmēaung f. *too exhaustive consideration*, CP 97¹⁷.

ofersmītan *to smear over*, LCD 67b.

ofersprǣc f. *loquacity*, CP.

ofersprǣce *talkative, tale-bearing*, Æ,CP.

ofersprǣdan *to overlay, cover*, RB 84²³.

oferspreca m. *one who talks too much*, OEG 28⁹.

ofersprecan⁵ *to say too much*, LPs : *be abusive*.

ofersprēce=ofersprǣce

ofersprecol *talking too much, tattling, in-discreet*, CP.

ofersprecolnes f. *talkativeness*, CP 308¹⁶.

oferstǣlan *to confute, convict, convince*, Æ, CP.

oferstæppan⁶ *to* ' *over-step,' cross*, LPs : *exceed*, KC.

oferstandan⁶ *to stand over*, BH 308²⁵.

ofersteall m. *opposition*, ÆH 1·534²⁰.

oferstealla m. *survivor*, MH 210²⁸.

oferstellan *to jump over*, BH 400²².

ofersteppan=oferstæppan

oferstīgan¹ *to climb over, mount, scale, sur-mount, overcome*, AO; Æ,CP : *surpass, excel, exceed*, BH; Æ,CP. [' *oversty'*]

oferstige m. *astonishment*, ÆL 23⁵⁵⁵.

oferstīgendlic *superlative*, ÆGR 15¹⁸.

oferstigennes *passing over*, OEG 405.

oferswimman³ *to swim over or across*, B 2367. [' *overswim'*]

oferswingan³ ' *transverberare'!* GD 344³³.

oferswīðan (ȳ) wv. and sv¹ *to overpower, overcome, conquer, vanquish*, Æ,AO,CP : *excel, surpass*.

oferswīðe adv. *over-much, excessively*, Chr. [' *overswithe'*]

oferswīðend m. *vanquisher*, ÆL 30¹²⁶.

oferswīðestre f. ' *victrix,'* WW 224³⁹.

oferswīðnes f. *pressure, distress*, NG.

oferswīðrian *to prevail, conquer*, LPs,RB.

oferswīðung f. *pressure, distress*, NG.

oferswōgan⁷ *to cover, choke*, BL 203⁹.

oferswȳðan=oferswīðan

ofersylfrian (AO)=oferseolfrian

ofersȳman (=īe) *to overload, oppress*, RB.

ofertæl n. *odd number*, LCD 1·288⁸.

ofertæle *superstitious*, Sc 218¹⁰.

ofertalian *to confute, convince*, RWH 3²⁸.

oferteldan³ *to cover over*, Ex 81.

ofertēon² *to draw over, cover*, Æ : *finish*, WW 209³⁵.

ofertogennes f. *the condition of being covered*.

ofertrahtnian *to treat of*, ÆH 1·202′.

ofertredan *to tread down*, GPH. [' *over-tread'*]

ofertrūwa m. *over-confidence*, LL 180,8⁷. [' *overtrow'*]

ofertrūwian *to trust too much*, CP,W.

oferðearf f. *great need, extreme distress*, W.

oferðearfa m. *one in great need*, CR 153.

oferðeccan *to cover over, hide*, Æ.

oferðencan *to think over, reflect*, GD.

oferðēon¹,³ *to excel, surpass*, Æ,CP.

oferðōht *thought over, considered*, GD 316²⁰.

oferðrēawian (ā³) ' *increpare,'* EPs 67³¹.

oferðryccednes (i) f. *pressure*, CPs 31⁷.

oferðrymm m. *excessive power*, DD 52.

oferufa *upon, above*, NG.

oferwacian *to watch over*, Æ. [' *overwake'*]

oferwadan⁶ *to wade across*, AO 72³³. [' *over-wade'*]

oferwealdan⁷ *to get the better of*, LL 454,7.

oferwealdend m. *over-lord, ruler*, EL 1236.

oferweaxan⁶ *to overgrow, overspread*, Æ,Bl. [' *overwax'*]

oferweder n. *storm, tempest*, CHR 794 E.

oferwelig *very rich,* NC314.
oferwenian *to be proud, become insolent or presumptuous,* Sc,GL.
oferweorc n. *sarcophagus, tomb,* Æ,OEG. ['*overwork*']
oferweorpan³ *to throw over, overthrow, CP,* Lcd : *throw down, assault,* LL56,11¹ : *cast something over another, sprinkle : stumble?* B1543. ['*overwarp*']
oferwīgan *to overcome,* SOL299.
oferwillan⁷ *to boil down : boil over,* LCD. [weallan]
oferwinnan³ *to contend with, overcome, subdue,* Æ,*AO*; CP. ['*overwin*']
oferwintran *to go through the winter, WW* 97¹¹. ['*overwinter*']
oferwist f. *gluttony, excess,* CP,LL.
oferwistlic *supersubstantial,* MtL6¹¹.
oferwlencan *to be very wealthy,* AO44¹². [wlanc]
oferwlencu f. *excessive riches,* GU389.
oferwrecan⁵ *to overwhelm,* WW35¹⁴.
oferwrēon¹,² *to cover over, conceal, hide, VPs :* clothe, Mt. ['*overwry*']
oferwrigels n. *covering,* GL.
oferwrit n. *epistle,* MtLp10¹ : *superscription,* LkR23³⁸.
oferwriten *superscription,* Mtp12².
oferwrīðan *to wrap round,* LCD49a.
oferwyllan=oferwillan
oferwyrcan *to cover over, overlay, Sol;* Æ, AO. ['*overwork*']
oferwyrðe *very worthy,* A11·171.
oferyld (W147¹⁷)=oferyldu
oferyldu (=ie) f. *extreme old age,* MFH170.
oferyrnan³ (=ie) *to go or run over,* Æ,*Lcd :* '*overrun*,' *cover over, overwhelm,* Æ,BH : *run past, cross.*
oferȳð f. *overwhelming wave,* SPs34²⁵.
ofesc f. *border?* KC3·393¹⁰.
ofest=efest, ofost
ofestan (e¹) *to hasten,* RBL.
ofetrip? n. *harvest,* ZDPh36·550.
ofet(t) (æ) n. *fruit, legume, Gen,Gl.* ['*ovet*']
ofeweard=ufeweard; ofǣran=āfǣran
offaran⁶ *to intercept, overtake, fall upon, attack,* Æ,AO. hindan o. *to intercept from behind, cut off retreat,* AO.
offeallan⁷ *to fall upon, cut off, kill, destroy, end,* Æ,*Chr;* AO : *fall away from, be lost to,* LL144,6. hine offēoll *committed suicide,* CHR962A. ['*offall*']
offellan=offyllan
offēran *to overtake (an enemy),* Æ,CHR.
offerenda m. *psalm or anthem sung during the offertory,* ÆP168¹⁵; ANS84·5²⁹.
offerian *to carry off,* B1583.
offēstre f. *nurse not living in the house? foster-mother?* CC10²².

offlēogan³ *to fly away* (Swt).
±offrian *to '*offer*,' sacrifice, bring an oblation,* Æ,*AO,VPs;* CP. [*L.* offerre]
offringclāð m. *offertory cloth,* NC314.
offringdagas mpl. *offering days,* OEG40²³.
offringdisc m. *offering-dish, paten,* Ct.
offringhlāf m. *shew-bread,* Mt12⁴.
offringsang m. *hymn while an offering is made,* ÆH1·218⁹; ÆP214²³.
offringsceat m. *offering-napkin, KC.* [v. '*offering*']
offrung f. *presenting to God, oblation, sacrifice,* Æ,*Mt :* thing presented, '*offering*,' Æ. [offrung- v. also offring-]
offrunghūs n. *house of sacrifice,* NC 314.
offrungspic n. *sacrificial bacon,* ÆL25⁹².
offyligan *to follow up,* LkLR1³.
offyllan (e;=ie) *to strike down, destroy, kill,* BH.
of-gān anv., pret. -ēode; -gangan⁷ *to demand, require, exact, extort,* Æ : *attain, obtain, acquire, gain,* Æ : *start from, begin.* ['*ofgo*']
ofgangen-e, -lic *derivative,* ÆGR.
ofgefen (Cp)=ofgifen pp. of ofgiefan.
ofgeorn *elated,* HGL.
ofgēotan² *to moisten, soak, steep,* Æ : *quench,* Æ : *pour out,* JnL2²⁵.
ofgestīgnes f. *descent,* MtLp6¹.
ofgiefan⁵ (i, y) *to give up, resign, leave, quit, desert,* AO. [giefan]
ofhabban *to hold back,* Ex9².
ofhæccan *to hack off,* LL.
ofhagian *to be inconvenient,* W275⁵.
ofhealdan⁷ *to withhold, retain,* Chr1035c. ['*ofhold*']
ofhearmian (impers.) *to cause grief,* JUD11¹.
ofhende *lost, absent,* MET25³⁴.
ofheran (RWH59¹⁶)=ofhieran
ofhingrian (=y²) *to be hungry,* Æ(3⁵⁵¹). ['*ofhungered*']
ofhnītan *to gore to death,* LL32,21.
ofhrēosan² *to overwhelm, cover over,* Æ : *fall down, fall headlong,* Æ.
ofhrēowan² *to cause or feel pity,* Æ. ['*arewe*']
ofhwylfan *to roll away,* ARHy2¹². [v. '*whelve*']
ofhyrian *to imitate,* GD120¹⁴.
ofirnan³ *to overtake,* Æ,Bo : *tire with running,* Æ. ['*ofrun*']
oflǣtan⁷ *to let go, lay aside, leave behind : let flow,* Bo66²⁹.
oflǣte (ā, ē) f. *oblation, offering, Ps : sacramental wafer,* Æ,Lcd. ['*oflete*'; *L.* oblata]
oflǣthlāf m. *bread used for the sacrament,* GD343¹⁵.
oflangian *to long,* Æ. ['*oflonged*']
oflāte (*VPs*)=oflǣte

oflecgan *to lay down*, PPs 68[1].

ofleogan[2] *to lie, be false*, PPs 17[43].

oflēte=oflǣte

oflicgan[5] *to overlay* (*a child*), *LL.* ['*oflie*']

oflician (w. d.) *to displease, be displeasing to, Æ.*

oflinnan[3] *to cease, stop*, BL 247[8] : *desist* (*from*).

oflongian=oflangian

oflystan *to fill with desire, please, Æ,Bo.* pp. of-lysted, -lyst *desirous of, pleased with.* ['*oflust*']

ofmanian *to exact* (*a fine*), LL 201,1.

ofmunan swv. *to remember, recollect,* CP.

ofmyrðrian *to murder,* CHR 979 E.

ofn=ofen

ofnēadian *to obtain by force, extort,* TC 295[22].

ofnet n? *closed vessel?* (BT), *small vessel?* LCD 11b. [ofn]

ofniman[4] *to fail,* LL (170[6]).

ofor=(1) eofor; (2) ufor; (3) ofer; ōfor=ōfer

ofost f. *haste, speed, zeal, Æ.* adv. -līce. on ofoste, of(e)stum *speedily, hastily.*

ofr (GL)=hofer

ofrǣcan *to reach, obtain,* LL 333 col 2. [v. '*ofreach*']

ōfres gs. of ōfer.

ofrian, ofrung (AO)=offrian, offrung

ofrīdan[1] *to overtake by riding, overtake, Æ, Chr.* ['*ofride*']

ofsacan[6] *to deny a charge, LL* 108B, n 5. ['*ofsake*']

ofscacan[6] *to shudder, OEG* 4160. [v. '*shake*']

ofsceamian (a) *to put to shame, Æ,Bo.* ['*ofshame*']

ofscēotan[2] *to shoot down, hit, kill, Æ,AO,* CP. pp. ofscoten *elf-struck* (*of cattle seized with sudden disease*).

ofscleacnes (APs 43[22])=ofslegennes

ofscotian *to shoot down,* AO : *spear,* AA 23[11].

ofsendan *to summon, Chr* 1048. ['*ofsend*']

ofsēon[5] *to see, behold, Æ.* ['*ofsee*']

ofsetenes f. *siege,* WW 458[28] : *sitting down,* EPs 138[1] (ob-).

ofsetnian *to besiege,* NC 349.

ofsettan (æ) *to beset, oppress, afflict, Hept, Lcd; Æ.* ['*ofset*']

ofsettung f. *pressure,* Sc 143[5].

ofsittan[5] *to press down, repress, oppress, Æ,* CP : *occupy, Hept,Bo;* CP : *hedge in, compass about, besiege.* ['*ofsit*']

ofslēan[6] *to strike off or out, cut off, destroy :* *strike down, kill, AO,BH,Lcd; Æ,CP.* ['*ofslay*']

ofslegennes f. *slaughter,* JRVPs 43[22].

ofslītan[1] *to bite* (*of a serpent*), NUM 21[9] (GR).

ofsmorian *to suffocate, strangle,* AO.

ofsnīðan[1] *to cut off, kill, Æ.*

ofsprǣc f. *locution, utterance,* HGL 460.

ofspring m. '*offspring,*' *descendants, posterity, Æ,KC.*

ofspyrian *to trace out,* LL 96,17.

ofst=ofost

ofstǣnan *to stone, kill,* APT 26[24].

ofstæppan[6] *to trample upon,* JOS 10[24].

ofstan=ofestan

ofstandan[6] *to remain, persist, continue, Lcd;* Æ : *restore, make restitution.* ['*ofstand*']

ofstede adv. *immediately,* Sc 193[12].

ofstende *hastening,* CM 186.

ofstician *to pierce, stab* (*to death*), *transfix,* AO.

ofstig *swift,* GPH 392.

ofstīgan *to descend,* NG : *ascend,* MtL : *depart,* MtL.

ofstingan[3] *to pierce, stab* (*to death*), *AO,Chr;* Æ,CP. ['*ofsting*']

ofstint (=ofstent) pres. 3 sg. of ofstandan.

ofstlīce=ofostlīce

ofstofen *impelled,* PPs.

ofstum v. ofost.

ofswelgan[3] *to swallow up,* Bo 46[15]n.

ofswerian *to abjure, deny on oath,* LL.

ofswingan[3] *to scourge* (*to death*), AO 154[8].

ofswȳðan (=ī) *to overcome,* LHy.

oft adv. comp. oftor, superl. oftost *often, frequently, CP,G;* Æ. oftost symle *continually.* o. and gelome *diligently.* ['*oft*']

oftacan[2] *to overtake,* NC 325.

oftalu f. *rejoinder, verdict against a claim,* TC 302[22] (v. LL 3·226).

oftēon[2] *to withhold, take away, withdraw, Æ,* CP.

oftfēore *requiring many journeys to carry,* v. ES 43·312.

ofthrǣd-=oftrǣd-

oftige m. *withholding,* LL.

oftorfian *to stone to death, Æ,AO.*

oftrǣde *often or always available : frequent,* Bo 136[17].

oftrǣdlic *frequent,* AO. adv. -līce, CP.

oftredan[5] *to tread down, trample on, Æ.* ['*oftread*']

oftredan *to tread to death,* AO 260[18]. ['*oftread*']

oftsīð m. *frequent occasion,* AO 290[29]. on oftsīðas *frequently,* CHR 979 C.

oftðwēal n. *frequent washing,* NC 314.

oftyrfan *to stone,* AO 172[28].

ofðǣnan *to be too moist,* LCD.

ofðe *or,* OEG 11[177] and n. [=oððe]

ofðecgan *to destroy,* GEN 2002.

ofðefian *to dry up?* ÆL 34[144].

ofðencan *to recall to mind,* CP 349[10]; VH 18.

ofðennan=ofðǣnan

ofðincð pres. 3 sg. of ofðyncan.

ofðīnan *to be too moist,* HL 204[319].

of-ðreccan (KGL), -ðriccan=ofðryccan

ofðringan³ to throng, press upon, ÆH,Mk.

ofðryccan (e, i) to press, squeeze, Æ : oppress, afflict, repress, destroy, Æ : occupy forcibly.

ofðryc(ced)nes f. trouble, oppression, CP.

ofðryscan to repress, subdue, CP.

ofðrysm(i)an to choke, stifle, Mk4¹⁹. [ðrosm]

ofðylman to choke, suffocate, NC314.

ofðyncan (impers.) to give offence, insult, vex, displease, weary, grieve, Æ,AO,B,Bo, CP,LL. ['ofthink']

ofðyrstan to suffer from thirst, be thirsty, thirst (for), Hept,Soul; Æ. ['athirst,' 'of-thirst']

ofðystrian to obscure, SPs73²¹. [ðēostrian]

ofunnan swv. to begrudge, deny, envy, Æ, CP.

ofweard (MFH170)=æfweard

ofweorpan³ to stone (to death), kill by a missile, Æ,AO.

ofworpian to kill (by stoning), LL.

ofwundrian to be astonished, Æ.

ōfyrit (WW385³⁹)=āfȳred pp. of āfȳran.

ōga m. fear, terror, dread, Æ : terrible object, Æ. [ege]

ōgengel m. bar, bolt, WW459¹⁰.

ō-hilde (e², y²), -heald sloping, inclined, GL.

ōhsta=ōcusta

ōht I. f. persecution, enmity. ōhte grettan to profane, GD235⁶. [FTP9,558] II.= āwuht

ohtrip v. ofetrip.

ō-hwǣr, -hwæðer=ā-hwǣr, -hwæðer

ōhwanon=āhwonan; ōhylde=ōhilde

ōl pret. 3 sg. of alan.

ōlǣc-=ōlecc-

ōlǣcung f. 'conspiratio,' OEG4955 (=ān-?).

olbend=olfend

±ōleccan (æ, i) to soothe, caress, flatter : please, charm, propitiate, CP. [leccan]

ōleccere, ōlecere m. flatterer, CP,WW.

ōleccung (æ) f. soothing, flattery, persuasion, allurement, charm, CP.

ōlectend m. flatterer, Cp1519. [=ōleccend]

ōlehtung f. flattery, GD : indulgence, MFH 170 (ōlect-).

ōlfæt=ālfæt

olfend m., olfenda m., olfende f. camel, Bl, Mt; CP. ['olfend'; L. elephantem]

olfendmyre f. she-camel, GEN32¹⁵.

ōlicc-=ōlecc-

oll n. contumely, contempt, scorn, insult, Æ. on oll 'nequicquam,' OEG2000.

ollonc, ollunc, ollung (LWS; A)=andlang

ōlðwong m. strap, WW379³².

ōlyhtword n. flattering speech, BL99²⁶. [ōleccan]

m m. rust, Æ.

m-=am-

oma? m. ome? f. a liquid measure, v. NC 314. [L. (h)ama]

ōman fp. eruptions of the skin, erysipelas, LCD. [cp. healsōme]

omb-=amb-

ōmcynn n. corrupt humour, LCD31a.

omer (a¹, e¹) a bird, 'scorellus,' GL.

ōmian to become rusty, Sc196⁵.

ōmiddan=onmiddan

ōmig rusty, rust-eaten, rust-coloured : in-flammatory, LCD.

ōmihte inflammatory, LCD.

ompella=ampella; ompre=ampre I.

on I. prep. (w. d., instr., and a.) (local, etc.) 'ON,' upon, on to (but ofer is more com-mon), up to, among, AO,CP : in, into, within, Æ : (temporal) in, during, at, on, about, Æ,AO : against, towards, AO : ac-cording to, in accordance with, in respect to, Æ : for, in exchange for. II. adv. on, CP : forward, onward : continuously, Æ (forð on). on riht rightly. on ǣr adv. formerly. on ān continuously, in concert : at once, forthwith. III. pres. 3 sg. of unnan. IV. (M)=ond, and

on- I. often meaningless, and only rarely= prep. on. II.=an-. III.=un-. IV.=in-

onādōn anv. to put on, ÆL7¹⁵⁶.

onǣht f. possession, CVPs2⁸.

onǣlan to set fire to, ignite, heat, inspire, incite, inflame, burn, consume, Chr (an-), Gen,Sol; Æ,CP. ['anneal(ed)']

onǣlend m. 'incensor,' GPH399.

onǣlet n. lightning, LPs143⁶.

onǣr adv. formerly. [on, ǣr]

onæðele (w. d.) natural to, MET13⁵¹.

onāfæstnian to make fast, bind, LPs9¹⁶.

onāhebban⁶ to lift up, exalt, CP56¹⁹.

onāl n. burning : incense, what is burnt, Ps.

onārīsan¹ to rise up (against), ERPs.

onarn pret. 3 sg. of oniernan.

onāsāwan⁷ to implant, instil, MFH170.

onāscunung=onscunung

onāsendan to send into, implant in, impart to, CM203.

onāsendednes (æ³) f. 'immissio,' LPs77⁴⁹.

onāsetednes (æ³) f. a laying on (of hands), NC 349.

onāsettan to set upon, place on, impress upon, Æ,CM.

onāslagen beaten (of metal), LPs97⁶.

onāswēgan to sound forth, LPs28³.

onāwinnan³ to fight against, LPs34¹; 55².

onbæc adv. backwards, back, behind, G,Ps.

onbæcling (e) adv. backward, behind. o. gewend having one's back turned, Æ.

onbærnan to kindle, ignite, heat, excite, in-spire, inflame, burn, AO,CP.

onbærn-ing (JPs65¹⁵), -nes (SPs) f. incense.

onbǣru f. *self-restraint?* Gu 1027.
onbāsnung f. *expectation*, DR 4³⁴.
onbeblāwan¹ *to blow upon*, LPs 104¹⁹.
onbecling (EPs)=onbæcling
onbecuman=oncuman
onbecyme m. *approach*, Sc 211⁸.
onbēgan=onbīgan
onbēgnes (=īe) f. *bending, curvature*, WW.
onbeht=ambiht
onbelǣdan *to inflict upon*, WW 90.
onbēn f. *imprecation*, BH 104³.
onbēodan² *to command, order*, AO : *announce, proclaim*, Æ,AO.
onbeornan³ *to set fire to*, Ex : *inflame*, Lcd.
onbēotend *threatening, impending*, DR 53².
onberan⁴ I. *to carry off, plunder* : *diminish, weaken.* II. *to be situated?* GD 98¹⁴.
onbergan=onbyrgan
onbescēawung f. *inspection, examination*, Sc 66¹⁰.
onbescēofan² *to thrust out*, WW 220¹⁹, ²¹.
onbeslagen *inflicted*, Æ.
onbestǣlan *to convict of crime*, LL 30,15.
onbestingan=inbestingan; onbid=anbid
onbīdan¹ *to remain, wait*, B : w. g. *wait for, await, expect*, AO : *attend upon, wait on.* ['*onbide*']
onbīgan (ē;=īe) *to subdue, subjugate*, Bl, Ps.
onbiht=ambiht
onbindan³ *to unbind, untie, loosen* : *release*, CP : *disclose.*
onbirgan=onbyrgan
onbītan¹ (w. g.) *to taste of, partake of, feed upon*, AA,LL.
onblǣst m. *onrush, attack*, EHy 5⁸.
onblǣstan *to break in*, WW 428¹.
onblandan³ *to mingle*, An 675.
onblāwan⁷ *to blow on or into, inspire, breathe* : *puff up.*
onblāwing f. *breathing upon*, JnL p 8⁶(in-).
onblāwnes f. *inspiration*, Bl 7²⁶.
onblinnan (MFH 118)=āblinnan
onblōtan⁴ *to sacrifice, kill a victim*, Gen 2933.
onborgian *to borrow*, CC 9¹¹⁷.
onbran=onbarn pret. 3 sg. of onbeornan.
on-bregdan, -brēdan³ tr. and intr. *to move, start up* : *burst open.*
onbring m. *instigation*, LL.
onbringelle f. *instigation*, ÆL 23b²⁹¹.
onbrosnung f. *decay, corruption*, EPs 29¹⁰.
onbryce m. *inroad*, OEG 2480.
±onbryrdan (āb-, inb-) *to excite, inspire, incite, encourage*, Æ,CP. onbryrd *excited, fired, ardent* : *contrite.* [brord]
onbryrding f. *incitement*, WW 419⁴².
onbryrdnes (e²) f. *inspiration, incitement, ardour*, Æ : *remorse, contrition.*

onbūgan²,¹ *to bend* : *bow, submit, yield to, agree with*, Bl,Mt; Æ,AO : *bend aside, deviate.* ['*onbow*']
onbūtan prep. (w. d. a.) and adv. '*about*,' *round about*, Æ : *round, around*, CP. adv. phr. west o. faran *to go west about.* [=ābūtan]
onbyhtscealc=ambihtscealc
onbyrdan=anbyrdan
onbyrgan I. (e, i) *to taste, eat*, Æ. II. *to be surety*, v. OEG 7⁹⁹.
onbyrging f. *tasting*, Lcd 1·136¹².
onbyrhtan *to illuminate*, Bl 105³¹.
onbyrignes f. *tasting*, Bl 209¹².
oncelg- (N)=oncīg-
oncennan *to bear, bring forth*, ÆT,KGl.
oncer=ancor
oncierran (e, i, y) *to turn, alter, change, transform* : *turn off or away, avert, prevent* : *turn oneself, go.*
oncīgan (ei²;=īe) *to call upon, invoke*, DR.
oncīgnes, oncīgung (ei) f. *invocation*, DR.
onclēow=anclēow
onclifian (eo, y) *to adhere, stick to, persist in*, GD,RPs.
onclyfiende *sticking to, tenacious*, Ct.
onclypian *to call upon*, Gen 4²⁶ (Gr).
on-cnǣwe, -cnāwe *known, recognised*, EPs 31⁵.
oncnāwan⁷ *to understand, know, perceive, observe*, Ma ; Æ,CP : *acknowledge, confess, disclose*, Æ. ['*acknow*']
oncnāwednes (RWH 92⁹)=oncnāwennes
oncnāwend m. *one who knows*, A 11·119.
on-cnāwennes (Æ),-cnāwnes (CP),-cnāwung (Sc) f. *acknowledgment, knowledge.*
oncnyssan *to cast down, afflict*, CPVPs.
oncnyttan=uncnyttan
oncor=ancor; ōncra=āncra
oncunnan swv. *to know*, Gl : *reproach, blame, accuse*, CP.
oncunnes f. *accusation*, JVPs; BH 212¹⁵.
oncunning f. *accusation*, BH 212¹⁵(b).
oncwealdan *to slay*, EPs 61⁴.
oncweðan⁵ *to answer, resound, echo*, Æ : *protest.*
oncyrran=oncierran; oncyrrāp=ancorrāp
oncȳðan *to make known*, TC 117¹.
oncȳðdǣd f. *hurtful deed*, An 1181.
oncȳðig *conscious, understanding*, EL 725 : *known*, ZDA 33-73¹².
oncȳðð† f. *pain, distress of mind*, B.
ond=and
ondǣlan *to infuse*, DR,LkL.
ondǣlend m. *one who imparts, infuser*, LkL.
onde-=ande-; onder-=under-
onderslic, ondeslic (DR)=ondrysenlic
ondesn, ondesnes f. *fear*, DR.
ondgit=andgiet; ondlēan=andlēan

ondliota=ondwleota, andwlita
ondlong=andlang; ondo (NG)=anda
ondōn anv. I. *to undo, open.* [=un-] II. *to put on (clothes)*, CM390; Sc83⁶.
ondōung f. *injection*, LCD97b.
on-drǣdan⁷ (and wv.) pret. 3 sg. -drēd, -drǣd, -dreord (A), also -drǣdde, pp. -drǣd (tr.) *to dread, fear, B,Chr,Mt* : (refl.) *be afraid, El,Lk.* ['*adread*']
ondrǣdendlic *fearful, terrible, Æ.*
ondrǣding f. *dread, fear, terror*, AO.
ondrencan *to intoxicate*, GUTH62²⁰ : *fill with water*, JPs64¹¹.
ondresn=ondrysnu
ondrincan³ (w. g.) *to drink*, BH.
ondrislic=ondrysenlic
ondruncnian *to become intoxicated*, EPs35⁹.
on-drysenlic, -drys(n)lic *terrible*, BH,MH. adv. -līce *reverently, with fear*, VH18.
ondrysne (and-) *terrible*, AO : *feared, venerated, venerable.*
ondrysnlic=ondrysenlic
ondrysnu (and-) f. *fear*, CP : *respect, reverence*, BL : *etiquette*, B1796.
ondrystlic=ondrysenlic
onds-=ands-
ondūne *down*, MH214¹¹.
ondw-=andw-
one=ono
onealdian *to grow old*, SPs31³.
oneardian *to inhabit*, CSPs (=in-).
oneardiend *inhabitant, indweller*, GD,PPs.
onefen, onefn=onemn
on-ēgan, -ēgnan (oe) *to fear, dread.* [ōga]
onēhting f. *persecution*, OEG2974.
onemn I. prep. (w. d.) *abreast of, alongside of, by, near, during, Æ,B,Ma*; AO. ['*anent*'] II. adv. *together, exactly, directly.* o. ðǣm *at the same time.*
onemnðrōwigan *to sympathise*, ÆL23b²⁴³.
onerian *to plough up, Æ,CP.*
onerning f. *attack*, DR36¹. [iernan]
ōnettan *to hasten, hurry forward, be quick, Æ* : *be busy, brisk : anticipate, Æ,CP* : (+) *get quickly, seize, occupy.*
ōnettung f. *precipitation*, CP455¹⁵.
oneða†=anda
onēðgung f. *breathing on*, ERPs17¹⁶.
onfægnian *to fawn on*, Bo102¹⁵.
onfæreld n. *going on, progress, journey : going in, entrance : attack, assault*, Sc212⁵.
onfæstan *to make fast*, GD224¹⁶.
onfæstnian (e²) *to pierce*, Jn,SPs.
onfæðmnes f. *embrace*, BL7²⁶.
onfangend m. *receiver*, ES9·37.
onfangennes f. *reception, acceptance, Æ.*
onfealdan⁷ *to unfold*, GD,MH.
onfeall (e) m. *swelling*, Lcd. ['*onfall*']
onfeallende ptc. *rushing on, overwhelming.*

onfehtan (VPs)=onfeohtan; onfell=onfeall
onfeng I.=andfeng. II. pret. 3 sg. of onfōn.
onfeohtan³ (e) *to attack, assault, fight with*, CHR.
onfillende (WW420¹⁹)=onfeallende
onfilte (WW)=anfilte
onfindan³ (but occl. wk. pret. onfunde) *to find out, learn, perceive, feel, notice, observe, discover*, CP : *experience, suffer.*
onfindend m. *discoverer*, GPH391.
onflǣscnes f. *incarnation*, BL81²⁹; BHy2⁴¹.
onflyge m., onflygen n. *infectious disease* (BT), LCD.
onfōn⁷ *to take, receive, accept, BH,Lcd,Mt*; Æ : *stand sponsor, Chr : harbour, favour unrighteously, LL : take hold of : undertake, (a duty) undergo (a rite), Bl : begin : conceive, Ps.* onfangenum gebede *after engaging in prayer, Æ.* ['*fang*,' '*onfang*']
onfōnd m. *undertaker, supporter*, Ps,AS14⁶?
onfōndlic (an-) *to be received*, CHRD110⁸.
onfongenes=onfangennes
onforan I. prep. *before (time), at the beginning of, Chr.* II. adv. *before, in front of, Ps.* ['*afore*']
onfordōn ptc. *destroyed*, LPs101²¹.
onforeweard-um, -an adv. *in front, in the first line, in the fore part, above all, Æ*; A5·455.
onforht=anforht
onforhtian *to be afraid, fear, Æ,GL.*
onforwyrd n. *destruction*, CSPs.
onfundelnes f. *experience*, LCD.
onfunden *experienced*, AS14⁶.
onfundennes f. *explanation : trial, experiment, experience.* [onfindan]
onga=anga; ongǣgn, ongǣn=ongēan
ongalan⁶ *to recite (a charm)*, LCD3·42¹⁸, S²Ps57⁶.
ongalend m. *enchanter*, BLPs57⁶.
ongalnes f. *song*, BRPs70⁶.
ongān I.=ongēan. II. anv. *to approach, enter into*, ES38·20 : *attack*, ES41·325.
ongang (o²) m. *entrance, incursion, assault, attack : worship*, BH106¹⁴.
ongangan⁷=ongān; onge=enge
on-gēan (ā, ē), -geagn (æ, e) I. prep. *towards, against, opposite to, contrary to, Æ*; AO,CP : *against, in exchange for.* II. adv. *opposite, back, Æ : 'AGAIN.'* eft o. *back again.* o. ðæt *on the other hand, on the contrary.*
ongēancyme m. *return, Æ.*
ongēancyrrendlic *relative*, ÆGR231¹⁷.
ongēanfealdan⁷ *to fold or roll back*, Sc148¹¹.
ongēanfēran (agēan-) *to return*, CHR1070.
ongēanflōwende *ebbing and flowing*, v. OEG 2363.
ongēanhworfennes f. *obstacle*, OEG2713.

ongēanhwyrf (ag-) m. *return*, HGL419.
ongēanhwyrfan (ag-) *to turn again, return*.
ongēanlecgan *to lay up, store up*, Sc156[6].
ongēansprecend m. *one who reproaches*, RSPs43[17].
ongēanweard *going back or towards*, AO : *near*, BK4. adv. -weardes, Æ.
ongēanweardlic *adversative*. adv. -lice, ÆGR.
ongēanwerian *to revile in return*, RB17[13]. [wyrigan]
ongēanwinnende *resisting*, APT2[4].
ongēanwiðerian *to oppose*, Sc33[20].
ongēanwyrdnes f. *opposition*, OEG3975.
ongeboren *in-born*, OEG4648,2[360].
ongebringan *to bring upon* : *impose*, CM36 : *enjoin*, CM1185 : *incline, induce*, ÆL25[549].
ongebyrigean (V²Ps33[9])=onbyrgan I.
ongecīgan *to call upon, invoke*, RHy1[4].
ongecīgung (ei³) f. *invocation*, DR99[13].
ongecoplīce=ungecoplice
onge-fæstnian, -festnian (Ps)=onfæstnian
ongefeht n. *attack*, DR. [feoht]
ongeflogen *attacked by disease*, LCD1·86'. [cp. onflygen]
on-gegen, -gegn=ongēan
ongehrēosan² *to rush upon, fall upon*, WW 419[6].
ongehȳðnes f. *advantage, profit*, LL476,12.
ongel, Ongel=angel I., Angel
ongelǣdan=ingelǣdan
ongelic (NG) I. *like*. II. *likeness*. adv. -lice, AO.
ongelīcnes f. *form, pattern*, Mt p14[20].
ongelihtan (AS2²)=onlihtan
on-gemang, -gemong prep. (w. d.) and adv. *among, during*, CP : *meanwhile*, CM. o. ðisum, ðǣm *meanwhile*.
ongemet=ungemet
ongēn, ongend=ongēan
ongenǣman *to take away* (*from*), GUTH14[11].
ongeotan=ongietan
ongēotan *to infuse, impregnate*, GD51[14].
ongēotung f. *pouring in*, LCD88a.
on-gerwan, pp. -gered (VPs)=ongierwan
ongesēon=onsēon
ongesetenes f. *knowledge*, BH474[15].
ongeslēan[6] *to slay*, BH44[17].
ongespanan¹ *to draw on, allure*, WW421[22].
onget-=ongiet-
ongetǣcan *to enjoin*, CM363.
ongetimbran *to build up*, AO.
ongeðwǣre=ungeðwǣre
ongewinn n. *assault*, Sc33[17].
ongewiss=ungewiss
ongewrigennes (GD139¹)=onwrigennes
ongieldan³ (i) *to atone for, be punished for, pay* (*the penalty*) *for*, AO : *pay, offer* (*gifts, sacrifice*). [*Ger.* entgelten]

ongien=onginn
ongierwan (e, i, y) pret. -girede I. *to unclothe, divest, strip*, Æ (=un-). II. *to clothe*, EPs131[16].
ongietan[5] (e, eo, i, y) *to grasp, seize* : *understand, learn, recognise, know, distinguish, judge, consider, Mt*; AO,CP : *see, perceive* : *discover* : *hear* : *feel, experience* : *know carnally*. ['*anget*']
ongietenes f. *knowledge, understanding*, BH : *meaning*, GUTH80[22].
ongifan[5] (æ) *to give back*, Æ : *forgive*.
ongildan=ongieldan
onginn=anginn
onginnan³ *to begin, attempt, endeavour, try hard*, Æ,G; AO,CP (This vb. is often used periphrastically w. another vb. in the inf., to denote the simple action of the latter. The compound is best translated by the historical aorist of the second vb.) : *attack, assail* : *act*, ÆL (āg-). ['*ongin*']
onginnendlic *inchoative*, ÆGR.
onginnes f. *undertaking*, BH,WW.
on-girwan=ongierwan
ongit=andgiet; ongit-=ongiet-
Ongle (AO), Onglisc=Angle, Englisc
ongnora? ongnere=angnere
Ongol=Angel; ongong=ongang
ongratað? '*arridet*,' OEG33² (v. BTs).
ongris-, ongrys-=angris-
ongrynt? '*arridet*,' OEG33² (v. BTs).
ongrype m. *attack*, W187².
ongryrelic *horrible*, GUTH36[24].
ongseta=angseta; ongunnenes=onginnes
ongy-=ongi-
ongyrdan *to unbuckle, unfasten*, ÆL; BH 196[28]. ['*ungird*']
ongyrnð '*inrogat*,' Sc10[4].
ongytan=ongietan
ongyte f. *inpouring*, ÆH1·362'.
onhādian (LL66,21)=unhādian
onhǣldan (VPs)=onhieldan
onhǣle *secret, concealed, hidden*, CR896.
onhǣtan *to heat, inflame*, AO,CP.
onhagian (impers.) *to be possible or convenient, be fitting, suit, please*, Æ,CP : *be at leisure*.
onhātan¹† *to promise*, JUL.
onhātian *to become hot*, WW.
onhāwian *to behold*, ÆL3[261].
onhealdan[7] (an-) *to keep* (*peace*), MET11[42].
onhēaw m. *trunk of tree, block of wood for hewing on*, WW.
onhebban[6] (occl. wk. pret. onhefde) *to raise up, erect, lift up, exalt, Bl*; Æ : *leaven* : *begin* : *take away*. ['*onheave*']
onhefednes (an-) f. *exaltation*, RB23².
onheld-=onhield-
onhergian *to harass*, CP73[18].

onheri-=onhyri-
onhetting f. *persecution,* OEG 2¹³⁰.
onhicgan=onhycgan
onhieldan (CP) (i²) *to bend, bend down, lean, recline, incline* : *decline, sink* : *fall away,* CPs 118¹⁰².
onhieldednes (e², y²) f. *declining,* CVPs 72⁴.
onhigian *to attack, despoil,* OEG.
onhindan, onhinder adv. *behind, backward.*
onhinderling adv. *back,* PPs.
onhiscan=onhyscan
onhlidan¹ *to open, reveal, unclose* : *appear.*
onhlinian *to lean on,* GL.
onhnigan¹ *to bend down, bow, worship.*
onhnigenes f. *adoration,* LF 56⁵.
onhohsnian *to detest?* (BT), *put an end to?* B 1944.
onhon⁷ *to hang, crucify,* AO.
onhræran=onhreran; onhræs=onres
onhreodan² *to adorn* (or? onreodan=*redden*), GEN 2931.
onhreosan² *to fall upon, rush upon,* GD,Ps.
onhreran *to move, disturb, arouse, excite,* CP.
onhrinan¹ (w. g. or d.) *to touch, lay hold of,* Æ,CP.
onhrine m. *touch, contact,* LCD 1·328¹.
onhrop m. *importunity,* Æ : *reproach,* LPs 68²⁰.
onhryre *attack,* OEG 50⁷² (onri-).
onhupian *to step back, retire,* CP 441²⁸.
onhwelan⁴ *to bellow back, resound,* WW 528³⁹.
onhweorfan³ *to change, turn, reverse,* CP.
onhwerfan (y²;=ie) *to turn, change, turn round.*
onhwerfednes (æ) f. *change,* AS 9³.
onhycgan (i²) *to consider,* DA 473.
onhyldan=onhieldan
onhyrdan† *to strengthen, encourage.* [heard]
onhyrenes f. *imitation,* CP,GD.
onhyr-gend, -iend (e, i;=ie) m. *emulator, imitator,* GD,GL.
onhyrian (e) *to emulate, imitate,* CP.
onhyring (e) f. *imitation, zeal,* Æ,CP.
onhyrsumian *to be busied with,* RB 71¹⁷.
onhyscan (i) *to mock at, vilify, reproach* : *detest* : *deceive.* [husc]
oniernan³ (y²) (†) *to give way, open (of a door)* : '*currere,*' BPs 118³² : '*incurrere,*' LL 410,3⁵ : *pour forth,* VH 18.
oninnan prep. (w. d.) and adv. *within, into, among.*
onlæc (Cp 1725)=onleac, pret. 3 sg. of onlucan.
onlæccan *to reproach,* EPs 105⁷.
onlædan=inlædan
onlænan *to lend, grant, let, lease,* CP.
onlæpnes (BH 128²³)=anlipnes
onlætan (an-) *to relax, permit,* RB.

onlang=andlang; onlec=anlec
onlecgende (*salve*) *to be applied,* LCD.
onlegen f. *poultice,* LCD.
onleoht-=onliht-
onleon¹† *to lend, grant, give,* WW.
onleoðian=onliðigan
onles-=onlies-
onlic (an-) *like, resembling, similar, Mt;* CP. adv. -lice, AO,CP. ['*anlike*']
+onlician (an-; -lican, GD 75⁴) *to compare* : *make like, simulate.*
onlicnes f. *resemblance, likeness, similitude, Gen.* : *picture, image, idol, WW;* AO,CP : *parable* : *stature, form.* ['*anlikeness*']
+onlicung (an-) f. *likeness,* CHRD 71¹³.
onliesan (e, y) *to loosen, set free, release,* CP.
onliesednes (i²) f. *remission (of sins),* AHy 9⁷⁷.
onliesend (e, y) m. *liberator,* CPs 39¹⁸ : *redeemer,* GD.
onliesendlic (y) *absolvable,* GD 345².
onliesnes (e) f. *deliverance,* BL,GD.
onligan (in-) *to inflame,* JPs 104¹⁹.
onlihtan (eo, y) *to illuminate, give light to, enlighten, Bl,Bo;* CP : *restore to sight* : *shine.* ['*onlight*']
onlihtednes=onlihtnes
onlihtend m. *enlightener,* PPs 26¹.
onlihting f. *illumination, enlightenment,* Æ.
onlihtnes f. *illumination,* BH,Ps.
onliðian (eo) *to loosen, relax,* GD.
onliðigan *to become pliant, yield,* SOL 356.
onlocian *to look on, behold,* Æ,CP.
onlociend m. *onlooker, spectator,* Æ.
onlong=andlang
onlucan² (=un-) *to unlock, open, unfold, reveal, disclose,* CP.
onlutan² *to bow, incline, bend down,* CP.
onlutung f. '*involucrum,*' GPH 402.
only-=onli-; onlys-=onlies-
onmædla=anmedla
onmælan *to speak to,* DA 210.
onman v. onmunan.
onmang (Æ)=ongemang
onmearca m. *inscription,* MkL 12¹⁶ (MkR in-).
onmearcung (e²) f. *inscription,* NG.
onmedan *to presume, take upon oneself?* RD 56¹⁵.
onmedla=anmedla
onmeltan³? *to soften,* PPs 88³⁸.
onmetan I. *to paint, cover over?* PPs 88⁴⁶. II. *to come upon, find out,* EPs 114³.
onmiddan prep. (w. d.) *amid, in the midst, at the middle of,* Æ.
onmitta=anmitta; onmod=anmod
onmunan swv. pres. 3 sg. onman, pret. onmunde *to esteem, think worthy of, consider entitled to,* CP : refl. *care for, wish* : *remember* : *remind,* B 2640.

onmyrran *to mar, disturb*, TC390'.
onn=ann, pres. 3 sg. of unnan.
onnhīgan (WW255¹¹)=onhnīgan
onniman⁴ *to receive, take*, PPs.
onnytt=unnytt
ono=heonu
onoeðung (VPs)=oneðung
onōrettan† *to perform with effort, accomplish.*
onorðung f. *inspiration, inbreathing*, LPs, Sc.
onoða (WW)=anda
onpennian *to open*, CP277⁸.
onrād f. *riding on horseback*, LCD68b.
onræfniendlic=unræfniendlic
onrǣs m. *onrush, assault, attack*, Æ,CP.
onrǣsan I. *to rush (on)*, VPs. ['onrese']
II. nap. of wk. sb. *irruptions*, WW.
onrǣsend m. *attacker*, LPs17⁴⁰.
onrēaflan *to strip (of)*, A12·505 (=un-).
onred m. *name of a plant*, LCD.
onrēodan v. onhrēodan; onrettan=orrettan
onrid n. *riding horse*, CC23²⁵.
onrīdan¹ *to ride (on a raid, etc.)*, CHR871A.
onriht *right, lawful, proper : owned by?*
Ex358. adv. *aright*, Æ. also -līce, BL43¹⁶.
onrihtwīsnes=unrihtwīsnes
onrīptīd f. *harvest-time*, ES39·352.
onrīsan (Æ)=ārīsan ['onrise']
onryne m. *course : incursion, assault*, LCD.
onsacan⁶ *to contest, dispute, strive against, resist, repel : (†) attack : refuse, deny, contradict, refute : exculpate, excuse oneself : renounce.*
onsæc I. *denying : denied : excused.* II. (LL24,41Ld)=andsæc
onsǣgan† *to prostrate*, DD,Gu.
onsǣgd-=onsǣged-
onsǣge *assailing, attacking*, B,CC,W. [sīgan]
onsǣgednes (e) f. *sacrifice, offering, Æ : oblation, (sacrificial) victim.*
onsǣgnes f. *holocaust, sacrifice*, BLPs65¹⁵.
onsǣgung f. *sacrifice*, WW.
onsǣlan *to untie, loosen*, B,BL. [=unsǣlan]
onsæt I. pret. 3 sg. of onsittan. II.=onset
onsǣtnes f. *snare*, DR121¹⁹.
onsǣtnung f. *snare*, DR147⁷.
onsagu f. *affirmation, accusation, reproach*, Mt; Æ. ['onsaw']
onsand f. *sending against*, VPs. ['onsand']
onsang m. *incantation*, GD73²⁶.
onsāwan⁷ *to sow : introduce into, implant*, CM658.
onsceacan⁶ (a) *to shake, shake off, remove*, GL.
onsceacnes f. *excuse*, EPs. [=onsacnes, Swt]
onsceamian=ofsceamian
onscendan *to confound, put to shame*, GD.

onsceon-=onscun-
onsceortian *to grow short*, MH104²³.
onscēotan² (un-) *to open*, GL.
onscillan (=y²) *to give back a sound, resound*, OEG8²⁶⁵.
onscōgan (an-) *to unshoe*, CP. pp. onscōd *unshod.* [=un-]
onscrȳdan *to clothe*, EPs,Sc.
onscunian (a¹, eo², y²) *to shun, avoid, fear, detest, hate, LL; Æ,CP : put away, reject, despise : irritate.* ['ashun']
on-scuniendlic (CP), -scunigendlic (Æ), -scunodlic *hateful, detestable.*
onscunigend m. *hater*, BL111²⁹.
onscunung f. *execration, abomination : exasperation*, Ps.
onscynian=onscunian
onscyte m. *attack, assault*, Æ.
onseacan (Cp665)=onsceacan
onsēcan *require, exact*, Jul. ['onseek']
onsecgan *to renounce, deny : offer sacrifice*, AO : *impute*, Æ : *inform*, Æ.
onsecgend m. *sacrificer*, LL.
onsēgednes=onsǣgednes
onsēn (VPs)=ansīen
onsendan *to send out, send forth, transmit, yield up*, AO,CP : *offer to*, VH.
onsēon I. (sv⁵) *to see, look on, behold, regard, take notice of*, AO. II. (A)=ansīen
on-set, -setl, n. *a sitting on, riding on*, GD 183.
onset(e)nes f. *laying on (of hands)*, MH84² : *constitution, founding.*
onsettan *to impose*, CP : *oppress, bear down.*
onsīcan¹ *to sigh, groan*, Bo.
onsīen I. (ȳ)† f. *lack, want.* II.=ansīen
onsīgan¹ *to sink, decline, descend : approach, impend*, Æ : *assail*, Æ.
onsit=onset
onsittan I. sv⁵ *to seat oneself in, occupy*, Æ : *oppress.* II. sv⁵ *to fear, dread* (=ond-).
onsittend m. *rider*, CHy4¹.
onslǣge m. *blow*, WW. [slege]
onslǣpan⁷ and wv. *to go to sleep, sleep*, BH.
onslāpan=onslǣpan
onslūpan⁷ *to unloose*, GD221²³. [=un-]
onsmyrung f. *anointing*, CHRD80¹⁹.
onsnǣsan (LL69,36) v. snǣsan.
onsnīðan¹ *to cut up*, LCD (ES43·321).
onsond=onsand
onspǣc f. *imputation, charge, claim*, LL.
onspannan⁷ *to unfasten, unbind, unloose, open, disclose, release.* [=un-]
onspeca (an-) m. *accuser*, CHRD62²⁶ : *claimant*, LL138,1³.
onspecend m. *accuser, plaintiff*, TC169.
onspillend m. *player*, A13·28,29.
onspornan=onspurnan
onspornend (=un-) *not stumbling*, Sc187⁸.

onsprǣc f. *speech, discourse*, GD332⁹ (an-).
onspreccan *to enliven*, Rɪᴍ9?
onsprecend=onspecend
onspringan³ *to spring forth, originate, rise, burst forth, burst asunder.*
onsprungennes f. *eclipse*, WW225³⁹.
onspurnan³ *to strike against, stumble*, WW 420³⁹.
onstæl m. *order, arrangement*, Gᴜ796.
onstǣlan *to impute to, accuse of*, MFH170.
onstæpe (e) m. *ingress*, ESPs67²⁶ (=in-).
onstæppan⁶ *to walk, go*, Lᴄᴅ,SPs (=in-).
onstal (=ea?) m. *provision, supply*, CP4¹.
onstāl m? *charge, reproof*, OEG.
onstandende *urgent, persistent*, Sc111¹⁴.
onstede=unstede
onstellan *to institute, create, originate, establish, give the example of*, *Bl*; AO,CP. [' onstell']
onstēpan (=īe) *to raise*, †Hy4³⁸.
onstīgend m. *mounted man*, VHy4¹.
onsting m. *claim, authority, jurisdiction, right of intervention*, Ct.
onstingan *to be angry (with)?* RBL115¹⁶.
onstīðian *to harden*, JnLR12⁴⁰.
onstregdan³ (and wk.) (i²) *to sprinkle*, BJVPs 50⁹.
onstydfullnes f. *instability*, DR. [=uni-]
onstȳran *to govern*, BH276¹¹ (v.l.).
onstyr-ednes, -enes f. *movement*, BH,Ps.
onstyrian *to move, rouse, disturb, stir, agitate, excite*, CP.
onsund=ansund
onsun-dran, -dron, -drum adv. *singly, separately, apart*, Gen,Mk : *privately* : *especially.* [' asunder']
onsundrian=āsyndrian
onswāpan⁷ *to sweep on, blow on*, Gʟ : *sweep away, banish.*
onswarian=andswarian
onswebban *to put to sleep, bury*, WW.
onswīfan¹ *to swing forward, turn against* : *push off, put aside, turn away.*
onswīðlic *mighty, loud*, ÆL31²⁸¹.
onswōgan=inswōgan
onswornod *confused*, NC315.
onsymbelnes f. *celebration (of mass)*, BH 112⁸.
onsȳn=ansīen, onsīen I.
onsyngian=unsyngian
ontalu f. *claim at law*, TC302²² (v. LL 3·226).
ontēnan (KGʟ65⁵)=ontȳnan
ontendan *to kindle, set fire to, inflame*, Æ, Lᴄᴅ,LL. ['tind,' 'ontend']
ontendnes (y) f. *burning, fire*, Æ : *inflammation*, Æ : *incitement, fuel*, Æ : *passion.*
ontēon² *to draw to oneself, assume, undertake*, CP : *pull, pull out* : *untie* (=un-).

ontēona m. *injury, oppression*, ERPs102⁶.
ontige m. *claim, usurpation*, RB140⁹.
ontiht-=ontyht-
ontimber *material*, Æ : *cause, occasion*, Æ.
ontimbernes f. *material*, MFH171: *teaching, edification.*
ontimbr-an, -ian, *to instruct*, BH.
ontre=antre
ontrēowan *to entrust, confide*, Dᴀ269?
ontrym-ian, -man '*invalescere*,' NG.
ontȳdran *to nourish, foster*, AO182²⁶.
ontȳdre '*sine foetu*,' *effete*, WW. [=ortȳdre?]
ontygnes f. *accusation*, LL22,37.
ontyhtan (ɪ) *to urge on, incite*, B3086 : *be intent on.*
ontyhting (i) f. *attention, application, aim, intention, instigation*, Sᴄ.
ontȳnan (ē) *to open, reveal, display*, CP. [tūn]
ontyndnes=ontendnes
ontȳnnes f. *opening*, Bʟ93²⁴.
onðǣslic (Sc33²⁰)=unðǣslic
onðenian *to stretch*, EPs63³.
onðēon¹,³† *to be useful, succeed, prosper.*
onðēowian *to serve*, CM473.
onðicgan *to eat of, partake of*, VH18.
±onðracian (a-, an-, and-) *to fear, dread*, Æ.
onðracung (an-) f. *fear, awe*, LPs34²⁶.
on-ðrǣce, -ðrǣclic (an-) *formidable, dreadful*, Æ.
onðrēagung f. *reproach*, ÆL23b⁶⁷².
onðrecan⁵ refl. *to fear*, Gᴜᴛʜ132²⁰⁸.
onðringan³ *to press on or forward*, AO : *move, be moved?* Gᴜ1300.
onðunian *to swell up? move round?* Rᴅ41⁹¹ : *exceed bounds.*
onðwægennes f. *washing*, HL13¹³⁸,¹⁵⁴.
onðwēan⁶ (in-) *to wash*, BH,GD.
onu=heonu
onufan prep. (w. d.) and adv. *above, upon, on*, Jᴜᴅ; AO : *beyond, after.* [' anoven']
onunder (an-) *under*, MFH171.
onuppan I. prep. (w. d.) *upon, on*, CP. II. adv. *in addition, besides.*
onūtan *out of doors*, Lᴄᴅ106b.
onwacan⁶ *to awake*, AO : *arise, be born.*
onwaccan f. *incitement, arousing*, DR74¹².
onwacnian=onwæcnian
onwadan⁶ *to penetrate into, attack, seize, occupy.*
onwǣcan *to weaken, shake (a resolution), soften, mollify*, CP. [wāc]
onwǣcenes f. *arousing*, GD337³³.
on-wæcnan, -wæcnian (e) *to awake, CP* : *arise, spring, be born* (=āwæcnan). [' awaken']
onwǣld (N)=onweald
onwæmme=unwemme; onwær- =unwær-

onwæstm m. *increase*, DR69[9] : *branch*, PPs.
[ōwæstm]

onwæterig=unwæterig

onwald, onwalh=onweald, onwealg

onwarian *to guard oneself against*, MFH
171.

onwealcan[7] *to roll, roll round*, LCD 1·246[10].

onweald (a[1], a[2]) **I.** mfn. *authority, power,
rule, sway, command, AO,Lk*; CP : *jurisdiction, territory*, CP. **II.** adj. *mighty,
powerful.* ['*onwald*']

onwealda (an-) m. *ruler, governor, sovereign* :
the Lord, God.

+onwealdian (an-; æ[2]) *to have dominion
over, get possession of*, LPs,LkLR.

onwealdig (a[1], a[2]) *powerful*, Bo 108[18].

onwealdnes f. *power, possession*, ERPs 2[8].

onwealg, onwealh *whole, sound, entire, uninjured, safe*, AO.

onwealglīce (an-) *wholly, completely*, CP
220[22].

onwealhnes f. *soundness, wholeness, purity,
modesty, chastity.*

onweard (=and-) adj. *acting against, opposed to*, Æ.

onwecnian=onwæcnian

onweg (aweg) adv. '*away*,' *forth, out, off,
onward, along*, B,Chr.

onwegācyr(red)nes (=ie[4]) f. *apostasy*, BH
176 (v.l.).

onwegādrīfan[1] *to drive away*, VPs.

onwegādrīfennes f. *a driving away*, GD
185[13].

onwegāfirran *to remove away*, VHy.

onwegālǣdnes f. *removal*, BH446[16].

onwegāscūfan[2] *to push away*, VPs.

onwegāwendan *to remove*, VPs.

onwegfǣreld n. *departure*, GD 119[26].

onweggewit n. *mental aberration*, VPs
115[11].

onweggewitennes f. *departure*, BH170[10].

onwegoncernes=onwegācyrrednes

onwegpullian *to pull away*, ES 43·339.

onwemme=unwemme

onwendan *to change, exchange* : *upset, end,
overturn, turn aside, avert*, VPs : *change for
the better, amend* : *change for the worse,
pervert* : *transgress* : *deprive* : *return.*

onwendedlic *changeable*, LCD 3·164[8].

on-wendednes, -wendnes f. *movement,
change, alteration*, VPs.

onweorpan[3] (in-) *cast in one's teeth, accuse* :
turn or throw aside : *begin the web.*

onweorpnes f. *onpouring*, BH118[5].

onwēstan=āwēstan

onwīcan[1] *to yield, give way*, WW.

onwille *wished for, agreeable*, Gu700.

onwindan[3] *unwind, loosen* : *retreat*, AN
531.

onwinnan[3] *to attack, assail*, Æ.

onwist f. *habitation*, Ex18.

onwlite=andwlite

onworpennes f. *enticement, allurement, inspiration*, HL200[164].

onwrecan=āwrecan

onwrēon[1,2] *to uncover, unfold, display,
explain, reveal*, Æ,CP.

on-wrig(en)nes, -wrihnes f. *revelation, exposure, exposition*, Æ. [wrēon]

onwrīting f. *inscription*, Lk20[24]. ['*on-
writing*']

onwrītung=onwrīðung

onwrīðan *to unbind, unwrap* (JUD173)=
unwrīðan.

onwrīðod pp. *supported*, BF198[23].

onwrīðung f. *ligament, bandage*, WW439[13]
(onwrīt-).

onwunian *to inhabit, remain*, Ps.

onwunung f. *dwelling-place* : *assiduity*,
OEG75.

onwurpan=onweorpan

onwyllan *to cause to boil, inflame*, Gu362.

onwylwan *to roll up, roll together*, EHy
2[12].

onȳðan *to pour in*, Sc200[7].

onȳwan (=īe) *to show, manifest* : refl. *appear.*

open '*OPEN*,' *exposed*, AO : *evident, well-
known, public, manifest, plain, clear*, AO :
open to re-trial, LL10,9.

openǣrs m. *medlar*, WW137[36]. ['*openarse*']

openere m. *opener*, BF152[3].

±openian *to* '*open*,' *open up, disclose, declare, reveal, expound*, Æ,BH,Ps; CP :
(+) intr. *become manifest* : (+) *be open to,
exposed to.*

openlic *open, public*, WW. adv. -līce
'*openly*,' *manifestly, plainly, clearly, unreservedly*, Bl,Bo,RB.

opennes f. *openness, publicity*, OEG : *manifestation*, ÆL23b[42].

±openung f. *opening, disclosure, manifestation*, Bl,W.

oportanie=aprōtane

ōr† n. *beginning, origin* : *front*, An,B.
['*ore*,' cp. ord]

or prefix (lit. '*out of*'=L. ex-) is privative,
as in orsorg, orwēna; or denotes origin,
antiquity, as in oreald. [*Ger.* ur-]

ōra **I.** m. *border, bank, shore*, CHR; Mdf.
II. m. '*ore*,' *unwrought metal*, BH,Ps,WW :
brass, ÆGr,Cp,CP. **III.** *a coin of Danish
origin*, LkL,LL (v. 2·601). ['*ora*']

oraðȝ=oroð

orblēde *bloodless*, WW397[29]. [blōd]

orc **I.** m. *pitcher, crock, cup*, B,GL. [*Late
L.* orca; *L.* urceus] **II.** m. *demon*, GL.
[*L.* orcus]

or-cēape, -cēapes, -cēapunga, -cēapungum adv. *gratis, without cause.*

orc-eard, -erd *(Æ,Lcd)*=ortgeard

orcēas *inviolable, unimpugned, unassailed,* GL.

orcēasnes f. *immunity, purity,* GL.

orcerdlēh f. *orchard,* HGL. [ortgeard, lēah]

orcerdweard m. *gardener,* WW 333²⁵.

orcgeard, orcird=ortgeard

orcnǣwe (ā) *evident, well-known.*

orcnēas mp. *monsters,* B 112. [*L.* Orcus]

orcðyrs m. *monster of hell, Orcus,* WW.

orcyrd=ortgeard

ord m. *point, spear-point, spear, Æ,B,CP : source, beginning, Æ,CP : front, vanguard, Æ : chief, prince;* in pl. *first men, the flower.* ['*ord*']

ordǣle *not participating, free from,* WW.

ordāl (ē) mn. '*ordeal*,' LL. [*Ger.* urteil]

ordālīsen n. *iron used in an ordeal,* LL 388,1.

ordbana m. *murderer,* GEN 1097.

ordceard=ortgeard ; **ordēl**=ordāl

ordfruma m. *fount, source, Æ : author, creator, instigator,* AO : (†) *chief, prince.*

ordfrymm (e²) *original,* ES 49·352.

ordstæpe m. *spear-stab, wound,* RD 71¹⁶.

ordwyga m. *warrior,* WALD 1⁶.

-ōre v. īsen-ō.

oreald *very old,* Bo 102¹⁸. [*Ger.* uralt]

ōred-=ōret-

orel n. *robe, garment, mantle, veil, Æ,*GL. [*L.* orarium]

oreldo=oryldu

orene I. *excessive,* v. SF 157 : *harmful.* **II.** n. *excess : injury?* LCD 3·16⁵ (orne).

orenlīce *excessively,* MFH 171.

ōret† m. *contest, battle.*

ōret-=orret(t)-

ōretfeld m. *place of contest,* OEG 8⁵⁰.

ōretla m. *contumely, insult,* GD 200¹⁶.

ōretlof n. *triumph,* CM 497.

ōret-mæcg† (e³), -mæcga (WW) m. *champion, warrior.*

ōretstōw f. *wrestling place, place of contest,* OEG.

ōrett-=ōret-

ōretta† m. *champion, warrior, hero.*

oreð=oroð ; **oreðian**=orðian

orf n. *cattle, live stock, Æ,Chr,LL.* ['*orf*']

orfcwealm (a²) m. *cattle-plague, murrain,* CHR,W.

orfcynn (i²) n. *cattle, Æ.*

orfeorme (y) (†) *destitute of, lacking :* (†) *empty, useless : squalid, filthy.*

orfeormnes f. *squalor, filthiness,* Cp 488s.

orfgebitt n. *grazing,* WW 149³³.

orfiermu f. *squalor,* OET 96⁹³³.

orfyrme=orfeorme

orfyrmð *refuse,* OEG 609.

organ m. *canticle, song, voice,* SOL.

organa? organe? f., organ-an, -on pl. *musical instrument, Æ,ApT,Ps.* ['*organ*'; *L.* organum]

organdrēam (APs 150⁴)=orgeldrēam

organe f. *marjoram, Lcd.* ['*organ*'; *L.* origanum]

organian=orgnian

organystre *player on an instrument,* GEN 4²¹.

orgeate=orgyte

orgel (o²) *pride, WW.* ['*orgel*']

orgeldrēam m. *sound of a musical instrument, Bl.* [v. '*orgle*']

orgellic *ignominious,* CP. adv. -līce *proudly, insolently, scornfully, Æ.*

orgello (A 11·98)=orgel

orgelnes f. *pride,* OEG 1108. [v. '*orgel*']

orgelword n. *arrogant speech,* ÆH 2·248¹¹.

orgete=orgyte

orgilde *not having discharged a payment (of* '*wergeld*'*),* LL.

orglīce=orgellīce

orgnian *to sing to an instrumental accompaniment,* ÆGR 181².

orgol=orgel

orgyte (ea, e) *well-known, manifest,* AO.

orh-=org-; **orhlættre**=orleahtre

orhlȳte *without lot or share in, destitute of, Æ.*

oriege *out of sight, not visible,* ANS 98·128.

orl m.=orel n.

orlæg† (e) n. *fate,* DA,DD.

orleahter m. '*discrimen,*' *lack of vice or defect,* v. ES 37·179 : *danger,* CHRD 2⁸.

orleahtre *blameless,* B,BL.

orleg=orlæg

orlegcēap m. *battle-booty?* GEN 1994.

orlege I. n. *strife, war.* **II.** adj. *hostile.*

orlegfrom *keen in battle,* RD 21¹⁵.

orleggīfre (æ) *fond of strife,* GEN 2287.

orleghwīl† f. *war-time,* B.

orlegnīð† m. *war, hostility,* GEN.

orlegsceaft f. '*supplicium*'? SOL 456? (GK).

orlegstund f. *time of adversity,* SOL 374.

orlegweorc n. *battle,* GEN 2020.

ormǣte I. (ā, ē) adj. *boundless, huge, excessive, intense, Æ,Chr;* AO. **II.** adv. ['*ormete*'; metan]

ormǣtlic *excessive,* CHR 1117 : *tremendous,* WYN 148. adv. -līce.

ormǣtnes f. *excess, immensity, Æ.*

or-mēte, -mette=ormǣte

ormōd *despondent, despairing, hopeless,* Bo, Hept; Æ,CP. ['*ormod*']

ormōdnes f. *desperation, despair,* CP.

orn=arn pret. 3 sg. of iernan.

orn-=oren-

ornest n. *trial by battle,* LL.

oroð n. *breath, breathing, snorting,* B,GL.

orped *adult, active, Bf.* ['*orped*'] adv. -līce *boldly* : *clearly, definitely.*
orrest f. *battle, combat,* CHR. [*ON.* orrusta]
orretscipe m. *infamy,* WW.
±orrettan *to put to confusion, disgrace.*
orsāwle *lifeless, dead,* ÆL.
orsceattinga *gratuitously,* BH242⁷.
orsorg (w. g.) *unconcerned, without care or anxiety, safe,* CP. [*OHG.* ursorg]
orsorglic (w. g.) *secure,* CP. adv. -līce *carelessly, rashly,* Æ,CP : *without anxiety or hindrance* : *securely, safely,* CP.
orsorgnes f. *security, prosperity,* CP : *carelessness,* CHRD50⁴.
orsorh=orsorg
ortgeard (*CP*), orce(a)rd (*Æ*) m. *garden,* 'ORCHARD*.'
ortgeard-=orcerd-; ortrēowe=ortrīewe
ortrēownes (ȳ) f. *diffidence, mistrust,* BL, GD.
ortrīewan (y) *to despair (of)* : (+) *doubt, disbelieve.*
ortrīewe (ēo, ȳ) *despairing, hopeless, AO,W* : *treacherous, faithless.* ['*ortrow*']
±ortrūwian w. g. *to despair, doubt, Æ.* ['*ortrow*']
ortrūwung f. *despair,* Sc131³,⁴.
ortrȳw-=ortrīew-
ortȳdre *barren,* A11·2⁴².
orð (KGL)=oroð
orðanc I. mn. *intelligence, understanding, mind* : *cleverness, skill* : *skilful work, mechanical art, Æ.* [*OHG.* urdank] II. adj. *ingenious, skilful.*
orðancbend (o²) f. *cunning band,* RD 43¹⁵.
orðances *thoughtlessly,* SOL164.
orðanclic *ingenious,* GD269¹³.
orðancpil (o²) m. *ploughshare?* RD22¹².
orðancscipe m. *mechanical art,* GL.
orðancum *skilfully,* B,GL.
orðian *to breathe, gasp, Æ* : *long for, aspire to, Æ.* [oroð]
orðonc (CP)=orðanc
orðung f. *breathing, breath, Æ* : *pore.*
oruð=oroð
orwearde adv. *unguarded,* B3127.
orweg *trackless?* A19·110.
orwegnes f. *inaccessibility,* WW220³⁴.
orwegstīg f. *out-of-the-way track,* WW.
orwēna (indecl. adj.)=orwēne
+orwēnan *to despair,* Æ,GD.
orwēne (w. g.) *hopeless, despairing of, Æ* : *despaired of, desperate.*
orwēnnes f. *despair,* Æ,LL.
orwīge *not fighting, unwarlike, cowardly* : *not liable to the legal consequences (of homicide),* LL76,42⁵,⁷.
orwīte=orwīge

orwurð n. *ignominy,* CPs82¹⁷.
orwyrð (VPs), orwyrðu f. *shame, dishonour* : *abuse.*
+orwyrðan *to disgrace,* GL.
+orwyrðe (-de) *traduced,* WW51²³.
orwyrðlic *shameful,* MH156²¹.
oryldu f. *great age.* [ieldo]
ōs m., gp. ēsa *a divinity, god* : *name of the rune for* o.
oser '*vimen,*' *osier,* OEG10².
ōsle f. '*merula,*' '*ouzel,*' *blackbird, Cp,Ep, WW.* [amsel]
ōsogen (WW501³³)=āsogen pp. of āsugan.
ōst m. *protuberance, knot, lump,* GL,MH.
osterhlāf m. *oyster-patty,* LCD79a.
osterscyll (o²) f. *oyster-shell,* LCD1·338¹⁶.
ōstig, ōstiht *knotty, rough, scaly,* GL.
ostre f. *oyster,* WW. [*L.* ostrea]
ostor-=oster-
ot I. (VPs)=æt. II.=oð
oter (*KC*)=otor
oterhola m. *otter's hole,* KC3·23'.
otor, otr (*Ep*), ottor m. '*otter,*' *WW.*
otsperning (KGL70¹⁶)=ætspornung
oð I. prep. w. a. and (rarely) d. *to, up to, as far as* : *until,* Æ,AO,CP. oð ðisum *up to now,* ES43·166. II. conj. *until.* III. as prefix. usu. denotes departure, separation, as in oðfeallan, oðwendan.
oðberan† *to bear away, carry off* : *bring.*
oðberstan³ *to break away, escape,* KC,LL.
oð-brēdan, -bregdan³ *to snatch away, carry off, rescue, remove, withdraw, Gu;* AO. ['*atbraid*']
oðclīfan¹ *to cleave to, stick, adhere,* CR1267.
oðcwelan⁴ *to die,* LL112,53.
oðcyrran (=ie) *to be perverted,* JUL338.
oðdōn anv. *to put out (eyes),* LL32,19.
oðēawan=oðīewan
oðēcan *to add to,* VPs68²⁷. [ēac]
oðēhtian *to drive away? dispossess?* LCD 1·384¹⁵ (A52·118).
ōðel=ēðel; oðēowan=oðīewan
ōðer I. (+ at KC6·155⁹) pron. sb. or adj. (always strong) *one of two, Æ,AO* : *second, Æ* : 'OTHER' : *something else, anything else* : *alternate, next* : *remaining, rest, AO* : *further, existing besides, Æ* : *another* : (in pl.) *the rest, the others.* ōðer...ōðer *the one...the other, Æ, CP* : *other...than, CP.* ōðer oððe...oððe *either...or.* ōðer healf *one and a half.* II. ('*aut*')=āhwæðer. comp. adv. ōðerlīcor *otherwise,* RB87¹⁹. ['*otherliker*'] III. *word, speech* ('*eloquium*'), PPs118³⁸. [*ON.* ōðr]
ōðergēara adv. *next year,* LCD.
ōðerhwīle *sometimes,* BF118²⁹.
ōðerlucor (RWH77⁷)=ōðerlīcor
oðēwan=oðīewan

oðfæstan† *to inflict upon*, EL,SAT : *set to* (*a task*), *entrust, commit*, CP.

oðfaran⁶ w. d. *to flee from*, *Ex.* ['*atfare*']

oðfeallan¹ *to fall off, decline, decay*, CP : *fall away from, be lost to, be wanting, fail* : *cease to concern.*

oðfēolan³ *to cleave, adhere*, WW416²⁴.

oðfeorrian *to take away*, LCD1·384⁴.

oðferian *to take away, bear off* : *save* (*life*).

oðflēogan² *to fly away*, PH347.

oðflēon² (w. d.) *to flee away, escape*, Æ,AO.

oðflītan¹ *to gain by legal process*, TC169'.

oðgān anv. *to go away, escape*, B2934.

oðglīdan¹ *to glide away, escape*, SOL401.

oðgrīpan¹ *to rescue*, BH408²⁷.

oðhealdan⁷ *to keep back*, CP. ['*athold*']

oðhebban⁶ *to raise, exalt, lift up*, CP.

oðhelde=oðhylde

oðhlēapan⁷ *to escape*, LL218,1¹¹.

oðhrīnan¹ *to touch*, HL16²²⁸.

oðhȳdan *to hide from*, AO94¹¹.

oðhylde (e) *contented*, LCD.

ōðian=ēðian

oðiernan³ *to run away*, LL,MET.

oðiewan (ē, ēa, ēo, ī, ȳ) tr. *to show*, Gen; CP: *show oneself, appear*, *El.* ['*atew*']

oðiewodnes f. *manifestation*, RWH67² (=ætēow-).

oðlǣdan *to lead away, carry off, snatch from, withdraw*, Ps. ['*atlead*']

oðlengan *to belong, pertain*, WYN49,68.

oðrān=oðhrān pret. 3 sg. of oðhrīnan.

oðrīdan¹ *to ride, proceed*, HELL40.

oðrinnan³ *to run off, escape*, Met20¹³⁸. [v. '*atrin*']

oðrōwan⁷ *to escape by rowing*, CHR897A.

oðsacan⁶ (w. g.) *to deny, abjure*, AO.

oðscacan⁶ *to escape*, LL177,6³.

oðscēotan² *to escape, slip off, turn aside*, Æ.

oðscūfan² intr. *to move off*, PH168.

ōðsperning f. *stumbling-block*, KGL.

oðspurnan³ (eo) *to dash against*, BL,KGL.

oðstandan⁶ *to stand fixed, remain, cease*, AO : *stand behind*, Æ : *perplex, hinder.*

oðstillan *to stop*, LCD1·82⁵.

oðswerian⁶ *to abjure, deny on oath*, AO,LL.

oðswīgan *to become silent*, OET631.

oðswimman³ (y) *to escape by swimming*, CHR915D.

oðtēon² *to take away*, LCD87a.

oððæt conj. *until* (or two words).

oððe, oðða conj. *or* : *and*, ANS151·79. oððe...oððe *either...or*, BH ['OTHER'] : (=oð ðe) *until.*

oððēodan *to sever, dismember*, AN1423.

oððet (KGL61¹⁹)=oððæt

oððīcgan⁵ *to take away*, EX338.

oððingian *to obtain by unfair means, usurp*, LL(412⁹).

oððo (BH66²⁰), oððon (HL,LL) conj. *or.* [=oððe]

oððringan³ *to deprive of*, AO : *drive out*, GD.

oðwendan *to turn away, divert, deprive of*, Gen403. ['*atwend*']

oðwindan³ *to escape, get away*, CHR897A.

oðwītan¹ *to charge with, blame, reproach with, taunt*, AO,CP.

oðwyrcan *to harm*, LCD1·384⁵.

oðȳwan=oðīewan

ōwæstm m. *shoot, branch, twig*, GL,PS.

ōwana (N)=āhwonan

ō-web, -wef (ā) n. *woof, weft*, Cp,WW. ['*abb*']

ōwēr, ōwern (BH)=āhwǣr; ōwiht=āwiht

ōwisc f. *edge*, KC3·388²⁵.

ōwðer=āhwæðer; ōwul=āwel

oxa m. nap. oxan, œxen, exen, dp. ox(n)um '*ox*,' *Ct,JnL,Rd,VPs,WW*; CP.

oxancealf n. *ox-calf*, LEVC1³.

oxangang m. *an eighth of a '*plough-land*,'* hide, BC3·370. ['*oxgang*']

oxanhyrde m. *herdsman*, OEG,WW.

oxanslyppe f. '*oxlip*,' Lcd.

ōxn f. *arm-pit*, WW.

oxnahyrde=oxanhyrde

oxnalybb n. *ox-heal* (*plant*), LCD.

ōxta=ōcusta; oxum v. oxa.

P

pād f. *covering, coat, cloak*, WW.

paddanīeg f. *toad-meadow, frog-island*, BC 2·246⁶.

padde, pade f. *toad, frog*, Chr1137; BC 2·377¹⁶. ['*pad*']

pǣca m. *deceiver*, BAS40²¹.

pǣcan *to cheat, deceive*, RB,W.

pægel m. *gill, small measure, wine vessel*, WW124² (A8·450). [v. '*pail*']

pǣl m. *javelin* (v. OEG19³).

pæll (e) m. *silk robe, cloak*, ÆGr : '*pall*,' *hanging, covering*, ÆH : *purple garment, purple*, BH,WW. [L. pallium]

pællen (e) *of costly stuff, purple*, Æ. ['*pallen*']

pællerēad v. fellerēad; pǣlm=palm

pæneg, pæning=pening; -pǣran v. for-p.

pærl? '*enula*' ('*gemmula*'? Wülker), ÆGR 304⁷.

pǣtīg=(prætig), prættig

pæð (a) mfn. nap. paðas '*path*,' *track*, Ct, Ex,Gl,Ps; Æ : *valley*, LkL.

pæððan *to traverse, travel over, pass along*, Met,Rd. ['*path*']

pāl m. '*pole*,' *stake, post*, WW334² : *spade.* [L. palus]

palendse (AO), palentse, pal(l)ente f., palent (Æ) m. *palace.* [Late L. palantium]

palentlic *of a palace, palatial*, WW342[7].
palester=palstr
pallium m. *pallium*, CHR804 : *splendid garment*, ÆL36[160]. [*L*.]
palm (æ), palma (ea) m. '*palm*'-*tree*, *Æ*, *DR,JnL,VPs* : *palm-branch*, *Æ*.
palm-æppel, -appel m. *date*, WW.
palmbearu m. *palm-grove*, WW488[13].
palm-dæg (Æ), -sunnandæg (*Lk*19[29]) m. '*Palm Sunday*.'
palm-trēo, -trēow m. '*palm-tree*,' *Æ,JnL*.
palmtwig n. *palm-twig, palm-branch*, *Æ*.
+**palmtwigian**† *to deck with palm-branches*.
palmwuce f. *week of which Palm Sunday is the first day*.
palstr, palster sb. *prick, point, spike*, GL.
palðer (AA39[15]), pandher (PA12) m. *panther*.
panic m. *a kind of millet*, LCD.
panmete m. *cooked food*, WW409[9].
panne (o) f. '*pan*,' *CP,WW*.
pāpa m. '*pope*,' *BH*; Æ,CP. [*L*. papa]
pāpanhād m. *papal office*, *Æ*. ['*popehood*']
pāpdōm m. *papacy*, CHR592.
paper m? *papyrus*, WW523[7].
papig=popig
papolstān (o[1], e[2]) m. *pebble*, *Æ,OEG*. ['*pebblestone*'; *L*. papula]
pāp-seld, -setl n. *papacy*, BL205[20].
paradīs m. *Paradise*, HEX512.
paralisin ds. of sb. *paralysis*, ÆL25[724].
-parian v. ā-p.
part m. '*part*,' *ÆGr*. [*L*. partem]
passion f. nap. passione *the part of the gospel containing the account of Christ's passion*, OET444[37].
pað, paðu=pæð
pāwa m. pāwe f. *peacock, peahen*, *ÆGr,Ep*, *Lcd,WW*. ['*po*'; *Lat*. pavo]
pēa m. *peafowl*, *Ph*312. ['*pea*']
peall '*defrutum*' (sc. *vinum*), OEG (v. ES 37·184).
peaneg=pening
pear-roc, -ruc m. '*clatrum*,' *fence by which a space is enclosed*, *Gl* : *enclosure, enclosed land*, *Bo,Chr,KC*; ÆL. ['*parrock*']
pecg m? *pig?* BC3·223[22] (pygg? v. SKED).
pell, pellen=pæll, pællen
pellican m. '*pelican*,' *Ps*101[5].
pen=penn
pending, pene(n)g, penig=pening
pening m. '*PENNY**,' *coin, money*, *Æ,LL* (v. 2·614) : *pennyweight*, Lcd.
pening-hwyrfere, -mangere m. *money-changer*, WW.
peningslæht (=i[3]) m. *coining money*, MtL 17[25].
peningwǣg f. *pennyweight*, LCD47b.
peningweorð (u[3]) n. *pennyworth, Lcd,KC*; Æ.

penn m. '*pen*,' *fold, BC*; Mdf. [*L*.]
pennig, penning=pening
pentecosten m. '*Pentecost*,' *Æ,Bf,Chr*.
pēo=pīe
peonie f. '*peony*,' *Lcd*1·168[14]. [*L*.]
peorð m. *name of the rune for* p, *chessman?* RUN38.
peose (piose, pyose)=pise; **pere**=peru
perewōs n. *pear-juice, perry*, WW128[20].
perfince=perwince
pernex m. *a supposed bird?* (mistranslation of *L*. pernix), RD41[66].
per-sic, -soc, -suc m. *peach*, LCD. [*L*. persicum]
Persisc *Persian*, Æ.
persoctrēow n. *peach-tree*, WW138[1].
peru f. '*pear*,' *ÆGr*. [*L*. pirum]
perwince f. '*periwinkle*' (*plant*), WW.
petersilie f. '*parsley*,' *Lcd*. [*Ger*. petersilie]
pētig=(prǣtig), prættig; **peððan**=pæððan
philosoph m. *philosopher*, AO.
pic n. '*pitch*,' *Ep,Sc*; Æ. [*L*. picem]
pīc m. *point, pointed tool, pick, pickaxe*, *Cp,WW*. ['*pike*']
picen *pitchy, of pitch*, BL,DHY.
picgbrēad? (picbred) '*glans*,' *mast, pig's food*, WW139[35]. [v. '*pig*']
+**pīcian** *to cover with* '*pitch*,' *Lcd*10a.
picung f. '*stigmata*,' *pricking*, *Cp*572s. ['*picking*']
pīe f. *parasite*, GL.
pierisc *Pierian*, A31·535.
pigment, pihment (y) *drug*, LCD. [*L*.]
pihten *part of a loom*, OEG. [*L*. pecten]
pīl m. *a pointed object, spike, nail, shaft, stake, Æ,Chr* : *arrow, dart, javelin* : pl. *hairs of plants, Lcd*1·304[1]. ['*pile*'; *L*. pilum]
pilce=pylece; **pile**=pyle
pīle f. *mortar*, CP. [*L*. pila]
pilece=pylece
+**pīled** *spiked, spiky*, ÆH.
pīlere m. *one who pounds in a mortar*, WW 141[19].
pilian (y[1]) *to peel, skin*, LCD3·114[13].
±**pīlian** *to pound in a mortar*, Ex16[14],WW 114[25].
pilsāpe f. '*silotrum*,' *soap for removing hair?* WW127[36],(NP8·204).
pīlstæf m. *pestle*, CP267[2].
pīl-stampe f.,-stoccm.,pīlstre f. *pestle*, WW.
pīn f. *pain, anguish, torture*. [*L*. poena]
pīnbēam m. *pine-tree*, Æ. [v. '*pine*']
pinca=pynca
pīnecwalu m? n? *torture*, W241[13].
pīnere m. *tormentor*, GPH,NG.
pinewincle=winewincle
pingan=pyngan
pīn-hnutu f. ds. -hnyte *fir-cone, Lcd*. ['*pine-nut*']

±**pīnian** _to torture, torment, AO,MtL_; Æ,CP. ['_pine_'; _L._ poena]

pinn sb. '_pin_,' _peg, Bf_ : _pen_, Mt p 2¹⁷.

pinnan obl. case of wk. sb. pinne? _flask, bottle_, WW 97¹⁰.

pīnnes f. _pain, torture_, TC 369'.

pinsian _to weigh, consider, examine, reflect_, CP. [_L._ pensare]

pintel '_penis_,' WW 292¹ᵉ ['_pintle_']

pīntrēow n. '_pine-tree Lcd_; ÆL.

pīn-trēowen, -trȳwen _of or belonging to a pine-tree_, LCD.

pīnung f. _torment, punishment_, Æ,AO.

pīnungtōl n. _instrument of torture_, Æ.

pionie (OEG 56⁴¹⁸)=peonie; **piose**—pise

pīpdrēam m. _piping_, LCD 3·208²².

pīpe f. '_pipe_,' _tube, Lcd_; Mdf : _wind instrument_, W,WW : _channel_, KC3·380². [_L._]

pipeneale f. _pimpernel_ (Swt).

piper=pipor

pīpere m. '_piper_,' _MtR,WW_.

pīpian _to_ '_pipe_' (_blow an instrument_), NC (ZDA 34·234).

piplian (y) _to show eruptions, break out in pimples_, LCD.

pīplic _musical_, OEG 1644.

pipor (e²) m. '_pepper_,' _Æ,Lcd_. [_L._ piper]

piporcorn n. '_pepper-corn_,' _Lcd_.

piporcwyrn f. _pepper mill_, ANS 84·325.

piporhorn (e) m. _horn for pepper_, LL 455,17.

±**pip(o)rian** _to season with_ '_pepper_,' _Lcd_.

Pirenisc _Pyrrhenian_, A 31·535.

pirge (GL)=pirie

pirgrāf m. _pear-orchard_, KC 5·284'.

pirie, pirige (Æ) f. _pear-tree_.

pīs _heavy_, NG. [_L._ pensum]

pise f. (eo, io, y) _pea_, _Cp,Lcd,WW_. ['_pease*_']

pisle f. _warm chamber?_ WW 186¹⁰. [_Low L._ pisalis]

pīslic _heavy_, NG. adv. -līce.

pistel=pistol

pistol m. _letter_, Æ : _apostolic letter_, Æ. ['_pistle_'; _L._ epistola]

pistolbōc f. _book of the epistles_, LL. [v. '_pistle_']

pistolclāð m. _vestment worn by the epistoler_, BC 3·366'.

pistolrǣdere m. _epistle-reader, sub-deacon_, CM.

pistolrǣding f. _a lesson in the church service_, Æ. [v. '_pistle_']

pistolrocc (e²) m. _vestment worn by the epistoler_, TC 429²².

pitt=pytt

piða wm. _inward part_, '_pith_,' _Bo_; CP.

placunis (wlacunis)=wlæcnes

plæce f. _open space, street_, DR,MtLR. ['_place_'; _L._ platea]

---

plæg-=pleg-; **plæse**, plætse=plæce

plætt m. _slap, smack_, ÆH 2·248'.

plættan _to buffet, smack_, Jn 19³. ['_plat_']

plagian=plegian

planēta _chasuble_ (BTs). [v. '_planet_']

plante f. '_plant_,' _shoot, CP,VPs_. [_L._ planta]

±**plantian** _to_ '_plant_,' _Æ,CP,VPs_.

plantsticca m. _dibble_, WW 106¹⁷.

plantung f. '_planting_,' _WW_ : _plant, Mt_.

plaster I. n. '_plaster_' (_as medicament_), DD, Lcd. [_L._ emplastrum] II.=palster

-platian v. ā-pl.

+**platod** _plated_ (_of gold_), OEG 11⁶¹.

platung f. _metal plate_, WW 196²⁴. [v. '_plate_']

pleagian=plegian

plega (a, æ) m. _quick motion, movement, exercise_, _Chr,Cp,Cr,Gen,WW_ : '_play_,' _festivity, drama, game, sport, AO,Bl_; Æ : _battle_, _B_ : _gear for games_, APT 12¹⁷ : _applause_.

plegan, ±**plegian** (a, æ, eo) (pres. occly. strong) _to move rapidly, An,Gen : exercise, occupy or busy oneself, Bo,Bl,LL_ : '_play_,' _sport with, amuse_ ò_neself, dance, CP,MtL_ : _contend, fight : play on an instrument, Ps_ : _clap the hands, applaud, El,VPs : make sport of, mock, Æ : cohabit_ (_with_), _Rd 43²_.

plegemann=plegmann

plegende '_playing_,' _Shr_.

plegere m. '_player_,' _WW 108⁹_.

plegestōw=plegstōw

plegestre f. _female athlete_, OEG 4735.

pleghūs n. '_playhouse_,' _theatre_, OEG 1752.

plegian=plegan

pleglic (GL) _athletic : scenic : comic_.

plegmann m. _gymnosophist, athlete_, GL.

plegol _playful, jocular_, ÆL 21²⁹² : _wanton_, CHRD 54²².

plegscip n. _small vessel_, WW 181⁴⁰.

plegscyld (e²) m. _play-shield, small shield_, GL.

plegstede m. _playground_, KC 6·244⁸.

plegstōw f. _playground, gymnasium, amphitheatre, Lcd,WW_. ['_playstow_']

plēo ds. of pleoh.

pleogan=plegan

pleoh n. gs. plēos _danger, risk, harm_, Æ,AO, CP : _responsibility_, LL 70,36².

plēolic _dangerous, hurtful, hazardous_, Æ, AO.

plēon⁵ (w. g.) _to expose to danger, adventure oneself_, CP.

plett f? _fold_, NG. [_L._ plecta]

plice v. plyccan.

plicettan? _to play with_, v. NC 315.

plicgan _to scrape, scratch_, GPH 396.

pliht m. _peril, risk, danger, damage, VPs, WW_; Æ. tō plihte _dangerously_. [pleon ; '_plight_']

plihtan *to imperil, compromise, LL.* [*'plight'*]
plihtere m. *look-out man at the prow,* OEG.
plihtlic *perilous, dangerous,* LCD,WW.
ploccian=pluccian
plōg, plōh m. *what a yoke of oxen could plough in a day, a plough-land, Lcd.* [*'plough'*]
plont-=plant-
plot *'plot' of ground, LL* 400,3 (v. 3·237).
pluccian *to 'pluck,' tear, Æ,Mt,WW.*
plūm f. *down?* Cp 1600 (v. A 47·248).
plūmblǣd f. *plum,* LCD 86a.
plūme f. *'plum,' Æ,Cp : plum-tree, Cp,Ep, Erf;* Mdf.
plūmfeðer f. *down,* ES 9·39. [*L.* pluma]
plūmsēaw (ē²) n. *plum-juice,* LCD 3·114'.
plūmslā f. *wild plum, sloe,* WW 139⁴.
plūmtrēow n. *'plum-tree,' Lcd;* ÆGR.
plyccan *only in plice 2 sg. subj.* (*IM* 122) *and plyce (imperat.)* (*IM* 127) *to pluck, pull, snatch,* NC 315. [*'plitch'*]
plyhtlic=plihtlic
plȳme f. *plum, plum-tree,* GL. [*L.* *prunea]
pocādl f. *eruptive disease, pox,* LCD.
pocc m. *'pock,' blister, pustule, ulcer, Lcd.*
pocca (*LkL*)=pohha
pohha, poh(ch)a m. *pocket, bag, CP,MkL.* [*'pough'*]
pohhede *baggy, RB.* [*'pough'*]
pōl m. *'pool,' CP,JnL;* Æ; Mdf.
pōlbǣr f. *pasture-land by a pool,* KC (MLR 19·203).
polente? f. *parched corn, Æ.* [*'polenta'; L.*]
pollegie f. *pennyroyal,* LCD. [*L.* pulegium]
pollup m. *scourge?* (BT), LL (278').
pon-=pan-; **pond**=pynd
popæg (Cp)=popig
popelstān (*OEG* 1815)=papolstān
popig m? *'poppy,' Gl,WW.*
popul *poplar?* KC 3·219⁸ (v. BT).
por, porr, porlēac n. *leek, Æ.* [*L.* porrum]
port I. mn. *'port,' harbour, AO : town (esp. with market rights or with a harbour), BH, Chr,LG,LL;* Mdf. [*L.* portus] II. m. *portal, door, gate, entrance, MtL,Ps;* Mdf. [*'port'; L.* porta]
portcwēne f. *prostitute,* NG.
porte f.=port II.
portgeat n. *city gate, Æ,WW.*
portgerēfa m. *'port-reeve,' mayor, Æ,Ct,LL, WW.*
portgeriht n. *town-due,* KC 3·138¹⁰.
portherpað *main road to a town,* KC 3·453'.
±**portian** *to bray (in a mortar),* CP.
portic mn. *portico, porch, vestibule, sanctuary, chapel, BH,Jn;* Æ. [*'portic'*]
portmann m. *townsman, Æ,WW.* [*'portman'*]
portstrǣt f. *public road,* KC.

portweall m. *city wall, Æ.*
portweg *public road,* KC 6·81¹.
port-wer (DR), -weora (KC) m. *citizen* (=-wara).
±**pos** n. *cold in head, Lcd.* [*'pose'*]
posa (NG)=pusa
poshlīwe *a kind of shelter?* KC 3·82².
posl, postling m. *pellet, pill,* LCD.
post m. *'post,' Æ,WW.* [*L.* postis]
postol m. *apostle, LkR.* [*'postle'*]
potian *to push, butt, goad, Æ,W.* [*'pote'*]
pott m. *'pot,' Lcd* 1·378' (v. late).
pottere m. *'potter,' BC* 3·49'.
prætt m. nap. prattas *trick, craft, art, Æ,W, ZDA.* [*'prat'*]
prættig (e) *tricky, sly, cunning, wily, astute, WW;* Æ. [*'pretty'*]
prafost (ā¹? o¹, a², e²) m. *officer, 'provost' (of a monastery), KC,MH,RB;* Æ. [*L.* propos(i)tus]
prafostfolgoð m. *order or rank of provost,* RB 126⁶.
prafostscīr f. *provostship,* RB 124¹⁶.
pranga v. wranga.
prass m. *noise, tumult, ÆL.*
prattas v. prætt; **prēan**=prēon
prēde=prȳte
prēdicere m. *preacher,* ÆGR 276¹.
prēdician *to preach,* Lk 8¹.
prēdicung f. *preaching,* NC 315.
prēon m. *'fibula,' pin, brooch, TC,WW.* [*'preen'*]
prēost (ēa, ē, īo) m. *'priest,' presbyter, BH, LL,Mt,Nic,WW;* AO,CP.
prēostgesamnung f. *community of priests,* NC 315.
prēosthād m. *'priesthood,' BH,OEG;* Æ,CP.
prēosthēap m. *body of priests,* GD 302²⁵.
prēosthīred (ȳ²) m. *body of priests,* CHRD.
prēostlagu f. *ecclesiastical law, canon law,* LL 380,2³.
prēostlic *'priestly,' canonical, Chrd* 89³⁷; CM 667.
prēostlīf n. *priests' quarters, monastery, ÆL* 31⁸⁴⁶.
prēostrēaf n. *priestly garment,* CHRD 64²⁷.
prēostregol m. *canonical rule,* CHRD.
prēostscȳr f. *parish, LL.* [*'priestshire'*]
prēowthwīl f. *twinkling of an eye, moment, Æ.*
press f. *press (for clothes),* LL 455,15.
prica m., price f. *'prick,' point, spot, dot, Æ, Lcd,Mt : small portion of space or time, Æ, Bf.*
-priccan v. ā-p.
pricel, pricels m. *'prickle,' goad, point, Lk, OEG : jot, tittle, MtL,LkL.*
±**prician** tr. *to pierce, Æ : prick out* : intr. *'prick,' sting, Sc :* (+) *point out,* BF.

pricmælum adv. *point by point*, Bf112³⁰.
pricðorn m. *thorn-tree*, KC3·436¹⁶.
pricung f. *'pricking,' remorse*, Æ2·88²².
prīm n? *the first hour (6 a.m.)* : *the service held at 6 a.m., 'prime,'* RB,WW. [L. prima (sc. hora)]
prīmsang m. *prime-song, service of prime*, Chrd,LL.
princ? *twinkling of an eye, moment*, v. OEG 2369.
prior m. *'prior,' Chr,TC*. [L.]
prīt=prȳt
-prīwan v. be-pr.
prodbor (prot-) n. *auger?* MtR.
profast=prafost
prōfian *to assume to be, take for*, LL. [L. probare]
profost=prafost
prūd, prūt *'proud*,' arrogant*, OEG,Sc.
prutene (ū?) f. *southern-wood, wormwood*, Lcd. [L. abrotanum]
prūtian *to be 'proud,' Chrd*.
prūtlic *haughty*. adv. -līce *proudly, pompously, magnificently* : *confidently*, Bf150¹⁴.
prūtscipe m. *arrogance, pride*, Gl,Ps.
prūtswongor *overburdened with pride*, W 257¹² (v.l.).
prūtung f. *pride, arrogance*, OEG. [v. 'proud']
prȳde=prȳte; **prȳdecere**=prēdicere
prȳt(o), prȳte f. *'pride,' haughtiness, pomp*, Æ,LL,OEG,W.
psaltere (Lcd)=saltere
psealm (WW), psalm=sealm
pūca m. *goblin*, OEG23². ['puck']
pūcel m. *goblin*, GPH394²⁴². ['puckle']
pucian *to poke, creep*, GPH397.
pudd m. *ditch*, GPH399.
puduc m. *wart*, GPH396.
pull mf. *pool, creek*, KC (v. GBG). [Keltic]
pullian *to 'pull,' draw, AA* : *pluck off (wool)*, Lcd3·176.
pūlsper n. *reed*, MtL11⁷ (v. A39·364).
pumic m? *pumice*, Lcd38a. [L. pumicem]
pumicstān m. *pumice-stone*, WW148³.
pund n. *'pound' (in weight or in money), pint*, Bf,Ct,G,Lcd; Æ,AO : *weight*, Wyn 43. [L. pondo]
pundar, pundor=pundur
pundere m. *one who weighs*, MtLp2³.
pundern n. *pair of scales* : *plumb-line*, OEG.
punderngend m? *one who weighs* (BTs), KGl545.
pundfald a *'pinfold,' pound*, BC.
pundmǣte adj. *of a pound weight*, RB63¹⁶.
pundur n. *weight, plumb-line*, Cp264D. [L. pondere]
pundwǣg f. *pound weight, measure (of corn)*, LL.

pūnere m. *'pounder,' pestle*, Sc95¹⁹.
pung m. *purse, Cp.* ['pung']
pungetung f. *pricking*, Lcd. [pyngan]
±pūnian *to 'pound,' beat, bruise*, Lcd,Sc.
punt *'punt,'* WW. [L. ponto]
pūr *bittern? sea-gull?* WW116,285. ['purre']
purlamb n. *lamb without blemish*, Ex12⁵.
purpl, purple (JnL)=purpure
purpure f., purpur (WW152²⁰) *purple, a purple garment*, AO,Mk; CP. ['purpur']
purpuren *purple*, WW151²⁴. ['purpurine']
purs *'purse,'* OEG18ʙ³⁶. [late L. bursa]
pusa (o) m. *bag, scrip*, NG.
puslian *to pick out*, Lcd127a.
-pūte v. ǣle-p.
pūtung f. *instigation*, Chrd62²⁷. ['putting']
pȳcan *to 'pick,' Chr*796F?
pyff m. *a 'puff' of wind*, Bo47²⁶ (Napier).
pyffan, pret. pyfte *to puff, blow*, v. OEG 1886.
pyhment=pigment; **pyl-**=pil-
pylce (A7·30)=pylece
pyle (i) m. *'pillow,'* Æ,AO,CP,Lcd. [L. pulvinum]
pylece f. *a warm fur garment, robe, pelisse*, A,WW. ['pilch']
pylewer *pillow*, OEG56¹⁶. ['pilliver']
pyll=pull
pylu (OEG29⁴), pylwe=pyle
pynca (i) m. *point*, OEG3683. [pyngan]
pynd? sb. *cistern? lake?* Rim49.
+pyndan *to impound, shut up*, CP276. ['pind']
pynding f. *dam*, CP276. [v. 'pind']
pyngan (i) *to prick*, CP. ['ping'; L. pungere]
pypelian=piplian
pyretre f. *pellitory*, Lcd3·12¹⁹. [L. pyrethrum]
pyrie, pyrige=pirie, pirige
pyrtan *to strike, beat*, GPH401.
pyse (Æ)=pise
pysecynn n. *sort of pea*, Lcd71a.
pȳtan *to put out (eyes)*, Chr796F?
pytt m. *'pit,' hole, well, grave*, AO,Ct,G,LL; CP; Mdf : *pustule*. [L. puteus]
pytted *'pitted,' dented, marked* (of a sword), EC225'.
pyttel (i) m. *hawk, kite*, WW.

Q

qu- is usually written cw-, which see.

R

rā m. nap. rān *'roe,' roebuck*, BH,Gl,Lcd; Mdf.
rabbian *to rage*, W84¹¹.
raca m. *'rake,' Bf, Gl*; GD192.

racca m. *part of the rigging of a ship*, WW.
racente f. *chain, fetter, Bl,Bo,Sc*; AO.
['*rackan*']
+racentēagian *to chain*, ÆL31³⁵.
racen-tēah f. gs. -tēage *chain, fetter, Bl*; Æ.
['*rakenteie*']
racete=racente
racetēage *(Mk)*=racentēah
raclan (w. d.) *to rule, govern, control* : *go forward, move, CP,W* : *hasten*, NR28²⁵.
['*rake*']
raciend m. *speaker, orator*, GD265¹².
rācing *(JnL)*=rǣcing
racu I. f. *exposition, explanation, observation* : *reason, argument* : *account, narrative,* Æ,CP : *rhetoric* : *comedy*. [reccan] II. f.
(LL455¹⁵)=raca
rād I. f. *ride, riding, expedition, journey, BH, Bo,Lcd* : *raid, Chr,LL* : *modulation,* RUN5 : *name of the rune for* r. ['*road*'; rīdan]
II. pret. 3 sg. of rīdan. III. m.=rǣd
+rād I. n. *reckoning, account* : *condition, stipulation,* AO : *intention* : *reason, wisdom, discernment,* Æ,AO : *accuracy*. ðus +r. *such, of this kind*. hū +rādes *how*. II. adj. *conditioned, circumstanced, disposed, adapted, CP* : *wise, clever, skilful, Bo;* AO : *straight, Guth*. +rāde sprǣc *prose*.
-rād v. brand-r.
rādcniht m. *tenant holding subject to service on horseback,* v. LL1·73. ['*radknight*']
rade=hraðe; +rādegian=+rādian
rādehere, rādhere=rǣdehere
radelod *having straight branches?* BC3·44.
rādhors n. *riding-horse, HL.* ['*roadhorse*']
radian=hradian
+rādian (eg, ig) *to reckon with, arrange,* Bo 96¹⁵ : *call to account*.
+rādlic *proper, fitting,* Æ. adv. -līce, *intelligently, clearly*.
+rādod *intelligent,* LCD3·196⁷.
rador=rodor
radost=hraðost, v. hraðe.
rādpytt m. *draw-well?* RD59¹⁵.
+rādscipe m. *discretion,* MET22⁴⁸.
rādstefn f. *message taken by a mounted man,* LL456,3. [cp. rādcniht]
rādumbel=rāradumbla
rādwērig *weary of travelling,* RD21¹⁴.
ræc=rec; ræcan, ræccan=reccan
rǣcan I. *to* 'REACH' *out, stretch out,* Æ,CP : *offer, present, give, grant,* Æ : *procure?* (Lieb), LL447⁶ and 3·249 : *extend* (intr.).
II.=hrǣcan
+rǣcan '*reach,*' *attain, overtake, Bl,Sat* : *give* : *obtain, seize, take, get, gain, Chr;* AO : *address, speak to,* AO : *handle, deal with* : *strike*.
ræcc m. *setter* (dog), WW276⁴. ['*rache*']

ræce f. *(Cp)*=raca; ræced=reced
rǣcing f. '*reaching,*' *holding out, presenting, JnL* : *seizing, capture,* DR (hr-).
rǣd=hrǣd
rǣd I. (ā, ē) m. *advice, counsel,* Æ : *resolution, deliberation, plan, way, design,* Æ, AO : *council, conspiracy,* Æ : *decree, ordinance,* CP : *wisdom, sense, reason, intelligence,* Æ : *gain, profit, benefit, good fortune, remedy,* Æ : *help* : *power, might*. tō rǣde +niman *resolve,* AO. tō rǣde ðincan *seem advisable*. ['REDE'] II. adj. =rēad. III. (ē) n. *reading lesson,* NG.
±rǣdan (ē) pret. 3 sg. reord, rēd; also wv. *to advise, counsel, persuade,* Æ : *consult, discuss, deliberate, plot, design,* Æ, AO : *decree, decide,* Æ : *rule, guide, have control over, possess* : *arrange* : *equip, provide for* : *bring, deliver* (goods) : *have an idea, guess, forebode,* Æ : *read, explain,* Æ : *learn by reading* : *put in order, BH* : *help*. ['READ,' 'REDE']
rǣdbana (ē) m. *accessory to a murder,* LL.
rǣdbora (ē) m. *adviser, counsellor,* Æ : (Roman) *consul*.
rǣdda m. *robin,* WW44¹⁸. [rēad]
rǣdde wk. pret. 3 sg. of rǣdan.
rǣde (ē) I. adj. (±) *prepared, ready, ready for riding* (horse), PPs : *skilled, simple*. ['*i-rede*'] II. n. (+) *trappings, armour, accoutrements, ornaments*. III. f. *reading, lesson,* RB18⁹. IV. (+) *design, device?* EL1054,1108.
rǣdecempa m. *horse-soldier,* WW228³⁹.
rǣdefæsting f. *entertainment of the king's visitors, or of his messengers when riding on his business,* KC2·60'.
rǣdegafol n. *rent paid in one payment* (in *money or in kind*), LL118,67.
rǣdehere m. *mounted troop, cavalry,* AO.
+rǣdelīce=+rǣdlīce; rǣdelle=rǣdelse
rǣdels mf., rǣdelse (ē) f. *enigma,* '*riddle,*' Æ : *consideration, discussion* : *imagination, conjecture, interpretation*.
rǣdemann m. *horseman,* PPs32¹⁵.
rǣden (ē) f. *condition, terms, stipulation,* Æ : *rule, government, direction* : *estimation,* WW.
±rǣdend m. *controller, disposer, ruler* : *diviner,* Sc75¹².
rǣdendlic *relating to a decree,* WW387, 494.
rǣdengewrit n. *written agreement,* TC168¹².
rǣdere m. '*reader,*' '*lector*' (ecclesiastical order), Bf,RB,LL : *scholar, diviner, expounder, interpreter,* OEG.
rǣdescamol m. *couch, reading-desk?* WW.
rǣdesmann m. *counsellor, adviser* : *steward,* EC. ['*redesman*']

rǣdewiga m. *horse-soldier*, WW228³⁸.
rǣdfæst *resolute, wise*, Æ.
rǣdfæstnes f. *reasonableness*, LL(306¹⁹).
rǣdfindende *giving counsel*, WW383⁸.
rǣdgeðeaht n. *deliberation, counsel*, EL, W.
rǣdgifa m. *counsellor, councillor*, CHR,LL : *consul*.
rǣdgift '*consulatus*,' '*senatus*,' GL.
rǣdhors n. *riding-horse*, Æ(8²³³).
rǣdhycgende *knowing, wise*, FT26.
rǣdic (e) m. '*radish*,' Lcd,WW. [L. radicem]
rǣdin=rǣden
rǣding I. f. '*reading*,' *a reading (passage read), lesson, narrative*, Æ,CP,RB : *consideration, consultation, counselling*, Æ (100²⁷⁰); (+) WW383²⁵. II.=rǣden
rǣdingboc f. *lectionary, book of the lessons*.
rǣdinggewrit (WW115¹⁰)=rǣdengewrit
rǣdinggrād m. *steps to lectern*, NC316.
rǣdingscam-ol (-ul) m. *ambo, rostrum, lectern, reading-desk*, OEG (=rǣdescamol).
rǣdistre f. *female reader*, GL.
rǣdlēas (ē) *ill-advised, unwise, helpless, rash, in disorder*, Chr,Da : *wretched, bad, miserable*. ['*redeless*']
rǣdlic *expedient, advisable, wise*, AO,CP. adv. -līce *wisely, prudently, skilfully, cunningly*, CP,HL : *deliberately, on purpose : fully, explicitly*, GD102¹⁹. ['*redly*']
rǣdlīce=hrǣdlīce
rǣdmægen n. *productive force*, RIM10? (or? rādmægen).
rǣdnes=hrǣdnes
±**rǣdnes** f. *agreement : decree : condition : definition, decision*.
rǣdo f. (RB62¹⁵n)=rǣd III.
+**rǣdod** *harnessed, caparisoned*, Æ (cp. +rǣde).
rǣdrīpe=hrǣdrīpe
rǣdsnotter *clever, sage*, AN473.
rǣdðeahtende† ptc. *taking counsel*, EL.
rǣdðeahtere m. *counsellor*, AO72,256.
rǣdðeahtung f. *counsel, advice*, AO154²⁷.
rǣdwита (AO)=hrǣdwǣn (or? rǣd-=rād-).
rǣdwita m. *counsellor, adviser*, DD299.
rǣdystre=rǣdistre; **rǣf**=rēaf
+**rǣt** *brought home to, convicted of*, LL66,32.
ræfen=hræfn
ræfn-an, -ian (GD) *to perform, do : undergo*.
ræfs-=reps-
ræfter (e, ea) m. *rafter, beam*, BH,GL.
rǣge (ā) f. *roe*, GL,Lcd. [rā]
rǣgel=hrægl
rǣgerēose f. *spinal muscles*, Lcd.
rǣghār *grey (with lichen)*, RUIN10. [ragu]
rægl=hrægl; **rægn**=rēgn
rægolfæst=regolfæst; **rægu**=ragu

rǣhte pret. 3 sg. of rǣcan.
ræm=hræfn; -**rǣman** v. ā-r.
rænc=renco; **ræng-**=reng-·
ræp pret. 3 sg. of repan.
rǣpan (ȳ) (±) *to bind, fetter, capture, enslave : yoke together*, ÆL31⁷⁸⁵.
rǣping=rǣpling
rǣpling m. *prisoner, criminal*, Æ. [rǣpan]
rǣplingweard (ē) *warder*, WW111¹⁰.
rǣps=reps
+**rǣptan** *to bind, fetter*, Bo112¹.
rǣran *to 'rear,' raise, build, create*, BH,Gen : *lift up, elevate, promote*, Bl : *establish, begin, commit, do*, Cr,W ; CP : *arouse, excite, stir up*, Rd. [rīsan]
rǣs m. *rush, leap, jump, running*, Æ,Cr, LG (hr-) : *onrush, storm, attack*, Æ,B. ['*rese*']
rǣsan *to rush, hasten*, CP : *enter on rashly : rush upon, attack*, B,Bl,MH. ['*rese*']
rǣsbora† m. *counsellor, leader, guide*.
ræsc m. *shower*, OEG3974.
ræscan *to vibrate, quiver*, DHy94¹.
ræscettan *to crackle, creak, coruscate*, DD, WW. ['*reschette*']
rǣsian=rǣswian
ræsn n. *plank, beam, wall-plate, raising piece*, Æ,WW. ['*rasen*']
ræst=rest
rǣswa† m. *leader, counsellor, ruler, guide : chief, prince, king*.
rǣswan, rǣswian *to think, consider, conjecture, suspect*, CP.
rǣswum dp. of *rǣs? or rǣsu? f. or *rǣswa? *suggestion, deliberation, counsel*, Az126.
rǣswung f. *reasoning, conjecture*, GL.
ræt m. '*rat*,' WW118⁴¹.
rǣt pres. 3 sg. of rǣdan.
ræð-=hræð-; **ræðe**=hraðe
rǣðe=rēðe
+**rǣðle**=+rǣde
rǣw I. (±) (ā, ēa) f. *row, line : succession*, Lcd : *hedgerow*. [v. '*rew*' and Mdf] II.= hrǣw
+**rǣwed**, +rǣwe(n), +rǣwod *arranged in rows*, WW.
-**rāflan** v. ā-r.; **rāge**=rǣge
raggig *shaggy, bristly, rough*, OEG. ['*raggy*']
ragofinc=ragufinc
ragu (æ) f. *lichen*, Æ,Lcd.
ragufinc (ea¹) m. *name of a bird, kind of finch*, WW.
rāha [Cp]=rā
rāhdēor n. *roe-buck*, Æ,Lcd. ['*roedeer*']
rāhhege m. *deer-fence*, KC3·77'.
rāhte=rǣhte pret. sg. of rǣcan.
ram=ramm; **ramesa**=hramsa
ramgealla m. *ram-gall (plant)*, Lcd.

ramm (o) m. '*ram*' (*sheep*), *Æ,VPs* : (*engine of war*), *Æ,CP* : (*zodiacal sign*), *Bf.*

ran pret. 3 sg. of rinnan.

rān I. n. *open robbery, rapine.* [*ON.*] II. pret. 3 sg. of rīnan. III. nap. of rā.

ranc *froward, proud, overbearing, Æ* : *noble, brave, strong, Chr* : *ostentatious* : *full-grown, mature, ÆL*35²². ['*rank*'] adv. -līce *boldly, confidently* : *ostentatiously, showily, LL.* ['*rankly*']

rancstrēt f. *straight road? splendid road?* GEN2112.

rand (o) m. *border, edge? KC* : (†) *boss of shield, rim of shield* : (†) *shield, buckler, B.* [v. '*rand*']

rand-bēag, -bēah m. *boss (of a shield), shield, Æ,*GL.

randburg f. *fortified city?* JUL19 : *shield-wall of waves (in the Red Sea),* Ex463?

randgebeorh n. *protecting shield of waves (in the Red Sea),* Ex296.

randhæbbend (o¹) m. *shield-bearer, warrior,* B861.

rand-wīga†, -wīgend†, -wīggend m. *shield-warrior, man at arms.*

rānn=rān III.

rāp I. m. '*ROPE*,' *cord, cable,* AO,CP. II. pret. 3 sg. of rīpan.

rāpgenga m. *rope-dancer,* WW408²⁵.

rāpincel n. (*small rope*), *cord, string,* GL.

rāplic adj. *of rope,* GPH399.

+rār n. *roaring, howling,* MH16²⁰.

rāradumbla m., rāredumle f. *bittern,* GL. [*Ger.* rohrdommel]

rārian *to* '*roar,*' *bellow, cry, lament, mourn, Æ,MH,MtL.*

rārung f. '*roaring,*' *howling, bellowing, WW.*

rās pret. 3 sg. of rīsan.

rāsettan† *to rage (of fire),* CR, MET. [rǣsan]

rāsian *to explore,* B2283.

ratian=hratian

raðe=hraðe

rāw (*Lcd*89b)=rǣw ['*row*']

+rāwan *to arrange in line,* WW.

raxan *to stretch oneself, Guth.* ['*rax*']

rēac pret. 3 sg. of rēocan.

rēad I. '*RED,*' *Æ,CP*; (*of gold*), *Æ.* II. pret. 3 sg. of rēodan.

rēada pl. *small intestines, WW*159³⁸ : *tonsil,* LCD. ['*read*']

rēadbasu (e²) *reddish purple,* LL.

rēade adv. *with red colour,* LCD.

rēadfāh *red of hue,* RUIN10.

rēadgoldlæfer f. *plating of (red) gold,* OEG 1070.

rēadian *to be or become* '*red,*' *Lcd,MtR*; *Æ.*

rēadlēaf *red-leaved,* BC; Mdf.

rēadlesc '*rubricata*' (*pellis*), v. OEG5324.

rēadnes f. '*redness,*' *BH,Bl*; *Æ.*

rēadstalede *red-stalked,* LCD1·378'.

rēaf (ē) n. *plunder, booty, spoil, LkL,Ps* : *garment, armour, vestment, Mt; Æ.* ['*reaf,*' '*reif*']

+rēafa=+rēfa

rēafere m. *robber, plunderer, Æ,Bo,Lk*; AO, CP. ['*reaver*']

-rēafetian v. wīn-(h)r.

rēafgend m. *robber,* KC3·350²⁶.

±rēaflan I. *to rob, plunder, take by force, waste, ravage, Æ,Bo,B,G,VPs,W*; AO : *carry off, remove, transport,* CP : (+) *strip,* NG. ['*reave*'] II. *to robe,* ÆP126¹⁰.

rēaflgende *rapacious, ÆL.* ['*reaving*']

rēaflāc nm. *robbery, rapine, ÆH* : *plunder, booty, Bo.* ['*reflac*']

rēaflol *rapacious,* LCD,GL.

rēaflolnes f. *rapacity,* OEG.

reafter=ræfter

rēafung f. *spoliation, plundering,* AO84²¹.

reagufinc (GL)=ragufinc

reahte pret. 3 sg. of reccan.

reahtigan *to dispute, discuss,* AO130²⁶.

rēam I. m. *cream, Lcd*113b. ['*ream*'] II.= hrēam

rēama=rēoma

rēamwīn? n. *a kind of wine,* OEG. [cp. *Fr.* vin crémant]

rēat pret. 3 sg. of rēotan.

rēaðe=rēðe; rēaw=rǣw

rēawde=hrēawde, pret. of hrēawan.

rēc m. *smoke, Gen,Ps.* ['*reek*']

+rec I. n. *rule, government* : *decree* : *explanation.* II. n. *tumult,* MtL27²⁴ (? for ungerec). III. *a small vessel, brigantine?* WW 30,432.

recan⁵ *to bring, convey,* WW420¹⁸ : (+) *go, move, rush.*

±rēcan I. pret. 3 sg. rēhte *to fumigate, expose to smoke, Lcd* : *burn incense,* GL. [v. '*reek*'] II.=reccan II.

reccan I. *to stretch, tend, go, CP* : *extend, hold out to, give* : (±) *instruct, explain, interpret, Æ* : *tell, narrate, B,Bo,G* : *quote* : *correct, reprove,* AO : (+) *to wield (authority), give judgment, decide, direct, control, Æ,CP* : (+) *prove* : (+) *count, reckon, Æ.* ['*recche*'] II. (rēcan) *to take care of, be interested in, Æ,B,Bo,Cr* : *care for, Mk* : *care, desire (to do something), Bo, Lcd,LL,MkL,WW.* ['*reck*']

recce- (CP), recci-=rēce-

-recce v. earfoð-r.

+reccelic=+reclic

rēccelīest (e³, ea³, i³) f. *carelessness, negligence,* CP.

reccend m. *ruler, guide, Æ,AO.*

reccend(d)ōm m. *governance, oversight,* CP.

reccenes=+recenes

reccere m. *teacher, ruler, director,* CP : *interpreter,* MtLp2¹³.
reccing f. *narrative,* ÆL30³⁷⁵.
reced nm. *building, house, palace, hall* : '*triclinium,*' OEG.
recedlic (æ) *palatial,* WW.
±recednes f. *narrative, history,* Æ : *interpretation* : *direction, correction.* ānfeald +r. *prose.*
recedōm=reccendōm
rēcel (v. MFH 171)=rēcels
rēcelēas '*reckless,*' *careless, negligent,* BH, Bo,Cp,W.
rēcelēasian *to neglect,* W. ['*reckless*']
rēcelēaslīce adv. *heedlessly, carelessly, inattentively,* CP (rēcce-), HL. ['*recklessly*']
rēcelēasnes f. '*recklessness,*' *carelessness, negligence,* LL,W; Æ.
rēce-lēast, -līestu=rēccelīest
rēcels (ī, ȳ) m. *incense, frankincense,* MtL, Lcd,Lk; Æ. ['*rekels*'; rēc]
rēcelsbūc (ȳ) m. *censer,* WW.
rēcelsfæt (i) n. *censer,* Æ. ['*rekelsfat*']
rēcelsian *to perfume with incense,* Lcd.
rēcelsrēoce f. *burning of incense,* FBO75¹⁹.
recen *ready, prompt, quick, Wa* : *rapid, violent, Cr,Ps.* ['*reken*']
recendōm=reccendōm
recene (i, y) adv. *instantly, quickly,* Æ.
+recenes f. *narrative, interpretation* : *direction, correction.*
recenian *to pay* : (+) *explain, recount, relate,* Ex525. ['*reckon*']
recenlīce (o²) adv. *immediately, forthwith,* G ['*rekenly*']
recennes *coming together?* WW381⁷ : *going?* BHB436¹⁵.
rēcetung (VPs)=hrǣcetung
+recnes f. *direction, inclination,* EPs138³.
recnian=recenian
recon I. *remuneration,* Gl. II.=recen
recse=risce; recyd=reced
+recu=+rec-
rēd I.=rǣd. II. pret. 3 sg. of rǣdan.
red-; rēd-=rǣd-; rǣd-; rēde=rēðe
redestān m.'*synophites,*'*red ochre?* WW47¹⁵.
+redian (æ) *to reach* : *discover,* W: *effect.*
rēdon pret. pl. of rǣdan.
±rēfa (usu. +) m. *high official,* '*reeve,*' *steward, sheriff, count* ('*comes*'), *prefect, consul,* BH,Ct,Mk,MH.
+rēfærn n. *court-house,* MH124¹³.
+rēfland n. *land held by a reeve,* BC.
+rēfmǣd f. *reeve's meadow,* Ct. [v. '*reeve*']
+rēfmann m. *official, courtier,* GD308·315.
refsan=repsan

+rēfscipe m. *reeve's office, stewardship,* Æ : *consulate,* WW371,495. ['*reeveship*']
+rēfscīr f. *steward's office, prefecture,* OEG.
refter (ē?)=ræfter
regellic=regollic; regen-=regn-, rēn-
regn (rēn; Æ,MH) m. '*rain,*' *VPs* : *showers of rain, Bl.*
regn-=rēn-; regnan=rīnan
regnheard *very hard,* B326. (cp. regnðēof)
regnian I. *to* '*rain,*' *MtR5⁴⁵.* II.=rēnian
regnðēoft m. *downright thief.* [FTp335]
regol (eo) m. *rule, regulation, canon, law, standard, pattern,* Æ : *monastic code of rules,* Æ : *ruler (instrument).* [L. regula]
regolbryce m. *breach of rules,* W166²².
regolfæst (æ) *rigid, strict, adhering to monastic rules,* Men44.
regolian *to draw lines with a ruler,* NC316.
regollagu f. *monastic law,* LL266,25.
regollic *according to rules, canonical, regular.* adv. -līce.
regollīf (eo) m. *life according to ecclesiastical rules,* BH,LL.
regolsticca m. *rule, ruler (instrument),* Æ.
regolðēaw m. *discipline of (monastic) rule,* A10·144¹²⁵.
regolweard m. *regulator, director, ruler, abbot, provost,* BH.
regul=regol; reht (VPs)=riht
rehte pret. 3 sg. of reccan.
rēhte pret. 3 sg. of rēcan II.
relicgang m. *visiting of relics,* MH62,72.
reliquias. mpl. *relics of saints* (reliquium is used in sg.), MFH171.
reliquiasōcn f. *visit to a shrine,* MFH172.
rēman=rȳman
remian *to mend,* v. NC317.
Rēmisc *Roman,* JnL18¹².
remm-=hremm-; remn=hræfn
rempan *to be hasty, precipitate,* CP149¹².
rēn (AO,CP)=regn
+rēn (ī) n. *ornament,* CP : *building,* NG.
rēnboga m. '*rainbow,*' Æ.
renc, renco (æ) f. *pride, ostentation,* LL,W.
rendan *to* '*rend,*' *tear, cut down,* LG.
rendegn (Erf1137)=ærnðegn
+rendrian *to peel,* Lcd25a.
rēndropa m. '*raindrop,*' Lcd3·278'.
rene=ryne
+rēne I. (ī) n. *ornament,* CP : *instrument* : *building,* NG. II. (±)=±ryne
renel (KGl)=rynel; reng=regn
renge (y) f. *spider, spider's web,* Ps. [L. aranea]
rengwyrm (æ) m. *intestinal worm,* Lcd.
±rēnian *to prepare* : (+) *arrange, set in order, mend, set (trap)* : (+) *adorn.* +r. tō bismere *humiliate, degrade,* AO. [*regnian; Goth. raginōn]

rēniend m. *revealer*, EL880.
rēnig (*Lcd,Rd*), rēnlic (Æ) '*rainy*.'
+rennan *to coagulate*, EPs67¹⁶.
rēnscūr m. '*rain-shower*,' Æ.
rēnsnægl m. *snail*, OEG23²⁰.
+rēnung (regn-) f. *arranging*, WW371¹⁹.
rēnwæter n. '*rain-water*,' *Lcd*.
renweard m. *house-guardian*, B770. [ærn]
rēnwyrm m. *earthworm*, *WW*. ['*rainworm*']
rēo (1)=rēowe; (2)=hrēoh
rēoc *savage, furious*, B122.
rēocan I. sv² intr. *to emit vapour, steam or smoke*, '*reek*,' *Lcd,Ps*; Æ : *stink*. II. (WW 244³⁶)=rēcan
rēocende (ē) *smoking, steaming*, Æ,*Jud*, *MtL*. ['*reeking*']
rēod I. '*red*,' *ruddy*, Æ,*Erf,MH*. ['*reod*'] II. n. *red colour*, WW. III.=hrēod
rēodan² *to redden, stain with blood* : (†) *kill?*
reodian *to sift? search out?* (=redian? ES 51·184), EL1239.
rēodian=rēadian
rēodmūða m. '*faseacus*' (*bird*), WW234²⁵
rēodnæsc (WW38¹³)?=rēadlesc
rēofan² (only in pp. rofen) *to rend, break*, Ex463.
reogol=regol
reohhe f. '*ray*,' *thornback?* *WW*181⁶.
+rēohnung=+rēnung; reoht=riht
rēol=hrēol; reoma=rima
rēoma (ēa) m. *membrane, ligament*, *Lcd*, *WW*. ['*rim*']
rēon I.=rēowon pret. pl. of rōwan. II. *lament*, HELL6.
rēone asm. of rēo(we).
±rēonian *to conspire, plot*, Æ.
rēonig† *mournful, sad, gloomy*, EL.
rēonigmōd† *mournful, weary*.
±rēonung f. *whispering, muttering, conspiracy*, ÆL,AO : *astrology*, OEG. [rūn]
reopa m. *bundle of corn, sheaf*, *VPs*. ['*reap*']
reopan (VPs)=repan; reopian=ripian
±reord† I. fn. *voice*, B,Cr,Ps : *language, speech*, ÆL. ['*rerde*'] II. f. *sustenance, food* : *meal, feast*. III. pret. 3 sg. of rǣdan.
reordan=reordian II.
reordberend† m. *man*, CR.
+reorddæg m. *feast-day*, ÆL23b⁷⁵³.
+reordglēawnes f. *skill in singing*, LPs32³.
reordhūs n. *eating room, refectory*, MkL14¹⁵.
reordian I. *to speak, discourse*, B,Cr,Gen : *read*. ['*rerde*'] II. (±) *to feed, refresh, entertain, feast*.
+reordnes f. *food, feasting, banquet* : *satiety*.
±reordung f. *refection, meal*, Æ.
+reordunghūs n. *refectory*, WW328³².
+reordungtīd f. *meal-time*, GD145¹³.
reosan '*pissli*,' *name of a plant?* WW300⁵.
+rēosan=+hrēosan; -rēose v. rǣge-r.

rēost *rest* (part of a plough), *CP,WW*. ['*reest*']
rēotan²† *to weep, mourn, wail*.
rēote v. rētu.
rēotig *mournful, sad, tearful*, RD1¹⁰.
rēow I.=hrēoh. II. pret. 3 sg. of rōwan.
rēowe f. *covering, rug, blanket, mantle*, BH, LL. [=rȳhe]
rēowlic=hrēowlic; rēowot=rēwet
rep-=hrep-
repan⁵ *to reap*, CHR,VPs.
repel m. *staff, rod*, GD20²⁶ (v. ES37·192).
reps m. *response* (*in a church service*), Æ, RB. [*L.* responsorium]
repsan (æ) *to reprove, blame*, GL.
repsung (æ) f. I. *a division of the night*, BF 122²¹ (hr-). II. *reproving*, GL. [=*ræfsung]
repung=hrepung; rēran=rǣran
+rerding=+reordung; resce=risce
rēsele f. *answer, solution*, RD40²⁸. [=*rǣsele]
rēsian=rǣswian
+resp *convicted of*, LL (v.l. for +rǣf).
respons *response*, LL(140²¹).
rest (æ) f. '*REST*,' *quiet, repose, sleep*, Æ : (±) *resting-place, bed, couch* : *grave*.
±resta f. *bedfellow, consort, wife*, Æ.
restan (absol. and refl.) *to* '*REST*,' *repose*, Æ : (+) *give rest to, lodge* : (w. g.) *rest from, remain, lie*, Æ.
rēstan *to rejoice, exult?* PPs113⁴.
restbedd n. *bed, couch*, PPs131³.
rest-dæg (æ), reste-, resten- (Æ) m. *day of rest, Sabbath day*, CP,G. ['*restday*']
restengēar n. *year of rest from work*, LEV 25⁵.
restgemāna m. *cohabitation*, BL,LCD.
resthūs n. *chamber*, APs,BH.
restlēas '*restless*,' *without rest*, RB121¹⁴.
+restscipe m. *cohabitation*, BH76²⁷.
rēsung (CP)=rǣswung
±rētan *to delight, cheer, comfort*, CP. [rōt]
rētend m. *comforter*, W257⁴.
rētu f. (only in d. rēote) *joy*, B2457.
reðe *righteous, just*, PPs (or ?=rēðe).
rēðe (of persons) *fierce, cruel, violent, harsh, severe*, Æ,B,BH : (of things) *terrible, dreadful*, Bl,Bo,CP : *zealous*, CP. ['*rethe*']
rēðegian=rēðian
reðehygdig *right-minded*, ALM2.
rēðeman m. *usurer* (GK), PPs108¹¹. [*Goth.* raðjo?]
rēðemōd† *savage, cruel, fierce, indignant*.
rēðen *wild*, ÆL10¹⁰² (cp. AS96).
rēð-ian, -igian *to rage, be fierce*, Æ,GD.
rēðig *fierce*, WW402²³.
rēðigmōd *savage, fierce*, MET25¹⁷.
rēðlic *fierce, cruel, deadly*. adv. -līce *violently*.

rēðnes f. *cruelty, severity, harshness, Bl,CP;* AO : *savageness, ferocity, BH,Lcd;* CP : *zeal,* CP : *storminess,* LkL8²⁴ (hr-). ['*retheness*']

±**rēðra** m. *rower, sailor,* GL.

+**rēðre** *constant,* CP306¹⁵.

±**rēðru** np. *oars,* GD,HL.

rēðscipe m. *fury, anger,* WW245¹⁷.

rēwet, rēwut n. *rowing,* Æ : *rowing-boat, vessel,* Æ. [rōwan]

rex m. inserted for 'cyning' at EL610, 1042.

riaht (K)=riht I.

rib, ribb n. '*rib,*' Æ,Cp,MH,*Soul;* AO.

ribbe f. *hound's-tongue, ribwort, Ep,Lcd, WW.* ['*rib*']

ribbspāca np. *rib-spokes, the brisket?* (BT), WW265²⁴.

rīca m. *influential man, ruler,* Æ.

rīcan (BDS16³⁶⁷)=rēcan (*riecan)

rīcceter, rīccetere (Æ)=rīceter

rīce I. *strong, powerful, Da;* LCD : *great, mighty, of high rank, Æ,BH,MH;* AO,CP : '*rich,*' Æ,BH,Bo,Lk. **II.** n. *rule, reign, power, might, authority, empire, Æ,Bl,Cr, MH;* AO. fōn tō rīce *to ascend the throne : kingdom, nation, diocese, B;* AO,CP : *reign (period of time).* ['*riche*']

rīcedōm n. *kingly rule,* W125⁹. ['*richdom*']

rīcels=rēcels; **ricen-**=recen-

rīceter, rīcetere n. *force, might, power, rule, dominion, glory, greatness,* CP : *ambition,* Æ : *tyranny, oppression, violence : arrogance,* ÆL32²³³.

ricg, ricig=hrycg

rīclic *sumptuous,* AS39⁴. adv. -līce *powerfully, Æ,CP : sumptuously, Lk.* ['*richly*']

ricone=recene; **rics**=risc

rīcsere m. *ruler,* DR113³.

rīcsian *to bear rule, reign, govern, tyrannize,* Æ,AO,CP : *dominate, prevail.*

rīcsiend m. *ruler,* DR102⁸.

rīcsung f. *domination,* DR174¹⁰.

+**rid** n. *riding,* WW229².

-**rīda** v. brand-r, tot-r.

rīdan¹ (±) *to '* ride*,' AO : move about, swing, rock, ride (at anchor) : float, sail, Gen : chafe (of fetters) :* (+) *ride over, occupy (a country), seize :* (+) *ride up to.* tō handa gerīdan *to bring into a person's power or possession.*

ridda m. *rider, horseman, horse-soldier,* Æ.

-**rīdel** v. for(e)-r.

rīdehere m. *mounted force,* OEG2⁴⁴⁴.

rīdend m. *rider, cavalier,* B2457.

rīdere m. '*rider,*' *trooper, knight, Chr*1085L.

ridesoht f? *fever,* NG. [hrið? suht?]

rīdusende *swinging,* GL.

rīdwiga m. *horse-soldier,* WW110²⁸.

riece=rīce; **rieht**=riht; **rif**=hrif

rīf *violent, fierce, ravenous, noxious,* AA.

+**rif** n. *seizing, catch (of fish) : number caught.*

+**rīf** *garment,* WW107¹¹ (v. NC295).

-**rife** v. hege-r.

rīfe *abundant,* Lcd3·164²¹. ['*rife*']

rifelede *wrinkled,* OEG18b⁷⁸. ['*rivelled*']

rifeling m. *shoe or sandal of raw hide, WW* 125. ['*rivelling*']

rifelung f. *wrinkle,* A32·506.

+**riflan** *to wrinkle,* ÆH1·614¹⁴.

rift, rifte (y) n. *cloak, veil, curtain, Æ,Cp, MtL.* ['*rift*']

rifter m. *reaping-hook, sickle, scythe,* GL.

riftre, riftere (y) m. *reaper,* Æ,GL.

rige=ryge; **rignan**=rīnan

rīhsian=rīcsian

±**riht** (æ, e, eo, y) **I.** n. *(what is straight),* 'RIGHT,' *equity, justice, law, canon, rule, Æ,CP : cause, legal action, Æ : a right, privilege, CP : correctness, truth.* on r.; mid rihte *rightly, correctly, properly : what is due, duty, obligation, CP : reckoning, account.* **II.** adj. *straight, erect, direct :* 'RIGHT,' *proper, fair, just, equitable, lawful, permissible : upright, righteous : true, correct : fitting, appropriate : real, genuine : right (as opposed to left).*

rihtæðelcwēn f. *lawful wife,* W298¹⁸.

rihtæðelo (y) npl. *true nobility,* Bo,MET.

rihtǣw f. *lawful wedlock,* W : *lawful wife,* LL.

±**rihtan** (e, y) *to make straight : set right, amend, correct, rebuke,* Æ : *guide, govern, direct, rule : set up, assign, restore, replace, erect.* ['RIGHT']

rihtandaga m. *proper (fixed) day,* LL.

rihtandswaru f. *retort, reproof,* PPs37¹⁴.

rihtcynecynn (y¹) n. *legitimate royal family,* AO.

rihtcyning m. *lawful king,* BH360¹⁴.

rihtcynn n. *true stock,* W13⁶.

rihtdōm *just judgment,* LL320,15b.

rihtdōnde ptc. *doing what is right,* BL.

rihte adv. 'RIGHT,' *due, straight (of direction, as in right on, due east), outright, CP : precisely, exactly, just, AO : rightly, duly, well, correctly, truly, properly, fairly, justly : directly, immediately, Æ.* ðǣr rihte *thereupon, straightway.*

+**rihte** n. *right, due, Æ,Chr*(1074L) : *religious rite, office,* ÆL. +rihtu pl. *last offices.* on +r. *straight on.* up on +r. *upright.* ['*i-riht*']

rihtbred n. *measure, rule, square,* WW.

rihtend m. *director, ruler, leader, guide,* Bo, GD.

rihtendebyrdnes f. *right order,* NC317.

rihtere m. *director, ruler,* Bo. ['*righter*']

rihtes (e) adv. *right, straight,* KC3·392⁶.

rihtfædrencynn (e, y) n. *direct paternal descent or pedigree.*

rihtfæsten n. *duly ordained fast,* LL 132,8.

rihtfæstendæg m. *duly appointed fast-day,* Æ.

rihtfæstentíd f. *duly appointed time of fasting,* Æ.

rihtfremmende (y)† *acting rightly.*

rihtful *'rightful,' honourable,* CHR 1100 L.

rihtgebroðru mpl. *brethren,* DR 57⁴.

rihtgefég n. *proper joint,* GD 248²⁶.

rihtgefremed *catholic, orthodox,* BH 456¹⁵.

rihtgegylda m. *duly appointed member of a guild,* TC 606¹⁴.

rihtgehātan⁷ *to pledge oneself, swear,* RPs 14⁴.

rihtgehīwan pl. *lawfully married persons,* LL 22 n16.

rihtgeléafful *orthodox,* BH,LL.

rihtgeléaffulnes f. *right belief,* ÆL 23b⁶⁹⁷.

rihtgeléaflīce adv. *in an orthodox manner,* CM 1167.

rihtgelӯfed (ē³) ptc. *orthodox, catholic.*

rihtgelӯfende *believing rightly, faithful,* BL.

rihtgemæcca m. *lawful husband,* LL.

rihtgemǣre=rihtlandgemǣre

rihtgemet n. *proper measure,* NC 317.

rihtgesamhīwan pl. *lawfully married persons,* LL 22,38.

rihtgescēad n. *right understanding,* GD 56².

rihtgeset *duly appointed, canonical,* CM 412.

rihtgesetednes f. *right ordinance,* NC 317.

rihtgesetnes f. *rightful office,* Bo 12¹³.

rihtgesinscipe *lawful wedlock,* LL.

+rihtgeswinc *lawful work,* CHRD 70³.

rihtgeðancod *right-minded,* LPs.

rihtgewitt (y) n. *right mind,* MH 192²².

rihtgewittig *in one's right mind,* GD 245²².

rihtgifu f. *irrevocable gift,* LL 366,81; 385.

rihthǣmed (y¹) n. *lawful wedlock,* CP.

rihthāmscyld m. *legal means of protection to a homestead?* LL 5,32 and v. ANS 115·389 (but v. BTs).

rihthāmsōcn f. *actual* 'hāmsōcn' (v. hāmsōcn), LL 614,49⁵⁸.

rihthand f. *right hand,* NIC 492; 508.

rihthanddǣda m. *actual perpetrator,* LL 188,1³.

rihtheort *righteous, just,* CPVPs.

rihthīwa (y¹) m. *lawful consort,* CP.

rihthlāford m. *rightful lord,* LL.

rihthlāforddōm m. *lawful authority,* CHR 918 c.

rihthlāfordhyldo (e⁵) f. *loyalty,* W.

rihting f. *action of guiding aright, direction, order, rule, guidance,* Æ,RB : *correction, reproof,* Æ : *body of rights, privilege? privileged district?* CHR 963 E : *'regularis' (in computation),* BF 30¹⁹. ['righting']

±rihtlǣcan *to make straight, put right, rectify, set in order,* RB,W : *direct.* ['rightleche']

rihtlǣce m. *duly qualified physician,* W 12¹².

rihtlǣcung (y) f. *criticism, correction,* Æ,CP.

rihtlagu f. *regular legal ordinance,* W.

rihtlandgemǣre n. *lawful boundary (of land),* KC.

rihtlic (y) *right, proper, just, fit, righteous,* Æ : *adapted, fitted.* adv. -līce *justly, uprightly, virtuously,* Æ : *properly,* 'RIGHTLY,' *regularly* : *correctly, precisely,* CP.

rihtlīcettere m. *downright hypocrite,* W 54¹⁴.

rihtlīf n. *right life, regular union (of married people),* LCD 3·176'.

rihtlīflād m. *right way of life,* GD 336¹.

rihtliðlic *articulate,* WW 355⁸.

rihtmēdrencynn (e¹, oe²) n. *direct mother's line,* OET 651.

rihtmēterfers n. *correct hexameter verse,* BF 100⁷.

rihtmunuc m. *true monk,* RB 73¹⁹.

rihtnama m. *correct name,* ÆL 23⁵⁴⁷.

rihtnes (e) f. *'rightness,' rectitude, equity,* Ps : *perpendicularity, straightness,* WW : *reckoning, account,* MtL : (+) *correction.*

rihtnorðanwind (y¹) m. *north wind,* AO 17¹⁷.

rihtraciend m. *expounder of righteousness (the preacher, Ecclesiastes),* GD 264²⁷.

rihtracu (y) f. *correct account,* TC 170⁴ : *right reason,* GD 262.

+rihtreccan *to guide, show rightly,* AS 26¹⁶.

rihtregol m. *right rule, canon,* LL,OEG.

rihtryne m. *right or straight course,* Bo, MET.

rihtscīr (LL 252,21)=rihtscriftscīr

rihtscrīfend m. *jurisconsult, lawyer,* WW.

rihtscriftscīr f. *properly assigned district of a confessor, parish,* LL 240,12¹.

rihtscylling m. *shilling of sterling money,* LL (222⁷).

rihtscytte (y) *sure of aim,* CRA 51.

rihtsinscipe *lawful wedlock,* Æ (1·148).

rihtsmēaung (e¹) f. *right reasoning or argument,* MtL p 9¹⁰.

rihtspell (y) n. *true discourse,* CP 9¹⁰.

rihtstefn f. *ordinary voice,* GD 28²⁸.

riht-tīd (BH 206²⁰) f., -tima (Bo 12¹³) m. *proper time.*

riht-ðēow, -ðēowa m. *lawful slave,* GD 180⁶.

rihtungōrēd m. *plumb-line,* WW 150⁴¹.

rihtweg m. *right way,* W.

rihtwer m. *lawful husband* : *legally correct* 'wergild,' LL 466; 467.

rihtwestende (y¹) m. *extreme western limit,* AO 8³².

rihtwīf n. *lawful wife,* LL 348,54¹.

rihtwillende *wishing to do right,* Bo 11¹⁷.

rihtwīs *'righteous,' just,* Bl,Bo,Chr,VPs; CP : *right, justifiable, Bl.*

rihtwīsend m. *Sadducee*, Mt3⁷.

±rihtwīsian to make '*righteous*,' *justify*, Lk, VPs; Æ : *direct aright, rule*.

rihtwīslic (y¹) *righteous*, CP. adv. -līce *rightly, reasonably*, Bo. ['*righteously*']

rihtwīsnes f. '*righteousness*,' *justice*, Mt; CP : *rightness, reason* : *righteous acts*, Æ.

+rihtwīsung (e) f. *justification*, VPs88³².

rihtwrītere m. *correct writer*, Gl.

rihtwuldriende *orthodox*, BHb310³³.

rihtwyrðe *proper, fitting*, AS13²².

rihtymbren n. *duly appointed Embertide*, W117.

rihtymbrendagas mp. *duly appointed Ember days*, W117.

rīm-=hrīm-

±rīm n. *number, counting, reckoning*, Chr, Cr,VPs; Æ,AO,CP. ['*rime*']

rima m. '*rim*,' *verge, border, coast*, Cp,WW.

rīman (±) to *count, number, reckon*, AO,Ps; Æ : *tell, enumerate, relate*, CP : *account, esteem as*. ['*rime*']

rīmāð m. *oath by a number of persons*, LL 154,9.

+rīmbōc *calendar*, ÆH1·98'.

±rīmcræft m. *arithmetic, reckoning, computation* : *calendar*, ÆL10¹.

rīmcræftig *skilled in reckoning*, BF.

rīmcræftiga m. *one skilful at figures*, BF42¹².

-rīme v. earfoð-r.; rīmforst=hrīmforst

rīmge-tæl, -telʈ n. *number*, Gen.

+rīmian to *calculate*, A8·307⁴⁰ (v.l.+rūnian at BF70²⁴).

rimpan v. hrimpan.

rīmre m. *reckoner, calculator*, BF70¹⁷.

+rīmtæl (HR13¹¹)=rimgetæl

rīmtalu f. *number*, El820.

+rīn (NG)==+rēn

rīnan¹ (and wv.) impers. and intr. *to rain*, Æ,Bl,Mt : *to send down, or fall, like rain*, Lk,VPs : (+) *to wet with rain*, WW379¹⁵. ['*rine*']

+rīnan=+hrīnan

rinc m. *man, warrior, hero*, B,Cr,Met. ['*rink*']

rincgetæl n. *number of men*, Ex234.

rincsetl (HGl489)=hringsetl

rind, rinde f. '*rind*,' *bark, outside*, Bo,Cr, Lcd; CP : *crust*, Æ.

-rindan, -rindran v. be-r.

rindeclifer f. *wood-pecker? nut-hatch?* WW 427²⁹.

rinden *of bark*, GPH390.

rindlēas *having no bark*, WW190³¹.

rīne=rȳne; ring=hring; rīning=hrīning

±rinnan³ to '*run*,*' *flow*, Chr,Cr,Ps,Sat : (+) *run together, blend, coagulate*, Cp. [=iernan]

rinnelle f. *runnel, rivulet, stream*. [=rynele]

rinning (y) f. *rennet*, WW128⁴³ : (+) *coagulation*, Lcd1·292⁸. ['*running*']

±rīp (ȳ) n. *harvest*, BH,Chr,Mt : *cut corn, sheaf* : *ripeness, maturity*, PPs118¹⁴⁷. ['*ripe*,' '*reap*']

rīpan I. (±) (ēo, ȳ) to '*reap*,*' Æ,AO,Chr, CP,G. II. (AS10⁵)=rīpian

+rīpan (hr-) *to rob*, G,W.

rīpe '*ripe*,' *mature*, BH,Bo.

rīpemann m. *reaper*, MtL (hr-). ['*reapman*']

rīpere m. '*reaper*,' Mt.

rīpian (ēo) to *become '*ripe*,' ripen*, Æ,Bf.

rīpīsern n. *sickle*, MtLR4²⁹.

rīpnes f. '*ripeness*,' *harvest*, LPs.

rippel? *a coppice?* (BTs), Ct.

riptere=riftere

rīptīma m. *time of harvest*, Mt. ['*reaptime*']

rīpung f. *ripening, ripeness, maturity*, Bf, RB,VPs. ['*riping*']

+rīs n. *fury*, WW43⁶.

±rīsan¹ I. (usu. +) to '*rise*,' *stand up*, Ps : *rise together*, DR25¹ : *be fit, be proper*, Æ, Gu. ['*irise*'] II. *to seize, carry off*.

risc, risce (e;=y) f. '*rush*,' Cp; Mdf. [L.]

riscbedd n. *bed of rushes*, EC. [v. '*rush*']

riscen *made of rushes*, Æ. ['*rushen*']

rischealh (y¹) *rushy corner? rushy slope?* BC1·183². [v. '*rush*']

risciht *rushy*, KC.

risclēac n. *rush leek, rush garlic*, WW356³⁶.

riscrīðig *rushy stream*, KC.

riscðȳfel m. *rush-bed*, Ct,Gl.

risen-=risn-

+risen *seizure*-, Guth78⁵. ['*rīsan*']

rīsende? *rapacious*, Bl225¹⁷.

+risenlic *convenient, suitable, becoming, honest, honourable*, AO,CP. adv. -līce.

risiendum '*odorato*'? OEG23⁴.

+rislic *equal to, like*, BHca450³.

±risne I. *fit, meet, proper, convenient*. II. n. (usu. pl.) *what is fitting, dignity, honour*, AO.

+risnes f. *congruity*, WW383¹⁶.

+risnian *to agree, accord*, WW336³⁷.

risoda m. *rheum*, Lcd (Harl) 1b.

rīt pres. 3 sg. of rīdan.

rīð f. *favour, indulgence*, Sc224⁷.

rīð fm., (±) rīðe f. *rivulet, stream*, Æ,Bo, CP; Mdf. ['*rithe*']

rīðfald m. *cattle-pen, cow-shed*, WW195³⁴. [hrīð-]

rīðig n. *streamlet*, Mdf.

rīðða=ryðða; rix (Æ,BH)=risc

+rīxian=rīcsian; rō=rōw II.

rocc m. *over-garment, rochet*, Lcd,WW. [Ger. rock]

roc(c)ettan *to eructate, belch forth, utter*, NG, VPs.

roccian *to rock (a child)* RWH137¹³.
rōd I. f. *'rood,' cross, gallows,* Æ,Bl,G,MH,
VHy; CP : *crucifix, Chr : rood (land
measure), BC : plot of land of a square
rod, BC,EC* (v. GBG and Mdf).
rōdbīgenga m. *worshipper of the cross,* WW
216¹⁶.
rōdbora m. *cross-bearer,* GPH389.
rodd m? *'rod,' stick (to beat with),* HL15¹¹⁹.
rōdehengen f. *hanging, crucifixion,* Æ.
roden (B1151?) pp. of rēodan.
roder=rodor
rōdetācen n. *sign of the cross,* Æ.
rōdewyrðe *deserving hanging,* HL18³⁸⁹.
+rōdfæstnian *to crucify* (BT).
rodor (a) m., gs. rod(o)res *ether, sky, heavens,
firmament,* Æ,CP.
rodorbeorht *heaven-bright,* DA369.
rodorcyning† m. *king of heaven,* EL.
rodorlic *of the heavens, heavenly, celestial,*
Æ.
rodorlīhtung (roder-) f. *dawn,* LPs.
rodorstōl (a¹) m. *heavenly throne,* GEN749.
rodortorht *heavenly-bright,* GEN1416.
rodortungol n. *star of heaven,* GEN1667.
rōdwurðiend m. *cross-worshipper,* HGL
403³⁰.
roeðe (Cp,NG)=rēðe
rōf I. † *vigorous, strong, brave, noble, renowned.*
II. ? *array, number,* BH(Sch) 699 n83.
rofen pp. of rēofan; **rōflēas**=hrōflēas
roglan *to flourish,* GnE119.
rōhte pret. 3 sg. of rēcan.
rom=ramm
Rōm (Bl,Bo), Rōmeburg (AO) f. *'Rome.'*
Rōmān-e, -an pl. *Romans,* AO.
rōmānisc *Roman,* Æ,AO.
romēi *sooty,* WW10³¹ (BTs). [=hrūmig]
Rōm-feoh, -gesceot (LL) n., -penig (LL,
Shr,W) m. *'Rome-penny,' 'Romescot,'
Peter's pence.*
rōmian (w. g.) *to possess?* GEN350.
romm=ramm
Rōmwalh (u¹) m. *Roman.* [wealh]
Rōm-ware (AO), -waran pl. *inhabitants of
Rome, Romans.*
rond=rand
rop I.? *broth,* WW272⁹. **II.**=ropp
rōp *liberal,* RD58³.
rōpnes f. *liberality,* WW.
ropp m. *intestines,* Lcd,WW (hr-). ['rope']
ropwærc m. *colic,* WW211¹².
rōrend=rōwend
rōsbedd *rose-bed,* OEG23⁸.
+rōscian (o?FTP353)=rōstian
rōse, rose f. *'rose,'* Æ,Bf,Bl,Bo,MH. [L.
rosa]
rōsen *made of roses,* Lcd : *rose-coloured, rosy,*
Æ,ZDA. ['rosen']

+rōsod *of roses,* OEG3278,
rōst=rūst
+rōstian *to roast, dry,* WW.
rot=hrot
rōt *glad, cheerful, bright,* RIM : *noble, excellent,* Æ.
rōt(e)? *'root,'* NC318.
rōtfæst ('root-fast'), *firmly established,* Chr
1127.
rōthwīl f. *time of refreshing,* PPs.
±**rōtian** *to 'rot,' putrefy,* Æ,Bf,CP,Lcd.
rōtlīce *gladly, cheerfully,* BH348⁸.
rōtnes f. *gladness,* DR : *refuge, protection,*
Pss.
+rōtsian *to comfort, gladden,* CP417⁹.
rōtsung f. *refuge, protection, comfort,* EPs
9¹⁰.
rotung f. *corruption, ulcer,* WW114¹⁴.
[rotian]
rōðer I. m. *rower, sailor,* CP. [rōwan]
II.=rōðor
roðhund m. *mastiff,* WW. [ryðða]
rōðor n., gs. rōðres *oar, scull,* CP,WW.
['rudder']
rōðra=rēðra
rōw I. *quiet, calm, gentle, soft, mild,* CP.
II. f. *quietness, rest,* Gu. ['row']
±**rōwan⁷** pret. pl. rēowon, rēon *to go by
water, 'row,' sail, swim,* LkL (hr-), WW;
Æ.
rōwend m. *rower,* CP : *sailor,* Æ.
rōwett=rēwet
rōwing f. *'rowing,'* NG.
rōwnes f. *rowing,* BH384²².
rudduc m. *robin,* WW. ['ruddock']
rūde I. m. *scabbiness, scab,* WW161¹⁴
(=*hrūda? A30·253). **II.** f. *rue.* [L. ruta]
rudig *rubicund, 'ruddy,'* OEG2932.
rudon pret. pl. of rēodan.
rudu f. *red colour,* ApT : *ruddy complexion,*
WW : *red cosmetic,* ÆL. ['rud']
rues=ryges gs. of ryge; **rūg**=rūh
rugern m. *month of rye-harvest, August?*
LL12 Pro.
rūh gs. rūwes *'rough*,' Guth,Rd;* Æ : *coarse
(of cloth),* DHy,WW : *hairy, shaggy,* Æ :
undressed, untanned, WW.
ruhha? m. *ray (fish),* NC324 (suhha).
['rough']
rūm I. adj. (±) *roomy, wide, long, spacious,
ample, large, liberal,* B,Bo,Mt,VPs; Æ,
CP : *unoccupied : unfettered, open, unrestricted, loose : noble, august.* **II.** m. (±)
space (extent or time), 'room,' Gen,Lk :
scope, opportunity, B,Met. *on +rum at
large, apart.*
rūma *stumbling-block,* A41·102²⁰.
+ruma† m. *space, place.*
rūman=rȳman

rūme (once +) adv. *widely, spaciously, roomily, amply, liberally, extensively, abundantly, Gen,Lcd : light-heartedly : in detail,* JUL314. [*'room'*]
rūmed-=rūmmōd-
rūmgāl *revelling in release from confinement* (*Noah's dove*), GEN1466. adv. -līce *widely,* NC318.
rūmgifa (eo²) m. *bountiful giver,* BH194³³.
rūmgiful (y²) *bountiful,* Æ,CP.
rūmgifulnes (eo², y²) f. *liberality, bounty, profusion,* Æ.
rūmheort *large-hearted, generous,* B : *free from care,* RB. adv. -līce, VH.
rūmheortnes f. *liberality,* LL,W.
rūmian *to become clear of obstructions,* Lcd 1·76¹³. [*'room'*]
rūmlic *benign, liberal : plentiful,* Æ. adv. ±rūmlīce *at large, fully, kindly, liberally, abundantly,* Æ,Bl,MtL. [*'roomly'*]
rūmmōd *liberal, lavish, kind,* CP.
rūmmōdlic *ample, large, full, liberal, gracious.* adv. -līce.
rūmmōdnes f. *large-heartedness, liberality, kindness,* CP.
rūmnes f. *breadth, abundance,* Æ.
rūmōd=rūmmōd
rūmor adv. comp. *still further,* GEN.
+rumpen=+hrumpen v. hrimpan.
rūmwelle *spacious,* MtL7¹³.
rūn f. *mystery, secrecy, secret, El,JnL : counsel, consultation, B,KC,Wa : (secret) council : runic character, letter, BH : writing, An,Da.* [*'roun'*]
+rūna m. *counsellor, confidant,* GL.
rūncofa m. *chamber of secrets, breast, bosom,* MET22⁵⁹.
rūncræftig *skilled in mysteries,* DA734.
rūnere m. *whisperer, tale-bearer,* Æ. [*'rouner'*]
rūnian (+at BF70²⁴) *to whisper, murmur, talk secrets, conspire,* Æ,Ps,Sol. [*'round'*]
rūniende *whispering,* WW441. [*'rouning'*]
runl *foul? running?* LCD3·36¹⁷. [?=*hrunol]
rūnlic *mystical,* MtLp5¹¹.
-runn v. cȳs-gerunn.
+runnen pp. of +rinnan.
+runnenes f. *that has been cooled or congealed,* GPH398.
rūnstæf m. *runic letter, rune,* Æ,B. [*'rune-stave'*]
rūnung f. *whispering, wheedling,* Æ. [*'rouning'*]
rūnwita† m. *adviser, counsellor, wise man.*
rūst m. *'rust,' Cp,MtL,RB : moral canker,* CP,HL.
rūstig *'rusty,'* AO251²¹.
rūte=rūde
rūwa m., rūwe f. *covering, tapestry,* W.

rūwes v. rūh.
rūxlan (MtR9²³)=hrūxlian
rȳan=rȳn
ryc-, rȳc-=rec-, rēc-
rȳcð pres. 3 sg. of rēocan.
rȳd (LL192,2B)=rād I.
+ryddan *to clear (land),* AS39⁵.
+rȳde *prepared, ready? easy?* RD64¹⁵.
ryden n. *name of a plant,* LCD122a.
rȳderian v. ā-r.
rȳe=rȳhe
rȳfe *'rife,' frequent,* Lcd 3·164²¹.
ryft (i, e) n. *covering, veil, curtain, cloak,* CP.
ryge (i) m. *'rye,' Cp.*
rygen (i) *made of rye,* Lcd. [*'ryen'*]
rȳhe f. *rug, blanket,* GL. [=rēowe]
ryht=riht; rȳm-=rīm-
±rȳman (ē) *to clear, open up, An,B,Lk,Met, W : widen, extend, prolong, enlarge, Æ,CP : make room, retire, yield, Æ.* [*'rime'; rūm*]
rȳmet n. *room, space, extent, Æ : comfort, benefit.*
rȳmetlēast f. *want of room,* ÆH1·34²².
rȳmð f. *amplitude,* CM18.
rȳn, rȳnan *to roar, rage,* BO.
ryne (e) mn. *running, onward course, Æ,Bf, Bo,VHy; AO : flux, flow (water, blood), Lk; Æ : period of time, cycle, course of life : expanse, extent : orbit.* [*'rune'*]
±rȳne n. *mystery, dark saying : mystic rite : sacrament : sacramental elements,* Æ.
rynegiest m. *running spirit (=lightning)? rain-foe?* (Tupper), RD4⁵⁸.
-rȳnegu v. hel-r.
rynel I. (e) m. *runnel, stream, Bl,GD,VPs.* [*'rindle'*] II. *runner, messenger,* Æ.
rynele f.=rynel I.
±rȳn(e)lic *secret, mystical : figurative, sacramental.* adv. -līce.
rynelīce? *'cursim,'* OEG7⁹⁰.
rȳnemann m. *one skilled in mysteries,* RD43¹³.
rynestrong *strong in running,* RD20⁷.
ryneswift† *swift in running,* MET.
ryneðrāg f. *space of time,* GU184.
rynewǣn† m. *swift vehicle, chariot,* PPs19⁷.
ryng-=reng-
±rȳnig *good in counsel?* CRA51. [rūn]
ryniga? m. *liquid that runs off?* LCD.
rynning f. *rennet,* WW128⁴³.
+rynning=+rinning
rȳnstæf (RWH119³⁶)=rūnstæf; rȳp=rīp
+rynu (Æ)=+ryne
+rȳpan I. *to spoil, plunder, rob, Chr,MtL, LL,W.* [*'ripe'*] II. pl. *sheaves,* CSPs. III.=rēpan. IV.=rīpan
rȳpere m. *robber, plunderer,* LL,W.
rȳping m. *plunder, spoliation,* OEG3149. [*'riping'*]

ryplen? *made of broom*, GPH399 (A31·536).
ryps=reps; **-rŷric** v. sǣ-r.; **rysc-**=risc-
rysel, rysl (Æ), rys(e)le (hl-) m. *lard, fat* :
resin, LCD210¹³ : *abdomen*, WW159⁶ (cp.
ryselwærc).
ryselwærc *pain in the stomach*, LCD115b.
+rysen-, +rysn-=+risn-
rŷsig (OEG8³³⁷)=hrīsig
ryt *rubbish for burning, underwood*, LL
36,27 (v. 3·46).
rȳð I.=rīð. **II.** pres. 3 sg. of rȳn.
rȳðer=hrīðer
ryðða (i) m. *a species of dog, mastiff*, Æ,
WW. [*Ger*. rüde]

S

sā m. *tub, bucket, Gl.* [*ON*. sār; v. '*say*']
saban m? *sheet*, WW502³³.
sac=(1) sacu; (2) sæc
saca nap. of sacu.
±saca m. *opponent, foe*, B,BH.
sacan⁶ *to struggle, dispute, disagree, wrangle,
fight : accuse, blame, bring a criminal or
civil action against any one, lay claim to*,
LL.
sacc (æ) m. '*sack*,' *bag*, Æ. [*L*. saccus]
sācerd mf. *priest, priestess*, Æ,CP. [*L*.]
sācerdbana m. *priest-slayer*, W.
sācerdgerīsne *befitting a priest*, BH206¹².
sācerdhād m. *priesthood*, CP.
sācerdland n. *land allotted to priests*, GEN
47²⁶.
sācerdlic *sacerdotal, priestly*, Æ,BH.
sācerhād=sācerdhād
sacful *quarrelsome, contentious*, Æ. ['*sak-
ful*']
sacian *to wrangle, strive*, Æ.
saclēas *innocent*, LL : *unmolested, safe, Chr,
KC,MtL*. ['*sackless*']
sacu f. (oblique cases often have sæc-) (±)
*conflict, strife, war, battle, feud, sedition,
dispute*, Æ,B,LL; AO : *reproof : affliction,
persecution, trial : sin, fault*, B,Ph :
prosecution, lawsuit, action. s. and sōcn
*jurisdiction, right of holding a court for
criminal and civil matters*, LL (v. 2·455).
['*sake*']
sad- v. sæd.
sāda m. *snare, cord, halter*, NG,PPs. [cp.
Ger. saite]
sadel=sadol
±sadelian *to* '*saddle*,' Æ, KC. ['*saddled*']
sadian *to be sated, get wearied, Bo* : (+)
satiate, fill, Ps. ['*sade*'; sæd]
sadol (e², u²) m. '*saddle*,' *B*; GD.
sadolbeorht *with ornamented saddle*, B2175.
sadolboga (u²) m. '*saddle-bow*,' WW.

sadolfelg f. *pommel of a saddle*, GL.
Saducēisc *Sadducean*; as sb. m. *Sadducee*.
sadul=sadol
sǣ mf. often indecl. but also gs. sǣs, sǣwe,
sēo; nap. sǣs, gp. sǣwa, dp. sǣwum,
sǣ(u)m *sheet of water*, '*sea*,' *lake, pool, Æ,
B,Bo,G,Lcd,VPs.*
sǣǣl m. *sea-eel*, WW447³⁶.
sǣælfen f. *sea-elf, naiad*, WW.
sǣbāt† f. '*sea-boat*,' *vessel, ship, B*.
sǣbeorg m. *cliff by the sea : mountain of
waves?* AN308.
sǣbrōga m. *sea-terror*, SOL84¹³.
sǣburg f. *seaport town*, MtL4¹³.
sǣc I. *offensive, odious : guilty.* **II.** (KGL
61²²)=sacc
sǣc-, sǣc-=sec- (and v. sacu), sēc-
sǣcc I.† f. *strife, contest.* [sacan] **II.** m.
sackcloth, Æ. ['*sack*';=sacc]
sǣcce pres. 1 sg. of sācan.
sǣccing m. *sacking, pallet*, Mk6⁵⁵ (v. NED).
sǣcdōm=sceacdōm
sǣceaster f. *seaport town*, MtR4¹³.
sǣceosol m. *sea-sand, shingle*, GEN32¹²,
WW147⁴¹.
sǣcerd=sacerd; **sǣcgen**=segen
sǣcir m. *sea-ebbing*, Ex291.
sǣclian (*Chr*)=sīclian
sǣclif n. *cliff by the sea, Bo.* ['*seacliff*']
sǣcocc m. *cockle*, WW94¹⁴.
sǣcol n. *jet*, WW416². ['*seacoal*']
sǣcyning m. *sea-king*, B2382.
sǣcysul=sǣceosol
sǣd (occl. sad- in obl. cases) w. g. *sated with,
weary of, satiated, filled, full, Ps,Rd.* ['*sad*']
sǣd (ē) n., nap. sǣd, sǣdu '*seed*,' *Mk,VPs*;
Æ,CP : *fruit, offspring, posterity, MkL,
VPs : sowing, Met*; Æ : *growth*.
sǣdberende *seed-bearing*, Æ.
sǣdcynn n. *kind of seed*, LL,WW.
sǣde pret. 3 sg. of secgan.
sǣdēor m. *sea-monster*, LCD,MH.
sǣdere m. *sower*, Æ,MkL. ['*seeder*']
sǣdian *to sow*, MtL13⁸ : *provide seed*, LL
450,10.
sǣdlēap m. *sower's basket, Bf.* ['*seedlip*']
sǣdlic *belonging to seed, seminal*, DR146⁸.
sǣdnað m. *sowing*, WW147⁴.
sǣdnes f. *satiety*, GPH391.
sǣdraca m. *sea-dragon*, B,GL.
sǣdtīma m. *seed-time*, HEXC226.
sǣearm m. *arm of the sea*, AO22⁴.
sǣelfen=sǣælfen
sǣfæreld n. *passage of the (Red) sea*, AO
38³³.
sǣfæsten f. *watery stronghold, ocean*, Ex127.
sǣ-faroð, -fearoð† m. *sea-coast*.
Sǣfern f. *Severn*, CHR. [*L*. Sabrina]
sǣfisc m. '*sea-fish*,' *Cr*.

sæflōd mn. *tide, inundation, flood, flow of the sea, flood-tide, AO* : *flow of a river,* VH : (†) *sea.* ['*seaflood*']

sæflota m. (*sea-floater*), *ship*, AN 381.

sæfōr f. *sea-voyage,* SEAF 42.

±**sægan** *to cause to sink, settle* : *cause to fall, fell, destroy.* [sīgan]

sægd-=sæged-

sægde pret. 3 sg. of secgan.

sægdig (N)=sægde ic

sægēap *spacious* (*ship*), B 1896 (v. ES 64·211).

±**sægednes** f. *sacrifice,* MkLR 12³³; APs 65¹³ : *mystery,* MtL 13¹¹ (gd-).

sægemǣre n. *sea-coast,* G.

±**sægen**=+segen

sægenga m. *ship,* B : *sailor,* BF 156³¹.

sægeset m. *coast region,* GL.

sægl=sigel; **sægnian**=segnian

sægon pret. pl. of sēon.

sægrund m. *sea-bottom, abyss,* Æ,CP.

sæh=seah

sæhealf f. *side next the sea, seaside,* Æ,CHR.

sæhengest m. *sea-horse, ship,* AN 488 : *hippopotamus,* WW.

sǣhete m. *surging of the sea,* BH 384²⁴.

sæholm m. *ocean,* AN 529.

sæht=seht

sæhund m. *sea-dog, sea-beast,* OEG 26⁶¹.

sæl n. nap. salu *room, hall, castle,* B,Rd. ['*sale*']

sæl (ē) **I.** mf. (occl. dp. sālum) *time, season, opportunity, occasion, condition, position,* Lcd; Æ,AO : *prosperity, happiness, joy, B.* on sǣlum *happy*; '*gaudete,*' GD 202⁶. tō sǣles *in due time,* NR 39. ['*sele*'] **II.**– sēl II.

sǣlāc† n. *sea-gift, sea-spoil,* B.

sǣlād† f. *sea-way, sea-voyage.*

sǣlāf f. *sea-leavings, jetsam,* Ex 584.

±**sǣlan** **I.** (ē) *to take place, happen,* CP : *succeed,* GD 202⁶. [sǣl I.] **II.**† *to tie, bind, fetter, fasten* : *curb, restrain, confine.* [sāl]

sǣland n. *coast, maritime district,* TC 308¹.

sæld=seld

sælen **I.** *made of willow,* WW 518⁶. [sealh] **II.**=selen

sǣleoda=sǣlida

sǣlēoð n. *song at sea, rowers' song,* WW 379⁹.

-sæleða v. sealt-s.

sǣlic *of the sea, marine,* Æ.

sǣlida m. *seafarer, sailor* : *pirate.* [līðan]

±**sǣlig** (+ exc. at LL 300A) *fortuitous,* OEG 4185 : *happy, prosperous, AO,Bo,Gen*; CP. ['*i-seli*']

+**sǣlige** *happily,* WW 407²³.

+**sǣliglic** (ē) *happy, blessed, fortunate.* adv. -līce, *Bo,DR.* ['*seelily*']

+**sǣlignes** f. *happiness,* (*good*) *fortune,* CP : *occurrence.*

sǣ-līðend, -līðende† m. *sailor.*

+**sǣllic**=+sǣliglic

sǣlmerige f. *brine,* ÆGR 192¹⁸. [*L.* *salmoria; *Gk.* ἀλμυρίς]

+**sǣlnes** f. *occurrence,* GL.

+**sǣltan** (NG)=syltan

sæltna m. *name of a bird, bunting? robin?* WW 44¹⁷.

sǣlð f. *dwelling, house,* GEN 785.

±**sǣlð** (ȳ) f. (usu. in pl.) *hap, fortune* : *happiness, prosperity, blessing, Bo*; Æ,CP. ['*i-selth*']

sǣlwang (o²)† m. *fertile plain.*

sǣm v. sǣ; **sǣma**=sēma

+**sǣman**=+sīeman

sǣmann m. '*seaman,*' *pirate, viking, B.*

sǣmearh† m. *sea-horse, ship,* E 2.

sǣmend=sēmend

sǣmest superl. (of *sǣme?) *worst.*

sǣmestre=sēamestre

sǣmēðe *weary from a sea-voyage,* B 325.

sǣminte f. *sea-mint,* WW.

sǣmninga=samnunga

sǣmra comp. (of *sǣme?) *worse, inferior, weaker.*

sǣmtinges=samtinges

sǣn (ē) *maritime, marine,* OEG 6²³, 8¹²⁸.

sǣnaca m. *sea-vessel, ship,* HU 26.

sǣnæs m. *cape, promontory,* B,GL.

sǣncgan=sengan; **sǣndan**=sendan

sǣne (often w. g.) *slack, lazy, careless, negligent, dull, cowardly.*

sǣnet n. *net for sea-fishing,* WW 336²⁰.

sǣngan–sengan; **sōnian**–segnian

sǣnig *maritime, marine,* A 13·32.

sǣostre f. *sea-oyster,* WE 63¹⁷.

sǣp (e) n. '*sap,*' *juice, Cr,WW.*

sǣp (ÆL 3¹⁶²)=sēap

sǣpig '*sappy,*' *juicy, succulent,* OEG 16¹.

sǣppe f. *spruce fir,* WW 269¹⁴. [*L.* *sappinum; *Fr.* sapin]

sǣpspōn f. *a shaving with sap in it,* LCD 106b.

sǣre=sāre

sǣrima m. *sea-shore, coast, Chr.* ['*searim*']

sǣrinc† m. *seaman, pirate, viking.*

sǣrōf *hardy at sea,* CRA 56.

sǣrwian=searwian

sǣrȳric m. *sea-reed?* (GK); *an ait?* (BT), WH 10.

sǣs=sess; **sǣs** v. sǣ.

sǣsceaða m. *pirate,* WW 469⁶.

sǣscell f. '*sea-shell,*' MH 18²³.

sǣsīð m. *sea-voyage,* B 1149.

sǣ-snægl, -snæl m. '*sea-snail,*' WW.

sǣsteorra m. *guiding star* (*for sailors*), HL. ['*seastar*'] sæster=sester

sǣstrand n. 'sea-strand,' foreshore, ÆH.

sǣstrēam, as mpl. waters of the sea, An. ['seastream']

sǣswalwe (hǣ-) f. sand-martin, WW7²⁸.

sæt pret. 3 sg. of sittan.

sǣt f. lurking-place : snare, gin? LL445,2. [sittan]

+sæt n. act of sitting, MkLp5¹⁴.

sǣta m? holding of land, EC447¹⁸.

-sǣta (ē) v. burg-s.

sǣtan=sǣtian; -sǣte v. an(d)-s.

sǣte f. house, KC3·79¹⁵.

+sǣte (ē) n. snare, ambush, DR37¹⁰.

Sǣterdæg=Sǣtern(es)dæg

sǣt-ere, -nere (ē) m. waylayer, robber : spy : seditious one, seducer (the devil), CP.

Sǣtern-dæg, Sǣter(n)es- m. 'Saturday,' BH,Bl,Lk. [L. Saturni dies]

Sǣterniht f. Friday night, ÆH1·216²⁷.

sǣtian (ē) (w. g.) to lie in wait for, plot against, CP. [sittan]

sǣtil, sǣtl=setl; sǣtn-=sǣt-

+sǣtnes=+setnes

sǣton pret. pl. of sittan.

sǣtung (ē) f. ambush, trap, plot, snare, CP : sedition.

sǣð (ÆL36²⁹⁵)=sēað

sǣðēof v. hēahsǣðēof.

sǣðerie=saturege; sǣðnes=sēðnes

sǣðrenewudu = sūðernewudu; sǣum v. sǣ.

sǣupwearp jetsam, TC421'.

sǣwǣg m. sea-wave, DA384.

sǣwǣter n. 'sea-water,' Lcd10b.

sǣwan=sāwan

sǣwār n. sea-weed, WW135²¹. ['seaware']

sǣwaroð n. sea-shore, beach, Az,Bo.

sǣwe v. sǣ.

sǣweall† m.'sea-wall,'sea-shore,beach, cliff, B : wall of water (in the Red Sea).

sǣweard m. coast-warden, B,LL.

sǣweg m. path through the sea, Ps8⁸. ['seaway']

sǣwērig† weary from a sea-voyage, An. ['seaweary']

sǣwet n. sowing, BH. [sāwan]

sǣwīcing m. sea-viking, Ex333.

sǣwiht f. marine animal, BH26⁶.

sǣwinewincle f? periwinkle (shell-fish), Lcd90a.

sǣwong m. sea-shore, beach, B1964.

sǣwð pres. 3 sg. of sāwan.

sǣwudu m. vessel, ship, B226.

sǣwum v. sǣ.

sǣwylm m. sea-surf, billow, B393.

sæx (GL)=seax

sǣȳð f. sea-wave, RUN,WW.

safene, safine f. savine (a kind of juniper), Lcd. [L. sabina]

saftriende ptc. rheumy, WW161³⁴ (MLR 19·203).

sāg I. a sinking, RD79⁵ (or ?sagol). II. pret. 3 sg. of sīgan.

saga I. imperat. of secgan. II. m. story, narrative, ÆL7¹⁹³. III. m.=sagu II.

+saga n. narrative, LkL1¹.

sagast pres. 2 sg., sagað pres. 3 sg., sagode pret. 3 sg. of secgan.

sāgol (e²) m. (sāgl- in obl. cases) club, cudgel, stick, staff, pole, AO,GD,Mt; Æ,CP. ['sowel']

-sagol v. lēas-, sōð-, wǣr-s.

sagu (±) I. f. 'saw,' saying, report, story, tradition, tale, Lk,WW; Æ : presage, prophecy : witness, testimony. [secgan] II. f. 'saw' (tool), Bf,WW.

sāh I. pret. 3 sg. of sīgan. II. pret. 3 sg. of sēon II.

sahl-=sealh-; sāhl=sāgol; saht=seht

sāl mf. bond, rope, cord, rein, collar, B,Gen. ['sole'; Ger. seil]

sala m. act of selling, 'sale,' WW.

salb (Ep)=sealf; salch=sealh

salde=sealde pret. 3 sg. of sellan.

salf (Cp)=sealf

salfie, salfige f. sage, Lcd. [L. salvia]

salh (Gl), salig=sealh

salletan to sing psalms, play on, or sing to, the harp, PPs104². [L. psallere]

salm-=sealm-

sālnes f. silence, Bf122²². [cp. Goth. silan]

salo=salu; salor=solor

salowigpād=salwigpād

salt=sealt

saltere (ea) m. 'psalter*,' collection of psalms, service-book containing the psalms, Æ,BH,Ct,LL : psaltery, Lcd (ps-). [L. psalterium]

salthaga m. robin redbreast? WW286¹¹.

salu I. (ea) dark, dusky, Rd. ['sallow'] II. nap. of sæl.

salubrūn (ea¹, o²) dark brown, FIN37.

sālum v. sǣl.

saluneb dark-complexioned, RD50⁵.

salupād dark-coated, RD58³.

saluwigpād=salwigpād

salwed ptc. darkened, painted black (with pitch), GEN1481.

salwigfeðera having dark plumage, GEN1448.

salwigpād† having dark plumage.

sālwong=sǣlwang

sam conj. whether, or. sam...sam whether... or, AO. sam ge...sam ge; sam ðe...sam ðe whether...or.

sam- (=together) denotes union, combination, or agreement. [ON. sam-]

sām- (=half-) denotes a partial or imperfect condition. [L. semi-]

sama=same v. swā.
samad-=samod-
sāmbærned half-burnt, OEG.
sāmboren born out of due time, WW356[2].
sāmbryce m. partial breach (of rules, laws, etc.), LL468,9.
sām-cwic, -cucu (o[1]) half-dead, Æ,AO
same only in swā s. (swā) in like manner also, as, CP.
samed=samod
samen (o[1]) adv. together, JnR.
sāmgrēne half-green, immature, WW405[4].
sāmgung young, CM123. [geong]
sāmhāl unwell, weakly, W273[10].
samheort unanimous, PPs149[1].
±samhīwan pl. members of the same household, married persons, CP.
samhwylc pron. some, BL,LL.
sāmlǣred half-taught, badly instructed, Æ.
samlīce together, at the same time, SOL 148[18].
samlinga=samnunga
sāmlocen half-closed, NC318.
sammǣle agreed, accordant, united, CHR, LL.
sāmmelt half-digested, LCD69b.
±samnian to assemble, meet, collect, unite, join, gather together, (tr.) Da,Lcd; (refl.) CHR : (intr.) Ps : glean. ['sam']
samninga=samnunga
±samnung (o) f. (but occl. gs. samnunges), union, congregation, meeting, assembly, council, MkL; Æ,CP : collection : union in marriage. ['samening']
samnunga (æ, e, o) adv. forthwith, immediately, suddenly. [=semninga]
samnungcwide (o[1]) collect, DR2[1].
samod (o[1]) I. adv. simultaneously, at the same time, together, Æ,AO : entirely, Æ : also, as well, too. II. prep. (w. d.) together with, at (of time), Æ. [Ger. sammt]
samodcumend flocking together, CM282.
samodeard (o[1], u[2]) m. common home, GU 1346.
samodfæst joined together, CR1581.
samodgang continuous, GD170[23] (v. NC 318).
samodgeflit (o[1]) n. strife, WW382[38].
samodgesīð m. comrade, GPH400.
samodherian (o[1]) to praise together, RPs 116[1].
samodhering f. praising, ES40·302.
+samodlǣcan to bring together, RPs112[8].
samodlīce adv. together, CHR1123.
samodrynelas mpl. 'concurrentes,' BF46[1].
samodsīðian to accompany, MFH137[18].
samodsprǣc f. colloquy, conversation, CM 511.
samodswēgende consonantal, ÆGR5[17].

samodtang continuous, successive, v. NC 318.
samodðyrlic (o[1]) adj. concordant, WW378[40].
samodwellung (o[1]) f. welding together, WW 380[44]. [weallan]
samodwist f. a being one with, GD224[4].
samodwunung f. common residence, living together, LL(422').
samodwyrcende co-operating, WW384[12].
sāmra=sǣmra
samrād harmonious, united, MET11[96].
samrǣden f. married state, CP19[18].
sāmsoden half-cooked, LL(166[2]n).
sāmstorfen half-dead, GPH401.
sāmswǣled half-burnt, OEG4388.
samswēge (u[1]) adj. sounding in unison.
samtinges (æ[1], e[1], e[2]) adv. all at once, immediately, forthwith, Æ.
samðe conj. in phrase samðe...samðe...as well...as... ('tam'... 'quam'...), CM,SC, etc. [sam]
sāmweaxen half-grown, NC319.
samwinnende ptc. contending together, WW 211[7].
sāmwīs stupid, dull, foolish, CP. adv. -līce.
samwist† f. living together, cohabitation, GL.
sāmworht unfinished, CHR.
samwrǣdnes f. union, combination, BO114[4].
sāmwyrcan to half do a thing, LL350,61[1].
sanc I. pret. 3 sg. of sincan. II.=sang
sanct m. holy person, saint, Æ. [L. sanctus]
sand (o) I. f. action of sending, embassy, mission, deputation, Æ : message : (also m.) messenger, ambassador, KC : sending, service, course of food, repast, mess, victuals, Gl; Æ. ['sand'; sendan] II. n. 'sand,' gravel, Æ,MtR,VPs; AO; Mdf : sandy shore, sea-shore, beach.
sandbeorg m. sand-hill, sand-bank, BO,KC.
sandceosol m. sand, gravel, Æ.
sandcorn n. grain of sand, Æ.
sandful sandy, SC223[13].
sandgeweorp (u[3]) n. sand-bank, quicksand, WW.
sandgewyrpe n. sand-heap, KC6·228'.
sandgrot n. grain of sand, HELL117.
sand-hlið n., nap. -hleoðu sandy slope, hillock, AN236.
sandhof n. sand-house, barrow, grave, GU 1169.
sandhricg m. sand-bank, ÆGR75[8].
sandhyll (o[1]) m. 'sand-hill,' Cp.
sandig 'sandy,' Lcd.
sandiht (o) sandy, dusty, AO.
sandland (o[1], o[2]) n. sandy shore, GU1308.
sandpytt m. sand-pit, ÆL35[325].
sandrid n. quicksand, WW183[7].
sandsēað m. sand-pit, KC.

sang (o) **I.** m. *noise, 'song,' singing, B,Bo, Cr,LkL* : *psalm, poem, lay, Bl,CP,VPs.* **II.** pret. 3 sg. of singan.

sangbōc f. *singing-book, service-book, KC, LL.* ['*songbook*']

sangcræft m. *art of singing, composing poetry, or playing an instrument, BH,PH.*

sangdrēam m. '*cantilena,' song, music,* CM 638.

sangere (o) m. *singer, poet, BH,Bl.* ['*songer*']

sangestre f. *songstress, ÆGr.* ['*songster*']

sangpīpe f. *pipe,* GPH389²⁶.

-sānian v. a-s. [sǣne]

sann pret. 3 sg. of sinnan.

sāp f? *amber, unguent,* GL.

sāpbox m. *resin-box? soap-box?* LL455,17.

sāpe f. '*soap,' salve, Lcd,WW* ; Æ.

sār **I.** n. *bodily pain, sickness* : *wound, 'SORE,' raw place* : *suffering, sorrow, affliction, Bo,Chr.* **II.** adj. *sore, sad, grievous, painful, wounding, CP.*

Sar(a)cene (o², i³) pl. *Saracens,* AO,DR.

Saracenisc adj. *Saracen, Æ.*

sārbenn† f. *painful sore or wound.*

sārbōt f. *compensation for wounding,* LL 500,10¹.

Sarc-=Sarac-

sārclāð m. *bandage,* WW.

sārcrene (ē²?) *sore, tender,* Lcd65b.

sārcwide† m. *taunt, reproach* : *lament.*

sāre (ǣ) adv. *sorely, heavily, grievously, bitterly, B,Cr,Gen,Ps* : *painfully, B.* ['*sore*']

sārege *grief, trouble,* RWH88¹³.

sārettan *to grieve, lament, complain, CP.*

sārferhð *sorrowful,* GEN2244.

sarga m. *trumpet, clarion,* GL.

sārgian (±) *to cause pain, afflict, wound, grieve* : *be pained, suffer, languish, CP.* [sārig]

sārgung f. *lamentation, grief,* Sc,W.

sārian *to become painful, CP* : *grieve, be sad, feel sorry for,* BH.

sārig '*sorry,' grieved, sorrowful, Æ,B,Bo, Cr,Ps.*

sārigcierm (e³) m. *wailing,* MFH128⁸.

sārigferhð† *sad-hearted.*

sāriglic *sad,* GD290⁶.

sārigmōd *dejected, mournful, B.* ['*sorry-mood*']

sārignes f. *sadness, grief, Æ,Chr.* ['*sorriness*']

sārlic *grievous, sad, doleful, painful, lamentable, bitter, Æ,B,Bo,Bl.* adv. -līce '*sorely,' grievously, mournfully, bitterly, painfully, Æ,Bl,Bo,Jul;* CP.

sārnes f. *affliction, distress, suffering, pain, grief, Æ.* ['*soreness*']

sārsēofung f. *complaint,* WW488³⁶.

sārslege† m. *painful blow,* JUL.

sārspell n. *sad story, complaint,* MH16³.

sārstæf m. *cutting word, abuse,* GU 205.

sārung=sārgung; sarw-=searw-

sār-wracu† f., gds. -wræce *grievous persecution, sore tribulation.*

sārwylm m. *pain, illness,* GU1123.

saturege f. *savory (plant), Lcd147a,WW.* ['*satureie'; L.*]

sāul=sāwol

±sāwan⁷ *to* '*sow*,' strew seed, implant, Æ* : *disseminate, CP.*

sāwel=sāwol

+sāwelod *having a soul, G* : *endowed with life,* LL.

sāwend, sāwere (*Mt*) m. '*sower.*'

+sawenlic=+sewenlic

sāwl (CP), sāwle=sāwol

sāwlian *to expire, Æ.*

sāwlung (e²) f. *dying, Shr.* ['*souling*']

sā-wol (-wel, -wul, -wl) f., gs. sāwle '*soul,' life, Æ,B,Bl,Bo,Ps;* CP : *spirit, Bl,Chr* : *living being, Æ.*

sāwolberend m. *human being,* B1004 (wl).

sāwolcund (e) *spiritual,* GU288.

sāwoldrēor† n. *life-blood.*

sāwolgedāl† n. *death.*

sāwolgesceot=sāwolscot

sāwolhord (e², wl)† n. *life, body.*

sāwolhūs† n. *(soul-house), body,* GU.

sāwollēas *soulless, lifeless, Æ.*

sāwol-sceat (e²), -scot m. *payment to the church on the death of a person,* LL.

sāwolðearf f. *soul's need,* TC474 (wl).

sāwon pret. pl. of sēon.

sāwul=sāwol

sca-, scā-, v. also scea-, scēa-.

scāda m. *crown of head, PPs67²¹.* ['*shode*']

+scādwyrt (ēa) f. *oxeye,* Lcd 103a,WW 50².

scæ-; scǣ-=scea-, sce-; scēa-

scæc (e) *fetters,* JGPh1·329. [*Du.* schake]

scæftamund=sceaftmund

scæfð=sceafoða

scæm-=scam-

scænan **I.** (±) (ē, ēa) *to break, wrench open, shatter, Æ.* ['*shene*'] **II.** (+) *to render brilliant?* SOL222 (GK).

+scæninges f. *collision,* WW384¹⁰.

scæp=scēap; scæptlō (Cp)=sceaftlō

scær=scear I. and II.

scæron pret. pl. of scieran.

scǣð **I.** (*Gen*)=scēað. **II.**=scegð

scafa m. *plane, Ep,LL.* ['*shave*']

±scafan⁶ (a, æ, ea) *to* '*shave,' scrape, polish, Cp,BH.*

scǣffōt *splay-footed,* GL.

scalde=sceolde pret. 3 sg. of sculan.

scaldhūlas pl. *reed, sedge,* WW37[15] (v. ES 43·320).

scaldōȳfel=scealdōȳfel +scaldwyrt (WW278[25])=+scādwyrt

scamel=scamol

scamfæst '*shamefast,*' *modest, CP.*

scamful (eo) *modest, DR.* ['*shameful*']

scamian (ea, eo, o) (w. g.) *to be ashamed, blush, B,CP* : (impers., w. a. of pers. and g. of thing) *cause shame, Æ,CP.* ['*shame*']

scamlēas '*shameless,*' *impudent, immodest, CP.*

scamlēaslic *shameless, CP.* adv. -līce '*shamelessly,*' *CP.*

scamlēast (ea[1]) f. *impudence, shamelessness, immodesty,* GL,Mk.

scamlic (æ, ea) *shameful, disgraceful, OEG;* AO : *modest.* ['*shamely*'] adv. -līce, *CP.*

scamlim n. *private member,* GPH390, WW 535[31]?

scamol (æ[1], e[1], ea[1], eo[1], o[1]; e[2], u[2]) m. *stool, footstool, bench, table (of money-changers), Bl,VPs.* ['*shamble*']

scamu (ea, eo, o) f. '*shame,*' *confusion, Cp, Lk* : *disgrace, dishonour, Cr* : *insult, MkR* : *shameful circumstance, WW* : *modesty, CP* : *private parts, Gen,WW.* s. dōn *to inflict injury.*

scamul=scamol

scamung (ea) f. *disgrace,* LRPs68[20].

scān pret. 3 sg. of scīnan.

scanca m. '*shank,*' *shin, leg, G,Ph,Gl,Sol, WW* : *ham? LL* (sconc).

scancbend (scang-) m. *garter,* WW152[39].

scancforad (e[3]) *broken-legged, CP,LCD.*

scancgebeorg f. *leg-greave,* WW535[9].

scancgegirela m. *anklet, garter,* WW467[29].

scanclīra m. *calf of the leg,* WW266[4].

scand I. (ea, eo, o) f. *ignominy, shame, confusion, disgrace, Chr,Cr* : *scandal, disgraceful thing, CP.* II. m. *wretch, impostor, recreant, buffoon, Æ,WW.* III. f. *bad woman, ÆL.* ['*shond*']

scandful *shameful, disgraceful, MH.* ['*shondfull*']

scandhūs m. *house of ill fame,* MH26[24].

scandlic (ea, o) *shameful, disgraceful, vile, unchaste, Bo;* Æ,AO. ['*shondly*'] adv. -līce *shamefully, obscenely* : *insultingly.*

scandlicnes (o) f. *shame, disgrace, CP* : *disgraceful act.*

scandlufiende *loving shamefully,* LCD 1·lxi[4].

scandword (ea) n. *abusive, blasphemous or obscene language,* W255[15].

scandwyrde *slanderous,* AB34[10].

scang-=scanc-; +scāp-=+scēap-

+scapen pp. of scieppan.

scapu-lare n., -larie f. *scapulary,* RB.

scar-=scear-; scaδ-=sceaδ-

scēab (Cp)=scēaf; sceaba=scafa

sceabb (æ, e) m. '*scab,*' *CP,Lcd.* ['*shab*']

sceabbede *purulent, having sores or scabs, OEG.* ['*shabbed*']

sceacan[6] (tr. and intr.) *to* '*SHAKE,*' *move quickly to and fro, brandish* : *go, glide, hasten, flee, depart, Æ* : *pass from, proceed, CP.*

sceacdōm (æ) m. *flight,* GEN31[20].

sceacel (e) m. '*shackle,*' *WW* : *plectrum.*

scēacere m. *robber,* NG. [*Ger.* schächer]

sceacga m. *rough hair, wool, etc., WW.* ['*shag*']

sceacgede *hairy, shaggy,* WW.

sceaclīne (WW182[26])=sceatlīne

sceacnes f. '*excussio,*' EPs140[4].

sceacul=sceacel

scead (a, æ, e) n. *shadow, shade* : *shelter, protection* : *stye,* Cp1954 (ES43·326).

+scēad (ā) I. n. *separation, distinction, LkL* : *discretion, understanding, argument, Æ; CP* : *reason, ÆP142[11]* : *reckoning, account, statement, Mt* : *accuracy* : *art, manner, method.* ['*shed*'] II. *reasonable, prudent* : *calculated,* GL.

±scēadan[7] (ā, ē) (tr. and intr.) *to divide, separate, part, Soul;* LCD : *discriminate, decide, determine, appoint* : *differ* : *scatter,* '*shed,*' *Lcd* : *expound* : *decree* : *write down.*

sceadd m. '*shad*' *(fish),* KC6·147[19].

sceaddgenge *seasonable for shad,* KC6·147[18].

scēadelīce=scēadlīce

+scēadenlīce *severally,* WW491[36].

scēadenmǣl *damascened (sword),* B1939.

scēadsealf f. *salve or powder (for the head?),* LCD.

sceadew-=sceadw-

sceadiht *shady,* CVHy5[3].

sceadlic *shady,* OEG2885.

+scēadlic *reasonable, discreet, wise, accurate, CP.* adv. -līce.

+scēadnes '*auctoritas,*' CHRD13[18].

sceadu (a) f., gs. scead(u)we, sceade '*shade,*' *shadow, darkness, Ex,Ps,Sol; CP* : *shady place, arbour, Lcd* : *shelter* : *scene,* v. OEG 2885.

sceadugeard m. *shady place,* Cp79T.

sceadugenga m. *wanderer in darkness,* B 703.

sceaduhelm (a[1]) m. *darkness,* B650.

sceadwian (a[1]) *to protect,* LPs90[4]. ['*shadow*']

sceadwig *shady,* RHy5[3].

±scēadwīs (ā)*sagacious, intelligent, rational, reasonable, wise, Æ.* adv. -līce, *clearly,* AO60[9].

+scēadwīslic (RBL14[1])=+scēadwīs

scēadwīsnes f. *sagacity, reason* : *discrimination, discretion* : *separation,* VH : *reckoning.*

sceadwung f. *overshadowing, Lcd*; Æ : *something giving shade*, OEG438. ['*shadowing*']
scēaf I. m. '*sheaf*,' *bundle, Æ,Lcd*; CP.
II. pret. 3 sg. of scūfan.
sceaf-=scaf-
scēafmǣlum adv. *into bundles*, Mt13³⁰.
sceaf(o)ða m. *chip, shaving, slip, scraping*, BH.
sceaft (æ, e) m. *staff, pole,* '*shaft*,' *Met,WW* : *spear-shaft, spear, Æ*; CP.
±sceaft fmn., nap. -tu, -ta, -te, tas *created being, creature, Bo*; Æ,CP : *origin, creation, construction, existence, Bo*; Æ,CP : (+) *dispensation, destiny, fate*, CP : (+) *condition, nature.* ['*shaft*']
sceaft-lō, pl. -lōn *spear-strap*, Cp (sce(a)pt-).
sceaftmund (æ) f. *span, LL.* ['*shaftment*']
sceaftriht(e) adv. *in a straight line*, CC54.
sceafð=sceafoða
sceaga (a) m. *copse, Ct*; Mdf. ['*shaw*']
sceagod=sceacgede
sceal pres. 1 and 3 sg. of sculan.
scealc m. *servant, retainer, soldier, subject, member of a crew, Ps* : *man, youth, B.* ['*shalk*']
sceald *shallow, BC*1·593 (v. PST1895–8, 532 and '*shoal*').
scealde=sceolde pret. 2 sg. of sculan.
scealdðȳfel (a¹) m. *thicket*, GD100; 212.
scealfor f., scealfra (Æ) m. *diver (bird), cormorant.* [cp. *OHG.* scarbo]
scealga (y) m. *a fish, roach? rudd?* WW. ['*shallow*']
-scealian v. ā-s.
sceall=sceal pres. 1 and 3 sg. of sculan.
sceallan pl. '*testiculi*,' LCD.
scealtu=scealt ðu (pres. 2 sg. of sculan, and pron. 2 pers.).
scealu (a) f. *shell, husk, Ep* : *scale (of a balance), Æ* : *dish*, KC. ['*shale*']
scēam m. *pale grey or white horse?* RD23⁴. [*Ger.* schimmel]
sceam-=scam-
scēan pret. 3 sg. of scīnan.
scēanan=scēnan
sceanc-=scanc-
sceand=scand
+sceandnes (ÆL)=+scendnes
scēanfeld=scīnfeld
scēap (ǣ, ē, ī) n. '*sheep*,' *CP,G,RB,VPs*, WW.
+sceap (a) n., nap. -pu '*shape*,' *form, created being, creature, El,Gen,WW* : *creation* : *dispensation, fate* : *condition* : *sex*, DR51⁴ : (±) '*genitalia*,' A11·2.
-sceap v. for-s.
scēapǣtere (ǣ¹, ī¹; e²) m. *sheep's carcase*, LL449,8.
sceapen pp. of scieppan.

scēapen adj. *of a sheep*, LCD.
+sceapennes f. *creation, formation, Æ.*
scēaphām m. *sheepfold*, EC373'.
scēapheord (y²) f. *flock of sheep*, Ex12³².
scēapheorden n. *shed*, WW185¹⁵.
+sceaphwīl (æ) f. *fated hour*, B26.
scēaphyrde (i) m. '*shepherd*.' (W; Æ).
scēaplic *of a sheep*, OEG118⁷.
+sceaplīce *ably, fitly*, BHCA324⁴.
scēapscearu (ē) f. *sheep-shearing*, GEN38¹².
-sceapung v. for-s.
scēapwǣsce f. *place for washing sheep*, Ct.
scēapwīc n. *sheepfold*, KC3·405⁵.
scear I. (æ, e) mn. *ploughshare, Cp,Sc.* ['*share*'] II. pret. 3 sg. of scieran.
scēara=scēarra
scearbēam m. *wood to which the ploughshare is fixed*, WW196²⁸. [v. '*share*']
sceard I. n. *incision, cleft, gap, Ct* : *potsherd*, GPH. ['*shard*'] II. adj. *cut, mutilated, gashed, notched, hacked* : (w. g.) *bereft of.*
±scearfian *to cut off, scrape, shred*, LCD, LkL.
scearflian *to scrape*, LCD1·184'.
scearfung f. *scraping, scarifying*, LCD.
scearian (a) *to allot*, KC.
scearn (æ, e) n. *dung, muck, Æ,Lcd,VPs.* ['*sharn*']
scearnbudda m. *dung-beetle*, ÆGr308¹n. ['*sharnbud*']
scearn-wibba (æ, e) -wifel (-fifel, WW) m. *dung-beetle.*
scēaron=scǣron pret. pl. of scieran.
scearp (a, æ) '*sharp*,' *pointed, prickly, Lcd, Soul,VPs* : *acute, keen, active, shrewd, Æ, Bo,Lcd* : *severe, rough, harsh, AO,Hell, Lcd* : *biting, bitter, acid, Lcd* : *brave.* [scieran]
scearpe I. adv. *sharply, keenly, Hex,Ps*; Æ. ['*sharp*'] II. f. *scarification*, LCD.
scearpecged '*sharp-edged*,' Æ.
scearpian *to score, scarify*, LCD.
scearplic *sharp, severe, effectual.* adv. -līce '*sharply*,' *acutely, keenly*, CP : *painfully, severely, OET,W* : *effectually*, CM192 : *attentively, Bf* : *quickly*, WW.
scearpnes f. '*sharpness*,' *acuteness, keen observation, Bo,Cp,CP*; Æ : *tartness, pungency, acidity, Lcd,W*; Æ : *effrontery*, GD : *efficacy.*
scearpnumol *effective*, LCD.
scearpsīene *keen-sighted*, Bo72,73.
scearpsmēawung f. *argument*, G.
scearpðanc(ful)līce adv. *efficaciously*, Sc.
scearpðancol *quick-witted, keen*, LCD3·440'.
scearpung f. *scarifying*, LCD.
scēarra fpl. *shears, scissors, CP,Gl,LL.* ['*shear*']
scearseax (e, i, ie, y) n. *razor*, CP.

scearu I. (a, æ, y) f. *shearing, shaving, tonsure,* Æ. II. (a) f. *'share'-bone, groin,* Lcd,WW.

scearwund? *wounded in the groin,* LL6, 63.

scēat I. m. *corner, angle, edge, point, promontory,* Mdf : *quarter, district, region, surface (of the earth)* : *lap, bosom, fold,* CP : *napkin, sheet, covering, cloak, garment,* CP : *inlet, creek,* BH90²⁷. [*Ger. schoss*] II. pret. 3 sg. of scēotan.

scēata m. *angle, corner,* AO : *bosom, lap, lower part of a sail* : *napkin.* [*Ger.* schote]

scēatcod m. *wallet,* WW107⁵. [codd]

sceatlīne f. *sheet by which a sail is trimmed to the wind,* WW288²⁴.

sceatt (æ,.e) m. *property, treasure, coin, money, wealth,* LL : *payment, price, tribute, bribe, reward,* Æ : *rent, mortgage-money : money of account, denarius, twentieth part of a shilling* (Kent), v. LL2·634. ['*sceat*']

sceatwyrpan *to make the payment to the bridegroom on which the bride passes into his power from that of the father,* WW386¹ (v. ES42·170).

scēað (æ, ē) f. *'sheath,'* Æ,*Gen,JnL* (ēæ) : *spike, nail,* JnL20²⁵? [cp. hornscēað]

sceaða (a) m. *injurious person, criminal, thief, assassin, B Mt;* Æ : (†) *warrior, antagonist : fiend, devil : injury,* Gen549. ['*scathe*']

sceaðan=sceððan

sceaðe f. *injury,* VH19.

socaðel f. *shuttle? weaver's slay?* LL455,15,1 (v. ANS115,165).

sceaðenes=sceðnes

sceaðful *hurtful,* GD209. ['*scatheful*']

±sceaðian *to injure, spoil, steal,* Æ.

sceaðig (æ) *injurious,* ÆGr63¹⁵.

sceaððignes f. *injury, harm,* Wyn35.

sceaðung f. *injury, damage,* TC138¹⁸,VH.

scēawendspræc f. *buffoonery,* WW533⁴.

scēawendwīse f. *buffoon's song,* Rd9⁹.

scēawere m. *spectator, observer, watchman, spy, B;* Æ,CP : *mirror, NC.* ['*shower*']

±scēawian *to look, gaze, see, behold, observe, B;* Æ,AO,CP : *inspect, examine, scrutinize, Chr,Lk;* Æ,AO,CP : *have respect to, look favourably on,* Æ : *look out, look for, choose,* Æ : *decree, grant, exhibit, display,* Gen. ['*show*']

scēawigend m? *spectator,* OEG,AA2¹⁴.

scēawung (ā) f. *seeing, surveying, inspection, scrutiny, examination, contemplation,* AO, CP : *respect, regard : show, spectacle, appearance, Bl,MkL : toll on exposure of goods.* ['*showing*']

scēawungstōw f. *place of observation,* Æ (1·210).

sceb=sceabb; **scēb**=scēaf; **scec**=scæc

scecel=sceacel; **sced**=scead

scēd pret. 3 sg. of scēadan.

scef-=sceaf-, scyf-

scegð (æ, ei) mf. *vessel, ship,* Chr,MH (v. WC137n). [*ON.* skeið]

scegōmann (æ) m. *sailor, pirate, viking,* Æ.

scehð=scegð; **scelŏ-**=scegŏ-

scel=(1) sceal; (2) sciell

sceld=(1) scield; (2) scyld I.

sceld-=scild-, scyld-; **scele**=scelle

scelēge (Gl)=sceolhēge

scelfan³ (=ie) *to totter, shake,* LL. [*ON.* skialfa]

scelfor=scealfor

scell I.=sceal. II.=sciell

scelle (=ie) *cutting off, separation* Cp777c: *discretion* RWH145⁴ (v. FM100).

scemel=scamol; **scēnan**=scænan

scenc (æ) m. (±) *drink, draught,* Lcd,MtL : *cup,* CM959. ['*shench*']

±scencan (æ) *to pour out, give drink, B,LPs, Sc;* Æ,CP. ['*shench*']

scencingcuppe f. *jug,* TC536⁷.

scendan I. (±, i, ie, y) *to put to shame, confound, discomfit, AO,VPs;* CP : *blame,* CP : *corrupt, injure, Cr,DR : disgrace, insult.* ['*shend*'] II.=scyndan I.

scendle f. *reproach,* LkLR11⁸.

+scendnes (æ, e, ea, i, y) f. *shame, confusion,* Æ,Ps. ['*shendness*']

+scendŏ f. *confusion,* VPs108²⁹.

scendung f. *reproach, affliction,* DR,LkL.

scēne=scīene; **scēnfeld**=scīnfeld

scennum dp. of sb. *pommel of sword-hilt? plate of metal on pommel?* B1694.

+scento, +scendŏo (VPs) f. *shame, confusion.*

scēo I. *cloud?* Rd4⁴¹. II.=scēoh, scōh

sceo-; scēo-=scọ-, scu-; scō-, scū-

scēoc pret. 3 sg. of sceacan.

scēod I.=scōd pret. 3 sg. of sceŏðan. II. pp. of scōgan.

scēofan=scūfan; **scēogan** (CP)=scōgan

scēoh I. *'shy,' timid,* Rim43. II.=scōh

scēohmōd *timid,* Jul672.

sceol (*sceolh) *squinting, awry,* WW. [*Ger.* scheel]

sceolan=sculan; **sceoldan**=scieldan

sceolh-ēge, -ē(a)gede (y) *squinting,* Æ.

sceolu=scolu; **sceom-**=scam-

scēon (±) I.† *to fall (to), occur, happen : go quickly, fly.* II.=scōgan

scēon-=scīen-

scēona gp. of scēoh.

sceonc=scanc-; **sceond**=scand

sceop=scop

scēop pret. 3 sg. of scieppan.

sceoppa m. *booth,* Lk21¹. ['*shop*']

sceoppend=scieppend
sceopu nap. of scip.
scēor=scūr; sceoran=scieran
sceorf (u, y) n. '*scurf*,' *BH* : *a skin disease*,
  Lcd : (+) *irritation of the stomach*, Lcd.
sceorfan³ *to scarify, gnaw*, AO : (+) *scrape*,
  shred.
sceorfe(n)de (u¹) *rough, scabby*, Lcd 56a,
  65b.
sceorian=scorian
sceorp (o) n. *ornament, clothing*, AO : *equipment, fittings (for a ship?)*, LL 444,1.
±sceorpan³ *to scrape, gnaw*, Lcd.
sceort=scort
scēos gs., nap. of scēoh, scōh.
sceot=scot
±scēot *ready, quick*, RB 97¹⁶.
sceota m. '*shoat*,' *trout*, WW 94.
±scēotan² *to* 'SHOOT,' *hurl missiles, cast,
  Æ : strike, hit, push, thrust, AO : run, rush,
  dart, press forward, Æ : contribute, pay :
  refer to, appeal to, Æ : allot, assign : befall,
  fall to, happen*, CHRD.
scēotend† m. *bowman, warrior*.
sceoton=scuton pret. pl. of scēotan.
sceoða=sceaða
scep=scyp I.; scep-=sciep-
+scep=+sceap; scēp (*VPs*)=scēap
scepen I. pp. of scieppan.   II.=scipen.
  III. (N)=scieppend
sceppe f. *a dry measure*, NC 319.   [*ON.*
  skeppa]
sceptlōh, sceptōg (GL)=sceaftlō
scer=scear; scer-=scear-, scier-, scir-
scerero (OET)=scēarra
scer(n)icge (=ie) f. *actress, female jester*, A,
  MH,RD (sciren-).
+scert (OEG 130)=scyrt, pp. of scyrtan.
sceruru=scēarra
-scerwen v. ealu-s, medu-s.
scēt=scēat pret. 3 sg. of scēotan.
scēte=scȳte; scetel (KGL)=scyttel
scett=sceatt; scēð=(1) scēað; (2) scegð
scēððǣd (æ) f. *injurious deed, crime*, WW.
sceð-nes, -enes f. *hurt, injury*, BH.
±scēððan⁶ and wv. (ea, y) *to scathe, injure,
  hurt, crush, oppress, disturb*. [sceaða]
scēððend† m. *adversary*, DR.
+scēððendlic *hurtful*, DR 118¹⁶.
scēððu f. *hurt, injury*, Lcd 1·342'.
scēowrǣc *hurtful, wicked*, BL 161³³.
sceu-, scēu-=scu-, scū-
scēwyrhta=sceowyrhta
scīa m. *shin, leg*, GL.
sciccels, sciccel (y) m. *coat, mantle, cloak*,
  Æ.
sciccing m. *mantle, cloak, cape*, GL.
scīd n. *thin slip of wood, shingle, billet*, Gl.
  ['*shide*']

scīdhrēac m. *rick or heap of firewood*, EC
  351¹⁰.
scīdweall m. *wooden palings*, WW 146²⁸
+scīe=+scȳ
-scīelan (ȳ) v. be-s.
scield (e, i, y) m. '*shield*,' *B,VPs* : *protector,
  Bl,Ph* : (±) *protection, defence*, AO,CP :
  part of a bird's plumage? PH 308.
scield- v. also scild-.
±scieldan (i, eo, y) *to protect*, '*shield*'
  ('*i-shield*'), *guard, defend, defend oneself*,
  Æ,B,Bl,Bo,Lcd,VPs; AO,CP.   +scieldod
  furnished with shields, Bl.
sciele (CP) pres. sg. subj. of sculan.
sciell I. f. '*shell*,' *Cp,MH,OEG* : *shell-fish* :
  scale, Æ,AO,CP. [scalu]   II. (y) *sonorous,
  shrill*, *Rim* 27.   ['*shill*']
sciellfisc (i, y) m. '*shell-fish*,' *Bo*.
-sciellig (y) v. stān-s.
scielliht (e) *having a shell*, Lcd.
sciendan=scendan
sciene (ē, ēo, ī, ȳ) *beautiful, B,Cr,Gen,Pa,
  Ph* : *bright, brilliant, light, Cr.*   ['*sheen*']
scīenes (ēo, ī, ȳ) f. *suggestion, instigation*,
  CP.   [scȳan]
scienn=scinn, scīn
scienð pres. 3 sg. of scīnan.
±scieppan⁶ (e, i, y) *to create, form*, '*shape*'
  ('*i-shape*'), *make*, Gen : *order, destine,
  arrange, adjudge, assign, B,Wy*; AO.
±Scieppend (y) m. *Creator, B*; CP.   ['*shep-
  pend*']
±scieran⁴ (æ, e, eo, i) *to cleave, hew, cut, An,
  B* : *cut hair, Æ,CP* : *receive tonsure, Guth* :
  '*shear*' *sheep, BC.* pp. scoren *abrupt*,
  CP 215⁸.
scierden (e) adj. *of sherds*, GPH 400. [sceard]
sciering (e) f. *shearing, shaving*, CM 610.
±scierpan (e, y) I. *to deck, clothe, equip*, ÆL.
  [sceorp] II. *to sharpen, LL,VPs* : *rouse,
  invigorate, strengthen*.   +scierpt *acute
  (accent)*, BF 184¹.   ['*sharp*']
+scierpla (i, y) *clothing, garments*, An,
  BL.
+scierpiendlīce (y¹) *fittingly*, BHB 324⁴.
scierseax=scearseax
scīet pres. 3 sg. of scēotan.
scīete (ē, ī, ȳ) f. *cloth, towel, shroud, Æ,BH,
  Cp,Mk,WW.*   ['*sheet*']
scīfe=scyfe
±scīftan (y) *to divide, distribute, allot,
  appoint, LL* : *place, order, arrange, LL,W.*
  ['*shift*']
scilbrung=scylfrung
scild=scield; scild-=scyld-
scildburh† (e, y) f. *shield-wall, phalanx* :
  roof of shields, testudo : *place of refuge*,
  SAT 309.
scilden f. *protection*, WW 52¹⁷.

±scild-end, -ere (ie, y) m. *protector, defender*, Ps.

scildfreca (y¹) m. *warrior*, B1033.

scildhete m. *foe*, An85. [scyld]

scildhrēoða (y¹, e², ea²) m. *shield, buckler* : *testudo, phalanx.*

±scildnes (ie) f. *defence, protection*, CP.

scildtruma (y¹) m. *testudo, phalanx, company (of troops)*, Æ,OEG. ['sheltron']

scildung (y¹) f. *protection*, Æ,DR.

scildweall (y¹) m. *wall of shields*, B3118.

scildwiga (y¹) m. *warrior*, B288.

scildwyrhta (y¹) m. *shield-maker*, Ct,LL.

scile (CP) pres. subj. of sculan.

scilfix=scielfisc

scilfor *yellow, golden*, OEG.

scill=sciell

scilling (y) m. *'shilling' (consisting of a varying number of pence), silver coin*, Æ, G,LL (v. 2·640),*WW.*

scillingrīm n. *count of shillings*, Wid92.

scīma m. *ray, light, brightness, effulgence, splendour*, CP : *twilight, gloom.* [scīnan]

scimerian (y) *to 'shimmer', glisten, shine*, NC319; OEG23⁵¹.

scīmian *to shine, glisten*, ÆGr,LkL : *grow dusky, dim, be dazzled, bleared*, Æ. ['shim']

scīn=scinn

scīnan¹ (ȳ) *to* 'SHINE,' *flash*, Æ,CP : *be resplendent* : (+) *shine upon, illuminate.*

scinbān n. *'shin-bone,' WW.*

scinccing (OET p. 26)=sciccing

+scincio np. *the fat about the kidneys*, Lcd.

scind-=sccnd-

scindel m. *a shingle*, KC6·33'.

scīndlāc=scinlāc

scīnefrian *to glitter*, WW348¹⁹.

scīnelāc=scinnlāc

scīnende (ȳ) *'shining,' MH,WW* : *eminent, distinguished, BH.*

scīnendlic *shining*, LPs18⁹.

scīnfeld (ēa) m. *Elysian fields, Tempe.*

scinhosu f. *greave*, OEG.

scinn I. n., scinna m. *spectre, illusion, phantom, evil spirit*, CP : *magical image*, ÆL36⁴⁰⁴. II. n. *skin*, Chr1075,WW 427²⁷?

scinncræft (y) m. *sorcery, magic*, AO.

scinncræftiga m.*sorcerer*,GD27¹⁵; LL248,7.

scinnere m. *magician*, Gl.

scīnnes I. f. *radiance*, MkL13²⁴. II.= scīenes

scinngedwola m. *phantom*, WW455¹¹.

scinngelāc n. *jugglery, magical practices*, An767.

scinnhīw n. *spectre, illusion, phantasm*, Æ.

scinnlāc I. n. *sorcery, magic* : *apparition, spectre, delusion, superstition* : *frenzy, rage*, AO. II.=scinnlǣce I.

scinnlǣca (ā²) m. *wizard, magician*, AO.

scinnlǣce I. *magical, spectral*, AO. II. f. *sorceress, witch.*

scinnlic (y) *spectral*, NC320.

scinnsēoc *spectre-haunted*, Lcd1·364⁴.

scīnu (y) f. *'shin,' WW.*

scip (y) n. *'ship,' BH,Bo,Chr,Cp*; AO,CP.

scīp=scēap

scipāc f. *oak for shipbuilding*, KC.

scipbroc n. *hardship on ship-board*, Bl173⁶.

scipbrucol (y) *destructive to shipping*, GPH 401⁹.

scipbryce m. *right to claim wreckage*, KC 4·208. ['shipbreche']

scipbȳme (y) f. *ship's trumpet*, GPH391.

scipcræft m. *naval force*, Chr1048d.

scipdrincende *shipwrecked*, DR61¹⁶.

scipe I. m. *pay, wage, WW*; ÆL31⁵⁵ : *position, rank.* ['shipe'] II. (+) n. *fate*, B2570?

scipehere=sciphere

scipen (e, y) f. '*scippon,' stall, cattle-shed*, BH,LL.

scipere (y) m. *shipman, sailor*, Chr. ['shipper']

scipfǣreld n. *voyage*, Æ,GD273¹⁸.

scipfǣt n. *a vessel in the form of a ship*, WW124⁸.

scipfarend (y) m. *sailor*, BH(Sch)261²

scipfērend m. *sailor*, An250.

scipfierd f. *naval expedition, fleet*, AO.

scipflota m. *sailor, pirate*, Chr937a.

scipforðung f. *equipment of ships*, LL314'.

scipfultum m. *naval aid*, Chr1049c.

scipfylleð *private jurisdiction exercised over a group of three hundreds*, KC6·240 (v.BT).

scipfyrd=scipfierd

scipfyrdung f. *fleet, naval expedition*, Chr, LL.

scipfyrð(r)ung f. *equipment of ships*, LL.

scipgebroc n. *shipwreck*, AO,CP.

scipgefeoht (y) n. *naval battle*, GPH389.

scipgefēre n. *sailing*, BH150².

scipgetāwu f. *tackling of a ship*, WW181²⁴.

scipgyld n. *ship-tax, ship-money*, TC307²⁴.

sciphamor m. *hammer for giving a signal to rowers*, WW.

sciphere m. *naval force, fleet (usu. hostile), squadron*, AO,Chr : *crew of a warship.*

scipherelic *naval*, HGl406⁴⁰.

sciphlǣder f. *ship's ladder*, WW.

sciphlǣst (y) m. *ship-load, crew*, AO,CP : *ship of burden.*

sciphlāford m. *ship-master, skipper*, WW 181²¹.

sciplan *to take 'ship,' embark* : (±) *man or equip a ship*, Chr.

scipincel n. *little ship*, WW.

scipplǎd (y) f. *journeying by sea*, BH198²⁹.

sciplæst=sciphlæst
sciplic *naval*, GL,HL 199¹²⁷.
sciplið n. *naval force*, CHR 1055 C.
sciplīðend m. *seaman* : *voyager*, ÆL 33¹⁸⁸.
sciplīðende ptc. *sailing*, WW.
scipmǣrls m. *ship's rope, cable*, WW.
scipmann (y) m. *'shipman,' sailor, rower,* BH,*Chr* : *one who goes on trading voyages.*
scipp-=sciepp-
sciprāp m. *ship's rope, cable*, AO.
sciprēōra (y¹) m. *rower, sailor*, GPH.
sciprōðor n. *ship's oar or rudder*, WW 455¹⁸.
sciprōwend m. *rower, sailor*, WW 455¹⁴.
scipryne m. *passage for ships,* TC 341¹⁶.
scipsetl n. *bench for rowers*, WW.
scipsōcn f. (KC 6·240') i.q. scipfylleð.
scipsteall (y) m. *place for ships*, BC 3·316¹⁶.
scipstēora m. *steerman, pilot*, CP.
scipsteorra m. *pole-star*, LCD 3·270'.
scip-stīera, -stȳra=scipstēora
scip-tearo, -ter, n., gs. -tearos; scip-t(e)ara, -te(o)ra m. (*ship-tar*), *bitumen, pitch*, LCD.
sciptoll n. *passage money*, ÆL 30¹⁶⁷.
scipwealh m. *servant whose service is connected with ships?* (BT) ; *one liable to serve in the fleet?* (Swt), EC 376¹⁵.
scipweard m. *ship-master*, AN 297.
scipwered n. *crew*, WW 451¹⁷.
scipwīsan (on) adv. *like a ship*, AA,Æ.
scipwrǣc *jetsam*, KC 4·146.
scipwyrhta m. *'shipwright,'* WW 112⁵.
scīr I. (ȳ) f. *office, appointment, charge, authority, supremacy*, AO,*Cp*,LL (+ at DR 187⁹) ; CP : *district, diocese, see, province, 'shire,' parish*, AO,*Gl*,LL ; Æ : *tribe.* II. adj. *bright, gleaming, shining, resplendent*, B, *Bo* : *clear, translucent, Cr,* WW : *pure, unmixed*, B,*Bo* : *white*, Jn 4³⁵. [*'shire'*]
sciran=scieran
scīran (ȳ) *to make clear, say, tell, declare*, B, CP : *arrange, determine, decide, decree, act in authority*, CP, (+) LkL 16² : (±) *clear from, get rid of*, AO,CP.
scīrbasu *bright purple*, WW 193¹².
scīrbisceop m. *bishop of a diocese*, WW 173³⁰.
scīre I. adv. *brightly*, *An* : *clearly* : *mightily*, *Cr* 1142. [*'shire'*] II. *'peribolum,' enclosure, curtilage*, WW 184²².
scīre-=scīr-
scīrecg *keen-edged*, LCD 1·390⁷.
scīrenicge (RD 9⁹)=scernicge
scīresmann=scīrmann
scīrfemūs (=ie) f. *shrew* (*mouse*), WW 477¹⁶. [sceorfan]
scīrgemōt n. *shire-moot*, LL,TC.
scīrgerēfa m. *'sheriff,'* KC.

scīrgesceat (ȳ) n. *property of a see*, KC 3·327².
scīrham *clad in bright mail*, B 1895.
±scīrian (e, y) *to ordain, appoint* : *allot, assign, grant* : (+) *mark off, count, reckon.*
scīriendlic (y) *derivative*, WW 222²³.
scīrigmann=scīrmann
scīrlett n. *piece or measure of land*, EC 239⁹.
scīrmǣled *brightly adorned*, JUD 230.
scīrmann (ȳ) m. *governor of a shire, prefect, sheriff, steward, procurator, official, KC* ; Æ,CP ; v. LL 2·649 : *inhabitant of a district, Æ.* [*'shireman'*]
scīrnes f. *elucidation*, WW 279²³.
scīrp-=scierp- ; scīrseax=scearseax
scīrðegen m. *thane of a shire*, BC 1·544⁸.
scīrung f. *separation, rejection*, RB 109²¹.
scīr-wæter (scyr-) n. *water forming a boundary*, CHR 656 E. [scieran]
scīrwered *bright?* Gu 1262.
scīrwita m. *chief man of a shire*, W. -scītan¹ v. be-sc.
scīte=scȳte ; scītefinger=scytefinger
scitol *purgative*, LCD 66a.
scitte f. *purging, Lcd.* [*'shit'*]
scittels (Æ)=scyttels
scl-(GL)=sl-
scmēgende (VPs)=smēagende pres. ptc. of smēagan.
scnīcend (GL)=snīcend pres. ptc. of snīcan.
scō=scōh ; sco-=sceo-
scōas=scōs v. scōh ; scobl=scofl
scōc pret. 3 sg. of sceacan.
scocca=scucca
scocha (=scohha) *'lenocinium,'* Ep 579.
scōcnyll m. *signal for putting on shoes*, ANS 84·10.
scōd I. pret. 3 sg. of sceððan. II. v. scōgan.
scōere m. *shoemaker, Gl.* [*'shoer'*]
scōf pret. 3 sg. of sceafan.
scofen pp. of scufan.
scofettan *to drive hither and thither*, CP 169¹³.
scofl f. *'shovel,' Cp,Ep*,LL.
scōgan pp. sc(ē)od *to 'shoe,'* Æ,CP.
scōh, scō, scēo m. gs. nap. sc(ē)os, gp. sc(ē)one, dp. sc(ē)on, scōum *'shoe,' Bf,G, Mt,WW.*
scōhere=scōere
scōhnægl m. *shoe-nail*, WW.
scōhðēn (ēo) m. *shoe-cleaner*, RBL 91⁹.
scōh-ðwang, -ðong m. *'shoe-thong,' boot-lace, Jn.*
scōhwyrhta (ēo, ēoh) m. *shoemaker, leather-worker*, GD 322,WW 97⁵.
scōian=scōgan
scōl f. *'school,'* Æ,BH,*Lcd* ; AO.
+scola I. m. *debtor*, WW 15²⁸. [sceal] II. *companion*, OEG 2271n. [scolu]

+scōla m. *fellow-student*, OEG 2271.
scolde pret. 3 sg. of sculan.
scōlere m. '*scholar*,' *learner*, Bf,LL.
scolh (WW 241¹³)=seolh
scōliere (Bf 54²⁷)=scōlere
scōlmann m. *scholar*, WW 314²⁹ : *client*, 163⁴⁴.
scolu I. (eo) f. *troop, host, multitude* : *shoal* (*of fishes*), A 13·418. II.=scōl
scom-=scam-
scōmhylte (scomm-?) n. *brushwood, copse, thicket*, WW 411³.
scōmlic *short*, MH 98¹³.
scōn=scēon v. scēoh; scon-=scan-
scop (eo) m. *singer, poet, B,Bo*; AO. ['*scop*']
scōp pret. 3 sg. of scieppan.
scopcræft m. *poetry*, ÆGr 215⁹.
scopgereord (eo¹) n. *poetical language*, BH.
scoplēoð n. *poem*, AO.
scoplic *poetic*, OEG 119.
scora m. *hairy garment*, WW 278¹.
scoren pp. of scieran.
scorian (eo) I. *to refuse*, Æ. II. *to jut out*, GD 213⁵.
scorp=sceorp
scort (eo, y) '*short*,' *not long, not tall, Bo, GD,Lcd* : *brief, Æ,Bf,Bl,Bo,CP*.
scortian (eo) *to become* '*short*,' *shorten*, Lcd : (±) *run short, fail*.
scortlic (eo) *brief*, Sc 214¹⁶. adv. -līce '*shortly*,' *briefly, soon, AO,LPs,ZDA* ; Æ.
scortnes (eo) f. '*shortness*,' *small amount* : *summary, abstract*, ÆGr : *short space of time*.
scortwyrplic (eo) *shortly coming to pass*, Lcd 3·156⁹.
scoru a '*score*,' NC 320. [scoren; scieran]
scōs gs. of scōh.
±scot (eo) n. '*shot*,' *shooting*, OEG; AO : *darting, rapid motion, Men* : *what is shot forth, AO,CP* : (+) *scot, payment* : *private apartment, sanctum, chancel*, Æ.
+scota m. *fellow-soldier*, WW 15,207.
scoten pp. of scēotan.
+scotfeoht n. *shooting, battle*, PPs.
scotfrēo *scot-free, free of tribute*, KC.
±scotian (eo) (tr. and intr.) *to move rapidly, shoot, hurl a javelin*, Æ.
scotlīra m. *calf of the leg*, Lcd.
scotspere n. *dart, javelin*, HGL 405.
Scottas mpl. *the Scots, BH,Chr; Æ,CP*. ['*Scot*']
scotung (eo) f. *missile* : *shooting* : *darting, flashing*, Lcd 3·280'.
scōum v. scōh.
scōung f. *provision of shoes*, LL 450,10.
-scrād v. scrīðend-s.
scrādung=scrēadung
scræb m. *cormorant? ibis?* Cp 1311.

±scræf (ea, e) n. [obl. cases occly. have scraf-] *cave, cavern, hole, pit, Æ,CP* : *hovel, Æ* : *den*, MtR 21¹³.
+scrǣpe=+scrēpe
scrætte f. *adulteress, prostitute*, Gl. [*L.* scratta]
scrǣwa=scrēawa
scrāf pret. 3 sg. of scrīfan.
scraf- v. scræf.
scrallettan† intr. *to sound loudly*.
scranc pret. 3 sg. of scrincan.
scrapian *to scrape, IM.* ['*shrape*']
scrāð pret. 3 sg. of scrīðan.
scrēad(e) f. '*shred*,' *cutting, scrap*, WW.
±scrēadian *to* '*shred*,' *peel, prune, cut off, Æ*.
scrēadung (ā) f. *shred, cutting, fragment, MtL* : *pruning, trimming*, WW. ['*shredding*']
scrēadungīsen n. *pruning-knife*, WW. [v. '*shredding*']
scrēaf=scræf
scrēawa m. '*shrew*' (*mouse*), Gl.
screb=scræb; scrēc=scrīc
scref=scræf
scremman *to cause to stumble*, Lev 19¹⁴.
±screncan *to cause to stumble, ensnare, deceive, CP,Ps* : (+) *cause to shrink or shrivel, MtL* 13⁶. ['*shrench*']
+scrence *withered, dry*, LkL 6⁸.
+screncednes f. *tripping up*, CVPs 40¹⁰.
screodu v. scrid; +scrēope=+scrēpe
screopu=screpu
screpan⁵ (i,y) *to scrape, scratch, Cp,Lcd, MkR* : *prepare*, LF 47'. ['*screpe*']
scrēpan *to become dry, withered*, MkR 9¹⁸.
scrēpe (ǣ, ēo) I. n. (+) *advantage*. II. (±) *suitable, adapted, fit*. adv. -līce.
+scrēpnes (oe) f. *convenience*, Cp 568.
screpu (eo) f. *strigil, curry-comb*, Gl.
scrēwa=scrēawa; scrīban (Gl)=scrīfan
scrīc (ē, ū) *shrike, missel-thrush?* Gl.
scrid I. n. nap. screodu *vehicle, chariot, litter*. II. *quick, fleet*, An 496.
scrīdan=scrȳdan
scride m. *course, orbit*, Met 28¹¹.
scridon pret. pl. of scrīðan.
scridwǣn m. *chariot* : *curule chair*, Bo.
scridwīsa m. *charioteer*, WW 150¹⁴.
+scrif n. *judgment, edict*, WW : *ceremony*, WW.
±scrīfan¹ *prescribe, ordain, allot, assign, impose* (*punishment*), LL; Æ : *hear confession*, '*shrive*,' LL : *receive absolution* : *have regard to, be troubled about, care for*, CP.
scrifen ptc? *painted?* Rim 13.
scrift m. *prescribed penalty or penance*, LL : *absolution*, LL : *confessor, CP,Cr*; Æ : *judge*. tō scrifte gān *to go to confession*, LL,W. ['*shrift*']

scriftbōc f. *book of penances, or on penance,* LL,W.

scriftscīr f. *confessor's area of jurisdiction* : *diocese,* LL164,26.

scriftsprǣc f. *confession,* LL.

scrimman[3] *to shrink,* Lcd2b. ['shrim']

scrīn (ȳ) n. *chest, coffer, ark,* Æ,*Jn* :'*shrine,*' Æ : *cage (for criminals).* [*L.* scrinium]

±scrincan[3] *to 'shrink,' contract, shrivel up, wither, pine away,* Æ,AO,Lcd.

scrind f. *swift course?* PPs103²⁴.

scringan=scrincan; **-scripel** (y) v. ēar-s.

scrīpen, scrīpende '*austerus,*' LkLR19²¹.

scripeð (*Cp*) pres. 3 sg. of screpan.

scritta m. *hermaphrodite,* WW161¹¹. (v. FTp473).

scrið (v. OEG2185)=scrid I.

scrīðan[1] *to go, move, glide,* B,Gu. ['scrithe']

scrīðe m. *course,* MET28¹¹.

-scrīðol v. wīd-s.; **scroepe,** scrōpe=scrēpe

scrofel n? *scrofula,* Lcd182a.

scrūc=scrīc

scrūd n., ds. scrȳd *clothing, dress* : *garment, vestment,* Æ,Chr,WW. ['shroud']

scrūd-=scrūt-

scrūdelshūs n. *sacristy, vestry,* ANS84¹⁵. [scrȳdan]

scrūdfeoh n.*money for buying clothes,* NC320.

scrūdfultum m. *grant towards providing clothes,* Ct.

scrūdland n. *land bequeathed as provision for clothing,* TC329¹⁹.

scrūdwaru f. *garb,* LL.

scruf [*Lcd*]=sceorf

scruncon pret. pl. of scrincan.

scrūtnere (ūd) m. *examiner,* CHRD88³³.

scrūtnian (ūd) *to examine, scrutinize, consider,* Æ.

scrūtnung (ūd) f. *search, investigation,* Lcd, ERPs.

scrybb d. *scrub, brushwood,* TC525²².

scrȳd v. scrūd.

±scrȳdan (ī) *to clothe, dress,* Æ,Bl,Lk,Mt. ['shride']

scryft=scrift

scrynce *withered,* JnL5³.

scrypan=screpan

scua m. *shadow, shade, darkness* : *protection.*

scucca (eo) m. *sprite, evil spirit, demon,* B, Bo,Mt : *the devil.* ['shuck']

scuccen (eo) *devilish,* NC319.

scuccgyld (eu¹) n. *idol,* PPs105²⁶.

scūdan[2] *to run, hurry?* Gu828.

scūfan[2] (ēo) *to 'SHOVE*,' thrust, push,* Æ : *push with violence, urge, impel,* CP : *push out, expel, deliver up* : (†) *display* : (intr.) *to move, go.*

sculan anv. pres. 1 sing. sce(a)l(l), scal, pl. sculon (eo), pret. sc(e)olde, sc(e)alde *to be*

obliged ('SHALL*,' *have to, must, must needs, am bound to, ought to),* Æ,AO,CP : *owe.*

scul-dor, -dra m., nap. -dru, -dra, +scyldru, -dre '*shoulder,*' Bl,Ep,Lcd,LG.

sculdorhrægl n. *cape,* WW327²⁴.

sculdorwærc m. *pain in the shoulders,* LCD.

sculdur=sculdor

scule pres. subj. of sculan.

sculthēta (WW)=scyldlǣta

±scunian (y) *to 'shun,' avoid,* Guth : *be afraid,* DR : (tr.) *abhor,* TC.

scunung f. *abomination,* LHy6²³ (? for on-s.).

scūr (ēo) m. (f) '*shower,' storm, tempest, trouble, commotion, breeze,* An,LkR,Ps; CP : †*shower of blows or missiles,* El,Jud 79.

scūra† m. *shower (of rain).*

scūrbeorg f. *roof,* RUIN5.

scūrboga m. *rainbow,* GEN1540.

±scurf=sceorf

scūrfāh *rainy, stormy,* A9·369; MFH172.

scūrheard† *made hard by blows (epithet of a sword).*

scūrsceadu f. *protection against storms,* GEN 813.

scutel I. m. *dish, platter,* WW280²². ['scuttle'] II.=scytel

scuton pret. pl. of scēotan.

scuwa=scua

+scȳ npl. *pair of shoes,* Æ,Ps.

scȳan? scȳn? *to suggest, persuade, prompt, incite, tempt,* BH,MtR.

scyccel, scyccels=sciccels

scydd m. *twist on a hill-side?* (Earle): *alluvial ground?* (BT),KC.

scȳde pret. 3 sg. of scēon and scȳan, scȳn.

scyfe (e, i) m. *shove, pushing, precipitation, furtherance, instigation,* CP. tō +sc. *headlong.*

scyfel(e) f. *woman's hood, head-dress,* GL.

scȳft pres. 3 sg. of scūfan.

scyftan=sciftan

+scȳgean *to furnish with shoes,* TC616'.

scyhhan (ES43·318)=scyn I.

scyhtan *to impel, prompt, urge,* GEN898; Gu98.

scyl=sciell

scylcen f. *female servant, slave, concubine,* ÆH2·162'. [scealc]

±scyld I. (e) fm. *offence, fault, crime, guilt, sin,* CP : *obligation, liability, due, debt,* CP. [sculan; *Ger.* schuld] II.=scield

scyld-=scield-, scild-

+scyldan *to accuse,* LL156,11.

scyldfrecu f. *wicked craving,* GEN898.

scyldful *sinful, guilty,* Æ.

scyldg-=scyldig-

scyld-hata, -hete† m. *enemy.*

scyldian=(1) scyldigian; (2) scyldan

scyldig (e, i) (usu. w. g.) *guilty, criminal, sinful, Æ,B*; CP : *liable, responsible, in debt to,* CP. ealdres sc. *having forfeited his life.* [' *shildy* ']

scyldigian *to sin* : (+) *place in the position of a criminal, render liable to punishment.*

scyldignes f. *guilt,* DR 42,103.

scyldigung f. *sum demanded as* 'wergeld,' LL 156,11.

scyld-læta [-hæta? cp. sculthēta] m. *bailiff,* WW 230²⁰.

scyldlēas *guiltless,* LCD.

scyldo=scyld I.

+**scyldru** v. sculdor; **scyldu**=scyld I.

scyldung=(1) scildung; (2) scyldigung

scyldwīte n. *fine for a crime of violence,* LL 567,38.

scyldwreccende ptc. *avenging sin,* CR 1161.

scyldwyrcende† *evil-doing.*

scyle pres. subj. of sculan.

scylēagede=sceolhēgede

scylf m. *crag, ledge, shelf,* Mdf : *pinnacle, turret, tower,* Æ.

-**scylfan** v. ā-s.

scylfe m. *shelf, floor,* GEN 1306.

scylfig *rocky,* OEG (scylp-).

scylfisc=sciellfisc; **scylfor**=scilfor

scylfrung (i) f. *shaking, swinging?* BL 99³⁴; WW 516¹⁶ (-brong).

scylfð pres. 3 sg. of scelfan.

scylga=scealga

scylian (=ie) *to separate, part, divide off.* sc. of male *to pay off, discharge,* Chr 1049. [' *shill* ']

scyll=sciell

scyllan (=ie) *to resound, sound loudly,* WW; OEG 4890. [' *shill* ']

scylling=scilling; **scylp**=scylf

scyltumend m. *helper,* PPs 27⁸.

scylun (N)=sculon pres. pl. of sculan.

scymrian=scimerian

scȳn I. *to* ' *shy*,' ÆL 31⁹⁷¹. II. v. scȳan.

scȳn-=scīn-, scinn-

±**scyndan** I. (e) (tr., intr.) *to hurry, hasten, drive forward, impel* : *incite, exhort,* CP. II.=scendan

scyndel m. *disreputable person,* BF 130²².

scyndendlīce adv. *hastily,* WW.

scyndnes f. *persuasion, prompting,* GD.

+**scyndnes**=+scandnes; **scȳne**=scīene

scȳnes, scȳnnes=scīenes

+**scynian** (DR 32⁵)=scunian

scynn n. *skin, fur,* CHR 1075 D. [ON.]

scynu (WW 307²⁷)=scinu

scyp I. m. *patch,* v. ES 43·316. II. (Chr 1048)=scip

scypen=scipen

scypian *to take shape,* LCD 3·146¹⁵.

scypp-=sciepp-

scyr-=scear-, scier-, scir-; **scȳr**=scīr

±**scyrdan** *to harm, injure, destroy,* AN,LL. [sceard]

+**scȳrdan**=+scrȳdan; **scyrf**=sceorf

scyrft *scarifying? scraping?* Cp 130 s.

scyrfð pres. 3 sg. of sceorfan.

scȳrmǣlum adv. *stormily,* Bo 47²⁵. [scūr]

scyrp-=scierp-

±**scyrtan** (e) tr. *to shorten,* AO : intr. *run short, decrease, fail.* [sccort]

scyrte f. *skirt,* GPH 393. [' *shirt* ']

scyrtest superl. of scort.

scyrting f. *shortening, abstract, epitome,* ÆH 2·460⁶.

scyrtra comp. of scort.

scȳt pres. 3 sg. of scēotan.

scyte (ē) m. *shooting, hurling,* AO : *stroke, blow, ZDA* : *dart.* [' *shute* '; scēotan]

scȳte f. (ē;=īe) ' *sheet*,' *linen cloth, BH,Cp, Mk.* [scēat]

scytefinger m. *forefinger,* LL,WW.

scyte-heald, -healden *inclined, sloping, precipitous,* GL.

scytel I. (u) m. *dart, arrow, Erf,Ps* : *tongue of a balance.* [' *shuttle* '] II. (=i) m. *excrement.* [scītan]

scytelfinger=scytefinger; **scytels**=scyttel

scyterǣs m. *headlong rush,* WW 426⁷.

scytere m. *shooter,* KC.

scytheald=scyteheald

scytta m. *shooter, archer,* Æ,AO.

scyttan (usu. for-sc.) *to bolt,* ' *shut* ' *to,* Æ : *discharge, pay off.*

scyttel, scyttels (e, i) m. *bolt, bar, Æ,Bl,W, ZDA.* [' *shuttle* '; scēotan]

Scyttisc I. *Scotch, Irish.* II. *Irish or Scotch language.* [Scottas]

scyðða=sceðða

sē m., sēo f., ðæt n. pers. (dem.) pron. *he, she, it, that, this* : rel. pron. *who, which* : def. art. 'THE*.' II.=sǣ. III.=swā

sēa (OET)=sēaw; **sēad** (NG)=sēod

sēada=sēaða; **seafian** (NG)=seofian

seah pret. 3 sg. of sēon.

seaht=seht I.; **seal**=sealh

sealde pret. 3 sg. of sellan.

±**sealdnes** (a) f. *act of giving,* WW 389³⁵ : *grant, gift,* KC 2·5³².

sēales gs. of sealh.

sealf (a) f. ' *salve*,' *ointment, unguent, medicament, Lcd,Mk*; CP.

sealfbox (e) m. *salve-box,* G,BK.

sealfcynn n. *an unguent,* WW 351³⁰.

sealfe=sealf; **sealfer-**=seolfor-

±**sealfian** *to* ' *salve*,' *anoint, Erf,WW.*

sealfie=salfie

sealf-lǣcnung, -lǣcung (*WW*114¹⁶) f. *curing by unguents, pharmacy.* [v. '*leeching*']

sealh (a) m., gs. sēales *willow, Gl,Lcd,Ps*; Mdf. ['*sallow*']

sealhangra m. *willow-hanger*, KC6·234¹⁷.

sealhrind f. *willow-bark*, LCD.

sealhyrst m. *willow-copse*, KC5·256'.

seallan=sellan

sealm (a, eo) m. '*psalm**,' *song, RB,Ps*; Æ, CP.

sealma (e) m. *bed, couch*, B,GL.

sealmcwide m. *psalm*, LPs97⁵.

sealmfæt n. only in phr. 'on sealmfatum,' '*in vasis psalmorum*'! PPs70²⁰.

sealmgetæl n. *number of psalms*, RB.

sealm-glīg, -glīw n. *psaltery, psalmody*, LRPs.

sealmian *to play an accompaniment on the harp*, Ps107¹. ['*psalm*']

sealmlēoð n. *psalm*, BLPs56⁹.

sealmlof n. *psalm*, LPs.

sealmloflan *to sing psalms*, LPs104².

sealmsang m. *psalm* : *composition or singing of psalms*, Æ : *psaltery*, CPs32² : *one of the canonical hours*, GD.

sealmsangere m. *psalmist*, CHRD112¹².

sealmsangmǣrsung f. *psalm-singing in the canonical hours*, ÆL23b³⁶.

sealmscop (eo²) m. *psalmist*, Æ,CP.

sealmtraht m. *exposition of psalms*, Æ (3²⁹⁷).

sealmwyrhta m. *psalmist*, Æ. ['*psalm-wright*']

sealobrūn=salubrūn

sealt I. n. '*salt*,' *Lcd,MtL*; CP. **II.** adj. *salt, briny*, *Cr*; AO,CP. [v. Mdf]

sealtan⁷ (a) *to* '*salt*,' *Æ,G,IM,Lcd*.

sealtbrōc (a) m. *brook running from salt-works?* KC3·206³⁰.

sealtere I. m. '*salter*,' *salt-worker*, *WW*; Æ. **II.** (CM362,679)=saltere

sealtern n. *salt-works*, BC. ['*saltern*']

sealtfæt n. *salt-cellar*, *LL,WW*. ['*saltfat*']

sealthālgung (a) f. *consecration of salt*, OET 587.

sealtherpað (a) m. *road to salt-works*, KC 3·206'.

sealthūs n. '*salt-house*,' *WW*.

sealtian (a) *to dance*, Lk7³². [*L.* saltare]

sealticge f. *dancer*, MH156¹⁴.

sealting f. *dancing*, CHRD79¹.

sealtlēaf n. '*mozicia*,' WW (?-lēap, NP 7·215).

sealtmere m. *brackish pond*, EC449'.

sealtnes (a) f. '*saltness*,' *VPs*.

sealtrod *track with willows*, KC3·236'.

sealtsæleða (y¹) m. *saltness*, LPs106³⁴; RPs.

sealtsēað m. *saline spring*, BH26²².

sealtstān m. *rock-salt*, *Lcd*1·374¹⁴ : *pillar of salt*, *Gen*; Æ. ['*saltstone*']

sealtstrǣt f. *road to salt-works*, KC.

sealtwīc n. *a place where salt is sold*, KC.

sealtwylle (a) f. *salt spring*, KC,LG. ['*saltwell*']

sealtӯð† f. *salt wave, sea-wave*.

sēam I. (ēo) m. *burden, load, Æ,LkL,LkR* : *bag* : *harness of a beast of burden*, Æ : *duty of furnishing beasts of burden*. ['*seam*'] **II.** m. '*seam*,' *suture, junction, Æ,WW*.

sēamere I. m. *beast of burden, mule*, WW. [*L.* sagmarius] **II.** m. *tailor*, Æ. [sēam II.]

sēamestre f. *sempstress*, (*also of males*) *sewer, tailor, Æ,KC,WW*. ['*seamster*']

sēamhors n. *pack-horse*, WW119⁴².

sēampending m. *toll of a penny a load*, KC.

sēamsadol m. *pack-saddle*, WW119⁴¹.

sēamsticca m. *an appliance used in weaving*, LL455,15¹.

sēap pret. 3 sg. of sūpan.

sēar *dry*, '*sere*,' *barren*, *GPH*402⁶⁹.

seara-, seare-=searo-; **sēargian**=sārgian

sēarian *to become sere, wither*, Shr. ['*sear*']

searo (searu) n. *art, skill, cleverness, cunning* : *device, trick, snare, ambuscade, plot, treachery, Æ,AO,CP* : *work of art, cunning device, engine (of war)* : *armour, war-gear, trappings*.

searobend m. *artistic clasp*, B2086.

searobunden *cunningly fastened*, RD56⁴.

searocǣg f. *insidious key*, GU1118.

searocēap n. *artistic object*, RD33⁷.

searocēne *very bold*, PPs100¹⁰.

searocræft m. *artifice, treachery, wile*, Æ : *artistic skill, art* : *engine, instrument (of torture)*, Æ.

searocræftig† *skilful, cunning*.

searo *fears secret path?* RIM65 (ES65·189).

searofāh *variegated, cunningly inlaid*, B 1444.

searogemme=searogimm

searogimm m. *curious gem*, B,Ps.

searogrim *fierce, formidable*, B594.

searohæbbend† m. *warrior*.

searohwīt n. *brilliant whiteness*, RIM67.

searolic *artistic, ingenious*. adv. -līce.

searomete m. *dainty, delicacy*, NC321.

searonet n. *armour-net, corslet*, B406 : *ensnaring net*, AN64; 945.

searonīð† m. *treachery, strife, battle*, B.

searopīl m. *artistic javelin*, RD87².

searorūn f. *mystery*, CREAT15.

searosǣled *cleverly bound*, RD24¹⁶.

searoðanc m. *sagacity, ingenuity, skill*, CP : *cunning, artifice.*

searoðancol† *shrewd, wise*, JUD.

searowrenc (y¹, a²) m. *artifice, trick*, AO.

searowundor n. *strange object*, B920.

searu=searo; **searw-** v. searo.

searwian (a, æ) *to be deceitful, dissimulate, cheat.*

searwum (dp. of searo) *skilfully.*

searwung=sierwung

seatul, seatl (NG)=setl

sēaŏ I. (æ) m. *hole, pit, MkL*; CP; Mdf : *well, cistern, spring, fountain, lake,* Mdf. ['*seath*'; sēoŏan] **II.** pret. 3 sg. of sēoŏan.

sēaŏa m. *heartburn?* LCD 21a.

sēaw m. *sap, juice, moisture, Gl,Lcd.* ['*sew*'] +**sēaw** *succulent,* LCD 95b : *soaked,* LCD 86²⁰.

seax (æ, e) n. *knife, hip-knife, short sword, dirk, dagger, Æ,B,Cp*; CP. ['*sax*']

seaxbenn (siex-) f. *dagger-wound,* B 2904.

Seaxe, Seaxanmpl.(gp. Seaxna) *Saxons,* AO.

Seaxland (e) n. *England,* SHR 16⁴.

±**sēcan I.** *to search for,* '*seek*' ('*i-seche*'), *inquire, ask for, look for, Æ : try, strive after, long for, wish, desire,* CP. s. on, tō *look to for, expect from,* CP : *visit, go to, AO; Æ : approach, attain to : get : attack, pursue, follow, Chr;* AO : *go, move, proceed, Æ.* **II.** (KGL)=sȳcan

secce (B 600)=sæcce, gs. of sacu.

secful (KGL)=sacful

secg I. m. (n) '*sedge*,' *reed, rush, flag, Gl, Lcd,WW*; Mdf. **II.**† f. *sword.* **III.**† m. *man, warrior, hero, B.* ['*segge*'] **IV.** m. *ocean,* OET.

secga m. *sayer, informant,* LL 396,4.

±**secgan** (æ) *to* '*say*' ('*i-seggen*'), *speak, inform, utter, declare, tell, recite, Æ*; AO, CP : *signify, mean, Æ : explain, discuss : attribute to :* (+) *avoid?* LkL p 3⁸. s. on *accuse of, charge with, Æ.*

secge f. *speech,* CR 190.

secgend m. *speaker, narrator,* CP,BH.

secggan=secgan

secggescēre? f. *grasshopper,* Cp 464.

secgihtig *sedgy,* WW 200²⁷.

secglēac n. *sedge-leek, rush-garlic,* LCD.

secgplega m. *sword-play, battle,* AN 1355.

secgrōf *brave?* (GK), *troop?* (FTP 347), RUIN 27.

secgscāra? m. *landrail, corncrake,* WW 287¹¹ and N.

sēcnes f. *visiting,* LkR 19⁴⁴ (oe).

sēd (VPs)=sǣd

+**sēdan** *to satisfy,* PPs 106⁸. [sæd]

sēde=sægde pret. 3 sg. of secgan.

sedinglīne=stedinglīne

±**sedl** (NG)=setl

sefa (eo) m. *mind, spirit, understanding, heart,* †CP 9¹⁰.

sēfer-=sȳfer-; **seflan**=seofian

sēfre=sȳfre

sēft comp. adv. *more softly.*

±**sēfte** *soft, pleasant, comfortable, easy : gentle, mild : effeminate, luxurious.*

sēftēadig *prosperous,* SEAF 56.

sēftlic *luxurious,* AS 39⁴.

sēftnes f. *rest, quietness, peace, Æ,AO.*

segc-=secg-; **segel**=segl

segen I. (æ) (±) f. *conversation, speech, statement, Æ,AO : premonition, prophecy, AO : report, story, legend.* sēo hālga +s. *Holy Writ.* **II.**=segn

+**segenlic**=+sewenlic; **segg**=secg

segl I. mn. '*sail*,' *AO,Bo,MH*; Æ : *veil, curtain,* CR 1139 : *pillar of cloud,* Ex. **II.**=sigel

±**seg-lan**, -lian *to* '*sail*' : (+) *equip with a sail.*

seglbōsm m. *bellying sail,* GL.

seglgerǣde n. *sail-tackle,* TC 549¹⁷.

seglgyrd (e²) mf. *sail-yard, yard, cross-pole, Cp,WW.*

seglian=seglan

seglrād f. (*sail-road*), *sea,* B 1429.

seglrōd f. *sail-rod, sail-yard.* [v. '*rood*']

seglung f. '*sailing*,' *BH.*

segn mn. *sign, mark, token, Gen : ensign, banner, B,BH.* ['*senye*'; *L.* signum]

segnberend m. *warrior,* RD 41²⁰.

segnbora m. *standard-bearer,* BL,WW.

segncyning m. *king before whom a banner is borne* (BT), Ex 172.

segne f. '*seine*,' *drag-net, Ex,JnL.*

+**segnes** f. *expression,* ÆL 23b⁷³.

±**segnian** (æn) *to make the sign of the cross, cross oneself, consecrate, bless, Æ,BH.* ['*sain*']

segnung f. *blessing, consecration,* BH,GD.

sēgon=sāwon pret. pl. of sēon.

seh (VPs)=seoh imperat. of sēon.

seht I. (ea) mf. *settlement, arrangement, agreement, KC : friendship, peace, BH.* **II.** adj. *reconciled, agreed, at peace, BC.* ['*saught*']

±**sehtian** *to conciliate, settle,* LL. ['*saught*']

±**sehtlian** (a, æ) *to reconcile, to come to an agreement,* CHR.

±**sehtnes** f. *agreement, reconciliation, peace, Æ,Chr.* ['*saughtness*']

sēhŏ=sēcŏ pres. 3 sg. of sēcan.

±**sehŏe** [=seh ŏu] interj. *behold!*

seigl, seign=segl, segn

seim *fat, EPs* 62⁶. ['*seam*'; *Late L.* sagimen]

seista=siexta; **sel** sn.=sǣl

sēl I. adj. comp. sēlra (*Mt*), sēlla (*B*), sȳlla, superl. sēlest (*Lk*), sēlost *good, great, excellent, clever, skilful,* AO : *noble, honourable : fitting, fit, advisable : sound, healthy, happy, prosperous.* [v. '*sele*'] **II.** (æ) comp. adv. (also sēlor) superl. sēlost *better, more effectually, rather, sooner, in preference, Æ,CP.* [sæl]

sēlan (OET,Ct)=sǣlan I. **selcūŏ**=seldcūŏ

seld† (æ) **I.** n. *hall, palace, residence.* **II.** n. *seat, throne, daïs, VPs.* ['*seld*']

+selda† *comrade, retainer.*

seldan adv., comp. seld(n)or, superl. seldost '*seldom,*' *rarely, CP;* Æ.

seldcūð *unusual, rare, strange, novel, Bo;* Æ : *various, WW.* ['*selcouth*']

seldcyme m. *infrequent coming,* Rᴅ 1¹⁴.

selde f. *vestibule,* WW 183⁹⁹.

selden *few, rare,* Sc 197¹⁸.

seldguma m. *retainer?* B 249.

seld-hwanne (CP), -hwænne (Æ) adv. *seldom, rarely.*

seldlic *rare, strange, wondrous, B* (syll-), *Met* (sell-) : *select, choice, excellent.* adv. -līce, *Sol;* Æ. ['*selly*']

seldnor, seldor, seldost v. seldan.

seldon=seldan

seldsīene *rare, extraordinary, unfamiliar, AO,KC?* (- synde). ['*seldseen*']

seldun (*CP*), seldum (*Sol*)=seldan

sele† m. *hall, house, dwelling, prison,* KC. [*Ger.* saal]

+sele m. *tabernacle,* EPs 14¹.

seledrēam† m. *hall-joy, festivity.*

seleful n. *hall-goblet,* B 619.

selegesceot n. '*tabernaculum,*' *tent, lodging-place, nest,* M. [*Ger.* geschoss]

selegyst m. *hall-guest,* B 1545.

selen (y) f. *grant, gift :* tribute, MkL p 5¹ : *munificence,* OEG. [sellan]

±selenes f. *tradition :* (+) *giving,* DR.

selerædend† m. *hall ruler or possessor.*

selerest f. *bed in hall,* B 690.

selescot=selegesceot

selesecg m. *retainer,* Wᴀ 34.

selest pres. 2 sg., seleð pres. 3 sg. of sellan.

sēlest v. sēl.

seleðegn m. *retainer, attendant,* B 1794.

seleweard m. *hall-warden,* B 667.

self I. (eo, i, y) pron. (str. and wk.) '*self,*' *AO,CP : own.* mid him selfum *by himself.* adj. *same, CP.* **II.**=sealf

selfǣta (y) m. *cannibal,* Aɴ 175.

selfǣte f. *a plant, wild oat?* Lᴄᴅ.

selfbana (o²) m. *a suicide,* Gʟ.

selfcwala (y) *a suicide,* MFH 172.

selfcwalu (y) f. *suicide,* Wʏ 56.

selfdēma, self-dēmere (RB), -dēmende (OEG 58¹⁹) (y) m. '*sarabaita,*' *monk living subject only to his own rules.*

selfdōm m. *independence* (Swt).

selfe v. swā.

selflic (y) *spontaneous, voluntary,* OEG.

selflīce I. n. *self-love,* '*amour propre,*' *pride, vanity, CP :* egotism, CP 25⁷. **II.** adj. *egotistic, puffed up, vain, CP.*

selfmyrðra (y) m. *one who takes his own life,* WW 424²⁵.

selfmyrðrung (y) f. *suicide (action).*

selfren=seolfren

selfsceafte *not begotten,* Gᴇɴ 523.

selfswēgend (y) m. *vowel.*

selfwealdlīce (eo¹, e²) *arbitrarily,* GD 289⁵, v.l.

selfwendlīce=selfwillendlīce

selfwill n. *own will, free-will, Bo,Met.* ['*selfwill*']

selfwille (y) *spontaneous, voluntary.* adv. -willes, Æ,RB. ['*selfwill*']

selfwillende *voluntary,* LPs 67¹⁰.

selfwillendlīce (eo¹) *following one's own will, arbitrarily,* GD 289⁵.

selian=sylian; **sēlig**=sǣlig

sēlla=sēlra, v. sēl.

±sellan (ea, i, ie, y) (w. d. pers. and a. thing) *to give, furnish, supply, lend,* Æ,B, Mt; AO,CP : *surrender, give up, betray,* Æ, JnL : *entrust, deliver to, appoint, allot :* lay by, hide, WW 212⁴¹ : '*sell**,' Æ,Jn : *promise.* āð s. *make oath, swear,* LL.

sellen=selen

sellend (y) m. *giver,* Æ : *betrayer,* MkLR 14⁴⁴.

sellendlic adj. *to be given,* Cʜʀᴅ 102.

sellic=seldlic; **selma** (Gʟ)=sealma

selmerige=sælmerige; **selnes**=selenes

sēlor, sēlost, sēlra v. sēl; **selt-**=sylt-

selð pres. 3 sg. of sellan; **sēlð**=sǣlð

+sēm n. *reconciliation,* LL 10,10.

sēma (ī, y) m. *arbitrator, judge,* ÆGʀ, GD.

±sēman I. *to smooth over, put right, settle, reconcile, pacify, AO,Chr,LL.* ['*seem,*' '*i-seme*'] **II.**=sīeman

sēmann (Rᴜɴ 45)=sǣmann

sēmend (ǣ) m. *conciliator, arbitrator,* LL.

sēmestre=sēamestre

semian=seomian; **semle**=simble

semnendlic *sudden,* GD 235⁴. adv. -līce *by chance.*

semninga (M)=samnunga

semtinges=samtinges; **senap**=senep

±sencan, tr. *to sink, plunge (in water), submerge, drown.* [sincan]

send f. *gift,* RB 87¹¹.

sendan I. (±) *to '*send*' ('i-send'), send forth, despatch, B,BH,Bl,CP,MtL;* Æ,AO : *impel, drive,* MkL : *throw, hurl, cast, VPs :* put, place, lay : *utter.* **II.** *to feast,* B 600? [sand]

senderlīce (KGʟ 74²⁷)=synderlīce

senderlīpe (HGʟ)=synderlīpe

sendlic adj. *about to be sent (on a journey),* RBL 113⁴.

sendnes f. *sending,* WW.

+sēne=+sīene

senep m. *mustard,* Gl,Lᴄᴅ. [*L.* sinapi]

senepsæd n. *mustard-seed*, LCD 3·88¹⁵.

sengan (æ) *to 'singe,' burn slightly*, LL 449,6² : *afflict*, RPs 30¹⁰.

sēnian=segnian; **senn** (HGL 519)=synn

senop=senep; **senoð** (CHR)=sinoð

senscipe=sinscipe

senst, sent=sendest, sendeð pres. 2 and 3 sg. of sendan.

senu=seonu

sēo I. f. gas. sēo(n) *pupil (of eye)*, Æ. **II.** pron. v. sē. [v. '*she*'] **III.** gs. of sǣ. **IV.** pres. 1 sg. of sēon. **V.** pres. 2 sg. subj. of bēon (wesan).

sēoc '*sick,' ill, diseased, feeble, weak*, Bl,Bo, Chr; Æ,CP : (†) *wounded* : *morally sick, corrupt, Jul,RB* : *sad, troubled, FAp,Gu.*

sēocan I. *to be ill, fall ill, ANS*117·25; GD. ['*sick*'] **II.**=sēcan

sēoclian=sīclian

sēocmōd *infirm of mind*, CHRD 23⁹.

sēocnes f. '*sickness,' disease*, LL,W : a *disease*, Lcd 3·126'.

sēod (ēa) m. *scrip, purse, bag*, Æ,GL.

seodo, seodu=sidu; **seofa**=sefa

seofafald (DR)=seofonfeald

seofan, seofen=seofon; **seofeð-**=seofoð-

seoflan (e, ea, i, y) *to sigh, lament*, CP.

seofon '*SEVEN,' Æ,AO.*

seofonfeald '*seven-fold,' Æ,Bf,RB.*

seofonfealdlīce adv. *seven times*, VPs.

seofongetel (e²) *the number seven*, OEG 1533.

seofonlēafe f. *tormentilla, setfoil (plant)*, LCD 1·232¹.

seofonnihte adj. *seven days old*, LCD : *lasting seven days*, Æ.

seofon-tēoða (AO), -ᴌe(ᴜ)g(e)ða '*seven-teenth,' BH.*

seofontīene (y³) '*seventeen,' BH; AO.*

seofontīenenihte *seventeen days old*, LCD 3·180.

seofontīenewintre *seventeen years old*, AO 190³⁰.

seofontīene=seofontīene

seofonwintre (y) *seven years old*, Æ,B,BH.

seofoða I. '*seventh,' Bl,Mt*; Æ,AO,CP. **II.**=sifeða

seofoðe *seventhly*, LL 158,18.

seofung f. *lamentation*, Bo,MET. [seofian]

seoh imperat. of sēon.

seohhe f. *sieve*, LL,WW. [sēon II.]

seohhian *to drain, filter*, ÆP 172²¹, (+) ES 49·353.

seohter m., seohtre (i) f. *drain, ditch*, Ct (Mdf).

seolc, seol-oc, -uc (io) m. '*silk,' silken cloth*, Bo,Lcd.

-seolcan v. ā-s.

seolcen (i) '*silken,' made of silk*, Bo,WW; Æ.

seolcwyrm m. '*silkworm,' WW.*

sēoles v. seolh; **seolf** (VPs)=self

seolfer=seolfor; **seolfern**=seolfren

seolfor (i, io, u, y) n., gs. seolfres '*SILVER,' CP; Æ.*

seolforfæt n. *silver vessel*, BH 252¹⁶.

seolforgewiht (y) m. *silver-weight*, LCD 3·92¹⁴.

seolforhammen *plated with silver*, EC 225'.

seolfor-hilt, -hilted (TC) '*silver-hilted.'*

seolforsmið m. '*silversmith,' WW.*

seolforstycce m. *piece of silver*, A 11·8³.

seolfren (e, i, y) *made of silver*, '*silvern,' Bo,Chr,Met.*

seolfring (y) m. *silver coin*, Æ.

seolh m., gs. sēoles '*seal,' AO,Lcd,WW.*

seolhbæð n. *seal's bath, sea*, RD 11¹¹.

seolhpæð ? n? *seal's path, sea, ocean*, AN 1710.

seolm (WW 101¹⁶)=sealm

seoloc, seoluc=seolc; **seolofr-**=seolfr-

seoloð (io¹, e²) m. *sea*, B 2367?

seolufr-=seolfor-, seolfr-; **sēom**=sēam I.

seomian† (e) *to be tired, lie at rest, tarry, continue, stand* : *hang, swing, sway* : *lower (as a cloud)* : *lay wait for*, B 161.

sēomint (WW 136³¹?)=sǣminte

sēon I. (±) sv⁵ *to 'see*'* ('*i-see'), look, behold*, B,G,Ps,Rd : *observe, perceive, understand, know, Cr,Ps* : *inspect, visit* : *experience, suffer, B,Cr* : *appear*, BF 86⁸ : (pass) *seem* : (+) *provide*, OET 175¹³. sih ðe *lo! behold!* **II.** sv¹ (tr.) *to strain, filter*, Æ,AO : (intr.) *run, ooze, trickle, drop, drip*, Æ,AO, Lcd. ['*syʒe,' 'sying'*] **III.** v. sco. **IV.**=sīen

seon-=sin-

seondon=sind pres. pl. ind. of wesan.

sēonian *to languish*, GD 284² . [OHG. siunōn]

seono (e¹, i¹; io¹, u²) f. '*sinew,' B,Lcd; AN.*

seonobend f. *sinew-band?* DEOR 6.

seonobenn f. *injury to a sinew*, WY 19.

seonod=sinoð

seonodolg n. *injury to a sinew*, AN 1408.

seonoð=sinoð

seonu=seono; **seonwe** gs. of seono.

seorðan³ *to lie with*, MtL 5²⁷. [ON?]

seorwum (Cp)=searwum, dp. of searo.

sēoslig *afflicted*, GU 899. [sūsl]

sēota=sǣta; **seotl**=setl

seotol=(1) setl; (2) sweotol

seotu nap. of set.

±**sēoðan²** (ȳ) '*seethe,' boil*, Lcd : *be troubled in mind, brood*, B : *afflict, disturb.*

seoððan=siððan

-sēoung (ēu) v. eag-s.

sēow pret. 3 sg. of sāwan.

sēowan, sēowian (ī, īo, ȳ) *to 'sew,' knit together, link, unite*, Æ,Cp,Mk.

seox=siex; **seoxter**=sester

sep (*GPH*391)=sǣp

sēpan† *to instruct.*

serc m., serce f. (y) '*sark*,' *shirt*, B,WW : *corslet, coat of mail.*

serede=sierwde pret. 3 sg. of sierwan.

Sēremōnað *June*, MEN. [v. '*siere*']

serew-, serw-=searw-, sierw-

serð=seorð, imperat. of seorðan.

sescle f. *sixth part*, BF192²,⁴. [*L.* sextula]

sess m. *place for sitting, seat, bench*, B,Cp.

sessian *to grow calm*, AN453.

sesta=siexta

sester (eo, y) m. *a certain measure of bulk*, Æ : *vessel, pitcher*, Æ. [*L.* sextarius]

-sestre v. twī-s.

±set n. *seat, habitation* : *entrenchment, camp, stall, fold* : *setting (of the sun)*. [sittan]

sēt-=sǣt-

sete imperat. of settan.

+setednes=+setnes; setel (CP)=setl

seten I. f. *set, shoot, slip*, VPs : *plantation* : *occupied (tilled?) land*, LL118,68. II. pp. of sittan.

+setenes=+setnes

+setennes f. *sitting*, VPs138².

sētere=sǣtere; Seterndæg=Sǣterndæg

setgong=setlgang

sethrægl n. *covering for a seat*, Ct,WW.

sētian=sǣtian; setin (GL)=seten

setl (æ, ea, eo, i, o) n. *seat, stall, sitting, place, residence*, Æ,B,BH,CP : *throne, see* : *siege*, AO. tō setle gān *to set (of the sun)*, Æ. ['*settle*']

+setl n. *assembly*, OEG1753.

+setla (æ) m. *one sitting beside*, ÆL2²³⁷ : *assessor, fellow-judge*, OEG56²⁰.

setlan *to* '*settle*' (*cause to sit*), *place, put, Whale.*

setlgang m. *setting, sinking*, Æ.

setlgangende ptc. *setting*, BH476¹³.

setlhrægel n. *seat-cover*, Ct.

setlrād f. *setting, sinking*, Ex109.

setlung f. *sitting, setting*, Æ,Ps.

sētn-=sǣt(n)-

±setnes (+ exc. in N) f. *foundation, creation, construction*, MtL : *position, size, extent* : *institution, law, ordinance, decree, will, Æ, BH,Mk* : *instruction* : *record, narrative* : *sentence, paragraph, figure of speech, composition.* ['*i-setness*']

setol=setl

sēton=sǣton pret. pl. of sittan.

setrægel (IM)=sethrægl

settan (±) *to make to sit*, '*SET*,' *lay, put, deposit, place, fix*, Æ; CP : *occupy, set or put down*, Æ : (±) *appoint, assign, institute, prepare, ordain, create, form, make, found, build, Æ,AO* : *sow, plant, Cp,Cr,Gen*,

MtL : *settle* (tr. and intr.), *abate, subside, sink* : *compose, compile, write*, Æ : *add* : *translate* : (+) *people, garrison* : *be situated* : *set off* : *lay in wait*, LPs9³⁰. s. ūt *issue, send forth, dismiss.* s. of *displace, depose.* sīð s. *travel, journey.* ±s. wið, ongean *compare.* s. tō gafole *let land.* [sittan]

+settednes (CHRD)=+setnes

settend m. *creator, ordainer*, DA333.

+settendlic *appointed, canonical*, CM362.

sēttere=sǣtere

setðorn m. *a kind of tree*, EC291'.

+setu† np. v. +set.

±sēðan *to affirm, testify*, Æ : *prove.* [sōð]

seðel (NG)=setl

±sēðend m. *asserter, affirmer*, WW.

+sēðnes (ǣ) f. *affirmation*, ByH8'.

seððe=sehðe

±sēðung f. *affirmation, proof*, Æ.

sēw=sēow pret. 3 sg. of sāwan.

sēw-=sǣw-

sewen=sawen pp. of sēon.

+sewenlic *visible*, Æ,Bo. adv. -līce *evidently.*

sex (NG)=(1) siex; (2) seax

Sexland=Seaxland; sexta=siexta

sī 3 p. sg. pres. subj. of wesan.

sibǣðeling m. *related noble*, B2708.

sibb (y) (v. LL2·651) f. *relationship*, AO,B, Chr; Æ : *love, friendship* : *peace, happiness*, BH,Chr,VPs; AO,CP. ['*sib*']

±sibb *related, akin*, B,LkL,W. as sb. *kinsman, kinswoman*, W,Soul. ['*sib*,' '*i-sib*']

sibb-=sib-

sibbecoss m. *kiss of peace*, ES33·176.

sibbegedriht=sibgedryht

±sibbian (y) *to bring together, conciliate, reconcile*, Æ,CP.

sibbs-=sibs-

sibcwide (y) m. *pacific speech*, LEAS29.

sibfæc n. *degree of affinity*, LL.

sibgebyrd f. *blood-relationship*, GEN1901.

sibgedryht† f. *related band* : *peaceful host.*

sibgemāgas mpl. *blood-relations*, Ex386.

sibgeornes f. *pacific disposition, friendship, love*, W.

sibge-sihð, -syhð f. *vision of peace* (lit. trans. of '*Hierosolyma*'), Ps.

sibi (GL) sibian=sife, seofian

sibleger n. *incest*, LL,W.

siblic *of peace, peaceable*, Æ : *related.* adv. -līce.

±sibling m. *relative, kinsman*, Æ. ['*sibling*']

siblufu† f. *friendship, love.*

+sibnes f. *affinity, relationship*, WW345¹⁶.

sibrēden f. *affinity, relationship*, Chr1127. ['*sibred*']

±sibsum *peace-loving, peaceable, friendly*, CP. adv. -līce. [v. '*i-sibb*']

+**sibsumian** to reconcile, be reconciled, Æ.
sibsumnes f. peace, concord, Chr; CP : brotherly love. ['sibsomeness']
+**sibsumung** f. peace-making, WW172⁴¹.
sibun (Cp)=seofon
sīc n. small stream, BC; Mdf. ['sitch']
sīcan I. (sv¹) to sigh, yearn for, AO,PPs. ['siche'] II.=sȳcan
siccet-, siccett-, siccit-=sicett-
sicclian=sīclian
sice m. sigh, Lcd1·388¹¹. ['siche']
sicel=sicol; **sīcelian**=sīclian
sicer-=sicor-
sicerian to trickle, penetrate, ooze, CP437¹⁴. ['sicker']
sicettan to sigh, groan, mourn, CP.
sicettung f. sighing, sigh, sob, lamentation, Æ.
sīcle sick, ill, ANS129·21.
±**sīclian** (ǣ, ē, ēo, ȳ) to sicken, become ill or weak, Lcd; ÆL. ['sickle'; sēoc]
sicol (u²) m. 'sickle,' Bf,Mk,WW.
sicor sure, certain, trustworthy, A : secure, CP. ['sicker']
sicorlīce (e²) with full certainty, NC321 (=RWH145¹²); FM99. ['sickerly']
sicornes f. certainty, NC321. ['sickerness']
sīd ample, wide, broad, large, vast, An,B, Gen,LL. ['side']
sīdādl f. pain in the side, pleurisy, WW 112³².
sīdan adv. wīdan and s. far and wide, BC. [v. 'side']
sīde I. adv. amply, widely, extensively, OEG. s. and wīde far and wide, El. ['side'] II. (±) f. 'SIDE,' Æ,CP. III. f. silk. [L. seta]
sīdece m. pain in the side, LCD172a.
sideful (y) decorous, modest, pure, virtuous, honest, Æ. ['sedeful'] adv. -līce.
sidefulnes f. virtue, modesty, ÆL.
sidelic sober, discreet, GPH389.
sidelīce adv. fitly, suitable, CP153.
siden v. ælf-s.
sīden made of silk, OEG3161,2.
sīdewāre f. zedoary, LCD137b. [Late L.]
sīdfæōme, sīdfæōmed† wide-bosomed, capacious (of a ship), B. [v. 'side']
sīdfeaxe, sīdfeaxode long-haired, Æ. [v. 'side']
sīdfolc† n. great people or number of people.
sīdhealf f. a large place, APs17²⁰.
sīdian intr. to extend? RIM65. [sīd]
+**sidian** (y) to arrange, set right, order. [sidu]
sīdland† n. extensive land, GEN.
sīdlingweg m. sidelong way, road that runs obliquely? (BT),KC3·446'.
sido=sidu
sīdrand m. broad shield, B1289.

sidu (eo) m., gds. sida custom, practice, manner, habit, rite, CP: manners, morality, good conduct, purity, CP. [Ger. sitte]
sidung (y) f. rule, regulation, GPH398.
sīdung (ȳ) f. augmentation, growth, BF64²⁹.
sīdwærc m. pain in the side, GD,LCD.
sīdweg† m. long road : (in pl.) distance.
sīdwyrm (ȳ) m. silk-worm, WW.
sīe pres. 1 sg. subj. of wesan (bēon).
siehst pres. 2 sg., siehð pres. 3 sg. of sēon.
+**siehð**=+siht; **sielf**=self; **siellan**=sellan
siellic=seldlic
±**sīeman** (ǣ, ē, ȳ) to load, burden, Æ,LkL. ['seam']
siemble=simble
sīen I. (ēo, ī, ȳ) f. power of sight, sight, vision, Jul,Lcd : pupil, eye. ['sene'] II. (=sīn) pl. pres. subj. of wesan.
siendon, sient (=sindon, sind) pl. pres. of wesan.
+**sīene** (ē, ī, ȳ) seen, visible, evident, plain, B. ['sene'] adv. plainly.
+**sīenelic** (ē, ȳ) visible, BH216¹⁴,VH. adv. -līce.
sierce=serce
sīere 'sere,' dry, withered, BC1·515²². [sēarian]
sierian=sierwan
±**sierwan** (i, y) to plan, devise, contrive : plot, lay snares for, entrap, CP : put on armour : (+) fit out, arm, equip, MA159. [searu]
sierwung (ea, y) f. plotting, artifice, trap, snare, treachery, Æ.
sieððan=siððan
siex (c, eo, i, y) 'SIX,' AO. For comps. v. also six-.
siexbenn=seaxbenn
siexfeald 'six-fold,' WW.
siexhund six hundred, AO; WID. [v. 'six']
siexta (e, i, y) 'sixth,' AO,Chr,LG,MH.
siexte (y) sixthly, LL158,17.
siextig (e, i, y) 'sixty,' AO,Bl,LG.
sife (y) n. 'sieve,' Cp,Lcd,WW.
sifeða (eo, y) m. and fpl. siftings, chaff, bran : tares, rubbish.
sifian=seofian; **sifiða**=sifeða; **sīfre**=sȳfre
siftan (e, y) to 'sift,' Æ,Bo,Cp.
sifun=seofon
sig=sī 3 p. sing. pres. subj. of wesan (bēon).
+**sig** n. victory, DR28².
sīgan¹ I. (±) to sink, set (of the sun), B,Bo, Chr : decline, CP : descend, fall, fall down, Æ : move, advance, go, go to, approach, B, Chr. sāh ūt came out, Æ. II.=sēon II.
sigbēh (NG)=sigebēah; **sigdi** (Ep)=sīðe
sige I. (y) m. victory, success, triumph, Æ, AO,CHR. II. m. sinking, setting (of the sun), MET13⁵⁶. [sīgan]

sige-bēacn, -bēacen n. *banner, Æ : emblem of victory, trophy, cross (of Christ)*, EL.
sigebēah m. *victor's circlet, crown*, BH.
sigebēam† m. *tree of victory, cross.*
sigebearn† n. *victor-child (Christ)*, EL.
sigebeorht *victorious*, BL203'.`
sigebeorn m. *victorious hero*, FIN38.
sigebrōðor m. *victorious brother*, AN183.
sigebўme f. *trump of victory*, Ex565.
sigecempa m. *victorious champion*, PPs 50¹⁰.
sigecwēn† f. *victorious queen*, EL.
sigedēma† m. *victorious judge.*
sigedryhten† m. *lord of victory, God.*
sigeēadig *victorious*, B1557.
sigefæst *victorious, triumphant, Æ.*
±**sigefæstan** (e³) *to triumph : crown as victor.*
sīgefæstnes f. *triumph, victory*, Ps.
sigefest=sigefæst
sigefolc† n. *victorious people.*
sigegealdor (y¹) n. *victory-bringing charm*, Lcd 1·388¹³. ['*sigalder*']
sigegefeoht n. *victory*, BH158⁶.
sigegyrd f. *victory-bringing rod*, LCD.
sigehrēmig† (ǣ) *rejoicing in victory.*
sigehrēð f. *fame gained by victory? confidence or joy of victory?* B490 (v. Klb143).
sigehrēðig† *victorious, triumphant.*
sigehwīl f. *hour of victory*, B2710.
sigel I.† (æ, e) m? n? *sun : name of the rune for* s. **II.**=sigil. **III.** f.=sigle I.
sigelbeorht† *sun-bright, brilliant*, MEN.
sigele=sigle
sigelēan n. *reward of victory*, EL,HGL.
sigelēas† *not victorious, defeated.*
sigelēoð† n. *song of victory.*
Sigelhearwa m. *Ethiopian*, VPs.
sigel-hweorfa m., -hwe(o)rfe f. *heliotrope.*
sigelic *victorious*, WW.
sigeltorht *radiant*, AN1248.
Sigel-waras, -ware pl. *Ethiopians*, MH.
sigemēce m. *victorious sword*, CR1531.
sīgend m. *wave*, WW. [sīgan]
siger m. *glutton*, OET72⁵⁶⁸.
siger-=sigor-
sigerēaf n. *triumphal robe*, WW153¹⁵.
sigerian I. *to be gluttonous*, WW489¹⁴. **II.**=sigorian
sigerīce† *victorious, triumphant*, Ex.
sigerōf† *victorious, triumphant.*
sigesceorp n. *ornament of victory*, GN136.
sigesīð (i²) m. *successful expedition*, OET.
sigespēd† f. *success*, AN,EL.
sigetācen n. *emblem of victory, sign.*
sigetīber n. *sacrifice for victory*, Ex402.
sigetorht *brilliant in victory*, SAT240.
sigetūdor n. *dominating race*, GU838.
sigeðēod† f. *victorious people*, B.

sigeðrēat m. *victorious troop*, CR844.
sigeðūf? m. *triumphal banner*, JUD201.
sigewǣpen n. *victorious weapon*, B804.
sigewang† m. *field of victory.*
sigewīf n. *victorious woman*, LCD1·384'.
+**sigfæstnian** *to be crowned as victor*, G.
sigi-=sige-
sigil, sigl n. *fibula, buckle, brooch, gem.* [cp. sigle]
sigirian=sigorian
siglan *to 'sail,'* AO.
sigle I. n. *necklace, collar.* II. f. *rye, black spelt*, LCD48a. [L. secale]
sigor (y) m. *victory, triumph, Æ.* [sige]
sigorbēacen n. *emblem of victory*, EL985.
sigorbeorht *triumphant*, CR10.
sigorcynn n. *victorious race*, EL755.
sigorēadig† *victorious.*
sigorfæst *victorious*, GD,GU.
sigorfæstnes (siger-) f. *victory*, A11·173.
sigorian (e) *to be victorious, triumph over, Æ.*
sigorlēan† n. *reward of victory.*
sigorlic *triumphal*, GL.
sigorspēd† f. *good fortune in war.*
sigortācen n. *convincing sign*, GU1089.
sigortīfer n. *offering for victory*, JUL255.
sigorweorc m. *deed of victory*, Ex316.
sigorwuldor n. *glory of victory*, GU93.
sigrian=sigorian
sigriend m. *victor*, DHy38³.
sigsonte f. *a plant*, LCD27b, 39a.
sigðe=sīðe; **sih**=seoh; **sihsta**=siexta
+**siht** (ie, y) f. *faculty or act of sight, Æ,Bo, Mk*; CP : *aspect : what is seen, vision, apparition.* ['*i-sight*']
-siht, -sihte v. blōd-, ūt-s.
sihte *marshy?* KC3·430'.
+**sīhte**=+sўhte pret. 3 sg. of +sўcan.
sihtre=seohtre
sihð I. f. *thing seen, vision*, JnL,MkL. ['*sight*'] II. pres. 3 sg. of sēon. III. (+)= +siht
sīhð pres. 3 sg. of sīgan.
+**sihðe** (BPs53⁶)=+sehðe
+**sihðnes** f. *vision*, MtL p7⁷.
silcen=seolcen; **silf**=self, seolf
-silfran v. be-s.
Sīlhearwa (Æ)=Sigelhearwa
sillan=sellan; **silofr**=seolfor
sīma I. m. *band, chain*, GEN765. II.=sēma
simbel I. (on) adv. *always, continually*†, AO. [cp. simbles] II.=simble
simbelfarende *roving, nomadic*, AO26¹⁶.
simbelgefēra (y¹) m. *constant companion*, MET11⁵⁰.
simble (e, y) adv. *ever, for ever, always, constantly, continually, continuously.* oftost s. *continually.*
simbles adv. *ever, always*, AN64.

simblian (y) *to frequent*, DR15¹⁰.

simb-lunga, -linga (siml-) *continually, constantly*, DR.

simel=(1) simbel adv.; (2) symbel

simeringwyrt=symeringwyrt

siml, siml-=simbel, simbl-

sīn I. (ȳ) refl. possess. pron. *his, her, its, their*. II.=sīen. III. plur. pres. subj. of wesan.

sin- (y) prefix, *perpetual, permanent, lasting, infinite, immense*.

sinað-=seonoð-, sinoð-

sinbyrnende *ever burning*, MET8⁵².

sinc (y)† n. *treasure, riches, gold, valuables, jewel*.

sincald *perpetually cold*, Ex472.

sincaldu f. *perpetual cold*, PH17.

±**sincan**³ *to 'sink,' become submerged, MtR : subside, Gen : digest easily, act as aperient?* Lcd81b.

sincbrytta m. *distributor of treasure, prince*, A3·71¹⁷.

sincfæt† n. *precious vessel, precious setting*.

sincfāg† *richly adorned*.

sincgestrēon† n. *treasure, jewel*.

sincgewǣge n. *abundance of treasure*, RIM17.

sinc-giefa, -gifa† m. *giver of treasure, ruler, chief, lord, king*.

sincgifu f. *gift of treasure*, AN1511.

sincgim m. *valuable gem, jewel*, EL264.

sincgyfa=sincgiefa

sinchroden† ptc. *adorned with costly ornaments*.

sincmāððum m. *treasure*, B2193.

sincstān m. *precious stone*, MET21²¹.

sincōego† f. *receipt of treasure*. [ðicgan]

sincweorðung† f. *costly gift*.

sind plur. pres. indic. of wesan.

sinder (y) n. *'cinder,' dross, scoria, slag*, Cp,WW ; CP.

sinder-=sundor-; **sinderlice**=synderlice

sinderōm m. *rust*, WW402⁴¹.

sindon plur. pres. indic. of wesan.

sindor=sinder

sindorlīpes (RB)=sundorlīpes

sindrēam† m. *everlasting joy*.

sindrig (Æ)=syndrig; +**sīne**=+sīene

sineht *sinewy*, Lcd91a. [seono]

sine-wealt, -weald (eo¹, y¹, æ²), *round, globular, concave*, Æ : *circular, cylindrical*. [sin-]

sinewealtian *to be unsteady*, WW515³¹.

sinewealtnes f. *roundness, globularity*, Lcd, WW.

sinewind *artery*, WW352²⁵. [seonu]

sinfrēa m. *overlord, husband*, B1934.

sinfulle f. *house-leek*, Lcd,WW.

singal *perpetual, everlasting*, Æ,CP : *continuous, constant*, Æ : *daily*.

singala, singale(s) adv. *always, continually*.

singalflōwende ptc. *ever-flowing*, WW177³⁶.

+**singalian** (y) *to continue*, ACPs88⁵¹.

singallic *incessant, continual*, CP61²¹. adv. (±) -līce.

+**singallician** *to continue*, JPs88⁵¹,140⁶.

singalnes f. *perseverance, assiduity*, OEG.

singalrene m. *constant flow*, HGL418. [ryne]

±**singan**³ (y) *to 'SING,' celebrate in song*, AO, CP : *crow, sing (of birds)*, Æ : *chant, intone : read, recite, narrate* : (*of things) sound, resound, ring, clank*, CP.

+**singe** (=+sinie?) f. *wife*, JUL54. [cp. sinig]

singendlic *that may be sung*, LVPs118⁵⁴.

sing-ere, -estre=sang-ere, -estre

singian (Æ)=syngian

singrēne (y) I. f. *house-leek, periwinkle*, Lcd. ['sengreen'] II. adj. *evergreen : uncooked (of vegetables)*.

singrim adj. *exceeding fierce*, JUL230.

sinhere m. *huge army*, B2936.

sinhīg-=sinhīw-

±**sin-hīwan**, -hīgan npl. *wedded couple*, Æ, CP.

+**sinhīwen** (synn-) *married*, HL,W.

sinhīwscipe m. *permanent tie (marriage)*, Bo50¹.

sinhwurf-=sinhwyrf-

sinhwyrfel *round*, BL.

sinhwyrfende ptc. *round*, OEG114.

+**sinig** *marriage*, DR108⁷.

+**sinigan**, sinigian *to marry*, NG.

+**sinigscipe**=sinscipe

+**sinlīce** (y) adv. *often*, RB127ᵘ : *diligently*, 97¹⁴.

sinn=synn

sinnan³† (w. g.) *to meditate upon, think of, care about : cease?* [Ger. sinnen]

sinnig=synnig

sinnihte† (y¹, ea²) n. *eternal night*. adv. -nihtes *in continual night, night after night*.

sinnīð m. *perpetual misery*, RIM52.

sinop=senep

sinoð (e, eo, y) f. *synod, council, meeting, assembly*. [L. synodus]

sinoðbōc (e, eo, y) f. *record of the decrees of a synod, canon law*, LL46,49⁸.

sinoðdōm (eo) m. *decree of a synod*, EL552.

sinoðlic *synodical*, BH.

sinoðstōw (eo¹, a²) f. *meeting-place, place where a synod is held*, BH102⁵.

sinowalt=sinewealt

sinrǣden f. (*continuing state*), *marriage*, CP.

±**sinscipe** (e, y) m. *cohabitation, marriage*, Æ,CP : (+) *married couple*, CP.

+**sinsciplic** (y) *conjugal*, CHRD,LL(440⁶).

+**sinscippend** *married*, GD218⁴.

sinsnǣd f. *large piece*, B743.

sinsorg f. *perpetual grief*, WIF45.

sint=sind plur. pres. indic. of wesan.

sintre(n)dende ptc. *round*, OEG. [v. '*trend*']

sintryndel (y¹, æ²) adj. *circular, globular*, LCD,WW.

sinðyrstende ptc. (w. g.) *ever-thirsting*, AO 130³¹.

sinu=seono

sinuwealt, sinwealt=sinewealt

sinwrǣnnes (y) f. *constant lechery*, WW 113²².

sīo=sēo; siodo=sidu; siofa=sefa

siogor (AA)=sigor

siol-=seol-, sel-

sioloð m? *water? sea?* B2367 (v. Klb).

sion '*laber*,' *a marsh plant?* Lcd 1·254. ['*sion*']

sīon=sēon II.; sipian=sypian

sīpian *to sink low, wane, decline*, LCD 3·151 (v. A31·538).

sīr=siger; sirew-, sirw-=searw-, sierw-

sisemūs f. *dormouse*, WW.

sīst=sīhst pres. 2 sg. of sēon I.

sit pres. 3 sg. of sittan.

sitl=setl

±sittan⁵ *to* 'SIT,' *sit down, recline, rest*, Æ; AO,CP : *remain, continue, be situated*, AO : *settle, encamp, dwell, occupy, possess*, Chr : *abide, reside*, AO : *lie in wait, besiege, invest*, Chr : *preside over*, Æ; CP : †*perch, roost* : (+) *sit out, finish*. on cnēowum s. *kneel*, AO. wið earm +s. lean. on s. (1) *assail, attack*; (2) *press on, weigh down*, Æ.

sīð (ȳ) I. m. *going, motion, journey, errand* : *departure, death* : *expedition, undertaking, enterprise* : *road, way* : *time, turn, occasion*, Æ; AO. on ānne s. *at one and the same time*. ōðre sīðe...ōðre sīðe *on one occasion ..on another* : *conduct, way of life, manner*, Æ : *fate, destiny, experience, hap, fortune*, Æ. ['SITHE'] II. adv. *late, afterwards*, G. comp. sīð, sīðor *later*. ǣr and s. *always*. ne ǣr ne s. *never*. ǣr oððe s. *ever* : a comp. adj. sīðra *late, later*, and a superl. sīð(e)-mest, sīðest *latest, last* are formed from sīð. æt sīðestan *at last, finally*. ['*sithe*'] III. prep. and conj. *after*. s. ðam *after, afterwards*. [*Ger.* seit] IV. (±)=±sihð pres. 3 sg. of sēon I.

+sīð I. m. (rare ds. +sīðan) *comrade, companion* : (†) *follower, retainer, warrior* : *count, thane*. II. n. *company*, v. LL 2·427; 446.

sīðberend m. *reaper*, WW235³. [sīðe]

sīðbōc f. *itinerary*, OEG 2023.

sīðboda m. *herald of departure (the pillar of cloud)*, Ex250.

sīðboren ptc. *late-born*, VPs,WW.

+sīðcund *fit to rank as a thane*, BH,LL.

+sīðcundlic *intimate*, BH 120³³ (v.l.).

sīðdagas mpl. *later times*, EL639.

sīðe m. '*scythe*,' Æ,Gl.

sīðemest, sīðest v. sīð II.

sīðfæt (Æ,CP), sīðfat mn. *way, journey, voyage, expedition* : *path, road, course*, Æ : *experience, conduct* : *period of time*.

sīðfrom† *ready for a journey*.

sīðgeomor *travel-weary*, FAP1.

sīðian *to go, depart, travel, wander*, Æ,B. ['*sithe*']

+sīðlic=+sīðcundlic

sīðlīce adv. *lately, after a time*, ÆH.

+sīðmægen n. *band of warriors*, GNE89.

+sīðmann=+sīð

sīðmest, sīðor, sīðra v. sīð II.

+sīðrǣden f. *troop*, WW206²¹.

+sīðscipe m. *fellowship, society*, BH.

sīðstapel *step, track*, LPs16⁵.

sīðð=sīð

sīðða adv. and conj. *afterwards*, JnL,LkL. ['*sith*']

sīððan, sīððon (eo, y) I. adv. *since, afterwards, from now on, hereafter, further, then, thereupon, after, later*, Æ. II. conj. *as soon as, when, since, after that, inasmuch as*. sīððan...sīððan *when...then*. III. prep. (w. a.) (LWS) *after*. ['SITHEN'; sīð, ðam]

sīðweg (GU859)=sīdweg

sīðwerod n. *travelling troop*, GEN2114.

±sīðwīf n. *noble lady*, GD,MH.

sīwan=sīwian

siwen pp. of sēon II.

siwen-īge, -igge, -ēge *blear-eyed*, GPH,CP 67.

±sīwian (ēo, ȳ) *to sew, mend, patch* : *knit together, unite*.

six=siex; six-; v. also siex-.

sixecge *six-sided, hexagonal*, WW.

sixfēte (y) adj. *of six (poetical) feet*, BF 192⁸.

sixgylde *entitled to six-fold compensation*, LL3,1.

sixhynde *belonging to the class whose* '*wergeld*' *was 600 shillings*, LL.

sixhyndeman (e¹, y¹) m. *one of the* sixhynde *class*, LL30,39.

sixhyrnede (e²) *having six angles*, WW179¹³.

sixnihte *six days old*, LCD.

sixteogoða '*sixtieth*,' ÆGr,RB.

sixtēoða (e¹, ȳ²) '*sixteenth*,' MH,ÆGr.

sixtigǣre *60-oared ship*. [ār]

sixtigfeald '*sixty-fold*,' ÆGr.

sixtigwintre *sixty years old*, Æ (GEN).

sixtÿne (y¹, e²) '*sixteen*,' Bf,MH.

sixtÿnenihte *sixteen days old*, LCD.

sixtÿnewintre *sixteen years old*, MH190,192.

slā=slāh
slacful (=æ) *lazy*, GL,LCD.
slacian=sleacian
slād pret. 3 sg. of slīdan.
slæ-=slea-; **slǣ**=slēa
-slæccan v. ā-sl.
slæd (a, e, ea) n. *valley, glade, AO*; Mdf. ['*slade*']
-slǣfan v. tō-s.
slæg-=sleg-
slæge m., slæget n.=slege
slægen pp. of slēan.
slǣgu (ē) f. *lethargy*, GL (v. A33·387).
slæht=slieht
slæhtan *to strike, slay*, NG. [*Ger.* schlachten]
+**slæhte** pret. 3 sg. of +sleccan.
slæhð=sliehð pres. 3 sg. of slēan.
slǣp I. (ā, ē, ēa) m. '*SLEEP*,' *Æ,CP* : *sleepiness, inactivity, CP* : *death*. **II.** m? *slippery place?* KC.
±**slǣpan**⁷ (ē, ā) pret. 3 sg. slēp, slēap; also wk. slǣpte, slēpte, slēpde *to* '*SLEEP*,' CP : *be benumbed, motionless, inactive, Æ,CP* : *lie with, Æ* : *rest in the grave, die, Æ*.
slǣpbǣre *soporific*, LCD 1·284'.
slǣpdrenc (æ²) m. *sleeping draught*, LCD 146b.
slǣpere m. *sleeper*, ÆL 1·23¹.
slǣpern (ā, ē, y²;=æ²) n. *dormitory*.
slǣping *sleeping*, APs 3⁶.
slǣplēas *sleepless*, GPH 399.
slǣplēast f. *sleeplessness, Æ*.
slǣpnes f. *sleepiness*, HL 14¹⁰⁶.
slǣpor *drowsy, sleepy*, SOL 258¹.
slǣpwērig *weary and sleepy*, RD 5⁵.
slǣpyrn=slǣpærn
slǣt=sliehð pres. 3 sg. of slēan.
slǣtan *to bait (a boar)*, ÆL 12⁷². ['*sleat*']
slǣting f. *right of hunting*, Chr 1087. ['*sleating*']
slǣw=slāw; **-slǣwan** v. ā-s.
slǣwð (ē) f. *sloth, indolence, Æ,Bo*; CP. ['*sleuth*'; slāw]
slāg=slāh
slaga m. *slayer, homicide, Æ,CP* : *executioner*, ÆL 12²³?
slagen pp. of slēan.
slagu=slægu
slāh, slāg f. '*sloe*' (*fruit of the blackthorn*), *Cp,Lcd,WW*; Mdf.
slahe=slēa
slāhðorn m. *blackthorn*, *Cp,Lcd*; Mdf. ['*sloethorn*']
slāhðornragu f. *blackthorn, lichen*, LCD 54a.
slāhðornrind f. *blackthorn bark*, LCD.
slān I. (K,N)=slēan. **II.** gs. of slā (slāh).
slanc pret. 3 sg. of slincan.
slang pret. 3 sg. of slingan.

slāp=slǣp; **slāpel**=slāpol
slāpfulnes f. *lethargy*, WW 541⁴²?
slāpian *to become sleepy*, CP.
slāpol *somnolent, lethargic*, RB,ÆGR 305⁷.
slāpolnes (e²) f. *somnolence, lethargy, Æ*.
slāpornes f. *lethargy*, A 11·98.
slāpul=slāpol
slar-ege, -ie f. '*clary*' (*plant*), *Lcd,WW*.
slāt pret. 3 sg. of slītan.
slāw '*SLOW*,' *sluggish, torpid, lazy, CP*.
slāwerm (KGL 80²²)=slāwyrm
slāwian *to be slow, sluggish, Æ*.
slāwlīce adv. '*slowly*,' *sluggishly, A,CP*.
slāwyrm m. '*slow-worm*,' *snake, Gl,Sc*.
slēa f. '*slay*,' *weaver's reed, WW*. [slēan; cp. slege]
sleac (v. A 39·366) '*SLACK*,' *remiss, lax, sluggish, indolent, languid, Æ,CP* : *slow, gentle, easy, Æ*.
sleacian *to delay, retard, slacken, relax efforts, Æ*. ['*slake*']
sleaclic *slow, languid, idle*, HGL 472. adv. -līce.
sleacmōdnes f. *slackness, laziness*, BYH 40²⁷.
sleacnes (e) f. *slowness, Æ,Bf,Lcd* : *remissness, laziness, CP*. ['*slackness*']
sleacornes f. *laziness*, A 11·98⁴⁰.
sleaht=slieht
slēan⁶ *to strike, beat, stamp, coin (money), forge (weapons), Æ* : *throw, cast* : *sting (snake)* : *pitch (tent), Æ* : *strike across (country), dash, break, rush, come quickly, Æ* : '*SLAY*,*' *kill, Æ,AO,CP*. wæl +s. *to slaughter* : *cast into chains* : (+) *strike down* : *play (harp, etc.)* : (+) *gain by fighting, win, conquer*.
slēap I. pret. 3 sg. of slǣpan. **II.** pret. 3 sg. of slūpan. **III.**=slēp
slēaw=slāw; **slēbescōh**=slēfescōh
slec-=sleac-
+**sleccan** *to weaken, disable*, CR 149. [sleac]
slecg f. ('*sledge*'-)*hammer, mallet, Nar,WW*; Æ.
slecgettan *to beat, throb*, LCD 82b.
slecgwyrhta m. *metal-worker*, GENC 4²².
sled=slæd; **slēf**=slīefe
slēfan *to slip (clothes) on, Guth*. +slēfed *furnished with sleeves*. ['*sleve*']
slēfescōh m. *slipper*, GL (slēbe-).
slēflēas=slīeflēas
slege (æ) m. *beating, blow, stroke, Æ* : *slaying, slaughter, murder, Æ,AO,CP* : *crash, impact, clap (of thunder)* : *destruction, defeat*, AO : (*weaver's*) '*slay*,*' WW 188⁵. [slēan]
slegebȳtl m. *beetle, hammer*, LCD 122b.
slegefǣge *doomed to perish*, JUD 247.
slegel m. *plectrum*, WW 466²³.

slegen pp. of slēan.

sleghrȳðer (slægr-) n. *cattle for slaughter*, NC321.

slegnēat (æ¹, ǣ²) n. *cattle for slaughter*, TC 105⁴.

slēgu=slǣgu

sleh=sleah imperat. of slēan.

sleht=slieht

slehð=sliehð pres. 3 sg. of slēan.

slēow=slīw

slēp I. (VPs)=slǣp. **II.** pret. 3 sg. of slǣpan.

slēp-=slǣp-

slēpan=(1) slǣpan; (2) (MET9⁵⁵). slȳpan

sleð (VPs)=sliehð pres. 3 sg. of slēan.

slēwð=slǣwð; **slī** (GL)=slīw

slic (ī?) n. *beater, mallet, hammer*, LL455,15. WW75¹⁶.

-slicod (y) v. nīg-s.

slid (APs34⁶)=slidor I.

slīdan¹ to ' *slide**,' *glide, slip, fall, fall down,* Guth : *fail, err, lapse,* Sol : *pass away, be transitory or unstable.*

sliddor=slidor

slide m. *sliding, slip, fall,* Æ,CP.

sliderian=slidrian

slidor I. *slippery,* Ps,Run. ['*slidder*'] **II.** n? *slippery place,* WW.

slidornes f. *slippery place, slipperiness,* BlPs. ['*slidderness*']

slidrian to *slip, slide,* CP,PPs. ['*sliddern*']

slīefe (ē, ī, ȳ) f. ' *sleeve*,' Æ,Bl,LL,RB.

slīeflēas (ē, ȳ) ' *sleeveless*,' RB,WW.

slieht (æ, ea, e, i, y) m. *stroke, slaughter, murder, death,* AO,HL : *animals for slaughter* : (+) †*battle.* ['*sleight*'; slēan]

sliehtswȳn (y¹) n. *pig for killing,* LL.

sliehð pres. 3 sg. of slēan.

slīf, slife=slīefe; **-slīfan** v. tō-s.

slifer *slippery,* HGL405.

sliht (AO,Æ)=slieht

-slihtes v. eorð-s.

slihð pres. 3 sg. of slēan.

slīm n. ' *slime*,' CPs,WW.

slincan³ to *slink, creep, crawl,* AA,DD.

slincend mn. *reptile,* Æ (GEN).

slingan³ to *worm, twist oneself, creep into.* [Ger. schlingen]

slipa=slypa

slipeg, slipig *slimy,* LCD.

slipor *slippery, filthy,* Sc : *unsteady, shifty,* Æ. ['*slipper*']

slipornes f. *filthiness,* DHy36⁸. ['*slipperness*']

+slit n. *rending, biting, bite,* Æ : *something to be torn or rent* : *backbiting, calumny.*

±slītan¹ to *slit, tear, split, shiver, rend to pieces, divide* : *bite, sting, wound,* CP : *backbite,* CP. [v. '*slit*,' '*slite*']

slitcwealm m. *death by rending,* LL(166n).

slite I. m. *slit, rent, tear, bite.* **II.** f? *cyclamen.*

sliten m. *schismatic, heretic,* MtLp8⁹.

slītendlic *gorging,* WW437⁵.

slītere m. *gorger, glutton,* WW : *destroyer,* W235²⁴.

+slitglīw n. *raillery,* WW372³².

slitnes f. *desolation, destruction, tearing up,* LL,MtL.

slītol *biting, pungent,* GPH394.

slītung f. *tearing, biting,* DEUT,LCD.

slīðan¹ to *injure, wound,* GNE202.

slīðe† I. adj. *savage, fierce, dire, cruel, hard, hurtful, perilous.* **II.** adv. *savagely.*

slīðelic *abominable,* EPs105¹⁹.

slīðen *cruel, hard, evil,* B,Bo.

slīðheard† (e²) *cruel, severe, savage.*

slīðhende *with fell paw,* GNE177.

slīðnes f. *abomination?* EPs105³⁶.

slīw m. *a fish, tench, mullet,* GL.

slōg I. pret. 3 sg. of slēan. **II.**=slōh I.

slōh I. mfn., gs. slō(ge)s, slō; das. slō(h) '*slough*,' *mire,* BH,W. **II.** pret. 3 sg. of slēan.

-slop v. ofer-s; **slopen** pp. of slūpan.

slota m. *morsel,* Sc153¹².

slūma m. *slumber,* DD,Gu. ['*sloom*']

slūmere m. *sleeper,* NC322.

sluncon pret. pl. of slincan.

slūpan² to *slip, glide, move softly,* Ex,LL.

slȳf=slīef; **slyht**=slieht

slyhð=sliehð pres. 3 sg. of slēan.

slypa m. *slime, paste, pulp,* Lcd. ['*slip*']

slȳpan (ē;=īe) to *slip (on or off),* A9·32¹⁵⁸.

slȳpescōh m. *slipper,* WW277²⁹.

slyppe f. *paste,* LCD163a.

slȳpræsn n. *sliding beam?* WW237¹. [ræsn]

slȳpð pres. 3 sg. of slūpan.

±smacian to *coax, flatter, allure, seduce,* HGL476; OEG3005.

smæc m. ' *smack*,' *taste,* WW : *scent, odour,* WW.

±smæccan to *taste,* ÆGr. ['*smatch*']

smæl I. (often smal- in obl. cases) sup. smalost, smælst '*SMALL*' : *thin, slender, narrow,* AO : *fine,* CP. **II.** v. hēafodsmæl.

smæle=smale

smæleðerm (A13·323)=smælðearme

smæll (=ie) m. *slap, smack,* JnL. ['*small*']

smælðearmas (y²) mp. *small intestines,* LCD.

smælðearme n. *lower abdomen,* CP.

smǣr (smǣre?) m. *lip,* GL,LCD.

smǣre-=smeoru-

smǣte *pure, refined,* Cp,MH; Æ. ['*smeat*']

smǣtegold n. *pure gold,* WW.

smǣtegylden adj. *of pure gold,* WW.

smal- v. smæl.

smale *finely, into small pieces,* Bo : *softly (not loudly).* ['*small*']

smalian *to become thin*, LCD 2a (Harl.).
smalum *little by little*, OEG 1553.
smalung f. *reducing (of flesh)*, LCD 98a.
smāt pret. 3 sg. of smītan.
smēac pret. 3 sg. of smēocan.
smēade pret. 3 sg. of smēagan.
smēag- v. smēah.
±smēagan, smēan (ē) *to think, think out, reflect, meditate on, deliberate,* Æ,CP : *examine, penetrate, scrutinize, look closely into,* Æ : *suppose* : *seek (opportunity).*
smēagelegen (? v. OEG 4142n) f. *syllogism.*
smēagendlic *meditative,* ÆGR 211⁶. adv. -līce *accurately,* GD 172¹⁴.
smēagung=smēaung
smēah I. adj. (smēag- in obl. cases) *sagacious, acute, subtle* : *penetrating.* II. pret. 3 sg. of smūgan.
+smēah n. *intrigue,* CHR 1094.
smēalic *searching, exhaustive, careful,* CP : *exquisite, choice.* adv. -līce *closely, thoroughly, accurately,* Æ,CP : *subtlely.*
smēalicnes f. *subtlety,* CHRD 98³⁵.
smēamete m. *delicacy (food),* BHCHRD.
smēan, smēang=smēagan, smēaung
smearcian (e) *to smile,* Bo; Æ. ['*smirk*']
smeart *smarting, painful,* W 295¹⁰. ['*smart*']
smeartung (e) f. *tickling,* A 8·450.
smēað I. f. *meditation,* SPs 118⁷⁷. II. pres. 3 sg. of smēagan.
smēaðanclīce adv. *in detail,* BF 78¹².
smēa-ðancol, -ðancollic *subtle.* adv. -e, -līce *exactly, thoroughly, studiously,* Æ.
smēaðancolnes f. *strictness,* ÆH 2·80'.
±smēaung (ē) f. *reflection, thought,* CP : *inquiry, search* : *intention, effort* : *intrigue* : *interpretation,* RWH 21²⁹.
smēawrenc m. *cunning device,* TC 339⁸ (smēh-).
smēawung=smēaung
smēawyrhta m. *skilled artisan,* LL 455,16.
smēawyrm m. *intestinal worm,* LCD.
smec=smæc; smēc=smīc
smedma (eo) m. *fine flour, pollen meal,* Gl, Lcd; Æ. ['*smeddum*']
smedmen adj. *of fine flour,* Sc 154¹.
smēgan=smēagan
smēgawyrm=smēawyrm
smēh=smēah
smelt I. (y) m. *sardine,* '*smelt*,' Cp. II.= smolt
smelting (i, y) f. *amber,* ÆL.
smēocan² *to emit smoke,* Æ,Lcd WW : *fumigate,* Lcd. ['*smeek*']
smeoduma=smedma
smēoh=smēah; smeolt=smolt
smeortan³ *to '*smart*,'* AO 36³⁰ (or ? fȳr- smeortende=*smarting like fire*).
smeortung (e) f. *smarting,* WW 114³.

smeoru (e), smeoruw n. *ointment, fat, grease, lard, tallow, suet,* CP,VPs. ['*smear*']
smeorumangestre (e¹, e²) f. *butter-woman,* LL.
smeorusealf (e¹, a²) f. *unguent,* LCD 55b.
smeoruðearm (æ¹, e¹) m. *entrail,* WW.
smeoruwig (e¹, e²) *rich, fat,* LCD 79a.
smeoruwyrt f. '*smearwort*,' Cp,Lcd.
smeoðian=smiðian
smer-=smear-, smeor-, smir-, smier-
smēr=smǣr; smera=smeoru
smere-=smeoru-
smerian *to laugh to scorn,* MtL 9²⁴.
smeringwyrt f. *name of a plant,* '*crispa, victoriola*,' WW 135¹. [cp. smeoruwyrt]
smeruwan=smierwan
smerwung=smirung; smēte-=smǣte-
±smēðan *to smooth, soften, polish,* CP : *appease, soothe,* CP.
smeðe (RB)=smiððe
smēðe *smooth, polished, soft,* Cp,JnL,Lk; Æ,AO,CP : *suave, agreeable,* CP : *not harsh (of the voice),* VHy : *lenitive.* ['*smeeth*']
±smēðian *to smoothen,* Lcd,OEG : *become smooth.* ['*smeeth*']
smēðnes f. *smoothness, smooth place,* Æ, WW. ['*smeethness*']
smēung=smēaung
smīc (ē, ȳ) m. *vapour, smoke,* Æ,AO,Bo, PPs,VHy. ['*smeech*'; '*switch*']
smīcan (ē) *to smoke, fumigate,* LCD,Ps. [smēocan]
smicer *beauteous, elegant, fair, tasteful,* Cp, Shr,TC. ['*smicker*'] adv. -ere, CP.
smicernes f. *smartness,* WW 416³¹.
+smicerod *well-fashioned,* WW 406²¹.
smicor=smicer; smidema=smedma
smīec=smīc
±smierwan (e, i, y) *to '*smear,*' anoint, salve,* Bf,Bl,G,VPs (smirian); CP. [smeoru] For comps. v. smir-.
smilte=smylte
smilting=smelting
smirels (e, y) m. *ointment, salve,* Æ,LL. ['*smerles*']
smirenes (e, y) f. *ointment, unguent,* LCD, LG.
smirewan, smirian=smierwan
smiringele (y¹) m. *anointing oil,* Ex 29²¹.
smirung (e, y) f. *ointment, unguent,* HL, Lcd : *unction* : *smearing, greasing.* [smeoru]
smirwan=smierwan; smirwung=smirung
smītan¹ *to daub, smear, soil, pollute, defile,* Æ,Cp,Lcd. ['*smite*']
smitte f. *smudge, smut, blot,* OEG,RB : *pollution.* ['*smit*']
±smittian *to befoul, pollute,* WW : *infect,* OEG. ['*smit*']

smiÐ m. *handicraftsman,* '*smith,*' *black-smith, armourer, carpenter, Æ,B,MtL.*
smiÐbelg (y²) m. *smith's bellows,* SOL85¹³.
smiÐcræft m. *manual art,* BH442¹⁶.
smiÐcræftega m. *skilled workman,* GEN 1084.
smiÐian (eo) *to forge, fabricate, design, Æ, OEG.* ['*smith*']
smiÐlīce adv. *dexterously,* WW.
smiÐÐe (smeÐe) f. *smithy, forge, Æ,BH,RB.* ['*smithe*']
smoc m. '*smock,*' *shift, WW.*
smoca m. '*smoke,*' *LPs,Nar* (cc).
smocen pp. of smēocan.
smocian *to emit* '*smoke,*' *Æ,LPs : fumigate, Lcd.*
-smogu v. ǣ-s.; -smoh v. in-s.
smolt I. (e, eo) *mild, peaceful, still, gentle, MtL.* ['*smolt*'] II. *lard, fat, CM,NC.* ['*smolt*']
smolte=smylte
smoltlīce adv. *gently,* RWH146²⁶.
smorian *to strangle, choke, suffocate, Cp, MtR.* ['*smore*']
smōÐ '*smooth,*' *serene, calm, Sc6*'; ES9·40.
smucon pret. pl. of smēorcan.
smūgan² *to creep, Æ.* [*Ger.* schmiegen]
smūgendlic *creeping,* LPs68³⁵.
smȳc=smīc
smȳcÐ pres. 3 sg. of smēocan.
smygel, smygels m. *retreat, burrow,* GL.
smyllan (=ie) *to crack* (*a whip*), GPH 388.
smylt=smelt
+smyltan *to appease,* BH386¹² : *assuage,* LCD.
smylte I. *mild, peaceable, calm, CP : cheerful : prosperous.* II. adv. *softly.* [smolt]
smyltelic=smyltlic
smylting (Æ)=smelting
smyltlic *tranquil, serene,* DR,MH.
smyltnes f. *tranquillity, peace, quiet, silence, CP : gentleness, smoothness, mildness, composure, placidity, CP : evening calm.*
smyr-=smier-, smir-
smytte=smitte; snā=snāw
snaca m. '*snake,*' *serpent, Lk,W.*
snacc m. *a small vessel, war-ship, Chr.* ['*snack*']
snād=snǣd II.
-snæcce v. twī-s.
snǣd I. m. *handle of a scythe, ÆH*2·162. ['*snead*'] II. (ā) m. *detached area of woodland, Ct* (Mdf). III. f. *piece, morsel, slice, portion of food, Æ,Lcd.* ['*snede*'; snīdan]
±snǣdan I. (ē) *to cut, slice, lop off, hew, Ln,CP,MtR.* ['*sned*'; snīÐan] II. *to eat, take a meal,* CHR1048.
snǣdel (GL)=snǣdelÐearm

snǣdelÐearm m. *great gut,* GL,LCD.
snǣding f. *meal, snack,* CM,RBL.
snǣdinghūs n. *cook's shop,* WW185¹.
snǣdingscēap n. *sheep for slaughter,* PPs 43²³.
snǣdmǣlum adv. *bit by bit,* LCD127a.
snægl (e), snægel m. '*snail,*' *Cp,Lcd,WW.*
snǣl=snægl; snǣs=snās
snǣsan (or? onsnǣsan) *to run through, pierce, spit,* LL69,36. [snās]
snǣÐfeld m. *a defined tract of pasture or woodland* (v. Mdf). [snǣd]
snās (ǣ) f. *spit, skewer,* WW237¹⁷ and N.
snāÐ I. pret. 3 sg. of snīÐan. II.(?) n? *killing* (v. OEG3070).
snāw, snāwa (MkL9³) m. '*snow,*' *Bl,Chr, Met,VPs : snow-storm, Bo.*
snāwceald *icy-cold,* MET29⁸.
snāwgebland n. *snow-storm,* AO186³⁴.
snāwhwīt *snow-white, Æ.*
snāwig '*snowy,*' *Lcd.*
snāwīt=snāwhwīt
snāwlic *snowy,* LCD,WW.
sneare, snearh f. '*snare,*' *OEG.*
snēdan=snǣdan; snēl, sneg(e)l=snægl
snell *smart, ready, rapid, keen, fresh, brisk, active, strong, bold, An,B,Cra,Ph;* AO. ['*snell*']
snellic *smart, ready, quick, rapid, bold.* adv. -līce, *Wy.* ['*snelly*']
snellscipe m. *quickness, boldness,* CHR1057D.
snelnes f. *agility,* APT13⁷.
snēomet adv. *quickly, speedily, swiftly : immediately, at once.*
+sneorcan³ (e) *to shrivel, dry up,* VPs30¹³.
snēowan⁷ (ō)† *to hasten, go.*
snērt f. *harpstring,* Ln. [cp. *Ger.* schnur]
+snerc pret. of sneorcan.
snīcan¹ *to sneak along, creep, crawl, CP,Lcd.* ['*snike*']
snid I. (±) n. *slice : cutting : slaughter.* [*Ger.* schnitt] II. m. *saw,* CP.
snide I. m. *incision : slaughter,* ES13·27⁹. II.=snid II.
sniden pp., snidon pret. pl. of snīÐan.
snidīsen n. *lancet,* LCD78a.
snirian=snyrian
snīte f. *snipe, Cp,WW.* ['*snite*']
±snīÐan¹ *to cut, lance, CP : cut off, amputate, CP : hew down, slay, kill, Æ; CP : mow, reap.* ['*snithe*']
snīÐstrēo *carline thistle?* (BT), *chopped straw?* (JGPh1·328),Cp358s.
snīÐung f. *incision, wound,* LCD : *slaughter,* WW.
snīwan *to snow, AA,BH,Cp; Æ.* ['*snew*']
snōca m. *nook? inlet?* BC3·141' (v. Mdf).
snōd f. *hood, head-dress, fillet, Æ.*
snoffa m. '*nausea,*' *CM*50.

snofl *phlegm, mucus*, LCD 9a.
snoflig *full of phlegm*, Bf 12¹⁸.
snofol=snofl
snoru f. *daughter-in-law*, Æ,AO. [*Ger.* schnur]
+snot n. *mucus*, LCD 20b.
snotor, snoter *clever, prudent, intelligent, discerning*, Bl,Chr,MtL; Æ,CP. [*'snoter'*]
snotorlic (e²) *philosophic, wise, clever*. adv. -līce.
snotornes (e²) f. *wisdom, prudence*, Æ.
snotorscipe m. *ratiocination, reason, reasonableness*, OEG 3215; 2¹⁷².
-snotorung (e²) v. word-s.
snotorwyrde *wise of speech, plausible*, W 107¹.
snotter, snottor, snottra (wk.)=snotor
snōwan=snēowan
snūd I. adj. *quickly approaching*, CR 842. II. n? *speed*, AN 267.
snūde† adv. *quickly, at once*, NG.
snyflung f. *mucus from the nose*, NC 322. [*'snivelling'*]
snyrian† *to hasten, hurry*.
snyring *sharp rock*, WW 371²².
snȳtan *to blow the nose*, NC 322. [*'snite'*]
-snȳtels v. candel-s.
snyteru=snyttru
snȳting f. *blowing of nose*, WW 162. [*'sniting'*]
snytre *clever, wise*, GEN 2808.
snytrian *to be clever, wise*, SOL.
snytro, snytru=snyttru
±snyttru f. (often in pl.) *wisdom, cleverness, prudence, sagacity, intelligence*, AO,CP.
snyttrucræft† m. *wisdom, sagacity*.
snyttruhūs n. *house of wisdom*, PPs 77⁶⁰.
snyttrum adv. *cunningly, wisely*, B,PPs.
snyðian *to go nose or beak forwards (of a plough)*, RD 22⁶.
-snyðian, -snyððan v. be-s.
soc I. (±) n. *suck, sucking*, Æ. [*'sock'*] II. m. *soakings*, Mdf.
sōc I. pret. 3 sg. of sacan. II.=sōcn
socc m. *'sock,' light shoe, slipper*, Cp,RB. [*L.* soccus]
socian *to 'soak,'* Lcd. [sūcan]
sōcn f. *seeking, question, inquiry, case, cause : visit, resort*, Æ,W : *attack*, B 1777 : *refuge, asylum, sanctuary*, Æ : *the exercise of judicial power, jurisdiction, right of inquisition, right of taking fines, revenue* (v. sacu), KC,LL (v. 2·454) : *district in which a 'socn' was exercised* (EHR 27·20). [*'soken'*]
sōcnes=sēcnes
+sod n. *cooking, boiling*, GL : *trial*, CP 267¹⁹.
soden pp. of sēoðan.
sodomitisc *sodomitish*, A 11·101³².

sōfte I. (=sēfte) adj. *'soft,' mild, gentle*, Æ : *quiet, calm, tranquil, undisturbed*, Æ : *luxurious* : *agreeable*, A 9·28. II. adv. Gen,Lcd,Met.
sōftnes f. *ease, comfort* : *'softness,' luxury*, Æ.
sogeða (o²) m. *hiccough, eructation*, LCD.
sōht pp., sōhte pret. 3 sg. of sēcan.
sol I. n. *mud, wet sand, wallowing-place, slough*, CP. II. *a wooden halter or collar for beasts*, WW 462³¹. [v. *'sole'*]
sōl n. *sun*, PPs 120⁶.
solar=solor
sōlate f. *sunflower, heliotrope*, LCD.
sole f. *shoe, sandal*, WW 125²⁵. [*L.*]
solere=solor
solian *to soil, become defiled*, Rim 67. [*'sole'*]
sōlmerca m. *sundial*, NC 350.
Solmōnað m. *February*, MEN,MH.
solor m. *loft, upper room*, CP,Ph : *'palatium,' hall, dwelling*, GD 248¹⁴ : *raised platform*, OEG 2²¹¹. [*'sollar'*; *L.* solarium]
solsece (æ²) f. *heliotrope*, LCD,WW. [*L.* solsequia]
som=sam; sōm-=sām-
sōm f. *arbitration, agreement, reconciliation*, Æ,LL. [*'some'*]
+sōm *unanimous, peaceable, friendly*, Æ.
somn-=samn-; somod=samod
somw-=samw-
sōn m. *sound, music*, CP. be sōne *aloud, loudly*. [*L.* sonus]
sōna adv. *'soon,' directly, forthwith, immediately, at once*, Chr,CP. s. swā *as soon as, when*, CP.
sonc=sanc pret. of sincan.
sōncræft m. *music*, A 13·38³⁰⁶.
sond=sand
song I.=sang pret. 3 sg. of singan. II. sb. *bed*, NG. [*ON.* sæng] III. *grape*, EHy 6³².
sonwald (NG)=sinewealt
sopa m. *'sup,' sip*, Lcd. [*'sope'*]
sopcuppe f. *sop-cup*, TC.
sopp *'offula,' 'sop,'* OEG 61¹⁰.
soppian *to soak, 'sop,'* Lcd 86a.
sore *mote*, MtL 7³.
sorg f. (occl. gs. in -es) *'sorrow,' pain, grief, trouble, care, distress, anxiety*, B,Bl,Bo,Cr; CP.
sorgbyrðen f. *load of sorrow*, AN 1534.
sorgcearig† *anxious, sorrowful*, B.
sorgcearu f. *sorrow, anxiety*, Gu 939.'
sorgful *'sorrowful,' sad, anxious, careful*, Æ,B,CP : *distressing, doleful*, B,Ph.
sorgian (pres. ptc. sorgende) *to 'sorrow,' care, grieve, be sorry for, be anxious about*, B,Bl,Bo; CP.
sorglēas *free from sorrow or care*, CR,LL.
sorglēast (h) f. *security*, LCD.

sorglēoð† (h) *dirge*, B.
sorglic *miserable*. adv. -līce, *CAS*. ['*sorrowly*']
sorglufu f. *sad love*, DEOR 16.
sorgstafas mp. *anxiety, care*, JUL 660.
sorgung f. '*sorrowing*,' W 114⁴.
sorgwīte (h) n. *grievous torment*, W 187².
sorgword (h) m. *lamentation*, GEN 789.
sorgwylm (æ²)† m. *wave of sorrow*.
sorh=sorg
sorig *sorry*, CP 227⁸.
sot=sott
sōt n. (*what settles down*), '*soot*,' *Cp,Lcd*.
sotel, sotl, sotol=setl
sotman m. *foolish man*, ÆLD 17¹⁰¹.
sotscipe m. *dulness, folly*, WW 171³³. ['*sotship*']
sott I. adj. *foolish, dull, stupid*. **II.** m. *dullard, fool, Bf.* open sott *downright fool*, Æ. ['*sot*']
sottian *to be foolish*, ByH 80¹¹.
sōð I. n. *truth, justice, righteousness, rectitude, CP : reality, certainty*. tō sōðe, tō sōðum *in truth, truly, truthfully, accurately*. tō sōðan, ðurh sōð *verily, in truth*. **II.** adj. *true, genuine, real*, AO,CP : *just, righteous*. ['SOOTH'] **III.**=L. pro- *in compounds, in* DR *and* NG.
sōðbora? m. *soothsayer, astrologer*, CHR 975A.
sōð-cwed, -cweden *veracious*, NG.
sōðcwide m. *true speech, truth, just saying : proverb*, NG.
Sōðcyning† m. *King of truth, God*.
sōðe adv. *truly, really, accurately, truthfully, rightly*, B,PPs. ['*sooth*']
sōðes adv. *verily, Mt*. [v. '*sooth*']
Sōðfæder m. *Father of truth, God*, CR 103.
sōðfæst (e²) *true, trustworthy, honest, Bl, Chr,Cr,OET,VPs : just, righteous, JnL, PPs*. ['*soothfast*']
±**sōðfæstian** *to justify*, NG.
sōðfæstlic (e) *true, sincere*, AN 876. adv. -līce *truly, honestly*, OET 452. ['*soothfastly*']
sōðfæstnes f. *truth, truthfulness, fairness, fidelity, Bf,Bl,Bo,CP,VPs : justice*. ['*soothfastness*']
sōðfest=sōðfæst
sōðfylgan '*prosequi*,' DR 29¹⁸.
sōðgid (ie²)† n. *true report*.
sōðhweðere conj. *nevertheless*, NG.
±**sōðian** *to prove true, bear witness to*, LL, NG. ['*soothe*'; '*i-sothe*']
sōðlic adj. *true, truthful, real, genuine, right, Bo*. -līce adv. *truly, indeed, really, certainly, Bl,El,G,VPs*. conj. *for, now, then, but, CP*. ['*soothly*']
sōðlufu f. *lovingkindness*, RWH 93²².
sōðsagol *truthful*, ÆGR,GD.

sōðsagu f. *truth, W : true story, MtL*. ['*soothsaw*']
sōðsecgan *to speak the truth*, BL.
sōðsecgendlīce *truly, genuinely*, GD 185¹⁷.
sōðsegen (æ²) f. *true statement*, ÆH.
sōðspǣce *truthful*, W 72¹⁶ E.
sōðspell n. *true story, history*, MtL p 7².
sōðsprǣc f. *true saying*, DR 171¹⁸.
sōðtācen n. *prodigy*, DR 43¹⁶.
sōðða (*JnL,LkL*)=siðða
sōðword† n. *true word*, PPs.
spāca m. '*spoke*' (*of wheel, etc.*), Bo : '*spoke-bone*' (*radius*), WW.
spade=spadu; **spādl**=spātl
spadu (æ) f. '*spade*,' *Æ,Gl,LL*. [L. spatha]
spæc I. pret. 3 sg. of specan. **II.** n. *small branch, tendril*, WW.
spǣc=sprǣc
spǣclēas '*speechless*,' GPH 398⁷².
spænð pres. 3 sg. of spanan.
spær *sparing*, Sc 52⁶.
spær-=spear-
spǣren adj. *of plaster*, GL.
spǣrhende (y²) *sparing*, ÆGR.
spærian (N)=sparian
spærlic (e) adj. *sparing*, HGL 494. adv. -līce.
spærlīra (e, ea, eo) m. *calf of leg*, Æ. ['*sparlire*']
spærlīred *with a thick calf*, WW 161²⁷.
spærnes f. *frugality, nearness*, DR,GL.
spærstān m. *gypsum, chalk*, WW. ['*sparstone*']
spǣtan *to* '*spit*,' *spew*, G; Æ,CP. ['*spete*']
spǣtl=spātl
spǣtl(i)an *to spit*, BH : *foam at the mouth*, WW.
spǣtung f. *spitting*, LCD 65a.
spala m. *substitute*, LL 484,2¹.
spāld (*El*)=spātl. ['*spold*']
spaldur *balsam*, GL (v. ES 37·186).
span=spann
+**span** n. *suggestion, persuasion, allurement*, CP.
±**spanan**⁷ *to draw on, allure, seduce, mislead, persuade, instigate*, Æ,AO,CP.
span-e, -u, pl. -a, -an f. *teat*, LCD,WW.
spanere (o) m. *seducer, enticer*, WW.
±**spang** fn. *clasp, buckle*, GEN. [*Ger.* spange]
spann I. f. '*span*' (*measure*), BH,WW. **II.** pret. 3 sg. of spinnan.
+**spann** n. *fastening, band, buckle, yoke*, CP.
±**spannan**⁷ *to join, link, fasten, attach*, CP.
spannung f. *span*, WW.
-spanung (i²) v. for-, lēas-s.
sparcian=spearcian
±**sparian** *to* '*spare*,' *be indulgent or merciful to, save, BH,CP,Shr,VPs : use sparingly, not to use, Æ : forbear, abstain from, BH, CP*.

+**sparrian** *to shut, bar,* MtL6[6].

sparwa=spearwa

spātl (ǣ) n. *spittle, saliva,* CP,Lcd,NG. ['*spattle*']

spātlian *to spit out,* WW162. ['*spattle*']

spātlung f. *what is spit out, spittle,* WW162. ['*spattling*']

spāŏl=spātl

spāw pret. 3 sg. of spīwan.

speaft (MkL8[23])=speoft; **speara**=spearwa

spearca (æ, e) m. '*spark,*' Bf,Bo,Cp,MH; CP.

spearcian *to throw out sparks, sparkle,* SAT 78? (v. OEG4029).

spearewa=spearwa

spearhafoc m. *sparrow-hawk,* Cp,WW. ['*spar-hawk*']

spearlīr-=spærlīr-

spearn pret. 3 sg. of spurnan.

spearnes=spærnes

spearnlian *to spurn, kick, sprawl,* Æ,GL.

spearwa I. m. '*sparrow,*' BH,Chr,Cp,Ps. II. m. *calf (of the leg),* GL (cp. spærlīra).

spec=spic; **spēc**=spǣc, sprǣc

specan=sprecan

specca m. '*speck,*' *spot,* Cp,Lcd,WW.

specfāh *spotted, blotched,* Cp22.

sped '*glaucoma,*' *sticky moisture, phlegm, rheum,* Cp,OEG. ['*spade*']

spēd f. *luck, success, prosperity,* Cp,El, PPs : *riches, wealth, abundance,* Cr,Gen; AO : *opportunity, power, faculty,* Bl,PPs : (only in dp. spēdum) '*speed,*' *quickness,* Gen. on s. *fluently, skilfully : offspring?* PPs103[16]. [spōwan]

±**spēdan** w. d. *to prosper, succeed,* Chr,Ma. ['*speed*']

spēddropa m. *useful drop (ink),* RD27[8].

spediende *suffering from* 'sped,' WW.

spēdig *lucky, prosperous, rich,* AO : *plenteous, abundant : powerful.*

+**spēdiglīce** adv. *prosperously,* LPs44[5].

spēdignes f. *opulence,* OEG3605.

spēdlīce adv. *effectually, effectively,* PPs.

+**spēdsumian** *to prosper,* OEG3630.

spēdum v. spēd; **spel**=spell

spelc m? *splint,* Lcd. ['*spelk*']

spelcan *to fasten with splints,* Lcd. ['*spelk*']

speld n., nap. speld, speldru *ember, torch,* OEG,WW. ['*speld*']

+**spelia** m. *vicar, substitute, representative, deputy.*

spelian *to be substitute for, represent,* Æ,RB. ['*spele*']

speliend m. *substitute, representative,* Æ,GR.

speling f. *deputyship,* RB10[12].

spell n. *narrative, history, story, fable,* Bo : *speech, discourse, homily,* Æ,B,Bo,Da,Lcd; AO,CP : *message, news : statement, observation.* ['*spell*' and v. Mdf]

spellbōc f. *book of sermons,* TC430[21].

spellboda m. *messenger, ambassador, angel speaker : prophet.* [beodan]

spellcwide m. *historical narrative,* AO100[12].

±**spellian** *to speak, discourse, talk,* Bo,Lcd, LkL; Æ : *announce, relate, proclaim,* Met : *conspire,* GD106[1]. ['*spell*']

spellstōw f. *place of proclamations,* Ct.

spellung f. *speech, conversation, narrative, discourse,* Æ.

spelt I. m. '*spelt,*' *corn,* WW. [L.] II. '*planca,*' *board of a book,* WW164. ['*spelt*']

spelter (LCD3·136)=spaldur

-**spendan** v. ā-, for-s.

spendung f. '*spending,*' ÆH556[29].

spēnn (=spēonn) pret. 3 sg. of spannan.

spennels m. *clasp,* WW238[34].

spenst pres. 2 sg., spenð pres. 3 sg. of spanan.

speoft (MkR8[23]; MtL27[30]) redupl. pret. of *spatan? to spit.* [v. ANS141·176]

+**speoftian** *to spit upon,* LkL18[32]. [ES 38·34]

spēon pret. 3 sg. of spanan, spannan.

Spēonisc *Spanish,* ÆL37[1].

speoru (GL) nap. of spere.

speorulīra=spærlīra

spēow pret. 3 sg. of spōwan.

spēow-=spīw-; **sper-**=spær-, spear-, spyr-

spere n., nap. spe(o)ru '*spear,*' *javelin, lance,* Æ,AO,Chr,CP,Cp,LG : *stitching pain,* LCD175a.

sperebrōga m. *terror at spears,* RD18[4].

sperehand f. *male line of descent,* BC3·340[19].

sperehealf f. *male line of descent,* TC491[20].

sperelēas *without a (spear-)head,* WW143[7].

sperenŏ n. *battle,* GEN2059.

speresceaft (æ[3]) m. '*spear-shaft,*' GD14[27].

sperewyrt (speru-) f. '*spearwort,*' *elecampane,* Lcd,WW.

speriend (WW66[20])=spyrigend

+**sperod** *armed with a spear,* ÆGR,BL.

spic n. *fat bacon,* Lcd,OET; Æ. ['*spick*']

spīce f., spīca m. *aromatic herb, spice?* BL, LCD. [L. species]

spichūs n. *larder,* GL,LCD.

spīcing m. *spike, nail,* ANS125[51].

spicmāse f. *titmouse,* WW286[15].

spigettan *to spit,* Æ,Bo.

spilæg '*spilagius*' (*spalangius?*), a venomous insect, DR125[15].

spilc=spelc

spild m. *annihilation, ruin,* CP.

spildan *to waste, ruin, destroy,* AN,JnL.

spildsīŏ m. *destructive expedition,* Ex153.

spilian *to sport, play,* LL,WW. ['*spile*']

±**spillan** *to destroy, mutilate, kill,* LG : *waste, DR* : '*spill*' (*blood*), Nic.

spillere m. *parasite, jester,* OEG679.

spilling f. *waste*, CHR999E.

spilð (GL)=spild

spind sb. *fat*, WW.

spindel=sprindel

spinel f., gs. spinle *'spindle,'* Cp,LL : *the thread on a spindle?* OEG17³⁷.

spinelhealf (nl) f. *female line of descent*, TC491²¹.

spinge=spynge; **spinil**, spinl=spinel

-spinn v. in-s.

±**spinnan³** *to 'spin,'* Æ,Cp,Lcd,MtR : *twist, writhe*, Æ.

spīr *spike, blade*, LCD99b.

spircan (y) *to sparkle*, Æ,GL.

spircing (y) *sprinkling*, GPH398.

spitel m. *small spade, dibble*, LL; GD201²⁰. ['*spittle*']

spittan *to dig in with a spud*, LL454,10.

±**spittan** *to 'spit,'* LkR,MtR,MkL.

spittian *to spit (for cooking)* (Swt).

spitu f. *'spit' (cooking)*, Æ,HL.

spiðra? m. *spider*, LCD53b.

spīwan¹ *to spit, spit out, 'spew,' vomit*, Æ, Bl,Chr,CP,Jul,MH.

spiwdrenc (i²) m. *liquid emetic*, LCD.

spiwe m. *vomiting*, LCD22b.

spiwedrenc=spiwdrenc

spīwere m. *one who spews*, WW108⁴. ['*spewer*']

spiweða=spiwða

spiwian (io) *to spew, spit up* (w. d.), JUL476.

spīwing (ēo) f. '*spewing*,' WW.

spiwol *emetic*, LCD.

spiwða (eo) m. *vomiting, vomit*, Æ.

splātan? *to split*, v. ES49·156.

splin=spinl

splott m. *spot, blot : patch (of land)*, Æ.

+**splottod** *spotted*, TC537'.

spōn I. m. *sliver, chip, shaving*, BH,Cp,Lcd. ['*spoon*'] II. pret. 3 sg. of spanan.

+**spon**, spong=+span, spang

sponge f. '*sponge*,' Mt.

sponn=spann

spor n. *spoor, track, trail, footprint*, CP : *trace, vestige*. [Ger. spur]

spor-=spur-

sporettan¹ *to kick*, CVHy6¹⁵.

sporetung f. *kicking*, EHy6¹⁵.

spornettan *to spurn, kick*, WW.

sporning f. *stumbling-block*, Sc134⁵. [v. '*spurning*']

sporwrecel? m. *what is tracked after being driven off?* (BT),TC172'.

±**spōwan⁷** *to succeed, thrive*, Æ,AO,CP : (impers.) *profit, avail, help*, Æ.

spōwendlīce adv. *prosperously*, PPs.

spracen n. *berry-bearing alder*, LCD,WW.

spræc I. n. *shoot, slip*, WW44²⁹. II. pret. 3 sg. of sprecan.

spr&ēc (ē) f. *language*, Æ : 'SPEECH,' *power of speech*, CP : *statement, narrative, fable, discourse, conversation*, Æ,CP : *eloquence*, Æ : *report, rumour : decision, judgment : charge, suit*, CP : *point, question : place for speaking*, NG.

spræcan=sprecan

spr&ēccyn n. *mode of speech*, BH486¹.

spr&ēce f. *talk, discourse*, Bo137¹.

+**spr&ēce** *eloquent, affable*, Æ,BH.

+**spr&ēcelic** *incapable of being used alone (of the inseparable prepositions)*, ÆGR.

spr&ēcful *talkative*, LPs139¹².

spr&ēchūs n. *senate-house, curia : auditorium*, WW : *guest-quarters (in a monastery)*, ÆL 31⁸⁴⁷. ['*speech-house*']

spr&ēcon pret. pl. of sprecan.

spr&ēdan *to spread* : (+) *stretch forth, extend*.

spr&ēdung f. *propagation*, DR109².

spr&ēngan=sprengan

spranc=sprang

spranca m. *shoot, slip, branch*, Gl. ['*spronk*']

sprang pret. 3 sg. of springan.

sprangettan *to quiver*, MP1·610; WW 473².

sprēawlian *to 'sprawl,' move convulsively*, GPH,OEG.

+**sprec** n. *faculty of speech : talk, discussion*.

sprēc=spr&ēc

±**spreca** m. *spokesman, councillor*, Æ.

±**sprecan¹** *to 'SPEAK*,' say, utter, make a speech*, Æ,AO,CP : *converse, converse with*, Æ : *declare, tell of* : (+) *agree*, AO. sp. on *lay claim to*.

+**sprecendlic** (spec-) *that should be spoken*, Sc123².

sprēcern n. *place for speaking*, NG. [spr&ēc, ærn]

sprecolnes (spec-) f. *loquacity*, Sc170¹⁵.

sprecul *talkative*, SPs139¹².

sprengan (æ) (±) *to scatter, strew, sprinkle, sow*, Æ,LL : *spring, break, burst, split*. sp. on *administer a clyster*. [causative of springan; '*sprenge*']

sprenging (i) f. *sprinkling*, CM388.

sprēot m. *pole, pike, spear*, Cp,TC,WW. ['*sprit*']

spretting=sprytting

spreulian (OEG50³⁴)=sprēawlian

spreut (GL)=sprēot

spricð pres. 3 sg. of sprecan.

sprincel m. *basket-snare (for catching fish)*, WW (v. ES43·322; FM200).

sprind *vigorous, strong*, OEG,Sol. ['*sprind*'; springan]

-sprindlad v. ā-s.

sprindlīce adv. *vigorously*, OEG738.

spring (y) m. '*spring,' source*, BC : *sprinkling : ulcer : flux*.

±**springan**[3] *to jump, leap, 'spring,' burst forth, rise*, B,Bo,G,Ma,MH; Æ : *spread, be diffused, grow*, Æ,Bf : *want, lack*, VH.

springd=sprind; **springing**=sprenging

springwyrt f. *caper-plant*, LCD.

+**sprintan** *to emit, utter*, JnL p 187[12].

spritting=sprytting

sprota m., sprot(t) n. *sprout. twig*, OEG, WW : *peg*. ['*sprote*']

sprott m. *sprat*, ÆL,Bf,NC. ['*sprot*']

sprungen pp., sprungon pret. pl. of springan.

-**sprūtan** v. ā-, geond-s.

sprycð pres. 3 sg. of sprecan.

spryng=spring; **sprȳtan**=spryttan

sprytle f. *chip*, BH 204[56] (v.l.).

spryttan *to sprout, come forth, spring, germinate, yield fruit*, BH,Lcd; Æ : *incite*. ['*sprit*']

sprytting (e, i) f. *shoot, sprout : increase*, CM 381.

spunnen pp., spunnon pret. pl. of spinnan.

spur-=spor-

spura (o) m. *spur*, Æ,Gl.

spure f. *heel*, EPs 48[5].

spurleðer n. *spur-strap*, WW 97[10].

±**spurnan**[3] (o) *to strike against, kick*, PPs : '*spurn,*' *reject*, Æ : *stumble*.

spurnere (o) m. *fuller*, ÆGR 35[2].

spurul (=*spurnul?) *given to kicking or trampling?* OET.

spylian v. ā-s.

spynge (i), spyncge f. *sponge*, AO. [*L.* spongia]

spyrc-=spirc-

spyrd m. '*stadium,' race-course*, NG.

spyremann (e[1]) m. *tracker*, TC 172'.

±**spyrian** (i) *to make a track, go, pursue, travel, journey*, CP : *follow out, ask about, investigate*, BH,Bo. ['*speer*'; spor]

spyrigend m. *investigator, inquirer*, SOL 140.

spyrnan *to stumble*, RWH 94[22].

spyrran (e;=ie) *to strike*, AA 22[8].

spyrring f. *striking*, OEG.

spyrte (e, i) f. *wicker basket, eel-basket*, Æ. [*L.* sporta]

spyrung f. *asking, investigation*, OEG 5214.

staca m. *pin, 'stake,'* AO,Lcd; Æ.

stacan (stagan) *to pierce with a stake, spit* (or ?*roast*, ES 40·242), IM 124[71].

stacung f. *the piercing of an effigy by a '* staca*' (a method of injury by witchcraft)*, LL.

stæde-=stede-

stæf m., nap. stafas '*staff,' stick, rod*, Æ,Bo, Cp,LPs,CP : *pastoral staff* : (often in pl.) *letter, character, writing*, Æ,Bo,WW : *document* : (in pl.) *letters, literature, learning*.

stæfad=stafod

stæfcræft m. *grammar*, Æ : (in pl.) *learning*, BH.

stæfcræftig *lettered*, OEG.

stæfcyst f. *letters, learning from books*, Æ.

stæfgefég n. *syllable*, ÆGR : *letters*, LSPs 70[15].

+**stæflæred** *instructed, lettered*, LCD.

stæfleahtor m. *grammatical fault*, OEG 5467.

stæfleornere m. *student*, OEG 3126.

stæflic *literary : literal*, Æ. ['*staffly*']

stæfliðere f. *sling, 'balista,'* GL.

stæfn=stefn

stæfplega m. *literary game*, GL.

stæfræw f. *row of letters, line of writing*, ÆL 23b[767] : *alphabet*, BH 484[27].

stæfróf *alphabet*, WW 397[14].

stæfsweord n. '*dolon,' lance? javelin?* WW. ['*staffsword*']

stæfwīs (e) *lettered, learned*, LCD 3·186'.

stæfwrītere=stærwrītere

stæg n. I. '*stay*' (*rope*), WW 288[26]. II. *pool, pond*. [*L.* stagnum]

-**stægan** v. ā-st.

stægan *steep*, CR, GL. [stigan]

stæger I. fn? '*stair,' staircase*, Æ,WW. [stigan] II. (BYH 110[18])=stægel

stægl=stægel

stæl I. n. *place, spot. on* stale *in place of, instead of. on* stale béon *stand in* (*good*) *stead, be a help to*, AO 232[23] : *situation, condition*. [*Ger.* stelle] II. pret. 3 sg. of stelan.

stæl=staðol; **stæla**=stela

±**stælan** *to found, institute, carry on : confess, admit*, VH. synne st. *to institute sin*, i.e. *enter on a conflict*, MEN 287 : (w. d.) *put upon, impute to, accuse of, charge with* : (†) *avenge*. [=*stæðlian=staðolian]

stæle=stale ds. of stalu.

stælg=stægel

stælgiest m. *thievish stranger*, RD 48[5].

stælherige m. *predatory army*, CP,CHR. [stelan]

stælhrān m. *decoy-reindeer*, AO 18[11].

stæll=steall; **stællan**=stiellan

+**stællan** *to stall, stable*, MH 20[1].

stælon pret. pl. of stelan.

stæltihtle f. *charge of stealing*, LL.

stælðing n. *theft*, CHRD 19[16]. [stelan]

stælwierðe *serviceable*, CP,Chr,Shr. [staðol; '*stalworth*']

stælwyrt f. *water-starwort*, WW 299[5].

+**stæn-**=+sten-

stæn-=stænen-, stān-

stænan (±) *to stone*, Mt; Æ,CP : *adorn with precious stones*, EL 151. ['*steen*']

stænc=stenc

stǣne f. *pitcher, jug*, WW 415[18]. ['*stean*']

stǣnen *made of stone, stony, Bl,G,MH*; Æ, AO,CP. ['*stonen*']
stǣner *stony ground*, NG.
stæng=steng
stǣnlíc *stony*, Lᴄᴅ 1·216'.
stǣning f. *stoning*, Æ,MH.
stæpe (a, e) m. usu. nap. nap. stapas (stæpan, RPs139⁵) *going, gait*, '*step*,' *pace, Ps,Rd, W*; Æ,CP : *spoor: power of locomotion: short distance, measure of length, MtR,WW* : *step, stair, Æ,VPs* : *pedestal, socket, HL* 199 : *grade, degree, Æ.* in stæpe *instantly*.
stæpegong (e) m. *stepping, going*, Rɪᴍ 22.
stæpmǣlum adv. *step by step, by degrees, gradually*, CP.
±**stæppan⁶** (e) *to* ' sᴛᴇᴘ,' *go, advance, Æ,CP*; AO.
stæppescōh (e) m. *slipper*, WW.
stær m., nap. staras *starling, Cp,MtL.* ['*stare*']
stǣr (ē) n. *story, history, narrative*, BH. [v. A 37·56 and LF 161]
stærblind *stone-blind, Cp.* ['*stareblind*']
stærcedferhð=stercedferhð
stǣreblind (*Shr*)=stærblind
stǣrleornere? m. *student of history*, v. OEG 4145n.
stǣrlíce adv. *historically*, OEG 2³¹⁰.
stærling m. '*starling,*' ZDA 33·241⁵⁴.
stærn=stearn
stǣrtractere m. *commentator, historian*, WW 207¹.
stǣrwrítere m. *historian*, AO.
stæð n. occl. gds. staðe, nap. staðas *shore, river-bank, AO,Chr*; Æ,CP. ['*staith*']
stæðfæst *firm, stable*, Cʀ 981.
stæðhlýpe I. (ē) *sloping, precipitous.* II. f. *a steep place*, GD 95¹⁶.
stæðhlýplíce adv. *steeply*, Bʟ 207²⁰.
stæðswealwe f. *sand-martin*, Lᴄᴅ,WW.
stæððan *to support*, Rᴅ 4⁷⁴.
±**stæððíg** *staid, serious*, Æ.
±**stæððígnes** f. *staidness, seriousness*, Æ,CP.
stæðweall m. *barrier of the shore*, Gᴇɴ 1376.
stæðwyrt f. *a plant*, Lᴄᴅ 29a.
stafas nap. of stæf.
staflan *to dictate*, Æ.
stafod (æ, e) *striped*, Ep,Erf.
stāg pret. 3 sg. of stīgan.
stagan=stacan?
stagga m. *stag, LL* 624,24. ['*stag*']
stāh pret. 3 sg. of stīgan.
stal=steall
+**stāl** n. *plaint, accusation, confession?* MFH 163,VH : *contention*, GD 329¹⁵.
+**stala** m. *accessory in theft*, LL 100,25¹.
stalað=staðol
stald=steald; **stale** v. stæl.
stālern n. *court of law*, WW.

staleð-=staðol-
stalgong m. *stealthy going*, Gᴜ 1113.
stalian *to go stealthily*, AO : (±) *steal, Æ.*
±**stālian** *to establish, confirm, strengthen* : *make an accusation*, LL 110ʙ¹. [=staðolian]
stall=steall
stalu I. (±) f. *stealing, robbery, theft, Bl, MtL*; Æ : *stolen article* : *fine for stealing.* ['*stale*'] II. *wood to which harp-strings are fixed?* WW 203³⁶. [v. '*stale*']
stalung f. *stealing, robbery*, AO.
stam (o) *stammering*, Gʟ.
stamera m. *stammerer*, EC 226'.
stamerian (omr-) *to* '*stammer,*' GPH,HL.
stammetan (o) *to stammer*, WW 447³⁰.
stamor *stammering*, Gʟ.
stān m. (and n. in NG) 'sᴛᴏɴᴇ,' *rock* : *gem*, CP : *calculus* : *milestone* (v. Mdf).
stānæx (e²) f. *stone-workers' axe?* WW.
stānbæð n. *vapour bath made by water poured on to heated stones* (BT), Lᴄᴅ.
stānbeorg m. *rocky elevation*, B,Ct.
stānberende *stony*, WW 427³⁶.
stānbill n. *tool for working stone*, WW 447³³.
stānboga† m. *rocky arch*, B.
stānbrycg f. *stone bridge*, Ct,WW.
stānbucca m. *mountain goat*, ÆGʀ 68⁵.
stānburg f. *town or fort of stone*, Gᴇɴ; Mdf.
stanc I. pret. 3 sg. of stincan. II. sb. *sprinkling*, WW.
stāncarr m. *rock*, DR 19¹¹.
stānceastel (i²) m. *walled enclosure? heap of stones?* Ct (v. GBG).
stānceosel (i², y²) m. *sand*, GᴇɴC 22¹⁷,OEG.
stān-clif n., nap. -clifu, -cleofu (B) *rock, cliff, crag*, GD.
stānclūd m. *rock*, Æ,CP.
stāncnoll m. *rocky knoll*, EC 248¹⁷.
stāncræftiga m. *clever stone-worker*, MH 202¹⁴.
stancrian *to sprinkle*, WW 162⁴⁶.
stāncrop m. '*stone-crop*' (*plant*), Lᴄᴅ.
stāncynn n. *kind of stone*, VH,ZDA 34·233.
stāncysel=stānceosel
stāncyst(en) *chestnut-tree*, KC 4·8²². [L. castanea]
stand (o) m. *delay*, MkLR 6³⁵. [v. '*stand*']
±**standan⁶** (o) *to* 'sᴛᴀɴᴅ*' ('*i-stand*'), *occupy a place, stand firm, Æ,AO,CP* : *congeal*, Lᴄᴅ 35b : *remain, continue, abide*, AO, CP : *stand good, be valid, be, exist, take place, Æ,CP: oppose, resist attack : reprove* : *stand still, stop, Æ* : (†) *appear, flash out* : *arise, come* : (†) *be present to, come upon* (*of fear*). ne s. tō ahte *be of no account*, W 82n. (+) *stand up, keep one's feet, Bo* : (+) *attack, assail, ÆL* : (+) *perform.* s. on *consist* : *depend on.*

stāndenu *stony valley*, KC3·383.
stāneht=stānihte; **stānex**=stānæx
stān-fæt n., nap. -fatu *stone vessel*, G,
WAL.
stānfāh† *stone-paven*.
stānflōr m. *paving-stone, tessella*, OEG14³.
[cp. flōrstān]
stang pret. 3 sg. of stingan.
stāngaderung f. *stone wall*, ERPs61³.
stāngeat n. *opening between rocks*, Ct.
stāngedelf n. *stone-quarry*, KC.
stāngefeall n. *heap of stones*, MH212²¹.
stāngefōg n. *stone-laying*, EL1021.
stāngella (i²) m. *'staniel,' pelican, VPs,WW*.
stāngetimbre n. *masonry*, WW441⁶.
stāngeweorc n. *art of building : stone-work,
masonry, Æ.*
stān-gripe m., dp. -greopum *handful of
stones?* EL824.
stānhege m. *stone fence, wall*, LPs79¹³.
stānhīfet (Ct)=stānhȳwet
stānhlinc m. *stony ridge*, KC.
stān-hliþ† n., nap. -hliðu, -hleoðu *rocky
slope, cliff, rock.*
stānhof n. *stone building*, RUIN39.
stānhol n. *hole in a rock*, AA8,33.
stānhricg m. *rocky ridge*, OEG5465.
stānhȳpe f. *stone-heap*, KC3·431⁹.
stānhȳwet n. *stone-quarry*, WW112¹⁰.
stānig (ǣ) '*stony,' rocky, MtR*; AO.
stāniht (ǣ) I. adj. *stony, rocky*, AO. II. n.
stony ground (Swt).
stānincel n. *little stone*, A13·31⁸⁶.
stānlesung f. *building with loose stones*, WW
117³⁴. [lesan]
stānlīm m. *cement, mortar*, WW205⁹.
stānmerce m. *parsley*, WW.
stānrocc m. *high rock, obelisk*, GL.
stānscalu f. *shale*, EC306¹⁸.
stānscræf n. *rocky cave*, MH.
stānscylf m. *rugged rock*, HGL449.
stānscylig *shaly, stony*, Mk4⁵. [sciell]
stānsticce n. *bit of stone*, WW376¹⁸.
stānstrǣt f. *paved road*, TC525²¹.
stāntorr m. *stone tower : crag, rock*, GD
12.
stānweall m. '*stone wall,' VPs*; Æ.
stānweg m. *paved road*, BC1·417'.
stānweorc n. '*stone-work,' RWH43¹⁷ : stone
structure, Æ.*
stānwong m. *stony plain*, RD88⁶.
stānwurma m. *mineral colour*, OEG1061.
stānwurðung f. *worship of stones*, LL.
stānwyrht? f. *stone structure*, WW341¹⁰.
stānwyrhta m. *stone-mason*, GL.
stapa m. *grasshopper, locust*, WW.
stapas v. stæpe; **stapel**=stapol
stapela m. *post, stake*, LL387,4².
stapen pp. of steppan.

stapol m., nap. stapolas, staplas *basis, trunk
of a tree, post, prop, support, stay, pillar,
column, An,MtL,WW : threshold? B*926 :
market and court? (v. EC466n) : *steps up
to a house door*, WW126⁸. ['*staple'*; v.
Mdf]
stapolweg m. *staked-out road?* KC5·281²³.
-stapplian v. under-s.; **stapul**=stapol
staras v. stær; **starc**=stearc
stareblind=stærblind
±starian *to* '*stare,' gaze, ÆL,B.*
staþ- v. stæð; **staþel**=staðol
staðol (ea¹, c², u²) m. *base, foundation,
support, BH,WW*; AO,CP : *station, position, state, condition*, CP : *stability, security :
firmament, heavens : underside of a turf,
Lcd : estate, farm*, GD222. ['*staddle*';
standan]
staðolǣht f. *real estate*, RIM22.
staðolfæst *fixed, firm, steadfast, Bo,MtL.*
['*stathelfast'*]
staðolfæstlic *steadfast, firm*, Æ. adv. -līce.
staðolfæstnes (ea) f. *stability*, Æ,GD.
+**staðol-fæst(n)ian**, -festian (ea¹, u²) *to
make firm, establish.*
staðolfæstnung f. *foundation*, LPs136⁷.
±**staðolian** (e²) *to fix, found, establish, Bl :
confirm, make steadfast, strengthen.* ['*sta-
thel'*]
+**staðoliend** (e²) m. *founder*, LPs47².
±**staðolung** f. *foundation, settlement : ordinance*, RB112²⁴.
staðolwang† m. *settling place.*
staðol=staðol; **steaf-**=stæf-
+**steal** n. *structure, frame*, WA110.
stealc† *lofty, steep, precipitous*, RD.
-stealcian v. be-s.
stealcung f. *act of going stealthily*, ÆH.
['*stalking'*]
steald pret. 3 sg. of stellan.
+**steald†** n. *dwelling, habitation.*
stealdan⁷ *to possess, own*, RIM22.
steall (a) mn. *standing, place, position, state,
WW : 'stall' (for cattle), stable, Cp*; Æ :
fishing ground.
-stealla v. eaxl-, hand-, ofer-s.
steallere (a) m. *marshal, constable*, CHR,
KC.
-steallian v. forð-s.
stēam (ē, īe) m. '*steam,' moisture, exhalation, Æ,Lcd,Pa : steaming fluid, blood,
ROOD62.
stēap I. *precipitous, deep : high, lofty, B,
Rd : prominent, projecting, Æ : upright?
B*2566 : *bright, brilliant, Gn,Sol.* ['*steep'*] II.
(ēo) m. *stoup, beaker, flagon.*
stēap-=stēop-
stēaphēah *very high*, RD264.
stēapol m. *cairn?* Ct (Swt).

stearc (a) *stiff, rigid, obstinate, Æ,El : stern, severe, hard, Æ : harsh, rough, strong, violent, impetuous, WW.* ['*stark*']

stearcferð *harsh, stern,* JUL636.

stearcheard *excessive,* DD200?

stearcheort† *stout-hearted,* B.

stearcian *to stiffen, become hard,* GPH402⁵⁶. ['*stark*']

stearclīce adv. *stoutly, strongly, vigorously,* Chr1016D : *strictly,* CHRD54²⁶. ['*starkly*']

stearcmōd *stubborn,* CHRD8²⁷.

stearm (NG)=storm

stearn (æ, e) m. *sea-swallow? tern?* Gl,Seaf. ['*stern*']

stearra (DR)=steorra

steartlian *to kick, struggle,* OEG. ['*startle*']

stea-ðel, -ðul=staðol

steb=stybb; **stebn** (GL)=stefn

stēda m. *stud-horse, stallion, Æ : entire camel.* ['*steed*']

stede (y) m. *place, site, position, station, Æ, Bo,Ct,Lcd,RB;* CP; Mdf : *firmness, standing, stability, steadfastness, fixity, Æ : strangury.* of s. *immediately.* [standan; '*stead*']

stedefæst '*steadfast,' steady, firm,* Ma,LL; ÆL.

stedefæstnes (styd-) f. *constancy,* DR50².

stedeheard† *firm, strong,* JUD223 (or ?steðe-).

stedelēas *unsteady, unstable,* ÆL.

stedewang† m. *field, plain.*

stedewist f. *steadiness,* HGL530⁴.

+stēdhors n. *stud-horse, stallion,* BH 138CA¹.

stedig *sterile,* Æ,LPs.

+stedigian (e²) *to stand still,* ÆL31²⁴².

stedignes f. *sterility,* ERSPs34¹².

stedinglīne f. *stay (ship's rope),* WW.

stef-=stæf-, staf-; **stefen**=stefn I.

stefn (æ) I. f. *voice, sound,* Æ,CP. II. m. *message, summons, turn (of military service), time : a body of men who take a turn at work, the English military force?* (BT), KC5·121'. nīwan stefne *anew, again.* III. m. '*stem,' trunk,* Bo,Sol : *foundation, root,* Bo : *prow or stern of a vessel,* B,WW. [stæf]

stefna† (æ) m. *prow or stern of a ship,* An. ['*stem*']

stefnan I. (±) *to institute, arrange, regulate : alternate.* II. (+) *to provide with a fringe,* CM288.

stefnbyrd f. *control,* CREAT45.

stefnelof n. '*vociferatio,*' LPs26⁶.

stefnettan (mn) *to stand firm,* MA122.

stefnhlōw (mn) *vocalic,* BF100¹⁶.

±stefnian (w. d.) *to summon,* CHR, MFH 163.

stefning (mn) f. *border, hem,* WW : *turn, shift,* CHR894.

stefnmǣlum (mm) *alternately,* CM280.

stela (æ, eo) m. *stalk : support,* ÆT.

±stelan⁴ *to 'steal,' rob,* Æ,Cp,LG,LL.

stēle (GL)=stȳle

stellan I. (y) *to place, put, set (example),* AO,CP. +stelled bēon mid *have an attack of,* GD. ['*stell*'] II.=stiellan

stelmēle m. *handled vessel,* LL455,17.

stelscofl (eo¹) f. *shovel with (long) handle?* GPH400⁴⁹⁸.

stem-=stefn-

stēm=stēam; **stēm-**=stīem-

steming=stemning

stemn (CP)=stefn

stempan *to pound,* LCD1·378'.

stempingīsern n. *stamping-iron,* WW.

+sten (æ) n. *groaning,* PPs30¹¹.

stenan *to groan,* PPs37⁹ : *rattle, clash,* EL 151.

stēnan=stǣnan

stenc m. *odour, Æ,BH,Bl : scent, fragrance,* CP : '*stench,' stink,* Æ,AO,BH. [stincan]

±stencan I. *to scatter : afflict?* PPs43³. II. *to stink,* JnL. ['*stench*'] III. *to pant,* HGL.

stencbǣre *stinking,* BH48¹⁷.

stencbrengende *odoriferous,* DR77'.

+stence (æ) *odoriferous,* LCD1·282'.

stencfæt n., pl. -fatu *smelling bottle,* OEG 8²⁹⁹.

±stencnes f. *odour,* DR.

stenecian *to pant,* OEG6⁵. [stenan]

steng m. *stake, pole, bar, rod, staff, cudgel,* Cp,LG,MH; CP. ['*sting*'; v. Mdf]

stent pres. 3 sg. of standan.

steol-=stel-

stēold pret. 3 sg. of stealdan.

stēop-=stēap

stēopbearn n. *orphan, Æ.* ['*stepbairn*']

stēopcild (ē, ēa) n. *orphan, unprotected one,* Bl,Jn. ['*stepchild*']

stēopdohtor (ē) f. '*step-daughter,*' WW, RWH139¹².

stēopfæder m. '*step-father,*' AO,Ep.

stēopmōdor f. '*step-mother,*' AO,Cp.

stēopsunu m. '*step-son,*' AO,Cp,WW.

stēor I. (ȳ) f. *steering, direction, guidance, Æ,BH : rule, regulation, Æ : restraint, discipline, correction, Æ,CP : penalty, fine, punishment, Æ,CP.* ['*steer*'] II. m. '*steer,' bullock, young cow,* Gl.

stēora (īe, īo, ȳ) m. *steersman, pilot, guider, director,* CP. ['*steer*']

stēoran=stīeran

stēorbord n. '*starboard,*' AO.

stēore f. *direction, discipline,* LL.

stēorend (ȳ) m. *corrector, director, ruler,* AN.

stēorere m. *steersman,* CP431³¹.

stēoresmann (*LL*)=stēormann ['*steers-man*']
steorfa m. *pestilence : carrion*, LL.
steorfan³ *to die*, ÆH. ['*starve*']
steorglēaw *clever at astronomy*, OEG.
stēorlēas *not under control or rule, wild, profligate, foolish*, Bo. ['*steerless*']
stēorlēaslīc *unmanageable*, GD 289¹⁰.
stēormann m. *pilot, master of a ship*, Æ. ['*steerman*']
stēornægl m. *handle of a helm*, WW 312⁴?
steornede *having a bold forehead?* WW. [cp. *Ger.* stirn]
stēoroxa m. *steer*, WW 120²⁶.
steorra m. '*star*,' *Chr,Lcd,VPs*.
stēorrēōra m. *steersman, master of a ship*, BL.
stēor-rōðer, -rōðor n. '*rudder*,' *Cp*; CP.
steorscēawere m. *astronomer, astrologer*, WW.
stēorscēofol f. *rudder*, WW.
stēorsetl n. *steersman's seat, after-part of a ship*, Æ.
stēorsprēc (=æ) *reproof*, RPs 37¹⁵.
stēorstefn m. *stern (of ship)*, WW 482¹⁵.
steort (e) sm. *tail, Cp,Bo : spit of land, cape : plough-tail*. ['*start*']
stēor-weorð, -wierðe *blameworthy, reprehensible*, CP 194,195³.
steorwigle n. *astrology*, GL.
steorwiglere m. *mathematician, astrologer*, OEG 55⁸.
steorwiglung f. *astrology*, A 13·33¹⁴¹.
step-=stæp-; stēp-=stēop-
stēpan† I. (±) *to erect, raise : elevate, exalt, honour, adorn, enrich :* (+) *help, support*. [stēap] II. (±) *to initiate, consecrate*, WW.
stēpel=stīpel
stēr=stær
stēran I. *to burn incense : fumigate*, Æ,Lcd. ['*stere*'] II.=stīeran
stercedferhð† (æ) *stout of heart, determined, bold, brave*.
stēring f. *incense*, OEG 1512.
stermelda m. *informer? complainant?* LL 9,5; v. 2·202.
stern=stearn; sterra (N)=steorra
stert=steort; sterung=styrung
stēða (WW)=stēda
steðeheard? *hardened on the anvil*, JUD 223 (v. ES 64·212).
stēup- (Ep)=stēop-
stī-=stig-; stīc-=stycce-
stīcādl f. *pain in the side, stitch*, WW 112²².
sticca m. '*stick*,' *Lcd : peg, pointer : spoon*, Lcd.
sticce I. n. *sticky matter*, LCD. II.=stycce
sticcian=stician
±stice m. *sting, prick, puncture, stab*, CP, LL : '*stitch*,' *pain in the side*, Lcd.

sticel I. m. *prick, goad, thorn*, CP. II.= sticol
sticels (Æ)=sticel
sticfōdder n. *case for spoons? or made of twigs?* LL 455,17.
stician (y) (±) tr. *to 'stick,' prick, stab, transfix, goad, gouge out, AO,BH,MH*; CP : *kill :* intr. *stick, inhere, be placed, lie, remain fixed, be hampered*, Æ,Bo; CP : *project*, KC.
sticmǣlum (Æ)=styccemǣlum
stic-ol, -ul *lofty, sharp, abrupt, steep*, Æ : *arduous, rough : scaly : biting*, GPH 417.
sticolnes (y²) f. *height*, OEG 4437.
stictǣnel m. *basket*, WW 403².
sticung f. *pricking, goading, stabbing*, AO.
sticwærc m. *stitch in the side*, WW 112²¹.
sticwyrt f. *agrimony*, WW 136²¹.
stīegan=stīgan
stiell m. *jump, leap, spring*, CR 720-736.
±stiellan I. (æ, e, i, y) *to leap, rush : attack*, GD. II. (y) *to make stalls for cattle? or to put them in stalls?* LL 454,11¹³.
stiem=stēam
stīeman (ē, ȳ) *to emit vapour, 'steam,' exhale (odour)*, Æ,Ph. [stēam]
stieme (ī) *a plant?* LCD 3·32¹⁹?
stīeming (ē) f. *fragrance*, OEG.
stiep m. *downfall?* GEN 60?
-stīepan (ē, ēa, ēo, ȳ) v. ā-s.
stīera=stēora
±stīeran (ēo, ī, ȳ) *to 'steer,' guide, direct, govern, rule*, Æ,BH,Bo,CP : (w. d. or g.) *restrain, correct, reprove, punish*, Bl,Lcd, MkL; Æ,AO,CP. [stēor]
-stierfan (æ, e, y) v. ā-s.
stiern-=styrn-
stiernes (ȳ) f. *discipline*, Æ.
stiernlīce (CP) v. styrnlīce.
stīf *rigid, 'stiff*,' GPH 394.
stīfearh m. *little pig (kept in a sty)*, LL 449,7. [stig]
stīflan *to be or become rigid*, ÆGR.
stīfician=stȳfecian
stīfig *steep*, BC (Mdf).
stig n. *sty, pen : hall*, Ct,GL.
stīg fm. *narrow path, way, footpath, track, road, course, line*, B,G,Ps. ['*sty*']
±stīgan¹ *to move, go, reach : go up, spring up, ascend, rise, mount, scale*, Bo,VPs; AO,CP : *go down, descend*, Æ,CP. ['*sty*']
stige m. *ascent, descent*, MEN 64.
stig-el (-ol) f. '*stile*,' *Ct,GD* 24.
stigelhamm m. *enclosure reached by a stile*, KC 5·289².
stīgend I. m. *stye (on the eye)*, WW 114¹⁰. ['*styan*'] II. m. *sailor*, v. OEG 32n.
stigian *to shut into a 'sty*,' Bf.
stīgnes f. *descent*, LkL 19³⁷.

stigráp m. '*stirrup*,' *WW*.

stigu=stig

stig-weard, -wita=stī-weard, -wita

stihl=stigel

+stiht n. *dispensation, provision*, VH 20.

stihtan (±) *to rule, direct, arrange, order, ordain*, AO,CP : *instigate*. [*Ger.* stiften]

stihtend (y) m. *disposer*, JUL419 : *protector*, RPs 58¹².

stihtere m. *director, ruler*, CP391²² : *steward*, GD221¹⁹.

stihtian (CP)=stihtan

±stihtung f. *arrangement, direction, dispensation, providence*, AO.

stīhð pres. 3 sg. of stīgan.

stileð=stylð pres. 3 sg. of stelan.

±stillan (y) I. *to be still, have rest, Ma* : (w. d. or a.) '*still*' ('*i-still*'), *quiet, calm, appease, hush, An,BH,Gen,LL* : *stop, restrain, abate, relieve, Lcd*. II.=stiellan

stille adj. adv. '*STILL*,' *quiet, calm, stable, fixed* : *gentle, Æ*; CP : *silent, Æ* : *secret*.

stilles=stilnes

stillīce adv. *silently*, CM266.

stil(l)nes (AO,CP) f. '*stillness*,' *quiet, Æ, Bo* : *silence, HL* : *peace*, AO,CP : *release, relaxation*, CP.

stīme=stīeme

stincan³ *to emit a smell*, '*stink*,' *exhale, ÆGr, Cp,Lcd*; AO : *sniff*, B2289 : *rise (of dust, vapour, etc.)*, RD30¹².

+stincan³ tr. *to smell*, CP : *have the sense of smell*, PPs. ['*i-stink*']

sting (y) m. '*sting*,' *puncture, thrust, BH, Guth*.

stingan³ I. *to* '*sting*,' *stab, pierce, push through, thrust, Bo,Ma*; CP. *st.* on *lay claim to, usurp*. II.=stincan

stintan=styntan; stīora=stēora

stiorc=stirc

stīpel (ē, ȳ) m. '*steeple*,' *tower, Æ,Mt*. [stēap]

stīpere m. *post, prop*, WW 126¹¹.

+stīr-=+stȳr; stir-=styr-

stīran=stīeran; stīráp=stigráp

stirc (io, y) n. *calf, Æ,Gl*.

stirgan=styrian; stitian=stihtan

stīð *stiff, thick, rigid, hard, firm, strong, CP* : *resolute, brave, Æ* : *stubborn, unrelenting, austere, strict, fierce, harsh, cruel, CP*; Æ. ['*stith*']

stīðe I. adv. *very much, strongly, well* : *harshly, strictly, severely, bitterly, Gen*; Æ. ['*stith*'] II. f. *name of a plant*, LCD160b.

stīðecg *stiff-edged*, RD88¹⁴.

stīðferhð† *determined, stern*.

stīðhycgende† (-hug-) *determined, resolute, brave* : *stern, obstinate*.

stīðhȳdig† *determined, resolute*.

stīðhygd *determined, resolute*, JUL654.

+stīðian *to become hard* : *become strong, grow up, mature, Æ* : *make firm*, CP.

stīðlic *firm, stout, strong, hard* : *decided* : *harsh, stern, severe*, Æ,CP. adv. -līce *forcibly*, BF94¹³.

stīðmægen n. *powerful force*, DD114.

stīðmōd† *resolute, brave, firm, unflinching, stubborn, stern, severe*.

stīðnes f. *hardness, rigidity, strictness, severity, rigour, Æ* : *firmness, constancy, Æ*.

stīðweg m. *rough way*, RD4³⁵.

stīweard m. '*steward*,' *housekeeper, guardian, WW*. [stig-]

stīwita m. *housekeeper? householder?* GEN 2079; RD4¹⁰.

stoc n. *place, house, dwelling*, GD (v. ES 37·191). ['*stoke*']

stocc m. '*stock*,' *stump, stake, post, log, Æ, Bl,OET*; Mdf : *stocks* : *trumpet, MtL*6².

stoccen *made of logs?* KC3·73'.

stoclīf n. *dwelling-place, city*, AS.

stocweard m. *citizen*, OEG5272.

stocwīc n. *dwelling-place*, GD172⁴.

stod mf. *post*, WW106³³.

-stod v. wealh-s.

stōd I. f. '*stud*' (*of horses*), KC,WW; Mdf. II. pret. 3 sg. of standan.

stōdfald m. *stud-fold, paddock*, Ct.

stōdhors n. *stud-horse, stallion*, BH138¹. [v. '*steed*']

stodla m. (*weaver's*) *slay*, LL455,15¹.

stōdmyre (e²) f. *brood-mare*, LL58,16. ['*studmare*']

stōdon pret. pl. of standan.

stōdðēof m. *horse-stealer*, LL54,9².

stofa, stofu, mf. *bath-room*, GL. [v. '*stove*']

stofbæð (u¹) n. *vapour-bath*, LCD.

stofn mf. *trunk, stem, branch, shoot*, OEG, WW : *progeny*, OEG : *station, position*. ['*stoven*']

+stogen pp. of +stīgan at MFB208.

stōl m. '*stool*,' *chair, seat, CP,Cp,G,Gen, Lcd,LL* : *throne* : *bishop's see*.

stole fn. '*stole*,' *long outer garment, DR, NG*. [L.]

stolen pp. of stelan.

stom=stam

stonc=stanc pret. 3 sg. of stincan.

stond=stand

stōp pret. 3 sg. of steppan.

stōpel m. *footprint*, BL127.

stoppa m. *bucket, pail*, GD,Gl. ['*stop*']

-stoppian v. for-s. ['*stop*']

stōr I. m. *incense, frankincense, Æ*. [L. storax] II. *strong, great, Chr* 1085. ['*stour*']

storc m. '*stork*,' *Æ,Gl*.

stōr-cille, -cyl(le) f. *censer, Æ*.

störfæt n. *censer*, IM 120¹⁴.

storm m. *tempest, 'storm,'* Lcd,LG,VPs : (†) *rush, onrush, attack, tumult, disturbance*, An,B; CP.

stormig *stormy*, OEG?,RWH66¹⁵ (storem-).

stormsæ *stormy sea*, Bo 115²².

störsæp n. *resin*, OEG4027.

störsticca m. *rod for stirring the incense in the censer?* (BT), EC 250,21.

stot m. *a kind of horse*, v. NC 323. [*'stot'*]

stöw f. *spot, site, station, locality, position*, B,Bo; Æ,AO,CP; Mdf : (*holy*) *place*, LL. [*'stow'*]

stöwigan *to retain, restrain*, Cp 1713.

stöwlic *local, limited by space*, Æ. adv. -līce *as regards place*, Æ.

strāc pret. 3 sg. of strīcan.

strācian *to 'stroke,'* CP,Lcd.

strācung f. *stroking*, WW 179⁹.

strād (1) pret. 3 sg. of strīdan; (2)=strēad

stræc (ǣ? e) **I.** *firm, strict, severe, stern, rigid, obstinate, hard*, Æ,CP : *strenuous, vehement, violent*, Æ. [streccan] **II.** n. *rigour* : *violence, force*, Æ.

stræclic *strict*, CP. adv. -līce *strictly, severely, vehemently, violently*, CP.

stræcnes (e) f. *pertinacity* : *rigidity, rigour*, GD.

stræde f. *pace*, MtL5⁴¹.

strædon pret. pl. of strēdan.

strægd pret. 3 sg. of stregdan.

strægdnes f. *aspersion*, BH446¹⁵.

strægl=strǣl II.

strǣl I. fm. *arrow, dart, missile.* [*Ger.* strahl] **II.** f. *curtain, quilt, matting, bed, Gl.* [*'strail'*]

strǣlbora m. *archer*, WW.

strǣle f.=strǣl I.

strǣlian *to shoot* (*an arrow*), RPs 63⁵.

strǣlwyrt f. *name of a plant*, LCD 36b.

strǣngð (VPs)=strengð

strǣt I. f. *'street,' high road*, B,Ct,G,OET; Æ,CP; Mdf. [*L.* strata (via)] **II.** f. *bed*, CPs. [*L.* stratum]

strǣtlanu f. *street*, NC 323.

strǣtweard (ē) f. *waywarden*, LL.

strand n. *'strand,' sea-shore*, G,KC; Æ.

strang (o) comp. strengra, superl. strengest (from strenge) *'STRONG,' powerful, able, firm, bold, brave*, Æ,CP : *constant, resolute, strenuous* : *strict, severe*, AO ; CP : *arduous* : *violent.*

strange adv. comp. strangor, superl. strangost *strongly, violently, furiously, severely*, BH,Met. [*'strong'*]

stranghynde *strong of hand*, ÆT473.

±**strangian** *to strengthen, confirm*, Æ,Bl; AO,CP : *be strong, prevail*, Æ,VPs : *press* (*after*) RWH86²⁵. [*'strong'*]

stranglic *strong, stout, firm, solid, sound, robust*, Æ : *severe.* adv. -līce *strongly, firmly, stoutly, boldly, bravely*, Æ,CP : *fiercely, violently*, MH.

strangmöd *resolute*, RB 138²⁸.

strangnes f. *strength, power, force*, Lk, Ps.

±**strangung** f. *strengthening, quickening, nourishing*, Æ : *vigour*, Æ.

strapulas mp. *breeches*, WW 125².

strāwberige=strēawberige

strē (N), strēa=strēaw

streac=stearc

strēad pret. 3 sg. of strūdan.

streaht pp. of streccan.

strēal=strǣl

strēam m. *'stream,' flood, current, river*, Bl, Bo,G,GD,Lcd; AO,CP : (†) pl. *sea.*

strēamfaru f. *rush of water*, An 1578.

strēamgewinn n. *strife of waters*, RD4²⁶.

strēamlic *of water*, ÆH1·444¹⁰.

strēamracu f. *water-course, channel*, An, WW.

strēamrād f. *course of a stream*, GL : *sea-path*, CRA.

strēamrynes adv. *flowing like a stream*, Æ.

strēamstæð n. *shore*, GEN 1434.

strēamweall m. *shore*, GEN 1494.

strēamwelm m. *surging stream*, An 495.

strēaw (ē, ēo) n. *'straw,' hay*, Æ,Lcd.

strēaw-berige, -beriewīse f. *'strawberry,'* Lcd,WW.

strēawian=strewian; **strec** (Æ)=stræc

strec-=stræc-

streccan (±) *to stretch* (*'i-stretche'*), *spread out, prostrate*, BH,G,Lcd : *reach, extend*, Æ.

streccanmöd *persistent*, ÆP 80¹⁰.

strecednes f. *bed, couch*, LPs.

streclic=stræclic

strēdan³ (and wv); pret. 3 sg. strēdde, pp. strēded, strēd)=stregdan

strēgan *to strew*, Seaf 97. [*'stray'*]

stregdan³ (and wv.) pret. strǣgd, strugdon (wk. stregde), pp. strogden (wk. stregd, strēdd) *to strew, sprinkle. disperse. scatter. straggle* : *to spread, extend.*

strēgl=strǣl II.

strehte pret. 3 sg. of streccan.

strēl=strǣl; **strēn**=strēowen

strēnan=strīenan

streng I. m. *'string,' cord, rope, ligature, sinew*, An,AS,B,G,Lcd. in pl. *tackle, rigging* : *lineage, race.* **II.**=strengu

+**strengan** *to strengthen*, LkL. +strenged *formed, made*, OEG 46⁸.

strenge *severe*, GEN 60. [v. strang]

strengel m. *ruler, chief*, B 3115. [strang]

strengest (AO,CP) v. strang.

strenglic *strong, firm*, GEN 273. adv. -līce.

strengra (*Bo*; Æ,AO,CP) v. strang. ['*strenger*']

strengð, strengðu f. 'STRENGTH,' *force, vigour* : *ability, superiority* : *firmness, fortitude, Æ* : *manhood, mature years* : *violence, ApT*.

strengu f. *strength, power, vigour, ability, B,VPs*; CP : *firmness, fortitude, CP : virtue*. ['*strengh*']

strenð (KGL)=strengð

strēon I. (±) n. *gain, acquisition, property, treasure, AO,LG,WW*; Æ,CP : *traffic, usury* : *procreation, Æ*. ['*i-streon*,' v. '*strain*'] II.=strēowen

strēonan=strīenan

+**strēones** (ēu) f. *petty gain*, GPH 389.

+**strēonful** *costly, valuable, precious, Æ.*

strēow=strēaw

strēowen (ē) f. *resting-place, couch, bed*, BH.

strēowian=strewian

strēownes f. *mattress, bedding*, BL 227.

strēt I. pres. 3 sg. of strēdan. II.=strǣt

strēw=strēaw; **strēwen**=strēowen

±**strewian** (ēa, ēo) *to* '*strew*,' *scatter, Bl*; CP.

strewung f. *what one lies on, bedding*, LPs 131³.

±**stric** n. *plague? strife? sedition?* LCD,LL,W.

strica m. *stroke, line, mark, Æ*. ['*streak*']

±**strīcan**[1] *to pass lightly over the surface, stroke, rub, wipe*, Lcd : *move, go, run, Met*. ['*strike*']

stricel m. I. *fount, breast*, GL. II. *implement for smoothing corn in a measure? rope?* (ES 43·325), Cp 266 T.

strīchrægl n. *a cloth for wiping?* CC 23²¹.

+**strician** *to knit together, mend*, MtL 4²¹.

strīdan[1] *to* '*stride*,' Gl. up on s. *mount* (*a horse*), GD 81²⁰.

stride m. '*stride*,' *step*, Cp 134 P.

±**strīenan** (ēo, ī, ȳ) *to acquire, gain, amass*, CP : *beget, AO,Mt*; CP : *increase, augment?* CP. ['*strene*']

+**strīenendlic** (e, y) *begetting*, OEG : *genitive*, ÆGR.

strigdeð pres. 3 sg. of stregdan.

strīman⁴ *to resist, oppose*, Cp.

strīna (=īe) m. *acquirer*, v. OEG 27¹.

strīnan=strīenan

strīnend (ēo;=īe) m. *acquirer*, ES 39·352.

-**strīpan** (y) v. be-s.

stripligan '*perfringere*'? v. OEG 46²¹.

strīð m. *strife, struggle, fight, contest, dispute, contention* : *opposition, antagonism*, HEXC 328 D. [*OS.*]

stroccian *to stroke*, NC 323.

+**strod** n. *plunder, robbery*, BH : *confiscation*, WW.

strōd n. *marshy land* (*covered with bushes or trees?*) BC (Mdf); PST 95/98,537.

stroden pp. of strūdan.

strōden, strogden pp. of stregdan.

±**strogdnes** f. *scattering, sprinkling*, DR.

strong=strang

strop '*struppus*,' (*oar-*)*thong, strap*, WW 181⁴². ['*strop*']

strosle (GD 100¹⁹)=ðrosle

-**strowennes** v. ā-s.

+**strud** (GD 162³²)=+strod

±**strūdan**² *to ravage, spoil, plunder, carry off.*

strūdend m. *robber* : *money-lender*, WW.

strūdere m. *robber*, GL,VH.

strūdgendlīce *greedily*, CHRD 108¹⁸.

±**strūdian** *to plunder*, NC 296,324.

strūdung f. *spoliation, robbery*, LL,W.

strugde (NG) wk. pret. 3 sg. of stregdan.

strūta (WW)=strȳta

strūtian *to stand out stiffly, struggle*, ÆL 32²⁰⁸. ['*strut*']

strūtnian (ÆL 23²⁶³)=scrūtnian

+**strȳdan** *to rob, deprive*, LL.

+**strȳdd**=+strēdd pp. of stregdan.

strȳdere=strȳndere

strȳn-=strīen-, strīn-

strȳnd (=īe) f. *generation, line of inheritance, race, stock, tribe, BH,DR,LG* : *gain*, WW 488³⁰. ['*strind*']

strȳndan *to waste*, WW.

strȳndere m. *squanderer, prodigal*, WW.

+**strynge** m. *wrestler*, WW 465⁴⁰.

strȳta (ū) m. *ostrich*, WW 48⁸⁷. [*L.* struthio]

stubb=stybb

stūc *heap*, ES 11·512.

studdan *to look after, be careful for,* RWH 136¹⁷.

studding f. *care, trouble, labour*, MFB 107 and n.

studu f., gs. stude, ds. styde (also indecl. in sg.), nap. styde *column, pillar, post, buttress, BH,WW*. ['*stud*']

stufbæð=stofbæð

stulor *stealthy, stolen, Æ*. adv. -līce, Æ.

+**stun** n. *din, crash, whirlwind*, CR,WW.

stuncen pp., stuncon pret. pl. of stincan.

stund f. *short space of time, moment, period, time, An,Met* : *hard time, Rd* : *hour* : *signal.* stunde *now, at once, from time to time* (v. also stundum). ['*stound*']

+**stund** n. *noise*, GUTH 36²⁸ (=+stun).

-**stundian** v. ā-s.

stundmǣlum adv. *from time to time, gradually, Æ* : *time after time, alternately, Æ,ZDA*. ['*stoundmeal*']

stundum adv. *from time to time, at times, Æ* : *with effort, laboriously, eagerly, fiercely, Æ.* [dp. of stund]

stungen pp., stungon pret. pl. of stingan.

stunian *to crash, resound, roar* : *impinge, dash.*

stunra (KGL69³¹)=stuntra gp. of stunt.
stunt *dull, stupid, foolish*, Æ.
stuntlic *stupid, foolish*, Æ. adv. -līce, Æ.
stuntnes f. *stupidity, folly*, Æ.
stuntscipe m. *foolishness*, Mk7²².
stuntspræc f. *silly talk* (BT).
stuntspræce *talking foolishly*, Sc97¹⁰.
stuntwyrde *talking foolishly*, W72¹⁷.
stūpian *to ' stoop,' AO : slope*, Lcd.
sturtende (DR57¹²)=styrtende
stūt m. *gnat*, WW. [*'stout'*]
stuðansceaft m. *prop*, AS1¹,¹⁰.
stuðu=studu
stybb m.   *stump, ÆGr,KC,WW*; Mdf.
[*'stub'*]
stycce (i) n. *piece, portion, bit, fragment*, Æ :
mite (small piece of money). ymbe st. *after
a short time*. [*Ger.* stück]
styccemælum adv. *piecemeal, little by little,
by degrees, gradually : to bits, to pieces,
AO : here and there*, AO.
stycian=stician
styde I.=stede. II. v. studu.
styfician (i¹) *to root up, extirpate*, Lcd3·184'.
styficlēah *a clearing in a wood*, BC3·694¹⁰
(v. PST95/98·541).
styficung (e²) f. *clearing (land)?* Ct.
styhtan=stihtan
stȳlan (=ie) *to harden, attemper*, Cr679.
[*'steeled'*]
stȳle (ē) n. *'steel,' B,Gl.*
stȳlecg *steel-edged*, B1533.
stȳlen† *of steel, hard as steel, Sol*; VH.
[*'steelen'*]
styll=stiell
styllan (1)=stiellan; (2)=stillan
±styltan *to be amazed, dazed, hesitate*, NG.
stylð pres. 3 sg. of stelan.
stȳman=stīeman; styng=sting
stynt=stent pres. 3 sg. of standan.
styntan *to make dull, stupefy*, Cp89H. [stunt]
+stynðo *coercion*, NC296.
stȳpel=stīpel
stȳr=stēor; styra=styria
stȳran=(1) stīeran; (2) stēran
styrc=stirc; stȳrend=stēorend
styrenes f. *power of motion, movement : disturbance, tumult : (+) tribulation*, DR.
styrfig adj. *belonging to an animal which
died of disease*, LL. [storfe]
styrfð pres. 3 sg. of steorfan.
styrgan=styrian
styria, styr(i)ga (i) m. *name of a fish,
sturgeon*, Gl. [*Ger.* stör]
±styrian (i) *to 'STIR,' move* (tr. and intr.),
rouse, agitate, excite, urge, CP : *cause : tell,
rehearse*, B873.
styric=stirc
styrigendlic *moving*, Æ : *mobile*, GD149³¹.

styring=styrung
styrman *to storm, roar, rage, cry out, shout*,
B,BH,Bo. [*'sturme'*]
styrne (=ie) *'stern,' grave, strict, hard,
severe, cruel*, Gen,Gl,W.
styrnenga adv. *inexorably*, Sol282.
styrnlic (ie) *hard, severe, harsh.* adv. -līce,
CP.
styrnmōd *stern of mood*, Jud227.
styrtan *to ' start,' leap up.* only in pres. ptc.
sturtende (=styrtende), DR57¹².
styrung (e) f. *moving, motion, Bf,Bo,G*; CP :
disturbance, commotion, G : exercise.
[*'stirring'*]
styðe ds. and nap. of stuðu (studu).
sū f. *sow.* [=sugu]
suā=swā
subdīacon m. *subdeacon*, Æ,BH.
sūcan² *to 'suck,' Æ,Lk,PPs,VHy.*
sucga=sugga; sucht-, suct-=suht-
sudon pret. pl. of sēoðan.
sue-=swe-
sufel, suf(o)l n. *relish eaten with bread* (v.
LL2·754), Jn,RB. [*'sowl'*]
+sufel, sufl adj. *with a relish added to it?
(of bread)*, Ct,LL.
suflmete m. *delicacy, relish*, GD201²⁶.
sufon (Bf48⁹)=seofon
sūftlēre=swiftlēre
sūgan² *to suck, suck in*, CP : *have hiccough?*
Lcd.
sugga m. *a kind of bird, titlark? wagtail?* Gl.
±sugian *to be or become silent*, AO. [cp.
swīgian]
sugu f. *'sow,' Cp,CP*; Æ.
suht (y) f. *illness*, Gen472.
suhterga† m. *brother's son, nephew : uncle's
son, cousin*, WW.
suhtergefæderan, suhtorfædran† mp. *uncle
and nephew.*
suhtriga=suhterga
suindr- (NG)=syndr-
sūl (Æ), sulh (AO) sfm., gs. sūle(s), ds. sylg
(CP), syl(h), as. sūl, sulh; nap. sylh, syll
(Æ), gp. sūla, dp. sūlum *plough*, Lcd,LG :
furrow, gully : a measure of land (Mdf).
[*'sullow'*]
sūlerēost *rest (part of a plough)*, WW219⁶.
sulf=sufl
sulfer, sulfern (DR)=seolfor, seolfren
sulhæcer m. *a strip of land for ploughing*,
LL450,9¹.
sulhælmesse f. *ecclesiastical tax on ploughed
land*, LL.
sulhandla m. *plough tail*, WW. [v. 'sullow']
sulhbēam m. *plough tail*, WW. [v. 'beam']
sulhgang m. *the land which can be gone over
by one plough in a day*, W170³⁷.
sulhgesīdu np. *ploughing tackle*, LL455¹⁷.

sulhgetēog n. *ploughing implements*, LCD 1·400¹⁹. [cp. *Ger.* zeug]

sulhgeweorc n. *plough-making*, GEN 1086.

sulhhæbbere m. *ploughman*, WW 495¹⁹.

sūlincel n. *small furrow*, WW 348³³.

sull, suluh=sūl

sulung n. *in Kent, the fiscal unit corresponding to the hide (or carucate in other counties)* (NED) Ct,LL. ['*suling*']

sum indef. pron. (used substantively w. g.) *a certain one, some one, something, one.* sixa s. *one of six* : (used adjectivally) *a certain*, 'SOME,' *any*, Æ,AO. sume...sume *some...others.* hit...sum...sum...*part of it...the rest...* : (used adverbially) *about.* s. hund *about a hundred.* sumes, s. on dǣle *to some extent, somewhat.*

sumar, sumer=sumor

sumdǣl *somewhat, some portion. Cp.* ['*somedeal*']

sūmnes f. *delay*, MtL 25¹⁹. [cp. *Ger.* versäumnis]

sumor m., gs. sumeres, ds. sumera, sumere '*summer*,' Bo,Chr,Gn,Ph,VPs; AO.

sumorbōc=sumorrǣdingbōc

sumorhāt n. *summer heat*, RIM 67.

sumorhǣte f. *summer heat*, AO,RB.

sumorhūs n. *summer-house*, ÆL 36⁹⁸.

sumorlǣcan *to draw on towards summer*, ÆH 1·614.

sumorlang† *summer-long, of the length of a summer's day.*

sumorlic *of summer*, Lcd,WW. ['*summerly*']

sumorlida I. m. *summer army or expedition (one which only comes for the summer)*, CHR 871. [liðan] II. (=-loda) m. *shoot, twig*, WW 450³⁰ (v. A 13·330).

sumormæsse f. *midsummer* (Swt).

sumorrǣdingbōc (e²) f. *summer lectionary*, TC 430¹⁶.

sumorselde f. *summer-house*, WW 184¹.

sumsende *swishing (of rain)*, RD 4⁴⁷.

sumswēge=samswēge

sumur=sumor

sunbēam mf. '*sunbeam*,' Æ : *sunshine.*

sunbearu m. *sunny grove*, PH 33.

sunbeorht *bright with sunshine*, PH 436.

sunbryne m. *sunburn*, LCD.

suncen pp., suncon pret. pl. of sincan.

sund n. *swimming*, Æ,B,AO : *capacity for swimming* : (†) *sea, ocean, water.* ['*sound*']

+sund *sound* ('*i-sound*'), *safe, whole, uninjured, healthy, prosperous*, Æ,B.

sundampre (o²) *dock (plant)*, LCD 44a.

sund-būende†, -buend mp. *sea-dwellers, man, mankind.*

sundcorn n. *saxifrage*, LCD,WW.

sundēaw *rosemary? sundew?* WW 301⁷.

+sundelic (WW 496²⁴)=+syndiglic

sunder=sundor

sunderanweald m. *monarchy*, ES 11·66.

sunderboren *reckoned apart*, OEG 26¹⁷.

sunderfolgoð m. *official teachership*, AO 286⁵.

sunder-frēodōm, -frēols m. *privilege*, Ct.

sunderlīpes *separately, specially*, OEG,RBL. ['*sunderlepes*']

sundermǣlum *separately, singly*, OEG.

sundermēd f. *private meadow*, Ct.

sunderstōw f. *special place*, Bo 80².

+sundful *sound, whole, healthy* : *prosperous*, Æ,Ps. ['*i-sundfull*']

+sundfullian *to prosper*, Ps.

+sundfullic *sound, safe, sure.* adv. -līce *safely, prosperously*, Æ.

±sundfulnes f. *health, prosperity*, Æ,Bo,CP: *safety*, ByH 126⁸.

sundgebland n. *commingled sea, surge*, B 1450.

sundgyrd (e²) f. *sounding-rod*, WW.

sundhelm† m. *covering of water, sea*, RD.

sundhengest† m. *sea-horse, ship*, CR.

sundhwæt *good at swimming*, WHALE 57.

+sundig (y) *favourable*, BH 386¹³Ca.

+sund(ig)lic (y) *prosperous*, BH : *safe*, GD 348¹⁰ : *healthy.* adv. -līce.

sundlīne f. *sounding-line, lead*, WW.

sundmere m. *swimming-bath*, WW.

sundnytt f. *use of the power of swimming*, B 2360.

sundor adv. *asunder, apart* : *severally* : *differently.*

sundor- v. also sunder-, synder-.

sundorcræft m. *special power or capacity.*

sundorcræftiglīce *with special skill*, BHCA 324³.

sundorcȳððu f. *special knowledge* LL (322³²).

sundorfeoh n. *private property*, Ct.

sundorgecynd n. *special quality*, PA 30.

sundorgenga m. *solitary (animal)*, BL 199⁵.

sundorgerēfland n. *land reserved to the jurisdiction of a* 'gerēfa'? WW 421¹¹.

sundorgifu f. *special gift, privilege*, Bo,GL.

sundorhālga m. *Pharisee*, Æ.

sundorland n. *private property*, GD,WW.

sundorlic *special*, Bo; CP 409¹⁰. adv. -līce *apart*, Æ,Bo,LG. ['*sunderly*']

sundorlīf n. *life in seclusion*, BH 294⁴.

sundormæsse f. *separate mass, special mass*, BK 27'; RSL 11·486.

sundornotu f. *special office*, LL 456,2.

sundornytt f. *special use, office, or service*, CP.

sundorriht n. *special right, privilege*, WW.

sundorseld (u²) n. *special seat, throne*, VPs.

sundorsetl n. *hermitage*, GUTH.

sundorsprǣc f. *private conversation, private conference,* Æ,AO,CP.

sundor-weorðung, -weorðmynt f. *special honour, prerogative.*

sundorwīc n. *separate dwelling,* BH262[14].

sundorwine m. *bosom friend,* FT29.

sundorwīs *specially wise,* EL588.

sundorwundor n. *special wonder,* MOD2.

sundoryrfe n. *private inheritance,* PPs 67[10].

sundplega† m. *sporting in the waves, bathing.*

sundrāp m. *sounding line, lead,* WW358[17].

sundreced n. *sea-house, ark,* GEN1335.

+**sundrian**=+syndrian. [*'sunder'*]

sundrum (on) adv. *singly, separately, apart: continuously,* CM211.

sundur=sundor

sundwudu† m. (*sea-wood*), *ship.*

suner (MtR)=sunor

sunfeld m. *Elysian fields,* SOL (K),WW.

sunfolgend *'solisequia,' marigold? heliotrope?* GL.

sunganges adv. *moving with the sun,* LL.

sungen pp. of (1) singan; (2) swingan.

sungīhte *solstice,* MH104[19],[21].

sungon pret. pl. of singan.

sunhāt *'soliflua,'* OEG56[205].

sunlic *solar, of the sun,* Æ.

sunna m. *'SUN,'* Æ.

Sunnadæg (N)=sunnandæg

Sunnanǣfen m. *eve of Sunday, Saturday.* [*Ger.* Sonnabend]

sunnancorn *gromel* (*plant*), LCD1·314[18]?

Sunnandæg m. *'Sunday*,' Bl,G,LL;* Æ.

sunnanlēoma m. *ray of light, sunbeam,* GD 171,172.

Sunnanmergen m. *Sunday morning,* ÆL 31[1371].

Sunnanniht f. *Saturday night,* Æ *: Sunday,* LL52,5[5].

sunnanscīma m. *sunshine,* MFH173.

sunnansetlgong m. *sunset,* CHR773.

Sunnanūhta m. *Sunday morning* (*early*), *early service time,* Æ,LL.

sunnb-=sunb-

sunne f. *'SUN,'* Æ,AO,CP.

sunnebēam=sunbēam

sunnelēoma (RWH147[11])=sunnanlēoma

sunnon pret. pl. of sinnan.

sunnu=sunne

sunor (e²) fn. *herd of swine,* NG.

sunsceadu f. *veil,* WW239[19].

sunscīene *radiant,* JUL229.

sunscīn *mirror,* WW519[4].

sunset n. *west,* NG.

sunstede m. *solstice,* BF,LCD.

sunsunu? m. *grandson,* v. LL460,11n.

sunu m., gds. suna *'SON,' descendant,* Æ *: the Son : young of animals.*

sunucennicge f. *mother,* DR.

sunusunu=sunsunu

sunwlitig *fair with sunshine,* GNC7.

±**sūpan**² *to swallow, sip, taste, 'sup,' drink,* Æ,CP,Lcd,LG,Ps : (+) *sop up, absorb.*

sūr *'sour,' tart, acid,* BC,Lcd : *made sour, fermented,* Lcd,WW.

sūre f. *sorrel,* LCD,GL.

sūr-ēagede, -ēg(ed)e, -īge *blear-eyed,* Æ. -**sūrian** v. ā-s.

sūr-milsc, -melsc, -melst adj. *half sour and half sweet* (*apple*).

sūrnes f. *'sourness,'* WW347[35].

sūsel=sūsl

sūsl nf. *misery, torment, torture,* Æ,AO.

sūslbona m. *devil,* SAT640.

sūslcwalu (-sel-) f. *painful death,* W.

sūslhof n. *place of torment,* †Hy10[31].

sūslstede (sel-) m. *place of torment, hell,* OEG56[184].

suster=sweostor; **sutel**=sweotol

sūtere m. *shoemaker,* Æ. [*'souter'; L.*]

-**sūtian** v. be-s.; **sutol,** sutul=sweotol

sūð* I. adj. comp. sūð(er)ra, sȳðer(r)a, superl. sūðmest *'SOUTH,' southern,* AO.
II. adv. comp. sūðor, sȳð *southwards, south,* AO,CP.

sūðan adv. *from the south,* CP *: on or in the south,* AO. be s. (w. d.), wið s. (w. a.) *south of.*

sūðanēastan adv. *in or from the south-east: to the south-east,* AO.

sūðanēastanwind m. *south-east wind,* WW 144.

sūðanēasterne *south-eastern,* LPs.

Sūðanhymbre mp. *Mercians,* CHR.

sūðanweard=sūðeweard

sūðanwestan adv. *from the south-west,* WW.

sūðanwestan-wind, -winda m. *a south-west wind.*

sūðanwesterne *south-western,* Bo10[13].

sūðanwind m. *south wind,* WW.

sūðdǣl m. *southern region, the south,* Æ, VPs; AO. [*'southdeal'*]

sūðduru f. *south door,* BL201[15].

sūðēast adv. *'south-east,' AO,Chr.*

sūðēastende m. *south-east end,* Bo67[31].

sūðēasterne *south-eastern,* ÆGR8².

sūðecg f. *southern edge,* KC.

sūðende m. *south end,* KC5·86'.

Sūðengle pl. *South Anglians, people of southern England,* LL.

sūðerige *'satirion'* (*plant*), WW137¹. [*L.* satureia?]

sūðerne *'southern,' southerly,* Æ,Bo,Lcd, MtL.

sūðernewudu m. *'southernwood,' wormwood,* Lcd.

sūðerra v. sūð.

sūðeweard adj. *southward, south, southern,* AO.

sūðfolc n. *southern nation or people, Suffolk,* CHR,LCD.

sūðfōr f. *journey south, pilgrimage to Rome,* BC 1·446.

sūðgārsecg m. *southern ocean,* AO.

sūðgemǣre n. *southern border,* AO.

sūðheald† *inclining southwards.*

sūðhealf f. *south side, AO;* Æ. ['*southhalf'*]

Sūðhymbre mpl. *Mercians,* CHR.

sūðland n. *southern land or shore, Æ,Chr.* ['*southland*']

sūðmǣgð f. *southern province,* BH.

sūðmann† m. *man from the south,* GEN.

sūðmest '*southmost,' AO.*

Sūðmyrce (e) pl. *southern Mercians,* BH 238³⁴.

sūðor v. sūð.

sūðportic m. *south porch,* CHR 1036.

sūðra v. sūð.

sūðrihte (y) adv. *due south,* AO.

sūðrima m. *south coast,* CHR.

sūðrodor (a²) m. *southern sky,* PH.

Sūðsǣ mf. *south sea, English Channel,* Æ.

Sūð-seaxan, -seaxe pl. *South-Saxons, people of Sussex : Sussex,* CHR.

sūðstæð n. *south coast,* CHR 897A.

sūðwāg m. *south wall,* Æ,BL.

sūðweard adv. *towards the south, southwards, AO,Lcd.* ['*southward'*]

sūðweardes adv. '*southwards,' Met.*

sūðweg m. *southern country,* Ex 155.

sūðwest I. m. *the south-west, Chr.* II. adv. '*south-west,' AO.*

sūðwesterne '*south-western,' ApT.*

sūðwind m. *south wind,* Ex 289.

suwian (LWS)=sugian

swā (ǣ, ē) I. adv. and conj. (w. ind. or subj.) *so as, consequently, just as, so far as, in such wise, in this or that way, thus, so that, provided that,* Æ. swā swā *so as, just as, so that.* swā same (swā) *in like manner : therefore, on that account : as, like :* (w. comparatives) *the.* swā...swā *the...the : where : when, so soon, as soon : although, unless, yet : if, as if.* II. pron. '*SO*,' *the same, such, that.* swā hwā swā *whosoever.* swā hwǣr swā *wherever.* bi swā hwaðerre efes swā *on whichever side.* swā ilce= swilce. swā selfe *in the same way.* ēac swā *also.* swā hwilc swā *whosoever.* swā...ne *though...not.* swā...swā *whether...or ; either ...or.* swā ðēah *nevertheless, yet, however.*

swāc pret. 3 sg. of swīcan.

swǣ=swā

swæc (CP), swæcc (e) m. *flavour, taste : smell, odour, fragrance.*

+swæccan (e) *to smell* (tr.), DD 206; (intr.) ARPs 113¹⁴; ÆGR 221 T⁹.

swæcehēow '*insania'?* RPs 39⁵ (v. ES 38·22).

swæf pret. 3 sg. of swefan.

swǣfan? *to burn,* MET 8⁴⁷.

swæfen=swefn; swæflen=sweflen

swæg=swēg; swægl=swegl

±swǣlan (tr.) *to burn, Cr,LPs.* ['*sweal'*]

swælc=swilc

swǣm m. *trifler, idler,* BF : *vain object,* CHRD.

-swǣman v. ā-s.; swǣncan=swencan

swǣp *enticement, persuasion, deceit* (v. OEG 2894n).

+swǣpa (ā, ē) pl. *sweepings, rubbish,* GL. [swāpan]

swǣpels (VPs) m? swǣpelse f. *robe, garment.*

swǣpig *fraudulent,* OEG 2894.

swǣr I. (ā, ē) *heavy, sad, Ps :* *oppressive, grievous, Cr,Gen :* *sluggish, inactive, weak, Cp,LG.* II. n. *sadness, trouble,* MFH 173. ['*sweer'*]

swǣrbyrd? f. *difficult birth?* LCD 185a.

swǣre† (ā) *grievously, oppressively.*

+swǣre=swǣr

+swǣred *oppressed, weighed down,* LCD 3·120′.

swǣrlic (ā) *grievous, heavy, Æ.* adv. -līce, Æ.

swǣrmōd *indolent, sluggish,* W 257.

swǣrmōdnes (ā) f. *dulness, stupidity,* CP 149¹⁵.

swǣrnes (ā) f. *heaviness, Æ :* *sluggishness, Bo.* ['*sweerness'*]

swǣrt (WW 257³)=sweart

±swǣs (ē) *intimate, special, favourite, dear, beloved : own : agreeable, gentle, benevolent : sweet, sugary.*

+swǣse *blandly, pleasantly,* WW 196¹².

swǣsenddagas mpl. *ides (in Roman calendar),* WW.

swǣsende (ē) n. (mostly used in pl. swǣsendu) *food, meal, dinner, banquet, dainties : blandishments,* WW 61²⁶.

swǣsing-=swǣsend-

±swǣslǣcan (ē¹) *to wheedle,* WW 61,196.

swǣslic *kind, friendly, agreeable, pleasant.* adv. -līce *kindly : properly : plausibly.*

±swǣsnes f. *wheedling, Æ : pleasure.*

+swǣsscipe m. *companionship,* NC 296.

swǣsung f. *lenitive, soothing application,* WW 241²⁴.

swǣswyrde *fair spoken,* WW 190³⁵.

±swǣtan *to sweat, exude, Æ,AO,BH,Lcd, Nar : labour, toil, CP : bleed,* CROSS 20 : *weld,* A 22·395 : (+) *oppress,* CPs 93⁵. [swāt]

swǣð (e) n., nap. swaðu *footprint, track,* CP : *trace, vestige,* CP. [cp. swaðu f.]

swæðel=sweðel

swæðelyne 'pinguis,' OEG 27³².

swæðer pron. whichever, whosoever, CP. [swā, hwæðer]

+swæðian to trace out, investigate, EPs 138³.

swæðlæcan to search out, visit, CHy 9⁶⁸.

swæðorian=swaðrian, sweðrian

swæðu=swaðu

swāf pret. 3 sg. of swīfan.

swāhwætswā pron. whatsoever.

swāhwæðer pron. whichever, LL.

swal(e)wo—swcalwc; swālīc—swilc

swaloð=sweoloð

swāmian to become dark, Gu 1069.

swamm (o) I. m. fungus, mushroom, Æ : sponge. [Ger. schwamm] II. pret. 3 sg. of swimman.

swan (o) m. 'swan,' Ep,Ph,WW.

swān m. herdsman, swineherd, peasant, Chr, Ep : (†) swain, youth, man, warrior. ['swon']

swanc pret. 3 sg. of swincan.

swancor† slender, trim, lithe, supple : languishing, weak, PPs 118⁸¹.

swang pret. 3 sg. of swingan.

swāngerēfa m. swineherd, reeve, officer set over the depasturing of swine in forests, Ct.

swangettung f. movement, agitation, NC 324.

swangor (o) heavy, inert, BH,W.

swangornes (o) f. sloth, laziness, CP.

swanrād f. swan's-road, sea, B 200.

swānriht n. law as to swineherds, LL 449,6¹.

swānsteorra m. evening star, Cp 145 U.

+swāpa=+swǣpa

±swāpan⁷ to sweep, drive, swing. rush (of wind), ÆGr,Bo,Ex,LPs : sweep up, take possession of, AO. ['swope']

swār=swǣr

swarc-=swearc-

-swarian (e, eo, o) v. and-s.

swarn-=sworn-; swart=sweart

swās=swǣs

swāt I. (ō) m? n? (+ at Lcd 3·98¹⁷) 'sweat,' perspiration, exudation, Æ,CP,Lk : (†) blood : foam, LkR9³⁹ : toil : labour, Bl; Æ. ['swote'] II. (+) sweaty, sweating, Lcd.

swatan (ā?) pl. beer, WW.

swātclāð m. 'sudarium,' napkin, ÆP 178².

swātfāh† blood-stained, bloody.

swātig sweaty, AO : (†) gory. ['swoty']

swātighlēor with sweaty brow, Gen 934 (or ? two words).

swātlīn n. napkin, CP.

swātswaðu f. gory track, B 2946.

swātðyrel n. pore of the skin, WW 159¹³.

swaðeah adv. however, yet, nevertheless.

swaðeahhwæðre adv. however, Æ.

swaðer=swæðer

swaðian to swathe, wrap up, RWH 137¹³.

swaðorian, swaðrian=sweðrian

swaðu (æ, e) f. footstep, track, pathway, B, Bo,MH : trace, vestige, BH : scar, Shr. ['swath'; cp. swæð]

swaðul m? flame, B 782.

swaðum (in) dp. bandages, WW 484¹⁷. ['swathe']

swē=swā ; swealewe=swealwe

swealg, swealh pret. 3 sg. of swelgan.

swealt pret. 3 sg. of sweltan.

swealwe (a, o) f. 'swallow,' Ep,Gu,Lcd.

swearc pret. 3 sg. of sweorcan.

swearcian to become dark, ÆH 2·258¹⁵.

swearcmōdnes (a) f. pusillanimity, LPs 54⁹.

swearcung (a) f. darkness, RPs 17²⁹.

sweard m. hide, rind, skin, Gl. ['sward']

+swearf (Lcd)=+sweorf

swearm m. 'swarm,' multitude, Gl.

sweart swarthy, black, dark, B,Lcd; Æ : gloomy : evil, infamous, Æ,Jul. ['swart']

sweartbyrd (æ¹) a dismal birth, Lcd 3·66'.

swearte† adv. miserably, evilly.

swearthæwen dark-blue, purple, violet, WW 376²⁴.

±sweartian to become black, Æ,Lcd : make black. ['swart']

sweartlāst with black tracks, Rd 27¹¹.

sweartnes f. blackness, black substance, Gl. ['swartness']

sweartung f. darkness, EPs 17²⁹.

swearð (G)=sweard ['swarth']

±swebban to put to sleep, lull, G : (†) kill, Æ,B. ['sweve']

swec (KGl)=swæc

swefan⁵ to sleep, slumber, rest, B,Cp : (†) sleep in death : cease, Ex. ['sweve']

swefecere m. sleeper, Chrd 26².

swefecung f. sleep, Chrd 31⁴.

swefed pp. of swebban.

swefel (æ) m. sulphur, Æ. [Ger. schwefel]

swefelrēc m. sulphurous smoke, VPs 107⁷.

swefen=swefn

swefet=sweofot

swefeð pres. 3 sg. of swebban.

+sweflan to put to sleep, lull, appease, Æ. ['sweve']

swefl=swefel

sweflen sulphurous, of brimstone, Æ,AO.

sweflennes (eo) f. sulphurousness, MFH 123³.

sweflenrēc (APs)=swefelrēc

sweflsweart sulphurous? WW 49²⁰.

sweflörosm m. sulphurous smoke,ERSPs 107⁷.

swefn n. (often pl.) sleep, Gen; Æ,AO : dream, vision, CP,Da,LG. ['sweven']

swefnian (w. nom. pers.) to dream, Lcd : (+)(w. acc. pers.) appear in a dream. ['sweven'] swefni(g)end m. *dreamer*, GEN 37¹⁹.

swefnracu f. *interpretation of dreams*, LL (154²⁹).

swefnreccere m. *interpreter of dreams*, WW 366¹².

swefot=sweofot

swēg (æ) m. *sound*, Æ,AO,CP : *noise, clamour, tumult* : *melody, harmony, tone*, Æ : *voice* : *musical instrument* : '*persona*,' Sc. [swōgan]

swēgan *to make a noise, sound, roar, crash*, Æ : *import, signify*, Æ. ['swey']

swēgcræft m. *musicians' art, music*, APT 16.

swēgdynn m. *noise, crash*, CR 955.

±swēge *sonorous, harmonious*, ÆL.

swegel=swegl

swēgendlic adj. *vocal, vowel*, ÆGR 6¹⁵.

sweger f. *mother-in-law*, Æ. [*Ger.* schwieger]

swēgesweard m. *organist* (*!*) JGPh 1·64.

swēghlēoðor† m. *sound, melody*.

swēging f. *sound, clang, roar*, Lk,WW.

swegl† (æ) I. n. *sky, heavens, ether* : *the sun* : *music?* II.=segl

sweglbefalden *ether-begirt*, SAT 588.

sweglbeorht *ether-bright, radiant*, GU 1187.

sweglbōsm m. *heaven, sky*, GEN 9 (pl.).

sweglcondel f. *heaven's candle, sun*, PH 108.

sweglcyning† m. *King of heaven*.

swegldrēam† m. *music*.

swegle† I. adj. *bright, ether-like, clear, brilliant, splendid*. II. adv. *clearly, brightly*.

sweglhorn m. *kind of musical instrument*, GL. [cp. *Goth.* swiglōn]

swēglic *sonorous*, CM 675.

sweglrād f. *modulation, music*, RIM 29.

swegltorht† *heavenly-bright*.

sweglwered (gel-) *ether-clad*, B 606.

sweglwuldor n. *heavenly glory*, GU 1160.

sweglwundor n. *heavenly wonder*, GU 1292.

swegr=sweger

+swegra=+swigra

+swēgsumlīce? *unanimously*, HL 18¹⁶².

swehor (GL)=swēor

sweig (KGL 88⁴)=swēg

sweigð=swēgeð pres. 3 sg. of swēgan.

+swel=+swell

swelan⁴ *to burn, be burnt up* : *inflame (of wound)*.

swelc (Bo,LG,OET ; AO,CP)=swilc. [v. 'such']

swelca m. *pustule*, WW 112¹⁷.

swelce=swilce

+swelg n. *abyss, whirlpool*, GL. ['swallow']

±swelgan³ *to* '*swallow*,' *incorporate, absorb, imbibe, devour*, Lcd,LL.

swelgend (y) fmn. (±) *whirlpool, vortex, gulf, abyss*, CP : *glutton, drunkard, debauchee*, AO.

swelgendnes f. *whirlpool*, WW 373².

swelgere m. *glutton*, WW 102¹⁵. ['swallower']

swelgnes f. *whirlpool*, WW 510¹⁸.

swelhð=swelgð pres. 3 sg. of swelgan.

sweliend=swelgend

+swell n. *swelling, tumour, boil*, Æ,LCD.

±swellan³ *to* '*swell*,' B,Lcd.

swellende *burning*, OEG 377⁸.

swelling f. *swelling*, EL 245.

±sweltan³ (i, y) *to die, perish*, Æ,B,Bo; AO, CP. ['swelt']

sweltendlic *about to die*, Lk,Sc.

-swemman v. be-s.

±swenc m. *trouble, tribulation, toil* : (+) *temptation*, LkL,Nar. ['swench']

±swencan (æ) *to vex, distress, trouble, afflict, torment, oppress*, B,Bl,Bo,G; Æ,CP. [causative of swincan; '*swenche*']

+swenc-ednes, -ennes, -nes (AA) f. *trouble, affliction, toil*, Æ.

sweng m. *stroke, blow, cut, thrust*, B,El. ['sweng']

swengan *to shake, shatter*, Gl : *swing, rush, fly out*, HL. ['swenge'; causative of swingan]

sweocol (CP)=swicol; sweofl-=swefl-

sweofot (e) n. *sleep*, B. ['swevet']

swēogian=swīgian; sweolce=swilce

Swēoland n. *Sweden*, AO 19².

sweoloð (a, o) m. *burning heat, glow, fire, flame*. [swelan]

sweoloðhāt (o¹) *burning hot*, OEG 56²⁰².

sweolung? f. *inflammation*, LCD 76b (sweop-).

Swēon pl. *Swedes*, AO,B,CHR.

swēop pret. 3 sg. of swāpan.

sweop-=swip-

sweopung v. sweolung.

swēor I. (ē, ȳ) mf. *pillar, column, prop*, CP : *bolt, bar*, ES 37·183. II. m. *father-in-law*, Æ,AO,CP : (±) *cousin*. [*Ger.* schwäher] III.=swōr pret. of swerian.

swēora (ī, īo, ū, ȳ) m. *neck, nape*, Bo,Bl; AO,CP. ['swire']

swēorbān n. *neck-bone, neck*, VHy. ['swirebone']

swēorbēag (u) m. *neck-band, necklace, collar, torque*, Æ.

+sweorc (o) n. *cloud, darkness, mist*, GEN, VPs.

±sweorcan³ *to grow dark, darken* (intr.), *become overcast, be obscured*, An : *be troubled, sad, become grievous, troublesome, angry*, B,Met; ÆL : *fall out (of mind)*, JPs 30¹³. ['swerk']

sweorcendferhð *sombre, sad*, JUD 269.

+sweorcenes (o, cn) f. *gloom*, LL (400⁹).

swēorclāð m. *neckcloiñ*, WW 210³⁶.

swēorcops m. *yoke, pillory, Gl.* [v. '*cops*']
swēorcoðu f. *quinsy,* LCD.
sweord (o, u, y) n. '*sword,' Æ,B,Bl,Fin,G;* AO,CP.
sweordbealo n. *sword-bale,* B1147.
sweordberende '*sword-bearing,' Gen* 1060.
sweordbite m. *sword-wound,* JUL603.
sweordbora (u, y) m. *sword-bearer, swordsman, Æ.*
sweordfætels m. *sword-belt,* ÆL23¹⁷⁸.
sweordfreca m. *swordsman, warrior,* B1468.
sweordgenīðla m. *sworded foe,* EL1181.
sweordgeswing (y¹) n. *sword-brandishing,* JUD240.
sweordgifu (y¹) f. *gift of swords,* B2884.
sweordgripe m. *sword-attack,* JUL488.
sweordhwīta (u, y) m. *sword-furbisher,* LL.
sweordlēoma (u¹) m. *flashing of swords,* FIN35.
+sweordod (u) *provided with a sword, ÆGr, NC.* ['*sworded*']
sweordplega m. *fighting, Wal22.* ['*swordplay*']
sweordrǣs m. *attack,* AP59.
sweordslege m. *sword-thrust,* JUL671.
sweordtīge m. *sword-drawing,* LPs9⁷.
sweordwegende (u¹) *sword-bearing,* LCD 3·204'.
sweordwīgend m. *warrior,* Ex260.
sweordwund *wounded with the sword,* WAL7.
sweordwyrhta (u¹) m. *sword-maker?* LCD 3·194¹⁰.
+sweorf (ea, y) n. *filings,* LCD.
±sweorfan³ *to file or grind away, polish, wipe, rub, scour.*
swēorhnitu f. *nit which lives on the neck of animals, tick,* WW.
Swēorīce n. *Sweden,* B.
swēorracentēh (ū¹) f. *neck-chain,* WW107³⁴.
swēorrōd (ū¹) f. *cross worn on the neck, EC* 250¹¹. [v. '*rood*']
swēorscacul m. *yoke, pillory,* WW116⁹.
swēortēag (ē) f. *collar,* GL.
+swēoru (ī, ȳ) np. *hills,* PPs.
swēorwærc m. *pain in the neck,* LCD.
sweostor (e, i, u, y) f. indecl. in sg., nap. sweoster, sweostra, sweostru '*SISTER,' Æ,AO : nun.*
+sweos-tor, -tra, -tru fp. *sisters,* AO.
+sweosternu *bearn children of sisters, cousins.*
sweostorbearn n. *sister's child, nephew, niece,* WW452².
sweostorsunu m. *sister's son, nephew, BH, Chr.* [v. '*sister*']
swēot† n. *troop, army, company, body, swarm.*
sweota? sweote? '*scrotum,'* LCD, v. A 30·134.

sweotel=sweotol
sweotol (i, u, y) *distinct, clear, evident, manifest, open, public, B,Bl,CP,OEG;* AO. ['*sutel*']
sweotole (e, o, u) adv. *clearly, precisely, plainly, openly, visibly,* CP.
±sweotolian (e, u, y) *to show, reveal, make manifest, Mt; Æ : become manifest, GK : state, explain, prove.* ['*sutele*']
sweotollīc (u¹, y¹) *clear, distinct.* adv. -līce *clearly, precisely, plainly, visibly, openly, Æ,BH.* ['*suteliche*']
±sweotolung (i, u, y) f. *manifestation, Epiphany : definition, explanation, exposition, declaration, Æ : written testimony, evidence.*
±sweotolungdæg (e, u) m. *Epiphany, Æ.*
sweotul=sweotol
Swēoðēod f. *Swedes, Sweden,* B,CHR.
sweoðerian=sweðrian
sweoðol I. m? *heat, flame,* B3145. [cp. swaðul] II.=sweðel
swēowian=swīgian; +swēpa=+swǣpa
swēr=(1) swār; (2) sweger; (3) swēor
+swerian⁶ (but occl. wk. pret. swerede) *to* '*SWEAR,' Æ;* AO,CP : *swear in (to an office) : speak?* SOL425. [*Ger.* schwören]
swerigendlīc *jurative, used in swearing (of certain adverbs),* ÆGR227.
swertling m. *titlark? warbler?* WW131¹⁵.
swēs=swǣs; swester (N)=sweostor
±swētan *to make sweet, sweeten, Jul,Lcd;* Æ,CP.
swēte I. adj. '*SWEET,' pure, fragrant, pleasant, agreeable,* AO,CP : *beloved, dear : fresh (not salt).* II. n. *sweetness, sweet.* [swōt]
swetelian (KGL)=sweotolian
swētian *to be sweet,* CP425¹⁴.
+swētlǣcan *to batten,* RPs65¹⁵.
swētlīce *sweetly, pleasantly,* BH486⁴.
swētmete m. *sweetmeat, dainty,* CP41¹⁵.
swētnes f. *sweetness, fragrance, BH,CP : pleasantness, BH : kindliness, goodness, Ps : something sweet, Cp*524A.
swetole=sweotole
swētwēge *agreeable (of sound),* DHy58⁸.
swētwyrde *smooth-spoken,* WW : *stuttering,* WW.
sweð=swæð
sweðel (æ, eo) m. *swaddling band, bandage, binding, G,Gl.* ['*sweddle*']
sweðerian=sweðrian; -sweðian v. be-.
sweðolian *to relent, be appeased,* CHR1123.
±sweðrian (a, æ, eo, i) *to retire, vanish, melt away, abate, dwindle, decrease, subside.*
+sweðrung (æ) f. *failure,* LCD.
sweðu=swaðu

sweðung f. *poultice*, CHRD,LCD.

swic n. *illusion*, CM441 : *deceit, treachery*, AO. ['*swike*']

+swic n. *offence*, MtR,WW : *snare*, OEG 127². : *cessation*.

swica m. *deceiver, traitor, betrayer*, Chr,G. ['*swike*']

±swican¹ (†) *to wander* : (†) *depart* : (w. g.) *cease from, yield, give way*, AO,CP : (w. d.) *fail, fall short, be wanting, abandon, desert, turn traitor*, AO : *deceive*, Æ. ūt s. *go forth.* from s. *fall off, rebel.* ['SWIKE,' 'I-SWIKE']

swicc m. (BH430⁴)=swæcc

swiccræft m. *treachery*, G,LL.

swicdōm m. *fraud, deception, deceit*, AO, Chr; Æ : *betrayal, treason* : *scandal, offence.* ['*swikedom*']

swice I. m. (†) *escape, end* : (†) *procrastination, delay*, GU1007 : *offence, snare, treachery, deceit*, AO. ['*swike*'] II. adj. *fallacious, deceitful.* III. f. *trap, snare*, GL. ['*swike*'] IV.=swicc

+swicednes=+swicennes

swicend m. *deceiver*, HL18³⁹,⁸⁷.

+swicennes f. *abstention, cessation*, Æ : *repentance.*

swicful *fraudulent, deceitful*, OEG. ['*swikeful*']

swician *to wander* : *be treacherous, deceive, cheat*, Æ : *blaspheme* : *cause to offend.*

+swicing f. *intermission, cessation*, CM 103.

±swicn f. *purgation, clearance, discharge*, LL.

+swicnan *to clear* (*of a charge*), LL.

swicol *guileful, false, deceitful*, Æ,Lcd. ['*swikel*']

swicollic *fraudulent, deceiving, deceptive, causing to stumble.* adv. -līce.

swicolnes f. *deceit*, W. ['*swikelness*']

+swicu f. *cessation*, RB148¹²³n.

swicung f. *deceit, fraud, deception*, A,Lcd : *stumbling-block, offence.* ['*swiking*']

swīfan¹ *to revolve, sweep, wend* : *intervene*, EC164. [*Ger.* schweifen]

+swifornes=+swipornes

swift (y) '*swift,' quick*, Æ,B,Bo,CP,GD; AO. adv. -līce, Æ,LPs,W. ['*swiftly*']

swiftlēre (u, y) m. *slipper*, Æ. [*L.* subtalaris]

swiftnes f. *swiftness, speed*, Bo,Ps.

swiftu f. *swiftness*, MET.28³.

swīgan=swīgian

swīgdagas mp. *days of silence* (*last three days of Holy Week*), Æ. [v. '*swie*']

swīge, swigge I. f. *silence, stillness, rest*, Æ, CP. II. adj. *still, quiet, silent, taciturn*, CP.

swīgen f. *silence*, ÆH2·532⁴.

swīgeniht f. *night of silence*, ÆP154³ (v. swīgdagas).

±swīgian (ȳ; ī, ēo, ū) *to be or become silent, keep silence, be quiet, still*, B,BH; CP. ['*swie*']

swīgiendlīce adv. *silently*, HL18³¹¹.

swīglīce *silently*, GENC24²¹.

swīglung f. *silence*, ANS84·3. (or ? swīglunga *silently*)

swīgmæsse f. *silent mass*, NC324. ['*swimesse*']

swīgnes f. *time of silence*, WW211⁴².

+swigra (e) m. *sister's son, nephew, cousin.*

swīgtīma (swīt-) m. *silent time, eventide, early part of the night*, BF122²².

swīgūht m. *dawn of the days of silence* (v. swīgdagas), ANS84·7.

±swīgung f. *silence* : *time of silence* : *delay*, NG.

swilc (æ, e, y) pron. (used substantively) *such a one, he, the same*, Æ : (used adjectivally) 'SUCH,' CP : (as relative) *which*, Æ. swilc...hwilc *such...as*; *so...as.* swilc...swilc *so much* (*many*)...*as*; *as much* (*many*)...*as*, Æ. ['*swilk,*' v. '*such*']

swilce (e, eo, y) adv. and conj. (w. ind.) *just as, as, in like manner, in such manner, likewise, resembling, thus* : (w. subj.) *as if, as though* : *also, moreover, too*, Bo. ['*such*']

swilchwugu *some...or other*, ÆL23b⁷⁶⁶.

swilcnes f. '*qualitas,' nature*, Lcd,RB. ['*suchness*']

swile=swyle

swilian, swillan *to* '*swill,' wash, wash out, gargle*, Cp,Lcd,Ps.

swil(l)ing f. '*swilling,' wash, gargle*, Lcd.

swilt=swylt

swiltan=sweltan

swilð pres. 3 sg. of swellan.

swīlunge=swīglunga

swīma m. *vertigo, dizziness* : *swoon*, Cr,Jud, Lcd; Æ. ['*swime*']

swīmæsse=swīgmæsse

±swimman³ (y) *to* '*swim,' float*, AA,Æ,B, Lcd,Rd,Wa.

swimmendlic (y) *able to swim*, ÆGR55³.

swīn (ȳ) n. *wild-boar, pig, hog*, pl. '*swine,*' Bo,Cp,G,Rd; CP; Mdf : *boar-image* (*on a helmet*), B.

+swin n. *song, melody*, PH137.

±swinc n. *toil, work, effort*, Æ,Ps : *hardship*, Gen : *the produce of labour*, W229⁷. ['*swing,*' '*swink,*' '*i-swinch*']

±swincan³ *to labour, work at, strive, struggle*, Æ,B; CP : *be in trouble* : *languish.* ['*swink*']

+swincdagas mp. *days of tribulation*, SEAF 2.

+swincednes (EPs17¹⁹)=+swencednes

±swincful *toilsome, painful, disastrous*, Bo; Æ. ['*swinkful*']

+**swincfulnes** f. *tribulation*, LPs 33⁷ : *trouble*, Sc 60¹¹.

±**swinclēas** (y) *without toil*, ÆH 2·364⁹. ['*swinkless*']

swinclic *laborious*, W 294¹⁸.

+**swincnes** f. *hardship*, *trial*, CHRD,GUTH.

swind=spind

swindan³ *to vanish, consume, pine away, languish*, BH,Ps. ['*swind*']

swīnen adj. *pig's, swine's*, LCD,Ps.

+**swing**† I. n. *surge, fluctuation.* II.= +swinc

swingan³ I. *to beat, strike, smack, whip, scourge, flog, chastise, afflict*, Æ,B,Bl,Cp, Lcd; AO,CP. '*swing*' *oneself, fly*, B 2264. sw. on twā *to divide by a blow.* II. (Æ,Ps)= swincan

swinge (y) f. *stroke, blow, stripe : chastisement*, CP.

swingell f. (often swingel-, swingl- in obl. cases); swingel(l)e f. *whip, scourge, rod*, Æ : *stroke, stripe, blow : affliction*, CP.

swingere m. *striker, scourger*, RD 28⁷.

swinglung f. *dizziness*, Lcd,WW. ['*swingling*']

swīnhaga m. *pig-pen*, KC.

swīnhyrde (ī) m. '*swineherd*,' ZDA 33·239²¹.

swīnin (GL)=swīnen

swīnlic *swinish*, WW 508²⁹?

swīnlīc n. *boar-image* (*on a helmet*), B 1452.

swinn m. *melody*, OEG.

swīnnes f. *pork food*, EPs 16¹⁴.

swīnsceadu *pannage*, TC 263⁷ (v. BTs).

swinsian (y) *to sound melodiously, make melody, sing*.

swinsung f. *sound, melody, harmony*, BH, GL.

swinsungcræft m. *music*, WW 442¹².

swinsweg? *melody* (v. OEG xxxiii).

swipa m., swipe f.=swipu

swipian† (eo) *to whip, scourge, beat*.

±**swipor** *cunning*, BH,SOL.

+**swipor-e**, -līce *cunningly*, Ps.

+**swipornes** (e²) f. *wile, cunning*, HL,MkR.

swippan=swipian

swipu (eo, o) f. *whip, stick, scourge*, Gl,RG, Sol : *chastisement, affliction.* ['*swepe*']

swir-, swīr-=sweor-, swēor-

+**swirga**, +swiria=+swigra

swirman (=ie) *to swarm*, LCD 1·384'.

swister=sweostor

swital, switel, switol=sweotol

swītīma=swīgtīma

swīð (ȳ) *strong, mighty, powerful, active : severe, violent.* comp. swiðre *right* (*hand, side, etc.*).

±**swīðan** [wv. and sv¹? cp. unforswiðen] *to strengthen, establish, support : use force against*, Æ (v. A 36·66).

swīðe (ȳ) adv. *very much, exceedingly, severely, violently, fiercely*, B,Bl,Chr,G; AO,CP. comp. swiðor *more, rather*. superl. swiðost *most, especially, exceedingly* : *almost, nearly*. for swiðe, swiðe swiðe *very much, very severely*, CP. ['*swith*']

swīðfæstnes f. *violence*, LL (138 n4).

swīðfeorm *rich, fruitful : violent*, RD.

swīðfeormende *becoming violent*, WW 374¹¹.

swīðferhð† (y) *bold, brave, rash.*

=**swīðfrom** *very strong, vigorous.* adv. -līce.

swīðhrēownes f. *remorse*, MFH 173.

swīðhwæt *very active*, RUN 5.

swīðhycgende (i)† *bold-minded*, B.

swīðian *to become strong : prevail : fix*, WW.

swīðlæt *very lax*, LL (318').

swīðlic *intense, excessive, severe, violent*, Æ : *immense*, Æ : *effective.* adv. -līce, Bo,G. ['*swithly*']

swīðlicnes f. *excess*, RBL 73⁷.

swīðmihtig *very mighty*, PPs 85¹³.

swīðmōd† *stout-hearted, brave : insolent, arrogant*.

swīðmōdnes f. *magnanimity*, A 11·173, SOL 150⁴.

swīðnes f. *excess, violence*, CM 458.

swīðor comp. of swiðe.

swīðra comp. of swīð, Lcd,LG. ['*swither*']

swīðrian=sweðrian

swīðrian *to avail, become strong, prevail*, Æ.

swīðsnel *very quick, agile*, CRA 82.

swīðspecende (ȳ) *talkative*, OEG 56¹⁴⁰.

swīðsprecel *talkative*, LPs 11⁴.

swīðstincende *strong-smelling*, WW 408¹⁸.

swīðstrang *very strong*, BH 38⁶B.

swīðstrēme *having a strong current, rapid*, BH 38⁶.

swīðswēge *strong-sounding, heroic*, OEG.

swīður=swīðor comp. of swīðe.

swiung f. *spasm, cramp*, WW 112¹⁹.

swīung=swigung

swodrian *to be fast asleep*, SPs 3⁵. ['*swother*']

swoeg=swēg; **swoesendu**=swǣsendu

swoetnes (GL,VPs)=swētnes

swōg (VPs)=swēg

swōgan⁷ *to sound, roar, howl, rustle, whistle, rattle*, Cr,Gen. ['*sough*']

+**swogen** *in a swoon, silenced, dead*, Æ,Lcd. ['*swow(n)*']

+**swogennes** v. in-s.

+**swōgung** f. *swooning*, Lcd. ['*swowing*']

swol n. *heat, burning, flame, glow.* [swelan; Ger. schwül]

swoleð=sweoloð

swolgen pp. of swelgan.

swolgettan *to gargle, wash the throat*, LCD.

swolig f. *burning*, LCD,WW.
swollen (*Ep*) pp. of swellan.
swoloð, swoloða (OEG 23⁵⁵)=sweoloð
swolten pp. of sweltan.
swoluð (*Æ*)=sweoloð; swolwe=swealwe
swom=swamm I. and II.; swon=swan
swoncor=swancor
swong=swang pret. 3 sg. of swingan.
swongor=swangor; swonrād=swanrād
+swōpe *sweepings, refuse*, Ln 111¹⁵.
swopu (NG)=swipu
swor (Ex 239)=spor
swōr I. pret. 3 sg. of swerian. II.=sār.
 III.=sweor
swōra=sweora; sworc=sweorc
sworcen pp. of sweorcan.
sword=sweord
sworen pp. of swerian.
swōretendlic *short-winded*, WW 355⁹.
swōrettan *to breathe hard, pant, yawn, sigh*,
 Æ.
swōret-ung, -tung f. *hard breathing, panting,
 sobbing, sighing, moaning*, *Æ*.
sworfen pp. of sweorfan.
swornian (a) *to coagulate*, GL.
swōron pret. pl. of swerian.
swostor=sweostor
swōt I. *sweet*, *JnL,Nar,OEG*. adv. swōte
 ÆGr. ['*soot*'] II.=swāt
swōtlic *savoury, sweet*, CP 311⁸. adv.
 -..ce.
swōtmete m. *sweetmeat, dainty*, Bo 33²³.
swōtnes f. *sweetness*, *DR,Shr*. ['*sootness*']
swotol=sweotol
swōt-stence (WW 341⁵), -stencende (DR)
 sweet-smelling.
swoðung=sweðung
+swōwung=+swōgung
swūgian (CP)=swigian; swulc=swilc
swulgon pret. pl. of swelgan.
swulton pret. pl. of sweltan.
swulung=sulung
swuncon pret. pl. of swincan.
-swundennes v. ā-s.
swur-, swūr-=sweor-, sweor-
swust-er, -or, -ur (*Æ*)=sweostor
swut-el-, -ol-, -ul-=sweotol-
swūwian=swigian; swyc-=swic-
swyft=swift; swȳg-=swīg-
swȳge=swige; swyl-=swil-
swyle (i) m. *tumour, swelling*. [swellan]
swyliend=swelgend
swylt† (i) m. *death*. [sweltan]
swylt-=swelt-
swyltcwalu† f. *agony of death*, AN.
swyltdæg† m. *death-day*.
swyltdēað m. *death*, PPs 55¹¹.
swylthwīl† f. *hour of death*, PH.
swym-=swim-; swȳn=swīn

swyn-=swin-; swyp- (N)=swip-
swȳr=sweor; swyrd=sweord
+swyrf=+sweorf
swyrfð pres. 3 sg. of sweorfan.
+swȳsnes=+swǣsnes; swyster=sweostor
swytel, swytol=sweotol; swȳð=swīð
swȳwian=sūgian, swīgian
sȳ=sīe pres. subj. of bēon.
syb, sybb=sibb
±sȳcan (ē, ī) *to suckle* : *wean*, ASPs 130².
 [sūcan]
syce (i, ī?) *sucking*, OEG 57⁸.
sȳclian=sīclian
sycomer m. *sycamore*, BK 4.
sȳcð pres. 3 sg. of sūcan; sȳcan.
+syd n. *wallowing-place*, WW 146¹⁵. [sēo-
 ðan]
sȳd=sīd; +sydian=+sidian
syde m. *a decoction*, LCD 1·280³. [sēoðan]
syfan=seofon; syfe=sife
sȳferǣte *abstemious*, RB 119²⁵.
sȳferlic (ē) *neat, cleanly, pure, sober,
 moderate*. adv. -līce.
sȳferlicnes f. *purity*, VH 20.
sȳferne asm. of sȳfre.
sȳfernes f. *cleanliness, purity, sobriety,
 moderation*, *Æ*.
syfeða=seofoða; syfian=seofian
+syflan *to provide with relishes, flavour*, TC,
 W. [sufl]
syflige (RBL), syfling (*Æ*) f. *food, pap,
 broth, soup* : *seasoning, relish*.
syfol=sufel; syfon=seofon
sȳfre (ē, ī) *clean, pure, chaste, sober,
 abstinent, temperate*, *Æ*. [*Ger*. sauber]
syftan=siftan
syge I. m. *sight, aspect*, FT 64? II.=sige I.
sygel=sigel; sygor=sigor
syh=seoh imperat. of sēon; syht=suht
syhð pres. 3 sg. of sēon I. and II.
+syhð=+sihð
+syhðe (BPs 120⁴)=+sehðe; syl=syle
sȳl I. f. *column, pillar, support*, AO. [*Ger*.
 säule] II. ds. of sūl, sulh.
sȳla m. *ploughman*, OEG 2357. [sulh]
sȳlæx f. *a kind of axe*, WW 379³³ (v. ES
 43·327).
syle, sylen *miry place, wallowing-place*,
 OEG. [sol]
sylen=selen
syleð pres. 3 sg. of syllan; sylf=self
sylfer, sylfor, sylfur (M)=seolfor
sylfren (*Æ*)=seolfren
sylfwill- (*Æ*)=selfwill-
sylg ds., sylh ds. and nap. of sūl, sulh.
Sȳlhearwa=Sigelhearwa
±sylhð(e) n. *team of oxen*. [sulh]
sylian (e) *to sully, soil, pollute*, CP,Met.
 ['*sule*']

syll I. f. '*sill*,' *threshold, foundation, base, basis*, Æ,B,CP. II. nap. of sulh.

sylla m. *giver*, RBL25⁶. [sellan]

sȳlla (DEOR6)=sēlla (sēlra) v. sēl I.

syllan (Æ)=sellan; sylle=syll I.

syllend (Æ)=sellend; syllic=seldlic

sylofr, sylofren=seolfor, seolfren

sȳlra=sēlra v. sēl I.

±syltan (æ, e;=ie) *to salt, season*, Æ. [sealt]

sylu f. *bog, miry place*, Ct.

sȳma=sēma; sȳman=sieman

symbel I. n. *feast-day, festivity, revel, feast*, AO : (†) *festival, holy day* : *solemn office*. II.=simbel

symbelcalic (i) m. *chalice*, TC515¹⁸.

symbelcennes f. *feast of a nativity*, DR.

symbeldæg m. *feast-day, festival, holiday*, Æ.

symbele=simble

symbelgāl *wanton with feasting, drunk*, DD 79.

symbelgereord n. *feasting, carousal*, SOL 407.

symbelgifa m. *giver of feasts*, AN1419.

symbelhūs n. *guest-chamber*, LkLR22¹².

symbelian=symblian

symbellic *festive* : *solemn*. adv. -lice *solemnly*, DR,RBL.

symbelmōnaðlic adj. *of a festival month?* WW375³⁸.

symbelnes f. *festival, feasting, festivity*, Æ : *festal character*, BF84² : *solemn assembly, solemn office*.

symbeltīd f. *festival-time*, DR.

symbelwērig *weary with feasting*, GEN 2640.

symbelwlonc *elated with feasting*, MOD 40.

symbelwynn f. *joy of feasting*, B1782.

symblan *to feast, banquet*, CP.

symble (Æ)=simble adv.

symblian (i) *to feast, carouse*, CP.

symel=symbel

symeringwyrt f. *violet*, WW322⁹.

syml=symbel I.; syml-=simbl-

'symnenlic=semnendlic; syn=synn

sȳn I.=sīen f. II.=sīn, sīen pres. pl. subj. of wesan (bēon). III.=sīn I.

syn- v. also sin-, synn-.

syna=suna gs. of sunu.

synbend m. *bond of sin*, NIC504²³.

synbōt f. *penance*, LL(316').

synbryne m? *burning ardour of sin*, MFH 143¹⁸.

synbyrðen f. *burden of sin*, BL,CR.

synbysig *guilt-haunted*, B2227.

syncræft m. *evil art?* BYH102³⁰.

synd=sind pres. pl. ind. of wesan (bēon).

+synd-=+sund-

syndǣd f. *sinful deed*, PPs,W.

syndan=sendan

synder-=sundor-

synderǣ (u²) f. *special law*, DR190¹⁰.

synderlic (e¹, i¹) *singular, separate, special, peculiar, private*, Bo,CP : *remote*. adv. -lice Æ, BH, Bo, MkL. ['*sunderly*']

synderlicnes f. *separateness, separation, seclusion*, OEG : *singularity, special excellence*, GD286¹¹.

synder-lipe, -lȳpe, -lȳpig *peculiar, special*. adv. -lipes (ȳ), OEG,RB. ['*sunderlepes*']

+syndgian *to make to prosper*, BH320¹².

syndig *skilled in swimming*, CRA58.

+syndig *favourable*, BH386¹³.

+syndiglic (del-) *prosperous*, BH388¹⁸.

syndir-=synder-

+syndlǣcan (synt-) *to cause to prosper*, RPs117²⁵.

syndolh n. *deadly wound*, B817 (or=sin-?).

syndon=sindon pres. pl. ind. of wesan (bēon).

Syndonisc *Indian*, MFH173, NIC592. [*L. Gk.*]

syndra? m., syndre? f.=sinder

±syndrian (u) *to '*sunder,' *separate, divide*, KC,LG,Sc.

syndrig (i) *separate, single*, PPs : '*sundry,*' *various, distinct*, Æ,BH : *special, private, peculiar, exceptional, particular*, Æ; AO, CP : *characteristic* : (distributive) *one each*. [*sundor*]

syndrige adv. *separately, specially, apart, alone*, LG. ['*sundry*']

syndrigendlic *discretive*, ÆGR229⁷.

syndriglic *special, peculiar*, BH. adv. -licc *specially* : *separately*, BH. ['*sundrily*']

syndrung v. ā-s.

syndurǣ=synderǣ

synew-=sinew-; and v. seonu.

synfāh *sin-stained*, CR1083.

±syngian *to sin, transgress, err*, Æ,CP.

syngrigendlic=syndrigendlic

syngrin (y²) f. *snare of sin, harm*, W.

syngung f. *transgression*, HL12¹³⁷. ['*sinning*']

synleahter m. *stain of sin*, W134²⁴.

synlēas '*sinless*,' *guiltless, innocent*, CP,Jn, W.

synlēaw *injury caused by sin*, W165²⁵.

synlic *sinful, foul, wicked*. adv. -lice.

+synlice=+sinlice

synn (e, i) f. (†) *injury, mischief, enmity, feud* : '*sin*,' *guilt, crime*, Bl,Bo,Chr,G,Sc, VPs; CP.

synn- see also syn-.

synnadæg (N)=sunnandæg

synnecge f. *female sinner*, MH126⁴.

synneðõht *sinful thought*, BYH136¹³.

synnful 'sinful,' guilty, wicked, corrupt, Bl, LG,VPs; CP.

synngiend m. sinner, EPs 111¹⁰.

+synnian to commit adultery, NG.

synnig guilty, punishable, criminal : sinful, CP.

synnlust m. desire to sin, Æ.

synoð=seonoð

synrǣs m. temptation, LL (284⁹).

synrūst m. canker of sin, CR 1321.

syn-sceaða, -scaða† m. sin-stained wretch, sinful outrager, VH 20.

synscyldig wicked, DD 168.

synt=sind pres. pl. ind. of wesan (bēon).

+synt-=+synd-

±synto f. soundness, health : prosperity, welfare, salvation. [gesund]

synwracu† f. punishment for sin.

synwund f. wound of sin, CR,LL.

synwyrcende† sinning.

sypan=sypian

sype m. wetting, act of soaking through, Bo. ['sipe']

sypian (i) to absorb, drink in, Lcd 94b. ['sipe']

sȳpian=sīpian; sypo, syppo=swipu

syrc m., syrce f.=serc, serce

syre=searwe, v. searo; sȳre=sīere

syredon=sier(w)edon pret. pl. of sierwan.

syretung f. lurking place, WW 440⁶. [searu]

syrewrenc=searowrenc

syrewung=searwung

syrfe f. service-tree, EC 373¹¹. [L. sorbus]

syrftrēow n. service-tree, KC 3·379'.

syric, syrice=serc, serce

sȳring f. sour milk, buttermilk, LL,WW. [sūr]

Syrisc Syrian, ÆL 18⁴⁰².

syrode=sierwde pret. 3 sg. of sierwan.

syru=searo

syrwa=searwa gp. of searo.

syr-wan, -wian (Æ)=sierwan

Syrware mpl. Syrians, PH 166.

syrwung=sierwung

syrwwrenc=searowrenc; syster=sester

syt-=sit-

sȳð I.=sīð. II. v. sūð adv. III. pres. 3 sg. of sēoðan.

sȳð-=sīð-; sȳðan=siððan

sȳðerra (BC,Lcd) v. sūð. ['souther']

sȳðst pres. 2 sg. of sēoðan.

sȳððan=siððan; sȳwian=sēowian

syx, syx-=siex, siex-, six-

T

tā I. f. 'toe,' Cp,LL,WW. II. f. (Æ)=tān m.

tabele, tablu, tabul, f., tabula m.=tabule

tabule f. 'table,' BH : a wooden hammer, or piece of wood struck as a signal for assemb-

ling monks, CM : writing tablet, Bf : gaming table, Gl : table of the law. [L.]

tacan⁶ to 'take,' seize, Chr 1072,1076. t. on to touch.

+taccian to tame, subdue, GPH 402 (= +ðaccian).

tācen, tācn n., nap. tācen, tācnu 'TOKEN,' symbol, sign, signal, mark, indication, suggestion, Æ,CP : portent, marvel, wonder, miracle : evidence, proof : standard, banner.

tācen-=tācn-

tācencircol m. indiction, TC 126³.

tācnan (Cp)=tǣcnan

tācnberend m. standard-bearer, ÆGR 27¹⁵.

tācnbora m. standard-bearer : guide, APT.

±tācnian to mark, indicate : betoken, denote, signify, represent, Bl,Bo; AO,CP : symbolise, ÆH,Bl : portend : demonstrate, express. ['token']

+tācni(g)endlic typical, emblematic, ÆH 2·278¹⁴; ÆP 122¹⁷.

±tācnung f. sign, presage, token, signal, Bo : manifestation, signification, type, Bo,BH : indication, symptom, proof : dispensation, AO 60¹ : phase (of moon), zodiacal sign, ANS 145·256. ['tokening']

tācon, tācun=tācen

tācor, tācur m. brother-in-law, Æ.

tāde, tādi(g)e f. 'toad,' WW.

tǣbere a weaving tool? tenterhook? WW 294¹⁷.

tǣcan, pret. tǣhte to transfer, translate, Æ. [ON. taka]

±tǣcan to show, declare, demonstrate, Æ, AO : 'TEACH*' ('i-tæche'), instruct, train, Æ; CP : assign, prescribe, direct, Æ,CP : warn : persuade, MtR 28¹⁴. +t. fram dismiss, LL 162,22.

tǣcing f. teaching, instruction, Æ : doctrine : direction, injunction, command, rule.

tǣcnan to mark by a token, denote, designate, mark out. [Ger. zeichnen]

-tǣcne v. earfoð-t.

tǣcnend m. index-finger, A 13·329, WW 426³⁸.

tǣcnian=tācnian

tǣcning f. demonstration, proof, Bo 90¹.

tæfl, tæfel (e²) fn. cube, die, game with dice or tables, Gl,Wy. [L. tabula; v. 'tavel']

tæfl-an, -ian to gamble, Gl. ['tavel']

tæfle adj. given to dice-playing, GNE 185.

tæflere m. gambler, WW. [v. 'tavel']

tæflstān m. gambling-stone, die, Gl. [v. 'tavel']

tæflung f. gaming, playing at dice, NC 325.

tǣg (A)=tēag

tægel, tægl (e) m. 'tail,' LL,WW; Æ.

tæglhǣr n. hair of the tail, LCD 1·360'.

tægðian (M)=teogoðian

tæherian (NG)=tēarian

tæhher (NG)=tēar

tǣhte pret. 3 sg. of tǣcan.

tæl (a, e) n. *number,* Æ.

tǣl (ā) f. *blame, reproach, calumny, abuse,* CP,WW : *blasphemy* : *disgrace.* ['*tele*']

+**tæl** I. (e, ea) n., nap. +talu *number, series,* Æ,LG : *numeral,* ÆGR : *number of people, tribe* : *catalogue,* WW 418³⁶ : *reckoning, estimation, opinion.* ['*tel,*' '*i-tel*'] II. adj. np. +tale *swift, ready,* PPs 56⁵ : *competent,* WW 505³. [v. '*tall*']

tæla=tela

±**tǣlan** (ē) *to blame, censure, scold, reprove, reproach, accuse,* Æ,AO,CP : *speak ill of, slander, insult, deride,* Bo,LRG,LL,WW : *despise, maltreat: dispute.* ['*tele*']

tælberend=telgberend

+**tælcircul** m. *cycle, series,* WW 204⁴².

+**tælcræft** (e) m. *arithmetic,* OEG 3117.

+**tæld**=+teld; -**tǣle** v. lēof-, un-t.

tǣlend m. *slanderer, backbiter* : *mocker, scoffer* : *reprover.*

tǣlende *censorious, slanderous,* BL,LL.

tǣlere (ē) m. *derider, scoffer,* KGL 75¹⁶.

+**tælfæst** *measurable,* LPs 38⁶.

tælfers (e¹) n. '*versus catalecticus,*' OEG 127.

+**tælful** *numerous,* Sc 231¹⁰.

tǣlful (ā) *blameworthy,* CHRD 67³⁶.

tælg=telg

tǣlhlehter m. *derision,* WW 172⁴. [hleahtor]

tælian=talian

tǣling f. *reproof,* CP : *derogation* : *slander, derision.*

tælla (GPH 394)=telga; **tællan**=tellan

tǣllēas *blameless,* CP. adv. -līce, CP.

tǣllic (ā) *blameworthy* : *slanderous, blasphemous.* adv. -līce *reprehensibly* : *shamelessly?* CHRD 70⁵.

tælmearc f. *date, period,* GU 849. [talu]

tælmet n. *measure, portion,* AN 113. [talu]

tǣlnes (ē) f. *blame, reproof,* CP : *derogation* : *slander, calumny, insult.*

+**tælrīm** n. *order, succession,* SOL 38.

±**tælsum** *in numbers, rhythmic,* OEG.

tǣlweorð-=tǣlwierð-

æl-wierðe, -wierðlic *reprehensible, blameworthy,* CP. adv. -līce.

ǣlwierðlicnes (eo²) f. *blameableness,* CP 52¹⁵.

-**tælwīs** (e) *skilled in arithmetic,* BF 112⁹, WW 207⁴⁰.

ǣlwyrd-, tǣlwyrð-=tǣlwierð-

ǣman=tīeman

æmespīle f. *sieve-frame, sieve-stand? sieve-stake?* LL 455,17 and 3·255. [v. '*temse*']

emian (GD 11⁹)=temian

ēnel (ē¹, ī²) m. *wicker basket,* Æ,Gl. ['*teanel*'; tān]

tǣnen *made of twigs,* OEG. [tān]

tæng-=teng-; **tǣnil**=tǣnel

tæppa m. '*tap,*' *spigot,* IM.

tæppe f? *strip of stuff or cloth,* '*tape,*' WW 107³³.

tæpp-ed, -et n. *figured cloth, tapestry, carpet,* TC,WW. ['*tapet*']

tæppelbred n. *footstool,* NG.

tæppere m. *tapster, tavern-keeper,* Sc,WW. ['*tapper*']

tæppestre f. *tapstress, female tavern-keeper,* ÆGr. ['*tapster*']

tœppet=tæpped

tæppian *to open* (*a cask*)? *furnish it with a tap or spout?* IM 125. ['*tap*']

tæppilbred=tæppelbred

tær pret. 3 sg. of teran; **tǣr**=tēar

tǣsan (±) *to pull, tear, comb, card,* Lcd : (†) *wound, injure, assault:* (+) *influence,* CP 297¹⁸. ['*tease*']

±**tǣse** I. *pleasant,* Met : *convenient, suitable,* B. ['*i-tase*'] II. (+) n. *advantage, convenience,* CP 387 : *useful thing, implement.*

tǣsel f. '*teasel*' (*plant*), Lcd 1·282¹⁵.

+**tǣslic** *convenient.* adv. -līce *conveniently* : *gently, softly, smoothly,* CP.

tæslīce (NG)=ðæslīce

+**tǣsnes** f. *advantage, convenience,* WW.

tæso=tēosu

+**tǣsu**=+tǣse II.

tǣtan *to gladden, cheer,* WY 4.

tætteca m? *rag, tatter, shred?* Æ,KC (v. BT).

tǣð=teð, v. tōð.

-**tǣwe** (ēo) v. æl-t.

tāh pret. 3 sg. of tēon II.

+**tāh** n. *teaching,* RIM 2 (ES 65·188).

tāhe (GL)=tā

tāhspura m. *spur, tip of toe?* WW 197¹⁴.

tāhte=tæhte pret. 3 sg. of tǣcan.

tal (N)=talu; **tāl**=tǣl; **tala**=tela

tald=teald pp. of tellan.

+**tale** v. tæl.

talente f. '*talent*' (*money of account*), AO. [L.]

±**talian** (æ) *to count, calculate, reckon, account, consider, think, esteem, value,* BH,CP,LG,W : *argue,* CP : *tell, relate,* LG; Æ : *impute, assign,* Æ,BH. (=tellan.) ['*tale*']

+**talscipe** m. *multitude,* NG.

talt-=tealt-

talu f. '*tale,*' *series, calculation* : *list,* WW : *statement, deposition, relation, communication, narrative,* Æ,KC : *fable, tale, story* : *accusation, action at law* (v. LL 3·226).

+**talu** v. +tæl.

tālwyrð-=tǣlwierð-

tam '*tame,*' Æ,Bo,WW : *tractable, gentle, mild,* Bo,Gn.

tama m. *tameness*, Bo,MET.

tamcian *to tame, soothe*, CHRD 96¹⁸.

-tamcol v. un-t.

tān I. m. *twig, rod, switch, branch* : *rod of divination*. **II.** *shooting? spreading?* GEN 2360. **III.** pl. of tā.

tānede *diseased in the toes?* WW 161²⁸.

±tang, tange (o) f. (sg. and pl.) *pincers, 'tongs,' forceps, Æ,BH,Bf,Gl*; Æ.

+tang (w. d.) *in contact with* (=pret. 3 sg. of +tingan). adv. +tange (o), RIM 42?

+tanglīce *together*, RB 47¹⁵.

tānhlyta m. *soothsayer, augur, diviner*, WW 189³. [tān, hlot]

tānhlytere m. *soothsayer, diviner*, WW 183³².

+tanned *tanned*, WW 118⁷. ['tanned']

tannere m. *'tanner,'* KC 2·411'.

taper (*Lcd,WW*)=tapor

taperæx f. *small axe*, CHR 1031A, CC 28¹⁶. [*ON.* taparöx]

tapor (ea¹; e², u²) m. *lamp-wick, 'taper,' candle, CP* : *a feeble light*, PH 114. [*Keltic?*]

taporberend m. *acolyte*, GL.

taran v. teoru.

targa? m., **targe?** f. *small shield, buckler*, KC. [v. *'targe'*]

+targed *furnished with a shield*, OEG 2259.

taru? f. *tear, rent*, WW 416²⁷. [teran]

tasol, tasul (GL)=teosel; **-tāwere** v. flæsc-t.

±tāwian *to prepare, make ready, make* : *till, cultivate, BH* : *harass, afflict, insult, Æ, AO.* t. tō bysmore *outrage, profane, Æ,W.* ['taw']

+tāw-u, -a np. *apparatus, implements* : *genitalia*, LCD 26a.

te-=tō-; **tēa** (NG)=tīen

+tēad (ē) pp. of +tēon and +tēagan.

tēafor I. n. *red, red lead, vermilion, purple*, WW. [v. *'tiver'*] **II.** meaning doubtful, or ? tēaforgēap (v. GK), RUIN 31.

tēag (ǣ, ē) **I.** f. *cord, band, thong, fetter, Cr*, WW. ['tie'] **II.** *case, chest, Æ,WW* : *enclosure, BC.* [*'tye'*]

+tēagan (ē) pret. +tēde, pp. +tēad *to make, prepare, dress, till*.

teagor (*Gu*)=tēar

tēah I. pret. 3 sg. of tēon I. and II. **II.**= tēag

teal-=tal-, tæl-, tel-

tēal-=tǣl-; +teald=+teld

tealde pret. 3 sg. of tellan; **tealgor**=telgor

tealt *unstable, precarious, Run,W.* ['tealt']

tealt(r)ian (a) *to totter, shake, stumble, waver* : *be untrustworthy* : *amble*. [cp. *Ger.* zelter]

tēam (ē) m. *descendant, family, race, line, Æ,Mk,TC* : *child-bearing, Æ* : *brood, Æ* : *company, band, Æ* : *'team' (of horses, oxen,*

etc.), *WW* : *vouching to warranty, right of jurisdiction in matters of warranty, EC,LL.*

+tēama (ȳ) m. *warrantor, surety*, LL.

tēaman=tīeman

tēamful *fruitful, LPs,WW.* [v. *'teemful'*]

tēamian=tīeman

tēampōl m. *breeding pool*, EC 322'.

tēan- (A)=tēon-; **teaper** (K)=tapor

tēapor (*Lcd*)=tēafor

tēar m. *drop, Cr,Lcd* : *'tear*',' B,Bl*; CP : *what is distilled from anything in drops, 'nectar,' WW*; CM.

tearflian *to turn, roll, wallow*, Mk 9²⁰.

tēargēotende *tear-shedding, tearful*, NIC 508¹⁵.

tēarian (tǣherian, ē¹) *to weep, JnL.* ['tear']

tēarig *tearful*, HGL : *watery*, LCD 125a.

tēarighlēor *with tearful cheeks*, GEN 2274.

tearn (WW 286⁷)=stearn; **tearos** v. teoru.

teart *sharp, rough, severe, Æ,OEG.* ['tart'; tær pret. of teran]

teartlic *sharp, rough, Æ.* adv. -līce, OEG. ['tartly']

teartnes f. *sharpness, roughness, hardness, OEG*; Æ. ['tartness']

teartnumol *biting, effectual*, LCD 1·152³.

teaslīce (NG)=ðæslīce

tēað=tēoð pres. pl. of tēon I. and II.

tebl, tebl-, tebil-=tæfl, tæfl-

tēc-=tæc-; **tēd-**=tīed-; **+tēd**=+tēad

tēde pret. of tēagan.

tēder=tȳder; **tēdr-**=tīed(e)r-, tȳdr-

tefel, tefil=tæfl

tēfrung (=īe) f. *picture*, AS 21⁴.

tēg=tēag; **tēgan**=(1) tīegan; (2) tēagan

tēge=tīge; **tegl**=tægl; **tēgð**=tēoð-

tēh=tēah pret. 3 sg. of tēon.

teherian (A)=tēarian

tehher, teher (*NG*)=tēar

tēhton=tǣhton pret. pl. of tǣcan.

teissu (LkL)=teosu; **+tel**=+tæl; **tēl-**=tǣl-

tela (i, ea, eo) **I.** adv. *well, fitly, properly, rightly, very, good, CP* : *prosperously, beneficially.* **II.** interj. *well! good!*

±teld n. *tent, pavilion, tabernacle, Æ,BH, TC.* ['teld']

+teldgehlīwung f. *tabernacle*, BF 74¹⁴.

teldian *to spread (net), set (trap), Cp,PPs* : *entrap.* ['teld']

teldsticca m. *tent-peg*, JUD 4²¹,²².

+teldung f. *tabernacle*, EPs 18⁵; 77⁶⁰.

+teldwurðung f. *feast of tabernacles*, WW 107¹⁷.

teldwyrhta m. *tent-maker*, ÆH 1·392'.

telede=tealde pret. 3 sg. of tellan.

+telfers (OEG)=tælfers

telg (æ) m. *dye, colour, tincture*, BH,GL.

telga m. *twig, branch, bough, shoot, CP* : *pole, stock*, EC 95'.

+telg-an, -ian *to dye*, WW.
telgberend *yielding a dye*, WW462¹⁹.
telge f.=telga
telgestre (æ¹) m. *dyer*, GD342³.
telgian I. *to put forth branches*, RIM34.
II.=talian. III.=telgan
telgor mf., telgra m., telgre f. *twig, branch, shoot*, Æ,Gl,Lcd. [v. '*tiller*']
telgung f. *dye, purple dye*, WW.
telian=tilian
±tellan (æ, ea) *to* 'TELL' ('*i-telle*'), *reckon, count, number, compute, calculate*, Æ : *account, estimate, consider, think, esteem, believe, CP : charge against, impute to : assign: state, recount, enumerate, announce, relate, Æ.* t. gelīc *compare*. [talu]
-tellendlic v. un-t.
teltrē, teltrēo n. *weaving-tool? tenterhook? tent-peg?* WW.
+telwīs *skilled in reckoning*, BF112⁹.
tēm=tēam; tema=tama
tēman=tīeman
tēmbyrst m. *failure to secure a voucher*, EC 202¹. [tēam]
Temes, Temese f. *river Thames*, AO. [*L.* Tamisia]
±temesian (i²) *to sift*, MkL. ['*temse*']
±temian *to tame, subdue*, Æ,CP,Lcd,LG : (+) *suffer, permit*, ÆL23⁸¹⁰. ['*teme*']
tempel, templ n. '*temple*,' Æ,Bl,CP,G,VPs. [*L.* templum]
tempel-=templ-
tempelgeat n. *temple-door*, W49²⁵.
tempelhūs n. *temple*, BYH118²⁴.
templgeweorc n. *structure of the temple*, W277²⁵.
templhālgung f. *dedication of the temple*, OEG40³⁶.
templic adj. *of a temple*, OEG.
±temprian v. *to '*temper*,' moderate*, Æ,Gl, Sc : *cure, heal*, Æ : *control, curb*, Æ (refl.), Lcd. [*Lat.*]
temprung f. *tempering, moderation*, Sc.
tēn (VPs)=tīen; tēnan=tȳnan
-tendan (y) v. ā-, for-, on-t.
tender=tynder
tend-ing, -ling f. *burning, stinging*, NC,GD. [v. '*tind*']
tēne=tīen; tēnel (Ep)=tǣnel
±tengan (æ) *to press towards, hasten*, Æ. āweg t. *get away, get off.* +t. on *assail*, AO.
+tenge *near to, resting on : oppressing, burdensome*, AO.
tēnil=tǣnel
tennan *to lure, coax?* WY4?
tēo pres. 1 sg. of tēon I. and II.
teochian=teohhian
tēode pret. of tēon III., tēogan, teohhian.

teofenian† *to join, put together*, CREAT.
tēofor=tēafor
tēofrian *to appoint?* PPs117²¹.
tēogan=teohhian
teogeða, teogoða=tēoða
teogoðian *to '*tithe*,' grant or pay tithes*, Æ, CP,G : *divide by ten*, Æ.
teoh fm., gds. teohhe *race : band, troop, company, society*. [*Ger.* zeche]
tēoh imperat. of tēon.
+tēoh n. *matter, material, universe?* RIM2.
teohhe v. teoh.
±teohhian (i, io) *to determine, intend, propose*, Æ,CP : *consider, think, judge, estimate*. [*OHG.* gizehōn]
+teohhung f. *arrangement, ordering*, HL 13⁶⁹.
teohhian=teohhian; teol-=tel-, til-
teolðyrl n. '*foramen*,' '*fenestra*,' OEG.
teom (MtR21⁵)=tam
tēon I. (±) sv² *to pull, tug, draw, drag, row (boat)*, CP : *draw together : withdraw, take*, LL356,70 : *entice, allure, induce, lead, bring*, CP : *bring up, educate*, Æ : *bring to, attract*, AO : *arrogate*, CP : *bring forth, produce*, Æ : *restrain*, LL : *betake oneself to, go, roam :* (+) *dispute*, NG : (+) *string up, play (instrument)*, ÆGR49¹⁴. ['TEE*,' '*i-teon*'; *teohan] II. sv¹ (but forms belonging to tēon I. often found) *accuse, censure*, Æ,LL; AO : *proceed against successfully*, ANS144·253. ['*tee*'; *tīhan] III. wv. (±) *to prepare, furnish forth, arrange, adorn, deck : produce, work, do, create, make*, Æ : *settle, fix, establish, constitute, ordain.* [=teohhian] IV. num.= tīen. V. n.=tēona. VI.=dēon (v. JAW19).
tēona m. *injury, hurt, wrong*, Bl,Mt; AO : *accusation, reproach, insult, contumely*, Æ, AO,CP : *anger, grief : malice*, Æ : *enmity, hostility*. ['*teen*']
tēoncwide† m. *hurtful speech : blasphemy*.
tēoncwidian *to slander, calumniate*, GL.
tēond I. m. *accuser*, LL. II. *drawer*, BH 288¹⁴.
tēone f.=tēona
tēonere m. *slanderer*, LPs71⁴.
tēonful *slanderous, evil, rebellious, painful*, SPs,W; Æ. ['*teenful*']
tēonhete† m. *malicious hate*.
tēonian (ȳ) *to injure, irritate*, LPs : *slander*. ['*teen*']
tēonlēas *free from suffering*, MFH174.
tēonlēg† m. *destroying flame*.
tēonlic *destructive, shameful, hurtful.* adv. -līce.
tēonrǣden (e²) f. *abuse, wrong, injury, humiliation*, Æ.

tēonsmið m. *evil-doer*, Gu176.

tēontig=hundtēontig

tēonword n. *reproach, abuse, calumny*, Æ, Lcd.

±**tēorian** *to fail, cease, become weary, be tired, exhausted, Gl,Lcd,LL,PPs* : '*tire,*' *weary, exhaust, PPs.* [teran]

±**tēorigendlic** *failing, defective*, Sc181⁴, ByH56¹⁵.

teoro=teoru

+**tēorodnes** f. *debility, weariness*, Gl.

teors m. '*calamus,*' '*veretrum,*' *Lcd,WW.* ['*tarse*']

teoru (e) n., occl. gs. tearos and wk. a. taran '*tar,*' *bitumen, distillation from a tree, resin, gum, balsam, Gl,Lcd* : *wax from the ear.*

±**tēorung** f. *exhaustion, weariness*, Æ.

teosel (a, e) m. *die* ('*tessera*'). [*L.*]

teosu (æ, e) f. *harm, injury, ruin, wrong.*

teosuspræc f. *harmful speech*, PPs139¹¹.

teosuword (teso-) n. *calumny, harmful speech*, NC.

teoswian (e) *to injure, harm*, Sol94.

tēoð pres. pl. of tēon I. and II.

tēoða (ē) '*TENTH,*' *Æ,AO,Chr.* tēoðan dǣl *tenth part.* [teogeða]

tēoðe *tenthly*, LL181,10.

±**tēoðian** *to divide by ten, tithe*, Æ : *take a tenth* : *give tithes, Æ,BC,CP,G.*

tēoðing=tēoðung

tēoðingdæg m. *tithing day, tenth day*, Æ.

tēoðingealdor m. *ruler over ten, dean, captain of ten*, RB.

tēoðingmann m. '*tithing-man,*' *headborough*, LL : *captain of ten*, Æ.

tēoðung f. *division into ten, decimation, tenth part, tithe,* '*tithing,*' *Æ,Lk,LL* : *band of ten men, LL.*

tēoðungcēap m. *tithe*, Bl39¹¹.

tēoðunggeorn *diligent in paying tithes*, A 12·518²⁶.

tēoðungland n. *land set apart for tithes*, LL 2·750.

tēoðungsceatt m. *tithing-money, tithes*, Bl, LL.

tēowlic=tōwlic

teped (*KGl*), tepet=tæpped; **tēr** (*Lcd*)=tēar

+**ter** n. *tearing, laceration* : *thing torn* : *tumult, discord.*

±**teran⁴** (ea, eo) *to* '*TEAR*,*' *lacerate.*

terdnes (A 13·34)=teartnes

tergan=tirgan

termen (i²) m. *term, end*, Bf,Lcd. [*L.*]

tero, teru (*Ep,WW*)=teoru

tes-=teos-; +**tēse**=+tǣse

teter m. '*tetter,*' *skin eruption, eczema, ring-worm, CP,Gl,Lcd,Sc.*

teting=tyhting; **tēð** v. tōð.

tēða=tēoða; **-tewestre** v. wull-t.

+**tēðed** *toothed*, AA31⁷.

TĪ=Tīw; **tīan** (N)=tēon III.

tīber† n. *offering, sacrifice, victim*, Gen.

tībernes f. *sacrificing, destruction*, AO50¹⁸.

ticcen (y) n. *kid, Æ,MtL.* ['*ticchen*']

ticgen (NG)=ticcen

ticgende *proudly adorned*, OEG.

ticia m. '*tick*' (*insect*), *Gl.*

tictator m. *dictator*, AO70³. [*L.*]

tīd f. *time, period, season, while* : *hour* : *feast-day, festal-tide* : *canonical hour or service.* on tīde *at the proper time.* ['*TIDE*']

tīdan (±) *to betide, happen, Bo,LL* : *fall to* (*one's lot*), *BC.* ['*tide,*' '*i-tide*']

tīdanðēnung=tīdðēnung

tīdd-=tīd-, tȳd-

tīddæg† m. *lifetime.*

tīdelīce=tīdlīce

tīdembwlātend=tīdymbwlātend

tīder=tīedre

tīdfara m. *one who travels at his own convenience?* Cr1674 (or ?two words).

tīdgenge *having a monthly course, periodical*, GPH392.

tīdlic *timely, seasonable, opportune*, AO : *temporal* : *temporary.* adv. -līce.

tīdlicnes f. *opportunity, fit time*, NG.

tīdran=tȳdran

tīdre=tīedre

tīdrēn m. *timely rain*, Deut28¹².

±**tīdrian** (ȳ) *to become feeble, weak* : *decay.*

tīdsang mn. *canonical hours, lauds*, Æ.

tīdscēawere m. *astrologer*, WW176⁴.

tīdscriptor m. *chronographer, chronicler*, WW204¹⁷ (hybrid word).

tīdðēnung f. *service at one of the canonical hours*, FBO.

tīdum adv. *at times, occasionally.*

tīdung f. (usu. pl.) *event, tidings, news*, Chr. ['*tiding*']

tīdwrītere m. *chronicler*, Gl.

tīdwurdung f. *service at one of the canonical hours*, HL11⁶⁷.

tīdymbwlātend (e²) m. *astrologer*, Lcd.

tīeder=tīedre

tīederlic (ē, ī, ȳ) *weak*, CP.

tīedernes (ē, ī, ȳ) *frailty* (*of body or soul*), CP.

tīedran=tȳdran

tīedre (ē, ī, ȳ) *weak, frail, infirm*, CP : *fainthearted* : *fleeting.*

±**tīegan** (ē, ī, ȳ) *to* '*tie*,*' *bind, Æ*; CP : *join, connect, ÆGr.* [tēag]

tīegle=tigle; **tieht-**=tyht-

tīehð pres. 3 sg. of tēon I. and II.

tīel-=til-; **tīema**=tīma

tīeman (ǣ, ē, ī, ȳ) *to bring forth, engender, beget, propagate, Æ,W* : *make answerable for another person, call as witness, Æ,Bas* : (±) *vouch to warranty, LL.* ['*teem*'; tēam]

+tĪeme I. (ē, ȳ) *suitable.* II. (ȳ) *team, yoke,* Æ.

tĪen (ē, ī, ȳ) num. ' TEN,' *CP.*

tĪenambre (ȳ) *holding ten ambers,* LCD 32b.

tĪenbebod (ē) n. *decalogue,* OEG 11¹⁰⁸

tĪenfeald (ȳ) *ten-fold,* Æ.

tĪengewintred (ȳ) *ten years old,* LL 19,27 H.

tĪennihte (ȳ) *ten days old,* BF 162¹³.

tĪenstrenge (ē, ī) *ten-stringed,* VPs.

tĪenwintre (ȳ) *ten years old,* Æ : *ten years long,* AO.

tier *heap?* (GK), *drop?* (Sedgef.), MET 20⁸¹.

tīfe f. *bitch,* LCD 64a.

tĪfer=tiber

-tĪg (ē, ȳ) v. fore-, forð-t.; Tīg=Tiw

tĪgan=tīegan; tige=tyge

tigel, tigele (o²) f. *earthen vessel, crock, pot, potsherd* : ' *tile,*' *brick,* AO; Mdf : *slabs for roofing, Cp,Lcd,VPs.*

tigelærne f. *tile kiln? house of brick?* KC 3·130'.

tigelen *made of pot, earthenware,* SPs 2⁹.

tigelfāg *tile-adorned,* AN 842.

tigelgetel n. *tale of bricks,* Ex 5¹⁹.

tigelgeweorc n. *brick-making,* Æ.

tigellēah m *brick-field,* KC 5·267²¹.

tigelstān m. *tile,* ES 11·66. [' *tilestone*']

tigelwyrhta (y) m. *brick-maker, potter.*

tigen pp. of tēon II.

tiger pl. tigras ' *tiger,*' Æ,Nar.

tīging f. *tie, connection.* ÆGR 14¹⁴. [tīgan]

tigl=(1) tigel; (2) tygel

tigle f. ' *muraenula,*' *sea-mullet?* WW 180³⁰.

tigle, tigol(e)=tigcl, tigclc

tigon pret. pl. of tēon II.

tĪgrisc *of a tiger,* A 4·161.

tigðian (AO)=tiðian

-tigu v. egeðgetigu [egðe]; tigule=tigele

tihian=teohhian

tiht (y) m. *charge, crime,* LL,WW. [tēon II.]

tihtan I. (y) *to accuse,* LL. [tēon II.] II.= tyhtan

tihtbysig *involved in accusations, of bad reputation,* v. LL 2·305 and ANS 144·253.

tihtle (y) f. *accusation, suit, charge,* AO.

tihtlian *to accuse, charge,* LL.

tĪhð pres. 3 sg. of tēon II.

til I. *good, apt, suitable, useful, profitable* : *excellent* : *brave* : *abounding.* II.† n. *goodness, fitness.* III. n.=till. IV. prep. *to, MtL,OET.* [' *till*']

tila=tela

tilen (eo) f. *endeavour,* GD 194¹².

tilfremmende *well-doing,* RD 60⁷.

tilgan=tilian; tili (OET)=twilic

tilia, tilig(e)a (y) m. *tiller, workman, hind, labourer, farmer, husbandman, Mt;* Æ. [' *tilie*']

tilian (eo, y) *to aim at, aspire to, strive after, try, endeavour,* Æ; CP : (±) *procure, obtain, gain, provide,* Æ : *exert oneself, work, make, generate,* Æ,CP : *tend, cherish, cultivate,* ' TILL,' *plough,* CP : *trade, traffic,* Æ : (±) *treat, cure.*

tiligea=tilia

tiling=tilung

till† n. *station, standing-place.*

till-=til-, tyll-

+tillan *to touch, attain,* Æ.

tillic† adj. *fit, good,* RD. adv. -līce.

tilmōdig† *well-disposed, kind, good.*

±tilð, tilðe (y) f. ' *tilth,*' *labour, husbandry, LL,W* : *crop, harvest,* LL : *gain, profit,* OEG.

tilung (eo, ie, io, y) f. *acquisition, procuring* : *care, solicitude* : *occupation, work, performance,* CP : *tending, culture, husbandry,* Æ : *produce, gain, income,* Æ.

tĪma m. ' TIME,' *period, space of time,* Æ, AO : *lifetime,* Æ : *fixed time,* Æ,AO,CP : *favourable time, opportunity,* CP : *a metrical unit, Bf.*

tĪman=tieman

±timber n. ' *timber,*' *building material,* LL : *act of building* : *building, structure,* BH, Lcd,MtL,VPs : *trees, woods,* AO. [v. Mdf]

timbergeweorc n. *cutting timber,* BC 1·344⁹.

+timberhālgung f. *feast of tabernacles,* OEG 56²⁸⁷.

timberhrycg m. *wooded ridge?* KC.

timberland (y¹, o³) n. *land given for repairing and maintaining buildings* : *land on which to grow timber* (BTs), KC 5·236¹².

+timbernes f. *building up, edification,* MFH 124.

timbor I. *a revolving borer, auger?* WW 273⁸. II. =timber

±timbran, timbrian *to build, construct, erect,* BH,CP,G,Gen,LL : *effect, do,* AO,CP; Æ : *edify, instruct* : *cut* ' *timber.*'

+tim-bre n., -bru f. *building, structure,* Æ, AO.

timbr(i)end mf. *builder,* BH,GD.

±timbrung f. *act of building,* Æ : *structure* : *edification.*

+tĪmian (ȳ) *to happen, fall out,* Æ,BF.

tĪmlīce *quickly, soon,* ÆT 12.

timpana m. *timbrel,* Æ,CP,VPs. [' *tympan*']

timpestre f. *female timbrel-player,* LPs 67²⁶.

timple f. *a weaver's instrument,* LL 455,15¹ (cp. ātimplian).

tin I. n. ' *tin,*' *CP.* II. f. *beam, rafter,* GL. III.=tinen

tĪn num.=tīen

tinclian *to tickle,* Sc 52,88.

+tinclic=+tyngelic

tind m. *spike, beak, prong, tooth of a fork,* *Cp,Ep,Sol.* ['*tine*']

tindig *spiked,* WW116¹².

tindiht *forked, jagged, beaked,* Gl,MH.

tindre=tyndre

tinen *made of tin, ÆGr.* ['*tinnen*']

+**ting,** tinge=+tyng, tynge

+**tingan³** *to press against,* An138.

+**tingcræft** m. '*mechanica,*' *rhetoric,* HGl 479.

-**tīning** v. gafol-t.

tinn *beam,* A19·491.

tinnan *to stretch,* Gl : *desire, long for? burn?* Rim54.

tinnen=tinen

tinstrenge=tīenstrenge

tinterg=tintreg

tinterðegn=tintregðegn

tintreg (*AO; Æ*) n., **tintrega** m. *torture, torment, punishment,* *AO,Lk,W.* ['*tintregh*']

tintreganlic=tintreglic

tintregend (terg) m. *torturer,* WW341¹⁹.

±**tintregian** *to torment, torture, punish, Æ,* AO.

tintreglic *full of torment, infernal,* BH346¹².

tintregstōw f. *place of torment,* Guth38⁴.

tintregðegn m. *torturer, executioner,* MtR, WW.

tintregung f. *torture, punishment, Æ,*WW.

tintrian (AO)=tintregian

tio-=teo-; **tiol-**=tel-, til-

tīr (ȳ) m. (†) *fame, glory, honour, ornament* : *name of the rune for* t : *name of a planet and a god* (*Mars*), Run17.

tīrēadig† *glorious, famous.*

tīrfæst† *glorious, famous.*

tīrfruma m. *prince of glory,* Cr206.

tirgan (e, y;=ie) *to worry, exasperate, pain, provoke, excite, Gl,Gu.* ['*tar*']

tirging (y) f. '*zelus,*' *provocation,* BlPs.

tīrlēas *inglorious, infamous,* B843.

tīrmeahtig† *of glorious might.*

tirð pres. 3 sg. of teran.

tīrwine m. (*famous*) *follower, retainer,* Met 25²¹.

tit, tite=titt

±**tītelian** *to indicate by a written mark, entitle, ascribe, Æ : appoint,* LL. [*L.*]

tītelung f. '*recapitulatio,*' *a giving of titles or headings,* OEG1153.

titolose '*tidulosa*' (*plant*), OEG56⁴²⁵.

titt m. '*teat,*' *nipple, breast,* Lcd,LkLR.

tittstrycel m. *teat,* WW158⁴⁴.

tītul m. '*title,*' *superscription,* MkL15²⁶. [*L.*]

tīð I. f. *assent, permission* : *giving, grant, boon, favour, concession, Æ,BH* (tigð). **tīðe** fremian *to grant.* ['*tithe*'] II. pres. 3 sg. of tēon I. and II.

tīða m., **tīðe** f. (only in phr. t. bēon, weorðan) *sharer in, receiver, grantee, BH,Mt.* ['*tithe*']

±**tīðian** (often w. g. thing and d. pers.) *to give, bestow, grant, permit, Æ,AO.* ['TITHE']

tīðing=tēoðung

tīðrian (ȳ) *to be favourable* (*to*), RWH66¹³.

+**tīung** f. *preparation, arrangement,* Cp 684a.

tīurung=tēorung

Tīw *Tiw* (*northern god of war*), *Mars,* Gl, MH : *name of the rune for* t.

Tīwesdæg m. '*Tuesday,*' *Bf*; RB.

Tīwesniht f. *Monday night,* Lcd.

tō I. prep. **α** (w. d.) (motion) 'to,' *into, Æ,AO,CP.* tō emnes *abreast of* : (rest) *at* : (figurative direction, object of verb) *conducing to, to.* fōn tō rīce *to ascend the throne* : (definition, destination) *for, as a.* wyrcan tō wīte *to contrive as a punishment* : *in accordance with, according to* : (time) *at.* tō midre niht *at midnight.* tō dæg *to-day.* tō langum fyrste *for a long time* : (with gerunds) *to express purpose, etc.* **β** (w. g.) (of time) *at.* II. adv. *besides, also, Bo* : '*too,*' *excessively, Bl,Cr* : *thereto* : *towards, in the direction of* : *in addition, besides.* adverbial phrases;—tō ðām (ðǣm), tō ðæs (1) *so* (adeo), *to such an extent.* (2) *to that end.* (3) *moreover, however.* tō hwæs *whither.* tō ðām ðæt, tō ðȳ ðæt *in order that.* tō ðon ðæt *until.* tō ðæs ðe *when, where.* tō hwon, tō hwȳ *for what, wherefore.* tō sōðum *truly.* tō ðearfe *according to what is needed.* ðǣr tō ēacan *in addition thereto.* ne tō wuhte *by no means.* tō him *next or nearest to him.*

tō- prefix I. with accent (stress) it has the meaning of adv. tō (as in tōcweðan, tōbringan, tōcuman). [*Ger.* zu-] II. without accent=*asunder* (as in tōbrecan). [*Ger.* zer-]

tōætȳcan (ē³) *to increase,* BH112¹. [ēac]

tōætȳcnes f. *increase,* BH226ca³¹.

tōāmearcian *to mark out, assign,* Sc29⁵.

tōbēdan *to elevate, exalt,* Bf144²,LPs36³⁵.

tōbēatan⁷ *to beat severely, destroy by beating,* *AO,Chr.* ['*tobeat*']

tōbefealdan⁷ *to fold together,* WW343¹⁰.

tōbeflōwan⁷ *to flow up to,* LPs61¹¹.

tōbegietan⁵ *to acquire, purchase,* EHy4¹⁶.

tōbelimpan³ (impers.) *it belongs, behoves,* Bl49¹.

tōberan⁴ *to carry, remove, carry off, purloin,* *Bl* : *scatter, dissipate, distract, destroy* : *swell,* CP : *separate.* ['*tobear*']

tōberennes f. *difference,* WW390²⁷.

tōberstan³ (intr.) *to burst apart, go to pieces,* Æ,*AO* : (tr.) *cause to burst apart, shatter,* Æ. [' *toburst* ']

tōberstung f. *bursting,* LCD74a.

tōbīgend *bowing down, tottering,* WW386³⁰.

tōblǣdan *to inflate, puff up,* Sc82¹⁰ : *dilate, enlarge,* LHy3¹.

tōblāwan⁷ *to blow to pieces, blast, scatter,* Æ : *puff up, inflate, distend,* Lcd. [' *toblow* ']

tōblāwennes f. *inflation,* ÆH1·86¹³.

tōborstennes f. *abscess,* LCD1·322'.

tōbrǣdan *to spread abroad, disperse, scatter,* AO,CP : *spread out, extend,* Bo,*Mt*; Æ : *open, dilate* : *multiply.* [' *tobrede* ']

tōbrǣd(ed)nes f. *broadness, breadth,* Ps.

tōbrecan⁴ *to break in pieces, break up, shatter, destroy, ruin, wreck, overthrow, annul,* Æ, Bo,*Lcd*; AO,CP : *diffuse* : *break through, violate, force, KC*; Æ,AO : *interrupt.* [' *tobreak* ']

tōbrēdan I.=tōbregdan. II.=tōbrǣdan

tōbregdan³ *tear in pieces, wrench apart, rend, lacerate,* AO,*MtR* : *distract* : *cast off, shake off* : *turn to, turn about.* slǣpe tōb. *awake, wake up.* [' *tobraid* ']

tōbrengnes f. *oblation, offering,* EPs39⁷.

tōbrittian=tōbrȳtan

tōbrocenlic *brittle, fragile,* W263¹³.

tōbrȳs-an, -ian *to bruise, shatter, crush, break to pieces, Mt*; Æ. [' *tobruise* ']

tōbrȳtan *to break in pieces, destroy,* Æ : *be repentant.* [' *tobryt* ']

tōbrȳtednes f. *contrition, sorrow,* LPs.

tōbrȳtendlic *brittle, fragile,* WW242¹².

tōbryting f. *crushing, contrition,* Sc82¹².

tōbryttian=tōbrȳtan

tōc pret. 3 sg. of tacan.

tōceorfan³ *to cut, cut to pieces, cut off, cut away,* Æ,*MkL*. [' *tocarve* ']

tōcēowan² *to bite to pieces, chew, eat,* Æ. [' *tochew* ']

tōch=tōh

tōcime=tōcyme

tōcīnan¹ *to split open, cleave asunder, splinter, crack,* Cp,*Lcd*; Æ. [' *tochine* ']

tōcirhūs n. *lodging-house, inn,* WW147²⁵.

tōclǣfan *to split, cleave,* OEG18b³⁸.

tōclēofan² *to cleave asunder, split, divide,* Æ,*Bo*. [' *tocleave* ']

tōcleofian=toclifian

tōcliflan *to cleave to, adhere, stick to,* BPs.

tōclifrian *to be torn in pieces, scratched about,* Æ.

tōclip-=tōclyp-

tōclypigendlic *vocative, used in calling,* ÆGR241¹⁵.

tōclypung f. *calling upon, invocation,* Æ.

tōcnāwan⁷ *to know, acknowledge, recognise, distinguish, discern,* Æ,CP.

tōcnāw(en)nes f. *understanding, discernment,* ÆH2·362'; GD311¹¹.

tōcnyssan *to shake,* RB121⁶.

tōcuman⁴ *to come, arrive,* CP.

tōcwæs-cednes (RPs105³⁰), -tednes (SPs) f. *trembling, shaking, shattering.*

tōcweðan⁵ *to forbid, interdict„ prohibit,* Æ.

tōcwīsan=tōcwȳsan

tōcwylman *to torment,* HL12⁵⁶.

tōcwȳsan *to crush utterly, grind to pieces, bruise, destroy* : *be crushed,* Æ.

tōcwȳsednes f. *crushed condition,* Æ : *contrition,* GD125¹¹.

tōcyme m. *coming, advent, arrival,* Æ,*Bl,* CP. [' *tocome* ']

tōcyrcanwerd *towards church,* ÆL31⁹⁰².

tōcyrran (intr.) *to part, separate,* CHR.

tōdæg, tōdæge adv. ' *to-day,* ' Æ,*CP*; AO.

tōdæl=tōdāl

tōdǣlan (ē) tr. and intr. *to divide, separate, scatter, disperse,* Æ,*AO*,Bo,*Chr,W* : *dismember, cut off, destroy* : *distribute,* Æ : *discriminate, distinguish* : *be divided* : *express, utter,* CPs. [' *todeal* ']

tōdǣledlīce adv. *separately, distinctly, diversely,* ÆGR.

tōdǣlednes f. *division* : *severance, separation* : *difference, intermission, respite, cessation,* Æ.

tōdǣlendlic *separable, distinct.* adv. -līce.

tōdǣlnes f. *division, separation,* CP.

tōdāl n. *partition, division, separation,* Æ : *difference, distinction, discretion,* Æ : *dispersion* : ' *comma,* ' *dividing point, clause, section, period.*

tōdēlan (KGL)=tōdǣlan

tōdēman *to decide, judge, sentence, determine.*

tōdihtnian *to dispose, arrange,* BLPs82⁶.

tōdōn anv. *to apply, put to, add,* LCD : *divide, separate, distinguish,* Hex,*LL* : *undo, open, unbind,* PPs. [' *todo* ']

tōdrǣfan *to scatter, disperse, separate, drive out or apart,* BH,*Mt*; Æ. [' *todreve* ']

tō-drǣfednes (Æ), -drǣfnes (JnL) f. *dispersion, scattering.*

tōdrēosan² *to be destroyed, perish, decay, MH.* [' *todrese* ']

tōdrīfan¹ *to scatter, disperse, drive away,* B, JnL; Æ : *destroy, repel.* [' *todrive* ']

tōdwæscan† *to put out, extinguish.*

tōēacan prep. and adv. *besides, moreover, also,* Æ,AO,CP.

tōēcan=tōēacan; **tōēcnes**=tōīecnes

tōefenes, tōemnes (AO) prep. (d.) *alongside.*

tōendebyrdnes f. *order, series,* BH216²⁰.

toeð (VPs)=teð

tōēðlan *to inspire,* GD270¹³.

tōfæng=tōfeng

tōfær n. *departure, decease,* LkL9³¹.

tōfaran⁶ intr. *to be scattered, disperse, separate, disappear, Gen,Lcd*; AO. [*'to-fare'*]

tōfealdan⁷ *to come to land* (trans. of *L.* 'applicare'), ÆGR 138⁹.

tōfeallan⁷ *to fall down, collapse, AO* : *fall apart, fall off, Æ.* [*'tofall'*]

tōfeng I. (?) m. *grip, seizure*, LPs 123⁶. II. pret. 3 sg. of tōfōn.

tōfēran *to go in different directions, separate, disperse, Æ* : *deal out, distribute, Æ.*

tōferian *to scatter, disperse, get rid of* : *put off* : *digest*, RB 32¹⁴.

tōfēsian *to drive away, rout*, W 132,133.

tōflēam m. *refuge*, RPs 93²².

tō-flēon, -flēogan² *to be dispersed, fly apart, burst, Lcd.* [*'tofly'*]

tōflēotan² *to carry away by a flood, Chr* 1097. [*'tofleet'*]

tōflōwan⁷ *to flow down or apart, be split, melt, Æ,CP* : *flow away, ebb* : *flow to, pour in* : *distract,* CP.

tōflōw-(ed)nes, -en(d)nes f. *flowing, flux, Æ* : *diffusion*, GD 94²¹.

tō-foran (e³, o³) prep. (w. d.) (time and place) *before, BH,Chr,G* : (superiority) *above, over, beyond, Æ,Bo* : *besides, ÆH* 2·584'. [*'tofore'*]

tōforlǣtan⁷ *to dismiss,* OEG 605.

tōforlǣtennes f. *intermission,* ÆH,RBL.

toft m. *homestead, site of a house, Ct,Lcd*; LL 400. [*'toft'*]

tōfyllan *to smite in pieces,* PPs 67²¹.

+tog n. *tugging, contraction, spasm, cramp,* Lcd : pl. *traces (of a horse),* ÆL 31⁹⁷³.

tōgædereweard adv. *towards one another,* AO.

tō-gædre, -gædere, -gadere adv. '*together,' An,BC,Mt.* tōg. gān, fōn, cuman *to engage in battle,* Chr. [gaderian]

tōgægnes=tōgegnes, tōgēanes

tōgǣlan *to profane, defile,* LPs 88³²·

tōgǣnan *to say, affirm,* LPs 93⁴.

tōgān anv. pret. 3 sg. tōēode *to go to or into* : (impers. w. g.) *come to pass, happen* : *separate, part, depart, Æ,HR.* [*'togo'*]

tōgang m. *approach, access, attack,* CM,Lcd.

tōgangan⁷ *to go away, pass away, BH,Rd.* [*'togang'*]

tōgēan prep. w. d. *towards, MkL* (-eægn). [*'togains'*]

tōgēanes prep. w. d. and a.; adv. *in opposition to, against, B,Chr,SPs* : *towards, to, Æ,Bl,MkL* : *before,* CP : *in return, in reply.* him tōg. *to meet him, Chr,MtL.* [*'togains'*]

tōgēare adv. *in this year,* BF 156¹⁷.

tōgeclīflan (eo, y)=tōclīflan

tōgecorennes f. *adoption,* DR 29¹⁴.

tōgeēcan=tōgeīecan

tōgeefnan? *to associate with, join oneself to?* AS 39⁶. [MS tōgeenan]

tōgegnes=tōgēanes

tōgehlytto f. *fellowship, union,* DR 109¹⁵.

tōgeīecan *to add to, increase,* BF,GD.

tōgeīecendlic (ī³) *added to, adjectival, adjective,* ÆGR.

tōgeīht pp. of tōgeīecan.

tōgeīhtnes f. *addition, increment,* BF 46³³.

tōgeladung f. *assembly,* MFH 174.

tōgelǣstan (e³) *to accompany,* WW 365⁴¹.

tōgelan⁴ *to diffuse,* GD 192¹⁸.

tōgelaðung f. *concourse,* MFH 173.

tōgelēstan=tōgelǣstan

tōgelicgende *belonging,* KC 3·350¹.

togen pp. of tēon I. (and occly. II.).

tōgenēalǣcan=tōnealǣcan

tōgēnes=tōgēanes

tōgengan *to separate,* GEN 841.

-tōgennes v. ofer-t., ðurh-t.

tōgēotan² *to pour away, spill* : *spread* : *exhaust.*

tōgescēadan⁷ *to expound, interpret,* LkR 24²⁷.

tōgescofen (CP) pp. of tōscūfan.

tōgesettan *to put to,* RPs 9³⁹.

tōgetēon²·¹ *to draw towards, attract,* BPs.

togettan impers. *to twitch, be spasmodic,* Lcd 81a. [togian]

tōgeðēodan (īe, ȳ) *to adhere, cling to* : *adjoin,* BH 56³⁰.

tōgewegen *applied,* BH.

tōgewunod *accustomed,* AS 23¹⁹.

tōgeȳcan=tōgeīecan

togian *to draw, drag,* HL 15³⁰⁸. [*'tow'*]

tōgife, tōgifes adv. *freely, gratis.*

togīnan¹ *to be opened, split, gape, yawn.* [cp. *Ger.* gähnen]

tōglīdan¹ *to glide away, split, slip, fall asunder, vanish, B,Met.* [*'toglide'*]

tōgolen pret. of tōgelan.

tōgotennes f. *pouring out, effusion, shedding, spreading,* Lcd.

+togu np. *traces (of a horse),* ÆL 31⁹⁷³.

togung f. *tugging, twitch, spasm,* Lcd.

tōh '*tough,' Cp,Ep* : *tenacious, sticky, Lcd.*

tōhaccian *to hack to pieces, Æ* (3¹⁸⁶). [*'tohack'*]

tōhǣlan *to emasculate, weaken,* MFH 174.

tōheald (a², y²) adj. and adv. *inclined, forward, in advance.*

tōhēawan⁷ *to hew in pieces, Æ,Chr.* [*'tohew'*]

tōhīgung f. *result, effect,* DR.

tōhiht=tōhyht

tohl=tōl

tōhladan⁶ *to scatter, disperse, destroy* (or ? *tōhlacan), GEN 1693.

tōhlēotan[2] *to divide by lot*, BL,PPs.

tōhlic *tough, tenacious.* adv. -līce, GL.

tōhlīdan[1] *to split, open, spring apart, burst, gape, break*, AO.

tohlīne f. *tow-line*, WW. [togian]

tōhlocen=tōlocen pp. of tōlūcan.

tōhlystend m. *listener*, CP96.

tōhnescan *to soften*, LCD 94a.

tōhopa m. *hope, Bo,PPs*; CP. ['*tohope*']

tōhopung f. *faith, trust*, ÆL23[155].

tōhrēosan[2] *to fall to pieces, decay, BH,W*; ÆL. ['*toreose*']

tōhrēran *to break, shake to pieces, destroy*, GL.

tōhricod ptc. *cut off, dispersed*, GPH 398, 399.

tōhrȳran *to shake in pieces*, v. OEG2261.

+toht n. *battle array, battle*, MA 104.

tohte† f. *fight, conflict, battle, campaign.*

tōhuntian *to hunt*, WE65[7].

tōhwega adv. and sb. *somewhat, some, a little.*

tōhweorfan[3] *to go away, separate, scatter, disperse*, CHR.

tōhwon adv. *wherefore, why : to which (point), to what extent, how far, how long : to which end, for what purpose or reason.*

tōhwyrfan (=ie[2]) *to overturn*, LPs117[13].

tōhyht m. *hope, refuge, consolation*, RUN.

tōhyld=tōheald

tōīecan (ē[2], ȳ[2]) *to increase*, BH112[1]B.

tōīecnes (ē[2]) f. *increase*, BH226[31].

tōiernan[3] *to run to, run together : flow away, be dispersed : run hither and thither, wander about.*

tōirnan=tōiernan; toi=toll

tōl n. '*tool,' instrument, implement*, Æ,Bo, LL : *weapon*, ZDA 9·424.

tōlǣgon pret. pl. of tōlicgan.

tōlǣtan[7] *to disperse, relax, release*, CP.

tōlǣtennes f. *despondency*, LCD 1·262[3].

tolcendlīce adv. *wantonly*, GPH401.

tolcettende '*indruticans*,' v. OEG1218.

tolcetung f. *wanton excitement*, OEG.

tōleoðian=tōliðian; tōlēs-=tōlȳs-

tolfrēo '*toll-free*,' KC4·209[19].

tolgetung=tolcetung; tōlic=tōhlic

tōlicgan[5] *to lie or extend in different directions, separate, part, divide*, AO,BC. ['*tolie*']

tōliðian (eo) *to dismember, separate*, Æ : *relax, cancel*, GD349[28].

toll mn. *impost, 'toll,' tribute*, Chr,EC,G, Gl : *passage-money*, Æ : *rent*, Æ : *act or right of taking toll*, Æ.

tollere m. *tax-gatherer, publican*, Æ,WW. ['*toller*']

tollsceam-ol, -ul m. *seat of custom, treasury*,

tollscīr f. *taxing district*, ÆH2·468'.

toln f. *toll, custom, duty, TC.* ['*tolne*']

tolnere m. *tax-gatherer*, WW. ['*tolner*']

tōlōcian *to belong to*, CC22[7].

tolsetl n. *place of toll or custom*, Æ.

tōlūcan[2] *to pull apart, dislocate, destroy, BH.* ['*tolouk*']

tōlȳsan (ē;=īe) *to dissolve, loosen, relax*, Æ : *unhinge, separate, break open.*

tōlȳs(ed)nes (ē) f. *loosing, dissolution, dispersion, destruction, release, dismissal : desolation*, GD : *death.*

tōlȳsend m. *destroyer*, WW220[13].

tōlȳsendlic *destructive*, LPs119[4].

tōlȳsing (ē) f. *loosing, release, redemption : destruction*, LCD 3·206[20].

tom=tam

tōm adj. w. g. *free from, Cr*1211. ['*toom*']

tōmǣldan *to hinder by speech*, DD26. [meldian]

tōmearcian *to distinguish, describe, note down, enrol*, G,SPs.

tōmearcodnes f. *enumeration, census, enrolment*, Lk2[2].

tō-mergen, -merigen (Æ)=tōmorgen

tōmetan[5] *to mete out*, LPs107[8].

tōmiddes prep. (w. d.) *amidst, among, in the midst of, Æ,Jn*; AO,CP. adv. *into the midst, B,Lcd*. ['*tomids*']

tōmorgen adv. *to-morrow, Bf,CP.* ['*tomorn*']

tōn dsmn. of tōh.

tōnama m. *surname, MkL*; Æ. ['*toname*']

+tōnamlan *to name besides, surname*, LKL6[14] (tor-).

tōnēalǣcan *to approach*, Pss.

tōnemnan *to distinguish by name, name*, AO.

tōnēolīcan=tōnēalǣcan

tong, tonge=tang, tange

tonian *to thunder*, ÆGR138[3].

tonice=tunece

tōniman[4] *separate, take apart : take away.*

tōnom-=tōnam-

top I. m. '*top' (highest part), WW*143[25] : *tassel, tuft.* II. '*top' (plaything)? ball? ApT* 13[13].

toppa m. *thread, tuft?* OEG23[45].

tor=torr

tōrǣcan (pret. 3 sg. tōrǣhte) *to join, put together*, OEG4489.

tōrǣndan=tōrendan; toranēage=torenīge

tōrbegete (o?) *hard to get*, LCD43b.

torcht, torct-=torht, torht-

torcul n. *wine-press*, MtR21[33]. [L.]

torcyrre *hard to convert*, MH110[15].

tord n. *piece of excrement, dung, filth*, LCD.

tordwifel m. *dung-beetle*, LCD.

toren pp. of teran.

tōrendan (æ) *to rend apart, tear in pieces,* MkL,PPs. ['*torend'*]

toren-ēage, -īg(g)e, -īege *blear-eyed,* CP.

tōrēosan=tōhrēosan

±torflan *to throw, cast missiles, shoot, stone,* Mk; Æ : *be tossed,* NC326. ['*torve'*]

torfung f. *throwing, casting (of stones),* AO.

torht I. n. *clearness, brightness.* II. adj. *bright, radiant, beautiful, splendid, noble, illustrious,* Ph. ['*torht'*] adv. -e *brightly, clearly : beautifully, splendidly.*

torhtian *to show,* Cp216I.

torhtlīc† *bright, clear, radiant, glorious.* adv. -līce.

torhtmōd† *glorious, noble.*

torhtnes f. *radiance, splendour,* GL,LCD.

tōrinnan (CP)=tōiernan

torn I. n. *anger, indignation : grief, misery, suffering, pain.* [*Ger.* zorn] II. adj. *bitter, cruel, grievous.*

+tornamian=+tōnamian

torncwide† m. *offensive speech.*

torne† adv. *indignantly, insultingly, bitterly, grievously.*

torngemōt n. *battle,* B1140.

torngenīōla† m. *angry opponent.*

tornīge=torenīge

tornlic *sorrowful, grievous,* PPs125⁵.

tornmōd *angry,* GU621.

tornsorg f. *sorrow, care,* FT76.

tornword n. *offensive expression,* CR172.

tornwracu f. *revenge,* GU272.

tornwyrdan *to be incensed?* AO54².

toroc *grub, weevil?* WW224³⁸ (ES41·164).

tōroren=tōhroren pp. of tōhrēosan.

torr m. '*tower,' watch-tower,* CP,MtL; AO : *rock, crag,* Mdf. [*L.* turris; v. ES41·102]

torrian *to tower,* ByH130¹³.

tōryne m. *running together, concourse,* ES 39·353.

tōrȳpan *to scratch,* EC164¹⁸.

tōsǣlan (impers., w. d. pers. and g. thing) *to be unsuccessful, fail : lack, want.*

tōsamne=tōsomne

tōsāwan⁷ *to strew, scatter, spread,* Æ.

tosca m. *frog, toad,* DR,PPs.

tōscacan=tōsceacan

tōscād-=tōscēad-

tōscægde v. tōscecgan.

tōscǣnan *to break in pieces, break,* Æ,JnL, MkLR. ['*toshene'*]

tōscarian=tōscearian

tōsceacan⁶ (a) *to shake in pieces,* WW : *drive asunder, drive away, shake off,* Æ. ['*to-shake'*]

tōscēacerian *to scatter,* ÆL23²⁴.

tōscēad n. *distinction, difference,* Æ,CP.

tōscēadan⁷ (ā) *to part, separate, scatter, divide : set at variance,* CP : *discern, discriminate, distinguish, decide,* Æ,Bo; CP : *differ : express,* LPs. ['*toshed'*]

tōscēadednes f. *separation,* MFH101.

tōscēadend m. *divider, separator,* WW223³⁰.

tōscēadenes (ā) f. *separation, distinction,* HL158¹⁶².

tōscearian (a²) *to scatter,* APs67².

tōscecgan (æ) *to be separate, differ,* BH 160²⁵n.

tōscelian=tōscylian

tōscendan *to destroy,* GD121²⁴.

tōscēotan² intr. *to spring apart, disperse,* Æ. ['*toshoot'*]

tōscerian (KGL)=tōscirian

tōscirian (e, y) *to divide, distribute,* MFH : *detach, separate,* GL : *distinguish,* CHRD.

tōscrīðan² *to flow apart, disperse,* MET20⁹³.

tōscūfan² *to push apart, scatter : impel, incite,* CP : *do away, remove.*

tōscyftan (=i) *to divide, distribute,* Chr. ['*toshift'*]

tōscyl-lan, -ian (e) tr. and intr. *to separate, divide,* NC351.

tōscyrian=tōscirian

tōsendan (tr.) *to send to : send apart, send out, disperse.*

tōsēoðan² *to boil thoroughly,* LCD.

tōsetednes f. *disposition,* EPs72⁷.

tōsettan *to dispose,* PSS,BL.

tōsēðan? *to test, prove,* AS7¹¹.

tōsīgan¹ *to wear out, be threadbare,* Æ.

tōsittan⁵ *to be separated,* AO14¹⁸.

tōslacian *to slacken, relax,* WW73¹⁰.

tōslǣfan *to cut up,* NR32².

tōslēan⁶ *to strike in pieces, destroy,* Æ,AO. Gl : *drive away,* RB18³,⁴. ['*toslay'*]

tōslīfan¹ *to split,* WW.

tōslītan¹ *to tear asunder, rend, wound, break open, open,* Æ,CP : *interrupt : separate, scatter, destroy,* CP : *distract : be different,* NG.

tōslitnes (y²) f. *laceration,* BH : *division,* NG.

tōslūpan² *to slip away, be relaxed, fall to pieces, open, dissolve,* Æ,CP : *melt (with fear) : be paralysed.* tōslopen *relaxed, loose, dissolute.*

tōslūping f. *dissolving, dissolution,* Sc68⁸.

tōsmēagan *to inquire into, consider,* Bo148⁵.

tōsnǣdan *to cut up,* NR28⁵.

tōsnīðan¹ *to cut asunder, cut up : cut off amputate.*

tōsōcn f. *visiting,* CHRD67³⁶.

tōsōcnes f. *pursuit,* DR28¹⁸.

tōsōcnung f. *pursuit,* DR81⁷.

tōsomne adv. *together,* Æ,AO,Bl; CP. t. cuman *to engage in battle.* ['*tosame'*]

tōsomnian *to collect together, bring together,* BH 230[7].

tōsōðan adv. *in sooth, in truth* (or ? two words).

tōspræc f. *speaking to* (*another*), *conversation,* Æ,CP.

tōsprædan *to spread out,* IM; Æ. [*'tospread'*]

tōspringan[3] *to spring apart, fly asunder, crack,* Æ. [*'tospring'*]

tōsprytting f. *inciting,* CHR 1101.

tosta=tosca

tōstæncan=tōstencan

tōstandan[6] *to be put off, not to occur : stand apart, differ from, be discordant,* Æ.

tōstencan (æ) *to scatter, disperse, drive apart, drag along,* Æ,CP : *nullify, destroy : perish,* SPs 82[9].

tō-stencednes (Æ), -stenc(en)nes, f. *dispersion, dissolution, destruction.*

tōstencend m. *prodigal,* LCD.

tōsteng-=tōstenc-

tōstician *to pierce,* AO 128[14].

tōstihtan *to order, arrange,* CPs 111[5].

tōstincan[3] *to distinguish by smell,* ÆH 2·372'.

tōstingan[3] *to thrust in, pierce,* LCD.

tō-stregdan, -strēdan[3] (and wv.) *to scatter, dissipate, disperse,* CP : *distract : destroy.*

tōstrēt (CP) pres. 3 sg. of tōstregdan.

tōsundrian *to separate,* LHY 7[8].

tōswāpan[7]† *to disperse.*

tōswellan[3] *to swell out,* Æ. [*'toswell'*]

tōswengan *to drive asunder, destroy.* [swingan]

tōsweorcan[3] *to obscure,* OEG 1737.

tōswīfan[1] intr. *to separate,* MET 11[36].

tōsyndrian *to sunder, separate, divide : discriminate.*

+tot n. *pomp, parade, vainglory,* ÆH.

tōtalu f. *reputation,* DR 102[3].

tōtellan *to distinguish,* MET 16[15].

tōtēon[2],[1] *to draw asunder, pull apart, rend, destroy,* AO : *take to oneself, claim for oneself,* LL (or ? tō prep.).

tōteran[4] *to tear in pieces, bite, lacerate, cut out,* Æ,AO,CP : *destroy : harass* (*mind*).

tōtian *to peep out, stick out,* CP 105[5]. [*'toot'*]

tōtihting f. *instigation,* CHR 1094.

tōtorfian *to cast about, toss,* Mt 14[24].

tōtræglian *to pull to pieces, strip,* GPH 396[267].

tōtredan[5] *to tread to pieces?* GL.

totrida m. *swing?* GL,WW 276[27].

tōtwǣman (ē, ēa, ȳ) *to separate, divide, dissever,* AO : *distinguish : break up, break in pieces, dissolve : scatter : defer, postpone,* LL 298,17[2] : *divorce,* CHR 958 D. [*'totweme'*]

tōtwǣmednes f. *separation, distinction,* W 194[22].

tō-twē(a)man, -twȳman=tōtwǣman

tōð m., ds. and nap. tēð, occl. ds. tōðe and nap. tōð(as) *'tooth*,*'* Cp,Guth,Lcd,LL, MtR,VPs; AO : *tusk,* WW 397[27]. tōðum ontȳnan *to utter.*

tōðece (æ[2]) m. *toothache,* AS 41[4].

tōðenednes f. *stretching, distension,* OEG 5452.

tōðēnian *to attend upon, serve,* Sc 102[9].

tōðening f. *distension,* OEG 2[476].

tōðēnung f. *administration,* CM 1185.

tōðerscan[3] *to dash in pieces,* CHR 1009.

tōðgār m. *tooth-pick,* LCD 13b.

tōðindan[3] *to swell up, inflate, puff up,* Æ : *be arrogant.*

tōðlēas *toothless,* GPH 394.

tōðmægen n. *strength of tusks,* GNC 20.

tōðrǣstan *to crush, destroy,* CPs 106[16].

tōðreoma=tōðrima; **tōðrescan**=tōðerscan

tōðrima (eo[2]) m. *enclosure of teeth, gum,* LCD.

tōðringan *to drive asunder,* RD 4[27].

tōðsealf f. *tooth-salve,* LCD.

tōðsticca m. *tooth-pick,* WW 219[3].

tōðunden pp. of tōðindan.

tōðundenes f. *the state of being puffed up, arrogance,* Æ.

tōðundenlic *arrogant.* adv. -līce, RB.

tōðunian *to astonish,* WW 346[22].

tōðwærc m. *toothache,* LCD.

tōðwīnan[1] *to disappear,* HL 15[200]. [dwīnan]

tōðwyrm m. *a worm in the teeth,* LCD 19a.

tōwælede pret. sg. of *tōwieltan to roll to,* MkL 15[46].

tō-ward, -wardes=tō-weard, -weardes

towcræft m. *spinning,* HL 10[339].

tōweard I. adj. *facing, approaching, impending,* BH,Bl,Lcd : *future,* Æ,Bl,Bo, Mk. **II.** prep. (w. d., g.) *towards,* AO,CP. **III.** adv. *towards, forwards.* [*'toward,' 'towards'*]

tōweardes=tōweard II., III.

tōweardlic *in the future,* Æ. adv. -līce, BH 368[21].

tōweardnes f. *future, time to come,* BH,BL.

tōweaxan[7] *to grow apart,* NR 22.

tōweccan *to arouse, excite,* B 2948.

tōwegan[5] *disperse, scatter,* PH 184.

tōwendan *to overthrow, subvert, destroy,* Æ, AO. [*'towend'*]

tōweorpan[3] (e, u, y) *to cast down, break in pieces, dissipate, blot out, destroy,* Æ,Bo, Mt; AO,CP : *throw out,* CP. [*'towarp'*]

tōwerd=tōweard; **tōwerpan**=tōweorpan

tō-wesnes (CP), -wesenes, -westnes (BH) f. *dissolution : separation, discord, dissension.*

towettan *to associate with,* LL (322').

towhūs n. *tow-house, spinning-house or chamber,* WW 186²⁹. [FTP 166]
tōwieltan v. tōwælede
tōwītan *to depart, pass away,* ByH 90².
tō-wiðere, -wiðre prep. (w. d., a.) *against,* Ex : *in answer to,* CR.
towlic *belonging to thread.* t. weorc *material for spinning,* WW.
towmȳderce f. *tow-chest? work-box?* TC 538²¹.
tōword (VPs)=tōweard
tōworpednes=tōworpennes
tōworp(en)nes f. *subversion, destruction, desolation,* Æ,CP : *dispersion : expulsion.*
tōwrecan † *to drive asunder, scatter, dissipate.*
tōwrītan⁵ *to describe,* OEG 1065.
tōwritennes f. *writing down, description,* Æ.
tōwrīðan¹ *to twist apart, distort,* ÆGR 155¹⁵.
towtōl n. *spinning implement,* LL 455,15¹.
tōwunderlic '*admirabilis,*' SPs 41⁴.
tōwurpan (Æ)=tōweorpan
tōwyrd I. f. *opportunity,* BH 52²¹. **II.=** tōweard
tōwyrpan=tōweorpan
tōwyrpendlic *destructible,* GPH 394.
tōwyrpnes=tōworpennes
toxa (OEG 1858)=tosca
tōȳcan=tōīecan ; **tōyrnan**=tōiernan
tracter *funnel,* NC 351. [*L.* trajectorium]
træd pret. 3 sg., **trǣdon** pret. pl. of tredan.
trǣf n., nap. tr(e)afu *tent, pavilion : dwelling, building,* AN 844.
trǣglian *to pluck, pull,* GPH 398.
trǣndel=trendel ; **trǣppe**=treppe
trafu v. trǣf.
trāg I.† adj. *evil, mean, bad.* **II.** f. *evil, affliction,* EL 668.
trāge adv. *evilly, cruelly,* PPs 108²⁰.
-trāglīce v. un-t.
traht m. *text, passage : exposition, treatise, commentary,* Æ. [*L.* tractus]
trahtað m. *commentary,* WW. [*L.*]
trahtbōc f. *(religious) treatise, commentary,* Æ. [trahtian]
traht-ere, -nere (Æ) m. *expounder, commentator, expositor.*
±traht-ian, -nian (Æ) *to treat, comment on, expound, consider : interpret, translate,* NG. [*L.*]
trahtnung, trahtung f. *explanation, exposition, commentary,* Æ.
trāisc *tragic,* BH 154³.
tramet m. *page (of a book),* ÆGR.
trandende (o¹) *precipitous, steep,* Cp 805 P.
trappe=treppe ; **tratung**=trahtung
trē (NG), **trēa** (VPs)=trēow I.
treaflice *grievously,* PPs 102⁶.
treafu v. trǣf.

±trēagian *to sew together, mend,* OEG.
treaht-=traht- ; **trēawa**=trēowa
+tred n. *crowd,* WW 209¹⁰.
±tredan⁵ (eo) tr. and intr. *to* '*tread*,*' step on, trample, B,CP,G,PPs* ; Æ,AO : *traverse, pass over, enter upon, roam through, B.*
treddan *to tread on, trample,* WW : *investigate,* PPs.
tredde f. *press (for wine, etc.),* GD.
treddian† *to tread, step, walk,* B.
trede *fit to tread on, firm,* CR 1166.
tredel m. *step,* WW 117⁶ : *sole of foot,* LL 438,21. ['*treadle*']
tredend m. *treader,* WW 197⁹.
trefet '*trivet,*' *tripod,* BC 3·367'.
trēg (WW 281³⁵)=trīg
trega m. *misfortune, misery, trouble, grief, pain, Gen,Met,RB.* ['*tray*']
tregian *to trouble, harass, vex,* EPs,W.
+tregian *to feel repugnance at,* A 2·358.
treht-=traht- ; **trem**=trym
tremegan=trymian, trymman
tremes=trymes ; **tremm-**=trymm- **-tremman** v. wið-t.
trendan *to turn round, revolve, roll,* A 1·285. ['*trend*']
trendel (æ, y) n. *sphere, circle, ring, orb, Æ,Bf,Chr,Lcd : circus.* ['*trendle*']
trendeled (y¹, y²) *made round,* WW 152⁵. [v. '*trindle*']
trendelnes f. *circuit, surrounding space,* RPs 11⁹ (u¹).
-trendlian v. ā-t. ; **trēo**=trēow
treodan (VPs)=tredan ; **trēoð**=trēowð
trēow I. n. (nap. trēowu, trēow) '*tree*,*' Æ, BH,CP,VPs* ; Mdf : *wood, timber, BH : beam, log, stake, stick, AO,Bl* ; CP : *wood, grove : tree of the cross, cross, Rood.* **II.** f. (ū, ȳ) *truth, fidelity, faith, trust, belief : pledge, promise, agreement, treaty : favour, grace, kindness.* [*Ger.* treue] **III.=**trēowe
trēowa (AO,CP)=trūwa
trēowan=trīewan
trēowan (ē, ī, īe, ȳ) trans. w. d. *to believe, trust in, hope, be confident, rely (on), B,Bo, Gen :* intr. *trust, PPs :* refl. *exculpate oneself, LL :* (+) *persuade, suggest,* AO : *make true or credible : be faithful (to) : confederate (with),* GL. ['*trow*']
trēowcynn n. *species of tree,* Æ.
trēowe I. (ē, ī, īe, ū, ȳ) '*true*' ('*i-treowe*'), *faithful, honest, trustworthy, B,Chr,Gen, Gu,LL,WW* ; AO : *genuine.* **II.=**trēow II.
trēowen (ī, ȳ) *of a tree, of wood, wooden, Lcd,WW 125²⁸* ; Æ. ['*treen*']
±trēowfæst *true, faithful, MtL,PPs* ; Æ. ['*truefast*']
+trēowfæstnian *to be trusty,* MtL p 4¹².

trēowfēging f. *joining together (of boards)*, WW 206³⁴.

trēowfugol m. *forest bird*, Gu 707.

±**trēowful** *faithful, trusty, true.* adv. -līce.

+**trēowfulnes** f. *'Israel'!* RPs 21²⁵; Hy 7⁸³.

trēowgeðofta† m. *faithful comrade*, AA 45⁴.

trēowgeweorc n. *wood-work, a structure of timber*, BH 272⁵.

trēowgewrid n. *thicket of trees*, Guth 20⁷.

trēowian=trēowan

±**trēowlēas** *faithless, treacherous, false*, CP : *unbelieving*.

trēowlēasnes f. *treachery, faithlessness*, BH : *unbelief, heresy*, GD.

trēowlic *true, faithful, trusty : safe.* adv. -līce, PPs : *confidently*, GL. ['*truly*']

trēowloga m. *pledge-breaker*, B 2847.

trēowlufu f. '*true love*,' Cr 538.

±**trēownes** (ē) f. *object of trust*, Bo 149²⁵,VH. ['*trueness*']

trēowrǣden f. *state of fidelity*, Gen 2305.

±**trēowsian** (ȳ) *to plight one's faith*, Chr, LL : *exculpate oneself.* ['*treouse*']

trēowsteall n. *grove, plantation*, EC,KC.

trēowstede m. *grove*, WW 149¹⁷.

trēowteru (trēot-) n. *tree-tar, resin*, WW.

±**trēowð** (īe, ȳ) f. '*truth*,' *veracity*, AO : *troth, faith, fidelity, Æ,AO : pledge, covenant, Æ.*

trēowðrāg f. *time for faithfulness, fidelity*, Rim 57.

trēowufæst=trēowfæst

trēowwæstm m. *produce of trees*, Chr.

trēowweorðung f. *tree-worshipping*, LL.

trēowwyrhta (ȳ) m. *wood-worker, carpenter*.

trēowwyrm m. *cankerworm, caterpillar*, CJVPs 77⁴⁶.

treppan I. *to '*trap*,' KGl 211. **II.** *to tread*, KGl 144.

treppe (a, æ) f. '*trap*,' *snare*, WW.

tret (KGl) pres. 3 sg. of tredan.

trēu=trēo, trēow

trēw=trēow

tribulian=trifulian

+**tricce** *contented*, RB 109⁷.

trideð, triedeð=tredeð, tritt pres. 3 sg. of tredan.

trīew-=trēow-

trifelung f. *grinding, pounding, stamping*, WW 423²⁵.

trifet (KGl), **trifot** (GL) sb. *tribute.* [L. tributum]

±**trifulian** *to break, bruise, stamp.* [L. tribulare]

trīg (ē) n. *wooden board, '*tray*,' Lcd.

trilidi=ðriliðe; **trim-**=trym-

trimilchi=ðrimeolce

trinda? m., **trinde**? f. *round lump, ball*, Lcd 139b.

trindhyrst m. *circular copse?* (Swt), KC 2·411′ (? place-name).

tringan³ *press*, APs 103³³ (?*twingan, BT).

trīo-=trēo-, trēow-

trit, tritt pres. 3 sg. of tredan.

trīw=trēow

trochscip=trogscip

trod n., trodu f. *track, trace*, B,LL. ['*trod*'; tredan]

trog m. *hollow vessel, '*trough*,' tray, BC,Gl, JnL,Lcd : canoe, boat*, AO.

trōg (NG)=drōg pret. 3 sg. of dragan.

troghryceg *ridge where there is a water-trough?* EC 447²⁰.

trogscip n. *a kind of boat*, WW.

troh (LWS)=trog; **trōh**=ðrōh

trondende *precipitous, steep*, Cp 805 P.

tropere m. *a book containing verses sung at certain festivals before the Introit*, IM,TC. [*Late* L. troparium]

trūa=trūwa, trēowa

±**trucian** *to fail, run short, Æ : deceive, disappoint.* ['*troke*']

trūg-=trūw-

trūgon (NG)=drōgon pret. pl. of dragan.

trūht (u?) *trout, Æ.* [L. tructa]

trum *firm, fixed, secure, strong, sound, vigorous, active, Æ,CP : trustworthy*, Bf 172²⁰.

+**trum**† n. *legion, army, host*, WW.

truma m. (±) *legion, troop, AO; Æ : regular order, array*, AO. ['*trume*']

+**trumian** *to grow strong, recover health, amend*, BH : *make strong.*

truming=trymming

trumlic *firm, durable, substantial, sound*, CP : *confirming, exhorting.* adv. -līce, *considerably*, Bf 80².

trumnað m. *confirmation*, Gu 729.

trumnes f. *soundness, health*, CP : *firmness, strength, stability, Æ : sureness, reliability : the firmament, heavens : confirmation, support.*

trundulnes=trendelnes

trūs (u?) m. *brushwood (for fuel)*, KC. ['*trouse*']

trūð m. *trumpeter, buffoon, actor, Æ.*

trūðhorn m. *trumpet, clarion*, GL.

trūw=trēow

±**trūwa** (ēo, ȳ) m. *fidelity, faith, confidence, trust, belief : pledge, promise, agreement, covenant : protection.*

+**trūwe**=+trēowe

±**trūwian** (ȳ) occl. pret. trūwde *to trust, Æ,CP : inspire with trust*, WW 243⁶ : *persuade*, AO : *exculpate oneself*, LL. ['TROW']

+trūwung f. *prop, stay, confidence,* CPs 88[19].
+tryccan *to confide, trust,* JnL 16[33].
tryddian=treddian
trydeð=tredeð, tritt pres. 3 sg. of tredan.
trym† (e) n. *small piece, short length.* fōtes t. *a foot's length.*
trym-=trum-, trymm-
+trym n. *firmament,* PPs 71[16].
+trymednes (LPs 104[16])=+trymnes
try-mes (*Mt*) mf., -messe f., -messa m. *a drachm weight : an English coin* (v. LL 2·683) : *a Roman coin* ('*tremissis*'=3 *denarii*), LG. ['*thrimsa*']
trymian, trymman (e) *to strengthen, fortify, confirm, comfort, exhort, incite,* CP,*Chr* : *set in order, arrange, prepare, array, arm,* AO : *become strong : be arrayed : give* (*hostages*) : *testify, attest.* ['TRIM']
-trymig, -trymmig v. un-t.
trymmend m. *supporter,* PPs : *one who makes an agreement,* GL.
trymmendlic *hortatory, encouraging,* BH,GL.
±trymming f. *confirmation, strengthening, encouragement,* Æ : *support, prop : edification,* Æ : *ordinance :* (+) *fortress,* KGL 67[4].
±trymnes f. *firmness, solidity : firmament, prop, support : confirmation, strengthening, encouragement : exhortation, instruction : arrangement, setting in order.* [trumnes]
tryms=trymes
trymð (i) f. *strength, support, staff, prop,* AS,LPs.
tryndel=trendel
trȳw=trēow; trȳw-=trēow-
tu=ðu; Tū=Tīw; tū=twā
tua=tuwa; tuā=twā
tube f. *trumpet,* GPH 391. [*L.* tuba]
±tūcian *to disturb, ill-treat, torment, punish,* Æ,*Bo,Met* : (+) *bedeck,* PPs 44[11] (? a mistake for +tunecian, IF 48·262). ['*tuck*']
tud? mn., tudu f? *shield,* OEG 5025 (cp. 747n).
tūdder, tūddor=tūdor
tūddorfōster m. *nourishment of offspring,* WW 219[17].
tūddorful *prolific, fruitful,* GL.
tūddorspēd f. *fertility,* GEN 2752.
tūddortēonde† *begetting issue.*
tūddres gs. of tūddor.
tūdor, tūder n. *offspring, descendant, issue,* Æ,CP,*Lcd,WW* : *fruit.* ['*tudder*']
tūdorfæst *fertile,* WW 400[35].
tūdornes f. *offspring,* OEG 3849 (tydder-).
tugon pret. pl. of tēon.
tui-=twi-
tulge comp. tylg, superl. tylgest *strongly, firmly, well.*
tumbere m. *tumbler, dancer, player,* ÆGR 35[6].

tumbian *to tumble, leap, dance,* G. ['*tumb*']
tumbing f. *dancing,* CHRD 79[1].
tūn m. *enclosure, garden, field, yard, Chr, Gl,G,Lcd* : *farm, manor,* BC,*LL* : *homestead, dwelling, house, mansion, BH,MH*; AO,CP : *group of houses, village, 'town,' Æ,Gl,JnL,KC,MH,* v. LL 2·352. on tūn gān *to appear to men,* BF,MEN. [v. Mdf]
tūn-cerse (æ[2]) f., -cressa m. *garden-cress, nasturtium, Cp,Ep,Lcd.* ['*towncress*']
tūncirce f. *church in a '*tūn,' TC.
tunder=tynder
tunece f. *under-garment, tunic, coat, toga,* Æ,AO. [*L.* tunica]
+tunecod *clothed in a toga,* GPH 393 (v. also IF 48·262).
tūnesman (*LL*)=tūnmann. ['*townsman*']
tunge f. (m) '*tongue,*' Æ,BH,CP,*Lcd* : *speech, language, CP,Mk,RB.*
tūngebūr m. *inhabitant, resident,* GL.
tungel=tungol
tungele? *talkative,* OEG 56[139].
tūngerēfa m. *town-reeve, bailiff,* Æ : *prætor.*
tungeðrum *tongue-ligament,* Lcd. [v. '*thrum*']
tungful *talkative,* Sc 81[9].
tungilsinwyrt=tunsingwyrt
tungle ds. of tungol.
tunglen *starry,* DHy. [tungol]
tunglere m. *astrologer,* GL.
tungol (e[2], u[2]) nm., nap. tunglu, tungol and (late) tunglan *luminary, star, planet, constellation,* Æ,AO.
tungolǣ (e[2]) f. *astronomy,* OEG.
tungolbǣre (e[2]) *covered with stars,* OEG.
tungolcræft (e[2]) m. *star-craft, astronomy,* Æ.
tungolcræft(i)ga (e[2], u[2]) m. *magician, astrologer.*
tungolcræftwīse (e[2]) f. *astronomy,* WW 346[2].
tungolgescēad (e[2]) n. *astrology,* GL.
tungolgim m. (*bright*) *star,* CR 1151.
tungolsprǣc f. *astrology,* HGL.
tungolwītega m. *star prophet, astrologer,* Æ.
tungul=tungol
tungwōd *sharp-tongued,* Sc 223[13].
tūnhōfe f. *ground ivy,* Lcd 123a. ['*tunhoof*']
tunice=tunece
tūnincel n. *small property, small farm,* GL.
tuningwyrt=tunsingwyrt
tūnland n. *land forming a '*tūn' or manor,* EC 445[6].
tūnlic *rustic,* WW 127[15].
tūnmann m. *villager, rustic, villein,* Æ,WW. ['*townman*']
tūnmelde f. *orach (plant),* WW 215[33].
tunne f. '*tun,*' *cask, barrel, BC,Cp*; Æ.
tunnebotm m. *bottom of a cask, drum?* WW 123[10].
tūnprēost m. *village priest,* CHR 870 F.

tūnrǣd m. *town council*, ÆL30²⁹⁷.

tūnscipe m. *'township,' population of a village, BH,LL.*

tūnscīr f. *administration of an estate, stewardship*, Lk16.

tunsingwyrt f. *white hellebore*, LCD.

tūnsōcn f. *'villarum jura regalia,' legal jurisdiction over a village*, TC308⁷ (v. LL 2·455).

tūnsteall m. *farm-stead, farm-yard?* KC.

tūnstede m. *farm-stead?* WW144²⁶.

tunuce=tunece

tūnweg m. *'privata via,' by-road*, KC, WW.

tūnyncel=tūnincel

tūr m. *'tower,' fortress, Chr* 1097.

turf f., gds. tyrf *'turf,' sod, soil, Chr,Cp, Guth,Lcd : greensward, BH,WW.*

turfhaga m. *grassy plot* (or ?=tyrfhaga A 35·141), EL830.

turfhlēow n. *covering of turf*, KC3·15′.

turflan=torfian

turl *ladle*, Cp290T. [*L.* trulla]

turnian *to turn, revolve*, Æ,LCD.

turnigendlic *revolving*, A6·12n.

turning f. *rotation*, W253¹⁴.

turtla m., turtle f. *'turtle'-dove, G,Ps;* Æ. [*L.* turtur]

turtur m. *turtle-dove, Bl,LG,VPs.* [*'turtur'*]

tūsc m. *grinder, canine tooth, Guth,Lcd,LL.* [*'tusk'*]

tuu=tū, twā; Tuu=Tīw

tuwa (Æ,AO,CP), tuwwa (=twiwa) adv. *twice.*

tūx=tūsc

tūxel, tūxl m. *tusk, canine or molar tooth, Lcd.* [*'tuscle'*]

twā I. (tū, v. twēgen), *Æ,AO.* [*'two'*] II. adv. *twice.* tū swā lang(e) *twice as long.*

twa-=twi-

twaddung? twædding f. *adulation*, CHRD.

twǣde num. *two parts out of three, two-thirds*, LCD. [twā]

+twǣfan w. g. *to separate from, deprive of :* hinder : w. a. *put an end to.*

twǣgen (M)=twēgen

twælf (M)=twelf

twǣm v. twēgen.

±twǣman (ē) *to divide into two, separate, Bf,W : cause to cease, adjust, settle : defer, postpone*, LL242¹⁹. [*'tweme'*]

twǣmendlīce adv. *alternately, separately*, OEG1368.

twǣming f. *parting, division, separation*, Æ : *distinction*, Æ.

twǣonung=twēonung; twām v. twēgen.

+twanc n. *collusion, deception*, OEG1517.

twānihte *two days old*, LCD.

twe-=twi-

twēgen num. nom. nom. m.; nom. f. twā; nom. n. tū, twā; gen. mfn. twēg(e)a, twēgra; dat. twǣm, twām *two,* Æ; AO,CP. tū swā lang *twice as long.* t. and t., twām and twām *in parties of two each.* [*'TWAIN'*]

twēgentig (oe; NG)=twēntig

twelf *'TWELVE,'* CP.

twelffeald *twelve-fold*, ÆH.

twelfgylde *twelve-fold*, LL3,1.

twelfhund *twelve hundred*, LL.

twelfhynde adj. *belonging to the class whose 'wergild' was* 1200 *shillings*, LL.

twelfnihte *twelve days old*, LCD3·178′.

twelfta I. *'twelfth,' An,Lcd,MH;* AO. II.=Twelftadæg

Twelftadæg m. *Twelfth day*, LL296,17.

Twelftamæsseǣfen *Eve of the Epiphany*, CHR1066.

twelfte, *twelfthly, in the twelfth place*, LL 182,12.

twelftig=hundtwelftig

twelfwintre *twelve years old*, CP.

twēman=twǣman

twengan *to pinch*, IM. [*'twinge'*]

twēntig *'TWENTY,' Æ,AO.*

twēntigfeald *twenty-fold*, ÆGR.

twentiggēare *twenty years old*, ÆL32³⁷.

twēntigoða (io³, o³, u³) *'twentieth,' Lcd,MH;* Æ,AO.

twēntigwintre *twenty years old*, W3¹.

±twēo m. *doubt, ambiguity*, Æ,AO,CP.

tweo-=twi-, twy-; twēogan=twēon

twēogende *doubting*, BH.

twēogendlic *doubtful, uncertain*, AO. adv. -līce.

tweolf=twelf

twēolic (ī, ȳ) *doubtful, ambiguous, equivocal.* adv. -līce, AO,CP.

±twēon I. pret. sg. twēode *to doubt, hesitate*, AO,CP : (impers. w. a. of pers.) *seem doubtful.* II. (ī, ȳ) m. *doubt*, Bo.

twēona m. *doubt*, VH21.

twēonelēoht n. *twilight*, WW175²⁴.

±twēonian (ȳ) (pers. and impersonal) *to doubt, be uncertain, hesitate*, CP.

twēonigend, twēoniendlic (ī, ȳ) *doubtful, expressing doubt*, Æ. adv. -līce *perhaps.*

twēonol (ȳ) *doubtful*, Sc,WW.

twēontig=twēntig

twēonullēoht (WW175³⁹)=twēonelēoht

twēonum in phr. *'be* (sǣm, etc.) twēonum,' *between* (*the seas, etc.*).

twēonung (ī, ȳ) f. *doubt, scruple*, Æ.

+tweosa=+twisa; twēoung=twēonung

tweowa=tuwa; twi, twia=tuwa

twī=twig n.

twi- prefix with meaning *two, double.* [*Ger.* zwie-]

twibēte adj. *subject to double compensation*, LL.

twibill n. (*two-edged*) *axe, Guth,WW*; Æ. ['*twibill*']

twibille *double-edged*, WW 141²⁷.

twibleoh *twice-dyed, double-dyed*, CP : *biform*, CHRD 78⁶.

twibōte (adj. and adv.)=twibēte

twibrowen (y) *twice-brewed*, LCD 45b.

-twicce (æ) v. angel-t.

twiccen=twicen

twiccere m. *one who divided up the food in a monastery*, WW 127³³.

twiccian *to pluck, gather* : *catch hold of, Lcd, Shr,WW*. ['*twick*']

twi-cen, -cene, -cyne (y¹) f. *junction of roads*.

twicere=twiccere

twidæglic (a², y²) *lasting two days*, BH 350³².

twidæl m. *two-thirds*, LCD.

twidǣlan *to divide into two* : *differ*, Sc.

twidēagod *twice-dyed*, OEG 1060.

-twidig v. lang-t.; **twie-**=twi-

twi-ecge, -ecgede *two-edged*, BH,Ps.

twiendlīce *doubtingly*, GUTH 70. [twēon]

±**twi-feald** (Æ), -fald (CP) *two-fold, double, ambiguous, BH,CP*. ['*twifold*']

±**twifeald-an**, -ian (y¹, y²) *to double*, Æ.

twifealdlic (a) adj. *two-fold, double*. adv. -līce, *Æ,Mt*. ['*twifoldly*']

twifealdnes (ie) f. *duplicity*, CP : *irresolution*, CP 307³ : *duplication*, BF 174¹⁶.

twifēre *accessible by two ways*, WW 194³⁰.

twiferlǣcan (y) *to dissociate*, Sc 6⁸.

twifēte (eo, y) *two-footed*, ÆGR.

twifeŏerede *as if with two wings, forked*, ÆGR 288¹¹.

twifingre (y) *two fingers thick*, LL 110, 49³.

twifyldan=twifealdan

twifyrclian (y¹, e²) *to branch off, deviate from*, ÆGR 288¹⁰ : *split into two*.

twifyrede *two-furrowed*, ÆGR 288¹¹.

twig n. '*twig*,' *branch, shoot, small tree, LG*; Æ,CP.

twig-=twi-; **twiga**=(1) twig; (2) tuwa

twigærede (y) *cloven*, ÆGR 288¹¹.

twīgan=twēogan, twēon

twigea=tuwa; **twigedēagod**=twidēagod

twigilde (adj. adv. and ? sb.) *paying double, liable to a double fine*, LL.

twīh num. (acc.) only in phrase 'mid unc twīh' *between us two*, GEN 2253. [cp. *Goth.* tweihnai]

twihēafdede (y) *double-headed*, ÆGR.

twiheolor f. *balance*, Cp 140B.

twihinde=twihynde

twihīw(ed)e (ēo) *of two colours or shapes*.

twihīwian *to dissimulate*, Sc 44⁸.

twihlidede *having two openings*, ÆGR 288⁶ (y).

twihwēole *two-wheeled*, LCD.

twihwyrft m. *double period*, OEG 2513.

twihynde I. *having* '*wergild*' *of 200 shillings*. **II.** *a* '*wergild*' *of 200 shillings*, LL.

twihyndeman m. *man of the* '*twihynde*' *class*, LL 601,87⁴.

twiicce=twiecge

twilæpped *with two lappets*, WW 153¹⁷.

twilafte *two-edged*, WW 194³⁵.

twilibrocen *woven of threads of two colours?* TC 537²³ (v. WC 113⁷). [twilic]

twilic *double, woven of double thread, Gl*. ['*twilly*']

twīlic=twēolic

twimylte *twice-melted*, OEG 4462.

twīn I. n. *double thread, twist*, '*twine*,' *linen-thread, linen, (byssus), CP,Gl,Lk*. **II.**= twēon II.

twinclian *to* '*twinkle*,' *wink, Bo,CP*.

twinebbe (y) *having two faces*, GPH 397⁴⁴⁸.

twīnen *of linen*, OEG.

twing? sb. *cluster*, HGL 496.

twingan v. tringan.

twīnigend-=twēonigend-

twinihte (y) *two days old*, LCD 27b.

twinn '*twin*,' *two-fold, double, two by two, Gl*.

+**twinn** m. *twin*. pl. '*twins*,' *triplets*, MH, SHR.

+**twinnes** (y) f. *junction*, BF 176⁴.

twīnung=twēonung

twīnwyrm, m. '*buprestis*,' *small insect*, WW 122²⁷.

twio=tweo

twirǣde (io, y) *uncertain* : *disagreeing, Bo, Mt*. ['*twirede*']

twirǣdnes (y¹, e²) f. *disagreement, discord, sedition*, Æ.

+**twis** *having the same parents*, GL.

+**twisa** m. *twin*, Æ.

twisceatte adv. *to the extent of a double payment*, LL 84,66¹.

twiscyldig *liable to a double penalty*, LL 90 H.

twiseht (y) *disunited, discordant*, Sc 192¹³.

twisehtan (y) *to disagree*, LCD 3·204', ANS 125·56²⁹⁵.

twisehtnes f. *dissension, disagreement*, Sc 6¹².

twiseltōŏ *with forked teeth?* WW 108¹⁵.

twisestre *containing two sesters*, JnL 2⁶ (mg).

twisla m. *confluence, junction, BC*; KC 5·198'. ['*twisel*']

twislian *to fork, divide into two, KC*. ['*twisel*,' '*twisled*']

twisliht *forked, branched*, KC.

twislung f. *division, partition*, Lcd 3·436³ : *difference*, CHRD. ['*twisling*']

twisnæcce *double-pointed, cloven*, ÆGR 288¹¹.

twisnēse *double-pointed, cloven,* GPH393⁷³.
twisprǣc f. *double speech, deceit, detraction.*
twisprǣce *double-tongued, deceitful, detracting,* Æ.
twisprǣcnes (y) f. *double speech, detraction.*
twisprecan *to murmur,* NG.
twispunnen *twice-spun,* CP83²³.
-twist v. candel-, mæst-t.
twistrenge *two-stringed,* ÆGR288¹⁰.
twitælged *double-dyed,* GL,VPs.
twi-ðrāwen, -ðrǣwen *twice thrown or twisted, twice woven,* CP.
twiwa=tuwa
twiwǣg f. *pair of scales,* WW194²⁸.
twiweg m. *junction of two roads,* WW177¹³.
twi-wintre, -winter adj. *two years old,* Æ.
twiwyrdig *ambiguous,* AO.
twoelf=twelf
twōgon=ðwōgon pret. pl. of ðwēan.
twuga, twuwa, twuwu=tuwa
twux=tusc; twy-=twi-
twȳ=twēo
twȳgean=twēogan, twēon I.
twȳlic (Æ)=twēolic; twȳn=twēon
twynihte=twinihte
twyspēcnes=twisprǣcnes
tȳ pres. 1 sg. of tȳn.
tyccen=ticcen; tycht-, tyct-=tyht-
tȳd (1)=tīd; (2) pp. of tȳn.
tȳd-=tīd-
+tȳd, tydd *skilled, learned.*
tydd-=tīd-, tūd-, tȳd-
tȳdde I. pret. 3 sg. of tȳn. II.=tīðde pret. 3 sg. of tīðian.
tȳde pret. sg. of tȳn.
tȳdernes (ydd) f. *branch,* OEG3849.
+tȳdnes f. *edification,* CHRD58⁸.
±tȳdran *to bring forth, produce, beget, propagate : be prolific.* [tūdor]
tȳdred *provided with offspring,* PPs143¹⁷.
tȳdrian=(1) tīdrian; (2) tȳdran
tȳdriend m. *propagator,* WW238²².
tȳdrung f. *propagation, production : branch,* ÆGR216¹⁵. [tūdor]
tyg-=tig-
tȳg=tēag
tyge (i) m. *drawing together, pulling, tug, pull* Æ : *leading (water)* : *draught (of water)* : *inference, statement,* Æ. [tēag, tīegan]
tygehōc (i¹) m. *hook for pulling,* LL455,15.
tygehorn (i) m. *cupping-horn,* LCD46a.
tygel m. *pulling-rope, rein,* Æ,WW. ['tial']
tygele f. '*murenula,' lamprey?* WW.
tygðian=tīðian; tyhhian=teohhian
tȳhst pres. 2 sg. of tēon.
tyht I. (i) m. *instruction, training, habit, Bo* : *going, course, motion, progress, El* : *region,* GU1255. ['tight'; tēon] II.=tiht

tyht-=tiht-
±tyhtan I. (i) (+) *to stretch, draw, pull, CM* : *invite, incite, instigate, provoke, talk over, persuade, attract, lead astray, seduce, Æ* : (+) *teach, train, PPs.* ['tight'; tēon I.]
II.=tihtan
tyhten f. *incitement, excitement,* GL. [tēon I.]
tyhtend m. *inciter, instigator,* GL.
tyhtendlic (i) *persuading, hortatory,* Æ.
tyhtere (i) m. *inciter, enticer,* WW.
tyhting (i) f. *incitement, impulse, instigation,. exhortation, suggestion, instruction, advice,.* Æ : *enticement, allurement, Æ.* ['tighting']
tyhtnes (i) f. *inward impulse, instinct, conviction,* WW.
tȳhð pres. 3 sg. of tēon.
tyl=til
tyldsyle f. *tent,* WW187⁴. [teld]
tylg, tylgest v. tulge; -tyllan v. for-t.
tȳm=tēam; tȳm-=tēam-, tīm-; tyma= tama
tȳman (Æ)=tīeman
tymb-=timb-
±tȳn I. *to instruct, teach,* Æ,AO. II. (Æ)=tīen
tȳn-=tīen-
±tȳnan I. *to hedge in, fence, enclose, shut, A,BH,LG,LL.* ['tine'] II. (=īe) *to irritate, vex, trouble, Bas,Bl,LL* : *insult, revile,* Æ. ['teen']
tyncen n. *bladder?* AO72³⁰.
tynder (e, i, u) f. '*tinder,' fuel, Bo,Gl,Sc;* Æ : *cautery.* [tyndan]
tyndercynn n. *combustible,* WW.
tyndig=tindig; tyndre, tyndren=tynder
+tȳne n. *entrance, court,* PPs115⁸.
±tynge I. adj. *fluent, eloquent : skilful.* II. adv. (also -līce) *courteously,* OEG2853.
+tyng(e)lic *polished, elegant, rhetorical.* adv. -līce.
+tyngnes (i) f. *fluency, eloquence,* Æ,CP : *skill,* BF14²².
-tȳning v. æcer-t.; gafol-t.
tyntreg=tintreg
tyr-, tȳr- v. also tir-, tīr-.
-tyran (=īe) v. be-t.
tȳran (=īe) *to shed tears,* Æ : *run with water* (eyes), LCD. [tēar]
tyrdelu, tyrdlu npl. *droppings, small pieces of excrement, Lcd.* ['treddle']
tȳrende *having watery eyes, Lcd.* ['tear']
tyrewa=tyrwa; tyrf v. turf.
+tyrfan *to strike, afflict,* GD29⁹. [torfian]
tyrfhaga f. *hoe, mattock,* LN17².
tȳrgan=tēorian
tȳriāca m. (*treacle), sovereign remedy,* LCD, WW. [L. theriacum; Gk. θηριακός]
tȳrian=tēorian
tyrnan *to turn, move round, revolve,* Æ. [L. tornare]

tyrngeat n. *turnstile*, KC3·405⁴.

tyrning (u) f. *turning round, rotation*, OEG : *rotundity, roundness*, OEG : *crookedness, deceit*, OEG56⁸⁶.

tyro=teoru

tyrð pres. 3 sg. of teran.

tyrwa m., tyrwe f. '*tar,' resin, Æ*. [=teoru]

tyr-wan, -wian I. (e, i;=ie) *to harass, vex, LPs*. ['*tar'*] II. *to '*tar,' B 295 : *to make like tar*, LCD 140a.

tysca m. *buzzard*, WW 259¹².

tyslian *to put on*, CM 260,ES8·62⁵.

tyslung f. *dressing*, ES8·62⁶.

tysse f. *coarse cloth*, JGPh 1·63. [*OHG*. zussa]

tȳtan *to sparkle, shine*, DD45.

tytt=titt; tȳð=tīð; tȳw-=tīw-

Ð

ðā I. adv. and conj. *then, at that time, Æ, AO,CP* : *after that time, thereupon, AO, Jul* : *when, at the time that, whilst, during, AO,B,Bl,Ps* : *there, where*, CHR : *seeing that, inasmuch as, if, when, since, as, because*. ðā ðā *when*. ðā...ðā *then...when*. ðā hwīle ðe *while, whilst, so long as*. ðā gīet v. ðāgīet. ['*tho*'] II. asf. and nap. of sē. ðā ðe *which*.

ðaca I. (±) m. *roof, covering*. II. gp. of ðæc.

±ðaccian *to clap, pat, stroke, touch gently, CP,Shr* : *smack, beat*, GD : *tame?* GPH 402. ['*thack'*]

ðacele=ðæcele

ðacian *to thatch*, LL 454,10. ['*thack'*]

ðacum dp. of ðæc.

ðadder (*JnL* 7³⁵)=ðider

ðæc I. (ea) n. *covering, roof of a building, Chr,MtR,PPs* : *thatch, Æ,BH*. ['*thack'*] II.=ðec pron. (das. of ðu).

ðæccille (N)=ðæcele; ðæcce f.=ðæc I.

ðæcele (e) f. *torch, lamp, light*, AA,NG. [=fæcele]

ðæcen=ðecen; ðæcile=ðæcele

ðæctigile f. *roof-tile*, Cp571.

ðæder, ðædres=ðider

ðæderlendisc (MH 178²⁵n)=ðiderlēodisc

+ðæf w. g. *agreeing to, consenting to, admitting* : *contented*.

ðæf (*JnR*)=ðēof; ðæfet-=ðafet-

ðæge mnp. pron. *they, those, them, Lk,Jn, Sol*. ['*thaie'*]

ðægen, ðægn=ðegen, ðegn

ðægon pret. pl. of ðicgan.

ðǣh (N)=ðēah I. and II.

ðæht (N)=ðeaht

ðǣm (ā, ē) dsmn. and dp. of sē pron. be ðǣm, on ðǣm *thereon, therein*. ēac ðǣm *in addition to this, besides this, also, moreover*. ǣr ðǣm ðe *before*. æfter ðǣm *after*,

later, next, after that (fashion). for ðǣm (ðe) *therefore, on that account, for that reason, because*. on ðǣm ðe *in this, in that*.

ðǣn=ðegn

ðǣnan *to moisten*, GD,LCD.

ðǣncan=ðencan; ðǣncung=ðancung

ðǣne=ðone asm. of sē.

ðǣnian=ðānian

ðǣnnan=ðennan; ðǣnne=ðonne

ðǣr (ē) adv. and conj. 'THERE*,' *thither, yonder* : *where, whither* : *then* : *when* : *though, if, so far as, whilst, provided that* : *in that respect*. ðǣr ðǣr *where, wherever*. ðǣr...of *therefrom*. ðǣr wið *in regard to that*.

ðǣra gp. of sē, sēo, ðæt.

ðǣrābūtan *about that place, ÆL*. ['*thereabout*']

ðǣræfter adv. '*thereafter,' CP,Lcd,Mt*.

ðǣræt '*thereat,' BH* 282⁶.

ðǣran *to dry*, HL13¹⁰³.

ðǣr-big, -bie adv. '*thereby,' thus, CP* 42,43¹⁴.

ðǣrbinnan (o³) adv. *therein, Æ,AO*.

ðǣrbufan *besides that*, CP52¹⁰.

ðǣre gdf. of sē.

ðǣrf=(1) ðearf; (2) ðeorf; ðǣrf-=ðearf-

ðǣrforan conj. *before that, Æ*.

ðǣrh=ðurh

ðǣrin '*therein,' wherein, Met*.

ðǣrinne (ē) *therein*, CP. ['*thereinne*']

ðǣrle=ðearle

ðǣrmid adv. *therewith, Æ,Bo*. ['*theremid*']

ðǣrnēhst *next to that*, LL280,2¹.

ðǣrnian *to lose?* CHR 1119 (v. MFH 174).

ðǣrof adv. '*thereof,' of that, Lcd*.

ðǣrofer *over or above that, CP,G*. ['*thereover*']

ðǣron adv. *therein, Æ,CP* : '*thereon,' Bl* : *thereinto, thereof*.

ðǣronbūtan (*Chr*)=ðǣreābūtan

ðǣronemn *alongside*, ÆP 164¹⁸.

ðǣrongēn adv. *on the contrary*, W 248²¹. ['*thereagain*']

ðǣronuppan adv. *thereupon, Æ*.

ðǣrrihte, ðǣrrihtes (ā, ē) adv *thereupon, forthwith, instantly, immediately, straightway, Æ,Bl,DHy*. ['*thereright(s)*']

ðǣrsc pret. 3 sg. of ðerscan.

ðǣrscan (NG)=ðerscan

ðǣrsc-wald, -wold=ðerscold

ðǣrst (SPs 74⁸)=ðærst

ðǣrtō adv. '*thereto,' to it, to that place, Æ* : *besides, Æ,BH* : *for that purpose, Æ* : *belonging to, Æ*.

ðǣrtōēacan adv. *besides, in addition to that, ÆH* 2·84⁸. ['*thereteken*']

ðǣrtōgēanes adv. *on the contrary, in opposition thereto, Æ* : *in exchange for, TC* 436¹⁷. ['*theretoyens*']

ðǣrðǣr adv. *wherever,* Æ.
ðǣrunder adv. *beneath, CP.* ['*thereunder*']
ðǣruppan *thereon, ÆL*30²⁰⁰. ['*thereup*']
ðǣrūt, ðǣrūte adv. *outside, without, AO, CP,Mk.* ['*thereout*']
ðǣrwið adv. *against, in exchange for,* Æ : '*therewith,' Bo.*
ðǣrymbe adv. *thereabout, on that point,* W 273¹.
ðǣrymbūtan *thereabouts,* Bн,Bo.
ðæs I. adv. (gs. of ðæt) *afterwards, AO,Chr : thence : accordingly, according as,* Æ : *therefore, because, CP : therefore, wherefore, because, that : as, according as; provided;* (to express proportion) *the* (*more, etc.*), *CP.* tō ðæs *to that point, to that degree.* ðæs ðe *since, after, afterwards, the more, CP,Mt.* ['THES'] II. gs. of sē and ðæt.
±ðæslǣcan *to agree with, be suitable,* Gl.
ðæslic I. adj. *suitable, congruous,* Æ : *harmonious : fair, elegant.* II.=ðyllic
ðæslīce adv. *opportunely, suitably, aptly, after this manner, similarly, thus,* Æ,AO.
ðæslicnes f. *fitness, convenience,* ÆH 1·326'.
ðæsma m. *leaven, yeast,* RB10¹⁸.
ðæsternes=ðēostornes
ðæsðe=ðæs ðe v. ðæs.
ðæt I. conj. and adv. '*THAT,' so that, in order that, after that, then, thence.* ðæt ðe *that.* II. nas. of sē, ðæt. ['THAT*']
ðætte I. pron. *which, that which.* II. conj. *that, so that, in order that.* tō ðon ðætte *so that.* [ðæt ðe]
+ðafa I. m. *favourer, supporter, helper, CP.* II. adj. (cpve +ðafera) *agreeing, consenting, acquiescing.*
ðafetere, ðafettere m. *one who acquiesces in, or condones, what is wrong, CP.*
+ðafettan (æ, ea) *to consent,* EHy6²⁷.
±ðafian (ea) *to allow, suffer, endure, permit, tolerate, BH,Bo,Ct,G,LL,W;* CP : *approve, consent to, submit to,* AO,CP. [' (*i*)-*thave*']
ðaforlic=ðaroflic, ðearflic
+ðafsum *consenting, agreeing,* MtL5²⁵.
+ðafsumnes f. *consent, agreement,* Mt pref. 14¹⁴.
±ðafung f. *permission, consent,* Æ.
ðāg, ðāh pret. 3 sg. of ðicgan, ðēon.
ðage=ðæge
ðāgēn=ðe āgēn *who again,* BL167⁶.
ðāgīet, ðāgȳt adv. *still : yet.*
ðāgon pret. pl. of ðicgan.
ðāh=ðēah; ðām=ðæm
ðamettan *to clap* (*the hands*)? APs97⁸.
ðan=ðon adv.
ðān I. adj. *moist, irrigated,* WW. II. n. *irrigated land.* [ðīnan] III. (LWS)=ðæm
ðanan=ðanon

±ðanc (o) m. *thought, reflection, sentiment, idea,* Æ : *mind, will, purpose : grace, mercy, favour, pardon : thanks, gratitude, CP;* AO, CP : *pleasure, satisfaction, CP : reward, recompense,* Gu442. Gode ð. *thanks* (*be*) *to God.* Godes ðances *through the mercy of God.* Drihtnes ðances *according to the will of the Lord.* mīnes ðances *by my favour, of my own will.* on ð. *willingly, gladly.* an ðance *acceptable, pleasant,* AO. dēofla ðonces *in honour of devils,* AO. tōðance *for the sake of* ['THANK']
+ðanc mn. *thought, mind, Lk.* ['*i-thank*']
ðances adv. *thankfully, gladly : voluntarily, gratis, BC,Bo,Chr.* [v. '*thank*']
ðancful adj. (+) *thoughtful, ingenious, clever : 'thankful,' Bl : contented, satisfied, BH,WW : pleasing, agreeable, CM : energetic, spirited.* adv. -līce '*thankfully,*' ÆL30¹⁴⁴.
ðanchycgende *thoughtful,* B2235.
±ðancian (o) (w. g. thing and d. pers.) *to thank, give thanks,* Æ; CP : *recompense, reward :* (w. i.) *rejoice.* ['THANK']
+ðancmetian *to think over, deliberate,* Gen 1917. [metgian]
ðanc-metung (o¹, eo²), -metegung f. *deliberation, thought,* BH88⁴ (v.l.).
±ðancol *thoughtful, mindful : prudent, wise :* (+) *desirous :* (+) *suppliant.*
ðancolmōd† *thoughtful, considerate, prudent, wise, attentive.*
ðanc-snot(t)or† *wise, prudent, ingenious.*
ðancung f. '*thanking,' thanksgiving,* Æ,AO, Jnl.
ðanc-weorð, -weorðlic (u², y²) *thankworthy, acceptable : thankful, grateful : memorable.* adv. -līce *gladly, willingly,* CP.
ðancword n. *thanks,* Wid137.
ðanc-wurð, -wyrð(e)=ðancweorð
ðand pret. 3 sg. of ðindan.
ðane (KGL)=ðone
ðanēcan ðe (o¹) adv. *whenever, as often as,* Bo.
+ðang n. *growth,* Sol180¹² (or ?=+ðanc, BTac).
ðānian (ǣ) *to be or become moist, moisten,* WW.
ðanne=ðonne
ðanon (CP), ðanone (o¹, a²) adv. *from that time or place, thence, away : whence, from which, of which, CP.* ðanon...ðanon *thence...whence : then, thereupon, henceforth : by which, through that.* ['THENNE']
ðanonforð (o¹, a²) adv. *after that, then, thenceforward,* OET,W.
ðanonweard adv. *departing thence,* Bo103⁷.
ðanun=ðanon
ðar-=ðear-, ðer-; ðār=ðǣr

ðāra I.=ðǣr. II. gp. of sē, sēo, ðæt.
ðas=ðæs gsmn. of sē.
ðās I. afs. and nap. of ðēs. ['those'] II.
nap. of ðāw=ðēow
ðassum (N)=ðissum, dmns. of ðēs.
ðat=ðæt; ðāðā v. ðā.
ðāw I.=ðēaw I. II.=ðēow
+ðāwenian=+ðwǣnan
ðāwian to 'thaw,' Lcd3·274'.
ðe I. rel. pron. (when govd. by a prep. the
prep. follows) who, which, that. ðe is often
associated by attraction with pers. pronouns. ðe ic I. ðe we we. ðe...his whose.
sē ðe his he whose. II. conj. when : or :
(=ðā) then : (=ðǣr) where, EL717 : (with
comparatives) than. hwǣðer ðe...ðe whether...or. ðe...ðe the...or, either...or. III.
art. the (indecl.), CHR963E and late. IV.
particle added to ðēah, for ðǣm, ðæs, etc.,
without affecting their meaning. V. das.
of ðu. ['THEE']
ðē=ðȳ; ðēa (NG)=ðēow
ðeac=ðæc; ðeaca=ðaca
ðēada (VPs)=ðēoda gp. of ðēod I.
ðēadōm (DR)=ðēowdōm
ðēaf (NG)=ðēof; ðeafian=ðafian
ðeah pret. 3 sg. of ðicgan.
ðēah I. (ē) conj. and adv. 'though*,' although, even if, that, however, nevertheless, yet, still, Bl,Bo : whether, Bo. ð. ðe
although. swā ð. nevertheless, yet. ð....ð.
although, still, yet. II. pret. 3 sg. of ðēon.
ðēah-hwæðere, -hweðre adv. yet, moreover,
however, nevertheless, but, Bl,CP. swā ð.
yet, nevertheless. ['thoughwhether']
ðeaht n. counsel, advice, design, Æ. [ðencan]
+ðeaht fn. thought, consideration, counsel,
advice, direction : design, contrivance,
scheme, Æ,CP : council, assembly, Æ.
+ðeahta m. adviser, counsellor, WW99⁵.
ðeahte pret. 3 sg. of ðeccan.
+ðeahtend m. counsellor, WW.
+ðeahtendlic deliberative, LL12.
±ðeahtere m. counsellor, BH.
±ðeahtian to ponder, consider, deliberate
upon, take counsel, Æ,CP : agree, MtL18¹⁹.
±ðeahtung (æ) f. counsel, consultation, GD,
NG.
ðēahðe=ðēah ðe
ðēana adv. nevertheless, yet. swā ð. however.
ðēara=ðāra, gmfp. of ðæt.
ðearf I. (a, e, y) f. need, necessity, want,
behoof, B,Lcd; CP. tō ðearfe as is needed,
according to what is needed : benefit, profit,
advantage, utility, Æ : trouble, hardship,
privation, distress, danger : duty, employment. ['tharf'] II. needful, necessary.
III.=ðeorf. IV. pres. 3 sg. of ðurfan.

ðearfa (æ, eo) I. m. poor man, pauper,
beggar, Æ,CP. II.destitute,poor, needy, Æ.
+ðearfan to be in want, SOL268⁷³.
ðearfednes f. poverty, BH.
ðearf-end, -igend (o) m. poor man, BK.
ðearfende needy, in want, poor, CP.
ðearfendlic needy, poor, miserable, APT,
GD.
ðearfendnes=ðearfednes
ðearfian to starve, be in need, want, PPs
71¹³. [Ger. darben]
+ðearfian to impose necessity, B1103.
ðearflēas adj. without cause or need, Æ.
adv. -lēase.
ðearflic profitable, useful, convenient, necessary, Æ. adv. -lice.
ðearflicnes f. want, poverty, GL,Sc.
ðearl adj. vigorous, strong, severe, strict,
harsh, violent, heavy, excessive. adv.
ðearle. swiðe ðearle with all their might.
ðearlic severe, cruel, harsh, violent, grievous.
adv. -lice, CP.
ðearlmōd† stern, severe, violent, strong,
mighty, JUD.
ðearlwis strict, severe, relentless, CP.
ðearlwislic severe, GD. adv. -lice, CP.
ðearlwisnes f. severity, strictness, BH,GD.
ðearlwȳs-=ðearlwis-
ðearm (a, e) m. gut, entrail, Æ,Gl. ['tharm']
ðearm(ge)wind n. windpipe (=windðearm),
OET509 (v. ES43·332).
ðearmgyrd m. girdle, belt, WW220¹.
ðearsc=ðærsc pret. 3 sg. of ðerscan.
ðearsm (BH426²⁴)=ðrosm
ðēat pret. 3 sg. of ðēotan.
ðēatan=ðēotan
ðēater m? theatre, AO154².
ðēatscipe (N)=ðēodscipe
ðēaw I. m. usage, custom, habit, conduct,
disposition, AO,B,JnL; CP : (in pl.)
virtues, (good) manners, morals, morality,
Æ,AO,Bo,Bl; CP. ['thew'] II.=ðēow
+ðeawe customary, usual, GD142³³.
ðēawfæst decorous, moral, virtuous, honourable, LL : gentle, CRA.
ðēawfæstlice correctly, ÆL5²²².
ðēawfæstnes f. obedience, discipline, Æ.
ðēawful moral, virtuous, W250⁴.
ðēawian I.=ðēowian. II. (+) to bring up
well, Æ.
ðēawlēas ill-mannered, ÆH2·380¹¹.
ðēawlic customary, Æ : decent, moral, Æ :
figurative. adv. -lice.
+ðēawod well-mannered, moral, Æ.
ðēb- (GL)=ðēof-
ðec das. of ðu. ['thee']
ðeccan (±) to cover, cover over, conceal, B,
Gen,Lcd,PPs : (†) swallow up? ['thatch']
ðeccbryce m. tile, HGL459⁴².

ðeccend m. *protector, defender*, PPs 70.
ðecele=ðæcele
ðecen f. *thatch, tile, covering, roof* : (fig.) *house*, Æ. [ðeccan]
ðecest pres. 2 sg. of ðeccan.
ðecgan I. *to consume*, LCD. II. obl. case of sb? *receptacle?* (BT) or=ðeccan? (Lieb.), LL 454,10.
+ðēd=+ðēod
ðēde pret. of ðēon (ðȳwan).
ðēf=ðēof
ðēfanðorn, ðefonðorn (APs 57¹⁰), ðēfeðorn =ðȳfeðorn
ðefel *mulled wine?* OEG 104.
ðēfel=ðȳfel
ðeflan *to pant, heave, palpitate*, HGL.
ðeften (HGl 461⁵⁶)=ðyften; ðēfð=ðīefð
ðegan *to serve*, GU 140.
ðegen I.=ðegn. II. pp. of ðicgan.
ðegen-=ðegn-, ðēn-
ðegeð 3 p. sg. pres. of ðecgan.
ðegh (GL)=ðēoh; ðegin=ðegn
ðegn (æ) [v. LL 456; 2·680] m. *servant, minister, retainer, vassal, follower, disciple*, AO,CP : *freeman, master* (*as opposed to slave*) : *courtier, noble* (*official, as distinguished from hereditary*), Æ : (†) *military attendant, warrior, hero*, AO. ['THANE']
ðegn- v. also ðēn-.
ðegnboren (ðegen-) *well-born*, LL.
ðegngylde n. *legal money value of a thane*, W 162¹⁰.
ðegnhyse m. *attendant, retainer*, WW.
±ðegnian (æ, ën) (w. d.) *to serve, minister, wait on*, B,BH,Bl,G; CP : *supply another with anything* : *perform* (*an office*). ['theine']
ðegnlagu f. *rights, duties or privileges of a thane*, LL,W.
ðegnlic *noble, brave, loyal*, Æ. adv. -līce.
ðegnrǣden f. *thaneship, service*, BL,GL.
ðegnriht n. *rights or privileges of a thane*, LL.
ðegnscipe m. *service, duty* : *ability*, AO : *manliness, valour*, AO : *body of retainers*.
ðegnscolu f. *band of vassals*, WW 371⁷.
ðegnsorh f. *sorrow for loss of thanes*, B 131.
ðegnung=ðēn-ung, -ing
ðegnweorud n. *band of followers*, CR 751.
ðegnwer m. *thane's* 'wergild,' LL.
ðego=ðegu
ðēgon=ðǣgon pret. pl. of ðicgan
-ðegu v. bēah-, wīn-ð.; ðeh (A)=ðec
ðēh I.=ðēoh I. II. (A,K)=ðēah
ðeht=ðeaht
ðel, ðell n. *board, plank*, (*metal*) *plate*, AA, W. [*Ger.* diele]
ðelbrycg f. *bridge of planks*, Ct.
ðelcræft=ðylcræft

ðellfæsten n. *fastness made of planks, ship, ark*, GEN 1482.
ðellian=ðilian
ðelma m. *noose, snare*, HGL 429¹⁷.
-ðelu v. buruh-, benc-ð. ['theal']
ðēm=ðǣm; ðēn=ðegn
±ðencan I. *to* 'THINK*' ('*i-thenche*'), *imagine, think of, meditate, reason, consider*, Æ; AO,CP : *remember, recollect, CP* : *intend, purpose, attempt, devise*, AO : *learn* : *wish, desire, long for*. [ðanc] II. =ðyncan
ðencendlic *thoughtful*, MFH 174.
ðende=ðenden; ðēnde=ðēonde
ðenden conj. and adv. *meanwhile, while, as long as, until*.
ðene=ðone
ðēnest f. *service, entertainment*, CHR 1054 D. [*Ger.* dienst]
ðēnestmann (ēo¹) m. *serving-man, retainer*, CHR 656 E.
ðēnestre f. *servant, handmaiden*, OEG 1358.
ðeng=ðegn
ðengel† m. *prince, king, lord, ruler*.
ðenian=ðennan
ðēnian (Æ,CP)=ðegnian
ðēnigmann=ðēningmann
ðēningfæt n. *serving-vessel*, RB 59.
ðēninggāst m. *ministering spirit*, ÆH 1·510¹⁵.
ðēninghūs n. *workshop*, GPH 394.
ðēningmann m. *serving-man*, Æ,CP.
ðēnisc (*religious*) *service*, EC 265⁷?
±ðennan (æ) *to stretch out, extend*, LCD, PPs : *prostrate* : *exert oneself* : *spread the fame of, magnify*, OEG. ['thin']
ðenning f. *stretching, extension*, A 11·172.
+ðēnsum *obedient, helpful, useful*, Æ. [ðegen]
ðēnung (ðegn-) *service, ministry*, BH,Bl, Bo; CP : (pl.) *attendants, retinue* : *use* : *church service, mass-book* : *meal-time, meal*, Æ. ['theining']
ðēnungbōc f. *book for divine service, mass-book*, ÆH 1·98' : *Leviticus*, ÆT 286².
ðēnungwerod n. *body of serving-men*, MH 218¹².
ðēo I.=ðēow m. II. ds. of ðēoh. III.= sēo II. IV. pres. 1 sg. of ðēon.
ðēod I. f. *people, nation, tribe*, Chr,Hy,Lk; AO,CP; Mdf : *region, country, province*, Bo : *men, war-troop, retainers* : (in pl.) *Gentiles*, Æ,MtR : *language*. ['thede'] II. *fellowship*, RB.
+ðēod pp. of +ðēon, ðȳwan.
±ðēodan (ī, īe, ȳ) *to join, associate* (*with*), *attach or subject oneself to*, Æ,CP : *come to, be near* : (+) *engage in* : (+) *translate*. ð. fram *separate*.

ðēodbealu† n. *public calamity*.
ðēodbūende† mp. *earth-dwellers, mortals*.
ðēodcwēn f. *queen, empress*, EL 1156.
ðēodcyning m. *monarch* : (†) *God*.
ðēode pret. 3 sg. of ðēon.
+ðēode n. *speech, language*, AO,CP : *nation* : *translation, Æ* : *meaning*.
ðēodegsa m. *general terror*, CR 834.
ðēoden m. *chief of a tribe, ruler, prince, king* : *God, Christ*. [ðēod]
ðēodend m. *translator*, OEG 15⁶.
+ðēodendlic *copulative*, ÆGR 259¹.
ðēodengedāl n. *separation from one's lord (through his death)*, GU 1324.
ðēodenhold† *faithful to one's lord*.
ðēodenlēas *without a ruler or chief, lordless*, B 1103.
ðēoden-māðm (-mādm) m. *treasure given by a prince*, GEN 409.
ðēodenstōl† m. *throne*.
ðēodeorðe f. *inhabited earth*, W 240¹⁵.
ðēodfēond m. *public enemy*, W.
ðēodfruma m. *prince, ruler*, MET 29⁹⁴.
ðēodgestrēon n. *people's treasure, great possession*, B 44; 1218.
ðēodguma† m. *man, warrior, retainer*, JUD.
ðēodhere m. *national army, host*, GEN 2160.
-ðēodig, -ðēodig-lic, -nes v. el-ð.
ðēodisc I.† n. *speech, language*, MET. II. adj. *Gentile*, OEG 8³⁵⁰. [*Ger.* deutsch]
+ðēodlǣcan *to adhere, cleave to*, LPs 24²¹.
ðēodland n. *inhabited land, district, country, empire* : *the continent*.
ðēodlic *national*, ÆGR 65⁶.
+ðēodlic *social, intimate*, WW 212⁶.
ðēodlīcetere m. *public deceiver, arch-hypocrite*, W 54¹⁸.
ðēodloga m. *arch-liar*, W.
ðēodmægen n. *troop, host*, Ex 342.
±ðēodnes f. (+) *joining, suture* : *conjunction, association, society* : (+) *conjugation*, ÆGR : (+) *translation*.
±ðēodrǣden f. *intercourse, fellowship, Æ*.
ðēodsceaða† m. *public pest, criminal*, W.
ðēodscipe (+ in VH) m. I. *nation, people, community, population*. II. *connection, association* : *discipline, training, teaching, instruction, testimony* : *learning, erudition*, CP : *administration, law, authority* : *conduct*.
ðēodstefn m. *tribe, nation*, PPs 83¹⁰.
+ðēodsumnes f. *agreement*, LkL p 8¹.
ðēodðrēa f? m? *general distress*, B 178.
ðēodwiga m. *great warrior*, PA 38.
ðēodwita m. *learned man* : *senator, Æ*.
ðēodwundor n. *great wonder*, CR 1155.
ðēof I. (ǣ, ēa) m., *criminal, 'thief,' robber*, G,LL,OET. II. f. *theft*, RBL 19¹².

ðēofdenn n. *robber's cave*, KC 3·15'.
ðēofend (only found in pl.?) f. *thieving, theft*.
ðēofet=ðiefð
ðēofeðorn=ðȳfeðorn
ðēoffeng m. *seizure of thieves by an owner on his own land* : *right to fines payable on conviction for theft?* TC (v. BT).
ðēofgild n. *payment for theft*, LL.
±ðēoflan *to 'thieve,' steal*, LL,TC.
ðēofmann m. *robber, brigand*, AO,ÆP.
ðēofsceaða m. *robber*, v. ANS 129·24 n 6.
ðēofsceolu=ðēofscolu
ðēofscip (ðeb-) n. *pirate-ship*, Ep. [v. 'thief']
ðēofscolu f. *band of robbers*, Bo 33¹⁰.
ðēofscyldig f. *guilty of theft*, LL 226'.
ðēofslege m. *slaying of a thief*, LL 97.
ðēofsliht m. *slaying of a thief*, LL 104B.
ðēofstolen ptc. *stolen*, LL.
ðēofð=ðiefð
ðēofung f. *thieving*, NC 327.
ðēofunt (NG)=ðēofend
ðēofwracu f. *punishment for theft*, LL 174.
ðēoging f. *increase, profit* : *advance, progress*.
ðēoh I. (ē, ī) n. (gs. ðēos, ds. ðēo; gp. ðēona) *'thigh,' hip*, AO,Gl,Lcd,MH. II. imperat. of ðēon.
ðēohece m. *pain in the thigh*, LCD.
ðēohgelǣte n. *thigh-joint*, LCD.
ðēohgeweald np. *'genitalia,'* LCD.
ðēohhweorfa m. *knee-cap*, LCD.
ðēohscanca m. *thigh-bone*, LCD,WW.
ðēohseax (æ²) n. *hip-sword, short sword, dirk*, WW.
ðēohwræc m. *pain in the thigh*, LCD 1·354'.
±ðēon I. (sv¹,³) *to thrive, prosper, flourish, grow, increase, ripen, Æ,B,Bl,Bo,Lk,Sc* : *be profitable, to become or be great, succeed, excel*, CP : *lengthen (of days)*. +ðogen *adult*. ['*thee,' 'i-thee'*] II. (wv.)=ðȳwan. III. (wv.)† *to perform, do*. IV. (+) *to receive, take*.
ðēona v. ðēoh; ðēonan=ðanon
ðēonde pres. ptc. of ðēon.
ðeonen=ðanon; ðēonest=ðēnest
ðēonyð=ðēownyd
ðēor m? *inflammation?* LCD.
ðēorādl f. *inflammation? blistering heat?* LCD.
ðeorcung=deorcung
ðēordrenc m. *a drink used for inflammation*, LCD.
ðēorf (æ, e, o) I. adj. *unleavened, Æ,G,WW* : *fresh? skim? (milk)*, LCD. II. n. *unleavened bread, Æ*. ['*tharf'*]
ðeorfa=ðearfa
ðeorfdagas mp. *days of unleavened bread*, BF 168³³.

ðeorfhlāf m. loaf of unleavened bread, Æ.
ðeorfling m. unleavened bread, WW 348²⁸. ['tharfling']
ðeorfnes f. freedom from leaven, purity, Æ.
ðeorfsymbel n. feast of unleavened bread, Ex 23¹⁴.
ðeorgerid n. inflammation? LCD 187a.
ðeorscwold=ðerscold
ðĕorwǣrc m. inflammatory disease? LCD 45b.
ðeorwenn f. inflammatory tumour or blister, carbuncle, LCD 123a.
ðeorwyrm m. inflammatory (parasitic) worm, LCD 45a.
ðeorwyrt f. fleabane, LCD.
ðēos I. dem. pron., nom. fem. this. v. ðēs. II. gs. of ðēoh. III. gs. of (ðēo=)ðēow.
ðeossa, ðeossum=ðissa, ðisum
ðēoster=ðēostor
ðēostor, ðēostre (īe, ī, ȳ) dark, gloomy, B, BH,PPs : sad, mournful. ['thester']
ðēostorcofa† m. dark chamber.
ðēostorful (ȳ) dark, dusky, Æ,Mt. [v. 'thester']
ðēostorfulnes (ē, ȳ) f. darkness, OEG.
ðēostorlic (e²) obscure, dark, Æ. ['thesterly']
ðēostorloca m. tomb, EL485.
ðēostornes (ǣ, ī, ȳ) f. darkness, AO,Bo. ['thesterness']
ðēostre=ðēostor, ðēostru
±ðēostrian (ȳ) to grow dark, become dim, be eclipsed, Æ,BH : darken, obscure, Bo,MkL. ['thester']
ðēostrig (ȳ) dark, obscure, blinded, GD,Mk. ['thestri']
ðēostru f. (ī, īe, ȳ), ðēostre n. (often in pl.) darkness, gloom, B,BH,CP,Mt; Æ. ['thester']
ðēostrung (ȳ) f. twilight, gloom, GUTH 36¹⁴.
ðeosum=ðisum
+ðēot I. n. howling, GUTH 48⁴. II. pres. 3 sg. of +ðēodan.
ðēotan². (ēa, ū) to roar, howl, Æ,Bo,Met : sound forth, resound, murmur, WW. ['theoten']
ðēote f. torrent, fountain, cataract, waterfall : conduit, pipe, Æ. [ðēotan]
ðēow I. fm. servant, slave, AO,CP,DR,G. II. adj. servile, Æ,AO,Bo,W. ['theow']
ðēowa m. (Æ,CP)=ðēow I.
+ðēowa m. enslaved person, v. MFH104.
ðēowæt=ðēowot
ðēowan I. (ē, ī, ȳ) to press, impress, force, Æ : thrust, pierce, stab : crush, push, oppress, check : threaten. II.=ðēowian
ðēowatdōm=ðēowotdōm
ðēow-boren, -berde not free-born, born in servitude.

ðēowcnapa m. bondservant, ÆH 2·510'.
ðēowdōm (ēa) m. slavery, servitude, service, vassalage, subjection, Æ,AO,DR; CP : divine service. ['theowdom']
ðēowdōmhād m. service, BH 480¹⁰.
ðēowe f. female slave, handmaiden, BH, MtL (ī). ['theow']
ðēowen, ðēowene=ðēowe
ðēowet (Æ)=ðēowot, ðēowt-
ðēowhād m. servitude, service, BH.
ðēowian I. (±) (ē, ēa) (w. d.) occl. pret. ðēowde to serve, minister to, be subject to, Bo,Lk,Mt; AO,CP : enslave, give over into slavery, Æ. ['theow'] II.=ðȳn. III. (+) V²Ps 140⁴=+ðēodan
ðēowin=ðēowe
ðēowincel (īo) n. little servant, CVHy3³.
ðēowing (ȳ) f. threat, reproof, GD 238¹⁷.
ðēowlic servile, ÆGR55¹n.
ðēowmann m. servant, ByH 134²⁰.
ðēowne as. of ðēowen.
ðēownȳd (ē²)† f. serfdom, slavery, DA.
ðēowot n. service, ministry, servitude, bondage, Æ,AO,CP.
ðēowotdōm m. service, CP 2¹⁰.
+ðēowtian to bring into captivity, RWH 141¹⁶.
ðēowracian to threaten, menace, SPs 102⁹.
ðēowracu (Æ)=ðēowwracu
+ðēowrǣden (RB)=ðēodrǣden
ðēowtlic of a slave, servile, Æ.
ðēowtling (wet) m. servant, slave, Æ.
ðēowtscipe m. service, ÆL23b²⁶.
ðēowð=ðēoïð, ðīefð
ðēowu=ðēowe; ðēowut=ðēowot
ðēowwracu f. commination, threat, threatening, Æ.
ðeox hunting-spear, HGL423.
ðēr=ðǣr
ðeran to rush, Cp150J.
ðerc-, ðercs-=ðersc-
ðerc(c)an (WW)=ðerscan
ðerexwold=ðerscold; ðerf=ðeort
ðerflicnes (KGL)=ðearflicnes
ðerh (NG)=ðurh
ðērinne=ðǣrinne; ðērrihte=ðǣrrihte
+ðersc n. thrashing, beating, GD.
±ðerscan³ (a, æ, ea, i, y) to thresh, 'THRASH*', beat, strike, CP.
ðerscel (y) f. flail, WW. ['threshel']
ðerscelflōr f. threshing-floor, Mt3¹²·
ðerscing f. thrashing, DR40¹⁵.
ðersc-old, -wald, -wold, ðerx(w)old (æ, eo, i, y) m. 'threshold,' border, limit, Æ,BH, Bl,Bo,Lcd,WW.
ðes=ðæs
ðēs (e?) m., ðēos f., ðis n. dem. pron. 'THIS.' beforan ðissum, ǣr ðissum before this, formerly.

ðester-=ðeostor-; ðestrian=ðeostrian
ðet, ðette=ðæt, ðætte
ðew-=ðeow-; ðī=ðȳ
ðīada (VPs134¹⁵)=ðeoda gp. of ðeod.
+ðian=+ðeon IV.
ðicce I. adj. 'THICK,' viscous, solid, AO : dense, stiff, CP : numerous, abundant, AO : hazy, gloomy, Æ : deep, AO. II. adv. thickly, closely, Bo,Lcd,WW : often, frequently, Gen 684. III. (VPs28⁹)=ðiccet.
ðiccet n. thick bushes, 'thicket,' SPs. [ðicce]
ðiccian tr., intr. to thicken, Æ,WW : crowd together, Shr. ['thick']
ðiccnes=ðicnes
ðiccol, ðiccul fat, corpulent, WW.
ðicfeald dense, OEG278.
+ðicfyldan to make dense, GL.
±ðicgan⁵ (and wv. in WS) (a, æ, e, ea) to take, receive, accept, Chr,Lcd : partake of, consume, taste, eat, drink, Mk; AO,CP. ['thig']
ðiclīce thickly, often, continually, frequently, in large numbers, AO.
ðicnes f. 'thickness,' density, viscosity, hardness, GD,Lcd, SPs : depth : anything thick or heavy (as clouds or rain), LPs,ZDA : darkness : thicket.
ðīd-=ðeod-; ðīdan=ðyddan
ðider (æ, y) adv. on that side, 'THITHER*,' whither, Æ; AO,CP. hider and ð. or. hidres ðidres (ðædres) hither and thither, CP : where, wherever.
ðidercyme m. a coming hither, NC327.
ðidergeond thither, Æ.
ðiderinn (y¹, y²) adv. therein, into that place.
ðiderlēodisc to that people, native, MH178²⁵.
ðiderweard, ðiderweardes adv. 'thitherwards,' thither, Æ,AO,Bo.
ðidres=ðider; ðīed-=ðeod-
ðieder (CP)=ðider; ðīef-=ðeof-
ðīefefeoh n. stolen goods, LL100,25¹.
ðīefð (ē, ēo, ȳ) f. 'theft,' Lcd,LL : stolen goods, LL (ðēoft). [ðēof]
+ðiegen=+ðigen; ðīen=ðȳn
ðīende=ðeonde; ðīenen=ðīnen
ðienga=ðinga gp. of ðing.
ðīestr-=ðēostr-; ðīī-=ðīef-, ðȳf-
ðigde, ðigede pret. 1, 3 sg. of ðicgan.
ðigen I. f. receiving, taking (of food or drink), eating, Æ : food or drink, Æ. [ðicgan] II. pp. of ðeon I. and ðicgan.
ðigeð pres. 3 sg. of ðicgan.
ðignen=ðīnen
ðīgon pret. pl. of ðeon I.
ðīh=ðēoh
ðīhsl=ðīsl
-ðīht v. maga-ð., mete-ð. and 'thight.'
ðihtig=ðyhtig
ðīhð pres. 3 sg. of ðeon I.

ðīl-=ðyl-
ðilian (e, y) to lay with planks, board over, Æ. [Ger. dielen]
ðilic=ðyllic
ðilling f. boarding, floor : table, GD97⁴.
ðille n. thin board, plank, flooring, GL. [Ger. diele]
ðillian=ðilian; ðillic=ðyllic
ðimiama m. incense, Æ. [L. thymiama]
ðīn I. gs. of ðu. II. adj. pron. 'THINE,' thy. III.=ðigen I.
ðīnan to grow moist, LCD13b.
ðinc=ðing
ðincan=(1) ðyncan; (2) ðencan
+ðincðo=+ðyncðo
+ðind n. swelling, LCD,WW.
ðindan³ to swell, swell up, Æ : (wrongly, through confusion betw. 'tabescere' and 'tumescere') melt, pass away, PPs111⁹, 118¹⁵⁸ : be angry.
ðīnen f. maid-servant, handmaid, Æ : midwife, Æ. [ðegn]
ðing n. 'THING,' creature, Æ : object, property, Æ : cause, motive, reason, Æ : lawsuit : event, affair, act, deed, enterprise, Æ, CP : condition, circumstances, Æ : contest, discussion, meeting, council, assembly : court of justice, v. LL2·449 : point, respect. mid nānum ðingum adv. not at all. for his ðingum for his sake. for ðisum ðingum for this reason. be fullum ðingum abundantly. ænige ðinga anyhow, in any way, somehow. raðost ðinga at the earliest. ælces ðinges entirely, in every respect.
ðingan to invite, address? GL.
+ðingan I. sv³ to thrive. II.=ðingian
+ðinge n. meeting, council : arrangement, agreement, covenant : intercession : fate.
±ðingere m. advocate, intercessor, mediator, priest, GL,CP.
ðingestre f. female advocate, mediatrix, HL 10⁶⁹⁸.
ðinggemearc n.† reckoning of time, allotted time.
ðingian (w. d.) to beg, pray, ask, intercede for, LL,Sat; CP : covenant, conciliate, compound with, settle : prescribe : (refl.) reconcile oneself (with) : determine, purpose, design, arrange : talk, harangue. ['thing']
ðinglēas free (from sin or crime), LL412.
ðingrǣden f. intercession, pleading, mediation, intervention, Æ.
+ðingsceat m. ransom, CP339¹⁰.
ðingstede† m. place of assembly.
ðingstōw f. meeting-place, place of council : place where ways meet, village : market.
+ðingð f. intercession, agreement : court where claims are settled? (BTs), LL228,1¹.
+ðingðo=+ðyncðo

ðingum adv. (instr. pl. of ðing) *purposely*.
±ðingung f. *advocacy, intercession, mediation*, Æ,CP.
ðinn-=ðynn-
ðinne asm. of ðin II.
ðinnen=ðinen
ðinra=ðynra comp. of ðynne.
ðinra gp. of ðin II.
ðint pres. 3 sg. of ðindan.
ðio, ðio-=ðeo, ðeo-
ðir f. *a female servant*, JnLR18¹⁷. [ON. ðir]
ðird- (NG)=ðrid-
ðire=ðinre gdsf. of ðin II.
ðirel=ðyrel; ðirl-=ðyrl-
ðirnet=ðyrniht
ðirsceflōr, ðirscelflōr=ðerscelflōr
ðirsceð pres. 3 sg. of ðerscan.
ðirscwald=ðerscold; ðirst=ðurst
ðis v. ðes; ðisa=ðissa gp. of ðes.
ðisan=ðisum dsmn. of ðes.
ðises gsmn. of ðes.
ðīsl f., ðīsle f. *waggon-pole, pole, shaft*. [Ger. deichsel]
ðislic=ðyllic; ðism=dism
ðisne as. of ðes.
ðison=ðisum dsmn. of ðes.
ðissa gp., ðisse, ðissere gdsf.; ðisson, ðissum dsmn. and dp. of ðēs.
ðistel (y¹) m. '*thistle*,' Gl,WW; Mdf.
ðistelgeblæd n. *blister caused by thistle*, Lcd162b.
ðistellēag m. *thistle-covered meadow?* KC 5·265²².
ðisteltwige f. *a kind of bird, goldfinch? linnet?* GL.
ðisternes (CP)=ðēostornes
ðistr-=ðēostr-
ðistra m. *trace, article of harness?* WW.
ðisum dsmn. and dp. of ðēs.
ðiðer=ðider
ðiustra '*ambulas*' (*amplas?*) Cp535A.
ðīw-=ðȳw-, ðēow-; ðīxl (GL)=ðīsl
ðō f. *clay, loam*, GL. [Ger. ton]
ðōcerian, ðocrian *to run up and down*, WW.
ðōddettan *to strike, push*, W.
ðōden (ō?) n. *whirlwind, high wind, whirlpool*, Æ,Cp,CP,Chr. ['*thode*']
ðōdor=ðōðor
ðoft, ðofte f. *bench for rowers*, WW. ['*thoft*']
+ðofta m. *comrade, mate*, Æ,AO : *follower, client*.
+ðoftian *to join, unite, associate* (wið), AO.
±ðoftræden f. *fellowship*, Æ.
±ðoftscipe m. *companionship*, W : *alliance* CP : *intimacy*, Chrd67³⁴.
+ðogen *adult* : *virtuous, excellent*. [pp. of ðēon]
ðōh (GL)=tōh

ðōhe f. *clay*, GL (=ðō).
±ðōht (+exc. N) mn. *process of thinking*, '*thought*' : *mind* : *a thought, idea, purpose* : *decree* : *compassion, 'viscera*,' LkLR 1⁷⁸. [ðencan]
+ðohta=+ðofta
ðōhte pret. 3 sg. of ðencan.
+ðōhtung f. *counsel*, ZDA21·189.
ðōiht *clayey*, WW348¹¹.
ðol m. '*thole*,' *oar-pin*, Cp,WW.
ðolebyrde *patient*, Sc. ['*tholeburde*']
ðolebyrdnes f. *endurance*, Sc3⁸(i²). ['*tholeburdness*']
ðolemōd=ðolmōd
±ðolian *to suffer, endure, undergo*. B,CP, Gen,MkL; AO : *allow*, KC : *persevere, hold out* (intr.), *remain, survive* : (w. g.) *to lose, lack, forfeit, dispense with*, Æ. ['*thole*']
ðoll=ðol
ðolle f. *saucepan*, OEG4115.
ðolmōd I. *forbearing, patient*, Æ,HL,Sc, OEG. II. m. *patience?* ÆL16³³⁴D. ['*tholemode*']
ðolmōdnes f. *forbearance, patience*, Æ. ['*tholemodeness*']
ðolo-=ðol(e)-
ðolung f. *passion*, Sc.
ðon I. instr. sing. of sē. II. adv. *then, now* : *thence* : (in negative clauses, with comparatives) *in comparison with* : *inasmuch as, when*. æfter ðon *after that*. ær ðon *before that* (antequam). nō ðon lange... *not long until*..., tō ðon *to that extent, so that, after that*. III. (VPs)=ðonne
ðōn=ðǣm; ðonan=ðanon; ðonc-=ðanc
ðone asm. of sē *the, that*.
ðonēcan=ðanēcan; ðonen=ðanon
ðong=ðanc
ðonne (a, æ) adv. and conj. THEN*, AO; CP : *therefore, wherefore* : *yet* : *while, when* : *thereafter, henceforth* : *rather than*, Ps : *since* : *although* : (with comparatives) '*than*,' Æ,CP. ðonne...ðonne *when...then*. ð. hwæðere *yet, nevertheless*. ð. gȳt *as yet, even*. ð. ðe *since*.
ðonon=ðanon
Ðor m. *Thor*, W; Lcd.
ðorf (NG)=ðeorf
ðorfæst *useful*, DR,LkR. [ðearf]
ðorfend=ðearfend
ðorfnian v. ðornian.
ðorfte pret. 3 sg. of ðurfan.
ðorh (VPs)=ðurh; ðorhniht=ðorniht
ðorlēas *useless*, NG. [ðearf]
ðorn m. '*thorn*,' *thorn-bush*, Æ,Bo,Cr,G,Gl; CP; Mdf : *name of the rune for* ð, Run.
ðorngeblæd n. *blister caused by a thorn*, Lcd 162b.
ðornian *to lose*, v. MFH174. [for ðorfnian?]

ðornig '*thorny*,' *Æ,W.*
ðorn-iht, -eht(e) *thorny*, GL,KC.
ðorning m. *thorny place*, BC1·480[8] (Mdf).
ðornrind f. *thorn-bark*, LCD19a.
ðorof (*MtL*)=ðeorf
ðorp (ðrop) m. *farm* : *village*, Chr,Gl. ['*thorp*']
ðorscen pp. of ðerscan.
ðost m. *dung*, Lcd. ['*thost*']
+ðōt=+ðēot
ðoterian (o²) *to cry, howl, lament*, Æ.
ðoterung f. *groaning, wailing*, Æ.
ðotor-, ðotr-=ðoter-
ðōð (CHR1135)=ðēah I.
ðōðor, ðōðer m. *ball*, AS,GL.
ðox=dox; ðrā=ðrēa
+ðracen *hardy*, WW108[25].
ðracian *to fear, dread, shun*, RHy9[50].
ðracu† f., gs. ðræce *pressure, fury, storm, violence* : *onrush, attack*.
±ðræc (usu. +) n. *throng* : *pressure, force, violence* : *equipment*, OEG.
ðræcful? (e) *strong*, RPs58[4].
ðræcheard *brave in battle*, EL123.
ðræchwīl f. *time of misery*, JUL554.
ðræcian=ðracian
ðræcrōf *keen in fight*, GEN2030.
ðræcswald=ðerscold
ðræcwīg m. *violent combat*, EX182.
ðræcwudu (e¹) m. *spear*, B1246.
ðrǣd (ē) m. '*thread*,' *Bo,Cp,Lcd*; Æ.
+ðræf n. *pressure*, CHRD12[6]. (*or* +ðrafu)
+ðræf (on) *unanimously* (Swt).
ðræft n. *contentiousness*, MOD42.
ðrægan† *to run*, EL.
ðræging=ðrēagung
ðrǣl (ēa) m. *serf*, '*thrall*,' LL,NG.
ðrǣlriht n. *serf's right*, W158[15].
ðrǣs (ē) *fringe, hem*, GL.
ðrǣscan=ðræstan; ðrǣsce (Cp)=ðrysce
ðrǣst=dærst
±ðrǣstan *to writhe, twist, press, force*, BH : *crush, oppress, torment, constrain, bind*, GL : *destroy*. [v. '*threst*,' '*i-thrast*']
+ðrǣstednes f. *contrition*, GD : *crushing*, WW.
ðrǣstnes f. *trouble, pain, grief* : (+) *contrition*.
ðrǣstung f. *affliction, torment*, CP317[7].
ðrǣwen=ðrāwen pp. of ðrāwan.
ðrǣwung=ðrēagung; ðrǣxwold=ðerscold
ðraflan *to restrain, reprove*, CP : *urge, push, press*, Æ : *demand*, CHRD12[10].
+ðrafu? f. *compulsion*, CHRD12[6].
ðrafung f. *reproof, correction*, CP.
ðrāg f. *space of time, time, while, period, season*, Gen,Jul : *occasion*, B,Bl,Bo : *evil times* : *paroxysm*. ðrāge *for a time, some time, long time*. ðrāgum *at times, some-*

times. ealle ðrāge *all the time, continually*. ['*throw*']
ðrāgbysig *long busy?* RD5¹.
ðrāglic (ðrah-) *long-continued*, MFH175.
ðrāgmǣlum† *at times, sometimes*.
ðrāh=ðrāg; ðrāll=ðrēal, ðræl
ðrang pret. 3 sg. of ðringan.
+ðrang n. *throng, crowd, tumult*, MA299.
±ðrāwan[7] *to turn, twist, curl*, Æ,Gl; CP : *rack*. ['*throw*']
ðrāwere m. *perverse person*, APs17[27].
ðrāwingspinl f. *crisping-pin*, OEG.
ðrāwu (GL)=ðrēa; ðrē=ðrēo
ðrēa I. mfn. *threat, menace, abuse*, CP : *rebuke, castigation* : *oppression, attack* : *calamity, throe*. [ðrēowan] II. imperat. of ðrēagan.
ðreacs=ðreax
ðrēade pret. 1, 3 sg. of ðrēagan.
±ðrēagan, ðrēawian (ē) *to rebuke, chastise, correct, punish*, CP,Mt; Æ : *threaten, menace* : *attack, oppress, torture, afflict, vex, harass*. ['*threa*']
ðrēagend m. *reprover*, OEG5380.
ðrēagung (ǣ, ēaw-) f. *threatening, reproof, correction*, Æ,CP.
ðreahs=ðreax
ðrēal I. f. *discipline, correction, punishment*, Æ : *reproof* : *threat*. II.=ðrǣl
ðrēalic† *severe, terrible, calamitous*, GEN.
ðrēan (Æ)=ðrēagan; ðrēanēd=ðrēanīed
ðrēang=ðrēagung
ðrēanīed (ē², y²)† f. *affliction, misery, distress, calamity*.
ðrēanīedla (ē², ȳ²)† m. *affliction, misfortune*.
ðrēanīedlic *calamitous*, JUL128.
ðrēanȳd=ðrēanied
ðrēap m. *troop, band*, DD,DHy,OEG.
ðrēapian *to reprove, correct*, CP165[17]. ['*threap*']
ðrēapung f. *reproof*, CP167[14]. ['*threaping*']
ðrēaswinge f. *chastisement*, APs37[18].
ðrēat I. (ēo) m. *press, crowd, throng, host, troop*, B,El,Mk : *oppression, coercion, calamity, Bl,Jul : threatening?* Æ. ['*threat*'] II. pret. 3 sg. of ðrēotan.
ðrēatend m. *violent person*, MtL.
ðrēatian *to urge, press, force, attack, harass*, Æ,Cp,MH,MtL : *threaten*, PPs : *reprove, rebuke, check*, PPs; Æ,CP. ['*threat*']
ðrēatmǣlum (ē) adv. *in swarms*, WW31[27].
ðrēatnes f. *affliction, tribulation*, MFH117.
ðrēatnian (Æ)=ðrēatian ['*threaten*']
ðrēatung f. *threatening, compulsion, ill-usage*, AO : *correction, reproof*, CP.
ðrēaung=ðrēagung
ðrēaw pret. 3 sg. of ðrēowan.
ðrēawend=ðrōwend
ðrēaweorc n. *misery*, GEN737. [*OS.*]

ðrēawian, ðrēawung=ðrēag-ian, -ung

ðreax (e) *rottenness, rubbish, refuse*, BAS 48²⁰; ÆL35¹⁵⁰. [*ON.* ðrekkr; v. ES43·332]

ðrec=ðræc

ðrece m. *force, violence*, W : *weariness*, LPs. [ðracu]

ðrecswald=ðerscold; ðrēd (*Cp*)=ðrǣd

ðrefe *a measure of corn or fodder*, BC 3·367. ['*thrave*']

+ðrēgan=+ðrēan; ðrēgian=ðrǣgan

ðrehtig=ðrohtig; ðremm=ðrymm

ðrēo v. ðrīe; ðreo-=ðri-

ðreodian (y) *to think over, deliberate* : *meditate* : (+) *resolve*, GD.

ðreodung (i) f. *deliberation, consideration*, BH : *scruple, hesitation*, W.

ðreohtig=ðrohtig

ðreohund n. *three hundred*, Æ.

ðreohundwintre *of the age of three hundred years*, GEN 5¹³.

ðreom v. ðrīe.

ðrēoniht f. *period of three days*, PA38.

ðrēora v. ðrīe

ðrēostru=ðēostru; ðrēot=ðrēat

ðrēotan² *to vex, weary*, AS47².

ðrēotēoða (ȳ) '*thirteenth*,' Æ,MH (-tegða), Mt; AO.

ðrēotīne (ē², ȳ²) '*thirteen*,' BH,Men.

ðrēotīnegeare *thirteen years old*, MH216¹⁶.

ðrēott-=ðrēot-

ðrēow I. pret. 3 sg. of ðrāwan. II.=ðrīe

ðrēowian=ðrōwian; ðreoxwold=ðerscold

ðrep? '*fornix*,' Ln34⁵⁹ (drep).

ðrepel=ðrypel; ðrerēore=ðrirēðre

ðrēs-=ðrǣs; ðrescan=ðerscan

ðrescold, ðrescwald=ðerscold

ðrēst-=ðrǣst-; ðrēt=(1) ðrēat; (2) ðrǣd

ðrēung=ðrēaung; ðrex=ðreax

ðrex-=ðersc-; ðrī=ðrīe; ðria=ðriwa

ðribeddod (y) *three-bedded, having three couches*, WW184²⁴.

ðriccan=ðryccan

ðridæglic (eo, y) *lasting three days*, BH 350³².

ðridǣled (eo, y) *tripartite*, OEG.

ðridda (y) num. adj. '*third**,' Bl,Cr,Lcd, LG; AO,CP. ðridde healf *two and a half*.

ðriddandǣl m. *third part*, LL.

ðridung=ðreodung

ðrīe (ī, ȳ) num. nam.; nafn. ðrēo; gmfn. ðrēora; dmfn. ðrim (ðreom) '*THREE**.'

ðrie-=ðri-; ðrīeste=ðrīste adv.

ðrīetan *to weary* : *force*, Bo.

ðrifeald '*three-fold*,' Æ,RB.

ðrifealdlic *three-fold, triple.* adv. -lice *in three ways*, LL. ['*threefoldly*']

ðrifeoðor=ðrifeðor

ðrifēte '*three-footed*,' ÆGr.

ðrifeðor *triangular*, GL.

ðrifingre (y) *three fingers broad or thick*, LL 110,49³.

ðriflēre (y) *three-storied*, ÆH 2·70¹⁷.

ðri-fotede, -fotad (y) '*three-footed*,' WW.

ðrifyldan (=ie) *to triplicate*, ÆGR287⁴.

ðrifyrede *three-furrowed*, ÆGR288¹²n.

ðrig=ðrīe; ðriga=ðriwa

ðrigǣrede (eo¹) *three-pronged*, ÆGR288¹⁰.

ðrigēare *three years old* : *space of three years*.

ðrigylde I. adj. *subject to three-fold payment, or compensation*, LL. II. adv. LL.

ðrihēafdede (y) '*three-headed*,' ÆGr67¹¹.

ðrihing=ðriðing

ðrihīwede (y) *having three forms*, ÆGR 287¹⁰.

ðrihlidede (y) *having three openings*, ÆGR 288⁶.

ðri-hyrne, -hyrnede (eo) *three-cornered*, Æ, LCD.

ðrilēfe (y) *three-leaved.* as sb.=*trefoil? wood-sorrel?* WW133²². ['*threeleaf*']

ðrilen (WW151³⁴, y), ðrilig, ðrili adj. *woven with three threads*, Gl; LV. ['*thrile*']

ðrilic (y) *triple, three-fold*, VHy.

ðrilīðe n. *year with an extra month* (*a third, named* līða), v. BT.

ðrim I.=ðrymm. II. v. ðrīe.

ðrim-=ðrym-

ðrimen (y) *a third part*, LCD47a.

Ðri-meolce, -milce n. *May*, MH.

ðrimilcemōnað (y¹, y²) m. *May*, MEN (v. CHRp276).

ðrims, ðrimse=trymes; ðrindan=ðrintan

ðrinen (y) *three-fold*, CM.

Ðrines f. *Trinity*, Æ,BH,Bl,Cr,DR. ['*three-ness*,' '*thrinness*']

+ðring (y) n. *crowd, pressure, commotion*, An; ÆL. ['*thring*']

±ðringan³ *to press, squeeze, crowd upon, throng, press forward, rush on, hasten, advance*, AO : *oppress* : (+) *pinch* (*with cold*) : *gain* (*by force*). ['*THRING**']

ðrinihte *three days old*, LCD.

ðrinlic *three-fold*, NC327.

ðrinna *three-fold, three times*, LL. ['*thrin*']

Ðrinnes (Æ)=Ðrines

ðrintan³ *to swell*, MOD24.

ðrīo=ðrēo, v. ðrīe.

ðriostr-(KGL)=ðēostr-

ðrirēðre *with three rows of oars.* as sb. *trireme*, AO (īe).

ðrisce=ðrysce; ðriscelflōr=ðerscelflōr

ðriscȳte (y¹) *triangular*, AO. [scēat]

ðrislite (ie) *tripod, three-forked*, A4·151.

ðrisnæcce (y¹, e²) *three-forked*, ÆGR288¹².

ðrīsnes=ðrīstnes

ðrīst, ðrīste I. adj. *daring, rash, bold* : *audacious, shameless*, CP,W. II. adv. *boldly, daringly.* ['*thriste*'; *Ger.* dreist] ðrīstelic=ðrīstiglic

ðrīstful *presumptuous*, CM369.

ðrīsthycgende† *brave-minded*.

ðrīsthȳdig† *bold, valorous*, B.

+ðrīstian *to dare, presume*, BH,LL.

ðrīstiglic *rash, bold, daring*. adv. -līce.

±ðrīstlǣcan *to presume, dare*, CP.

ðrīstlǣcnes f. *boldness*, GD.

+ðrīstlǣcung f. *presumption*, MFH164.

ðrīstlēasnes f. *want of boldness?* A11·101.

ðrīstlic *bold*, MFH. adv. -līce.

ðrīstling m. *bold person?* (BT), *thrush* (Mdf), EC450¹⁵.

ðrīstlong *very long?* (or=ðrīstling?) BC 3·618.

ðrīstnes f. *rashness, boldness*, CM,Sc.

ðrīstra=ðīstra

ðrīstrenge (eo, y) *three-stringed*, ÆGR288¹⁰.

ðrīt (Æ) pres. 3 sg. of ðrīetan.

ðrītig 'THIRTY,' Æ; AO,CP.

ðrītigfeald 'thirty-fold,' Mt.

ðrītigoða (ēo, ȳ, tt) 'thirtieth,' ÆGr,BH,Mt.

ðrītigwintre *thirty years old*, Æ.

ðrīttēoða=ðrēotēoða

ðrittig=ðrītig; ðrīð=ðrȳð

ðrīðing *third part of a county*, 'riding,' LL.

ðrīðinggerēfa m. *governor or sheriff of a* 'ðrīðing,' LL.

ðriwa adv. *thrice*, Mk,RB; AO. ['thrie']

ðriwin-tre, -tra, -ter *three years old*, WW. [v. 'thrinter']

ðroc n. *table*, Mk11¹⁵ : *piece of wood on which the ploughshare is fixed*, WW219⁶. ['throck']

ðroehtig=ðrohtig

ðrōh I. 'rancor,' GL. II. 'rancidus,' OEG.

ðroht† I. m. *exertion, labour, endurance, toil, trouble, suffering*. II. adj. *dire, troublesome, tormenting*.

ðrohtheard† *strong in enduring*, AN,EL : *hard to endure*, EL.

ðrohtig (e? eo) *enduring, persistent, persevering, laborious*.

ðrong=ðrang pret. 3 sg. of ðringan.

ðrop=ðorp; ðrosle=ðrostle

ðrosm m. *smoke, vapour*, Æ.

ðrosmig *vaporous, smoky*, W138²⁶.

ðrostle (ō?) f. 'throstle,' *thrush*, BC,Cp,GD.

ðrota (WW306¹³)=ðrote

ðrotbolla m. *gullet, windpipe, larynx*, Æ, Gl,LL. ['throatboll']

ðrote, ðrotu f. 'throat,' Æ,Bo,WW.

ðroten pp. of ðrēotan.

ðrotu (Æ)=ðrote; ðrōung=ðrōwung

ðrōwend m. *serpent, scorpion, basilisk*, Æ.

ðrōwend-=ðrōwiend-

ðrōwere m. *sufferer, martyr*, DR,LCD.

ðrōwerhād, ðrōwethād m. *martyrdom*, GD.

±ðrōwian (o?) *to endure, suffer, die*, Æ,B, Bl,Bo; AO,CP : *pay for, atone for* : *sympathise*. ['throw']

ðrōwiendhād (e²) m. *martyrdom*, GD231⁸c.

ðrōw-iendlic, -igendlic *suffering, enduring, passive*, Æ. ð. dēað *apoplexy*.

ðrōwung f. *suffering : passion, martyrdom*, Æ,CP : *painful symptom : anniversary of martyrdom*. ['throwing']

ðrōwungrǣding f. *reading about martyrs, martyrology*, CM286.

ðrōwung-tīd f., -tīma n. *time of suffering*, Æ.

+ðrūen pp. of ðweran.

ðrūh fmn. *pipe, trough*, Gl,MH : *chest* : *tomb, coffin*, Æ,BH ['through']

ðrum=ðrim v. ðrie.

-ðrum v. tunge-ð. ['thrum']

ðrungen pp., ðrungon pret. pl. of ðringan.

ðrustfell n. *leprosy*, Cp103B.

-ðrūt v. fisc-ð.

ðrūtigende *strutting, bouncing*, Æ : *threatening*, ÆL10²⁷³.

ðruton pret. pl. of ðrēotan.

ðrūtung *anger, pride : threatening*, ÆL7⁷⁶.

ðrūðhorn=truðhorn; ðrȳ=ðrīe, ðrī

ðryan=ðryn

±ðryccan pret., ðrycte, ðryhte (tr.) *to trample on, crush, oppress, afflict, repress*, Bo; CP : (intr.) *press, push*, Gu. ['thrutch']

±ðryccednes f. *distress, trouble*, RWH67³².

ðrycnes f. *tribulation, affliction*, MtR.

ðryd-=ðrid-, ðreod-; ðrȳd-=ðrȳð-

+ðrȳde pret. 3 sg. of +ðrȳn.

ðrȳh=ðrūh

ðryhte pret. 3 sg. of ðryccan.

ðryl=ðyrl, ðyrel

+ðrȳl n. *crowd, multitude*, ÆL23⁹². [ðrȳn]

ðrym=ðrymm

ðrymcyme m. *glorious coming*, Gu1230.

ðrymcyning† m. *glorious king, king of glory, God*.

ðrymdōm m. *glory*, W254¹⁴D.

ðrymen=ðrimen

ðrymfæst† *glorious, illustrious, noble, mighty*.

ðrymful† *glorious, majestic, peerless*.

ðrymilce=ðrimeolce

ðrymlic *glorious, magnificent*, AO : *powerful, mighty*. adv. -līce.

ðrymm m. *multitude, host, troop*, ÆL,Cr : *torrent : force, power, might, ability : glory, majesty, splendour*, Bl. ['thrum']

ðrymma m. *brave man, hero*, AN1141.

ðrymme, ðrymmum adv. *powerfully, violently*.

ðrymrīce n. *realm of glory, heaven*, BL105¹¹.

ðrymsa=trymes

ðrym-seld n., -setl (Æ) n. *seat of honour, throne*.

ðrymsittende† ptc. *sitting in glory, dwelling in heaven,* AN.

ðrymwealdend I. adj. *all-ruling,* Æ. II. m. *lord of glory.*

+ðrȳn *to press, bind,* v. NC328 : *repress* : *express.*

ðrync (AO76³⁴)=drinc imperat. of drincan.

ðrynen=ðrinen; Ðrynes=Ðrines

ðryng sb. *conduit, channel?* (=ðring?) WW 198¹⁴.

Ðrynnes (Æ)=Ðrines; ðryosm=ðrosm

ðrȳpel (ē) m. *instrument of torture, cross?* WW225⁴¹. [ðrēapian].

ðrȳpelūf *'eculeus,' 'catasta,'* WW180¹³.

+ðryscan *to weigh down, afflict, oppress,* CP. [ðerscan]

ðrysce (æ, i) *'thrush,'* WW.

ðryscel-=ðerscel-

±ðrysman, +ðrysmian *to press, oppress, stifle,* AO. [ðrosm]

ðryssce=ðrysce; ðrȳst=ðrīst

ðrȳst-=ðēost-

ðrȳt pres. 3 sg. of ðrēotan.

ðrȳð† f. (often in pl.) *might, power, force, strength* : *majesty, glory, splendour* : *multitude, troop, host.*

ðrȳðærn n. *noble house, palace,* B657.

ðrȳðbearn n. *strong youth,* AN494.

ðrȳðbord n. *strong shield,* EL151.

ðrȳðcyning m. *king of glory, God,* AN436.

+ðrȳðed *mighty,* PH486.

ðrȳðful (†) *strong, brave* : *splendid, glorious,* VH.

ðrȳðfullian (ðrȳð-) *to fill up,* RPs130¹.

ðrȳðgesteald n.*noble dwelling, palace,* CR354.

ðrȳðig *mighty, strong,* GEN1986?

ðrȳðlic *strong, valiant,* B. adv. -līce (?), B.

ðrȳðo=ðrȳð

ðrȳðswȳð† n. *mighty, powerful,* B.

ðrȳðu=ðrȳð

ðrȳðum† *very, violently.*

ðrȳðweorc n. *mighty work,* AN774.

ðrȳðword n. *lofty discourse,* B643.

ðu (ū) pron. 2 pers., gs. ðīn, das. ðe, ðec; dual n. git, gīt, g. incer, d. inc, a. incit, inc; np. gē, gīe. gp. ēower, dp. ēow, ap. ēowic, ēow *'THOU*.'*

ðūf m. *tuft* : *banner, standard, crest.* [L. tufa]

+ðūf *thriving, luxuriant,* WW.

ðūfbǣre *leafy,* OEG2222.

ðūfeðistel=ðūðistel

ðūflan *to shoot forth, grow luxuriantly,* WW 408².

ðūfig *leafy,* WW408³.

ðūft m. *thicket,* WW408¹⁴.

ðugon pret. pl. of ðēon.

+ðūhslan *to make misty, dark,* W137⁹.

ðūhte pret. 3 sg. of ðyncan.

+ðuhtsum *abundant,* MH138¹⁵.

ðullic=ðyllic

ðūma m. *'thumb,'* Ep,Lcd,LL.

ðumle sbpl. *entrails,* Cp210u.

+ðun n. *loud noise,* PPs,WW.

ðunar=ðunor

ðunden pp. of ðindan.

ðunelic=ðunorlic

ðuner, ðuner-=ðunor, ðun(o)r-

ðung m. *a poisonous plant, wolf's-bane, aconite, nightshade?* GL.

+ðungen *full grown, thriven* : *competent, excellent, distinguished, virtuous,* ÆL. as sb. *notable, king's thane.* [pp. of ðēon]

+ðungenlīce adv. *virtuously, soberly,* WW.

±ðungennes f. *growth, maturity* : *goodness, excellence, virtue, perfection.*

ðunian *to stand out, be prominent* : *be proud* : *roar, thunder, crash, groan.*

ðunnung=ðūnung; ðunnur=ðunor

ðunor (e², u²) m., gs. ðun(o)res *'thunder,'* AO,Cp,Jn,Rd : *thunder-clap,* Lcd : *the god Thunder, Thor* : *Jupiter.*

ðunor-=ðunr-

ðunorbodu f. *sea-bream?* WW180³⁴.

ðunorclǣfre f. *bugle (plant),* LCD.

ðunorlic (e²) *thundery,* OEG.

ðunorrād f. *thunder, thundering,* Æ.

ðunorrādlic *thundering,* HGL451⁴⁶.

ðunorrādstefn f. *voice of thunder,* PPs76¹⁴.

ðunorwyrt f. *thunder-wort, houseleek,* LCD.

Ðunresdæg m. *'Thursday,'* LL.

ðunreslege m. *thunder-clap,* RWH83,85.

Ðunresniht f. *Thursday eve, Wednesday night.*

±ðunrian *to 'thunder,'* Bo,Jn (impers.) : PPs (pers.).

ðunring f. *thundering,* CHR1085.

ðunung f. *creaking, noise, din,* WW.

ðunur, ðunur-=ðunor, ðun(o)r-

ðun-wang (e, o), -wange (æ, e) f. (n?) *temple (of the head),* Æ,WW. [*'thunwang'*]

Ður=Ðor

ðuren=ðworen pp. of ðweran.

Ðuresdæg=Ðunresdæg

ðurfan swv. pres. 1, 3 sg. ðearf, pl. ðurfon, pret. sg. ðorfte; subj. pres. ðurfe, ðyrfe *to need, be required* : *must, have occasion to,* CP : *want, be needy* : *be under an obligation, owe.* [*'THARF*'; ðearf]

ðurg=ðurh prep.

ðurh (e, o) I. prep. (w. d. a. g.) (space) *'THROUGH'* (*'thorough'*), G : (time) *through, during,* PPs : (causal : agent, means, instrument) *through, by, by means of, in consequence of, because of.* ðurh ealle *entirely* : (manner) *in, with, by, in conformity with* : *for the sake of, in the name of* : (end, aim) *with a view to, on behalf of.* II. adv. *through, throughout.*

ðūrh=ðrūh
ðurharn pret. 3 sg. of ðurhiernan.
ðurhbeorht *very bright, transparent, radiant, clear,* Æ.
ðurhbiter *very bitter, sour, perverse,* CERPs 77⁸.
ðurhblāwan⁷ *to inspire, animate,* CM370.
ðurhborian *to bore through,* AA29¹⁷.
ðurhbrecan⁴ *to break through,* Æ,B.
ðurhbregdan³ *to draw through, transport.*
ðurhbrengan *to bring through,* LPs77¹³.
ðurhbrūcan² *to enjoy fully,* WW98¹.
ðurhburnen *thoroughly burnt,* LCD165b.
ðurhclǣnsian *to cleanse thoroughly,* MtR3¹².
ðurhcrēopan² *to creep or pass through,* Bo93⁵.
ðurhdelfan³ *to dig through, pierce,* Æ.
ðurhdrencan (æ²) *to saturate,* RWH138¹⁷.
ðurhdrēogan² *to work through, accomplish, pass (time),* CM.
ðurhdrīfan¹ *to drive or push through, strike : pierce, perforate : penetrate, imbue.*
ðurhdūfan² *to dive through,* B1619.
ðurhendian (e¹) *to accomplish, perfect,* LL 411,2².
ðurhetan⁵† *to eat through, consume,* WW.
ðurhfær n. *secret place,* Sc39².
ðurhfǣreld '*transitus,*' V²Ps143¹⁴.
ðurhfæstnian *to transfix,* JnLR19³⁷.
ðurhfaran⁶ *to pass through, traverse, penetrate, pierce,* CP.
ðurhfarennes f. *inner chamber,* ASPs104²⁸.
ðurhfēran *to pass through, traverse, penetrate,* BH. [' *thoroughfare*']
ðurhfēre I. *penetrable.* II. n. *secret chamber,* MkL24³⁶.
ðurhflēon² *to fly through,* BH136¹.
ðurhfōn⁷ *to penetrate,* B1504.
ðurh-gān anv., pret. -ēode *to go through, pass through, penetrate,* Æ. [' *throughgo*']
ðurhgangan⁷=ðurhgān
ðurhgefeht (o¹) n. *war,* Cp205ₚ.
ðurhgēotan² *to fill entirely, imbue, saturate, impregnate,* BH,W.
ðurhglēdan *to heat through,* DA244.
ðurhhǣlan *to heal thoroughly,* LCD.
ðurhhālig *most holy,* CHRD,GL.
ðurhhefig *very heavy,* GD104²⁶.
ðurhholod *bored through,* OEG4035.
ðurhhwīt *quite white,* WW163⁶.
ðurhiernan³ *to run through, pierce,* Æ,WW.
ðurhlǣran *to persuade,* Sc38¹².
ðurhlǣred *very learned, skilled,* WW118²³.
ðurhlāð *very hateful,* WW130²⁸.
ðurhlēor-an, -ian *to penetrate,* GD : *pass through,* JVPs.
ðurhleornian *to learn thoroughly,* GD136⁴.
ðurhlōcung f. *preface, introduction,* WW 172³⁸.

ðurhrǣsan *to rush through,* RD4³⁶.
ðurhscēotan² *to shoot through, pierce,* Æ,AO.
ðurhscīnan (ȳ) *to shine through, be transparent,* WW148⁷. [' *throughshine*']
ðurhscīnendlic *illustrious, splendid,* LPs 15⁶.
ðurhscrīðan¹ *to go through, traverse,* BF4³⁰ : *examine, consider :* þry into, BF142¹¹.
ðurhscyldig *very guilty,* ÆL11³²¹.
ðurhscȳne *transparent,* WW148⁷.
ðurhsēcan *to search through, inquire thoroughly into,* Sc209³. [' *throughseek*']
ðurhsēon⁵ *to look through, examine :* penetrate, Bo. [' *thoroughsee*']
ðurhslēan⁶ *to strike or pierce through,* Æ : *attack, afflict, kill.*
ðurhsmēagan *to search thoroughly, investigate, think out,* CHR,MH.
ðurhsmūgan² *to pierce, bore through, eat through : go through carefully or slowly.*
ðurhsmyrian *to smear, anoint,* W229³.
ðurhspēdig *very rich,* ÆH1·502⁸.
ðurhstandan *to continue,* GD200⁸.
ðurhsticcian (o¹) *to transfix,* JnL19³⁷.
ðurhstingan³ *to pierce through, thrust through, prick,* Æ; CP. [' *throughsting*']
ðurhstrang *very strong,* OEG50²⁵.
ðurhswimman³ *to swim through,* WW52¹.
ðurhswīðan *to prevail,* LPs51⁹.
ðurhswōgan *to penetrate,* BH430⁵ (v.l.).
ðurhsȳne (=īe) *limpid, transparent,* OEG 23³⁵.
ðurhtēon² *to carry or put through :* finish, *fulfil, carry out, effect,* Æ,AO,CP : *draw, drag : continue : afford : undergo.*
ðurhtogennes f. *a religious reading at monastic meal-times,* RBL118⁷.
ðurhtrymman (e¹) *to confirm,* JnLR10²⁵.
ðurhðrāwan *to twist through,* LCD.
ðurh-ðyddan, -ðȳn *to pierce, thrust through,* Æ.
ðurhðyrel (i²) *pierced through, perforated,* LL.
ðurh-ðyrelian (CP), -ðyrlian *to pierce, penetrate.*
ðurhunrot *very sad,* ZDA33·238¹¹.
ðurhūt prep. (w. a. CHR) adv. *right through,* Æ. [' *throughout*']
ðurhwacian *to keep vigil,* BL227⁷.
ðurhwacol (e⁸, u³) *wide-awake, sleepless,* Æ.
ðurhwadan⁶ *to penetrate, go through, bore, pierce.*
ðurhwæccan *to keep vigil,* LkL6¹².
ðurhwæcendlic *very vigilant,* ÆL23b⁴³.
ðurhwǣt *thoroughly wet,* ÆP172¹⁸.
ðurhwerod *quite sweet, very sweet,* GL.
ðurhwlītan¹† *to look through, see,* CR.
ðurhwrecan⁵ *to thrust through,* HL,WW.

ðurhwundian *to pierce through, wound badly,* LL 82,61¹.

ðurhwunenes f. *perseverance,* MFH 176.

ðurhwunian *to abide continuously, remain, continue, settle down,* Æ,AO,CP : *persevere, hold out, be steadfast,* CP.

ðurhwunigendlic *constant, continued.* adv. -līce.

ðurhwunol *perpetual,* CHRD 92¹⁷.

ðurhwunung f. *perseverance, persistency,* RB,Sc : *continued residence,* RB.

Ðurresdæg=Ðunresdæg

ðurruc m. *small ship? hold of a ship? WW* 181³⁵. [v. '*thurrock*']

ðurscon pret. pl. of ðerscan.

Ðursdæg (*Jn*)=Ðunresdæg

ðurst (y) m. '*thirst,*' *Bf,Lcd*; Æ,AO,VPs.

ðurstig (y) '*thirsty,*' *PPs,Mt*; Æ : *thirsting after, greedy, Bo.*

ðuru=duru; ðuruh=ðurh

ðus adv. '*THUS,*' *in this way : as follows : to this extent* (qualifying adjs.), Æ.

ðūsend num. (sbn., always followed by gen.) '*thousand,*' *Æ,AO,Chr*; CP.

ðūsend-ealdor, -ealdorman m. *captain of a thousand men,* v. OEG 4747.

ðūsendfeald '*thousand-fold,*' *Æ,W.*

ðūsendgerīm n. *computation by thousands,* SOL 290.

ðūsendgetel n. *a thousand,* ÆGR 284⁴.

ðūsendhīwe *multiform,* WW 101¹.

ðūsendlic adj. *of a thousand,* BL,WW.

ðūsendmæle? adj. *a thousand each, a thousand,* PPs,WW.

ðūsendmælum† adv. *in thousands,* SAT.

ðūsendmann m. *captain of a thousand,* Æ.

ðūsendrīca m. *chief of a thousand,* WW 110¹¹.

ðūsent-=ðūsend-; ðuslic=ðyllic

ðuss=ðus; ðūtan=ðēotan

ðūðistel m. *sow-thistle, Gl.* ['*thowthistle*']

+ðūxsian (DOM 105)=+ðūhsian

ðwā (NG)=ðwēa pres. 1 sg. of ðwēan.

ðwægen pp. of ðwēan.

ðwæl=ðwēal

ðwæle? (ē) f. *fillet? towel?* v. OEG 53²⁶.

±ðwænan *to soften, moisten,* BH,CP,LCD.

ðwæng=ðwang; ðwær-=ðwēr-

±ðwære (usu. +) *united, concordant, harmonious,* Æ : *compliant, obedient : agreeable, pleasant, gentle : peaceful : prosperous.* adv. -līce.

±ðwær-ian, -læcan¹ (ē) *to agree, consent to : reconcile : suit, fit.*

+ðwærlic *agreeing, harmonious : symmetrical,* BF 180¹. adv. -līce *gently.*

±ðwærnes f. *concord, peace,* CP : *gentleness.*

+ðwærung f. *consent,* Sc 228¹².

ðwagen rare pp. of ðwēan.

ðwāh (A)=ðwēah imperat. of ðwēan.

ðwang (æ, e) mf. '*thong,*' *band, strap, cord,* Æ,G,WW : *phylactery, MtL,R.*

ðwār-=ðwēr-; ðwarm=ðwearm

ðwastrian *to whisper,* HL 18³⁸¹.

ðwāt pret. 3 sg. of ðwītan.

ðwēa pres. 1 sg. of ðwēan.

ðwēal (æ, ē) n. *washing, bath, laver,* CP,JnL 12³ : *soap,* ES 43·334 : *ointment.* [*Goth.* ðwahl]

±ðwēan⁶ *to wash, cleanse,* Æ,CP : *anoint,* MtL 6¹⁷.

ðwearm m? *cutting tool,* GL.

ðwēhl=ðwēal; ðwēle=ðwæle

ðwēnan=ðwænan; ðweng (NG)=ðwang

ðwēor, ðweorg=ðweorh

+ðwēor v. buter-geð.

ðwēora m. *depravity : perversity,* CP 222⁸.

ðwēores adv. (gen. of ðweorh) *athwart, transversely, obliquely,* AO : *perversely.*

ðweorh adj., gmn. ðwēores *cross, transverse, bent, crooked : adverse : angry : perverse, depraved,* CP.

ðweorh-fero, -furu, -fyri *cross-furrow,* GL.

ðweorhtēme=ðweortīeme

ðweorian=ðweran

±ðwēorian *to oppose, thwart, be opposed to or far from.*

ðwēorlic *perverse, contrary, adverse,* Æ : *reversed, out of order.* adv. -līce *insolently,* GD.

±ðwēornes (ȳ) f. *perversity, frowardness, obstinacy, depravity,* Æ.

ðweorscipe m. *perversity,* CP 269⁶.

ðweortīeme (ē², ī², ȳ²) *contentious, perverse, wicked,* CP.

ðweoton (BH 204³²)=ðwiton pret. pl. of ðwītan.

ðwēr, ðwerh=ðweorh

±ðweran⁴ *to stir, churn* : (†) *beat, forge, render malleable, soften.*

ðwēre (æ) *pestle,* OET 102,103.

ðwihð (ie) pres. 3 sg. of ðwēan.

ðwīnan *to decrease, lessen,* LCD.

+ðwinglod *fastened up?* (BT), HL 18²¹⁸.

ðwīr=ðweorh

ðwiril m. *handle of a churn, whisk,* WW 280³¹. [ðweran]

+ðwit n. *cuttings,* BH 204³² (v.l.). [ðwītan]

ðwītan¹ *to cut, whittle, cut off, cut out,* BH, Lcd. ['*thwite*']

ðwōg, ðwōh pret. 3 sg., ðwogen pp. of ðwēan.

ðwong=ðwang

ðworen pp. of ðweran.

+ðwōrnes=+ðwēornes; ðwurh=ðweorh

ðwyhð pres. 3 sg. of ðwēan.

ðwȳr (Æ), ðwȳr-=ðweorh, ðwēor-

ðwȳrs=ðwēores
ðȳ I. pron. (instr. sing. of sē, ðæt). æfter ðȳ
after (that), later. II. conj. and adv. because, since, on that account : therefore, CP,
Lcd : then : (with comparatives) the. ðȳ...
ðȳ the...the. mid ðȳ while, when. tō ðȳ
ðæt for the purpose that, in order that. for
ðȳ ðe because. ðȳ lǣs (ðe) lest. ['thy']
ðȳan=ðȳn; ðȳc-=ðic-
ðȳdan=ðēodan
ðȳddan to strike, stab, Æ,CP : thrust, press,
Æ. ['thud']
+ðȳde (īe) good, virtuous, CRA 68.
ðȳder=ðider; ðȳf=ðēof
ðȳfel m. shrub, bush, copse, thicket, Æ,Lcd,
LPs,WW. ['thyvel'; ðūf]
ðȳfeðorn y? (ē, ēo, ī) m. hawthorn?
bramble? Gl,Lcd. ['thevethorn']
ðȳflen? (or ? ryplen) bushy, GPH 399⁴⁵⁷.
ðȳften f. handmaid, OEG. ['thuften']
ðȳfð=ðīefð; ðȳgan=ðȳn
+ðȳht pleasing, RIM 18.
ðȳhtig (i) strong, B1558.
ðȳhð pres. 3 sg. of ðēon.
ðȳlǣs conj. lest. ðȳ lǣs ðe lest.
ðȳlc=ðyllic
ðȳlcræft (e) m. elocution, rhetoric, OEG.
±ðȳld (usu. +) nf. patience, LkLR. ['thild']
±ðȳldelic patient. adv. -līce patiently,
quietly.
+ðȳld-ian, -(i)gian to be patient, bear, endure,
CP: give in, agree, OEG3237 : wait for, Ps.
±ðȳldig (usu. +) adj. patient, DR; Æ,CP.
[v. 'thild'] adv. -līce.
+ðȳldmōd patient, W72⁷.
+ðȳldmōdnes f. patience, NC297.
+ðȳldo (u²)=+ðȳld
+ðȳldum patiently, steadfastly, B1705.
ðȳle m. speaker, orator : jester, WW385³.
ðȳlian (Æ)=ðilian; ðȳling=ðiling
+ðȳll n. air, breeze, DR121¹⁸.
ðȳllan to calm, assuage, BH.
ðȳllic pron. such, such a, Æ,AO,CP.
['thellich']
+ðȳllic 'densus,' OEG5⁴ (?=+ðiclic; or
+ðȳllic, from ðȳn).
+ðȳlmed brought down, abashed, LPs19⁹.
ðȳmel m. thumbstall, 'thimble,' Lcd.
ðȳmele adj. of the thickness of a thumb, LL
110,49³.
ðȳn (1)=ðīn; (2) (±)=ðȳwan, ðēowan
±ðȳncan (i) (impers. w. d.) pret. 3 sg. ðūhte
to appear, seem, CP; AO. mē ðyncð
methinks. him ðūhte it seemed good to
him. ['THINK*']
±ðȳneðo (i) f. dignity, rank, office, Æ,CP :
meeting, assembly, court of justice, LL :
private arrangement (to defeat justice),
LL112,52.

ðȳnden=ðenden
+ðȳnge=+ðinge
±ðȳngo progress, promotion, N.
ðȳnhlǣne wasted, shrunk, WW446²¹.
ðȳnne (i) 'thin,' BH,Lcd,RB : lean, Lcd,
WW : not dense, Æ,BC : fluid, tenuous,
BH,Lcd,Met : weak, poor, BH,Lcd.
ðȳnnes (i) f. lack of density, tenuity, fluidity,
Lcd73b : poverty, feebleness (of sight),
Lcd1·134. ['thinness']
±ðȳnnian (i) to 'thin,' make thin, lessen,
dilute, Æ,Gl,Lcd : become thin, ÆL.
ðȳnnol (u²) lean, thin, WW172¹⁶.
ðȳnnung, ðȳnung f. 'thinning,' act of
making thin, Lcd98a.
ðȳnwefen thin woven, WW439³⁴.
ðȳrel (ȳ?) I. n. hole, opening, aperture, perforation, BH,MtL,Sc,WW. II. adj. pierced,
perforated, full of holes, CP. ['thirl']
ðȳrelhūs n. turner's workshop, WW185³¹
(ðryl-).
ðȳrelian=ðyrlian
ðȳrelung f. piercing, CP153²⁵.
ðȳrelwamb with pierced belly, RD79¹¹.
ðȳrf=ðearf
ðȳrfe subj. pres. sing. of ðurfan.
ðȳrl=ðyrel
ðȳrlian (i) to perforate, pierce, excavate, Æ,
WW. ['thirl']
-ðȳrlic v. samod-ð.; ðȳrn=ðorn
ðȳrne f. thorn-bush, bramble, Æ; Mdf.
ðȳrnen thorny, of thorns, Æ,CP. ['thornen']
ðȳrnet n. thorn, bramble, thorn-thicket, OEG.
ðȳrniht, ðȳrnihte thorny, LCD.
ðȳrran to dry, render dry, RD29⁴.
ðȳrre withered : dry, Lcd. [Ger. dürr]
ðȳrs m. giant, demon, wizard, B,Cp; Mdf.
['thurse']
ðȳrscel==ðerscel
ðȳrscð pres. 3 sg. of ðerscan.
ðȳrscwold=ðerscold
ðȳrst=ðurst
+ðȳrst thirsty, MH170⁶.
ðȳrstan (pers. and impers.) to 'thirst,' thirst
after, AO,CP,G,Lcd,Sc. [ðurst]
+ðȳrstgian=+ðrīstian
ðȳs instr. smn. of ðēs.
ðȳs-=ðis-; ðȳslic=ðyllic
ðȳsma=disma
-ðȳssa v. brim-ð.
ðȳster=ðeostor; ðȳstr-=ðeostr-
ðȳt, ðȳtt pres. 3 sg. of ðēotan.
-ðȳtan v. ā-ð. [OHG. dōzōn]
ðȳðel (LPs79¹¹)=ðȳfel
ðȳðer=ðider; ðȳw-=ðēow-
±ðȳwan to press, impress, Æ : stab, pierce :
crush, push, oppress, check : threaten.
+ðȳwe=+ðēawe
ðȳwð=ðīefð

U

uce, ucu=wuce, wucu
ūder n. '_udder,_' WW 61[16].
udu (N)=wudu
ūf I. m. _owl,_ GL : _vulture,_ ÆGR 48[17]n. II.
m. _uvula,_ WW.
ufa=ufan
ufan (o) adv. _from above,_ Æ,AO,CP : _over,
above, on high,_ CP. on u.; u. on ðæt
besides. on u. hærfest _in late autumn._ on u.
midne winter _after Christmas._ [_Ger._ oben]
ufancumende _coming from above,_ GD 285[6].
ufancund _from above, supreme, divine,_ CP.
ufane=ufan
ufanweard adj. (often used w. d. as a prep.)
highest, topmost, Æ. ufanweardum _above,
at the top._
ufemest (superl. of uferra, ufor) _highest,
uppermost, topmost,_ Æ. ['_ovemest_']
ufen=ufan
ufenan, ufenon I. adv. _from above, Chr,Jn,
W._ II. prep. _over and above, DD._ on
ufenan _upon the top of._ ['_ovenon_']
ufera=uferra
±uferian (of-) _to delay, put off,_ Æ : (+)
raise up, elevate, BK 8 : _extol, honour,_ Æ.
[ufor]
uferor (u³) _higher,_ OEG 5058.
uferra comp. adj. _above, higher, upper, BH_ ;
CP : _outer, Lcd,WW_ : _after_ (of time), _later,
future, AO,Lcd_ ; CP. ['_over,_' '_uver_']
uferung f. _delay,_ GD 245[8].
ufeweard I. adj. _upward, ascending, upper,
higher up,_ Æ,CP : _later._ II. sb. _upper part,
outside,_ Æ.
ufewerd=ufeweard ; uffrian=uferian
ufon=ufan
ufor adv. _higher, further away, further up,_
Æ,CP : _later, posterior, subsequent._
ufora=uferra ; ufur=ufor
uf-weard, -werd=ufeweard
uht=wuht=wiht fn.
ūht m., ūhte f. _twilight, dusk, early morning,
dawn,_ Lcd : _nocturns._ on ūhtan _at day-
break, B,Bl._ tō ūhtes _towards dawn._
['_ughten_']
ūhtantīd=ūhttīd
ūhtantīma m. _time of nocturns,_ BTK 194[14].
ūhtcearu f. _sorrow at dawn,_ WIF 7.
ūhtentīd=ūhttīd
ūhtfloga m. _twilight-flier, dragon,_ B 2760.
ūhtgebed n. _morning prayer, matins,_ GUTH,
WW.
ūhthlem m. _crash at dawn,_ B 2007.
ūhtlic I. _morning, matutinal, of matins,_ BH.
II.=ūtlic
ūhtsang m. _morning song, matins, BH,RB_ :
nocturns. ['_uhtsong_']

ūhtsanglic _nocturnal, used at nocturns,_ CM
1014.
ūhtsceaða m. _twilight foe,_ B 2271.
ūhttīd f. _twilight, early morning, dawn, BH._
[v. '_ughten_']
ūhtðegnung f. _matins,_ WW 129[33].
ūhtwæcca f. _night watch, vigils,_ RB 40[10].
ūle f. '_owl,_' Æ,Cp.
ulf (JnL 10[12])=wulf
ulmtrēow n. _elm tree,_ WW 138[12]. ['_ulm-
tree_'; _L._]
ultur m. _vulture,_ Bo 102[33].
ūma m. _a weaver's beam,_ WW.
umb, umbe=ymb, ymbe
umbor n. _infant,_ GNE 31.
umborwesende† _being a child,_ B.
un- I negative or pejorative prefix. II.
occasionally=on- (prefix expressing reversal of a previous action) as in unbindan.
unābeden neg. ptc. _unbidden,_ Æ.
unābēgendlic=unābȳgendlic
unāberendlic _unbearable,_ Æ,CP. adv. -līce.
unāberiende _unbearable,_ LCD 3·260[23]n.
unābēt=ungebēt
unābindendlic _indissoluble,_ Bo.
unāblinn n. _irrepressible state, unceasing
presence,_ GUTH 46[10].
unāblinnend-e, -lic _unceasing, perpetual._
adv. -līce, Æ,AO,CP.
unāboht=ungeboht
unābrecendlic _inextricable,_ WW 419[2].
unābȳgendlic (ē) _inflexible,_ WW 421[30].
unācenned _unbegotten,_ ÆH 1·464'.
unācnycendlic _that cannot be untied or
loosened,_ DR 108[10]. [cnyccan]
un-ācumendlic (Æ), -ācumenlic _unbearable,
unattainable, impossible._
unācumenlicnes f. _unbearableness,_ RBL
114[9].
unācwencedlic _unquenchable,_ G.
unādrūgod _undried, not dried,·not hardened,_
CP 383[32].
unādrysn-ende, -en(d)lic _unquenchable,_ NG.
un-ādwǣsced, -ādwǣscendlic, -ādwēscedlic
inextinguishable, unquenchable, Æ.
unǣaðe=unēaðe
unǣfastlīce=unǣwfæstlīce
unǣm(et)ta m. _want of leisure, work, occupation, hindrance,_ CHRD,LL.
unǣmtigian _to deprive of leisure,_ AS 36[19].
unǣrh=unearg
unǣsecgenlic (EPs 100[6])=unāsēðendlic?
unǣt f. _gluttony,_ DEUT 21[20].
unǣtspornen _not hindered,_ GD 60[26].
unǣðelboren _not of noble birth, low-born,_ Æ.
unǣðele _of low birth, ignoble, base,_ CP.
unǣðelian (an-) _to degrade, debase,_ Bo,MET.
unǣðelīce adv. _ignobly, basely,_ BH 442[11].

unæðelnes f. *ignobility*, GD 151²⁴.
unǣwfæstlīce adv. *irreverently* : *unlawfully*.
unǣwisc (ē) '*pudicus*,' WW 291²⁵.
unāfandod *untried*, AS 32¹⁹.
unāfe(o)htendlic (æ³) *what cannot be contended against, inevitable*, DR,WW.
unāfīled *undefiled*, LPs 17³¹.
unāfūliende=unfūliende
unāfunden *undiscovered*, Æ : *untried*.
unā-fylledlic, -fyllendlic *that cannot be filled, insatiable*, Æ. adv. -līce.
unāga m. *one who owns nothing*, PPs 112⁶.
unāgǣledlīce *unremittingly*, BL 121⁵.
unāgān adj. *not lapsed, in force*, KC.
unāgelȳfed=unālȳfed
unāgen *not one's own or under one's control, precarious*, CP.
unāgifen *unpaid*, TC 201′.
unāgunnen *without a beginning*, ÆH.
unāhefendlic *unbearable*, MFH 176.
un-ālīef-, -lē(a)f-=unālȳf-
unālogen *not false, true*, NC 328.
un-ālȳfed (CP), -lȳfe(n)dlic (īe) *not allowed, unlawful, illicit*. adv. -līce *unlawfully, without permission*, Sc.
unālȳfednes (ē³;=īe) f. *what is forbidden, licentiousness*, BH.
unālȳsendlic *without remission*, ÆH 1·500′.
unāmælt *unmelted*, GL.
unāmānsumod *not excommunicated, in church fellowship*, Æ.
un-āmeten, -metenlic, -metgod *unmeasured, unbounded, immeasurable, immense*, Æ, RPs.
unan-=unon-
unandcȳðignes (o²) f. *ignorance*, JVPs 24⁷.
unandergilde *irreplaceable, invaluable*, Bo 27²⁰.
unandett *unconfessed*, W 71⁷.
unand-gittol, -gytful *unintelligent, incapable, ignorant, foolish*.
unandhēfe (-hoife) *insupportable*, MtR 23⁴.
unandweard *not present, absent*, ÆH 1·128¹⁷.
unandwendlic=unāwende(n)dlic
unandwīs *unskilful*, WW.
unānrǣdnes f. *inconstancy*, BL 31³⁴.
unāpīnedlīce adv. *with impunity*, DR 113¹⁵.
unār f. *dishonour*, AO.
un-āræf(n)ed, -āræfne(n)dlic *not permissible, impracticable*, Æ : *intolerable*. adv. -līce.
unāreccendlic *unexplainable, wonderful*, Sc 26¹⁵.
unārefnendlic (VPs)=unāræfnendlic
unāreht *unexplained*, Bo 77¹⁶.
+unārian *to dishonour*, AO,CP.
unārīmed adj. *unnumbered, countless, innumerable*, AO.

unārīme(n)dlic *innumerable, immeasurable*, AO. adv. -līce, AO.
unārlic *dishonourable, dishonest, disgraceful* : *contrary to what is fitting, unnatural (of a will)*, WW. adv. -līce *dishonourably* : *unmercifully*.
unarodscipe f. *remissness, cowardice*, CP 149¹⁵.
unārwurðian (eo) *to dishonour*, ÆH 1·442′.
unārwurðlic *dishonourable*, CHRD 63²⁴.
unārwyrðnes f. *irreverence, indignity*, Sc 224¹.
unārȳmed=unārīmed
unāsæcgendlic=unāsecgendlic
unāsædd=unāsedd
unāscended *unhurt*, DR.
unāscruncen *not withered, undecayed*, DR 24¹⁶.
unāscyrigendlic *inseparable*, ÆH 1·326²⁷.
unāscyrod *not separated*, WW 253³.
unāsecgende *unspeakable, ineffable*, BH 264³⁰.
unāsecgendlic *indescribable, unspeakable, ineffable*, Æ. adv. -līce.
unāsedd *unsatisfied, unsatiated*, GL.
unāsēðenlic (KGL), -āsēðendlic *insatiable*.
unāsīwod (ēo) *unsewed, without seam*, Jn 19²³.
unāsmēagendlic *inconceivable, inscrutable, unsearchable*, Æ.
unāsolcenlīce *diligently*, RB 20¹⁹.
unāspring-ende, -endlic (GD) *unfailing*.
un-āspyriendlic (e³, o³) *unsearchable*, GD, WW.
unāstīðod *not hardened, not firm*, CP 383³².
unāstyr-ed, -od *unmoved*, GD.
un-āstyriende, -āstyri(g)endlic adj. *immovable, firm* : *motionless*, Æ.
unāsundrodlic *inseparable*, DR.
unāswundenlīce adv. *diligently*, BH.
unātaladlic (N)=unātellendlic
unāteald (SCR 28³²)=unteald
unātellendlic (ea) *innumerable*, CHR.
unātemed *barbarous*, BH.
unātemedlic *untameable, wild, fierce*, BH 162²⁸.
unātēoriende *indefatigable*, OEG.
unātēorigendlic *lasting, permanent, unceasing*, Æ : *indefatigable, unwearied*. adv. -līce.
unātēorod *unwearied*, OEG 2373.
un-ātēriend-, -toriend-=unātēorigend-
unātwēogendlīce=untwēogendlīce
unāðrēotend *unwearied, assiduous, persistent*, CR 388.
unāðroten *unwearied, indefatigable, vigorous*, CP 171⁹. adv. -līce, CP.
unāwægendlic *unshaken*, TC 319⁹.
unā-wæscen, -waxen *unwashed*, WW 190, 439.

unāwemmed (ALRSPs), -lic (DR) *un-stained, spotless.*

unāwemmednes f. *incorruption,* Bf 168²¹.

unā-wend, -wended(lic) *unchangeable, un-changed, inviolate* : *unmoved.*

unāwendend-e (MET), -lic (Æ) *unchange-able, unceasing.* adv. *-līce.*

unāwerded (oe;=ie) *unhurt,* N.

unāwīdlod *undefiled,* DR 24¹⁶.

unāwriten *unwritten,* Æ.

un-bældo, -bældu=unbieldo

unbærende=unberende; unbald=unbeald

unbealaful *guiltless, innocent,* W.

unbeald (a) *cowardly, timid, weak, irre-solute, distrustful, CP,Jul.* ['unbold']

unbealu n. *innocence,* PPs 100².

unbeboht *unsold,* AO 18¹⁰.

unbebyriged *unburied,* GD,W.

unbecēas *incontestable,* LL 112,53¹.

unbecrafod *unquestioned, not subject to claims,* LL 358,72.

unbecweden *unbequeathed,* TC.

unbeden '*unbidden,*' LL (386).

unbe-fangenlic, -feonglic (BHCA 224¹⁹) *un-intelligible, incomprehensible,* Æ.

unbefliten *undisputed,* EC 69'.

unbefohten *unopposed, unattacked,* MA 57.

unbefōndlic *incomprehensible,* BHo 224¹⁹.

unbegān *untilled,* LCD : *unadorned,* HGL 435.

unbegrīpendlic *incomprehensible,* BL.

unbegunnen *without a beginning,* Æ. ['un-begun']

unbehēafdod *not beheaded,* ÆL 23¹⁸⁵.

unbehēfe *not suitable, inconvenient,* WW 508³⁴.

unbehelendlīce adv. *without concealment,* W 138³.

unbehelod *uncovered, naked,* GENC 9²¹.

unbehrēowsigende *unrepenting,*ÆH 1·500¹⁵.

unbelimp=ungelimp

unbeorhte (y) *not brightly,* Bo.

unberēafigendlic *never to be taken away,* ÆL 23b²⁴³.

unberende *unbearable* : *unfruitful, barren,* Æ,LG,VPs. ['unbearing']

unberendlic *unbearable,* LCD 3·260²³.

unberendnes (eo²) f. *barrenness,* DR, VPs.

unbermed *unleavened, unfermented.* [beor-ma]

unbesacen (æ²) *undisputed,* LL.

unbesænged=unbesenged

unbescēawod *improvident, inconsiderate,* GL,Sc. adv. *-līce.*

unbescoren *unshorn,* RB 135²⁹.

unbesenged *not singed, unburnt,* W 25¹⁹.

unbesēondlic (BH 224¹⁹)=unbefōndlic?

unbesmiten *undefiled, pure, spotless,* Æ.

unbesorh *unconcerned, not interested,* ÆH 2·486⁹.

unbēted *uncompensated, unexpiated, un-atoned,* CR 1312.

unbeðōhte adv. *unthinkingly,* CP 434².

unbeweddod *unbetrothed, unmarried,* Æ.

unbewelled *not boiled away,* LCD 93b. [weallan]

unbiddende *not praying,* ÆH 1·156⁴.

unbieldo (æ) f. *want of boldness, diffidence, timidity,* CP.

unbilewit (y²) *harsh,* OEG 56²³².

unbindan³ *to* '*unbind,*' *loosen,* LG; Æ : *pay* (NG; trans. of '*solvere*'). [=onbindan]

unbiscopod *not confirmed by a bishop,* LL, W. ['*unbishoped*']

unbiðyrfe† *useless, idle, vain.*

unblēoh *clean, bright,* DD, PPs.

unbletsung f. *curse,* LL (310').

unblinnendlīce *incessantly,* BH 34⁶.

unbliss f. *sorrow, affliction,* Æ.

+unblissian *to make unhappy,* NC 297.

unblīðe *joyless, sad, sorrowful,* CP : *un-friendly.*

unblīðemēde *sad of heart,* MtL 26³⁷.

unblōdig *bloodless,* GPH 395¹⁶.

unblonden *unmixed,* DR 68¹⁵.

unboht '*unbought,*' *free,* NG.

unboren '*unborn,*' Æ,CP.

unbrād *narrow,* Ct,LCD.

unbrǣce† *unbreakable, indestructible.*

un-brece, -brice=unbryce; unbrīece=un-brȳce.

unbrocheard *delicate, tender,* Bo,WW.

unbrosn-igendlic (Æ), -endlic (GD) *inde-structible, incorruptible.*

unbrosnodlīce *incorruptibly,* GD 348²³.

unbrosnung f. *incorruptibility,* Æ.

unbryce† *unbreakable* : *indestructible, ever-lasting.* [brecan]

unbrȳce (īe) *useless,* GL,PPs. [brūcan]

unbrȳde *honestly,* LL 400,2.

unbunden (LL, Rd) pp. of unbindan.

unbȳed *uninhabited desert,* NG.

unbȳergo np. *uninhabited places,* DR 1⁹ (? for unbȳencg, MLR 18·273).

unbyrged '*unburied,*' MH 28²¹.

unbyrhte=unbeorhte

unbyrnende *without burning,* B 2548.

unc pers. pron. (d. a. dual) *us two.*

uncænned=unācenned

uncǣfscipe m. *sloth, neglect,* CHR 47.

uncamprōf *unwarlike,* GPH 399.

uncapitulod *without headings* (*to chapters*), LL (204¹).

uncēap(ed) *gratuitous, gratis,* MtL 10⁸.

uncēapunga *gratuitously,* DA 746.

uncēas(t) n? *oath of reconciliation,* LL 104,35.

uncenned=unācenned

uncer I. g. dual of pers. pron. *of us two.* II. poss. pron. *belonging to us two.*

uncet=unc

unclǣmod *unsmeared*, GPH 398.

unclǣne '*unclean*,' *BH,Bl,Cr,LG,WW*.

unclǣnlic *unclean, impure*, *DR*. adv. -līce, *ÆH*. ['*uncleanly*']

unclǣnnes f. *uncleanness, impurity*, *AO, CP,DR,Mt,OEG*.

unclǣno f. *uncleanness*, NG.

±unclǣnsian *to soil, pollute*, AO,CP.

unclǣnsod *unpurified, CP*. ['*uncleansed*']

unclēn-=unclǣn-

uncnyttan *to unbind, untie, loosen*, *Lk*; Æ. ['*unknit*']

uncoren *evil, reprobate*, VH 21.

un-coða m., -coðu f. *disease*, Æ : *plague*, CHRD 70[7].

uncræft m. *evil practice*, LL,W.

uncræftig *helpless*, DD 239.

uncrafod (LL 232,14)=unbecrafod

uncre gdf. of uncer II.

uncristen *infidel*, BHo 306[23]. ['*unchristian*']

uncumlīðe *inhospitable*, W 257[14].

uncūð *unknown, strange, unusual, Æ,AO* : *uncertain, Æ,CP* : *unfriendly, unkind, rough*. ['*uncouth*']

uncūða m. *stranger*, Jn 10[5].

uncūðlic *unknown*. adv. -līce *in an unfriendly manner, unkindly*, LL. ['*uncouthly*']

uncūðnes f. *strangeness*, GD 278[15].

uncwaciende *firmly*, CP 41[7].

uncweden (*unsaid*), *revoked*, WW 114[45].

uncwēme *not pleasing*, MFH 176. ['*unqueme*']

uncweðende *speechless, dumb*, Bo,SOLK.

uncwisse *dumb*, BH 290[12].

uncwyd(d) *uncontested, undisputed*, LL.

uncȳme *unseemly, mean, paltry, poor*, BH, BL.

uncynde *unnatural*, Bo 91[21]B.

un-cynn, -cynlic (Bo) *unsuitable, improper*.

uncȳpe *gratuitous*, WW 514[31].

uncȳped=uncēaped

un-cyst, -cyste f. *mistake, error* : *vice, wickedness, crime, Æ,CP* : *stinginess, parsimony, Æ* : *disease*, LCD. [cēosan]

uncystig *mean, stingy, niggardly, Æ*, CP.

uncȳð=uncūð

uncȳðig *ignorant, unacquainted with* : *devoid of*, GU 1199.

un-cȳðð, -cȳððu f. *ignorance, Æ,CP* : *foreign country*.

undǣd f. *wicked deed, crime*, W.

undæftelīce=ungedæftlīce

un-dǣled, -dǣld *undivided*, Bo.

undēaded *not deadened*, LCD 3a.

undēadlic *immortal, for all eternity, Æ,DR*. adv. -līce. ['*undeadly*']

undēadlicnes f. *immortality, Æ*. ['*undeadliness*']

undēagollīce=undēogollīce

undearnunga adv. *openly*, LL.

undēað-=undēad-

undēaw *without dew*, LCD 35a.

undeclīnigendlic *indeclinable*, ÆGR.

undēd=undǣd

undēogollīce (ēa, ī) adv. *plainly, clearly*, CP.

undēop *shallow, low*, CP.

undēopðancol *shallow, silly*, ÆH 1·286′.

undēor=undēore I.

undēore I. adj. *cheap, CP,WW*. ['*undear*'] II. adv. *cheaply*.

undeornunga=undearnunga

under I. prep. w. d. and a. '*UNDER*,' *beneath, Æ* : *among, AO* : *before, in the presence of* : *under the shelter of*, CHR : *in the service of, in subjection to, under the rule of, Æ,AO,Chr* : *during, AO,Chr* : *by means of, by*. swerian u. God *to swear by God*. u. bæc=underbæc. II. adv. *beneath, below, underneath, Æ,B,Chr,MH*.

underāgendlic adj. '*subnixus*,' DR 182[16].

underandfōnd (o³, oe⁴) '*susceptor*,' DR 193[6].

under-bæc, -bæcling adv. *backwards, back, behind, Æ*,CP.

underbēgan *to subject*, DR. [bīegan]

underbeginnan³ *to undertake, purpose*, ÆT 76[7].

underberan⁴ *to support, endure, DR,Sc*. ['*underbear*']

under-brǣdan, -bregdan *to spread under*, WE.

underbūgan² *to submit (to)*, Æ.

underburg f. *suburb*, DEUT 32[32].

underburhware mp. *dwellers in a suburb* (BT).

undercerran *to overturn, subvert*, LkLR 23[2]. [cierran]

undercing=undercyning

undercrammian *to stuff between, fill out underneath*, ÆH 1·430⁴.

undercrēopan² *to be secretly grasped, seized by something, Æ* : *penetrate, undermine*, GD.

undercuman⁴ *to assist*, DR.

undercyn(in)g m. *under-king, viceroy, Æ*.

underdelf n. *undermining*, ASPs 79[17].

underdelfan³ *to dig under, undermine, break through, Æ,Lk*. ['*underdelve*']

underdīacon m. *subdeacon*, LL.

underdōn anv. *to put under*, LEV 1[12].

underdrencan *to choke by drowning*, MkL 5[13].

underdrifennes f. *subjection*, LkL p 6[16].

underēade (N)=underēode, pret. 3 sg. of undergān.

undereoton (Ruin6)=undereten pp. of underetan.

underetan[5] *to eat underneath, undermine, subvert,* Bo27[2].

underfang '*susceptor,*' SPs.

underfangelnes=underfangenes

underfangen (pp. of underfōn) *neophyte,* ÆL31[730].

underfang-enes, -elnes f. *undertaking, assumption : reception, hospitality,* GD 76[22].

underfealdan '*subdere,*' EHy6[30].

underfeng I. m. *undertaking, taking in hand,* CP23[22]. **II.** pret. 3 sg. of underfōn.

underflōwan[7] *to flow under,* Rd11[2].

underfolgoð m. *subordinate office,* AO286[5]c.

underfōn *to receive, obtain, take, accept,* Æ, AO,CP : *take in, entertain : take up, undertake, assume, adopt, Æ,AO,CP : submit to, undergo, Æ : steal.* ['underfo']

underfōnd m. *one who takes anything in charge,* LPs.

underfōnlic *to be received,* RBL97[8].

underfyligan '*subsequi,*' LkL23[55].

undergān anv. *to* '*undergo*' : *undermine, ruin,* Lcd.

undergangan[7]=undergān

undergend-=under(i)gend-

undergeoc *under the yoke, tame,* MkL21[5].

undergerēfa m. '*proconsul,*' *deputy-governor,* Æ.

undergereord=underngereord

undergesett *placed under,* GD307[12].

undergestandan[0] *to stand under,* LL108,44.

undergeðēoded *subject,* LL88′.

undergeðēodnes=underðēodnes

undergietan[5] (i, y) *to note, mark, understand, perceive, Æ,AO,Chr,Mt.* ['underyete']

underginnan[0] *to begin, undertake,* ÆT76[7]n.

undergitan (Æ)=undergietan

undergynnan=underginnan

undergytan (Æ)=undergietan

underhebban[6] *to bear, support, lift,* NG.

underhlystan '*subaudire,*' *to supply an omitted word,* ÆGr151.

underhlystung f. *the act of supplying an omitted word,* ÆGr151.

underhnīgan[1] *to submit to, undergo, Æ,CP : succumb to, sink under.*

underholung f. '*suffossum,*' LV[2]Ps79[17].

underhwītel m. *under-garment,* WW187[21].

underhwrǣdel=underwrǣdel

underi-ende, -gende, -gendlic *inoffensive, harmless,* AO.

underiernan[3] *to run under* : '*succurrere,*' Dr43[8].

underlǣttēow m. *consul,* AO68[2]c.

underlecgan *to* '*underlay,*' *prop, support,* Æ,CP.

underlicgan[5] *to* '*underlie,*' *to be subject to, give way to, Æ,CP,RB.*

underlihtan *to alleviate,* DR.

underling m. *underling, inferior,* HL,KC.

underlūtan[2] *to bow or bend under : support, sustain,* CP.

undermete=undernmete

undern m. *morning (from* 9.0 *a.m. to* 12.0 *noon) : the third hour* (=9.0 *a.m.*; *later,* 11.0 *a.m.*), *Lcd; Æ : service at the third hour,* RB. ['undern']

underne=undierne

underneoðan (y[3]) adv. *underneath,* AO.

underngereord m. *morning meal, breakfast,* AO.

underngeweorc n. *breakfast,* GD66[12].

underngi(e)fl n. *repast, breakfast,* CP322[19].

underniman[4] *to take in, receive, comprehend, understand, Æ : blame, be indignant at : take upon oneself, Æ : steal,* Lcd. ['undernim']

undernīðemest *lowest of all,* Met20[35].

undernmǣl n. *morning-time, Æ,B.* ['undermeal']

undernmete m. *morning meal, breakfast,* AO.

undernrest f. *morning rest,* MH42[6].

undernsang m. *tierce (religious service about* 9.0 *a.m.*), RB,LL.

undernswǣsendu np. *early meal,* BH164[30].

underntīd f. *the third hour* (=9.0 *a.m.*), *noon, morning-time, BH,Mt; Æ : tierce.* ['underntide']

undernyðan (Æ)=underneoðan

underondfōnd—underandfōnd

underplantian '*supplantare,*' Sc,SPs.

undersang=undernsang

underscēotan[2] *to prop up, sustain, support,* CP : *intercept, pass under.*

underscyte m. *passage underneath, transit, Æ : brake, drag-chain,* OEG50[15].

undersēcan *to examine, investigate, scrutinize, CP.* ['underseek']

undersettan '*supponere,*' LPs36[24]?

undersingan[3] '*succinere,*' ÆGr181[2].

undersittan[5] '*subsidere,*' ÆGr157[5].

undersmūgan[2] *to creep under, surprise,* RB.

understandan[6] (o[3]) *to* '*UNDERSTAND,*' *perceive, Æ; CP : observe, notice, take for granted, ÆL23b[186] : subsistere,' DR.*

understandennes (o[3]) f. '*substantia,*' DR 31[20].

understanding f. '*understanding,*' Sc221[13].

understapplian '*supplantare,*' LPs16[13].

understaðolfǣst=unstaðolfǣst

understingan[3] *to prop up, support,* CP113[11].

understond-=understand-

understrēdan *to strew under,* MH18[21].

understrēowed *underlaid,* ÆL37[201].

undersyrc m. *undershirt*, WW379³⁰. [serce]

undertíd (*Chrd*)=underntíd

undertōdal f. *secondary division*, ÆGR291⁵.

undertunge f. '*sublingua*,' *part under or behind the tongue, tongue-ligament*, WW 264¹⁷ (or ? two words, Cp,LPs9²⁸; 65¹⁷).

undertungeðrum *tongue-ligament*, Lcd. [v. '*thrum*']

underðencan (æ³) *to consider*, CP49²³ : (refl.) *change one's mind, repent*, LL438,22.

underðēnian *to serve under*, Sc5⁶.

underðēod *subjected, subject* : *assistant, suffragan*.

underðēodan (īe, ȳ) *to subjoin, add* : *subjugate, subject, subdue, reduce, degrade*, Æ, CP : *support*, OEG4339.

under-ðēodendlic, -ðēodenlic *subjunctive*, ÆGR.

underðēodnes (ī³) f. *subjection, submission, obedience*, Æ : '*supplantatio*,' EPs40¹⁰.

underðēow m. *subject, slave*, AO.

underðīedan (AO,CP)=underðēodan

underðīednes (ī³)=underðēodnes

underðȳdan=underðēodan

underweaxan⁶ '*succrescere*,' Sc104⁸.

underwedd n. *deposit, pledge*, Æ.

underwendan '*subvertere*,' Sc196⁶.

underweorpan '*subjicere*,' EPs143².

underwrǣdel m? *waistband*, WW153¹.

underwreðian (eo, i, y) *to support, sustain, uphold, strengthen, establish*, Æ,CP.

underwreðung f. *propping up, support, sustentation*, Sc,WW.

underwrītan *to write at the foot of, subscribe*, BH312³⁰.

under-wriðian, -wryðian=underwreðian

underwyrtwalian '*supplantare*,' EPs17⁴⁰.

underȳcan (īe) *to add*, CM385²⁹².

underyrnan=underiernan

undierne (e, i, y) I. *open, manifest, clearly known* : *public, nuncupatory*. II. adv.

undīgollīce=undēogollīce

undīlegod *unerased*, CP423²³.

undolfen *untilled*, GD202⁴.

undōm m. *unjust judgment, injustice*, W.

undōmlīce *indiscreetly*, Sc202¹⁵.

undōn anv. *to* '*undo*,' *open, loosen, separate*, Æ,AO : *cancel, discharge, abrogate, destroy*, LG.

undrēfed *untroubled, undisturbed, undefiled*, CP31³.

undrifen *not driven or tossed*, LL222,2.

undruncen *sober*, CP295⁸.

undrysnende *inextinguishable*, MtL3¹².

undȳre=undēore

undyrne=undierne

unēacen (ē) *barren*, OEG27³¹.

unēacniendlic *unfruitful, sterile*, OEG1030.

unearfoðlīce adv. *without difficulty*, OEG.

un-earg, -earh (Æ), -earhlic (Æ) *not cowardly, dauntless, bold, brave*.

unēaðe (y) I. adj. *not easy, difficult, hard, disagreeable, grievous*, Æ,An,WW. II. adv. *not easily, hardly*, Bo,Chr,LG, WW : *unwillingly*, Æ,BH : *scarcely, only just*, Æ. ['*uneath*']

unēaðelic *difficult, hard, impossible* : *troublesome*, Nic611'. adv. -līce.

unēaðelicnes (ā², ǣ², ē², ȳ²) f. *difficulty*, BH 296²¹.

unēað-lǣ(c)ne, -lācne *not easily cured*, Lcd.

unēaðmylte *indigestible*, Lcd82b.

unēaðnes (ē, īe) f. *difficulty, inconvenience, trouble, worry*, Æ : *severity, harshness*.

unēawfæstlīce=unǣwfæstlīce

un-efn, -efen(lic) *unequal, unlike*, Cr : *anomalous, irregular*, ÆGR. adv. -efne, Ps. ['*uneven*']

un-ēmetta, -ēmota=unǣmta

unemn=unefn

unendebyrdlīce *in a disorderly manner*, CP.

unered *unploughed, uncultivated*, WW147³.

unēstful *ungracious*, WW191¹⁷.

unēð-=unēað-, unīeð-

unēwisc=unǣwisc

unfǣcne (ā) *without malice, sincere, honest, faithful*, B,LL.

unfæderlīce adv. *in an unfatherly manner*, W106⁶.

unfǣge† *not fated to die*, B.

unfæger *not beautiful, unlovable, deformed, ugly, hideous*, B,Bo,Bl. ['*unfair*']

unfægernes (e) *ugliness, disfigurement*, GD 279¹⁵ : *abomination*, MtL24¹⁵.

unfǣglic *not fatal*, Bo107²⁹.

unfǣgre (ǣ) adv. *unfairly, foully*, Gen. ['*unfair*']

unfǣhð f. *peace* (*dropping of a feud*), LL 100,28.

unfǣle *wicked, unlovely, unholy, evil*, Gen, Mk,WW. ['*unfele*']

unfæst *not fixed, not firm, loose, unsteady, tottering*, Bo,CP. ['*unfast*']

unfæstende *not fasting*, LL(252¹).

unfæstlīce adv. *not firmly, vaguely, indistinctly*, CP156¹³.

+**unfæstnian** *to unfasten*, MFH165.

unfæstrǣd *unstable, inconstant*, CP.

unfæstrǣdnes f. *inconstancy*, CP.

unfæsð-=unfæst-

unfāh *exempt from hostility, not under a ban*, LL186,1¹.

unfealdan⁷ *to unfold, open*, G,GD : *explain*, Sc.

unfeax *without hair, bald* (Swt).

unfēcne=unfǣcne

unfēferig *not feverish*, Lcd1·164'.

unfeger-=unfæger-

unfēlende '*unfeeling*,' *insensible*, Lcd 99a.

unfenge *not acceptable*, MFH 176.

un-feor, -feorr adv. *not far from, near*.

unfeormigende (on-) *inexpiable*, ÆL 23b⁴²⁶.

unfēre *disabled, invalided*, CHR 1055.

unfērnes f. *impotence, infirmity*, RWH 137¹².

unflitme? *unreservedly?* B 1097.

un-flycge, -fligge *unfledged*, OEG 28¹³.

unforbærned *unburnt*, Æ,AO.

unforboden *unforbidden, lawful*, Æ.

unforbūgendlīc *unavoidable*. adv. -līce *without turning away*, ÆL 23b⁴³¹.

unforburnen *unburnt*, ÆH 2·480⁷.

unforcūð *reputable, good, honourable, noble, brave*, CP. adv. -līce. [fracoð]

unfordytt *unobstructed*, OEG 3613.

unforebyrdig *impatient*, Sc 8¹³.

unfored (od) *unbroken*, Æ.

unforedlic (o³) *indissoluble*, OEG.

unforescēawod *hasty, unconsidered*, HExC 387.

unforescēawodlic *hasty, precipitate*, WW 426⁸. adv. (v. unforsc-).

unforfeored *unbroken?* WW 231³³.

unforgifen *unforgiven*, CP : *not given in marriage*.

unforgifende (y³) *unforgiving*, GD 320¹.

unforgitende *unforgetting, mindful*, GUTH 76²².

unforgolden *unpaid*, LEV 19¹³.

unforhæfednes (fd) f. *incontinence*, CP.

unforhladen *unexhausted*, WW 255³⁹.

unforht adj. *fearless, bold*. adv. -e, -līce.

unforhtigende *fearless*, ÆH 2·140'.

unforhtlēasnes? *fear, timidity*, VH 21.

unforhtmōd *fearless*, ÆH.

unforlǣten (ē) *not left*, NG.

unformolsnod neg. ptc. *uncorrupted, undecayed*, Æ.

unformolten *unconsumed*, ÆH 1·488⁷.

unforod=unfored

unforrot-edlic (HGL), -iendig (ÆP 14⁷), -iendlic (OEG) *incorruptible*.

unforscēawodlīce *unawares*, WW 92¹⁰ : *inconsiderately, hastily*, ÆH.

unfor-spornen, -spurned *not hindered*, GD 60²⁸.

unforswǣled *unburnt*, ÆH 2·20¹⁵.

unforswīgod *not passed over in silence*, ÆL 23b³⁵.

unforswȳðed *unconquered*, AA 3¹¹.

unfortredde sb. *the plant which cannot be killed by treading, polygonum aviculare, knot-grass*.

unfortreden *not destroyed by treading*, LCD 3·299'.

unforwandigendlīce adv. *unhesitatingly, boldly*, ApT 21⁹.

unforwandodlīc adj. *unhesitating, fearless*, CP. adv. -līce *recklessly*, CP : *unswervingly*.

unforwealwod *unwithered*, BL 73²⁵.

unforwordenlīc (u³) *undecayed*, OEG 60.

unforworht I. *innocent*. II. *unrestricted, free*, KC.

unforwyrded *undecayed*, NC 351.

un-fracodlīce, -fracoðlīce *honourably, becomingly, fitly*, Bo.

unfratewod *unadorned, unpolished*, GPH 396. [frætwian]

unfremful *unprofitable*, Æ,GL.

unfremu f. *damage, hurt*, GEN.

unfrēondlīce *unkindly*, Gen 2689. ['*unfriendly*']

unfricgende *unquestioning*, GEN 2649.

unfrið m. *breach of peace, enmity, war*, AO : *state of being outside the king's peace*.

unfriðflota m. *hostile fleet*, CHR 1000 E.

unfriðhere m. *hostile army*, CHR.

unfriðland n. *hostile land*, LL 222,3¹.

unfriðmann m. *alien enemy*, LL 222,3³.

unfriðscip n. *hostile ship*, CHR,LL.

unfrōd *young, inexperienced*, B 2821.

unfrōforlīce *uncontestably*, OEG 56¹⁸⁷?

unfrom† *inert*, B,PPs.

unfūl '*insulsum*' MkLR 9⁵⁰.

unfulfremed *imperfect*, Æ.

unfulfremednes f. *imperfection*, CP.

unfulfremming f. *imperfection*, LPs 138¹⁶.

un-fūllende (HGL), -fūliendlic (OEG) *incorruptible*.

unfullod *unbaptized*, LL.

unfulworht *imperfect, unfinished*, RB 20³.

unfyrn adv. *not long ago*, BL : *soon*, GD.

ungǣnge *useless, vain*, MtR 15⁶.

ungan=ongan pret. 3 sg. of onginnan.

ungeǣndod=ungeendod

ungeǣsce *unheard of*, GD 284²⁰.

un-geǣwed (-iǣwed) *unmarried*, OEG 5248.

ungeandett *without confession*, W 135³².

ungeaplīce *carelessly, unskilfully*, CHRD 123⁹.

ungēara adv. *not long ago, lately, recently* : *soon, shortly*.

ungearo=ungearu

ungearu, gsm. ungear(o)wes *unready, disinclined, unprepared, untilled*, AO,CP. on ungearwe *unawares*, AO.

ungearuwitolnes f. *dulness of mind*, GD 331¹⁵.

ungearwyrd *not respected*, WW 421³².

ungeāðe=unēaðe

ungeāxod *unasked*, ÆH 1·428⁶.

ungebarde=ungebierde

ungebēaten *unbeaten, unwrought*, Ln 23⁵.

ungebēgendlic=ungebīgendlic

ungebeorhlīce *rashly? intemperately?* ÆH 2·322²⁶.

unge-bēt(ed), -bett *unatoned for*, CP : *unacquitted*, EC 217¹⁰.

ungebierde (a, y) *beardless*, GL.
ungebīged *unbent*, OEG 2977.
ungebīgendlic *inflexible, rigid* : *indeclinable*, ÆGR.
ungebleoh *of different colours, unlike*, ÆGR.
ungeblētsod *unblessed*, JUL 492.
ungeblȳged *intrepid*, GU 913. [bleoh]
ungeboden *without being summoned*, TC.
ungeboht *unbought, unbribed*, LL 398,8.
ungeboren *yet unborn*, LL 126 Pro.
ungebrocen *unbroken*, WW 398³².
ungebrocod *uninjured*, ÆH 1·464⁶.
ungebrosnendlic *undecaying*, BH,GD.
ungebrosnod *uncorrupted, undecayed*, Æ.
ungebrosnung f. *incorruption*, SC 71².
ungebunden *unbound*, ÆGR 14¹³; GD 214¹⁶.
ungebyrde I. *uncongenial*, BO 92²². **II.**=ungebierde
ungebyrded *inviolate*, GD 199⁴.
ungebyredlic *incongruous*, DR 179¹⁷.
ungecindelic=ungecyndelic
ungeclǣnsod *unclean, impure*, Æ.
ungecnāwen *unknown*, APT 17¹³.
ungecnyrdnes f. *negligence, indifference, idleness*, ÆH 2·552'.
ungecoplic *unsuitable, unbefitting, troublesome*. adv. -līce, SC 80¹⁴.
ungecoren *reprobate*. u. āð *oath taken by a body of persons generally* (*opposed to* cyreāð), LL.
ungecost *reprobate*, BH 480⁴.
ungecwēme *unpleasing, disagreeable*, SC 38¹⁵.
ungecyd *unsaid, not declared*, LL 212,9.
ungecynde *unnatural*, BO : *alien*, CHR.
unge-cyndelic, -cyndlic, -cynelic *unnatural, monstrous, terrible*. adv. -līce.
ungecyrred *unconverted*, LCD 3·442¹.
ungedæftelīce=ungedæftlīce
ungedæftenlic=ungedafenlic
ungedæftlīce adv. *unseasonably*, CP 97¹⁶.
ungedæftnes f. *untimely intervention or interruption*, CP 97¹⁹.
ungedafenlic *improper, unseemly*, Æ : *unseasonable, troublesome*, CP (v. A 33·272). adv. -līce *improperly, unduly, unreasonably, unjustly, unsuitably*.
ungedafenlicnes f. *unfitness, inconvenience*, CPs 9²².
ungedafniendlic (HGL 492)=ungedafenlic
ungedallic *infinite, without end*, GD 337¹¹.
ungedēfe *improper, not fitting, disagreeable*. adv. -līce.
unge-dēfelic, -dēflic=ungedafenlic
unge-dered, -derod (Æ) *unhurt, uninjured, unmolested*.
ungederstig=ungedyrstig
ungedrehtlīce adv. *indefatigably*, WW 428³.

ungedrȳme *inharmonious, discordant*, CHRD 57¹². [drēam]
ungedwimorlīce *clearly, without any delusion*, NC 328.
ungedyrstig *timid*, CP 209¹⁰.
ungeeahtendlic (a³, æ³) *estimable*, BH,GD.
ungeended=ungeendod
ungeendigendlic *infinitive*, ÆGR : *infinite*.
unge-endod (CP), -endodlic *unending, endless, infinite, boundless*.
ungefæd (a) *indiscretion*, CHRD 13¹⁴.
ungefǣglic=unfǣglic; **ungefǣr-**=ungefēr-
ungefandod *untried, having no experience*, CP 407,409.
ungefaren *impassable, without a road*, BLPs.
ungefēa m. *unhappiness*, NC 328.
ungefēalīce *miserably*, CHR 755.
ungefēge *unfit, improper*, WW 191²².
unge-fēle, -fēled *without feeling*, LCD.
ungefēre I. *impassable* : *impenetrable, inaccessible*, CP. **II.** adv. *impassably*.
ungefēred *inaccessible*, AA 30⁷.
ungefērenlic *difficult, trackless*, AA 25⁹.
ungefērlic *unsocial, internecine*. adv. -līce *in civil war*.
ungefērne *impassable*, VPs (oe).
ungefeðered *not feathered*, WW 427¹⁶.
unge-fōg, -fōh **I.** *immoderate, excessive*, Æ : *overbearing, presumptuous, unbending*, Æ. **II.** n. *excess*, CHRD 70¹⁶. adv. -fōge *excessively*, AO.
unge-fōglic (AO), -fōhlic *fierce, strong* : *immense*. adv. -līce.
ungefrǣg-e, -elic *unheard of, unusual, inconceivable*. adv. -līce.
ungefrætwod *unadorned*, WW 419¹¹.
ungefrēdelīce adv. *callously*, CP 265¹⁶.
ungefrēglīce=ungefrǣglīce
ungefremed *unfinished*, LL,WW.
ungefremmung (on-) f. *imperfection*, RPs 138¹⁶.
ungefullod I. *unfulfilled*, RD 60¹⁴. [fullian] **II.**=ungefulwod
ungefulwod *unbaptized*, Æ,BL.
unge-fyld (BO), -fylle(n)d(lic) *insatiable*.
ungefynde *worthless, barren?* CP 411¹⁹.
ungefyrn adv. *not long hence, not long ago, not long after*, Æ.
ungegearwe=ungearwe v. ungearu.
unge-gearwod (DR), -gerad (MtR) *not clothed*.
ungeglenged *unadorned*, OEG 1210.
ungegrēt *ungreeted*, GUTH 22²⁰.
ungehādod *not ordained, not belonging to an order* (used of men and women), IM 127¹⁸.
un-gehǣlendlic, -gehǣledlic *incurable*, VHy.
ungehǣmed *unmarried*, OEG 1174.
ungehǣplic *unsuitable, unfit*, A 8·452.
ungehālgod *unhallowed, unconsecrated*, Æ.

ungehāten *unpromised, unbidden*, BL 189²⁷.

ungehēafdod *not having come to a head*, LCD 1·92'.

ungehealdsum *unchaste*, Æ. adv. -līce.

ungehealdsumnes f. *incontinence, unchastity*, KC,LL.

ungehealtsum=ungehealdsum

ungehefegod *not pregnant*, OEG 27³¹.

ungehende (æ³) *remote*, HL 12⁸.

ungehendnes f. *remoteness, distance*, ÆGR 14¹⁹.

ungeheort *disheartened*, ÆL 23⁶².

ungehēred=ungehȳred

unge-hīersum (CP), -hīrsum (Æ) *disobedient, rebellious*.

ungehīrsumnes (ȳ) f. *disobedience*, Æ,VH.

ungehīrsumod (ȳ) *disobedient*, RBL 12⁸.

unge-hīwod, -hīwodlic *unformed, not fashioned, unshapen : unfeigned, genuine*.

ungehlēoðor *inharmonious*, WW 224⁷.

ungehrepod *untouched*, Æ.

ungehrinen *untouched*, BH,GD.

ungehwǣde *much*, LCD 53b.

ungehwǣrnes=ungeðwǣrnes

ungehȳr-=unge-hīer-, -hīr-

ungehȳred (ē³) *unheard of, untold*, BH 40³³.

ungehȳrnes f. *hardness of hearing, deafness*, LCD.

ungehyrt *disheartened, fearful*, W 192²⁴.

ungel m. *fat, tallow, suet*, Æ.

ungelācnod *unhealed*, GUTH 66¹⁶.

ungelādod *not acquitted*, EC 217¹⁰.

ungelæccendlic *unreprovable*, Sc 119¹¹.

ungelǣred *untaught, illiterate, unlearned, ignorant, rude*, Æ,CP. adv. -līce.

ungelǣredlic *unteachable*, GD 110²¹.

ungelǣrednes f. *unskilfulness, ignorance*, CP.

ungelaðod *uninvited*, ÆH 1·128¹⁸.

ungelēaf *unbelieving*, PPs 67¹⁹.

ungelēafa m. *unbelief*, BL,CHR.

ungelēafful *unbelieving*, CP : *incredible*, OEG.

ungelēaffullic *unbelieving : incredible*. adv. -līce.

ungelēaffulnes f. *unbelief*, BL,G.

ungelēaflic *incredible*, Æ.

ungelēafsum *unbelieving*, BH.

ungelēafsumnes f. *unbelief, infidelity, heathenism*, BH 70²⁵.

ungelēf-=ungelīf-; ungelēofa=ungelēafa

ungelīc *unlike, different, dissimilar, diverse*, Æ,Bo,Bl,OEG; CP. adv. -līce. ['*uniliche,' 'unilike*']

ungelīca m. *one unlike others*, ÆL 7²⁸.

ungelīcian *to displease*, Æ (94⁶⁶).

ungelīclic *improper*, GUTH 12¹⁷. adv. -līce, LCD 59a.

ungelīcnes f. *unlikeness, difference*, CP.

ungelīef-=ungelīf-

ungelīfed (ȳ) I. *unbelieving*, Æ. II. *illicit*, BH 2·229.

ungelīf-edlic, -endlic (īe, ȳ) *incredible, extraordinary*. adv. -līce.

unge-līfen, -līfende (e³, y³) *unbelieving*, NG.

ungelīfend (ē) m. *unbeliever*, NG.

ungelīfnes (ē) f. *unbelief*, NG.

ungeligen=ungelygen

ungelimp nm. *mishap, misfortune*, Æ.

ungelimplic *inconvenient, unfortunate, disastrous*, Æ : *abnormal, unreasonable*. adv. -līce.

ungelȳf-=ungelīf-

ungelygen *not lying, true*, LL.

ungēm-=ungȳm-

ungemaca m. '*impar,' not a match*, ÆGR.

ungemæc *unlike*, GD 91¹⁵; WW 223³⁵.

ungemæt=ungemet

ungemǣte I. *immense, extraordinary*, CHR 1115. ['*unimete*'] II. adv. *immensely*.

ungemǣtlic *excessive*, AO 28²⁷.

ungemēde *unbearable, unpleasant*, MOD 25.

ungemēdnes f. *adversity*, DR 63¹³.

ungemeltnes f. *indigestion*, LCD 68b.

ungemenged *unmixed, pure*, BO 100³¹.

ungemet n. *excess, superfluity : immensity : want of moderation*, Bo,Lcd. ['*unimete*']

ungemet *not met with, unknown*, OEG 2488.

ungemete I. adj. *huge*, GD 12⁹. II. adv. *excessively, immeasurably, immoderately, extremely*, B,Ps. ['*unimete*']

ungemetegod (Æ)=ungemetgod

ungemetelice=ungemetlice

ungemetes=ungemete II.

ungemetfæst *not moderate, intemperate, excessive : very firm*, MET 7³³.

ungemetfæstnes f. *excess, intemperance*, BO 109⁹.

ungemetgod *out of due proportion, excessive*, CP : *unbridled, intemperate*.

ungemetgung f. *excess*, Æ,CP.

ungemetigende *intemperate, unrestrained*, VH 22.

ungemetlic *immeasurable, immense*, AO : *excessive, immoderate, violent*. adv. -līce, AO,CP.

ungemetnes f. *extravagance*, OET 180³.

ungemetum adv.=ungemete

ungemīdlod *unrestrained, unbridled*, Æ, CHRD.

ungemiht *without strength, weak*, BO 108⁵n.

ungemihtig=unmihtig

ungemindig=ungemyndig

ungemōd *discordant, dissentient, quarrelsome*, CP.

ungemōdignes f. *contentiousness*, W 8¹⁵n.

ungemōdnes f. *strife*, CP 344⁹.

ungemolsnod *undecayed*, MH 78¹.

ungemunecod *not made a monk*, LL (142⁴).
ungemylt *undigested*, Lᴄᴅ 2a (Harl).
ungemynd f. *madness*, Lᴄᴅ.
ungemyndig (w. g.) *unmindful, forgetful, heedless (of)*, Æ.
ungenæmnendlic *unknown?* GD 341¹³.
ungenīdd (ē, īe) *uncompelled*, AO,CP.
ungeocian *to 'unyoke,'* ÆGr 277³.
ungeonbyrded=ungebyrded
ungeorne *negligently* : *unwillingly*, AO.
ungeornful *indifferent, remiss, slothful*, CP.
ungerād I. (w. g.) *ignorant, foolish, unskilled, unfit*, Æ,CP : (w. d.) *at variance, wrong, discordant, dissentient*, Æ,AO : *ill-conditioned, rude*, Æ. II. n. *discord*, CP : *folly*, Æ.
ungerādnes (æ) *disagreement*, Lᴄᴅ.
ungerǣd=ungerād
ungerǣde *foolish*, MFH 176.
ungerǣdlic *unteachable, ignorant, rough*, GD 110¹¹. adv. -līce *sharply, roughly, violently*.
ungerǣdnes f. *disagreement, sedition*, AO.
ungerǣdod *without harness*, KC.
ungerec n. *tumult*, BH,MtR 27²⁴.
ungereccan *to clear oneself of an accusation*, LL 168,1².
ungereclic *unruly, unrestrained*, Bʟ 19⁶. adv. -līce *confusedly, recklessly*.
ungerēdelīce=ungerǣdlīce
ungerēnod *not ornamented*, TC 515'. [regn-]
ungereord *uninstructed, barbarous*, WW 193³.
ungereord(ed)lic *insatiable*, CVPs 100⁵.
ungereordod *unfed, empty*, ÆL 19⁹¹.
ungerepod=ungehrepod
ungerian=ungierwan; **ungeriht**=unriht
ungeriht *uncorrected, unreformed*, Cʜʀᴅ.
ungerīm I. n. *countless number, host*, Æ. II. *countless, untold*, Æ.
unge-rīmlic, -rīmed(lic) *countless, untold*.
ungerinen=ungehrinen
ungerinselīce=ungerisenlīce
ungerīped *immature, too early*, Æ.
ungerisedlīce=ungerisenlīce
ungerīsende *indecent*, OEG 3673.
ungerisene I. *unseemly, improper* : *incongruous, inconvenient.* II.=ungerisnu
ungerisenlic *unbecoming, improper*, CP. adv. -līce, CP.
ungerīsnes (uni-) f. *impropriety*, HGʟ 507.
ungerisnu n. (often pl.) *inconvenience* : *impropriety, indignity, disgrace*, AO.
ungerōtsian=unrōtsian
ungerwan=ungierwan
ungerȳde I. *rough, boisterous*, W 137⁷. II. n. *rough place*, Lk 3⁵.
ungerȳdelic *rough, violent*, GD 265²; LV 47. adv. -līce *suddenly, impetuously*, Æ.

ungerȳdnes f. *noise, tumult*, Sᴄ 82².
ungesadelod=unsadelod
ungesælig *unhappy, unfortunate*, Æ,AO, CP. adv. -līce *unhappily* : *wickedly*.
ungesælignes f. *unhappiness, misfortune*, BH,Bʟ.
ungesællīce=ungesæliglīce
ungesælō f. *trouble, misfortune, unhappiness, sorrow*, CP.
ungesawen=ungesewen
ungescaðignes=ungescešðignes
ungescēad I. n. *want of intelligence, senselessness.* II. adj. *unreasonable*, Lᴄᴅ : *excessive*, VH. III. adv. *exceedingly*, Dᴀ 243.
ungescēadlic *unreasonable, indiscreet.* adv. -līce *unreasonably, absurdly*.
ungescēadwīs(lic) *unintelligent, irrational, imprudent, foolish*, Æ,CP. adv. -līce.
ungescēadwīsnes f. *want of intelligence, indiscretion, folly, ignorance*, CP.
ungesce(a)pen *uncreated, unformed*, Æ.
ungescended *unhurt*, DR 146¹¹.
ungesceððed *unhurt*, BH 218²⁵.
ungesceððignes (a, æ) f. *innocence*, ÆH.
ungescrēpe (æ) I. n. *an inconvenience*, BH 382⁹. II. *inconvenient, useless*, BH,WW.
ungescrēpnes (æ) f. *discomfort*, BH 322³⁰.
ungescrōp n. *an inconvenience* BHᴄ 382⁹.
ungesegenlic=ungesewenlic
ungeseht adj. *at variance*, FM 358²⁸.
ungesēl-=ungesæl-; **ungesēne**=ungesȳne
ungesēnod *not signed with the cross*, Soʟ 148¹⁰. [segn]
ungesēonde *blind*, Lᴄᴅ 1·368'.
ungeseowenlic=ungesewenlic
unge-sewen, -sewen(d)lic *unseen, invisible*, Æ,CP. adv. -līce.
ungesibb *not related*, Rᴅ,Soʟ : *unfriendly, hostile*, Bʟ,BH.
ungesibsum *quarrelsome, contentious*, CP.
ungesibsumnes f. *quarrelsomeness, discord*, CP 351¹.
ungesilt=unsealt
ungesoden *unsodden, unboiled*, Lᴄᴅ.
ungesom *at variance*, ÆH 1·478'.
ungespēdig=unspēdig
ungestæððe-=ungestæððig-
ungestæððig *unsteady, inconstant, unstable, fickle*, CP. adv. -līce.
ungestæððignes f. *inconstancy, frivolity*, CP.
ungestrēon n. *ill-gotten treasure*, W 183⁹.
ungestroden *not subject to confiscation*, LL 12,4¹.
ungesund *unsound, faulty*, RWH 105².
ungesundlīce *excessively, exceedingly*, GD 15².
ungeswēge *inharmonious, dissonant, discordant, out of tune, harsh*, Gʟ.
ungeswenced *unceasing*, NC 329.

ungeswencedlic *unwearying*, BH436[16].
ungeswīcende *unceasing*, A2·357.
ungeswīcendlīce *incessantly*, Sc.
ungeswuncen *not laboured over, not well done*, WW430[11].
ungesylt=unsealt
ungesȳne (ē) *unseen, invisible*, WW17[46].
ungesȳnelic *invisible*, BL,W.
ungetǣse I. n. *trouble, hardship, severity*, CP. **II.** adj. *troublesome, inconvenient*.
ungetǣslīce adv. *inconveniently*, AS30[10].
ungetǣsnes f. *unsuitableness, inconvenience*, WW419[38].
ungetel *innumerable* (BT).
ungetemed=unātemed
ungetemprung f. *inclemency*, CM461.
ungetēori(g)endlic *inexhaustible.* adv. -*līce incessantly*, LL.
ungetēorod *unfailing*, Æ : *unwearied*, CHRD.
ungetēse=ungetǣse II.
unge-tīmu f? -tīme n? *evil time, adversity, mishàp*, AO,GD.
ungetinge (Æ), **ungetingful** (GPH) *not eloquent.* [tunge]
ungetogen *uneducated*, Æ. ['untowen']
ungetrēowe (ī, īe, ū, ȳ) *untrue, faithless*, Æ.
ungetrēownes f. *unbelief*, CP447[6] : *faithlessness*, GD160[5].
ungetrēowsian=untrēowsian
ungetrēowð f. *unfaithfulness, treachery*, W 160[6].
ungetrum *weak, infirm*, Bo132[32].
unge-trūw-, -trȳw-=un(ge)trēow-
ungetwǣre (WW248[17])=ungeðwǣre
ungetwēogendlīce (GD231[21]) = untwēogendlīce.
unge-tȳd, -tȳdd *ignorant, untaught, unskilful*, CP.
ungetȳred=ungetēorod
ungeðǣslic *unfit, improper, unseemly*, WW 191[23].
ungeðanc mn. *evil thought*, W.
ungeðancful *unthankful, ungrateful*, W241[4].
ungeðeaht n. *evil counsel*, RB118[10].
ungeðeahtendlīce *hastily*, BH124[13].
ungeðēawe adv. *not customary*, GUTH72[17].
ungeðēawfæst *ill-regulated*, RBL14[16].
ungeðēod *disunited, separate*, GEN1698.
ungeðinged *unexpected*, CP317[13],VH.
ungeðungen *base*, NAR42[12].
ungeðwǣre I. *disagreeing, quarrelsome, troublesome, stubborn, vexatious, undutiful, irreverent*, Æ,CP. **II.** n. *disturbance*, MtR 265.
ungeðwǣrian *to ǝe discordant, disagree, be at variance with*, Æ.
ungeðwǣrlic *inharmonious, discordant*, RB 19[2] : *hostile*, GD349. adv. -*līce peevishly*.

ungeðwǣrnes f. *disturbance, quarrel, discord*, AO : *violence*, BH144[27].
ungeðwēre=ungeðwǣre
ungeðyld fn. *impatience*, CP. [ðolian; Ger. ungeduld]
ungeðyldelīce adv. *impatiently*, Bo.
ungeðyldig *impatient*, Æ,CP.
ungeðylð=ungeðyld
ungeðyre '*discensor*'? Cp283[D].
ungewæder=ungewider
ungewæm-=ungewem-
ungewǣpnod *without weapons, unarmed*, Æ.
ungewealden *disordered (of the stomach)*, LCD : *involuntary, unwilling*, VH.
un-gewealdes, -gewaldes adv. *involuntarily, by chance*, CP.
ungeweaxen *immature*, WW352[27].
ungeweder=ungewider
un-gewemmed (Æ), -gewemmedlic *unspotted, unblemished, undefiled, uninjured.* adv. -*līce uncorruptly*, BH276[20].
ungewem(med)nes f. *freedom (from stain)*.
ungewende(n)dlic *immovable*, GD,LCD.
ungewendnes f. *unchangeableness* (Swt).
ungewēned *unexpected*, LCD.
ungewēnedlic *unhoped for*, GD347[14].
ungewēnendlic *incalculable*, GD284[20].
un-gewērged, -gewērigod *unwearied, untiring*.
un-gewidere n., gs. -gewidres *bad weather, storm*.
ungewiderung f. *bad weather*, CHR1086.
ungewild (y) *unsubdued*, OEG.
ungewilde (y) *not subject to, independent of*, AO : *untamed, unbridled.* [geweald]
ungewildelic (y) *unyielding*, ÆH2·92[2].
ungewill *displeasing*, CHR.
ungewilles *undesignedly*, LL31,21[13].
ungewintred *immature, young*, LL18,26.
ungewirhtum=ungewyrhtum
ungewis=ungewiss
ungewislic *unaccustomed*, Bo15[22]n.
ungewīsnes f. *uncertainty, ignorance*, BH.
ungewiss I. n. *uncertainty, ignorance*, Æ, AO : *unconsciousness* : *ignominy, shame*, SPs82[15]. **II.** adj. *uncertain*, Æ,CP : *unwise, ignorant, inexperienced* : *doubtful*, Æ : *causing shame, shameful*, KGL75[10].
ungewisses *unconsciously, involuntarily*, CP.
ungewītendlic *permanent, imperishable*, ÆL 34[298]. adv. -*līce permanently, perpetually*, CP441[21].
ungewitfæstnes f. *madness*, LCD82b.
ungewitful *unwise, senseless, mad*, CP.
ungewitfulnes f. *madness*, CP185[1].
ungewitlic *stupid, foolish*, LCD65a.
ungewitnes f. *folly*, GD95[23] (v. BTs).

ungewītnigendlīce *freely, with impunity,* ÆGR 233⁶n.
ungewītnod *unpunished,* Æ,CP.
ungewitt n. *folly, madness,* Æ.
ungewittig *irrational, foolish, mad,* Æ.
ungewittiglīce (-witte-) *unwisely, foolishly, madly,* GD 2; 104.
ungewittignes f. *folly, madness,* GD 163; 247.
ungewlitig *not bright, dull,* AS 31¹⁹.
±**ungewlitigian** *to disfigure,* AS.
ungeworht *unformed, unfinished,* Æ.
ungewriten *unwritten,* WW.
ungewuna I. m. *evil habit, vice,* CP 169⁹.
II. *unusual,* Æ : *uninhabited,* Æ.
ungewunelic *unusual, strange,* Æ. [*Ger.* ungewöhnlich] adv. -līce, Æ.
ungewuniendlic *uninhabitable,* Lᴄᴅ.
ungewyder=ungewider
ungewyld-=ungewild-
ungewylles=unwilles
ungewynelic=ungewunelic
ungewyrded *uninjured,* Pʜ 181.
ungewyrhtum (be) adv. phr. *without a cause,* CVPs.
ungier-wan, -ian (e, i, y) *to unclothe, divest of.*
ungifre *pernicious,* Gᴇɴ 2470.
ungifu f. *evil gift,* W 52,58.
unginne *not great or broad,* GɴE 206.
ungl=ungel; **unglad**=unglæd
unglæd (a) *cheerless, dull,* Bo 14¹⁴. [' *unglad* ']
unglædlic *implacable,* GPH 392 : *cheerless,* VH 22.
unglædnes f. '*imperitia,*' WW 423²⁹. [mistake for unglēawnes?]
unglǣw=unglēaw
unglēaw *ignorant, foolish, unwise,* Æ. adv. -līce, CP.
unglēawnes f. *want of discernment, folly, ignorance,* Pᴀ 70.
unglēawscīpe m. *folly,* Sc 83¹⁶.
unglenged=ungeglenged
ungnȳðe (ē) *not niggardly, not sparing, liberal.* adv. -līce, GD.
ungōd I. adj. *not good,* Lᴄd. [' *ungood* '] II. n. *evil.*
ungor=hungor
ungrǣdiglīce *abundantly,* GD 175¹.
ungrāpigende *not grasping,* ÆH 1·366'.
ungrēne *not green, bare of grass,* Gᴇɴ 117.
ungrīpendlic *irreprehensible,* EPs 18⁸.
ungrund *vast,* Ex 508.
ungrynde *bottomless,* Rɪᴍ 49.
ungyfeðe *unaccorded,* B 2921.
un-gyld, -gylde n. *excessive tax,* Cʜʀ. [gieldan]

ungylda m. *one who is not a member of a guild,* TC 606¹⁶.
ungylde adv. *not entitled to compensation,* LL.
ungyltig *innocent,* AO 184⁹.
un-gȳmen, -gȳming f. *carelessness,* BH.
ungȳmende (ē) *careless,* BH 434⁵.
ungyrdan=ongyrdan
ungyrian=ungierwan
ungystlīðe (=ie) *inhospitable,* NC 329.
unhādian (on-) *to unfrock, divest of holy orders,* LL.
unhādod=ungehādod
unhādung f. '*exordinatio,*' RBL 110⁸.
unhǣl=unhāl, unhǣlu
+**unhǣlan** *to weaken, debilitate,* Sc 51¹⁰.
unhǣlð f. *ill-health, weakness, infirmity.*
unhǣlu f. *sickness, unsoundness,* AO,Chrd, LL,MtL : *mischief, evil,* B,Bғ. [' *unheal* ']
unhǣmed *unmarried,* WW 530¹⁹.
unhǣr=unhār
unhāl *sick, ill, weak,* Æ,Bo; CP. [' *unwhole* ']
unhālgod *unhallowed, unconsecrated,* Æ.
unhālian *to pine away,* BPs 118¹³⁹.
unhālig (ǣ) ' *unholy,*' *profane,* ELPs 42¹.
un-hālwende (RHy), -hālwendlic (Æ) *incurable, deadly* : *unprofitable.*
unhandworht *not made with hands,* Mk 14⁵⁸.
unhār (=an-) *hoary, grizzled,* B 357.
unhēah (ē) *not high, low,* Æ.
unhēanlīce *valiantly,* Cʜʀ 755 : *not inadequately,* GD 43²⁵.
unhearmgeorn *inoffensive,* ÆH 2·44²⁰.
unhēarsumnes=unhīersumnes
un-hēg, -hēh=unhēah
unhelde (Cʜʀ 1095)=unhyldo
unhelian *to uncover, reveal,* Lk 12². [' *unhele* ']
un-hēor-, -hēr-=unhīer-
unhered *unpraised, not celebrated,* Bo 68²⁴.
unherigendlic *not praiseworthy,* ÆH 2·406¹⁷.
unhetol *peaceable,* NC 329.
unhīere (ē, ēo, ȳ) I. *horrible, monstrous, fierce, wild, tempestuous.* II. adv. *horribly.*
unhīerlic *wild, fierce, savage, gloomy.* adv. -līce (GD 161¹⁰).
unhīersum (ȳ) *disobedient,* Gᴜᴛʜ 12¹⁴. adv. -līce.
unhīersumnes (ȳ) f. *disobedience,* CP.
unhierwan (y²) *to calumniate,* Wᴄ 70¹⁵.
unhīredwist f. *unfamiliarity,* Sc 203¹³.
unhīwe *formless,* GPH 399²⁵⁹.
unhīwed *not feigned,* OEG.
unhlēowe *unfriendly, chill,* Ex 494.
unhlīdan (Æ)=onhlīdan
unhlīs(e) *infamous, disreputable,* KGL 68⁴².
unhlīsa m. *ill-fame, discredit, dishonour,* Æ.
unhlīsbǣre *disreputable,* WW 354¹⁷.

unhlīsēadig *infamous*, WW420[15].
unhlīsful *infamous*, GL.
unhlīsig *infamous*, KGL56[5].
unhlitme *very unhappily*, B1129 (or ?= unflitme).
unhlūd *not loud*, GD85[5].
unhlȳs-=unhlīs-
unhnēaw† *generous, liberal*.
unhoga *foolish*, MkL7[18].
unhold *disloyal, unfriendly, hostile*, Æ,BH. ['*unhold*']
unholda m. *monster, devil*, CR762.
unhrǣdsprǣce *slow of speech*, Ex6[30].
unhrēoflig *not leprous*, ÆH1·124'.
unhrōr *without motion*, Bo146[26].
unhūfed *bareheaded*, OEG4466.
unhwearfiende *unchangeable, fixed*, Bo20[29].
unhwīlen† *eternal*.
unhȳdig *ignorant, foolish*, AN,Bo.
unhȳhst=unhēhst superl. of unhēah.
unhyldo (e) f. *displeasure, disfavour, unfriendliness*, CP. [*Ger.* unhuld]
unhyr-=onhyr-
unhȳr-=unhīer-
unhȳðig† *unhappy*, AN,GU.
uni-=unge-
unīeð adv. (comp.) *with greater difficulty, more hardly*, CP. [ēað]
unīeð-=unēað-
unin-seglian, -sæglian (Æ) *to unseal*.
unīðe=unīeðe; uniucian=ungeocian
unlāb=unlāf
unlācnigendlic *incurable*, LCD1·262[1].
unlācnod *unhealed*, CP61[4].
unlǣce m. *bad physician*, LCD60b.
un-lǣd, -lǣde *poor, miserable, wretched, unhappy, unfortunate : accursed, wicked : straying? (of cattle)*.
unlǣdlic *miserable*, NC329. adv. -līce.
unlǣgne=unlīegne
unlǣne *permanent*, W264[18].
unlǣred *unlearned, untaught, ignorant*, CP.
unlǣrednes=ungelǣredne;
unlæt *unwearied, indefatigable*, WW.
unlǣttu f. *sin*, GD289. [unlǣd]
unlāf f. *posthumous child*, WW.
unlagu f. *abuse of law, bad law, oppression, injustice*, LL. æt unlagum *unlawfully*. ['*unlaw*']
unland m. *desert, waste : counterfeit, supposed land*, WH13.
unlandāgende m. *not owning land*, LL112.
unlār f. *bad teaching*, LL,W.
unlaðod (ByH26[23])=ungelaðod
unlēafful=ungelēafful
unleahtorwyrðe *not culpable*, PPs18[7].
unlēanod *unpaid*, EC148[4].
unlēas *not false, true : truthful*. adv. -līce.
unlēcð=unlȳcð pres. 3 sg. of unlūcan.

unlēfedlic=unlȳfendlic; unlēgne=unlīegne
unlēof† *not dear, hated*.
unleoðuwāc (e[3]) *inflexible, rigid, stubborn*.
unleoðuwācnes f. *inflexibility*, WW.
unlēsan=unlīesan; unlib-=unlyb-
unlic=ungelic
unlīchamlic *incorporeal*, Æ,GD.
unlīcð (Æ)=unlȳcð pres. 3 sg. of unlūcan.
unlīcwyrðe *displeasing*, ÆL23b[374].
unlīefed=unālȳfed
unlīegne (ǣ, ē) *not to be questioned*, LL.
unlīesan (ē, ȳ) *to unloose*, Æ : *set free, put on a free footing*.
unlīf n. *death*, MFH176.
unlīfes *dead*, ÆL18[203].
unlifi(g)ende (y) *lifeless, dead*. [libban]
unliss? (hl-) *disfavour*, OET464 (v. ANS 142·254).
unlītel=unlȳtel
unlīðe *ungentle, harsh, severe*, Æ.
unlīðowāc=unleoðuwāc
unlofod *unpraised*, PR62.
unlond=unland
unlūcan[2] *to unlock, open*, Chrd; Æ. ['*unlouk*']
unlust m. *evil desire, lust, sensuality*, Æ : *disinclination, weariness, laziness*, Æ,Sol : *nausea*, LCD. [*Ger.* unlust]
+unlustian *to loathe*, BL59[8].
unlyb-ba m., -be f. *poisonous drug, poison*, Æ : *witchcraft*, Æ. [lybb]
unlybbende (MH164[21])=unlifigende
unlybwyrhta m. *worker with spells or poisons, wizard*, Æ.
unlȳfednes=unālīefednes
unlȳfendlic *illicit, unlawful*, ZDA31[8].
unlȳfigende=unlifigende
unlyft f. *bad air*, LCD6a.
unlygen *unlying, truthful*, LL156,12.
unlȳsan (Æ)=unlīesan
unlȳt n. *a great deal*, PPs61[9].
unlȳtel *not small, much, great, very large*.
unmǣdlīce=unmǣðlīce
unmǣg? m. *evil kinsman? alien?* WALD2[23].
unmǣge *not akin*, PPs68[8].
unmǣgel=unmeagol
unmǣgnes f. *weariness*, WW224[14].
unmǣgðlīce=unmǣðlīce
unmǣht- (N)=unmiht-
unmǣle *unspotted, immaculate, pure, virgin*.
unmǣne *not criminal, honest, innocent, truthful : free (from)*.
un-mǣre, -mǣrlic *inglorious*, Bo.
unmǣte *excessive, immense, great, vast*, BH; Æ : *countless, innumerable*. ['*unmeet*']
unmǣtlic (ē) *enormous*, AA6[3],22[4].
unmǣtnes f. *vastness, excessive greatness*, BH.
unmǣð f. *transgression, sin*, HL13·234.

unmǣðful *immoderate, excessive*, NC329.
unmǣðlic *excessive*, Æ. adv. -līce *excessively*, Æ : *unmercifully, cruelly*, Æ.
un-maga m., -magu f. *needy person, dependant, orphan*, LL.
unmanig *not many, few*, GUTH,BH.
unmann m. *monster, wicked man*, Æ : *hero*, GUTH12²⁷.
un-meagol, -meahl *insipid*, WW.
unmeaht=unmiht
unmedome (e³, u³) *incompetent, unfit, unworthy*, Æ,CP.
unmedomlīce adv. *negligently, carelessly*, LL.
unmeht=unmiht
unmeltung f. *indigestion*, LCD95a.
unmendlinga=unmyndlinga
unmēne=unmǣne
unmenged *unmixed*, WW.
unmenn nap. of unmann.
unmennisclic *inhuman*, Bo70²⁶.
unmēt-=unmǣt-
unmicel (y²) *little, small*, GD.
unmīdlod *unrestrained, unbridled*, CP.
unmidome=unmedome
unmiht (ie) I. f. *weakness*, CP. ['*unmiht*'] II. (æ) *impossible*, MtL.
+unmihtan *to deprive of strength*, ÆL25⁷⁷¹.
un-mihtelic, -mihtlic *impossible*, G.
unmihtig (æ, e) *weak, powerless*, Æ,Bo : *impossible*, NG. ['*unmighty*']
unmihtiglic (æ) *weak*, LCD : *impossible*, LkLR.
unmihtignes f. *weakness*, LCD.
unmilde *not meek, harsh*, BH100²⁹. ['*unmild*']
unmildheort *merciless*, Æ.
unmilts f. *severity, anger*, Ct.
unmiltsigendlic *unpardonable*, ÆT78⁶³. [milts]
unmiltsung f. *hardness of heart*, AO64¹⁶.
unmirigð=unmyrhð
unmōd n. *depression*, LCD65a.
unmōdig *humble*, CP : *timid*.
unmolsniendlic *uncorrupted*, OEG60.
un-monig, -moneg=unmanig
unmurn *untroubled*, PPs75⁴.
unmurnlīce† adv. *unpityingly, without sorrowing*.
unmycel=unmicel
unmyhtig=unmihtig; unmylts-=unmilts-
unmyndgian=unmynegian
unmynd-linga, -lenga, -lunga adv. *unawares, unexpectedly*, Æ,AO : *undesignedly*.
unmynegian *to overlook, not to demand*, LL 382,43.
unmyrge *unpleasant? sad?* WW211¹⁶.
unmyrhð f. *sadness*, W148⁹,VH.
unna m.=unne

±unnan pres. 1 sing. an(n), on(n), pl. unnon; pret. sg. ūðe, pp. ±unnen swv. w. d. pers. and g. *thing to grant, allow, bestow, give*, B,Bo,CP,Chr,G,Ps; AO,Æ : *be glad to see, wish, desire*, AO,Ps. un-nendre handa *voluntarily*. ['(*i*)-*unne*']
unne f. *favour, approval, permission, consent* : *grant* : *liberality*.
unnēah adj. adv. *not near, far, away from*.
un-nēde, -nēdig=unnīedig
unnēdelīce (GD346⁹; JAW55,56)=ungnȳðelīce
unnēg, unnēh=unnēah
unnend m. *one who grants*, DR5⁵.
unnet=unnyt
unnīed-ig, -enga adv. *without compulsion or restraint, willingly*, CP. [nēad]
unnit=unnyt II.
unnīðing m. *honest man* (*not an outlaw*), CHR1087; v. ANS117·22.
un-nyt, -nytt I. adj. *useless, unprofitable*, Æ,CP. II. m. *unprofitableness, emptiness, vanity, folly* : *useless thing*.
unnytenes=unnytnes
unnytlic *useless, unprofitable, foolish*, CP. adv. -līce.
unnytlicnes f. *uselessness*, LCD.
unnytnes f. *unprofitableness, frivolity, emptiness*, LL,W.
unnytwyrðe *unprofitable, useless*, Æ,CP. adv. -wurðlīce, Æ.
unnȳðones? f. *peace, freedom from hate*, VH 23.
unofercumen *unsubdued*, GL.
unoferfēre (oe⁴) *impassable*, GL.
unoferhrēfed *not roofed in*, BL125²¹.
unoferswīð-ed, -edlic, -ende, -endlic *unconquerable, invincible*.
unoferwin-nene (WW), -nendlic (AO) *invincible*.
unoferwrigen *not covered*, ÆL23b²⁰⁹.
unoferwunnen *unconquered*, AO156²⁸.
unoferwunnendlic=unoferwinnendlic
unoflinnedlīce *unceasingly*, NC329.
unofslegen *not killed*, ÆH2·544'.
unondcȳðignes f. *ignorance*, JVPs24⁷.
unondgetful=unandgittol
unongunnen *without a beginning*, ByH80²³.
unonlȳsendlic *unpardonable*, GD348⁴.
unonstyred *unmoved*, GD270⁹n.
unonstyrigendlic *motionless*, GD225⁴.
unonwend-endlic, -edlic *unchangeable, constant, immovable*. adv. -līce.
unorne *old, worn out, decrepit*, Ma256. ['*unorn*']
unornlic *old, worn*, Jos9⁵.
unplēolic *not dangerous, safe*, Æ. adv. -līce.
unrǣd m. *folly, foolish plan* : *crime, mischief, injury, plot, treachery*, Æ,AO.

unræden f. *ill-considered act*, GEN 982.
unrædfæst *unreliable, incompetent*, ÆP 212¹⁵.
unrædfæstlíce *unwisely, rashly*, ÆL 18⁴⁵⁶.
unrædlic *thoughtless*, BL 99²¹. adv. -líce, Æ.
unrædsíð m. *foolish enterprise*, RD 12⁴.
unræfniendlic *intolerable*, SPs 123⁴ (on-).
unreht=unriht
unrehthæmdere=unrihthæmere
unreordlic v. ungereordlic
±unrētan *to make sad*, AO. [rōt]
unrētu f. *sadness, disquiet, anxiety*, AA 46⁹.
unrēðe *not cruel, gentle*, ÆH 2·44'.
unríce *poor*, LL,RB.
unriht (e, y) **I.** n. *wrong, sin, vice, wickedness, evil*, Æ,B,Bo,Chr : *injustice, oppression*, Bo,LL; Æ : *wrong act*, Bo. **II.** adj. *wrong, unrighteous, wicked, false* : *unlawful*, Bo,Ps. ['*unright*']
unrihtcræfing f. *unjust claim*, TC.
unrihtcyst f. *vice*, LL (262').
unrihtdǣd f. *evil doing*, BH,W.
unrihtdǣde *iniquitous*, LPs 9²⁴.
unrihtdēma m. *unjust judge*, W.
unrihtdōm m. *iniquity*, DA 183.
unrihtdōnd m. *evildoer*, BL 63¹⁵.
unrihte *unjustly, wrongly*, B,Ps. ['*unright*']
unrihtfēoung f. *unrighteous hate*, MET 27¹.
unrihtful *unrighteous, wicked*, NC 329.
unrihtgestrēon n. *unrighteous gain*, BL 63⁸.
unrihtgestrod n. *ill-gotten booty*, NC 330.
unrihtgewill n. *evil desire*, Bo 9²³.
unrihtgewilnung (y)=unrihtwillnung
unrihtgilp m. *vainglory*, LL (262').
unrihtgītsung f. *wrongful greed*, BL,Bo.
unrihthǣman *to fornicate, commit adultery.*
unrihthǣmdere (VPs 49¹⁸)=unrihthǣmere
unrihthǣmed **I.** n. *fornication, adultery.* **II.** adj. *adulterous.*
unrihthǣmedfremmere m. *adulterer*, NC 330.
unrihthǣmend m. *adulterer*, BL 63.
unrihthǣmere m. *fornicator, adulterer*, Æ.
unrihthǣmeð=unrihthǣmed I.
unrihthēmere (KGL)=unrihthǣmere
unrihtlic (e, y) *unrighteous, wrongful, wicked*, Æ. adv. -líce, MH,RB. ['*unrightly*']
unrihtlust m. *unlawful desire*, Bo 19²⁰,VH.
unrihtlyblác nm. *unlawful magic*, W 253¹¹.
unrihtnes (e²) f. *wrong, wickedness*, BL.
unrihttíd f. *improper occasion*, MFH 177.
unrihtweorc n. *secular work done on Sunday*, LL (130²⁵).
unrihtwíf n. *unlawful consort, mistress*, TC 373'.
unrihtwífung f. *unlawful wedlock*, BH 116³.
unrihtwillend (y²) m. *evil-disposed person*, CP 89²².

unrihtwillnung f. *unlawful desire, lust, ambition*, CP.
unrihtwís '*unrighteous,*' *wrong, unjust*, Bl, Bo,G,VPs; Æ,CP. adv. -líce, CP. ['*unrighteously*']
unrihtwísnes (e, y) f. *injustice,* '*unrighteousness,*' *iniquity*, Bf,VPs; Æ,CP.
unrihtwísu f. *unrighteousness*, BL,Ps.
unrihtwrígels n. *covering of error*, BL 105³⁰.
unrihtwyrcend m. *evildoer*, BL.
unrihtwyrhta (y) m. *evildoer*, CP.
unrím **I.** n. *countless number, huge host, large quantity, mass.* **II.**=unríme
unríme *countless, innumerable*, BH.
unrímfolc n. *countless number (of people)*, CP 51¹².
unrímgōd? n. *incalculable good*, BH 94¹⁹.
unrípe *immature,* '*unripe,*' *WW.*
unrōt *sad, dejected*, Æ,CP : *displeased, angry.*
unrōtian *to become sad* : (±) *make sad.*
unrōtlic *sad, gloomy*, MtL. adv. -líce, MtR 16³.
unrōtmōd *sad-hearted*, BL 113¹².
unrōtnes f. *sadness, contrition, disquietude*, Æ,CP.
±unrōtsian *to be or become sad, be grieved*, Æ : *make sad.*
unrūh *smooth, without seams*, JnLR 19²³.
unryht (AO,CP)=unriht
unrȳne m. *diarrhœa*, LCD 1·172¹².
unsac *not accused, innocent*, LCD 3·288⁶.
unsadelod *not saddled*, LL.
unsǣd *unsated, insatiable*, PPs 100⁵.
unsǣd **I.** n. *evil seed*, W 40²³. **II.** *not said*, ÆH. ['*unsaid*']
unsæht=unseht
unsǣl m. *unhappiness*, W 236²⁶. ['*unsele*']
unsǣlan *to untie, unfasten*, WW.
unsǣle *wicked*, WW 421²³. ['*unsele*']
unsǣlig *unfortunate, unhappy, wretched*, Jul,W : *mischievous, pernicious*, Gen 637 : *wicked*, An. ['*unseely*']
unsǣlð f. *unhappiness, misfortune, adversity, misery*, Bo,Ps; CP. ['*unselth*']
unsǣpig *sapless*, ÆH 1·102⁴.
unsalt=unsealt
unsamwrǣde *contrary, incongruous*, Bo 106⁶.
unsār *painless*, AO,CP.
unsāwen *unsown*, LL 450,10.
unscǣðed=ungesceðed
unscǣðful (e, ea) *innocent.* adv. -líce, CP.
unscǣðfulnes (ea, e) f. *innocence*, CP.
unscǣðð-ednes, -ignes (e) f. *harmlessness, innocence*, Æ.
unscǣðð-ende (e²), -ig *innocent, harmless*, Æ,BH.

unscamfæst *impudent, shameless,* GL.
unscamfulnes (eo²) f. *shamelessness, immodesty,* MkL7²⁰.
unscamig *unashamed,* JUL552.
unscamlic *shameless, immodest,* Æ. adv.
-līce.
unscað-=unscæð(ð)-
un-scēad(e)līce *unreasonably,* RB54¹³.
unscēadwīslic *unreasonable,* ÆH2·210'.
unsceaft f. *monster?* RD88³².
unsceam-=unscam-
unsceapen *uncreated, unformed,* ByH72²⁰, RHy54¹³.
unscearp *not sharp (of wine),* LCD.
unscearpnes f. *dulness,* BH402²⁹.
unscearpsȳne *not sharp-sighted,* LCD11b.
unsceað-=unscæð-
unscelleht (=ie) *not having a shell,* LCD33b.
unscellīce *without discrimination, recklessly?* RWH141³ (v. scelle).
unscende (y)† *blameless, glorious.*
un-scende, scendende *uninjured, uncorrupted.*
unscennan *to unharness,* WW91¹³.
unscēod=unscōd pp. of unscōgan.
unscēogan=unscōgan
unsceom- (NG)=unscam-
unscēotan (WW190³⁰)=onscēotan
unsceð-=unscæð-; **unscildig**=unscyldig
unscirped *unclothed,* MtL22¹¹.
unscōgan (ēo) *to unshoe.* pp. unscōd '*unshod,*' Æ,CP.
unscom-=unscam-
unscoren *unshorn,* CM,WW.
unscortende *not failing,* LkLR12³³.
unscrȳdan (ē², ī²) *to put off (clothes), undress, uncover, strip, deprive of,* Æ. unscrȳdd pp. *naked.* [scrūd]
unscyld f. *innocency,* SPs40¹³.
unscyldgung f. *innocence,* ERPs17²⁵.
unscyldig (i) *guiltless, innocent,* Æ,CP : *not responsible.*
unscyldiglic *excusable,* BL189³². adv. -līce *innocently,* BK12.
unscyldignes f. *innocence,* Ps.
unscynde=unscende
unscȳrdan=unscrȳdan
unscyttan *to undo, unbolt,* ÆL31⁸⁶³.
unscyðende=unscæððende
unseald *ungiven,* HL10⁴⁹⁵.
unsealt (a, y) *unsalted, insipid,* G,WW.
unsēfernes=unsȳfernes
unsefful *senseless,* RHy6³¹. [sefa]
unsegenlic (ByH6,8)=unsewenlic
unseglian *to unseal,* RWH78³³.
unseht I. mfn. *discord, disagreement, quarrel.* **II.** adj. *not agreed, hostile,* Chr. ['*unsaught*']
unsehtnes f. *discord, quarrel,* NC330. ['*unsaughtness*']

un-seldan, -seldon (Æ) *not seldom, repeatedly, frequently,* LL. ['*unselde*']
unsēofene *not sighing,* MFH177.
unsewenlic *invisible,* Bo138².
unsibb f. *dissension, contention, war, strife,* AO.
unsibbian *to disagree,* WW.
unsibsumnes f. *anxiety,* JnL p6¹.
unsideful *immodest, unchaste,* WW.
unsidefullnes f. *immodesty,* OEH300'.
unsidelīce *immodestly, indecorously,* CHRD 60³⁴.
unsidu m. *bad custom, vice, impurity, unseemliness.* [*Ger.* unsitte]
unsīf-=unsȳf-
unsigefæst *not victorious,* ÆL18⁴⁴.
unsingian=unsyngian
unsīð m. *unfortunate journey or expedition, misfortune, mishap,* Æ.
unslǣpig *sleepless,* WW427¹⁵.
unslāw (ǣ, ēa) *not slow, active,* Æ,W. ['*unslow*'] adv. -līce, CP381¹.
unsleac *not remiss, active, diligent,* WW. adv. -līce, RB20¹⁸.
unslēaw=unslāw
unslid? unslit (Cp33s) n. *fat, grease, tallow.* [*Ger.* unschlitt; or ?=unsylt]
unslitten *untorn,* JnL19²³.
unslȳped *open, loosed,* W83⁹.
unsmǣðe=unsmēðe
unsmeoruwig *not greasy,* LCD106b (smerig).
unsmēðe *not smooth, uneven, rough, scabby,* WW.
unsmēðnes f. *roughness,* WW.
unsmōð=unsmēðe
unsnotor (e³) *unwise,* ÆGR. adv. -līce.
unsnotornes (y², e³) f. *folly : wickedness,* LPs.
unsnott-=unsnot-
unsnyttru† f. *folly, ignorance.*
unsnyttrum† adv. *foolishly.*
unsoden *uncooked,* Lcd. ['*unsodden*']
unsōfte *harshly, bitterly, severely, violently,* Gu,Lcd; Æ : *with difficulty, hardly, scarcely : uncomfortably.* ['*unsoft*']
unsōftlīce *harshly,* ÆH1·434⁷.
unsōm f. *disagreement,* LL.
unsorh *free from care,* BL217²⁹.
unsōð I. adj. *untrue, false.* **II.** n. *falsehood.*
unsōðfæst *untruthful : unjust, unrighteous.*
unsōðfæstnes f. *injustice, unrighteousness.*
+**unsōðian** *to falsify, disprove,* LL202,320.
unsōðsag-ol, -ul *untruthful,* Æ.
unspannan⁷ *to unfasten,* WW231³⁵.
unspecende=unsprecende
unspēd f. *want, poverty,* LG,Ps. ['*unspeed*']
unspēdig *poor,* Æ,AO : *not fertile,* GEN 962.

unspiwol *that stops vomiting?* LCD.
unspornend=onspornend
unsprecende *not able to speak,* Æ.
unstæfwīs *illiterate,* GPH393.
unstæðöïg *unstable, irregular, weak, frivol ous, wanton,* Æ.
unstæðöïgnes f. *instability, inconstancy, wantonness,* Æ.
unstaðolfæst *unstable, unenduring, weak, fickle,* Æ.
unstaðolfæstnes f. *instability, weakness, fickleness,* Æ.
unstenc m. *stench, stink,* DD,W.
+unstill-an, -ian *to disturb, agitate,* RB.
unstille *moving, changeable, restless, inquiet, uneasy,* CP.
unstil(l)nes f. *agitation, restlessness, disturbance, disquiet, trouble, disorder, tumult,* Æ,AO.
unstrang *weak, infirm, feeble, MH,RB;* Æ. ['*unstrong*']
unstrenge *weak,* ÆH2·390'.
unstydful *inconstant, apostate,* DR121¹⁰. [=unstede-]
unstydfullnes (on-) f. *instability,* DR.
unstyrendlic *immovable, hard to carry,* MtL 23⁴.
unstyriende *immovable, stationary,* Bo.
unswǣs *unpleasant, disagreeable, uncongenial.* adv. -swǣse.
unswǣslic *ungentle, cruel,* JUD65. [swǣs]
unswefn n. *bad dream,* LCD3·288'.
unsweotol *imperceptible, indistinct,* Bo, MET.
unswēte *not sweet : foul, GD,Lcd.* ['*unsweet*']
unswicen *unbetrayed, unharmed, safe,* CHR 1048.
un-swicende, -swiciende *true, faithful,* CHR.
unswicol *trustworthy, true,* GL,W.
unswīð *not strong,* LCD. adv. -swīðe *sluggishly,* OEG56⁸³.
unsydeful=unsideful
unsȳferlic *impure,* BL43¹⁷.
unsȳfernes f. *impurity, foulness,* BH.
unsȳfre (ī) I. adj. *impure, unclean, filthy.* II. adv. *filthily,* CR1484?
unsylt=unsealt
unsyngian *to exculpate,* LL98,21¹.
unsynnig *guiltless, innocent, Æ : undeserved.*
unsynnum adv. *guiltlessly,* B1072.
untǣle *blameless, faultless,* Æ.
untǣled *unblamed,* CP351²⁰.
untǣllic (ā) *blameless, immaculate, undefiled, praiseworthy.* adv. -līce, Æ,CP.
untǣl-wierðe (y³) *blameless,* CP. adv. -wierðlīce.
untæslic=unðæslic; untāl-=untǣl-
untala (NG)=untela

untamcul *untameable,* GPH397.
unteala=untela
unteald *uncounted,* LCD3·264¹¹.
untealt *stable, steady,* CHR897D.
untela adv. *not well, amiss, badly, ill, improperly, wrongly,* CP.
untellendlic *indescribable* (Swt).
untemed *untamed, CPs,WW.* ['*untemed*']
untēmende=untȳmende
untēnan (KGL)=ontȳnan
untēogoðad *untithed,* CP439²⁹.
unteola=untela
untēorig *untiring, unceasing,* MET28¹⁷.
untīdǣt *untimely eating,* NC330.
untīdfyl f. *untimely eating or drinking,* W46¹⁴.
untīdgewidere n. *unseasonable weather,* CHR1095.
untīdlic *unseasonable,* AO. adv. -līce.
untīdspǣc f. *untimely speech,* LL(322⁹).
untīdweorc n. *work at an improper time* (*e.g. on Sunday*), W.
untīena (AO)=ontēona
untīgan *to '*untie,*' loosen, unchain, G;* Æ. [tēag]
untilad *destitute,* Bo16¹².
untīma m. *unseasonableness, wrong time, Æ,CP : bad time, misfortune,* W297⁷. ['*untime*']
untimber *worthless material?* (BTs), MFH 176 (or ?=on-t.).
untīme *ill-timed, unfortunate,* Æ. ['*untime*']
untīmnes f. *evil times,* W207¹⁸.
untīnan=ontȳnan
untōbrocen *unbroken,* Æ.
untōclofen *uncloven,* ÆL25⁴⁵.
untōdǣled *undivided, individual, indivisible, inseparable,* BF,Bo.
untōdǣl(ed)lic *inseparable, indivisible,* Æ. adv. -līce.
untōdǣl(ed)nes f. *undividedness,* BF118¹.
untō-dǣl(end)-, dāl-, -dēlen=untōdǣled-
untogen *untied, loose,* GD222³.
untōlǣtendlīce *incessantly,* GD117²³.
untō-lēsende, -lȳsende *that cannot be loosed, inextricable,* WW.
untōlȳsendlic *unforgivable,* GD342²⁶.
untōsceacen *unshaken,* TC.
untōslegen *unshattered,* AS22²³.
untōsliten *untorn, uninjured,* CP.
untōsprecendlic *ineffable,* TC.
untōtwǣmed *undivided,* ÆH.
untōworpenlic (e², a⁴) *inviolable,* OEG11¹⁵³.
untrāglīce *frankly,* EL410.
untrēow=untrēowð
untrēowe (ī, ȳ) '*untrue,*' *unfaithful,* LL.
untrēowfǣst (ī, ȳ) *unfaithful, unreliable,* GPH,NIC475²⁸.

untrēowlīce *faithlessly, AO.* ['*untruly*']
untrēownes f. *unfaithfulness,* GD 160⁵.
untrēowsian *to defraud, deceive,* CP : *offend,*
G.
untrēowð f. *unfaithfulness, treachery, AO.*
untrum *infirm, weakly, sick, ill, BH,Bl,*
VPs; Æ,CP. ['*untrum*']
untrumhād m. *infirm state,* BH 78²⁸.
untrumian *to be or become sick or infirm* :
make weak, Æ.
untrumlic *infirm, weak,* NUM 13²⁰.
untrumnes f. *weakness, sickliness, infirmity,*
illness, Chr,CP,Mt; Æ,AO.
untrymed *unconfirmed (by a bishop),* LL
(140¹⁹).
un-trymig, -trymmig *sick, infirm,* NG.
untrymigan *to become weak,* JnL 6².
untrymmigo f. *illness,* MtL 10¹.
untrymnes=untrumnes
untrymð f. *weakness, illness,* LL,PPs.
untrȳw-=untrēow-
untwēgendlīce=untwēogendlīce
untwēo m. *certainty,* CR 961.
untwēod *undoubting,* AN 1244.
untweofeald=untwiefeald
untwēogende *unhesitating, not doubting,*
CP.
untwēogendlic *indubitable, certain.* adv.
-līce *indubitably, unhesitatingly, undoubt-*
ingly, AO,CP.
untwēolic (ī) *undoubted,* OEG. adv. -līce
certainly, with certainty, Æ.
untwēonde=untwēogende
untwēon(d)līce=untwēogendlīce
untwēonigend (ȳ) *undoubting,* A 9·115⁴⁵.
untwī-, untwȳ-=untwēo-, untwie-
untwie-feald, -feld *not double,* CP : *not*
double-minded, without duplicity, sincere,
CP.
untȳd *unskilful, inexperienced,* CP.
untȳddre=untȳdre; untȳdlic=untīdlic
untȳdre I. *firm, unbending,* AN 1254. II. m.
monster, B 111.
untȳdrende *barren,* LCD 33b.
untȳgian=untīgan
untȳgða *unsuccessful (in getting one's wish),*
CP 257¹⁸.
untȳmende *barren, unfruitful, Æ.* [tīeman]
untȳnan=ontȳnan
untȳned *unfenced,* LL 106,40.
unðærfe in phr. 'unðærfe ðing' '*nequa-*
quam,' MtL 2⁶. [unðearf]
unðæslic *inappropriate, unseemly, unbe-*
coming, absurd, Æ. adv. -līce, Æ.
unðæslicnes f. *impropriety,* ÆH 2·316⁸.
unðæslicu f. *incongruity,* RB 124¹³.
unðanc m. *ingratitude, disinclination, dis-*
pleasure, AO,Sol; Æ,CP : evil intention,
an ill turn, ApT,Chr,CP; Æ. unðances

unwillingly, compulsorily, AO, Chr,LL.
['*unthank*']
unðancful *unthankful,* CP,GD.
unðanc-ol, -ul *ungrateful,* NC 330.
unðanc-wurðe, -wyrðe *ungrateful* : *not*
acceptable, disagreeable, Æ.
unðancwyrðlīce *ungratefully,* NC 330.
unðearf f. *damage, hurt, detriment, ruin,*
Æ.
unðearfes *without a cause,* PPs 13⁶.
unðēaw m. *vice, sin, fault, CP; Æ.* ['*un-*
thew']
unðēawfæst *disorderly, ill-mannered, dis-*
solute, Æ. adv. -līce.
unðēawful *uncontrolled, disorderly,* WW.
unðinged *unexpected, sudden,* CP.
unðingod *unatoned for,* CP 423³⁵.
unðolemōdnes f. *impatience, A.* ['*unthole-*
moodness']
unðoligendlic *intolerable,* Sc 208¹⁴.
unðorfæst *unprofitable,* DR 179¹⁷.
un-ðrīste, -ðrīeste *diffident,* CP.
unðrōwendlicnes f. *impassibility,* ZDA
31·14.
unðrōwigendlic *unsuffering, Æ.*
unðurhscēotendlic *impenetrable,* LCD.
unðurhtogen *unperformed,* CP 329¹⁴.
unðwægen=unðwogen
unðwǣre=ungeðwǣre
+unðwǣrian *to disagree, Æ,CP.*
unðwǣrnes f. (ē) *discord, division,* CHR.
un-ðwean, -ðwagen, -ðwægen, -ðwegen,
-ðwēn=unðwogen
unðwērnes=unðwǣrnes
unðwogen *unwashed,* G.
unðyhtig *weak,* OET 107.
unðyldig=ungeðyldig
unðyldicnes f. *difficulty,* BH 2·340.
unwāclic† *steadfast, strong, noble, splendid.*
adv. -līce.
unwǣded (ē) *not clothed,* MtL 22¹¹.
unwǣder=unweder
unwælgrim *gentle, merciful,* GD 133⁶.
unwæm-=unwem-
unwær (-war- in obl. cases) *incautious, care-*
less, unthinking, foolish, Æ,Bl,CP :
unaware, unexpected. on un-wær, -waran,
-warum *unawares, unexpectedly, Chr.*
['*unware*']
unwæres (o¹, a²) *unawares, suddenly, Chr.*
['*unwares*']
unwærlic *unwary, heedless,* CP. adv. -līce,
AO,Bl,Chr; CP. ['*unwarely*']
unwærnes f. *heedlessness,* W 297⁷.
unwærscipe m. *folly,* ÆH 1·68⁴.
unwæscen '*unwashen,*' Lcd 41b.
unwæstm mfn. *barrenness,* W : *tare, weed,*
NG.
unwæstmbǣre *unfruitful, barren, Æ,CP.*

unwæstm-bærnes (Æ,AO), -berendnes (Æ) f. *unfruitfulness, barrenness, sterility.*
unwæstmberendlic *sterile,* WE54⁹.
unwæstmfæst *barren,* BL163⁶.
unwæstmfæstnes f. *barrenness,* BL163¹⁷.
unwæterig *dry, desert, Lk.* ['*unwatery*']
unwandiende *unhesitating,* CP381²⁵.
unwar- v. unwær.
unwarnod '*unwarned,*' LL382³³.
unwealden *involuntary,* VH23.
unwealt *steady, stable,* CHR897.
unwearnum† adv. *irresistibly : suddenly, in a moment.*
unwearð=unweorð
unweaxen† *not grown up, young.*
unwēded=unwǣded
unweder n. *unfavourable season, bad weather, storm, Chrd, LG;* Æ. ['*unweather*']
unwederlīce adv. *tempestuously,* Mt16³.
unweg=onweg
unwegen *not weighed,* LCD1·376⁷.
unwemlic *unsullied, pure,* WW522³⁵.
un-wemme(d) *unblemished, unstained, uninjured, Æ,DR,Ps : inviolate.* ['*unwemmed*']
unwemmend m. *innocent man,* REPs 36¹⁸ (on-).
unwemming f. *incorruptibility, incorruption,* Sc41¹⁰.
unwemmu (æ²) f. *spotlessness,* RWH136³⁵.
unwemnes f. *purity,* HL18⁴²².
unwended=unāwended
+unwendnes=onwendnes
unwēne *unexpected : hopeless,* Æ.
unwēned *unexpected, unhoped for,* AA,Sc.
unwēnlic adj. *unpromising, hopeless, desperate,* AO,CP. adv. -līce *unexpectedly, by chance,* GD88¹⁷.
unwēnunga *unexpectedly,* Bo140¹⁰.
unwēod n. *ill weed,* W92¹⁹.
unweoder=unweder
unweorcheard *delicate, weakly, infirm,* RB 75⁸.
unweorclic (o) *unsuitable for work,* BF122²⁴.
un-weorð (u, y), -wierðe (u) adj. adv. *unworthy, Æ : poor, mean, of low estate, AO, Chrd,RB : worthless : contemptible, ignoble, Bo.* ['*unworth*']
±unweorðian (o, u) *to slight, treat with contempt, dishonour, Æ,LG;* CP : *become worthless, vile, dishonour oneself.* ['*unworth*']
unweorðlic (u) *unworthy, dishonourable,* AO : *unimportant, humble,* CP. adv. -līce *unworthily, dishonourably, ignominiously,* AO,CP : *indignantly.*
unweorðnes f. *slight, contempt, disgrace,* AO,CP.

unweorðscipe m. *dishonour, disgrace, Bo : indignation,* CP222⁹. ['*unworship*']
unweorðung (u) f. *disgrace : indignation,* CP222¹² : *dishonouring,* CHRD40.
unweotod=unwitod
unwer (KGL)=unwær
unwered *unprotected,* GEN812.
unwērig *unwearying, indefatigable, persistent, AO, Lcd;* Æ. ['*unweary*']
unwerlīce=unwærlīce
unwerod *not sweet,* CP447¹⁹.
unwestm=unwæstm; unweðer=unweder
unwīd *not wide,* NC330.
unwidere n. *bad weather,* W.
unwidlod *unpolluted,* DR90¹⁷.
unwierðe=unweorð
unwīese=unwīse, unwīslīce
unwilla m. *repugnance, displeasure, Æ,AO, LL,Sol,WW.* ['*unwill*']
unwillan=unwillum
unwillende '*unwilling,*' *involuntary, CP : averse (to), HL.*
unwilles adv. *unwillingly, involuntarily, reluctantly,* Æ.
unwillum adv. *unwillingly, reluctantly.* his unwillum *against his will, AO : involuntarily, unintentionally.*
unwilsumlīce adv. *involuntarily, against one's will,* BH442²³.
unwindan³ (=on-) *to unwind, uncover,* Æ.
unwine m. *foe, enemy,* CHR,Ct.
unwinsum=unwynsum
unwīs '*unwise,*' *foolish, ignorant, uninformed, Bl,VPs;* CP : *insane,* GD.
unwīsdōm m. '*unwisdom,*' *imprudence, folly, ignorance, CP,VPs.*
unwīse=unwīslīce
unwīslic *foolish.* adv. -līce, *CP,Lcd;* Æ. ['*unwisely*']
unwīsnes f. *ignorance : wickedness,* DR.
unwita m. *witless person, ignoramus,* LL.
unwitende '*unwitting,*' *ignorant, AO.*
unwītnigendlīce *without punishment, with impunity,* ÆGR233⁶.
unwītnod *unpunished,* CP.
unwītnung f. *impunity,* Sc235⁵.
unwītod (io, u) *uncertain,* DR,GNE.
unwittig *unconscious, ignorant, stupid, Æ.* ['*unwitty*']
unwittignes f. *folly,* GD163³⁴.
unwittol *ignorant,* Sc80¹².
unwitweorc n. *evil work,* BL111². [?inwit-]
unwiðerweard *friendly,* CP361²⁰.
unwiðerweardlic *not discordant,* NC330.
unwiðmetenes f. *incomparability,* OEG587.
unwiðmetenlic *not comparable, incomparable,* Æ. adv. -līce.
unwlite m. *dishonour,* WW.
unwliteg=unwlitig

±**unwlitegian** *to become disfigured*, CP : *disfigure, transform*, CP.

unwlitegung f. *disfigurement*, WW 391[5].

unwlitig *unsightly, deformed, disfigured, illfavoured*, Æ.

unwlitignes f. *disfigurement*, BH 384[4].

unworclic=unweorclic

unword n. *abuse, slander*, AB 34·10.

unworht v. ungeworht.

unworðian=unweorðian

unwrænc=unwrenc

unwrǣne *not lustful*, LCD.

unwrǣst(e) (ē) *feeble, weakly, evil, AO, Chr* : *unsteady, untrustworthy, Chr.* ['*unwrast*']

unwrǣstlīce adv. *incongruously, inaccurately*, BF 186[25]. ['*unwrastly*']

unwrecen *unpunished, unavenged*, B,Bo.

unwrenc (æ) m. *vice, evil design, CP,W.* ['*unwrench*']

unwrēon[1,2] *to uncover, reveal, Æ,Bf,G,VPs.* ['*unwry*']

unwrēst=unwrǣst

unwrig-ednes, -ennes f. *uncovering, revelation*, RBL 42[16].

unwrigen *open, unconcealed*, MFH 101[7] (pp. of unwrēon).

unwriten *unwritten*, Bo.

unwrītere m. *incorrect copyist*, ÆGR 3[24](= ÆT 80[120]).

unwrīðan *to untwist, unbind*, CP.

unwunden I. *not wound*, WW 187[30]. **II.** pp. of unwindan.

unwundod '*unwounded*,' Gen 183.

unwuniendlic *uninhabitable*, LCD 3·262[2].

unwurð=unweorð; **unwuted**=unwitod

unwynsum *unpleasant*, Æ.

unwynsumnes f. *unpleasantness*, Æ.

unwyrcan *to undo, destroy*, A 11·113.

unwyrd f. *misfortune, trouble*, Bo,LCD.

unwyrht f. *ill-doing*, Bo 123[32].

unwyrtrumian *to root out*, MtL 13[29].

unwyrð-=unweorð-; **unwyrðe**=unwierðe

unymb-fangen,-fangenlic *incomprehensible*, GD.

unymbwendedlic *unalterable*, DR 164[16].

unymbwriten *not circumscribed*, GD 268[24].

unȳð-=unēað-

unȳðgian *to trouble*, EPs 34[15].

ūp adv. '*up*,' Æ,CP : *up stream, up country (inland), AO,Chr* : *upwards.* lǣtan ūp *to put ashore.* ūp forlǣtan *divide.*

ūpāblāwan[7] *to blow up, be in eruption (of a volcano)*, ÆL 8[222].

ūpābrecan[4] *to break out or through, boil up*, Æ.

ūp-ābregdan, -ābrēdan[3] *to lift up, raise up, exalt, Æ,CP : expand*, BF 70[11].

ūpāfangnes f. *reception, assumption*, A 5·464.

ūpāhæf-=ūpāhaf-

ūpāhafenlīce (æ) adv. *arrogantly*, OEG 667.

ūpāhafennes f. *exultation. presumption, arrogance, pride*, CP : *uplifting. elevation*, Æ.

ūpāhafu *lifting up*, CHRD 30[21].

ūpāhebban[6] *to lift up, raise up, exalt*, Æ,CP : *rise in the air, fly.*

ūpāhefedlīce *arrogantly*, HGL 422[8].

ūp-āhefednes (Æ), -āhefennes=ūpāhafennes

ūpāhōn[7] *to hang up*, Æ.

ūpāmȳlan? *to come to light, appear*, HGL 463 (v. OEG 4784).

ūpārǣran *to raise up, lift up, exalt*, AO,CP : *excite* : *introduce*, BF 122[16].

ūpāreccan *to erect, raise, build*, VPs.

ūpārīsan[1] *to rise up*, CP.

ūpārisnes f. *resurrection*, EHy 14[6].

ūpāspringan[3] *to spring up, arise*, BF 84[11].

ūpāspringnes (u[3]) f. *uprising*, BF,LPs 102[12].

ūpāspryttan *to sprout forth, germinate*, BF 58[1].

ūpāstīgan[1] *to rise, ascend*, Æ,CP.

ūpā-stigen(nes), -stīgnes f. *ascent, ascension, means of going up.*

Ūpāstīgnestīd f. *Ascension-tide*, VH 23.

ūpāstreccan *to uplift*, CM 38.

ūpātēon[2,1] *to draw up, bring up, rear* : *draw out, pull out, pluck up* : *lift up, place in an upright position*, Æ.

ūpāðenian *to elevate, lift up*, CP.

ūp-āweallan, -āwallan[7] *to well up, steam up, boil up*, Æ.

ūpāwegan[5] *to lift up, support*, Æ.

ūpāwendan *to turn upwards, raise*, Æ. pp. ūpāwend *supine*, ÆGr.

ūpbrēdan[3] *to reproach with, upbraid*, W 248[9].

ūpcuman[4] *to come up, arise.*

ūpcund *from above, heavenly*, CP.

ūpcyme m. *rising, origin, source*, DA,VPs.

ūpeard m. *land above, heaven*, GU 1051.

ūpende m. *upper end*, Bo,KC.

ūpengel† m. *heavenly angel.*

ūpēode pret. 3 sg. of ūpgān.

ūpfæreld n? *ascension*, ÆH 1·444[1].

ūpfeax *bald in front*, WW 276[32].

ūpfēgan *to erect*, CP.

ūpfēran *to go forth, spring forth*, GPH 401.

ūpferian *to carry up, to raise*, Sc 130[7].

ūp-flēogan (Æ), -flēon[2] *to fly up.*

ūpflēring f. *upper floor (of house)*, Æ.

ūpflōr fm., ūpflōre f. *upper chamber or story, garret*, Æ.

ūpflugon pret. pl. of ūpflēogan.

ūpgān anv. *to go up* : *make to go up, raise* : *rise (of sun)*, GUTH 148[41].

ūpgang m. *rising, sunrise*, Æ : *going up approach, ascent* : *landing, going inland.*

úpganga m. *landing*, MA 87.
úpgebrēdan (W 249³)=úpbrēdan
úpgemynd n. *contemplation of things above*, AN 1066.
úpgēotan² *to well up*, GUTH 131¹⁹⁹.
úpgodu np. *the gods above, heathen gods*, WW 497²⁵.
úpgong=úpgang
úphafenes=úpāhafennes
úphēafod n. *upper end*, KC 6·79¹⁰.
úphēah *uplifted, tall, high, elevated : sublime, noble, upright.*
úpheald n. *support*, KC 4·232⁵. [*'uphold'*]
úphebban (JRsVPs)=úpāhebban
úphebbe f. *water-hen, coot*, PPs 103¹⁷.
úphebbing f. *uprising*, LkL 8⁸.
úp-hefenes (VPs), -hefnes=úpāhafennes
úpheofon m. *heaven above, sky*, BH,W.
úphladan⁶ *to draw up*, HGL 418.
úphūs n. *upper room*, WW 384³.
úpland n. *country (as opposed to town)*, CHR 1087.
úplang (o²) *upright, erect : tall*, AA 33⁴.
úplegen f. *hair-pin*, WW 223¹⁶.
úplendisc *from the uplands, rural, rustic, from beyond the town*, Æ. [úpland]
úplic *upper, supreme, lofty, sublime, heavenly, celestial*, Æ,CP.
úplyft fnm. *upper air, ether, sky*, BTK 196,198.
úpnes f. *height*, LPs 103³.
úpniman⁴ *to raise up*, EHy 3⁸.
upon=uppan; upp=úp
uppan (o²) prep. (w. d. and a.) *on, upon, up to, against*, Æ,Chr,G,RB : (time) *on, after*, Chr,G : *in addition to.* wið u. *above.* on u. *against.*
+uppan=+yppan
uppe I. adv. *above, aloft, up, inland*, CP. u. on *upon.* II.=yppe
uppe-=úp-
uppian *to rise up, swell*, CP 277⁷.
uppl-=úpl-
uppon=uppan
úprador=úprodor
úprǣcan *to reach up*, BL 223¹⁰.
úpriht *upright, erect*, Æ : *face upwards*, OEG 2157. adv. -rihte *straight up*, KC.
úprine=úpryne
úprocettan *to belch up*, EPs 118¹⁷¹.
úp-roder, -rodor† m. *upper heavens, ether, firmament*, Ex.
úpryne m. *ascent, rising (of sun)*, BH,Bo.
úpsittan⁵ '*residere*,' ÆGr.
úpspring (u²) m. *rising up, origin, birth*, Æ : *what springs up.*
úpsprungennes f. *eclipse*, BH 240²⁰ʙ.
úpstandende '*upstanding*,' *erect*, Lcd,WW 154.

úpstīgan¹ *to move up, rise, ascend*, Cr,Jn 1⁵¹. [*'upsty'*]
úpstīge m. *ascent, ascension*, Æ : *staircase*, GD 170²⁴.
úpstīgend m. *one who mounts up, rider*, DR; CHy 4¹.
úptēon² *to draw up*, AA 24¹³.
úpþyddan *to swell up*, GUTH 131¹⁹⁷.
úpwǣg=úpweg
úpwæstm m. *stature*, StC 68¹⁸.
úpware mp. *inhabitants of heaven*, WW 355²⁹.
úpweallan⁷ *to boil up*, AO.
úpweard, úpweardes adv. *up*, '*upward(s)*,' Æ : *towards heaven : backwards (in time)*, Bf 156¹⁶.
úpweg† m. *ascent, ascension.*
úpyrnan³ (eo;=ie) *to run up, grow, increase : rise.*
úpyrne=úpryne
úr m. *bison, aurochs : name of the rune for* u. [*Ger.* auer]
úre I. possess. pron. 'OUR,' *ours*, Æ,AO, CP. II. gp. of ic.
úrelendisc *of our country*, ÆGR 93¹⁷.
úrigfeðere† *dewy-winged.*
úriglāst *leaving a damp track*, WY 29.
úrne asm. of úre I.
urnen pp., urnon pret. pl. of iernan.
úron=úrum dsmn. and dp. of úre I.
ús dap. of pers. pron. ic '*us*.'
úser I. poss. pron. gen. ússes *our*. II. gp. of ic.
úsic, úsig, úsih=ús; ússe=úre; ússer= úser
ússes v. úscr; ússic=úsic, ús
ússpīung f. *expectoration*, WW 113⁹. [út, spīwung]
ússum dsn. of úser.
út adv. '*out*,' AO,BH,Bo,G,Lcd : *without, outside.*
úta- (N)=útan-
útāberstan³ *to burst out, burst forth*, CP.
útābrecan⁴ *to break out*, Æ.
útācnyssan *to drive out*, ERPs 35¹³.
útacumen=útancumen
útacund *extraneous, external, foreign*, NG.
útacunda m. *stranger*, LkL 17¹⁸.
útacymen=útancymen
útādelfan³ *to dig out*, ÆGR.
útādōn anv. *to do out, put out*, Æ.
útādrǣfan *to drive out, expel, destroy*, Æ.
útādrīfan¹ *to drive out, disperse, dispel*, LL.
útǣðmian (ē) *to breathe out*, MFH 122⁸.
útāfaran⁶ *to come forth, go out, depart*, CP.
útāflōwan=útflōwan
útālǣdan *to lead out*, LL,VPs : *produce : release*, VH.
útālēoran *to cause to depart, flee away*, CVPs 51⁷.

ūtāmǣr-an, -ian *to drive out, expel, depopulate*, BH.

utan=wuton

ūtan adv. *from outside, An,Chr* : *on the outside, without, Bo,Gen.* ūtan landes *abroad, PPs* 64⁸. ['*outen*']

ūtanbordes adv. *from abroad*, CP 3¹¹.

ūtan-cumen, -cymen I. *foreign, strange, AO, W; Æ* : *belonging to another.* ['*outcome*'] II. m. *stranger, foreigner.*

ūtane adv. *from without, outwards, outside, externally*, CP : *abroad*, AO 164¹⁴.

ūtanlandes v. ūtan.

ūtanweard *external, outside, WW.* ['*outward*']

ūtānȳdan *to drive out, expel*, RPs 43³.

ūtanymbstandnes (o⁴) f. *surrounding*, JPs 140³.

ūtascēotan² *to sprout forth, burst forth*, CP : *to pierce out*, AO.

ūtāsellan *to grant outright*, KC 6·154'.

ūtāslēan⁶ *to strike outwards, break out*, CP.

ūtāslīdan¹ *to slip forwards, fall (into)*, GPH 388.

ūtāspīwan⁴ *to spew forth*, CP 447¹⁷,¹⁹.

ūtātēon²,¹ *to draw out, Æ.*

ūtātȳnan *to exclude*, VPs.

ūtāðȳdan *to thrust out, cast out, Æ.*

ūtaweard (NG)=ūtanweard

ūtāwindan³ *to slip forwards, fall (into)*, GPH 388.

ūtberstan=ūtāberstan

ūtcumen=ūtancumen

ūtcwealm (a, æ) m. *utter destruction, extirpation*, Cp 461r.

ūtcȳðan *to promulgate, announce*, A 4·166.

ūtdrǣf f. *decree of expulsion*, ÆL 21⁸⁵.

ūtdrǣfere m. *driver out*, WW 172⁴⁶.

ūtdragan⁶ *to remove*, LL 454,9.

ūtdrīfan¹ *to drive out or away, expel, scatter, disperse.*

ūte adv. *out, without, outside, abroad*, BH, Chr,LL,Mt; Æ : *out.* ['*oute*']

ūtemest=ȳtemest

ūten, ūtene=ūtan, ūtane

ūtera, ūterra adj. (ȳ) (comp.) *outer, exterior, external*, BH,LL,Ps,Sc; AO,CP. superl. ȳtemest *uttermost, utmost, extreme, last.*

ūterlic (o²) *external*, MFB 102: *material*, 125.

ūtermere m. *outer sea, open sea*, CHR 897A.

ūteweard adj. *external,* '*outward,*' *outside, extreme, last*, Chr. as sb. *outward part, exterior*, LG. on ūteweardan *on the outside, outwardly.*

ūteweardum *outwards*, Chr 893. ['*outward*']

ūtfær n. *going out, exit, departure, Æ.*

ūtfǣreld n. *exodus, going out*, Æ,AO.

ūtfangeneðeof *right of judging thieves caught outside one's jurisdiction, and of taking fines for the crime*, Ct. [v. '*outfangthief*']

ūtfaru f. *going out, Æ,RB.* ['*outfare*']

ūtflōwan⁷ *to flow out, Æ,CP* : *scatter, be dispersed*, EHy 5⁶.

ūtfōr f. *evacuation (from body)*, LCD 6a.

ūtforlǣtan *to cast out, Æ,AO,CP.*

ūtfūs *ready to start*, B 33.

ūtgān anv. *to go out*, CP.

ūt-gānde, -gangende *outgoing*, CD.

ūtgang (eo, o) m. *going out, departure, exit, exodus* : *latter part, Guth, MtL, VPs* : *privy* : *dejecta, excrement*, LCD : '*anus.*' ['*outgang*']

ūtgangan⁷=ūtgān

ūtgārsecg m. *remotest sea*, CREAT 70.

ūtgefeoht n. *external war*, BH 47² (Schipper).

ūtgegān=ūtgān; **ūtgelǣdan**=ūtlǣdan

ūtgemǣre n. *extreme or remotest limit*, PPs.

ūtgenga m. *exit*, MtR 22⁹.

ūtgēð (KGL) pres. 3 sg. of ūtgān.

ūtgong=ūtgang

ūthealf f. *outer side*, WW 153⁴⁵.

ūthere m. *foreign army*, CHR.

ūthlēap n. *fine for a man escaping from his lord*, TC.

±**ūtian** *to put out, expel, LL* : *alienate (property).* ['*out*']

ūtirning (io) f. *flux*, MkL 5²⁵.

ūtlād f. *right of passage outwards by water*, EC 344 : *assembling (of material)*? AS 2⁷.

ūtlǣdan *to lead out, bring out*, LL 54,8¹.

ūtlǣdnes (ē) f. '*abductio,*' EHy 6³⁶.

ūtlænda=ūtlenda; **ūtlændisc**=ūtlendisc

ūtlǣs f. *out-pastures*, KC 6·214.

ūtlaga m. '*outlaw,*' *Æ,W.*

±**ūtlagian** *to* '*outlaw,*' *banish*, Chr.

ūtlagu? f. *outlawry*, LL. [*ON.* útlagi]

ūtlah *outlawed*, CHR,LL.

ūtland n. *foreign land, PPs* : *outlying land (granted to tenants), TC* 502. ['*outland*']

ūtlec=ūtlic

ūtlednes=ūtlǣdnes

ūtlenda m. *foreigner, stranger, alien*, GL.

ūtlende=ūtlendisc

ūtlendisc (æ) I. *strange, foreign, Æ,Chr.* II. m. *foreigner, stranger.* ['*outlandish*']

ūtlēoran *to go out, pass*, GD.

ūtlic *foreign*, BH : *remote*, CHRD 61.

ūtmǣran *to proclaim, announce*, AA 49¹⁰.

ūt-mǣst, -mest=ȳtemest

uton=wuton; **ūton**=ūtan

ūtone=ūtane

ūtor (comp. of ūte) adv. *beyond, outside.*

ūtrǣsan *to rush out*, CHR.

ūtre=ūterre f. and n. of ūterra.

ūtrīdan¹ *to ride or go away*, LL 210,8.

ūtrine=ūtryne

ūt-roccettan, -roccian *to belch out*, EJPs.

ūtryne m. *running away, issue, exit, outlet*, Ps,Sc : *what runs out*, Lcd.

ūtsang=ūhtsang

ūtscēotan[2] *to abut on*, EC121[8] : *suffer to escape, aid the escape of*, LL194,6[1].

ūtscūfan[2] *to push out, shut out, exclude*, Æ.

ūtscyte m. *outfall, outlet, exit*, Æ.

ūtscytling m. *stranger, foreigner*, Sc200[4].

ūt-siht, -sihte f. *flux, diarrhœa*, Æ,AO.

ūtsihtādl f. *diarrhœa, dysentery*, Lcd.

ūtsīon[1] *to issue out*, AO38[7].

ūtsīð m. *going out, departure : death*, Gu.

ūtspīwung v. ūsspīung.

utter, uttor=ūtor; **uttermæst**=ȳtemest

utun=wuton

ūtwæpnedmann m. *stranger*, BH354[25].

ūtwærc m. *dysentery?* Lcd.

ūtwald m. *outlying wood*, EC289[17].

ūtwaru f. *foreign defence*, LL.

ūtweallan[7] *to well out, flow forth*, AA41[17].

ūtweard adj. *outside of, going away, striving to get out*, B. ['*outward*']

ūtweardes adv. '*outwards*,' CP.

ūtweorc=ūtwærc

ūtwīcing m. *sea-rover*, Chr1098.

ūtyrnende *diuretic, purgative, diarrhœic*, Lcd.

ūtyrning (io[2]) f. *flux*, MkL5[25].

ūð- intensive prefix.

ūðe pret. sg. of unnan.

ūðgende=ūðgenge

ūðgenge *fugitive, alien, fleeting, vanishing, departing*, B,BH.

ūðmǣte *huge*, MH76[1]n.

ūðon pret. pl. of unnan.

ūðuta=ūðwita; **ūðweot-**=ūðwit-

ūðwita (eo[2], u[2]) m. *scholar, sage, philosopher, scribe, Pharisee*, Æ.

ūðwitegung f. *philosophy*, Æ.

ūðwitelic=ūðwitlic

ūðwitian *to study philosophy*, ÆGr146[2].

ūðwitlic *philosophical, academical*, WW.

ūðwuta (NG)=ūðwita; **ūðwyt-**=ūðwit-

V

vīpere f. *viper*, MtR23[33].

W

wā I. (see also wēa) m. '*woe*,' *affliction, misery, evil*, AO,CP; Æ. **II.** interj. (occly. governs d.) *woe! alas!* CP. wā lā, wā lā wā, wei lā wei *ah! oh! alas!* Æ,Bo,LPs. ['*wellaway*,' '*wellawo*']

wāc I. adj. *weak, soft, feeble, effeminate, cowardly, timid, pliant*, Æ,CP,Wa : *slender, frail : insignificant, mean, poor*, TC; Æ : *bad, vile.* ['*woke*'] **II.** n. *weakness*, LL. **III.** pret. 3 sg. of wīcan.

wac-=wæc-

wacan[6]† *to awake, arise, be born, originate.* [v. '*wake*']

waccor=wacor

wāce *weakly, slowly, negligently*, LL.

wacel=wacol

wacen (æ[1], ea[1], a[2], o[2], u[2]) f. *wakefulness : watching, vigil : division of the night*, NG : *incentive*, DR63[15].

wacian (æ, e) *to be awake or active, keep awake, watch*, Æ,CP. ['*WAKE*']

wācian *to become weak, languish :* (±) *waver, be cowardly, flinch, Chr,Ma.* ['*woke*']

waciende *watching, vigilant.*

wāclic *weakly, mean, vile, insignificant, trifling*, Æ. adv. -līce, Æ,Met. ['*wokely*']

wācmōd n. *faint-hearted, cowardly*, CP : *weak-minded, irresolute*, Æ.

wācmōdnes f. *weakness (of mind or body), cowardice*, CP.

wācnes f. *weakness, insignificance*, Æ, OEG. ['*wokeness*']

wacnian=wæcnan

wacol *awake, vigilant, watchful, attentive*, Æ. adv. -līce, Æ.

wacon=wacen

wacor *watchful, vigilant*, LL; CP. ['*waker*'] adv. -līce, CP.

wacsan=wascan

wācscipe m. *weakness, slackness*, LL208,1[5].

-wacu v. niht-w.; **wacul**=wacol

wācung f. *vigilance*, GD.

wād I. n. '*woad*,' ÆGr,Gl,Lcd; Mdf. **II.** (?) *drag-net*, OEG61[15] (v. A31·528).

wad- v. wæd.

wadan[6] *to go, move, stride, advance*, An,B : '*wade*,' *Ma*; AO : (+) *traverse, pervade, Ma.*

wadom=waðum

wādsǣd n. *woad-seed*, LL454,12.

wādspitl m. *woad-dibble*, LL455,15. [v. '*spittle*']

wadu? v. wād II.

wadung f. *travelling, going*, Æ.

wǣ (N,VPs)=wā; **wǣarhrōd**=weargrōd

wǣb, wǣbb=webb; **wǣc-**=wāc-

±wǣcan *to weaken, oppress, trouble*, BH. [wāc]

wæccan (±) *to* '*watch*,' *wake*, DR. [=wacian]

wæcce f. '*watch*,' *vigil, wakefulness*, Æ,Bo, Bl,Lcd,Lk; CP.

wæccen=wacen

wæccende *watchful, awake*, B,Bl,Chrd,LL. ['*watch(ing)*']

wæccendlíce *watchfully*, GD 242¹⁴.

wæccer=wacor

+**wæcednes** f. *weakness*, ÆH 2·552'.

wæcen=wacen; **wæcg** (GL)=wecg

wæclan=wacian

wæcnan, wæcnian [v. also wacan] *to come into being, awake, come forth, spring from, arise, be born*, B. ['waken']

±**wæd** n. [usu. pl.; wad- in obl. cases] *ford, water, sea, ocean*.

wæd f. *robe, dress, apparel, clothing, garment, covering*, Æ,Bo,Da : *sail*, ES 40·326. ['weed']

wæd-=wēd-

wædbrēc (ā) fp. *breeches*, GEN 3⁷.

wædd=wedd; ±**wæde** n.=wæd f.

wædelnes (ē) f. *poverty*, CP.

wæden=waden pp. of wadan.

wæden *of woad, bluish, purple*, OEG. [wād]

wæder=weder

wæderáp m. *stay, halyard*; pl. *rigging*, WW 515¹⁵.

+**wædian** *to clothe, dress, equip, furnish*, G.

wædl (ē, ēð) f. *poverty, Bo*; CP : *barrenness*, AO. ['waedle']

wædla (ē) *poor, destitute, VPs.* as sb.= *beggar, poor man, VPs*; Æ,CP. ['waedle']

wædle=wædl

wædlian *to be poor, destitute, beg*, Æ.

wæd-lig (Æ), -ligend (GD) *poor*.

wædling m. *poor person*, JPs 87¹⁶.

wædlnes=wædelnes

wædlung f. *poverty, want*, Æ : *begging*, Æ.

wædo=wād

wæf pret. 3 sg. of wefan.

+**wæf**=+wef

wæfan *to clothe*, W 119⁶.

wæfels (ē) mn. *covering, mantle, cloak, dress, clothing, garment*, Æ.

wæfergange f. *spider*, CPs 89⁹. [wefan]

wæfergeornnes f. *eagerness for sight-seeing*, LL (wǣfereorn-).

wæferhūs n. *amphitheatre*, ÆL 24⁴⁹.

wæferlic *of a theatre, theatrical*, OEG 62.

wæfernes f. *show, pomp, pageant*, OEG 4465.

wæfer-sēn, -sēon=wǣfersȳn

wæfersolor m. '*pulpitum*,' *stage*, OEG 3458.

wæferstōw (ēa) f. *theatre*, LCD.

wæfersȳn (ē³, ēo³, ī³, īe³) f. *spectacle, sight, show, display*, Æ. [wāfian]

wæflian *to speak foolishly*, v. NC 333.

wæfon pret. pl. of wefan.

wæfre *unstable, unsteady, wavering, wandering, restless* : *flickering, expiring*.

wæfs=wæps

wæfð, wæft f. *show, spectacle*, Bo,MET.

wæfung (GL)=wāfung

wæg I. m.=weg. II. pret. 3 sg. of wegan.

wǣg (ā, ē) I. m. *motion* : *water* : *wave, billow, flood, sea*. [wegan] II. (±)=wǣge. III.=wāg. IV.=hwæg

wǣgan=wegan

±**wǣgan** (ē) *to trouble, afflict*, CP : *deceive, falsify*, Æ : (+) *frustrate*, DOM 115.

wǣgbora m. *child of the waves?* B 1440.

wǣgbord n. *ship, vessel*, GEN 1340.

wǣgdēor n. *sea-animal*, CR 988.

wǣgdropa m. *water-drop, tear*, GU 1030.

wǣge I. f. *weight, scales, balance*, Æ,Sc, VPs,WW ['weigh'] : 'wey' (*of cheese, wool*, etc.), BC,LL : '*pensum*,' *burden*. II.† (ē) n. *cup, chalice*.

+**wǣge** n. *weight, measure*, LCD.

wægel (WW 124²)=pægel?

wægen=wægn; **wægenðīxl**=wægneðīxl

wægescalu=wǣgscalu

wǣgetunge f. *tongue of a balance*, WW 148¹⁹.

wǣgfær n. *sea-voyage*, AN 925.

wǣgfæt n. *water-vessel, clouds*, RD 4³⁷.

wǣgfaru f. *track in the sea*, EX 298.

wǣgflota† m. (*wave-floater*), *ship*.

wǣghengest† m. *ship*.

wǣgholm m. *sea, ocean*, B 217.

wǣglæst=weglēast

wǣglīðend† m. *sea-farer, sailor*.

wǣglīðende† *seafaring*.

wægn (wægen, wǣn) m. *carriage, 'wain,' waggon, chariot, cart, vehicle*, B,Cp. Carles wǣn; wǣnes ðīxl *the constellation of the Great Bear*, Bo. [wegan]

-**wægnan** v. be-w.

wægnere (æn) m. *waggoner*, WW.

wǣgnere m. *enticer*, WW 436¹². [wǣgnian]

wægnest=wegnest

wægnfaru f. *chariot-journey*, WW.

wægngehrado (æn) *waggon-plank*, WW 267³³.

wægngèrefa (æn) m. '*carpentarius*,' *waggon-master?* WW.

wægngewǣde (æn) n. *waggon-cover*, LL 455,17.

+**wǣgnian** *to deceive* : *condemn*, CHRD 97.

wægnscilling m. *tax on waggons*, TC 138¹².

wægntrēow (æn) n. *log given to the carter of a load of wood*, LL 453,21⁴.

wægnðol (æn) *cart-pin?* WW 343³⁹.

wægnweg (æn) m. *cart-road*, KC.

wægnwyrhta (æn) m. '*carpentarius*,' *cartwright*, WW. ['wainwright']

wǣgon pret. pl. of wegan.

wǣgpundern n. *weighing-machine*, LL.

wǣgráp? m. *wave-rope, wave-bond* (*ice*), B 1611. [or? wǣlráp]

wǣgryft=wāgrift

wǣgscalu f. *scale of a balance*, WW 437¹⁹. [scealu; Ger. wagschale]

wǣgstæð n. *sea-shore*, RD23².
wǣgstrēam m. *current*, Ex311.
wōgsweord n. *sword with wavy pattern*, B1489.
wǣgðel† n. *ship, vessel*.
wǣgðrēa f. *peril of the sea*, GEN1490.
wǣgðrēat m. *deluge*, GEN1352.
+wǣht pp. of +wǣcan and +wǣgan.
wǣl I. n. [nap. walu] *slaughter, carnage*, BH; AO. w. +slēan *to slaughter* : *field of battle* : (usu. in pl.) *dead bodies*, AO. ['*wal*'] II. m.=wiell. III.=wel
wǣl mn. *whirlpool, eddy, pool*, Æ,CP : *ocean, sea, river, flood.* ['*weel*']
wæl-=wel-; wǣl-=wēal-
wæla=wela
±wǣlan *to afflict, vex, torment*, GU,MtR.
wǣlbedd† n. *slaughter-bed.*
wǣlbend f. *band of destruction*, B1936.
wǣlbenn f. *deadly wound*, Ex491.
wǣlblēat *deadly-pale?* B2725.
wǣlceald *deadly-cold*, SOL468.
wǣlcēasega m. *carrion-picker* (*raven*), Ex164.
wǣlclomm m. *deadly fetter*, GEN2128.
wǣlcræft m. *deadly power*, RD87¹¹.
wǣlcwealm m. *violent death*, RD2⁸.
wæl-cyrige, -cyrie f. (*chooser of the slain*), *witch, sorceress*, Gl,Nar. ['*walkyrie*']
+wǣldan (*MkLR*)=+wieldan
wǣldēað m. *death in battle, violent death*, B695.
wǣldrēor† n. *blood of battle, battle-gore*, GEN.
wǣlegian=weligian; wǣler=weler
wǣlfǣhð f. *deadly feud*, B2028.
wǣlfæðm m. *deadly embrace*, Ex480.
wǣlfāg *blood-stained*, B1128.
wǣlfeall=wælfill
wǣlfel *greedy for corpses, ghoulish*, EL53.
wǣlfeld m. *battlefield*, CHR937.
wǣlfill m. *slaughter, death, destruction*, GEN.
wǣlfūs *awaiting death*, B2420.
wǣlfyll=wælfill
wǣlfyllo f. *fill of slaughter*, B125.
wǣlfȳr† n. *deadly fire* : *funeral pyre*, B.
wǣlgǣst† m. *murderous sprite*, B.
wǣlgār† m. *deadly spear.*
wǣlgenga m. *sea-monster?* OEG5⁴¹; 8³⁰⁵.
wǣlgīfre† *bloodthirsty, murderous.*
wǣlgimm m. *death-bringing gem?* RD21⁴.
wǣlgrǣdig *flesh-eating, cannibal*, AN135.
wǣlgrim *fierce, violent, bloody, cruel* : *fateful, dire.* adv. -līce, AO.
wǣlgrimnes f. *cruelty, torture*, GD.
wǣlgryre m. *deadly horror*, Ex137.
wǣlhere m. *slaughtering army*, GEN1983.
wǣlhlem m. *death-stroke*, B2969.
wǣlhlence† f. *coat of mail.*

wǣlhrēow (ēa²) *cruel, fierce, savage, bloodthirsty*, CP.
wǣlhrēowlic *cruel*, VH. adv. -līce.
wǣlhrēownes f. *cruelty, ferocity, atrocity, slaughter*, Æ,CP.
wǣlhwelp m. *destroying hound*, RD16²³.
wǣlig=welig; wǣlisc=wielisc
wǣll=weall; wǣll-=wæl-
wǣlla=willa II.; wǣllan (N)=willan
wǣlle (VPs)=wille; wǣlm=wielm
wǣlmist† m. *mist of death.*
wǣlnett n. *death-net*, Ex202.
wǣlnīð† m. *deadly hostility, war.*
wǣlnot m. *baleful inscription*, SOL101.
wǣlpīl m. *deadly arrow, dart*, GU1127.
wǣlrǣs† m. *deadly onslaught*, B.
wǣlrǣst=wælrest; wǣlrǣw=wælhrēow
wǣlrāp? m. *flood-fetter* (*ice*), B1610?
wǣlrēaf n. *spoil from the slain* : *act of spoiling the slain*, LL.
wǣlrēc m. *deadly reek*, B2661.
wǣlregn (ll) m. *deluge*, GEN1350.
wǣlrēow=wælhrēow
wǣlrest (æ²)† f. *bed of slaughter, grave.*
wǣlrūn f. *murderous song?* EL28.
wǣlsc=wielisc
wǣlsceaft m. *deadly spear*, B398.
wǣlscel n? *carnage*, JUD313.
wǣlseax n. *dagger*, B2703.
wǣlsliht (ea, i, y) m. *slaughter, carnage*, Chr : (†) *combat.* [v. '*wal*']
wǣlslihta m. *murderer, slayer*, GD254²².
wǣlslītende *corpse-biting*, W187¹⁴ : *deadly-biting*, W241¹².
wǣlspere n *deadly spear*, MU322; LCD175b. [v. '*wal*']
wǣlsteng m. *spear-shaft*, B1638.
wǣlstōw f. *place of slaughter, battlefield*, AO. āgan wǣlstōwe geweald *to obtain possession of the battlefield, conquer.*
wǣlstrǣl mf. *deadly shaft*, GU1260.
wǣlstrēam m. *deadly flood*, GEN1301.
wǣlsweng m. *deadly thrust*, GEN987.
wǣlt *part of thigh, sinew*, LL7,68. [weald]
wǣltan=wyltan
wǣlwang m. *field of the slain*, AN1227.
wǣlweg (SEAF63)=hwælweg
wǣlwulf† m. *warrior*, MA : *cannibal*, AN.
wǣlwyrt=wēalwyrt (or ? wæl- v. '*wallwort*').
wǣm=(1) wamm; (2) hwamm
wǣm-=wem-
wǣmbede *big-bellied*, WW161²². [wamb]
wǣmman=wemman
wǣmn (LWS)=wǣpen
wǣmnian=wǣpnian; wǣmst-=wæstm-
wǣn=wenn; wǣn-=wen-
wǣn=wægn; wǣnan=wēnan
wǣnes=(1) wācnes; (2) wōhnes

wæng, wænge=wang, wange

wænunga=wēnunga; **wǣpan**=wēpan

wǣpen n. (nap. wǣp(e)n, wǣp(e)nu) *'weapon,' sword, B,Chr*; pl. *arms, Bo, Gu,VPs*; Æ,AO,CP : *membrum virile, WW.*

wǣpenbora m. *weapon-bearer, warrior, knight,* Æ.

wǣpend, wǣpened=wǣpned

wǣpen(ge)tæc n. *wapentake' (subdivision of a riding),* LL.

wǣpengeðræc n. *clash of spears?* DR 168³.

wǣpengewrixl(e) n. *hostile encounter,* CHR, W.

wǣpenhād=wǣpnedhād

wǣpenhete m. *armed hate,* AP80.

wǣpenhūs n. *armoury,* WW348¹³.

wǣpenlēas *unarmed,* Æ,OEG. [*'weapon-less'*]

wǣpenlic *male,* WW.

wǣpenstrǣl fm. *arrow,* PPs56⁵.

wǣpentæc=wǣpengetæc

wǣpenðracu† f. *storm of weapons.*

wǣpenðrǣge *weapon, equipment?* CRA61?

wǣpenwīfestre=wǣpnedwifestre

wǣpenwiga m. *armed warrior,* RD15¹.

wǣpmann (Æ, *'wapman'*)=wǣpnedmann

wǣpn=wǣpen; **wǣpnahūs**=wǣpenhūs

wǣpned I. adj. *male,* AO. II. m. *male person.*

wǣpnedbearn n. *male child,* BH76⁸.

wǣpnedcild n. *male child,* Æ,LCD.

wǣpnedcynn n. *male sex,* Æ.

wǣpnedhād m. *male sex,* Æ : *sexual power,* GD26³⁰.

wǣpnedhand f. *male line,* TC491'.

wǣpnedhealf f. *male line,* TC491¹⁶.

wǣpnedmann m. *male, man,* AO.

wǣpnedwīfestre f. *hermaphrodite,* WW.

±**wǣpnian** (mn) *to arm,* Æ,Chr; CP. [*'weapon'*]

wǣpnmann=wǣpnedmann

+**wǣpnu** np. *arms,* LPs45¹⁰.

±**wǣpnung** f. *armour,* Æ : *army.*

wǣps m. *'wasp,'* Gl; Æ. [L. *vespa*]

wǣr I. (napm. ware) *wary, cautious, prudent,* Æ,CP : (w. g.) *aware of,* Æ,Chr : *ready, prepared, attentive.* [*'ware'*] II.† n. *sea, ocean.* [ON. *verr*] III.=wer. IV.= wearr

wǣr I. adj. *true, correct,* GEN681. II. f. *faith, fidelity : keeping, protection : agreement, treaty, compact, pledge, covenant : bond (of friendship).*

+**wǣr** wg. *'aware' (of), watchful, on one's guard,* Chr1095.

wǣr-=war-, wear-, wer-, wier-, wyr-

wǣran=werian

wǣrc (wræc) m. *pain, suffering, anguish,* BH,Lcd (A; often confused with WS. weorc. v. JAW52). [*'wark'*]

wǣrcan *to be in pain,* Lcd. [*'wark'*]

wǣrcsār (e) n. *pain,* MkR13⁸.

wǣre=wer II.

wǣre I.=wǣr II. II. pret. 2 sg. of wesan.

wǣrfæst† (e²) *honourable, faithful, trusty.*

wǣrg=wērig

wǣr-genga, -ganga (ē¹)† wm. *one seeking protection, stranger* (or ?=wer-).

wǣrigian=wērgian

+**wǣrlǣcan** *to warn,* Æ.

±**wǣrlan** *to go, pass by,* DR,NG.

wǣrlēas† *faithless, perfidious.*

wǣrlic I. *careful, wary, circumspect,* El,LL, WW. [*'warely'*] adv. -līce, Æ,CP. II.= werlic

wǣrlīce adv. *truly,* GEN652?

wǣrlicnes f. *wariness,* HL13²⁶³. [*'wareliness'*]

wǣrloga† m. *troth-breaker, traitor, liar, devil.* [*'WARLOCK'*; lēogan]

wǣrlot n. *craftiness, deceit,* WW354³¹.

wǣrna=wrenna

wǣrnes I. f. *wariness, caution,* Bl. [*'wareness'*] II.=weargnes

wǣron pret. pl. of wesan.

wǣrnung=wiernung

wǣrsagol *cautious in speech,* W72¹⁷.

wǣrscipe m. *cunning, caution, prudence,* Bo; AO,CP. [*'warship'*]

wǣrstlic=wrǣstlic

wǣrword n. *word of warning,* WW.

wǣrwyrde *cautious in speech,* FT57.

wǣs pret. 1, 3 sg. of wesan.

wǣsc f. *ablution, washing,* CM441. [v. *'wash'*]

+**wǣsc** n. only in wǣtera +w. *'alluvium,'* WW179³⁵,187⁸. [v. *'wash'*]

-**wǣsce** v. scēap-w.

wǣscen=wascen pp. of wascan.

wǣscern n. *washing-place,* WW185².

wǣscestre f. *washer, house-keeper, 'presbytera,'* GD276. m. at GD191²³ (*'fullo'*). [*'washester'*]

wǣschūs n. *'wash-house,' bath-house,* ZDA 31·13³²³.

wǣscing m. *washing, ablution,* Ct.

wǣsend=wāsend ; -**wǣsma** v. here-w.

wǣsp=wǣps; **wǣst**=west

wǣst-=wēst-; **wǣstem-**=wæstm-

wǣstling m. *sheet, blanket,* GL.

wǣstm (e) mn. (nap. wæst-mas, -me) *growth, increase : plant, produce, offspring, fruit, Bo,Bl,G*; Æ,CP : *result, benefit, product : interest, usury : abundance : stature, form, figure, B,G.* [*'wastum'*]

wǣstmaseten f. *planting,* Mt15¹³.

wæstmbǣre *fruitful,* Æ,CP.

+wæstmbǣrian *to be or make fruitful,* WW.

wæstmbǣrnes (io) f. *fruitfulness,* Æ.

wæstmbǣro f. *fruitfulness,* AO58²⁰.

wæstmberende *fertile,* AO.

wæstmberendnes f. *fertility,* BH74³⁰B.

wæstme f.=wæstm

wæstmfǣst *fruitful,* ANS122²⁴⁷.

wæstmian *to grow, increase, bear fruit,* BL, LG.

wæstmlēas *unfruitful, RG;* Æ. ['wastum-less']

wæstmlīc *fruitful,* DR18¹³.

wæstmsceatt m. *interest, usury,* Ps,WW.

wæsŏm=wæstm

wǣt (ā, ē) I. adj. 'WET,' *moist, rainy,* Æ; AO. II. n. *moisture,* Bo : *liquid, drink,* RB; Æ. ǣt and w. *food and drink,* Æ.

wǣta m. *wetness, moisture, humours, fluid, water, CP,Bl,G;* Æ : *drink,* Æ : *sap : urine.* ['wete']

±wǣtan *to 'wet,' moisten, water,* Gu,Lcd, Rd : *become wet : bedew, VPs.*

wǣte f.=wǣta m.

wǣter (e) n. (gs. wætres, wæteres) 'WATER,' *Æ,CP;* Mdf : *sea.*

wǣterādl f. *dropsy,* LCD.

wǣter-ǣdre, -ǣddre f. *spring of water, source,* Æ.

wǣterælfādl f. *a disease,* LCD.

wǣterælfen f. *water-elf,* WW457⁸.

wǣter-berend (OEG871), -berere (WW) m. *water-bearer, sutler, camp-follower.*

wǣterbōh m. *succulent shoot, sprig,* WW149²⁵.

wǣterbolla m. *dropsy,* LCD.

wǣterbrōga† m. *frightful flood,* AN.

wǣterbūc m. *water-pot, pitcher,* Æ.

wǣterbucca m. *water-spider,* WW122⁴.

wǣterburne f. *water-stream,* DD3.

wǣterbyden f. *bucket, cask,* WW503¹⁴.

wǣterclāð m. *towel,* RB59⁷.

wǣtercrōg m. *water-pot,* WW484²⁸.

wǣtercrūce f. *water-pot,* Cp283ʊ.

wǣtercynn n. *water, form or kind of water,* VH23.

wǣterdrinc m. *a drink of water,* NC331. [v. 'water']

wǣter-egsa, -egesa† m. *water-terror.*

wǣterelfen=wǣterælfen

wǣterfæsten n. *water-fastness, place protected by water,* CHR894A.

wǣter-fæt n., nap. -fatu *water-pot, flagon,* Jn; Æ. [v. 'water']

wǣterflaxe f. *water-pitcher,* Mk14¹³. [v. 'flask']

wǣterflōd m. 'water-flood,' *inundation, deluge, AO;* Æ.

wǣterfrocga m. *water-frog,* CHRD96²⁷. [v. 'water']

wǣterful *dropsical,* WW.

wǣterfyrhtnes f. *hydrophobia,* WW112²⁴.

wǣtergāt f. *water-spider,* WW122⁴.

wǣtergeblǣd n. *watery pustule?* LCD162b.

wǣtergefeall n. 'waterfall,' *CC*116.

wǣtergelād n. *conduit,* WW339⁴.

wǣtergelǣt n. *aqueduct,* WW211¹³.

wǣtergesceaft f. *nature of water,* GD220¹⁷.

wǣtergewǣsc n. 'alluvium,' WW187¹.

wǣtergrund m. *sea-bottom, depth,* PPs106²³.

wǣtergyte m. 'Aquarius' *(sign of the Zodiac),* LCD3·246⁴.

wǣterhæfern m. *crab,* LCD16b.

wǣterhālgung f. *consecration of water,* DR117¹.

wǣterhelm m. *covering of ice,* GNE74?

±wǣterian *to 'water,' moisten, irrigate, supply water (to),* Æ,Ps,CP : *lead (cattle) to water,* Æ (Gen).

wǣterig 'watery,' *watered,* Æ,Lcd,WW.

wǣterlēas 'waterless,' *Æ* (Gen),LG.

wǣterlēast f. *want of water,* Æ(9¹⁷⁷).

wǣterlic *aquatic,* GPH394.

wǣtermēle (ǣ³) m. *bowl, basin,* ÆGR.

wǣternǣdre f. *water-snake,* WW.

wǣterordāl n. *water-ordeal,* LL388,2.

wǣterpund n. 'norma, libella aquatica,' WW150⁸⁷.

wǣterpytt m. 'water-pit,' *well,* Æ.

wǣterrīðe? f. *conduit* (v. OEG1714n).

wǣterscēat m. *napkin, towel,* WW127³.

wǣter-scipe (Æ,CP), -scype m. *sheet of water, waters : conduit.*

wǣterscÿte f. *towel, napkin,* Æ.

wǣtersēað m. *cistern : pool, lake,* GD112¹⁷.

wǣtersēoc *dropsical, G;* Æ. ['watersick']

wǣtersēocnes f. *dropsy,* Æ,LCD.

wǣterslǣd n. *watery glade,* KC.

wǣterspryng m. *water-spring,* DA386.

wǣtersteall m. *standing water, pond,* GUTH205.

wǣterstefn f. *voice of waters,* PPs92⁴.

wǣterstoppa m. *bucket,* GD11²².

wǣterstrēam m. *river,* OEG,Ps. ['water-stream']

wǣtertīge m. *canal, aqueduct,* HGL418⁵⁰.

wǣterðēote f. *conduit, flood-gate, torrent, cataract,* Æ.

wǣter-ðīsa, -ðissa m. *whale,* WH50 : *ship,* Gu1303.

wǣterðrūh f. *water-pipe, conduit,* GL.

wǣterðrÿð f. *rush of waters,* PPs106²².

wǣterung f. 'watering,' *providing with water, carriage of water,* Æ.

wǣterwǣdlnes f. *dearth of water,* ÆL23b⁵³⁸.

wǣterweg m. *watercourse, KC,WW.* ['waterway']

wæterwrīte f. '*clepsydra*,' *water-clock*, WW 378³⁹.

wæterwyll m. *spring, fountain*, LL312,5¹.

wæterwyrt f. *water star-wort*, LCD. ['*water-wort*']

wæterȳð f. *billow*, B2242.

wætian *to be wet*, WW447¹.

wætig (GPH389)=pætig

wætla m. *swathe, bandage*, LCD78a.

wætnes (ē) f. *moisture*, LkL8⁶. ['*wetness*']

wætrian=wæterian; **wætter** (N)=wæter

wætung f. *wetting, moisture*, LCD.

wæð n. *ford*, CHR1073D. [*ON*. vað] **-wæða** v. here-w.

wæðan *to wander, roam about* : *hunt*. [wāð]

wæðeburne f. *fishing stream?* BC (Mdf).

wæðelnes=wædelnes; **wæðl**=wædl

wæwærðlic *serious?* BF192³⁰. adv. (e², y²) -līce *confidently? plausibly?* BF6¹⁸,W169¹.

wæx (N)=weax

wæx=wēox pret. 3 sg. of weaxan.

wæxð pres. 3 sg. of wascan.

wafian *to 'wave*,' Æ,Lcd.

wāfian *to be agitated, astonished, amazed, gaze at, wonder at, admire*, Æ : *hesitate*.

wāfiende '*theatralis*,' '*visibilis*,' OEG233.

wāforlic=wǣferlic

wāfung (ǣ, ē) f. *spectacle, display, pageantry, sight*, Æ : *astonishment*, Æ. [wāfian]

wāfungstede m. *place for shows, theatre*, WW.

wāfungstōw f. *place for shows, theatre*, LCD 3·206¹⁶.

wǣg I. (ǣ) m. *wall*, Æ,AO,B,Bl; CP. ['*wough*'] II.=wǣg I.

wāghrægel n. *tapestry, vail*, NG.

wagian *to move, shake, swing, totter*, Æ,Bo, Cp,Rd. ['*waw*']

wagn=wægn

wāgon=wǣgon pret. pl. of wegan.

wāgrift (e, y) n. *tapestry, vail, curtain*, Æ.

wāgðeorl *doorway?* LPs61⁴. [ðyrel]

wāgðyling (wāh-) f. *wainscoting*, WW147³¹. [wāg, ðille]

wagung f. *moving, shaking*, LCD.

wāh I. *fine*, LCD101b (IF48·264). II. (Æ,Bo)=wāg

wāh-=wāg-

wahsan=wascan; **wal**=wæl.

wal-=wæl-, weal-; **wala** (N)=wela I.

wālā! wālāwā! interj. (w. g.) v. wā.

walan v. walu I.; **Wālas**=Wēalas

walc-=wealc-

wal-crigge, -cyrge=wælcyrige

walcspinl (o¹) f. *curling-iron, crisping-pin*, WW198¹; OEG26⁷⁰.

wald (BC,Jud) ['*wold*']=weald

wald-=weald-

walde (CP443¹¹)=wolde

waldenīge *blue or grey-eyed, wall-eyed*, Erf 1166.

waldmora=wēalhmora

Wāle (=ēa) f. *Welshwoman, female slave*, RD.

waled *striped*, WW416²³. ['*waled*']

waler (DR)=weler; **walh**=wealh

wālic *woful, lamentable*, SAT100.

wall (VPs)=weall

wallað (DR)=pres. pl. of wællan, willan.

walm (N)=wielm

walu I. f. *ridge, bank*, KC : *rib, comb* (*of helmet*), B1031? : *weal, mark of a blow*, OEG. ['*wale*'] II. v. wæl I.

wālwyrt=wēalwyrt; **wam**=wamm

wamb (o) f. *belly, stomach*, LG,Ps,Rd,WW; Æ,CP : *bowels*, Lcd : *heart*, VHy : '*womb*,' LG,VPs : *hollow*, BC,Rd.

wambādl f. *stomach-ache*, LCD81a.

wambhord n. *contents of the belly*, RD18¹⁰.

wambscyldig? *gluttonous?* v. NC331.

wambsēoc *having pain in the stomach*, LCD.

wamcwide (o)† *shameful speech, curse, blasphemy*.

wamdǣd (o)† f. *deed of shame, crime*.

wamfreht (o) n. *sinful divination*, WW.

wamful† *impure, shameful, sinful, bad*.

wamlust (o) m. *allurement, enticement*, A 13·28; OEG7³⁷.

wamm (o) I. mn. *stain, spot, scar*, B,KGl : *disgrace, defect, defilement, sin, evil, crime* : *injury, loss, hurt, misfortune*. ['*wam*'] II. adj. *shameful, bad*.

wamsceaða (o)† m. *sin-stained foe, devil*.

wamscyldig (o) *sinful, criminal*, GEN949.

wamwlite (o) m. *wound in the face*, LL.

wamwyrcende (o) *worker of sin*, CR1093.

wan I. (o) (usu. undecl. and used predicatively) *wanting, deficient, lacking, absent*, BH,Bl,Cr,VPs; CP. ānes wan ðe ðritig *or* ānes wana ðrittigum *twenty-nine*. ['*wane*'] II. pret. 3 sg. of winnan. III.= wann

wan- expresses privation or negation.

wana I. m. *lack, want, deficiency*, Bo,Gl; Æ. w. bēon *to lack, fail*, Æ. ['*wane*'] II.= wan I.

+wana *lacking, wanting*, MtL19²⁰. ['*wane*']

wanǣht (o) f. *want, poverty*, †Hy4¹⁰³.

wananbēam m. *spindle-tree*, GL.

wancol (e) *unstable, unsteady, tottering, vacillating, weak*, Bo. ['*wankle*']

wand I. pret. 3 sg. of windan. II. f? *mole* (*animal*), Gl. ['*want*']

+wand n. *fear*, RB68⁸ : *hesitation, scruple*. būtan gewande '*incunctanter*,' CHRD52²⁵. [windan]

wandeweorpe (u³) f. *mole* (*animal*), Æ.

wandian (o) *to hesitate, flinch, desist from, omit, neglect,* Æ,Bl,CP : *fear, stand in awe,* Æ : *have regard to, care for.* ['*wonde*']
wandlung f. *changeableness,* Bo 15²⁷.
-wandodlīce v. unfor-w.
wandrian *to* '*wander,*' *roam, fly round, hover,* Bo,CP,Fin,LL : *change : stray, err.*
wandung f. **I.** *feeling of respect,* CHRD 61³⁴. **II.** *turning aside,* CHRD 99¹⁹.
wand-wurp, -wyrp=wandeweorpe
wanfāh (o) *dark-hued,* RD 53⁶.
wanfeax (o) *dark-haired,* RD 13⁸.
wanfōta m. *pelican,* WW 287¹⁰.
wanfȳr (o) n. *lurid flame,* CR 966.
wang I. (o) m. *plain, mead, field, place,* B, Bl,Ph : *world.* ['*wong*'] **II.** m.=wange
wangbeard m. *whisker,* LCD 73a.
wange (e, o) n. *jaw, cheek,* Æ,Lcd,RG. ['*wang*']
wangere m. *pillow, bolster,* BH,WW. ['*wanger*']
wangstede† m. *place, locality,* RWH 67¹².
wangtōð m. *molar, grinder,* LL,WW. ['*wangtooth*']
wangturf f. *meadow-turf,* LCD 1·400⁷.
wanhæf-=wanhaf-
+wanhǣlan *to weaken,* Æ.
wanhǣlð f. *weakness, sickness,* Sc 54¹⁹.
wanhǣw (o) *bluish,* WW 376²³.
wanhafa m. *poor man,* SPs 85¹.
wanhafol *needy,* ÆL.
wan-hafolnes, -haf(e)nes (æ²) f. *want, hunger.*
wanhāl *unsound, weak, ill, maimed,* Æ, CP.
+wanhālian *to make weak,* HL 12⁵¹.
wanhālnes f. *weakness, ill-health,* RB,Sc.
wanhlȳte *having no share in, free from,* WW 398³³.
wanhoga m. *thoughtless one, fool,* SOL.
wan-hygd, -hȳd† f. *carelessness, recklessness, daring.*
wanhygdig (hȳdig)† *careless, rash.*
±wanian *to diminish* (tr.), *lessen, curtail, injure, impair, take from,* Ct,Rd; Æ,AO : *infringe, annul : diminish* (intr.), *dwindle, decline, fade, decay,* B,Chr,Chrd,Jn; Æ, CP : '*wane*' (moon), Bl.
wānian *to complain, bewail, lament, bemoan,* B,Cr,Jul; AO. ['*wone*']
wan-iendlic, -gendlic *diminutive,* ÆGr.
wann I. (o) *dark, dusky, lurid,* B,Gl,Met. ['*wan*'] **II.** pret. 3 sg. of winnan.
wannhāl=wanhāl
wannian *to become dark-coloured, turn black,* NC 332 : *become discoloured?* ÆP 178¹¹ ['*wan*']
wanniht *wan, pale, livid,* WW 431²¹.
wansǣlig (o¹)† *unhappy.*

wansceaft (o¹)† f. *misery, misfortune.*
wansceaf-ta m. (or -te f.) *a disease,* LCD.
wansorȳd *poorly clad,* ÆH 2·500¹⁷.
wansēoc '*commitialis*'? v. OEG 4937.
wansian *to diminish,* Chr 656 E. ['*wanze*']
wanspēd f. *poverty, want,* AO,Sc. ['*wanspeed*']
wanspēdig *poor, indigent,* Æ. ['*wanspeedy*']
wanung (o) f. *waning, decrease, deprivation, diminution, loss, injury, weakening,* Æ, BH,Lcd.
wānung f. *howling, lamentation,* Æ,LG. ['*wonung*']
wanwegende *waning* (moon), LCD.
wāpe (a²?) *napkin, towel?* IM 122²³.
wapelian, wapolian *to bubble, froth, exhale, emit, pour forth,* GL.
wapul m? *bubble, froth,* WW.
war=wearr
wār I. n. *sea-weed,* Gl : *sand.* ['*ware*'] **II.**=wǣr
wara, gs. of waru.
-waran v. burg-, ceaster-, eorð-w.
waras (N)=weras nap. of wer I.
-waras v. burg-, eorð-w.
warað=waroð
ward=(1) weard; (2) wearð (weorðan)
-ware v. burg-, eorð-, ceaster-w.
waren-=warn-; **warht**=worht
warian I. *to be wary, beware,* Gen,KGl,LL : (±) *guard, protect, defend : warn,* Gl; CP : (†) *hold, possess, attend :* (†) *inhabit.* ['*ware*'] **II.** *to make a treaty* (with), BH.
wārig *woody, dirty,* GnE 99.
wāriht *full of sea-weed,* GL.
waritrēo=weargtrēow
warnian (ea, are) (±) *to* '*warn,*' *caution,* Æ, Chr,Lcd,W : (±) *take warning, take heed, guard oneself against,* Æ,Lk; CP : *deny* (oneself, etc.). ['*wearn*']
warnung (ea) f. '*warning*' : *foresight, caution,* Æ,Cr,Sol.
waroð (a¹, ea¹, e¹, a², e², u²) n. *shore, strand, beach,* B,Met,Ps. ['*warth*']
wāroð n. *alga, sea-weed,* RD 41⁴⁹.
waroðfaruð m. *surf,* AN 197.
waroðgewinn (u²) n. *surf,* AN 439.
warp=wearp I.; **warr**=wearr
warpenig v. weardpening
warscipe=wærscipe
warð I. (N)=waroð. **II.** (N)=wearð pret. 3 sg. of weorðan.
waru I. f. '*ware,*' *article of merchandise,* Æ, WW. **II.** f. *shelter, protection, care, custody, guard, defence, vindication,* AO,Gu; Æ. ['*ware*']
-waru v. burg-, ciric-, eorð-w.
waruð, wāruð=waroð, wāroð

was=wæs; -wāsa v. wudu-w.
wascan⁶ (æ; acs, a(c)x) to 'wash,' cleanse,
Æ,BH,G,TC : bathe, lave.
wāse (v. OEG 1818) f. mire, marsh, Gl.
['ooze']
wāsend (ǣ) m. 'weasand,' windpipe, gullet,
Gl,Lcd.
wāsescite f. cuttlefish, WW 181⁷. [wāse,
scēotan]
wāst pres. 2 sg. of witan.
wāt I. pres. 3 sg. of witan. II. pret. 3 sg.
of witan. III.=wǣt
watel (o², u²) m. 'wattle,' hurdle, covering :
(pl.) thatching, BH,Gl,LkL.
water=wæter; watol=watel
watr-=wætr-, wæter-
watul=watel
wāð† f. wandering, journey : pursuit, hunt,
hunting, chase, MET 27¹³.
wāðan? to wander, flee, GUTH 113n.
waðema=waðuma
wāðol wandering? or m. full moon? FIN 8?
wað-um, -uma† m. wave, flood, stream, sea.
wāwa ['wowe'; ÆGr,Gen]=wēa
wāwan⁷ to blow (of wind), RD 41⁸¹.
waxan=(1) wascan; (2) weaxan
waxgeorn=weaxgeorn
we (ē) pron. (1st pers. plur.) g. ūser, d. ūs,
acc. ūs(ic) 'WE.'
wēa m. misfortune, evil, harm, trouble :
grief, woe, misery : sin, wickedness.
weacen=wacen
wēacwānian to lament, SAT 320.
wēadǣd† f. evil deed.
wēadhōc (Ep 887)=wēodhōc
weadu (K)=wudu
wēafod=wēofod; weag=weg
wēagesīð m. companion in trouble, W.
weagian=wagian
weahte pret. 3 sg. of weccan.
weahxan=weaxan
weal=(1) weall; (2) wæl
wēal=wealh; weal-=weall-, wel-
wēalāf† f. wretched remnant.
wēaland=wēalland
Wēalas (pl. of wealh) the 'Welsh,' Chr,LL :
Wales. West Wē(a)las West-Welsh,
Cornish.
+wealc n. rolling, tossing motion : attack,
CHR 1100.
wealca (a) m. †billow, rolling wave : light
floating garment.
wealcan⁷ (±) to move round, revolve, roll,
toss, Gl; CP : fluctuate : revolve in one's
mind, discuss, scheme, reflect, Æ,CP : roll
together : (+) go, traverse, Gl. ['walk']
wealcere m. fuller, WW 407²⁹. ['walker']
±wealcian (a) to curl, OEG 26⁶⁹ : roll up,
HGL 489⁵⁶.

wealcol mobile, not firmly fixed, GPH 399⁴⁴¹.
wealcspinl (a, o) f. crisping-pin, OEG,WW.
Wēalcynn n. the Welsh kin, EC 146'.
weald I. (a) m. weald, forest, wood, grove,
BC,Chr,Jud; AO : bushes, foliage, GEN
846. ['wold'] II. m. power, dominion,
mastery, AO (usu. +) : groin, LCD 1·12⁹.
III. powerful, RB 117⁵. IV. conj. in case.
w. ðeah perhaps, possibly, ÆH. ['wald']
+weald (a) n. might, power, possession, A,
B,Rood : control, command, dominion, AO,
Bl : bridle : protection : subjection : groin :
pudenda : muscles of the neck? LL 88,77.
(his) gewealdes of his own accord, in-
tentionally, LL. ['wield']
±wealdan⁷ (a) w. g. d. (instr.) and a. to rule,
control, determine, direct, command, govern,
possess, AO,CP : 'WIELD*' (a weapon),
exercise : cause, bring about, CP.
wealdbǣr f. place affording mast for swine,
EC 60²³.
+wealden I. adj. subject (to), easily con-
trolled : inconsiderable, small, AO,CP. II.
adv. moderately.
wealdend (a) I. m. leader, controller, ruler,
lord, king (often of God), B,Bo. ['wald-
end'] II. f. female ruler.
±wealdende ruling, powerful, Æ,Cr. ['wielding']
Wealdendgod m. Lord God, PPs.
+wealdendlīce powerfully, PPs 135¹⁶.
wealdendras late nap. of wealdend.
+wealdenmōd self-controlled, CRA 70.
wealdes (usu. +) of one's own accord,
voluntarily, CP 198²².
wealdgenga m. robber, thief, ÆT 1089.
±wealdleðer n. rein, bridle, Æ.
wealdmoru=wēalhmoru
wealdnes (a) f. rule, VPs 144¹³.
wealdswaðu (a¹) f. forest-track, B 1403.
weale=wale; wēales v. wealh.
wealfæsten=weallfæsten
wealg nauseous? CP 447¹⁸. ['wallow']
wealgat=weallgeat
wealh (a) m. (gs. weales) foreigner, stranger,
slave : Briton, Welshman : shameless
person, HGL 527²².
wealhāt boiling hot, red-hot, Lcd 96a.
['wallhot']
wealhbaso f. foreign red, vermilion, GL.
Wealhcynn n. men of Wales, Britons, CHR.
wealhen=wielen
wealhfæreld (a) n. a force which patrolled
the Welsh border? KC 2·60'.
wealh-gefēra, -gerēfa m. commander of the
'wealhfæreld,' CHR 897A.
wealhhāfoc m. foreign hawk, falcon, AA,
GL.
wealhhnutu (a) f. 'walnut,' WW 452³⁴.

wealhisc=wīelisc

wealh-moru, -more (a¹) f., -mora m. *carrot, parsnip*, LCD,WW.

wealhstod m. *interpreter, translator*, Æ,CP : *mediator*, CP.

Wealhðēod f. *Welsh nation*, LL.

wealhwyrt [v. '*wallwort*']=wēalwyrt

weallan *to be defiant*, ÆL12⁴⁸.

wēalic *woeful, sorrowful*, WY12.

weall I. (a, æ) m. 'WALL,' *dike, earthwork, rampart, dam*, Æ; AO,CP; Mdf : (†) *rocky shore, cliff*. II. f. *fervour*, HGL465. III.= wæl. IV.=wiell

weallan⁷ (±) *to be agitated, rage, toss, well, bubble, seethe, foam, be hot, boil*, AO,B, Lcd; CP : *swarm*, Æ,WW : *flow*, Æ. ūp w. *to rise (of a river)*, AO. ['*wall*']

wēalland n. *foreign country*, GEN2706 (weal-) : *Normandy*, CHR1040E. [wealh]

Wēallas=Wēalas

weallclif n. *sea-cliff*, B3132.

wealldīc f. *a walled ditch?* KC5·346¹⁹.

wealldor n. *door in a wall*, CR328.

+wealled=+weallod

weallende *boiling, raging*, Æ,B : *fervid, ardent, energetic, fiery : swarming (with vermin)*, Æ,WW. [v. '*wall*,' '*walling*']

weallfæsten n. *walled place, rampart, fortification, fortress.*

weallgeat† n. *rampart-gate, postern.*

weallgebrec n. *wall-breaking, act of making a breach*, AO134³⁰.

weallgeweorc n. *building of a wall*, Æ : *destruction of walls*, ÆGR12⁵.

weallian *to go abroad, travel, wander : go as pilgrim*, LL. ['*wall*']

weallīm m. *cement, mortar*, GEN11³.

wēallisc=wīelisc

+weallod *walled, Num.* [v. '*wall*']

weallstān† m. *stone used in building*, Cr, Ruin. ['*wallstone*']

weallstaðol (e³) m. *interpreter, translator*, RWH41³³ (wealh-?).

weallsteall m. *wall-place, foundation?* WA88.

weallstēap† *steep as a wall*, GEN.

weallstilling (y) m. *repair of walls* (v. BT).

weallstōw=wælstōw

weallōrǣd (a¹) m. *plumb-line*, WW522²⁷.

weallung (a, y) f. *agitation, fervour, zeal.*

weallwala† m. *part of a house-wall? foundation?* RUIN21.

weallweg (a¹) m. *walled road?* Ct.

weallwyrhta m. *mason*, GL.

weallwyrt=wealwyrt

wēal-mora, -more=wealhmoru

wealnes (CPs)=wealdnes

wealowian=wealwian

wealsāda m. *cord (for binding captives)?* PPs139⁵. [wealh]

wealstilling (y²)=weallstilling

wealstod=wealhstod

wealt=wielt pres. 3 sg. of wealdan.

wealte f. *a ring*, Erf1105.

wealweorc n. *masonry*, Æ.

wealwian I. (a, y) *to roll* (intr.), Bo,BH, CP : *roll* (tr.). ['*wallow*'] II. *to dry up, shrivel, wither, decay*, Bo. ['*wallow*']

wealword n. *defiant word*, A11·98³⁷. [wealh]

wealwyrt (a, æ) f. *dwarf elder*, Cp,Lcd. ['*wallwort*']

wēamēt, wēamētto f. *passion, anger*, Æ.

wēamōd *ill-humoured, angry*, CP. ['*wemod*']

wēamōdnes f. *anger, impatience*, Æ,CP.

weaps=wæps

wear=(1) wearr; (2) hwer

wear-=wær-

wearas=weras npl. of wer.

wearc=wærc

weard I. fm. *watching, 'ward,' protection, guardianship*, Æ,B; AO,CP : *advance post*, AO : *waiting for, lurking, ambuscade*. II. m. *keeper, watchman, guard, guardian, protector*, B,Bl; AO : (†) *lord, king* : (†) *possessor*. III. adv. *towards, to.* wið... weard *towards*. IV.=wearð. V. '*sandix*,' v. A30·249.

weardian *to watch, guard, keep, protect, preserve*, LL,Ps : *hold, possess, occupy, inhabit : rule, govern*, Da665. lāst w. *keep the track of, follow closely.* swaðe w. *remain behind.* leger w. *keep one's bed.* ['*ward*']

weardmann m. *watchman, guard, patrol*, Æ.

weardpening? (warp-) m. *rent paid in lieu of military service*, Ct1087? ['*wardpenny*']

weardseld, weardsetl (Æ) n. *guardhouse, watch-tower.*

weardsteall m. *watch-tower*, WW.

weardwīte n. *penalty for not keeping guard*, TC411³¹. ['*wardwite*']

wearf I. (EC202¹⁵)=wearp pret. 3 sg. of weorpan. II.=hwearf

wearg (e) I. m. *(wolf), accursed one, outlaw, felon, criminal*, Rood,WW; Æ. ['*wary*'] II. (-erig, -yrig) adj. *wicked, cursed, wretched.* [ON. vargr]

weargberende *villainous*, WW407²⁷.

weargbrǣde (-geb-) f. *a warty eruption, impetigo, stye in the eye, tetter, ringworm, mole, freckle*, Lcd,WW. ['*waribreed*']

wearglīc (ere-, eri-) *wretched.* adv. -līce (y¹).

weargnes (æ, e, y) f. *evil*, MtL,PPs.

weargrōd f. *scaffold, gallows*, GL.

weargtreafu (rht) np. *hell*, EL927.

weargtrēow (ari-) n. *gallows*, KC. ['*warytree*']

weargung (e) f. *misery*, EPs 87¹⁹.

wearh I.=wearg. **II.**=wearr

wēariht=wearriht

wearm '*warm,*' *Bo,Met,Rd*; Æ,CP. adv. -e, *Lcd.*

wearmelle=wurmille

±**wearmian** *to become or make* '*warm,*' Æ, *BH,G,HL,Ph,Rd*; CP.

wearmlic *warm*, DA 350.

wearmnes f. *warmth*, ÆL 11¹⁶⁰. ['*warmness*']

wearn I. f. *reluctance, repugnance, refusal, denial*, CP : *resistance : reproaches, abuse.* [waru] **II.**=worn

wearn-=warn-, wearrn-

wearnmǣlum (ē) adv. *in troops*, WW 25¹. [worn]

wearnwīslīce adv. *obstinately*, WW.

wearod, wearoð=waroð

wearp I. (a) m. '*warp,*' *threads stretched lengthwise in a loom*, *Cp,Rd* : *twig, osier.* **II.** pret. 3 sg. of weorpan.

wearpfæt n. *basket*, WW. ['*warpfat*']

wearr (a, æ, eo) m. *callosity*, *Cp,Lcd.* ['*warre*']

wearrig (Æ), wearriht *warty, knotty.*

wearrihtnes f. *roughness (of skin)*, GL.

wearrnes (wearn-) f. *knottiness* (Swt).

wearscipe (AS 69¹⁵)=wærscipe?

weart, wearte (a, e) f. '*wart,*' *Cp,Lcd.*

weartere (æ) m. *occupier, dweller*, CHR 565. [weard]

wearð I. n.=weorð. **II.** pret. 3 sg. of weorðan. **III.**=waroð

wearð-=weorð-

wēas adv. *by chance, accidentally*, CP. mid w. *by chance.*

weasc-=wæsc-

wēasgelimp n. *chance occurrence*, WW 410¹⁰.

wēaspell n. *evil tidings*, B 1315.

weastern (CHR 1015)=western

weastm=wæstm

wēatācen† n. *sign of grief.*

wēaðearf f. *woeful need*, WIF 10.

weax (e) n. '*wax,*' *BC,Bl,Ps*; AO.

weaxæppel m. *ball of wax*, SOL 150³³.

±**weaxan** (e) **I.** sv⁷ *to* 'WAX,' *grow, be fruitful, increase, become powerful, flourish*, Æ, *CP*; AO. **II.**=wascan

weaxberende m. *candle-bearer, acolyte*, DR 195⁸ (io²).

weaxbred (e) n. *writing-tablet*, Æ,RB : *diagram, table*, BF 180³⁰. ['*waxbred*']

weaxcandel (e¹, o²) f. '*wax candle,*' *Cp,WW.*

weaxen (e¹) **I.** *waxen, made of wax?* LCD. **II.** pp. of weaxan.

weaxgeorn (a) *very greedy*, WW 102¹³.

weaxgesceot n. *payment in wax*, W 171¹.

weaxhlāf m. *wax tablet*, LCD.

weaxhlāfsealf f. *wax salve*, LCD 92b.

±**weaxnes** f. *increase, growth : interest, usury.*

weaxscot=weaxgesceot

weaxsealf (e) f. *wax salve*, LCD,WW.

weaxung f. *growth, increase*, Bf 138¹⁹. ['*waxing*']

web, webb n. '*web,*' *weft : woven work, tapestry*, *B,Cp,Sc*; Æ. [wefan]

webba m. *weaver*, WW. ['*webbe*']

webbēam m. *weaver's beam*, WW : *treadle of a loom*, WW. ['*webbeam*']

webbestre f. *female weaver*, WW 188¹¹. ['*webster*']

webbgeweorc n. *weaving*, HL,MH.

webbian *to contrive, devise*, AN,BL,EL.

webbung (hw) f. *plotting, conspiracy*, OEG 2975 : '*scena*' (=wāfung? v. OEG 2920).

webgerēðru np. *weaver's tool*, WW 294¹⁶.

webgerod n. *weaver's implement*, Cp 1988.

webhōc m. *weaver's comb, reed?* WW.

weblic *pertaining to a weaver*, GL.

websceaft m. *weaver's beam*, WW 293³⁹.

webtāwa m. *thread, line*, WW 433⁸.

web-tēag (æ¹, ǣ²) f. *weaving-thread*, OET 615.

wēbung (Cp 180s)=wāfung

webwyrhta m. *fuller*, MH.

wecca=wēoca

weccan (±) *to awaken, arouse*, B,BH,CP, Cr : *call up, bring forth, produce : recall : exhort, encourage : move, set in motion : kindle.* ['*wecche*']

weccend m. *instigator*, GPH 393.

wēce=wāc I.

wecedrenc m. *emetic*, LCD.

wecg m. '*wedge,*' *Cp,Sc* : *mass of metal, lump*, Æ : *piece of money*, Æ,BH,WW.

weccgan *to move, agitate, drive hither and thither*, *Met,Ps* : *be moved*. ['*weigh*']

wecian (VPs)=wacian

wecnian=wæcnian

wed=wedd

wēd=wǣd

+**wēd I.** n. *fury, rage, foolishness, madness.* [wōd] **II.** (ZDA 31·9¹⁶⁸) pp. of wēn.

±**wēdan** (ǣ) *to be or become mad, rage*, Æ, *BH,G*; AO,CP. ['*wede*']

wēd-beorge, -berge=wēdeberge

wedbrice=wedbryce

wedbrōðor m. *pledged brother (in a brotherhood of compact, not of blood)*, CHR. [wedd]

wedbryce m. *treachery*, W. [? v. '*wed*']

wedd n. *pledge, agreement, covenant, security*, *B,Bl,Chr*; Æ,AO,CP : *dowry*, WW. ['*wed*']

+**weddian** *engage, pledge oneself, covenant, promise, vow*, *Lk,LL* : *give to wife, betroth* : '*wed,*' *marry*, *Chrd,LL.*

weddung f. *pledging, betrothal,* Nic474³³. ['*wedding*']

wēde I. *raging, mad,* LcD,LkL. [wōd] II. (A)=wǣde

+wēde n. *fury, rage, madness,* Æ. [wōd]

wēdeberge f. *hellebore,* LCD,GL.

wēdehund m. *mad dog,* LCD,MET.

wēdelnes (VPs)=wǣdelnes

wēden (MFH178)=wǣden

wēdend *raving,* Bo,Cp. [v. '*wede*']

wēden(d)sēoc *mad,* GD135n; 223.

wēdenheort I. *mad, insane,* WW. II. n. *madness.*

wēdenheortnes f. *madness, frenzy,* CP.

weder I. n. 'WEATHER,' *air,* AO : *sky, firmament* : *breeze, storm, tempest.* II.=weðer

+weder=+wider

wederblāc *bleached by the weather,* A8·449.

wederburg f. *exposed town,* AN1699.

wedercandel f. *sun,* PH187.

wederdæg m. *day of fine weather,* Az96.

wederfest *weather-bound,* CHR1046E.

wederian *to exhibit a change of weather,* LCD.

wedertācen n. *sun,* Gu1267.

+wederu=+wideru

wederung (æ) f. (*bad*) *weather,* Chr1085. ['*weathering*']

wederwolcen n. *cloud,* Ex75.

wedewe=wuduwe

+wedfæstan (wet-) *to pledge,* Cp635s.

wēding f. *madness,* GD164²⁷; WW409³⁸.

wēdl-=wǣdl-

wedlāc n. *pledge, plighted troth,* '*wedlock*,' GL.

wedloga m. *violator of agreement, traitor.*

+wef n *woof, web,* WW490⁹⁸ : *text, context?* BF172¹¹.

wēf-=wāf-, wǣf-, wēof-

wefan⁵ (eo) (±) *to* '*weave*,' BH,LPs, WW; Æ : *devise, contrive, arrange.*

wefl I. f. *woof, warp,* GL : *an implement for weaving, shuttle?* LL455,15 and 3·254. II.=wifel

weft, wefta m. '*weft*,' A9·263.

weg I. (æ) m. 'WAY,' *direction,* AO; Æ : *path, road, highway,* Mdf : *journey,* Æ : *course of action,* CP. ealne w. (ealneg) adv. *always.* on w. (āweg) adv. *away.* be...wege *on the way* (*to*). II.=wæg II.

wēg=(1) wǣge; (2) wīg

weg-=onweg-; wēg-=wǣg-

wegan⁵ (±) *to carry,* B,Nar : *support, sustain, bear, bring,* CP : *move* : *wear,* BH, CP : (±) '*weigh*,' *measure,* ÆGr,Lcd,W.

+wegan *to fight,* B2400.

weg-brāde, -brǣde (Æ) f. '*way-bread*,' *plantain, dock,* Gl,Lcd.

wegfarende (ǣ, ē) '*wayfaring*,' ÆL.

wegfērend m. *wayfarer, traveller,* Bo,GD.

wegfērende *wayfaring,* ÆH,GD. ['*wayfering*']

wegfōr f. *travel, journey,* WW423³³.

wegg=wecg

weggedāl n. *road-dividing, cross-way,* GL.

weggelǣte fn. *junction of roads,* Gl. ['*wayleet*']

weggē-sīð? -sīða? (v. OEG861) *travelling companion.*

weggewit n. *aberration* (*of mind*), CPs115¹¹.

weg-lā interj. '*euge!*' PPs69⁴. [=wā lā]

weglēas *out of the way, erroneous* : *without a road,* WW. ['*wayless*']

weglēast (ī²) f. *trackless place, wilderness,* ARSPs106⁴⁰.

wegnest (ǣ¹) n. *food for a journey,* HL : *viaticum,* BH.

wegrēaf n. *highway robbery,* LL.

wegtwiflung f. *branching of roads,* WW179¹⁶. [=-twislung]

wegu f. *vehicle,* GD314²⁵.

wegur (WW143¹³)=wīgār

wehsan=weaxan

wehte pret. 3 sg. of weccan

wei v. wā; weig-=weg

wel I. adv. (comp. bet) 'WELL,' *abundantly,* Æ,CP : *very, very easily, very much* : *fully, quite,* Æ : *nearly* : *pleonastic* (*as in* ēac w.=*also*), *sometimes*=*indeed, to be sure.* tō w. *too well.* w. nēah *nearly, almost.* w. hwǣr, w. gehwǣr *for the most part, nearly everywhere.* wella *alas!* (cp. wā lā). II.=wæl. III.=wiell. IV.=wiel

wel-=hwel-, wæl-, weal-, wiel-

wela (a, ea, eo) m. '*weal,*' *prosperity, happiness, riches* (*often in* pl.), BH,Bo,Bl,G, Gen; AO,CP.

Wēland m. *the Smith-God, Northern Vulcan.*

welbescēawod *discreet, considerate,* RB, WW.

welboren '*well-born*,' *noble,* Æ,LG.

welcn=wolcen

weldǣd (ē²) f. *good deed, benefit, kindness,* Ph. ['*weldede*']

weldōn anv. *to do well,* CP : *benefit, satisfy, please,* MtL15¹⁵.

weldōnd (ōe) m. *benefactor,* GL,DR.

weldōnnes f. *well-doing, kindness,* DR13¹⁷.

weleg=welig

welena gp. of wela.

weler (eo) mf. *lip,* Æ,CP.

weleðig *rich,* ANS128·299.

welfremming f. *good deed, benefit,* DR187¹⁷.

welfremnes f. *benefit,* DR.

welg=welig

welga=weliga wm. of welig adj.

welgā interj. *hail!* WW25²³.

welgeboren=welboren

welgecwēme *well-pleasing,* SPs,VH.

welgecwēmedlic *well-pleasing*, SPs.
welgecwēmnes f. *favour*, DR.
welgedōn *well-done, good, beneficent*, CP.
welgehwǣr=welhwǣr
welgelīcian *to please well* : *be well pleased*, AO,CVPs.
welgelīcwirðe *well pleased, acceptable*, VPs 118¹⁰⁸.
welgelīcwirōnes f. *good pleasure*, VPs 140⁷.
welgespring=wyllspring
welgestemned *having a good voice*, ANS 84·6.
welgetȳd *well-instructed*, ES 39·354.
welgewende *thriving*, MFH 178.
welgian=weligian
welhǣwen *beautifully coloured*, CP 411²⁸.
welhrēowlīce=wælhrēowlīce
welhwā †pron. *each, every*.
±**welhwǣr** adv. *(nearly) everywhere*, CP.
±**welhwilc**† (e, y) pron. *each, any, nearly every*.
welig I. *well-to-do, rich, prosperous*, AO,B, WW; CP. ['*wealy*'] II. m. '*willow*,' LCD, LG.
±**weligian** *to be prosperous, abound* : *enrich*, Æ. [v. '*awelgien*']
weligstedende (woegl-) *making rich*, DR 99⁹.
well=(1) *will*; (2) *wel*; **wella**=wiella
wellā=wā lā; **welle**=wille
wellende (VPs)=willende pres. ptc. of willan.
wellere *bosom, fold, hollow*, WW.
wellibbende (y²) *living well, well conducted, reputable*, CP.
wellīcian *to please well*, MFH 178.
wellīcung f. *agreeableness*, EPs 68¹⁴.
wellīcwyrðe (u³) *well-pleasing*, BCPs 146¹⁰.
wellyrge (GL)=wælcyrige
welm(a)=wielm(a)
-welm v. fōt-w.; **Wēlond**=Wēland
welor=weler; **welp**=hwelp
welrēab (Ep,Erf 642)=wælrēaf
welrūmlīce adv. *graciously*, DR.
welrummōd *gracious*, DR 12²⁰.
wel-spring, -sprynge (CP)=wyll(ge)spring
welstincende *fragrant*, CP 439³³.
welswēgende *melodious*, SPs 150⁵.
welt, welð=wielt, wielð pres. 3 sg. of wealdan, weallan.
welðungen† *honoured, in high repute*.
weluc=weoloc
welung f. *revolution (of a wheel)*, OEG 28³⁰. [wielwan]
welweorðe *of high esteem*, LCD 3·432'.
welwilled-=welwillend-
welwillende *well-wishing, benevolent, kindly, good*, Æ,Chrd; CP. ['*well-willing*']
welwillendlīce *benevolently, lovingly, kindly*.

wel-wille(n)dnes, -wilnes f. *benevolence, good-will, kindness*, Æ. ['*wellwillingness*']
wel-wyll-, -wylle(n)d-=welwillend-
welwyrcend m. *well-doer*, BL 137¹⁴.
welwyrcende *well-doing*, AS.
wem=wamm
wēman *to sound, be heard*, AN 740 : *announce*, AN 1480 : (±) *persuade, convince, lead astray*.
wēmend m. *herald, declarer*, EL 880.
wēmere m. *procurer*, WW 171²⁸.
±**wemman** (æ) *to defile, besmirch, profane, injure, ill-treat, destroy*, BH,Lk,LL,Ps; Æ, CP : *abuse, revile*. [v. '*wem*,' '*awem*']
+**wemmedlic** *corruptible*, ÆL 2·348⁸. adv. -līce, WW.
+**wemmednes** f. *defilement*, Æ.
±**wemmend** m. *adulterer, fornicator*, OEG.
+**wemmendlic** *seducing, corrupting*, OEG 2912.
±**wemming** m. *defilement, blemishing, spoiling*, OEG : (+) *profanation*. ['*wemming*']
+**wemmodlīce** (æ) adv. *corruptly*, WW 89².
wemnes=wemmednes
wen=(1) wynn; (2) wenn
wēn I. fm. (n?) *belief, hope, opinion, expectation, supposition*, Bo : *probability*, B : *estimation*. w. is ðæt *perhaps*, Bl,CP : *name of the rune for* w. ['*ween*'] II.= wægn
+**wēn** *to bend, twist*, NC 297 (A 14·139).
wēna m. *hope, opinion, expectation, idea, fancy*, CP.
±**wēnan** (w. g. or a.) *to* '*WEEN*,' *fancy, imagine, believe, think*, Æ; CP : *expect, hope*, Æ,AO,CP : *fear (for), despair (of)* : *esteem* : *wonder*, ES 37·191.
wenbȳl m. *boil, carbuncle*, LCD.
wencel I. (i) n. *child*, Bas,GD. ['*wenchel*'] II.=wancol
wend m. *what turns up, an event*, Bo,TC.
+**wend**=+wind
±**wendan** *to turn, direct*, Æ,CP : '*WEND*' *one's way, go*, Æ,AO : *return : change, alter, vary, restore*, Æ : *happen : convert : translate*, CP. w. on *to turn against*. [windan]
wēnde pret. 3 sg. of wēnan.
Wendelsǣ mf. *Mediterranean Sea*, AO.
-wenden v. ed-w.
wendend m. *that which turns round*, WW 489¹².
wendende *movable, revolving*, Sc 97⁴.
wendere m. *translator, interpreter*, OEG 5259.
Wendle† mp. *Vandals*.
wendung f. *change, turning, rotation*, CP, Sc. ['*wending*']
+**wēne** *perhaps*, MkR 14² (oe).

wēnendlic *to be hoped for,* GD 269¹⁴.

wēnere=wǣgnere

wēnestu=wēnstu; weng=wang

±wenian *to accustom, habituate, inure, train,*
ÆCP : *entertain, treat* : (+) *tame* : *break
off, 'wean' from, RB.* w. mid wynnum
treat kindly. w. tō wiste *feast, entertain.*

wēninga=wēnunga

wēnlic *comely, Æ* : '*conveniens*,' MkL. adv.
-līce *handsomely,* Bғ44⁸.

wenn I. mf. '*wen,' tumour, Lcd,WW.* II.
(K)=wynn

wennan=wenian

wenncīcen n. *little wen,* ZDA31·46.

wennsealf (wen-) f. *wen-salve, ointment for
a tumour,* Lᴄᴅ.

wenspryng m. '*nævus,' mole,* WW451¹⁹.

wēnstu=wēnst ðu, pres. 2 sing. of
wēnan.

wensum=wynsum

went pres. 3 sg. of wendan.

Wentas, Wente, Went-Sǣte, -Sǣtas mp.
people of Gwent (roughly=Monmouth-
shire).

wēnð pres. 3 sing. of wēnan.

wēnung f. *expectation, hope, BH*; AO112¹² :
doubt. ['*weening*']

wēn-unga, -unge (ǣ) adv. *possibly, perhaps,
by chance, Æ.*

wenwyrt f. *crowfoot? lesser celandine?
darnel?* Lᴄᴅ.

wēo (Rᴅ57⁵)=wōh? or wēa?

wēobed, wēobud=wēofod

wēoce f. *lamp or candle-'wick,' IM.*

wēocs=wēox pret. 3 sg. of weaxan.

wēocson pret. pl. of wacsan (=wascan).

wēocsteall (ES11·64)=wēohsteall

weocu=wucu

wēod n. *herb, grass, G*; CP : '*weed,' Bo.*

weodewe=wuduwe

wēodhōc m. '*weed-hook,' hoe, Cp*; LL
455,15.

wēodian *to 'weed,'* LL454,9.

wēodmōnað m. *August,* Mᴇɴ,MH.

weodo, weodu=wudu

weoduma=weotoma

wēodung f. '*weeding,'* WW105³.

weofan (VPs)=wefan

wēofod (e²) nm. *altar, CP,Mt,RB.* ['*weved*']

wēofodbōt f. *fine for injuring a priest, which
was applied in support of the altar,* v. LL
2·276.

wēofodheorð (wībed-) m. *altar-hearth,*
GD.

wēofodhrægl (wīgbed-) n. *altar-cover,* BH
90².

wēofod-scēat (Æ), -scēata m. *altar-cloth.*

wēofodsteall m. *place of the altar,* LL
(254n).

wēofod-ðegn, -ðēn m. *altar-attendant, priest.*

wēofodðēnung f. *altar-service,* LL380,2.

wēofodwiglere (wīgbed-) m. *soothsayer,*
WW108¹⁰.

+weofu pl. of +wef.

wēofud=wēofod

weofung f. *weaving,* WW490³⁸.

wēog=wīg

weogas=wegas nap. of weg.

wēoh=wīg

wēohse=wēox pret. 3 sg. of weaxan.

wēohsteall m. *place of the altar, sanctuary,
choir,* LL.

weol=weoll; weol- (A)=wel-

weolc I. pret. 3 sg. of wealcan. II.=weoloc

weolcn=wolcen

weolc-rēad, weolcen-=weolocrēad

weold pret. 3 sg. of wealdan.

weoll pret. 3 sg. of weallan.

weolm=wielm

weolme (=ea) f. *choice, pick of one's fellow-
creatures,* Cʀ445.

weoloc (e, i, y) m. '*whelk,' cockle, murex,
BH,Gl* : (*purple*) *dye from the murex.*

weolocbasu *purple,* Gʟ.

weolocrēad *shell-fish red, scarlet, purple,*
BH,Gʟ.

weolocscyll (e³) f. *whelk, cockle, shell-fish,*
BH.

weoloctælg m. *purple dye,* WW. [telg]

weolt pret. 3 sg. of wealtan.

weoning (WW234²²)=meoning

wēop pret. 3 sg. of wēpan.

wēop-=wēp-; weor=wer I.

woorad=wcrod

weorc (e, o) n. '*WORK,' labour, action, deed,
Æ,CP* : *exercise* : (†) *affliction, suffering
pain, trouble, distress* (v. JAW52) : *fortification.* weorcum *with difficulty.*

+weorc n. *work, workmanship, labour, construction* : *structure, edifice, Æ* : *military
work, fortification.*

weorc- v. also wyrc-.

weorccræft m. *mechanics,* OEG55⁶.

weorcdǣd (oe¹, ē²) f. *action, operation,* DR
125¹⁸.

weorcdæg m. *work-day,* CM,RB.

weorce I.† adj. *painful, bitter, difficult, hard.*
II. adv. *hardly, with difficulty,* Jᴜʟ.

weorcful *active,* Sc169¹ : *industrious,* OEG
55⁶.

weorcgerēfa m. *foreman, overseer, Æ.*

-weorcheard, -weorclic v. un-w.

weorchūs (e) n. *workshop,* WW.

+weorclic *pertaining to work,* OEG1042.

weorcmann (e) m. '*workman,' Bo,LG.*

weorcnýten n. *working cattle,* LL26n.

weorcrǣden f. *corvée-work,* EC377¹.

weorcsige m. *success in work,* Lᴄᴅ1·388'.

weorcstān m. *hewn stone*, Æ.
weorcsum *painful*, GEN 594.
weorcðēow† mf. *servant, slave*, GEN.
weorcuhta m. *hour of matins on a non-festival day*, NC 332 (cp. mæsseuhta).
weorcum v. weorc.
weorcwyrðe *fit for work, able-bodied*, MFH 178.
weord=wyrd
weordungdæg (WW 206³²)=weorðungdæg
weored=werod I.; **weorel.** -world
weoren pp. of weosan.
weorf n. *beast of burden* (v. CC 129), *cattle*.
weorf-=hweorf-
weorfemeoluc? f. *milk from wild cattle?* LCD 102a (MS ðeorfe-).
weorftord (-oruf-) m. *dung of cattle*, PPs 112⁶.
weorht=worht pp. of wyrcean.
+**weorht**=+wyrht; **weorlan**=werian
weorld (BL)=woruld; **weorm**=wyrm
weormlan=wearmian; **weorn**=worn
weornan=wiernan
±**weornlan** (u) *to pine away, become weak, fade, wither, destroy*, Æ.
weorod=werod I. and II.
weorold=woruld
+**weorp** n. *throwing, dashing, tossing*, AN 306 : *what is thrown up*.
±**weorpan** (o, u, y) I. sv³ *to throw, cast, cast down, cast away*, Bo,G; Æ,AO,CP : *throw off, out, expel* : *throw upon* : *open*, ÆL : *drive away*, Jn : *sprinkle*, B,Lcd : *hit*, Bo : (+) *reach by throwing*, CP. w. tō handa *to hand over*. w. handa on *lay hands on* (*a person*) : (w. d. pers.) *charge with, accuse of*. [*'warp'*] II.=wierpan
weorpere m. *thrower, caster*, Rd 28⁷. [*'warper'*]
weorpian *to pine away*, ERPs 38¹².
weorras (Cp 161c)=wearras, nap. of wearr.
weort=wyrt; **weorteard**=ortgeard
weorð I. (e, ea, i, o, u, y) n. *'worth,' value, amount, price, purchase-money, ransom*, AO,G,VPs; CP. II. (ie, o, u, y) adj. *worth*, LL : *worthy, honoured, noble, honourable, of high rank*, Æ,BC,Bo; CP : *valued, dear, precious*, AO,CP : *fit, capable*. III.= worð I.
±**weorðan³** (u, y) *to become, get, be* (passive auxiliary), *be done, be made*, CP : *happen, come to pass, arise, take place, settle* : (+) impers. *get on with, please, agree*, AO,Chr : *think of, occur to*. [*'WORTH,' 'i-worth'*]
weorðe=weorð, wierðe
weorðere m. *worshipper*, JnL.
weorðful (u¹) *worthy, honourable, honoured, glorious, good*, B,G,Chr,Lcd. [*'worthful'*]
weorðfullic (u) *worthy, honoured, honourable, distinguished*, CP. adv. -līce, AO.

weorðfulnes f. *dignity, honour*, AO.
weorðgeorn *desirous of honour, high-souled*.
±**weorðian** (o, u, y) *to esteem, honour, worship, distinguish, celebrate, exalt, praise*, AO,CP : *adorn, deck* : *enrich, reward*. [*'WORTH,' 'i-wurthi'*]
-**weorðiend** v. rōd-w.
weorðig=worðig
weorðlēas (u) *worthless*, WW 130²⁰.
weorðlic (u, y) *important, valuable, splendid*, Æ,AO,Chr,Jul : *worthy, estimable, honourable, distinguished, exalted*, Bo,Chr : *fit, becoming*. adv. -līce. [*'worthly'*]
weorðlicnes f. *worthiness, honour, estimation*.
weorðmetednes (u¹) *'adinventio,'* SPs 76¹².
weorð-mynd, -mynt (u) fmn. *honour, dignity, glory*, AO,CP : *mark of distinction*.
weorðnes (e, ie, o, u, y) f. *worth, estimation* : *splendour, rank, honour* : *integrity*.
weorðscipe (o, u) m. *worth, respect, honour, dignity, glory*, Æ; AO,CP : *advantage, good* : *distinction* (*in behaviour*), LL. [*'worship'*]
weorððearfa (u¹, y¹) *poor man*, BK 12.
weorðung f. *honouring, distinction, honour, glory*, CP,LG : *celebration, worship*, Æ : *excellence* : *ornament*. [*'worthing'*]
weorðungdæg m. *day for bestowal of honours or offices, festival*, BK 23.
weorðungstōw f. *place of worship, the Tabernacle*, Æ.
weoruc=weorc; **weorud**=werod
weoruf=weorf; **weoruld**=woruld
wēos gs. and nap. of wēoh.
weos-=wes-
weosnian=wisnian
weot-=wit-; **weotod**=witod
wēoðel=wēðel, wǣdl
wēoðerweard=wiðerweard
weoðo-, wēoðo-=wiðo-, wīðo-
wēox pret. 3 sg. of weaxan.
weoxian *to cleanse?* A 9·261,262.
±**wēpan⁷** *to 'weep,' complain, bewail, mourn over, deplore*, Æ,BH,CP,G,MH.
wēpen=wǣp(e)n
wēpende adj. *'weeping,'* Æ,BH,Ps.
wēpendlic *deplorable, mournful*, CHR. adv. -līce.
wēpman=wǣpnedmann
wēpn, wēpned=wǣpen, wǣpned
wēpnian=wǣpnian
wer I. m. *male being* : *man* : *husband*, Æ, AO : (†) *hero*. [*'WERE'*] II. m. *the legal money-equivalent of a person's life, a man's legal value* (=wergild), LL. III. m. *'weir,' dam, fish-trap*, CP,Ct; Mdf : *catch, draught*. [werian] IV. (or were?) *troop, band*, WW, ÆL 30¹⁹⁵.

wēr=wǣr II.; **weran**=werian
werbēam m. *warrior*, Ex486.
wer-borg, -borh m. *pledge for the payment of* 'wergild,' LL.
werc (GL,VPs)=weorc
wercan=wyrcan
wercyn n. *human race, tribe*, RIM61.
werdan=wierdan; **were**=wer
wēre (M)=wǣre II.
wered=werod; **wēreg**=wērig
weregan (KGL)=wiergan
werfǣhðō f. *feud by which* 'wer' *is incurred, breach of the peace*, LL.
werfan=hwierfan
werg=(1) wearg; (2) wyr(i)g
wergan (A)=(1) wiergan; (2) werian I.
wērgan wk. ds. of wērig.
wergeld=wergild; **wergend**=weriend
wērgenga=wǣrgenga; **wergian**=wiergan
±**wērgian** to 'weary,' exhaust, be or become tired, BH,GD; Æ,AO,CP.
wergild (æ¹, e², i², y²) n. *compensation, value of a man's life* (v. LL2·731). ['*wergeld*']
wergildðēof m. *thief who might be redeemed by payment of his* 'wergild,' BC,LL. ['*wergeldthief*']
wergnes=weargnes
wergulu f. *crab-apple*, LCD3·34¹⁴ (v. BTs and MP24·220).
wērgum dsmn. of wērig.
wergyld=wergild
werhād m. *male sex, virility, manhood*, Æ.
werhbrǣde=weargbrǣde
werhta=wyrhta
wērī—wērig
±**werian** (æ) I. *to guard, keep, defend*, AO : ward off, hinder, prevent, forbid : restrain : occupy, inhabit, GU322 : *dam up*, CP469³. ['WERE'] II. *to clothe, cover over : put on, 'wear,' use*, AO,Chr,LL : stock (land). III. (+) *to make an alliance*, BH52¹⁹.
wērian=wērgian
weriend m. *defender*, Æ,W.
werig=wearg, wyrig
wērig 'WEARY,' tired, exhausted, miserable, sad, AO,CP : *unfortunate*. [wōr]
werigcweðan=wyrgcweðan
werigen=werian
werigend=weriend
wērigferhð† adj. *weary, cast down*.
wērigian=wērgian
wērigmōd† *weary, cast down*.
werignes=wyrignes
wērignes f. '*weariness*,' BH.
werilic=werlic; **wērines**=wērignes
wering f. *weir, dam*, CP277⁸.
werlād f. *clearing by the oaths of a number of men according to a man's* 'wer,' LL.
werlēas *without a husband*, LL.

werlic *male, masculine*, ÆGR : *manly : marital*. adv. -līce, Æ.
wērloga=wǣrloga; **werm-**=wearm-
wermǣgð† f. *tribe, nation*, GEN.
wermet n. *man's measure, stature*, WW.
wermōd m. *wormwood, absinthe*, Æ.
wern-=wearn-, wiern-
werna (Cp)=wrenna
wernæg(e)l m. *(man's nail?), wart, tumour*, Æ. ['*warnel*']
werod (eo¹, e²) I. n. [nap. werodu, werod] *throng, company, band, multitude*, Bl,Cp, G; Æ : *host, army, troop, legion*, Æ,AO. ['*wered*'] II. *sweet*, Æ. III.† n. *sweet drink, mead*.
werodian *to grow sweet*, Bo51⁴.
+**werodlǣcan** (e²) *to make sweet or pleasant*, Sc196⁵.
werodlēst f. *lack of fighters*, EL63.
werodlīce adv. *sweetly*, CM887.
werodnes f. *sweetness, pleasantness*, Æ.
werold=woruld
wēron (M)=wǣron pret. pl. of wesan.
weroð=waroð
werp f. *recovery (from sickness)*, CP457¹⁶. [=wyrpe]
werpan=weorpan
werrēaf n. *civil clothing*, CHRD.
werrest (BL)=wierrest
werscipe=wǣrscipe
werse, werst=wierse, wierrest
werstede m. *place of a weir*, EC246¹⁰.
wert (KGL)=wyrt; **werte**=wearte
wer-tihtle, -tyhtle f. *charge involving the penalty of* 'wer,' *homicide*, LL.
werð=wierð pres. 3 sg. of weorðan.
werðēod† f. *folk, people, nation*.
werðnes (K)=weorðnes; **werud**=werod
weruld=woruld; **wērun** (NG)=wǣron
werwulf (-rew-) m. '*werewolf*,' fiend, LL.
wes (VPs)=wæs pret. 3 sg. of wesan.
wēsa m. *drunkard*, WW84⁵. [wōs]
wesan anv. pres. 1 sg. eom, bēo, 2 eart, bist, 3 is, við; pl. sind(on); bēoð; pret. wæs, wǣron; subj. pres. sīe, sȳ, bēo; sīn, bēon; pret. wǣre, wǣren *to* 'BE'* : *happen*. v. also bēon.
+**wesan** *to strive, contend*, SOL181. [cp. +wosa]
±**wēsan** *to soak, macerate : ooze*, LCD : *dye*, OEG5196. ['*weese*']
wesand=wesend; **wesc**=wæsc
wēse *moist, macerated*, LCD3·292⁶. [wōs]
wesend (eo) m. *bison*, GL.
wesendhorn m. *bison's horn*, TC536¹.
wesendlīce *essentially*, GD336; 337.
wesing f. '*confectio,*' '*debilitatio,*' v. OEG 1857.

wesle, weosule (*Gl*) f. *'weasel,' Æ,LL.*
+wesnes f. *dissension,* BH 274⁵.
wesp=wæps
west adv. *westwards, 'west,' in a westerly direction, Bo,Chr,Ct,Ma;* AO.
westan, westane adv. *from the west, Gen, Lcd;* AO. be westan (prep. w. d.) *west of.* ['*westan*']
±**wēstan** *to lay waste, ravage, AO,PPs.* ['*weste*']
westanhealf=westhealf
westannorðan *north-west (wind),* OEG.
westansūðan *south-west,* AO.
westansūðanwind m. *south-west wind,* CVPs 77²⁶.
westanweard *westward,* AA 38¹⁶.
westanwind m. *west wind,* AO 17¹⁵.
West-Centingas mp. *people of West Kent,* CHR 999.
westdæl m. *west quarter, western part, Bl, VPs;* AO. ['*westdeal*']
West-Dene mp. *West Danes,* B.
wēste *waste, barren, desolate, deserted, uninhabited, empty, B,BH,G,VPs.* wēste land *waste land, desert,* EHR 1912. ['*weste*']
westem (VPs)=wæstm
westema v. westerne
wēsten I. nmf. *waste, wilderness, desert, Æ, AO,CP.* **II.** adj. *waste, desolate, Æ.*
westende m. *'west end,' AO,Chr.*
wēstengryre m. *terror of the desert,* Ex 117.
wēstensetla m. *hermit, anchorite, MH,RB.*
wēstenstaðol m. *waste place,* RUIN 28.
westenwind=westanwind
wēstern (LG; '*western*')=wēsten
westerne '*western,' westerly, BH,Chr,Gl.* wester(r)a *more westerly;* westema, westmest (AO) *most westerly.*
westeweard=westweard
westhealf f. *west side, AO,Chr.* ['*westhalf*']
wēstig (oe) *waste, deserted, desert, NG,RG.* ['*westy*']
westlang adv. *extending westwards,* KC.
westm (VPs)=wæstm
westmearc f. *western boundary,* OET 484.
westmest (*AO,BC,KC;* '*westmost*') v. westerne.
wēstnes f. *desolation : desert place,* EPs 77¹⁹.
westnorðlang adv. *extending north-westwards,* AO 22¹⁷.
westnorðwind m. *north-west wind,* WW.
westra (*BC;* '*wester*')=westerra; v. westerne.
westrīce n. *western kingdom, AO,CHR.*
westrihtes (y²) adv. *due west, westwards,* AO.
westrodor† m. *western (=evening) sky.*
westsǣ f. *western sea, AO,BH.*

West-Seaxe, -Seaxan mp. *West Saxons : Wessex.*
westsūðende m. *south-west extremity,* AO 8²³.
westsūðwind m. *south-west wind,* WW.
westu=wes ðu, 2 pers. imperat. of wesan.
West-Wēalas mp. *Cornishmen,* CHR.
westwe(a)rd I. adv. *westwards, Chr,Lcd.* ['*westward*'] **II.** adj. *westerly, AO,Ct.*
westweg m. *western way,* PPs 74⁶.
westwind m. *'west wind,'* BH 458¹⁷.
wesule=wesle
wēt I. pres. 3 sg. of wēdan. **II.** adj.=wæt
wet-, wēt-=wæt-, wǣt-
weterēdre=wæterǣdre
+**wetfǣstan**=+wedfæstan
wetma=wituma
wēðan *to assuage, make calm,* PPs 106²⁸.
wēðe *sweet, mild, pleasant,* BH,CR.
weðel *swathe, bandage,* WW 22¹⁴.
wēðel=wēðl, wǣdl; **wēðelnes**=wǣdelnes
weðer I. m. *'wether' sheep, ram, Æ,GD.* **II.**=weder I.
weðerwynde=wiðewinde; **wēðl**=wǣdl
±**wēðnes** f. *suavity, mildness, DR,PPs.*
wex (VPs)=weax; **wexe**=weax
wēxon=wēoxon pret. pl. of weaxan.
wh-=hw-
wī I.=wīg. **II.** (K)=weg
wiaht (K)=wiht
wiarald, wiaruld (K)=woruld
wibba m. *crawling thing, beetle,* WW 121²⁵.
wībed (VPs)=wēofod
wiber=wifer; **wibil** (GL)=wifel
wībora=wīgbora
wīc nf. *dwelling-place, lodging, habitation, house, mansion, B,BH,Gen; CP : village, town, Bl,Mk : in pl. entrenchments, camp, castle, fortress : street, lane : bay, creek.* ['*wick*'; v. Mdf]
wic-=wuc-
±**wīcan¹** *to yield, give way, fall down,* B,Ex.
wīcbora=wīgbora
wicca I. m. *wizard, magician, soothsayer, astrologer, LL,WW.* ['*witch*'] **II.**=wicga
wicce (y) f. *'witch,' Æ,OEG.*
wiccecræft m. *'witchcraft,' magic, OEG,LL.*
wiccedōm m. *witchcraft,* BK 20; HL 11¹²³. ['*witchdom*']
wiccian *to use witchcraft,* LL. ['*witch*']
wiccræft (CRA 70)=wiccecræft? or wicgcræft (*skill with horses*)? (BT).
wiccung f. *enchantment,* LL. ['*witching*']
wiccungdōm m. *witchcraft,* DA 121.
wicdæg=wucdæg
wice I. mf. *'wych'-elm, Gl,Lcd.* **II.** (*Chr, BH*)=wuce. **III.**=weoce.
wice f. *office, function, Æ : officer,* CHR 1120. ['*wike*']
wīceard m. *dwelling-place,* GU 907.

wīceng=wīcing
wīcfreoðu f. _protection of a dwelling_, GnE129.
wicg (y) n. _horse_, B (v. rare in prose). ['_widge_']
wicga m. _insect, beetle_, Lcd,WW.
wīcgefēra (Chr897a)=wīcgerēfa
wīcgerēfa m. _bailiff, reeve of a_ 'wīc' _or vill_, Chr897bcd : '_publicanus,_' _tax-gatherer_, WW.
wicgung=wiccung
wīcherpað m. _a public road to a_ 'wīc' (BT), KC3·418[26].
±wīcian _to dwell, lodge, rest in_, WW; Æ, AO : _encamp, bivouac_, CP : _harbour, anchor_, AO. ['_wick_']
wīcing m. _pirate, viking_, AO.
wīcingsceaðe f. _piracy_, Gl.
wīcnera, wīcnere (Æ) m. _steward, bailiff_, A, ZDA. ['_wickner_']
wīcnian _to attend upon_, Æ,RB127[3].
wīcscēawere m. _provider of a home_, Bl163[12].
wīcsteall m. _camping-place_, Ex92.
wīcstede† m. _dwelling_, B.
wīcstōw f. _dwelling-place, residence_ : _camp, encampment_, Æ,AO.
wīctūn m. _vestibule, court_, PPs.
wicðēn=wucðegn; wicu=wucu; wid=wið
wīd '_wide_,' _vast, broad, long_, Æ; AO,CP. w. and sīd _far and wide._ tō wīdan ealdre, tō wīdan fēore, wīdan fyrhð _for ever._
wīdan adv. _from far_ (v. also wīd), KC. ['_widen_']
wīdbrād _wide-spreading_, Gen643.
wīdcūð adj. _widely known, celebrated_, Æ.
wīde (once+) adv. _widely, afar, far and_ '_wide,_' Æ,AO,CP. sīde and w. _far and wide._ ['wide']
wīdefeorh†=wīdeferð
wīdefeorlic (wīder-) _eternal_, WW117[21].
wīde-ferhð†, -fyrhð I. mn. (_long life_), _long duration, long time._ II. adv. _always._
wider-=wiðer-
+wi-dere pl. -d(e)ru n. _weather (good or bad), storm, tempest_, AO. [weder]
+widerian (impers.) _to be fine weather_, LL 454,12.
widewe=wuduwe
wīdfæðme† _ample, extensive_, An.
wīdfarend m. _wanderer_, CP315[4].
wīdfeorh=wīdeferhð
wīdfērende† _coming from afar._
wīdferhð=wīdeferhð
wīdfloga† m. _wide-flier (of a dragon)_, B.
wīdfolc n. _great nation_, Gen1638?
wīdgal=wīdgil
wīdgangol _wandering, roving_, CP.
wīdgenge _wandering (monk)_, OEG58[10].
wīd-gil, -gill (e, ie) _wide-spread, broad, extensive_, Æ,CP : _wandering_, GD.

wīdgilnes f. _amplitude, spaciousness_, Æ.
wīdgongel=wīdgangol; wīdgyl=wīdgil
wīdhergan _to extol_, CP439[34].
wīdian _to become wider_, GD315.
wīdl mn? _impurity, filth, defilement_, GD, WW.
wīdland† n. _extensive country_, Gen.
wīdlāst† I. _far-wandering._ II. m. _long wandering, long way or road_, Rd.
±wīdlian _to defile, pollute, profane_, LL, NG.
±wīdmǣran=±wīdmǣrsian
wīdmǣre _celebrated, well-known_, AO,CP.
±wīdmǣrsian (tr., intr.) _to spread abroad, divulge_, Æ : _celebrate._
wīdmǣrsung f. _proclamation_, Sc96[11].
wīdmērsian=wīdmǣrsian
wīdnes f. _width_, WE60[18].
wīdobān=wiðobān
widor=weder; widor-=wider-
wīdor comp. of wīd.
wīdrynig _far-flowing_, An1509.
wīdsǣ mf. _open sea, ocean_, Æ,AO.
wīdsceop adj. _widely distributed_, Pa6.
wīdscofen _scattered far and wide_, B936.
wīdscrīðol _erratic, wandering_, Chrd,LL.
wīdsīð† m. _long journey_ : _far-traveller._
wīððil (DR98[12])=wīdl; widu=wudu
widuw-, widw-=wuduw-
wīdwegas† mp. _distant regions._
wiebel=wēofod; wiebel=wifel
wiece=wuce; Wieht=Wiht
wiel (e) m. _slave, servant_, Æ.
wiel- v. also wil-, wyl-.
+wield (i, eo) _power, control_, AO. ['_wield_']
±wieldan (æ, i, y) _to have power over, control_, CP : _tame, subdue, conquer, seize_, Chr,CP : (+) _compel_, LL265,15 : (+) _temper._ [v. '_wield*_']
wielde I. (±) (y) _powerful, victorious_, Æ,AO, GD. II. _in the power of, under the control of_, Æ.
+wieldend (y) _subduer_, GPH391.
wielding (y) f. _domination, rule_, LPs.
wielede pret. 3 sg. of wielwan.
wielen (i, y) f. _foreign woman, female slave_, AO.
wielincel n. _little servant, slave_, GPH401.
wielisc (æ, e, ea, i, y) _foreign_ : _British (not Anglo-Saxon)_, BC,Chr,LL : '_Welsh_' : _not free, servile._ [wealh]
wiell, wiella m., wielle (AO) f. (e, i, y) '_well_,' _fountain, spring_, CP; Mdf. [weallan] For comps. v. wyll-.
wielle=wille pres. 3 sg. of willan.
wielm (a, æ, e, eo, i, y) m. _boiling, swelling, sur , billow, current, stream_, An,B,BH,CP, Jul : _burning, flame, inflammation_ : _fervour ardour, zeal_, CP. ['_walm_'; weallan]

wielma (e) m. *inflammation*, LCD 31a (v. A 46·227).

wielmfȳr (æ) n. *blazing fire*, CR 932.

wielmhāt (y) *burning hot*, Gen 2584. [v. '*walm*']

wieln-=wiln-

wielt I. pres. 3 sg. of wealdan. II.=wielð

wielð pres. 3 sg. of weallan.

wien-=win-

wieoldon=weoldon pret. pl. of wealdan.

±wierdan, +wierdlian (e, i, y) *to spoil, injure, destroy, violate, obstruct*, Bo,Cp, LG,Ps. ['*werde*']

wierding (oe, y) f. *bodily injury*, DR, LL 410,3⁵ : *blemish*, OEG 649.

wierdnes (oe) f. *injury, vice*, DR.

wiergan (æ, e, i, iri, yri, y) *to abuse, outlaw, condemn, curse, proscribe*, Æ,CP,G,Gl : *blaspheme*, Æ : *do evil*. [For compounds v. wyrg-, wyrig-] ['*wary*']

wiergen v. grund-w.

wiernan (e, i, y) (w. g. of thing and d. of pers.) *to withhold, be sparing of, deny, refuse, reject, decline*, AO,CP : *forbid, prevent from*. ['*WARN*']

wiernung (æ) f. *refusal*, LL 152,3. ['*warning*']

wierp m. *cast, throw, shot, blow*, AO.

±wierpan (æ, y) *to recover from illness, get better*, CP.

wierpð pres. 3 sg. of weorpan.

wierrest (superl. of yfel) '*worst*,' Æ,Bl,Bo, CP,G,Ps.

wiers (y) adv. '*WORSE*,' CP.

wiersa m., wierse fn. (comp. of yfel '*WORSE*,' CP. [For comps. v. wyrs-]

wierst=wierrest

wierð pres. 3 sg. of weorðan.

wierðe (Bl,CP,G; '*wurthe*')=weorð

wīese=wīse pl. of wīs.

wieste=wiste, v. witan.

wiet-, wīet-=wit-, wīt-

wiexð pres. 3 sg. of weaxan.

wīf n. *woman, female, lady*, BH,Bl,Cp,LG; Æ,AO,CP : '*wife*,' Bo,Mt; Æ,AO,CP.

+wīf I. n. *fate, fortune*. [wefan] II. n. *a disease of the eye*, LCD 3·292².

wīfcild n. *female child*, BH 76⁹.

wīfcynn n. *womankind, female sex*, BH,Bl. ['*wifkin*']

wīfcȳððu f. *company of a woman? intercourse with a woman?* CHR 755A.

+wīfe=+wif

wīfel I. m. '*weevil*,' *beetle*, Cp,Rd. II. (HGl; '*wifle*')=wifer

wīfer *missile, arrow, dart*, v. OEG 1103.

wīfērend (KGL)=wegfērend

wīffæst *bound to a wife, married*, LL 348,54.

wīffex n. *woman's hair*, WW. [feax]

wīffrēond m. *female friend*, LkLR 15⁹.

wīfgāl *licentious, unchaste*, CP 453³⁰.

wīfgemædla m. *woman's fury*, LCD 122b.

wīfgemāna m. *intercourse with a woman*, LCD 1·336.

wīfgeornes f. *adultery*, MtL 15¹⁹.

wīfgifta fp. *dowry, outfit? marriage?* JUL 38.

wīfhād m. *womanhood*, Æ : *female sex*, Æ.

wīfhand f. *female inheritor, female side*, Ct.

wīfhealf f. *woman's* (*i.e. mother's*) *side*, CHR p 3'.

wīfhearpe f. *timbrel*, CPs 150⁴.

wīfhīred n. *nunnery*, GD 27⁸.

wīfhrægel n. *woman's clothing*, GD 212¹⁰.

±wīfian *to take a wife, marry* (*of the man*), Æ,Bo,LL. ['*wive*'; '*i-wive*']

wīflāc n. *cohabitation, fornication*, LL.

wīflēas *unmarried*, LL (190⁸). ['*wifeless*']

wīflēast f. *lack of women*, ÆL 10²¹⁶.

wīflic *womanly, feminine, female*, AO,BH, Gl. adv. -līce. ['*wifely*']

wīflufu† f. *love for a woman*.

wīfmann (o²) m. '*woman*,' Æ,AO,BH,LG; CP : *female servant*.

wīfmyne m. *love for a woman*, GEN 1861.

-wifre v. gange-w.

+wifsǣlig *fortunate*, WW 496⁸.

wīfscrūd n. *woman's clothing*, ÆP 142; TC 530.

wift=weft

wīfðegn m. *procurer*, WW.

wīfðing n. *marriage, cohabitation*, LCD,LL. ['*wifthing*']

±wīfung f. *marrying* (*of the man*), *wedlock*, Æ.

wig (KGL)=weg.

wīg I. n. *strife, contest, war, battle*, Æ,AO, CP : *valour* : *military force, army*, Æ. II. (wīh, wēoh)† n. *idol, image*.

wiga m. *fighter*, An,Men : *man*. ['*wye*']

wīgan¹ *to fight, make war*, Æ,B.

wīgār m. *spear, lance*, WW 143¹². [wīg, gār]

wīgbǣre *warlike*, WW 193¹⁸.

wīgbealu n. *war-bale*, B 2046.

wīgbed=wēofod

wīgbill n. *sword*, B 1607.

wīgblāc *bravely caparisoned*, Ex 204.

wīgblēd? m. *luck in war*, RIM 26 (wilbec).

wīgbora m. *fighter*, ÆGR 27¹⁶.

wīgbord† n. *shield*, B,Ex.

wīgcræft m. *war-power, art of war*, AO.

wīgcræftig *strong in battle*, B 1811.

wīgcyng=wīcing

wīgcyrm m. *noise of battle*, GEN 1990

wīgelung=wīglung

wīgend† m. *warrior, fighter*.

wīgende *fighting*, Æ.

wīgfreca† m. *warrior*.

wīgfruma† m. *war-chief*.

wigg=(1) wīg I.; (2) wicg; **wigga**=wicga
wiggebed=wēofod; **wiggend**=wīgend
wiggetāwe fp. *war-gear*, B368. [wīg, geatwe]
wiggild (wīh-) n. *idol*, DAN,NC.
wiggryre m. *war-terror*, B1284.
wighaga† m. *war-hedge*, *phalanx*.
wigheafola m. *helmet*, B2661.
wigheap m. *troop of warriors*, B477.
wigheard *brave in battle*, MA,OEG.
wighete m. *hostility*, B2121.
wighryre m. *slaughter, defeat*, B1619.
wighūs n. *battlement, tower*, AO,CP : *turret (on an elephant's back)*, ÆL25⁵⁶⁰.
wighyrst f. *war-gear, accoutrements*, RUIN 35.
wigian *to fight*, LL132,6⁵.
wigle n. *divination*, A,OEG. ['wiel']
wiglēoð n. *war-cry, battle-signal*, Ex221.
wiglere m. *soothsayer, wizard*, Æ. ['wielare']
wiglian *to take auspices, divine*, Æ,LCD.
wiglic *warlike*, Ex,Gl. adv. -līce.
±**wiglung** f. *soothsaying, augury, witchcraft, sorcery*, Æ,WW (wīl-). [v. 'wiel']
wigmann m. *warrior*, LL,W.
wignoð m. *warfare, war*, WW442¹?
wigol *divining, foreboding*, WW133².
wigplega† m. *war-play, battle*.
wigrād (ō) f. *war-path*, GEN2084.
wigrǣden f. *state of war, battle*, WALD1²².
wigsigor† m. *victory in a battle*.
wigsīð m. *military expedition*, GEN2094.
wigsmið I. m. *maker of idols*, PPs113¹². II.† m. *warrior*.
wigspēd† f. *success in war*.
wigspere n. *war-spear, dart*, WW143¹⁴.
wigsteall n. *rampart, entrenchment*, LV,GL.
wigstrang *mighty in war*, WW360³⁶.
wigtrod n. *path of an army*, Ex491 (or ? wigrod *battle-pole*, Sedgefield).
wigðracu† f. *onslaught in battle, attack*.
wigðrīst *bold in battle*, JUL432.
wigwægn m. *war chariot*, AO38.
wigwǣpen n. *weapon of war*, W170⁸.
wigweorðung† (ēoh¹) f. *idol-worship*.
wīh=wīg; **wīhaga**=wīghaga
wīhian=wōhhian
wihst pres. 2 sg. of weaxan.
wiht I. (u, y) fn. 'WIGHT,' *person, creature, being* : *whit, thing, something, anything*. II. adv. *at all*. ne w., nǣnig w. *not at all*. nān w. *no whit*. III. *(+)* f. *weighing, 'weight,'* Lcd,LL.
Wiht f. *Isle of Wight*, CHR. [L. Vectis]
wihte adv. (d. instr. of wiht) *at all*.
±**wihte** n. *'weight,'* Lcd.
wihtga=wītega
Wihtland n. *Isle of Wight*, BH,CHR.

wihtmearc f. *plumb-line*, OEG3005.
Wiht-sǣtan, -sǣte mp. *inhabitants of the Isle of Wight*, BH52⁴.
Wihtware mp. *inhabitants of the Isle of Wight*, CHR.
wīhūs=wīghūs; **wīl**=wiell
wīl n. *'wile,' trick*, CHR1128.
wil-=wiel-, wigl-, will-, wyll-
wila (y) *'catenarum,'* v. OEG3560n and 7²⁵⁷.
wīlāwei=wā lā wā
wīlbec m. *stream of tears*, RIM26. [or? winbrec (*war's alarms*) ES65·189]
+**wilbod** n. *commandment*, WW191²².
wilboda m. *messenger of joy, angel*, GU1220.
+**wilcō** n. *rolling, tossing*, JPs88¹⁰. [wealcan]
wilcuma I. m. *'welcome' guest*, B,DHy,Sat. II.=wilcume
wilcume interj. *'welcome!'* GD,LG,WW.
±**wilcumian** *to 'welcome,' greet*, Æ,Mt.
wild? *wild*, OEG4706n.
wild-=wield-
wildæg m. *day of joy*, CR459.
wilddēor n. (occl. dp. wildrum) *wild beast*, Bo,Bl,VPs; AO : *deer, reindeer*. ['wilddeer']
wilddēorcyn n. *species of wild beasts*, RWH57¹⁵.
wilddēoren *like wild beasts, fierce*, Sc99⁷.
wilddēorlic *savage*, CP. adv. -līce.
wilde I. 'WILD,' *untamed, uncontrolled*, A, AO : *uncultivated, desert*, AO. II. adv.
+**wilde**=+wielde
wildēar (N), wil(de)dēor, wilder, wildor= wilddēor
wildefȳr n. *lightning*, CHR : *erysipelas*, WW.
wildeswīn m. *wild boar*, ANS129·44.
wildgōs f. *wild goose*, WW364¹.
-wildian v. ā-w.
wildrum v. wilddēor.
wile pres. 3 sg. of willan.
+**wile**=+will
wileg(e)=wilige
wilewīse=wiligwīse
wilfægen *fain, glad*, Æ.
wilfullīce adv. *willingly*, Gl. ['wilfully']
wilgæst (e²) m. *welcome guest*, MOD7.
wilgedryht† f. *willing band*.
wilgehlēða m. *intimate companion*, RD15³. [hlōð]
wilgeofa=wilgiefa
wilgesīð† m. *willing companion*.
wilgest=wilgæst
wilgestealla=willgestealla
wilgiefa† (eo, i) m. *gracious giver, king*.
wilhrēmig *rejoicing in satisfied desire*, WW 376²⁶.
wilhrēðig *exultant*, EL1117.
wilia=wiliga; **wilian** (Æ)=wylwan

±**wilian** (y) *to connect, bind*, Sc 11⁸; W.

wilie=(1) wilige; (2) wielle

wiliga m., wilige (y) f. *basket*, *Æ,Mk,WW*.
[*'willy'*]

wiligwīse (wile-) *basket-wise*, Bl 125²¹.

wiliht (y) *full of willows*, Ct.

wīlisc=wīelisc

will (1) n.=willa m.; (2)=wiell
+**will** n. *will, wish, desire*, *Bo*; AO,CP.
[*'i-will'*]

will-=wiell-, wyll-

willa m. I.*mind*, '*WILL*,' *determination, purpose*, *Æ*,CP. sylfes willum *of one's own accord* : *desire, wish, request* : *joy, delight, pleasure* : *desirable thing, valuable.* **II.** (æ, e, y) *fountain, spring*.

willan (y) anv. pres. 1, 3 sg. ind. and subj. wile, wille, wielle, pret. wolde *to* '*WILL**,' *be willing, wish, desire*, *Æ,AO*,CP : (denoting habit, repetition) *to be used to*, *Æ* : *to be about to* : (sign of the future tense) *shall, will*, *Æ,CP*.

willcuma=wilcuma

willen I. *willing, desirous*, AS 63²⁴. **II.**= wyllen

-willen v. dol-w.

wīllendlic (BH)=hwīlwendlic

willendlīce adv. '*willingly*,' *WW*; VH.

willes adv. *willingly, voluntarily*, *Æ*.

willfægen=wilfægen

willgebrōðor mp. *brothers*, Gen 971.

willgesīð=wilgesīð

willge-steald, -steall n. *riches, wealth*, Gen 2146? (or ? willgestealla m. *willing companion*).

willgesweostor fp. *sisters*, Gen 2607.

willgeðofta m. *pleasant companion*, Gen 2026.

±**willian** *to wish, desire*, *Bo*,Ps.

willic (y) *from a fountain*, WW. [wiell]

willīce (y) adv. *willingly, voluntarily*, *CM*. [*'willy'*]

willnung=wilnung

willsele m. *pleasant dwelling*, Ph 213.

willsīð=wilsīð

willspell† n. *good tidings*, El.

willsum=wilsum

willung f. *desire*, BH. [*'willing'*]

willwong m. *pleasant plain*, Ph 89.

willwyrdan *to be complaisant*, AB 34·10.

wilm=wielm

wiln (Æ)=wielen
+**wilnes** f. *desire, wish*, LPs 20³.

±**wilnian** (w. g. or a.) *to wish, long for, desire, will*, *An,B,Bo,Chr,CP,G*; AO : *beg for, supplicate, entreat, petition for* : *tend towards*, CP. [*'wilne'*]

±**wilniendlic** *desirable* : *capable of desire*, ÆL 1⁹⁷ : (+) *unbridled*, ÆH 2·398'.

±**wilnung** f. *desire, longing (good or bad)*, AO,CP. [*'wilning'*]

wiloc=weoloc

Wil-sǣte, -sǣtan mp. *people o Wilts* : *Wiltshire*, Chr.

wilsc=wīelisc .

wilsīð m. *desired journey*, An,BH.

wilsum(lic) *desirable, delightful* : *ready, willing, voluntary, spontaneous* : *devoted.* adv. -līce.

±**wilsumnes** f. *willingness, devotion*, BH : *free-will offering*, LRPs : *vow*.

wilt I. pres. 2 sg. of willan. **II.** pres. 3 sg. of wealdan.

wiltīðe *having obtained one's wish, glad*, OEG 2219³⁵⁸⁹.

wilð pres. 3 sg. of weallan.

wilðegu f. *agreeable food*, An 153.

wiluc-=weoloc-

wiluncel (GPH 401)=wielincel

wīlwendlic=hwīlwendlic

wimman, wīman=wīfmann

wimpel (win-) m. '*wimple*,' *covering for the neck, cloak*, Gl.

win=winn

wīn n. '*wine*,' *B,Bl,OET,WW*; CP. [L.]

wīnærn n. *tavern, cellar*, Gl : *drinking hall, wine hall*, B 655.

wīnbælg=wīnbelg

wīnbēam m. *vine*, WW.

wīnbeger n. *grape*, NG.

wīnbelg (æ) m. *(leather) bottle for wine*, Mt. [v. '*belly*']

wīn-berge, -beri(g)e f. *whortle-berry*, OEG : '*wine-berry*' ('*whimberry*'), *grape*, *G,WW*.

wīnbōh m. *vine-shoot, vine*, Æ.

wīnbrytta m. *wine-seller, inn-keeper*, WW.

wīnburg† f. *festive city* : *walled vineyard, castle*.

wīnbyrele m. *inn-keeper*, WW 377⁴.

wincan=wincian

wince f. '*winch*,' *pulley*, WW 416⁶.

wincel I. m. *corner*, Ct. [Ger. winkel] **II.**=wencel

wincettan *to wink*, PPs 34¹⁹.

wincian *to close one's eyes, blink*, Æ,CP. [*'wink'*]

winclo=wenclu, nap. of wencel.

wīnclyster n. *cluster of grapes*, OEG 18ʙ³.

wīncole *wine vat*, WW 439³⁰.

wīncynn n. *wine*, NC 333.

wind m. '*WIND*,' *CP*; Æ,AO.
+**wind** n. *winding thing, winding path*, WW : *woven thing*.

windǣddre f. *windpipe*, WW.

±**windæg†** m. *day of strife or toil*.

±**windan**³ (tr.) *to* '*WIND*,' *plait, curl, twist* : *unwind* : *whirl, brandish, swing* : (intr.) *turn, fly, leap, start, roll, slip, go*, *Æ,CP*;

AO : *busy oneself with*, Bo 18¹⁸ : *delay,
hesitate*, Gu 265 : *roll up* : *repair*, AS (v.
NED).

windbǣre (ē²) *windy*, OEG 43¹⁰.

windbland (o²) n. *blast of wind*, B 3146.

+**winde** *blowing*, BH 202⁷.

-**winde** v. ed-, næddre-, wudu-w.

windecræft=wyndecræft

windel m. *basket*, Æ,CP. ['*windle*']

windelocc m. *curly lock*, WW.

windelstān m. *tower with a winding staircase*, (BT),WW 145¹⁷.

windelstrēaw n. '*windle-straw*,' Lcd,WW.

windeltrēow n. *oleaster, willow*, WW.

wind-fona, -gefonna m. *winnowing fan*,
LkLR.

windfylled *blown down*, LL 452,19.

windgeard m. *home of the winds, sea*, B 1224?

windgereste f. *resting-place of the winds*,
B 2456?

windhladen (æ²) *windy*, ANS 120·297.

windig '*windy*,' *breezy*, Æ,B,Lcd,Lk.

windiht (GPH)=wundiht; **windil**=windel

windiuscoful=windscofl

windles gs. of windel.

windong=windung

windrǣs m. *storm of wind*, MkL 4³⁷.

wīndrinc (e, y) m. *wine-drink, wine*, PPs;
Æ. [v. '*wine*']

wīndruncen *elate, intoxicated with wine*, Da,
RBL.

windscofl f. *fan*, WW 478²⁵.

windsele m.† (*windy hall*), *hell*, Sat.

windswingel f. (*wind-whip*), *fan*, WW 154¹⁰.

windumǣr (wudu-?) f. *echo*, WW 474⁸.

windung I. f. *winnowing, chaff, tares, straw*,
NG. II. f. *something woven, hurdle*, WW.
['*winding*']

windwian wv. *to fan*, '*winnow*,' MH,VPs.

windwig=windig

windwigceaf n. *chaff*, OEG 2439.

windwigsyfe n. *winnowing-sieve, fan*, WW
141¹¹.

wine† m. [occl. gp. winig(e)a] *friend, protector, lord*, B : *retainer*, B,Chr. ['*wine*']

wīneard=wīngeard

wine-dryhten (i³)† m., gen. -dryhtnes
friendly lord, lord and friend.

wīnegeard=wīngeard

winegēomor *mourning for friends*, B 2239.

winelēas† *friendless*.

winemǣg† m. *dear kinsman*.

wīnern=wīnærn

winescipe m. *friendship*, Gu,WW.

winestre=winstre

winetrēow f. *conjugal fidelity*, Hu 50.

wineðearfende† *friendless*.

winewincle f. *periwinkle* (*shell-fish*), Lcd,
WW.

wīnfæt n. *wine-vessel, wine-vat*, WW.

+**win-ful**, -fullic *laborious, tedious, hard*,
BH,GD. adv. -līce.

wīngāl† *flushed or intoxicated with wine*.

wīngeard m. *vineyard*, Bl,Bo,Chr : *vine?*
WW. ['*winyard*']

wīngeardbōg m. *vine-tendril*, WW 118³.

wīngeardhōc m. *vine-tendril*, WW 201³¹.

wīngeardhring m. *cluster of fruit*, WW
213¹⁷.

wīngeardseax n. *vine pruning-knife*, WW
234⁴⁴.

wīngeardwealh (wīneard-) m. *worker in a
vineyard*, Chrd 68².

wīngedrinc n.(†) *wine-drinking, drinking
bout* : *wine*, WW.

wīngerd=wīngeard

wīngetredde=wīntredde

wīngyrd=wīngeard

wīnhāte f. *invitation to wine*, Jud 8.

wīn(h)**rēafetian** *to gather grapes*, LPs 79¹³.

wīnhūs n. *wine-house, tavern*, Gl,LL.

winiga, winigea v. wine.

wining (eo, y) m. *leg-band, garter*, IM,WW.

wīnland n. *wine-growing country*, Chrd 15²¹.
['*wineland*']

wīnlēaf n. *vine-leaf*, OEG 18b⁷³.

wīnlic *vinous, like wine*, Æ.

wīnmere m. *wine-vat*, WW 439³⁰.

±**winn** n. *toil, labour, trouble, hardship*, BH,
Lk : *profit, gain*, PPs : *conflict, strife, war*,
Bo,Gen; AO. ['*win*,' '*i-win*']

±**winna** m. *enemy, adversary*, Æ,CP.

winnan³ (y) *to labour, toil, trouble oneself* :
resist, oppose, contradict, Bo : *fight, strive,
struggle, rage*, B,Bl. on w. *attack* : (+) *conquer, obtain, gain*, Chr,Met,Nar : *endure,
bear, suffer* : *be ill*. ['*win*'; '*i-win*']

winnend m. *fighter* Gl.

+**winnesful**=+winful

±**winnstow** f. *wrestling place*, WW.

winnung=windung; **winpel**=wimpel

wīnreced† n. *wine hall*.

wīnreopan⁵ (=e²) *to gather in the vintage*,
VPs 79¹³.

wīnsǣd *satiated with* '*wine*,' Jud 71.

wīnsæl n. *wine-hall*, Wa 78.

wīnsele† n. *wine-hall*.

wīnsester m. *wine-vessel*, WW 122³¹. [L.]

winstōw=winnstōw

winstre I. adj. *left*, Æ,CP. II. f. *left
hand*.

winsum=wynsum

wint pres. 3 sg. of windan.

wīntæppere m. *wine-tapster, tavern-keeper*,
OEG 2652. [v. '*wine*']

winter mn. [ds. wintra; nap. wintru,
winter] '*WINTER*,' Æ,AO,CP : pl. (in com-
puting time) *years*, Æ,AO,CP.

winterbiter† *bitterly cold.*
winterburna m. *winter-torrent,* BC,LG.
['*winterbourne*']
wintercealdt *wintry-cold.*
wintercearig *winter-sad, sad with years?*
WA 24.
winterdæg m. '*winter day,*' Bo.
winterdûn f. *hill on which sheep were kept in winter?* LL 453,1.
winterfeorm f. *Christmas feast,* LL 452,21⁴.
Winterfylleð *October,* MEN,MH.
wintergegong m. *fate,* WW 406⁶.
wintergerīm† n. *number of years.*
wintergetel n. *number of years,* CHR 973A.
wintergewǣde n. *garment of winter, snow,* PH. [v. '*winter*']
wintergew(e)orp n. *snow-storm,* PH 57.
winterhûs n. '*winter-house,*' ÆL 36⁹⁸.
winterig=wintrig
winterlǣcan *to grow wintry,* CHR,LCD.
winterlic *wintry, winter, Æ.* ['*winterly*']
winterrǣdingbōc f. *lectionary for the winter,* TC 430¹⁶.
winterrīm=wintergerīm
wintersæt=wintersetl
winterscûr m. *winter-shower,* Ph 18. [v. '*winter*']
winterseld=wintersetl
wintersetl n. *winter-quarters,* AO; CHR. [v. '*winter*']
wintersteal m. *stallion a year old,* LL 378,7.
winterstund f. *winter-hour, short time, year?* GEN 370.
wintersufel n. *food for winter,* LL 450,9. [v. '*winter*']
wintertīd f. *winter-time, Æ,BH.* ['*wintertide*']
wintīber n. *wine-offering, libation,* WW 130¹³ (-tīfer).
+wintīd f. *time of affliction,* GD 210¹⁵.
wintra v. winter.
-wintre v. ān-, twi-w., etc.
+wintred *grown up, adult, CP : aged, AO, LL.* ['*wintered*']
wīntredde f. *winepress,* OEG 2647.
wintreg=wintrig
wīntrēow n. *vine, LG; Æ.* ['*winetree*']
wīntrēowig adj. *of the vine,* GPH 390.
wintrig '*wintry,*' AO,Bo.
wīntrog m. *wine-vessel,* MtL 21³³. [v. '*wine*']
wīntunne f. *wine-cask* (or ? *wīntûn winehouse*), ÆP 19¹. [v. '*wine*']
wīntwig n. *vine-twig,* WW.
winð pres. 3 sg. of winnan.
wīnðegu† f. *banquet of wine.*
wīnwircend m. *vine-dresser,* Mt pref. 19³.
+winworuld f. *world of care,* GU 829.

wīnwringe f. *winepress,* Mt,GL.
wio-=weo-, wi-, wu-; wīohbed=wēofod
wīpian *to* '*wipe,*' *cleanse, Æ,Lcd,RB.*
wīr I.† m. '*wire,*' *metal thread, wire-ornament, B,Rd.* II. (ȳ) m. *myrtle,* GL; Mdf.
wir-=wear-, wier-, wyr-
wīrboga m. *twisted wire?* RD 15³.
wirc-=weorc-, wyrc-
wird-=wierd-
+wīred *made of wire,* TC 537'.
wirg- (Æ)=wierg-, wyr(i)g-
wīrgrǣfe? f. *myrtle-grove,* WW.
wirian=wiergan
wirig-=wierg-, wyr(i)g-
wirman (WW 399¹⁶)=wyrman
wīrpð pres. 3 sg. of weorpan.
wīrtrēow n. *myrtle,* LCD,WW.
wīrtrēowen (y¹, ȳ²) adj. *myrtle,* LCD 1·236¹.
wirtruma=wyrtruma
wirð I.=weorð I. II.=wierð pres. 3 sg. of weorðan.
wirðe=worð I.
wīs I. adj. '*WISE,*' *learned, Æ,AO,CP : sagacious, cunning : sane : prudent, discreet, experienced, Æ,AO,CP.* as sb. *wise man, CP.* II.=wīse I.
+wis=+wiss
wīsa† m. *leader, director.*
wīsan=wesan; wīsan (DAN 35)=wīsian
wīsbōc f. *instructive book?* PPs 138¹⁴.
wīsc- (Æ)=wȳsc-
wīsce n. *meadow liable to floods, BC,KC;* PST 95/98,542. ['*wish*']
wischere m. *diviner?* ÆL 21⁴⁶⁶.
wīsdōm m. '*wisdom,*' *knowledge, learning : experience, B,Bo,G,LL; Æ,CP.*
wīse I. f. '*WISE,*' *way, fashion, custom, habit, manner, Æ,CP : testamentary disposition : business, affair, thing, matter, Æ,CP : condition, state, circumstance, AO,CP : reason, cause, Æ : direction : melody, MEN 70 : idiom.* II. adv. *wisely.* III. (ȳ) f. *sprout, stalk, Lcd,Rd,WW.* ['*wise*']
wīs-fæst, -fæstlic (PPs) *wise, sagacious, discreet, learned, intelligent.*
+wīsfullīce *knowingly,* GD 95³¹.
wīshycgende *wise, sagacious,* B 2716.
wīshȳdig† *wise, discreet, sagacious,* GEN.
±wīsian (w. d. or a.) *to direct, instruct, guide, lead, B; Æ,CP : point out, show, Gen.* ['*i-wisse*']
wislic *certain, sure, true, PPs.* ['*wisly*'] adv. (±) -līce *certainly, truly, Lcd,Lk,PPs : moreover.* ['*iwisliche,*' '*wisely*']
wīslic *wise, sagacious, prudent, BH,W; Æ, AO.* adv. -līce, *Bo,CP,Gen,LL,Met.* ['*wisely*']
wisligan=hwistlian
wīsnes f. *teaching,* LCD 3·82².

wisnian *to dry up, wither, waste away,* BL. [weornian]

+**wiss I.** n. *what is certain, certainty, surety,* Æ. **II.** adj. *certain, sure, trustworthy, BH, Bo,Guth,Nic : knowing.* tō (ge)wissan (Æ, OEG), gewissum; mid gewisse *especially, certainly, RB,HL.* ['*wis,*' '*i-wis*']

wiss-=wis-

wisse=wiste pret. 3 sg. of witan.

wĭssefa m. *wise-souled man,* SOL 438?

wissian (Æ,W; '*wis*')=wīsian

±**wissian** *to direct, instruct, guide, Æ,Gen : point out, show,* Æ. ['*i-wisse*']

wiss-iend, -igend m. *governor, director : driver (of chariot),* Æ.

+**wisslīce**=+wislīce

wisste=wiste pret. 3 sg. of witan.

wissum (tō) adv. *altogether, completely,* OEG.

±**wissung** f. *showing, instruction, guidance, Æ,LL : certainty : rule, regulation, government,* Æ. ['*wissing,*' '*iwisse*']

wist f. *being, existence : well-being, abundance, plenty : provision, nourishment, subsistence, food, meal, feast, delicacy,* Æ,CP. [wesan]

wiste pret. 3 sg. of witan.

wīstfæstlic=wīsfæstlic

wistful *productive,* CHR 1112.

±**wistfulgend** m. *banqueter,* EPs 41[5].

±**wistfullian** *to feast,* Æ.

wistfullīce adv. *luxuriously,* WW 513[6].

wistfulnes f. *good cheer,* BAS 50[25].

±**wistfullung** f. *feasting,* OEG.

wistfyllo f. *fill of food,* B 734.

wistgifende *fertile,* WW 457[25].

+**wistian** *to feast,* G.

wistl-=hwistl-

+**wistlǣcan** *to feast, banquet,* G.

wist-mete m., nap. -mettas, *sustenance,* ÆL 23b[582].

wiston pret. pl. of witan.

wisōlung=hwistlung

wīswylle *wise in purpose,* PPs 118[40].

wīswyrdan *to be wise in speech,* A 13·38.

wīswyrde *prudent in speech,* W 72[18].

wit I. pron. 1 pers. (nom. dual), gs. uncer, d. unc. acc. unc(it) *we two, B,Mt*; CP. wit Æthered *Æthered and I.* ['*wit*'] **II.** (±)=witt

±**wita** (eo, ie, u) m. *sage, philosopher, wise man, adviser, councillor, elder, senator* (v. LL 2·737), *Æ,BH,LG*; AO : *witness, BH, LG; Æ,CP : accomplice.* ['*wite*'; witan]

±**witan** (eo, y) swv. pres. 1, 3 sg. wāt, 2 wāst, pl. witon, subj. pres. sg. wite, pl. wit-en, -on; pret. sg. wiste, pp. witen *to be aware of or conscious of, know, understand,* AO,CP : *observe, perceive :* (+)

ascertain, learn. andan w. *dislike.* incan w. (tō) *to have a grudge (against).* ege w. *to fear.* dōn tō witanne *to cause to know, inform.* ['WIT*'; '*i-wite*']

±**wītan**[1] **I.** *to guard, keep : look after, Lcd, LL.* ['*wite*[2]'] **II.** *to impute or ascribe to, accuse, reproach, blame,* AO,B,Bo. ['*wite*[1]'] **III.** *to depart, go, go out, AO, Met : leave off : pass away, die* (often forðgew.), *Æ,CP.* ['*wite*[3]']

wīte n. *punishment, torture, plague, injury, Bo,Gen,VPs; CP : penalty, fine, LL : contribution, in money or food, to sustenance of king or his officers,* LL 356,69[2] : *woe, misery, distress.* ['*wite*']

wītebend† mf. *bonds of torture or punishment,* AN.

wītebrōga m. *tormenting dread,* W.

wītedlīce=witodlīce

wītedōm (BH)=wītegdōm.

wītedōmlic *prophetic,* GUTH.

wītefæst *penally enslaved,* TC.

wīt-ega, -(i)ga m. *wise man : lawyer,* NG : *prophet, soothsayer, CP,LG : prophecy.* [wītan; '*witie*']

wītegeard? m. *amphitheatre,* v. OEG 3333.

wītegdōm (i[2]) m. *prophecy, prediction : divination,* DA.

wītegestre f. *prophetess,* ÆT 715,Lk 2[36].

±**wītegian** *to prophesy, predict, Æ,LG;* AO. ['*witie*']

wītegung f. *prophecy, divination, Æ,LG.* ['*witieng*']

wītegungbōc f. *book of prophecy,* ÆL.

wītehrægl n. *penitential garb, sackcloth,* PPs 68[11].

wītehūs n. *torture-house, prison, hell : amphitheatre (as place of torture and martyrdom),* OEG.

wītel=hwītel

wītelāc† n. *punishment.*

wītelēas *without punishment or fine,* LL 360,73[4]. adv. -līce *with impunity,* TF 109[26].

wītelēast f. *freedom from punishment or fine,* Swt.

wītelic *toilsome, carking,* MFH 178 : *penal,* GD 330; 332.

witelīce (GD 102[24])=witodlīce

witenagemōt n. *meeting of the wise men, national council, Æ,Chr.* ['*witenagemot*'; wita]

+**wītende** *transitory,* MFH 165.

wītendlic=wītigendlic

+**wītendlic** *transitory, perishable,* Æ,CP.

wītendlīce=witodlīce

+**wit-endnes** (G), -ennes f. *departure, death,* BH,MH.

wīterǣden f. *punishment, fine, BC,LL.* ['*witereden*']

+witerian *to inform*, RWH 135[18]. [witter]

wītern n. *prison*, WW 199[31]. [ærn]

wītescræf n. *pit of torment, hell*, SAT 691.

wīt(e)steng m. *pole used for torture*, OEG.

wītestōw f. *place of torment or execution*, BH.

wīteswinge f. *scourging, punishment*, GEN 1864.

wīteðēow adj. and sbm. *man reduced to slavery by the law*, Ct,LL.

witewyrðe *punishable*, GD 208[5].

+witfæst *of sound mind*, GUTH 66[17].

wītg-=wīteg-

-witian v. be-w., uð-w.

wītiendlic=wītigendlic; witig=wittig

wītig-=wīteg-

wītigende (ByH 102[26])=+wītende

wīt-igendlic, -t(i)endlic *prophetic*, OEG.

wītiglic *punitive, of punishment*, GD.

wītingstōw=wītnungstōw

±witlēas *foolish, mad*, Lcd,Met. ['witless']

witlēasnes f. *want of intelligence, folly*, OEG 47[3]. ['witlessness']

±witlēast f. *folly, madness*, Æ. [witt]

+witloca m. *mind*, MET,CP 469[2].

witmæreswyrt f. *spoonwort?* LCD 12a.

wītnere m. *tormentor, torturer*, Æ.

±witnes f. *knowledge, 'witness,' testimony*, Bl,Bo,DR,G : *a witness*, CP. nīwa gew. *the New Testament.* ['i-witness']

+witnian *to confess*, ÆH 2·124[22] (or ? +wītnian).

±wītnian *to punish, chastise, torture, afflict*, Æ,AO,CP.

wītnigend m. *punisher*, EPs 78[11].

wītnung f. *torment, torture, punishment, purgatory*, Æ.

wītnungstōw f. *place of punishment, purgatory*, ÆH.

witod=witodlīce

witodlic *certain, sure*, LkR 20[6] (wutud-); adv. and conj. -līce *truly, for, verily, certainly, undoubtedly, indeed, thus, but, and, therefore, wherefore*, Æ,AO,CP. [witan]

-witol v. fore-w.

witolnes f. *wisdom*, GD 331[15]. [witan]

witon I. pres. pl. of witan. II.=wuton

wītrod=wīgtrod

+witscipe m. *evidence, knowledge*, BH. ['witship']

±witsēoc *possessed, insane*, Æ.

±witt n. *understanding, intellect, sense*, Æ, B,Bo,Lk,Met : *knowledge, consciousness : conscience*, CP. ['wit,' 'i-wit']

+witt-=+wit-

witter *wise, prudent*, CHR 1067 D. [ON. vitr]

±wittig† *wise*, B,Cra,Ex,LL : *sagacious, reasonable : skilful*, Cra,OEG : *conscious, in one's right mind*, Æ. adv. -līce. ['witty']

wittignes f. *intelligence*, OEG 78 (wytti-).

wittol=witol

wītu nap. of wīte.

witud=witod

wituma (e, eo, y) m. *dowry* (v. LL 2·739).

witumbora m. *bridesman, paranymph*, OEG 1774.

wītungstōw=wītnungstōw

wītword n. *written evidence, will, covenant*, LL,TC. ['witword']

wið I. prep. (w. a.) WITH, *by, near, against, beside, at, through* : (w. d.) *from (separation)*, *with (opposition)*, *for, in return for, on condition of, beside, near, opposite* : (w. g.) *towards, to, at, against.* w. ēastan (1) adv. *to the east*; (2) prep. *east of.* w. ūp *upwards, above.* w. ðān ðe *because, in consideration of, provided that.* wið...weard prep. (w. a.) *towards.* II. conj. *until.*

wiðæftan I. adv. *from behind, behind, after*, AO. II. prep. *behind, at*, Æ.

wiðblāwan[7] *to blow away*, CP 439[24].

wið-bregdan[3], -brēdan[3] *to withhold, restrain, withstand, oppose*, Æ,CP : *take away*, GD 203[5].

wiðcēosan[2] *to reject*, Ps. pp. wiðcoren *rejected, reprobate, outcast*, BH,MH.

wiðcostian 'reprobare,' EPs 32[10].

wiðcwædenes=wiðcwedennes

wiðcwedennes f. *contradiction*, CHR,Ps.

wiðcwedolnes=wiðercwedolnes

wiðcweðan[5] *to speak against, contradict, gainsay, oppose, resist*, Æ : *forbid, refuse, deny : reject, renounce*, CP.

wiðcweðenes=wiðcwedennes

wiðdrīfan[1] *to repel, drive off*, PPs.

wiðe-=wiðig-

wiðēadon (N)=wiðēodon pret. pl. of wiðgān.

wiðēastan *eastward, eastwards*, AO.

wiðeftan=wiðæftan

wiðer I. prep. and adv. *against.* II. adj. *hostile*, GPH 394. ['wither']

wiðerbersta m. *adversary*, SOL 86[5].

wiðerbreca (a[3], eo[3], o[3], u[3]) m. *adversary* : *the devil, Satan.*

wiðerbrocian *to oppose*, CVPs.

wiðerbrōga m. *adversary, the devil*, CR 564.

wiðerbruca=wiðerbreca

wiðercerran *to turn against, prance* (Swt). [cp. wiðercyr]

wiðercora m. *adversary, rebel, apostate, sinner*, Æ.

wiðercoren *rejected, reprobate, wicked*, Æ.

wiðercorenes f. *reprobation*, ÆH 2·290[19].

wiðercwednes (CP 143[20])=wiðercwidennes

wiðercwedol *opposing, contradicting*, Ps.

wiðercwedolnes f. *contradiction*, GL.

wiðercwedung f. *contradiction*, SPs51⁴.

wiðercweð-=wiðercwed-

wiðercweðan⁵ *to withstand*, LPs.

wiðercwida (y) m. *contradicter*, OEG1893 : *opposer, rebel*, WW110²³.

wiðercwiddian (y³) *to murmur*, LPs40⁸.

wiðercwide m. *contradiction*, PPs : *opposition, resistance*, LL.

wiðercwidel-=wiðercwedol-

wiðercwidennes (e³, y³) *contradiction*, LPs.

wiðercwyd-=wiðer-cwed-, -cwid-

wiðercyr m. *rearing (of a horse)*, EL926.

wiðerdūne (ē³, y³) *narrow? uphill? steep?* (BTs), Mt7¹⁴.

-wiðere v. tō-w.

wiðerfeoht-=wiðfeoht-

wiðerflita m. *opponent, adversary*, AO,CP.

wiðerhabban *to resist*, PPs72²⁰.

wiðerhlinian *to lean against*, GL.

wiðer-hycgende, -hȳdig *refractory, perverse, antagonistic, hostile*. as sb. *rival, adversary*.

wiðerian *to resist, oppose, struggle against*, Æ : *irritate, provoke* : *be provoked*. ['*wither*']

wiðerlǣcan (y¹, ē³) *to deprive*, EPs83¹³.

wiðerlēan† n. *requital* : *compensation*.

wiðerling m. *opponent, adversary*, EHy4⁷. ['*witherling*']

wiðermāl n. *counter-plea, defence*, CHR1052.

wiðermēde *perverse, antagonistic*.

wiðermēdnes (oe) f. *perversity*, DR : *adversity*, DR.

wiðermēdo f. *antagonism*, GEN : *perversity*, PPs : *adversity*, DR.

wiðermetan⁵ *to compare*, WW.

wiðermōd *unwilling, contrary*, CP212⁷.

wiðermōdnes f. *adversity*, CP83¹⁹.

wiðermoednes (DR)=wiðermēdnes

wiðerrǣde *contrary, opposed, adverse, perverse, rebellious*, Æ : *disadvantageous* : *disagreeable, unpleasant*.

wiðerrǣdlic *contrary, adverse*, ÆGR264¹.

wiðerrǣdnes f. *opposition, discord, variance, disadvantage, adversity*, Æ.

wiðerrǣhtes (=rihtes) adv. *opposite*, B 3039.

wiðerriht n. *recompense*, WW118¹².

wiðersaca m. *adversary, enemy*, Mt,RB; Æ : *betrayer* : *apostate*, Æ. ['*withersake*']

wiðersacian *to renounce, become apostate*, OEG : *blaspheme*.

wiðersacung f. *apostasy*, GL : *blasphemy*, Sc.

wiðersæc I. n. *contradiction, hostility, opposition*, Æ : *apostasy*. [*sacan*] II. *unfavourable*, LCD97a.

wiðersprecend m. *a contradicter*, CHRD41²⁹.

wiðerstæger *steep*, WW.

wiðerstandan⁶ *to resist*, EPs16⁸.

wiðersteall (a³) m. *resistance, opposition*, Æ.

wiðersȳnes adv. *backwards*, BL93¹⁹.

wiðertalu f. *defence*, ÆH1·530⁶ (v. LL 3·226).

wiðertihtle f. *counter-charge*, LL.

wiðertrod† n. *return, retreat*.

wiðertȳme *troublesome, grievous*, LPs34¹³ : *contrary*, BF174¹.

wiðerweard *contrary, perverse, adverse, Bo, G* : *rebellious, hostile, Bl*; AO,CP : *inconsistent* : *unfavourable, noxious, bad*. ['*witherward*']

wiðerwearda m. *adversary*, BL,LPs17²⁷.

wiðerweardian (o³) *to oppose*, SPs.

wiðerweardlic *contrary, inimical, perverse*, Æ. adv. -līce.

wiðerweardnes f. *opposition, perversity, arrogance, enmity, CP*; Æ : *adversity, calamity, trouble*, CP. ['*witherwardness*']

wiðerwengel m. *adversary*, ARHy4⁷, RPs 73¹⁰.

wiðerwenning f. *controversy*, Sc146¹⁵. [*winnan*]

wiðer-werd-, -wi(e)rd-=wiðerweard-

wiðerwinn n. *contest*, OEG2³.

wiðerwinna m. *opponent, rival, adversary, enemy*, Æ,CP; AO. ['*witherwin*']

wiðerwinnan³ *to revolt*, GPH389.

+wiðerwordian=+wiðerweardian

wiðerwyrd=wiðerweard

wiðewinde=wiðowinde

wiðfaran⁶ *to come off, escape*, Ex573.

wiðfeohtan³ *to fight against, rebel*, BH, WW.

wiðfeohtend m. *adversary*, BH,CP.

wiðfēolan³ *to apply oneself to*, BH.

wiðferian† *to rescue, redeem*, PPs.

wiðflita=wiðerflita

wiðfon⁷ (w. d.) *to grasp at, clutch*, B760.

wiðforan I. prep. *before, in the presence of*. II. adv. *before, previously*.

wið-gān anv., -gangan⁷ *to go against, oppose* : *pass away, vanish, disappear*.

wiðgehæftan=wiðhæftan

wiðgemetnes f. *comparison*, BH430²⁰.

wiðgeondan prep. *beyond*, Mt3⁵.

wiðgrīpan¹ *to grapple with*, B2521.

wiðgȳnan *to reject*, ÆL23⁵⁴¹.

wiðhabban (æ²) (w. d.) *to oppose, resist, restrain, hold out*, AO.

wiðhæftan *to restrain*, A7·12.

wiðheardian *to harden*, ARSPs94⁸.

wiðhindan adv. *behind*, Æ.

wið-hogian (w. g.) *to disregard, reject*, GEN 2864.

wiðhycgan† *to reject, despise, scorn*.

wiðī-=wiðig-

wiðig, wiði(g)e m. *withe, 'withy,' willow, BC*; Æ (Mdf) : *band, fetter, fillet, garland*.

wiðigrǣw f. *hedgerow*, KC. [v. '*rew*']

wīðigrind f. *willow bark*, LCD 37a.

wīðing-=wiðig-

wiðinnan I. adv. *'within,' from within*, Æ, Ps. II. prep. (w. d. a.) *within*.

wið-inne, -innen, -innon=wiðinnan I.

wiðir- (N)=wiðer-; wīðl (GD)=wīdl

wiðlǽdan *to lead away, remove, rescue*, Ps.

wiðlǽdnes f. *abduction*, Ps (BT).

wīðlan (N)=wīdlian

wiðlīcgan⁵ *to oppose, resist*, CHR, CHRD.

wiðmetan⁵ *to compare with, liken to*, Æ.

wiðmētednes f. *invention, device*, SPs.

wiðmeten(d)līc *comparative (in grammar)*, ÆGR.

wiðmetennes f. *comparison*, Æ.

wiðmeting f. *comparison*, SC.

wið-neoðan (Æ), -niðan, -nyðan adv. *below, underneath, beneath*.

wiðobān (wido-) n. *collar-bone*, LCD,LL.

wiðobend (eo¹) *woodbine*, Lcd 113b. ['*withbind*']

wiðone (BL)=wið ðone

wiðor-=wiðer-

wiðowinde f. *convolvulus, woodbine*, Gl,Lcd. ['*withwind*']

wiðrǽde=wiðerrǽde

wiðret n. *resistance, opposition*, B. ['*wither*']

wiðrēotan² *to abhor? resist?* EL369 (GK).

wiðrian=wiðerian

wiðsacan⁶ *to forsake, abandon, renounce, refuse, deny*, Bl,G; Æ,AO,CP : *oppose, strive against*, AO.

wiðsacendlīc *used in negations*, ÆGR 226³.

wiðsacung f. *denial, renunciation*, Sc 60¹⁴.

wiðsceorian (o²) *to refuse*, CP 59¹².

wiðscrīðel=widscrīðol

wiðscūfan² *to thrust back, refute, repel*, BH.

wiðsecgan *to renounce*, DR. ['*withsay*']

wiðsēon⁵ *to rebel, rise against*, AO.

wiðsetnes f. *opposition*, GL.

wiðsettan *to withstand, resist*, HL,LPs : *condemn*, RWH 137²¹. ['*withset*']

wiðslēan⁶ *to oppose, bring to naught*, Æ, CP.

wiðsprecan⁵ *to contradict, gainsay : converse*, AS : *revile : speak with*, GD 345⁸.

wiðspurnan³ *to hit against*, MtL 4⁶.

wiðstæppan⁶ *to step or go out of*, Ps.

wiðstandan⁶ (w. d.) *to 'withstand,' resist, oppose*, Æ,Bl,Bo,Lcd,LG,Wa; AO,CP : *be lacking*, LL 102,31.

wiðsteall=wiðersteall

wiðsteppan=wiðstæppan

wiðstond-=wiðstand-

wiðstunian *to dash against*, LCD 160b.

wiðstyllan *to retreat*, WW 17²⁶.

wiðstyltan *to hesitate, doubt*, MtL 21²¹.

wiðtēon² *to take away : restrain*, CP.

wiðtremman *to step back*, CP 441²⁷.

wiððe f. *cord, band, thong, fetter*, Æ,WW. ['*withe*'; v. also wīðig]

wiððer-=wiðer-

wiððingian *to be reconciled to*, MFH 178.

wiððir (DR 168²)=wiðer

wiððyddan *to blunt*, v. OEG 4235.

wiðufan I. prep. (w. d.) *above*. II. adv. *before, previously*.

wið-uppan, -uppan adv. *above*.

wiðūtan I. prep. (w. d.) *outside of*, AO,LL, Mt : *except*, Lcd : '*without*.' II. adv. *from outside, outside*, HL.

wiðweorpan³† *to reject, repudiate*.

wiðwestan *to the west of*, AO 8¹².

wiðwinde=wiðowinde

wiðwinnan³ *to fight against, oppose*, AO, CP.

wiðwiðerian *to resist, withstand*, GD 117¹⁹.

wixlan (N)=wrixlan

wixð=wiexð pres. 3 sg. of weaxan.

±wlacian *to become lukewarm, be tepid*, Æ, CP.

wlaco, wlacu, wlæc *tepid, lukewarm, cool*, CP. ['*wlak*']

wlacunes=wlæcnes; wlæc v. wlaco.

wlæce n. *tepidity*, GPH 397.

wlæclīc *lukewarm*. adv. -līce.

wlæclīce (PPs 148⁵)=wræclīce

wlæcnes f. *lukewarmness*, CP.

wlæffetere m. *stammerer*, GPH 403.

wlæffian (ea) *to stammer, speak indistinctly*, Chrd 74¹¹. ['*wlaffe*']

wlænc=wlanc, wlenc

wlænco=wlenco

wlæta=wlætta

+wlætan *to defile, debase*, Bo 114²³.

wlætlīce=wlæclīce

wlætta m. *loathing, nausea, eructation, heartburn*, Lcd,RB; Æ : *an object of loathing : disfigurement*, OEG 4461. ['*wlat*']

wlætung (ā, ē) f. *nausea*, Cp,Lcd : *disfigurement*, OEG 4461. ['*wlating*']

wlanc (æ, o) *stately, splendid, lofty, magnificent, rich*, B,Ph : *boastful, arrogant, proud*, B. ['*wlonk*']

wlancian *to become proud or boastful, exult*, GL.

wlanclic adj. *proud, arrogant*. adv. -līce, GL.

wlāt pret. 3 sg. of wlītan.

wlātere m. *spectator*, CHRD 96²⁴.

-wlātful v. neb-w.

wlātian I.† *to gaze, look upon, behold*. [wlītan] II. (impers.) *to loathe*, Æ,Lcd. ['*wlate*']

wlātung I. f. *sight, spectacle*, CHRD 79⁴. II.=wlǣt(t)ung

wleaffian=wlæffian

±wleccan *to make tepid*, CP. [wlæc]

wlenc, wlenco (AO,CP), wlencu f. *pride, arrogance, haughtiness* : *glory, pomp, splendour*, AO,CP : (†) *bravado* : *prosperity, riches, wealth*. [wlanc]

+**wlencan** *to enrich, exalt*, EL,TC,VH.

wlēttung=wlǣtung

wlisp, wlips (Æ) *lisping*.

-**wlispian** v. ā-wl.

wlita m. *countenance*, GL.

wlītan¹† *to gaze, look, observe*.

wlite m. *brightness* : *appearance, form, aspect, look, countenance*, LG : *beauty, splendour*, Bl,VPs; Æ : *adornment*, CP. ['wlite']

wliteandet? n. *confession of splendour*, PPs 103².

wlitebeorht† *beauteous*.

wliteful *beautiful*, Sc 21⁸.

wliteg-=wlitig-

wlitelēas *ugly*, AN 1171.

wlitelīce *handsomely*, BL 205⁶.

wlitescīne (ē³, ȳ³) † *lovely, beautiful*, LPs 80⁴.

wlitesēon f. *sight, spectacle*, B 1650.

wlitetorht† *brilliant, lovely*.

wlitewamm (o³) m. *disfigurement of the face*.

wliteweorð n. *legal value of a man's life, ransom*, GD 179²¹.

wlitig *radiant, beautiful, fair, comely*, Æ; CP. adv. -ige, -iglīce. ['wliti']

wlitigfæst *of enduring beauty*, PH 125.

±**wlitigian** *to beautify, adorn* : *become beautiful*, SEAF 49 : *form, fashion*, PSS.

wlitignes f *beauty, splendour*, BL.

wlitu=wlite; **wlō**=wlōh

wlōh f., dp. wlō(u)m *fringe, ornament, tuft* : *bit*, GU 1127.

+**wlōh** *adorned*, GEN 1789.

wlonc=wlanc

wlott *spot, blemish*, OEG 648?

wlōum v. wlōh.

wlyt-=wlit-; **wō**=wōh

wōc pret. of wacan (v. 'wake').

wōcer=wōcor

wōcie, wōcige *noose*, OEG 962; 3560.

wōclic=wōhlic

wōcor† f. (gs. wōcre) *increase, growth* : *offspring, progeny, posterity, race* : *usury*

wocorlīce=wacorlīce

wōcs=wōsc pret. 3 sg. of wascan.

wōd I. adj. *senseless, mad, raging*, AS,Chr, Cp,G,Lcd; AO : *blasphemous*. ['wood'] II. pret. 3 sg. of wadan.

wōda I. m. *madman*, Æ. II. m. *storm, flood? danger?* TC 341⁸.

wodawistle=wodewistle

woddor n. *throat, gullet?* SOL 95.

wōddrēam m. '*dæmonium*,' RPs 95⁵ (v. ES 38²⁵).

wōdelic=wōdlic

Wōden m. *Woden* : *Mercury*, WW.

wōdendrēam m. *madness*, WW 245¹⁰. ['widdendream']

Wōdenesdæg=Wōdnesdæg

wōdewistle f. *hemlock*, GL.

wōd-frec, -fræc *madly ravenous*, LL,W.

wōdheortnes f. *madness*, MFH 178.

wōdian=wēdan

wōdlic *foolish, mad, furious*, Æ. adv. -līce *madly, furiously*, Æ,Bas,HL : *blasphemously*. ['woodly']

wōdnes f. *madness, frenzy, folly*, Æ.

Wōdnes gs. of Wōden.

Wōdnesdæg m. *Woden's day*, '*Wednesday*,' G.

Wōdnesniht f. *Tuesday night*, LL,W. [v. '*Wednesday*']

wōdōm=wōhdōm

wōdon pret. pl. of wadan.

wōdscinn n. *madness, folly*, W 80³.

wōdscipe m. *insanity*, WW 245¹².

wōdsēoc *mad*, GD 135¹.

wōdðrāg f. *paroxysm, madness, fury*, CP.

woecan (N)=wæccan

woerc- (N)=weorc-; **woerd-**=wird-

wofflan *to shout, rave, blaspheme*, Æ.

woffung f. *madness, raving*, GD : *blasphemy*, Lk 24¹¹.

wōg=wōh

wōgere m. '*wooer*,' *suitor, sweetheart*, Æ, Chrd.

wōgerlic *amorous*, CHRD 78³⁴.

wōgian *to* '*woo*,' *court, marry*, Æ,Sc,TC.

wogung f. '*wooing*,' ÆL 7³⁰¹.

wōh I. n. *bending, crookedness* : *error, mistake*, Æ : *perversity, wrong, iniquity, depravity*. on w. *wrongly, wickedly*. ['wough'] II. adj. *bent, awry, twisted, crooked* : *uneven, rough* : *wrong, perverse, evil, depraved, bad, unjust*, CP : *false* (*weight*), W 70³. on wōn *wrongfully, in error*. ['wough']

wōhbogen† *bent, crooked*.

wōhcēapung f. *fine for illegal trafficking*, KC 5·143²².

wōhdǣd f. *wrong deed, crime*, BL,GD.

wōhdōm m. *unjust judgment*, BF 242⁶ (ōd).

wōhfōted *having deformed feet*, WW 161³⁰.

wōhfremmend m. *evildoer*, MET 9³⁶.

wōhful *wicked*, NG.

wōhfulnes f. *wickedness*, NG.

wōhgeorn *inclined to evil*, W 183⁸.

wōhgestrēon n. *ill-gotten property*, W.

wōhgod n. *false god, idol*, PPs 78⁵⁸.

wōhhǣmed n. *fornication, adultery*, CP.

wōhhǣmend m. *fornicator, adulterer*, CP.

wōhhǣmere m. *fornicator, adulterer*, CP 401³⁰.

wōhhandede *maimed (of the hands),* WW 161²⁹.

wōhhian? *to speak wildly, rave?* GD 314⁷.

wōhlic *perverse, wrong, unjust, evil.* adv. -līce, Æ.

wōhnes f. *crookedness, crooked place,* Æ : *wrong, error* : *wickedness,* Æ.

wōhs, wōhson=wōsc, wōscon pret. 3 sg. and pret. pl. of wascan.

wōhsum *evil,* DR 27⁹ (wōg-).

wōl mfn. *pestilence, mortality, disease,* AO, CP.

wōlbǣrnes f. *calamity, pest,* AO 62³⁴.

wōlberende *pestilential, pernicious,* CP.

wōlberendlic *pestilential,* CHR 1086.

wōlbryne m. *pestilence,* AO 86²⁴.

wolc (WW 175²⁰)=wolcen

wolc-=walc-, wolcen-

wolcen nm. (nap. wolcnu) '*convolutio,' ball, lump,* PPs 147⁵ : *cloud,* B,Bl,Chr,CP,G, VPs : *sky, heavens.* ['*welkin'*]

wolcenfaru† f. *scudding of clouds.*

wolcengehnāst n. *meeting of clouds (in a storm),* RD 4⁶⁰.

wolcenrēad=weolocrēad

wolcenwyrcende? ptc. *cloud-making (Centaurs),* WW 456²⁴.

wolcn=wolcen; **wolcrēad**=weolocrēad

wolcspinl=walcspinl

wol-cyrge, -cyrige=wælcyrige

wold=weald

wōldæg m. *day of pestilence,* RUIN 26.

wōldberendlic=wōlberendlic

wol-de, -don pret. 3 sg. and pret. pl. of willan.

wōlgewinn n. *calamitous war,* AO 64¹⁵.

wōlic=wōhlic

wollentēare *streaming with tears,* B 3032.

-wolma v. fōt-w.; **wom**=wam(m)

wōm I.=wōgum dp. of wōh, adj. II.= wōma

wōma m. *noise, howling, tumult* : *terror, alarm.* swefnes w. *dream-tumult, vision* : *eloquence?* OEG 8b¹⁰.

woman *to infringe,* EC 151¹⁶ : (+) w. d. pers. and g. thing *deprive of,* EC 151¹⁷. [*wamm*]

won I.=wan, wann. II. pret. 3 sg. of winnan.

wōn I. wk. gdsn. and dpmn. of wōh. II.= hwōn

won-=wan-

wōna gp. of wōh II.

wondor=wundor

wōnes=wōhnes; **wong**=wang

wōp I. m. *cry, shrieking, weeping, lamentation,* B,G; Æ,CP. ['*wop*'] II.=wēop pret. 3 sg. of wēpan.

wōpdropa m. *tear,* SOL 283.

wōpen pp. of wēpan.

wōperian *to weep,* HL 18³².

wōpig *sad, lamenting,* ÆL.

wōplēoð n. *dirge, elegy,* OEG 3504.

wōplic *tearful, sad,* Æ. adv. -līce.

wōpstōw f. *place of mourning,* Æ.

wōr=wōs, wāse

wōra gp. of wōh.

worc=weorc

word I. n. '*WORD,' speech, sentence, statement, Æ* : *command, order* : *subject of talk, story, news, report,* Æ,AO : *fame, Æ* : *promise* : *verb, Æ* : (*incarnate*) *Word.* II. *rod,* CPs : (*gooseberry*) *bush?* LkL 6⁴⁴ (v. ES 38·340; 40·152). III.=werod

word-bēot† n., -bēotung (HU 14) f. *promise.*

wordcærse (WW 416⁸)=worðigcærse?

wordcennend m. *the begetter of the Word,* GPH 389.

wordcræft† m. *poetic art, eloquence, El.* [v. '*word*']

word-cwide (e, y), -cwyðe m. *words, speech, language, utterance.*

worden pp. of weorðan.

wordes adv. *with words, verbally, orally.*

wordfæst *true to one's word, true,* OEH 301¹³.

wordful *talkative, verbose, fluent,* Sc.

wordgebēot=wordbēot

word-gecwide (æ³) n., -gecweodu np. *verbal agreement,* LL,TC.

wordgemearc n. *definition or limitation by words,* GEN 2355.

wordgcrўne† n. *dark saying.*

wordglēaw *skilful in words,* DA 418.

wordgydd m. *lay, dirge,* B 3173.

wordhlēoðor† n. *voice, speech.*

wordhord† n. *treasury of words.*

wordig '*wordy,' verbose,* OEG 1416.

wordlāc n. *speech,* LPs 18⁴.

wordlār f. *teaching,* CHRD 53²².

wordlatu f. *delay in speech?* AN 1519.

wordlaðu† f. *conversation, speech.*

wordlēan n. *reward for song,* RD 78⁹.

wordlian (u¹) *to talk, commune,* BF : *conspire,* GD 106¹.

wordliend m. *speaker,* OEG 2321.

wordloc n. *art of logic,* WW 388¹¹.

wordloca m. (*word-hoard*), *speech,* AN 470.

wordloga m. *deceiver, liar,* W 40¹⁰.

wordlung n. *talk, discourse* : *empty talk.*

wordmittung f. '*collatio,*' WW 178³⁵.

wordpredicung f. *preaching,* CHRD 66²³.

wordrian=wordlian

wordriht n. *suitable word,* B 2631 : *spoken law,* Ex 3.

wordsāwere m. *rhetorician,* CP 97⁴.

wordsige m. *success in speech,* LCD 1·188'.

wordsnoter (o³) *eloquent, wise in words.*

wordsnoterlic *philosophical, learned,* OEG 2270.

wordsnoterung f. *sophism,* OEG 2268.

wordsomnere m. *enumeration, catalogue,* WW 212²⁷.

wordsomnung f. *'collatio,'* WW 178³⁵.

wordsprecende *able to speak,* VH 24.

wordwīsa m. *sophist,* WW 493³⁰.

wordwrītere=wyrdwrītere

wordwynsum *affable,* WW 191²¹.

wōre dsf. of wōh.

worf=weorf; **worflan**=woſſian

wōrhana m. *moor-cock, cock-pheasant,* GL.

wōrhenn f. *hen pheasant,* WW.

wōrhona=wōrhana

worht pp. *(Bl; 'ywrought'),* worhte pret. 3 sg. of wyrcan.

wōrht-=wrōht-

wōrigan *to roam, wander,* Æ : *move round, totter, crumble to pieces.* [wōr, wērig]

world=woruld; **worm**=wyrm

wormōd=wermōd

worms (u, rsm) nm. *matter, pus, virus, Ep,* Lcd; AO,CP. *['worsum']*

worn (ea, eo) m. *large amount, number* : *troop, company, multitude, crowd* : *progeny.*

worngehāt n. *promise of numerous offspring,* GEN 2364?

wornlust=wamlust

worod=werod; **woroht**=wrōht

worold (AO,CP)=woruld

worpan=weorpan

worpen pp. of weorpan.

worpian *to cast, throw, pelt,* CP,EL.

worsm=worms; **wort**=wyrt

worð I. (eo, u) nm. *court, courtyard, curtilage, farm,* Mdf : *street.* **II.**=waroð

worð-=weorð-

worðig (eo, u, y) m. *enclosed homestead, curtilage, farm,* Æ,CP; Mdf : *street.*

worðigcærse f. *name of a plant,* LCD 3·303.

worðignetele f. *nettle,* LCD 44a.

worōscipe=weorðscipe; **worud**=werod I.

woruftord=weorftord

woruld (e¹, eo¹, ia¹; o²) f. *'WORLD,' age, AO, CP* : *men, humanity* : *way of life, life* : *long period of time, cycle, eternity.* tō worulde, ā on worulda world, in woruld worulde *world without end, for ever.*

woruldǣht f. *worldly possessions,* BH, LL.

woruldafol (-el) n. *secular or worldly power,* LL,W (ES 45·161).

woruldār f. *worldly honour,* CP : *secular property.*

woruldbearn n. *man,* RD 81²⁷.

woruldbebod n. *universal command, edict,* VH 24.

woruldbisgu f. *worldly occupation,* LL.

woruldbisgung (eo¹, y²) f. *worldly business* : *worldly misery, trouble.*

woruldbismer (o²) nm. *worldly reproach,* CP 61¹⁰.

woruldbliss f. *worldly bliss,* GU 135.

woruldbōt f. *compensation prescribed by the secular power,* LL 128,2.

woruld-broc n., *-bryce* (o²) m. *worldly trouble,* CP 259² : *use for secular purposes,* MH 136⁹.

woruldbūend† m. *world-dweller.*

woruldcamp m. *secular warfare,* ÆP 140⁴.

woruldcandel f. *sun,* B 1965.

woruldcearu (a³) f. *worldly care,* Æ.

woruldcempa m. *earthly soldier,* ÆL.

woruldcræft m. *secular art,* Æ. in pl. *world's hosts,* DA 362 (MP 26·434).

woruldcræftig *skilled in secular arts,* ÆP 128²⁵.

woruldcræft(ig)a m. *secular artificer,* ÆP 128¹⁰.

woruldcund *worldly, secular,* CP. adv. -līce, CP.

woruldcyning† m. *earthly king,* Æ.

worulddǣd f. *worldly business,* LL (414').

worulddēad *dead,* PPs 142¹.

worulddēma m. *secular judge,* LL.

worulddōm m. *secular judgment,* Æ.

worulddrēam† m. *earthly joy.*

worulddrihten m. *world's lord, God,* MET 29¹.

woruldduguð† f. *worldly riches,* GEN.

woruldearfoð† n. *earthly misery,* MET.

woruldege m. *earthly fear,* LL (310¹⁹).

woruldende m. *end of the world,* B 3083.

woruldfægernes f. *earthly beauty,* MH 34⁶

woruldfeoh n. *earthly goods, wealth,* GEN 2142.

woruldfolgað m. *worldly occupation,* BL.

woruldfrætwung (world-) f. *worldly ornament,* BL 125³⁶.

woruldfrēond (ȳ³) m. *friend in this world,* W.

woruldfrið m. *worldly peace,* LL 220,1.

woruldfruma m. *primeval man, patriarch,* GUTH 12²⁸.

woruldgālnes f. *lust of pleasure,* W 219¹⁴.

woruldgebyrd n. *worldly origin,* BH.

woruldgedāl n. *death,* EL 581.

woruldgefeoht (o²) n. *earthly fight,* MH 36²⁶.

woruldgeflit n. *dispute, lawsuit?* LCD 3·174'.

woruldgerǣdnes (eo¹) f. *secular ordinance,* LL.

woruldgeriht n. *worldly justice, secular right or due,* LL 210,2¹.

woruldgerȳsnu np. *secular customs,* LL.

woruldgesǣlig *prosperous,* MA 219.

woruldgesǣlða (o²) fp. *worldly fortune,* AO.

woruldgesceaft† f. *creature of this world* : *world.*

woruldgestrēon† n. *worldly riches.*
woruldgeswinc (o²) n. *earthly toil, misery,* CP.
woruldgeðincð f. *worldly honour, dignity,* GD,W.
woruldgeðōht (world-) mn. *worldly thought,* BL15¹⁴.
woruldgewinn n. *earthly war,* ÆL25⁸³².
woruldgewritu np. *secular writings,* BH.
woruldgewuna m. *customary law,* LL206,1a.
woruldgielp (i³, y³) mn. *pride of this world, glory,* CP.
woruldgifu f. *worldly gift,* BH,CHR.
woruldgītsere m. *coveter of worldly things,* MET14¹.
woruldgītsung f. *covetousness,* BO,MET.
woruldglenge m. *worldly pomp,* BL,LL.
woruldgōd n. *worldly good,* BO,BH.
woruldgylp (Æ)=woruldgielp
woruldgyrla (o²) m. *secular garment,* CHRD 96¹¹.
woruldhād m. *secular state,* BH,GD.
woruldhlāford m. *secular lord,* CP.
woruldhlīsa m. *worldly fame,* ÆH2·566⁶.
woruldhremming (o²) f. *worldly hindrance,* CHRD75³⁵,101⁴.
woruldhyht m. *earthly joy,* Az136.
woruldlǣce m. *earthly physician,* ÆH 1·472¹³.
woruld-lagu f., **-laga** m. *civil law,* LL,W.
woruldlēan n. *earthly reward,* LL(422¹²).
woruldlic *earthly,* Æ,Bo : '*worldly,*' *secular,* MH; Æ. adv. **-līce** *temporally.*
woruldlīf n. *life in this world* : *secular life,* BH.
woruldlufu f. *love of this world,* Æ.
woruldlust m. *worldly pleasure,* Bo.
woruldmǣg m. *earthly kinsman,* GEN2178.
woruldman m. *human being, man of the world, layman,* Cr,Met; Æ,CP. ['*worldman*']
woruldmēd f. *earthly reward,* LL(422¹⁴).
woruldnēod f. *temporal need,* LL267,32.
woruldnytt f. *worldly use or profit,* GEN, LCD.
woruldprȳdo f. *worldly pride,* Lcd3·428', ByH124³. [v. '*pride*']
woruldrǣden f. *way of the world,* B1143 (v. MLN25·113).
woruldrīca m. *great man,* Æ.
woruldrīce I. n. *earthly kingdom,* CP : *world-realm, world.* ['*worldriche*'] II. adj. *having worldly power or riches.*
woruldrīcetere (o²) n. *worldly power,* CHRD 68³⁴.
woruldriht (y³) n. *secular or civil law* : *God's law for the world.*
woruldsacu f. *worldly strife,* W170⁹.
woruldsǣlða fp. *earthly blessings,* Bo.

woruldscamu (ea³) f. *public disgrace,* LL,W.
woruldsceaft† f. *earthly creature,* Az.
woruldscēat m. *part of the world, region.*
woruldscēawung f. *worldly sight,* CHRD76³⁰.
woruldscipe m. *worldly matter, CP.* ['*worldship*']
woruldscīr (world-) f. *life in the world* (*i.e. not monastic*), *worldly affairs* GD3⁷.
woruldscrift (eo¹, y³) m. *confessor,* ByH 132¹.
woruldsnotor *world-wise* : *scientific,* MH 44²⁵.
woruldsorg f. *earthly care,* CP,Bo.
woruldspēd f. *worldly wealth, success in the world,* CP.
woruldspēdig *rich in this world,* CP333².
woruldsprǣc f. *worldly talk,* LL.
woruldstēor f. *secular penalty,* LL258,51.
woruldstrang *having worldly power,* NC334.
woruldstrengu f. *physical strength,* RD27².
woruldstrūdere m. *spoliator, robber,* LL,W.
woruldstund *sojourn upon earth,* EL363.
woruldðearf f. *this world's needs,* BH.
woruldðearfa m. *poor man,* PPs69⁶.
woruldðearfende *poor in worldly goods,* CR 1351.
woruldðēaw m. *worldly affair,* Bo7¹³.
woruld-ðegen, -ðegn, -ðēn m. *earthly or secular servant,* LL.
woruldðēnung (o²) f. *secular office,* NC334.
woruldðēowdōm m. *secular service,* CHR963.
woruldðing (o²) n. *worldly affair, thing,* Æ, AO,CP : *earthly riches.*
woruldðrymm m. *worldly glory,* ByH124⁵ (world-).
woruldwǣpn (o²) n. *earthly weapon,* BL213⁴.
woruldwǣter n. *ocean, sea,* SOL186'.
woruldwela m. *worldly wealth,* CP.
woruldwelig *rich in worldly goods,* NC335.
woruldweorc n. *secular work,* LL : *mechanics.*
woruldweorðscipe m. *worldly honour,* LL.
woruldwīdl n. *world-filth,* CR1007.
woruldwīg n. *worldly contest,* LL.
woruldwilla m. *earthly good,* Bo24².
woruldwilnung f. *earthly desire,* CP.
woruldwīs (o²) *worldly-wise,* CP : *learned,* CP.
woruldwīsdōm m. *worldly wisdom, science,* Æ.
woruldwīse f. *custom of the world,* MH68⁹B.
woruldwita m. *learned layman, sage,* LL.
woruldwīte n. *punishment, fine,* CR,LL.
woruldwlenco f. *magnificence, ostentation,* CP.
woruldwrenc (o²) m. *worldly cunning,* CP.
woruldwuldor n. *worldly glory,* CHRD66²⁰.
woruldwuniende (o²) *dwelling,* MET13¹⁷.
woruldyrmðu f. *earthly wretchedness,* AO.
wōrung f. *wandering, roving,* Æ,MFH179.

wōs I. n. *sap, juice, Lcd.* ['*ooze*'] II. gs. of wōh.

+wosa m. *conversation, intercourse, DR.*

wōsan (NG)=wēsan

wōsc pret. 3 sg., wōscon pret. pl. of wascan.

wōse=wāse

wōsig *juicy, moist, Lcd.*

-wost v. fore-w.

wōð† f. *sound, noise : voice, song, poetry : eloquence.*

wōðbora† m. *orator, speaker, seer, prophet, poet, singer.*

wōðcræft† m. *art of speech or song.*

-woðe v. got-w.

wōðgiefu f. *gift of song,* Rd 32⁸.

wōðsong m. *song,* Cr 46.

wōum dp. of wōh, adj.

wōx I. pret. 3 sg. of weaxan. II.=wōsc

wracian I. *to be in exile, wander, travel.* II. *to carry on, prosecute,* AO 50²¹.

wraclīce=wræclīce

wracnian (æ) *to be a wanderer, traveller, pilgrim, Æ.*

wraco=wracu

wracu (e) f. (g. often wræce) *revenge, vengeance, persecution, enmity,* B,BH,G, LL,VPs,W; AO,CP : *punishment, penalty,* AO,CP : *cruelty, misery, distress, torture, pain, Ph*; AO. on ðā wrace *in retaliation.* ['*wrake*']

wræc I. (e) n(f?) *misery,* CP : *vengeance, persecution, BH,Bl : exile.* ['*wrack*'] II. *what is driven,* OET 37⁶². III. pret. 3 sg. of wrecan. IV.=wærc (A; v. JAW 52)

wræca=wræcca; wræcan=wrecan

wræcca (e) m. '*wretch,*' *Jul*; CP : *fugitive, outcast, exile,* B,Bo,Chr; AO : *adventurer, stranger : sojourner.*

wræccan=wrecan; wræce v. wracu.

wræcend=wrecend

wræcfæc n. *time of exile, banishment, misery,* Rim 64.

wræcful *wretched, miserable, ÆH.*

wræchwīl f. *time of exile or distress,* Ph 527.

wræclāst† (e) m. *path of exile.*

wræclāstian *to banish,* WW.

wræclic adj. *foreign : strange, unfamiliar, extraordinary : wretched, exiled.* adv. -līce.

wræclic=wrætlic

wræc-mæcg†, -mæcga (Jul 260) m. *exile, outcast, miserable man.*

wræcmon m. *fugitive,* Ex 137.

wræcnes=wrecnes

wræcnian=wracnian

wrǣcon pret. pl. of wrecan.

wræcscipe (e) m. *exile,* Bl,EPs 119⁵.

wræcsetl n. *place of exile,* Gu 267.

wræcsīð m. *journey of exile or peril, pilgrimage,* Æ : *exile, persecution,* Æ,AO : *misery.*

wræcsīðian *to wander, travel abroad, be in exile,* Æ.

wræcstōw f. *place of exile or punishment,* Bo, Gen.

wræcwīte n. *punishment,* Bl 5.

wræcworuld f. *miserable world,* W 1²,VH.

wrǣd f. *band, bandage, wreath,* CP : *bundle : band, flock.* [wrīðan]

wrǣdmǣlum adv. *in companies,* WW 411⁴².

wrǣg-=wrēg-

wrǣne (ē) *unbridled, loose, lustful,* AO.

wrænna (Æ)=wrenna

wrǣnnes f. *luxury, lust, wantonness,* AO, CP.

wrǣnsa m. *wantonness,* OEG 2347.

wrǣnscipe (ē) m. *wantonness,* OEG 5290.

wrǣnsian *to be wanton,* NC 335.

wrǣsnan *to alter, change, modulate,* Rd 25¹.

wrǣst (ā) *firm, able, strong, excellent : delicate.* adv. -e.

wrǣstan I. (±) *to '*wrest,*' bend, twist, twang,* Sol,Wy. II. *to be or make elegant?* WW.

wrǣstlere m. '*wrestler,*' WW 431²⁶.

wrǣstlic I. *pertaining to wrestling,* WW. II. (ā) *delicate, elegant,* WW.

wrǣstliend *wrestler,* WW 431²⁵. [wrǣstan]

wrǣstlung f. '*wrestling,*' *struggling,* GD, OEG.

wræt=wrætt; wrǣt=wrǣtt

wrætbaso (e¹) *red,* Gl. [wrætte]

wrǣteread *red,* Lcd 111b.

wrǣtlic *artistic, ornamental : curious, wondrous, rare.* adv. -līce. [wrætt]

wrætt m., wrætte f. *rubea tinctoria? crosswort? hellebore?* Lcd,WW (A 30·248).

wrætt† f. *ornament, work of art, jewel.*

wrǣð I.=wrǣd. II.=wrǣððo

±wrǣðan (ē) *to anger,* ByH 112¹² : *get angry, be angry,* DR : *resist violently,* Lcd 3·212⁴.

wrǣðian=wreðian; wrǣðo=wrǣððo

wrǣð-studu, -stuðu (e) f. *column, pillar, support,* BH,W.

wrǣððo, wrǣð(ð)u (ā) f. '*wrath,*' *anger, indignation,* DR,Leofric Missal,NG.

wræxlian=wraxlian

wrāh pret. 3 sg. of wrēon.

wrang (o) I. n. '*wrong,*' *injustice,* LL,W. II. *rough, uneven,* KC. III. pret. 3 sg. of wringan.

wranga (pr-) *hold of a ship,* WW. ['*wrong*']

wrangwīs *rough, uneven,* OEG 1770.

wrāsen (ǣ) f. *band, tie, chain,* WW 34²⁴.

wrāst=wrǣst

wrāt pret. 3 sg. of wrītan.

wrǣ I. adj. 'WROTH,' furious, angry, hostile, AO : terrible, horrible : grievous, harsh, bitter, malignant, evil, cruel. adv. -e, Bo, G,Gu,Ps. ['wrothe'] II. f. cruelty : hardship. [wrīðan] III.=wrǣd. IV. pret. 3 sg. of wrīðan.
+wrāðian (refl.) to be angry, Chr1070,RG. ['wroth,' 'iwrathe']
wrāðlic† grievous, severe, bitter. adv. -līce, B. ['wrothly']
wrāðmōd† angry, GEN.
wrāðscræf n. pit of misery, hell, RD41⁴¹.
wrāðða=wrǣðða
wraðu† f. prop, help, support, maintenance, BH.
+wraxl? wrestling-place, gymnasium, OEG 18b⁶⁸?
wraxlere m. wrestler, OEG.
wraxlian to wrestle, Æ. ['wraxle']
wraxliende wrestling, contending, striving, Æ.
wraxlung f. 'wrestling,' WW150⁸. ['wraxling']
wrēah pret. 3 sg. of wrēon; wrec=wræc
wrecan⁵ (eo) to drive, impel, push : press forward, advance : fulfil, accomplish : utter, deliver, pronounce : expel, banish, persecute, CP : (±) 'WREAK,' revenge, avenge, punish, CP; AO.
wreccan I. to awake, arouse, Æ,CP. ['wrecche'] II.=wrecan
-wrecel v. spor-w.
wrecend m. avenger, B,LL.
wrecnes (æ) f. vengeance, NG : wickedness, BHCA70¹².
wrecscip (æ?) 'actuaria'? ES43·336.
wrecu (VPs)=wracu
±wrēgan I.† to excite, stir up. II. to accuse, impeach, Æ,Chr,Cp,MH. ['wray']
+wrēgednes f. accusation, ES62·114².
wrēgend m. accuser, BH,GL.
±wrēgendlic accusative, ÆGR22²⁰.
wrēgere m. accuser, informer, Æ. ['wrayer']
wrēgistre (ǣ) f. female accuser, ÆL2²⁰⁸.
wrēgung f. accusation, ÆGr. ['wraying']
wrēhte pret. 3 sg. of wrēgan.
wrehtend m. instigator, WW420²⁹.
wrēhtend m. accuser, KGL73²³.
wrēn-=wrǣn-
wrenc m. wile, stratagem, trick, deceit, Bo, Sc; AO : (†) modulation, melody, song. ['wrench']
wrencan to twist, IM : spin intrigues, devise plots, MOD33. ['wrench']
wrenna (æ) m., wrenne f. 'wren,' Cp,WW.
wreocan=wrecan
wreogan (M)=wrigon pret. pl. of wrēon.
±wrēon¹,² to cover, clothe, envelop, conceal, hide, Gen,Lcd,LG,LL : protect, defend, Gen, Rd. ['wry']

wrēotan=rēotan; wreotian=writian
wreotu nap. of writ.
wrēoð=(1) wrǣd; (2) wrǣðða
wreoðenhilt with twisted hilt, B1699. [=*wriðenhilt]
wreoðian=wreðian; wrēoðian=wrīdian
wretbasu=wrǣtbaso
±wreðian to support, sustain, uphold, Bo, GD; CP. ['wrethe']
wreðstudu=wrǣðstudu
wrīanne (N)=wrēonne gerund of wrēon I.
wricð, wriceð pres. 3 sg. of wrecan.
wrid m. shoot, plant, bush, BC,Gl,Lcd; Mdf. ['wride']
+wrid I. n. thicket? GUTH. II. husk, WW 412³.
wrīdan¹ to grow, thrive, flourish, GEN,LCD.
wriden pp. of (1) wrīdan; (2) wrīðan.
wrīdian† grow, flourish, spring up, AA.
wriecð=wricð pres. 3 sg. of wrecan.
wriexl=wrixl
wrigelnes f. covering, JPs60⁵.
wrigels mn. covering, cloak, veil, HL,VPs. ['wriels']
wrigen pp., wrigon pret. pl. of wrēon.
wrigennes (gn-) f. a covering, EPs60⁵.
wrigian to go, turn, twist, bend, Bo,Rd : strive, struggle, press forward, endeavour, venture, Bo. ['wry']
wrīhst pres. 2 sg., wrīhð pres. 3 sg. of wrēon.
+wrinclian to wind about, KC4·34⁹. +wrinclod serrated, GPH39⁸.
+wring n. liquor, drink, WW128¹⁷.
wringan³ to 'wring,' twist : (±) squeeze, press out, Æ,Bo,GD,Lcd.
wringe f. (oil-)press, GD250¹⁵. ['wring']
wringhwǣg n? strained whey, LL451,16.
+wrisc=+wrixl; wrislan=wrixlan
wrist f. 'wrist,' LL386,2.
±writ n. letter, book, treatise, Ph : scripture, writing, DR,LG : 'writ' ('i-writ'), charter, document, deed, AO,Bl : 'stilus,' GPH402.
±wrītan¹ (ȳ) to incise, engrave, 'WRITE,' draw, Æ,Chr,CP; AO : bestow by writing.
writbred n. writing tablet, MH,WW.
-wrīte v. wæter-w.; -writennes v. tō-w.
±wrītere m. 'writer,' scribe, author, portrayer, painter, Æ,Bf,Bo,CP,Mt : secretary, CP,GD.
writeȳren (MH146¹²)=writīren
writian I. (eo) to chirp, chatter, v. OEG37³. II. to cut? draw a figure? ES8·478.
wrīting f. writing, SPs44².
wrītingfeðer f. pen, EPs44².
wrītingīsen n. style, pen, MH146¹²c.
writīren (ȳ²) n. writing instrument, style, MH146¹².
+writrǣden f. written agreement, WW217⁷.

writseax n. *style, pen,* MtLp2¹⁸.

writt-=wrīt-

+**wrið** n. *strap, thong,* WW143¹³? (v. A 8·451).

wriða m. *band, thong, bridle, Æ,Sc : collar, ring, Æ,Rd.* ['*wreath*']

±**wrīðan¹** (ȳ) I. *to twist, ÆGr : wrap, bind up, bind, tie, fasten, fetter, check, BC,LL : vex, torture, Æ.* ['*writhe*'] II.=wrīdan

+**wrīðelian** *to bind?* OEG23⁷?

wriðels m. *band, fillet, bandage,* WW411¹⁷.

+**wriðennes** f. *binding,* LCD.

wrīðian=wrīdian

+**wrīðing** f. *binding,* Sc202¹³.

wrix(i)endlic *mutual,* GD2⁷. adv. -līce *turn about, one by one, by turns, in turn,* CP.

wrixl f., **wrixla** m. *change, exchange, barter,* CP.

+**wrixl,** +**wrixle** n. *turn, change : exchange, purchase, intercourse : requital : office.*

wrixlan (±) *to change, barter, exchange, reciprocate, lend,* AO. wordum w. *converse :* (+) *recompense, requite :* (+) *obtain,* CP.

+**wrixle** *alternate : vicarious,* GL.

wrixlian=wrixlan

+**wrixlic** *alternating,* OEG2¹³⁵.

±**wrixlung** f. *change,* BF120²⁰ : *loan,* WW 115,449.

wroegan=wrēgan

wrogen pp. of wrēon.

wroht=worht pp. of wyrcan.

wrōht I. f. *blame, reproach, accusation, slander : fault, crime, sin, injustice, Æ : strife, enmity, anger, contention, dispute,* AO,CP : *hurt, injury, calamity, misery.* [wrēgan] II. m. *tale-bearer,* ÆGR217².

wrōhtberend m. *accuser,* APs,WW.

wrōhtbora m. *accuser, monster,* WW : *the devil,* CR.

wrōhtdropa m. *criminal bloodshed,* GnE196.

wrōhtgeorn *contentious,* CP357.

wrōhtgetēme n. *series of crimes?* (BT),GEN 45.

wrōhtian *to do harm?* HL15¹⁰⁵.

wrōhtlāc n. *calumny,* W160⁵n.

wrōhtsāwere m. *sower of strife,* CP359.

wrōhtscipe m. *crime,* GEN1672.

wrōhtsmið† m. *worker of evil, evildoer.*

wrōhtspitel *slanderous,* EGL. [spittan]

wrōhtstæf m. *accusation,* EL926 : *injury,* RD72¹²,¹⁴.

wrong (WW201³⁵)=wrang II.

wrōt m. *snout, elephant's trunk, Cp,WW.* ['*wroot*']

wrōtan⁷ *to root up, Cp,Ps,Rd.* ['*wroot*']

wrugon pret. pl. of wrēon.

wrungen pp. of wringan.

wrycð pres. 3 sg. of wrecan.

wryhta=wyrhta

wrȳhð=wrīhð pret. 3 sg. of wrēon.

+**wryndan** (MtL7²⁵)=+gryndan

wrȳt-=wrīt-

wrȳte (CM56⁸³)=prȳte

wrȳðan=wrīðan

wucaðēn=wucðegn

wuc-dæg, wuce-, wicu- m. '*week-day,*' BH; Æ.

wuce=wucu

wucðegn (i¹) m. *monk or priest appointed for a week's duty, weekly servant,* CM,RB.

wucðēnung f. *service for a week,* RB59,60.

wucu (i, ie, io) f. '*week,*' *Bf,Lcd,RB ;* AO,CP.

wucubōt f. *penance lasting a week,* LL (278¹²).

wucweorc (i¹) n. (*compulsory*) *work for a week, by a tenant, KC,LL.* ['*weekwork*']

wude=wudu

wudere m. *wood-man, wood-carrier,* WW 371⁵. ['*wooder*']

wudewe=wuduwe

wudian *to cut wood, Æ,W.*

wudig *wooded, having trees,* Az120.

wudigere, wudiere (WW; '*woodyer*')= wudere

wudiht *thick* (*with trees*), *forest-like,* GPH 402.

wudo-=wudu-

wudu (i, io) m., gs. wuda, wudes; nap. wudas, wuda '*wood,*' *forest, grove, BC,CP, LL,VPs; Æ,AO;* Mdf : *tree, B,Cp,Ph : the Cross, Rood : wood, timber, Bo,CP,Gn :* (†) *ship,* B : *spear-shaft,* B398.

wuduœlfen (ₑ³) f. *wood-elf, dryad,* WW.

wuduæppel f. *wild apple, crab,* LCD71a.

wudubǣr f. *woodland pasture,* KC.

wudubǣre *wood-bearing,* OEG1806.

wudubǣrnett n. *burning of wood,* LL16,12; 24n².

wudubāt n. *wooden boat,* AN907.

wudubēam† m. *forest tree.*

wudubearo m. *forest, grove,* AA,W.

wudu-bend, -bind m.=wudubinde

wudubill n. *hatchet, Cp;* GD. ['*woodbill*']

wudubinde I. (-bindle) f. '*woodbine,*' *convolvulus, Gl,Lcd,LG.* II. f. *bundle of sticks,* OET35¹⁸.

wudubior (=bora?) m. *wood-carrier,* HGL 427.

wudublǣd† (-blēd) f. *forest blossom.*

wudubucca m. *wild buck, wild goat,* LCD.

wudubyrðra m. *wood-carrier, camp-follower,* OEG869.

wuducerfille f. *wood-chervil, cow-parsley,* GL.

wuducocc m. '*woodcock,*' *Gl.*

wuducroft m. *a croft with trees on it?* (BT) KC3·376⁶.

wuduculfre m. *wood-pigeon*, WW.

wuducūnelle f. *wild thyme*, LCD.

wuducynn n. *an aromatic (?) wood*, JnL12³.

wududocce f. *wild dock, sorrel*, LCD.

wuduelfen=wuduælfen

wudufæsten n. *place protected by woods, woodfastness* : *ship*.

wudufald *a fold in a wood*, KC.

wudufeld m. *wooded plain*, PPs131⁶.

wudufeoh n. *forest-tax*, LCD.

wudufille=wuducerfille

wudufīn f. *pile of wood*, ÆGR.

wudufugol m. *forest bird, wild fowl*, BO, MET.

wudugāt f. *wild goat*, LCD.

wudugehæg n. *woodland pasture* (BTs), KC3·176¹.

wuduhēawere m. *wood-cutter*, Æ. [v. '*wood*']

wuduherpað m. *public path through a wood*, KC3·213².

wuduhīewet n. *illegal cutting of wood*, LL 567,37.

wuduholt n. *forest, wood, grove*, PH.

wuduhona m. *woodcock*, WW38⁸.

wuduhrofe=wudurofe

wuduhunig n. *wild honey*, Mk; Æ. [v. '*wood*']

wudulād f. *carting wood*, LL452,21⁴.

wudu-lǣs f., gs. -lǣswe *wood-pasture, run (for cattle) in a wood*, Ct.

wuduland n. '*woodland,*' BC.

wudu-leahtric, -lectric m. *wood-lettuce, wild sleepwort*, LCD.

wudulēswe=wudulæswe

wudulic adj. *woody, wooded, wild*, Æ,WW.

wudumǣr (ē³) f. *wood-nymph, echo*, GL.

wudumann m. *woodman*, KC3·275⁹.

wudumerce m. *wild parsley, wood-mint*, LCD. [v. '*wood*']

wudung f. *getting of wood*, Æ : *right of estovers*, KC. ['*wooding*']

wudurǣden f. *wood-regulation, right of estovers*, LL.

wudurēc m. *smoke from a funeral pyre*, B 3144.

wudurima m. *border of a wood*, KC3·34¹⁵.

wudurofe f. '*woodruff,*' Lcd,WW.

wudurose f. *wild rose*, LCD34b?

wudusnīte f. *wood-snipe*, WW.

wudusūræppel f. *crab-apple?* LCD160a.

wudutelga m. *branch of a tree*, SOL421.

wudutrēow n. *forest tree*, LL,W.

wuduðistle m. *wood-thistle*, LCD.

wuduwa (wyde-) m. *widower*, LL. ['*widow*']

wuduwald m. *forest*, WW426³⁵.

wuduwanhād n. *state of a woman who has not a husband, chastity,* '*widowhood,*' CP, HL.

wuduwāsa m. *faun, satyr*, WW. ['*woodwose*']

wuduwe (i, eo, y¹; e²) f. '*widow,*' Chr,G,Ps.

wuduweard m. *forester*, LL452,19. ['*woodward*']

wudu-weax n., -weaxe f. *wood-waxen, genista tinctoria*, Lcd. ['*woodwax*']

wuduwēsten mn. *wild forest*, CHRp5n.

wuduwinde f. *woodbine*, GL.

wuduwyrt f. *plant which grows in woods*, BL59³.

wudwe=wuduwe

wuhhung f. *rage, fury, madness* : (pl.) *the Furies*.

wuht AO,CP=wiht; **wuhung**=wuhhung

wul=wull; **wulder**=wuldor

wuldor n. *glory, splendour, honour*, Bo,VPs; Æ,CP : *praise, thanks* : *heaven*, EL. ['*wulder*']

wuldor-bēag, -bēah m. *crown of glory*, Æ.

±**wuldorbēagian** *to crown*, ÆH.

wuldorblǣd m. *glorious success*, JUD156.

wuldorcyning m.† *King of Glory, God.*

wuldordrēam m. *heavenly rapture*, MFH.

Wuldorfæder† m. *Glorious Father.*

wuldorfæst *glorious.* adv. -fæste, -fæstlīce.

wuldorfæstlīcnes f. *glory*, Æ.

wuldorful *glorious*, Æ : *vainglorious*, SC.

±**wuldorfullian** *to glorify*, Æ.

wuldorfullīce adv. *gloriously*, ÆH.

wuldorgāst m. *angel*, GEN2912.

wuldorgeflogena m. *one who has fled from glory, devil*, LCD3·36¹⁵.

wuldorgesteald† np. *glorious possessions, realms of glory.*

wuldorgeweorc n. *wondrous work*, ES 43·167.

wuldorgifu† (eo) f. *glorious gift, grace.*

wuldorgim m. *glorious jewel, sun*, RD81²⁰.

Wuldorgod m. *Glorious God*, BHB344⁸.

wuldorhama† (o³) m. *garb of glory.*

wuldorhēap m? *glorious troop*, NC335.

wuldorhelm m. *crown of glory*, BL.

wuldorlēan† n. *glorious reward.*

wuldorlic† *glorious*, BL,Ps. adv. -līce.

wuldormāga m. *heir of heaven*, GU1067.

wuldormago m. *heir of heaven*, GU1267.

wuldormicel *gloriously great*, †Hy7⁹⁴.

wuldornytting f. *glorious service*, RD81¹⁹.

wuldorsang m. *glorious song*, MFH114¹⁰.

wuldorspēd f. *glorious wealth*, GEN87.

wuldorspēdig *glorious*, AN428.

wuldortān m. *plant with medicinal virtues?* (BT), LCD3·34'.

wuldortorht† *gloriously bright, clear, brilliant, illustrious.*

wuldorðrymm m. *heavenly glory*, AN,BL.

wuldorweorud n. *heavenly host*, CR285.

wuldorword n. *glorious word*, †Hy7⁴⁶.

wuldrian (±) *to glorify, praise, extol,* Æ : *boast, brag,* Æ : *live in glory,* Æ.

wuldrig *glorious,* DR.

wuldrung f. *glorying, boasting,* Sc,DR.

wuldur=wuldor

wulf m. *(he-)'wolf,'* Cp,LG,Wy; Æ,AO, CP; Mdf : *wolfish person, devil,* Cr, MH.

wulfescamb m. *wild teasel,* Lcd,WW.

wulfeshēafod n. *head of a wolf,* Lcd : *outlaw,* LL (v. NED). [*'wolfshead'*]

wulfestǣsel f. *(wolf's) teasel,* Lcd.

wulfhaga m. *shelter from wolves?* CC53.

wulfhēafodtrēo m. *cross, gallows?* Rd56[12].

wulfheort† *wolf-hearted, cruel,* Da.

wulf-hlið n., nap. *-hleoðu hillside inhabited by wolves,* B1358.

wulfhol n. *wolf's hole,* WW.

wulflȳs n. *fleece of wool,* WW198[26].

wulfmod=wullmod

wulfpytt m. *wolf's hole?* BC,KC.

wulfsēað m. *wolf's hole,* KC3·264[5].

wulfslæd n. *valley of wolves,* KC3·456[6].

wull f. *'wool,'* Gl,Lcd,VPs; Æ.

wullcamb m. *comb for wool,* LL454,15[1]. [*'woolcomb'*]

wullcnoppa (?hn-) m. *tuft of wool,* WW.

wulle=wull

wullen (KC; *'woollen'*)=wyllen

wullian *to wipe with wool,* Lcd1·356'.

wullmod m? *distaff,* Gl.

wulltewestre f. *wool-carder,* Lcd.

wulluc *cover, wrapper,* A31·65.

wullwǣga f. *scales for wool,* WW148[21].

+**wun**=+wuna

±**wuna** I. m. (usu. +) *habit, custom, practice, rite, Bo;* Æ. *on gew. habban to be accustomed to,* CP. [*'i-wune'*] II. (+) *wonted, customary, usual, Chr,LG.* [*'wone'*]

wund I. f. *'wound,' sore, ulcer, B,BH,Cr, Lcd,RB;* CP : *wounding, injury,* Æ. II. adj. *wounded, sore,* AO.

wundel f. *wound,* LL,RB.

wundelīce=wundorlīce

wunden (B; *'wounden'*) pp. of windan.

wundenfeax *with twisted mane,* B1400.

wundenhals *with twisted prow,* B298.

wundenlocc† *with braided locks.*

wundenmǣl *etched, damascened (of a sword),* B1531.

wundenstefna m. *ship with curved or wreathed prow,* B220.

wunder=wundor

±**wundian** *to 'wound,'* Æ,CP,Chr,LL,Ps; AO.

wundiend *'vulnerator,'* ERHy6[42].

wundiht, *wundig ulcerous, full of sores,* GPH.

wundle=wundel

wundlic *wounding, wound-inflicting,* GPH 402[51].

wundon pret. pl. of windan.

wundor (often confused with wuldor) n. (gs. wundres) *'WONDER,' miracle, marvel, portent, horror,* Æ; AO,CP : *wondrous thing, monster.*

wundorāgræfen *wondrously graven,* An712.

wundorbēacen n. *strange sign,* PPs73[5].

wundorbebod n. *strange order,* B1747.

wundorblēo n. *wondrous hue,* Cr1140.

wundorclam n. *strange bond,* Cr310.

wundorcræft† m. *miraculous power.*

wundororœftiglīce *with wondrous skill,* BH 324[3]o.

wundordǣd f. *wondrous deed,* Bl.

wundordēað m. *wondrous death,* B3037.

wundoreardung f. *wondrous dwelling.* VH24.

wundorfæt (e[2]) n. *wondrous vessel,* B1162.

wundorful (e[2]) *'wonderful,' OEG;* Æ. adv. -līce.

wundorgehwyrft (e[4]) *wondrous turn,* GPH 390.

wundorgeweorc=wundorweorc

wundorgiefu f. *wondrous endowment,* Wy72.

wundorhǣlo (u[2]) f. *wondrous healing,* BH 446[12].

wundorhūs? n. *'solarium,' upper room,* GD 119[26].

+**wundorlǣcan** *to make wonderful, magnify,* SPs16[8].

wundorlic *wonderful, remarkable, strange, AO,Bl;* Æ,CP. adv. -līce, Æ,CP,Lcd. [*'wonderly'*]

wundormāðm m. *wonderful treasure,* B2173

wundorsēon f. *wonderful sight,* B995.

wundorsmið m. *skilled smith,* B1681.

wundortācen n. *miracle,* PPs104[23].

wundorweorc n. *'wonder-work,' miracle,* An,Bl.

wundorworuld f. *wonderful world,* Rd40[17].

wundorwyrd f. *wonderful event,* El1071.

wundres v. wundor.

±**wundrian** (w. g.) *to 'wonder,' be astonished (at),* Bl,Bo,G,Ph; Æ,AO,CP : *admire : make wonderful, magnify.*

wundrigendlic *expressing wonder,* ÆGr 241[16].

wundrum adv. (d. of wundor) *wonderfully, strangely, terribly.*

wundrung f. *wonder, astonishment, admiration,* Æ,Cr : *spectacle,* OEG4370. [*'wondering'*]

wundspring m. *ulcerous wound,* Lcd1·356'.

wundswaðu (e) f. *scar,* VPs37[6].

wundur=wundor

wundwīte n. *compensation for wounding,* LL76H.

+**wunelic** *usual, customary,* Æ,CP : *accustomed* (*to*), *adapted* (*to*). adv. -līce, BH. ['*i-wuneliche*']

wunenes, wununes f. *dwelling, habitation* : *perseverance,* DR. [wunian]

wungynde=wuniende pres. ptc. of wunian.

wunian (±) *to inhabit, dwell, abide, exist,* B, Bl,Cp,G; AO,CP : (+) *remain, continue, stand,* Æ,B,Bl; AO,CP : (±) *be used to, be wont to,* ÆGr : (+) *habituate oneself to,* CP73¹⁴. ['*wone*']

wuniendlic *perpetually,* GD264⁷.

wunigend m. *inhabitant,* RBL5¹¹.

+**wunlic**=+wunelic; **wunn**=wynn

wunnen pp., wunnon pret. pl. of winnan.

+**wunod** *domiciled,* GUTH9²³.

wunones=wunenes; **wunsum**=wynsum

wununes=wunenes

wunung f. *act of dwelling, living,* Bl,RB : *dwelling, habitation,* Æ,HL. ['*wonning*']

wunungstōw f. *abiding-place,* GD31¹⁹.

wuraðo (N)=wræððo; **wurcan**=wyrcan

wurd=(1) wyrd; (2) word

wurdon pret. pl. of weorðan.

wurht, wurhton=worhte pret. sg., worhton pret. pl. of wyrcan.

wurm=wyrm

wurma m., wurme f. *murex, purple-fish* : *any dye, woad, purple* : *a plant used for dyeing.*

wur-mille, -mele (ea¹) f. *wild marjoram,* GL.

wurms=worms; **wurnian**=weornian

wurpan=weorpan

wurpul *that which throws down,* GL.

wursm=worms; **wurst**=wierrest

wurt=wyrt; **wurð**=weorð

wurðe=weorð(e), wierðe; **wurðig**=worðig

wūscbearn n. (*dear*) *little child,* JnL13³³. [wȳscan]

wūso (JnR13³³)=wūscbearn

wussung=wissung; **wuta**=wita

wutan=wuton

wutedlīce, wutodlíce (NG)=witodlíce

wuton 1 pers. pl. subj. of wītan *to go.* used to introduce an imperative or hortatory clause *let us...! come!* CP.

wutu (M), wutum, wutun (N)=wuton

wutudlīce=witodlíce

wūðwuta (DR)=ūðwita; **wȳc**=wīc

wyc-=wic-; **wȳd**=wīd; **wyd-**=wud-

wyder-=wiðer-; **wȳf-**=wīf-

wyglere=wiglere; **wyht**=wiht

wyl-=weal-, wel-, wi(e)l-; **wȳl-**=wīel-

wylcð pres. 3 sg. of wealcan.

wylf f. *she-wolf,* OET.

wylfen I. adj. *wolfish,* DEOR,OEG. **II.** f. *she-wolf, fury,* Lcd; GL. ['*wolfen*']

wylian=wylwan

wȳliscmoru=wēalmoru

wyll I. f. *wool,* LL(166n⁴). **II.**=wiell

wyllan (æ, e;=ie) *to boil,* Lcd. ['*well*']

wylleburne †f. *spring.*

wyllecærse (i) *watercress,* Lcd,WW. ['*wellcress*']

wyllen (i) *made of wool, woollen.*

wyllestrēam m. *running water,* Ph. ['*wellstream*']

wyllewæter n. *spring water,* Lcd. ['*wellwater*']

wylleweg *road to a well or spring,* KC 5·150¹².

wyllflōd (i) *flood, deluge,* GEN1412.

wyllgespring n. *spring,* BH,PH.

wyllspring(e) (e¹, i¹) m. *spring,* Æ,CP, WW. ['*wellspring*']

wyloc=weoloc; **wyn**=wynn

±**wyltan** (æ, e;=ie) *to roll.*

wylw-an, -ian (e, i;=ie) *to roll, roll together* : *compound, join.*

wyn-=win-, winn-; **wȳn-**=wīn-

wynbēam m. *tree of gladness, holy cross,* EL844.

wynburh f. *delightful town,* PPs127².

wyncondel f. *pleasant light, sun,* Gu1186.

wyndæg† m. *day of gladness.*

+**wynde** n. *weaving,* GL.

wyndecræft m. *art of embroidery,* GL.

wyndle f. *wound,* LL381,23.

wyndrēam m. *jubilation, joyful sound,* Ps.

wyndrēamnes f. *jubilation,* LPs150⁵.

wyndrian=wundrian; **wyne**=wine

wynele m. *gladdening oil,* PPs108¹⁸.

wynfæst (e) *joyful,* PsC50¹⁹.

wyngesīð m. *pleasant companion,* PPs100³.

wyngrāf mn. *delightful grove,* PPs94¹³.

wynigað=wunigað pres. pl. of wunian.

wynland† (o²) n. *land of delight.*

wynlēas† *joyless.*

wynlic *pleasant, beautiful, joyful,* HL,Ph. adv. -līce, Ps. ['*winly*']

wynlust m. *sensual pleasure,* Æ.

wynmæg f. *winsome maiden,* Gu1319.

wynn f. (occl. late as. wyn) *joy, rapture, pleasure, delight, gladness,* B; AO. ['*win*']

wynn- v. also wyn-, win(n)-.

wynnum† *joyfully, beautifully.* [wynn]

wynpsalterium n. *psalm of joy,* PPs56¹⁰.

wynröd f. *blessed cross,* SOL235.

wynsang m. *joyful song,* W265³¹.

wynstaðol m. *joyous foundation,* RD92³.

wynsum (e, i; once +wuns-) '*winsome,*' *pleasant, delightful, joyful, merry,* B,MH, Ph; CP : *kindly,* BH.

+**wynsumian** *to rejoice, exult,* DR : *make glad, make pleasing.*

±**wynsumlic** adj. *pleasant, delightful* adv. -līce *pleasantly, happily* Æ

wynsumnes (i) f. *loveliness, pleasantness, rejoicing, Æ.*
wynwerod n. *'chorus,' joyous band,* GL.
wynwyrt f. *pleasant plant,* DD5.
wynyng=wining
wyorðmynd (BL)=weorðmynd
wȳr=wīr; **wyrc**=weorc
±**wyrcan** (e, eo, i) *to prepare, perform, do, make,* 'WORK*,' *construct, produce, effect,* Æ; AO,CP : *use (tools)* : *dispose, constitute* : *amount to* : (w. g.) *strive after* : *deserve, gain, win, acquire.* Eastron w. *to keep Easter, eat the passover.*
+**wyrce** n. *work* : *proceeds of work, perquisite,* LL449,7 (v. BTs).
wyrcend m. *worker, doer,* ÆH.
wyrcnes f. *work, operation,* BH.
wyrcta (Ep,MtL)=wyrhta
wyrcung f. *working, work,* DR.
±**wyrd** I. fn. *fate, chance, fortune, destiny,* B,Bo,Cp,Seaf; Æ,AO : *Fate, the Fates, Providence,* CP : *event, phenomenon, transaction, fact,* Bl,Cr : *deed* : (+) *condition* : *pleasure,* AO126³³. ['*weird*'; weorðan] II. f. *verbosity,* OEG1419.
wyrdan=wierdan
+**wyrde** I. n. *speech, conversation* : *ordinance.* II. *acknowledging, agreeing with,* CHR1055. III.=+wyrðe
+**wyrdelic** *historical, authentic,* Æ : *fortuitous,* OEG. adv. -līce *eloquently* : *accurately, verbatim* : *wisely,* OEG208.
+**wyrdelicnes** f. *eloquence,* A13·38³²¹.
wyrdgesceapum *by chance,* WW400²⁵.
+**wyrdignes** f. *eloquence,* OEG5488.
+**wyrdlian**=+wierdan
wyrdnes f. *condition, state,* Bo128n.
wyrdstæf m. *decree of fate,* Gu1325.
±**wyrdwrītere** m. *historian, chronicler,* Æ.
wyred=werod
wyregung=wyrgung
wyrest=wierrest; **wyrfan**=hwierfan
wyrg=wearg
wyrgan I. *to strangle,* Cp; Æ. ['*worry*'] II.=wiergan
wyrgcwedol (e;=ie) *ill-tongued, given to cursing.*
wyrgcwedolian (e) *to curse,* VPs.
wyrgcwedolnes (e¹, i²) f. *cursing,* Ps.
wyrged (æ) *the devil,* NG.
-**wyrgednes** v. ā-w.
wyrgels=wrigels; **wyrgelnes**=wyrgnes
wyrgend (e) m. *reviler, evildoer,* ÆL.
wyrgende *given to cursing,* W70¹⁸.
wyrgnes f. *abuse, cursing,* Æ,BH.
wyrgðu† (æ, e) f. *curse, condemnation, punishment* : *evil, wickedness.*
wyrgung (e) f. *curse, cursing, condemnation, banishment,* Æ.

+**wyrht** (eo) fn. *work, deed, service* : *desert, merit,* AO,CP : *transgression.* mid gewyrhtum *deservedly.*
wyrhta m. '*wright,*' *artist, labourer, worker, maker, creator,* Æ,Bl,Bo,G,LL; CP : (+) *fellow-worker* : (+) *accomplice.*
wyri-=wearg-; **wyrian**=wiergan
wyricean=wyrcan; **wyrig**=werig
wyrig-=wearg-, wyrg-
wyrld=woruld
wyrm (eo, o, u) I. m. *reptile, serpent, snake, dragon,* Æ,AO : '*WORM,*' *insect, mite* : *poor creature,* VPs. [wurma] II.=wearm
wyrma=wurma; **wyrmǣt**=wyrmǣte (I.)
wyrmǣte I. f. *attack of worms, worm-eaten state,* A,LCD. II. adj. *worm-eaten,* Lcd. ['*wormete*']
±**wyrman** (æ, e, i;=ie) *to warm, make warm.*
wyrmbaso *red, scarlet,* OET113⁶⁷.
wyrmcynn n. *serpent-kind, sort of serpent,* AO,B,G. ['*wormkin*']
wyrmella=wurmille
wyrmfāh *adorned with figures of snakes, damascened?* B1698.
wyrmgal(d)ere (u) m. *snake-charmer,* Æ.
wyrmgealdor n. *charm against snakes,* LCD148a.
wyrmgeard m. *abode of serpents,* SOL469.
wyrmgeblǣd n. *swelling from snake-bite? (or insect-bite?)* LCD162b.
wyrmhǣlsere m. *diviner by serpents,* WW441³⁵.
wyrmhīw n. *likeness of a serpent,* ÆL10¹⁰⁴.
wyrmhord n. *dragon's hoard,* B2222.
wyrming (æ, e;=ie) f. *warming,* BIIb196²⁷. [wearm]
wyrmlīc n. *form of a serpent,* WA.
wyrmmelu n. *worm-meal,* '*pulvis e vermibus confectus,*' LCD.
wyrmrēad (u¹) *purple, scarlet,* Æ.
wyrms nm. *virus, corrupt matter,* Æ.
±**wyrmsan** *to fester,* CP.
+**wyrms(ed)** *purulent,* LCD,WW.
wyrmsele m. *hall of serpents, hell,* JUD119.
wyrmshrǣcing f. *spitting up of matter,* WW113⁸?
±**wyrmsig** (u) *purulent,* WW.
wyrmslite m. *snake-bite,* W188¹.
wyrmsūtspīung f. *spitting up of matter,* WW113⁸?
wyrmwyrt f. *worm-wort,* LCD.
wyrn=wearn; **wyrnan**=wiernan
wyrp m. *a throw, cast,* Lk22⁴¹. ['*wurp*']
wyrpan=wierpan
wyrpe (e;=ie) f. *revolution, change, recovery, relief, improvement.* [weorpan]
+**wyrpe** n. *heap,* KC5·78'; Mdf.
wyrpel m. *jess (in falconry),* WY87 (v. ES 37·195).

-wyrplic v. scort-w.
wyrpst, wyrpð pres. 2 and 3 sg. of weorpan and wyrpan.
wyrrest=wierrest; wyrs=wiers
wyrshrǣcung=wyrmshrǣcing
wyrsian (=ie) *to get 'worse,'* Æ,*VPs,W.*
wyrslic (=ie) *bad, vile, mean,* RD,W.
wyrsm-=wyrms-
wyrst=(1) wrist; (2) wierrest
wyrt (e, i) f. I. *herb, vegetable, plant, spice,* CP,*Lcd,LG,VPs;* AO : *crop* : *root.* ['*wort*']
   II. '*wort' (brewing),* Lcd.
wyrtbedd m. *bed of herbs,* Lcd.
+wyrtbox f. *fragrant herb or perfume box,* OEG 8²⁹⁹.
wyrtbrǣð m. *fragrance,* Æ.
wyrtcynn n. *species of plant,* JnL,WW.
wyrtcynren n. *the vegetable world,* LPs 146⁸.
wyrtdrenc m. *herbal drink, medicine, Cp.* [v. '*drench*']
wyrteceddrenc m. *herbal acid drink,* Lcd 63b.
wyrtfæt n. *scent-bottle,* OEG.
wyrtforbor n. *restraint from action by the operation of herbs* (BT), Lcd 111b.
wyrtgælstre f. *witch who works with herbs,* Lcd 3·186¹¹.
wyrtgeard m. *(kitchen) garden,* CPs 143¹³.
wyrt-gemang (Æ) n., -gemangnes (e³) f. *mixture of herbs, spices, perfume.*
wyrtgyrd=wyrtgeard
±wyrtian *to season, spice, perfume,* Lcd, WW.
wyrtig *garden-like? full of herbs?* ÆL 30³¹².
wyrtmete m. *dish of herbs, pottage,* WW.
wyrt-rum, wyrt-(t)ruma m., -rume f. *root, root-stock,* CP : *origin, beginning, stock.* [v. CC 68]
±wyr(t)trumian *to take root* : *establish* : *root out,* DR.
wyrttūn, ±wyrttūn (Æ) m. *garden.*
wyrttūnhege f. *garden enclosure,* GD 67¹⁸.
wyrtung f. *a preparation of herbs,* Lcd 1·342'.
wyrtwala (i, eo, u¹; æ, e²) m. *root, stock,* Lcd : *base, lower part,* KC.
wyrtwalian (æ²) *to set, plant, root* : *root up,* ÆGr.
wyrtwalu f.=wyrtwala
wyrtweard m. *gardener,* GD 23; Jn 20¹⁵.
wyrtwela=wyrtwala
wyrð=weorð
wyrðan *to irrigate with manure,* A 36·77.
+wyrðan I. (=ie) *to value, appraise.* II.= +weorðan
wyrðe=weorð
+wyrðe (=ie) n. *bulk, contents, amount,* Lcd.
wyrðeland=yrðland

wyrðig I. *fitting, deserved,* AO 256¹¹. II.= worðig
wyrðing m. *fallow land? cultivated land?* WW 495²⁰.
wyruld-=woruld-; wys-=wis(s)-
±wȳscan (ī) (w. d. pers. and g. thing) *to* 'WISH,' Æ,*CP;* AO : (+) *adopt,* ÆH.
+wȳscednes f. *adoption,* RBL 11¹⁴.
+wȳscendlic *desirable,* CM 109 : *optative (mood),* ÆGr : *adoptive.* adv. -līce.
+wȳscing (ī) f. *adoption,* RB 10².
wȳsdōm (Æ)=wīsdōm; wyt=wit pron.
wyt-, wȳt-=wit-, wīt-; wytt=wit pron.
wytuma m. *paranymph,* A 13·30⁸². [= witumbora? (BT)]
wyð-=wið-
wyxð pres. 3 sg. of weaxan.

Y

yb (AA)=ymb
ybilberende (OEG 53¹⁶)=yfelberende
ȳcan, ȳcean=īecan
yce (WW 468²²)=hice
ȳce (ī) fm. *toad, frog,* Lcd,WW.
ȳcte pret. 3 sg. of ȳcan.
ȳdæges=īdæges
ȳddisc n? *household stuff, furniture, possessions,* Æ. [ēad]
ȳde=ēode; ȳdel=īdel; ydes=ides
ȳdisc=ȳddisc; ȳdl-=īdl-; yel-=iel-
yfæsdrype=yfesdrype
yfel I. adj. gsm. yfel(e)s *bad, ill,* Bl,*Lcd,Mt* : '*evil,' wicked, wretched,* Bl,*CP,Mt.* comp. wiersa, wyrsa *worse.* superl. wierrest(a), wiersta, weorsta, wyr(re)sta *worst,* Æ,AO. II. n. '*evil,' ill, wickedness, misery,* B,*Bl, CP,OET,RB,Ps.*
yfelādl f. '*cachexia,' consumption,* WW 113¹³.
yfelberende (ybil-) *bringer of evil tidings,* OEG 53¹⁶ (v. ANS 85·310).
yfelcund *evil, malignant,* LPs.
yfelcwedolian (ð) *to speak evil,* ERPs 36²².
yfel-cweðende, -cweðelgiende (EPs) *evil-speaking,* SPs 36²³.
yfeldǣd f. *ill deed, injury,* Æ.
yfeldǣda m. *evildoer,* ÆL.
yfeldǣde *evil-doing,* Æ,Lcd,Gl.
yfeldēma m. *wicked judge,* NC 335.
yfeldōnd m. *evildoer,* JnL 18³⁰.
yfeldōnde *evil-doing,* LL (424²⁰).
yfeldysig '*stultomalus,'* WW 165¹⁸.
yfele=yfle
yfelful *malicious, wicked,* A 11·116¹³.
yfelgiornes f. *malice, wickedness,* DR.
±yfelian *to inflict evil, hurt, wrong, injure,* Ps : *become bad, grow worse, suffer,* W. ['*evil*']

yfelic, yfellic *evil, bad* : *poor, mean* : *foul, ugly.* adv. -līce.

yfellǣrrende *persuading to evil*, GPH390.

yfellibbende *evil-living*, RBL118¹⁰.

yfelnes f. *wickedness, depravity, Æ*; CP. ['*evilness*']

yfelsacend (eo¹, u²) m. *blasphemer*, GD289²⁷.

±yfelsacian *to blaspheme*, BL189; GD289²⁷.

yfelsacung f. *calumny, blasphemy, Æ,*BL.

yfelsǣc (eo¹, u²) n? *blasphemy*, EL524.

±yfelsian (ebol-) *to blaspheme*, NG,WW.

yfel-sprǣce, -sprecende *evil-speaking*, Ps.

yfelsung (ebol-, eoful-) f. *blasphemy*, LL.

yfeltihtend m. *inciter to evil, Æ*H.

yfeltihtende *inciting to evil, Æ*H.

yfelwille *malevolent*, Sc196¹⁸.

yfelwillende *vicious, Æ,*CP.

yfelwillendnes f. *malice*, LPs.

yfelwilnian *to desire evil*, LPs.

yfelwoerc n. *evil deed*, DR103¹.

yfelwyrcende *evil-doing, Æ*L.

yfelwyrde *evil-speaking*, ES39·354.

yfemest superl. adj. *highest, uppermost*, CP. [ufan]

ȳfer v. ȳfre.

yfera=yferra; yferdrype=yfesdrype +yferian *to exalt*, LPs.

yferra comp. adj. *after, subsequent* : *higher.* [ufan]

yfes f.=efes

yfesdrype (æ²) m. '*eaves-drop*,' EC141¹⁶.

ȳfig=īfig

yfle adv. (comp. wirs) *evilly, badly, ill, wrongly, miserably, hurtfully, Bl,G,Gen, Ps,Rd.* ['*evil*']

±yflian=yfelian

yflung f. *injury*, GD197¹².

yfmest=yfemest

ȳfre? ȳfer? *escarpment?* BC,KC (v. GBG).

ȳgett=iggað

ȳgland=īegland; ȳgðelīce=īeðelīce

ȳhte=īhte; ȳl=īl; ylca (Æ)=ilca

ylcian=elcian; yld=ield; yle=ile

ylf, ylfe=ælf

ylfet, ylfetu, ylfette (Æ)=ilfetu

ylfig *raving, mad*, WW. [v. '*giddy*']

ylful (HGL529)=ieldful

ylp m. *elephant*, WW; Æ. ['*elp*']

ylpen-=elpen(d)-; ylpesbān=elpendbān

yltsta=ieldesta wk. masc. superl. of eald.

yltwist f? *catching of birds*, WW351⁶.

ym-=ymb(e)-; ymb=ymbe

ymb-=imb-

ymbærnan *to travel round*, BH28⁸.

ymbbegang=ymbgang

ymbberan⁴ *to surround*, JUL,MkLR.

ymbbīgnes (bebīg-) f. *bending round, bend, circuit, sweep (of a river)*, BH424¹⁰. [bīegan]

ymbbindan³ *to bind round*, MkL9⁴².

ymbcæflan *to embroider round, bedeck*, RPs 44¹⁵.

ymbceorfan³ *to circumcise*, NG.

ymbceorfnes f. *circumcision*, JnR7²³ (-cernes).

ymbcerr (=ie) m. *turning about, going, migration*, NG : *tergiversation, trickery*, DR.

ymbcerran=ymbcyrran

ymbclyccan *to enclose*, RPs16¹⁰ (ES38·25).

ymbclyppan (i) *to embrace, clasp, Æ*GR.

ymbclypping f. *embracing*, OEG4529 (emc-).

ymbcyme m. *assembly, convention*, LL12 (ymc-).

ymbcyrran (e²; =ie) *to turn round, go round, make the circuit of* : *overturn, change*, NG.

ymbdringend=ymbhringend

ymbe (e¹, u¹) I. prep. w. a. d. and adv. (of place) *around, about, at, upon, near, along* : (of time) *about, at, after, before.* ymb utan *about, by, around* : (causal, etc.) *about, in regard to, concerning, on account of, owing to.* ðæs y. lītel *soon after.* y. bēon *to set about a thing.* ['EMBE,' '*UMBE*'] II. (=i) n. *swarm of bees*, LCD1·384'; Mdf.

ymbe-=ymb-

ymbeaht mp. '*collatio*,' WW; OEG53²² (v. ES11·492).

ymbeardian *to dwell round*, VPs30¹⁴.

ymbebǣtan *to curb, restrain*, MET24³⁷.

ymbebēgnes=ymbbīgnes

ymbeornan=ymbiernan

ymbesprǣc f. *talk, remark, criticism, Æ.*

ymbe-ðanc, -ðonc, -ðanca m. *thought, reflection*, CP.

ymbeðencan=ymbðencan

ymbeðridian *to think about*, NC335.

ymb-fær (embef-) n., -færeld (Æ) nm. *journey round, circuit.*

ymbfæstnes f. *enclosure*, DR174⁹.

ymbfæstnung f. *monument, tomb*, JnL19⁴¹.

ymbfæðmian *to embrace*, SOL150'.

ymbfaran⁶ *to surround*, AO80²⁶ : *travel round*, GD490³.

ymbfaru (emf-) n. *circuit*, HGL422¹⁴.

ymbfeng I. m. *envelope, cover*, OEG468. II. pres. 3 sg. of ymbfōn.

ymbfēran *to go about, journey round*, AA 30¹⁰; GPH396.

ymbfōn⁷ *to surround, encompass, embrace, grasp, seize*, AO.

ymbfrætewian *to decorate, deck round*, LPs, W.

ymb-gān anv., -gangan⁷ *to go round, surround.*

ymbgang (eo²) m. *going about, circuit, circumference, surrounding belt*, AO.

ymbgearwian *to clothe, dress*, NG.
ymbgedelf n. *digging round*, ÆH 2·408¹¹.
ymb-gefrætwian, -gefretwian (VPs)=ymbfrætewian
ymbgeong (N)=ymbgang
ymbgerēnian *to deck round*, BLPs 143¹⁵.
ymb-gesett, -geseten *neighbouring*, BH 2·362.
ymbgesettan=ymbsettan
ymbgirdan=ymbgyrdan
ymbgong=ymbgang
ymbgyrdan (i) *to gird about, encircle, surround*, Æ.
ymbhabban *to surround*, AO : *include, contain : detain*.
ymbhaga (=i¹) m. *enclosure for bees*, LCD 1·395⁴. [ymbe II.]
ymbhaldan=ymbhealdan
ymbhammen *surrounded, covered*, WW 340¹⁴.
ymbhangen pp. of ymbhōn.
ymbhealdan⁷ *to encompass*, SAT 7.
ymbhēapian *to crowd about*, WW.
ymbhēdig=ymbhȳdig
ymbhegian *to hedge round*, ÆGR.
ymbhēpan=ymbhȳpan
ymbhīwan (WW 381²)=ymbhȳpan
ymbhlennan (emb-) *to surround*, OEG 24.
ymbhoga m. *care, anxiety, solicitude, consideration*, *Mt*; CP. [v. '*embe*']
ymbhogian *to be anxious about*, LPs.
ymbhōn⁷ *to surround, deck, clothe*, HL,W.
ymb-hringan *to surround, fence round*, CP : *wind round*, WW.
ymbhringend m. *attendant member of a retinue*, GL.
ymbhūung=ymbhȳwung
ymbhwearft=ymbhwyrft
ymbhweorfan³ (e², u²) *to turn round, revolve : go round, encompass : tend, cultivate*, CP.
ymbhweorfnes f. *change, revolution*, DR 37¹⁸.
ymbhweorft (e²)=ymbhwyrft
ymbhwerf- (u², y²)=ymbhweorf-
ymbhwyrft (e, ea, eo, i) m. *rotation, revolution, turn : circle, extent, environment, circuit, orbit*, Æ,CP : *circle of the earth, orb, globe, world*, Æ,AO : *region, district : cultivation*, Æ.
ymb-hȳde, -hȳdi-=ymbhȳdig-
ymbhȳdig *anxious, solicitous, careful, suspicious : to be observed, needing attention*, Æ. adv. -līce.
ymbhȳdiglic *anxious, careful, solicitous*. adv. -līce.
ymbhȳdignes f. *anxiety, solicitude*, ÆH.
ymbhygd f. *anxiety*, BL,GD.
ymbhygdig=ymbhȳdig
ymbhȳpan *to press round, assail*, BH,WW.

ymbhȳwung (-hūung) f. *circumcision*, JnL 7²².
ymbiernan³ (io, y) *to run round : surround*, MH.
ymblǣdan *to lead round*, OET (VHy 7¹⁸).
ymblǣrgian (emb-) *to provide with a rim, surround*, OEG 8³⁷⁷. [lǣrig]
ymblicgan⁵ *to surround, enclose*, AO.
ymblīðan *to sail round*, BH 408²⁵.
ymblōcian *to look round*, NG.
ymbloflan *to praise*, LPs 116¹.
ymblyt m. *circle, circuit, circumference*, SAT 7?
Ymbren n. '*Ember-'tide, Ember-day*, *Lk,LL*. [ymbryne]
Ymbrendæg m. *Ember-day*, BF,W.
ymbrene=ymbryne
Ymbrenfæsten n. *periodical fast (at Ember-tide)*, *LL*; Æ. [v. '*ember*']
Ymbrenwuce (i³) f. *Ember-week*, *LL* 78,43. [v. '*ember*']
Ymbrigdæg=Ymbrendæg
ymbrine=ymbryne
ymbryne (e², i²) m. *revolution, circuit, course, anniversary*, Æ : *lapse of time*, Æ.
ymbscēawian *to look round*, NG.
ymbscēawiendlīce adv. *circumspectly*, BH 450²¹.
ymbscēawung f. *looking round*, DR.
ymbscīnan¹ *to shine round*, ÆH.
ymbscrīðan¹ *to revolve about*, MET 20²⁰⁸.
ymbscrȳdan *to clothe*, Æ. [scrūd]
ymbscūwan *to screen, defend ('obumbrare')*, EPs 139⁸.
ymbscȳnan=ymbscīnan
ymbsēan (N)=ymbsēon II.
ymbsellan *to surround, enclose, beset*, Æ : *endue, clothe*, VH 24.
ymbsēon I. sv⁵ *to look round*. II. f. *beholding, regard*.
ymb-set, -setl n. *siege*, BH.
ymbsetennes f. *siege*, Ps.
ymbsetnung f. *sedition*, LkL : *siege*, GL.
ymbsett *neighbouring*, BH 362.
ymbsettan *to set round, surround, beset, encompass*, Æ : *plant*.
ymbsewen *circumspect*, GD 107¹¹.
ymb-sierwan, -sirwan pres. 3 sg. -sireð *to design, plot*, CP : *lay in wait for*.
ymbsittan⁵ *to set round, surround, invest, besiege*, Æ,AO,CP : *sit over, reflect upon*.
ymbsittend† m. *one living near, neighbour*.
ymbsmēagung (embe-) f. *consideration*, WW 165²⁸.
ymbsnāð, ymbsniden, pret. 3 sg. and pp. of ymbsnīðan.
ymbsnidennes f. *circumcision*, Æ.
ymbsnīðan¹ (em-) *to circumcise*, *Lk*; Æ. [v. '*embe*']

ymbspænning f. *allurement*, CHRD 66³³.
ymbspannan⁷ *to span or clasp round, embrace*, BH 392⁶.
ymbsprǣc f. *conversation, comment, criticism*, Æ.
ymbsprǣce *spoken about, well known*, MET 10⁵⁹.
ymbsprecan³ *to speak about*, Lk 19⁷.
ymbstandan⁶ *to stand around, surround*, Bo, BH.
ymbstandend m. *bystander*, Æ (emb-).
ymbstand(en)nes f. '*circumstantia*,' Pss.
ymbstocc (=i¹) m. *stump containing a swarm of bees*, KC 5·234.
ymbstrīcan *to smooth round*, LCD 36b.
ymbstyrian *to stir about, overturn*, LkL 15⁸.
ymbswǣpe f. *digression*, WW 5²⁸.
ymbswāpan⁷ *to sweep round, environ* : *envelop, clothe*.
ymbswāpe=ymbswǣpe
ymbswīfan¹ *to revolve round*, NC 352.
ymbsyllan=ymbsellan
ymbsyrwan=ymbsierwan
ymb-trymian, -trymman (Æ,CP) *to surround* : *fortify, protect*.
ymbtrymming m. *fortification*, Æ.
ymbtȳnan *to hedge round, surround*, MtR 21³³,W 146²⁷. [tūn]
ymbtyrnan *to turn round*, LCD : *surround*, WW.
ymbðeahtian *to consider, reflect*, CP.
ymbðencan *to think about, consider*, CP.
ymbðonc=ymbeðanc
ymbðreodian (embōryd-) *to deliberate*, GL.
ymbðreodung (i, y) f. *deliberation, consideration*, GL.
ymbðringan³ *to press round, throng about*, Ps,WW.
ymbðringend=ymbhringend
ymbðrydung=ymbðreodung
ymbūtan (e¹) prep. (w. a.) and adv. *around, about, outside, beyond, Mk*; AO,CP. [v. '*embe*']
ymbwǣfan *to clothe*, LPs 44¹⁵.
ymbwǣrian *to turn (oneself) about, turn towards*, NG.
ymbweaxan⁶ *to grow round, surround*, AO.
ymbwendan *to turn round* : *turn away, avert*.
ymbwendung f. *reviving* : *behaviour*, DR.
ymbweorpan³ *to surround*, AN 1555.
ymbwīcigan *to surround, beleaguer*, Ex 65.
ymbwindan³ *to clasp round, hold* : *wind round*.
ymbwlātian *to contemplate*, Æ 145¹².
ymbwlātung f. *contemplation*, ÆGR.
ymbwrītan¹ *to score round*, LCD 124a.
ymbwyrcan *to hedge in*, CP : *weave*, MtL 27²⁹.

ymbyrnan=ymbiernan
ymcyme=ymbcyme
ymel (æ, e) m. *weevil, mite, beetle, caterpillar*, ÆGR; GD.
ymele, ymle f. *scroll*, ÆL,WW.
ymen m. '*hymn*,' *sacred song, Bl,Ps*. [L. hymnus]
ymenbōc f. '*hymn-book*,' BH 484²³.
ymener (BC 3·660')=ymnere
ymensang m. *hymn*, GD,AJPs.
ymesēne *blind*, ÆH 1·418'.
ymest=yfemest; ymle (Æ)=ymele
ymmon, ymn=ymen
ymnere III. *hymn-book*, BC,KC 4·275'. ['*hymner*'; L. hymnarium]
ymnyttan=emnettan; ȳmon=ȳmen
ymryne=ymbryne; yn-=in-
ynce m. '*inch*,' LL,Sol. [L. uncia]
yndse f. *ounce*, AO : *piece of money, shekel*. [L. uncia]
yngrian=hyngrian; ynn-=inn-
ynnelēac (ene-, yne-, ynni-) n. *onion*, GL.
ynse, yntse (Æ)=yndse
yplen (WW)=ypplen
±yppan *to bring out, open, manifest, disclose, display, reveal, betray, BH,CP,WW* : *come forth, be disclosed* : (+) *utter*. ['*uppe*']
yppe I. (u) f. *upper room* : *raised place, high seat, tribune* : *stage, platform*, WW 150⁹.
II. *evident, known, open, manifest*.
ypping f. *manifestation* : *accumulation, extent, expanse?* Ex 498.
yppingīren (ip-) n. *crowbar?* LL 455,15 (or ? cippingīren ANS 115·164).
ypplen II. *top, height*, OEG 2862.
ypte pret. 3 sg. of yppan.
ȳr I.† m. *name of the rune for* y : *bow?* : *gold? horn?* RUN 27. II. n? *back of axe*, CHR,LCD.
yrcðu=iergðu; yrd=eard; yrd-=yrð-
ȳre I. m. *a coin of Danish origin*, BC 3·371². II.=ȳr
ȳren=īren
yreðweorh (JUL 90?)=ierreðweorh
yrf- v. also ierf-.
yrfan *to inherit* : *leave (by will)* : *honour with a funeral feast* (BTac), TC 611⁵.
yrfcwealm (a²) m.*murrain*, CHR 986 CE. [orf]
yrfebēc fp. *will, testament*, WW.
yrfecwealm=yrfcwealm
yrfeflit n. *dispute about an inheritance*, EC 145¹⁶.
yrfefyrst m. *legal formality or delay before entering on an inheritance*, WW 115³.
yrfegedāl n. *division of an inheritance*, Æ.
yrfegewrit (e¹) n. *will, testament, charter*, EC 145.
yrfehand (e¹) f. *natural successor*, EC 111¹⁴.
yrfelāf f. *bequest, inheritance* : *heir*, Ex 403.

yrfeland (ie) n. *inherited land*, CP.
yrfelēas (ie) *unprovided with cattle*, TC162'.
yrfe-numa, -nama (RWH53²⁰) mf. *heir, successor, Æ.*
yrfestōl† m. *hereditary seat, home.*
yrfeweard (ie) m. *heir, son*, AO,CP.
±yrfeweardian *to inherit*, CLSPs.
yrfeweardnes (ie) f. *heritage*, CP.
yrfeweardwrītere, yrfewrītend m. *will writer, testator, Æ.*
yrfweard-=yrfeweard-; +yrgan=eargian
yrgð, yrgðo, yrhðu=iergðu
yrm-=eorm-, ierm-; yrnan=iernan
yrre=ierre; yrs-=iers-
yrsebin f. *iron box*, LL455,17 (?=īsern, BT).
yrð (ea;=ie) f. *ploughing, tilling, LL : standing corn, crop, produce, BH.* ['*earth*']
yrðland (æ, ie) n. *arable land, KC,WW*; Æ. ['*earthland*']
yrðling (æ, e, eo, i) m. *husbandman, farmer, ploughman, WW*; Æ : *wagtail?* ANS 119·434. ['*earthling*']
yrðmearc f. *boundary of ploughed land*, KC.
yrðtilia=eorðtilia; ys=is, v. wesan.
ȳs=īs; ysel=esol; ysele=ysle
ȳsen, ȳsern=īsen, īsern
ysl, ysle f. *spark, ember, Æ.* ['*isel*']
yslende *glowing*, WW235²⁸.
ysope f., ysopo (indecl.) '*hyssop,*' *Æ,Lcd, VPs.*
ȳst f. *storm, tempest, hurricane*, AO,CP.
ȳstan *to storm, rage*, OEG.
ȳstas=ēstas np. of ēst.
ȳstig *stormy, of the storm*, LcD,PPs.
yt=itt pres. 3 sg. of etan.
ȳtan I. *to drive out, banish*, CHR1058D : *squander, dissipate*, RB55⁴. [ūt] II.= ūtan
Ytas=Iotas

ȳtemest superl. adj. *uttermost, extreme, last, Bo,DR,LG,VPs*; AO,CP. on ȳtemestum sīðe '*in extremis.*' ['*utmost*']
ȳtend m. *devastator*, WW232³⁷.
yteren *made of otter-skin*, AO18²¹. [otor]
ȳterra=ūterra
yteð=iteð pres. 3 sg. of etan.
ȳting f. *outing, journey, Æ,RB.*
ȳt-mest, -mæst=ȳtemest
ytst, ytt=itst pres. 2 sg., itt pres. 3 sg. of etan.
ȳttera, ȳttra=ūter(r)a
ȳð I. f. *wave, billow, flood, An,B*; Æ,CP : (†) *sea : liquid, water.* ['*ythe*'] II.=īeð
ȳð-=ēað-, īeð-
ȳðan=(1) īeðan; (2) ȳðgian
ȳðbord n. *ship? ship's side?* CRA57.
ȳðeg=ȳðig; ȳðegan=ȳðgian
ȳðfaru† f. *wave-course, flood.*
ȳðgebland† n. *wave-mixture, surge*, B.
ȳðgewinn† n. *wave-strife, life in the waves*, B.
ȳðgian *to fluctuate, flow, surge*, CP : *roar, rage.*
ȳðgung=ȳðung
ȳðhengest m. (*wave-horse*), *ship*, CHR1003E.
ȳðhof† n. *water-dwelling, ship.*
ȳðian (Æ)=ȳðgian
ȳðig *billowy, stormy*, ÆL16⁷⁰.
ȳðlād f. *sea-voyage*, B228.
ȳðlāf† f. *sand, shore, beach.*
ȳðlidt† n. *ship, vessel*, AN.
ȳðlida m. *wave-traverser, ship*, B198.
ȳðmearh† m. *sea-horse, ship.*
ȳðmere m. *ocean of waves*, PH94.
ȳðung f. *agitation, commotion, Æ* : *inundation, Æ.*
ȳðwōrigende *wandering on the waves*, WW 243³.
ȳwan, ȳwian=īewan

SUPPLEMENT

ADDITIONAL SIGN AND ABBREVIATIONS

: After an entry the colon indicates that the word is already in the main part of the dictionary and that a meaning given after the colon is believed to take precedence over the one given in the main part.

AHD   Die althochdeutschen Glossen, ed. E. Sievers and E. Steinmeyer, Bd. 1–4, Berlin, 1879–98.

AJP   American Journal of Philology.

ASPR   The Anglo-Saxon Poetic Records, 6 vols., ed. G. Krapp and E. Dobbie, New York, 1931–53.

BHW   The Homilies of Wulfstan, ed. D. Bethurum, Oxford, 1957.

BPG   The Old English Prudentius Glosses at Boulogne-sur-Mer, ed. H. Meritt, Stanford, 1959 (Stanford Studies in Language and Literature, 16).

CGL   Corpus Glossariorum Latinorum, 7 vols., ed. G. Goetz, Leipzig, 1888–1923.

CPC   The Peterborough Chronicle, ed. C. Clark, Oxford, 1958.

EGS   English and Germanic Studies.

EI   The Old English Exodus, ed. E. Irving, New Haven, 1953.

FF   Der Flussname Themse und seine Sippe, by Max Förster, Sitzungsberichte der Bayerischen Akademie der Wissenschaften, phil.-hist. Abt., Bd. 1, München, 1941.

FGR   Zur Geschichte des Reliquienkultus in Altengland, by Max Förster, Sitzungsberichte der Bayerischen Akademie der Wissenschaften, phil.-hist. Abt., Hft. 8, München, 1943.

FL   Fact and Lore about Old English Words, by H. Meritt, Stanford, 1954.

GAT   The Old English Apollonius of Tyre, ed. P. Goolden, Oxford, 1958.

GLL   Lehnbildungen und Lehnbedeutungen im Altenglischen, by H. Gneuss, Berlin, 1955.

HAW   Anglo-Saxon Writs, by F. Harmer, Manchester, 1952.

HBK   Kommentar zum Beowulf, by J. Hoops, Heidelberg, 1932.

HBS   Beowulfstudien, by J. Hoops, Anglistische Forschungen 74, Heidelberg, 1932.

HEW   Altenglisches Etymologisches Wörterbuch, by F. Holthausen, Heidelberg, 1934.

HSC   Studien zum altenglischen Computus, H. Henel, Beiträge zur Englischen Philologie 36, Leipzig, 1934.

JEGP-   Old English Glosses, Mostly Dry Point, by H. Meritt, to appear in JEGP.

JM   The Jespersen Miscellany, London, 1930.

JW   Wulfstanstudien, by K. Jost, Schweizer Anglistische Arbeiten, Bd. 23.

KCM   Catalogue of Manuscripts Containing Anglo-Saxon, by N. Ker, Oxford, 1957.

KF   One leaf of a Latin-Old English Glossary, now at the University of Kansas (see KCM 240).

KN   Untersuchungen einiger altenglischen Krankheitsnamen, by J. Geldner, Braunschweig, 1906.

KW   Die Wunder des Ostens, ed. F. Knappe, Berlin, 1906.

LCG   The Corpus Glossary, ed W. Lindsay, Cambridge, 1921.

MÆ   Medium Ævum.

MAG   The Battle of Maldon, ed. E. Gordon, London, 1937.

MNG   Notes on Some Old English Glosses in Aldhelm's De Laudibus Virginitatis, by T. Mustanoja. Bulletin de la Société Néophilologique de Helsinki, 51, 49–61 (1950).

SUPPLEMENTARY ABBREVIATIONS

MPS   The Poetical Dialogues of Solomon and Saturn, ed. R. Menner, New York, 1941 (MLA Monograph 13).

OEGC   Old English Glosses, A Collection, ed. H. Meritt, New York, 1945 (MLA General Series 16).

PM   Medicine in Anglo-Saxon Times, by J. Payne, Oxford, 1904.

RAC   Anglo-Saxon Charters, ed. A. Robertson, Cambridge, 1956.

RES   Review of English Studies.

SFF   Seasons for Fasting, ed. in ASPR 6, 98–104.

SHS   The Hymns in SPS.

SK   Lexicographical notes kindly sent to me by Sherman Kuhn.

SN   Studia Neophilologica.

SPS   The Salisbury Psalter, ed. C. and K. Sisam, EETS 242 (London, 1959).

TLG   The Later Genesis, ed. B. Timmer, Oxford, 1948.

VHF   Die Vercelli Homilien, 1 Hälfte, ed. Max Förster, Bibliothek d. ags. Prosa, Bd. 12 (Hamburg, 1932).

VLC   The Life of Saint Chad, ed. R. Vleeskruyer, Amsterdam, 1953.

VM   The Vercelli Manuscript (photostat reproduction), Rome, 1913.

WB   Beowulf, ed. C. Wrenn, revised ed. London, 1958.

YWES   The Year's Work in English Studies.

ADDITIONS TO DICTIONARY

abal *strength*, TLG 32, 499; v. afol
ābetēon *to accuse*, OEGC 4, 368
āblāwung: add *swelling*, LCD 18 a
āblegned: add LCD 3, 42, 25
ācǣglod: *locked with a key*, FL 2, A 1
accent m. *accent*, A 8, 333, 23
ācdrenc: lemma cirta = tiriaca, to which the part ac belongs?
āchangra m. *oak wood on a slope* (BTs)
ācholt m. *an oak wood* (BTs)
ācursian *to malign*, SPS 36, 8
ādihtian *to compose*, ASPR 6, 202, nn. 3–4
ādlberende *disease-bearing*, OEGC 8, 19
ādloma: = āðloga, FL 2, A 2
ādwollan *to degenerate*, OEGC 28, 234
æbbung: delete *gulf, bay*, FL 3, H 40
æcersplott m. *an acre* (BTs)
æcerweg m. *a field-road* (BTs)
āecgan? *to set on edge*, OEGC 30, 99, n.
ǣcin *a kind of law?*; lemma tabetum for tabletum? *a tablet of the law*, WW 279, 1 (printed wrongly cecin)
ǣfrelīce *in perpetuity*, ANS 111, 276
æfterfylgung: add *sect*, FL 2, B 20
æftergancnes,
   -gegencednes = æftergengnes, ÆL, 10, 219, v.l.
æfteronfōnd *one about to receive*, FL 3, A 1
ǣgmore: = angnere?
ǣgnian: = ængian, *to oppress?* (EI 265, n.)
± ǣlan: add [āl]

ǣlepe: delete, FL 2, B 2
ǣlere *fleabane?* FL 2, B 2
ælfisc? *elfish*, ES 38, 300; AHD 2, 162, 8
ælfsogoða: add *jaundice?*, KN 14
ǣlifn: *alum*, CGL 5, 343, 3 (Ep. Gl.); v. HEW s.v. ælefne
ǣmetla m. *one at leisure*, ASPR 3, 308, 183
ǣmynd: v. ANS 171, 22; HEW enters ǣmynde, *forgetfulness*
ǣmyrce: literally *not murky*, FL 3, D 1
ǣnetlīf n. *solitary life*, OEGC 9, 4; 10, 2
ǣrādl *early illness*, ASPR 3, 305, 31
ǣrǣt: *overeating*, HBS 20; for defence of *too early eating*, v. A 66, 17, n. 1
ǣreldo: delete, FL 3, A 2
ǣrglæd: *very kind?*, HBS 23
ǣrgōd: *very good*, HBS 20
ǣristhyht *hope of resurrection*, BH 220, 28
ǣrlēof: delete, FL 2, B 3
ǣrlyft: delete, FL 2, B 4
ærnignweg = ærneweg, BHB 398, 30
ǣsmæl: *contraction of the pupil*, LCD 2, 338, 1
æstel: *bookmark*, FGR 11, n. 3
æthȳd: delete, FL 3, I 1
ætrihte II: add ætrihtes, VHF 2, n. 3 a
ætstandan: add *to blight* (*crops*), CPC 1086, 20
āettan: delete, FL 2, B 59
ætwenian: add OEGC 28, 44 n.
ǣwiscberend: *middle finger* (lemma impudicus from Isid. *Etym.* 11, 1, 71)

æwul: delete, FL2, A11
æxfaru:=æscfaru, *military expedition*, FL 4, B1
Africanisc *African*, WW445, 39
āgan: add+(BTs)
āgānian *to gape*, GD216, 17
agen *ear of grain*, ANS117, 21
āgenland *land held in absolute possession?*, RAC p. 415
āgnian: delete *to enslave*; v. āgnian=ængian
āgniden: delete first entry; the word is a ptc.; v. LCG, D78
āheordan? *to set free (from captivity)*, WB2930 n.
āhīðend *a ravager*, WW412, 19
āhwettan *to drive away with a curse*, TLG31, 406
āhwilc: delete, FL2, A3
ahwlic *terrible*, FL2, A3
alb: read albe
aldgeddung *an old saying*, FL4, B2
alefne *alum*, WW134, 38; 146, 21; ms. efne to which should be added the al of lemma alumen; v. ælifn
ālendan *to lease*, RAC142, 24
Alexandrinesc *Alexandrian*, Mt p. 8, 13
allefne adj. or adv. *quite equal* or *universally*, RES8, 162
Alleluia m. *the Alleluia*, HSC40, n. 9
ālȳfednes? *granting*, FL3, H10
āmānsumung: add *Hermon*, KCM319a
amerian: delete, BPG580 note
āmerian: add BPG580
anbesettan *to inflict*, BPG608
anbeweorpan *to cast into*, BPG1000
anburge *sureties*, RAC p. 344
āncor: read ancor, HEW
andbicnian: add context of lcmma concerns dogs harassing a cat
andēages: delete, HBK
andfenge: add *receptacle*, OEG105
andfylstan *to aid*, SPS43, 26
andlang: add B2695, *by his side?* (ASPR4, 255) *related?* (HBK)
andrecefæt: delete, FL3, H4
āndrencefæt *a cup emptied at one swallow*, FL3, H4
andwliteful: *with grim look*, BPG382
ānhealfrūh *having one side rough*, FL3, H24
ānrǣde=ānrǣd, BTs
anspel: delete, FL3, A3
anstīg: v. FL3, I2
anstōr *incense*, GLL68
āntīd: v. HBK
anung:=andung? (FL2, A4)
ānwald *monarchy*, WW440, 25 (GLL40)
ānwalda? *lone ruler*, VHF112, n. 26
Arabisc *Arabian*, ÆGR65, 12

ārǣfsan *to intercept*, KF
ārfæst(i)an *to show mercy*, SPS102, 3
Arrianisc *Arian*, GD240, 8
arscamu: delete, ASPR5, 212
āscrīfan *to describe*, OEGC4, 255
āscyled *made manifest*, OEGC2, 212
āsēcendlic *to be sought*, LPs110, 2
āslīding: *a slip of the tongue*, BPG51
assedun *dun-coloured like an ass*, WW163, 16
Assirisc *Assyrian*, OEG26, 20
āstrīcan *to strike severely*, VHF4, 38
āstrogdnis *sprinkling*, GLL69; or āstregdnes, q.v.
āstrowenes: *spread?*, FL3, A4
āsyngian *to sin*, GLL73
ātendnes *incentive*, A65, 230
Athēnisc *Athenian* (BTs)
ātordrinca: delete; the part drincan is a verb at MH94, 20
ātorgeblǣd: add *abscess*, BTs
ātwiccian *to excerpt*, OEGC4, 222
āðȳtan: delete entry II; aðytið=aytið; v. OEG4080
āwǣgnian *to fail to perform, annul*, HAW458, 9
āwārnian: for ās-warnian read ā-swārnian
āwesnis *essence*, OEGC72, 1
āwilnian *to wish for*, VM67a, 15
āyttan: delete (FL2, B59)

bædan: add a query; v. FL5, A1
+bælcan: delete, FL6, A2
+bēran: for meaning exultare v. JEGP49, 298
bēerfōt: add W181, 1
bancoða: read bāncoða, *bone disease*, LCD2, 102, 16
bānloca: *muscle*, HBK p. 94
Barda m. *the Apennines*, AO186, 33; v. FL4, C1
bēag: add *treasured things*, B2635 (HBS p. 75); *a treasured thing (sword)*, B2041 (WB)
bēaghyrne: delete, FL3, H5
bēagian: only+, not±, GLL222
bealuhycgende: v. OEGC61, 52
bēansǣd: add RAC252, 15
bebbisc=hehbiscop?, FL2, A6
bebyrwan: delete, FL2, A7
becierran: add *to change*, VHF151, n. 11
bedbǣr: v. OEGC51, 5 n.
+bedgiht: *time for going to prayer*, FL4, D13
begǣn *to affirm*, CR1307 (ANS166, 82)
begietend: add VHF57, 47
begroren:=begnornende? (ASPR1, 232)
behleonian *to lean (something) against*, VHF42, n. 197
bellringestre f. *bellringer*, A76, 502

bemîðan: add WW218, 21 (FL2, B6)

bēn: add *favour*, B428 (ASPR4, 138)

bēogang: *flight of bees*, FL2, A8

bēolǣs *pasture with flowers for bees?* (BTs s.v. læs)

bēotung: add+, WW408, 35

+berbed: = +byrded, *bordered*, FL2, A26

berigeblæ *an instrument for forking barley?*, WW411, 25

besceadwung f. *overshadowing, Selmo,* LPs67, 15

bescēawodnes: add, interprets *Sion*

bescîrung glosses exordinatio, JEGP- v. unhâdung

besparrian: add OEGC48, 1

beswicfalle: two words, not a cpd., JEGP46, 415

besylcan *to exhaust*, EL697

betellan: add *to prove one's claim to*, HAW481, 31

betweohceorfan glosses intercidere, GLL 209

beðrāwan: add *(in making candles)*; v. BPG242

bid: read bid and add on bid wrecen, *brought to bay*, B2962

bīegan: add+, BTs

+bīgnes: = begegnes, FL2, A27

bigstandan *to stand by, help*, VHF35, n. 156

+bind: add *constipation*, WW232, 33

bisceopēðel *episcopal see*, BHB262, 11

bisceophādöenung f. *episcopal service*, BHB232, 16

bisceophālgung f. *consecration of a bishop*, BHB72, 16

bisceopwyrtil: add *betony*, A41, 139

biscopstæf *bishop's staff*, FGR76, 162

biterlic *sad, bitter*, ÆL23, 250

bitrum adv. *bitterly*, EL1244n. (ed. Gradon)

bizant m. *a coin*, BPG548

+blǣcan: add *to make pale*, FL6, A2

blǣce: add *psoriasis*, PM48, 134

blǣcern: *lantern*

bledu: v. heolorbledu

+blîðian: add+, SPS91, 5

blōdiorn *bloody flux*, MkL p. 3, 7

blōdorc *sacrificial vessel*, BPG673

blōdspîwung *spitting of blood*, OEGC73b, 24

blōdwracu f. *revenge for bloodshed*, VHF28, n. 123

bōccynn n. *a kind of book*, SOLK192, 8

bōcholt *a beechwood* (BTs)

bogefōdder: *case for the bow*, FL3, H6

bōhtimber: v. HEW

bōl *necklace*, LCG, M302 (HEW)

bordstæð: *the rigging of a ship*, ASPR2, 110, 442

borgwedd: prob. not a cpd.

brādian: add *to become broad*, W262, 7d

brādsweord *broadsword*, Jud. 317 (ASPR4, 289)

bræcdrenc: add+, and read WW351, 28

brǣdîsen: delete, FL3, D2

brand: add brand Healfdenes, *Hrothgar,* B1020 (WB)

breahtmung: *flickering (of the eyelids),* FL3, A5

brēdîsern: delete

bredîsern *tablet knife, writing instrument,* FL3, D2

+bregd: add *fabric*, BPG852

+bregdstafas: *cunning skill in letters*, MPS

brēmelðȳfel m. *a bramble-thicket* (BTs)

brēmelwudu *a bramble-wood* (BTs)

breneð: 3 sg. of brȳnan, *to make brown?* (ASPR6, 157, 43)

brēosa: a ghostword that came to life; v. MLN51, 331

brēostgyrd: delete?; v. prēostgyrd

brīdelgym *a bridle ornament*, OEGC28, 456

brimsa?: v. MLN51, 331

broht: = broð, FL2, A10

broðhund: = roðhund, FL4, A2

brūmiddel *intercilium*, KF

brūneða: read bruneða, HEW

brȳdan = bregdan, ÆGR176, 3d

+bryddan: v. MPS16 n.

bryrdnes: add+, *compunction*, GLL50

brȳtofta: delete; fol. 18r of Additional MS. 32, 246 reads brytgifta

bryðen: add WC p. 54, 10

bucheort *a tragelaph*, FL2, B29

buclic *like a goat* (gloss to tragicus) OEGC 28, 55

buf the interjection *buff*, FL4, E1 n.

būl: delete I after būla

būla: add DR4, 3; OEG8, 319

Bulgarisc *Bulgarian*, GD300, 21

burgende? *city boundary*, EL31 (ed. Gradon)

buterstoppa: add *churn?*

bȳl: delete the queries; add Mod. Eng. *bile* (HEW)

bylda: *builder* at CRA75

+byrd: to *fate* add MPS376 n.

byrdicge: prob. from same original gloss as byrding

byrdling: *offspring*, FL3, A7

byre: delete *storm*, BPG873

+byrgen: *grave*, WW277, 7 (FL2, A28)

byrst: add *a crash*, WW215, 27

byrstende: ptc. of berstan (BTs)

byrðincel n. *a little burden*, OEGC2, 193

cærswill m. *a spring where cress grows* (BTs)

caflwyrt: delete, FL2, A54

Caldisc *Chaldean*, OEGC28, 118

camp *a fetter*, PPs149, 8

cān: delete, ASPR5, 216, 79

Cananisc *of Canaan*, MkR3, 18

Cappadonisc *Cappadocian*, OEG2302

Carles wǣn *Charles' Wain*, LCD3, 270, 11

casebill: delete; v. cēasbill

cēacbora: *jugbearer?*; v. LCG A659 n.

cēacfull *a jugful*, LCD70b

cealccrundel *a chalk ravine* (BTs)

cealfwyrt: delete, FL2, A54

cēaptoln f. *toll on buying and selling*, HAW p. 78

cēasbill *a club associated with philosophical dispute*, BPG438 n.

ceasterwyrhta *city builder* (a mistaken glossing of polimitarium) WW469, 21

cecil:=cēcel; v. LCG S698 n.

cecin: delete; ms. æcin; v. ǣcin

cellod: cf. scutum cælatum?

cenep: add BPG947 n.; and to meaning *bit* add (*bristling with points*)

cenningstān: delete, FL4, A3

ceorcing: delete, BPG745 n.; v. ceorung

ceorung: add BPG745

ceoselstān: add *stone* (*disease*), WW113, 18; the lemma comes from Isid. *Etym.* 4, 7, 32

cicropisc: *Cecropean*; v. Isid. *Etym.* 9, 3, 16

+**cīd**: read ± cīd (v. gecīd in BTs)

cildild f. *childhood*, BF12, 7

Cillinesc *Cyllenian*, WW379, 4

cine I: read cīne (HEW)

cintōō: delete *front tooth* and add WW85, 10

circwyrhta m. *church-builder*, HAW p. 510

cist: delete *horn*, FL4, D5

clangettung *clangour*, MLN67, 554

clēot *a cleat*, LCG P411 (v. HEW)

clericmann m. *a clerk* (BTs)

clifhlēp: delete the query, FL4, A5

±**clifian**: add BPG982 n.

clifwyrt: *burdock?* (it is a glossary variant of clate)

clynian: delete entry I, BPG982

cnēorift: delete *kneehose*, FL4, D2

cnēosār *pain in the knee*, OEGC73c, 12

cocer: delete *spear*, NP1, 209

+**cōcnian**: add WW372, 12 (misprinted gerecanade)

cocrōd f. *a clearing for netting woodcocks* (BTs)

Cōferflōd *the river Chebar*, MPS20 n.

coltemǣre *boiled wine*, MNG54

cōlcwyld: delete, FL3, J3

+**collenferhtan**: *to enhearten*, FL6, A3

corcīō: delete; v. corncīō

+**corded**: delete the query, FL3, H18

corncīō *growth of grain*, FL2, A12; note also corwurm=cornwurm, OEG1064

cornwurma: add OEGC51, 7

corporale *a cloth for covering the Host*, FGR90

corōr *a whisk?*, LCG V93 (v. HEW)

costere: delete *spade, shovel*, FL2, B10; v. fostere

+**cow**: v. VHF97, n. 148

cræftbōc f. *commentary*, OEGC30, 88

crammingpohha: *a bag crammed with ill-gotten gains?*, FL4, A6

cranc *chronicle*, RAC250, 16

credic?:=cremdisc?, *a cream dish*, FL3, C1

crinc: read cinc? *derision*, FL4, D3

crismclāō *chrism-cloth, headband*, FGR90

crismsmyrels *anointment with holy oil*, FGR90

crīst: read crist, Förster, *Alteng. Lesebuch* 45

crompeht: add OEGC19, 1

+**crōwed**=+crōged, OEGC27, 21

cursian: delete *to plait*, FL2, A14; JEGP-

cūself: delete, BPG280 n.

cūter *chewing gum*, FL4, B4

cwecesand: read cwece sund, *lively strait of water?*, FL2, A15

cwedelian=wyrgcwedolian, GLL122

cwelderǣde: v. OEGC36, 10 n.

cwiccliende: for twincliende?, FL4, D4

Cwicelmingas *descendants of Cwicelm*, ÆGR15, 3

cynehelm: on the meaning *royal power* v. HAW477, n. to l. 24; add *garland*, GAT 26, 8 n.

cynesetl: add WW71, 6

cynestrǣt: for 71, 6 read 467, 7

cynewāōen: delete, WC14, 16n.

cyninge f. *a queen*, BL13, 1

cyningstān *an instrument used in casting dice*, WW150, 24 (FL4, A3)

cyningwīc *stately dwelling*, GnE107 (ASPR 3, 307, n. to 108)

cynling *clan*, ANS111, 276

+**cyrtan**: *to lop off*, BPG919

cyst: for meaning *picked host, company*, add EI229 n.; v. ciest in HEW

cytwer: *a basket-weir*; v. cietwer in HEW

dæg: add ǣr dæge ond æfter dæge, *in perpetuity*, HAW479, l. 10

dægmǣlspilu: delete; Additional MS. 32, 246, fol. 7r dægmeles-; add dægmǣles pil and dægmǣles pinn, ÆGR321, 6

dægword? *Chronicles*, Ex519 (ASPR1, 216, 519 n.)

dǣlnymendlic *participial*, ÆGR134, 20

+**dafenes** glosses oportuno at SPS144, 15

+**dāl**: add ± (BTs)

dalc: add Jos7, 21

dalisc: lemma dedalei taken as de dalei, FL3, K1

dalmatice: omit the query

daroðæsc? *spear*, EL140 (ASPR2, 134, n. to 140)

dað: delete, FL2, A16

dēagwyrmede: for assoc. with *gout* v. FL4, D6

dēawdrīas: delete, ASPR1, 224, 276

dēawwyrm: add *itch-mite*, *foot-worm*, PM44

delfīn: delete, FL2, B12

dengan: add CP461, 16 (FL3, F2)

dennian: v. ASPR6, 147, 12

dēog: v. WB850 n.

dēopðancenlīce = dēopðancollīce, RWH42, 3

+**deorflēas**: for GL read BPG1017 n.

dēð: delete entry II, FL6, A1

dīcsticce *stick supporting a dike*, FF772, n. 1

dīerlingðegn *favourite follower*, A73, 19

docga: add (*referring to cruel persons*), FL3, J4

dolhsmeltas: = dolhsweðlas?, FL2, A17

dōmesdæg = dōmdæg, VM3b 15; 114a 18

doxian: v. VHF100, n. 165

dracu f. *affliction*, W91, 7e

dragan: add *to suffer*, MLR27, 452

droht: *a pull at the oars*, WW486, 27; context of lemma remorum tractibus

dropa: delete the query (HEW)

+**dropa**: for assoc. with drop v. FL3, A13

dryhtdōm: delete; part dryht repeated from preceding dryhten, SK

dryncelēan: *entertainment given by the lord of the manor*, ANS127, 196

dryslic: read ondryslic, FL2, B41

dūstswerm: add *atoms*, FL4, A7

+**dwildæfterfolgung**: delete, FL2, B20

dwoligendlic *heretical*, GD239, 21, o

+**dyhtedum** adv. *splendidly*, OEGC62, 17

dȳst, **dȳð** = dēst, dēð, ÆGr3, 24d; 210, 1d; 212, 5d

ēabrycg f. *bridge over a river*, ÆL27, 53

ēad-: for eað- read ēað-

ēaganbyrhtm m. *a flash of the eye, moment*, VHF78, n. 41

ēaghyll: *the hairless prominence between and above the inner corners of the eyes*; lemma glebenus from glaber

ēaland: *maritime land* also at OEGC4, 199

ēalandcyning m. *island king*, BHB308, 8

ealdgeðungen *old and distinguished*, W99, 15

ealdhryðerflǣsc *meat that has been stored away*, WW127, 33; v. succidia at Isid. *Etym.* 20, 2, 24

ealdorlēas: *lacking a leader*, B15

ealdorlēas: *lifeless*, B1587

ealdwerig: read ealdorwērig? *fatally weary*, EI50 n.

ēalic *of a river*, OEGC28, 216

ealleðern *wholly of leather*, Additional MS. 32,246, fol. 12r; scetra: ealleþern scyldas; v. Isid. *Etym.* 18, 12, 5

eallhālgung: *all worship*, FL3, H25

ealuscerwen: *serving of bitter ale*, EGS4, 67ff.; v. also WB

eardere *a dweller*, SHS4, 15

eardlufu: delete the query (HBK)

eardrīce: delete; ms. eardwica

ēarede: add (*of a pitcher having* duas ansas, Isid. *Etym.* 20, 5, 3); cf. ansa: auris, CGL6, 73

earhwinnende *cowardly conquering* (*of a poisoned arrow*), VM133b, 23

earmheortnes *pity*, FL2, A38

earngēap: add *falcon*? (HEW)

earningland: *land for which service was rendered*?, WC p. 178, 21

ēarðyrel: in support of *ear-passage* v. FL3, J5

ēastān *a river-stone*?, LCD2, 218, 23

ēaðbelg m. *irritability*, VHF103, n. 176a

Ebrēisclīce adv. *in Hebrew*, JnI.19, 13

eceddrinca: delete; v. VM8a, 9 where the part drincan is a verb

ecgclif n. *steep shore*, B2893 (HBK)

edginnan *to begin again*, OEGC27, 35

edspellung f. *recapitulation*, OEGC20, 3

efengemetgian *to temper equally*, FL5, A5

efenhemman: delete, FL5, A5

Eficisc *of Ephesus*, FL3, H8

efne: delete *alum*; v. alefne

eftgān *to go*, GLL215

eftgewæxen *grown again*, LCD1, 378, 15

egnwirht: delete, FL5, A2

eiðe = egðe; printed ciþe at WW105, 2

eleberende *containing oil*, OEGC8, 17

elegrēofa: *tinder from residue of pressed olives*, FL3, A9

elleahtor *misuse of the letter l*, FL2, A20

elleoht: delete; v. elleahtor

ellheort *disheartened*; v. hellheort

ellhygd = elhygd, GD108, 4

emleahtor *misuse of the letter m*, FL2, A20

emleoht: delete; v. emleahtor

eoforhēafodsegn: read eoforhēafdod segn? *banner with a boar's head*; cf. geheafdod hring, *ring with a head*, WW152, 45; mycelheafdod, 161, 19; and Latin aper, *military banner*

eolene: = eolha, *elk*? BPG417 n.

eorle *the Eruli?*, WB6 n.

eorðgestrēon n. *earthly treasure*, W263, 24*d*

eorðryne *earthquake*, A73, 19 (ms. eorð-renas)

eotonweard: *watch against the monster*

ēowigendlic *demonstrative*, ÆGR231, 5, o

ern *grain, harvest*, ANS171, 19; v. rugern

esne: add *scholar*, FL3, H8

ēst: add *history? origin?*, B2157 (HBK)

ēstnes *bliss*, NP28, 49

ēt: for æt read ǣt

fācennes *deceitfulness*, JEGP-

fǣcnung *suspicion*, A65, 230

fǣdernama m. *surname*, RWH53, 21

fǣderrīce n. *heaven*, VM70*b*, 22

fǣrbifongen: add a query; not wholly legible

fǣrcumen *sudden*, OEGC9, 100

fǣrfrīge *with freedom to go*, JEGP33, 346

fǣrnes *suddenness*, JEGP-

fǣsting: for LL58, 7 read 58, 17

fæðel: delete, FL4, B5

fāg: add *tessellated*, WB725 n.

faldwyrðe *entitled to have his own fold*, HAW p. 476

falðing: *something that falls*; glossaries assoc. lemma moles with ruina

farendlic *pervious*, JEGP-

faul: *an expression used as a charm*

+**feallan**: add on lufe, *to fall in love*, GAT2, 10; 26, 22

fearhhama: *womb of a pig*, FL3, H12

fēawnes: add +, GLL188

feaxclāð: *band for the hair*

feaxēacan: delete, FL4, D7

feaxscēara: *hair shears*, FL3, H13

feht: add *shaggy pelt*, FL3, J6

felafricgende *well informed*, B2105 (HBS p. 119)

felarīce *very rich*, ÆH1, 582, 14

felasprecol = felaspecol, LCD3, 192, 22

felcyrf: add JEGP-

feltūngrēp: add *privy*, VHF146, n. 48

fenfugol: add (ms. fenfixas)

feohhord *treasury*, JEGP-

feohlufu f. *love of money*, BH(Sch)160, 13 (an elliptical compound)

fēolheard: *hard as a file*, MAG108 n.

fēondulf: on the authenticity of this word v. BPG617 n.

feorhcynn: *kinds of living creatures*, B2266 (ASPR4, 235)

feorhlegu *life* at B2800 (HBK)

feorhnest n. *provisions*, JEGP-

feorm: add *disposal*, WB451 n.

fēowergǣrede *four-pointed*, ÆGR288, 11

fēowerstrenge *four-stringed*, ÆGR288, 11 (bifidus taken as from fides)

fēowertȳnenihte *fourteen nights old*, BH206, 28

+**fēra**: for fera read fēra

ferhweard *guard of life*, B305 (EGS4, 67)

+**fērlǣcan**: add +, ÆGR191, 17, j

ferð *crowd*, WA54 (EGS4, 84)

fetelhilt: v. NP28, 43

feðerberende adj. *feathered*, OEGC28, 481

flah = feoh, OET446, 9

fīfmægen: *quintuple powers*, MPS136 n.; delete fīfel

fingerdocca: *foxglove?* OEGC70, 22 n.

fīrenðēof: delete, FL2, B16

fiscfell: = fiscwell, FL2, A21

fiscflōdu: not a cpd.? (ASPR6, 204)

flǣre: *one of the spreading sides at the end of the nose*, FL3, H15

flǣsccostnung f. *carnal desire*, KCM p. 120, 3

flǣsclīce adv. *carnally*, CP207, 16

flǣsctāwere: *butcher*

flǣðecomb: two separate words? (FL2, A22)

+**fīenod**: read +flerod, *flared?* (FL4, D14)

fleoðomum glosses flactris, WW239, 38; d. pl. of flēotham? *watery place*; note wætersteall to flactiris and cf. flōdham, wæterham

flind = flint, WW415, 10 (FL3, A11)

flocgian: v. BPG846 n.

flōdgrǣg *flood-grey*, GNC31 (ASPR6, 175)

flōdweard: *guardian of the flood?*, EI494 n.

flogoða: *venom*, BPG997

flustrian: *to flatter*, JEGP-

fnæs: delete ref. to WW425, 27, where fnasum is error for snasum; add LkL8, 44

fōder: delete *hatchet*, FL5, B1

fōdderbill *an instrument for cutting fodder*, FL5, B1

fōgclāð *a patch*, FL2, A24

foldgrǣg: delete; v. flōdgrǣg

foldwylm *earth-stream*, PH64; usually, but unnecessarily, emended (SK)

fonfȳr *firefang*, JEGP-

foraldung *old age*, OEGC28, 312

forbēn: on this nonce word cf. FL2, A23

forbīgels: delete, FL2, B18

forboren *restrained from the effect of herb, bewitched?*, LCD2, 114, 9; v. 2, 306, 12; KN19

forcinnan? *to destroy*, MPS107 n.

forcomplan? *to fight for*, BPG31 n.

ford: add *waterway*, B568 (HBS p. 99)

fordēad: *as if dead*, FL3, D3

fordēmednes: add GD345, 3

foreādihtian: delete; v. ādihtian

forebīcnung f. *prophecy*, ÆH1, 540, 26

forublǣsting: delete, FL4, D8

forecennednes *progeny*, SHS8, 50

foredēman *to prejudge*, RBL105, 6
forefǣger: read forfæger
forefengnes *a protective skirting (of woods)*, OEGC4, 28
forefrēfrend *proconsul*, DR190, 9*b*
foregesellan *to advance (money)*, BHB330, 6
foregielpan: delete (BTs)
forehālig: delete; v. NP28, 46
forelǣttēow *leader*, LkL22, 26
foresettendlic *prepositive*, ÆGR267, 6
foretimbrigende *enclosing, impeding* BH (Sch)552, 63
+**forewrit** *prologue*, KCM280, 4
forgebind n. *stricture?*, LCD1, 338, 3
forgiefednes *forgiveness*, GLL39
forgīeman: insert ī before ȳ
forgifung: *the nuptial gift before the morning gift*, FL3,H16
forgrindet: 3rd sing. pr. of forgrindan (LCGC776)
forhrædlīce adv. *too soon*, CP445, 1
forhtlēasnes f. *fearlessness*, VHF4, n. 13*a* (context calls for un-)
forhto *fear*, SPS88, 41
forlǣtu: v. VHF138, n. 6
forlētere *a forsaker*, LkL p. 9, 17
formǣlan *to negotiate*, ANS111, 280
forrǣpe *assart*, SN16, 33
forrēcelēasian *to neglect*, BTs
forscēotan: add *to advance money*, NP28, 45
forscired: based on same doc. as forscyrian
forsittan: add *to give out, fail*, B1767 (v. FL3,A5 n. 2)
forsuncen *faded out (of the written page)*, KF
forsweflan: *to kill, perish*, FL5,A3
fortīn n. *a portent*, FL4,B6
fortog: read innanfortog, LCD109*b*
fortogen: *griped*
forðāgān *to pass away*, Mt14, 15
forðāloten *prone*, A65, 230
forðātȳdred *propagated*, OEGC4, 91
forðegide *consumed*, SFF214 (v. Sisam, *Studies*, p. 57)
forðgelǣdan *to bring forth, cause to grow*, GLL232
forðhebban *to further*, GLL220
forðmid *at the same time*, FGR68
forðrǣsted *contrite*, GLL52
forðringan: preferably *drive out* at B1084 (HBK)
forðsecgan *to announce, proclaim*, GLL90
forðsendan *to send forth*, ÆL23*b*, 204
forðswebung *a killing?*, FL5,A3
forðtihtan *to persuade*, KCM p. 52, 8
forðtilian *to go on striving*, VM72*b*, 11

forðwegan *to further*, GLL220
forðyldegung *tolerance*, A65, 230
forðysmed:=forðrysmed
foryldu: context calls for *weariness* at BPG1030
fostere *a spade*, FL2,B10
fōtclāð: delete; v. fōgclāð
fōtgemet: delete *foot-fetter*, FL5,A5; add *a foot in measure*, HSC60
fōtgeswell n. *swelling of the foot*, LCD3, 70, 27
fōtlǣstlēas *soleless*, FL3,H32
fōtrāp: *rope by which the foot of a sail is tied*, JEGP46, 416
fōðorn: delete; ms. slit mid ðe foðorne= mid ðefoðorne; v. ðefeðorn at LCD3, 56, 27, and on the use of a thorn as a scalpel v. LCD2, 106, 5
framādrȳfan: add VHF69, 165
framāscūfan *to drive away*, VHF69, 163
frēahbeorhtian: add+, GLL103
frēawrāsn: *splendid band*, AJP62,338,n. 30
frēcenful *dangerous*, OEG628
fregen II: add ANS135, 399
fregensyllic: delete, ES36, 325; ANS135, 399
fregnðearle: delete; noun fregn and adverb ðearle; not a cpd.
frēols:add *charter of freedom*, HAW447,n. 5
Fresilc: read Fresisc
Frīandæg *Friday*, RBL43, 13
frigedōm m. *deliberation*, RBL97, 8
frihtere: WE61, 14 (ms. frif-)
frīs: *Frisian*, ASPR3, 306, 95
friðowang: *place of refuge* (WB)
fromācnȳslian *to degenerate*, OEGC30, 105
frumcenning m. *first-born*, SPS77, 51
frummeoluc: *beestings*, JEGP52, 372
frumtēam *first team (of animals harnessed in line)*, WW427, 31
frysca: quite possibly a form of fersc, *fresh, youthful*; v. buteonem at CGL6, 158 and butio glossed frysca, WW10, 8
fugeldoppe: two words?, A41, 111 n. 7
fulhealden: *sufficient, ample*; cf. German vollhaltig
fullhealden: delete; v. ful-
fullnes: read 111, 13 and v. SPS p. 37
fultumgestre f. *a helper*, A65, 230
fyrclian: *to fork into many rays*, EGS5, 84; CPC p. 81
fyrdhama: read fyrdhom (ASPR4, 196)
fyrdtiber: delete the query (FL3,H14)
fȳrencylle f. *lamp*, BHB476, 15
fyrgenhēafod? *mountain headland*, Charms 4, 27 (ASPR6, 213)
fȳrrace: a dubious word, doc. as ferrece; note Latin ferrea in glosses to lemma vatilla at CGL7, 395

fyrsrǣw f. *a row of furze* (BTs)
+**fyxan** *to trick*, FF792, n. 8; v. also JEGP33, 345, n. 25

gadinca: read gādinca, *maimed animal?*, FL4,B7
gæstlīðend *hospitable*, WE66, 12
gafolgyld: delete the query, BPG548 n.
galend *enchanter*, GLL97
gangtūn m. *latrine*, ÆL18, 379
gār: on the meaning at GEN316 v. FL4, B8 and NP39, 204
gāra: add *strip of cloth, saddle cloth*, WW332, 10
gāstgifu: read WW200, 18
gātaloc n. *goat-house*, WW275, 31
gealga: delete entry II; galgan at WW445, 35 and 499, 14=geallan; v. OEG2950
geallādl: add *jaundice*, KN7
gealpettan: delete *to live gluttonously?*, VHF76, n. 22
gēancyrrendlic *relative*, ÆGR231, 17j
gēansprecan *to contradict*, GLL124
gearofang *grappling hook?*, FL4,D12
Gēatisc? *of the Geats*, WB3150 n.
gefestre f. *a giver*, A76, 502
gēgan: v. FL3,A14
gēnde: delete=; add=gīnde, gȳnde at ÆL 25, 636c
gēoabbod m. *former abbot*, GDh41, 27
gēomagister m. *former teacher*, BHc410, 13
gēomēowle: only B2931
gēotend:=gēotendæder, FL2,B51
gēotenlic: for gegotenlic? BPG437 n.
gētan: delete grētan; v. HBK
gielphlæden: *laden with glorious words*, ASPR4, 159
gilddagas: delete *guild-days*; lemma ceremonia from Isid. *Etym.* 6, 19, 36
gildet *gelded*, WW120, 38; v. ðrysumer
gildfrēo *free of tax*, ANS111, 276
gildlic: delete *of a guild*; v. FL3,H25 n.
gildsetl n. *meeting-place of a guild*, FF792, n. 9
gilp: for doubt about meaning *dust, powder*, v. JEGP46, 419; add=grip, *furrow?*
gilte: add *barren pig*, LCD2, 88, 24
gimrodor:=gimhrōðor, *gem-splendour*, FL 3, A17
ginfæsten: delete, EI567 n.
+**gīscan**:=giscian?, *to yex*, FL3,A15
+**gite** *conscious*, OEGC28, 409
glæs: delete glæsas, BPG678
glēd: add *an instrument of torture*, FL4, D22
glemm: read W67, 18
glīwcynn: possibly for onclēow; v. JEGP 43, 438

glīwingman: *mocker*, FL4,A10
glōf: delete *pouch* (HBS p. 118)
gluto *glutton*, Ælfric's Colloquy, ed. Garmonsway, 297 n.
glyrende *looking askance*, FL3,J15; BPG 440
glȳs-=glēs-, ÆGR293, 13d
godcundlicnes=godcundnes, ÆL23b, 230g
godē-: read gode-
godgesprǣcen=godsprǣce; v. godgesprǣce in BTs
godwebben: v. VHF23, n. 103
goldhordhūs: *treasury*, not *privy*, FL4, D23; JEGP-
goldhwæt: v. WB3074n.
goldwreken *inlaid with gold*, WC p. 74, 7
gorettan: delete *pour forth, emit*, FL3,J16
gōseflǣsc n. *gooseflesh*, Klaeber, *Studies* (1929), p. 272
grammaticancræft=grammaticcræft, ÆL 35, 14
greðe: *a companion?*, FL3,C2
griffus *griffon*, MPS256
grimena: ms. grimena ðus rendering bruchus cuius=grime maðu ðæs?; v. grame ceaferas at corres. passage in PPs104, 30
grimhȳdig=gramhȳdig, VHF77, n. 38
grimman: v. WB306 n.
+**grindswile** *a swelling caused by friction, intertrigo*, KF
grinu: not necessarily a colour; v. FL2, A33
grīstra: *miller*; glosses cerealis pistor, WW 141, 4; 202, 29
grōwan: delete *become*, FL3,A18
grundwiergen: *accursed monster of the deep*, HBK
grunian: *to desire*, not *chew the cud*, FL3, E1; v. gruncian, BPG597
grytte: delete *spider*;=grytt, *dust*; aranea taken as arena (SK)
gullisc: *gilded*, MLN59, 111
gūðfrēa: delete; FL2,B25
gūðgeorn *tempting, looking for a quarrel*, OEGC60, 12
gūðmōd *of warlike mind* (Klb.); *warlike mind* (WB), B306
gūðmōdig: delete
Gūðmyrce: *warlike border-dwellers?* EI59 n.
gydenlic: *of a goddess*; add (from the same context) OEG3193; 7, 233; 8, 170
gyrdelbred: add (*carried in the purse?*) FL2,A34
gyrigyden f. *goddess of dress*, BPG670

hādswǣpa:=hādswæpe, *bridesmaid*
hæcce: *frontal*, rather than *crozier*, EGS5, 72, n. 22

hæcine: add, from Latin acinum, FL4, D24

hæfegītsung: delete, FL2, A35

hæferbīte: delete, FL4, D25

hæfergāt: delete; two words separated by point in Harley 3376

± hæftnīedan: only +

hǣlestre f. *saviour*, A65, 230

hǣmedrīm: *number of dallyings*, FL3, A20 + hǣrede *hairy*, ANS117, 24

hǣðenfeoh: delete, FL2, B26

hǣðenwēoh *idol*, JUL53 (emended to -feoh in Woolf's ed.)

hǣwmænged *mixed purple*, OEGC4, 12

hafenian: *to lift up*, MAG42 n.; B1573

hālettend: *forefinger*, FL2, A36

hālewǣge *a holy cup*, ANS171, 29

hālgungbōc: *book containing coronation liturgy*, ASPR6, LXXXIX

hālswurðung: read halswurðung, *neck ornament*, EI549 n.

hamorian: delete, BPG580

hand: add ymb hand, *at once*, BPG52; bām handum twām, *zealously*, ANS162, 230

handæx: add *hatchet*

handwyrm: add *itch-mite*, PM44

harasteorra: read hāra-, FL4, A11

hāredagas *dog days*, OEGC63, 17

hāreminte *white mint?*, A41, 140 n.

hārewyrt: delete WW135, 5 and v. A41, 140 n.

hāsgrumel *sounding hoarsely*, OEGC15, 2

hātlīce: add *vehemently*, BHT352, 21

hattefagol: add a query; v. BTs under hǣreanfagol

hāwung: *ability to see*, VHF99, n. 155 + hēafdod: add (*referring to a ring*)

hēafodbeorg: *protection for the head* at B1030

hēafodbryce *breaking of the skull*, LCD1, 150, 22

hēafodclāð: add *the cloth used for covering the head of a dead person*, ÆL31, 1425 (v. B445)

hēafodsegn: read eoforhēafdod segn?

hēafodslæge: *a head-stroke, beheading*, FL3, A21

hēafodsmæl: *part of a tunic* (BTs)

hēahdēma m. *high judge*, W254, 8d

hēahfexede a slavish gloss to alticomum (iubar), OEGC9, 35; v. hēahhelm in BTs and feaxede of a comet

hēahgræft: *prominent sculpture*, FL3, D6 + healddagas: v. FL3, H20

healdend: add + at LCD3, 192, 23

healfes hēafdes ece *migraine*, LCD2, 20, 21

healfgewriten *half-written* LkL, 16, 6 (FL3, D16)

healfhrūh: v. ānhealfrūh

healfhundisc *semi-canine*, WNL191x

healfrūh: delete

healhālgung: delete, FL3, H25

hēalic = ēalic, FL2, A37

heallðegn: = healðegn

healðegn: *occupier of the hall* at B142 (WB)

hēanhād: delete; two words—context for the glosses is ardui formam propositi; v. BTsII, 2b under hēah

hēap: add forloren hēap, *ruined troop*, ÆH1, 342, 25

heardhīðende *ravaging*, RD33, 7 (ASPR3, 340)

hearma: add netila = nitella, *dormouse*

hearmdæg: delete; v. Klb., 2nd supplement, p. 470

hearmheortnes: delete, FL2, A38

hearplic *of a harp*, OEGC7, 21; 8, 15

hebbendlic: delete; ms. oferhebbendlic

hegessugge: read hegesugge

hellegāst: delete†; add GD189, 26

hellemūð *mouth of hell*, RWH118, 4

hellepīn *hell-torment*, RWH75, 28

hellerūne: delete B163; v. helrūna

hellfenlic *like a fen of hell*, FL2, B27

hellheort: prob. for ellheort, *disheartened*; cf. ellhygd

hellwendlic: delete, FL2, B27

helpendrāp: influenced by opiferra = opisphora

helrūna: add *one knowing the mysteries of hell*

helung *covering*, SPS35, 8

hemman: delete, FL2, B28

hēofon: read heofon, *heaven*, EI46n.

heofonarīce = heofonrīce, VHF46, 32

heofonhæbbend: read WW355, 21

heofonhlytta = efenhlytta, GLL60

heofonhūs *ceiling*, WW29, 22; v. hūshefen (FL4, A15)

heortbucc: delete, FL2, B29

heorða: delete the query, FL4, C3

heoruwearg: *accursed foe*, Klb.

herehorn m. *trumpet*, ÆGR40, 7 n.

herescipe *troop*, SFF18

hergere? *plunderer*, OEGC28, 341n.

herian: add *to help*, B1833 (HBS)

hīa = hīe, NG

hice(māse): read hīce(māse), HEW

hiellan: delete, FL5, A4

hierdung: delete *restoring*, FL3, H29

higesynnig? *sinful*, SFF168; or hige, synnig man (Sisam, *Studies*, p. 51)

hig, hig *o, o*, WW91, 7

hildefrōfor *battle-comfort*, WAL II, 12 (ASPR6, 140)

hildelēoma: *battle-flame (sword)* B1143; *destructive flame (of the dragon)* B2583 (HBK) hiltlēas: v. FL3, H26

hīredcniht: v. WC p. 127

hīredgerēfa: v. FL3,H27

hīwian: add hīwian on, *to change to*, VHF101, n. 169

hīwiend *one who forms*, OEG365n.

hīwlic: *of marriage*, not *matronly*, JEGP46, 420

hīwspræc *artfully formed speech*, SPS39, 5 (ms. hwispræce); v. spæcehēow

hlæddisc: *dish laden with varied viands*, v. Isid. *Etym.* 20, 2, 8

hlæfde:=læfðe

hlæpewince: delete

hlāfhūs *Bethlehem* (*domus panis*), ÆH1,34, 15

hleg(i)ende: read hleg(l)ende

hlēohræscnes: v. hlēorhræscnes

hlēonian: delete, FL3,A22

hlēorhræscnes *a striking in the face*, FL6, A6

hlēoðrian: add *to bark*, WW378, 3

hlēowfæst: add *protected*, VHF143, 67

hlīdan:=liðian?, FL4,B12

hlīf m. *moon-shaped ornament*, OEGC55, 5

hlīpcumb *a valley with steep sides* (BTs)

hlōse: add *lewze*, FL4,D37

hnoc: delete, FL4,D28

hnot: add *hornless*, WW444, 19

hnylung: prob.=hlinung

hoferede: add *strumous*, ÆGR322, 1

hofrede:=hoferede, *hump-backed*, FL2, A41

hōh: add *headland*, WB3157 n.

hohfullīce *carefully*, RBL89, 6

hōl: *malice?, envy?*, BHW269, 57 n.

± holen *prince, protector*, MÆ12, 65

holstæf: delete, FL4,A12

hōn: delete *tendrils of a vine*, BTs

hōnende: read hōnede

+ hopp: delete *small bag*, FL3,D4

hoppetan: read hoppettan, LCD2, 352, 1; GD118, 25

hopscȳte: add WC p. 62, 22

hopsteort: read hōpsteort, FL4,D30

hordestre *stewardess*, A76, 502

horines *filth*, SHS6, 5

hornādl *a disease* (*connected with venery*), LCD60*b*

hornungbrōðor *bastard brother*, OEGC8, 13

hospan *to reproach*, SPS41, 11; 118, 42

hracca: delete, JEGP52, 373

+ hradod *quick*, A67, 126, n. 4

hræfnsweart *black as a raven*, VHF101, n. 168

hrægltalu: *supply of clothing*, RAC48, 26

hræglðēnestre f. *keeper of the robes*, A76, 502

hrandsparwa: delete?, FL2, A42

hrēodgyrd f. *reed used as fishing rod*, BPG 145

hrēðmann? *glorious warrior*, WB445 n.

hrēðsecg? *glorious warrior*, WB490 n.

hrīcian: add BPG722

hrimpan: *to wrinkle, contract*, FL3,D5

+ hrin: delete, FL6,A4

hrinde *frost-covered*, B1363 (HBK)

hring: on wopes hring cf. EGS2, 68ff.

hringgewindla: *the coil of a serpent*, FL3, A23

hrīstle:=hrīscl; v. LCG E10

hrōflēas: add *with no houses*, RAC p. 460

hrohian *to cough*, MÆ1, 208

hrohung *spitting*, MÆ11, 90

hrycigan:=hrīcian, BPG722

hrympel: delete the query; ms. hrympellum

hrȳmðe *noise*, A73, 23 n. 50

hūdenian: delete, FL3,F2

+ hūfud *with pontifical headband*, BPG674

hund: delete *sea-beast*, FL4,A13

hundesberie *nightshade?*; glosses uua canina, OEGC73*a*, 8

hunigæppel: *round cake made with honey*, FL4,A14

hunigsmæc m. *the taste of honey*, ASPR2, 60, 28

hunigtēaren: for GL read BPG123

hūnsporu: *part of the rigging of a ship?*; gloss to dolon, q.v. at Isid. *Etym.* 19, 3, 3; v. hūnðyrlu

hunu?: v. FL2,B30

hwelpian *to bring forth offspring*, OEGC61, 7

hwilpe: *yarwhilp*, YWES14, 77

hwītian: add *to make white*, VHF145, 86

hwītlēadtēafor *salve of white lead*, AB34, 115

hwītstōw *Lebanon* (BT)

hwol:=wolma, FL5,D1

hwȳorf *cattle*, FL2,B31

+ hȳdan: delete *to fasten with a rope?*, JM46

hȳdscip: *a ship made with hides*, FL3,H30

hȳge *the top of the gullet*, WW264, 16; 405, 10 (HEW)

± hyhtlīce *suitably*, VHF62 n. 61

+ hylced: *bent apart*, BPG764 n.

hylsung:=hwistlung, FL4,D32

hypsār *sciatica*, OEGC73*c*, 11

hȳreborg: prob. two words, each acc.

hyrsian: prob.=hȳrsumian, FL2,A43

hȳðscip:=hȳdscip

īdelbliss f. *vain joy*, ANS132, 330, 26

īdellust *vain desire*, KCM p. 120, 3

idig: ms. idge=igde, ecgede, *edged?*, FL3, D7

īegclif: delete; v. ecgclif
ierfa: read 446, 4
+iht *yoked together*, ÆGR289, 2
inbrecan *to break into*, BPG330 n.
inbrēdan: delete; v. inbrecan
incūð: add *wicked*, SN14, 216
indēpan: add +, BPG162
in(for)lǣtan *to let in*, VHF8 n. 26
ingebed: delete, FL2, A44
ingerǣcan *to give (something) in (to somebody)*, BPG235
inlād: for first entry subst. *toll on goods carried into market*, HAW477
inlendiscnes *habitation*, JEGP-
inmearg: delete, BPG665
innanfortog *gripe*, LCD2, 300, 27
innangund = innancund, LCD1, 196, 17
innanonfeal *internal swelling*, LCD2, 10, 11
innanwyrm *intestinal worm*, LCD1, 82, 22
insǣte: *of ambush*, FL3, H31
insceaft f. *internal generation*, MPS447 n.
inscūfan *to shove in*, VM135b, 18
±intimbrian *to edify*, VHF67, n. 85
inðer: delete, FL2, B32
inðicce: delete; ms. inðicce but *in* dotted for deletion
inwegan gloss to inlabi, GLL230
inweorpan *to begin (the weft)*, OEGC55, 9
inwrecg = inwærc, BPG1077 n.
inylma pl. of innylfe, BPG725
Iringes weg v. FL4, C4
Ispanisc *Spanish*, GD237, 21
istoria *history*, MPS4 n.

lāclic: delete, JW130, n. 3
lācnystre f. *physician*, A76, 502
lǣ *hair of the head*, WW263, 21; 368, 14 (FL3, H55)
+lǣdendlic: add ±, SPS97, 6
lǣfel: delete ref. to löffel
lǣfðe *a sprinkling*, FL4, D27
lǣlan?: add, v. ASPR2, 120
lǣtcumen *late*, OEGC27, 29
lahgewrit n. *rule*, KCM414, 12
lāmen = lǣmen, RWH76, 17
landefne: *the resources of the land*, CPC 1085, 12 n.
landgemirce: add *shore*, B209
langlīfe: read langlīf(e), ÆGR320, 1
langmōdlīce *patiently*, GLL113
lārfæsten: v. A66, 29 n. 4
latimer m. *interpreter*, EHy16, 5
lēad: add *an instrument of torture*, BPG344
lēafsele: *place for shade*, FL4, D34
lēasbrēden f. *falsehood*, ÆL17, 107 v.l.
lēasgespeca *a falsifier*, A65, 230
lēasōlæccere *false flatterer*, ÆGR303, 8
lēawfinger: v. FL4, D33
+led: = glēd

+legergield: v. FL4, D15
lengian: delete, MPS262 n.
lengtogra: positive langtog at OEGC27, 31
lent: delete?; v. BPG152 n.
lēoht: add *world*, TLG34, 310
leornestre f. *a student*, A76, 502
lēoðucræft: read leoðu-
leoðuwācunga: read liðewācung, *mitigation*, FL5, A5
lēpene *a basket*, RAC200, 9
lēwsa: add *misery*, WW202, 31 (FL4, D35)
Libanisc *of Lebanon*, OEGC28, 364
+licbisen *an imitation*, DR50, 4; *an imitator*, 12, 11
līgfȳr: add VPs28, 7 (SK)
ligrægel *a garment of varied hues*, WW126, 1 (FL4, D36)
limgesihð: read limgesīð, FL4, B13
līnsētcorn *a grain of linseed*, ASPR6, 128, 11
lið: add *point*, OEGC4, 111 n.
liðelēaf *camomile*, OEGC73c, 9 (lemma aviane = apiana)
liðerlic: v. FL3, J21
lodrung: read loðrung, *delusion*, A36, 71
lōf: *band*, MLN40, 411
lōhsceaft: v. HEW
lōse = hlōse, LCG F342
lufe wk. f. *loved home*, B1728 (WB)
lufen: *beloved home* (HBS111)
Lundonisc *of London*, VLC162, 11
lungencoðu f. *lung disease*, LCD1, 388, 1
lyftedor: v. EI251 n.
lyftwynn: *joyous air*, B3043 (HBK)
lyge: delete section III (FL2, A45)
lȳpenwyrhta: *basket maker*, AB29, 253
lȳtel: add lȳtlan ond lȳtlan, *little by little*, OEGC9, 69
lytwist? *deception*, FL2, A61

mādmōd: delete; v. vngemedemad
mǣdæcer m. *a meadow* (BTs)
mǣddic f. *a dike in a meadow* (BTs)
mǣdmann *mower*, FGR80, 4
mǣgdeneorðe f. *virgin soil*, NP28, 49
mǣgmann m. *clansman*, BH(Sch)115, 213
mǣgðblæd: read mǣgðblǣd, *glory of virginity*, BPG920 n.
mǣgðegesa? *viking*, GnE106 (ASPR3, 306)
mǣl: add 730 *meals in a year*, HSC67
mænibrǣde: v. FL3, H33
mænihīwe *multiform*, AJP59, 213
mǣrehwīt *pure white*, ANS132, 399
mǣr-hege: read mǣrhege
mǣrhlisa: delete? (FL3, A24)
mǣssandæg = mæssedæg, ÆL25, 203c
mǣssecapitel m. *chapter of the mass*, CM536
māgatoga? *pedagogue*, OEGC4, 117, n.

māhling *parent, kinsman*, ANS117, 21
Mailrosisc *of Melrose*, OEGC9, 22
+man: delete WW492, 20; add WE57, 15
mānfolm: *hand* (FL5,C1)
market: add *market rights*, HAW476, 16
masc *mash*, RAC198, 31
mealmstān: *sandstone* (HEW)
meduscerwen: v. EGS4, 74
meduwyrhta *brewer*, HAW508, 12; or=
mēdwyrhta?
Memfitisc *of Memphis*, OEGC28, 415
menescilling: add LCG L277
mēoning: delete, FL2,B35
meoring: *hindrance?*, EI63 n.
Merewīoing *the Merovingian*, B2921
metenīõing *food-niggard*, ANS117, 23
+metfæstlīce: add +, ÆGR294, 1, *j*
+methāt? *temperate*, A47, 51
mēõlg: add SFF228
micelnes: add +, GLL45
middangeardtōdǣlend *cosmographer* (BTs)
middelflēre: *the part of the nose between the
flaring sides at the end*, FL3,H15
middelsǣ *middle sea*, RAC160, 1
midfeorh adj. *middle-aged*, BH440, 31
midgetellan *to count, include*, A65, 230
midhilte: two words? lemma capulus at
Isid. *Etym.* 18, 6, 2 follows ensis glossed
hiltlēas sweord
milescian *to become mellow*, WW441, 28
min: add JEGP43, 441 ff.
mindōm: *pusillanimity* (FL4,D38)
mīnlic adj. *in my manner*, GD231, 17, 0
minnæn: delete, FL6,A7
misbēodan: add *to announce wrongly*,
ANS111, 280
misbregdan *to change*, JEGP-
misfēdan: v. GLL208
mīõgihlytto *fellowship*, DR93, 13
mōdhǣp: read mōdhēap, *bold host*, EI242 n.
mōdsēocnes: *fright, sadness*; v. cardiacus at
Isid. *Etym.* 4, 6, 4
mōdõrÿõo? *arrogance*, WB1931 n.
moisn: add OEGC28, 453
monighēowlic *multifarious*, OEGC4, 405
morgensēoc: for AN241 read ASPR3, 218,
96
mōrhop: *a hollow in the moor*; v. fenhop
and ASPR4, 140, 450
morõcwalu=morõorcwalu, VHF103, n.179
muntgīu *the Alps*, W152, 9
muscflēote: read mustflēoge; lemma bibi-
ones from Isid. *Etym.* 12, 8, 16 and
among words glossed fleoge
mūsere m. *mouse-hawk*, OEGC36, 14
mūsõēof *a thieving mouse*, WW408, 4
(FL3,A25)
mȳgõ=mǣgõ, KGL876
mylenoxa *a mill-ox*, RAC254, 7

myima: delete, BPG725
+myndblīõe: delete, FL2,A30
mynetīsen: for 447 read 477
mynna m. *intention*, ANS111, 276
mynsterõing n. *property of a monastery*,
RB56, 11n.
myrõu: or myrõe?, *murderous*, WB
+mȳtan= +mētan II, HGL525, 3

nacudwrāxler *gymnosophist*, KCM382; v.
Isid. *Etym.* 8, 6, 17
nægl: delete *spear*, FL3,A26
nǣnigõinga *not at all*, VHF148, 117
nǣrende: v. MPS330 n.
næsc: WW337, 3; LCD2, 104, 13
nāhwanan *not at all*, VHF11 n. 45
nāmrǣden: read namrǣden, *naming*, FL3,
A27
Nazarenisc *Nazarene*, Mk10, 47
nēahmynster=nēahnunmynster, BHB254,
10
nearoõanc: add *evil thought*, VHF51, 99
nēobedd: *bed of spirits*, in GEN (TLG36,
343)
nēodlaõu: *urgent summons*, WB
nēodspearuwa: delete *restless*, FL5,C2
+neorõ: delete, FL4,D17
netwerõlicnes *utility*, OEGC30, 20
Nicēnisc *Nicene* (BTs)
nīgecyrred: read OEG3477
nīgende=hnīgende?, RD8, 8 (ASPR3, 326)
nihtbutorflēoge: v. FL3,H35
nihtēage: *a disease of the eye*, WW114, 6;
456, 34 (v. FL3,H36)
nihterne adj. *nightly*, ANS132, 331
nip: delete, BPG838
niõer(ā)settan *to set down*, GLL238
niõerlǣtan *to lose heart*, ANS117, 22
niõerlang *stretching downward* (BTs)
nīõing: v. metenīõing, unnīõing
norõgārsecg m. *northern ocean*, BHB308,
35
Norõmandisc *Norman* (BTs)
norõweall m. *north wall*, RAC36, 8
nōõ: read nōw?, *ship*, at WH28 (FL2,A47)
nūhwænne *straightway*, VHF14, n. 57
nūna: prob. scribal error for nū õā occurring shortly before; infl. by following
naviculam
nūten=nīeten, VLC182, 218
nȳdgefēra *inevitable companion*, EL1260 n.
(ed. Gradon)
nȳdgylta *debtor*, GLL145
nȳfellan=nīwfyllan, *to fill anew*, SOLK85,
12
nytõearflic *useful*, HAW340, 14; 358, 8
nȳõan=nēõan, GD18, 10
nyõerāworpen *one who has been cast down*,
KCM169, 26

ōdencole: read ōdencolc, FL2, B63

oemseten: delete *shoot*, *slip*, FL4,D61

ofācennan *to generate*, KW63, 6

ofāstīgan *to descend*, GLL211

ofdūneāstīgan *to descend*, GLL211

ofer: add *without*, B685

oferberan *to carry over*, VHF31 n. 130

oferblissian glosses supergaudeant, SPS34, 19; 24

oferbrū: add LCD3, 186, 25

oferbrūwa m. *eyebrow*, ÆGR298, 3; WW263, 25

oferbrycg(i)an: add MPS297 n.

oferclif: delete, FL3,D10

oferdæg m. *remaining day (in computation)*, HSC55

oferfæst *transfixed*, LkL p. 11, 13

oferfeallan: add *to fall upon*, A73, 26

oferflēdnes *fluctuation, vacillation*, GLL138

ofergemet: v. VHF66 n. 81

ofergeswincfull *excessively troublesome*, CHR1097 (p. 234, 2)

oferhīgian: *overpower* (HBK)

oferhrēgan: delete, MPS297 n.

oferhrēosan *to fall*, SPS57, 9

oferhyrned: *having great horns?*, RUN 4 (ASPR6, 153, n. to 4)

ofermǣnan *to confute*, FL3,A28

ofermistian *to obscure*, OEGC4, 371

oferrǣdlīce *frequently*, RBL93, 4

ofersēam: *a special bag*, FL3,D11

ofersewenness *contempt* (BTs)

ofersiwenlic *contemptible*, CP208, 11 (v.l., p. 507, where read 208 for 206)

oferspyrian *to traverse*, OEGC28, 232

ofertælod p. ptc. of ofertalian, RWH70, 17

ofertredan: for GPH substitute ZDA20, 37

oferweorpan: delete the query after *stumble*

oferwēsnes *over-indulgence*, OEGC4, 259

oferwyrðe: delete, FL2,B37

oferyð: *wavering, vacillation* (GLL138)

ofetrip: delete, NP5, 352

offrettan *to devour*, MkL12, 40

ofgeorn: delete, FL2,B38

ofheran: read ofhēran,=ofhīeran, *to hear, overhear*, RWH59, 16

ofnet: ms. ofnete=on fæte, *in a jug?*

ofsittan: add *to sit upon*, B1545

ofspræc: delete, FL2,B39

oftrahtung *a pulling out*, LkL, p. 8, 10

ofōȳstrian: add Pembroke College MS. 312 (binding fragment)

ofwyrtrumian *to eradicate*, LkL17, 6

ōgengel:=ongegnel?, *opposite*, FL4,D42

ohtrip: read ōhtrīp, *forced work at harvest*, NP5, 352

ōlōwong: part ol may be from note indicating corrigia=colligia

onācenned *inborn?*, OEGC9, 68

onǣht: two words?, v. II under ǣht in BTs

onǣlend: prob. for p.ptc. of onǣlan, BPG 801

onāgēotan *to infuse*, GLL228

onāhōn *to hang on*, VHF31, n. 130a

onālihtan *to illuminate*, GLL33

onāslīdan *to fall away, fail*, GLL230

onbebringan *to bring upon*, VM107b, 21

onbefeallan *to fall upon*, BPG18

onberan: delete *to be situated*, MLR42, 358

onbesendan *to send to*, FGR65, n. 2

onbesmītan *to defile*, A66, 27

onbrosnung: delete, FL2,B40

ondegslic *terrible*, FL2,B41

ondlēanian *to grant*, FL3,A22

ongeador *together*, B1595

ongēanclyppan *to call back*, A65,230

ongēanryne *a course*, GLL216

ongēanstandan *to stand toward*, W252, 18

ongefealdan *to wrap*, OEGC61, 54

ongelīcnes: for 14, 20 read 17, 7; add *parable*, LkR4, 23

ongeniman *to take away*, WW397, 23

ongesendan *to send to*, FGR65, n. 2

onhiscend m. *a mocker*, OEGC2, 175

onīdlian *to empty*, SPS74, 9

onlūtung: *a lurking place*, BPG1011

onmeltan: delete, FL2,B42

onmētan: *to paint*, PPs88, 39

onnīed f. *oppression?*, EI139 n.

onopenian *to open*, SPS77, 23

onorðian *to inspire*, BPG200

onsǣlan: for B read B489?

onscægan *to deride*, MÆ1, 137

onsēcan: add B1942

onslīdan *to fall away, fail*, GLL230

onspǣtan *to spit on*, JEGP-; *to spew into*, WW526, 1 (onspec=onspet)

ontōblāwen *blown on*, BPG263

onweggewit: read onweggewite m. *departure* (SK)

orcðyrs: delete, HBS p. 19

orfgebitt: *food for cattle where there is no pasturage*, FL3,H38

orgel: for WW read W148, 32

orrest: *trial by battle*, EGS5, 85, n. 63; CPC p. 77

ōðer: delete *word, speech*, FL5,C3

oðhylde: delete, FL2,B43

pardus *a leopard*, AA123, 12

pēcung *deception*, OEGC24, 32

picgbrēad: v. FL4,A18

pilstre: delete, FL2,B44

pīpe: add *tube for drinking sacramental wine from chalice*, RAC226, 25 n.

plegian: add p. mid hondum, *to clap hands*, EL805 n. (ed. Gradon) plicettan: delete, BPG 682 n.

plicgan:=plyccan?, BPG 598 n.

plōgesland *ploughland*, RAC 164, 25

plyccan: add *to pluck with desire*, BPG 682

pocādl: add *smallpox*, PM 43, 130

prass: add *pomp*, W 148, 32; *proud array*, MA 68

preg m. *a pointed stick*; *pray*, OEGC 38, 3

prēostgyrd? *staff carried by member of clergy?*, FL 2, A 9

prodbor:=wrōhtbora?, FL 2, A 50

prologa *prologue*, MPS 89

pucian: delete, BPG 664 n.

pudd: *a sore, wound*, BPG 793 n.

puduc: *a little sore*, BPG 793 n.

purlamb: *a male lamb, a pur* (HEW)

pyfian *to blow*, BPG 664

pyrtan:=pȳtan?, BPG 934

+rādod: delete, A 67, 126 n. 4

+rǣcan: add *to wound*, FL 3, J 12

rǣdescamol: delete *couch* and add= rǣdingscamol, FL 3, D 12

rēada: delete *small intestines*; v. tolia at Isid. *Etym*. 11, 1, 57

+rec: delete entry III?; v. FL 2, A 31

+recenes: add *proof*, WW 381, 7 (context of lemma is testimoniorum congerie); add also BHB 436, 15 (lemma vocatio assoc. in glossaries with demonstrare)

recennes: delete; v. +recenes

recon: delete, FL 2, B 46

recondlic glosses numerosus, SPS 77 heading

redestān: read rēde-; delete the query and also read *sinopis*

regulares *regular days in computation*, HSC 53

reliquias: add r. rǣran, *to carry relics in procession*, FGR 7

+rēne: for *instrument, building* subst. *edification*, FL 6, A 4

rēniend: delete; ms. wemend

rēnlic *rainy*, BPG 964

rēodmūða: *parrot*, FL 4, D 43

rēstan: delete, FL 4, D 44

rīcehealdend *guardian of the kingdom*, A 67, 117 n. 12

+rid *food*, GD 323, 3; v. bedgerid

rīfnes *fierceness*, OEGC 4, 329

rihtgewittelic *rational*, SHS 15, 32; 37

±rīm: add *a calendar, numeral*, RAC 250, 13

rīpð *harvest*, OEGC 24, 23

risiendum: ptc. of hrisian, FL 4, B 14

rið: delete, FL 2, B 48

rōdetācen: add *crucifix*, VM 108a, 11

rōmian: *to try to obtain*, TLG 28, 360

+rōstian: read +roscian, JEGP 52, 373

rudian *to be ruddy* ES 8, 478, 60

rūma: delete, FL 2, B 49

+runnenes: delete, BPG 721

ryplen: delete the query, BPG 843

sadolfæt *harness?*, WC 80, 22 n.

sadolgāra *saddle cloth*, WC p. 74, 11 (there taken as *harness*); v. gāra

sǣdsworn *a coalescing of seed*, FL 4, D 45

sǣebbung *ebbing of the sea*, FL 3, H 40

sǣhund: v. FL 4, A 13

sǣlwāg? *hall*, AN 1493 (ASPR 2, 121)

sǣmearh: for E 2 read EL 228

sǣsteorra: add *title of Virgin Mary* (BTs)

±samhīwan: add *members of a guild?*, FF 792, n. 4

samodherigendlic glosses conlaudabilis, GLL 57

samodwellung: add (*of substance in the birth of a bee*) FL 3, A 30

sārcrene: v. cren in HEW

scǣgan *to jeer*, MÆ 1, 137

scamlim: read WW 532, 31 and delete the query; ms. scamescan lim=scame, scamlim

sceadugeard: v. FL 4, A 19

scēatcod: read sceattcod, *bag for provisions*, FL 4, D 46

sceaðe: read sceaðu, VHF 143, n. 33

scēawungstōw: add *Sion* (BTs)

scenc: add *cupful*, GD 127, 11

scencen *pig's shank*, FL 4, A 20; also scencel

scencingcuppe: v. WC p. 112

scennum: v. EGS 2, 75

scer *clear, undisputed* (*in legal terminology*) HAW 62, 10 n.

scīlfor: *glittering*, OEG 532 (v. FL 3, A 31)

scinncræftig *magical* (referring to Satan), A 65, 230

scinngedwola: delete, FL 3, A 32

scipberende *carrying ships*, OEGC 28, 321

scipgefeoht: v. BPG 89 n.

scipgefēre: read scipgefær (BTs)

scipwealh: *Welsh sailor*, RAC 204, 22 n.

scipwered: v. FL 4, B 15

scīrgesceat: delete; note the reading reported by Neil Ker at FF 784

scitte: add *diarrhoea* (BTs)

+scola: for *debtor* substitute *fellow-debtor*, MNG 55

+scōla: delete, MNG 56

scōm-: read scom; v. scamm in HEW

scoplic: for 119 read 199

scora: v. FL 4, D 47

scortwyrplic: *soon effecting an improvement?*, ES 60, 82

scrǣb: add OEGC 36, 17

scriccettan *to screech*, OEGC 15, 4

scriftæcer *land whose yield served as payment for a priest?*, RAC240, 4 n.

scrīpen: read scirpen?, *sharp*, FL4,C5

scufrægl *pullable curtains*, RAC194, 20 n.

scūrheard: for relation to regnheard v. WB p. 81

scylfrung: *glittering*, FL3,A31

scypgesceot *ship-scot*, HAW63, 2 n.

scȳr *a hut*, OEGC55, 1

scyte: delete *stroke, blow?*, v. FL3,A33

Scyððisc Scythian, ÆL7, 345

sealmbōc *psalter*, ÆH1, 604, 24

sealmfæt: v. FL5,C4

sealtlēaf: read sealtlēap, *salt basket*, FL4, A23

sēamtoln *toll on the packhorse load*, HAW 117, 4

sēftēadig: ms. eft eadig

selfǣte: *groundsel*; (senecio is glossed selbeza in OHG, gundswelga in OE)

± sellan: delete *lay by, hide*, FL5,B2

sendan: for *to feast* subst. *to put to death*, ASPR4, 147

sendnes: *Mass*, WW445, 34; 498, 39 (context missarum sacramentis)

seofonhīwe *septiform*, A65, 230

sēoðan: add *to seethe* (*wrath*), BPG478 n.

sepulcer *grave*, FGR70, n. 1

+ sēðedlic *probable*, OEGC28, 20

sīa = sēo, OET446; 447

sibgeleger = sibleger, W164, 5c

sicera m. *an intoxicating drink*, CHRD74, 6

sīcing f. *sighing*, OEGC30, 59

sidung: *arrangement* (*of the dining table*)?, BPG750 n.

sigehrēð: v. hrēðsecg

Sigelhearwa: = Sigelearpa, *sun-darkened?*, FL2,A40

siger: add *groundsel*, WW301, 24 (syr = siger; v. WW30, 39)

sigerīce *realm of victory*, EI27; 530

sinderhǣwe? *cinder-grey*, OEGC51, 4 n.

sinewind: delete, FL2,B51

Sionbeorg Sion, SN20, 202

sīðboren: the word misinterprets depost fetantes: v. GLL200

+ sīðscipe: add ±, BH246, 18 n.

sinulīra *muscle*, FL2,A51

sixecge: add sixecgede, ÆGR289, 5

slāpfulnes: delete; slapel at WW541, 42 incomplete for slapfulnis at 162, 19; but fol. 4r of Antwerp MS. 47 reads slapulnis

slidor: II, *slides for launching and pulling up ships*, WW182, 18

slitol: delete, BPG420 n.

slypton wk. pret. of slūpan?, VPs75, 6 (SK)

smēa *titbit?*, RAC74, 20 n.

smeringwyrt: = symeringwyrt, WW135, 1

smyllan: *to smack*, BPG4

snǣdan: add, a strongly urged (HBK) emendation for sendan at B600

snāð: delete entry II, MNG58

snyring: possibly for styrung, JEGP46, 424

snyttruhūs: add *Silo*, FL6,B4

sōcnman *sokeman*, HAW85, 13 n.

socða *broth, gruel*, FL4,D48

sol *dark, dirty*, FL4,D50

solcennes f. *laziness*, ANS117, 22

sore: delete, FL2,B52

sorgbyrðen: read sorgbryðen, *brew of sorrow*, ES67, 340

sōðlufu: two words? VHF54 n. 1a

sōðwundor n. *true wonder*, EI24; EL1121

spǣcehēow v. swæcehēow

spēd: delete *offspring*, FL6,A8

spircing: *sparkling*, BPG755

stæf: add *Sunday letter* (*in computation*) HSC47, n. 20

stæfplega: glosses ludus litterarius, LCG L289; WW433, 14 (context Ludi litterarii disciplina, Orosius 1, 18, 1)

stæfsweord: *swordstick*, FL3,H43

stæfwrītere: *grammarian*, WW372, 34; 414, 11; 487, 14

stǣna *stone jug*, MtL26, 7

+ stāl: add ±, VHF83, 113 n.

stānbryce *a piece of stone*, FL2,A53

stānbrycg: delete WW

stānfæt: add *jewelled sheath?* WAL II, 3 (ASPR6, 139)

Stānhenge *Stonehenge*, FF326, n. 2

stānwalu f. *a bank of stones* (BTs)

stānwyrht: delete WW341, 10 and add WW150, 32 (FL4,D51)

stānwyrhta: add WW341, 10 (FL4,D51)

± staðolfæstan = ± staðolfæstnian   ÆGR 192, 2

staðolnes *firmament*, GLL174

stelscofl: = stēorsceofl, BPG875 n.

stencan: delete *to afflict*, FL3,D14

stēordalc *steering pin, helm*, JEGP-

steornede: = steorrede

steorrede *starred* (*of a white mark on horse's forehead*) FL4,D52

stēða: delete; fol. 6r of Additional MS. 32246 reads steda

± stīgan: add hēanne bēam gestīgan, *to climb the high oak* (*to beat down acorns*) AJP66, 1–12

stīgend: add *rider*, GLL239

stincan: delete? *sniff*, B2289 (HBK)

stincan *to move rapidly?*, B2288 (HBK); RD29, 12 (ASPR4, 236, n. to B2288)

stondnis *substance*, OEGC72, 2

stōrsticca: *incense spoon*, RAC226, 32 n.

strecednes: *spreading*, FL4,B16

+strēones: delete, BPG 93

±strīc: *plague* at BHW 269, 57 n.

strīcel, I: *teat*, FL 3, A 35; BPG 155 n.

strīpligan:=plyccan?, BPG 598 n.

strȳnd: delete *gain*; gestreonde at WW 488, 30=gestreone; v. WW 190, 3

+strynge: = +styrung?, v. FL 3, A 16

stuntsprǣc: ms. stuntspæc

stȳcing f. *a clearing* (*of land*), FF 771 n. 8

styntan: add +, *to repress*, BPG 278

+stynðo: v. VHF 97, n. 144

sum: add *an important one*, WB glossary

sunboga *arc of the sun*, JEGP-

sunderboren: *born of disparate parents*, FL 4, D 53

sūðēasthealf f. *the south-east*, OEGC 4, 384

sūðerne: add *of southern make*, MAG 134 n.

swæcehēow: read spǣcehēow, *form of speech*, FL 6, A 9; note also hīwlīce spǣce in BTs

swǣfan: read swǣlan?

swǣrbyrd?: for LCD 185a subst. LCD 3, 66, 22; ms. swærtbyrde

swǣsenddagas: v. FL 4, A 25

swǣslic: add + (BTs)

swæðelyne: delete, FL 3, B 1

sweartbyrd: v. swǣrbyrd; for possible ref. to *blue baby* v. ANS 171, 33

swēgesweard: delete; ms. suge sweard (LCG U 222) *sow's hide*; v. vistilia at CGL 7, 423

sweglwered: *clothed with radiance* (HBK)

swolling: *swelling sail*, EL 245 n. (ed. Gradon); but a case can be made for ms. spellingum

swētwyrde: delete *stuttering*; add *lisping*, FL 4, A 26

swīnhege m. *a fence to keep swine from straying* (BTs)

swīnlic: delete the query; ms. swinlice

swiung: delete, JEGP-

swor:=swol?, EI 239 n.

swōrettan: add *to sigh* (*about something*), VHF 85, n. 75

sworian? *to sigh*, VHF 101, n. 168

swūrplætt m. *a stroke on the neck*, FL 2, B 53

swȳrige? *troublesome*, JM 49

syllestre f. *a giver*, A 76, 495 n.

sylting *seasoning*, KCM 94, ix

symbelbrēad *bread for a feast* (*of water and a loaf in the desert*) SFF 122

symbelmōnaðlic: delete the query, FL 4, D 54

symeringwyrt: *mallow?*, A 41, 139

+taccian: delete, BPG 1022 n.

+tācnigendlīce *figuratively*, ÆH 2, 114, 25

tæg tæg *te-hee*, FL 4, E 1

±tæl: delete *competent*, WW 505, 3; add *having mastery of*, WW 502, 3 (lemma competem=compotem)

tǣmespīle: *sieve-stake*, FF 463, n. 2

tala=talu, WW 204, 3 (FL 3, H 47)

tamcian: add +, BPG 1022 n.

tēafor: add *pigment, salve*, AB 34, 101

teltrē:=teldtrēow, *tent-peg*; v. claus · lignum tentorii, WW 205, 20

tēofrian: add: v. CP 153, 23

teolðyrl: *an opening in a beehive, service entrance*, FL 3, A 37

+tēwian *adorn*, W 262, 22 d

tīdfara: *one who goes at his allotted time?*, BPG 286 n.

tīmlic *suitable, of proper age*, BPG 922

Tīrisc *of Tyre*, OEGC 8, 14

tōætēacnes f. *increase*, BH 295, 12 (Sch)

tōætēacnian *to increase*, BH 295 n. (Sch)

tōātēon *to draw in*, GLL 243

tōāwrītan *glosses conscribere*, GLL 98

tōbesettan *to put to*, GLL 245

tōbringan *to bring to*, BPG 49

tōforlētan: add *to leave to*, VM 69 b, 7

tōgecīgan *to call to*, GLL 92

tōgegearwian *to prepare*, A 65, 230

tōgelǣdan *glosses adducere*, GLL 234

tōgelaðian *to invite along*, OEGC 60, 17

togeteohhian *glosses apponere*, GLL 245

tōgetēon *to draw in*, GLL 243

tōhāwiend *spectator*, JEGP 56, 65

tōhelpan *to help*, MkR 9, 24

tolcettende *talking vainly?*, BPG 931 n.

tōlīhtan *to illuminate*, GLL 33

tōlūtan *to incline to*, VHF 24, n. 106

tōlynnan *to take away* (BTs)

top: on the meaning *plaything*, v. GAT p. 52

tōrǣcan: *proffer*, VHF 37, n. 171; *to apply* (*fire in torture*), OEG 4489

toroc: the word is Celtic, like guohioc in same glossary

torr: with meaning *tower* this is a different word from torr, *rock*; v. HEW

tōsettan *to put to*, GLL 245; *to clamp*, BPG 302

tōspillan *to destroy*, SPS 82, 5

tōtræglian: v. BPG 602 n.

totrida: delete the query, FL 4, E 2

træglian: *tear apart, destroy*, BPG 602 n.

trēowlēasnes: add + (BT)

+trēownes: add *faithfulness*, VHF 99, 309

treppan: delete *to trap*, FL 2, B 54

treumbicin? *glosses* (mel) silvestre Mt 3, 4 (KCM p. 476, 6)

+trīowed *shafted*, WW 143, 5 (FL 3, H 21)

trogscip: *boat made from a hollowed log*, FL 3, H 49

trym: add ǣnge trym, *step by step*, FL 4, D 1

tube: delete, BPG 257 n.

tud: delete; v. tudenard

tudenard *a shield,* MNG 59

tunge: add on halre tungan, *unequivocally?,* *viva voce?,* RAC p. 284, n. 11

tungele: delete; v. tunggelælle

tunggelælle adj. *verbose,* FL 2, B 55

tūnstede: add, based on loca inter agros, Isid. *Etym.* 15, 2, 14

turfgret *turfpit,* WC 86, 19 n.

twelfmōnð *twelvemonth,* VM 108 a, 1

twentigesnihte *twenty nights old,* BHc 206, 30

twifingre: add *(of fat on swine)*

twihǣmed *one who marries twice,* KCM p. 93 c

twilafte: read twilǣste (FL 2, B 56)

twiman renders homo dubius, WE 55, 2

twing: delete, FL 2, B 57

twīnwyrm: read twinwyrm, FL 4, A 27

twiseltōð: *with two protruding front teeth,* FL 3, H 50

twisnēse: v. BPG 328 n.

tȳdrung *weakness, sterility,* OEG 1031

tyncen: *little tub,* FL 2, A 55

tȳrlāca: delete WW

± ðaccian: delete *to tame,* BPG 1022 n.

ðǣrgemang *thereamong,* BPG 54

ðamettan: very likely scribal error for ðafettan

ðearfendlīce *poorly,* VHF 128, n. 121

ðearflic: add *poor,* RBL 100, 4

ðearmgyrd: read WW 120, 1

ðeccbryce: delete?; v. OEG 2256 n.

ðelneðung *some kind of plant,* OEGC 73, 1

ðencan: add ± ðencan mid, *to remember someone with (a gift),* VHF 99, 314

ðēodfēond: *archfiend,* BHW 137, 52 n.

ðēodlāreow *great teacher,* SFF 96

+ ðicfyldan: *to make dense (the material for a fire), to pile up,* BPG 974

ðīstra: delete the query, A 76, 411–21

ðiustra: = ðēoster, FL 4, D 55

ðolle: *instrument on which a martyr was burned,* FL 3, A 38

ðornðȳfel m. *thorn bush,* FGR 69, n. 3

+ ðracen: *stout of frame,* FL 4, C 2

+ ðrǣsted *contrite,* GLL 53

ðrāg: add sume ðrāge, *at times,* OEGC 4, 381

ðrāgmǣl n. *unhappy time,* JUL 344 (ed. Woolf)

ðreclic *terrible,* SPS 95, 4

ðrepel *a torture instrument of three stakes,* FL 2, B 60

ðrifingre: add *(referring to the fat of swine)*

ðrihǣmed *one who marries thrice,* KCM p. 93 c

ðrīstlēasnes: delete, A 66, 31 n.

ðrosm: add BPG 760 n.

ðrōwungdæg m. *day of martyrdom,* Luick Festgabe (1925), p. 192

ðrūh: delete *chest,* BPG 867 n.

ðrydǣgðyrn *period of three days,* OEGC 7, 13

ðrymdōm: *glorious judgement*

ðrȳpel: delete; v. ðrepel

ðrȳpelūf: delete, FL 2, B 60

ðrysumer? *three years old,* WW 120, 38 (ms. triennis · þrywinter ł sumer gildeto(x))

ðunorbodu: v. FL 3, H 51

ðunorsliht m. *thunderstroke,* A 73, 25

ðurh: add, with inst. case, VHF 116, n. 43

ðurhlǣdan glosses perducere, SPS 77, 52

ðurhlonge? adv. *continuously,* GEN 307; v. TLG p. 38

ðurhrǣdan *to read through,* OEGC 28, 23

ðurhūtlīce adv. *thoroughly,* NP 28, 49

ðurhwunigendlic: add A 65, 230

ðurhwunungnes *perseverance,* SPS p. 37

ðweorhtimber *resolutely made,* JUL 550 n. (ed. Woolf)

ðwērian = ðwēorian, VHF 148, 117

ðȳflen: delete, BPG 843

ðȳfilg *brambly,* OEGC 30, 32

ðȳmele: add *(referring to the fat of swine)*

ðyrncin *kind of thorn,* FL 4, A 28

unǣtnes *affliction,* RAC p. 60, 8; unǣtnessa gebīdan, *to die*

unāhladen *unexhausted,* JEGP-

unāmyrred *uninjured,* ÆL 35, 285

unbecweden: add *uncontested,* RAC p. 92, 14

unbesprecen *uncontested,* RAC p. 60, 29

unbeðōht *unexpected,* JEGP-

unbȳergo: delete; ms. unbyengo, DR ed. Lindelöf, p. 206, n. 1

underbeðeodan *to subject,* JEGP-

underburhware: add SHS 6, 32

undergrīpan *to seize,* RWH 122, 23

underslīcende *slipping under,* JEGP 56, 65

underðeodan: add *to instruct,* VLC 172, 120 n.

+ unfæstnian: delete; see foll. word

± unfæstnod *not fixed in the mark (referring to an arrow),* VHF 104, n. 182

unforhtlēasnes?: v. forhtlēasnes

unforðōht *unexpected,* JEGP-

unfrōforlīce: no *un* in ms.

unfūl: read unful, *empty,* FL 4, D 56

ungearwyrd: delete, JEGP 52, 376

ungebierde: add WW 395, 16; OEG 7, 247

ungedōn *not done,* OEGC 28, 486

ungeearned *undeserved,* A 65, 230

ungefynde: *undeveloped,* FL 4, E 3

ungemēde: substitute ungemedemad, *unmeasured,* ASPR 3, 299, 25

ungemetlicnes *intemperance,* KF

ungenīwiendlic *unrenewable,* OEGC 28, 188

ungeorwyrd *unsullied*, JEGP 52, 377

ungescæōfulnes *innocence*, GLL 134

ungeōyre:=ungeōwǣre; lemma discensor
=dissensor, a glossary equivalent of
discordator, q.v. at WW 223, 10

ungewyldendlic *impatient*, OEGC 30, 18

unglēaw: add *very sharp?*, WB 2564 n.

unhālwendlic: add *not salutary*, ANS 122,
257, 7

unhlitme: *without casting lots?* ASPR 4,
177, 1128

unlǣdu *misery*, VHF 29, n. 124

unlagu: delete *bad law*, BHW 356, 16

unmiht: add *faintness?*, WW 199, 36

unmihtiglic: add *faint?*, LCD 2, 60, 8

unmihtiglīcnes *inability*, LCD 1, 56, 15

unmōdnes *pride*, A 66, 32, n. 4

unmyrge: delete the queries; v. colludium
at CGL 6, 231, where dolus might be taken
to equal dolor

unnīōing: add *liberal man*, ANS 117, 23

unorne: *simple*, MAG 256 n.

unrād f. *cruel raid*, CPC 1111, 6 n.

unrēone? *very sad*, VHF 92, n. 116a

unrihthād *improper manner*, VHF 76, 44 n.

unrihthǣming f. *fornication*, ANS 111, 280

unrihttīd: *time of evil*, VHF 94, n. 128

unrihtwilla *bad intention*, A 66, 28

unrīmgōd: *unnumbered good works*, ÆL 33,
241

unsǣle: delete; ms. unfǣle

unscæōōig *innocent*, ÆH 1, 512, 12

unsceandlīce *shamelessly*, ÆL 23b, 372

unsceōōiglīce *innocently*, FGR 80, 3

unseofene: read unseofiende

unsettan *to take down*, MkL 15, 36

unslid:=unsilt, *unsalted*; v. LCG P 400 and
LCD 3, 18, 5

untamcul: *invincible*, BPG 680 n.

untellendlic: add CPC 1137, 20

untīdlic: add *timeless*, BPG 452

untōdǣled: add *unshared*, VHF 33, n. 146

untōslopen *undissolved*, JEGP-

untrum: add +, ÆL 21, 187

unōurhfǣre *impenetrable*, OEGC 27, 25

ūpāhafen *exalted*, VHF 75, 34

ūpālūcan *to eradicate*, GLL 251

ūpfeax: *with bristling hair*, FL 4, D 57

ūpgelǣded *led up*, VM 135a, 24

ūpgodu: delete *heathen gods*, FL 3, A 40

ūphebbe: delete, FL 2, A 57

ūprǣran *to raise up*, GLL 249

ūpreccan *to erect*, GLL 250

ūpscīnan *to rise shiningly*, OEGC 62, 5

ūpsettan *to exalt*, SHS 8, 52

ūpspringan *to rise up*, Lk 1, 78

ūsspīung: delete; fol. 4 v of Additional
MS. 32, 246 reads wyrmsspiung

ūtāblegned *ulcerated*, LCD 2, 10, 5; 2, 98, 25

ūtālūcan *to pluck forth*, GLL 251

ūtāslīdan: *to slip out*, BPG 50 n.

ūtāwindan: *to slip out*, BPG 50 n.

ūtāwyrtrumian *to root out*, VM 75a, 5

ūtfaran *to go out*, SPS 145, 4

ūtfēolan *to get out*, VHF 95, 255, n. 130

ūtforlǣtan: add *to let out*, VHF 133, 57

ūtlād: for *right of passage* substitute *toll on
goods carried out of market*, HAW 477, 16

ūtofgān *to go out of*, VHF 39, n. 182

ūtyrnan *to have diarrhoea*, LCD 63 b

wād: add cpds. with beorh, denu, lond
(BT)

wǣgbora: add *wave-bearer?* (HBK)

wǣgel: delete the query

wǣgngerefa:=wǣgngefēra,   *wagon-com-
panion*; v. carpentarius, collegiatus at
CGL 6, 230

wǣgnōol: delete; v. wǣhōoll

wǣhōoll *battering ram*, FL 3, A 41

+ wǣlan: add MPS 143 n.

wǣlblēat: *deadly* (HBK)

wǣlgenga: read wǣlgenga and delete the
query, FL 4, A 29

wǣlkyrging renders gorgoneus, WE 55, 6

wǣpenbǣre *weapon-bearing*, OEGC 27, 11

wǣterbucca: v. FL 4, D 58

wǣtergāt: v. FL 4, D 58

wǣterlēod *fish*, OEGC 28, 386

wǣtersol *pool*, Jn 5, 2

wāgōeorl: *a break in a wall*; v. ōyrelung
ōæs wages, CP 153, 25

waled: *ridged*, FL 3, D 17

walu: *metal ridge on top of helmet, like that on
Sutton Hoo helmet* at B 1031; v. WB, p. 319

wambecoōu f. *stomach trouble*, LCD 87 b

wambegicōa m. *itching of the stomach*,
LCD 90a

wambewyrm *intestinal worm*, LCD 90a

wambscyldig: read wamscyldig, *sinful*,
VHF 93, n. 120

wancian *to waver*, RD 87, 7 (ASPR 3, 377)

wanfōta: v. Canopos at Isid. *Etym.* 12, 7, 26

wansēoc: *melancholic*, FL 4, D 59

wassen *vassal*, ANS 111, 277 (Celtic); v.
HAW p. 532

wēageslō: *companion in crime*, ASPR 4,
282, 16

+ wealc: add *military expedition*, ES 72, 10

wealcol: *rolling in the waves*, BPG 831

wealdweaxe *sinew*, OEGC 52, 12 n.

wealhwyrt: *elecampane*, A 41, 133 n. 6

weallstaōol: delete the query, FF 157, n. 1

weallwala: *wall panelling?*, AJP 62, 336

wealte: add *a snare*, BPG 138

wealword: v. A 66, 34 n.

weardstōw *watchtower*, OEGC 6, 1

wederāwendednes *variation of weather*, KF

wegend? *a bearer*, OEGC28, 294
wegtwiflung: fol. 19v of Additional MS. 32, 246 reads wegtwislung
wellere: WW278, 19, prob. equivalent to wellyrgae, *walkyrie?*, LCG S379 n.
wellwill *a spring*, KC5, 344, 29
wenncīcen: v. ANS171, 21
weolocbasu: add OEGC51, 6
weoning: = wining, FL2, B35
weorcland *land subject to labour services*, RAC166, 7 n.
+weorclic: delete, FL2, A32
weorf: = hwȳorf
weorŏðearfa: delete, ES62, 129
werbǣr f. *pasture land near a weir* (BTs)
werbēam: read wǣrbeam? *protecting pillar*, EI486 n.
±werian: add *discharge obligations on* (land), HAW p. 450, n. 3
werping *loss?* (gloss to iactura), ANS117, 23
wēstenlic *eremitic*, OEGC4, 140 ·
westrihte *westward*, OEGC4, 112 n.
weðel: delete, FL2, B62
wicðēnestre f. *weekly servant*, A76, 502
wīcung *lodging*, WW147, 26
wīdefeorlic: delete wīder; fol. 5v of Additional MS. 32, 246 reads widewīdl: add JEGP56, 66
wīdnes: add ÆH2, 578, 10
wīdu f. *width*, KW55, 13 (=WE60, 18c)
wielincel: delete, BPG925
wīfcȳ̄ððu: v. OEGC4, 79 n.
wifrian *to shake* (a weapon), OEGC25, 3
wiga *the Holy Spirit?*, EL937 n. (ed. Gradon)
wiglian: add+, GLL97
wīgnett? *gladiator's net*, FL2, A58
wīgnoð: delete the query, FL4, C8
willodlīce *willingly*, SPS53, 8
willung: add+, GLL109
wilnincel *a little female servant*, BPG925
wiluncel: delete; v. wilnincel
wilweg n. *desired way*, W252, 17
winclian? *to wink*, FL4, D4
wīncole: read wīncolc, FL2, B63
windiht: delete
wīngeard: delete the query after vine and add WW136, 36 (lemma brionia=vitem albam at Isid. Etym. 17, 9, 90)
wīngeardhring: *vine tendrils*, FL3, H56
wīnian *to pluck* (grapes), LkL6, 44
winnendlic *fighting*, MNG61
wiorðegend *worshipper*, EPs108, 11 (fenerator taken as venerator)
+wīred: add *ornamented*, KCM p. 163c; v. also WC14, 12 n.
wīsbōc: *book of wisdom*, GLL99
wīsnes: *wisdom*, VHF59, n. 35; +, *understanding*, LcD3, 82, 2

wītecyll *sack in which parricides were put to death*, FL4, D31
wītewyrðe: read wītewyrðe
witnesman *witness*, ANS111, 277
witod: = witodlīce, BHW139, 87
witodlīce: add+, W113, 13 n.; 119, 17 n.
wiðerstede *substitution*, JEGP-
wiðersȳnes: add *withershins*
wiðerung *obstinacy*, KCM p. 319a
wiðgehæftan *to fight against*, BPG822 n.
wiðig: cpds. with bed, brōc, ford, grāf, lēah, mǣd, mere, mōr, pōl, pytt, slǣd, ðȳfel (BT)
wiððingian: *to talk against, contradict*, VM65b, 6
+wixlan *to change*, MLR27, 453
wlæce: = wlæc?, BPG652 n.
wlǣtlic *foul*, OEGC28, 431
+wlencan: add±, VHF93, n. 118
wlita: delete, FL2, B64
wliteandet: delete the query, FL5, C4
wlitescēawung *Sion*, BH212, 11
wlitiglīce: add VHF39, 331b
wōdscinn: *mad trickery?*, BHW118, 34 n.
wordbebod *command*, VHF113, 52
wordcennend: v. BPG115 n.
wordclipinde *able to speak*, VHF88, n. 93a
wordriht: *statement of what is right according to law or custom*, WB2631 n.
woruldbebod: *secular edict*, VHF113, n. 30
woruldgeflit: delete the query (ANS134, 288)
woruldgeðingu *worldly things*, VM69b, 10
woruldhogu f. *worldly care*, BHW204, 82
wrǣtbaso: add OEGC51, 8
wraðo = wraðu?, FL2, A60
+wrinclod: *wrinkled?*, BPG750 n.
±writ: delete *stilus*, BPG1018 n.
wrōhtbora: delete *monster*
wuduclāte *a plant*, aristolochia OEGC73b, 9
wuducynn: *a kind of tree*, FL4, A31
wuduhætt *leafy top*, OEGC8, 16
wuldorbēacn *sign of glory*, A73, 18, n. 12
wuldorbēag: add *iris of the eye*, FL3, H58
wulfsēað: *pit in which wolves were trapped*, RAC4, 12 n.
wyrmsūtspīung: delete; ms. wyrmsspiung
wyrpendlic *suitable for throwing*, OEGC9, 12

yfelmynan *to consider wickedly*, SPS82, 4
yfelonbecweðende *persuading to evil*, BPG179
yltwist: v. lytwist
ymbeardung *dwelling around*, GLL214
yrsebin: read yrfebin, *fodder basket for cattle*, FGR55n.
ȳðwōrigende: *wave-wandering* (fish), FL3, K2